THE OXFORD HANDBOOK OF

POSTCOLONIAL STUDIES

THE OXFORD HANDBOOK OF

POSTCOLONIAL STUDIES

Edited by

GRAHAM HUGGAN

OXFORD
UNIVERSITY PRESS

UNIVERSITY PRESS

Great Clarendon Street, Oxford, OX2 6DP,
United Kingdom

Oxford University Press is a department of the University of Oxford.
It furthers the University's objective of excellence in research, scholarship,
and education by publishing worldwide. Oxford is a registered trade mark of
Oxford University Press in the UK and in certain other countries

Published in the United States of America by Oxford University Press
198 Madison Avenue, New York, NY 10016, United States of America

British Library Cataloguing in Publication Data
Data available

ISBN 978-0-19-958825-1

Printed and bound in Great Britain by
CPI Group (UK) Ltd, Croydon, CR0 4YY

Links to third party websites are provided by Oxford in good faith and
for information only. Oxford disclaims any responsibility for the materials
contained in any third party website referenced in this work.

CONTENTS

PART II   THE COLONIAL PRESENT

PART III   THEORY AND PRACTICE

PART IV   ACROSS THE DISCIPLINES

PART V   ACROSS THE WORLD

LIST OF CONTRIBUTORS

Ananda Abeysekara is Associate Professor in the Department of Religion and Culture at Virginia Tech (US). He is the author of *The Politics of Postsecular Religion: Mourning Secular Futures* (2008).

David Attwell, South African by birth, is Professor of English at the University of York (UK). He has published widely on J. M. Coetzee. His other books include *Rewriting Modernity: Studies in Black Literary History* (2005) and *The Cambridge History of South African Literature*, co-edited with Derek Attridge.

Susan Bassnett is an international expert on translation studies and holds a Chair in Comparative Literature at the University of Warwick (UK). With Harish Trivedi, she edited *Postcolonial Translation: Theory and Practice* (1999), and since then she has published numerous books and articles on aspects of translation, comparative and world literature. She is also well known as a journalist and writer.

Ali Behdad is John Charles Hillis Professor of Literature, Professor of English and Comparative Literature, and Chair of the English Department at UCLA (US). He is the author of *Belated Travelers: Orientalism in the Age of Colonial Dissolution* (1994) and *A Forgetful Nation: On Immigration and Cultural Identity in the US* (2001). He is the co-editor (with Dominic Thomas) of *A Companion to Comparative Literature* (2011), and is currently completing a manuscript on Orientalist photography.

Elleke Boehmer is Professor of World Literature in English at the University of Oxford (UK) and Professorial Governing Body Fellow at Wolfson College. Among her publications are *Colonial and Postcolonial Literature* (1995, 2005), *Empire, the National and the Postcolonial 1890–1920* (2002), *Stories of Women* (2005), and the biography *Nelson Mandela* (2008). She is also the editor of numerous volumes and the author of four acclaimed novels.

Timothy Brennan is Professor of English and Comparative Literature at the University of Minnesota (US). He is the author most recently of *Wars of Position: The Cultural Politics of Left and Right* (2006) and *Secular Devotion: Afro-Latin Music and Imperial Jazz* (2008). He is currently at work on a two-volume study entitled *Borrowed Light: Vico, Hegel and the Colonies* and *Avant-Gardes, Colonies, and Communists: Homiletic Realism and Imperial Form*.

Diana Brydon is Canada Research Chair in Globalization and Cultural Studies and Professor in the Department of English, Film, and Theatre at the University of Manitoba

(Canada). She is currently investigating transnational literacies and global democracy. Her co-edited book (with Marta Dvorak), *Crosstalk: Canadian and Global Imaginaries in Dialogue*, appeared in 2012.

Rey Chow is Anne Firor Scott Professor of Literature at Duke University (US), and serves on the board of around forty journals, book series, and research centres worldwide. Her scholarly writings, which have appeared in ten languages, include *The Rey Chow Reader* (2010) and *Entanglements, or Transmedial Thinking about Capture* (2012).

Nikita Dhawan is Junior Professor of Political Science for Gender/Postcolonial Studies and Director of the Frankfurt Research Center for Postcolonial Studies at Goethe University, Frankfurt (Germany). Her publications include *Impossible Speech: On the Politics of Silence and Violence* (2007) and *Decolonizing Enlightenment: Transnational Justice, Human Rights and Democracy in a Postcolonial World* (ed., 2013).

David Farrier is Lecturer in Modern and Contemporary Literature at the University of Edinburgh (UK). He is the author of *Unsettled Narratives: The Pacific Writings of Stevenson, Ellis, Melville and London* (2007) and *Postcolonial Asylum: Seeking Sanctuary Before the Law* (2011). He is also the editor of a special issue of *Moving Worlds* (12.2) on asylum narratives.

Simon Featherstone teaches Drama at De Montfort University in Leicester (UK). He is the author of *Postcolonial Cultures* (2005) and *Englishness: Twentieth-Century Popular Culture and the Forming of English Identity* (2009).

Charles Forsdick is James Barrow Professor of French at the University of Liverpool (UK). A specialist in the fields of travel writing, slavery, postcolonial literature, and French colonial history, he is the author of *Victor Segalen and the Aesthetics of Diversity* (2000) and *Travel in Twentieth-Century French and Francophone Cultures* (2005).

Leela Gandhi is Professor of English at the University of Chicago. She is a founding co-editor of the journal *Postcolonial Studies*. Her books include *Postcolonial Theory, Affective Communities, Measures of Home*, and the co-authored *England through Colonial Eyes*.

Priyamvada Gopal is Senior Lecturer in Postcolonial and Related Literatures at the Faculty of English, University of Cambridge (UK). In addition to several essays, she is the author of two monographs, *Literary Radicalism in India: Gender, Nation and the Transition to Independence* (2005) and *The Indian Novel in English: Nation, History and Narration* (2009). She has also edited, with Neil Lazarus, a special issue of *New Formations* (59) entitled 'After Iraq: Reframing Postcolonial Studies'.

Peter Hallward teaches at the Centre for Research of Modern European Philosophy at Kingston University London. He has written books on the philosophy of Alain Badiou and Gilles Deleuze, and is the author of *Damming the Flood: Haiti and the Politics of*

Containment (2007) and *Absolutely Postcolonial* (2001). His book on the Will of the People is forthcoming from Verso in 2013.

Waleed Hazbun is Associate Professor of International Relations at the American University of Beirut (Lebanon), where he directs the Center for Arab and Middle Eastern Studies. He is the author of *Beaches, Ruins, Resorts: The Politics of Tourism in the Arab World* (2008).

Barry Hindess, after working as a sociologist in Britain, learned to pass as a political scientist at Australian National University, where he is now an Emeritus Professor in the School of Politics and International Relations. His publications include papers on time, liberalism, and imperial rule, and *Discourses of Power: From Hobbes to Foucault* (1995), *Governing Australia* (ed. with Mitchell Dean, 1998), *Us and Them: Elites and Anti-elitism in Australia* (ed. with Marian Sawer, 2004), *Corruption: Expanding the Focus* (ed. with Manu Barcham and Peter Larmour, 2012).

Stephen Howe is Senior Research Fellow at the University of Bristol (UK) and co-editor of *The Journal of Imperial and Commonwealth History*. His books include *Anticolonialism in British Politics* (1993), *Ireland and Empire* (2000), *Empire: A Very Short Introduction* (2002), and the edited collection *New Imperial Histories* (2009). His *Intellectual Consequences of Decolonisation* is forthcoming with Oxford.

Graham Huggan is Chair of Commonwealth and Postcolonial Literatures in the School of English at the University of Leeds (UK). His publications include *The Postcolonial Exotic: Marketing the Margins* (2001), *Australian Literature: Postcolonialism, Racism, Transnationalism* (2007), and most recently, with Helen Tiffin, *Postcolonial Ecocriticism: Literature, Animals, Environment* (2010).

Dane Kennedy is Elmer Louis Kayser Professor of History and International Affairs at George Washington University (US). He has written extensively on Britain and its empire, colonialism in Africa and India, and imperial historiography. His latest book is *The Last Blank Spaces: Exploring Africa and Australia* (2013).

Michelle Keown is Senior Lecturer in English Literature at the University of Edinburgh. She is the author of *Postcolonial Pacific Writing: Representations of the Body* (2005) and *Pacific Islands Writing: The Postcolonial Literatures of Aotearoa/New Zealand and Oceania* (2007), and co-editor of *Comparing Postcolonial Diasporas* (2009).

Neil Lazarus is Professor of English and Comparative Literature at the University of Warwick (UK). He is the author most recently of *The Postcolonial Unconscious* (2011). Previous publications include *The Cambridge Companion to Postcolonial Literary Studies* (2004) and *Nationalism and Cultural Practice in the Postcolonial World* (1999).

John McLeod is Professor of Postcolonial and Diaspora Literatures at the University of Leeds (UK). He is the author of *Postcolonial London: Rewriting the Metropolis* (2004),

J. G. Farrell (2007), and *Beginning Postcolonialism* (2nd edn, 2010). He has edited *The Routledge Companion to Postcolonial Studies* and is on the editorial boards of *The Journal of Commonwealth Literature*, *The Journal of Postcolonial Writing*, and *Moving Worlds: A Journal of Transcultural Writings*. He has published over thirty essays on postcolonial, diasporic, and transcultural literatures.

Walter D. Mignolo is William H. Wannamaker Distinguished Professor and Director of the Center for Global Studies and the Humanities at Duke University (US). He has been working for the past twenty-five years on the formation and transformation of the modern/colonial world system and on the idea of western civilization. Among his major publications are *The Darker Side of the Renaissance: Literacy, Territoriality and Colonization* (1995), *Local Histories/Global Designs: Coloniality, Subaltern Knowledge and Border Thinking* (2000), and *The Idea of Latin America* (2005). His most recent publications are *The Darker Side of Western Modernity: Global Futures, Decolonial Options* (2011) and, with Madina Tlostanova, *Learning to Unlearn: Decolonial Reflections from Eurasia to the Americas* (2012).

Stephen Morton is Senior Lecturer in English at the University of Southampton (UK). His publications include *States of Emergency: Colonialism, Literature and Law* (2012), *Salman Rushdie: Fictions of Postcolonial Modernity* (2007), *Gayatri Spivak: Ethics, Subalternity and the Critique of Postcolonial Reason* (2006), and *Gayatri Chakravorty Spivak* (2003). He has also co-edited *Terror and the Postcolonial* (2009) and *Foucault in an Age of Terror* (2008), while articles have appeared in *Textual Practice*, *Public Culture*, *New Formations*, *Parallax*, and *Interventions*.

Dana Mount is Assistant Professor in English at Cape Breton University (Canada), where she teaches world and indigenous literature. Previous research has focused on the concept of everyday environmentalisms in postcolonial literature; she has also done work on the discourse surrounding water issues for the United Nations University Institute for Water, Environment, and Health.

Stuart Murray is Professor of Contemporary Literatures and Film at the University of Leeds (UK), where he is also Director of the multidisciplinary Leeds Centre for Medical Humanities. His postcolonial research interests are in the cultures of encounter and settlement in New Zealand and the Pacific, and in the history of postcolonial studies. He has written and edited four books on New Zealand literature and film, and is the co-editor of *What Postcolonial Theory Doesn't Say*, to appear with Routledge in 2014.

Susie O'Brien is Associate Professor of English and Cultural Studies at McMaster University (Canada). Her research is on postcolonial literature and the concept of resilience in postcolonial ecology and culture.

Ato Quayson is Professor of English and inaugural Director of the Centre for Diaspora and Transnational Studies at the University of Toronto (Canada). His publications include *Strategic Transformations in Nigerian Writing* (1997), *Postcolonialism: Theory,*

Practice or Process? (2000), *Calibrations: Reading for the Social* (2003), and *Aesthetic Nervousness: Disability and the Crisis of Representation* (2003). He has also edited the two-volume *Cambridge History of Postcolonial Literature* (2012) and is a Fellow of the Ghana Academy of Arts and Sciences.

Shalini Randeria is Chair of the Department of Social Anthropology/Sociology at the Graduate Institute of International and Development Studies in Geneva (Switzerland). She has been President of the European Association of Social Anthropologists (EASA) and a Fellow of the Institute of Advanced Study in Berlin (Germany). Her research interests are in the anthropology of law, state, globalization, and social movements. Her recent publications include the edited German-language volumes *Vom Imperialismus zum Empire* (2009) and *Jenseits von Eurozentrismus* (2012).

Pooja Rangan is Assistant Professor of Culture and Media in Eugene Lang College at the New School (US). She holds a PhD in Modern Culture and Media from Brown University, where her dissertation, 'Automatic Ethnography: Otherness, Indexicality, and Humanitarian Visual Media', was awarded the Marie J. Langlois Prize in 2012. Her work has appeared or is forthcoming in *Camera Obscura*, *South Asian Popular Culture*, *Interventions*, and *differences*.

Michael Rothberg is Professor of English and Conrad Humanities Scholar at the University of Illinois at Urbana-Champaign (US), where he also directs the Holocaust, Genocide, and Memory Studies Initiative. He is the author of *Multidirectional Memory: Remembering the Holocaust in the Age of Decolonization* (2009) and *Traumatic Realism: The Demands of Holocaust Representation* (2000). He has also co-edited *The Holocaust: Theoretical Readings* (2003), *Cary Nelson and the Struggle for the University: Poetry, Politics, and the Profession* (2009), and special issues of the journals *Criticism*, *Interventions*, *Occasion*, and *Yale French Studies*.

Salman Sayyid is Director of the International Centre for Muslim and Non-Muslim Understanding at the University of South Australia. He is the author of *A Fundamental Fear* and a co-editor of *A Postcolonial People* and *Thinking Through Islamophobia*. His wide-ranging publications have a decolonial thread running through them.

Frank Schulze-Engler is Professor of New Anglophone Literatures and Cultures and Director of the Centre for Interdisciplinary African Studies at Goethe University, Frankfurt (Germany). He is the co-editor of *African Literatures in the Eighties* (1993), *Crab Tracks: Progress and Process in Teaching the New Literatures in English* (2002), *Transcultural English Studies: Theories, Fictions, Realities* (2008), and *Beyond 'Other Cultures': Transcultural Perspectives on Teaching the New Literatures in English* (2011).

Patricia Seed is Professor of History at the University of California, Irvine (US). Included among her publications are *Ceremonies of Possession in Europe's Conquest of the New World*, *American Pentimento: The Invention of Indians and the Pursuit of Riches* (winner of the James A. Rawley Prize in Atlantic History), and the 1992 article 'Colonial and

Postcolonial Discourse' and its 2003 follow-up, 'More Colonial Discourse'. She is also the author of the *Oxford Map Companion to World History* (forthcoming, 2013).

Joanne Sharp is Professor of Geography at the University of Glasgow (UK). Her research interests are in the intersection of postcolonialism, development, and geopolitics. Recent publications include *Geographies of Postcolonialism: Spaces of Power and Representation* (2009) and *The Ashgate Companion to Critical Geopolitics* (2013), co-edited with K. Dodds and M. Kuus.

Stephen Slemon teaches postcolonial literatures and theory at the University of Alberta (Canada). His current research pertains to the social management of mountaineering, from the period of high colonialism to the present moment of mountaineering's global sprawl. Recent articles include 'Deception in High Places' (with Zac Robinson) in *The Canadian Alpine Journal* (2011), and 'The Brotherhood of the Rope: Commodification and Contradiction in the Mountaineering Community', in *Renegotiating Community: Interdisciplinary Perspectives, Global Contexts*, ed. Diana Brydon and William D. Coleman (2008).

Jo Smith (Kai Tahu, Kāti Mamoe, and Waitaha) teaches in the Media Studies Programme at Victoria University of Wellington (Aotearoa/New Zealand). Her published work examines the socio-political power of media technologies with a primary focus on how colonial histories inform contemporary media practices. While her home discipline is Film and Media Studies, she researches across three interrelated fields (Indigenous, Postcolonial, and Settler Colonial Studies) to ask new questions about the ways in which media technologies, institutions, and aesthetic practices help shape notions of identity, nationhood, and community.

Ann Laura Stoler is Willy Brandt Distinguished University Professor of Anthropology and Historical Studies at the New School for Social Research in New York (US). She is co-founder of the online journal *Political Concepts: A Critical Lexicon*, and has been a Visiting Professor at Birzeit University in Ramallah, the École Normale Supérieure and Paris VIII in Paris, and the School of Criticism and Theory at Cornell. Her books include *Race and the Education of Desire: Foucault's History of Sexuality and the Colonial Order of Things* (1995), *Carnal Knowledge and Imperial Power* (2002), *Along the Archival Grain* (2009), and several edited volumes. An interview with her appears in *Public Culture* (Fall 2012).

Tyler Stovall is Professor of French History at the University of California, Berkeley (US). His most recent books include *Paris and the Spirit of 1919* (2012) and *Black France/France noire*, co-edited with Trica Keaton and T. Denean Sharpley-Whiting. He is currently writing a transnational history of modern France.

Patricia Tuitt is Professor and Executive Dean in the School of Law at Birkbeck, University of London (UK). She is the author of numerous essays on international refugee law and of the 1996 monograph, *False Images: Law's Construction of the Refugee*.

She has also written widely in the field of postcolonial theory, notably in *Race, Law, Resistance* (2004).

Stephen Turner teaches in the English Department at the University of Auckland (Aotearoa/New Zealand). He has published numerous articles on the settlement and history of Aotearoa/New Zealand, particularly with regard to media and the politics of Indigeneity. He is currently working on a manuscript concerned with Indigenous law and settler society.

Daniel Vukovich (胡德) is an Associate Professor at Hong Kong University, where he teaches a range of courses in postcolonial, literary, and theoretical studies. He is the author of *China and Orientalism: Western Knowledge Production and the PRC* (2012) and has published numerous articles and chapters in the US, UK, and China, including in *China and New Left Visions* (2012). His current book project, *Seeing Like An Other State*, focuses on the consequences for political theory and 'science' of the rise of China and, perhaps, Vietnam.

GENERAL INTRODUCTION

GRAHAM HUGGAN

POSTCOLONIALISM AND REVOLUTION

Postcolonial criticism usually ends up running behind the history it sometimes attempts to anticipate. In 2011, as this volume was finally beginning to pick up pace, it was overtaken by the cascading series of events now popularly known as the 'Arab Spring' as these rushed in to claim global media attention. Although some journalists wasted no time in categorizing the successive uprisings in Tunisia, Egypt, Libya, and elsewhere as 'spontaneous [outbreaks], contagious and unforeseen ... apparently impossible beforehand [but] inevitable afterwards' (Black 2012: vii), less excitable accounts emphasized that there had been numerous antecedents and that the uprisings might best be seen within a larger historical pattern of national and transnational social movements registering the unfinished struggle against 'liberalized autocracy' in the Arab world (for a journalistic selection, see Manhire 2012; for historical context, also Brumberg 2002; El-Mahdi 2009; McAdam et al. 2001). Unsurprisingly, the events of the 'Arab Spring' were soon picked up by postcolonial critics, most of whom continued—problematically perhaps—to see their field as being closely attuned to worldwide liberation movements (see for example Al-Rahim 2011; Bamyeh 2011; Rooney 2011; for an earlier critique of the relationship between postcolonial and liberation theory, see also Parry 2004). As one of the most prominent among them, the UK-based literary/cultural critic Caroline Rooney remarked of unfolding events in Egypt, a 'postcolonial approach [generally] attempts to engage with questions of national self-determination through attending to the cultural forms in which a nation expresses itself, reflects on itself and critiques itself' (2011: 373)—questions raised by the coming to consciousness, not so much of the people as of Arab and western leaders, who were 'abruptly awakened themselves by those who [had been] awake all along, maintaining a vigilance for the right moment to seize' (373). National consciousness aside, Rooney's approach is best characterized as Saidean rather than Fanonian. Hence her view that the events of the 'Arab Spring' have powerfully combined to challenge the 'civilizationist' narrative of Islamic threat and the lazy association of a still-Orientalized Middle East with fundamentalism and the religiously grounded rejection of modernity; and hence her insistence that what is really at stake is 'the ongoing progressive struggle [to make] Egyptian modernity possible' and for Egyptians to be able to negotiate that modernity in their own terms (372; see also the essays by Hazbun and Mignolo in Parts II and I of this volume).

At the same time, the events of the 'Arab Spring' invited a re-reckoning of the view, still common among Marxist exponents in the field, that postcolonial criticism had long since turned its back on its liberationist origins, a state of affairs generally attributed to the poststructuralist 'turn' in the 1980s with which postcolonial studies was—depending on perspective—either summarily or presumptuously identified (for critical accounts of the 'turn' and its effect on postcolonial studies, see Brennan 2007; Lazarus 2011; Parry 2004; see also Part II of this volume). This view, however intemperately expressed, needs to be taken seriously. In a recent, characteristically passionate iteration in his book *The Postcolonial Unconscious* (2011), Neil Lazarus decries the 'anti-anti-liberationist' tendencies of postcolonial criticism, which may have succeeded in positioning itself against ingrained US anti-liberationism, but is still given to disavow liberationist discourse itself as historically anachronistic (10; see also Scott 2004 below). As Lazarus suggests, the empowering *revolutionary* vocabulary that once animated a generation of anti-colonial activists—Cabral, Césaire, Fanon—has fallen into disuse, and a diluted *revisionist* vocabulary has taken its place that responds to prevailing political sentiments. These sentiments, which Lazarus jointly links to the disappointments of the Bandung era, the collapse of Soviet communism, and the ascendancy of global neoliberalism, have had the effect of putting revolutionary anti-imperialism in the shade despite its obvious and enduring relevance to 'the intensification of imperialist social relations in the times and spaces of the [contemporary] postcolonial world' (17; see also Lazarus in this volume).

Although Lazarus does not mention him, the anthropologist David Scott provides a particularly good example of this revisionist impulse. Scott's coruscating account of the Haitian Revolution of 1797–1804, *Conscripts of Modernity* (2004), concerns itself with 'our [uncertain] present after the [irreparable] collapse of the social and political hopes that went into the anticolonial imagining and postcolonial making of national sovereignties' (1). The postcolonial present, says Scott, is a present 'after Bandung': it reflects the irreversible demise of the national-liberationist ideologies that flourished during the decolonization decades. Scott's book draws primarily on C. L. R. James's magisterial 1958 account of the Haitian Revolution, *The Black Jacobins*, which he legitimately sees as 'one of the great inaugural texts of the discourse of anticolonialism', just as the Revolution itself, encompassing 'the [great] revolutionary story of the self-emancipation of New World slaves', was one of the defining socio-political events in the making of the modern world (9; for further reflections on James, see also Featherstone in this volume). However, Scott then startlingly proceeds to turn the tables on conventional readings of James's text as a 'vindicationist narrative of revolutionary overcoming'; instead, seen from the vantage point of the present, *The Black Jacobins*, and in particular the story of its Romantic revolutionary hero Toussaint L'Ouverture, is dramatically reconfigured as a critical-revisionist account of our 'tragic' postcolonial times (14). For Scott, *revolution*, which once defined the 'very horizon of radical oppositional politics and haunted the imagination of modern intellectuals', has lost its force and has become 'enfeebled [as a] salient category in our oppositional political vocabulary' (65). What is left is *revisionism*, a more-or-less radical interpretative strategy that allows Scott to reread James's work in light of the 'tragedy of colonial enlightenment' in whose wake we westerners currently live, and in whose shadow we plaintively acknowledge that 'the critical languages in which we [previously] wagered our moral vision and political hope (including the languages of black emancipation and postcolonial critique) are no longer commensurate with the world they were meant to understand, engage, and overcome' (210).

The relationship between revolution and revisionism in Scott's text is made clear in an epilogue in which, in the last and perhaps most surprising of his moves, he compares James's largely celebratory view of the Haitian Revolution with the more sceptical position taken towards revolutions in general by the political philosopher Hannah Arendt. Scott's juxtaposition of James and Arendt is surprising in other ways: Arendt's classic 1963 study *On Revolution* is, after all, hardly notable for the attention it gives to Haiti, focusing almost exclusively as it does on the French and American revolutions as paradigmatic if markedly different examples of revolution in the modern age (1990 [1963]: 18). Both revolutions, Arendt argues, were linked sets of social and political events in which the idea of *freedom* was brought together with the idea of *novelty*. Modern revolution, in this sense, is not just about the pursuit of human freedom—the basis of all revolutions—but about the replacement of an old order by a new one: it describes the inexorably unfolding historical process by which 'members of the vast majority of mankind, the low and the poor, all those who had always lived in darkness and subjection to whatever powers there were, should rise and become the supreme sovereigns of the land' (40). Arendt points out, however, that most modern revolutions have conspicuously failed to provide a lasting basis for the political exercise of freedom: in sacrificing the political to the social, they have fought shy of producing the political foundations that might turn epic revolutionary struggle into the sustainable production of civil rights and liberties. Most modern revolutions—to put this another way—have been inspired by freedom but have missed the opportunity to found it; and it is this operative distinction, potentially tragic in its consequences, that Arendt sees as marking the political spirit of our times.

Scott's approach to revolution seems uncannily similar to Arendt's, even if he understandably stops short of endorsing her Eurocentrism. More to the point, he sees James's work as being similarly informed both by a 'tragic vision of freedom' and by the compensatory recognition that the great revolutionary traditions can still be remembered and retold (2004: 214). This compensatory recognition seems unlikely to impress those—Lazarus among them—who hold to James's revolutionary Marxism; nor, I should probably add, would it have been much likely to have impressed James himself. However, I do not think it should be mistaken for defeatism. Rather, it invites revisionism: a self-conscious revisiting of the past—including the colonial past—with a primary view to seeking inspiration from its revolutionary struggles, tempered by the secondary and sober realization that these struggles have most often failed to sustain the new social and political conditions they produced. Scott implicitly allies himself here with the political theorist Bernard Yack, whose revisionist views on revolution are part-inspired, as are his own, by the late twentieth-century collapse of Soviet communism. Yack associates a longer history of modern revolutionary thought with the teleological view that posits 'total revolution' as a powerful antidote to the 'dehumanizing ethos that shapes modern society', but ultimately finds the idea of 'total revolution' both illusory and nostalgic, born out of an agonized reflection on the failure of the French Revolution to achieve its social and political goals (1992: xii, 20). What Scott objects to, as does Yack, is not the idea of revolution itself but the uncritical narrative of overcoming that accompanies it: hence their joint emphasis on revisionism as a way of returning to the inspirational beginnings of revolution without necessarily endorsing its determinate ends.

Let me be clear here: I am not trying to claim the 'victory' of postcolonial revisionism, tragic or otherwise, over revolutionary Marxism; nor do I agree with Scott's dismal view that we currently live in a 'time of postcolonial crisis in which old horizons have collapsed or evaporated and new ones have not yet taken shape' (168). However, I also happen to disagree with the view taken by Lazarus and others that contemporary postcolonial criticism has cleared a space for itself by parting the ways with the revolutionary spirit that once drove it; and I disagree even more strongly with the view, expressed most forcefully by Benita Parry, that postcolonial criticism today is largely defined by the 'post-turn' tendency to 'disown liberation discourses and practices, and indeed anti-colonialist rhetoric and organization [of all kinds]' (2004: 75). Instead, it seems to me that the postcolonial field is torn, and has been for some time now, between competing revolutionary and revisionist impulses, and that much of the intellectual momentum it continues to generate is borne—explicitly or implicitly—out of the dialectical interaction between these. Indeed, I would go so far as to argue that the very vocabulary that Lazarus, Parry, and others want to reinstate—'liberation', 'revolution', 'decolonization', etc.—never disappeared from the postcolonial lexicon in the first place; on the contrary, its meanings are continually renegotiated in a complex revisionist process that allows the relationship between past and present, or what Scott elegantly calls 'the paradoxical inscription of pasts within the present', to be productively reassessed (2004: 169).

'Memory' has probably become the key term through which this process is instantiated (see Rothberg in Part III of this volume). But memory discourses, important though these are, are only part of postcolonialism's vast, internally diversified revisionist enterprise. For if postcolonial criticism returns restlessly to the colonial past, gauging it in and for itself as well as for its multiple secretions in the present, it also critiques the teleologies that continue to inform past–present relations (Enlightenment narratives of 'progress', 'end-of-ideology' arguments about globalization, etc.: for a thoroughgoing critique of these teleologies, see the chapters by Abeysekara and Hindess in Part IV of this volume; see also some of the essays in Part V). Similarly, postcolonial criticism reinvigorates the spirit of anti-colonial resistance—the revolutionary spirit, if you will—while simultaneously recognizing the need to modify the vocabularies that surround it. This does not mean that postcolonial criticism simply moves on, adapting itself to the trends and needs of the moment. There is a crucial difference between claiming that postcolonial studies has the capacity to generate 'new discourses of resistance' (Williams 2010: 88)—which seems fair enough—and blithely suggesting that the postcolonial field is now in the process of being 'rerouted', breaking new conceptual ground and adjusting its sights towards 'neocolonial imbalances' in the contemporary globalized world (Wilson et al. 2010: 1). Opportunistic presentism, to my mind, is as much a danger to the field as unreflective historicism; and it is for this reason among several others that postcolonial studies should be dutifully suspicious towards market-driven demands that it reinvent itself—not least because the incessant proclamation of the 'new', a sure sign of the intellectual branding prevalent under late capitalism, is part of a commodifying process it explicitly contests (Huggan 2001; also Brouillette 2007 and section 3 of this chapter). Rather, postcolonial criticism might do better to re-engage in the lively battle over its own intellectual and institutional origins without becoming a prisoner to self-reflexivity—a familiar if overdiagnosed problem—and without reacting, with an anger that is predictable as it is complicit, to the latest expedient announcement of its demise (Dirlik 2003; Loomba et al. 2005; Yaeger 2007). It should probably be clear by now that I think the best way for postcolonial critics to do this is to stay true to their own revisionist instincts: the crucial question remains, though, revisionism of what kind?

POSTCOLONIALISM AS CRITICAL REVISIONISM

I have been suggesting so far that while postcolonialism's revolutionary impetus holds open a theoretical debate about beginnings—a debate Arendt sees as being synonymous with revolution—its revisionist dimensions invite the practical reconsideration of endings (e.g. the question of liberation 'after independence', the question of affiliation and alignment 'after Bandung'). I want to examine this dialectical relationship further; but before I do so, a few preliminary observations on revisionism seem in order. While revisionism in its dictionary definition refers primarily to the theory or practice of revising one's view of a previously accepted political doctrine, the term is probably most relevant to postcolonial studies in its broader historical sense.[1] Historical

---

[1] Historical revisionism is, it seems to me, more intrinsic to the postcolonial field than its literary counterpart, critical rereading, which—partly as an effect of the alliance between postcolonialism and postmodernism—flourished during the 1980s and 1990s, the most obvious example being Ashcroft, Griffiths, and Tiffin's *The Empire Writes Back* (1989). For a while, it seemed as if postcolonial revisionism effectively meant *literary* revisionism: see Lee's confident assertion that 'most postcolonial projects have a common denominator: the critical rereading of texts in the Western canon that have been thought of as embodying universal and transhistorical values' (1997: 89). There are several by now familiar problems with this view: the assumption of a more or less transparent correlation between colonialism as a 'politico-economic reality' and colonialism as a 'system of cultural representation' (Lee 1997: 89); the use of literature as historical evidence; the tendency to reinscribe binary systems (e.g. through the now virtually defunct 'writing back' model); and the consolidation of postcolonialism as a predominantly 'reactive idiom' (Suleri 1992: 21; see also Lee 1997: 109). There are reactive tendencies as well, of course, in historical revisionism: the easy view, for example, that there are 'hegemonic' and 'counter-hegemonic' forms of historical writing or—an argument sometimes used by so-called 'anti-revisionist' historians—that solid bodies of historical evidence can be called upon that that resist or surpass ideology-driven attempts to recast them from a particular perspective. Postcolonial revisionism has not always avoided these traps, but it generally proceeds from the not unreasonable view that history is open to contending interpretations, and that such interpretations are 'inextricably associated with political agendas and social identities' from the start (Howe 2000: 232).

revisionism has had a bad press, and it is not hard to see the reasons. Revisionist history—it has been said often enough—is less likely to be progressive than reactionary; it is frequently accused of being biased or reductive; while, at another level, it is sometimes dismissed as tautological, i.e. all historicizing is revisionist in one way or another in so far as it takes 'a second look at what has already been otherwise', just as history attempts the impossible recuperation of that which is already lost (Radhakrishnan 2008: 69; see also Howe 2000).[2] At the same time, revisionist history is by definition quarrelsome, confrontational—qualities always likely to endear it to postcolonial scholars, whose interventionist stance on colonial history-making naturally inclines them to rub history against the grain (see Stoler and some of the other essays in Part I of this volume). Not that postcolonial revisionism is concerned with setting the record straight: it does not seek a corrective to the past so much as to trouble accepted versions of it; and it is adamant that the past, impinging as it does on the present, needs to be returned to again and again. But as the theorist R. Radhakrishnan (on whose work I am drawing here) suggests, there is a 'double-tongued truth [in] any revisionist vision' (2008: 75), one necessarily tied to the plurality of perspectives:

> The semantics of revisionism is necessarily double, and not just in the context of the antagonistic contact zone between subjugated and dominant knowledges, but in a broader theoretical sense as well. For example, how are the specific politics of feminist revisionism or postcolonial revisionism related to the general nature of revisionism as such? What are the differences between patriarchal dominant historiography as the object of a reading or brushing against the grain and the historiography of colonialism or that of normative heterosexuality or that of racism subjected to a similar antagonistic reading? What are the specific assumptions about nature, human nature, gender, race and ethnicity, and sexuality that drive the semantics of each revisionist project under the broad syntactic umbrella called revisionism as such? (76)

These are not rhetorical questions, but they point to the potential dilemma of an infinite regress of revisionism in which the plurality of possible perspectives stretches out ad infinitum to leave what Radhakrishnan calls, loosely following Foucault, a 'revisionist

---

[2] As Stephen Howe apologetically remarks near the beginning of an essay that paradoxically seeks to *recuperate* revisionism in the context of ultra-nationalist accounts of Irish and Israeli-Palestinian history: '"Revisionism" is an awful label, politically as well as historiographically. In different contexts … it has meant everything from people who think the English Civil War had short-term political causes rather than long-term social ones, to people who deny that Nazis murdered any Jews. It has meant maximalist or physical-force Zionists (Benjamin Netanyahu's ideological forebears) and Dublin journalists who disliked Charles Haughey. Meanwhile all historians are in some narrower sense revisionists, challenging previous accounts and interpretations with newer ones. Whether in academic contexts or political ones, the term might well be thought meaningless' (2000: 230). As Howe later makes clear, however, revisionism is not meaningless at all and can usefully counteract the very bias of which it is often accused; there are thus 'good' and 'bad' revisionisms, the latter of which require further revisionism—a point frequently made by postcolonial critics, two recent contexts being 'civilizationist' cultural analysis (Huntington) and 'revisionist' imperial history (Ferguson). I will come back to this point later in my discussion of the paradigmatically revisionist work of Edward Said.

politics of ongoing questions' with no discernible end in sight (76; see also Foucault 1970). Such 'open revisionism' is not necessarily a bad thing, but there is always the risk that it turn into the equivalent of a postmodern hall of mirrors in which historical truths, while rarely secure or guarantee-able, are held in permanent abeyance. As Radhakrishnan, otherwise sympathetic to this kind of poststructuralist approach, puts it in pithier language, 'is the look back towards the past necessary for the look forward into the future? [And if it is], which look towards the past is legitimate and historical, and which apocryphal and self-deluded?' (76).

Radhakrishnan turns, appropriately enough, to Fanon for support: Fanon the *revolutionary*, wedded to the cause of decolonization as a revolutionary practice—'a program of disorder ... which sets out to change the order of the world', he dramatically calls it (Fanon 1965 [1963]: 36)—but also Fanon the *revisionist*, 'both solicitous and suspicious of history', committed to mobilizing historical categories yet aware at the same time of the simultaneous elusiveness and ideological malleability of the historical past (Radhakrishnan 2008: 76). Perhaps the best way of understanding Fanon's revisionist programme, Radhakrishnan suggests, is to see it as an attempt to 'rediscover the native as the postcolonial African national' (77). Yet the 'native', as Fanon himself seems to admit, is neither the most solid nor the most reliable of categories; and the history he seeks to remake occupies equally insecure and violently contested ground (for a discussion of Fanon's 'native', see Farrier and Tuitt in this volume). Fanon's revisionism is revolutionary, we might say, in so far as it programmes an attempt to reverse the historically sanctioned structures of power on which colonialism founds itself: decolonization is not just liberation but revolution, pitting two implacable opponents against each other in a bloody struggle at the end of which—Fanon puts it in the strongest possible terms—'the last shall be first' (1965 [1963]: 37). But Fanon's revolution (which he makes clear is as much internal as external, as much psychically grounded as physically fought) is conducted at the same time in the watchful spirit of a revisionism that recognizes that there are not just contending perspectives on history but contending histories, each of which lays claim to the present; thus, while 'the native intellectual [can] repudiate the authority of colonial history, [he cannot abolish] its "given-ness"', and the project of postcolonial revisionism becomes a confrontational 'encounter with that history which is not one's own' (Radhakrishnan 2008: 78).

It is instructive here to compare Radhakrishnan's brief discussion with the more detailed analysis of Fanon to be found in Lazarus's previously mentioned book *The Postcolonial Unconscious*. This latter analysis takes up its place alongside what Lazarus calls a series of 'revisionary' readings of theorists central to postcolonial studies, with an unsurprising but understandable emphasis on Said and Fanon, the two most frequently cited 'founding figures' of the field (for different views on this, see the essays by Abeysekara and Brennan in this volume). 'Re-revisionary' is more appropriate in so far as Lazarus is eager to rebut poststructuralist readings of both figures in the name of a postmodernism-inspired 'postcolonialism' he relentlessly opposes. The ferocity of Lazarus's attack is understandable; for at stake in his view is nothing less than a 'dispute or battle over postcolonial meaning' in which 'Said' and 'Fanon' feature as catalytic agents for the transformative understanding of the postcolonial field (2011: 184).

As should already be apparent, Lazarus is less interested than Radhakrishnan in uncovering the revisionist tendencies embedded within Fanon's revolutionary thinking, and more concerned with mapping what looks suspiciously like a corrective, Marxist-liberationist reading onto previous critical accounts of Fanon's work. This path is opened up via a patient reading of David Macey's 2000 biography, *Fanon: A Life*, itself a revisionist text that, in Lazarus's words, 'breaks open the field into which it intervenes, enforcing in the process a reconfiguration not only of its boundaries but also of its internal arrangements and relations' (2011: 162). As Lazarus explains, the biography is divided into 'two conflicting and incompatible schemas' (163). The first of these is a liberationist Third-Worldism linked to 'the upsurge of revolutionary anticolonial nationalism in the post-1945 period'; the second ensues from what Lazarus calls 'the containment and rolling back of insurgent anticolonial nationalism by the imperialist powers [especially the United States] since 1975 or so … and the [corresponding] obsolescence of the earlier liberationist Third-Worldist ideologeme' (163; see also Lazarus in this volume). The first schema recuperates a 'revolutionary' Fanon, (although, as Macey shows, this celebratory vision needs to be complicated), while the second presents its revisionist, 'postcolonial' reverse image. In Macey's words,

> [If] 'Third Worldist' readings [have] largely ignored the Fanon of *Peau noire, masques blancs* [*Black Skin, White Masks*], post-colonial readings [have concentrated] almost exclusively on that text and studiously avoided the question of violence. The Third Worldist Fanon was an apocalyptic creature; the post-colonial Fanon worries about identity politics, and often about his own sexual identity, but he is no longer angry. (2000: 28, also quoted in Lazarus 2011: 165)

As the sardonic tone of this passage makes clear, Macey has little truck with the 'postcolonial' Fanon, a confusing, self-contradictory image he sees as being almost wilfully decontextualized—caricatured even—in the blind service of poststructuralist critique (2000: 27). Lazarus latches gleefully onto Macey's peremptory dismissal of postcolonialism's revisionist assessment of Fanon as a 'deconstructive critic of (western) humanism' (Lazarus 2011: 162), reserving particular scorn for his own *bête noire*, Homi Bhabha, whose polymorphous Fanon, like Henry Louis Gates's before it, seems impossible to square 'either with Fanon's actual writings or with the trajectory of Fanon's own career' (Lazarus 2011: 166; see also Bhabha 2005; Gates 1991).

Like Macey, Lazarus sides unequivocally with the 'revolutionary' Fanon, summarizing some of the main themes of his work as follows: 'revolutionary nationalist anticolonialism, violence and counter-violence, popular political mobilisation, the relation between party and people and between proletarian and peasant classes, the role of culture and ideology in the furtherance of the struggle, and the Algerian conflict and its relevance for and relation to "African" and "Third World" liberation struggles' (Lazarus 2011: 174). Unlike Macey, however, Lazarus energetically defends the contemporary relevance of these struggles. To some extent echoing Scott, Macey suggests that Fanon, for all the inspirational quality of his rage, 'does not speak for the tragic Algeria of today' (2000: 503). 'The themes of Third World solidarity and unity,' he continues, 'of a vision of pan-Africanism and of the liberating power of violence have not worn well. For a generation, Fanon was a prophet. He has become a witness to the process of decolonization but, whilst his discussion of racism remains valid, he has little to say about the outcome of that process' (503). Lazarus disagrees with this. As he points out, Fanon's influence—particularly his writings on nationalism and decolonization—continues to be apparent in a number of contemporary liberation struggles; and, to revisit my remarks about the 'Arab Spring' at the beginning, if postcolonial intellectuals across the Arab world and in support of recent events there have certainly read their Said, it also seems highly likely that they have read, and have reflected deeply on, their Fanon. More to the point, the general struggle against imperialism continues. As Lazarus concludes, the supposed 'new world order' of today has turned out not to be so different from the 'old' one it is often prematurely seen as supplanting (see Parts II and V of this volume); and contra Macey, he considers Fanon's committed struggle against this order to be as urgent for our times as it was for his (2011: 180–1).

It should be clear, I hope, that I am sympathetic to this; yet there are problems. For one, as Lazarus admits, the 'revolutionary' Fanon is no more transparent than the 'postcolonial' one; and for another, postcolonial criticism—despite Macey's and Lazarus's damaging portrayals of it—has been attuned to, if not necessarily persuaded by, the 'revolutionary' Fanon from the start. To return to Radhakrishnan, there is a sense in which Fanon remains theoretically suspicious of the very binary categories (colonizer/ colonized, master/slave, etc.) that are most practically useful to him; this is not necessarily to turn Fanon into a deconstructive critic, but rather to acknowledge that there is a crucial link between the *practical* (revolutionary) project of smashing 'the unequal historical conditions brought into existence by binarity' and the *theoretical* (revisionist) enterprise of 'dismantling the very structure of binarity itself' (Radhakrishnan 2008: 77; see also Part III of this volume). The main problem with Macey's approach to Fanon is that it reinstalls binarity even as it seeks to question it —a problem shared by Lazarus across the seemingly unbridgeable divide in their political viewpoints. The battle over Fanon, in both cases, turns out to be one over the legitimacy of revisionism. Revisionism, in this last sense, should not be confused with either renewal or return, though it should be understood as shuttling unceasingly between these. Rather, it is about the enunciative possibility of *reclamation* as a political speech act.[3] Lazarus's

---

[3.] Probably the best example of this form of critical revisionism is the dispersed (in both a geographical and methodological sense) 'rescue work' of the India-based Subaltern Studies Collective, one of whose primary aims is to revalidate histories of peasant struggle that are often conspicuously missing from official historical accounts. One of the problems of the SSC—although, to be fair, it is a problem that is explicitly recognized by many of its members—has been the tendency to work within European historical categories. For a useful recent critique of this tendency, see Gajarawala, who sees the SSC's 'project of recovery [as helping] to build a revolutionary historical consciousness' (2011: 586), but also points out the inappropriateness of such explicitly or implicitly linear historical categories for subaltern social groups, e.g. Dalits, whose collective sense of self and of historical emplacement seems to require a different understanding of historical knowledge than that provided in the SSC's revolutionary-cum-revisionist historical accounts.

revisionary reading reclaims Fanon with a practical view towards reusing him; Macey's memorializes Fanon in Arendt's tragic sense of imaginatively reclaiming the revolutionary spirit that he once embodied and is now at significant risk of being lost.

These alternative speech acts are not mutually exclusive. On the contrary, it is the dialectical interaction between them that guarantees postcolonialism's dynamic status as a self-perpetuating form of *critical revisionism*. Postcolonialism, we might then say, is a performative mode of critical revisionism, consistently directed at the colonial past and assessing its legacies for the present, but also intermittently focusing on those forms of colonialism that have surfaced more recently in the context of an increasingly globalized but incompletely decolonized world. This might add a certain methodological clarity to earlier, equally wholesale definitions of postcolonialism as 'a studied engagement with the experience of colonialism and its past and present effects, both at the level of ex-colonial societies as well as at the level of more general global developments thought to be the after-effects of empire' (Quayson 2000: 25). But it continues to leave us with a series of crucially unanswered questions: which kinds of revisionism are to be performed within the field, and how is their legitimacy to be measured? And if postcolonialism is best seen, as Radhakrishnan and others imply, in terms of a *combination* of revisionisms, which combination works best or will this necessarily depend on what particular object or process is being studied, what particular contingencies attach to it, and what broader institutional benefits derive from a particular intellectual task? There seems little point, in this last context, in arguing that postcolonial studies lacks institutional support when there has been plenty of evidence for some time now to suggest precisely the opposite; a better question to ask is whether it retains its critical edge under institutional conditions where it has so obviously been transformed into an intellectual orthodoxy or, as Homi Bhabha has said more generally of critical theory, in circumstances marked by the constitutive tension between 'institutional containment' and 'revisionary force' (1994: 32; for more critical views of this, see Dirlik 1994 and Huggan 2001). To ask this question another way: at what point does postcolonial revisionism merely recite as it reclaims; when do its histories from below and counter-canonical readings become all too easily predictable? And can it move beyond what Lazarus calls its 'fetishization' of representation: its theoretically inflected obsession with western systems of knowledge and belief and the translation of those systems into self-consuming artefacts; its dogged insistence on tracing the lines of control and power that underlie the production of colonial and postcolonial cultural texts? (Lazarus 2011: 114)

One perfectly serviceable answer to this is that it does not need to. What registers as obsession to some will doubtless look more like engagement, even commitment, to others, and it seems legitimate to argue that the postcolonial field, while long since relinquishing its earlier, text-based claims to be 'transgressive', has retained its oppositional capacity to harness a theoretically and historically informed analysis of the shifting politics of textual representation to the situational demands of contemporary cultural critique. 'Critical consciousness', Edward Said's capacious term, still seems the best one to encapsulate this, and Said's—to my mind—remains the most convincing attempt to

account for postcolonialism as a committed mode of revisionist knowledge, both rigorously self-aware and resolutely adversarial, that dedicates itself to the service of human
freedom in the context of a world historically conditioned by colonial relations of power.
Whether it is possible to square this kind of commitment with revolutionary solidarity
is another matter. Indeed, as Said would repeatedly insist throughout his work, especially in his reflections on the oppositional role of the intellectual, critical consciousness
should not be confused with solidarity. Thus, despite his lifelong commitment to the
Palestinian cause, he always argued that, as an independent intellectual, it was his duty
to forswear the kind of blind loyalty to liberationist causes that might short-circuit critical thinking. Intellectual support for liberation struggles was, he repeatedly affirmed,
vitally necessary. But the following passage (from *Representations of the Intellectual*) is
typical for the caveat it adds to this:

> Loyalty to [an oppressed] group's fight for survival cannot draw in the intellectual so
> far as to narcotize the critical sense, or reduce its imperatives, which are always to go
> beyond survival to questions of political liberation, to critiques of the leadership, to
> presenting alternatives that are too often marginalized or pushed aside as irrelevant
> to the main battle at hand. (1994: 41)

Clearer still is this passage, from an essay originally published in *The London Review of
Books* and later included in the 1999 collection *Letters in Transit*:

> For myself, I have been unable to live an uncommitted or suspended life: I have not
> hesitated to declare my affiliation with an extremely unpopular cause. On the other
> hand, I have always reserved the right to be critical, even when criticism conflicted
> with solidarity or with what others expected in the name of national loyalty. There
> is a definite, almost palpable discomfort to such a position, especially given the
> irreconcilability of the two constituencies, and the two lives they have required.
> (1999b: 108–9).

'Solidarity' is a troublesome term in Said's indissolubly mixed critical vocabulary. Thus,
while at times he seems almost to turn his back on it—'never solidarity before criticism'
is a well-known Said credo (1994: 32)—at others it becomes one of the foundational
principles in the broad, uncompromisingly confrontational but also unfailingly generous humanist vision he offers to a violently divided world (for different perspectives on
this, see Lazarus 2011 and Robbins 2004). So much is clear from the praise he showers
on Fanon and James, the former for the visionary power with which he was able to trace
an 'immense cultural shift from the terrain of nationalist independence to the theoretical domain of liberation' (1993: 324), and the latter for his inspirational capacity in
reaffirming the 'value of the epic struggle for human emancipation and enlightenment'
(1989: 126). In either case, Said stops short of endorsing revolutionary *violence* without
necessarily letting go of the idea of revolutionary *consciousness*, a term that also comes
into play in the 1995 re-edition of *Orientalism*, where he speaks, in proudly acknowledging the original's widespread influence, of a recent 'revolution of consciousness of

women, minorities and marginals so powerful as to affect mainstream thinking world-wide' (1995a: 350).

This 'revolution of consciousness' is a long way, of course, from the violent independence wars that inspired James and Fanon, and just as far from the class-based analyses that have underpinned Marxist revolutionary struggle. Rather, it corresponds to a humanistic enlargement of vision that Said relates, here as elsewhere in his work, to postcolonialism, the 'historical and political imperatives' of which are connected to 'emancipation [and] revisionist attitudes towards history and culture', indicating that the postcolonial field as a whole, for all its postmodernist prevarications, is marked by 'a general approach to universal concerns' (1995a: 351–2). This recuperative reading of postcolonialism is out of step with Said's earlier, stinging critiques of it (see for example Said 1986b, 1995b; also Williams 2001). What interests me here, though, is not the much commented-on inconsistency of Said's views but his direct association of postcolonialism with *revisionism*—a revisionism he clearly links to general liberationist principles if not to any particular revolutionary cause.

Revisionism, for Said, is not just a question of politically motivated rereading; it is a committed if non-partisan act in which cultural critique is brought into line with political engagement. This is not to be confused, though, with political *activism*. Said, in this sense, would most likely have disagreed with Robert Young's succinct working definition of postcolonialism as 'nam[ing] a politics and philosophy of activism that contests [contemporary conditions of cultural and economic] disparity, and so continues in a new way the anti-colonial struggles of the past' (Young 2003: 7). Said's stance comes closer, though, to Young's immediate qualification of this definition. For postcolonialism's activist potential, Young goes on to explain, does not usually consist—although it certainly can consist—of an incitement to direct material struggle; rather it registers an attempt to 'intervene, to force its alternative knowledges into the power structures of the west as well as the non-west' (2003: 7). Dubious binaries notwithstanding, Young's valid point is that the grounds for continuing anti-colonial struggle are as much epistemological as they are physical and material; relational too in so far as postcolonial theory is 'about relations between ideas and practices: relations of harmony, relations of conflict, generative relations between different peoples and their cultures [that underlie] a world that has been changed by struggle and which [the field's] practitioners intend to change further' if they can (Young 2003: 7; see also Part III of this volume).

The key word to my mind here is 'intervention'. As its intermediary status implies, intervention operates in the interstices between cultural critique and political advocacy: its primary goal is to raise general consciousness of injustice rather than to provide a specific rationale for struggle, armed or otherwise; and its baseline recognition is that while theory is no direct substitute for politics, theory and politics are inextricably entwined (see Boehmer in Part III of this volume). For Said, as for Young, postcolonialism is best understood as a sustained form of intellectual interventionism, at once individually committed to the parallel pursuits of freedom and justice and collectively driven by the will to change a flagrantly unequal, unevenly developed world. This oppositional tradition is linked, for both, to the inheritance of anti-colonial thought: to 'the radical legacy of its political determinations, its refusal to accept the status quo, its transformation of epistemologies, [and] its establishment of new forms of discursive and political power' (Young 2001: 428). Where the two most obviously part company is in their understanding of the foundational role of revolutionary violence in achieving social change, with Said tending to distance himself from the Fanonian views that Young explicitly embraces: that anti-colonial struggle is essentially a form of revolutionary war; that violence is intrinsic to it; and that the ongoing battle against colonialism is one against violence 'in its natural state' (Fanon 1965 [1963]: 48; see also Young 2001: 294–5).

As Young makes clear, however, this is by no means the *only* way of theorizing anti-colonial struggle—non-violent options are also possible.[4] 'Violence versus non-violence', he epigrammatically says, 'that [is] the anti-colonial question'; but as he then readily concedes, the reality of most twentieth- and twenty-first-century anti-colonial resistance movements, whether incorporated or not into national liberation struggles, is that violent and non-violent tactics have been strategically combined (2001: 296). This revised view again approaches that of Said, who, for all that his temperament is significantly more inclined to combative debate than bloody conflict, to the open-ended spirit of intellectual dissidence than goal-oriented programmes of revolutionary militancy, never goes quite so far as to dismiss the moral legitimacy of force (Said 1988, 1993; see also Brennan 2007; Parry 2001). That said, Said also repeatedly insists throughout his work that liberation struggles of both the present and the past, however heroically framed, are by no means immune from criticism, and that the ideologies of intractable difference that drive them consciously or unconsciously suppress the cross-cutting alliances and overlapping activities that are the marks of even the most irreconcilably polarized of human conflicts. 'Ideologies of difference', he typically complains in a blistering 1986 review essay on the Jewish American cultural critic Michael Walzer, 'are a great deal less satisfactory than impure genres, people, activities; separation and discrimination are often not as estimable as connecting and crossing over; moral and military victories are not always such wonderful things' (1986b: 106).

---

[4] Gandhi—who remains something of a forgotten figure in postcolonial criticism—is central to Young's argument here. Young counterpoints Gandhi and Fanon as complementary if profoundly different anti-colonial hero figures by showing that, while the latter moved 'from analysis of the disabling violence of colonialism to advocating military violence against the colonial regime', the former 'combined strategies of non-violent non-cooperation with a more widespread psychological resistance, arguing that they were both more ethical and more effective than any kind of violence' (2001: 323). While Young is careful not to dismiss either option, he implicitly suggests that non-violence needs to be de-idealized, and that it effectively worked in a 'negative dialectic with the perpetual possibility and reality of violence' in the India of Gandhi's time (324; see also McGonegal 2009). For a recent essay that *re*idealizes non-violence, associating it with Gandhi as a 'revolutionary' anti-colonial figure, see Trivedi (2011). While Trivedi not unreasonably argues that there continues to be a 'monumental mismatch' (547) between Gandhian legacies of non-violence and orthodox (Fanonian) postcolonial accounts of the role of violence in anti-colonial struggle, he somewhat spoils the point by assimilating the latter uncritically to 'Marxist discourse', thereby missing the revisionism that is integral to both.

Here, as so often in his work, Said's chosen emphasis is on the Israeli-Palestinian conflict, which he interprets in terms of morally competing, but also historically intersecting, national narratives. To offer wholehearted support for one, as Said unabashedly does, does not necessarily involve wholesale rejection of the other; indeed, as he goes on to suggest in a later essay, 'Israelis and Palestinians are now so intertwined through history, geography and political actuality that it seems to me absolute folly to try and plan the future of one without that of the other' (1999b: 19; see also Robbins 2004). Measured statements such as this have been eagerly latched upon as evidence of Said's broad humanistic support for intercultural reconciliation (see for example Bové 1993). Yet 'reconciliation' is not a term that features widely in Said's expansive cultural-political vocabulary; and most common when it does are pained assertions of its opposite ('The Zionist-Israeli narrative and the Palestinian one are irreconcilable ... and this irreconcilability was already quite obvious to several generations of early Zionist leaders and thinkers, as of course it was to all the Palestinians', 1999c: n.p.), or steely refusals to entertain the very possibility of reconciliation in circumstances where it smacks of moral compromise or political accommodationism ('I [have] learned from Adorno that reconciliation under duress is both cowardly and inauthentic: better a lost cause than a triumphant one, more satisfying a sense of the provisional and contingent than the proprietary solidity of permanent ownership ... I have [long since] accepted the irreconcilability of the various conflicting, or at least incompletely harmonized, aspects of what, cumulatively, I appear to have stood for', 1999a: 112–13).

One might argue here that 'reconciliation' (like 'solidarity') can mean very different things at different times in Said's work, and that its meanings can alter within the space of a few sentences. One might also reasonably expect from a critic one of whose most important books (*Culture and Imperialism*) ends with a chapter entitled 'Freedom from Domination in the Future', that the prospect of framing creative alternatives to intractable histories of separatist identity and conflict is an attractive one (Said 1993; see also Bové 1993; McGonegal 2009). 'Reconciliation', in this last sense, may yet be seen to emerge in Said's work as the utopian horizon of a sustained imaginative effort— a self-consciously revisionist attempt to narrativize shared histories and experiences which, moving beyond naturalized histories of conflict and antagonism, position themselves strategically against the automatic and repeating gestures of a 'politics of blame' (Said 1993: 19). As Paul Bové, whose ideas I have been parsing here, explains more fully,

> Said's understanding of shared experience calls forth narratives of common history that are ... the best hope for overcoming the stories of conflict, separation, and radical purity or identity that horrify the world and form the morbid and deadly cultures of radical nationalism. At the same time, this is no groundless hope. Said has understood two all-important things. [T]he first [of these] is historical: ... reconciliation is needed and possible [at a time when] division is doing its worst [*sic*] ... [while the] second is cultural: narratives have formed nations but now other narratives form relations across nations, against divisive commitments to identity and purity. Always Said's thinking moves in two directions because the realities he is trying to understand develop complexly, but not necessarily as contradictions.

Nationalisms form communities against imperial occupation; yet nationalisms threaten division and separation. So there is [in Said's words] 'a noticeable pull away from separatist nationalism toward a more integrative view of human community and human liberation'. (Bové 1993: 267–8)

If Bové's preliminary account of the reconciliatory aspects of Said's 'contrapuntal' thought is convincing, his subsequent, almost hysterical dismissal of its postcolonial dimensions is not. From Bové's scandalized liberal-humanist perspective, Said needs rescuing from the legion of leftist 'ideologues' and postcolonial 'opportunists' who see the promise of reconciliation as no more than a 'collaborationist sell-out', and whose collectively attributed aim is to 'weaken the vision of [his] work, to undermine the truths of complex historical experience and identities, [to] promote conflict (which, outside academia, is often truly murderous), and [to] impoverish human culture and so threaten the human species itself' (1993: 269). It seems worth pointing out that Said's friends, diverse though these are, have not generally tended to double as postcolonialism's enemies; and that the continuing battle over Said and other postcolonial critics has often been engaged most vigorously by those who seem to have had the least acquaintance with their work (for different if largely compatible versions of this argument, see Brennan 2007 and Huggan 2005). My larger point though has to do with reconciliation itself, which has recently become a lively debating point in postcolonial studies. What are we to make of this 'reconciliatory' strand in contemporary postcolonial theory and criticism, which seems initially at least to be so profoundly at odds with the field's revolutionary credentials? Are 'revolutionary' and 'reconciliatory' postcolonialisms mutually exclusive or does their negotiated relationship with critical revisionism offer a new, triangulated way of looking at and creatively accounting for the constitutive contradictions in the postcolonial field?

POSTCOLONIALISM AND RECONCILIATION

I have argued thus far that postcolonial theory and criticism might best be seen in terms of a linked set of not necessarily compatible revisionisms, which are as much creative engagements with the present as they are critical interrogations of the past. These revisionisms enter into a complex relationship with the history of revolutionary and liberationist thought, the dialectical aspects of which have neither been accepted nor appreciated; this relationship significantly complicates the manufactured binaries (poststructuralism versus Marxism, culturalism versus materialism, etc.) which—ironically to a greater degree than one might have thought would be the field's formative binary, the colonizer versus the colonized—have tended to dominate 'in-house' discussions of the nature and function of postcolonial studies to date. The introduction of a third term, 'reconciliation', risks muddying the waters further still, not least because it appears so out of step with postcolonialism's putatively radical credentials (for a lively exchange on the would-be radicalism of postcolonial thought, see the essays in Part III of this volume). Predictably, it is the field's Marxists who have been particularly scathing, seeing reconciliation as little more than an ideological smokescreen for dominant cultural and economic interests, an irresponsible escape from continuing historical obligations, and a politically expedient initiative to champion the supposedly reparative effects of negotiation, collaboration, and reciprocity in what remains a fundamentally divided and consequently *un*reconciled world. For materialist critics like Benita Parry, for instance, the consensus politics of reconciliation represents more of an obstacle to than a catalyst for social transformation: the symbolic possibilities of reconciliation should not be dismissed, but nor should they be prematurely celebrated, and 'our best hope for universal emancipation lies in remaining [discontented with the present] and unreconciled to the past' (2005: 25).

Non-Marxists too have shown considerable scepticism towards the usefulness of reconciliation as a sustainable idiom for postcolonial studies. The Australian-based cultural critic Simon During, for example, has provocatively opposed 'reconciliatory' to 'critical' postcolonialisms, seeing the postmodernist vocabulary (ambivalence, hybridity, mimicry, etc.) of the former as having long since passed its sell-by date, and suggesting that the necessary critique of 'reconciliatory' postcolonialism has led, not to a reconstituted postcolonial studies, but to a discernible and irreversible shift from postcolonial to global studies as more appropriate to the cross-disciplinary study of contemporary society and culture in today's intricately interconnected world (1998: 31–2). Needless to say, I disagree with During, if not necessarily with Parry, but the most interesting question in both cases is what 'reconciliation' actually stands for: what sense, if any, can be made out of such an apparently misleading and politically malleable term? A second question comes to the fore here: *why* has the term become so prominent and why is it now so often written about; why has there been what Jill Scott calls a veritable 'explosion of [academic publishing] in the areas of reconciliation, transitional justice, and conflict resolution' in areas such as philosophy, psychology, sociology, political science, literature, and law? (2010: n.p.). And a third: *how* can reconciliation be recuperated for postcolonial studies, and in what kind of relationship to revolutionary anti-colonial thought and postcolonial critical revisionism, which I am arguing here—against the grain perhaps—are the two dialectically interrelated paradigms that structure the postcolonial field?

Let me take these questions in turn, though for obvious reasons I will focus on the third one. As decent a working definition of reconciliation as any is that provided by the political theorists Brandon Hamber and Gráinne Kelly (2009), who see it as 'developing a mutual conciliatory accommodation between antagonistic or formerly antagonistic persons or groups', at the heart of which is 'the preparedness of people to anticipate a shared future' (287). This definition, while perhaps too general to be truly useful, has the advantage of separating reconciliation from forgiveness, which is usually understood as having a religious source; of seeing it as a pragmatic—and often difficult—process rather than as an ideal product; and of envisaging that process in dialogical, continually renegotiated and renegotiable terms. As Hamber and Kelly propose, reconciliation is—or at least should be—an engine of social, political, and economic change;

both material and symbolic, at once individual and collective, it aims to acknowledge without simultaneously drawing a line under the past (2009: 299; see also McGonegal 2009; Quinn 2009; J. Scott 2010).

It is not difficult to see why reconciliation processes, framed in these generous terms, should be attractive at a time when the language of apology, compensation, and redress has entered mainstream political vocabularies all over the world, and when the social and economic realities of globalization have arguably brought with them a heightened awareness of structural inequalities, systemic interdependencies, and the collective need for both theoretical and practical considerations of what it means to share space, but not necessarily values, in a technologically connected but politically and economically sep-arated world (for a discussion of the links between 'globalism' and 'global consciousness', see Part V of this volume). Nor is it difficult to see why these processes—many of which have colonial roots—should be of keen interest to postcolonial scholarship, operating as it currently is in the wake of an 'ethical turn' evidenced in the revived (rather than strictly new) attention to trauma theory, memory studies, critical cosmopolitanism, and the dis-course of human rights. Reconciliation also forms part of a revived interest in utopian thinking in postcolonial theory and criticism that takes in work as diverse as Derrida's treatises on the 'promises' of democracy and friendship; growing realizations of the con-ceptual limits of critique (see Abeysekara in this volume); a rethinking of commitment and community in future-oriented contexts; a shift from individual guilt to collective responsibility; and a reassessment of the productive role of the creative imagination in thinking what Julie McGonegal optimistically calls 'the possibility of a radically differ-ent future, a world beyond the politics of pain and despair enacted by colonialism and its various aftermaths' (2009: 14). Finally, however, it is not difficult to see why these processes should elicit considerable suspicion and why reconciliation's practical prob-lems might be seen as outweighing its idealistic promises: the legal problems of who adjudicates and who 'forgives'; the political problems of agency and authority; the his-torical problems of closure and teleology; and the overriding structural problem of how to bring about 'a radical revision to existing relations of inequality' (McGonegal 2009: 33) without previously securing the transformed material conditions that would seem necessary to bring such revised relations about (see Parry above).

An illustrative case study might be useful here. Like Parry, the Australian-based geog-rapher Jane Jacobs sees reconciliation as an impediment to change rather than a facilita-tor of it, concentrating her attack on the pre-Apology reconciliation debates in Australia (for a post-Apology update, though written in much the same vein, see Johnson 2011; see also Hindess in Part IV and, in a related if non-identical New Zealand context, Smith and Turner in Part IV of this volume). For Jacobs, the collective pursuit of reconcili-ation in postcolonial Australia is part of a state-sanctioned national narrative: it cor-responds, that is, to an official revisionist strategy of 'correcting the national sense of self' (2007: 208). Jacobs sees this strategy in terms of (1) a 're-indigenization' of national belonging and (2) an assimilative management of anti-colonial resistance, with both of these being similarly rephrased in postcolonial revisionist terms. Reconciliation, she suggests, 'may not stop certain uncomfortable "truths" [e.g. about Australia's colonial past] being told', but is designed to prevent these from getting too close and affecting 'the existing order of things' (217). Reconciliation, in other words, offers a *revisionist* but strictly *non-revolutionary* story of indigenous resistance, then reclaims that story—and by corollary its players—in the national interest: 'Reconciled (non-Aboriginal) Australia wants the grand moments of colonial triumph to be chastened by historically contained memories of Aboriginal opposition', but it also prefers its resistance in the past, as 'something that happened *then* but is remembered *now*' (216; her italics).[5]

Writing more than a decade later in the wake of Kevin Rudd's much-applauded official apology to indigenous Australians, Miranda Johnson recodes, but also reconfirms, this postcolonial revisionist narrative. What is being valued in post-Apology Australian reconciliation debates, Johnson suggests, is indigenous peoples' 'primordial attachment to place and community' in the face of historical injustice; what is *not* being valued is the political autonomy of indigenous peoples themselves (2011: 188). Reconciliation, seen this way, reinforces the political authority of the postcolonial settler state even as it claims to apologize to its victims; it performs what Lazarus might call the 'anti-anti-liberationist' gesture of appealing to an oppositional (anti-colonial) narrative of indigenous presence which is then repackaged in inclusive national (postcolonial) terms (2011: 199; see also Smith and Turner in Part II of this volume for a New Zealand variation on this assimilative method).

This smacks of 'bad' revisionism, as Howe might call it (see note 2), but that is not all it is. For, as Jacobs suggests, reconciliation processes in Australia and elsewhere have notably failed to corral indigenous resistance into the closely guarded national spaces of 'calm co-habitation' (208) their respective governments claim officially to be fashioning; instead, these failures have opened up alternative spaces of resistance, organized around plural identities and incommensurable differences, which can also be considered in ('good') revisionist terms. As Jacobs expresses it, 'Rather than reconciliation restructuring the parameters of national knowing into a new space of calm co-habitation, its actually producing a most contested politics of knowing and rights. Reconciliation may have as its goal a transcending of a more familiar oppositional politics, but it is at the same time generating new political articulations characterised by a range of significant reversals and inversions' (208). This fundamentally conflicted understanding of reconciliation is,

---

[5.] This is largely in keeping with Fanon's view that reconciliation is, by definition, incompatible with revolution: 'no conciliation is possible', he insists, in postcolonial societies where liberation and the revolutionary consciousness it succours can only be brought about after a violent struggle between two implacably opposed sides (1965 [1963]: 39). However, it might also help explain why most postcolonial approaches to reconciliation to date (the notable exception is South Africa) have focused on the relationship between indigenous and non-indigenous peoples in settler states (e.g. Australia, Canada, New Zealand) that have not recently experienced revolutionary violence or rupture. Reconciliation, in this sense, may be seen as part of state-sponsored national projects to hold revolution at bay or even to block the social processes that might make it possible. Such projects posit reconciliation as a revisionist process whereby the state accepts wrongdoing in the past while acknowledging the need to take reparative measures in the present. However, it is the state itself that organizes the conditions under which such measures are to be taken; state authority is implicitly reinforced by privileging the pursuit of *justice* over and against the pursuit of *freedom* that is intrinsic to revolutionary change.

it seems to me, much closer to the oppositional spirit of Said's work than Bové's accommodating liberal-humanist rendition of it; it also gives the lie to McGonegal's similarly consensus-based account of reconciliation as 'an entire project … of transforming the brutal conditions' that are the unbroken historical legacy of colonial relations of power (2009: 33).

McGonegal, at least, recognizes that this project is by definition 'ongoing and perpetually unfinished' (33), and that reconciliation, rather than presenting a morally superior alternative to violence, operates in constant tension with other, more directly confrontational resistance practices; in fact, there is a sense in which reconciliation can itself be seen (as Jacobs and Johnson appear to see it) as a form of violence in so far as it is 'forced or imposed by those occupying positions of [authority and] power' (33). Perhaps McGonegal's account of postcolonial reconciliation might itself be seen as performing a 'reconciliatory' move that mediates between apparently incompatible approaches to the subject: an idealist view in which reconciliation 'advocates situating truth relative to testimony, narrative, and memory in the interests of promoting justice' (181); a postmodernist view in which the value of truth itself is questioned; and a materialist view which acknowledges that the granting of 'forgiveness' and the possibility of rapprochement depend on the restoration of specific, historically and geographically situated forms of political autonomy without abandoning the general idea/ideal that reconciliation can provide a 'means of agency for the oppressed' (52, 55).

This composite revisionist view, I would argue, combines several of the contradictory narratives embedded within postcolonialism itself: the universal narrative of enlightenment and emancipation; the deconstructionist critique of it; and the 'new humanist' insistence that a shared planetary future can only be created by addressing and overturning the systemic inequalities that work together to impede human freedom in the modern world.[6] That modernity itself has helped create these inequalities is one of postcolonialism's givens; so too modernity's multilayered connections to the histories of capitalism and colonialism, which postcolonial critics, despite often significant ideological and methodological differences, all see as being symbiotically entwined (see Hindess and Mignolo in this volume). But if one of the few generally agreed-upon tasks of postcolonial

---

[6.] The role of humanism in postcolonial thought has been persistently contested. For poststructuralists, by and large, humanism is no longer a serviceable category, whilst for Marxists it needs to be critiqued for its arrogant assimilation to western imperial interests but reinstated in universal liberationist terms. For many of the latter, it also needs rescuing from the blandishments of 'posthumanism', which can alternately be seen as a sustainability-oriented recognition of the need to see the world in terms other than those that reinforce human domination and as a radical questioning, as much philosophical as biological, of the category of the 'human' itself (for different perspectives on this, see Brennan and Mount and O'Brien in Parts I and IV of this volume). Both the deconstructive and recuperative dimensions of postcolonialism have affiliations, though in markedly different ways, with the philosophical legacies of humanism, as do most of the field's significant figures: the ongoing battle over Fanon and Said mentioned above, for instance, is at least in part a battle over contending critical-theoretical interpretations of humanism's potential to provide the philosophical basis for a decolonized world.

studies has been to show that alternative understandings of modernity—alternative modernities—are possible, it seems there are many, not necessarily compatible ways of achieving this, just as there are many, not necessarily compatible postcolonialisms, each seeking energetically to intervene in the unfinished history of the modern world. Postcolonialisms, like the colonialisms they seek to contest, are volatile and fractured, dynamically but also uncontrollably plural (see Seed in Part I of this volume). At once belated and anticipatory, they offer often radically different ways of understanding the past as well as a myriad of alternative possible avenues to a necessarily uncertain future. Reconciliation-oriented postcolonialism stresses a negotiated path; its revolutionary counterpart insists on an embattled one. However, as I hope to have shown here, these are not mutually exclusive options, while both are refracted through the prism of critical revisionism. If revisionism, as I am riskily suggesting, is the default mode of postcolonial theory and criticism, then attempts to forge a 'new' postcolonial studies will by definition be stymied. But so too will attempts to move 'beyond' postcolonial studies, for even if particular *kinds* of revisionism will fall in and out of fashion, the general *practice* of revisionism, in restlessly shuttling between necessary return and desired renewal, offers a welcome critical bulwark against postcolonialism's negative trajectory from premature celebration (Shohat 1992) to premature demise (Yaeger 2007).

A revisionist approach to postcolonial studies will always run the risk of being seen as quaintly nostalgic, reprehensibly regressive even. (Before being accused of this myself, I should reiterate that I am using revisionism here to recuperate revolutionary ideas without necessarily rejecting their reconciliatory alternatives, and to show that *both* reconciliation *and* revolution are central to current understandings of the postcolonial field.) Notwithstanding, revisionism has the advantage of complicating the opposite (i.e. self-confidently progressivist) view, most likely to be endorsed by materialist critics, that the postcolonial field has made the transition from an earlier, text-based approach that dominated the first wave of postcolonial literary/cultural criticism in the 1980s and 1990s to the cross-disciplinary, interventionist model of the present day (see Mukherjee 2006; also Young 2003). Admittedly, this threefold model—multisited, multilingual, multidisciplinary—has a lot to be said for it (for further reflections on this model, see Huggan 2008). Indeed, some of the more discomforting questions it raises are explicitly addressed in this volume: what power, explanatory or otherwise, does postcolonialism's 'culturalist' vocabulary, indebted as it still is to one version or other of secular idealism, have in today's increasingly postsecular climate? Is the current, cross-disciplinary approach to postcolonial studies necessarily an improvement on the earlier, text-based model, or does it risk exacerbating postcolonialism's overgeneralizing tendencies, producing new conceptual and methodological confusions of its own? What kinds of regional comparisons are needed at a time when the earlier, largely nation-based approach of comparative postcolonial criticism no longer seems appropriate; whither postcolonialism in an increasingly fragmented, and transnationally configured, globalized world? Is there a danger, in focusing on contemporary experiences of colonialism and imperialism, of losing touch with their historical antecedents, or an equal-and-opposite temptation to merge the 'colonial present' (Gregory 2004) indiscriminately with the imperial past? Can the 'new' postcolonial studies liberate itself from 'older' tendencies to view empire as an all-encompassing concept-metaphor, or will it end up reproducing the figural understandings of, e.g., the 'exile' and the 'migrant' that were not particularly helpful in explaining historical processes of colonial dislocation and resettlement, and are no more useful in assessing the condition of their globalist, 'new imperialist' counterparts now? (Hardt and Negri 2000; Harvey 2003; see also Part II of this volume.) Can the 'new' postcolonial studies, in propagating a form of 'transnational literacy' (Spivak 1999), work towards opening up the linguistic range of its highly disparate subject matter, or will its latest encounters with globalization merely reinforce the hegemony of the one particular world language, English, in which the vast majority of its work continues to be conducted, even though it is precisely such linguistic/cultural hegemonies that the field makes it its business to contest?

These questions are no doubt useful, and several of the essays in this volume choose, directly or indirectly, to engage with them. However, two overriding questions still need to be asked: just how 'new' is the 'new' postcolonial studies? And is 'newness' such a vital category? To put my own view one last time: if postcolonial studies is to remain relevant to today's world—and I certainly believe it will—it will need to pay greater attention than ever to the various conflicted histories that inform it; while if its radical credentials are to be taken seriously—and I firmly believe they should—they will need to be more strongly connected than ever to the anti-colonial struggles of the past. Postcolonial studies, in this last sense, may be seen as defiantly *un*fashionable, even if, for perhaps understandable professional reasons, many of the field's current practitioners have strategically adjusted their sights to the realities of the contemporary globalized world. It also remains obstinately dedicated to what Timothy Brennan somewhat backhandedly calls a 'welcome intellectual generalism' (2008: 49; see also Brennan in Part I of this volume). The postcolonial, as Peter Hallward exasperatedly remarked more than a decade ago, may well 'present itself as a sort of general theory on the non-generalisable as such' (2001: ix), but surely this is the *point* of postcolonial studies, and while it is certainly true that postcolonial theory/criticism makes large, at times tendentious generalizations, this is the occupational hazard of any ambitiously comparative field. Nor is the postcolonial field, as Hallward implies, necessarily committed to seeking refuge in the specific or to reaching out, in spite of itself, to an extreme form of singularity through which specific cultural differences are somehow collapsed into an originary Difference that effectively transcends them all (Bhabha 1994; Hallward 2001). Rather, as Hallward grudgingly acknowledges, the postcolonial field wavers—unconvincingly at times— between the singular and the specific: between the wary but necessary acceptance of universal values and the close attention to those cultural particularities, and their abiding capacity for political manipulation, that universals (the 'human condition', the 'struggle for justice', etc.) are sometimes given to disguise. Postcolonialism, understood this way, registers a continuing obligation to complexity: it fervently supports the idea of a just world, but it is also aware of the ways in which this idea can be made and remade to serve particular sets of political and historical interests, not all of them egalitarian or beneficial; and in which the imperialisms of the present, to twist Aijaz Ahmad, may be ironically founded on the *anti*-colonialisms of the past (Ahmad 1992; see also Parts II and III of this volume).

This much is clear: 'postcolonial' is a troubled term in an embattled set of social and historical circumstances. There can be no doubting its slipperiness, its conceptual inadequacy in face of the immensity of its subject; but there can be no doubting either the compelling nature of its material and the social immediacy of its contemporary intellectual interests and continuing historical effects. To some extent, postcolonial studies amounts to the sum of its own internal differences. This is not a field one is likely to look to for methodological coherence or consensual politics, nor is it a field (despite the noticeable development of critical and theoretical orthodoxies, many of them situated at the cusp of Marxism and poststructuralism) that is likely to exhaust its own capacity for provocative debate. Postcolonialism, as a loose set of revisionist techniques, is both irrepressibly and incorrigibly combative, quarrelling with the world it wishes to transform but also, and no less obviously, bickering with itself. This is no less, of course, than one might expect of a field whose existence has been persistently fraught since its first institutional appearance in the 1980s, and the increasingly frequent allegation of whose replacement by emergent disciplines such as transnational cultural studies or globalization studies is so far from being the truth that it seems almost pointless to reject. What is closer to the truth, perhaps, is that terms such as 'postcolonial', 'transnational', and 'global' work better together than apart, and help collectively to explain the times we live in. This volume also suggests they help collectively to make predictions for the future and to assess the continuing significance of the past. Such predictions and assessments, like much else in the field, will likely remain speculative or hypothetical. One thing is for sure though: that postcolonial studies will continue to be relevant as long as colonialism—multiple colonialisms—exist in the current world order, even if the field's remit is, paradoxically, to play its utopian part in making colonialism and the imperialist ideologies that drive it a thing of the past.

Recent evidence suggests that there are grounds for hope—or hope at least that the struggle for emancipation will continue. At the time of writing, as the 'Arab Spring' continues to unfold, it seems tempting to reflect on the continuing viability of revolution. 'Tahrir Square', in the unabashedly romantic view of Egyptian novelist Alaa Al Aswany, 'became [for a time in 2011] like the Paris Commune. The authority of the regime collapsed as the authority of the people took its place' (2011: ix). But it is equally tempting to reflect on revolution's shortcomings or, perhaps better, on the perils of assuming revolutionary change before it has actually happened; and as the political commentator Olivier Roy has more cautiously suggested, ongoing events in Egypt are perhaps best understood in Arendtian terms as the 'politics of protest' rather than as 'the dawn of a new [political] regime' (2011: n.p.; also Arendt 1990 [1963] and the opening section of this essay above). Meanwhile, one could be forgiven for thinking that much of the world is at war: a highly selective list here might include civil wars in Afghanistan and Somalia; insurgencies in Sudan and Iraq; drug wars in Mexico and Colombia; and armed conflict—some but by no means all of it revolutionary—in Syria, Yemen, Chechyna, Nigeria, Kashmir, and West Papua. We might recall that Arendt's opening argument in

On Revolution (1963) was that the rest of the twentieth century would eventually see the eclipse of war by revolution, though she was canny enough to recognize that the one could easily blend into the other, and that violence was the most likely common denominator for both (1990 [1963]: 18). She was right, up to a point: a variety of revolutionary freedom struggles, most of them violent in the extreme, would go on to characterize much of the latter half of the twentieth century, and revolution has already made a defining mark on the new millennium. So too has war. The question of war, and the sometimes illusory freedoms it claims to protect, should trouble postcolonial studies far more than it has done, certainly far more than its own sometimes tedious internecine conflicts; but that should not stop the age-old pursuit of human freedom from being its primary and urgently necessary goal.

Graham Huggan, April 2012

REFERENCES

Ahmad, Aijaz (1992). *In Theory: Classes, Nations, Literatures.* London: Verso.

Al Aswany Alaa (2011). *On the State of Egypt: What Caused the Revolution*, trans. J. Wright. Edinburgh: Canongate.

Al-Rahim, Ahmed (2011). 'Whither Political Islam and the "Arab Spring"?' *The Hedgehog Review,* 13.3: 8–22.

Arendt, Hannah (1990 [1963]). *On Revolution.* London: Penguin.

Ashcroft, Bill, Gareth Griffiths, and Helen Tiffin (1989). *The Empire Writes Back: Theory and Practice in Post-Colonial Literatures.* London: Routledge.

Bamyeh, Mohammed (2011). 'Anarchist, Liberal, and Authoritarian Enlightenments—Notes from the Arab Spring', *Jadaliyya,* 30 July. Online source: <http://www.jadaliyya.com/pages/contributors/4687>, accessed 10 April 2012.

Bhabha, Homi (1994). *The Location of Culture.* London: Routledge.

Bhabha, Homi (2005). 'Foreword: Framing Fanon', in F. Fanon, *The Wretched of the Earth*, trans. C. Farrington. New York: Grove Press, vii–xlii.

Black, Ian (2012). 'Introduction', in Toby Manhire (ed.), *The Arab Spring: Rebellion, Revolution and a New World Order.* London: Guardian Books, vii–xiv.

Bové, Paul (1993). 'Hope and Reconciliation: A Review of Edward W. Said', *Boundary 2,* 20.2: 266–82.

Brennan, Timothy (2007). *Wars of Position: The Cultural Politics of Left and Right.* New York: Columbia University Press.

Brennan, Timothy (2008). 'Postcolonial Studies and Globalization Theory', in R. Krishnaswamy and J. C. Hawley (eds), *The Postcolonial and the Global.* Minneapolis: University of Minnesota Press, 37–53.

Brouillette, Sarah (2007). *Postcolonial Writers and the Global Literary Marketplace.* Basingstoke: Palgrave Macmillan.

Brumberg, D. (2002). 'Democratization in the Arab World? The Trap of Liberalized Autocracy', *Journal of Democracy,* 13.2: 56–68.

Dirlik, Arif (1994). 'The Postcolonial Aura: Third World Criticism in the Age of Global Capitalism', *Critical Inquiry,* 20.2: 328–56.

Dirlik, Arif (2003). 'Where Do We Go from Here? Marxism, Modernity and Postcolonial Studies', *Diaspora*, 12.3: 419–35.

During, Simon (1998). 'Postcolonialism and Globalisation: A Dialectical Relation After All?' *Postcolonial Studies*, 1.1: 31–47.

El-Mahdi, Radab (2009). 'The Democracy Movement: Cycles of Protest', in R. El-Mahdi and P. Marfleet (eds), *Egypt: The Moment of Change*. London: Zed Books, 87–102.

El-Mahdi, Radab and Philip Marfleet (eds) (2009). *Egypt: The Moment of Change*. London: Zed Books.

Fanon, Frantz (1965 [1963]). *The Wretched of the Earth*, trans. C. Farrington. New York: Grove Books.

Foucault, Michel (1970). *The Order of Things*. New York: Vintage.

Gajarawala, Toral Jatin (2011). 'Some Time between Revisionist and Revolutionary: Unreading History in Dalit Literature', *PMLA*, 126.3: 575–91.

Gates, Henry Louis, Jr (1991). 'Critical Fanonism', *Critical Inquiry*, 17.3: 457–70.

Gregory, Derek (2004). *The Colonial Present: Afghanistan, Israel/Palestine, Iraq*. Oxford: Blackwell.

Hallward, Peter (2001). *Absolutely Postcolonial: Writing between the Singular and the Specific*. Manchester: University of Manchester Press.

Hamber, Brandon and Gráinne Kelly (2009). 'Beyond Coexistence: Towards a Working Definition of Reconciliation', in J. R. Quinn (ed.), *Reconciliation(s): Transitional Justice in Postconflict Societies*. Montreal: McGill-Queen's University Press.

Hardt, Michael and Antonio Negri (2000). *Empire*. Cambridge, Mass.: Harvard University Press.

Howe, Stephen (2000). 'The Politics of Historical "Revisionism": Comparing Ireland and Israel/Palestine', *Past and Present*, 168.1: 227–53.

Huggan, Graham (2001). *The Postcolonial Exotic: Marketing the Margins*. London: Routledge.

Huggan, Graham (2005). '(Not) Reading *Orientalism*', *Research in African Literatures*, 36.3: 124–36.

Huggan, Graham (2008). *Interdisciplinary Measures: Literature and the Future of Postcolonial Studies*. Liverpool: University of Liverpool Press.

Jacobs, Jane M. (1997). 'Resisting Reconciliation: The Secret Geographies of (Post)colonial Australia', in S. Pile and M. Keith (eds), *Geographies of Resistance*. London: Routledge, 203–18.

James, C. L. R. (2001 [1958]). *The Black Jacobins: Toussaint L'ouverture and the San Domingo Revolution*. London: Penguin.

Johnson, Miranda (2011). 'Reconciliation, Indigeneity, and Postcolonial Nationhood in Settler States', *Postcolonial Studies*, 14.2: 187–201.

Lazarus, Neil (2011). *The Postcolonial Unconscious*. Cambridge: Cambridge University Press.

Lee, Kyung-Won (1997). 'Is the Glass Half-Empty or Half-Full? Rethinking the Problems of Postcolonial Revisionism', *Cultural Critique*, 36: 89–117.

Loomba, Ania, Suvir Kaul, Matti Bunzl, Antoinette Burton, and Jed Esty (eds) (2005). *Postcolonial Studies and Beyond*. Durham, NC: Duke University Press.

Macey, David (2000). *Frantz Fanon: A Life*. London: Granta.

Manhire, Toby (ed.) (2012). *The Arab Spring: Rebellion, Revolution and a New World Order*. London: Guardian Books.

McAdam, D., S. Tarrow, and C. Tilly (2001). *Dynamics of Contention*. Cambridge: Cambridge University Press.

McGonegal, Julie (2009). *Imagining Justice: The Politics of Postcolonial Forgiveness and Reconciliation*. Montreal: McGill-Queen's University Press.

Mukherjee, Pablo (2006). 'Surfing the Second Waves: Amitav Ghosh's Tide Country', *New Formations*, 59: 144–57.

Parry, Benita (2001). 'Overlapping Territories and Intertwined Histories: Edward Said's Postcolonial Cosmopolitanism', in P. Williams (ed.), *Edward Said*, vol. 3. London: Sage Publications, 335–61.

Parry, Benita (2004). *Postcolonial Studies: A Materialist Critique*. London: Routledge.

Parry, Benita (2005). 'Reconciliation and Remembrance', *Pretexts*, 5: 84–96.

Quayson, Ato (2000). *Postcolonialism: Theory, Practice or Process?* Cambridge: Polity Press.

Quinn, Joanna R. (ed.) (2009). *Reconciliation(s): Transitional Justice in Postconflict Societies*. Montreal: McGill-Queen's University.

Radhakrishnan, R. (2008). 'Revisionism and the Subject of History', in R. Krishnaswamy and J. C. Hawley (eds), *The Postcolonial and the Global*. Minneapolis: University of Minnesota Press, 69–81.

Robbins, Bruce (2004). 'Solidarity and Worldliness: For Edward Said', *Logos*, 3.1: 1–9.

Rooney, Caroline (2011). 'Egyptian Literary Culture and Egyptian Modernity: Introduction', *Journal of Postcolonial Writing*, 47.4: 369–76.

Roy, Olivier (2011). 'This is Not an Islamic Revolution', *New Statesman*, 15 February. Online source: <http://www.newstatesman.com/religion/2011/02/egypt-arab-tu ...>, accessed 10 April 2012.

Said, Edward W. (1986a). 'Intellectuals in the Post-Colonial World', *Salmagundi*, 71/2: 44–81.

Said, Edward W. (1986b). 'Michael Walzer's "Exodus and Revolution": A Canaanite Reading', *Grand Street*, 5.2: 86–106.

Said, Edward W. (1988). 'Identity, Negation and Violence', *New Left Review*, I.171: 46–60.

Said, Edward W. (1989). 'C. L. R. James: The Artist as Revolutionary', *New Left Review*, I.175: 126–8.

Said, Edward W. (1993). *Culture and Imperialism*. New York: Knopf.

Said, Edward W. (1994). *Representations of the Intellectual*. New York: Random House.

Said, Edward W. (1995a). *Orientalism*, 2nd edn. New York: Vintage.

Said, Edward W. (1995b). *The Politics of Dispossession*. New York: Vintage.

Said, Edward W. (1999a). 'Palestine: Memory, Invention and Space', in I. Abu-Lughod, R. Heacock, and K. Nashef (eds), *The Landscape of Palestine: Equivocal Poetry*. Birzeit: Birzeit University Publications, 3–20.

Said, Edward W. (1999b). 'No Reconciliation Allowed', in A. Aciman (ed.), *Letters of Transit: Reflections on Exile, Identity, Language, and Loss*. New York: The New Press, 87–114.

Said, Edward W. (1999c). 'Truth and Reconciliation', *Al-Ahram Weekly On-Line*, 14–20 January. Online source: <http://weekly.ahram.org.eg/1999/412/op2.htm>, accessed 10 April 2012.

Scott, David (2004). *Conscripts of Modernity: The Tragedy of Colonial Enlightenment*. Durham, NC: Duke University Press.

Scott, Jill (2010). *A Poetics of Forgiveness: Cultural Responses to Loss and Wrongdoing*. New York: Palgrave Macmillan.

Spivak, Gayatri Chakravorty (1999). *Critique of Postcolonial Reason: Toward a History of the Vanishing Present*. Cambridge, Mass.: Harvard University Press.

Shohat, Ella (1992). 'Notes on the Post-Colonial', *Social Text*, 31/32: 633–51.

Suleri, Sara (1992). *The Rhetoric of English India*. Chicago: University of Chicago Press.

Trivedi, Harish (2011). 'Revolutionary Non-Violence', *Interventions: International Journal of Postcolonial Studies*, 13.4: 521–49.

Williams, Patrick (2001). 'Nothing in the Post? Said and the Problem of Post-Colonial Intellectuals', in P. Williams (ed.), *Edward Said, vol. I*. London: Sage Publications, 314–34.

Williams, Patrick (2010). '"Outlines of a Better World": Rerouting Postcolonialism', in J. Wilson, C. Şandru, and S. Lawson Welsh (eds), *Rerouting the Postcolonial: New Directions for a New Millennium*. London: Routledge, 86–97.

Wilson, Janet, Cristina Şandru, and Sarah Lawson Welsh (eds) (2010). *Rerouting the Postcolonial: New Directions for a New Millennium*. London: Routledge.

Yack, Bernard (1992). *The Longing for Total Revolution: Philosophical Sources of Social Discontent from Rousseau to Marx and Nietzsche*. Berkeley: University of California Press.

Yaeger, Patricia (2007). 'Editor's Column: The End of Postcolonial Theory? A Roundtable with Sunil Agnani, Fernando Coronil, Gaurav Desai, Mamadou Diouf, Simon Gikandi, Susie Tharu, and Jennifer Wenzel', *PMLA*, 122.3: 633–51.

Young, Robert (2001). *Postcolonialism: An Historical Introduction*. Oxford: Blackwell.

Young, Robert (2003). *Postcolonialism: A Very Short Introduction*. Oxford: Oxford University Press.

PART I

THE IMPERIAL PAST

INTRODUCTION

GRAHAM HUGGAN

Bearing in mind Stephen Howe's exasperated claim that 'ideas about empire have [recently] seemed to spread and multiply beyond all control: imperialism, as a word, has gone imperial' (2002: 10), the opening section of the Handbook looks at different ways of envisaging empires and imperialisms, with an emphasis on broadly postcolonial approaches to the imperial past. While the section will offer different interpretations of empire, most of these are in accordance with Howe's broad-based definition of empire as a 'large, composite multi-ethnic political unit, usually created by conquest', and of imperialism as a sum of the 'attitudes and actions which create or uphold such political units'—attitudes and actions that imply indirect, as well as more direct, forms of authority and control (2002: 30).

Postcolonial approaches to empire are often less historical than they claim to be, which is why this section includes the work of prominent imperial historians as well as a variety of postcolonial literary/cultural critics whose work engages explicitly or implicitly with the imperial past. The phrase 'the imperial past' begs a series of other questions: whose past is it that is being referred to; what is meant by the adjective 'imperial'; and when does that past begin (and when does it end or can it reasonably be expected to end)? These questions are given extra resonance by the fact that empires past and present have been so culturally different, even if many of them have operated with similar politico-economic mechanisms and apparatuses of power. The section aims accordingly to look comparatively at empire, focusing on the largest European colonial empires: Britain's, to be sure, but also those of Spain and Portugal, France and the Netherlands. It will be asked to what extent these empires are historically circumscribed, what legacies they have left for the nations that founded them, and what continuities exist between the 'colonial present' (the heading of the Handbook's next section) and the imperial past.

It will also be asked to what extent empire is a world-historical phenomenon, as evident in Asia as it has been in Europe, though it will challenge the sweeping view that empire has operated as 'a default mode of political organization throughout much of history' (Van Steenkiste 2008; see also Darwin 2007)—a view which, in confusing the durability of the idea of empire with the inevitability of empires, subscribes to an ideological fatalism that postcolonial critics and theorists vigorously contest. Empires are neither 'inevitable' nor 'normal', and the violence they produce far outweighs any economic and political advantages to be derived from them. Nor are they consistent; as David Harvey among others points out, different empires have historically produced different imperialisms, some of them radically incompatible with one another, while different conceptions of empire—'hard' and 'soft', formal and informal, coercive and consensu-al—can easily become 'internalized [within] the same [political] space' (Harvey 2003: 5; see also Howe 2002; Said 1993).

Empires are *plural*: they may function simultaneously as economic engines, politi-cal units, and ideological vehicles, but they obviously exist in all shapes and sizes, are subject to a variety of often contradictory motives, and produce an equally wide array of different methods for controlling (and justifying the control of) others and for under-standing themselves. They are also *global*. Not all empires aspire to world domination, nor do they all constitute what the British imperial historian John Darwin (2009) calls a functionally interdependent 'world system'; but empires of the past are best understood in global terms as competing visions for the conquest and control of other people's ter-ritories and resources, just as empires of the present—whether seen or not in terms of an overriding 'capitalist imperialism' (Lazarus 2011)—consist in rival attempts to wrest control over the global economy that encompasses them all.

It seems only sensible to insist on political and, above all, economic understandings of empire and imperialism as instruments for predatory commercial interests, and the repeated failure to do so has been a charge laid, with depressing regularity, at postco-lonialism's door. Marxist critics such as Neil Lazarus, for example, have demonstrated increasing impatience with those postcolonial theorists (basically all those other than Marxists) who persist in seeing empire and imperialism in terms of processes of 'cul-tural and epistemological subjugation, whose material preconditions have been referred to only glancingly, if at all' (Lazarus 2011: 17; see also the General Introduction to this volume). Lazarus has a point, but surely empire and the imperialist ideologies that drive it need to be seen in *both* economic *and* cultural terms as well as in the relationship between them; strategic perceptions of cultural difference, after all, provided one of the primary 'moral' justifications for European economic expansion, and it is difficult to disagree with Edward Said that the battle over 'culture' has been central to the modern imperial experience—surfacing most recently in US-led 'civilizationism' (see Mignolo's and Sayyid's chapters in this section)—just as the various European colonial empires' economic 'pattern[s] of dominions [and] possessions laid the groundwork for what is now in effect a fully global world' (Said 1993: 4; see also Part V of this volume).

A second charge made by Lazarus in the same book (*The Postcolonial Unconscious*) is also worth examining here. Postcolonial studies, he suggests, has not only not been particularly effective in revealing either the long history of empire or the 'intensification of imperialist social relations' (2011: 16) that now obtains under current conditions of globalization; it has tended to *mystify* these relations, either by ignoring imperialism altogether or by falsely assuming its 'obsolescence' (16) by the time of the 1980s and 1990s, generally acknowledged to be the key decades in the discipline's own institutional growth. Again it seems necessary to qualify, without necessarily dismissing, this state-ment. There is little doubt that postcolonial studies can be seen as part of what is gen-erally referred to as the 'cultural turn' at European and, particularly, North American universities during the period in question—a turn often accompanied by rapt attention to the work of Continental poststructuralist thinkers: Derrida, Lacan, Foucault. Yet this—as Lazarus himself admits—is only part of the complex institutional history of postcolonial studies as a discipline, and even the most 'culturalist' of postcolonial critics have rarely subscribed either then or now to the demise, still less the obsolescence, of imperialism; on the contrary, it is the *continuity* of empire as both idea and practice that works, paradoxically no doubt, to guarantee the anti-colonial credentials of those working in the field.

For Lazarus, as for other postcolonial Marxists, imperialism is—as Lenin famously saw it—a particular stage in the development of global capitalism; failing to acknowledge this, however, is hardly tantamount to suggesting that imperialism is obsolete. It is true, nonetheless, that postcolonial critics have sometimes been reluctant to address the symbiotic relationship between imperialism, modernity, and global capitalism (though equally true that they have tended to focus on European rather than non-European imperialisms, and have not always been ready either to acknowledge that the long history of empire significantly pre-dates the emergence of capitalist imperialism in the west: see Sayyid below). Elaborate distinctions between 'imperialism' and 'colonialism', with one seen as pre-dating the other, will not help to solve the problem (see, for example, Boehmer 1995; Loomba 1999). What is needed, it seems, is a more methodical understanding of the imperial past as the product of a set of shifting historical conjunctures and relations—an understanding to which both imperial historians and postcolonial literary/cultural critics are well capable of contributing, precisely because of the significant differences in approach and method that their perhaps unduly compartmentalized disciplines entail (see Part IV of this volume).

It seems appropriate, then, that the chapters that follow in this section (and in other sections) represent a wide range of disciplines—history, literary/cultural studies, anthropology, sociology, philosophy—and that primacy is not given to any one of these; rather, close attention is paid to the relationship between them all. Postcolonial studies, after all, is a relational field investigating an equally relational subject—and a further axiom of empires is that they are always relational if not always systematic, despite their systematizing intent. Stephen Howe's critical definition of empire as a relational term that promiscuously refers to 'any and every type of relation between a more powerful state or society and a less powerful one' (2002: 13) comes to mind here; or Michael Doyle's, which sees empire as a 'relationship, formal or informal, in which one state controls the effective political sovereignty of another political society [whether] by force, or by political collaboration, or by economic, social, or cultural dependence' (Doyle 1986: 45; also quoted in Said 1993: 8).

Neither of these definitions is complete, nor should we expect it to be. Both definitions, for example, overlook the possibility of empires that are not necessarily extensions of state power. Hardt and Negri's all-embracing postmodern empire, while speculative and abstract, is one of these: a 'decentered and deterritorializing apparatus of rule', coextensive with if not reducible to globalization, it 'progressively incorporates the entire global realm within its open, expanding frontiers' (2000: xii). There is perhaps nothing particularly 'new' about the 'new imperialism' being argued for here, nor anything especially 'postmodern' about it either; rather, contemporary empire-building is driven, as it ever was, by the rival ideological demands of consent and conquest, and by the competing political and economic imperatives of territorial expansion and centralized power (Harvey 2003; see also Part II of this volume). That said, alternative philosophical conceptions of—and definitional disagreements around—empire are likely to continue as long as empire itself continues; ironically perhaps, one of the few things that historians and theorists of empire appear to agree on is that the imperial past is not past. That basic contradiction shadows this section, as it does other sections in this volume. But however empire is seen, and however imperialism is seen as operating, historical understandings of both empire and imperialism are as necessary today as they have ever been, partly as a way of assessing, appreciating, and, whenever and wherever necessary, contesting the multiple legacies of empire for the contemporary world.

The section begins with a chapter by the distinguished American anthropologist and historian Ann Laura Stoler, which raises the vexed issue of Enlightenment's relationship to empire. Stoler is critical of the persistence with which the Enlightenment has been posited as central to understandings of the European colonial empires, suggesting that these understandings—both of Enlightenment and empire as well as the relationship between them—have been far more plural and internally conflicted than is often taken to be the case. Plurality and conflict also apply to some of the governing assumptions surrounding Enlightenment and empire: the identification of empire with order and rationality; the preconception that these were based on shared and agreed-upon knowledge; and the designation of Enlightenment itself as the 'Age of Reason'—a designation belied by the central role of sentiment and the passions in Enlightenment thinking and in the 'colonial dispositions and ... practices [it] served'.

Stoler's particular focus is on the nineteenth-century Netherlands Indies. Here, Stoler's exemplary archival research—which has informed her work over several decades—reveals neither uniformity in colonial response nor unanimity in colonial method; instead, it shows 'how much is missed and amiss in how [Dutch colonial] mappings of the Enlightenment onto empire [were and still are] formed'. Uncertainty is at the heart of things; and Stoler's emphasis, accordingly, is on what she elegantly calls 'the unquiet minds of colonialisms' European practitioners to invoke ... history "in a minor key"'—a history that 'initiates a rereading of the anxious and anticipatory states that imperial governance engendered to better understand the regimes of security it produced and the expectant, affective economies on which imperial formations continue to depend'. Stoler does not contest that reason still held sway in the nineteenth-century Netherlands Indies, as elsewhere in Europe's far-flung and sharply differentiated colonies; but she insists that 'rational, scientific ways of knowing the world were insufficient for [imperial] governance', and that these proved incapable either of describing the 'temperament of rule' or of capturing how it worked.

It is the *messiness* of empire that emerges from Stoler's multi-layered account: the anxieties and insecurities it instilled; the hesitations and slippages it engendered; the moments of 'discernment when ... common sense and convention failed [colonial administrators], and what [they] thought they knew, and how they might know it, they found they did not'. Empire—in so far as it can be seen as singular at all—is less system-atic than it desires, and more fashioned by desire than its claim to detached rational-ity supposes; indeed, it is marked by a wide range of 'emotional registers of experience' that demonstrate, not just the affective force of imperial governance, but also the speed with which the social passions and sensibilities attached to it 'could traverse the colony and the globe'. These registers emphasize the interconnectedness, in European colonial regimes, of private and public spheres of influence; they also highlight what Stoler calls the 'lived epistemic spaces' in which colonial agents operated—fragile, often fearful sites in which their apprehension of things they could *not* see, and things they did *not* know, were imaginatively shaped.

Stoler ends by asserting the continuity of *déraison*, Foucault's expansive term for the instabilities that underlie even Reason's most self-assertive gestures, in contemporary imperial/colonial practices; 'unreason', she says, 'organized the political grammar of empire at its beginning' and now re-emerges in, e.g., the 'colonizing passions of relent-less Israeli incursions on Palestinian [territory]', or in the 'standard operating proce-dures' of the US presence in Iraq (see also Morton in Part II of this volume). This is a salutary reminder—one repeated throughout this volume—that fear and insecurity, not just of the world as it is but of how it might be imagined to be, lies at the spectral heart of any empire, just as what Ahmad (1992) calls the 'imperialisms of the present' are con-tinually shadowed by the 'colonialisms of the past'.

In the next chapter, the American historian Tyler Stovall brings to the surface what was already embedded in Stoler's work: namely that there has been an intellectual rift between postcolonial theory and imperial history, though theorists and historians alike, without necessarily settling their differences, have 'learned greatly from one another' in their respective analyses of the imperial past (see also Kennedy in Part IV of this volume). A further problem, Stovall suggests, is the immensity of the terrain that both postcolo-nial theorists and imperial historians cover, even within broadly national imperial enter-prises: Stovall's own focus is on the colonial empires of Britain and France. Comparison between these two empires, he suggests, has tended to focus on the differences between them, including 'contrasting processes of decolonization, economic versus political motivations for empire, [and] direct and indirect rule'. More recent work, however, has brought out similarities, e.g. in the relationship between empire and modernity or in the role played by liberal political thought in shaping the colonial encounter, and it is on this last set of connections that the subsequent argument of Stovall's chapter rests. His particular focus is on the rise of mass liberal democracy in both countries. This reveals the paradox that the age of mass democracy in Europe was also an age of imperialism—a contradiction that Stovall sees as being central to the modern world at large.

Stovall's emphasis, unlike Seed's in the chapter that immediately follows his, is on the European history of empires seen from the metropolitan rather than the colonial perspec-tive, though his wider aim is to 'broaden [imperial] history beyond the traditional focus on policymaking elites to consider how empire shaped the political culture of modern Britain and France themselves'. His argument turns on the transition from 'old' (monar-chical) to 'new' (liberal democratic) models of empire during the nineteenth century, with the latter model combining the humanitarian elements of the era of democratic revolution (e.g., anti-slavery) with an 'aggressive expansionism' based, not just on economic imperatives but on a consolidated view of social and cultural differences shaped by nineteenth-century European racial theory (see Gopal in Part II of this volume).

While Stovall shows that the emergent alliance of liberal democracy and the new imperialism was remarkable in both of the countries (Britain and France) that form the basis of his analysis, he takes care to point out the differences between them, e.g. in later decolonization patterns and the changing political demands of the working class. However, his analysis, by and large, focuses—riskily perhaps—on similarities between the two countries. These are brought together one last time in his conclusion, where he suggests some of the different ways—highlighted later by Michael Rothberg (see Part III of this volume)—in which the imperial past in both Britain and France is far from over, not least because the manufactured polarity between metropole and colony, often phrased in the exclusivist rhetoric of nation, persists. This, for Stovall, is at the heart of the postcolonial dilemma—one in which the global spread of democracy suggests more inclusive alternatives to nationalist imperialism while ushering in new, reintensified forms of cultural differentialism that suggest that, at best, 'the democratic project remains incomplete'.

While Patricia Seed's chapter, like Stovall's, focuses on similarities and differences between two former European colonial empires, in her case Spain's and Portugal's, it departs from it significantly by adopting a subaltern/indigenist rather than a metropolitan approach. 'Indigenism', for Seed, is a falsely homogenizing category created out of histories of invasion and conquest; like the colonialism to which it is yoked, it is 'not and never has been a singular noun'. Seed's focus, accordingly, is on separating out the important internal differences within these categories, and in exposing the equally variegated 'colonial fictions' by which the indigenous peoples of the Americas could be treated, depending on European political and economic priorities, as either fundamentally different or essentially the same. For Seed, it is the 'neocolonial formulation of principles governing the status of native peoples that defies American postcolonialism and marks its distinctiveness'—a particularly bald instance of the generally fine line that separates the 'colonial present' (see Part II of this volume) from the imperial past. Paradoxically, Seed sees the native-born elites of Spanish and Portuguese America, who have been understandably eager to distinguish themselves from their Iberian predecessors, as attempting to rationalize their privilege by glorifying a 'safely distant indigenous past'.

This particular instance of the colonial present is used to suggest that liberty rarely followed the transition to independence and the return of political power to indigenous communities in the Americas; nor, generally speaking, have the subsequent histories of postcolonial nations in other parts of the world offered an 'uplifting narrative about the removal of European power'. Postcolonial literature, Seed suggests, has supplied a critical alternative, although it is as well to be reminded that the vast majority of its subaltern perspectives have been fashioned by elites (see McLeod in Part IV and Dhawan and Randeria in Part V of this volume). Subaltern authors do exist, however, and Seed provides some compelling examples from the Spanish and Portuguese Americas. Some of these works are self-consciously informed by a cosmopolitan perspective that appeals to a broad international community but does not necessarily carry direct political consequences, and Seed duly provides a series of cautionary tales to show how, in the face of neocolonial political and economic authority, cosmopolitanism's 'forward momentum', defined as it is largely in cultural terms, 'comes to a screeching halt'.

Seed concludes by issuing a salutary reminder that the actual status of indigenous communities in the Americas and elsewhere is often markedly different from the heroic role assigned to them in the postcolonial cultural imaginary; in the Americas, she suggests, 'no reversal of the fundamental colonial project [has been possible], and … the cultural fictions of Indian identities remain entrenched'. Seed reminds us too that categories like 'subaltern' and 'indigenous', which continue to be mobilized by postcolonial critics for a variety of oppositional and emancipatory purposes, may also falsify the actual conditions and/or historical circumstances in which subaltern/indigenous peoples live.

Walter Mignolo's chapter, like Seed's, focuses on Latin America, but brings it into dialogue with the Latin countries of the European Union and the Islamic countries of North Africa and the Middle East. Also like Seed, Mignolo is interested in alternatives to more-or-less mainstream, European-centred versions of imperial history, seeing—as in much of his recent work—the need for a 'decolonial shift' centring on transverse relations between Islam, Latinity, and modernity in a globalized world.

One aspect of this shift is 'dewesternization': a deliberate challenge to those 'imperial/colonial metamorphoses of the west' that are inscribed within the history of capitalism, Christianity, and secularism. Mignolo takes neoliberalism to be the latest iteration of this continuing history, which, folded into the composite 'Eurocentrism', he understands as a 'general epistemic model that organizes subjectivity and knowledge, gender and sexuality, economy and the state'. Over and against this western model he posits the notion of a 'transmodern' world that both exposes the complicities between modernity and imperial/colonial power and works towards overcoming them. The 'decolonial shift', in this last sense, offers nothing less than a 'radical undoing of modernity/coloniality' that, setting its face against the binaries of post-'9/11' 'civilizationism', simultaneously opposes 'a five-hundred-year history of empire, capitalism, and modernity … in which coloniality [modernity's destructive underside] is conspicuously missing from accounts'.

A further aspect of the 'decolonial shift' reassesses the role played in the imperial past, and on into the colonial present, by the world's subaltern peoples, whose collective agency—demonstrated so clearly in the recent events of the 'Arab Spring'—can no longer be contained by a civil society that seeks to instrumentalize their revolutionary anger and political dissent (see also the General Introduction to this volume). This also shows the possibilities offered by transmodernity, in which modernity is openly 'confronted with other languages, religions, and histories that take it beyond the Greco-Roman and Christian legacies of the west'.

A third aspect of the 'decolonial shift' requires a renewed acknowledgement of the place of Islam *within* rather than *against* Europe and a corresponding recognition of the currents of justice, equality, and pluralism within Islamic thought. (Mignolo concedes here that the history of Islam is as likely to yield examples of authoritarian thinking and action.) 'Decolonial transmodernity' is not, however, an automatic championing of Islam anymore than it is an unquestioning celebration of the imperial achievements of western Christianity; rather, in analysing the complex tracery of historical connections *between* them, it seeks to articulate parallel world views to those of the west, to reveal the alternative epistemologies contained within western world views, and to highlight pluralistic, often localized understandings of human relations and interactions that contest, explicitly or implicitly, universal imperial ambitions of dominating the world. 'The single story of western civilization', Mignolo insists, is slowly but inexorably ending; and other narratives—those informed by the 'alternative trajectories' of decoloniality and dewesternization—are rapidly emerging to take its place.

Like Mignolo's chapter, Bobby Sayyid's complicates standard postcolonial accounts of the triangulation of capitalism, modernity, and empire by working to effect a 'decolonial shift' that disrupts the persistent European emphasis of each of these three elements while counteracting the historical telescoping of empire that tends to happen when the elements are combined. Also like Mignolo, Sayyid looks to the articulation of Islam and empire as a way of positing alternatives to Eurocentric understandings of empire and imperialism. But whereas Mignolo's primary concern is to use the decolonial shift to pave the way for a globally inflected, appropriately dewesternized 'transmodernity' (see above), Sayyid's is to demonstrate the historically and politically specific nature of Islamicate imperialism at a time when Muslims, and the master-signifier of Islam, are being ideologically co-opted into re-establishing the 'violent hierarchy' between the west and the non-west.

The main thrust of Sayyid's argument is that Islamicate empires (i.e. empires closely associated with, but not necessarily reducible to, Islam) have historically relied on the construction of a distinct Muslim identity—one, however, that is less racially exclusive than its European Christian (or secular) counterpart, which both philosophically underpins and politically reiterates the original European colonial order as 'a racist order [in which the] European colonial empires [functioned] as racial states'. The Islamicate empires, Sayyid insists, were not structured around the logic of racialization, but one of the main ideological features of post-'9/11' civilizationism has been the *re*-racialization of Muslims as latter-day predatory imperialists intent on the conquest of the west. Ironically, civilizationism has reinstantiated western (US-style) imperialism, organizing it around the coordinates of the 'war on terror', with consequences—as much epistemological as cultural and political—that suggest the powerful capacity of empires to persist even given what Sayyid calls the postcolonial 'temper of the times' (see Part II of this volume). At the same time, Islam's continued haunting of the west suggests 'the contingency at the heart of the western [imperial] enterprise'; and this contingency, which also exists at the heart of contemporary postcolonial studies, might help explain why present-day articulations of Islam and empire play as much to the tensions of the 'postcolonial imperial present' as they do to the Islamicate imperial past.

In the section's concluding chapter, Timothy Brennan maintains the theoretical emphasis of Sayyid's piece, but makes clear that its main contribution is to *philosophy*, which he distinguishes from 'jackdaw' theory by linking it to specific, readily identifiable intellectual traditions anchored in core philosophical texts. The tradition he focuses on is Hegelian, and its core text is Hegel's *Philosophy of Right* (sometimes seen as a tacit defence of colonialism). For these and other reasons, Hegel might seem a curious choice, but as Brennan points out, Hegel's critique of the Enlightenment (see also Stoler's opening chapter in this section), his openness to non-European traditions, and his indebtedness to French revolutionary thought, all indicate his relevance to twentieth-century anti-colonial thinking, while the political oppositionalism embedded in *Philosophy of Right*, in particular, suggests that—contrary to the popular view of Hegel as a conservative apologist—there are radical political implications to his work.

Brennan's careful reading of *Philosophy of Right* reveals further complicities between imperialism and capitalism, between political and ethical considerations of empire, and—with another nod to Stoler's earlier chapter—between 'the political institutions of colonialism [and] the structure of colonialist thought'. Brennan does not deny the 'cultural disparagement' to be found in Hegel, e.g. his robust belief in the differences between 'advanced' and 'backward' cultures. Notwithstanding, he insists that Hegel, seen from the vantage point of what he unequivocally calls the 'imperial present', provides 'philosophical resources [for] the [continuing] anti-colonial project', not least via Hegel's spirited defence of human beings as the sole power capable of resisting global inequality—a defence as necessary as it ever was in face of what Brennan sees as the fake universalism and 'cybernetic triumphalism' of our allegedly 'posthuman' times (for a different view, see Rangan and Chow in Part III of this volume; also Mount and O'Brien in Part IV).

As suggested above, Brennan's chapter returns us to several of Stoler's arguments at the beginning of this section: that the imperial past secretes itself into the present; that empires need to be philosophically as well as materially resisted; and that resources can be found for this resistance even in the most apparently unpromising places: the self-justifying colonial archive; the racist philosophical text. This is not to compartmentalize the imperial past or to collapse it for instrumental purposes into the present; rather, it is to insist on what Edward Said calls, in another context, reading against the grain of empire in whichever forms—physical or mental, material or symbolic—it continues to be found.

REFERENCES

Ahmad, Aijaz (1992). *In Theory: Nations, Classes, Literatures*. New York: Verso.

Boehmer, Elleke (1995). *Colonial and Postcolonial Literature: Migrant Metaphors*. London: Routledge.

Darwin, John (2007). *After Tamerlane: The Global History of Empire Since 1405*. London: Penguin.

Darwin, John (2009). *The Empire Project: The Rise and Fall of the British World-System 1830–1970*. Cambridge: Cambridge University Press.

Doyle, Michael W. (1986). *Empires*. Ithaca: Cornell University Press.

Hardt, Michael and Antonio Negri (2000). *Empire*. Cambridge, Mass.: Harvard University Press.

Harvey, David (2003). *The New Imperialism*. New York: Oxford University Press.

Howe, Stephen (2002). *Empire: A Very Short Introduction*. Oxford: Oxford University Press.

Lazarus, Neil (2011). *The Postcolonial Unconscious*. Cambridge: Cambridge University Press.

Loomba, Ania (1999). *Colonialism/Postcolonialism*. New York: Routledge.

Said, Edward W. (1993). *Culture and Imperialism*. New York: Knopf.

Van Steenkiste, Serge J. (2008). 'Invitation to Thoroughly Rethink European and Western Expansionism', review of J. Darwin, *After Tamerlane*. Online source: <http://www.amazon.com/review/R2RB9XURUQVAE7>, accessed 18 December 2012.

CHAPTER 1

···

REASON ASIDE

*Reflections on Enlightenment
and Empire*

···

ANN LAURA STOLER

INTRODUCTION

···

One need not be well versed in the field of colonial studies to attest that the glare of the Enlightenment pervades historiographies of nineteenth-century European imperial formations and their analytic space. Some notion of 'an Enlightenment project' (as Alasdair MacIntyre first called it) features as a core conceptual frame for understanding how and why what is commonly referred to as 'universal reason' and 'totalizing systems of knowledge' underwrote European colonial expansions and made possible the regimes that claimed sovereignties over the non-European world (MacIntyre 1984: esp. 51–78; see also Young 1990). It is in these terms that many students of empire have come to understand the subjects that imperial macropolities created and coerced, the agents they recruited, the dispositions they cultivated, and the domains they privileged for intervention. Implicit or explicit, 'the Enlightenment' is cast as an organizing principle for understanding the epistemological scaffolding of imperial governance—what political lessons we need to learn from its prescriptive mandates and its durable effects, and which of those commanding logics surreptitiously work on and through us so differentially now.

To whomever and whatever we may attribute inspiration (Kant or Hegel), or grant pride of place to account for the ubiquity of this 'turn', of which there are too many to name (Theodor Adorno and Max Horkheimer, Michel Foucault, Edward Said, Jean-François Lyotard, or the scripted narratives of scientific progress that some colonial architects rehearsed amongst themselves), 'the Enlightenment' with a capital E appears almost seamlessly to map onto the capital E of empire. For that master of Enlightenment scholarship, Jonathan Israel, it is a postmodern camp that has been guilty of portraying 'The Enlightenment' as 'biased, facile, self-deluded, over-optimistic, Eurocentric, imperialistic and ultimately destructive' (2006a: v).[1] Israel's assault aside, the Enlightenment has been far more pluralized by students of empire than his derisive statement would suggest. If anything it is the sprawling scope of the Enlightenment's impact and the features underscored to define its most prominent concerns that need qualification (Berman 1998).[2]

The choice of verb to describe the effect of the Enlightenment's precepts on imperial principles may be vague or precise. So too its attributed effects: the Enlightenment has been argued to provide the vehicle of imperial domination, buttress empire, inaugurate the exploratory verve that opened to its voracious agrarian enterprises and ambitious scientific projects, shape the dispositions of empire's practitioners, preen imperial arrogance, prime anti-colonial nationalist movements, and not least animate and justify the toxic mix of coercive and curative interventions and reforms that have served the installation of European sovereignties across the globe. The notion of 'Enlightenment-as-imperialism' and the 'epistemic violences' that fusion enabled (as Gayatri Spivak has charged) have dominated scholarship over the last few decades just as its imaginary is said to have once instrumentally colonized so much of the world (Williams and Chrisman 1994: 15).

In this chapter, I invite us to look more carefully at what this fit between imperial formations and Enlightenment precepts looks like, between the workings of one imperial body politic, that of the nineteenth- and early twentieth-century Netherlands Indies, and the loose cut of its Enlightenment clothes. At issue is *not* the discrepancy between prescription and practice alone, but rather what constituted the lived epistemic space in which different forms of knowledge were combined, contested, and implicitly compared. There are three underlying, if tacit, assumptions that deserve examination and that frame my concerns in what follows. One is the unquestioned identification of empire with a 'rule of reason'. That equation seems to take little account of what was often a more cobbled and messy colonial order of things that careened between standardization and arbitrary protocols, bureaucratic precisions and unrealistic visions, large-scale planning and gross failures of foresight. Not least, the conditions and practices of governance often contravened what a commitment to reason might otherwise have required and a commitment to rational knowledge would have disallowed. The second assumption is also tacit. It is one that leaves unquestioned whether European colonials shared a clarity

---

[1] Interestingly, Israel significantly tones down his dismissal of postmodern scholarship after *Enlightenment Contested* obviously had already gone to press, noting instead of its practitioners: 'their partially correct (but too narrow) critique', and thinking 'with' them rather than against them. See also Israel (2006b).

[2] Berman impatiently condemns those who insist on collaboration between Enlightenment and empire. By his account, students of empire have got it all wrong by endorsing 'a blanket refusal of reason—and, by extension of science, progress, and a normative universalism'.

(if not consensus) about the kinds of knowledge that mattered to them. I would argue that they did not. With respect to the making of social kinds, to the production of racial categories, and to the strategies of security and surveillance that empire's architects and agents so assiduously sought to put in place, their confidence was often compromised by a disquieted and uncertain epistemic space (Stoler 2009).

The third assumption, that the Enlightenment is best designated as 'the Age of Reason', is one largely shared among students of empire but not unique to them. At issue are the multiple implications of that convention for how imperial governance has been viewed by scholars: how the latter have understood the domains empire's practitioners saw as their proper province; which particular kinds of knowledge those practitioners deemed 'relevant'; and ultimately what they saw as being their requisite tasks to perform. I am not alone in arguing that an overarching commitment to reason in fact poorly describes the compendium of the Enlightenment's core considerations or the prevailing concerns of many of those taken as Enlightenment exemplars. Here I follow Albert Hirschman's and Susan James's compelling arguments that in matters of governance and statecraft, the sentiments and passions—mental states usually opposed to the rule of reason—were central both to Enlightenment thinking and, as I hope to show, to colonial dispositions and the practices they served (Hirschman 1977). Indeed, it was seventeenth-century French philosophers who understood that the art of governance entailed 'the art of knowing men' (James 1997: 2). It was John Locke, after all, author of what some have considered 'the "Bible" of the Enlightenment', who attended so finely and fiercely to those affective sensibilities that made one eligible to be a proper citizen (Morsberger 1996; see also Mehta 1992, esp. ch. IV). Hume identified the contagious quality of sentiments, and later Adam Smith worried over the problematic careers of the moral sentiments in usefully or abusively shaping a state's agendas and political priorities (Pinch 1996).

Under Dutch colonial rule, attention to sentiments marked out the domains targeted for scrutiny and surveillance, the attachments and proximities seen as problematic, the 'habits of heart' that were demanded for governance but might alternately undermine its fragile order. Efforts to assess other people's non-manifest 'interior states' and the kinds of affective and psychological knowledge on which those assessments relied, were both critical for identifying who and what constituted a present threat to the colonial polity and, as importantly, who might constitute a threat in the future. This was more than a pragmatic problem in the apparatus of governance. A limited capacity to recognize political sentiments and personal attachments *that could not be measured* was understood as one of the most vulnerable nodes in the craft of rule. As I argue here, efforts to discern affective differences permeated the seemingly benign and more brutal strategies of defence, security and segregation. Not least, it underwrote a quest for affective knowledge about intuitions and inclinations that would make more accessible bodily, tactile, and intimate sites for intervention and control (Stoler 2010b).

I address these questions through the archival field that I know best, that of the nineteenth-century Netherlands Indies. It would be easy to see such a specific focus as peculiar and unique.[3] The Indies architecture of authority was singular. But the epistemic predicaments it reveals and repeats were not. My concern is specific, my archive particular to the Indies, my aims both narrow and broad: to offer another inflection on imperial dispositions less tethered by the supremacy of reason, one that opens to alternative genealogies of the present. My focus is on the making of social categories and the conceptual work (both epistemological and political) that went into the ascription of racial kinds.

One might imagine such a domain to provide a contrived invitation to illustrate how the logic of scientific rationality was invoked to authorize such distinctions and to secure the rigid categories that cordoned off and clarified those who were white and inherently superior from those who were not. Indeed, nineteenth-century race sciences sought and claimed to have found universal laws of racial classification derived from biologically blatant patterns of human physical variation.[4] It is in this quintessential and critical space of race-making—on which colonial regimes were so vitally dependent—that the noisy, ambiguous qualities of human admixture called to question the knowledges on which those distinctions could and should be made. If Enlightenment precepts and concepts mattered, they did so not because they provided the firm percepts of colonial rule, nor because they were wholly convincing and exhaustive; on the contrary, it is precisely because they were understood at the time to offer inadequate sources of epistemic authority for the pedagogy of empire's governing tasks.

THE RULE OF REASON

Even if the Enlightenment has been a very important phase in our history, and in the development of political technology, I think we have to refer to much more remote processes if we want to understand how we have been trapped in our own history. (Foucault 1981: 228)

Progress, reason, scientific rationality, liberalism, and secularism are among those many political concepts (and the institutional formations they animated) claimed to bear genealogies rooted in Enlightenment thinking. Such thinking is claimed to have made it possible

---

[3.] According to Jonathan Israel, the Dutch Enlightenment had its strongest influence on the European Enlightenment and was of 'diminishing' importance and increasingly 'marginal' throughout the 18th century. Israel's notion that the establishment of the *Maatschappij tot Nut van 't Algemeen* (Society for the Public Good) was a significant example of Dutch Enlightenment projects is problematic. Not only was it an institution based on punitive care and coercive instruments of reform, it became one of the models for the children's agricultural colonies that some have called 'prisons in the fields'. See Israel (1995: 1038–66); on the Dutch Enlightenment in Java see Taylor (1983: 78–95); on the *Maatschappij tot Nut van 't Algemeen*, see Schauwers (2001: 298–328), also Stoler (2010b).

[4.] The histories that have been written with this story of racism are too many to list here. For one example, see Taguieff (1988).

for empire's advocates to conceive of their ventures as ennobling enterprises, to school its agents and architects to value their jobs as moral missions if not relish their bureaucratic tasks. Foundational Enlightenment priorities find in empire what Uday Mehta writes of liberalism, its iconic descendant, as the concrete space of its dreams (Mehta 1999: esp. Intro.; see also Gopal in Part II of this volume). In Partha Chatterjee's incisive account, it is the tyrannical universality of Reason that sets passions to work in its service while keeping 'itself in the background, untouched, unharmed … [and] unscathed' (1993: 168.) He locates 'the story of the Enlightenment in the colonies' in 'the hands of the policemen and … in the station house when the cunning of reason turns against "particular ethical values of the nation" (168). Gyan Prakash identifies the subtle ways in which scientific reason became "a multivalent sign" that exerted force in a wider social and political domain. In British India, reason was the syntax of reform for British colonials and Indian intellectuals. Universal Reason, he holds, was not only a means of rule adapted to other guises and other languages; science was "the grammar of modern power with its fullest expression in the state" (1999: 9). On the terrain of Latin America, Walter Mignolo tracks an earlier genealogy of imperial authority that also asserted a hegemonic epistemological imaginary': 'a planetary epistemological standard' that valued scientific authority and its credibility above other ways of knowing the world with Reason supporting a new global design (2000: 59; see also Mignolo in this section of the volume).

Central to these claims is identification not only of an imperial veneration of Reason and rational knowledge, but of empire as a crystalline and unspoken embodiment of the way both worked their way through the infrastructure of authority, the hierarchies of credibility and the prioritized policies in colonial relations. Colonial circumstances are said to have offered a new sense of, and sites for, the uses of rational knowledge to tame nature and control subject populations, fuelled by those with conviction in its power, in its transformative qualities, and in the pragmatics of governance, its efficacy and worth. Peter Gay reminds us in his much-lauded volume *The Enlightenment: The Science of Freedom* (1996), that it was Francis Bacon who, in breaking with the historical fatalism that preceded the Enlightenment, insisted that knowledge was power. It is students of colonialism who have attributed that insight, so differently mobilized, to Foucault. For Dipesh Chakrabarty (2000), the master narrative of the European Enlightenment has been, and continues to be, the silent referent that organized the Eurocentric epistemics of imperial knowledge production. As Partha Chatterjee (1993) has shown, India's elite nationalists shared its premises and were entrapped by it. Chakrabarty demonstrates how that narrative has enforced a pernicious teleology, a sequential temporality, and a form of historical progression that captured colonial agents, and more pointedly still governs our writing of history and continues unknowingly to bind us all.

If what falls under the Enlightenment project is sometimes encompassing and broad, it is the elevation of a parochial, local, and culture-bound sense of reason to a universal standard against which critical colonial studies has been rightly aimed—against epistemological commitments that have partitioned the world into unequally deserving and differentially capable social kinds, plotted on a grid that divides those who are either committed to and capable of reason from those who are not. As Dorinda Outram has put it, 'The Enlightenment itself often seemed to devote as much energy to designating entire social groups, such as women or peasants, as impervious to the voice of reason, as it did to constructing a better world for [some] human beings' (1995: 21–2). The deeper critique targets less implementation than the structural entailments of knowledge production itself.

Rethinkings of this tableau have come from within and outside the quarters of colonial historians. Sarkar Muthu (2003) contends that the foes of empire were among the most prominent Enlightenment intellectuals and that by eliminating those anti-imperial arguments from our purview we have diminished our own ability to track the diverse effects of its force. Gyan Prakash (1999) argues that India's colonized intellectuals mounted their assault by asserting 'another reason', thereby opening colonialism's 'normalizing myth ... to questioning and contention ... [and to] a space for the negotiation of science's status as truth' (72).[5] Richard Schweder (1984) attributes to his discipline (and my own), anthropology, a long-standing appreciation of cultural difference that refused the normative uniformity of mankind under the 'dictate of reason and evidence' (27–66).

No one who has spent time in French, British, Dutch, or German colonial archives would deny that scientific and technological inquiry and innovations were fundamental to the organizational apparatus of imperial ventures, or that colonial administrations called upon and encouraged European experts and amateurs of all kinds—botanists, economists, geographers, architects, doctors, epidemiologists—to ply their trade, refine their instruments, and indeed to imagine and to attempt to make of colonized places their comparative 'laboratories of modernity' on an unfettered scale (Pyenson 1980; Goss 2011). Still, after nearly three decades of work in the French and Dutch colonial archives, I am struck by how much is missed and amiss in how these mappings of the Enlightenment onto empire are framed. There seems something too readily unquestioned about the epistemic commitments that are supposed to have governed colonial visions, something too capacious in the ready line-up of governing practices with the Enlightenment's abstract claims.[6] I broach this issue by

---

[5] Aamir Mufti (2007) insists that it is a 'false perception to view the colonial reenactment of the modern bourgeois Enlightenment as entirely the imposition of an external (European) form' (24).

[6] Let me clear. My focus is not primarily on science and empire. I have no intention of contradicting the fine-grained historical work, in so many different colonial contexts, on the synergies of scientific and imperial pursuits across so many domains, as in Richard Grove's exemplary work, *Green Imperialism* (1995). And of course colonial bureaucracies across the globe drew on science to collect statistics, to dam up rice fields for export crops, to convert sugar beet machines into those for Javanese cane sugar, to conceive imperial maps (and reorder space to fit them) in the pursuit of imperial sovereignty, under the sign of giving 'value', and in the name of progress and profit, social welfare, and peace. Nor is my subject Enlightenment thinking among colonial subjects, popular or elite visionaries who appropriated its emancipatory lexicon of freedom for themselves. Others are pursing those projects with finesse. I think, among others, of David Scott's considered reading of Toussaint L'Ouverture and C. L. R. James's early attention to him, of Michel-Rolph Trouillot and Laurent Dubois' study of the French and Haitian revolutions, of Partha Chatterjee's rendition of a Bengali middle-class elite smitten with Enlightenment precepts, and of Akeel Bilgrami's treatment of Gandhi's prophetic warnings against a 'liberal democracy' that India's elite were so eager to embrace as part of the dissenting 'Radical Enlightenment'. See Scott 2004; James 2001; Trouillot 1995; Dubois 2004; Chatterjee 1995: 93–117; Bilgrami 2006.

examining the effects of what I call the 'epistemic politics' of empire—the constellation of conceptually articulated and inchoate understandings of what the arts and crafts of governance entailed in the late nineteenth-century and early twentieth-century Netherlands Indies—on the ways of knowing that guided its practitioners and on what made up the unstable coordinates of colonial common sense (Stoler 2008a). I am struck by how much is assumed about what colonial agents did, how they did it, and not least about how successfully they achieved—and how much they were convinced of—their taxonomic goals.

WHAT WE KNOW AND HOW WE KNOW IT

The science of order is the science of a lie. (Rancière 2004: 17)

'Reason', as we know too well, is an elusive, indeed moving target: mobile in meaning, unfettered by scale, historically contingent, radically altered by context.[7] In its movement between common noun and commanding concept, it may silently traverse the analytic heights of philosophy, detail the precise procedures of scientific enquiry, or ratify that which constitutes the thoughtful grounds for the most mundane acts. With a capital R it represents at once a European philosophical tradition of truth production, both the form and content of the kind of knowledge valorized in it. As a verb, 'to reason', it often loses its philosophical command and epistemic weight. As an adjective to modify an action considered 'reasoned' and 'reasonable', it parses shared understandings and prosaic requirements. As a modifier of 'knowledge', the adjective 'rational' stands in its place to indicate either subsumption by a set of norms and procedures or conceptual schemes already in place, independent of what any practitioner may find on the ground. If sometimes these different senses of the term are distinguished, they often were, and still are, not.[8] As students of empire have argued, the conflation of reason as a mental faculty, universal reason as a specific European logic, and reason—as opposed to emotion—as that which is required to make good judgements is no historical or

---

[7] As Talal Asad notes, when people make claims about the concept of rationality (and religion) it is not always clear what concept of rationality they are using. See his *Genealogies of Religion* (1993: 235) and footnotes 57 and 58 therein. On the use of a concept of rationality in current debates that is 'wider than mere scientific truth', see Chatterjee (1993), esp. 14–17; with respect to science as a 'multivalent sign' that 'penetrates the fabric of social life' in the history of Indian modernity, see also Prakash 1999: 7.

[8] Akeel Bilgrami offers one enabling way to clarify our use of the concept of rationality in this impacted epistemic and historical space, suggesting that we distinguish between a 'thin' sense of rationality as that which is 'uncontroversially possessed by all' and a 'thick' sense of rationality that 'owes to specific historical developments in outlook around the time of the rise of science and its implications for how to think ("rationally") about culture and politics and society'. It is the 'thick' notion of scientific rationality against which Gandhi's critiques were aimed, a position, Bilgrami argues, that he shared with many proponents of the Radical Enlightenment. See Bilgrami (2006) and the responses to it.

semantic accident.[9] Their interchangeability has been understood to form part of the unspoken epistemological matrix of European superiority, the Enlightenment's legacy, a conflation that helped secure the hierarchical racial order of the imperial world.

Still, the archival record for this period of Dutch rule in its colonial heartland of Java and Sumatra sits uneasily with a conception of a rule of reason as its operative frame. If 'reason' was 'the syntax of reform', it was a grammar that yielded neither a clear political semantics nor straightforward rules of application. Dipesh Chakrabarty notes that the task of examining European rationalism in the history of empire is 'a matter of documenting how its "reason," which was not always self-evident to everyone, has been made to look obvious far beyond the ground where it originated' (2000: 43). I would agree. Our points of entry and sites of query are complementary. But they are not the same. Chakrabarty's are posed against what he sees as the warped, constraining optic of European colonial archives and the unspoken logic and forms of history that underwrote their implicit truth claims. My points of entry are the documentary forms and the political content subjacently lodged within them. My sights turn more toward a history of what Gaston Bachelard once called 'epistemological detail', to those conceptual and political perturbations that disperse and hug close along—and on the ragged edges of—the European colonial archival grain (1940: 12).[10] Or to put it differently: threats to colonial common sense come in many forms: some 'breaches of self-evidence' are pressed by colonial subjects; others erupt from within the protocols of governance itself, those moments 'when the certainties are lost' among those Europeans we have taken to be Reason's disciples and advocates.[11]

The 'minor' histories, to which Dipesh Chakrabarty and I turn, converge and diverge as well. Both 'cast doubt on the "major"' and reflect on the ways in which the '"rationality" of the historian's methods necessarily makes [relationships to the past] "minor" or inferior, as something "nonrational" … as a result of, its own operation' (2000: 101). Chakrabarty's focus probes other ways of knowing 'subaltern pasts' excluded from what counts as history in a European mode. Mine rest with the unquiet minds of colonialisms' European practitioners to invoke what I think of as 'history in a minor key'. Such a history initiates a rereading of the anxious and anticipatory states that imperial governance engendered to better understand the regimes of security it produced and the expectant, affective economies on which imperial formations continue to depend.

My interest here is in the Dutch civil servants and in the social, industrial, legal, and medical technicians who worked directly for them or on the outskirts of their authority.

---

9. While much of the contrast was between reason and the authority of *religious* sentiments—of faith—it is the more general distinction between the calculus of reason and the capricious, unpredictable power of the sentiments that has had such lasting post-Enlightenment resonance.

10. The term 'epistemological detail' is actually Hans-Jörg Rheinberger's beautiful translation of Bachelard's methodological entreaty to turn away from '*un seul point de vue fixe*' and instead to imagine a 'method of arranged dispersion', '*une méthode d'analyse très fine*'. See Rheinberger (1997: 23).

11. 'A breach of self-evidence' is Michel Foucault's definition of a historical event. See Foucault (1994); also Foucault (1997: 143).

Both groups palpably struggled with the criteria to use in assigning racial categories and evaluating moral dangers and political threats, and with how to make convincing and credible their assessments. They questioned not the validity of empire so much as the kinds of knowledge that served what they were counted on to know. Epistemic clarity eluded them: what a deep confidence in a 'calculus of reason' and science as 'the measure of men' might be imagined to bestow (Adas 1989).

To say that what constituted 'reason' for them was not self-evident is not to suggest that they were closet anti-imperialists, renegades to European colonial society, or unheralded descendants of the counter-Enlightenment. On the contrary, they were, as Paul Rabinow once aptly called them, colonialism's 'social technicians'—both fledgling and seasoned bureaucratic agents of empire whose reports had to be comprehensible and convincing to their superiors about who was a danger, what threatened security, and what was a risk (1989: 13). To make credible their recommendations, they needed to be versed both in the categories that demonstrated a skilled adherence to the repertoire of narratives deemed appropriate, and in the selective choice of contexts that accorded with those conventions. Such prosaic features of reportage were subject to the 'political rationalities' of rule but never dictated by the mandates of 'reason' alone.

Who has a 'Fear of Phantoms'?

> A ruler who is himself enlightened has no fear of phantoms, yet who likewise has at hand a well-disciplined and numerous army to guarantee public security, may say what no republic would dare to say: Argue as much as you like and about whatever you like, but obey! (Kant, quoted in Asad 1993: 203)

Whether construed as a period, a 'cultural climate', an intellectual phenomenon, a political legacy, or a disposition toward the world in Kant's sense above, the work Enlightenment thinking has been enlisted to perform may account for both less than its evocation promises and than its accusers profess: less in that classificatory zeal is often taken as evidence of its definitive imprint on colonial epistemology; less in that historical emphasis on the regulative 'architectonics' of reason privileges prescriptive categories rather than the fractious epistemic work and uncertainties of those who wrestled with them.[12] As with any commanding term elevated to a concept, the Enlightenment is a 'point of condensation' that gathers in its components, as it draws in affiliate concepts that provide resonance and make it 'work' (Deleuze and Guattari 1994: 20). It prescribes a *directionality*, pre-empts and prompts certain lines of enquiry. Most importantly, it forecloses and precludes others. It promises access and legibility, generalizations that comfort as they bind and arrest.

[12.] On Kant's 'architectonics of reason', see Derrida (2005: 120).

Peter Gay, who has sought to remind us of the diverse and acrimonious currents within the Enlightenment, still celebrates it as a period marked by 'the recovery of nerve', a 'ubiquitous and irresistible' commitment to an 'ardent and unshackled spirit of inquiry' (1996: 11). Many historians might agree that nineteenth-century imperial projects relished that encyclopedic quest for knowledge and displayed that nerve, albeit in brash and destructive ways. But one might be equally struck by how much imperial management produced and displayed the opposite: a nervous reticence about what to know, distrust of civil servants who knew too much, a bureaucratic shuffling that regularly moved officials from one region or district to the next, favouring a bracketed know-how, stupefied states of ensured ignorance (as Avital Ronell 2002 might call them), and—ostensibly to curb collusion and corruption with local rulers—truncated local ties and thin familiarities. Local knowledge was filtered through and schooled in Dutch institutions in the Netherlands, a requirement for access to all but the lowest civil service positions. Only then was knowledge of Java brought back to Java. Valorized and relevant local knowledge, as I have long argued, could not be really local at all.

During the opening of East Sumatra's plantation belt in the 1870s such strategies served them poorly. In the final chapters of *Along the Archival Grain* (2009), I recount the story of the abrupt dismissal of a certain newly transferred district officer, Frans Carl Valck, who, confronted by an unprecedented series of murders of European planters in the months before his arrival, was unprepared (and some thought unhinged) by the multiple acts of violence in and around the estates but as much by the wooden categories in which he was schooled to make sense of them. Outraged at the false facts imparted by planters, he was ultimately undone by what he knew, what he asked, and what he did not then know about the principles of imperial disregard expected of civil servants stationed near the European estates (181–236). He gave native rumours credibility over the confected facts plied to him by planters committed to maintaining their unencumbered control. Valck was ousted from the service and excised from colonial hagiographic history for knowing both too little and too much.

The iconic Enlightenment motto 'dare to know' may have animated some of the new 'self-consciously scientific Orientalists' that Christopher Bayly describes in his study of British political intelligence in northern India in the 1790s (1996: 118). And Andrew Goss (2011) may be right that the 'floracrats' in Java who collected and classified plants 'strove for' an Enlightenment ideal of ordered knowledge. But such quests and bravado were hardly typical of Dutch colonial practice in the Netherlands Indies. Massive compilations of statistics, scientific initiatives, and political intelligence were joined with a circumspect disposition toward knowledge of the world in which colonial civil servants lived. Someone like Frans Carl Valck was not alone in having to reckon with the failure of what he was schooled to take as prevailing common sense. It proved to be a poor guide for when and from what he should have properly turned away. Trust, the backbone of civil service collegiality, was strained in a social environment where people could not be sure to belong to the legal (European) status they claimed or to be whom they morally claimed to be. Or perhaps distrust was more deeply carved into colonial relations among Europeans by the compounded illegitimacies of the profits and privileges accrued from their ventures.

The notion that the Enlightenment enforced a reduction to the 'calculability of the world' had more success in some domains of Indies administration than others. If the moral sciences were born of Enlightened Reason, the Dutch colonial archives tell other tales: ones in which the tools for delineating racial categories proved too blunt to do their work, inadequately sharpened to read those 'invisible ties', affective bonds and moral proclivities for which physical attributes provided poor access. Intuitions about comportment, habits, and affiliations filled in that with which more scientific criteria and measurements could not contend. If statistics was designed to subject social relations to the 'sweet despotism of reason', as Ian Hacking argues, it was a tool of limited use (1990: 35). It could not predict the political aspirations of those who threatened the state's projects nor could it identify the abnormally strong and wilful sentiments that coursed among them. It could not distinguish true Europeans from those who sought sundry means to claim that status. Not least, it could not identify those who would remain reliably loyal from those whose sentiments might turn them recalcitrant, stubbornly resistant to higher command, or subversive.

Let me underscore a critical point: at issue was not a 'failed' project of reason that nevertheless held dominant sway. There were successes and failures to be sure. My point is that rational, scientific ways of knowing the world were insufficient for governance. They were inadequate to describe the temperament of rule, nor did they capture how it worked. Priya Satia, in an incisive study of what she calls Britain's 'covert empire' in the Middle East, argues that intuitions guided intelligence strategies precisely because rational knowledge could not. This 'intuitive mode' may have been a 'radical departure from the dogged empiricism of earlier and contemporary efforts to gather information' within the British Empire, as she argues. Still, it was neither an invention emerging with the Great War nor was it specific to British intelligence operations as she repeatedly claims (Satia 2008: 6). Intuitive knowledge not only directed early twentieth-century spies on the edges of empire. In the Netherlands Indies, it also shaped the archives of security that document nineteenth-century imperial governance, the imagined and real threats on which those intuitions fed, and the intimate, secreted domains of bedroom and nursery into which the quest for 'security' invariably sought to reach (Stoler 1995, esp. ch. V). What separated grounded intuitions from extravagant fabrication was not always clear. However we might describe that space in between, it would not be captured by a commitment to 'rational knowledge'.

Nor was this the case just for the Indies. Thomas Richards argues that an 'epistemological paranoia' that 'conflated knowledge and terror' was the hallmark of a British 'corporate subject' in whom that paranoia 'can be seen as part of a larger and systematic phenomenology of rearmament'. Richards' insights about 'epistemological panic' draw on colonial fiction but these are descriptions that make sense of a much wider imperial phenomenon across the globe (1993: 14). From what was then the Netherlands Indies to South Asia, the 'supremacy of reason' might better be termed a fantasy of reason applied to the phantoms of empire.

Already figured as a key diacritic of the Enlightenment and of empire, as colonial historians we are quick to question the authority of Reason, but not its authority among colonial agents themselves. Doing so exposes equivocations that otherwise would have no rightful place. For example, if we take one common definition of 'rational knowledge' as that which allows one to order categories, recognize viable categories, and include or exclude members from them, its pre-eminent authority seems more tenuous, more fragile, less suited to bear its authoritative weight. Among empire's agents, category errors were rampant, markers of difference were fluid and vexed. Orphanage directors had only vague guidelines when confronted with light-skinned children who chose to stay with their native mothers or fathers. Colonial lawyers filled their briefs on the regulation of mixed marriage with dense footnoted exegeses on the barrage of claims to European rights and membership (or outright rejection of them) that laws could not help them assess.

'Rational knowledge' did not always fail its purveyors and practitioners, but in situations in which it did so, it tended to do so again and again. Decisions about who counted as a European and by what measure, whether racial attributes derived from the tainted milk of a native woman who was or was not an infant's mother, at what age a child of mixed parentage could be lost or redeemed as European, whether a Maltese or Italian in colonial Algeria was really French or merely 'neo-French' as the historian Pierre Nora once disparagingly called them (only designated as French by their 'identity papers', as he wrote), relied on multiple ways of apprehending and evaluating what Clifford Geertz once called 'the tonalities and temper' of the common sense of their social world (Nora 1961; see also Stoler 2011). Reasoning, as the philosopher Susan James asserts, is 'arduous'. By popular Enlightenment notions of reason, it was 'severe, rigorous, strict, exact, and above all *unpersuasive*' (1997: 215). In the Indies, intuitions and the 'considered thought' of common sense, conveyed in 'temper' and 'tonalities', could sometimes have more purchase in the grey borderlands of race and in the invisible networks of 'the enemy' that imperial intelligence was charged to trace (Geertz 1983: 84). Racialized exemptions and exclusions did not depend on a fixed set of essentialisms but on protean and strategic rearrangements of them (Stoler 1997). The Enlightenment notion of reason—which James describes as 'strict' and 'exact'—did not.

Intuition, as Aristotle imparted to his disciples, was the basis of reasoned wisdom, but colonial intuitions were turned to other ends. They emanated from an elaborately imagined world of potential enemies in the making, poised to storm their guarded privilege and sequestered space. What historians of science Lorraine Daston and Peter Galison call 'epistemic worries' were the constant concerns of governing agents (2007: 35). They were more aware than we, who feverishly cull their archived inscriptions, of their piecemeal knowledge and how much evaded what they were charged to count, measure, anticipate, and control.

If these tasks were usually seamlessly carried out, as my first distracted readings of the Dutch colonial archives' formulaic narratives seemed to suggest, in repeated returns I have come to see more the uneasy labour that could appear as surface tremors through tedious reports and rote refrains. Contexts were never givens. The choice of one rather than another could give credence to one set of truth claims, dismiss the validity of another, or frame the parameters and thus the 'causes' sought to explain an 'event'. Choices of context imply epistemic commitments, how they are contested and change. Whether the slashing of a European planter and his family was attributed to an Aceh-based Islamic assault on European rule or to the idiosyncratic passions of an abused and vengeful estate worker marshalled both different kinds of 'proof' and different ways of assessing mental states. What emerges as a choice of context indexes both how people imagine they know what they do and the affective grids of intelligibility on which they draw.

How words are used and repeated in these archives draws us close to this epistemic unease to broach something more than the strictures of bureaucratic conventions. Phrases and wording sometimes adhered to protocol; sometimes they marked falterings about the suitability and proper use of received designations. Such hesitancies unsettle the sure-footed criteria of what 'goes without saying' so central to the force of common sense and to the fictive clarities of a taxonomic state.

The intensity and density of the debates that crescendoed in the late nineteenth century around one particular social category, that of the *inlandsche kinderen* (who were neither natives [*inlandsche*] nor children [*kinderen*] as a literal translation would suggest), offers a 'paradigmatic' site of this unease, in the sense that Agamben understands a paradigm, where the contradictions are on the surface—acute and exposed (Agamben 2009: 18). What colonial agents had to say about the category of *inlandsche kinderen* (a designation that constantly slipped between 'poor whites', Indo-Europeans, déclassé Europeans born in the Indies, and those who were mixed and veered more toward native cultural sensibilities than European ones)—and who officials differently imagined they were—is a story about the making and unmaking of that crafted clustering in the Indies' racial history. But it is not about that alone. It is also about the competing intelligibilities that racial regimes called forth. Hesitancies about social labels and uncertainty about their use provide entry points to identify a 'breach of self-evidence'—Foucault's provocative definition, as we have seen, for a historical 'event'.[13] These are moments of discernment, when colonial common sense and convention failed them, when that which people thought they knew, and how they might know it, they found they did not.

Inlandsche kinderen was a mobile designation about social milieu, an appellate and a political fact. That many Eurasian children were raised in 'respectable' families made no difference to the reams of colonial literature, newspaper articles, and confidential official documents that worried incessantly about the micro-environments in which they lived: whether children were acquiring the dispositions and cultural competencies to be European or in the case of poor mixed-blood children, whether they were properly

---

[13.] Foucault's phrase is actually a '*rupture des évidences*', but I prefer Paul Rabinow's rendering of it as a '*breach* of self-evidence', which better captures than would a literal translation something between a 'break' and 'gap' and Foucault's identification of that which at one moment seems so obvious and at another no longer is so. See also Rabinow (2003: 41).

schooled in the unspoken rules that would limit their aspirations. Racialized perceptions and practices are rarely diminished or deterred by contrary empirical evidence. These are the complex social imaginaries that shape the emotional economies and sensory regimes by which people distinguish 'us' from 'them'.

Displaced histories are folded within the changing contours of who 'fitted' or refused the labels assigned to them. There is no colonial mindset lurking in the pen's shadow, no overarching *mentalité* floating in the ether of colonial space. We would do better as historians of colonial governance to attend to the ground lying between the resiliency and fragility of categories, to the moments when reasonings went awry, when the rubrics of 'poor whites' and 'mixed bloods' made little sense because people and things were not what and where they ought to be. Under such conditions the 'ought' could waver, either reassert its authority or dissolve in the face of its contradictions; a term might be abandoned, substituted, and changed. The contested epistemics of race emerge in these moments, the explicit and oblique ways of knowing on which the knowledge of social kinds relied. Social ontologies (and specifically racial ones) were reassembled and remade. Much of the provocation for *Along the Archival Grain* came from pausing when racial attributes once accepted as signature features of social membership were questioned or emphatically reaffirmed. Such unanticipated interruptions invite us to attend to what people did next. Some sought to press their queries further; others rapidly recoiled from their own doubts and disregarded what they saw or heard in favour of what they knew they were supposed to have witnessed, or what those they hoped and needed to trust, chose to report and said.

Epistemic labour is wedged within their narratives, sometimes slicing through received rubrics with uncensored turns of phrase, hesitant asides in marginalia, brash queries slashed across a page in the imperative or acquisitive tense. Confused assessments, parenthetic doubt about what might count as evidence, eyewitness accounts by those with dubious credentials, dismissed rumours laced with pertinent truth, contradictory testimonies called upon and quickly discarded—these are when words slip from their safe moorings to reappear unauthorized, inappropriate, and unrehearsed. In the epistemic politics of empire, it is not Enlightenment reason that guides their disquiet. Uncertainty provides the subjacent coordinates.

For the Indies, the Weberian model of rationally minded, bureaucratically driven state actors buttressed by accredited knowledge and scientific legitimacy, and backed by a monopoly on armed force demands modification. If homage to reason was a hallmark of rule, it was neither pervasive nor persuasive, nor yet its sole guiding force. As prominent in these colonial archives that range across public and secreted documents, official and private correspondence, and commissioned reports is not the rule of reason but what might be (mis)construed as its opposite—a discursive density around sentiments and their subversive tendencies, around sensibilities and their political consequences, around intuitive know-how, around assessments of affective dispositions and their beneficent and dangerous political effects.

I have fleshed out parts of this argument in *Along the Archival Grain* and will not do so here again. But it might useful to elaborate on some key points. The 'political rationalities' of Dutch rule—those strategically reasoned forms of administrative common sense that informed policy and practice—were grounded in schooling appropriate sentiments, in shaping appropriate and reasoned affect, in directing affective judgements, and in deterring those that collided with administrative control.

SENSIBILITIES IN POLITICAL RATIONALITIES

One defining feature attributed to the Enlightenment project was the normative guide it is said to have offered for subordinating individual passions to their rightful place in the social realm, and for the clear and principled distinctions it made between reasoned judgement and affective life. Both features have been subject in recent scholarship to critical re-evaluation. Students of seventeenth- and eighteenth-century philosophy are increasingly prepared to argue, as does Susan James, that the passions have been systematically ignored as a 'central topic [in] the heartland of early-modern [Enlightenment] philosophy' (1997: 25). It was Bacon who held that governance required knowing 'how affections are kindled, and incited; how pacified and refrained, how they disclose themselves, how they work, how they vary, how they gather and fortify, how they are enwrapped one within another'. Members of the Indies administration understood that well. Colonial statecraft took seriously the force of affect and strove for its mastery. The concern in seventeenth-century political thinking that states should be called upon to harness individual passions, to transform and civilize the sentiments of their subjects through counteracting ones, as Albert Hirschman recognized, was 'to prosper...as a major tenet of nineteenth-century liberalism' (1977: 19). It was also to flourish as a key diacritic in distinguishing race.

Hirschman's history of the passions suggests another genealogy. It would not be a history that starts with the supremacy of reason in the nineteenth century and then traces it back to the Enlightenment roots of rationality. It would rather set out one of equal force, and with as long a *durée*. It might register how much political theory and moral philosophy of the seventeenth and eighteenth centuries contested the role of the sentiments in issues of governance. As numerous philosophers of the period now insist, the sentiments and affections were not always opposed to reason but were its 'underbelly' (Gaukroger 1998). Our genealogy might look to that eighteenth-century 'culture of sensibility', which tied material power and moral weight to the taste and character of cultivated and lettered men.

Most importantly, it would not start with a clear-cut division between reason and sentiment as distinct and given conceptual realms. Rather, it would track how they were entangled, disassembled, and conjoined. It would trace that sustained oscillation and ambiguous distinction between the two, not the definitive dominance of the former and their pointed severance. It might go further and attend to those moments—and events—in which the two did not collide as separate recognizable faculties but inextricably meshed. It might start from an observation shared among many across the disciplines, that 'emotions' are not outside reason but privileged sources of critical judgement (Solomon 1988, 2004; see also Nussbaum 2001). It might pursue William Reddy's claim that modernity's early moments in the 'age of reason' could as accurately be characterized as an 'age of sentiments'.[14] It would register the work of sentiment in *constituting* both reason and political rationality in eighteenth-century philosophical debates. It might track the recursive features of that entangled political space.

Not least, it might allow us to work differently through the politics of the darker sentiments and sensibilities that imperial projects of the twentieth and twenty-first centuries continued to produce and on which they have continued to depend: anxiety, fear, and paranoia. These were fundamental to forging the technologies of security that cordoned off persons and space; that forced migration or restricted movement; and that legitimated expulsions, manhunts, and incarcerations. It is these affects that account for what Rob Nixon (2011) has called 'the slow violences' to which imperial polities adhered, violences that rational knowledge could not explain nor wholly help us comprehend.

Gertrude Himmelfarb argues that we have all been misled by imagining that the Enlightenment belonged to the French, or that their 'ideology of reason' faithfully captures what the Enlightenment was about. By her account, its more 'enlightened' expression emerged from the analytic and political impulses of British and Scottish moral philosophers with their attention to the 'social affections' (2005: 19). She is right to point to the affections but grossly misconstrues the sorts of political work those affections were enlisted to do. Her account of the beneficent virtues does not stray from Europe or the US. But the distribution of compassion, sympathy, and pity—who had them and to whom they were rightly directed—was pivotal to the workings of imperial formations. Each was part of the durable architecture of empire, with exacting exclusions and inequities structured through them. They charted the affective grid that separated true Europeans and their colonized others and provided the affective grounds on which racially distinguished 'benevolent' institutions were formed. Social hierarchies were created and bolstered by sympathy for empire's subjects (Rai 2002; see also Stoler 2006b). Pity demanded distance and preserved it as forcefully as did segregated housing, pools, and schools (Boltanski 1999).

Himmelfarb's chosen contemporary exemplar of an Enlightenment legacy makes precisely this point despite her own intention. She finds it alive and well in George W. Bush's solution to curb welfare and social services for the poor, what he called 'compassionate conservatism', an aggressively punitive social project that she praises for 'encourag[ing] the social affection of the one while respecting the moral dignity of the other'. On the contrary, compassionate conservatism was boldly marked by a racialized principle of distinction between those deserving of public welfare and those who were

---

[14.] William Reddy makes this argument explicit in his unpublished manuscript, 'The Emotional Common Sense of True Modernity', but more generally suggests such a rethinking in *The Navigation of Feeling* (2001) and *The Invisible Code* (1997). I thank him for allowing me to quote from this unpublished manuscript.

not. Not unlike Thomas Haskell's description of the principles that guided humanitarian sensibility in the early nineteenth century, sympathy provided 'an ethical shelter', a way of confining one's responsibility to a fraction of 'suffering humanity without feeling that we have thereby intended [to do so]' (Haskell 1985: Part 1: 352). That is the genealogy that should be tracked. As Hannah Arendt parsed pity, it is the pleasure of 'being sorry without being touched in the flesh' (1965: 80).

Partha Chatterjee has held that Reason with a capital R went 'untouched and unscathed' in the colonial project, following Hegel's lesson that because reason does not work directly on the subject or lower itself to becoming a particular thing, it cunningly makes the individual's passions work in its service. Some of the British colonial elite may indeed have seen empirical science as universal rational knowledge, free from prejudice and passion. But, as Johannes Fabian makes the case, the practices of British scientific explorers in Africa showed otherwise. In *Out of Our Minds* (2000), which he calls a 'critique of imperialist reason', Fabian argues that the accumulation of ethnographic knowledge was inseparable from the prejudices and passions that equally guided these men. Affective and emotional registers of experience were prerequisites, not hindrances to what they sought to know and how they were able to know it.[15]

If knowledge production among some scientific explorers was dependent on affective knowledge, the art of governance was as well. Like Hume, the Indies' governing elite saw the sentiments as contagious and portable. They pondered how far and fast social passions and political sensibilities could traverse the colony and globe. Dutch colonials wrote incessantly of the '*stille kracht*' (the hidden force of the Indies) that could destroy their collective project, the European community's security, an individual's sense of composure: what counted toward maintaining a European self and soul. This is not to rehearse *Heart of Darkness* but rather to underscore a point to which Edward Said hinted in his 1966 study of Conrad's letters. Conrad and those Europeans about whom he wrote did not live with the assurance of Reason at their backs, but with a troubled relationship to what they knew or, as Said put it, a 'problematic knowledge' of themselves. The 'syntax of reason' was found wanting, an impoverished grammar of intelligibility, for what they needed to do and act upon, and where they needed to locate themselves. It was not only then in the allegedly mystical, tradition-bound world of the colonized other where passions went amok and where people were animated by spectral fears and visions. Panivong Norindr (1996) is not alone in claiming that it was 'phantasmatic Indochina' rather than anything else that most French knew so well.

It was not just the failures of reason that disrupted the coherence of colonial agents and the policies they were charged to enforce. It was also an exuberant imaginary

[15.] It is hard not to notice that many of those most concerned with this relationship are eminent students of South Asian history and of the British Empire in particular. I would only note that just as our understanding of the gradated degrees of sovereignty on which imperial formations have been based do not coincide with the South Asian template, Dutch, French, US, German, and Spanish historiography has been far less bent on granting a rule of reason—or assaults on it—such a prominent place.

that produced a commitment to something else; what one might argue was a fundamental and frequent turn *away from reason* organized a spectrum of nervous, expectant, protective small and large-scale gestures: infeasible blueprints for colonial projects, improbable security measures, a continually shifting set of confinements, detentions, and displacements that were to reorder and bind the social and spatial partitions of their privileged, profitable, and insecure world, and could never do so enough.

EPISTEMIC PRACTICE

Recent thinking about the politics of epistemology and empire leaves little room to examine the *lived epistemic space* in which empire's architects and agents operated. What colonial actors imagined they could know and, more importantly, *what epistemic habits they developed to know it*, required competing, often implicit and changing epistemic frames. Rather than treating epistemology as a domain of the foundational, architectural, and fixed, I share a premise of historical and social epistemology: epistemic considerations are neither transcendent nor abstract. They are squarely of the colonial world. Treating epistemology as a navigational strategy alters field and ground and shapes what questions we ask. People sought to identify things they knew they could not see, 'racial membership' or political desires unavailable to ocular evidence. They sought to distinguish politically motivated passions from private ones, to know when the latter could turn into the former—and to know when they needed to act upon them.

In the Indies, the project and problems of the 'making up of people' pervaded the administrative archives, the Dutch-language press, and a century worth of colonial fiction; it also fed the epistemic anxieties that eddied around them. The production of social kinds entailed the codification of 'self-evident' measures to distinguish social privilege and political exclusion. In a colony where the legal stipulation for being granted European equivalent status entailed evidence of being 'at home' in a European milieu, what counted as adequate knowledge went beyond the preparatory courses for a civil service career. In distinguishing race, upbringing could be given more weight than paternity, comportment more credence than colour, and cultural competence more weight than birth. In this trained and strained social space, colonial agents relied on an intuitive reading of sensibilities more than science, on a measure of affective states—of affiliations and attachments—more than origins, and on assessments of moral civilities that were poorly secured by colour-based taxonomies or visual markers.

Surface perceptions were deemed unreliable, producing what the Dutch called 'fabricated' and 'fictive' Europeans, 'Europeans in disguise', and what French officials in Indochina most feared, natives and *métis* who 'fraudulently' were legally recognized and 'passed' as European. These categorical errors could only be accessed by another kind of knowledge of 'hidden properties' of human kinds and interior dispositions, of inclinations secreted in their depths, probabilistic predictions about the political consequences of people's affective and moral states.

This, I have argued, is the space of colonial governance where truth claims compete, crushed by the weight of convention or resilient in the immediate threat of the everyday, where certainties are put to the test and credibility wavers. Classical probability theory in the Enlightenment, as Lorraine Daston aptly reminds us, was designed to measure the incertitudes of a modernizing world (1988: 6). Colonial civil servants were charged to do the same. In Daston's reading it is not Reason but Uncertainty that is key. I would agree. As interpretative communities both depended on rules of reliability and trust, on a shared common sense about what was likely that did not always serve them well. The historian of science Hans-Jörg Rheinberger too reminds us that a defining feature of scientific inquiry was a shifting 'boundary between what is thought to be known and what is beyond imagination' (1997: 11). In the domain of governance, it is that expectant space in between which has produced improbable strategies of defence and security and ever more elaborately streamlined profiles of the enemy. New epistemic objects with political import are produced in that haze between what one does 'not quite yet know' and that for which there is not yet a name. The making of colonial categories occupies this epistemic space. New social objects were the archives' product and only then turned into subjects of enquiry and objects of documentation.

Because imagining what might be was as important as knowing what was, these archives of the visionary and the probable should command our attention. Marked by erratic movement in verbal tense, the conditional mood could powerfully reshape an immediate response, revise the present and near future, and refigure events that had long passed. Prolific in producing the feared, the unrealized and the ill-conceived, such visions provide traces of troubled social topographies and agitations of a peculiar kind that prompted infeasible plans (such as those that the fascist linked Fatherland's Club proposed to set up agricultural colonies for mixed-bloods on the Indies' fringe in New Guinea) that could not be carried out, and even if they were, could not be sustained (Stoler 2010b: 106–8). That political scientists today are able to posit a new obsession with the anticipatory future tense in contemporary security regimes as a hallmark of our current political moment belies more than an historical myopia. It does more than grossly truncate the historical depth of these imaginaries. It foreshortens the imperial coordinates of a quest to specify the interior states of those whose reasoned affects remain unintelligible to the sorts of reason defined by imperial control.[16] To follow these breaches and falterings renders the panoptic state based on rational knowledge a frail conceit. Even in such a quintessential product of bureaucracy and reasoned procedure as the state commission, preconceived protocols failed.

[16.] See for example, Colonomos (2010), who distinguishes today's security regimes from earlier ones and today's justification for 'preventive warfare' by justifications for the future.

For the European Pauperism commissions of 1901, proof of the difference between destitute whites and Indo-European paupers continually escaped the categories that field officers were directed to apply. 'Objective' data never told them enough. What they resorted to were conversant notions of who 'belonged' where, how people spoke to their young, sat, ate, and dressed. Neglect of children, indifference to work, succumbing to native standards were affective states not easily captured in numbers; condemnations of the sensory world in which poor whites lived shed more palpable and convincing evidence of what colonial agents already thought they knew about sorts of people and how race shaped their habits and inclinations. For such commissions on race, it is not science alone to which they turned but other ways of reading and rendering what distinguished social kinds. Both the Poor White Commissions of South Africa from the late 1920s and those of the Indies from 1900 and earlier, explicitly linked domestic relationships—between parent and child, nursemaid and infant—to the security of the state. Relations between people and everyday things—clothing, furnishings, room arrangements, and window-openings—were benchmarks of racialized distinctions. Eyewitness testimonies to intimacies of the home became data of a particular kind, critical to the state's audit of its commitment to the public good, to racial differentiation, and to its own viability (Stoler 2006a).

One is reminded of Max Weber's contention that bureaucracies excise those domains they cannot measure, by 'eliminating from official business love, hatred and all purely personal, irrational, and emotional elements which escape calculation' (Pugh 1990). But in the Dutch colonial bureaucracy such 'emotional elements' bore epistemic and political weight. To whom one expressed attachment vs. contempt, concern vs. indifference, respect or disdain provided cultural and legal 'proof' of who one really was, where one ranked and racially belonged. These were as much the grammar of rule as anything else. These were judgements and interpretations of the social and political world. They served as incisive markers of rank and the unstated rules of exemption.

Administrative anxiety was riveted on those affective states of European colonials which could not be easily gauged, on those neither within the state's reach to manage nor assess. An extraordinary public demonstration by European and Creole whites in Batavia in May 1848 (described at length in *Along the Archival Grain*), when family attachments threatened to crash against the demands for state loyalty, underscored how much those in charge of the city and the colony recognized that habits of the heart were both the subjects and objects of their political rationalities and could not be cordoned off. Such sentiments constituted the political, affected the internal workings of state, and shaped its course. Whether it was parental rage (at prolonged separation from their children who required schooling in Holland for elevated positions in the colonial civil service) or sentiments spawned by ferment in the streets of Paris and Amsterdam in the preceding months, were questions the authorities asked repeatedly among themselves. Again, a commitment to some notion of a universal reason proved insufficient to account for what those well-heeled among them would risk and demand.

CRITICAL HISTORY AS FIELDWORK
IN PHILOSOPHY

The French historian Robert Darnton once defined 'history in an ethnographic grain' as history that attends to 'thought about how they thought' (1984: 3). It is not a bad starting point for reflecting on the conceptual clusters that imperial governance promoted and what those convergences looked like on the ground. But if it is methodological traction we are after, then it is not when common sense operated that should draw our attention but when it failed. More purchase still might come by staying close to those 'epistemological details' to which people attend, to the conceptual and non-conceptual tools they create, to how they imagine they know the interior states of others. Such a venture might be captured by what Pierre Bourdieu and Paul Rabinow, following John Austin, have called 'fieldwork in philosophy'. For Bourdieu, that project entails a sociological mapping of the privileges on which elite knowledge formations draws, and on the exclusions that its procedures serve (Bourdieu 2000, 1990; Rabinow 2007; see also Austin 1957). Rabinow has pushed the venture further to identify the labour that goes into assembling 'knowledge-things' and to describe the practices that confer their authorization (2003: 85). In my view, 'fieldwork in philosophy' is equally about the making of ontologies and the inchoate processes that produce concept formation in lived epistemic space. It asks, historically and in our political present, how styles of political reasoning shift and endure, how structures of racial feeling are tacitly lived and framed (Williams 1977: 134). Fieldwork in philosophy, by my account, might track how new epistemic things emerge as responses to new political urgencies and historical contexts. Such an approach invites us to ask what methods colonial agents imagined were useful to make their worlds more intelligible, without assuming that reason rather than unarticulated sentiments and sensibilities were their guides.

SECURITY: BETWEEN REASON AND DÉRAISON

> Any reading of Dutch colonial literature astounds one with its obsessive concern with a (supposedly fragile) *orde*. (Anderson 1966: 98, emphasis mine)

These lines, written by the eminent Indonesianist scholar Benedict Anderson in an 1966 essay, would seem to warrant little rewriting. But when republished twenty-four years later, the crucial parenthetical phrase—'(supposedly fragile)'—disappeared, replaced by 'a menace of order' (1990: 133). For Anderson it might have been a trivial revision (with the snide adverbial remark 'supposedly fragile' perhaps excised as redundant given that reference to a Dutch 'obsessive concern' with order, already nailed the critique). But I would argue otherwise, that it is in the slippage between the adjectival phrase 'supposedly fragile' and the noun 'menace' where much of the workings of Dutch colonial governance operated and where colliding concerns over 'security' would reside. If '*rust en orde*' (peace and order) were keywords of the Dutch colonial state's vision of its tranquillizing task, what constituted a threat both exceeded its tools of measurement and was more incipient and veiled than its tools could assess. Implying that Dutch authorities only imagined their rule to be 'fragile' (as a rationale to justify its intelligence apparatus) flattens a more complicated story. It turns away from what we might learn from that troubled space about what Dutch authorities knew, and how they knew it. As Austin might have suggested in his 'Plea for Excuses', the phrase 'supposedly fragile' dismisses the question before it is asked. It obscures how reasons were crafted, how good Reason was affirmed, how much unreason informed not so much aberrant moments in the arts of governance as it did phantoms produced and fears circulated. Not least it glides past how violence rendered as an appropriate response when reasonably framed.

'*Rust en orde*' was an incantation and a political concept that drew other concepts into its frame and fold. Along with it came the invariable iteration of the threat to 'security' (*veiligheid*) and the fear of 'insecurity' (*onveiligheid*) that perhaps better captures the unquiet affective space that Dutch colonials inhabited and the shapes of the phantoms with which they lived. In the corridors of imperial authority and in the lives of Europeans who sought to be 'at home' in the colonies, security was a common noun that worked as a political concept: it could expand and extend, slide between scales, and not least create subjects—and their ascribed proclivities—to be defended against and contained.

We might return again here to Hans-Jörg Rheinberger's persuasive argument that new epistemic things are formed by 'a permanent process of reorientation and reshuffling of the boundary between what is thought to be known and what is beyond imagination' (1997: 11). 'Security' is an epistemic object that occupies such a conceptual and concrete space. As a feature of imperial governance, 'security' is put to work in multiple domains to call forth its object (see Sharp in Part II of this volume). The quest for security and the safeguarding of it could mobilize the deployment of Dutch battalions readied with arms on the outskirts of Batavia in 1848; it could produce a demand for treatises on colonial household management (minutely attentive to where servant quarters were placed and who cared for one's young). 'Security' hovered in the interstices of the legal codes that separated mixed-blood children from their native mothers, was splayed across the repeated commissions on impoverished whites. Not least, 'security' concerns blurred into the 'moral safety' of the young and confirmed the necessity of nurseries for European children for 'reasons of state'.[17]

Imperial practice and imperial knowledge were, in part, predicated on making common sense of the categories of persons against which society had to be defended and reshuffling this membership as situations changed. A broader genealogy of security as

---

[17.] I use the term 'reasons of state' here not with reference to a specific state apparatus of a particular moment in European history as does Foucault, but rather with reference to the connotation of the prevalent term used in colonial documents, '*rust en orde*'.

a concept would not be an inexorable teleology of the present. It would attend to how political common sense gets forged, how related histories are severed, how specific places are retooled with substitutable populations in them. Such a genealogy would ask how durabilities of empire shape the sensibilities and logics that underwrite the distribution of containments, displacements, and managed mobilities of our world today (Stoler 2008b; see also Part II of this volume).

THE UNDERSIDE OF REASON

As Ian Hacking writes in his preface to the new complete version of Foucault's *History of Madness* (2006), the key term of *déraison* quickly dropped out of the abridged French editions after 1961 and never appeared in the English translation at all. Hacking nevertheless argues that *déraison* was the central and elusive concept that defined Foucault's project.[18] If Hacking is tentative about what Foucault meant by it, he knows what it is not: neither the opposite of reason nor madness alone. But I think Foucault's treatment of *déraison* suggests something else, an analytic move that runs through much of Foucault's work. *Déraison* might be better understood not as a fixed noun with assigned attributes, but as a relational concept, a methodological entry point, a diagnostic of sorts that registers historical movements: the subtle shifts, imperceptible substitutions, and bold-faced reversals between that which was once deemed reasonable and then was not. *Déraison* seems to operate as a relational concept with respect to a changing norm, to those practices and perceptions that were once deemed reasonable and then slip to its outer shores. *Déraison* may be a way of marking that which recedes from and rejects convention's demands: when unquiet minds can no longer be trusted to be predictable; when they/we become unreliable guardians of common sense.

This relational quality of *déraison* is close to what Michel Serres too describes as central to Foucault's work: for Serres *déraison* works as a displacement that produces 'the closed insularity of reason' to track how that insularity 'slowly takes shape' (Serres 1997: 51). As Foucault expressed it,

> unreason slowly creeps back to that which condemns it, imposing a form of retrograde servitude upon it, where recognition of this unreason is the mark, the sign and almost the emblem of reason itself. (2006: 345)

Unreason then is not reason's opposite; rather, it is its repeatedly incited and verifying moment, shaped by its normative and changing truths. Nowhere is the force of Reason more vulnerable than at its centre, among its staunchest advocates. Architects of empire might be seen as those occupying this unstable but normalized place. To live in and off

---

[18.] See Hacking's foreword to Michel Foucault, *History of Madness* (2006); see also his 'Déraison' (2008).

empire entails a more complex set of psychic dispositions than often acknowledged. Imperial dispositions are marked by a negative space: one from where those with privilege and standing might excuse themselves. Unreason in these colonial archives is a distinguishing mark, ascribed to those off-guard, overworked, or overwrought states that produce uncommon, unauthorized critical reflections that emerge when one does not look away. But it may also index the presence of other forms of sensory, intuitive knowledge; structures of feeling that perforate the hyper-rationalized technologies that produce insecurity and defence.

Perhaps we need to apprehend history—with all due respect to Aristotle's distinction between historians who 'tell of things that have been' and poets 'of things as might be'—as a project that strives to locate imperial histories and the violence they condoned in the space in between. Such accounts would leave more room for the conditional, anticipatory tense that such polities engendered, an *unheimlich* world of those imagined to be possibly masking their intentions, potentially hiding their 'real' attachments: those whom empire's agents took their external and most proximate threats to be. Such an approach turns us from the ready-made synthesis of Reason to expansions, contractions, and reversals of its making. Concepts do not come fully hatched but, as Rheinberger notes, from 'spatio-temporal singularities', more like 'auxiliary organs of touch', smell and premonition in the flesh (1997: 14). Importantly, a history of such epistemic things arrives at no point of completion since there is 'no possibility of anticipating the future object constellations that accrue from it' (14).

The universals that have been considered to organize imperial taxonomies were breached from the start. Challenges came from those within radical strands of the Enlightenment, from those outside its direct orbit who reworked its principles for themselves, and from many more who never thought about it at all. Fanon was not alone in identifying colonialism and racism as European afflictions that would cut off its breath. Unreason organized the political grammar of empire at its beginning—and in so far as it has been concentrated in rationales for torture in the name of curbing violence, it re-emerges in the 'standard operating procedures' of the US presence in Iraq, and in the US Department of Homeland Security's billion-dollar initiatives to identify people's propensities for 'Violent Intent' (prior to any act) with 'non-invasive brainscans' and by calculating the tautness of their posture and body temperatures.[19] It takes privileged shelter in a colonizing Zionist reason that underwrites relentless Israeli incursions on Palestinian land, in the continued singling out of French citizens whose parents may be of North African origin, and in the US State Department's surreal endeavour to identify the attributes of a 'Universal Adversary'.[20] Such projects produce their predators and

[19.] See, for example, Sanfilippo and Nibbs (2007); Sample (2007); M. Richards (2007); Barrie (2008). See also *The Economist*, 'If Looks Could Kill: Surveillance Technology', 25 October 2008, and Morton in Part II of this volume.

[20.] National Planning Scenarios (Department of Homeland Security). Online source: <http:/www. globalsecurity/org/security/library/report/2004/hsc-lanning-scenarios-jul04.htm>, accessed 5 June 2010, page no longer available.

prey, ever more people assigned attributes relevant to security, which in turn amplify what the conceptual matrix around 'security' must broach and breach. Security regimes adhere to the protocols of common sense, sanctify what is normal, and recruit sensory intuitive knowledge as crucial features of intelligence expertise. The practices that flourish in the pursuit of 'things as they might be' have long undone the 'supremacy of reason' as a mark of the Enlightenment and a hallmark of empire, as they once looked and in the forms they manifest today.

References

Adas, Michael (1989). *Machines as the Measure of Men: Science, Technology, and Ideologies of Western Dominance.* Ithaca: Cornell University Press.

Agamben, Giorgio (2009). 'What is a Paradigm?', in *The Signature of All Things: On Method* trans. Luca D'Isanto with Kevin Attell. New York: Zone Books, 9–32.

Anderson, Benedict (1966). 'The Language of Indonesian Politics', *Indonesia*, 1: 89–116.

Anderson, Benedict (1990). 'The Language of Indonesian Politics', in *Language and Power: Exploring Political Cultures in Indonesia.* Ithaca: Cornell University Press, 123–51.

Arendt, Hannah (1965). *On Revolution.* New York: Vintage.

Asad, Talal (1993). *Genealogies of Religion.* Baltimore: Johns Hopkins University Press.

Austin, John (1957). 'A Plea for Excuses', *Proceedings of the Aristotelian Society (1956–1957).* Online source: <http://www.ditext.com/austin/plea.html>, accessed 24 March 2009.

Bachelard, Gaston (1940). *La philosophie du non.* Paris: PUF.

Barrie, Allison (2008). 'Homeland Security Detects Terrorist Threats by Reading Your Mind', Fox News.com, 23 September. Online source: <http://www.foxnews.com/story/0,2933,426485,00.html>, accessed 15 December 2012.

Bayly, Christopher (1996). *Empire and Information: Intelligence Gathering and Social Communication in India, 1780–1870.* Cambridge: Cambridge University Press.

Berman, Russell A. (1998). *Enlightenment or Empire: Colonial Discourse in German Culture.* London: University of Nebraska Press.

Bilgrami, Akeel (2006). 'Occidentalism, the Very Idea: An Essay on the Enlightenment and Enchantment', *Critical Inquiry*, 32.3: 381–411.

Boltanski, Luc (1999). 'The Politics of Pity', in *Distant Suffering: Morality, Media and Politics.* New York: Cambridge University Press, 3–19.

Bourdieu, Pierre (1990). 'Fieldwork in Philosophy', in *In Other Worlds: Essays Toward a Reflexive Sociology,* trans. M. Adamson. Stanford: Stanford University Press, 3–33.

Bourdieu, Pierre (2000). 'Critique of Scholastic Reason', in *Pascalian Meditations.* Stanford: Stanford University Press, 9–33.

Chakrabarty, Dipesh (2000). *Provincializing Europe: Postcolonial Thought and Historical Difference.* Princeton: Princeton University Press.

Chatterjee, Partha (1993). *Nationalist Thought and the Colonial World: A Derivative Discourse.* Minneapolis: University of Minnesota Press.

Chatterjee, Partha (ed.) (1995). *Texts of Power.* Minneapolis: University of Minnesota Press.

Colonomos, Ariel (2010). *Le Pari de la guerre: Guerre préventive, guerre juste?* Paris: Denoël.

Darnton, Robert (1984). *The Great Cat Massacre and Other Episodes in French Cultural History.* New York: Vintage.

Daston, Lorraine (1988). *Classical Probability in the Enlightenment.* Princeton: Princeton University Press.

Daston, Lorraine and Peter Galison (2007). *Objectivity*. New York: Zone Books.

Deleuze, Gilles and Félix Guattari (1994). 'What is a Concept?', in *What is Philosophy?* New York: Columbia University Press, 15–54.

Derrida, Jacques (2005). *Rogues: Two Essays on Reason*. Stanford: Stanford University Press.

Dubois, Laurent (2004). *A Colony of Citizens: Revolution and Slave Emancipation in the French Caribbean, 1787–1804*. Chapel Hill: University of North Carolina Press.

Fabian, Johannes (2000). *Out of Our Minds: Reason and Madness in the Exploration of Central Africa*. Berkeley: University of California Press.

Foucault, Michel (1981). 'Omnes et singulatim: Toward a Criticism of "Political Reason"'. The Tanner Lectures on Human Values, II. Salt Lake City: University of Utah Press.

Foucault, Michel (1994). 'Table Ronde du 20. Mai 1978', in *Dits et écrits*. Paris: Gallimard, 4–23.

Foucault, Michel (1997). 'For an Ethics of Discomfort', trans. Lysa Hochroth, in S. Lotringer (ed.), *The Politics of Truth*. New York: Semiotexte, 135–45.

Gaukroger, Stephen (ed.) (1998). *The Soft Underbelly of Reason: The Passions in the Seventeenth Century*. London: Routledge.

Gay, Peter (1996). *The Enlightenment: The Science of Freedom*. New York: Norton.

Geertz, Clifford (1983). 'Common Sense as a Cultural System', in *Local Knowledge*. New York: Basic Books, 73–93.

Goss, Andrew (2011). *The Floracrats: Science and the Failure of the Enlightenment in Modern Indonesia*. Madison: University of Wisconsin Press.

Grove, Richard (1995). *Green Imperialism: Colonial Expansion, Tropical Island Edens, and the Origins of Environmentalism, 1600–1860*. Cambridge: Cambridge University Press.

Hacking, Ian (1990). *The Taming of Chance*. Cambridge: Cambridge University Press.

Hacking, Ian (2006). 'Foreword' to M. Foucault, *History of Madness*. New York: Routledge, pp. ix–xii.

Hacking, Ian (2008). 'Déraison', in 'Foucault across the Disciplines' Conference, UCSC, 2 March 2008. Online source: <http://humweb.ucsc.edu/foucaultacrossthedisciplines/foucault.htm>, accessed 15 December 2012.

Haskell, Thomas (1985). 'Capitalism and the Origins of the Humanitarian Sensibility', parts 1 and 2, *American Historical Review*, 90.2/3: 339–61, 547–66.

Himmelfarb, Gertrude (2005). *The Roads to Modernity: The British, French, and American Enlightenments*. New York: Vintage.

Hirschman, Albert (1977). *The Passions and the Interests: Political Arguments for Capitalism Before its Triumph*. Princeton: Princeton University Press.

Israel, Jonathan (1995). *The Dutch Republic: Its Rise, Greatness, and Fall, 1477–1806*. Oxford: Clarendon.

Israel, Jonathan (2006a). *Enlightenment Contested: Philosophy, Modernity, and the Emancipation of Man, 1670–1752*. New York: Oxford University Press.

Israel, Jonathan (2006b). 'Enlightenment! Which Enlightenment?', *Journal of the History of Ideas*, 67.2: 523–45.

James, C. L. R. (2001). *The Black Jacobins*. New York: Penguin.

James, Susan (1997). *Passion and Action: The Emotions in Seventeenth-Century Philosophy*. New York: Oxford University Press.

MacIntyre, Alasdair (1984). *After Virtue*. Notre Dame: University of Notre Dame Press.

Mehta, Uday (1992). *The Anxiety of Freedom: Imagination and Individualism in Locke's Political Thought*. Ithaca: Cornell University Press.

Mehta, Uday (1999). *Liberalism and Empire: A Study in Nineteenth-Century British Liberal Thought*. Chicago: University of Chicago Press.

Mignolo, Walter D. (2000). *Local Histories/Global Designs: Coloniality, Subaltern Knowledges, and Border Thinking.* Princeton: Princeton University Press.

Morsberger, Katharine (1996). 'John Locke's *An Essay Concerning Human Understanding*: The "Bible" of the Enlightenment', *Studies in Eighteenth Century Culture*, 25: 1–19.

Mufti, Aamir (2007). *Enlightenment in the Colony: The Jewish Question and the Crisis of Postcolonial Culture.* Princeton: Princeton University Press.

Muthu, Sarkar (2003). *Enlightenment against Empire.* Princeton: Princeton University Press.

Nixon, Rob (2011). *Slow Violence and the Environmentalism of the Poor.* Cambridge, Mass.: Harvard University Press.

Nora, Pierre (1961). *Les Français d'Algérie.* Paris: René Juillard.

Norindr, Pavinong (1996). *Phantasmatic Indochina: French Colonial Ideology in Architecture, Film, and Literature.* Durham, NC: Duke University Press.

Nussbaum, Martha (2001). *Upheavals of Thought: The Intelligence of Emotions.* Cambridge: Cambridge University Press.

Outram, Dorinda (1995). *The Enlightenment.* New York: Cambridge University Press.

Pinch, Adela (1996). *Strange Fits of Passion: Epistemologies of Emotion, Hume to Austen.* Stanford: Stanford University Press.

Prakash, Gyan (1999). *Another Reason: Science in the Imagination of Modern India.* Princeton: Princeton University Press.

Pyenson, Lewis (1980). *Empire of Reason: Exact Sciences in Indonesia, 1840–1940.* Leiden: Brill.

Rabinow, Paul (1989). *French Modern: Norms and Forms of the Social Environment.* Cambridge, Mass.: MIT Press.

Rabinow, Paul (2003). *Antropos Today.* Princeton: Princeton University Press.

Rabinow, Paul (2007). 'Preface', Thirtieth Anniversary Edition, *Reflections on Fieldwork in Morocco.* Berkeley: University of California Press, xi–xxviii.

Rai, Amit (2002). *The Rule of Sympathy: Sentiment, Race and Power, 1750–1850.* New York: Palgrave.

Rancière, Jacques (2004). *The Philosopher and His Poor.* Durham, NC: Duke University Press.

Reddy, William (1997). *The Invisible Code: Honor and Sentiment in Pre-revolutionary France, 1814–1848.* Berkeley: University of California Press.

Reddy, William (2001). *The Navigation of Feeling: A Framework for the History of the Emotions.* New York: Cambridge University Press.

Rheinberger, Hans-Jörg (1997). *Toward a History of Epistemic Things: Synthesizing Protein in the Test Tube.* Stanford: Stanford University Press.

Richards, Michael (2007). 'Comments on "Project Hostile Intent Plans 'Non-Invasive' DHS Brainscan"', *The Register.* Online source: <http://www.theregister.co.uk/2007/08/09/no_not_the_mind_probe_again/>, accessed 1 October 2007.

Richards, Thomas (1993). *The Imperial Archive: Knowledge and the Fantasy of Empire.* London: Verso.

Ronell, Avital (2002). *Stupidity.* Urbana, Ill.: University of Illinois Press.

Said, Edward W. (1966). *Joseph Conrad and the Fiction of Autobiography.* Cambridge, Mass.: Harvard University Press.

Sample, Ian (2007). 'Security Firms Working on Devices to Spot Would-Be Terrorists in the Crowd', *The Guardian*, 9 August .

Sanfilippo, A. P. and F. G. Nibbs (2007). 'Violent Intent Modeling: Incorporating Cultural Knowledge into the Analytical Procedure'. Washington, DC: US Department of Energy.

Satia, Priya (2008). *Spies in Arabia: The Great War and the Cultural Foundations of Britain's Covert Empire in the Middle East.* New York: Oxford University Press.

Schauwers, Albert (2001). 'The "Benevolent" Colonies of Johannes van den Bosch: Continuities in the Administration of Poverty in the Netherlands and Indonesia', *Comparative Studies of Society and History,* 43.2: 298–328.

Schweder, Richard A. (1984). 'Anthropology's Romantic Rebellion Against the Enlightenment, or There's More to Thinking than Reason and Evidence', in R. Schweder and R. Levine (eds), *Culture Theory: Essays on Mind, Self and Emotion.* Cambridge: Cambridge University Press, 27–66.

Scott, David (2004). *Conscripts of Modernity: The Tragedy of Colonial Enlightenment.* Durham, NC: Duke University Press.

Serres, Michel (1997). 'The Geometry of the Incommensurable', in A. Davidson (ed.), *Foucault and His Interlocutors.* Chicago: University of Chicago Press, 36–56.

Solomon, Robert (1988). 'On Emotions as Judgments', *American Philsoophical Quarterly,* 25.2: 183–91.

Solomon, Robert (2004). *Thinking about Feeling.* New York: Oxford University Press.

Stoler, Ann Laura (1995). *Race and the Education of Desire.* Durham, NC: Duke University Press.

Stoler, Ann Laura (1997). 'Racial Histories and their Regimes of Truth', *Political Power and Social Theory,* 11: 893–97.

Stoler, Ann Laura (2006a). 'Degrees of Imperial Sovereignty', *Public Culture,* 18.1: 125–46.

Stoler, Ann Laura (ed.) (2006b). *Haunted by Empire.* Durham, NC: Duke University Press.

Stoler, Ann Laura (2008a). 'Epistemic Politics: Ontologies of Colonial Common Sense', *Philosophical Forum,* 39.3: 349–69.

Stoler, Ann Laura (2008b). 'Imperial Debris: Reflections on Ruins and Ruination', *Cultural Anthropology,* 23.2: 191–219.

Stoler, Ann Laura (2009). *Along the Archival Grain: Epistemic Anxieties and Colonial Common Sense.* Princeton: Princeton University Press.

Stoler, Ann Laura (2010a). 'The Imperial Modern: The Carceral Archipelago of Empire'. Keynote address delivered at CRASSH conference on 'The Political Life of Documents', University of Cambridge, January 2010.

Stoler, Ann Laura (2010b). 'Zones of the Intimate in Imperial Formations', preface to new edn of *Carnal Knowledge and Imperial Power.* Berkeley: University of California Press, ix–xxxiv.

Stoler, Ann Laura (2011). 'Colonial Aphasia: Race and Disabled Histories in France', *Public Culture,* 23.1: 121–56.

Taguieff, Pierre-André (1988). *La force du préjugé: Essai sur le racisme et ses doubles.* Paris: La Découverte.

Taylor, Jean (1983). *The Social World of Batavia.* Madison: University of Wisconsin Press.

Trouillot, Michel-Ralph (1995). *Silencing the Past.* Boston: Beacon Press.

Weber, Max (1990 [1924]). 'Legitimate Authority and Bureaucracy', in D. S. Pugh (ed.), *Organization Theory: Selected Readings,* 3rd edn. London: Penguin, 3–15.

Williams, Patrick and Laura Chrisman (eds) (1994). *Colonial Discourse and Post-Colonial Theory: A Reader.* New York: Columbia University Press.

Williams, Raymond (1977). *Marxism and Literature.* New York: Oxford University Press.

Young, Robert J. C. (1990). *White Mythologies: Writing History and the West.* London: Routledge.

CHAPTER 2

....

EMPIRES OF DEMOCRACY

....

TYLER STOVALL

INTRODUCTION

....

The relationship between postcolonial theory and imperial history has ranged from dialogue and intellectual cross-fertilization to conflict and incomprehension (see Kennedy in Part IV of this volume). Theorists like Robert Young have accused historians of misapplying normative categories from a reified vision of European history to other peoples, judging them wanting according to Eurocentric standards of progress (Young 1990; see also Chakrabarty 2000). Some historians have responded by challenging theorists' notions of history as simplistic and out of touch with contemporary innovations in historical methodology (Cooper 2005; Howe 2001). But at the same time, theorists and historians have learned greatly from one another. The work of postcolonial critics like Edward Said (1978) has played a seminal role in inspiring the new interest in imperial history, and the findings of historians have in turn enriched debates about colonial and postcolonial cultures. Finally, both perspectives are central to scholarly attempts to understand the many connections between the postcolonial present and the imperial past.

What does it mean to approach the history of empire and colonialism from a postcolonial perspective? In this chapter, I will do so by considering how some key themes of postcolonial theory map onto specific historical case studies, focusing on a comparison between two of the leading empires of modern times, those of Britain and France. The very idea of comparing two such vast imperial spaces represents a significant departure from the conventional empirical perspective of the historian; a brief essay on such a huge topic must of necessity take a broad-based thematic approach. Some crucial themes are the interrelations of colony and metropole, the intersection of the colonial and the postcolonial, and the politics of liberation embedded in both colonialist and anti-colonialist discourses, with my general aim being to examine how such broad ideas play out in the history of imperial Britain and France.

The colonial empires of Britain and France have generated immense bodies of scholarly literature for a variety of reasons (see for example Aldrich 1996; Levine 2007). One is their sheer size; in 1914 together they controlled approximately one third of the world's land surface, and they have left linguistic, cultural, and political legacies to an unprecedented array of peoples. Another reason is their central place in postcolonial theory, much of which has focused on the British experience in particular. As a result, at least during the modern era the Anglo-French experience has been central to imperial history. Although both colonial empires have a long history, they attained their greatest expanse and global significance during the years between the French Revolution and the Second World War. Their rise and fall coincided with but also crucially contributed to ideas of modernity, illustrating the truism that colonialism has been intrinsic to the making of the modern world (see Mignolo in this section of the volume).

Studies comparing the two empires have generally focused on the differences between them, e.g. contrasting processes of decolonization, economic versus political motivations for empire, direct versus indirect rule, the relative importance of empire to metropolitan populations, different attitudes toward race, sex, and miscegenation (Cooper 1996, 2005; Kahler 1984). More recently, however, studies have also considered what they have in common, looking for example at the relationship between empire and political modernity or at how liberalism in Britain and republicanism in France shaped the colonial encounter (Mehta 1999; Pitts 2005; Wilder 2005). This chapter shares that new perspective, exploring the history of these empires in relation to a key aspect of modernity, the rise of mass liberal democracy. At first glance, liberal democracy and empire would seem to have little to do with one another. After all, European colonialism to a large extent rested upon denying the rights of liberal citizenship and mass democracy to the peoples they controlled: the natives were subjects, not citizens; they were to be ruled over, not to rule themselves. Yet the age of mass democracy in Europe was also an age of imperialism (Cooper and Stoler 1997). This paradox was perhaps greatest in France, which as of 1870 managed to be both a republic and an empire at the same time. In Britain as well, though, the nineteenth century witnessed both the gradual expansion of the franchise at home and the empire abroad. The 1919 peace of Paris, which ended World War I, roundly condemned empires within Europe, seeking to replace them with democratic nation states, but just as consistently supported and extended principles of colonial rule outside Europe (Manela 2007; Morrow 2005). In the modern era, Britain and France have been at once leading democracies and leading colonial empires, a contradiction that has underscored their centrality to the modern world as a whole.

A classic explanation of this relationship is Vladimir Lenin's *Imperialism* (1917), which argued that the western prosperity that made mass democracy possible rested upon colonial exploitation. Similar views of the link between empire and working-class prosperity can be found in the ideology of social imperialism (Semmel 1960). Cecil Rhodes, for example, argued that imperial expansion constituted a key solution to working-class militancy and socialism by offering job prospects in the colonies and increasing prosperity at home. Another variant of this argument holds that pride in imperial conquest both reflected and facilitated the integration of the masses into liberal democratic political culture, so that traditions like Britain's Empire Day fostered working-class support for modern democracy in Europe (English 2006). In what follows, I take a less functionalist view of this relationship, emphasizing instead the interaction between the ideologies of liberal democracy and empire. In brief, I will suggest that in modern France and Britain not only did liberal ideas shape colonialism, but the colonial encounter also structured the notion and practice of liberal democracy itself.

Modernity and paradox are certainly no strangers to each other: the very idea of liberal democracy is itself paradoxical, combining two fundamentally different and frequently opposed political principles, liberty and equality (see Gopal in Part II of this volume). I want to explore the British and French empires as prominent examples of democratic imperialism, considering how this contradiction played out at different times in both Europe and its colonies. I will focus on three key areas. First, I will consider the transition from early modern to modern forms of empire, that is to say, from monarchical to liberal-democratic ideologies in both metropoles and colonies. The so-called age of democratic revolution had a crucial colonial dimension, and modern empires were as much its heirs as were modern democracies. For Britain and France in particular, albeit in very different ways, this was a foundational moment for both dimensions of national life. Second, I will outline the issue of empire and social difference. Several scholars have considered the relationship between race and class as illustrative of colonialism and its impact upon metropolitan societies, and an important literature has addressed the gendered character of imperial ventures. At the same time, the extension of the franchise to women, lower-class men, and people of colour has been key to the rise of mass democracy in both nations. Third, I will consider the history of decolonization and the definitive victory of socially informed democracy in Britain and France, two phenomena that happened at roughly the same time.

As the above makes clear, I am approaching the comparative study of empire from the point of view of the metropoles rather than that of the colonies. In so doing, I certainly do not intend to privilege European perspectives, and I have learned enormously from the wealth of historical studies on the experiences of the colonized, their adaptations and resistance to colonial rule, and the rise of anti-colonial nationalism. However, if one is to take seriously the idea that colonialism shaped Europe as well as its colonies, then one must analyse in detail the European history of empire; and here I hope to broaden this history beyond the traditional focus on policymaking elites to consider how empire shaped the political culture of modern Britain and France themselves. Throughout, I will consider the history of colonialism as both past and not: for if the British and French empires achieved their apogees in specific historical circumstances, these histories have obvious implications for the present. For example, a key aspect of western political culture, liberal mass democracy, is rooted in the heritage of empire. Recent deployments of the idea of liberal democracy as being seminal to western civilization underscore the importance of this relationship, demonstrating both its historical significance and its burning relevance today.

FROM OLD TO NEW EMPIRE

For both Britain and France, the first half of the nineteenth century represented a transition from one form of empire to another. Whereas the colonialism of the early modern

era had taken place under monarchical institutions and was dominated by mercantil-
ist economic practices, the new arose in the context of increasingly democratic states
organized around the idea of mass citizenship and liberal political economy. If the
first phase of empire reached its heights in the Caribbean and the Indian Ocean, the
second witnessed the scramble for Africa and increased incursions into East Asia and
the Pacific. Most notably, this transition took place during two seminal upheavals, the
French and Industrial Revolutions, movements originating in France and Britain but
gradually achieving global significance. This era witnessed the birth of modern liberal
democracy, and modern imperialism was its handmaiden in the colonies as well as in
Europe (Davis 1999; Hobsbawm 1996).

Challenges to slavery and the Atlantic slave trade were key to both transitions.
Whereas African slavery had constituted the core of the European empires of the early
modern era, increasing challenges to it by the end of the eighteenth century necessitated
a new imperial project. The decline and ultimate abolition of Atlantic slavery did not
concern the colonies alone; it went hand in hand with the rise of modern conceptions
of citizenship and the nation state. Enlightenment challenges to absolutism hammered
home the point that subjects were not free men, and that royal oppression equalled ser-
vitude. Only free men could end slavery and only the death of slavery could guarantee
freedom (Drescher 2009; Matthews 2006; Ryden 2009).

The existence of a crucial colonial and anti-slavery dimension to the era of democratic revolution does not necessarily explain, though, why the idea of empire not only
survived, but also reached an unprecedented extent in slavery's aftermath. Why did the
turbulent transition to the modern era bring about new forms of colonial control rather
than making people free? How, more specifically, did ideas of freedom and empire coincide and how did they together contribute to the rise of liberal democracy? Neither in
Britain nor in France did one form of empire lead automatically to the other; the fact
that they arose in different parts of the world suggests overlapping rather than sequential relationships. Nonetheless, the fact that this transition occurred during the first half
of the nineteenth century, and that the new imperial forms it involved adopted much of
the ideology of democracy, suggests an important connection. In short, the centrality of
liberalism to the modern empires of Britain and France arose to a significant extent out
of the cauldron of democratic revolution.

The French case is the most dramatic. Ever since C. L. R. James, generations of historians have analysed the relationship between the French and Haitian revolutions.
Although most have granted the link between the two, the question tends to have been
framed in terms of the impact of the former on the latter; very few have considered how
the slave uprising in Saint-Domingue, the most profitable colony in the world at the
time and a major contributor to France's economy, affected the course of the upheaval
in France. Yet it is clear that insurgent forces on both sides of the French Atlantic shared
a common belief in the republic as a force for liberation against despotism and slavery (battles between slave and French armies in both Saint-Domingue and Guadeloupe
presented the spectacle of antagonists both shouting 'Vive la république!'). The failure
of the Jacobin republic in Paris paralleled the failure of the revolutionary movement in

the greater Caribbean, leaving independent Haiti alone, vulnerable, and impoverished. Throughout the French Atlantic and beyond, struggles for democracy and against traditional forms of empire frequently marched together (James 1989; see also Fick 1990; Garraway 2008).

These parallels did not end with the French Revolution of 1789. Napoleon's overthrow of the revolutionary regime in France restored slavery in what remained of the French Caribbean, and it took another French revolution to abolish it once and for all. The combination of anti-slavery agitation in the metropole and threatened slave insurrections in Martinique and Guadeloupe meant that once the revolution triumphed in 1848, the new provisional government speedily put an end to bondage in the colonies. In the same brief period, France abolished forever both the monarchy and slavery; universal suffrage and citizenship came both to the people of the metropole and to those of the 'old colonies' (Jennings 2000).

If the Revolution of 1848 spelled the end of old forms of empire, the Revolution of 1830 marked the beginning of the new. In that year, French troops conquered Algeria, establishing the first colonial presence in Africa since Napoleon's abortive invasion of Egypt in 1798 and laying the cornerstone of the new imperial expansion of the late nineteenth century. The Algerian campaign also had an important anti-monarchical dimension: undertaken by the regime of Charles X in a futile effort to allay domestic discontent, in actual fact it facilitated the success of the 1830 Revolution by removing large numbers of royal troops from Paris at a crucial time (Abi-Mershed 2010; Lorcin 1995; Stora 2004). Yet three succeeding French regimes pursued the conquest of Algeria, which was not complete until the late 1850s, reflecting the growing embrace of imperialism by liberals in Britain and France alike. For Alexis de Tocqueville, the conquest of Algeria was justified by the struggle against despotism: France would free the Arabs from Turkish rule and bring them into the civilized world. As he noted in 1837, 'We need in Africa, just as in France, and even more than in France, essential guarantees to the individual living in society; nowhere is it more necessary to establish individual liberty, respect for property, and guarantees of all rights than in a colony' (quoted in Pitts 2005: 24). A determined opponent of slavery, Tocqueville's support of empire in Algeria—in his own mind at least—confirmed rather than contradicted the support of liberty that would eventually lead him to champion the emancipation decree of 1848.

For France, then, the principles of liberalism that brought the old empire to an end lay at the heart of its successor. It was no accident that the regime that made liberal democracy the dominant political system in the nation, the Third Republic, also presided over the greatest period of imperial expansion in French history. In shifting our perspective to imperial Britain we find similar relationships between 'old' and 'new' visions of empire. The rise of a mass-based anti-slavery movement constituted a central aspect of the age of democratic revolution in Britain. Far more than in France, British liberalism defined itself in the struggle against human bondage (Oldfield 1998). During the wars against Napoleon, for example, the British Navy not only fought to ensure the safety of national shipping but to suppress the Atlantic slave trade. The triumphs of liberalism at home went hand in hand with the struggles against slavery in the colonies: as Emilia

Viotti da Costa has shown in her history of Guyana's Demerara slave revolt of 1823, rebel slaves were both inspired by and in turn inspired the abolitionist faith of non-conformist missionaries (da Costa 1994). The abolition of slavery in Britain's colonies a year later inspired liberal organizations like the Anti-Corn Law league, whose battle against mercantilism would triumph during the next decade (Morgan 2009).

If British liberalism's forward-march in the early nineteenth century embraced the campaign against slavery, so too did campaigns for democracy include important colonial dimensions. Anti-slavery was a key factor in the non-conformist religious and political cultures that inspired so many movements for democratization in Victorian Britain; moreover, both the landmark 1832 and 1867 reform bills, which laid the basis for mass liberal democracy in Britain, were debated in the context of hopes and fears about West Indian slave emancipation and colonial revolt (Hall 2000, 2002; Holt 1992). Ultimately, as Catherine Hall and others have argued, democracy in Britain triumphed as a racialized system based on white privilege, which by definition was unavailable to the non-white masses of the colonies.

To an even greater extent than in the French case, the era of democratic revolution did not bring freedom to the British Empire: Jamaica and other colonies remained in thrall until the mid-twentieth century. Rather, the increasing dominance of liberalism in British political thought both transformed the rationale for empire and brought about the greatest expansion in its history. Yet in creating this vast new empire British liberalism was itself transformed, in a manner akin to the transformation that produced liberal mass democracy. One of the main bodies of historiography about the British Empire concerns what is popularly known as 'the imperialism of free trade': first formulated by Robinson and Gallagher and since explored by a number of economic historians, this approach underscores the role of British financial dominance in creating a large 'informal empire', one without annexations or colonies, in countries like China, Argentina, and the southern United States during the nineteenth century (Gallagher and Robinson 1953; see also Semmel 1970; Wolfe 1997). Such overseas dominance conformed much more closely to classic liberal ideology than did the spread of formal colonialism in the late nineteenth century, thus raising the question of why those committed to free trade and small government would end up creating the biggest political unit in world history.

In part, the British state extended formal imperial control in response to the failures of mercantilism. This happened most clearly in India, where the Indian Mutiny brought about the collapse of the venerable East India Company and the implementation of direct rule by the British crown (Bowen 2008; Herbert 2008; Spilsbury 2008). Also important was the perceived need, both strategically and economically, to annex colonies as a way of preventing European rivals from doing so and thereby shutting out British commerce altogether. But at the heart of the liberal imperial project, in both Britain and France, lay a concern with uplift and modernization, what the French would come to call *la mission civilisatrice* and Rudyard Kipling would immortalize as 'the white man's burden'. This concern linked the anti-slavery of the era of democratic revolution with the aggressive expansionism of the new imperialism. It was no accident that a major rationale for British and French conquests in sub-Saharan Africa was initially the effort to stamp out the slave trade by going upriver from the African coasts to root it out at its source in the interior of the continent (Coleman 2004; Klein 1998). Just as in Britain and France liberal democracy required the creation of an educated populace integrated into the acceptance of a liberal world view, so too in their colonies must the natives be 'civilized' to make democracy possible—at least some day. This orientation justified both the subjection of native peoples and the violation of certain basic liberal principles of governance and justice. In both metropoles and colonies, liberal democracy was neither purely liberal nor purely democratic, but a complex mixture of the two ideals (Conklin 1997).

Yet a key part of the story concerns an essential divergence. Whereas liberal democracy triumphed in imperial Britain and France, it did not in their colonies. Ultimately the leaders of Britain and France concluded that their colonial subjects were fundamentally different from them, in ways that both recalled and diverged from notions of difference in their own societies. This question of difference was to play a central role in the evolution of liberal empires into political units composed both of citizens and subjects, a question to which I turn below.

EMPIRE AND DIFFERENCE

As many scholars have noted, racial difference has been a central aspect of modern empire (Samson 2005). In recent years historical studies of colonialism have focused on questions of difference, not only racial but also concerning class and gender. The work of scholars like Ann Stoler (see the preceding essay in this volume) has been instrumental in broadening our understanding of how visions of the native as other have shaped the formation of social identities in both metropoles and colonies (Stoler 2002). At the same time, issues of difference played a major role in the rise of liberal democracy in both Britain and France, where the right to vote expanded progressively along lines determined by class and gender. In Britain, ever-larger segments of the popular classes were granted the franchise during the nineteenth century, whereas in France universal suffrage triumphed more dramatically as a result of the Revolution of 1848. In both cases, the enfranchisement of women represented the culmination of liberal democracy. And in both cases, although with some important differences, the expansion of democracy at home paralleled the growth of empires abroad, empires that steadfastly refused to enfranchise their subjects. To a significant extent, the racial other became the *doppelgänger* of liberal democracy, underscoring both its potential and its limits (Foot 2005; Huard 1991).

How did race, class, and gender intersect in the making of liberal democratic empire in Britain and France? In addressing this I will concentrate on contrasting visions of class in the home countries and visions of race in their colonies, exploring their similarities and differences. As historians like Susan Thorne have noted, discourses of class in nineteenth-century Britain owed not a little to images of savagery and race generated by the colonial encounter (Thorne 1997). At the same time, plans for 'civilizing' the natives were modelled after those aimed at improving the condition of the working classes at home. In both cases, gendered ideas of masculinity and femininity shaped ideas about how to make good citizens out of the untutored masses. Ultimately, in both countries liberal democracy rested on (1) the integration of the class other and (2) the exclusion of the racial other, for its accomplishment meant separating the two.

The history of European racial theory in the nineteenth century sheds some light on these intersections, for theorists often treated issues of race and class interchangeably. Whereas during the Enlightenment commentators on race had tended to portray differences between populations as mutable, in the nineteenth century European scholars increasingly saw racial distinctions as fixed and unchanging (Eze 1997; Mosse 1978). This squared with a more pessimistic perspective on class, and indeed on the whole classic liberal project. As individual upward mobility into the bourgeoisie declined after the mid-nineteenth century, the working classes seemed more than ever a separate stratum of society, in fact a separate race. The growing importance of nation states and national cultures in nineteenth-century Europe also fed upon and contributed to increasing social polarization, for which race became the ultimate metaphor. The view of nations as (antagonistic) races, a perspective that culminated in the First World War, also testified to the salience of race thinking in the making of modern Europe. Additionally, the rise of a more deterministic and mass-based Marxism after 1870 fed into notions of the working classes as the inassimilable other, the revolutionary barbarians lurking at civilization's gates.

While students of European racial theory have often focused on Germany, weaving a teleological narrative that leads inexorably to the Holocaust, these ideas also had a significant impact in Britain and France, dealing in both cases with class as well as race. In Britain, the 'social Darwinism' of Herbert Spencer and others represented liberalism at its most muscular. Based on the presumption that the dominance of the strong was essential to progress and the rule of civilization, social Darwinism quickly acquired a racial component. European triumphs over natives in Africa and Asia clearly showed the superiority of the former over the latter, and justified colonial rule as a means of improving the human condition in general. At the same time, social Darwinism argued that British workers had only themselves to blame for their misery, portraying class stratification as the consequence of innate inequalities of ability (Clark 1984; Hawkins 1997).

In France, meanwhile, Count Artur de Gobineau's *Essay on the Origins of Inequality* was a pioneering text of the new scientific racism of the nineteenth century. Gobineau's fears of racial degeneracy and miscegenation reflected anxieties about the revolutionary Parisian mob and its proletarian heirs, thus racializing concerns about modern society in general (Biddiss 1970). Spencer and Gobineau both rejected the belief in uplift that lay at the base of both liberal democracy and modern views of empire (Gobineau in fact opposed colonialism as leading to race mixing). In Britain and France, fears of mass culture and liberal democracy found expression in terms of race and class, underscoring the manifold connections between homeland and empire.

Visions of the colonial other also blended questions of race and class in the British and French colonies. Scholars have long debated the role played by race in motivating and justifying imperial rule. More recently, some have turned their attention to the ways in which European conceptions of class were played out in racial terms in the colonies. Benedict Anderson's concept of 'tropical Gothic' underscores the ways in which bourgeois white settlers in overseas colonies used racial superiority to carve out the aristocratic lifestyle they had always wanted but could not attain in Europe; while Ann Stoler and others have considered the problem of 'poor white' settlers in European colonies, individuals whose class and race positions contradicted each other and thus risked undermining central tenets of the colonial social order. In general, European ideas about class difference constituted one important model for racial distinctions in the colonies, just as ideas of race generated by the colonial encounter served as a template for the increasingly class-stratified societies of nineteenth-century Britain and France (Anderson 1991; Stoler 1989).

Yet whereas discourses of race and class often reflected similar anxieties in the nineteenth century, the French and British nation states ultimately integrated their working-class citizens while their empires tended not to assimilate their non-white inhabitants. For example, whereas both nations enacted and funded mandatory primary education for their metropolitan populations, offering not only basic levels of literacy but also a sense of belonging to the national community, they failed to provide the same educational opportunities to their colonial subjects. While in Britain and France upwardly mobile workers could find opportunities in politics, education, and administration, in the colonies those fortunate enough to obtain a European education usually found their career paths blocked by racial boundaries, either explicit or implicit. The increasing fear of the educated colonial subject, and in a similar vein of the mixed-race individual, underscored a hard-and-fast sense of racial separation in the colonies which was without parallel at home (Kelly and Kelly 2000; Segalla 2009; Seth 2007).

At the same time, the increasing channelling of working-class discontent into the routine political structures that made liberal democracy possible in both countries also rendered parallels between class in Europe and race in the colonies more tenuous by the late nineteenth century, in the era of the new imperialism. One finds nothing comparable to the interactions between the French and Haitian revolutions during this period. For many poor British and French citizens, the colonies offered a way of escaping the working-class condition in Europe: it is often said that Scots ran the British Empire, and residents of a similarly poor French province, Brittany, played an analogous role in imperial France (Fournier 2005; Fry 2001; White 2007). More generally, the emphasis on working-class respectability led at times to the image of the savage being used as a negative referent to underscore the justice of its political demands; and while Lenin's *Imperialism* noted how European economic prosperity to a significant degree rested on colonial exploitation, the political culture of liberal democracy depended to a large degree on the exclusion of the racialized colonial other as well (Kirk 1985; Rose 1992).

The history of Irish migration to Britain in the nineteenth century is an excellent example of the interactions between metropolitan ideas of class and colonial ideas of race. In many respects Britain's original colony, Ireland also furnished one of the first major colonial migrations in the history of modern Europe (Howe 2000; Kenny 2006).

Irish immigrants in early nineteenth-century Britain—and the Irish in general—were frequently racialized as non-white, and caricatures of the times depicted them as sharing the negative qualities commonly ascribed to those of African descent (de Nie 2004; Lebo 1976). Firmly placed at the bottom of the social hierarchy in Victorian London and other cities, the Irish represented a colonial population adrift in the metropole, utterly foreign and inassimilable despite being the product of centuries of English rule.

At the same time, Irish immigrants, who were almost all working class and poor, played a significant role in the formation of class consciousness in nineteenth-century Britain. Both directly and indirectly, Irish immigrants made important contributions to Chartism, often pushing it toward more radical and violent action (Epstein 1982; O'Higgins 1961); while half a century later, London's Irish figured prominently in the great dock strike of 1889. Participation in the strike was to win them new respectability for the social stratum to which they belonged, in effect helping to make them more 'English'; thus whereas during the early nineteenth century Irish working-class agitation was often viewed as analogous to that of uprooted peasants or even rebel slaves, by the century's end one could make out a new vision of the Irish in Britain, as increasingly acknowledged members of the British working class.

It is perhaps no accident that the integration of the Irish working class in Britain came at a time of imperial expansion in Africa and Asia. London's East End, the centre of the 1889 dock strike and a symbol of both Irish and working-class poverty, was also the great port that represented links with the overseas colonies. The rise of mass democracy in Britain and new imperial ambitions thus manifested themselves in the same urban setting; while, more broadly, the creation of a new colonial other facilitated—if only to a certain degree—the increased acceptance of the old (McClintock 1995).

A similar dynamic unfolded in late nineteenth-century France. Napoleon III's Second Empire replicated the complex blend of republicanism and imperialism pioneered by its more illustrious predecessor. It both reinforced the principle of universal suffrage, albeit in distorted form, and engaged in major imperial ventures, some successful (New Caledonia), some not (Mexico). Its successor, the Third Republic, not only became the longest-lived democratic regime in French history, enshrining the dominance of liberal democracy in the nation's political culture, but also oversaw France's greatest period of colonial expansion overseas. The new regime was born in the crisis of military defeat and revolution, dramatized above all by the fiery apocalypse of the Paris Commune, which represented the final major manifestation of the insurgent Parisian mob that had haunted French politics since 1789. The bloody defeat of the Communards definitively exorcised this threat, rendering the creation of a viable liberal democracy possible in the last quarter of the nineteenth century.

Conquest of the Commune by the forces of conservatism in 1871 was a victory for both liberal democracy and empire. The images of savagery that surrounded the Communards, most notably the portrayals of Communard women as incendiary Amazons, strongly suggested the triumph of civilization over barbarity. It is worth noting that a leading punishment for those insurgents who survived the government's vicious repression was deportation to the colonies: over 4,000 were sent to New

Caledonia alone. When in 1878 the indigenous peoples of the island staged a major revolt against the French, the bulk of the Communard exiles sided with the colonial authorities against the insurgents, some even taking up arms and joining the forces of order to suppress the Kanaks. As Alice Bullard has noted, in New Caledonia two visions of savagery, political and racial, confronted each other. A year later, the Communard veterans were allowed to return to France and the French state amnestied them in 1880. By abjuring their own insurgent traditions and taking up the cause of imperial authority, the former Communards symbolized the alliance of liberal democracy and empire that lay at the heart of the Third Republic (Bullard 2000).

Much of the work of that regime would consist of building the basis of liberal democracy or, as Eugene Weber has put it, of turning peasants into Frenchmen. In his classic 1976 study of national identity formation in late nineteenth-century France, Weber not only analysed the ways in which the French government brought rural inhabitants into the culture of the modern nation state, but also specifically contrasted its success in integrating peasants into national culture with its failure to do the same with the residents of the colonies. As Weber notes, analogies between the backwardness of the French provinces and the barbarity of Africa and Asia abounded, yet in the end France still made the former a part of the national community in fundamental ways that were not open to the colonized (Weber 1976).

This contrast goes deeper than a simple comparison between heavy investment in provincial primary education—to take one prominent example—versus the paltry sums devoted to colonial schooling. More importantly, it derives from the increasing belief in France that colonial subjects could not become French citizens; that race and culture made them irredeemably different. By the end of the nineteenth century, French theorists of colonialism were moving away from the doctrine of assimilation, which emphasized turning the natives into French citizens, to one of association, focusing on the 'preservation' of native cultures and multiple routes to civilization. Association had the benefit of validating different ways of life, but in the colonial context it ultimately constituted the abandonment of the idea that the colonized had a place in the national community of France. In an era of democratic expansion, one might dream of civilizing the white savages of the provinces, but the overseas natives were by and large fated to remain essentially other (Betts 1961).

In Britain and France, then, intersections of race and class both illustrated and facilitated the alliance between liberal democracy and the new imperialism. This alliance transcended the rise of popular imperialism (a significant phenomenon in Britain) at the turn of the century. Whereas these increasingly democratic nations were able to assimilate a critical mass of the metropolitan lower classes, the growing influence of scientific racism and the failures of liberal efforts overseas largely prevented the similar assimilation of the colonized. Consequently, imperial liberal democracy had a paradoxical cast—citizenship in the metropole, subjecthood in the colonies—and the difference was racial. While both class and race continued to interact as important markers of social identity and distinction in both centre and periphery of empire, the contrast between them was central not just to the imperial nation state but also to liberal democracy. For both France and Britain, the dawn of the twentieth century witnessed a new vision of democracy, one less liberal but more popular, and firmly rooted in the colonial encounter.

DECOLONIZATION AND THE RISE OF SOCIAL DEMOCRACY

No single issue looms larger in comparisons of the British and French empires than their differing histories of decolonization. While historians have largely debunked the notion that Britain granted independence to its colonies magnanimously and peacefully, pointing to the violence of partition in India and Palestine and the brutal repression of insurgencies in Kenya and Malaya, it remains true that London avoided the kinds of massive colonial wars experienced by Indochina and Algeria. So whereas the classic trope of a 'right' British way versus a 'wrong' French one may not hold water, still the two empires implemented decolonization in fundamentally different ways. Scholars have advanced a number of explanations for this difference, including France's greater humiliation during World War II, Britain's earlier experiences in peacefully granting self-rule to the white Dominion colonies, the greater strength of post-war British governments compared to the weakness of the French Fourth Republic, and the particularly radical nature of nationalist forces in Algeria and Indochina (Duara 2004; Kahler 1984; Smith 1978; Spruyt 2005).

For the purposes of this chapter, a key contrast lay in the attitudes of the working-class political left in both countries towards decolonization. Whereas in Britain the left overwhelmingly supported the end of empire and under the post-war Labour government implemented key aspects of the process, in France the left was divided on the question (and sharply divided in general). The French Socialists mostly supported colonialist agendas in both Indochina and Algeria, while the Communists largely (but not entirely, especially in Algeria) backed nationalist causes. In large part, while in Britain working-class political leaders embraced decolonization, in France it was imposed upon them (Gupta 1983; see also Kahler 1984).

What does this contrast, and the history of decolonization in general, reveal about the relationship between empire and liberal democracy? While formal colonialism ended differently in the two empires, in both cases it collapsed during the same period and in a similar political context: just as the rise of liberal democracy and the new imperialism were coterminous in Britain and France, so too were decolonization and the beginnings of social democracy. The parallel was closest in Britain, where the first majority-based Labour government, elected in 1945, presided over the granting of independence to India and Pakistan at the same time as it implemented a major expansion of welfare state policies. Yet in France, as well, the retreat from formal empire under the Fourth Republic took place at the same time as the dramatic growth of *l'état providence*. Social democracy, which blended the mass character of liberal democracy with the social-ist commitment to social equality or at least the guarantee of basic living standards, arose inexorably from the trauma of the Second World War, as did widespread decolo-nization (Dutton 2002; Lowe 1993; Noble 2009; Smith 2003). The question is, to what extent were these two phenomena not only coterminous but also interdependent; and if so, how?

The simplest answer was that European nations had to choose between investing in empire abroad or social benefits at home; according to this logic, funding the welfare state depended on abandoning the expense of colonial administration overseas. Such a response regarded empires as an economic burden rather than as a source of wealth, a perspective very different from that of the late nineteenth century. While there is much truth to this view, it is not the only story; for the massive recovery and increasing pros-perity of the late 1940s and 1950s in western Europe made it possible—as during the late Victorian era—for imperial states to have guns and butter at the same time (Springhall 2000). France, for example, pursued state expansion at the same time as it engaged in two major colonial wars, between 1946 and 1962; and, more strikingly, Britain sharply increased its economic exploitation of its African colonies after the war in response to American pressures on sterling, a move that helped spur nationalist demands for inde-pendence (Howe 1993: 145). The importance of post-war American hegemony also played an important role in forcing Anglo-French decolonization, as the Suez crisis of 1956 made clear, but at the same time France and Britain adopted many social welfare policies at odds with American ideals of triumphant capitalism.

A more useful approach consists in exploring the ideological relationship between decolonization and social democracy in mid-twentieth-century France and Britain. Certainly, the horrors of Hitler's Europe, horrors with definite parallels to the colonial encounter, discredited both racism and imperialism for the post-war world.[1] The strong affinities between anti-fascism in metropolitan politics and anti-colonialism overseas can also explain the end of empire within and without Europe. At the same time, the concatenation of these two events speaks to broader tensions within imperial liberal democracy. Social democracy represented a deepening of the idea of democratic society, one that called into question the idea that all men are equal in spite of major differences in material circumstance. It recognized that states must make provisions to ameliorate social differences, in contrast to the classic liberal idea that the universal embrace of its principles would ultimately make those differences disappear. In a similar vein, decolo-nization (especially when won violently by the colonized) affirmed the bankruptcy of liberal ideas about uplifting the natives. Whether this project had succeeded or failed, the widespread abandonment of formal empire meant it had effectively ceased to exist; and in both respects, the liberal democracy of the late nineteenth century no longer suited the conditions of the post-war world.

---

[1] Historians have debated the actual impact of Nazism and the Holocaust on the reaction against racism during and after World War II. See for example Barkan 1992; also Wolton 2000.

It is certainly possible that social democracy benefited from the end of the basic contradiction of imperial liberal democracy, the division between citizens and subjects based on geography and race. This also represented a deepening of the democratic ideal and of citizenship, paralleling that achieved by welfare state policies. This more profound emphasis on popular nationalism, the 'people's nation', rendered the old imperial democratic paradox increasingly unsustainable, yet since visions of the people by and large did not include colonial subjects decolonization became the *de facto* alternative to the untenable prospect of including them as equals in the national community.

Anti-colonial resistance was of course a constant of the imperial experience, making it difficult to pinpoint the beginnings of the movement toward decolonization. Clearly, however, the two world wars played a seminal role in mobilizing mass-based nationalism in the British and French colonies as well as undermining Europeans' abilities to hold on to increasingly recalcitrant populations. Both France and Britain called extensively upon imperial resources to fight the First World War, portraying it frequently in racialized terminology as a war for civilization against German barbarity. However, what would become a struggle for liberal democracy in Europe, especially after the first Russian Revolution and America's entry into the war, ended up by reaffirming and extending colonialism. This blatant contradiction was not lost upon colonial militants in 1919 who used what Erez Manela has called 'the Wilsonian moment' to organize a series of revolts against metropolitan authority and to begin the construction of mass nationalist movements. In the face of an imperial liberal democracy that continued to insist upon the difference between citizen and subject, leaders of the colonized began to adopt ideas of revolution (Manela 2007; see also Macmillan 2002).

The end of World War I was a period of socialist revolution at home as well, and not only the Russian Revolution, but also the turmoil in central Europe seemed for a time to call into question the survival of capitalism as a whole. Britain and France experienced the revolutionary contagion to a lesser extent than other parts of Europe, suggesting an interesting balance between stability at home and turmoil overseas. Nonetheless, the aftermath of the Great War witnessed challenges to imperial liberal democracy at home and abroad, mounted by both class and racial others; and, as during the era of democratic revolution over a century earlier, colonial and metropolitan activism marched to a similar beat (Lindemann 1974; Mitchell 1970).

This parallel was much stronger during World War II, leading directly to the collapse of France and Britain's formal empires after 1945. Recalling the similarities between eighteenth-century Jacobinism in France and her Caribbean colonies, the French resistance to Vichy and Nazi Germany strongly resembled anti-colonial movements in the overseas empires. Both emphasized a combination of nationalist fervour and radical, even revolutionary visions of society. Both the resistance in France (and elsewhere in occupied Europe) and movements like the Vietminh in Indochina fought on several fronts, confronting the foreign occupier but also indigenous social and political elites: victory for both consequently consisted in expelling the invader *and* in transforming the societies once liberation had been achieved.[2]

For France, the colonies played a more central role in national life during the Second World War than ever before. The German occupation of the metropole shifted the nation's centre of gravity to the empire, the primary battleground for the forces of Vichy and De Gaulle. In particular, Free France first assumed concrete shape in the colonies: the Gaullist flag first flew over imperial territory and Brazzaville in French Equatorial Africa became the first official capital of 'free' France. Moreover, the majority of Free French troops during the war were colonial subjects. To an unprecedented degree, therefore, core notions of freedom and of Frenchness became colonial as a result of the German occupation (Jennings 2001; Onana 2006; Thomas 1998). At the same time, the need to assert French national identity and France's ability to liberate herself in the face of crushing defeat led the leaders of Free France to underplay the colonial dimension of their movement, both at the time and in the construction of popular memory after the war. De Gaulle excluded colonial troops from taking part in the liberation of Paris in 1944, portrayed, in spite of the key participation of Spanish Republican exiles, as a uniquely 'French' affair).

The leaders of Free France and of the internal Resistance shared a commitment to a more inclusive, anti-fascist democracy, a vision that also lay at the base of the Fourth Republic's commitment to the welfare state. However, this emphasis on national unity and solidarity excluded the colonies, since they did not figure in official images of the 'real' France. Ultimately the empire could only serve France; it did not count as an integral, still less equal, part of the French nation. A more full-fledged democracy could either admit colonial subjects as full French citizens or let them pursue their own path, but the unequal imperial democracy of the pre-war era would no longer suffice. After 1945 France and her colonies would pursue both options, resulting in widespread (although incomplete) decolonization.

The 1946 constitution that established the Fourth Republic graphically illustrated the vision of post-war empire that rose out of the successful struggle against Vichy. Most notable for granting the franchise to women, the constitution also reformed the relationship between France and her colonies. First, it offered the 'old colonies' a choice between independence and full-fledged departmental status in France. The four colonies strongly opted for the latter choice, ultimately becoming a kind of postcolonial remnant of empire that represented a possible vision of a more inclusive France but also continued to illustrate some of the problems—economic, political, and cultural—of imperial dependency (Daniel and Constant 1997). Second, the constitution abolished the distinction between subject and citizen, making all residents of the French colonies citizens of France. This was not equal citizenship, however, but more closely resembled the old subject status under a new guise. Such reform did little to mollify the forces of

---

[2.] Unfortunately, few historians of Europe have studied the nexus between anti-fascism and anti-colonialism. See the classic discussions of this relationship by Césaire (1955) and Fanon (2002).

anti-colonial nationalism: fighting broke out in Indochina later that year, and wars of empire would dominate the history of the Fourth Republic more than any other regime in the nation's history (Rioux 1987).

At the same time, the Fourth Republic transformed French society and laid the foundations for the post-war welfare state. It created the first major social security system in the nation's history, nationalized large sectors of the economy, and invested heavily in education and housing, radically altering the skylines of Paris and other cities by building massive new public housing towers, the famous *HLMs*. The fact that France invested so heavily in social improvement while at the same time pursuing seemingly endless colonial warfare reflected the old imperial democratic paradox, but its failure to achieve both suggested that this paradox could not endure; that the new post-war France would have to choose between empire and modern democracy.

The sharp division of the French left after 1945 played a key role in shaping the relationship between social welfare and decolonization. Unlike Britain, where Labour essentially monopolized working-class and left politics, in France socialists and communists could both draw on mass support, but became increasingly hostile to one another with the onset of the Cold War. As long as the tenuous coalition known as 'tripartism' held, both parties advocated the reform rather than the abolition of French colonialism. However, the fact that France's first major struggle over empire after 1945 involved a war with the Vietminh, formally allied with the USSR and like the French communists in the Resistance combining nationalist and revolutionary ideology, forced the leaders of the PCF into a difficult position. As members of the tripartite coalition government, they were increasingly pressured to choose sides by the burgeoning Cold War, and the war in Indochina became more and more a marker of that choice. At the same time, the wage controls that had helped fund reconstruction provoked widespread discontent among the party's working-class base, forcing it to renounce the economic policies of its own coalition. By the end of 1947 these dual pressures, domestic and colonial, forced the PCF out of the coalition government and into the political wilderness for over a generation (Graham 1965; Williams 1964).

Social democracy in France would henceforth be built without the revolutionary left, which represented the loudest voice arguing for egalitarian reforms of the empire. After 1947, the French socialist leadership generally backed France's bloody and futile resistance to the end of formal empire, most notably supporting the policy of 'pacification' in Algeria. Ultimately, however, it became clear to the socialists, and the French people in general, that attempts to maintain colonial rule by force were not only ruinous economically but also, as the collapse of the Fourth Republic in 1958 made clear, a threat to democracy itself. If France wanted the new, socially progressive democracy, it had to abandon the empire. Although the new French Union seemed to promise a more democratic arrangement between France and her colonies, few were fooled by these appearances. De Gaulle's sudden abandonment of colonial rule in Africa during 1960 thus reflected the exhaustion provoked by the Algerian war, but also underscored Paris's rejection of a more egalitarian union, a *Eurafrique*, that some had proposed after 1945 (Marseille 1984; Ross 1995).

In short, the combination of social welfare and decolonization created a new vision of France: one more unified and prosperous, one better suited to the modern era. In spite of the many differences in decolonization patterns across the Channel, the same holds true for Britain. One contrast between the two nations' retreat from empire was that while traditionally Britain had been much more committed to a vision of itself as an imperial nation than France, after World War II she took the lead in relinquishing her colonies. In particular, changing attitudes within the Labour Party heralded a new day for the British Empire. Whereas party members embraced a variety of perspectives on empire, both pro- and anti-colonial, Labour had generally preferred the ideal of 'Little England' to the strains of social imperialism, in spite of popular pressures to the contrary. Moreover, by the interwar years party members had begun to develop significant contacts with nationalist and labour activists in the Empire, especially India and the Caribbean, as well as relationships with colonial expatriates in the metropole (Howe 1993; Gupta 2002).

The war years increased anti-colonial feeling substantially, both in the Labour Party and in Britain as a whole. Nazi submarine warfare in the Atlantic and Japanese victories in Asia had cut Britons off from their colonies, shown by as mundane a factor as the improved dental hygiene resulting from reductions in the supply of Caribbean sugar. More substantially, the reluctance of many colonial subjects to defend the British Empire, as they had done in World War I, caused consternation and even resentment at home: British politicians of all stripes roundly condemned the 1942 Quit India movement and local British authorities imprisoned Mohandas Gandhi and most of the Congress Party leadership for the duration of the war (Chakravarty 2002; Wolpert 2006). In sharp contrast to the French experience, during the Second World War many Britons came to regard the Empire as a liability rather than an asset, especially as they began to look beyond achieving victory to imagining the nature of democracy and social justice in their own country (Darwin 2006).

At the same time, the Labour Party moved towards a more consistent anti-colonial policy. In its 1942 conference it passed the Charter of Freedom for Colonial Peoples, modelled on the Atlantic Charter (Howe 1993: 137–8). By the war years, the party had embraced the principle of self-government for India, a principle that would become the centrepiece of the Labour government's decolonization strategy after 1945. As Partha Sarathi Gupta has noted, this commitment did not necessarily carry over to other parts of the Empire, notably Africa: Labour often drew a racial line between its brown and black colonies, and the idea of Indian self-rule in some respects seemed to turn that country into a Dominion along the lines of white former colonies like Canada and Australia. Nonetheless, when Labour came to power in 1945, in contrast to the tripartite governments that ruled France after its liberation, it came fully committed to national independence for the imperial jewel in the crown.

Labour's victory in 1945 represented not just a landslide victory for the left but a transformation of British politics. The party came to power with a solid majority, which was very different from the two weak coalition governments it had formed during the 1920s. Social democracy had clearly come to stay in Britain, and even after Labour lost a close election to the Conservatives in 1951, key elements of its vision endured. This was true of both colonial and social policy, underscoring the connection between decolonization and the welfare state. Labour did indeed grant independence to the new nations of the Indian subcontinent and to its former League of Nations mandates in the Middle East; however, it was the Conservatives, ostensibly the party of empire, who directed the decolonization of Africa and the Caribbean in the 1950s and 1960s. The war between British forces and communist insurgents in Malaya began under the Labour government, and successive Conservative governments pursued it vigorously. Whereas in France decolonization brought about the collapse of the Fourth Republic, in Britain it underscored the breadth of new attitudes toward empire (Goldsworthy 1971; Smith 1978).

Labour's implementation of welfare state policies was far more controversial and encountered sharp Conservative opposition. Building on the wartime Beveridge Report advocating universal health care, the Labour government passed the National Insurance Act (1946) and created the National Health Service (1948). It also moved to nationalize significant parts of the economy, starting with the Bank of England in 1946 and moving onto the railroads, coalmines, and iron and steel industries by the end of the decade. Unlike in France, welfare state policies in Britain seemed to benefit directly from the withdrawal from empire and the costs it entailed, with reduced government and military expenditure overseas bringing increased government investment in social benefits at home. The post-war British welfare state thus validated the arguments of those on the left who had charged imperialism with reducing domestic living standards and ultimately harming the welfare of 'Little England'. And while Conservatives derided the ideology of the welfare state, it remained central to British social policy until the government of Margaret Thatcher challenged it in the late 1970s. Like decolonization, the welfare state became a key aspect of the identity of Britain after 1945 (Hill 1993; Lowe 1993).

The relationship between the advent of social democracy and the retreat from empire thus underscores similarities in French and British decolonization, in contrast to the traditional emphasis on their differences. More specifically, it shows how a new, more inclusive, vision of mass democracy born in the cauldron of total war ultimately proved incompatible with the old imperial vision. Not only did many feel that the cost of empire and of imperial war in particular was hindering efforts to create a new society at home, but the principle of equality for all members of the national community could not accommodate radical disparities between colonizer and colonized. Given a choice between making the natives equal or setting them free, the logic of decolonization led inexorably to the latter.[3]

[3.] This of course raises the question of neocolonialism: did national independence really equal freedom or even the definitive end of empire for the colonies? The classic work on this question is Nkrumah (1965); see also Young (2001).

Conclusion: Postcolonial Society, Postcolonial History

This chapter has argued that France and Britain blended ideas of empire and mass liberal democracy during the modern era, so that the many intersections of the two ideas are key to any understanding of what Gary Wilder has termed the imperial nation state. In what remains, I want to explore the postcolonial dimensions of this basic issue. Historians and cultural theorists have often differed about the meaning of postcolonialism: whereas the former often define it as a specific period beginning with the end of widespread formal empires after 1945, the latter generally see it as a methodological and ultimately political approach to the study of society and culture (see Kennedy in Part IV of this volume). I will conclude by considering how the relationship between democracy and empire can be articulated by both visions of postcoloniality and thus illustrate the affinities between them.

If the rise of the welfare state in Britain and France paralleled the retreat from formal empire, so too did its decline correspond to the increasingly postcolonial nature of society in both countries. The great irony of decolonization is that it brought the empire home, in the form of immigrants from former colonies, to a much greater extent than anything that occurred during the period of formal imperial rule. By the 1980s both France and Britain had large communities of peoples of colonial origin, including many born in the metropole ('second-generation immigrants') who demanded full citizenship and equality. At the same time, the end of the post-war boom brought frontal assaults on social welfare, symbolized above all by Margaret Thatcher. Similar to the racialized attacks that are common in American politics, leading politicians in Britain and France made postcolonial migrants and their children central to their critiques of welfare state benefits. In both countries, National Front parties argued that the only way to uphold *l'état providence*, and by extension the very existence of the prosperous post-war working class, was to eliminate people of colour from it.

This latest articulation of the relationship between empire and democracy clearly indicates that the imperial past is by no means past, and that it and the postcolonial present have a good deal in common. Meanwhile, questions of colonial memory and nostalgia have loomed large in both Britain and France recently, showcasing conflicts over current political disputes and the nature of national identity (see Rothberg in Part III of this volume). In France, the last twenty years have witnessed a new level of attention to the history and memory of the Algerian war, but also, in sharp contrast to this, a vogue for colonial Indochina, '*Indo-chic*'. The 2005 attempt by the National Assembly to force schoolteachers only to give positive accounts of the nation's colonial past caused a firestorm of protest by historians, and the massive suburban riots that broke out at the end of that year showed how the conflicts of the colonial era had been reinscribed in postcolonial urban space. Britain, too, has seen extensive recent debates on the relationship between national identity and empire, which have explored not only the impact of the colonies on life in the metropole, but also the extent to which notions of 'Englishness' itself emerged from imperial encounter. A series of boisterous public challenges to the idea of 'multicultural' Britain as a betrayal of the nation's heritage has reflected tensions around race and the perceived threats to national identity posed by moves for European integration and globalization. In both countries, advocates of a more traditional sense of nation have frequently targeted the United States as a negative referent of racial plural- ism. Postcolonial scholarship has often found itself at ground zero in the transatlantic culture wars over the nation's soul.

Such current concerns underscore the importance of the relationship between empire and democracy, both past and present. The question of national identity is rooted in the rise of the democratic nation state in both France and Britain, so that the idea of the People assumes its most concrete appearance when wrapped in the national flag. Viewing the modern democratic nation through an imperial lens both challenges such ideas of democracy and suggests more inclusive alternatives. However, as long as the polarity between metropole and colony survives—even in its postcolonial manifesta- tions—the democratic project remains incomplete. Only when this is no longer the case can France and Britain claim to be truly postcolonial.

References

Abi-Mershed, Osama (2010). *Apostles of Modernity: Saint-Simonians and the Civilizing Mission in Algeria*. Stanford: Stanford University Press.

Aldrich, Robert (1996). *Greater France: A History of French Overseas Expansion*. Houndmills: Macmillan Press.

Anderson, Benedict (1991). *Imagined Communities: Reflections on the Origin and Spread of Nationalism*. New York: Verso.

Barkan, Elazar (1992). *The Retreat of Scientific Racism: Changing Concepts of Race in Britain and the United States between the World Wars*. Cambridge: Cambridge University Press.

Betts, Raymond (1961). *Assimilation and Association in French Colonial Theory*. New York: Columbia University Press.

Biddiss, Michael D. (1970). *Father of Racist Ideology: The Social and Political Thought of Count Gobineau*. New York: Weybright and Talley.

Bowen, H. V. (2008). *The Business of Empire: The East India Company and Imperial Britain, 1756–1837*. Princeton: Princeton University Press.

Bullard, Alice (2000). *Exile to Paradise: Savagery and Civilization in Paris and the South Pacific, 1790–1900*. Stanford: Stanford University Press.

Césaire, Aimé (1955). *Discours sur le colonialisme*. Paris: Présence Africaine.

Chakrabarty, Dipesh (2000). *Provincializing Europe: Postcolonial Thought and Historical Difference*. Princeton: Princeton University Press.

Chakravarty, Shachi (2002). *Quit India Movement: A Study*. Delhi: New Century Publications.

Clark, Linda (1984). *Social Darwinism in France*. Tuscaloosa: University of Alabama Press.

Coleman, Deirdre (2004). *Romantic Colonization and British Anti-Slavery*. New York: Cambridge University Press.

Conklin, Alice (1997). *A Mission to Civilize: The Republican Idea of Empire in France and West Africa, 1895–1930*. Stanford: Stanford University Press.

Cooper, Frederick (1996). *Decolonization and African Society: The Labor Question in French and British Africa*. Cambridge: Cambridge University Press.

Cooper, Frederick (2005). *Colonialism in Question: Theory, Knowledge, History*. Berkeley: University of California Press.

Cooper, F. and A. L. Stoler (eds) (1997). *Tensions of Empire: Colonial Cultures in a Bourgeois World*. Berkeley: University of California Press.

Da Costa, Emilia Viotti (1994). *Crowns of Glory, Tears of Blood: The Demerara Slave Rebellion of 1823*. New York: Oxford University Press.

Daniel, J. and F. Constant (eds) (1997). *Cinquante ans de départementalisation outremer*. Paris: L'Harmattan.

Darwin, John (2006). *The End of the British Empire: The Historical Debate*. London: Wiley Blackwell.

Davis, David Brion (1999). *The Problem of Slavery in the Age of Revolution*. New York: Oxford University Press.

De Nie, Michael (2004). *The Eternal Paddy: Irish Identity and the British Press, 1798–1882*. Madison: University of Wisconsin Press.

De Tocqueville, Alexis (2001). *Writings on Empire and Slavery*, ed. and trans. J. Pitts. Baltimore: Johns Hopkins University Press.

Drescher, Seymour (2009). *Abolition: A History of Slavery and Antislavery*. Cambridge: Cambridge University Press.

Duara, Prasenjit (ed.) (2004). *Decolonization: Perspectives from Now and Then*. New York: Routledge.

Dutton, Paul (2002). *Origins of the French Welfare State: The Struggle for Social Reform in France*. New York: Cambridge University Press.

English, Jim (2006). 'Empire Day in Britain, 1904–1958', *The Historical Journal*, 49.1: 247–76.

Epstein, James (1982). *Lion of Freedom: Feargus O'Connor and the Chartist Movement*. London: Croom Helm.

Eze, Emmanuel Chukwudi (ed.) (1997). *Race and the Enlightenment*. Cambridge, Mass.: Blackwell.

Fanon, Frantz (2002). *Les Damnés de la Terre*. Paris: La Découverte & Syros.

Fick, Carolyn (1990). *The Making of Haiti: The Saint-Domingue Revolution from Below*. Knoxville: University of Tennessee Press.

Foot, Paul (2005). *The Vote: How It Was Won and How It Was Undermined*. New York: Viking.

Fournier, Marcel (2005). *Les Bretons en Amérique française, 1504–2004*. Rennes: Les Portes du large.

Fry, Michael (2001). *The Scottish Empire*. East Lothian: Phantassie.

Gallagher, John and Ronald Robinson (1953). 'The Imperialism of Free Trade', *Economic History Review*, 6.1: 1–15.

Garraway, Doris (2008). *Tree of Liberty: Cultural Legacies of the Haitian Revolution in the Atlantic World*. Charlottesville: University of Virginia Press.

Goldsworthy, David (1971). *Colonial Issues in British Politics: From 'Colonial Development' to 'Wind of Change'*. Oxford: Clarendon Press.

Graham, Bruce D. (1965). *The French Socialists and Tripartism*. Toronto: University of Toronto Press.

Gupta, Partha Sarathi (1983). 'Imperialism and the Labour Government', in J. Winter (ed.), *The Working Class in Modern British History*. Cambridge: Cambridge University Press, 99–124.

Gupta, Partha Sarathi (2002). *Imperialism and the British Labour Movement, 1914–1964*. New Delhi: Sage.

Hall, Catherine (2000). 'The Rule of Difference: Gender, Class and Empire in the Making of the 1832 Reform Act', in I. Blom, K. Hagemann, and C. Hall (eds), *Gendered Nations: Nationalism and Gender Order in the Long 19th Century*. Oxford and New York: Berg, 107–36.

Hall, Catherine (2002). *Civilising Subjects: Metropole and Colony in the English Imagination 1830–1867*. Chicago: University of Chicago Press.

Hawkins, Mike (1997). *Social Darwinism in European and American Thought 1860–1945: Nature as Model and Nature as Threat*. Cambridge: Cambridge University Press.

Herbert, Christopher (2008). *War of No Pity: The India Mutiny and Victorian Trauma*. Princeton: Princeton University Press.

Hill, Michael (1993). *The Welfare State in Britain: A Political History since 1945*. Brookfield, Vt.: Edward Elgar Publishing.

Hobsbawm, Eric (1996). *Age of Revolution, 1789–1848*. New York: Vintage.

Holt, Thomas C. (1992). *The Problem of Freedom: Race, Labor and Politics in Jamaica and Britain 1832–1938*. Baltimore: Johns Hopkins University Press.

Howe, Stephen (1993). *Anticolonialism in British Politics: The Left and the End of Empire*. Oxford: Clarendon Press.

Howe, Stephen (2000). *Ireland and Empire: Colonial Legacies in Irish History and Culture*. New York: Oxford University Press.

Howe, Stephen (2001). 'The Slow Death and Strange Rebirths of Imperial History', *Journal of Imperial and Commonwealth History*, 29: 131–41.

Huard, Raymond (1991). *Le suffrage universel en France: 1848–1946*. Paris: Aubier.

James, C. L. R. (1989). *Black Jacobins: Toussaint L'Ouverture and the San Domingo Revolution*. New York: Vintage.

Jennings, Eric (2001). *Vichy in the Tropics: Petain's National Revolution in Madagascar, Guadeloupe and Indochina*. Stanford: Stanford University Press.

Jennings, Lawrence C. (2000). *French Anti-Slavery: The Movement for the Abolition of Slavery in France, 1802–1848*. Cambridge: Cambridge University Press.

Kahler, Miles (1984). *Decolonization in Britain and France: The Domestic Consequences of International Relations*. Princeton: Princeton University Press.

Kelly, Gail Paradise and David H. Kelly (2000). *French Colonial Education: Essays on Vietnam and West Africa*. New York: AMS Press.

Kenny, Kevin (ed.) (2006). *Ireland and the British Empire*. New York: Oxford University Press.

Kirk, Neville (1985). *The Growth of Working Class Reformism in Mid-Victorian England*. Urbana: University of Illinois Press.

Klein, Martin A. (1998). *Slavery and Colonial Rule in French West Africa*. New York: Cambridge University Press.

Lebo, Richard Ned (1976). *White Britain and Black Ireland: The Impact of Stereotypes on Colonial Policy*. Philadelphia: Institute for the Study of Human Issues.

Lenin, Vladimir (1996 [1917]). *Imperialism: The Highest Stage of Capitalism*. London: Pluto Press.

Levine, Philippa (2007). *The British Empire: Sunrise to Sunset*. Harlow: Pearson.

Lindemann, Albert S. (1974). *The 'Red Years': European Socialism versus Bolshevism, 1919–1921*. Berkeley: University of California Press.

Lorcin, Patricia M. E. (1995). *Imperial Identities: Stereotyping, Prejudice and Race in Colonial Algeria*. New York: St Martin's Press.

Lowe, Rodney (1993). *The Welfare State in Britain since 1945*. New York: St Martin's Press.

Macmillan, Margaret (2002). *Paris 1919: Six Months that Changed the World*. New York: Random House.

Manela, Erez (2007). *The Wilsonian Moment: Self-Determination and the International Origins of Anticolonial Nationalism*. Oxford: Oxford University Press.

Marseille, Jacques (1984). *Empire colonial et capitalism français: Histoire d'un divorce*. Paris: A. Michel.

Matthews, Gelien (2006). *Caribbean Slave Revolts and the British Abolitionist Movement*. Baton Rouge: Louisiana State University Press.

McClintock, Anne (1995). *Imperial Leather: Race, Gender, and Sexuality in the Colonial Conquest*. New York: Routledge.

Mehta, Uday Singh (1999). *Liberalism and Empire: A Study in 19th Century Liberal Thought*. Chicago: University of Chicago Press.

Mitchell, David (1970). *1919, Red Mirage: Year of Desperate Rebellion*. London: Cape.

Morgan, Simon (2009). 'The Anti-Corn Law League and British Anti-Slavery in Transatlantic Perspective, 1838–1846', *The Historical Journal*, 52.1: 87–107.

Morrow, John H. (2005). *The Great War: An Imperial History*. London: Routledge.

Mosse, George (1978). *Toward the Final Solution: A History of European Racism*. New York: H. Fertig.

Nkrumah, Kwame (1965). *Neocolonialism: The Last Stage of Imperialism*. New York: International Publishers.

Noble, Virginia (2009). *Inside the Welfare State*. New York: Routledge.

O'Higgins, R. (1961). 'The Irish Influence in the Chartist Movement', *Past and Present*, 1.20: 83–96.

Oldfield, J. R. (1998). *Popular Politics and British Anti-Slavery: The Mobilization of Public Opinion against the Slave Trade*. New York: St Martin's Press.

Onana, Charles (2006). *Noirs, Blancs, Beurs: Libérateurs de la France*. Paris: Duboiris.

Pitts, Jennifer (2005). *A Turn to Empire: The Rise of Imperial Liberalism in Britain and France*. Princeton: Princeton University Press.

Rioux, Jean-Pierre (1987). *The Fourth Republic, 1944–1958*. Cambridge: Cambridge University Press.

Rose, Sonya O. (1992). *Limited Livelihoods: Gender and Class in Nineteenth-Century England*. Berkeley: University of California Press.

Ross, Kristin (1995). *Fast Cars, Clean Bodies: Decolonization and the Reordering of French Culture*. Cambridge, Mass.: MIT Press.

Ryden, David (2009). West Indian Slavery and British Abolition, 1783–1897. Cambridge and New York: Cambridge University Press.

Said, Edward W. (1978). *Orientalism*. New York: Pantheon.

Samson, Jane (2005). *Race and Empire*. Harlow: Pearson.

Segalla, S. D. (2009). *The Moroccan Soul: French Education, Colonial Ethnology, and the Muslim Resistance, 1912–1956*. Lincoln: University of Nebraska Press.

Semmel, Bernard (1960). *Imperialism and Social Reform: English Social-Imperial Thought, 1865–1914*. Cambridge, Mass.: Harvard University Press.

Semmel, Bernard (1970). *The Rise of Free Trade Imperialism: Classical Political Economy, the Empire of Free Trade and Imperialism 1750–1850*. Cambridge: Cambridge University Press.

Seth, Sanjay (2007). *Subject Lessons: The Western Education of Colonial India*. Durham, NC: Duke University Press.

Smith, Timothy B. (2003). *Creating the Welfare State in France, 1880–1940*. Montreal: McGill-Queen's University Press.

Smith, Tony (1978). 'A Comparative Study of French and British Decolonization', *Comparative Studies in Society and History*, 20.1: 70–102.

Spilsbury, Julian (2008). *The Indian Mutiny*. London: Weidenfeld & Nicolson.

Springhall, John (2000). *Decolonization Since 1945: The Collapse of European Overseas Empires*. Basingstoke: Palgrave Macmillan.

Spruyt, Hendrik (2005). *Ending Empire: Contested Sovereignty and Territorial Partition*. Ithaca: Cornell University Press.

Stoler, Ann Laura (1989). 'Rethinking Colonial Categories: European Communities and the Boundaries of Rule', *Comparative Studies in Society and History*, 13.1: 134–61.

Stoler, Ann Laura (2002). *Carnal Knowledge and Imperial Power: Race and the Intimate in Colonial Rule*. Berkeley: University of California Press.

Stora, Benjamin (2004). *Algeria, 1830–2000: A Short History*. Ithaca: Cornell University Press.

Thomas, Martin (1998). *The French Empire at War, 1940–1945*. Manchester: Manchester University Press.

Thorne, Susan (1997). '"The Conversion of Englishman and the Conversion of the World Inseparable": Missionary Imperialism and the Language of Class in Early Industrial Britain', in F. Cooper and A. L. Stoler (eds), *Tensions of Empire: Colonial Cultures in a Bourgeois World*. Berkeley: University of California Press, 238–62.

Weber, Eugene (1976). *Peasants into Frenchmen: The Modernization of Rural France, 1870–1914*. Stanford: Stanford University Press.

White, Owen (2007). 'Priests into Frenchmen? Breton Missionaries in Côte d'Ivoire', *French Colonial History*, 8.7: 111–21.

Wilder, Gary (2005). *The French Imperial Nation-State: Negritude and Colonial Humanism between the Two World Wars*. Chicago: University of Chicago Press.

Williams, Philip (1964). *Crisis and Compromise: Politics in the Fourth Republic*. Hamden, Conn.: Anchor Books.

Wolfe, Patrick (1997) 'History and Imperialism: A Century of Theory, from Marx to Postcolonialism', *The American Historical Review*, 102.2: 399–402.

Wolpert, Stanley (2006). *Shameful Fight: The Last Years of the British Empire in India*. New York: Oxford University Press.

Wolton, Suke (2000). *Lord Hailey, the Colonial Office and the Politics of Race and Empire in the Second World War: The Loss of White Prestige*. New York: St Martin's Press.

Young, Robert J. C. (1990). *White Mythologies: Writing History and the West*. London: Routledge.

Young, Robert J. C. (2001). *Postcolonialism: An Historical Introduction*. Oxford: Blackwell Publishers.

CHAPTER 3

THE IMPERIAL PAST

Spain and Portugal in the New World

PATRICIA SEED

Two unique themes appear in postcolonial thinking from both Spanish and Portuguese America: indigenism and a tradition of subaltern people's own literature of critique. Of these two, the first subject remains formative, differentiating the New World from other places since colonial times. The second development uniquely distinguishes Iberian postcolonial writing. Recent cosmopolitanism has failed to dislodge either distinction. The first and most crucial feature, as well as the historically the most enduring, is indigenism.

'Indigenous' is a category of people created by invasion or conquest; it does not exist prior to the arrival of armed invaders from elsewhere. Only when outsiders or foreigners attack or overrun a place do people become 'natives'; there can be no 'natives' if neither foreigners nor outsiders are present to define that difference. Rather, that term is reserved for categories of people created as the result of armed assault, occupation, and the resettlement of outsiders. Hence efforts to try to define 'indigenous' as an autochthonous concept have foundered (Hamilton and Placas 2011: 249–52),[1] principally because the concept cannot be separated from its inception by means of encroachment or incursion.

In the Americas, diverse communities whose inhabitants considered themselves highly differentiated people were lumped together as 'natives' following European invasions. This label created the foundation for categories that allowed them to become fundamentally other, eventually incorporated, enslaved, or excluded according to political and cultural rules introduced by outsiders. With the overthrow of colonial regimes, signifying the ousting of the intruders, the question of the political future of the indigenous

[1.] Many of the popular definitions of 'indigenous' simply do not work when applied to the New World. Perry (1996: 8) argues that it denotes local populations in place before a state incorporated them—but that excludes the Inca and Aztec empires, which most certainly were states. The effort to declare the people they conquered as authentic indigenes formed part of the colonial strategy of Iberian colonialists to discredit the Incas, most notably in Peru beginning in 1570.

population emerged as a significant issue that remains debated everywhere and resolved nowhere.

Unlike anywhere else on the planet, the initial scope of the category of 'native' was staggering. When settlers (outsiders) arrived, they found thousands of different communities and languages, and several hundred million people. In short, the scale and diversity of the newfound 'natives' far exceeded anything that Africans, Asians, or Europeans had previously encountered. Within the ambit of the three interconnected continents of Africa, Asia, and Europe, outsiders episodically discovered and invaded isolated communities, but nothing on the scale or scope of the encounter with the people of the Americas had ever occurred. Nor would such an experience ever happen again on a similarly spectacular scale.

During the first seventy years following Columbus's accidental encounter with the inhabitants of the newly named Caribbean, Spanish and Portuguese explorers travelled along the coast of eastern Canada, through the southeastern United States from Florida to the Mississippi Valley, and south to Argentina and Chile. Portuguese and French arrivals journeyed along the coast of Brazil. The diversity and numbers of people who were to become 'natives' during these journeys was astonishing—from small nomadic communities to massive empires with elaborate state and record-keeping mechanisms.

During this first phase of contact, Europeans defined several hundred million people from a broad range of communities on two continents as 'indigenous'. In the second stage, commencing a decade or so after contact, foreign (European) governments began to rule, entrenching their political authority over these newly encountered people. This second phase, marking the period when 'indigenous' people were subordinated to the invaders throughout the Americas, became known as the colonial era. 'Natives' were transformed into 'Indians', the name by which indigenous people were reduced to a single collectivity, subject to the rule of outsiders during colonial governance. But not all the occupiers viewed the newly constituted 'Indians' with the same eyes, nor did they classify them identically.

Colonialism is not and never has been a singular noun. Rather, multiple colonialisms have differed in their political as well as their economic objectives. Every European power that governed natives in the New World imposed its own system of subordination; French, Dutch, Swedish, Spanish, Portuguese, and English outsiders on the mainland of the Americas ruled Indian communities very differently. However, three of these six invaders would defeat their European competitors and dominate the indigenes on the American continent for the next two to five hundred years: Spain, Portugal, and England. Hence their policies have had the most significant and enduring impact on indigenous people.[2]

Spain, Portugal, and England each subjected the formerly heterogeneous group of 'natives' according to fundamental premises for amassing wealth they brought with them, embedded in their own languages and histories. English-speaking colonialists

---

[2.] France controlled commerce with natives along the St Lawrence and Mississippi riverways for over a century, but when defeated by the British in 1763, their definitions of indigene vaporized.

(and later imperialists) sought native land while their Spanish- and Portuguese-speaking counterparts sought native labour. Under different colonialisms, 'natives' were stripped of their individuality and diversity as they were grouped together as 'Indians', economic factors of production for colonial powers.

To assist in this transition from separate peoples to factors of production, 'natives' were invented as communities that were morally and politically incapable of exercising dominion over the principal object of colonial economic desires. 'Indians' were not defined by any shared characteristic or behaviour of actual people; rather, they became identified by a colonial fiction, a synecdoche in which the conduct of some was converted into the identity of the many. More importantly, this misrepresentation smoothed the way for the profit-making ambitions of the invaders by permitting them to exercise whatever legal means existed in their country of origin to acquire wealth. Since not all invaders valued the same objectives, a fictionalized colonial identity materialized around distinct economic ambitions acceptable to each colonizing power. A single community would be defined differently depending upon which side of the colonial border it found itself (Seed 2003: 113–34).

In English-speaking colonies, 'Indians' were defined as incapable of owning their own land, while in Spanish- and Portuguese-speaking colonies they were viewed as needing to donate their labour for the salvation of their souls. In the English-speaking world, natives—including settled planters and farmers—were invented as 'hunters', since under traditional English law non-elite hunters lacked ownership rights over land. Thus the native farmers of Georgia were transformed into 'hunters' who could then be deprived of autonomy over their land. In the Spanish-speaking and Portuguese-speaking Americas, Indians would be invented as 'cannibals' because such depraved practices signified that they had to be put to work to prevent them from falling back into their amoral patterns of behaviour.[3] In this way, Englishmen justified dominion over land and Spaniards rationalized power over labour. Several centuries of neocolonial name-calling have failed to establish the moral or political superiority of either colonial economic fiction.

The arrival of independence in both Spanish- and English-speaking regions paved the way for similar continuities in rule. Throughout the continental Americas, liberation from colonial rule occurred during a similar time span and set the stage for distinctive parallels in the treatment of indigenes. The progression from colonial to postcolonial states on most of the American mainland occurred in a fifty-year time period between 1775 and 1825. On the North American side, the independence movement in the United States succeeded (largely aided by French support) a few decades earlier (1775–83) than in the Spanish-speaking areas. Between 1809 and 1825, all of the Spanish and Portuguese colonies on the mainland of the Americas emerged as independent. At first, the royalist forces (parallel to the US loyalists) defeated the insurgents, but by 1816, insurgents had gained their first permanent victories at both ends of the

---

[3] A similar narrative appeared to justify a variety of treatments inflicted by Portuguese settlers upon indigenous populations of the New World. The only significant difference lay in the organization and types of unfree labour imposed. See Vainfas (1995).

continent. By 1825, aided by political divisions in Spain, independence forces upended the royalists. In Brazil, an independent kingdom proclaimed in 1822 was followed by a war lasting only twenty-two months and ending with victory for the Brazilian side.

However, the end to colonialism followed a similar trajectory in Spanish, English, and Portuguese Americas, not simply because of the shared timing, but more profoundly because liberation throughout the Americas yielded power not to the region's indigenous people but rather to the colonizers' descendants. From the Arctic's frozen shores to the slashing winds of the southern ocean, power passed from English, Spanish, and later Portuguese rulers to the largely white but overseas-born offspring of colonizers, bypassing the continent's indigenous people entirely.

This situation contrasts sharply with the postcolonial fate of African and most Asian nations 150 years later, when political power came into the hands of one or more groups of indigenous people. Hence a profound and important difference separates the postcolonial Americas from the Asian and African experience. Deprived of a return to power by indigenous communities, the post-independence era in the Americas marked a much smaller break with the colonial past than elsewhere. In its place emerged a neocolonial reformulation of principles governing the status of native peoples that defines North and South American postcolonialism and marks its distinctiveness.[4]

Derek Gregory's insistence that we live in the 'colonial present', amid 'constellations of power, knowledge, and geography that ... continue to colonize lives all over the world' (2004: xv) describes the contemporary position of the people of the Americas who became indigenous with the arrival of the colonizers more profoundly than in other parts of the world where colonialism endured for far fewer centuries (see Part II of this volume). In the United States, neocolonial fictions of Indians as 'hunters' continued unchanged by the movement for independence of colonists. Within forty years of independence, when lawyers repeatedly pointed out that the Cherokees were cotton plantation owners and even slave-holding plantation owners as many settlers aspired to be, the Chief Justice of the United States responded that the facts mattered not at all. 'Indians were hunters', therefore the Cherokee plantation owners were hunters and could be removed from their property.[5] The invented colonial identity created for 'Indians' trumped all other considerations, including the reality of successful and prosperous indigenous agriculture.

Gregory's colonial present appears equally powerfully in the Spanish-speaking Americas, where the fictional identity was amoral cannibals. The charge continues to be employed in modern Spanish-speaking American nations. In 1992 at an international conference of indigenous NGOs, a prominent expert on the history of Brazilian Indians painted a romanticized portrait of the hard-pressed life of indigenous people

---

[4.] The only other countries with similar experience outside the Americas are Australia and New Zealand, both of which have fundamentally altered the neocolonial relationship, allowing power sharing with Aboriginal and Māori people beginning in the 1970s in New Zealand and the 1980s in Australia. See Hindess in Part IV of this volume; also Smith and Turner in Part II.

[5.] Johnson v McIntosh, 21 US 576.

prior to conquest. I raised the issue that romanticization did a disservice to the historical lives of these people and left the speaker vulnerable to exaggerated counter-charges of native barbarity. As the word cannibalism left my mouth, a well-known Mapuche activist interrupted. 'You cannot say that!' he shouted. 'That's what they [Chilean government officials] always use against us.' In seeking to deny autonomy to Mapuche communities, Chilean officials employ the same fictitious neocolonial rationale. Mapuches have never been cannibals anymore than hundreds of millions of other natives of the Spanish- (and Portuguese)-controlled Americas. But the mere mention of the word sufficed to bring the continuing power of colonial tropes into sharp focus.

While the economic ambitions behind the colonial fictions did not budge during independence, the cultural representations of indigenous cultures did undergo a transformation in a large section of the Americas. While these portrayals remained stubbornly stuck in the emergent nationalist literature of the English-speaking world, they shifted in the former Iberian colonies. During the build-up to independence in Spanish and Portuguese America, the accumulation of political and economic grievances that led to the declaration of war was accompanied by the emergence of a new intellectual rationale. Iberian New World writers began to invent a new political identity for themselves founded upon one of the irrefutable distinctions of the New World, ironically the existence of unique indigenous communities.

When Columbus and then the Spaniards encountered the New World, they came into contact for the first time with unique people and natural environments that no one in Africa, Asia, or Europe had ever seen or described before. From plants such as the tomato and chocolate, to animals such as the armadillo and American alligator, the New World contained natural wonders that were recounted and described in great detail for the European public. Although Europeans had long been fascinated by written accounts and images of 'other' people, customs, dress, and religion, the American setting and its inhabitants were unlike any that world had previously known. For emerging nationalist writers in the Iberian world, these distinctive traits and unique histories, many previously chronicled in European descriptions and histories, would serve as elements defining a uniquely American identity.

In the second half of the eighteenth century, composers of both history and fiction began to wax eloquent about the glories of the indigenous people whom the Spaniards had conquered. Archaeological investigations were launched into the monuments of indigenous art and architecture, and the discoveries celebrated at length in print. Long-neglected texts by early missionaries critical of colonial rule surfaced to be published and cited. Equally crucial accounts by early indigenous adopters of the Spanish language and second-generation (mixed-race) writers saw the light of day for the first time since their authors had sent them off to the Crown hundreds of years before. In Mexico, Francisco Xavier Clavigero mounted a defence of indigenous languages, retelling the history of the Aztecs or Nahuas as that of a great long-past civilization: his *History of Ancient Mexico* became a perennial best-seller during the nineteenth century (Claverigo 1987 [1780]). Although Peru resisted independence until the end, a suitable political mythology for an independent nation also emerged around historical indigenous themes, employing the romance of the name and the equally romantic vision of the lone holdout against Spanish rule—the original Tupac Amaru rebellion evoking the last military holdout against Spanish forces in the 1580s. In late eighteenth-century Peru, the mestizo leader of a pro-Indian rebellion, José Gabriel Condorcanqui, adopted the name of the leader of the last Inca holdout against the Spanish conquest, calling himself Túpac Amaru II. Such Indian uprisings against the government emerged as part of the political mythology of independence (Arciniegas 1992).

Likewise in Brazil, long-buried Portuguese accounts of indigenous people were uncovered in archives and published for the first time. Descriptions of indigenous customs and appearance by the early Portuguese religious emissaries to the New World appeared in print for the first time. For unlike Spaniards, who had published extensively on the New World, Portuguese arrivals had produced only a single volume. During the sixteenth century, Portuguese public attention focused on the far more lucrative and voluminous trade with Asia, about which there was no dearth of written material. When it came time for independence, however, Brazilian writers led by Francisco Varnhagen had first to locate, then to publish, accounts about natives that had never before seen the light of day (Sousa and Varnhagen 1851; see also Monteiro 2000).

However, search as they might, Brazil's authors could uncover no counterpart to the glories of historical Incas and the Aztecs, or even guerilla warriors such as the Araucanos. Instead, early nineteenth-century writers focused on a similar romantic theme of more recent genesis—the noble savage. The original coastal-dwelling Tupi people of Brazil were converted into the wise and knowledgeable inhabitants of a complex natural landscape from whom the Brazilians had learned. The nationalist identity of an independent Brazil could thus reside in the historical distinction of the noble savage who, having dispensed his knowledge, had safely disappeared.

These literary representations, however, dealt with the Indian past, not their present. The Aztec, Maya, and Inca empires had long since been crushed and all remnants of their power vanquished, leaving behind spectacular architecture and objects. Nor was the situation different in Brazil. For the image of the noble savage referred not to any of the then existing communities of Brazil, but rather to the largely extinct or assimilated Tupi people of the coast, many of whom had been decimated by the first waves of disease in the New World.

The glorification of the safely distant indigenous past emerged as part of the rationale by which largely white, overseas-born descendants of colonizers sought to rationalize their entitlement to the political privileges then held by the Spanish- and Lusitanian-born. By inventing a romanticized indigenous past for themselves, the native-born elites of Spanish and Portuguese America proclaimed their distinction from their Iberian-born competitors and predecessors while fixing their rights as the legitimate holders of political dominion (Seed 1991, 1993; see also Sommer 1991).[6] While laying the foundation for

---

[6.] Sommer characterizes the foundational fictions of Spanish American independence as national romances. While this aptly captures the tone of nationalist narratives, it misses the continuing neocolonial content and function of these tales with respect to indigenous people.

national distinctiveness around an invented connection with a safely historically remote past, the question of how to legitimate exploitation of the current living indigenous people presented something of a problem after the end of colonial rule.

Not long after achieving independence, several emerging nations of Spanish America abolished the nearly moribund colonial system of forced labour (*encomiendas*) in their territories. Closing the door on the colonial system deprived relatively few traditional families of their remaining quotas of unfree labour, but it also ensured that elites with more recently acquired fortunes were free to coerce labour, as opposed to only those with colonial familial connections. The new leadership's self-congratulatory liberation of indigenous people from their colonial status as 'Indians', in Mexico and elsewhere, only enabled their exploitation of their labour in other formats, including debt peonage.

Many newly independent Iberian states also moved quickly to abolish the colonial form of cultural and economic subjugation called tribute.[7] With its roots in a long-standing Islamic tradition of ritual degradation of conquered peoples, tribute also placed additional demands on 'Indians' to work in order to earn money to turn over to local government officials. Within two decades of independence, many of the independent states had abolished the dwindling amount of tribute handed over to public officials.

However, in the heavily indigenous Andean countries where governments still garnished considerable sums from native people, the end to collecting these amounts from unfree labour came excruciatingly slowly. Not until 1854 did Peru abolish Indian tribute, while in nearby Ecuador to the north and Chile to the south, the system ceased functioning only three years later. In neighbouring Bolivia, the profits of unfree labour continued to be collected until 1874. Furthermore, when Bolivian government leaders abolished tribute, they simultaneously attacked traditional indigenous landholding, ordering its transfer to mixed-race and other outside owners (Albornoz 1978: 169, 173; Platt 1982).

As the Bolivian example illustrates, the end to colonially instituted tribute payment formed part of a concerted effort to exploit traditional people and economies more openly, without depending upon the traditional category of 'Indian'. Colonial regimes of labour exploitation depended on individual and community identification of people as indigenous. Freed from the necessity to identify an individual as indigenous, land and mine owners could make demands on individuals of mixed racial origin as well, giving them freer access to labour.

However, the core of the colonial representations of Indians remained untouched. The Spanish narrative of triumphal moral conquest over groups of depraved people was not questioned, for it underpinned the continuing postcolonial political and economic domination of indigenous people. Images of purportedly aberrant behaviour by Tupi inhabitants of Brazil were similarly reinforced. In the Iberian Americas, the essential

---

[7] Abolition of tribute occurred with Independence in Colombia, Venezuela, Argentina, Paraguay, Mexico, Guatemala, and other Central American nations.

rationale for occupation of the New World and rights to dominion over its inhabitants—Christianization—remained free from challenge.[8] The continuing valuation of
Christianity over native religions and the continuing charges of amoral indigenous conduct serve to justify the continued postcolonial Iberian rule over the Americas, just as
the postcolonial fiction of 'hunters' functions to rationalize legal and political control
over the English-speaking Americas (Seed 2003: 163–78).

Colonialism bequeathed its political legacies of violence and profiteering to the independent states, and some of those states carry out governance practices resembling
those of their colonial predecessors. In this respect, the postcolonial Americas share
similar fates with many of the newly independent states of Africa. While postcolonial
discourse sometimes took a celebratory turn, buttressed by the proposition that that the
removal of European political authority in itself constituted a moral victory, for numerous African and Asian societies the promised emancipation never materialized despite
the return of political power to indigenous communities. The subsequent histories of
more than two dozen postcolonial nations offer little in the way of exemplary postcolonial rule. Dictatorships, continuing clan and ethnic hostilities, two failed states (western
Sahara and Somalia): all of these fail to offer any uplifting narrative about the removal of
European power.

More than two dozen Middle Eastern and African states—from Morocco to Iraq—
offer a cautionary tale about postcolonial benefits. Libya, Ethiopia, and Somalia were
freed from Italian colonialism; Jordan, Egypt, Iraq, Oman, Bahrain, Qatar, United Arab
Emirates, Dubai, and Kuwait emerged as independent of British rule as did the Sudan,
Zimbabwe, and Uganda; Lebanon, Algeria, Morocco, Mauritania, Senegal, Mali, Guinea,
Côte d'Ivoire, Burkina Faso, Benin, and Niger broke away from France, and Cameroon,
the Democratic Republic of Congo, Tanzania, and Namibia gained independence from
Belgium and Germany; while Angola, Guinea-Bissau, and Mozambique eventually
achieved freedom from the Portuguese. But political liberty has not always followed.

Despite the seizure of power by native-born elites rather than indigenes, the Spanish
and Portuguese Americas shared a frequently similar postcolonial experience, one more
in keeping with the frequent political turmoil and disturbances following liberation
from rule by outsiders. This period of struggle with dictatorship, tortures, executions,
and secret jails, however, has taken its toll for a considerably longer period of time than
in Africa and Asia, covering both the nineteenth and twentieth centuries.

The postcolonial era of the Spanish and Portuguese Americas initially involved the
removal of European overlords. However, by the second half of the nineteenth century,
tired of the ceaseless political wrangling, some writers tried to unearth something of
value from the earlier period. While few argued for a return to a neocolonial monarchy (the ill-fated expedition of Maximilian and Carlotta), others suggested reviving the

---

[8.] 'These savages [of Brazil] eat human flesh for food, something no other pagan nation does except
for vengeance in fights and ancient hatreds … [Their behaviour makes them] enemies of all human kind'
(Sousa and Varnhagen 1851: 79–80).

colonial era's mechanisms for resolving domestic political conflicts peacefully (Vicente Fidel López, *La novia del hereje* [1854] and Vicente Riva Palacio, *Monja y casada, virgen y martír* [1868] and *Martín Garatuza* [1868]). Others diagnosed a sense of aimlessness, lamenting post-independence anomie and expressing nostalgia for the lack of shared political goals emerging from the independence struggles (Alberto Blest Gana's *Durante la reconquista* [1897], Vicente Fidel Lopez's *La Loca de la guardia* [1897], and Nataniel Aguirre's *Juan de la Rosa* [1885]: see also Skinner 2006: 30–1).

During the twentieth century, brutal dictators and military governments prevailed in Argentina, Bolivia, Brazil, Chile, Guatemala, and Nicaragua, among others. Some of the continent's most effective writers exposed their abuses through fiction—often at a politically necessary distance from the events. Gabriel García Márquez's *El general en su laberinto*, Carlos Fuentes's *Cristóbal Nonato*, Abel Posse's *Los perros del paraíso*, Augusto Roa Bastos's *Yo El Supremo*, and Edgardo Rodríguez Juliá's *La noche oscura del Niño Avilés* all indicted authoritarian political rule.

In the second half of the twentieth century, almost 150 years after independence, post-colonial writers in Hispanic America began to criticize earlier narratives of nationalism. This change was facilitated in part by the long time period that had elapsed since the first such stories began to appear. But its more immediate roots lay in the appropriation of nationalist discourses by political and military dictators as vicious and ruthless as the despised former and increasingly distant colonial leadership. As those rationales were deployed to increasingly oppressive purposes, literature critical of the national narrative grew. Elena Poniatowska, for example, in *Hasta no verte Jesús Mío* (1969) employed a humble rural woman narrator to criticize the formerly untouchable nationalist revolution of 1910.

While literary figures have employed subaltern or indigenous narrators to criticize dictatorships, subalterns or indigenous people themselves can rarely be found in literature articulating their own critiques of the political and economic system. Postcolonial literature is usually composed by elites,[9] either in fiction, narrative, or in history recorded by literate elites, often according to a political or legal formula (see McLeod in Part IV). Senegal's Mariama Bâ, for example, wrote powerfully about the position of women abandoned by their husbands, but she, like many others writing in this genre came from an elite, educated family (Bâ 1982). Notably absent from postcolonial writings elsewhere are the voices of actual living subalterns themselves.

An enormous amount of writing has been poured into literature precisely around this question 'Can the subaltern speak?'[10] The way the question is posed presupposes, though, that the questioner herself is not subaltern, but rather belongs to a highly privileged elite. For a subaltern would ask 'can we speak?' (See Dhawan and Randeria in Part

---

[9.] Cambridge-educated Appiah's maternal grandfather, Stafford Cripps, was a member of the British House of Commons. Spivak, Guha, and other Indian intellectuals come from highly educated elite Bengali families.

[10.] The postcolonial discourse of the Indian circle often tends to focus upon literature or history written by elites. See Guha (1983); also Spivak (1988).

V of this volume.) In Spanish and Portuguese America, however, a critical postcolonial literature authored by subalterns emerged in the twentieth century. This genre of literature, often by women, began as a form of protest against economic oppression and exploitation in Spanish and Portuguese America. *Let Me Speak! Testimony of Domitila, a Woman of the Bolivian Mines* describes the labour exploitation in the Bolivian tin mines,[11] while Carolina de Jesus examines the life of poverty, scavenging for food in the *favelas* of São Paulo in *Child of the Dark*.[12]

It is axiomatic that subaltern speaking—more accurately, writing—is mediated by editors, who shape their narratives and transform their expressions into grammatically correct sentences. While the role of these intermediaries has been subjected to intensive scrutiny, the central voice behind the text is subaltern and often female. The effort by literate elites to popularize and disseminate subaltern and indigenous voices speaks to the existence of a populist trend not usually encountered elsewhere.

A second type of subaltern literature appeared in the 1970s and 1980s as many parts of Latin America once again became subject to ruthless military rule and dictatorships. In response to this savagery, new subaltern voices began to emerge, denouncing political brutality. The distinct form of postcolonial writing to cope with the fallout from the ferocity of military nationalism was called witnessing or, in Spanish, *testimonio*.[13] Witnessing became the best-known theme in postcolonial writing from Spanish America in the final decade of the twentieth century when the genre gained, however fleetingly, a central place for Spanish America on the international stage. In 1992 K'iche' Mayan Rigoberta Menchú was awarded the Nobel Peace Prize for her testimonial writing. In *I, Rigoberta Menchú*, her best-known work, she denounces the several major abuses of Guatemala's indigenous Mayan community including torture and executions by the Guatemalan military, and the ongoing exploitation of Mayan labour by wealthy landlords.[14]

In the controversy that followed, it emerged that several events and episodes that Menchú had described as happening to her were actually witnessed by her mother. Cruelties she described as personally suffering were certainly widespread in Guatemala in the 1970s and 1980s, but she herself did not suffer from those abuses—even though many around her did. In her 1984 story, Menchú claimed that she and her family had been forced to work as peons on a distant coastal plantation for eight months of the year, when her family was well off enough to escape that fate, and when most in her community could not (Arias and Stoll 2001). However, Menchú's unreliability as a narrator only marginally diminished her reputation.

[11.] For related efforts to create subaltern voices, see Pozas (1962).

[12.] The quasi-fictional version of the autobiographical account appeared first in *Juan de Chamula*, not a historical individual, but a composite Tzotzil individual describing the exploitative labouring conditions of Indians at the start of the twentieth century. See de Jesus (1962).

[13.] John Beverley has characterized this writing as 'bearing witness' and as 'bringing the subaltern voice … into civil society'. See Beverley (2004: xvii, 19).

[14.] See Menchú and Burgos-Debray (1984). The book's original German subtitle was telling: *Leben in Guatemala* (*Life in Guatemala*).

The popularity of Rigoberta Menchú's story outside of Guatemala rested in part upon a long-standing conception of Spanish America as the place where atrocities were committed. Bartolomé de Las Casas's devastating portrait of the cruelties committed by Spanish soldiers during the conquest of the New World has been avidly and popularly read in English and other languages since the second half of the sixteenth century (Maltby 1971; see also Mignolo in this section of the volume). Las Casas's enduring popularity lent credibility to narratives of brutal executions taking place in Spanish America.[15] Even when elements of Menchú's story were revealed not to have been personally witnessed by the narrator, the facts of government brutality had occurred as described, confirming international cultural suspicions of Iberian barbarism.

The second element buttressing her account was her authentic claim to K'iche' Mayan identity. Menchú was a member of a K'iche' community, as her ancestors had been for generations. In this respect she would claim, as no member of the ruling postcolonial elite could, the right to Mayan identity as a form of cultural property. While able to draw upon preconceptions of Iberian brutality and Mayan identity, Menchú's writings achieved their greatest influence through a phenomenon of relatively recent efflorescence. Cosmopolitanism—a belief in the shared morality of a single, united human community—created an opportunity for indigenous people to leap over nationalism to appeal to a broader international community (Appiah 2007). Menchú's appeal to cosmopolitan morality succeeded spectacularly with the awarding of a Nobel Peace Prize. That recognition thrust the formerly somewhat obscure writings of a K'iche' Mayan woman into the international spotlight and dragged along with it the previously ignored brutality of a nationalist military regime.

Rigoberta Menchú's successful appeal to cosmopolitanism finally put pressure on the Guatemalan government to accept an investigation into the violence. In Oslo, Norway in 1994, two years after her prize, terms were established for a truth and reconciliation commission called the Historical Clarification Commission (*Comisión para el Esclarecimiento Histórico*) to look into the cruelties that Menchú had denounced ten years before. Five years after the Oslo accords, a report, *Guatemala: Memory of Silence* was published, identifying 42,275 victims by name, over 80 per cent of them indigenous Maya murdered or disappeared by the military.[16]

Witnessing, whether in its autobiographical form or in the truth commissions that follow, gives voice to the victims but rarely results in actual consequences for the

---

[15.] It would be impossible to list the immense literature on the Black Legend here. Instead, the very first translations are Dutch, French, and then English. Bartolomé de las Casas, *Seer Cort Verhael Vande Destructie Van D'Indien ... In Brabantsche Tale ... Uyte Spaensche Ouergeset* (1578); Las Casas and Jacques Miggrode, *Tyrannies et Cruautez des Espagnols, Perpetrées és Indes Occidentales ... Traduictes par Iaques De Miggrode, Etc.* (Anvers: F. de Ravelenghien, 1579); Las Casas and M. M. S., *The Spanish Colonie, Or Briefe Chronicle of the Acts and Gestes of the Spaniardes in the West Indies, Called the Newe World, for the Space of XI. Yeeres ... Nowe First Translated into English, by M. M. S. B.L.* (London: For William Brome; imprinted by Thomas Dawson, 1583).

[16.] *Guatemala, Memoria del silencio: Tz'inil na 'tab'al; conclusiones y recomendaciones del Informe de la Comisión para El esclarecimiento Histórico* (Guatemala: Misión de Verificación de las Naciones Unidas en Guatemala, 2004).

perpetrators within the nation. The primary function of storytelling about evil is to bring it to the awareness of other people: members of the broader civil society. The story of evil is told, but not punished. Those implicated in political torture and murders of civilians during military dictatorships participate in the theatre of remorse staged for the benefit of the broader national public. Once staged, the rest of society moves on. Those who sit with these shattered souls as they recount their stories may be prepared to acknowledge the existence of evil, but having done so they then get on with their lives: an actual end to the abuses is not necessarily on the cards.

As a cultural form, the cosmopolitan imaginary has the power to give voice to victims but it does not carry political consequences with it. That arena belongs to political internationalism. The grounds for an international forum with consequences gained strength beginning in the 1960s as a set of organizations developed dedicated to ending abuses.[17] The International Criminal Court at The Hague (2002) has served this function, as does the Special Court for Sierra Leone, set up jointly by the government of Sierra Leone and the United Nations to prosecute war crimes. Both developed into means by which justice could be rendered where domestic political apparatuses remained corrupt or ineffective.[18] However, for the indigenous Maya of Guatemala, no such prosecution was possible.

Cosmopolitanism became the means by which subalterns could achieve a limited agency that had previously been denied them. In *Subalternity and Representation* John Beverley describes 'a project that is deconstructive of the claims of the nation [and] nationalism ... to represent the subaltern and [presents] new forms of collective political and cultural agency' (1999: 103). That new cultural agency, however, not merely deconstructs, but also operates outside the nation by finding support in cosmopolitanism, where it seeks recognition from a broader audience.

While cosmopolitanism may have given agency to an indigenous woman from Guatemala, its limitations have become increasingly apparent. In addition to the absence of mechanisms for political or economic justice, cosmopolitanism's forward momentum comes to a screeching halt in the face of both representations and institutions of postcolonial political and economic power. The first constraint on cosmopolitanism lies in the language of politics and economics inherited from colonialism. Ashcroft et al. (1995) postulate that language is the locus for postcolonial struggle. Language does remain an area of struggle, but principally in the battle for cultural power. Meanwhile, the language of economic and political power has remained resolutely colonial. Law and politics in the postcolonial states have largely remained in the hands of the colonial languages. The discussions in the Brazilian Congress of Deputies today remains in Portuguese, just as debates in the Canadian and US congress are in English and in the parallel elected bodies in the Hispanic Americas are in Spanish.

[17.] The foundation for this role by the United Nations was originally laid in the wake of the Second World War and the Universal Declaration of Human Rights (1948).

[18.] For justice on an individual level, the parallel development of non-governmental organizations such as Amnesty International (1961) and Human Rights Watch (1978) rescued individual victims of abuses.

Legal traditions embedded in the linguistic premises of each of these languages constrain political choices (Seed 2003).

The second crucial limitation of cosmopolitanism rests with the inescapable link between cultural representations and profit-making enterprises. The basic economic objectives of colonial settlers remain the same in the postcolonial era—land in the former English colonies, labour in the former Spanish colonies. As a consequence, the cultural fictions permitting the realization of colonial economic ambitions have remained untouched. Native Americans remain 'hunters', unable to earn revenue from agriculture or own land for profitable agriculture. Spanish American 'Indians' remain amoral, unable to escape excessive labour obligations. Nothing less than the political legitimacy of rule over the Americas is at stake; for if American Indian farmers had a right to their lands, then huge swathes of the southeastern United States would have to be restored to their rightful indigenous owners. Similarly, the economic fiction of amoral Indians would lead to calls for financial restitution to indigenous communities for uncompensated labour. Neither outcome is likely. In this way, the fundamental differences in economic identities assigned to 'Indians' in separate parts of the Americas remain untouched by postcolonial changes—and well beyond the reach of cosmopolitan discussions.

Finally, these national political and economic boundaries to cosmopolitanism also limit the possibilities for concerted international efforts among indigenous communities. In the past they have also created the grounds for miscommunication among groups of natives who have mistaken their mistreatment for a shared colonial experience. But separate economic ambitions have powered different colonialisms, resulting in different forms of destruction as well as creating the need for different remedies. For example, in the United States and other postcolonial Anglophone nations with indigenous populations, one of the continuingly powerful political arguments against intruders is the protection of their sacred religious sites. Such a position would not only be unthinkable in the Iberian Americas, but would constitute an open invitation to political repression. Iberian rule over America was founded on the premise that native religions are inherently and dangerously amoral. Hence the idea of defending sacred native grounds or sacred ceremonies would not only invite antagonism, but would only attract the kind of oppression (on moral premises) that indigenous communities in former Spanish colonies are most anxious to avoid.

Postcolonialism, in sum, differs in every part of the world because the apparently common starting point—opposition to colonialism—does not operate consistently across national and international borders. Differences are grounded not only in the obvious diversity of local circumstances but, equally importantly, in the different forms of colonialism itself. Similarly, colonialism does not operate and has never operated as a single phenomenon. Rather, multiple colonialisms have dominated in distinctively different ways, leaving traces of their presence in the form of shared political and economic convictions and postcolonial constraints upon indigenous communities. In the Americas, English-speaking colonialists (and, later, imperialists) focused their economic ambitions on land, depriving the indigenes they dominated of traditional dominion over their territories, while Spanish- and Portuguese-speaking settlers commandeered native labour to fulfil their economic desires. As a result, the postcolonial fates of natives subject to the same form of colonialism have also varied widely. Indigenous people in areas formerly ruled by Englishmen are profoundly shaped by the postcolonial preoccupation with reasserting hegemony over land, while those of their counterparts previously under Iberian rule are similarly formed by concern with freedom from onerous labour obligations. As a consequence, the nature of postcolonial literature has varied because political and economic traditions embedded in language and practice have differed, as well as the linguistic boundaries that have circumscribed both modes of support for colonial rule and modes of opposition.

While rulers of the immense geographic territory from Mexico south to Patagonia share nationalist sentiments with many other postcolonial nations, they all confront the distinctive, unresolved, and sometimes violent tensions over the role of indigenous people. Most societies of Hispanic and Lusophone America are multi-ethnic societies and struggle internally to situate the role of indigenous people in the postcolonial cultural imaginary as well as the actual status of indigenous communities. In the three Iberian America nations, the indigenous population remains the largest single ethnic group. Forty per cent of both Guatemala and Peru and 55 per cent of Bolivia consider themselves indigenous. In other post-Iberian colonial nations over half the inhabitants claim to be part-indigenous, ranging from 58 per cent of Colombians to 95 per cent of Paraguayans.[19] Only Argentina, Chile, Brazil, and Costa Rica have small indigenous populations and relatively few claimants to part-Indian ancestry, but both Brazil and Chile incorporate the indigenous past into the present nationalist imaginary.

While ending colonial rule in Africa and Asia signified a return of power to indigenous communities, in the Americas neocolonial elites retained political control, meaning that no reversal of the fundamental colonial project was possible, and that the cultural fictions of Indian identities would remain entrenched. It would be possible to overcome colonial fictions in Africa and Asia, but not the New World.

References

Albornoz, Nicolás Sánchez (1978). 'Tributo abolido, tributo repuesto. Invariantes socioeconómicas en la época republicana, in T. H. Donghi, *El ocaso del orden colonial en Hispanoamérica*. Buenos Aires: Sudamericana, HN110.5.A8 O23.

Appiah, Kwame Anthony (2007). *Cosmopolitanism: Ethics in a World of Strangers*. New York: Norton.

Arciniegas, Germán (1992). *Los comuneros*. Caracas: Fundación Biblioteca Ayacucho.

[19.] 58% of Colombians, 60% of Mexicans, 65% of Ecuadorans, 70% of Nicaraguans, 84% of Panamanians, 90% of El Salvadorans and Hondurans, and 95% of Paraguayans claim to be part-indigenous. Data from Venezuela is unavailable, since the question about ethnic identity has been dropped from the census since 1990 and research on the topic is discouraged. Estimates suggest that perhaps 50% of Venezuela would claim mixed Indian ancestry. Belize is a former British colony.

Arias, Arturo and David Stoll (2001). *The Rigoberta Menchú Controversy.* Minneapolis: University of Minnesota Press.

Ashcroft, Bill, Gareth Griffiths, and Helen Tiffin (eds) (1995). *The Post-Colonial Studies Reader.* London: Routledge.

Bâ, Mariama (1982). *So Long a Letter.* London: Virago.

Beverley, John (1999). *Subalternity and Representation: Arguments in Cultural Theory.* Durham, NC: Duke University Press.

Beverley, John (2004). *Testimonio: On the Politics of Truth.* Minneapolis: University of Minnesota Press.

Claverigo, Francisco Javier (1987 [1780]). *Historia Antigua de México.* Prólogo de Mariano Cuevas. México: Porrua.

De Jesus, Carolina (1962). *Child of the Dark: The Diary of Carolina Maria de Jesus.* New York: Dutton.

Gregory, Derek (2004). *The Colonial Present: Afghanistan, Palestine, and Iraq.* Malden, Mass.: Blackwell Publishing.

Guha, Ranajit (1983). *Elementary Aspects of Peasant Insurgency.* Delhi: Oxford University Press.

Hamilton, Jennifer A. and Aimee J. Placas (2011). 'Anthropology Becoming …? The 2010 Sociocultural Anthropology Year in Review', *American Anthropologist*, 113.2: 246–61.

The International Criminal Court (2002). 'Elements of Crimes', *Official Journal of the International Criminal Court.* The Hague: International Criminal Court.

Las Casas, Bartolomé de (1578). *Cort Verhaal Vande Destructie Van D'Indien … In Brabantsche Tale … Uyte Spaensche Ouergeset.* Place of publication unknown.

Las Casas, Bartolomé de and Jacques Miggrode (1579). *Tyrannies et Cruautez des Espagnols Perpetrées és Indes Occidentales … Traduictes par jacques De Miggrode, Etc.* Anvers: F. de Ravelenghien.

Las Casas, Bartolomé de and M. M. S. (1583). *The Spanish Colonie, Or Brief Chronicle of the Acts and Gestes of the Spaniardes in the West Indies, Called the Newe World, for the Space of XI Yeeres … Nowe First Translated into English, by M.M.S. B.L.* London: For William Brome; imprinted by Thomas Dawson.

Maltby, William S. (1971). *The Black Legend in England: The Development of Anti-Spanish Sentiment.* Durham, NC: Duke University Press.

Menchú, Rigoberta and Elisabeth Burgos-Debray (1984). *I, Rigoberta Menchú: An Indian Woman in Guatemala.* London: Verso.

Monteiro, John M. (2000). 'The Heathen Castes of Sixteenth-Century Portuguese America: Unity, Diversity, and the Invention of the Brazilian Indians', *Hispanic American Historical Review*, 80.4: 697–719.

Perry, Richard (1996). *From Time Immemorial: Indigenous People and State Systems.* Austin: University of Texas Press.

Platt, Tristan (1982). *Estado boliviano y ayllu andino: Tierra y tributo en el Norte de Potosí.* Lima: Instituto de Estudios Peruanos.

Pozas, Ricardo (1962). *Juan the Chamula: An Ethnological Re-creation of the Life of a Mexican Indian.* Berkeley: University of California Press.

Seed, Patricia (1991). 'Colonial and Postcolonial Discourses', *Latin American Research Review*, 26.3: 181–200.

Seed, Patricia (1993). 'More Colonial and Postcolonial Discourses', *Latin American Research Review*, 28.3: 146–52.

Seed, Patricia (2003). *American Pentimento: The Pursuit of Riches and the Invention of Indians*. Minneapolis: University of Minnesota Press.

Skinner, Lee J. (2006). *History Lessons: Refiguring the Nineteenth-Century Historical Novel in Spanish America*. Newark, Del.: Juan de la Cuesta.

Sommer, Doris (1991). *Foundational Fictions: The National Romances of Latin America*. Berkeley: University of California Press.

Sousa, Gabriel S. and Francisco A. Varnhagen (1851). *Tratado descritivo do Brazil em 1587.* Rio de Janeiro: Typographia Universal de Laemmert.

Spivak, Gayatri Chakravorty (1988). 'Can the Subaltern Speak?', in C. Nelson and L. Grossberg (eds), *Marxism and the Interpretation of Culture*. Urbana, Ill.: University of Illinois Press, 271–313.

Vainfas, Ronaldo (1995). *A heresia dos indios: Catolicismo e rebeldia no Brasil colonial*. São Paolo: Companhia das Letras.

CHAPTER 4

··

IMPERIAL/COLONIAL METAMORPHOSIS

A Decolonial Narrative, from the Ottoman Sultanate and Spanish Empire to the US and the EU

··

WALTER D. MIGNOLO

INTRODUCTION

··

This chapter is a shorter version of a paper originally given at the 'Islam, Latinity, Transmodernity' international conference held in Ankara and Istanbul, Turkey, 12–16 April 2005, and printed at the pre-publication stage.[1] At that time, the Academia de Latinidade, working in conjunction with UNESCO, was focusing on dialogues between the Latin countries of the European Union (France, Italy, Spain, Portugal) and the Islamic countries of North Africa and the Middle East. Participants in the conference included Gianni Vattimo, Edgard Morin, Mário Soares, and Federico Mayor. This was the period when Turkey's potential membership of the European Union was a hotly debated issue (with one part of the debate, especially in Turkey, being why Turkey should be included but Russia should not: Tlostanova 2005). My own contribution to the debate—significantly updated since then—was as a Latino of the margins, born outside Europe (Argentina) and currently living and working in the US.[2] My argument in 2005 would address the three keywords of the conference title—Islam, Latinity, transmodernity—but would twist the last of these to capture the sense of *decolonial*

---

[1] Online source: <http://www.alati.com.br/ing/publicacoes_2005_islam_latinite_transmodernite.html>, accessed 7 November 2012.

[2] For an updated argument, see Mignolo (2011).

transmodernity (Dussel 1998). To do this, it would prove necessary for me to tell a story that has often been invisible in both European and world history over the past five hundred years. The story, briefly, is that I do not see 'empire' from the global north but 'coloniality' from the global south (Levander and Mignolo 2011). This is linked to my personal history. I have lived in the US for more than thirty years, but my heart and my passport go in different pockets. When I arrived in the US in 1970s, I became a Hispanic; later, I metamorphosed into a Latino. The subject matter may be the same in both cases, but what is at stake is very different. Epistemology is a question of the heart that is then processed by the mind.

It would be impossible, not to mention ill-advised, to provide a global history of several empires and their interconnections in the space of a single essay. What I proposed in 2005, and what I now propose here, is to look instead at a few selected examples of the logic of coloniality behind many existing historical narratives. I will review and remap some basic principles of how imperial history has been and still continues to be written; I will then go on to speculate on how a shift in the geography of reasoning might contribute to exploring some of the hidden recesses that hegemonic (Eurocentric) versions of imperial history have overlooked. One example of such a shift might be to ask, instead of how 'corrupt' African states are, how illegal and unethical the western creation of African states was in the first place.[3] The particular shift I have in mind here is primarily *epistemic*; and it impinges, in a variety of ways I will proceed to illustrate, on the complex history of relations between Islam, Latinity, and modernity in a global world that has been made to build the foundations and serve the interests of western civilization since the sixteenth century. My main intention in making this shift is to reveal a hidden history—the history of *coloniality*—that lies behind the façade of western modernity. One way of bringing this history to light is through current debates on Europe and Eurocentrism; another is by clarifying the distinction between the *post*colonial and the *de*colonial; while still another is the particular form of critique of Eurocentrism I will refer to here as *dewesternization*. As I will show, decolonial and dewesternizing projects are uncoupled ('delinked') from rather than dependent on postmodernity.

EUROCENTRISM AND COLONIALITY

The debate on Eurocentrism has at least two dimensions, both of which operate within an internal debate from which the rest of the world is largely absent. The first strand of this debate is contained within the European history of ideas: that is to say, it is a debate between the defenders of European exceptionalism and their detractors. Two fairly recent examples here might include David Landes's *The Wealth and the Poverty of Nations* (1998), which makes the case for European exceptionalism,

---

[3.] I take this example from Chimamanda Ngozi Adichie (2009).

and John Hobson's *The Eastern Origins of Western Civilization* (2004), which mobilizes powerful counter-arguments to show that European exceptionalism (such as it exists) has historically been based on imperial expansion and violence, suggesting in the process that imagining possible worlds for the future depends on the stories of the past we tell.

Susan George has been one of the most vociferous advocates to date for what the European model has to offer the future of humanity, building her argument around ideological differences between France and the US (George 2004). Today (2012) it seems that the European Union has little to offer in terms of models for global futures. In any case, whether worlds of the future will follow the European or American model arguably makes little difference for those who continue to suffer from the 'colonial wound'—the modern imperial denigration and dispossession of non-European peoples, languages, cultures, and histories in both the present and the past. Both models offer alternatives within imperial/colonial metamorphoses of the west: the history of Christianity, capitalism, and secularism. This history also relates to the European Union, which I currently see—provocatively no doubt—as a subaltern empire operating according to the logic of an internal imperial difference between north and south which, emerging in the eighteenth century, has been translated more recently into a similar difference between the EU and the US (see also Schulze-Engler in Part V of this volume).

Here is where the second strand of the debate around Eurocentrism comes into focus. Supporters of George's idea of Europe as a world model and advocates for its US counterpart both conveniently forget that, put together, Europe and the US count as significantly less than half of the world's population. While it is true that the whole world today must contend in one way or another with neoliberal, neoconservative, and neosocialist ideals and ideologies, much more needs to be made of the *local* histories of world regions—Asia, Africa, South/Central America, and the Caribbean (SCAC). This last statement needs qualifying; for in arguing that more needs to be done, I do not mean more narrative in which analytical 'knowledge' resides in western Europe and the US and 'cultures' are situated in the rest of the world as so much raw material for that knowledge. In shifting the geography of reasoning, I do not intend to provide more information about the 'non-west' but rather to use non-modern (i.e. *neither* Christian *nor* liberal *nor* Marxist) ways of thinking to disrupt the single story of western epistemic modernity. (Whenever I make this argument, one of the counter-arguments I hear is: all well and good, but East and South East Asian states, e.g. China and Singapore, are using Confucianism to legitimate themselves. This is certainly true. Western monarchic states used Christianity, secular bourgeois states liberalism and Christianity, and Lenin and Mao Marxism: all of these were alternative means and mechanisms towards the legitimation of the state. There is no 'safe place', in sum, but the west remains the only civilization that for five hundred years succeeded in controlling and managing a single story, for all its staggering internal diversity: Catholic and Protestant, creationist and evolutionist, liberal and Marxist, modern and postmodern. Shifting the geography of reasoning effectively *means* there is no 'safe place': it means, for example, that liberalism and Confucianism can be used both to control and to liberate.)

Admittedly, Eurocentrism has not necessarily been the ostensible target of some of the most vocal recent criticism: in the case of the Zapatistas, for example, the target is more likely to be neoliberalism, while for members of the World Social Forum, it is globalization (see Dhawan and Randeria in Part V of this volume); and a particular, self-privileging western version of modernity continues to be denounced in the Middle East by followers of such influential twentieth-century thinkers as Ali Shariati (1980), Sayyid Qutb (2008), and, more recently in Morocco, the philosopher Mohammed Abed al-Jabri (see the 'Decolonial and dewesternizing Latinity' section of this essay). However, I submit that Eurocentrism is the master model of all subsequent variations, like neoliberalism and globalization or, perhaps better, globalism. For my purposes here, neoliberalism, globalism, and modernity will all be taken to be changing shades of Eurocentrism, which will be understood as a general epistemic model that regulates ontology, organizing subjectivity and knowledge, gender and sexuality, economy and the state. Eurocentrism, in short, consists of a series of self-justifying narratives of civilization and salvation, progress and development, which serve to rationalize the logic of expropriation and exploitation, and which simultaneously license the extension of poverty and the concentration of wealth.

Decolonial 'Delinking' from Eurocentrism: the Hidden History of Coloniality

To shift the geography of reasoning, to 'delink' from the single story of modernity, implies to start from coloniality and not from modernity; better yet, it asserts unequivocally that there is *no modernity without coloniality*. The coupling of modernity and coloniality unmasks the ruse of modernity's 'overcoming' of both tradition and colonialism. Simply put, coloniality cannot be overcome by modernity, because it is the other half of the story. Modernity might indeed have the capacity to overcome *colonialism*, but it cannot overcome *coloniality* precisely because coloniality is constitutive of it—it is part of the fabric of modernity itself.

In what follows, I want very briefly to trace the constitution and some aspects of the imperial/colonial metamorphoses that have structured coloniality from the sixteenth to the early twenty-first century. In sketching out these transformations, my general aim is to uncover a story that is not often told; that tends to go unseen unless we focus on coloniality. (Change your starting point, and you have a different story.) Let me begin with Suleiman the Magnificent, who was sultan between 1520 and 1566, and under whose governance the Ottoman Sultanate reached the apex of its power. Suleiman was a contemporary of Charles V of the Holy Roman Empire and Charles I of Castille, but it seems pointless to compare these figures, still less to rank them in importance, for the principal difference between them lies not in their coeval imperial authority but in the history that has unfolded since they ruled. After all, it was not the EU that, around a decade ago, wanted Turkey to join but the other way round; and it was the then Turkish leader Recep Tayyip Erdoğan who promptly turned the tables, opting to follow the dewesternizing trajectories of East/South East Asia and the Middle East instead. (If you start not from the EU but from Turkey, you have a different story.) The Ottoman Sultanate no longer exists of course, but Spain and Germany do; though it is becoming increasingly clear that dewesternizing projects of different kinds are taking hold. The consciousness that Turkey is 'the west of Asia' and that Asia is 'returning' (not 'rising') is also growing. It is clear that Turkey will never drink of the fountain of ancient Greece that once nourished Hegel's Spirit and that has often been taken to be the foundation of western civilization—in both modern and postmodern variants—itself. (However, equally possible in the context of Asia's 'return' is that this Spirit, now no longer trapped in its monumentalizing western narrative, has begun to travel east.) How is it that Suleiman the Magnificent and Charles I and V ruled over equally powerful Sultanate and Empire, but that it was Christendom and Europe that prevailed and not Islam and the Ottomans? What does this history mean to us all in today's world order? And why is it that while Ivan the Terrible began to build a similarly powerful empire around the time of Charles V and Suleiman the Magnificent, Russia is not a prospective candidate to join the EU while Turkey, for many people, is? (Tlostanova 2005)

One place we might turn for some answers is a map that Samuel Huntington originally produced as an accompaniment to the article that would later provide the foundation for his ill-judged book on the 'clash of civilizations' (Huntington 2002). The map features a dividing line that starts in the north and runs south over the frontier between Finland and Russia. It then scrolls down to Estonia, Latvia, and Lithuania, cutting Belarus and Ukraine in two, and continuing further to the middle of Romania where it makes a sharp right turn, cutting Bosnia in half and leaving Croatia in the west and Serbia in the south. To the east of this line, Huntington places Orthodox Christianity and Islam; while to the west is western Christianity. And with 1500—a similarly resonant moment for many anti-colonial resistance movements—Huntington also risks an establishing date. (1500, in fact, can be interpreted from two entirely different historical directions: a shift in the geography of reasoning allows us to decide which one of these to take.) For Huntington, the chronological line that divides modernity from tradition in time—that is, the *visible* history of western civilization—goes hand in hand with the line that separates modernity from barbarism in space—that is, the *invisible* history of coloniality, which functions as modern western civilization's 'darker' element. But if you start instead from the other side of Huntington's line, you have a different story: the beginning of a decolonial story. Decoloniality is not a project within the linear narrative of modernity according to which the 'post' signals the anxiety for novelty; on the contrary, it is a radical *undoing* of modernity/coloniality in order to build a world of differences without hierarchies: a polycentric rather than a unipolar world. If another world is possible after all, then the entire world will have to participate in its making. In this broad sense, it is not poststructuralism that lies behind decoloniality (as it does for postcoloniality), but rather the non-aligned politics of the 1955 Bandung conference and the decolonial thinking of

Frantz Fanon (Mignolo 2012b; Mignolo and Escobar 2009; see also Lazarus in Part III of this volume). The concept of 'transmodernity'—introduced by the Argentine philosopher Enrique Dussel within the genealogy of Latin American decolonial thought—can help us here insofar as it moves beyond both postmodernity and postcoloniality, both prefixes of which are trapped in modern ideologies of linear temporality. More needs to be said about this; but first let me comment a little further on the broader implications of Huntington's map.

A DECOLONIAL MAPPING OF A DIVIDED EUROPE

As I previously suggested, Huntington's temporal line, which is grounded in 1500, accompanies a spatial line separating western Christianity from Orthodox Christianity and Islam. The focus on Islam after '9/11' has been both justified and skilfully manipulated by the US government; however, the fall of the Soviet Union in 1989 as well as the fall of the twin towers in 2001 should serve to remind us that Orthodox Christianity is placed *together* with Islam on the 'wrong' side of Huntington's spatial line. Where does this double division come from? It might be helpful here to think of Byzantium, from where the transference of Roman power to Constantinople was enacted. The Byzantine Empire has had a lasting impact on a large number of modern nations, from Albania to Ukraine; and if Byzantium was a second Rome, Moscow was a third, named as such at the beginning of the sixteenth century.

Let me fill out these preliminary geopolitical thoughts by commenting on a 2004 essay by the former US ambassador to Romania, James C. Rosapepe, and by situating it in the wider context of both Huntington's and, before him, Hegel's ideologically charged divisions between the southern and eastern zones of Europe and what both of them saw as being Europe's heartland, the northwest. (Rosapepe's remarks should be understood in the early 1990s context of post-Soviet Romania and Romanians' since-fulfilled desires to join the EU.) Huntington's remapping largely follows Hegel's, coming as it does at the end of a two-hundred-year history that traced a path from the rise of British and other western European imperialisms in the nineteenth century to the fall of the Soviet Union not long before the dawn of the twenty-first. Not that this fall, or the change of hands by which the US took over the European imperial leadership after the Second World War, has necessarily altered the Hegelian world order. This order, first mapped in the famous introduction to Hegel's disquisition on the philosophy of history (1822), traces a tendentious geographical profile of Europe that ideologically divides the southern countries—Italy, Spain, and Portugal in particular—from their northern counterparts, notably England, France, and Germany. The north*west*, claims Hegel, is indisputably the 'centre of Europe'; the north*east*, however, he sees as coming 'only late into the series of historical States, and [as forming and perpetuating] the connection with Asia' (Hegel 1991 [1822]: 102). Hegel's geopolitical mapping corresponds largely with the geopolitical imaginary of Huntington's 'clash', though a distinction needs to be maintained between the clash of *civilizations*, which Rosapepe among others sees as being partly though not wholly motivated by religious differences, and the clash of *ideologies*, which he sees as being manifested in the 1989 fall of the Berlin Wall.

Rosapepe goes on to mention several other complicating factors. Orthodox Christian Greece, for example, is still regarded by many—including Huntington—as the cradle of western civilization and is a member of NATO and the European Union. (In 2012—the time of writing—we have learned that it is of little use to be the cradle of a civilization that has lost control of its own internal affairs.) Catholic Croatia, on the other hand, belongs to neither. And as Rosapepe remarks somewhat contradictorily of the ex-Soviet states of central and east Europe, 'all EU members are Protestant or Catholic, while the former Soviet republics are Orthodox or Muslim' (2004: 68). Huntington, it seems, is not describing a *historical* situation; rather, he is mapping a largely *imagined* geopolitical relation to a five-hundred-year history of empire, capitalism, and modernity—one in which coloniality is conspicuously missing from accounts.

Rosapepe brings another example, Turkey, into the picture towards the end of his article. Turkey's proposed candidacy for EU membership, he suggests, is

> generally painted as a difficult and defining challenge to Europe's future. The country is large, its population is growing fast, and it is Muslim. But in many ways, it is already quite integrated with the West. Turkey has been a NATO member and a market economy for decades; it has long and close trade and labor ties with Europe. Moreover, the United States supports EU membership for Turkey, as do many European countries. (2004: 72)

What is the long history that links Suleiman the Magnificent to a country that has been a NATO member for several decades and is now fully integrated into the market economy but not to the EU? And how is it that a Muslim country can be envisioned as joining the EU? But if Greece and Croatia are exceptions, then what is to prevent Turkey from being another one? As Rosapepe rightly insists, religion is not enough to understand where the 'Euro Curtain' is being located, or to dictate at any given time who is 'in' and who is 'out'. (These questions, though relevant at the time of the conference in Ankara/Istanbul, are arguably no longer relevant today. Turkey has begun to turn its face to the east; perhaps being 'the west of Asia' is more promising for the future that being 'the east of Europe'.)

What is beyond religion then? Nationalism and secular racism are as good candidates as any; and Immanuel Kant's excruciatingly stereotypical commentary on national profiles proves helpful in elucidating both. Kant begins in southern Europe:

> The Spaniards, who evolved from the mixture of European blood with Arabian (Moorish) blood, displays in his public and private behavior a certain solemnity ... The Spaniard's bad side is that he does not learn from foreigners; that he does not travel in order to get acquainted with other nations; that he is centuries behind in the sciences. He resists any reform; he is proud of not having to work; he is of a romantic quality of spirit, as the bullfight shows. (1996: 231)

He then goes on to speak about the east and north-east, with his targets this time being the Russians, the Poles, and the European Turks:

> Since Russia has not yet developed definite characteristics from its natural potential; since Poland no longer [has] characteristics; and since the nationals of European Turkey have never had a character, nor will ever attain what is necessary for definite national character, the descriptions of these nations' characters may properly be passed over here. (1996: 235)

In section four of *Observations on the Beautiful and the Sublime* (1764), Kant repeats his whirlwind tour of national characteristics. European national characters remain more or less the same here, but Kant omits the Russians, Poles and Turks and, instead, moves directly to the Arabs:

> If we cast a fleeting glance over the other parts of the world (that is, we are leaving Europe here), we find the Arab the noblest man in the Orient, yet of a feeling that degenerates very much into the adventurous ... His inflamed imagination presents things to him in unnatural and distorted images, and even the propagation of his religion was a great adventure. (1960: 109)

A scarcely less prejudicial view is that of the sixteenth-century Spanish historian and Dominican friar Bartolomé de Las Casas, who—typically for his time—saw the Ottomans as barbarians, although—untypically perhaps—he still recognized their achievement. The Ottomans' barbarity, for Las Casas, consisted not so much in their lack of social organization (the usual benchmark for barbarism) but rather in their having the 'wrong' religion and in their not writing in Roman alphabetic script (Mignolo and Tlostanova 2006). Here we see the early signs of *Latinity* emerging as a distinctive feature of western civilization. Latinity was entrenched within theology at the time, though it would become laic later on in France. In both guises, however, Latinity was an important element in the secular ideology of modernity, encompassing both Protestant France and the Catholic South (i.e. Italy, Spain, and Portugal). Two rough-and-ready stages can be borne in mind here: (1) the Renaissance moment of Latinity, which was Christian and Catholic (Las Casas); and (2) post-Enlightenment Latinity, which was mainly secular, although with a Christian background. Both stages had distinct bearings on the European relationship to Islam. In the first case, Latinity confronted Islam at the level of religion, in the second at the level of secularism and the separation of religion from the state. This is no doubt why Kant (who obviously did not belong to Latin Europe and considered himself as part of the continent's secular heartland) saw the Arabs as people with 'inflamed imaginations': the 'Spaniards of the Orient', exuberant and irrational, Kant compares them unfavourably to the Persians, who 'permit to their pleasure-prone disposition a tolerably kind interpretation of the Koran', and who are accomplished poets with refined taste (1960: 109–10).

One might well ask what happened to the Ottoman Sultanate, which, two centuries before Kant, was in full splendour. How, all of a sudden, did this most refined of people become the 'characterless' European Turks? One way of accounting for this astonishing downturn is through the colonial matrix of power hidden behind the triumphal rhetoric of modernity and civilization. For Kant, as for many of his contemporaries, the rhetoric of modernity (Enlightenment emancipation, economic growth in the heartlands of Europe) made them blind to their own palpably racist conviction of Europeans' superiority and mission over the rest of the world. What can be found here once again is a 'darker' side of modernity, *coloniality*, driven by the corrosive effects and damaging consequences of colonialism; and what can be extrapolated from it are those imperial/colonial *differences*, borne of the colonial wound suffered by non-European peoples, that underlie the modern histories of Europe and the US (Mignolo 2011).[4]

Beyond Kantian geopolitics and today's political corridors, stock markets, trade centres, and military bases are what Frantz Fanon once called the 'wretched of the earth': those considered as being below the line of their plain humanity, as being somehow 'defective' in their ethnicity, their language, or their faith (Fanon 2001 [1961]). The 'wretched' is an important category of decolonial thought that makes visible what the rhetoric of modernity conceals: modernity cannot be enjoyed without the production of the 'wretched'. (Start from the 'wretched' instead of the 'winners of history', and you have a different story.) What has been overlooked, in fact, in European intellectual history since at least the eighteenth century (but has come to the forefront at the beginning of the twenty-first) is that there is an irrevocable link between race, religion, economy, the national state, and the global reach of modernity/coloniality. This complex set of interrelations goes back to the origins of the colonial matrix of power: European 'discovery' and expansion; the emergence of Atlantic commercial circuits; and the historical foundation of capitalism and its indirect complicity with Christianity and racism—all of these are movements that register continuities with the present day. The question prompted by all of this is how to work towards a future in which modernity/coloniality can finally be overcome and Eurocentrism stripped of its global imperial ambitions. To illustrate what I mean by this, let me quickly set out three basic interpretative paradigms.

GLOBAL FUTURES, DECOLONIAL OPTIONS

The first is the mutation (metamorphosis) from modernity to *postmodernity* that was first articulated by European intellectuals, especially in France. This mutation took place within the parameters of the western 'civilizing mission': that is, in relation to the Greek and Roman linguistic and categorical foundations of knowledge, which were then translated into the six modern imperial European languages (Italian, Spanish, and Portuguese, which were predominant during the Renaissance; and English, German,

---

4. For an explanation of how imperial/colonial differences impinge on the current world order, see Mignolo (2012b).

and French, which were predominant during and after the Enlightenment and the Napoleonic Wars). The transition from the modern to the postmodern generally pre-supposes paradigmatic changes, but within the same *tradition*; however, I would rather see it as registering internal changes within the same *paradigm*.

The second concerns mutations between the parameters of different civilizations. I would describe these as *transcultural* mutations to underline the fact that they are taking place beyond the geopolitical space of western European history, and that they involve different languages and categories of thought than those embedded within European knowledge systems. (Start from local histories other than those of Europe, and you have a different story.) Such mutations point, in turn, to the possibilities offered by *transmodernity*—the march of modernity across its own epistemic bound-aries, with modernity becoming 'trans' rather than 'post' in the sense that is confronted with other languages, religions, and histories that take it beyond the Greco-Roman and Christian legacies of the west (Dussel 1998, 2002; see also Mignolo 2000). An expres-sion frequently associated with this paradigm is the 'dialogue of civilizations' originally proposed by Khatami in 2000 to counter Huntington, and later endorsed by Zapatero and Erdoğan after the events of 2001 (SETimes.com 2005). This paradigm is identified today with dewesternization.

The third and last involves a set of processes that might be best described as deco-lonial options and transmodern *pluriversality*—open processes that 'delink' from the totalitarian claims of modern universality. According to the decolonial option, local problems to be solved and global issues to be confronted relate alike to the ongoing process of undoing the colonial matrix of power. Without this decolonial step, trans-modernity (understood here in terms of decolonial pluriversality) will be little more than an attenuated form of Euro-imperialism, perhaps following the EU model (the traditional one, not the neoliberal variant that brought Europe to its knees in 2011–12), in which non-European subjectivities, while not necessarily excluded, will continue to be framed by the dominant European structure of knowledge, and non-European lan-guages, while unofficially recognized, will continue to all intents and purposes to play a second-class role. Why decolonial and pluriversal transmodernity? Because moder-nity is imperially *uni*versal: thus, to undo modernity/coloniality is to undo the belief that the world needs to be ordered and managed by universality (see Hindess in Part IV of this volume).

This accords with the situation we find ourselves in today: a single modernity pre-dominantly seen from the Euro-American perspective and involving a dizzying array of colonial experiences in at least three continents over at least five hundred years. From these continents, which are home to more than three quarters of the world's people, two principal trajectories are emerging: dewesternization and decoloniality (Chen 2010; Mahbubani 2008; Mignolo 2011). These two shifts entail looking at the history of Europe and the US from the experiences and memories of those touched by western expansionist imperatives: not only the ubiquitous wretched, but also a wide variety of non-western religious and educational institutions and non-western states (TV Multiversity 2011). The critical thought of Adorno/Horkheimer (1969) and their followers is the equivalent, in the internal history of Europe, of what dewesternization and decoloniality mean for the non-European world, which is no longer waiting—if it ever did—for the latest instructions from European postmodern philosophers on what and how to think. But though dewesternization and decoloniality have their point of origin outside Europe, they may still be applicable within it (see also Schulze-Engler in Part V of this volume). In this sense, the decolonial future of the EU and the US rests firmly in the hands of 'Third World' migrants. Whether Euro-American scholars will join these projects, and whether they will be able to do so without reproducing forms of 'modern' knowledge associated with coloniality, are open questions. Certainly, such projects are urgently needed at both ends of the colonial power spectrum to address the colonial woundsinflicted by imperial power, the racial matrix of which has historically affected non-European peoples at a different rate and on a different scale.

Meanwhile, China has become a major player—and not only economically. Albeit economically powerful, China has also been subject to racialization by western imperial knowledge (see Vukovich in Part V of this volume). (It is worth noting here that 'yellow' implicitly means 'not white'; it is white-controlled knowledge that has made the Chinese 'yellow', a rhetoric of racial slur that cuts across classes and national GNP.) One can hardly expect the histories of China or India, Bolivia or Tanzania, Russia or Uzbekistan, Algeria or Iran, to be easily subsumed within the world history of Hegel, or painlessly accommodated within the linear history of a Europe that is seen as having originated in Greece and as having reached as far as postmodernity (Chakrabarty 2000).

Alternatively, take the case of Creole elites in 'Latin' America, who are white and of European descent, but not Europeans. Seeing and feeling themselves to be different from Europeans (the Spaniards first, the French and British later), Creole elites have chosen to adopt Latinity (*Latinidad*) as their way of establishing difference-in-sameness with Europe. But for the region's many Indian and African peoples, *Latinidad* has not been an enabling concept, robbing them of the possibility of telling their own stories and consigning them instead to bit-part roles in the official accounts of European intellectuals and/or Creoles of European descent.

Similar processes obtain in the Middle East and North Africa. Sayyid Qutb states, for example, that:

> Humanity is standing today at the brink of an abyss, not because of the threat of annihilation hanging over its head—for this is just a symptom of the disease and not the disease itself—but because humanity is bankrupt in the realm of 'values', those values which foster true human progress and development. This is abundantly clear to the Western World, for the West can no longer provide the values necessary for the [flourishing of] humanity. (Qutb in Euben 1999: 55)

For Qutb, dewesternization and decoloniality are not questions of integration or recognition, but rather of equal participation in building global futures. I see Qutb's African perspective as being powerfully complementary to the diverse struggles of Indigenous (Indian) peoples, Afro-Caribbeans, Afro-South and Central Americans, Native Americans and Chicano/Latinos in North America, as well as those of mestizos and migrants in the Caribbean and South America (among the latter of whom I count myself).

What we are witnessing today are three major trajectories towards the future. The first of these is the historical expansion of Europe and the US in a process we might well describe as *rewesternization*. The foundation of the European Union and President Obama's foreign policy can both be seen as clear orientations to maintain western leadership (see Hazbun in Part II of this volume). Rewesternization has clearly been a prerogative of foreign policy for Obama after the debacle of the Bush-Cheney era, as the US and its European allies struggle to maintain world leadership and to manage the colonial matrix of power. More recently, the announcement of the 'American Pacific Century' is another step in that direction (Clinton 2012).

All of this is becoming increasingly difficult, however, not least because *dewesternization* processes intervene, failing notably to work to Euro-American instructions. The world is arguably reaching a mature age, having finally come to understand that its destiny cannot be decided from outside of its own divergent historical trajectories—trajectories in which local histories and their local consequences interact with global designs. In this conjuncture, border thinking emerges to nourish dewesternization processes (Arrighi 1994; Mignolo 2000).

A second vision of the future might be described as the 'mutual consent annexation' by which countries such as Lithuania, Poland, and Romania have joined the European Union. In this case, the project of rewesternization is enacted by the EU and endorsed by post-Soviet leaders. The old dream of belonging to Europe makes sense of course for countries either blighted by Soviet rule or looking to improve social and economic standards; and what European imperialism was certainly successful in creating, especially after the eighteenth century, was a desire for 'civilization' and 'lifestyle' that is still powerfully attractive today. The question is, what next? Europe will have its new frontiers, but these will still be frontiers; European 'core' countries and those invited to join the EU are thus involved in a double bind, neatly summarized by Rosapepe:

> The EU accession process is both a result and a cause of the New Europe's relative success in making the political and economic transition from the Soviet bloc. Part of the reason why 'they' have been invited to join the European Union is that they have done well in creating democratic status and re-orienting their economies to the market place. But, equally, part of the reason why they have done well is their expectation of EU membership. (2004: 72, quotation marks added)

This was said a decade ago, when neoliberalism was still a dream (at least for some) and not the nightmare it has turned into. And who are 'they'? Mainly political and economic leaders, supported by the media but also—we can well guess—by a significant majority of civil society, drawn by the desire to belong to Europe. But now look outside Europe: at Ukraine's Orange Revolution, for example, which was not only pro-Europe but pro-US; or at Lebanon, where political and economic ties with Europe have been established but the Euro-American opposition to Islam is not so easily overturned. Highly selective counter-examples such as these suggest that one way of imagining transmodernity is as a form of manifest destiny—as the inexorable process by which all opposition to western modernity will eventually be overcome.

Yet there are other possibilities, e.g. a future in which, although western contributions to human civilizations are recognized, Islamic countries will be in the hands of progressive leaders rather than radical fundamentalists or local agents of western capitalism in the 'non-west'. 'Fundamentalism' is not only a tendency outside Europe and the US; in 2012 we are well aware that it is everywhere. The control of knowledge and the rhetoric of modernity serve to disguise western fundamentalism, but there is a limit. This limit has been transgressed. Decolonial visions are proposing something radically different from the current raft of fundamentalisms: Christian, free-market, neoliberal, Marxist, Islamist. I am not saying that this entire system of ideas *is* fundamentalist; I am saying that it is not *immune* from fundamentalism. Decolonial visions, by contrast, are based on *options*, and options mean that there is no truth without parenthesis (one definition of fundamentalism) and that every truth is in parenthesis because there are nothing but options.

Decolonial and Dewesternizing Latinity

Before pulling the various strands of my argument together, let me make my own position clear here. I am neither a historian of Europe nor a scholar of Islam, and I certainly claim no great expertise in either. I am neither European nor Muslim but the Catholic-raised son of Italian immigrants to Argentina, currently residing as a 'Latino' in the US. I am neither a political theorist nor a social scientist; I now like to see myself as a decolonial scholar, born and educated in the 'Third World', and thinking at the crossroads of *Latinidad* in the US and in Latin America, double vantage points where its historical connections with Europe have been severed in the first case and sustained in the second. I write from my own personal and social experience, using the tools of academic scholarship to build my arguments. Let me now recapitulate these arguments, which revolve around a set of connections between Islam, Latinity, and modernity.[5]

I will deal first with the links between Latinity and the historical bases for Eurocentrism and, since the Renaissance, modernity/coloniality. The articulation of Latinity and modernity begins with what might be called the 'Constantine Legacy' through which Christianity was allied with empire. During the Renaissance, and particularly in the sixteenth century, Christianity was reinforced by its 'victories' over the Jews and Moors and consolidated through a global expansion of its spiritual and material interests. At the

---

[5] Latinity, it might be added here, is—like any other identity—based on memory, both individual and collective. Colonization of being operates to cut off those memories and attempts to integrate them into imperial memory. Imperial memory works in the same way as capitalism, which works to erase any other form of economy and which annexes land and people to the labour force. That is why colonization of knowledge goes hand in hand with colonization of being.

same time, the global expansion of Christianity broke the link between language and religion, paving the way for minority Christian populations in such Muslim countries as Lebanon and Indonesia.

This brings me to the second moment of Latinity in its secularized form and diversified in the various Romance languages of modern imperial Europe. It is during this time that Latinity and modernity/coloniality become deeply entangled in European imperial projects. During the nineteenth century, secular Latinity began to perform the unifying role that Catholicism had previously fulfilled in the so-called Latin countries, with France taking over the lead from Catholic Spain. At more or less the same time, Latinity became the imperial ideology, mainly in Spanish America but led by France. ('Latin' America is a French invention with the consent of Creoles of European descent, mainly of Spanish descent. 'Coloniality without colonies' continues to this day in South/Central America and in the Spanish Caribbean in the name of Latinity.)

The third moment, a breakaway from European Latin legacies, happens in the US. When 'Latinos' define themselves as such, the umbilical cord with Europe has been severed. We 'Latinos/as' link ourselves to the south of the US that was once the north of Mexico and with the rest of the subcontinent and the Caribbean Islands. In Argentina I was (and still am) an Italo-Argentinian, but in the US I am a Latino-American: two very different versions of *Latinidad* obtain here. The first attaches itself to the identity of white Creoles and immigrants who arrived in the Americas during the second half of the nineteenth century, propelled by the Industrial Revolution. Being Italo-Argentinian means I am 'white', but being a 'Latino-American' means that I am categorized as a person of 'colour'. Because Latinity in the US was rearticulated by colonial subalterns, a significant shift took place in subjectivity and therefore in epistemology.[6] *Latinidad* in the US has accordingly created links with other colonial-subaltern formations like 'Africanity' and 'Indigeneity'. In multiethnic cities like New York and Miami, Latinos and African Caribbeans have more in common than their skin colour or their place of origin: both communities are linked, rather, by the colonial wound, which allows for shared spaces of protest and contestation and above all for thinking 'otherwise', for the creation of border epistemologies.

Let me turn now to Latin–Islam relations. The expulsion of the Moors from the Iberian Peninsula produced a shift from the Islam and Latin/Roman relations that had obtained during the Middle Ages, to the Islam and Latin/Christian relations that would dominate the scene from the Renaissance on. This shift took place, not only within an internal history of the making of Europe, but also in relation to the 'externalities' of colonial expansion by which Europe and later the US affirmed and consolidated their increasingly confident sense of themselves. To speak of 'Latin–Islam' relations is perhaps an awkward way of phrasing this insofar as 'Latin' (today showing its secular face)

[6.] Colonial subalterns—different to Gramsci's ones—are explicitly racialized subjects: they are Fanon's 'wretched' in terms of class rather than race. This might explain why the modern wretched in Europe react against immigrants from North Africa and South Asia—immigrants who are seen as competing with them for their jobs.

hides its ties with Christianity and 'Islam' with Arabic, even though there is no one-to-one relationship between language and religion. It might be better in this sense to look at relations between Christian and Islamic religions, on the one hand, and at those between Latin and Arabic languages, on the other.

My second point is as much an epistemological as a linguistic issue. The Moroccan philosopher Mohammed Abed al-Jabri can be taken as the initial example here (see, for example, al-Jabri 1994). In al-Jabri's work, Arabic philosophy is accorded a long history and a wide geographical spread, but also a linear chronology; consequently missing from his account is a sense of the cross-cutting ties between Arabic and Latin and Arabic and Continental European philosophy—ties that enable a two-way transhistorical conversation between, say, Ibn Rushd in twelfth-century Seville and René Descartes in seventeenth-century Amsterdam. This transhistorical cut has two imperial moments beyond the history of philosophy proper. The first of these was the aforementioned expulsion of the Moors from the Iberian Peninsula at the end of the fifteenth century, which interrupted the translation flow from Arabic to Spanish and Latin; while the second was the displacement of the centre of Atlantic commerce from southern Europe (Seville) to northern Europe (Amsterdam). It is surely worth noting that it was at the time when Amsterdam had become a trade centre, when Holland had achieved its short-lived imperial dominance, and when Europe was in the middle of a religious war, that Descartes was in Amsterdam busily writing *Discours de la méthode* (1636). My larger claim here is that relations between Arabic Islam, Christian Latinity, and secular Latinity need to be understood *both* within a hegemonic epistemology based in Greek and Latin and historically deployed in the six imperial European languages of modernity, *and* within that complex historico-structural nexus which encompasses what we understand as modern imperialism/colonialism and capitalism today.

Towards a Decolonial Transmodernity[7]

How are we to think of transmodernity and decolonial pluriversality within this formidably knotted history? More specifically, how might we reimagine a history that is composed of interconnected historico-structural nodes rather than strung out on a line marked by a 'post', be that 'post' colonial or modern? (Start your story from the receiving end of western expansion, and you will soon get rid of the 'post'.) To begin, we might say that modernity goes hand in hand with the formation of a European identity emerging out of marginal western Christendom in the Middle Ages. In the sixteenth century, the Christian (Catholic) frontiers of Europe were mapped between Islam—the Ottoman Sultanate—and Orthodox (Slavic) Christianity—the Russian Czarate/Empire. Cutting rapidly to the eighteenth, European self-definition lay in the hands of northern

---

[7] I do not have space here to explain the contribution of dewesternization to the future transmodern world. I simply refer the reader to Mignolo (2011) and Mignolo (2012a, 2012b).

intellectuals and philosophers, separated from Islam by the buffer zone of the south-ern Balkan countries, protected from the Ottoman Sultanate by the Austro-Hungarian Empire, and having both Catherine and Peter the Great in their own (respectively French and German) hands. Modernity at this time was redefined, using the French Revolution as a reference point; and secularization, freedom, and democracy were increasingly seen as the irrevocable and irreversible destiny of mankind. Today, however, what is irrevers-ible is the process of dewesternization and decoloniality, engendered—in complex ways I cannot possibly detail here—by the consolidation and expansion of western civiliza-tion (imperial Christianity, patriarchy, racism, capitalism).

Within this admittedly sketchy historical frame, decolonial and pluriversal trans-modernity becomes subject to two radically different interpretations. One is shaped out of the celebratory refashioning of European identity via, e.g., the European Union. Perhaps it would be more appropriate to call this trajectory 'altermodernity' since the term is now in circulation. The other is seen from the perspective of the wretched of the earth: 'Third World' liberationist philosophies and other modern-day continuations of the decolonial shift (the Bandung Conference, 1955; Dussel 1998). In its first mean-ing, transmodernity implies the expansion of Europe from its 'core' towards 'peripheral' European countries, presupposing in the process that consent will be provided for these countries being annexed. In its second meaning, transmodernity implies the decoloni-zation of knowledge and being and the opening up of material and imaginative possi-bilities for an-other world.

In this last sense, decolonial transmodernity offers other ways of looking at the rela-tionship between Latinity and Islam. One radical version of this shift is the Moroccan intellectual Abdessalam Yassine's, for example in his provocative 2000 essay, *Winning the Modern World for Islam*. For Yassine,

> We are … face-to-face with modernity that eradicates, a modernist ideology which calls for 'disencumbering the way' so that 'enlightened humanity' might dispel the darkness of 'tradition'—a 'tradition' which, in the eyes of the West, is currently incarnate in the 'illuminati' of an obscurantist Islam. Modernity is thus a 'sacralization' of the natural law of reason, and a submission to all that it entails. To be modern, it is supposed, means one must rebel against the sacred, against the divine. Ideological modernism owes it to itself to have as its goal 'disencumbering the way'. This is rationalism's violent indictment of the irrational, it is the crushing argument against the tatters of tradition by armed and wealthy scientific technology.

How are we (I mean those of us who are engaged in this debate) to account for such an antagonistic view? We can try to ignore it or—what perhaps amounts to the same thing—assimilate it to 'civilizationist' theory by positing a spectrum of fundamental-isms with Huntington and Yassine at opposite poles. But this way of proceeding is hardly transmodern; rather, it is imperialist, and it also fails to acknowledge (though Yassine does) that racism is at stake. However, before ceding ground to radical views, it also seems worth looking at their liberal-progressive counterparts. The Muslim intellectual Ahmad S. Moussalli, for instance, has argued that as the basic doctrines of government and politics developed in the history of medieval Islam, they contained the seeds of modern liberal democracy and pluralism within them; thus, while the 'highest Islamic political institution, the caliphate, is mostly a history of authoritarian governments, the economic, social, political and intellectual history of Islam abounds with liberal doctrines and institutions' (Moussalli 2003: 286–7).

Moussalli's views arguably overlook the complicities between liberal thought and totalitarianism in the post-Enlightenment tradition, or the continuities between liberalism and neoliberalism on current political and economic terrain. Is there so much difference between the caliphate and other forms of so-called 'Asiatic despotism' and totalitarian regimes in the heart of Europe (Adolf Hitler), on Europe's imperial frontier (Josef Stalin), or on Europe's colonial peripheries (Augusto Pinochet, Saddam Hussein)? But what then *is* the difference? It is tempting to see it as being the privilege of a western modernity to offer solutions to others' problems. (Those who hold such beliefs have the tendency, even as they moralistically point to others' crises, to see themselves as having solved their own problems by themselves.) Moussalli is surely right, however, that the principles of justice and equality are as likely to be found in Islam as in the European 'discovery' of democracy in the eighteenth century—and that Islam is just as likely to yield examples of authoritarian thinking and action as well.

Two further examples can be drawn from the work of Farish A. Noor, another progressive Muslim intellectual to have addressed these issues. In Noor's first example, when a Palestinian mother cries amid the rubble of her home, searching for the buried bodies of her children, her pain is seen as being as 'exotic', even 'incomprehensible'; while in the second, when a Bosnian son bears his heart and threatens to avenge the death of his sibling, killed by murderous mercenaries, his call for justice is interpreted as an 'irrational' cry for blood. Noor concludes from these two examples that 'somehow the agony of Muslims is [being] presented [here] as … less than human' (2003: 325). Muslims, he goes on to assert, are often seen today as 'being radically different' and 'much of this is due to our own introvertedness, born and bred [as we are] in a climate of suspicion and frustrations' (326). This climate, however, is hardly new, nor are the racist anxieties that fuel it; and as I have been suggesting throughout this chapter, at least some of their seeds were planted in Christian discourse, mainly after the sixteenth century when the modern/colonial map was drawn.

What does all of this tell us about the relationship between Islam, Latinity, and modernity? I want to conclude by making three interrelated points:

(1) Islam can be understood in its relation to Latinity on two levels: the religious level of 'Islam proper' and the linguistic-epistemic level on which Arabic is the language of religion, science, and philosophy. Latinity, in both its Christian and its secular versions, is profoundly implicated in the making of the modern imperial/colonial world.

(2) Transmodernity, according to this narrative, has at least two completely different interpretations. In the first interpretation, the EU and the US will lead the new stage of planetary history, co-opting the rest of the world into their rewesternizing

projects, which are aimed at adapting the colonial matrix of power to current situations and demands. In the second, the time to be co-opted has passed; transmodernity implies instead that a single planetary model managed by a group of countries that holds less than one quarter of the world population is a no-longer-sustainable aberration. Two alternative trajectories come into the frame here: dewesternization and decoloniality.

(3) Dewesternization, similarly, has two not necessarily compatible trajectories. One is secular, while the other is based on official religion (e.g. in Iran and Indonesia). Decoloniality is likewise split between a secular trajectory and a spiritual one. Both trajectories may be seen to have emerged in the Bandung Conference. The secular trajectory has strong representation from Africans and African Caribbean politicians, activists, and intellectuals (Nkrumah, Fanon, Césaire), while its spiritual counterpart is exemplified in, inter alia, Native American liberation theology (Tinker 2004) and Islamic educational work (TV Multiversity 2011).

Given the circumstances in which this paper was first written, I chose to start with the Ottoman Sultanate. Today I could have started with the Opium War, but the basic line of argument would have been the same one. My main point has been to argue that the single story of western civilization is ending. It may survive for a while, but decolonial and dewesternizing narratives are underway to threaten it. These narratives are entangled with Europe, but they did not originate there. The Bandung Conference, which planted the seeds for both decoloniality and dewesternization, was not only a political event: it was an epistemic and ethical crossroads. Things have changed greatly in the world since the Ottoman Sultanate first fell victim to the single narrative of modernity/coloniality. In his opening address at Bandung, Sukarno reminded us all of the way forward: 'This is the first international conference of colored peoples in the history of mankind.'[8]

References

Adichie, Chimamanda Ngozi (2009). 'The Danger of a Single Story'. Online source: <http://www.youtube.com/watch?v=D9Ihs241zeg>, accessed 7 November 2012.

Al-Jabri, Mohammed Abed (1994). *Introduction à la critique de la raison arabe*. Paris: Éditions de la découverte.

Arrighi, Giovanni (1994). *The Long Twentieth Century*. London: Verso.

Clinton, Hillary (2012). 'America's Pacific Century'. Online source: <http://www.foreignpolicy.com/articles/2011/10/11/americas_pacific_century>, last accessed 7 November 2012.

Chakrabarty, Dipesh (2000). *Provincializing Europe: Postcolonial Thought and Historical Difference*. Princeton: Princeton University Press.

Chen, Kwan-hsing (2010). *Asia as Method: Toward Deimperialization*. Durham, NC: Duke University Press.

[8.] The quotation is from Wright (1956).

Dussel, Enrique (1998). *Postmodernidad y transmodernidad: Diálogos con la filosofía de Gianni Vattimo*. Mexico: Universidad Iberoamerica.

Dussel, Enrique (2002). 'World-System and "Trans"-Modernity'. *Nepantla: Views from the South*, 3.2: 222–44.

Euben, Roxanne L. (1999). *Enemy in the Mirror: Islamic Fundamentalism and the Limits of Modern Rationalism*. Princeton: Princeton University Press.

Fanon, Frantz (2001 [1961]). *The Wretched of the Earth*, trans. C. Farrington. London: Penguin.

George, Susan (2004). *Another World is Possible If*. London: Verso.

Hegel, Georg W. F. (1991 [1822]). *The Philosophy of History*, trans. J. Sibree. New York: Prometheus.

Hobson, John M. (2004). *The Eastern Origins of Western Civilization*. Cambridge: Cambridge University Press.

Horkheimer, Max and Theodor Adorno (1969). *Dialectic of Enlightenment*. New York: Continuum.

Huntington, Samuel P. (2002). *The Clash of Civilizations and the Making of World Order*. New York: Free Press.

Kant, Immanuel (1960). *Observations on the Beautiful and the Sublime*, trans. J. T. Goldthwait. Berkeley: University of California Press.

Kant, Immanuel (1996). *Anthropology from a Pragmatic Point of View*, trans. V. L. Dowdale. Carbondale: Southern Illinois University Press.

Khatami, Mohammed (2000). Round Table: Dialogue Among Civilizations,

United Nations, New York, 5 September. Online source: <http://www.unesco.org/dialogue/en/khatami.htm>, accessed 17 December 2012.

Landes, David (1999 [1998]). *The Wealth and Poverty of Nations*. Tunbridge Wells: Abacus Press.

Levander, Caroline and Mignolo, Walter (eds) (2011). 'The Global South and World Dis/Order'. Special issue of *The Global South*, 67.2.

Mahbubani, Kishore (2008). *The New Asian Hemisphere: The Irresistible Shift of Global Power to the East*. New York: Public Affairs.

Mignolo, Walter D. (2000). *Local Histories/Global Designs: Coloniality, Subaltern Knowledges, and Border Thinking*. Princeton: Princeton University Press.

Mignolo, Walter D. (2011). *The Darker Side of Western Modernity: Global Futures/Decolonial Options*. Durham, NC: Duke University Press.

Mignolo, Walter D. (2012a). 'Intraviews (II). An Interview with Christopher Mattison', Hong Kong Advanced Institute of Cross-Disciplinary Studies. Online source: <http://www6.cityu.edu.hk/hkaics/intraviews/wm2.html>, accessed 3 May 2012.

Mignolo, Walter D. (2012b). 'Delhi 2012: La desoccidentalización, los BRICS y la distribución racial del capital'. Online source: <http://waltermignolo.com/2012/04/21/dheli-2012-la-desoccidentalizacion-los-brics-y-la-distribucion-racial-del-capital/, accessed 3 May 2012.

Mignolo, Walter D. and Arturo Escobar (eds) (2009). *Globalization and the Decolonial Option*. New York: Routledge.

Mignolo, Walter D. and Madina V. Tlostanova (2006). 'Theorizing from the Borders: Shifting the Geo- and Body-Politics of Knowledge', *European Journal of Social Theory*, 9.2: 205–21.

Moussalli, Ahmad S. (2003). 'Islamic Democracy and Pluralism', in Omid Safi (ed.), *Progressive Muslims: On Justice, Gender and Pluralism*. Oxford: Oneworld, 286–305.

Noor, Farish A. (2003). 'What is the Victory of Islam? Toward a Different Understanding of the *Ummah* and Political Success in the Contemporary World', in Omid Safi (ed.), *Progressive Muslims: On Justice, Gender and Pluralism*. Oxford: Oneworld, 320–32.

Qutb, Sayyid (2008). *The Sayyid Qutb Reader: Selected Writings in Politics, Religion and Society*, ed. Albert J. Bergesen. New York: Routledge.

Rosapepe, James C. (2004). 'Beyond New Europe: Does A Euro Curtain Exist?' *Harvard International Review*, 3: 68–72.

SETimes.com (2005). 'Erdogan, Zapatero Launch Alliance of Civilisations Initiative', SETimes.com, 28 November. Online source: <http://setimes.com/cocoon/setimes/xhtml/en_GB/features/setimes/features/2005/11/28/feature-01>, accessed 17 December 2012.

Shari'ati, Ali (1980). *Marxism and Other Western Fallacies: An Islamic Critique*. Berkeley, Cal.: Mizan Press.

Tlostanova, Madina (2005). 'Seduced by Modernity: Why Turkey Can Be/Become Europe and Russia Cannot'. Paper given at the 2005 conference 'Islam, Latinity, Transmodernity'. Online source: <http://www.alati.com.br/ing/publicacoes_2005_islam_latinite_transmodernite.html>, accessed 1 September 2010.

Tinker, George (2004). *Spirit and Resistance: Political Theology and American Indian Liberation*. Kitchener: Fortress Press.

TV Multiversity (2011). 'Notes on Decolonizing Universities'. Online source: <http://tvmultiversity.blogspot.com/2011/07/notes-on-decolonising-universities-part.html>, accessed 3 May 2012.

Wright, Richard (1956). *The Color Curtain: Report on the Bandung Conference*. Oxford: University of Mississippi Press.

Yassine, Abdessalam (2000). *Winning the Modern World for Islam*, trans. Martin Jenni. New York: Justice and Spirituality Publications.

CHAPTER 5

....

EMPIRE, ISLAM, AND THE POSTCOLONIAL

....

SALMAN SAYYID

INTRODUCTION

....

One of the most persistent criticisms of postcolonialism is that it promotes an anti-pathy to imperialism that tends to focus on the experience of European colonial empires and neglects other, non-western instances of imperial hubris (see, for example, Howe 2002; see also the introduction to this section of the volume). The articulation of Islam and empire has not been subject to sustained postcolonial investigation; rather, the relationship between Muslims and imperialism has tended to be represented in terms of Muslim subjugation to European colonial rule. Postcolonial critics have largely avoided the discussion of Islamicate imperialism (Hodgson 1974).[1] There are good reasons for this. First, the most recent experience of Islamicate communities has been that of being European colonial subjects. By 1900, three out of four Muslims were living in European empires, while there were only four significant polities—the Ottoman domains, Persia, Morocco, and Afghanistan—outside of European control (Schulze 2000: 25, 23). Most of Muslimistan was affected by European colonial rule, and in this respect the Muslim story is not very different from stories of other non-western societies.[2] Islamicate soci-eties share a set of experiences common to what used to be described as the Third World: colonization, unequal exchanges, institutionalization of cultural inferiority, anti-colonial struggles, formal independence. It is easy to conclude from this that the dominant relationship between Islam and empire has been that of Muslim subjugation. Second, postcolonial studies has largely been focused on the European colonial enter-prise and its remaking of the world; other, prior imperial formations have not been at the forefront of postcolonial analysis.

---

[1] Hodgson (1974: 58) first introduced the term Islamicate which refers to social phenomena that are informed by Islam but were reducible to it.

[2] Muslimistan refers to countries 'dominated (either formally or informally) socially and culturally by the Islamicate' (Sayyid 2010: 3).

To put Islam and empire into conversation with the postcolonial is, at best, an ambivalent gesture. Such a conversation can be read as part of the heroically democratizing process by which the western canon has become less Eurocentric and more ecumenical; by which marginalized histories have been reclaimed and recovered; and by which the story of the west has come to feature characters who interrupt its privileged whiteness, marking out western plutocracies as intrinsically multicultural and post-racial in an increasingly interconnected world. According to this post-racial narrative, racialized differences in the west have only a cosmetic significance; racism proper is more likely to be located among non-western communities including non-western immigrants to western countries (Sayyid and Hesse 2008). This narrative often sets up a contrast between Islam and the west as the primary axis structuring contemporary social and cultural relations. The contrast between the imagined benevolence of western imperialism (past and present) and the attributed aridity of Islamicate imperialism restores the legitimacy of the western imperium, building a case for the necessity and desirability of continued American-led military action in the age of the 'war on terror', and institutionalizing the series of so-called 'humanitarian interventions' that have taken place in the aftermath of the Cold War (Cooper 2004; see also Part II of this volume).[3] On first reading, Muslims appear to be subjects of European colonialism or—what often amounts to the same thing—to require western regulation and protection; on the second, they appear as potential or actual imperialist heirs of rapacious and predatory empires. In this chapter, I want to explore this tension between subaltern and imperial readings of Islam and empire as these are disclosed in a postcolonial context.

Double Decolonization

There are many different ways of describing the postcolonial context in which the contemporary politics of Islam has emerged; for the purposes of this chapter, I want to emphasize two relatively recent developments that have eroded the 'violent hierarchy' between the west and the non-west, which constituted the colonial order. The first of these developments revolves around anti-colonial national liberation struggles, which did much to make European colonial regimes ungovernable by mobilizing sustained armed resistance. The second concerns the various civil rights struggles that have undermined the domestic status quo in western plutocracies. These two struggles can

---

[3.] Robert Cooper, a senior diplomat and advisor to the Blair government, was one of the early advocates of humanitarian intervention and other forms of liberal imperialism in the 1990s. The incongruity of such a position became explicit when Cooper found himself defending the Bahraini police against widespread protests against the Bahraini government during the so-called 'Arab Spring'. See Cooper (2004) for the case for liberal imperialism; see Gopal (Part II of this volume) for the case against. See also Hazbun (Part II) and the General Introduction to this volume for further reflections on the 'Arab Spring'.

be viewed together as two fronts of a single conflict in which western primacy and white privilege—always intimately linked—have been weakened and challenged. Both these developments benefited from the reordering of the international environment in the aftermath of the Second World War. The Cold War, by turning the planet into an arena for overtly ideological competition between two contending systems of belief and economic organization, provided both anti-colonial and civil rights struggles to potentially outflank their local opponents by widening their resistance beyond parameters set by the colonial order. One of the hallmarks of the colonial enframing of the world was the way in which it sought to establish a hermetically sealed border between the west and the rest (Hall 1992: 276–79), metropole and periphery, nation and empire. This border allowed figures as diverse as John Stuart Mill, Thomas Jefferson, Alexis de Tocqueville, and Lord Cromer to behave inconsistently, knowing that the contradictions of their own thoughts and actions could be rescued by recognizing the different logics that operated in the colonial divide. To give an example, Lord Cromer championed women's empowerment in Egypt by campaigning against the veil, and then became president of the National League for Opposing Woman Suffrage in England. Similarly, it was an ontological gap between the west and the rest that allowed Alexis de Tocqueville to praise religiosity in America and condemn it in Algeria (Richter 1963; see also Pitts 2000). Of course, these figures and many others like them were complex, as human beings are, and their lives showed the inconsistencies and slippages that are common to humanity. The point is not that they were hypocritical or cynical—they may or may not have been—but rather that these inconsistencies rested upon an assumption that empire and nation denoted not only two distinct political structures but rather two separate universes, so that it was quite possible to talk up democracy in Britain and France while ignoring the fact that a majority of the subjects of the British and French governments lacked basic political rights (see Stovall in this section of the volume).

Given the division between nation and empire that constituted western colonial order, it is not surprising that what Mignolo has described as the 'decolonial shift' occurred as the confluence of two struggles: civil rights and anti-colonial (Mignolo 2000; see also Mignolo in this section of the volume). This double decolonization of the international order and of the domestic spaces sustained by that order was made possible because of the way in which the mutual hostilities of the Cold War provided an ideological umbrella under which it was possible to challenge western supremacist discourse. The national liberation wars helped to speed up the dismantling of the European empires in Asia and Africa, while at the same time the ideological challenge posed by the Soviet Union created spaces that subaltern groups within western plutocracies could use to support their demands for civil rights (Krenn 1998; see also Tyner and Kruse 2004).[4]

---

[4] Krenn points to how Soviet Union propaganda focused on 'the Negro Question', using the subjugation of African Americans as an indictment of the USA itself. Similarly, African American politicians have attempted to take the plight of African Americans to the UN, thus blurring the distinction between domestic and foreign policies. See also Tyner and Kruse (2004).

The shift from the Cold War to the 'war on terror' has, however, consolidated the way in which the anti-colonial and civil rights struggles have recently become disaggregated. This consolidation is marked by the way in which western plutocracies increasingly represent themselves as being anti-racist, anti-patriarchal, and even anti-homophobic as compared to non-western communities, in particular those now organized around the signifier of Islam. In the age of the 'war on terror', Islam and its cognates provide a link between the domestic lack of social cohesion and external threats to national security. The tropes of rogue states and 'home-grown' terrorists populate the discourse of the 'war on terror' (see Morton in Part II of this volume).

Islam raises questions, then, that have geopolitical implications (rogue states and terrorist cells), cultural connotations (the balance between secularism and minority needs), and epistemological consequences (e.g. those encapsulated in the question: can the history of the world still be told as a scaled-up history of the west?). Meanwhile, the relationship between Islam and empire has shifted from an academic to a general cultural concern; for not only does the historical idea of an Islamicate empire provide a populist example of 'bad empire' to be contrasted with 'good' ones such as those of Britain and by extension the US (see Ferguson 2003 and 2004), but the aims of present-day Muslim minorities and movements can also be deciphered from a highly selective reading of Islamicate empires in the past. The image of a Saracen with a scimitar in one hand and the Qur'an in the other is a staple of Orientalism past and present. This image is often linked to the assumption that the spread of Islam was uniquely due to military dominance—an assumption that establishes the essentially violent character of the Muslim enterprise (past and present).

Currently, the most sustained and elaborate recycling of this image and its associated themes is found in what can be broadly described as neoconservatism.[5] Neoconservatism came to the fore as a project aimed at perpetuating the unipolar moment that followed the collapse of the Soviet Union and the unravelling of the Cold War. Neoconservatives saw a historic opportunity in the fall of the Soviet Empire to consolidate a Pax Americana that would forestall the possibility of any geopolitical rival emerging to challenge the United States (McGowan 2007: 124; see also the essays by Gopal and Hazbun in Part II of this volume). In this vision of an everlasting American future for the world, neoconservatives were responding to the process of double decolonization. According to neoconservative narratives, Islam (sometimes extremist Islam) is a totalitarian ideology set upon world domination and the reduction of all non-Muslims to a subjugated status (Burleigh 2008; Gray 2003). The 'bad empire' of Islam (in its various incarnations) sits alongside attempts to emphasize the moral superiority of the 'good empire' of Britain (or other more recent western imperial formations). In its attempt to privilege the British empire and, by extension, to justify American global hegemony, neoconservative discourse displaces the postcolonial

---

[5.] Many of those who are described as neoconservatives prefer the designation neo-Reaganite.

critique of imperialism onto imperial Islam, either explicitly or more implicitly (e.g. by arguing that the imperial sins of Islam are far greater than those of western empires, or that Atlantic slavery was a lesser evil than Saharan slavery, or that 'Muslim racism' is more racist than western racism).[6] There is, however, good reason to see in the Islamicate empires an imperialism that has its own specificity, and some of those specific features will now be recounted below.

IMPERIAL ISLAM

The beginnings of Islamicate empire are generally seen as lying in the organization of a state centred on Medina in the 620s. The Medina state was able to unify the Arabian Peninsula for the first (and to this day only) time through a process of military campaigns and diplomatic manoeuvres. This unification meant that Muslim armies came into conflict with the Roman and Persian empires, as the Arabian Peninsula was no longer a buffer zone patrolled by contending nomadic bands in the pay of Roman or Persian authorities. The challenge of the Medina state, however, was not purely geopolitical; it was also philosophical. By the time of the emergence of the Islamic state, the Mediterranean basin and Iranian plateau had been dominated not only by empires but the very idea of empire as a world state for millennia (Fowden 1993). The Roman and Persian empires were not just predominant in the region, but their predominance had been sedimented over centuries: they presented themselves as heirs to an imperial legacy that transcended its current dynastic configurations. The Persian imperial heritage has plausibly been traced from the imperial formations of the Assyrians of the sixth century BCE through the Babylonians, Achaemenids, Parthians, and Sassanids. In some cases, the homage to previous empires was self-conscious (e.g. the Sassanids presenting themselves as direct legitimate heirs to the Achaemenids), while in other cases it was implicit, e.g. the use of purple as a signifier of imperial dignity (Aro and Whiting 2000). The Roman Empire was philosophically grounded in the Roman republican tradition but was also linked via *imitatio Alexandri* to Persian imperial tropologies. Given the prestige of these empires and the pedigree of their imperial heritages, it would not be unreasonable to suppose that the 'barbarian' states on their periphery would aspire to become part of these imperial grand narratives. The Islamicate polity could have easily slipped into the niches carved out by ancient imperial legacies; but to a large extent the Islamicate

---

[6.] A number of generally unreliable accounts circulate on the Internet in which the victims of imperial Islam are numbered in their hundreds of millions as an attempt to illustrate the uniquely violent character of Islam and its adherents. Given the generalized awareness of the millions of deaths attributed to European colonialism, to make the case that Islam was particularly violent requires figures that top these. Of course, it goes without saying that such calculation of death and destruction is extremely difficult given our lack of documentation on demography in the distant past.

state did not do this, nor did the order that Muslim forces forged just rework existing imperial traditions.[7] This was remarkable since the Islamicate state's neighbours had one of the longest sustained traditions of imperial formations. The articulation of Islam and empire, however, did not simply produce another iteration of prevailing imperial traditions; it marked nothing less than the enunciation of a new semantic universe.

The emergence of empire founded by Muslim armies interrupted the dependence on the previously standard model of imperial narratives. In approximately one hundred years (from roughly 630 to 750), the Islamicate state conducted a series of military campaigns on a continental scale that would yield, up to that point, the largest empire in the world. Muslims conquered territories from Sind to Spain; in the process, they shattered the Persian Empire and captured the richest provinces of the Roman Empire. In purely spatial terms, the territory captured by Muslim armies was approximately 11 million square kilometres, making it twice the size of the previous largest empire (Taagepera 1978). The speed and the scale of the conquest signalled a dramatic jump in empire-building capacities. Not only did Muslim arms lay low empires that had been around for half a millennium; they did so without necessarily having any significant technological, fiscal, or demographic advantage over their enemies. The 'miracle' of Muslim military success has been explained either as divine verdict (in favour of the Muslims or against their enemies) or in more prosaic terms as the consequence of an implausible demographic explosion in the arid Arabian Peninsula or as the will to plunder. As Fred McGraw Donner (1981) has argued, however, all these explanations tend to discount the highly organized and disciplined structure of the Muslim conquests, the relative numerical weakness of their armies in relation to those of their opponents, and the absence of any significant superiority in weaponry. The success of the Muslim armies was ideological: that is, it was based on the construction of a Muslim political identity which could not be reduced to an Arab ethnicity or nomadic positionality.

The construction of a distinct Muslim identity is crucial to any understanding of the hundred-year jihad. In the name of Islam, armies were organized, defeats were endured, and victories sustained. The seasoned generals of the Roman and Persian empires, who had tried-and-trusted methods of dealing with nomadic border incursions, had nothing in their strategic repertoire to deal with Muslim armies that were largely immune to being bought off or being played off one faction against another. As Walter Kaegi observes: 'No Byzantine manual of statecraft or warfare offered advice on how to handle the appearance of a major prophet amidst the peoples who surrounded the empire' (2003: 230). They had no answer either to the way in which Muslim armies proved able to coordinate their actions across great distances with a relatively unified command structure, given the communications technology available at the time. Muslim identity

---

[7.] This is not to deny that the imperial traditions of the Roman and Persian empires had an influence on Islamicate empires in subsequent centuries or that the unfolding of the venture of Islam was not inflected through local traditions, but rather that the Muslims saw themselves as separate from previous empires. Contrast this with the jostling for imperial investiture among the Germanic successor states of the Roman Empire.

was reinforced by conquest and by subsequent occupations that saw not the garrisoning of ancient cities but the establishment of nearby garrison towns. This strategy helped limit the assimilation of Muslim identity into the rich, textured cultures of the Roman and Persian empires. It is not necessary here to follow the various permutations of the Islamicate polity and the multiple ways in which its centrifugal and centripetal tensions played themselves out regionally, dynastically, and denominationally. Nor is it necessary to argue that the semantic order inaugurated by the hundred-year jihad did not subsequently begin to be creolized, or to see in this process of creolization the recovery of a national essence underlying Islamization, e.g. the reaffirmation of a previously subjugated Persian or Indian identity. Rather, the Islamicate empires could be identified, despite all these internal differences and nuances, as those imperial formations in which the articulation of Islam as a master signifier was hegemonic.

Michael Doyle defines empire as 'a relationship, formal or informal, in which one state controls the effective sovereignty of another political society … Imperialism is simply the process of establishing or maintaining an empire' (1986: 45; see also the introduction to this section). Thus, the assessment of whether a particular entity is an empire or not turns, like most significant political projects, on the question of identity. To put this differently, an empire implies that there is a very sharp divide between society and state. England following the Norman Conquest was an empire to the extent that the Norman elite was clearly marked out from the large sections of the society over which it ruled. Doyle acknowledges this, seeing in what he calls the 'Caracallan threshold' the moment at which an empire transforms itself into a nation. This term refers to an edict of the Roman Emperor Caracalla in 212 CE that granted citizenship to all free adults, thereby formally ending the distinction between the privileged citizens of Rome and free (i.e. non-enslaved) subjects of the Roman Empire.[8] The difference between the metropolitan elite and peripheral subject population became to all intents and purposes eroded, so that the divisions between rulers and ruled did not refer to different ethnically marked populations. Islam not only legitimated Muslim conquests; it also constructed the identity of Muslims as the primary form of identification. Non-Muslim adult men, excluding priests and rabbis, were liable to pay a poll tax (justified by their exclusion from military service). This economic discrimination was matched by its social equivalent. For the most part, Muslim armies did not conquer autonomous communities with full political rights; rather they conquered communities that were part of other empires, communities that were under authoritarian rule. Becoming Muslim was an option that remained open to the subject population. There was no need to undergo an elaborate

[8.] This edict, however, was a culmination of practices that distinguished the Roman state from its near contemporaries including democratic Athens: Rome had been periodically willing to enfranchise populations it had defeated. As a consequence, Roman military expansion also led to expanded Roman citizenry, contrasting with the shortage of manpower that crippled the abilities of states like Sparta and Athens to maintain their imperial advantage. See Ian Morris's (2009) comparative analysis of the 'Greater Athenian state'. As Morris points out, the restrictive citizenship of some of the Hellenic city states significantly constrained their demographic resources.

apprenticeship, nor was there any specific barrier due to ethnicity or linguistic competence. Thus Islam, which supplied the Muslims with armies, discipline, endurance, and immunity from being subverted by their enemies, also made it difficult for Muslim rulers to erect effective barriers that would prevent their subjects from crossing the Caracallan threshold. The universalism and egalitarianism of Islam weakened the ability of Muslim rulers to sustain a permanent and rigid state of imperial privilege vis-à-vis conquered peoples. Crossing the Caracallan threshold means weakening the sense of 'foreignness between rulers and ruled' that is characteristic of imperial formations (Morris 2009: 132). The longevity of empires can be seen in some part as a function of the ability of imperial formations to allow their subjects to become 'citizens'. The Islamicate empires became engines for turning non-Muslims into Muslims, although the process was not swift and the reasons for individuals to become Muslims were no doubt overdetermined by a variety of factors.[9] The empires produced by the venture of Islam were ones in which (relative to historical precedents and contemporaries) the extractive impulse of imperial rule was tempered by the ever-present possibility of subjugated populations becoming Muslims (Parsons 2010).

Racism and Citizenship

One of the features of European colonial empires, in contrast to Islamicate enterprises, was that it remained difficult for non-European subjects to become citizens of the empires (see Stovall in this section of the volume). As a consequence, European colonial empires tended to be experienced as a form of distant authoritarian rule by the majority of the peoples they governed. The colour line that underwrote colonial order appeared permanent and rigid. Unlike the Roman, Chinese, or Islamicate empires (during most of their iterations) the ability of subjects of European colonial rule to become part of a 'ruling upper-class culture' was heavily restricted (Mann 1988 [1986]: 143; see also Vukovich in Part V of this volume). The authoritarianism of the colonial order existed despite claims made by imperialists and their supporters that European empires, because of their Enlightenment heritage, were uniquely capable of modernizing (i.e. civilizing) their non-western subjects. The trouble was that however much the 'natives' were civilized they were never civilized enough to become co-partners of the imperial enterprise. The emergence of racism as a distinct form of governmentality owed much to the challenge that Spanish rulers were confronted with following the elimination of the last sovereign Muslim polity in the Iberian Peninsula (Venn 2006: 62–72; see also Seed in this section of the volume). The Spanish authorities, confronted with a large population of

---

[9] See Bulliet's (1979) pioneering studies on the process of Islamization of the territories governed by Muslims. Bulliet suggests that for nearly 200 years the majority of people that Muslims ruled in Syria and Persia were non-Muslims. Conquest did not lead to immediate conversions (or reversions) to Islam.

Muslims and Jews who had been compelled to convert, instituted strategies of surveil-lance that had largely been absent from the large Eurasian empires. Attempts to police Muslim and Jewish conversions as being authentic or not, and the politicization of the population due to the conflict between the forces of the Reformation and those of the Counter-Reformation, produced innovations in techniques of surveillance and the extension of their scope beyond elite society to the general populace. The fragmentation of Christendom along confessional lines went hand in hand with the development of the early modern state with its panoply of administrative regulations and interventions. In the process, a means of conceptualizing the social emerged that came to be characterized by the regulation and disciplining of non-Europeanness with reference to Europeanness (Hesse 2011). As Barnor Hesse argues, race can

> be understood as having been historically and geographically constructed by European colonial derived regimes as a governing practice to distinguish between 'whiteness/Europeaness' and 'non-Europeaness/non-whiteness' in terms of regulations, affinities, spaces and discourses in modernity's colonies. In this racially constitutive and governmental sense populations colonized outside Europe were recruited, interpellated and allocated to these assemblages of territory, corporeality, culture, politics, religion, and obliged under law and practice to comport themselves within the social contours of their designated assemblage of race. (2011: 164)

The establishment of race as a regulatory practice based on the hierarchy between Europeanness and non-Europeanness provided the European colonial empires with a political identity that resolved one of the perennial problems confronting empire builders: that of the proconsul who 'goes native' (Mann 1988: 141–3). In the history of European colonialism, there are very few examples of European governors identify-ing with their colonial subjects to the extent that they were ready to break their iden-tification with Europeanness.[10] Thus, the development of race erected a barrier to the Caracallan threshold; it meant effectively that the European colonial order was a racist order and that European empires were racial states. The intertwining of the racial state and the modern state was forged in the crucible of the early modern European empires, which came to contain the two distinct spatial entities: the homeland and the conquered lands. Racialized differences came to be deployed as a means of enhancing the solidarity of imperial nations and of preventing their non-European subjugated populations from eroding the privileges of empire (Goldberg and Quayson 2002).

The Islamicate empires, with due caveats for the cruelty and venality that can be found in all human endeavours, were not structured around a logic of racialization. This does not mean these empires lacked a privileged elite, nor does it mean there was no humili-ation or violation of the subject populations, but it *does* mean that reading all imperial

---

[10.] There is an argument that the independence movements of the Americas did draw a distinction between themselves and Europe; however, they continued to privilege Europeanness vis-à-vis both the indigenous and enslaved African populations of the western hemisphere.

iterations through the prism of the European colonial enterprise is not particularly helpful. This is not to say that European colonialism was more vicious or more exploitative than other imperial structures—such accusations and counter-accusations are generally sterile—simply that empires founded in the wake of Europe's appropriation of the Americas were organized by different logics than previous empires (Schmitt 2003: 86–100). One of these logics was a deployment of race as the primary ontology of the social. It is important here to have a proper understanding of the empirical 'messiness' of deployment: confusion between philosophers and historians of a certain ilk arises on precisely on this issue (see Stoler in this section of the volume; also Kennedy in Part IV). Any generalization that ranges over 500 years (at least) and covers a number of large political entities (British, French, Spanish, Portuguese, Dutch, and Russian empires, just to name the most prominent in the story of European colonialism) is bound to be messy. There will always be evidence of good-natured colonial administrators who were not 'racist' (whatever that may mean, and it is often unclear what it does mean in such accounts) or who actually loved the indigenous colonial subjects and cared for them, but this does not mean that the logic of racism was absent from European colonial formations. European imperial formations were crucibles of both colonialism and racism. In fact, it would be difficult to separate the two, for racism was a category coined to describe the practices pioneered by Nazis in Germany in the 1930s in relation to Jews and Roma. The pioneering nature of Nazis in this regard was not in terms of innovative practices, since all these practices had all previously been present in the colonial empires of Britain, France, and the Netherlands; rather it was the application of policies of segregation, intimidation, and humiliation to populations present within Europe that earned the sobriquet of racism. Thus, the split between racism and colonialism came to echo the split between the west and the non-west. It was this racial logic, as much as the irruption of capitalism, the dawn of modernity, and the shift from continental to oceanic power, that was one of the key differences between European colonial empires that emerged in the post-Columbian universe and earlier empires. The Islamicate empires shared a series of overlapping features with other pre-modern imperial structures. The articulation of Islam and empire was a historical relationship, not an essential or necessary one. As such, it is not straightforward to read from the experience of European colonial empires and Islamicate empires.

ISLAM AND THE POSTCOLONIAL

One of the main effects of postcolonial critiques of European colonial enterprises has been to see similar logics and cruelties at work in all imperial formations, thus making all empires worthy of condemnation (Parsons 2010). Given the way in which Muslim political projects sit upon the cusp of this double decolonization, the historical critique of Islamicate empires joins the contemporary polemics of the place of Islam and

Muslims in the world. The record of the various heirs to the first Islamicate empire has become part of the attempt to see a violent essence at the heart of Islam. In particular, the Ottoman and Timurid (Mughal) empires are often presented today as examples of the baleful influence of Islam, while the lack of development in the Balkans is frequently attributed to the retardation imposed by 500 years of Ottoman rule (Ágoston 2007: 75). Similarly, the Muslim conquest of large parts of South Asia is very often presented as a major distortion of the intrinsic nature of the 'original native' societies of the region. Europe and South Asia are possibly the two regions most affected by Islamicate encounters that did not succumb to complete Islamization. The consolidation and formation of Indian and European identity is heavily based on the contrast with Islam. This may account for the way in which Islam can be mobilized as the antipode in opposition to which Europeanness and Indianness can be articulated without great effort, and Islamicate imperial formations can be presented correspondingly as exercises in alien rule.

Many Muslims today strive to disassociate themselves from Islam's imperial past by arguing for the disarticulation of Islam from its spatialization of power. To a large extent, these views echo postcolonial-inspired critiques of imperialism. Either there is a refusal to accept that Islam was an imperial formation or, if it was, then it is declared that it was no different from European colonial empires: in other words, that it was also characterized by a racialized form of governmentality. The historical instances of Islamicate empires haunt the contemporary world through assertions that demands by local Muslim communities for justice or for inclusion in the conversation of the nation are the thin end of the wedge that will result in the Muslim conquest of the west; this threat of a jihad to come is then used to mobilize support for a series of preventive crusades against nebulous 'Islamic' rogues and terror networks. The age of the 'war on terror' has opened up debates about a new configuration of the state that echoes more closely the imperial claims of the past rather than declarations of national sovereignty. Under the guise of humanitarian interventions and preventive war, however, we have seen the ostensible breakdown of the doctrine of national sovereignty and the possibility of a postcolonial (and post-racial) imperium. Since at least the Iranian Revolution, the United States and its allies have become increasingly involved in low-level 'counter-insurgency' operations in much of Muslimistan (see Hazbun in Part II of this volume). This postcolonial gunboat diplomacy initially saw the deployment of US military power to discipline and regulate activities within Muslimistan.[11] The launching of the 'war on terror' has since transformed this postcolonial gunboat diplomacy into full-scale colonial-style campaigns, including the US-led military invasions of Afghanistan and Iraq, while operations

---

[11.] The United States established Central Command in 1983 to coordinate military operations in the 'crescent of crisis', a region identified by President Carter's National Security Advisor Zbigniew Brzezinski as stretching along the shores of the Indian Ocean, and one in which fragile states were threatened with destabilization by elements hostile to western values. See *Time Magazine* (1979).

against or in the territories of Muslim countries such as Pakistan, Somalia, Libya, Iran, and Syria have resulted in the virtual recolonization of parts of Muslimistan.[12] It is in this 'new imperial' context that the articulation of Islam and empire is currently disclosed (Harvey 2003; see also Part II of this volume).

Living in the time of the 'war on terror'—a war whose continuity is marked not only by its persistence beyond the governments that initiated it, but also by its banal institutionalization in the international system—it is possible to discern the contours of empire represented not so much in terms of an opposition to the multitude, but rather as an opposition to terror (see Morton in Part II of this volume). This terror is incarnated in the bodies of Muslims, whose very appearance (both in terms of what they look like and that they are present) becomes problematic. From the introduction of legislation banning Muslim woman from wearing headscarves, to debates about the 'ethnic profiling' of potential terrorists in relation to how Muslim they look, these are simply outward symptoms of a deeper unease which cannot be simply reduced to the tangle of geopolitical, cultural, and epistemological factors that frame Muslims. At the heart of this war against terror is not a simple struggle against rogue states or violent extremists but rather an attempt to erase the contingency of the western enterprise. The European colonial empires were central to the process by which western cultural practices became hegemonic in the world. The appeal of the west, and its centrality in the world, were products not of its intrinsic qualities (e.g. claims of prosperity, democracy, and stability) but rather of its power over other empires. The world we live in was forged by the European colonial order. The effect of this exercise of collective imperium on a planetary scale was to demonstrate the contingency of all non-western formations. Thus it is easier for us to conduct a thought experiment like the one carried by Graham Fuller, once vice-chairman of the National Intelligence Council at the Central Intelligence Agency, who speculates in a recent book on a world without Islam. Fuller argues that many of the tensions and conflicts that are perceived to exist between the Islamicate and western (European) worlds would still exist even if there were no Islam, since the cause of these conflicts is the *longue durée* of geopolitics and not the nature of religious or ideological sentiment inherent in Islam itself. Islam, according to Fuller, cannot explain tensions in the Middle East (2010: 300); rather, it appears supplemental to the contemporary world. In other words, Fuller is able to imagine a world without Islam because Islam has a relationship with the contemporary world in which its contingency is fully disclosed. In contrast, it is perhaps not surprising that one of the most famous musings about a world in which Islam was necessary and absolute comes from the pen of Edward Gibbon, writing in the eighteenth century when European colonial power could be challenged and defeated by non-western regimes. Gibbons famously mused that the consequences of a Muslim victory at the battle of Tours (732 CE) would be the Islamization of northern

---

[12.] See Chandrasekaran (2007 [2006]) for descriptions of the high life of officials of the American Provisional Coalition Authority in occupied Baghdad. One of the most interesting things about Chadrasekaran's account is the similarity between the American occupation and earlier European colonial administrations in the way these officials comported themselves in relation to the 'natives'.

Europe and the emergence of Oxford as a bastion of Quranic teaching. Islam's role as a counterfactual foil to the story of Europe's rise to global ascendancy is not merely a matter of historical whimsy, but a very real possibility. For the Age of Europe ushered in by the European colonial empires often involved a direct challenge to Muslim authorities. European colonialism directly replaced or subverted Muslim rule in large parts of Asia and Africa. Colonialism replaced an Islamicate world system that stretched right across the Afro-Eurasian supercontinent. This replacement was both *epistemological*, with the unravelling of the power/knowledge complexes that were part of the Islamicate order, and *political* in so far as Muslim elites found their position undermined by the imposition of European rule. Thus, Islam emerges in contrast to Christendom in the formation of pre-modern identifications of Europe, and re-emerges as one major opponent of European colonialism; and now it appears as the cosmological enemy at the centre of the 'war on terror'. Despite many periods of *convivencia* and overlapping similarities between Islam and the west, the hegemonic sense of western identity often evokes a contrast with Islam and its cognates, which continually hints at the possibility of an alternative universe in which the contingency of Europe is revealed.

The postcolonial condition suggests that the relationship between Europe and the present is not necessary; it could have been otherwise and, even if we cannot imagine what a world without the European colonial venture would look like, we can still imagine that such an outcome might be possible. The haunting of the west by Islam hints precisely at such a possibility. Islam's articulation with empire suggests the possibility of an alternative world order in which Christendom/Europe are peripheral and threatened. The history of the articulation of Islam and empire points to the contingency at the heart of the western enterprise.

Empires have been the dominant form of the spatialization of power in human history (Mann 1988; Burbank and Cooper 2010). Beginning perhaps with Sargon's Akkadian hegemony and moving on to Assyria's elaboration of imperial techniques of governance and their Persian, Sinic, Indic, and Greco-Roman iterations, empire has dominated the political order of the cited cultures and agrarian economies of the Eurasian landmass (Mann 1988). The outburst of nationalism among people claiming a European heritage in the eighteenth and nineteenth centuries helped dismantle the continental empires of the Hohenzollerns, the Hapsburgs, and the Ottomans. The nationalist revolts of non-European peoples culminated in the twentieth century in the dismantling of the oceanic empires of Britain, France, and Holland. These struggles, which seem to have consigned the imperial form of spatialization of power to the past, have undoubtedly helped to consolidate postcolonial studies as a means of understanding the complex imbrications between empire, nation, and identity. Postcolonial approaches have focused mainly on European colonial empires and the legacy they bequeathed to the contemporary world. The nature of this legacy has become more complicated with the advent of the 'war on terror', which has made it possible to see the complex mutations by which empire persists even in an era when the temper of the times is postcolonial. The articulations of Islam and empire thus play on the tensions of a postcolonial imperial present as well as an Islamicate imperial past. In between these tensions the promise of a decolonial future glimmers.

REFERENCES

Ágoston, Gábor (2007). 'Information, Ideology and the Limits of Imperial Policy: Ottoman Grand Strategy in the Context of Ottoman-Habsburg Rivalry', in Virginia Askan and Daniel Goffman (eds), *The Early Modern Ottomans: Remapping the Empire*. Cambridge: Cambridge University Press, 75–103.

Aro, Sanna and R. M. Whiting (eds) (2000). *The Heirs of Assyria*. Helsinki: University of Helenski Press.

Bulliet, Richard (1979). *Conversion to Islam in the Medieval Period: An Essay in Quantitative History*. Cambridge, Mass.: Harvard University Press.

Burbank, Jane and Frederick Cooper (2010). *Empires in World History: Power and the Politics of Difference*. Princeton and Oxford: Princeton University Press.

Burleigh, Michael (2008). *Blood and Rage: A Cultural History of Terrorism*. London: Harper Collins.

Chandrasekaran, Rajiv (2007 [2006]). *Imperial Life in the Emerald City: Inside Iraq's Green Zone*. London: Gardeners Books.

Cooper, Robert (2004). *The Breaking of Nations: Order and Chaos in the 21st Century*. London: Atlantic Books.

Donner, Fred McGraw (1981). *The Early Islamic Conquests*. Princeton: Princeton University Press.

Doyle, Michael W. (1986). *Empires*. Ithaca and London: Cornell University Press.

Ferguson, Niall (2003). *Empire: How Britain Made the Modern World*. London: Allen Lane.

Fergusson, Niall (2004). *Colossus: The Rise and Fall of the American Empire*. London: Allen Lane.

Fowden, Garth (1993). *Empire to Commonwealth: Consequences of Monotheism in Late Antiquity*. Princeton: Princeton University Press.

Fuller, Graham E. (2010). *A World Without Islam*. New York: Little, Brown and Company.

Goldberg, David Theo and Ato Quayson (eds) (2002). *Relocating Postcolonialism*. Oxford: Blackwell Publishing.

Gray, John (2003). *Al-Qaeda and What it Means to be Modern*. London: Faber and Faber.

Hall, Stuart (1992). 'The West and the Rest: Discourse and Power', in Stuart Hall and Bram Gieben (eds), *Formations of Modernity: Understanding Modern Society An Introduction*. Cambridge: Polity Press, 275–320.

Harvey, David (2003). *The New Imperialism*. Oxford: Oxford University Press.

Hesse, Barnor (2011). 'Self-Fulfilling Prophecy: The Postracial Horizon', *South Atlantic Quarterly*, 110.1: 155–78.

Hodgson, Marshall (1974). *The Venture of Islam: Conscience and History in a World Civilization, vol. 1: The Classical Age of Islam*. Chicago: University of Chicago Press.

Howe, Stephen (2002). *Empire: A Very Short Introduction*. Oxford: Oxford University Press.

Kaegi, Walter (2003). *Heraclius, Emperor of Byzantium*. Cambridge: Cambridge University Press.

Krenn, Michael L. (1998). *Race and US Foreign Policy During the Cold War*. New York: Garland Press.

Mann, Michael (1988 [1986]). *The Sources of Social Power, vol. 1: A History of Power from the Beginning to A.D. 1760*. Cambridge: Cambridge University Press.

McGowan, John (2007). *American Liberalism: An Interpretation for Our Time*. Chapel Hill: University of North Carolina Press.

Mignolo, Walter D. (2000). *Local Histories/Global Designs: Coloniality, Subaltern Knowledges, and Border Thinking.* Princeton: Princeton University Press.

Morris, Ian (2009). 'The Greater Athenian State', in Ian Morris and Walter Scheidel (eds), *The Dynamics of Ancient Empires: State Power from Assyria to Byzantium.* New York: Oxford University Press, 99–177.

Parsons, Timothy (2010). *The Rule of Empires: Those Who Built Them, Those Who Endured Them, and Why They Always Fall.* Oxford: Oxford University Press.

Pitts, Jennifer (2000). 'Empire and Democracy: Tocqueville and the Algeria Question', *Journal of Political Philosophy,* 8.3: 295–318.

Richter, Melvin (1963). 'Tocqueville on Algeria', *The Review of Politics,* 25.3: 362–98.

Sayyid, S. (2010). 'Thinking Through Islamophobia', in S. Sayyid and Vakil Abdool-Karim (eds), *Thinking through Islamophobia: Global Perspectives.* New York: Columbia University Press, 1–4.

Sayyid, S. and Barnor Hesse (2008). 'Narrating the Postcolonial Political and the Immigrant Imaginary', in N. Ali, V. S. Kalra, and S. Sayyid (eds), *A Postcolonial People: South Asians in Britain.* New York: Columbia University Press, 13–31.

Schulze, Reinhard (2000). *A Modern History of the Islamic World.* New York: I. B. Tauris.

Taagepera, Rein (1978). 'Size and Duration of Empires: Systematics of Size', *Social Science Research,* 7: 108–27.

Time Magazine (1979). 'Iran: Crescent of Crisis', *Time Magazine,* 15 January.

Tyner, J. A. and R. J. Kruse, II (2004). 'The Geopolitics of Malcolm X', *Antipode,* 36.1: 24–42.

Venn, Couze (2006). *The Postcolonial Challenge: Towards Alternative Worlds.* London: Sage Publications.

Young, Robert J. C. (2001). *Postcolonialism: An Historical Introduction.* Oxford: Blackwell Publishing.

CHAPTER 6

....

HEGEL, EMPIRE, AND ANTI-COLONIAL THOUGHT

....

TIMOTHY BRENNAN

It is thus not too far-fetched to suggest that one could easily recast the story of post-war French philosophy (and recent American literary theory and criticism) as the story of Hegelianism by other means.

(Barnett 1998: 25)[1]

INTRODUCTION

....

We are, according to some, experiencing a 'vigorous ... Hegel revival' (Jameson 2009: 3). This return has been marked by a series of specifically postcolonial imperatives, not only in the obvious case of Susan Buck-Morss's *Hegel, Haiti, and Universal History* (2008), or Slavoj Žižek's neo-Hegelian writings on terrorist violence, the bombing of Serbia, and Islamophobia, but also in a whole array of scholarship in the last couple of decades that has set out to establish the relevance of critical theory— and Hegel's central place in it—to the study of empire (see for example Bartolovich 2002; Ganguly 2001, 2010; Kruger 2007; Losurdo 2004; Noyes 2003; Vásquez-Arroyo 2008). My colleagues in this section have variously addressed the imperial past via geography, history, social theory, and anthropology. My own contribution will be via *philosophy*—not 'theory', however, which I take to be distinctive only in its scattered, often idiosyncratic borrowings from or recombinations of earlier philosophical positions freed from their textual specificity. My aim, in part, is to get beyond the habit of excluding certain philosophical traditions in theory, and instead to revisit them as open questions.

---

[1] As Jon Stewart puts it in *The Hegel Myths and Legends*, 'the tradition that is inaugurated after Hegel is most accurately understood not as a new beginning or a radical break with the past but rather as something continuous with what preceded it' (1991: 307).

The Hegelian tradition is certainly one of these, perhaps the most significant of all, and it has a famously vexed relationship to the field. For postcolonial studies has always been deeply divided politically; there is no such thing as 'postcolonialism', in other words— the unitary formation that a few critics have tried to depict in arguing for a unique and coherent philosophical and political outlook. There are, instead, unstable alliances with clashing objectives, sharing only their resistance to empire and a commitment to tell a more inclusive, more truly global story. The war over Hegel could not be more central to the past and future of postcolonial studies itself—where the field came from and what it deliberately excludes. At different times and in different places, Hegel has been accused of an unsavoury deification of the state; of uncritically defending bourgeois property relations; of being a philosophical idealist; of overrating the internal life of an unprob-lematic, heroic subject; of adopting a coercive concept of universality; of imposing a reprehensible concept of historical *telos*; and of infamously conflating differences by way of a quasi-theological 'absolute spirit'.

But as an opening gesture—to reopen the case—what if we were to rethink the matter philosophically? It is Hegel, after all, who first historicizes Kant's attempt to grasp the limits of reason, and to move the static, a priori categories that have such great descrip-tive force in Kant into a dynamic intersubjective drama of self and alien other (Kainz 1996: 60).[2] It is Hegel who deploys, and in this form invents, a language of movement and volatility that implicitly disrupts accepted categories of social and natural status, and refuses to accept the ontological authority of the powerful and the powerless locked in an eternal, binary relationship. And it is Hegel who brings a geopolitical conscious-ness into the discourse of philosophical modernity, yoking together the destinies of centre and periphery by establishing the global nature of the historical encounter and by exposing the complicity between civilizational rhetoric and economic entwinement (Hegel 1977: 228–40; Hegel 1991: 245–9, 341–60; see also Part II of this volume). This powerful combination of ideas did not simply spring to life, as Hegel sardonically notes in *Phenomenology of Spirit* (1807), by way of 'absolute insight' in the reclusive lair of the philosopher-genius (1977: 574). It had a parentage, and along with the most immediate influences of Fichte and Schelling, whose hold on Hegel has been tirelessly commented on, there is a deeper borrowing of tropes of conflictual history, epic colonial migrations, and the marvel of the first laws that guides his gestures, especially in *Philosophy of Right* (1821). I would contend that these tropes come from Giambattista Vico, who has played a small—perhaps insufficient—role in postcolonial studies to date.[3]

---

[2]   See for example, his *Lectures on the Philosophy of History*: '[For Kant] outside us there are things-in-themselves devoid of space and time, while inside us there is a space that is not a space for anything, and a time which is not a time for any particular thing. What Kant fails to realize is that the universality of space and time does not prevent them from being *external* universals' (quoted in Kainz 1996: 60).

[3]   Edward Said's well-known attractions to Vico have, for the most part, been confined to two essays and to the final chapter of his critical study of modernist 'rupture' in *Beginnings* (1998). But they underlie a number of motifs in *Orientalism* (1978) as well, above all Vico's refusal to give primacy to any one race and his 'will and intention'—as Said puts it—to arrive at a brand of humanism based on a poetic (literary-critical) reading of human prehistory.

I am proceeding, then, from the premise that there has not just been a failure to recognize the affinities between Hegelian philosophy and anti-colonial theory, but also an
active effort to demote or marginalize the German philosopher—to 'overcome Hegel', as
Judith Butler puts it, or to perform a 'detour' away from Hegel, as Althusser advocated
much earlier (Butler 1999; Althusser 1976: 134). Gilles Deleuze puts it most bluntly:
'I most detested Hegelianism and dialectics' (1995: 6). Or consider the most telling
instance, because the most casual, in Spencer and Krauze's *Introducing Hegel*—one of a
widely read series of philosophical primers in 'graphic guide' form—which improbably
declares that 'one could write an intellectual history of our century without mentioning
Hegel' (Spencer and Krauze 1996: 157).[4]

Clarifying inheritances often involves factoring in this kind of antipathy, and viewing
antipathy itself as having a more than occasional relationship to theory, being rather a
defining part of it. This is presumably what Domenico Losurdo has in mind when he
writes that:

> The political history of interpretations has nothing to do with the 'history of effects'
> (*Wirkungsgeschichte*) so dear to Gadamer's hermeneutics. Yes, he does replace, by
> way of a truly priceless conciliatory strategy, the notion of a 'misunderstanding' with
> that of a 'dialogue' articulated between critics and text in various ways. However,
> the manner in which he disregards the notion of actual contradiction and the
> socio-political dimension of the hermeneutic debate is no less radical than the
> historiography we are criticizing here. (2004: 31)

In other words, political differences contribute an additional factor to the complexities of productive misreadings; the wilful occlusion of possibilities is one aspect of the
hermeneutic process that is not captured—is in fact obscured—by an aleatory reading
based on the invention of semantic indeterminacy.

Since we are speaking here of postcolonial studies, what of non-western philosophy,
which has at times played a prominent role within it? What for example of the African
vernacular thought of Wole Soyinka, or of those aspects of African philosophy treated
in important anthologies by Emmanuel Chukwudi Eze, Pieter Coetzee, and A. P. J.
Roux, among others, or in the pioneering work of Robert Farris Thompson? Similarly,

---

[4] Spencer and Krauze contend that Hegel was never very popular outside Berlin and that
Hegelianism remained a 'minority perspective' in a Germany dominated by Neo-Kantianism and
romanticism. This statement is partly valid, though only in a highly qualified sense, and is truer of
the mid- to late nineteenth century than the twentieth, which is presumably the 'our century' they are
referring to. They fail to mention the role of Hegelianism in the positivism that emerged from Hegel's
follower, Ludwig Feuerbach; the meteoric rise of social democracy in the political arena; or the effects of
Hegelian Marxism on the labour movement, on twentieth-century aesthetics, on *Kulturkritik*, and on the
disciplines of anthropology and sociology, which left-Hegelianism virtually invented. Only by restricting
Hegel to a school of academic philosophy can it be said that it dissipated, and even then, only until
neo-Hegelians appeared on the scene like Georg Lasson, Hermann Nohl in the interwar period, and of
course Georg Lukács. After that, Hegelianism of various sorts can be said to dominate philosophical
thinking in the century, as the Barnett epigraph suggests.

in syncretic neo-African philosophy in the Americas, we can find modes of address very different from the Continental traditions, in the studies of, among several others, Alfred Métraux, Lydia Cabrera, Fernando Ortiz, and Joan Dayan. Then there is the matter of religious philosophy, the role of which in recent criticism should not be discounted (see Abeysekara in Part IV of this volume): the influence of eastern traditions of dialectics, for instance, which shaped Mao's writings on peasant revolt, or the effects of *dvaita* and *advaita* philosophy, in their turn, which can be felt in the work of seminal Indian thinkers like M. K. Gandhi and Rabindranath Tagore. More recently, versions of religious thought outside the Continental tradition, or in tension with it, have been evident: examples here include Hinduism (which plays a significant part in the Heideggerian phase of Subaltern Studies), Islam in today's Secularism Studies, Zionism in a variety of academic contexts, the role of Jewish hermeneutic thought in deconstruction and Benjamin criticism, the influence of deistic Christianity on American Studies, and so forth. Even in Europe itself, the term 'Continental' ignores the significant Anglo-American contribution to philosophy, including positivism, British empiricism, analytic philosophy, and pragmatism.

The philosophical traditions deriving from Hegel, though, still retain their primacy—and this also means the anti-Hegelian (or differently Hegelian) core of what we today call 'theory'. This is in part because none of these ideas enter the humanities unaffected by the western traditions of philosophy; as Jean-Luc Nancy puts it, seemingly self-evidently, Hegel is 'the inaugural thinker of the contemporary world' (2002: 3). But even here we find a glaring paradox; for despite popular assumptions to the contrary, it is Hegel rather than, say, Husserl or Nietzsche, who gives an explicit theoretical space to non-western thought, and who provides an opening for scholars to explore such sources seriously. In *Phenomenology of Spirit*, for example, Hegel relativizes Christianity beyond recognition in section VII ('Religion'), tracing in anthropological fashion its rituals to pagan antecedents, and portraying Christ as an allegorical rendering of the necessary embodiment of the Spirit as 'subject'. Here, the entire conception of the Trinity is turned into a shadow of the workings of Mind in vivid passages, the primary purpose of which is to reveal that what Hegel means by 'God' is human self-consciousness (1977: 549). *Phenomenology of Spirit*, we should not forget, is the book in which Hegel excoriates the Enlightenment (he is thinking primarily of Spinoza) for its superficial rejection of religious faith as mere superstition, and who urges us to appreciate the counter-logics of the world's religions on their own terms—to recognize their profound philosophical achievement (1977: 487–581). In his *Lectures on the Philosophy of History*, meanwhile, he is very clear about saying that spirit or 'mind' is only a development of an idea invented in the Orient during those long millennia in which Europe was irrelevant, and he remarks that German culture relies for its thinking on the extraordinary early metaphysics of Vedantic philosophy. These fundamentally Herderian (and Vichian) points place Hegel within an intellectual lineage which is, to my knowledge, wholly neglected in postcolonial studies, and which provide some of the earliest justifications for treating seriously the non-Continental and non-western traditions of thought I outlined above, locating them within a common vision of the imperial past.

In this chapter, however, I have chosen to focus on Hegel's *Philosophy of Right*. Why this particular book? First, because it is Hegel's clearest political statement, proving important, even formative, for the thinking of those critics of empire that followed in his wake. For example, Marx's response to Hegel's study of Right (1844) establishes some of the principal motifs of relevance to postcolonial theory, suggesting why Marxism was able to produce the ideological armature, imagery, and analytical techniques of the first global movements against imperialism in the early twentieth century (Marx 1989). Second, because there is a tendency in the United States and Europe today to seek political guidance in, on the one hand, the philosophy of antiquity and, on the other, the Dutch or English Enlightenment.[5] Hegel, by contrast, is unthinkable without the French Revolution, his inspiration. Indeed, I would go so far as to suggest that there is an unstated political logic to those many rejections of Hegel today (Althusserian, Deleuzian, Derridean, Foucauldian) which seek to find their inspiration in a political theory earlier than, and so not informed by, that revolution. For thinkers such as these, the French Revolution raises uncomfortable issues of popular insurrection, active organizational forms, and militant agency that confound many of their emphases on the need to work in the interstices, on the powers of individual rather than institutional sovereignty, and on the ethical risks of representing others. Third, because it is most clearly in *Philosophy of Right* that Hegel brings the quotidian, practical, and visceral aspects of social life into philosophy; where all the dialectical language refined in his earlier theory reappears; and where its stakes are most clearly seen as they are applied to problems of labour, ownership, law, slavery, colonization, and political organizations. Fourth, because the characteristic slippage in contemporary political discourse from the political to the ethical (one of the features of our post-political age, not merely in the managerial emphases of neoliberalism but within radical theory itself), is anticipated and headed off by Hegel, who calls this ethics 'morality' and distinguishes it from a higher order of political commitment to the social, which he calls 'ethical life' (*Sittlichkeit*). Fifth, because *Philosophy of Right* is a late work, and therefore comes from that part of Hegel's career when he is typically seen to have become complacent and conservative, and even to have become an apologist for the Prussian state—thereby making it instructive to see the degree to which this is untrue, and to witness what I would argue is the consistency of his message with younger, more obviously liberationist, work. Sixth, because it is in this book above all that one can see that our assumptions about what Marx superseded in Hegel is often found in Hegel himself, and that what are commonly seen as the Marxist revisions of Hegel are often original Hegelian positions. And finally, because it is in *Philosophy of Right* that we see an unusual, highly original defence of the state form that is explicitly

---

[5.] Examples here include the many references to Attic Greece in Heidegger's essays on the world picture, the work of art, and 'dwelling' in the earth, as well as in Arendt's political philosophy; to Roman law in the political theory of Giorgio Agamben; or the uses of Polybius in Negri. In the second case, consider the arguments of Althusser and Deleuze that Spinoza was not simply an Enlightenment rationalist but a radical materialist and a revolutionary—a view that has achieved significant contemporary purchase.

divorced from any particular state. This knotty problem of state authority, coercive means, and legal restrictions more than any other vexes our current thinking about politics and theory in the humanities. As I have argued elsewhere, this thinking generally expresses itself in terms of an 'anarchist sublime' taking its cue from Nietzschean positions, which is to say from an aesthetic and bohemian space with an unexpected bearing on the colonial discourse of its time (Brennan 2010: 34–49; see also Brennan 2006: x–xiii, 145–232; Holub 1998).

It has become clear in the age of Ben Bernanke and Henry Paulson that it is not the state but the corporation that today assumes the unelected prerogatives of government, leaving the state paradoxically as the only leverage against privatization. Corporate power has reached this degree of strength only by taking over the state, as was once the dream of its Marxist nemeses. This point is exactly the one Hegel presciently makes in *Philosophy of Right* in discussing the growing dangers to life and art posed by an unregulated market (1977: 196–202; see also Hegel 1975a: 193–4). A strange convergence seems to exist between the book's anticipatory insights and its present rejected status, as though the one entailed the other and had a necessary relationship to it. In what follows, I want to give a possible reason why.

THE SUBJECT, THE HUMAN, THE STATE

Anti-colonial discourse begins by recognizing the other. It is in *Philosophy of Right* that the concept of the other is elaborated in the form of a political realism that is at the same time ethically ambitious and optimistic. As Hegel phrases it: 'While I *preserve* my subjectivity in implementing my ends ... in the course of this objectifying them I *at the same time* supersede this subjectivity in its *immediacy*, and hence in its character as my individual subjectivity' (1991: 112). In other words, my own subjecthood is null and void unless it grounds its life in the difference of the subject independent of my will (the other). Hegel proceeds to derive from this observation a series of 'oughts' (the 'good', the 'bad', conscience, obligation, duty, responsibility), but not in a normative fashion. These 'oughts' are neither based on religious or traditional moral grounds, nor are they the result of the imposition of the will of the sovereign; rather, Hegel derives them from what he calls the 'truth' of the concept of will. This is a crucial point, one often lost in the critique of system philosophies. Where this critique tends to see Hegel as a prudish moralizer, what is forgotten is that the persuasive links he establishes between apparently unlike dimensions (politics and ethics, self and other) are enabled only by his argument's systematic character, which links by incremental steps the processes of mind to law, communities, and associations. Self-realization is both a coming-to-understanding of what I am and a *realizing* of the self in the act of making my essential character as will determinate and external: 'my soul ... and my body are not separated ... I can withdraw into myself ... but this is *my* will; *for others*, I am in my body' (48).

For Hegel, the state is not simply a mechanism for enforcing abstract rights; it also has to agree in content with the 'inner necessity' of the good. These examples illustrate what Hegel means by 'universal'. What gradually sinks in is that the entire motivation for his methodology of proceeding from the abstract to the concrete is to give authority to political *opposition*. For Hegel, the poor are not poor naturally, but because they have been abused; they are the victims of injustice. This, I want to suggest, is where there has been a fundamental misunderstanding at work in Hegel's reception: for what appears to be a rejection on the grounds of his conservative, oversystematizing, and indeed annoyingly abstract dimensions is in fact a flight from the radical political implications of his work. Perhaps it is not Hegel's being an impediment to radical political change that is the cause of his rejection, but rather his enabling of a radical political change in which theory is true only when it becomes *reality*, for it cannot be true only in *thought*.

Recht ('right') in *Philosophy of Right* has various meanings. It can mean my rights to freedom, as in the phrase 'human rights'; or it can refer to law; or it can signify 'what is right' as opposed to what is wrong. Hegel's book can be seen, then, as being at once about the basis for social interaction as such (the rules, limitations, and *modi vivendi* of individuals in a collectivity); about the political and juridical forms possible when subjects attempt to make sense of, to arrange, or to codify this basis of social interaction; and about the principles that undergird these attempts. All three dimensions of the inquiry exist at the same time and are inextricable from one another.

Hegel's idealism (as distinct from materialism), though real, is of a special type: in his lexicon, for example, the 'Idea' (as distinct from the 'concept') only manifests itself in existence, in practicality, and in realization (1). His term for this is *actualization*, which does not simply mean the acting upon of an idea, or the turning of the idea into a physical presence, but the bringing of an idea to its completion by allowing its inner necessity to express itself. *Recht*, to put this in another way, is *the right I give myself through my own determination in the presence of the fact of others*. Agency is philosophically established on the grounds of subjectivity, but only in the sense that 'the subjective will determines itself as correspondingly objective, and hence as truly concrete' (106). The subject is 'the series of its actions' (124). What Hegel is emphasizing, in short, is a non-arbitrary arbitrariness. There is no 'out there' that steps into the human realm to provide an unshakeable foundation or to deliver a chiselled tablet of divine commands that establishes our right to be free. Right has no external source for its validation. Rather, we produce it from inside ourselves, and the will is—in a dialectical move—free only in so far as it demands freedom as its *right*.

The human being is, in Hegel's terms, 'wholly indeterminate'. He/she 'stands above his drives and can determine and posit them as [his/her] own'. Drives are 'part of nature', he readily concedes, but 'to posit this "I" depends upon my will, which therefore cannot appeal to the fact that the drive is grounded in nature' (11). In other words, the charge (made often enough) that Hegel is coercively normative, or that he polices desire, is almost exactly inverted. For rather than Spinoza or, later, Nietzsche—both of whom stand for the imprisonment of the subject in his/her drives and who affirm the complete absence of free will—it is Hegel who invokes the possibilities and open-endedness of actions implied by the freedom of will, which is 'wholly indeterminate'.

THE ANTI-COLONIAL PER SE

Hegel's account of colonization in *Philosophy of Right*, albeit brief, vividly evokes the *Machtpolitik* of market forces seeking a *deus ex machina* in order to resolve domestic overproduction (247–8). 'Despite an excess of wealth, civil society is not wealthy enough', Hegel laments. Labourers, robbed of their self-sufficiency and dignity, are drawn beyond the confines of their home country in search of the means required for subsistence (245). Earlier in the same text, Hegel had voiced his opposition to slavery for being contrary to the personhood of property, hence destructive of ethical existence—a phrase he spends over half of the book exploring under the name of '*Sittlichkeit*' (57, 66) or, in his idiosyncratic usage, the 'system of ethical life'. Hegel, in other words, is anticipating here what later commentators would eventually take for granted: that even if one were to take the dubious position that colonialism was not a direct source of European enrichment (as many critics of imperialism, including Marxists, have at times contended), nevertheless it brought out the worst in the peoples of the home country (Brenner 1977: 66). The colonial territories become a 'vast open field for acts of individual violence', he complains, a violence that is typically curtailed by laws prevailing at home. In this way, the colonies enable the endangered market to survive by extramural means—a view that Carl Siger would later make famous in *Essai sur la colonisation* (1907) (M. Chailley Bert, quoted in Siger 1907: 173).

Dispassionately delivered in a scientific tone, Hegel's tight linkage of the market and colonialism have been interpreted at times as a justification for colonialism, as though he were self-evidently in support of the absolute rights of private property. But if that were the case, why would he consider *bürgerliche Gesellschaft* ('bourgeois society') to be the malign author of exploitation; and why would he treat the unregulated acquisition of property as a form of theft, as he explicitly does in *Philosophy of Right*? At any rate, he concludes his brief comments on colonialism unambiguously: 'the liberation of the colonies itself proves to be of the greatest advantage to the mother state, just as the emancipation of slaves is of the greatest advantage to the master' (248).

Along with *Lectures on the Philosophy of History*, *Philosophy of Right* is, for all that, the book of Hegel's most frequently singled out as being offensive to the decentring of European value, giving voice to the marginal or protesting the legacies of colonial injustice. In fact, I have chosen to focus on this text in part for that very reason, although I should add that in the nature of Hegel's cumulative method of working—his tendency throughout his career to elaborate earlier arguments in new words, submitting them to different fields of depth and different structures in a process his commentators describe as the Hegelian 'system'—the core of his case in *Philosophy of Right* had already appeared as early as the Jena *System of Ethics* (1802–3) and especially in those middle-to-late sections of *Phenomenology* devoted to 'Spirit' (Hegel 1988; see also Hegel 1977: 437–85).

Still, *Philosophy of Right* is a special case since it is here, in the supposedly late, conservative Hegel (in a book published by Hegel in his own lifetime, and thus free of the dubious veracity of student lecture notes, which play a large if unacknowledged role in the wording of some the most egregious passages of the *Lectures in the History of Philosophy*) that one finds a direct treatment of what troubles contemporary theory most when reckoning with the left Hegelian tradition. This has always been the sticking point for liberal thought when it confronts the Marxism that apprenticed itself to Hegel's philosophy: namely, Hegel's bold and in some ways paradoxical defence of order, law, and the delimiting potential of the state as a curb on actions harmful to the social whole. These curbs would include what today is called 'regulation' but that Hegel himself also saw in ethical terms. It is here that we find the argument most clearly expressed that 'freedom' can be actualized only in a sovereignty that is governmental, not just individual. Hegel saw government, as did Vico before him, as a remarkably difficult and fortunate human achievement, not unlike the invention of fire by early *Homo sapiens*. Anthropologically—seen in terms of the transition of humans from bestiality to civilization—it represented a break or leap into a higher mode of existence; and only by tracing its gradual coming-to-form could one understand its current necessity. To put this in a related way, this problematic imposition from above was actually a collective creation, repressive and self-serving in many of its actual manifestations, but vital as a *potential* form that could be bent to more welcome ends and, exactly in this sense, 'rational'.

To express this idea in the manner most fitting for postcolonial theory—the manner embraced by the anti-colonial intellectuals of the immediate post-World War II era—his position is that freedom must be able to *defend itself*. This sovereignty-as-state nevertheless raised a series of ethical conundrums that Hegel works out over about two-thirds of the book. *Philosophy of Right*, then, can be seen among other things as a book of ethics; but it is not one that displaces politics as its more 'responsible' alternative, rather one that demonstrates the impossibility of being ethical without being political. To be good, for Hegel, requires having the means to effect. Politics ceases to become, as in Hobbes or later Nietzsche, the police—it does not descend into a brutal *Macht* politics pure and simple.

The book's contribution to anti-colonial thought can be seen most clearly in what it inspired and made possible. These are primarily the leads Marx followed while critiquing *Philosophy of Right*, supposing—not always successfully—that he was departing from it. It is, in fact, the only book of Hegel's that Marx systematically addresses, and some of the explosive anti-colonial implications of Marxism found in *Capital* and *Grundrisse*—which would provide inspiration for the anti-imperial movements of the period between 1905 and 1933, and then again in the former colonies themselves from 1947–79—are found in gestation in Marx's critique of the book, which, following Hegel himself, is conceived as a domestic *German* problem and not only a colonial one.[6] This

---

6. These leads include the international dimension of resistance, the necessarily global scale of capitalist accumulation, the creation of new taste markets in the colonies, the imperial strategy of exporting capital, the intentional underdevelopment of peripheral economies, the concept of wage slavery, the cosmopolitan character of (world) literature, and the ongoing war between the country and the city.

aspect of mutual entanglement and shared destiny permeates the writing of both figures and helps define their thinking. Hegel implicitly removes the conceptual barriers
between white and black, metropolitan and peripheral, by portraying colonialism as a
repercussive system, where the agent makes him/herself a victim by violating the norms
carefully established in their own polity.[7]

HEGEL'S POSTCOLONIAL RECEPTION

Dissenters within the field of postcolonial studies—those who have argued for a more
materialist approach to subjectivity, identity, and power—have been accused at times
of simply misreading the field; of failing to see that postcolonialism's critique was never
about the concrete project of dismantling colonialism but about the inscription of imperialism into philosophy; not about the political institutions of colonialism but about the
structure of colonialist thought; not about the mechanics of power but about the language and philosophy of empire. This would be another reason for turning to Hegel,
if only up to a point, since his work insists that these two realms of inquiry cannot be
binarized in this way; that they always implicate one another. By extrapolating from
his position, we are forced to consider whether this separation is itself an example of
the imperial 'inscription' often alluded to in postcolonial studies: a division of labour
that tears into two halves what the theory of totality expressed poignantly as a coherent
individual-universal.

Two influential attacks on Hegel from within postcolonial studies—by Tsenay
Serequeberhan and Robert Bernasconi, respectively—are worth looking at here in
order to allay the fear that I may be speaking at a tangent or overshooting the mark.
Serequeberhan explicitly takes up *Philosophy of Right*, proposing that Hegel's epistemological enthusiasm for the Idea justifies the enslavement of 'Negroes' and can be
distilled as an equation: 'the Idea (*Idee*) = colonialism'. He goes on to argue that Hegel
believed in the 'inherent desirability' of western 'colonial expansion' (2007: 64, 65,
93). Avoiding the more common procedure of alluding to Hegel negatively in passing, Serequeberhan methodically works through the logic and arguments of the text's
account of property, concluding that colonial expansion, seen by Hegel as a 'paradoxical contingent effect of the inner workings of Modernity', is for all that 'nicely dressed
up and packaged as the ontological necessity inscribed in the self-actualization of

---

7. The late sections of *Philosophy of Right* make this especially clear: 'In existence [*Dasein*] this *negative*
relation [*Beziehung*] of the state to itself thus appears as the relation of *another* to *another*, as if the
negative were something *external*. The existence [*Existenz*] of this negative relation therefore assumes the
shape of an event, of an involvement with contingent occurrences coming *from without*. Nevertheless,
this negative relation is the state's *own* highest moment—its actual infinity as the ideality of everything
finite within it' (§323, p. 360). Hegel specifically notes in the next entry that any 'sacrifice' demanded by
state sovereignty not be 'simply equated with civil society' (that is, the economy of private property).

Weltgeist.[8] Hegel, he argues, believes that 'a person has the right to take possession of "any and everything"' (2007: 67).

I have already discussed why this reading runs contrary to Hegel's meaning; in fact, he places severe constraints on owning, and regales owning for its own sake. But it is best to go beyond direct refutation to cast the argument in its broader context. 'Civil society' (*bürgerliche Gesellschaft*), as Hegel meant it, was the parallel power and authority of the market, the world of business, and the organizations that attend them. In this context, he analyses what he calls the 'system of needs'—work, the estates of trade and industry, colonization; justice, law, police, the corporation. These are the categories under which he organizes his argument; and this recognition on his part of a dual power situation in regard to the authority that governs society leads him, at times, to the conclusion that the market undermines values and destroys lives. He is the first modern philosopher to build a theory of *labour* into his system: episte-mology, ethics, ontology, and aesthetics are all intimately bound up with the question of labour for Hegel. It is Hegel, not Marx, who is the first to describe the 'alienation' (*Entäusserung*) of labour.

It is in *Philosophy of Right* that Hegel sets out to redefine the elements of business life, taking its terms back from the economists. He denies that property is sacred, that it must be protected even over human life; on the contrary, he argues that everyone must have property, especially the property-less, for without it their personality cannot be realized. For to possess objects as one's own is to hasten the reckoning with what one is not, and therefore to define the will by way of negation in the sense that that which has no will is owned. Notice how Hegel's argument is logically derived from earlier parts of his system, which is precisely what relieves it of its mere normativity; instead, its inexorable persua-sive force is the result of its being decoupled from individual choice by way of minute accretions in an argumentative process that coheres only as a system. The contemporary sensibility that informs this approach is clearest, perhaps, in Hegel's sceptical assessment of 'public opinion', the new authority just then being summoned by the representatives of an illusory market choice (1991: 318).[9] His account of colonization itself in the book, though glancing (248), is an accurate description of the brutality behind market forces and of the slavery upon which they depend (57).

[8.] Scholarly objections can be raised about Serequeberhan's project as well. For example, he enlists Herbert Marcuse in support of his argument that 'Hegel reproduces, on the level of thought, the imperious relations that Europe imposes on the non-European world'. Actually, Marcuse in *Reason and Revolution* (1986: 176) quotes Hegel to opposite effect, extensively commenting on Hegel's *Verhandlungen in der Versammlung der Landstände des Königreichs Württemberg im Jahr 1815 und 1816* in *Schriften zur Politik und Rechtsphilosophie* (199). Marcuse summarizes Hegel's views as follows: 'the old privileges of the estates have about as much basis in modern society as have 'sacrificial murder, slavery, feudal despotism, and countless other infamies.'

[9.] 'Public opinion therefore deserves to be *respected* as well as *despised*—despised for its concrete consciousness and expression, and respected for its essential basis, which appears in that concrete consciousness only in a more or less obscure manner … the first formal condition of achieving anything great or rational, either in actuality or in sciences, is to be independent of public opinion' (Hegel 1991: 355).

I stress this point since in recent readings of Hegel—notably Fredric Jameson's *Valences of the Dialectic* (2009)—the 'system' character of his work is sharply criticized, and the legacies of Franco-German 'theory' (as distinct from Hegelian 'philosophy') are held up as ethically superior for being open-ended and resistant to resolution (46–7). Serequeberhan falls into a curious literalism in reading Hegel because, philosophically, he is resistant to the system character of Hegel's mode of presentation. Hegel's attempt to explain the logic of the actual is mistaken for a theodicy of conquest, and the consequences are missed of Hegel's deliberate appropriation of 'ethics' for politics in the sense that Right as a universal ground of non-cynical political activity is, at the other end, portrayed as useless if not actualized by the organized force of a state. When Hegel writes, for example, that 'poverty is a problem for civil society because it is a necessary consequence of the workings of civil society that certain individuals be reduced to poverty', he is not justifying civil society, but saying that colonialism is the inevitable outgrowth of capitalist modernity, and that this is unacceptable.[10] Serequeberhan avers that Hegel wishes to exclude the poor from society, making them ineligible for justice (2007: 78), and yet Hegel defends theft by the poor (1991: 127), placing it higher than the right of secure property since the poor have been done a wrong and because 'what is law may differ in content from what is right in itself' (1991: 212). A person's own body, and the means to keep it alive, are possessions for Hegel, the very paradigm of property. To realize the right to property in this sense is in effect to curtail the right of the powerful to possess anything that would interfere with another's bodily right, not just to physical survival but to freedom.

Serequeberhan declares that his reading of Hegel is 'de-structive' in the sense of being based on the term *Destruktion* from Heidegger's *Being and Time* (1927) (Heidegger 1962: part 1, sec. 6). 'Such a de-structive reading', he writes, 'is a radical exegesis firmly implanted in the text that undermines the text from within and in terms of the central notions on which the text in question is grounded and in so doing reveals the hidden impulses articulated in the text' (2007: 28). I already alluded to this dubious practice of reading-as-creative-misreading when I quoted Losurdo on Gadamer (see my Introduction). Here it might well be wondered why, if one were only revealing what was hidden in the text itself, one would want to appeal to a word that suggests a violent dismantling, a taking apart, and implies a prior distrust and disparagement. And why, in a book that quite rightly speaks of 'the *beguiled* and *beguiling* service rendered European colonial expansion by the occidental tradition of philosophy' (93; emphasis mine), would one want to apprentice oneself to Heidegger or take him as one's guide in exposing the complicit Hegel? On the one side, we see a partisan of the French Revolution, an opponent of religious dogma, and a critic of landed property; on the other, a partisan of a genocidal one-party state founded on racial hierarchies whose *telos* is foreign conquest and enslavement and, more to the point,

---

[10.] The contradiction made so much of in Marx is forecast by Hegel himself: 'Work becomes mechanical until finally man is able to step aside and install machines in his place' (1991: §198).

whose philosophy disrupts agency and displaces the human from the conceptualization of being.

Similar problems arise in what is probably the best-known assault on Hegel within postcolonial theory: Robert Bernasconi's 'Hegel at the Court of the Ashanti' (1998). It is impossible to disagree with some of the accusations in the essay, and Bernasconi is undoubtedly effective at demonstrating Hegel's (or his students') redeployment of the offensive language and attitudes of sensationalist travel literature. But three aspects of the essay seem much more doubtful. First, Bernasconi does not raise the interpretative problem of achroamatic texts in general (that is, ones based on the notes of students and not written by the author him- or herself), nor does he clarify that the available editions of the *Lectures on the Philosophy of History* (he mentions three) are all posthumous. He notes that not all of the versions mention Africa, but does not say why. According to Duncan Forbes, Hegel taught the course five times, and kept gathering historical materials, revising his views, or simply dispensing with sections of his earlier lectures when he considered them insufficiently informed (Hegel 1975b: 5–9). Second, Bernasconi's essay is inexorably negative, overlooking those dimensions of the *Lectures on the Philosophy of History* that demonstrate cultural relativism and lend theoretical support to the decentring of Europe. For example, Hegel comments on the reliance of German culture on the innovations of Vedantic philosophy and Egypt, whose unparalleled civilization in antiquity arose from the inspirations of a kingdom founded by Ethiopians.

Egypt, says Hegel in *Science of Logic* (17), developed the mathematical sciences earlier than anyone (Hegel 1989). The anomalous relationship of Africa and Egypt in *Lectures on the Philosophy of History* has been explained, according to Bernasconi, by pointing out that Egypt is not treated as part of Africa at all by Hegel, but rather of Persia, in order to deny African cultural achievement. This is a gaffe on his part, however. Hegel's comments on Africa (as opposed to parts of Africa, like Egypt) are restricted to the Introduction only because the Introduction is dedicated to analysing *continents* geographically (he goes on to discuss North America and Asia, for instance, as a whole, without distinguishing among its various peoples or traditions). When he discusses Egypt in the next section, it is because there the organizational concept is different. The concept in that section is what survived and what did not from past empires (he argues that Egypt's 'marvels' survived, whereas Persia's did not). His discussion of Egypt in the company of other civilizations from the eastern Mediterranean world (Judea, Syria, Greece) is no more an attempt to sever egypt from Africa than to sever Greece from Europe or Syria from the near East. As I mention above, Egypt's civilization according to Hegel was prefigured and influenced by the Nubians to the south, which is still another way to appreciate that his point is not what Bernasconi ascribes to him.

Third, the essay's foundationalist thrust, which implies more than it says, strongly suggests that the reprehensible core of Hegel's lectures on history transcends that single work and instead characterizes every line of his entire oeuvre by hidden circuits of fealty. The essay title, for example, with its trope of the 'court' in which Africa is judged, is not taken from *Lectures on the Philosophy of History* but from *Philosophy of Right* (which Bernasconi conveniently fails to mention). More importantly, he fundamentally alters its meaning. The court of judgment (*Gericht*) that Hegel refers to in *Philosophy of Right* is precisely not one delivered by one people upon another, or one individual on another, as an exercise of spurious evaluation. His whole point in summoning the term is to distance himself sardonically from the contingent tastes of specific nations or races, since in the playing out of historical action, the meaning of the human can only find itself in the particular actualities that transpire in its name. What has been *done* as a way of demonstrating what humans *are*, he is saying, is the ultimate arbiter of history's meaning: 'This history of spirit is its own *deed*; for spirit is only what it does' (1991: 343).

By this flawed mode of presentation, Hegel and Hegelians are exposed as apologists for the European colonialist enterprise—not abstractly, but in practice as an actual process of conquest and subjugation. They stand condemned, not in the form of a collection of challenged statements, or in the lapses of an individual career, but in a whole lineage of thought stained by an inner complicity; and what is more, Hegel is not condemned by Bernasconi alone, nor yet by rival schools of European philosophy, but by the Ashanti, for whom he claims to be the spokesperson. We have to ask ourselves whether this kind of criticism is safely beyond the imposition of western structures of thought on Africa and its peoples—including the African scholars he cites in support—rather than precisely a product of western philosophy's immense anti-Hegelian resources, occurring as it does in a volume titled *Hegel after Derrida*. Bernasconi's suggestion to the contrary, no unanimity of opinion exists among scholars of African descent in regard to Hegel's views on colonialism and slavery. Many of Hegel's most enthusiastic supporters were and are African and Afro-Caribbean scholars and activists (see, for example, Aly Dienge 1978; Camara 2011; James 1980). The essentialism on which Bernasconi's argument is implicitly based dissolves, and the disputes he considers are not—as he suggests—based on race, but on *position*.

Hegel certainly believed that there were 'advanced' and 'backward' cultures—as did many of the independence-era intellectuals of Africa and Latin America, who continually stressed the importance of *development* (infrastructure, education, technical knowledge, literacy) to eliminate the impediments that 'backwardness' represented to their own sovereignty (Chilcote 1968; Hawkins 2010; Nyrere 1967; see also Sharp in Part II of this volume). The universalism that underlies his notion of the Absolute—to take another dimension of his thinking—was, as he himself puts it, 'world-historical', which is to say precisely *not* ethnocentric, but deliberately inclusive of a general human achievement: 'genius, talent, moral virtues, and sentiments, and piety', he writes in the *Lectures on the Philosophy of History*, are found in 'every zone, under all political constitutions and conditions' (1095). That he shared the cultural disparagement and even racism of Kant, Hume, Spinoza, and others is undeniable. That their project was to overcome the superstitions, blood-privileges, and violence of European autocracy does not excuse their fixation on reason versus the primitive or 'uncultured', but it does place it in a different light. Racism is racism, and cannot be temporized. On the other hand, the chief issue in this past for our imperial *present* should be what philosophical resources, if any, this legacy has given the anti-colonial project, and how that compares with its philosophical other.

There is a lack of balance, at the very least, in Bernasconi's argument. The hetero-doxy, not conformism, of Hegel's years of apprenticeship is neglected, and Hegel's early 'theological' writings in Berne are misperceived. He in fact indicts Christianity as the structural continuation of the tyranny of the Roman Empire, which took the Roman repression of foreign races and turned its silencing impulses 'inward' (Lukács 1966: 1–89). In the context of his attractions to the political openings provided by the French and Haitian revolutions, Hegel's intense study of Christianity in Berne ended up with his finding in Christianity an imperial impulse: a reactive mirror image of Roman repression.

But perhaps, in light of Bernasconi's critique of Hegel 'after Derrida', my response is too defensive. Today's supposedly post-Hegelian environment is, as we all know, domi-nated by poststructuralist challenges to the integrity of the subject, the viability of the human, and the false and illusory presence of speech. As a philosophical matter, privilege is given to the written, and to a peculiar, even imperious, authority; theories of know-ledge based on textuality seek to place the critic in a position of political prominence. A postcolonial reckoning with these ideas is long overdue. Can it really be denied that these familiar tenets of deconstruction derive ultimately from the early clerical writings of the great monotheisms (Judaism, Christianity, Islam)—the people of the 'book'—and find their initial authentication in the early CE among exegetes like Philo of Alexandria, rabbinical scholars, and the early fathers of the church in the eastern Mediterranean: the very laboratory and testing ground of what later became 'Europe'? How can we not recognize the devastating consequences to non-western cultural value that this subli-mation of writing, and the priority given to the written, the clerical, the rabbinical, and the hermeneutical (what Gramsci called the 'bookish', 1985: 273, 117–19, 122–3), have had over the oral and the vulgate? After all, these forms effectively diminish popular non-literary modes of artistic expression, literary realism, the vernacular, and directly didactic or educational cultural practices: in short, they persistently undervalue the aes-thetic core of the majority of work produced in the formerly and still colonized world (see Featherstone in Part III of this volume).

There is an oppressive ethno-religious weight, moreover, that lies behind their current proliferation in the academy, exacerbated by the upside-down claim that western phi-losophy is plagued by a privileging of the oral and the metaphysics of presence whereas it is the machinery of the *written* and its clerical, philological, new critical, and, finally, deconstructive fetish of the revelatory aspects of language that marks the violence of the west on the illiterate and the articulate. 'Is it conceivable', asks R. Radhakrishnan, 'that Derrida, Lacan, and Foucault may at best be distracting when applied to postcolonial-ity? Could there be other epistemic starting points for the elaboration of postcolonial complexity?' (Radhakrishnan 2003: 51). This kind of question may lie behind the shift in recent years to more recognizably militant and materialist inquiries: the recent turning away from the postcolonial emphasis of the 1980s and 1990s on texts, discourses, affect, identity, and migrancy to the more engaged and more conspicuously activist language of political movements, embattled immigrant communities, and contemporary wars (see Parts II and III of this volume).[11]

NON-EUROPE AND THE HUMAN

It was *Philosophy of Right* that inspired Marx to see Europe as stamped by its colonies and as sharing many of their features. In his response to the book, Marx curiously launches not into a discussion of 'right' and 'law' or the 'state' but into a diatribe on German 'backwardness' and the fight between the country and the city; European development abroad is seen for the first time as being intertwined with European underdevelopment at home. *The Communist Manifesto*'s brilliant descriptions of capitalism as inherently imperialist ('the discovery of America, the rounding of the Cape …') are a continuation of Marx's observations in his earlier engagement with Hegel's political theory, where he describes the mutual entanglements and interdependency of the colonies and Europe (Marx and Engels 1988 [1848]). He borrows Hegel's idea that self-realization as a species form mirrors political independence as a social need: that is, the link between the *alien* and the alienation of labour. Marx writes:

> The relation of industry, and of the world of wealth generally, to the political world is one of the chief problems of modern times … In Germany we are beginning to recognize the sovereignty of monopoly at home in order that it may be invested with sovereignty abroad. (57)

Self-realization is not possible without the enforcement mechanisms and protections of a state authority; and no state capable of representing the interests of the individuals that comprise it is possible under conditions of social backwardness. This is as true of Germany or Italy or Russia as it is of Senegal or Mexico.

The imperial present *in* the past is also a problem of critical theory, and theory—as distinct from philosophy—in the humanities is currently seeing a proliferating number of claims that we have entered a posthuman world. These claims, which inherit the same critiques of 'Man' that owe their force to the exclusion and disparagement of Hegel, have found at least three highly visible modes of expression in recent years: a posthumanism based on the figure of the animal or on the biotechnologically compromised uniqueness of the human body, and of the non-priority of a human species that has betrayed other animals by its ecological devastation and its undeserved mastery (see for example Agamben 2003; Gontier 1999; Haraway 2003; Wolfe 2003); the cybernetic triumphalism of thinking machines, and the argument that mind has now become inferior to artificial intelligence, which has separated itself entirely from human intervention,

---

[11.] Some examples of this new materialism in postcolonial theory include, for example, *Social Text*, 26.2 (2008); *Transition*, 99 (2008); and *Public Culture*, 21.1 (2009).

and now thinks for itself (Hayles 1999); and, finally, a version of the 'history of objects' that I alluded to before, what might be seen as a kind of 'green' misanthropy. In this last variant, we also find a romance with death, an act of purifying the inquiry by way of a desired oblivion of the social world as such by contemplating the happy end of the entire species (François 2007; see also Chakrabarty 2009).

Hegel's appeals to 'spirit' as a common species ground arouse suspicions of an ethnocentric imposition from above. There, too, the singularities of moments, locations, and beings seem irreducibly abstracted for service to a false and imperious European commonwealth of Mind. At such a stifling juncture, the posthuman enters as the exploder of all pretensions, clearing the path of misbegotten projects dedicated to an ever-elusive 'progress' whose very invocation sickens one as much as the human failures for which it serves as cover. The extremism of the gesture is evident, for we are no longer talking about false attributes or values of a cultural centre coercively dubbed 'universal' by Eurocentric sleight of hand—which is what the gesture effectively opposes—but about something much more far-reaching and fatal to colonized and colonizer alike—the baseline ability to think the 'human' at all. This gesture arguably contains within it a new universalism: a universally applicable absence, a blanketing global negation of the human self, which, while displacing an unwelcome hierarchical ordering of human types, eliminates every distinction among ideas, positions, beliefs, or situations, leaving nature to emerge as the ultimate quietism and final sanction for current unequal structures of power and value (see also Mount and O'Brien in Part IV of this volume).

In *this* setting, who is and who is not Eurocentric? It appears that our way of conceiving that charge is now belated. Hegel's strategy of conceptualizing the human was, I have argued, comprehensive. Despite first appearances, his depiction of the person was devoid of moralizing or religious transcendence; its colloquial idealism based itself on a self-circular, wilful act of subject-making. He described how this subject is brought along in his or her activity by inches, and according to a logic he/she effects in order to recognize a common destiny with other subjects that leads, haltingly and imperfectly, to the routine machinery of political and civic institutions as decisively communal solutions. By contrast, the discourses of the posthuman are peremptory, basing themselves on a homology with the latest theories of the metropolis's industries of science and technology. The posthuman announces itself as the only future—as the future the stubborn cannot accept because it is so *avant*, a natural future absent of will, given that even the movers and shakers of the technocratic elite do not control the global script they are busily rewriting. What better way, sensing their coming displacement by the emergent peripheral powers of China, India, and Brazil, than for these elites to re-establish their leadership *theoretically* in an act of prophetic suicide by effectively acquiescing to the claims of bioscience, informatics, and deep ecology in obliterating the human altogether? Whether this is a lament or a protest—whether it is a diagnosis of what science and a reckless corporate profit sector have forced them to conclude or whether it is a dystopian celebration that finally puts the human in its place—is, in the logic of their pastiche, impossible to detect. The return to Hegel today, at any rate, may offer a viable response to these non-options. Hegel's importance for postcolonial theory today is that he offers a persuasive intellectual portrait of the one power that can resist global inequality and stave off ecological catastrophe—the human being.

REFERENCES

Agamben, Giorgio (2003). *The Open: Man and Animal*. Stanford: Stanford University Press.

Althusser, Louis (1976). *Essays in Self-Criticism*. London: New Left Books.

Aly Dienge, Amada (1978). *Hegel, Marx, Engels et les problèmes de l'Afrique noire*. Dakar: Sankoré.

Barnett, Stuart (ed.) (1998). *Hegel after Derrida*. New York: Routledge.

Bartolovich, Crystal (2002). 'Figuring the (In)Visible as an Imperial *Weltstadt*: The Case of Benjamin's Moor', *Cultural Critique*, 52: 167–208.

Bernasconi, Robert (1998). 'Hegel at the Court of the Ashanti', in S. Barnett (ed.), *Hegel after Derrida*. New York: Routledge, 41–63.

Brennan, Timothy (2006). *Wars of Position: The Cultural Politics of Left and Right*. New York: Columbia University Press.

Brennan, Timothy (2010). 'Borrowed Light: Nietzsche and the Colonies', in V. Langbehn and M. Salama (eds), *German Colonialism: Race, the Holocaust, and Postwar Germany*. New York: Columbia University Press, 34–49.

Brenner, Robert (1977). 'The Origins of Capitalist Development: A Critique of Neo-Smithian Marxism', *New Left Review*, 104: 25–93.

Buck-Morss, Susan (2009 [2008]). *Hegel, Haiti, and Universal History*. Pittsburgh: University of Pittsburgh Press.

Butler, Judith (1999). 'Final Reflections on "Overcoming" Hegel', in *Subjects of Desire: Hegelian Reflections on Twentieth-Century France*. New York: Columbia University Press, 230–8.

Camara, Babacar (2011). *Reason in History: Hegel and Social Changes in Africa*. Lanham, Md.: Lexington Books.

Chakrabarty, Dipesh (2009). 'The Climate of History: Four Theses', *Cultural Inquiry*, 35: 197–222.

Chilcote, Ronald (1968). 'The Political Thought of Amilcar Cabral', *Journal of Modern African Studies*, 6.3: 373–88.

Deleuze, Gilles (1995). *Negotiations*, trans. M. Joughin. New York: Columbia University Press.

François, Anne-Lise (2007). *The Literature of Uncounted Experience*. Stanford: Stanford University Press.

Ganguly, Keya (2001). *States of Exception: Everyday Life and Postcolonial Identity*. Minneapolis: University of Minnesota Press.

Ganguly, Keya (2010). *Cinema, Emergence, and the Films of Satyajit Ray*. Berkeley: University of California Press.

Gontier, Thierry (1999). *L'homme et l'animal: La philosophie antique*. Paris: Presses universitaires de France.

Gramsci, Antonio (1985). 'On the Bookishness of Intellectuals', in *Selections from Cultural Writings*, ed. David Forgacs and Geoffrey Nowell-Smith, trans. William Boelhower (Cambridge, Mass.: Harvard University Press), 273, 117–19, 122–3.

Haraway, Donna (2003). *The Companion Species Manifesto: Dogs, People, and Significant Otherness*. Chicago: Prickly Paradigm Press.

Hawkins, Kirk A. (2010). *Venezuela's Chavismo and Populism in Comparative Perspective.* Cambridge: Cambridge University Press.

Hayles, Katharine (1999). *How We Became Posthuman: Virtual Bodies in Cybernetics, Literature, and Informatics.* Chicago: University of Chicago Press.

Hegel, G. W. F. (1975a). *Hegel's Aesthetics: Lectures on Fine Art,* vol. 1, trans. T. M. Knox. Oxford: Oxford University Press.

Hegel, G. W. F. (1975b). *Lectures on the Philosophy of World History,* trans. H. S. Nisbet. Cambridge: Cambridge University Press.

Hegel, G. W. F. (1977). *Phenomenology of Spirit,* trans. A. V. Miller. Oxford: Oxford University Press.

Hegel, G. W. F. (1988). *System of Ethical Life and First Philosophy of Spirit, Part III of System of Speculative Philosophy,* trans. and ed. H. S. Harris and T. M. Knox. Albany: State University of New York Press.

Hegel, G. W. F. (1989). *Hegel's Science of Logic,* trans. A. V. Miller. New York: Humanities Books.

Hegel, G. W. F. (1991). *Elements of the Philosophy of Right,* trans. and ed. A. Wood. Cambridge: Cambridge University Press.

Heidegger, Martin (1962). *Being and Time.* New York: Harper.

Holub, Robert C. (1998). 'Nietzsche's Colonialist Imagination: Nueva Germania, Good Europeanism, and Great Politics', in S. Friedrichsmeyer, S. Lennox, and S. Zantop (eds), *The Imperialist Imagination: German Colonialism and its Legacy.* Ann Arbor: University of Michigan Press, 33–50.

James, C. L. R. (1980). *Notes on Dialectic: Hegel, Marx, Lenin.* London: Allison & Busby.

Jameson, Fredric (2009). *Valences of the Dialectic.* London: Verso.

Kainz, Howard P. (1996). *An Introduction to Hegel.* Athens: Ohio University Press.

Kruger, Loren (2007). *Post-Imperial Brecht: Politics and Performance, East and South.* Cambridge: Cambridge University Press.

Losurdo, Domenico (2004). *Hegel and the Freedom of Moderns.* Durham, NC: Duke University Press.

Lukács, Georg (1966). *The Young Hegel: Studies in the Relation between Dialectics and Economics,* trans. R. Livingstone. Cambridge, Mass.: MIT Press.

Marcuse, Herbert (1986). *Reason and Revolution: Hegel and the Rise of Social Theory.* London: Routledge.

Marx, Karl (1989). 'Contribution to the Critique of Hegel's *Philosophy of Right*', in R. Tucker (ed.), *The Marx/Engels Reader.* New York: Norton, 18–36.

Marx, Karl and Friedrich Engels (1988 [1848]). *The Communist Manifesto.* New York: W. W. Norton.

Nancy, Jean-Luc (2002). *Hegel: The Restlessness of the Negative,* trans. J. Smith and S. Miller. Minnesota: University of Minnesota Press.

Noyes, John (2003). 'Hegel and the Fate of Negativity after Empire', in '*Postcolonialism Today: Theoretical Challenges and Pragmatic Issues*', Virtual Symposium. Toronto: Open Semiotics Resource Centre, 1–29.

Nyrere, Julius (1967). *The Arusha Declaration.* Dar es Salaam: Publicity Section, TANU.

Radhakrishnan, R. (2003). *Theory in an Uneven World.* Oxford: Blackwell.

Said, Edward W. (1978). *Orientalism.* New York: Vintage.

Said, Edward W. (1998). *Beginnings: Intention and Method.* London: Granta.

Serequeberhan, Tsenay (2007). *Contested Memory: The Icons of the Occidental Tradition.* Trenton, NJ: Africa World Press.

Siger, Carl (1907). *Essai sur la colonisation.* Paris: Societé de Mercure de France.

Spencer, Lloyd and Andrzej Krauze (1996). *Introducing Hegel.* New York: Totem Books.

Stewart, Jon (ed.) (1991). *The Hegel Myths and Legends.* Evanston: Northwestern University Press.

Vásquez-Arroyo, Antonio (2008). 'Universal History Disavowed: On Critical Theory and Postcolonialism', *Postcolonial Studies,* 11.4: 450–73.

Wolfe, Cary (2003). *Animal Rites: American Culture, the Discourse of Species, and Posthumanist Theory.* Chicago: University of Chicago Press.

....

IMPERIAL HISTORIES, POSTCOLONIAL THEORIES

STEPHEN HOWE

....

The relationship between postcolonial theory and historical studies began as, and in many quarters long remained, one that varied only from mutual indifference or incomprehension to active hostility. Even today, thirty years and more after the publication of postcolonialism's founding texts, and after profound transformations in the intellectual landscapes both of cultural and literary studies and of historical writing on empires and colonialisms, echoes of those misunderstandings and antagonisms can still be heard. And even as some of the old schisms have lost their former urgency, they have been supplemented or in part supplanted by newer ones. Heated debates are currently being conducted over the relevance of imperial pasts to the 'colonial present', especially in southwest Asia; over relations between Islamic pasts (and Islamist and indeed Islamophobic thought) and the discourses of imperialism and anti-imperialism; and over the usefulness or otherwise of postcolonialism for understanding the former Russian empire and the post-communist world. Meanwhile, *settler* colonialism is now increasingly understood as being fundamentally distinct from other forms of colonialism, even colonialism as such, while a combative 'decolonial' rhetoric has emerged from Latin America that diverges from, and claims a different lineage to, the postcolonial.

Several of these developments are represented, or at least alluded to, in the essays in this section. What these essays cannot fully do, within the format and the space constraints of this volume, is reflect the intensity and complexity of dispute over each of these intellectual trends, or indeed the sheer variety of relevant new work in imperial and (post)colonial studies, among historians and scholars in related fields. By the same token, this commentary cannot do more than gesture towards some of those evolving intellectual patterns, as they relate to the essays collected here.

Graham Huggan, in his Introduction to this section, aptly notes that '[p]ostcolonial approaches to empire are often less historical than they claim to be' and that 'postcolonial studies can be seen as part of what is generally referred to as the "cultural turn" at European and, particularly, North American universities'—a 'turn' often associated with enthusiasm for poststructuralist and (for a time) postmodernist thinkers, and sometimes with a then-fashionable New Historicism in literary studies. All of these features point towards reasons why so many historians responded with bafflement or dislike, as—in a distinct but overlapping pattern—did many Marxist or *marxisant* thinkers. Often, too, something simpler and more banal was at work: misapprehensions among or boundary-defence between academic disciplines (see Part IV of this volume). Historians in general tend to be seen, fairly or not, as predisposed by the very nature of their own discipline towards empiricism or positivism. Certainly most contemporary historians of empire, especially but not only in the Anglophone world, have had little taste for grand theory or anything with the odour of poststructuralist, postmodernism, epistemological relativism. They have tended to identify colonial and postcolonial cultural theories—also historical writing influenced by these, sometimes labelled the 'new imperial history'—with those voguish elements, and with an alleged disregard for historical specificity and precision (see also Kennedy in Part IV of this volume).

There was, it must be recognized, considerable warrant for such charges in the work of some of the key early postcolonialists—though the indictment stuck less firmly or fairly on Edward Said than on some others—and even more in that of their soon-numerous epigones. Too often, a handful of isolated colonial texts or incidents served as rather perfunctory prefaces to far-reaching declarations about a generalized 'colonial situation'. Three of the essential keywords of historical and social-scientific discourse seemed disconcertingly absent: 'evidence', 'context', and 'explanation'. Sometimes, not least in the writings of Gayatri Chakravorty Spivak, there was an alarming carelessness about empirical detail. Or, as with Homi K. Bhabha's immensely influential essays, there was what to many critics seemed a minimal awareness of the need to situate texts in the time and circumstances of their creation; and what to many historians seemed the methodological absurdity of basing general claims about colonial writing on a single, often notably unrepresentative, text. Bold, all-embracing suggestions about the colonial past were buttressed by citations from literary and psychoanalytic theory, but not by any investigation of concrete colonial circumstances. It all rested, such critics felt, on an unexamined exaggeration of colonialism's purposeful effectiveness. An exaggeration, moreover, with a disturbing political payoff: for even where, say, mimicry, or 'sly civility', were seen as subversive of the colonial project, they mounted their resistance entirely on ground previously defined by colonial culture itself. This failed to register the possibility—indeed the massively documented reality from a vast range of colonial situations—that the colonized had retained and adapted their own fairly autonomous discursive agendas, not necessarily either copying or overtly resisting, but synthesizing the old and the new, the indigenous and the imported.

The critique of such alleged tendencies was just one aspect of an often intense politicization of the relevant debates, where positions taken for or against a particular theoretical stance were often seen as being necessarily associated with political, even ethical, attitudes towards empire, its legacies, and its apparent twenty-first-century revival. In some eyes, the very category of 'history' was a case in point; thus, in his pioneering early work *White Mythologies* (1991), Robert J. C. Young argued that recourse to the notion of 'History' in critiques of poststructuralist thought posed as a solution something which itself was a problem. (It was a very Hegelian problem at that: as Brennan's essay here reminds us, a great deal of the evolution of anti- and postcolonial thought can well be seen as an extended dialogue with Hegel's ghost.) 'History', for Young, was identified with *historicism*: with teleological, rationalist, universalizing (and covertly imperializing) global narratives; and these in their turn were identified almost exclusively with Hegelian Marxism. The only alternative admitted was also a Marxist one: Althusserian structuralism. Hegel's legacy, Young argued, has dictated that the dominant discourses of 'History' remain obdurately Eurocentric. In particular, 'Marxism's universalizing narrative of the unfolding of a rational system of world history is simply a negative form of the history of European imperialism' (Young 1991: 2).

It is questionable whether the two lines of attack on universalist and historicist theories—the poststructuralist and the postcolonial—really mesh in Young's account or elsewhere in early postcolonial theory. The former was the more carefully traced; the latter remained too often a matter of political proclamation, a kind of *deus ex machina*. It was never concretely shown, either that there is a necessary connection between historicism, rationalism, Enlightenment thought, and imperialism, or that the former ordinarily or centrally operated to legitimize the latter. Instead, the relationship was simply assumed or asserted. As Stoler's chapter here suggests, both the Enlightenment and colonialism, and the relations between them, were far more complex, varied, and ambivalent than much postcolonialist writing, especially at the high tide of French-model anti-humanism, tended to proclaim. Many of us would tend now to greater scepticism over how fully or effectively poststructuralism broke from this imperializing legacy: if, for instance, Foucault was repeatedly (and in large part rightly) accused of ethnocentrism, Derrida was perhaps too often 'excused' on the rather tenuous basis of a few short, rather occasional essays such as 'Racism's Last Word'. It might be added (though the point cannot be further explored here) that similar criticisms would surely apply, with at least equal force, to the rather surprising current vogue in postcolonial scholarship for the ideas of Giorgio Agamben (see Part II of this volume). In general, though, there is today more widespread doubt about proclamations of unmediated, effective associations between theoretical work and political transformation than there was in the 1980s.

The subsequent trajectory of Robert Young's own work both exemplified and helped to facilitate wider trends. Since his early forays into postcolonial theory, Young has increasingly expressed his dissatisfaction with the abstraction and self-referentiality of much in that field, which itself has become a discourse in the strict and even pejorative sense. However, Young still defends the value of such work even while he scales down the apparent ambition of claims made on behalf of it, insisting that much criticism has involved 'a form of category mistake: the investigation of the discursive construction of colonialism does not seek to replace or exclude other forms of analysis, whether they be historical, geographical, economic, military or political … The contribution of colonial-discourse analysis is that it provides a significant framework for that other work by emphasizing that all perspectives on colonialism share and have to deal with a common discursive medium which was also that of colonialism itself' (1995: 163). This is not exactly a modest claim: that one particular, in some eyes rather esoteric kind of work must provide the framework for all others. Yet Young's writing has itself become ever more historical in focus over time, as well as more direct and concrete in its political ambitions (see especially Young 2001).

The political stakes continue to be seen as high by many participants in these debates, and indeed are often seen as having been heightened by global developments since September 2001 (developments which, it is sometimes suggested, themselves also fatally undermined much postcolonial theory in its early, high-theoretical mode). This is perhaps most evidently the case with two currents of thought represented in essays here: that of the 'decolonial turn' and that of arguing for particular, and particularly important, kinds of relationship between imperialism and Islam.

The central thrust of recent Latin American 'decolonial' thought, some of whose main themes are helpfully summarized here by Mignolo, is to urge the necessity for a 'decolonization of knowledge' more far-reaching than anything achieved by existing critical projects. This involves, inter alia, dismantling the seemingly inextricable bond forged long ago between modernity and 'coloniality', and uncovering the multiple ways in which a coloniality of being and thinking persists far beyond and long after the apparent ends of colonialism's political forms. It insists that history is not linear and singular but multiple, containing always innumerable simultaneous projects and possibilities, and espousing a 'transmodern' world vision that links together various sites of colonized conditions and consciousness around the globe. This is not the place for a substantive critique of that project, which has been energetically put forward by theorists like Aníbal Quijano, Enrique Dussel, and Arturo Escobar, as well as Mignolo himself. It certainly offers a bold and politically challenging alternative to a North Atlantic postcolonialism that is now widely seen as having reached a point of critical exhaustion. Yet one may register preliminary doubts over how effectively it might 'travel' beyond its Latin American points of origin, despite Mignolo's and others' strong claims for transverse relations among Latin, Muslim, and other sites of (de)colonial domination. Its main intellectual points of reference seem to remain, so far, very specific to the southern Americas and—ironically—to western Europe. No reader of Edward Said will need convincing of the point that 'travelling theories' often, perhaps inevitably, become distorted and run the risk of being disarmed during their migrations. That certainly seems to be the case in some recent appropriations of Indian, African, Middle Eastern, and other postcolonial debates by scholars in other locations. It remains to be seen whether decolonial thinking can escape that fate or move beyond the faults it shares with an earlier postcolonialism: excessive abstraction, rampant culturalism, and the ready tendency to indulge in sweeping global 'everything is colonial' rhetoric.

Some intriguing parallels may be found in claims recently made about the potential resources of Islamic—and Islamist—thought in relation to colonial pasts and presents. A part of that case may be found in Sayyid's essay here, and in his other recent work. Yet—as Sayyid is himself well aware—there are strong grounds for scepticism over whether, historically, there have either been distinctive or generic Islamicate forms or experiences of empire (either as empire builders or as colonized subjects) or a distinctive Islamic or Islamist form of anti-colonialism or anti-imperialism. Is there a body of thought that analyses imperialism (or colonialism, or neocolonialism, or indeed what for some is now a near-synonym, globalization) from a uniquely Islamic perspective, a body of thought with some continuity and coherence to it? My own basic answer to this is a pretty decisive 'no'.

It is important to note, of course, that globally influential thinkers about empire and colonialism have come from societies of Muslim majority and indeed sometimes from pious, Koranic backgrounds: the Egyptian economist Samir Amin, the Senegalese historian Cheikh Anta Diop, and the Pakistani political analyst Eqbal Ahmed are just three that come to mind. But such thinkers, it seems to me, have almost always been secularists and leftists and at times fierce critics of religious ideology. None have been Islamists. And certainly no Islamist—indeed very few Muslims—can be found in the 'canon' of anti-colonialist writers established by the postcolonial cultural studies industry. Indeed, I would suggest that the only really interesting or substantial thinkers about imperialism to have come from the ranks of those usually labelled Islamists—like al-Afghani, Qutb, or more recently Shari'ati—in fact derive those elements of interest, coherence, or originality in their thought from sources which are *not* specifically Islamic, let alone Islamist. There is an obvious danger here: that because of my own background and sympathies—because of my own western, secular intellectual formation—I may be incapable of discerning, let alone reacting positively to, the intellectual merits of arguments that draw on primarily religious resources or employ a religious idiom. Or—a closely related failing—it may be that my judgement that very few coherent or rigorous ideas about imperialism, or any other specifically political subject, are to be found in Islamist writings reflects only my own restricted, indeed ethnocentric, conception of the political. I can only say that I am keenly aware of those dangers. I have gone to the writings of people usually described as the most substantial Islamist political thinkers— al-Afghani or Maududi, Shariati or Qutb—in what I hope is a genuinely enquiring spirit. I expected to find there far more than I did. Mine was an experience of surprise, disappointment, and puzzlement at how thin these writings were. Opposition to imperialism, to America, Europe, or the west, has never been the main preoccupation of most Islamist thinkers and activists, or at least not until very recently. Many have had very little to say about empire beyond vague generalities; and almost none, with the possible exception of Shariati, has said anything very original or analytically powerful. Maududi, indeed, once argued that colonial rulers posed little real threat to Islam for their cultural impact was too superficial: it was their indigenous successors, with greater local knowledge, who were more of a threat (Maududi 1982 II: 5–6). Then there is an intriguing counter-argument, presented for instance by Marnia Lazreg (2000) in relation to Algeria, that Islamists turn 'colonialism' into an ahistorical, demonized category with which all their opponents and especially the postcolonial state are identified—but their own venture, so alien to the lived reality of Algerian Islam across centuries, is itself a project of cultural and psychological colonialism very like the French 'civilizing mission'.

The fascination of political Islam, in the context of (post)colonial counter-discourses, is that it stands virtually alone—and certainly in unique prominence—as a supposedly rival universalism to that (or those) of the west. A second striking feature is that, whereas Islamism evidently functions in many parts of the world as a form of, or perhaps a surrogate for, cultural nationalism, the central thrust of the ideology is determinedly anti-nationalist. But is 'Islam' a coherent or meaningful object of socio-political analysis in the first place? Responses to this basic question have exhibited—indeed have been the classic site of—the ideological battle in which western Orientalists have been accused by radical and Third World scholars of essentializing an ahistorical 'Islam'; but political Islamists have strongly asserted a profound socio-cultural unity, which counter-critics have in their turn argued reproduces both the stereotyping tropes of Orientalism and the fantasies of religious archaism. At worst, a mythical 'Islam' has been created from the combined efforts of the religion's bigoted foes and its self-proclaimed partisans. This 'Islam' seems to have acquired a kind of immunity from the demands of contextualization, of attention to internal diversity and change and to structural (including, though far from exclusively, economic) determination, which are posed to historical and social studies by almost all other ideological formations.

The Middle East may well be the region where, in recent years, the discourses of anti-imperialism, cultural nationalism, and identity politics have been most prevalent and most fiercely contested (see Part II of this volume). This intense contestation derives above all from the Arab–Israeli conflict; and it has had a secondary and derivative, but nonetheless powerful, impetus from the 'conflict about the conflict' that rages in western politics, academia, and the media. This secondary conflict has gained some of its ferocity from the fact that here, and almost uniquely, central tenets of the anti-imperialist worldnview have been deployed with force by both sides (though it has become ever weaker in the pro-Israeli camp as 'Jewish national liberation' has been supplanted by the rhetoric of 'western values' and, in the USA, neoconservatism). Out of it has come the most influential single body of writing about the culture of colonialism, that of Edward Said, while, more recently, massive western intervention in the Gulf has provided a peculiarly sharp focus for dispute over the contemporary meanings of imperialism. As far as the wider controversies over the politics of identity, race, culture, and 'Otherness' are concerned, the Middle East has involved three of the figures often viewed as the west's most seminal (some would suggest, *successively* seminal) 'Others': the Jew, the Arab, and the Muslim. And it is here, perhaps more than in any other of the multiple sites of dispute and contestation referenced in the essays in this section, that the diverse, contending political investments in the debate over postcolonialism and history will continue to exert their power for a long time to come.

References

Lazreg, Marnia (2000). 'Islamism and the Recolonization of Algeria', in Ali Abdullatif Ahmida (ed.), *Beyond Colonialism and Nationalism in the Maghreb.* New York: Palgrave Macmillan, 147–64.

Maududi, Abu'l A'la (1982). *Selected Speeches and Writings,* trans. S. Zakir Aijaz. 2 vols. Karachi: International Islamic Publishers.

Young, Robert J. C. (1991). *White Mythologies: Writing History and the West.* London: Routledge.

Young, Robert J. C. (1995). *Colonial Desire: Hybridity in Theory, Culture and Race.* London: Routledge.

Young, Robert J. C. (2001). *Postcolonialism: An Historical Introduction.* Oxford: Blackwell.

PART II

THE COLONIAL PRESENT

INTRODUCTION

GRAHAM HUGGAN

The Colonial Present (2004), the Canadian-based social geographer Derek Gregory's magisterial study of the 'war on terror' and its colonial antecedents, has been one of the most influential books of the last decade for postcolonial studies, with its influence spreading far beyond the discipline in which it originated. While it is indebted to Fanon and Said, still widely accepted today as being the two foundational figures for postcolonial criticism, *The Colonial Present* is very much a book for our times, and its underlying concerns—the 'new imperialism' (Harvey 2003), the global 'security mentality' (Duffield 2007), the post-Cold-War shift from geopolitical modes of state control to biopolitical modes of population containment—have helped bring postcolonial studies into animated conversation with the contemporary globalized world (see also Part V of this volume). Gregory's engagement with postcolonialism is oblique but never distancing or dismissive; thus, while he permits himself the routine put-down of describing the postcolonial in terms of its 'precocious prefix' (7), he also suggests that the force of the term has been in seeking to account for different colonialisms at different times, and for the 'heterogeneous temporalities' (7) through which multiple pasts condense into a single present, and the 'lazy separations between past, present and future' (7) are interrogated along with the western teleology that lends them ideological support (see Hindess in Part IV of this volume; also Brennan in Part I).

Four brief points can be made here about Gregory's book, each of which is taken up in more detail in subsequent essays in this section. First, the colonial present is associated with, but not reducible to, both earlier paradigms of neocolonialism and recent designations of the new imperialism. Like Fanon, still probably the most lucid analyst of neocolonialism, Gregory insists that the colonial world is violently divided, both physically and ideologically (Fanon 1961); and like Harvey, perhaps the most persuasive commentator on the new imperialism, he sees the contemporary world order in terms of a 'new global narrative in which the power to narrate is vested in a particular constellation of power and knowledge within the United States of America' (Gregory 2004: 16; see also Harvey 2003). However, unlike either Fanon or Harvey, Gregory locates the colonial present fair and square within a continuing global *modernity*—a colonial modernity that 'produces its other, verso to recto, as a way of at once producing and privileging itself' (4).

This ushers in my second point: that the colonial present is as much a *geographical* as a *historical* phenomenon. Produced and reinforced by Saidean 'imaginative geographies' that demarcate boundaries—less real than imagined—between self and other, 'their' space and 'ours', it contributes to a nested complex of 'architectures of enmity' that constitutes the world on which it claims to comment and reflect (Gregory 2004: 17; see also

Said 1978). These geographies operate within a culturally and economically globalized world in which space can expand as much as it contracts, and where what Gregory calls 'the proliferating partitions of colonial modernity' (252) become the means by which those ideologically differentiated zones that operate under the code words 'Afghanistan', 'Iraq', and 'Palestine'—his three main case studies in *The Colonial Present*—have been strategically refashioned in the wake of the 2001 terrorist attacks on Washington and New York (19).

Third, and as implied above, the 'war on terror' is—as Gregory himself puts it—'one of the central modalities through which the colonial present is articulated' (13). 'America', also a coded term, is of course very much at the centre of this; and indeed one of the axioms of *The Colonial Present* is that the United States, though by no means a new imperial power, has become emblematic of twenty-first-century capitalist imperialism, and that the two most immediate consequences of '9/11' have been to facilitate and consolidate American imperial outreach while producing a heightened, inevitably security-oriented projection of America as a 'homeland'—a fiercely protected national space (2004: 50; see also Harvey 2003; Smith 2003). To some extent, then, it might be said that Gregory's work has been representative of a shift in the object of postcolonial critique from European-derived to American-led imperialisms, or, to put this less charitably, that postcolonial critique has recently performed a slide from the paradoxical Eurocentrism of its 'first-wave' critical insights to the equally self-privileging Americo-centrism of its 'second-wave' global-capitalist debates (Mukherjee 2006; see also the General Introduction to this volume).

Less contentious, perhaps, is the evidence of a further shift from *geo*political to *bio*political considerations of imperial power in the context of what Mark Duffield calls the 'wider security mentality that is [currently] interconnecting the policing of international migration, the strengthening of homeland social cohesion, and the development of fragile states' in a radically unsettled, precariously interconnected world (2005: 157; see also Sharp in this section of the volume). Duffield is too hasty in spelling an end to 'the world of independent states', which he nostalgically links to a heroic era of decolonization, and in seeing this 'brave but short-lived world [as having] given way to what is perhaps the real heir of decolonization: an innovative, unstable and circulatory "world of peoples"' in which alliances are primarily biopolitical rather than geopolitical in their focus, even though geopolitics and biopolitics remain—as in earlier colonial periods—symbiotically entwined (143–4). More convincing, however, is his portrayal of the dangers and uncertainties that this fundamentally unstable world has created, and of the various protective actions—including those endorsed by what he provocatively but accurately calls a 'newly respectable' interventionist liberal imperialism—to which these dangers and uncertainties, sometimes strategically exaggerated, have given rise (144; see also Gopal in this section of the volume).

One of the tasks *The Colonial Present* sets itself is to engage critically with this particular modality of new imperialism and its profound biopolitical implications. And one strategy it employs is to foreground the work of the Italian political philosopher Giorgio Agamben, whose 'metaphysics of power' Gregory sees as informing the 'war on terror' in a number of different if interrelated ways: through the establishment of punitive 'non-places', e.g. Guantánamo Bay, where the procedures and regulations of international law can be disregarded (see Morton's chapter); through strategies of separation and containment in which Agamben's 'space of the exception' is given physical form; through mobile borders that justify continued practices of occupation and encroachment, suggesting that 'spaces of the exception [themselves] constantly move and multiply' (Gregory 2004: 128); and through the 'indiscriminate categorisation of whole populations [so as to legitimate] the indiscriminate use of violence against them' (143)—one example, this last, of the many ways in which sovereign power establishes the exclusionary basis it needs to protect and privilege itself.

Several chapters in this section of the volume are indebted, explicitly or implicitly, to Agamben, although they also test the limits of his theories, which can easily appear over-abstract and not sensitive enough—insensitive even—to situated knowledges of, or culturally specific ways of being in, the world (see, for example, Smith and Turner's chapter). It seems appropriate in this context that the lead-off chapter, Stephen Morton's, should turn at least in part to Agamben in order to explain how and why postcolonial criticism is increasingly moving to address concerns of biopolitical sovereignty, law, and human rights and the fractious relationship between these. This relationship, Morton usefully suggests, should be integral to any attempt to understand the workings of colonial power, both in the past and in the present, with his own case studies mostly being drawn, like Gregory's, from those militarized theatres of operations that are Afghanistan, Israel/Palestine, and Iraq.

Morton is particularly interested in what might be called genealogies of the colonial present in which contemporary truth claims (e.g. about terrorism) either disguise or distort the historical relationships behind them, and the perception of moral duty (e.g. in combating terrorism) may easily become the pretext for violent colonial intervention, as demonstrated in the siege of Gaza or the war in Iraq. Following Gregory following Agamben, Morton sees Guantánamo Bay—a paradigmatic space of exception—as a similarly leading instance of law in the greater service of colonial power and the wider context of the 'war on terror', citing Gregory's loose likening of Taliban fighters, al-Qaeda terrorists, and Afghan refugees and civilians to Agamben's exclusionary figures of 'bare life'. Parsing Gregory, Morton shows how detention camps such as Guantánamo Bay 'disclose the violent political foundations of the modern liberal-democratic nation-states' such as the US, thereby confirming Agamben's link between political sovereignty and the state of exception; it is through examples like these, Morton believes, that postcolonial studies can and must engage with colonial narratives of the law and the stereotypical cultural representations that underlie them—stereotypes that also inform present-day Islamophobia, which lazily and often dangerously associates Muslims with 'terrorism, Sharia law, the practice of veiling, and the preaching of global jihad'. Stereotypes like these may be rife, but they are socially and historically *situated*; and by insisting, Said-style, on the 'specific historical function of cultural representation in the maintenance of colonial sovereignty', Morton succeeds in suggesting both the possibilities opened up by postcolonialism's dialogue with Agamben and postcolonialism's role in pointing out the contextual limitations of Agamben's thought.

A further potential corrective to Agamben is issued by life-writers such as Moazzam Begg, whose 2006 prison memoir *Enemy Combatant* graphically describes the day-to-day realities of the author's life in a US detention camp, with these experiences implicitly being set against those decontextualized discourses of terrorism that collapse differences of place and history, e.g. in the creation and consolidation of exclusionary 'non-places' like Guantánamo or the ubiquitous 'security zones' of the West Bank. Protective spaces like these indicate that, in the colonial present, 'the control … of judicial order serves to legitimate military violence and occupation under the guise of [upholding] liberal values such as democracy and human rights'—a vivid instance of liberal intervention-ist imperialism in which the 'very discourse of human rights [is adopted] as a tech-nique of governmentality', and 'international law [works] to support western political hegemony'—as it continues to do in Afghanistan, Israel/Palestine, and, even after mili-tary withdrawal, Iraq. Drawing on other literary and cinematic examples such as Kamila Shamsie's epic novel *Burnt Shadows* (2009) or Annemarie Jacir's short film *Like Twenty Impossibles* (2003), Morton convincingly shows how imaginative work, while not solv-ing material problems, may yet offer creative alternatives to a colonial present in which humanitarianism serves military ends and state-sanctioned violence has become nor-mative; in such unpromising contexts, cultural narratives may 'shed light on the condi-tions of possibility for justice in a way that the law cannot'.

Liberal imperialism in the context of the colonial present is also the subject of Priya Gopal's pleasingly combative chapter, which sees a form of 'hard-headed liberalism'— at once justifying intervention in the name of freedom and licensing the restriction of freedoms—as refiguring the west's conflicted relationship to both the rest of the world and itself. Liberal imperialism, for Gopal, recasts empire in the language of democracy and human rights, draping itself in new ideological clothing; however, the connec-tion between liberal political thought and empire is hardly new, and indeed—as Uday Mehta pithily puts it in the context of the British Empire—'the liberal involvement with the British empire [was] coeval with liberalism itself' (quoted in Gopal below; see also Stovall in Part I of this volume).

Contemporary liberal imperialism, Gopal suggests in keeping with Gregory and Morton, is predominantly American despite its British antecedents. Making the case for a 'restitution of western civilizational values under the aegis of a relatively benign imperium', this kind of imperialism, despite the different forms it takes, shares several polemical credos: that '9/11' was a political turning point; that it irrevocably confirmed a new enemy in the shape of Islamic fundamentalism; and that Islamic fundamentalism— which is itself a form of imperialism—urgently needs to be countered and conquered by liberalism, which rests, and can only rest, in the simultaneously benevolent and belliger-ent hands of the US.

Gopal goes on to identify 'two complementary prototypes for the present-day liberal intelligentsia', which she calls—polemically in her turn—the Renegade Liberal Prophet and the Self-Representing Native Acolyte. The former (the late Christopher Hitchens is cited here as a prominent example) is a fierce advocate of American-based civilization-ist values; is hostile to 'old-school' anti-colonialism and multiculturalism; and claims to espouse a hard-headed, common-sensical attitude towards a deeply divided and dangerous world. The latter is perhaps best seen in the figure of the self-representing Muslim woman relaying her critical views of Islam back to the west and, in so doing, allaying western liberal anxieties about military intervention and the imposition of western values by accepting—or at least appearing to accept—that there is no logical alternative to these values, either in the democratic heartlands of America (their ultimate origin and repository) or in the benighted autocratic systems that regulate social mores 'at home'.

Gopal's primary example here is Azar Nafisi's popular memoir *Reading Lolita in Tehran* (2003), a heavily stylized account of everyday upper-middle-class life in post-Revolution Iran, whose coarse aims—only slightly sweetened by the book's refined worldly rhetoric—consist in exposing the continuing tyrannies of Islam while triumphantly claiming the moral high ground for the secular west. A second literary example—this time a male voice—is Khaled Hosseini's best-selling novel The *Kite Runner*, also published in 2003, which Gopal 'outs' as a redemptive morality tale doubling as a pro-American vehicle for liberal colonial discourse, and opposing a redeemable version of American 'flawed goodness' to 'geneaologically allied forms of evil' (one of the novel's several facile connections is between the Taliban and the Nazis) that are irredeemable and absolute.

One might object here that Gopal's angry rhetoric rehearses the same journalistic jingoism she seeks to expose, but her basic argument is surely a good one: that the relationship between liberalism and empire, which has deep historical roots, lies at the heart of the colonial present; and that latter-day liberal imperialism, combining as it does the cold logic of the market with the impassioned attack on 'illiberal' values worldwide, continues to justify what Hamid Dabashi calls the 'manufacturing [of] consent and [the] discarding [of] history at the speed of one major military operation every two years'—an object lesson in late-capitalist amnesia that postcolonial studies has not remembered particularly well either, and that it would do well to confront.

Jo Sharp's chapter addresses this amnesia head-on by examining what we might call—loosely adapting Gregory—the geopolitics of memory in the colonial present (Gregory 2004; see also Rothberg in Part III of this volume). Like Gregory, Sharp sees geopolitical issues in terms of their temporal as well as spatial components. She looks, accordingly, to trace some of the different ways in which colonial modernity produces and privileges itself by fashioning others through the multiple processes of colonial memory. These processes, she suggests (again following Gregory), can be broken down into two strands: colonial *nostalgia*, which 'idealizes the difference of the other'; and colonial *amnesia*, where 'otherness is seen as deviation, to be subjugated and controlled'. Most of the rest of Sharp's chapter is devoted to showing these two processes at work in recent constructions of Africa and African peoples in the context of the 'war on terror'. As she reminds us, the 'war on terror', popularly associated with the Middle East (see also Hazbun in this section), arguably has its origins on the African continent, with the simultaneous bombings of US embassies in Nairobi (Kenya) and Dar es Salaam (Tanzania) in August 1998. The bombings, instantly linked to al-Qaeda, produced an equally instant response, with violent US air strikes in Sudan and Afghanistan; causing extensive collateral damage in both cases, these led to localized arguments that America was effectively creating its own enemies 'through the interventionist and imperialist policies [it was enacting] around the world'.

Sharp's primary contention is that the 'war on terror' has rekindled a western geopolitical imaginary of Africa organized around the colonialist tropes of 'absence' and 'lack' and facilitated by colonial amnesia. This imaginary is linked in turn to what Sharp calls, following Duffield (2007) and others, the 'security-development nexus'. The threat of terrorism in Africa has led, particularly post-'9/11', to an intensification of security concerns and a clear linkage of these concerns to western development initiatives, with some of the classic tropes of colonial nostalgia (e.g. the white man's burden) re-emerging in the humanitarian discourses surrounding poverty reduction and foreign aid. At the same time, an increasing shift from geo- to biopolitical registers is evidenced in draconian regimes of development governance through which entire populations, seen *à la* Agamben to be 'beyond politics', are administratively managed; where routine violence is committed in 'civilizationist' interests; and where western governmental and non-governmental organizations become increasingly entangled in African state affairs.

As Sharp puts it starkly, development under these circumstances is 'first and foremost about the security of the west, about managing populations surplus to the needs of international capitalism "over there" from threatening the privileges of those who benefit from it "over here"'. This is not the only possible scenario, however, and Sharp ends, much as does Morton, by locating alternatives to the colonial present in, e.g., collaborative African reworkings of modernity or the shared communitarian hopes of the 'Arab Spring'. While recent instances such as these, as Sharp rightly warns, always run the risk of being romanticized, they still indicate the potential of a 'postcolonial ethics' to construct alternatives to a dominant western geopolitical imaginary of Africa that works towards perpetuating the colonial present by strategically forgetting the lessons of the colonial past.

Like Sharp, Waleed Hazbun—a political scientist by training—emphasizes security issues in the context of the 'war on terror'. For Hazbun, as for Sharp, the predominant geopolitical imaginary in this context is that of the US, which continues to steer global political events in its own national interests. His focus is on the Middle East, where Arab actors—even in the wake of the recent uprisings—have rarely been seen in American eyes as shaping the regional or international order. Hazbun provides a corrective account of the Obama administration's self-consciously 'progressive' reaction to recent events in Egypt and elsewhere, resituating this in the context of a liberal discourse driven, like the civilizationism it ostensibly opposes, by both residual and renewed fears of 'the rising power of Third World states' (see Gopal in this section; also Mignolo and Sayyid in Part I). The Obama administration, Hazbun suggests, may officially reject the Huntington thesis, but it still 'privileges US-dominated forms of global order, ignores their hierarchical power relations, and fails to fully recognize the agency of Middle East states and societies as actors in the international system'. This liberal order is still driven, Hazbun insists, by displaced forms of security-conscious neorealism that overlook the constitutive role of the US in *producing* insecurity in the Middle East. Following Gregory, Hazbun sees such an order as having clear colonial antecedents. Even Obama's recent, explicitly stated support for political self-determination in Egypt can be read within this larger context as the latest strategic attempt to 'craft a new narrative of American relations with the Arab world'. This 'new' narrative, on closer inspection, turns out not to be so new after all; and, like the ones it is conveniently imagined as replacing, it is driven by anxieties over the US's diminishing power to shape an increasingly multipolar world.

Hazbun ends by suggesting a way forward. Invoking Gregory again, he calls for genuinely new geopolitical imaginaries that are locally based, popularly driven, and democratically shared among a variety of national and transnational actors that are not necessarily beholden to the state (see also the General Introduction to this volume). These imaginaries, he concludes, are unlikely to find much favour with the US, which seems indisposed to developing a 'more inclusive regional security framework that might address the varied interests of both its allies and its rivals'. Whatever the case, a US-dominated liberal order seems likely only to increase the insecurity it claims to counter, leaving the US with some hard decisions to make about whether it wants to 'exert influence through persuasion and diplomacy', or whether it wants to (and can) return to the option it perhaps never fully abandoned in the first place, that of 'impos[ing] control through projecting power'.

The last two chapters in the section return to contemporary issues of biopolitics, invoking but also criticizing Agamben. David Farrier and Patricia Tuitt's chapter centres on the representation of modern-day refugees, whom they seem ready to see as matching Agamben's description of contemporary biopolitical relations, but only in so far as they also test the limits of a violent biopolitical order in which they, like the colonial present that contains them, are inextricably enmeshed. Farrier and Tuitt's contribution takes the innovative form of a dialogue between a literary critic (Farrier) and a legal scholar (Tuitt), and much of the chapter alternates, accordingly, between abstract considerations of legal theory and situated case studies drawn mostly from Australia and the UK. At times the two are conspicuously mismatched, but at others, they come together to perform a kind of critical montage that splices graphic images of, e.g., detention-camp lip sewing with cerebral considerations of the refugee as—to list just a few examples, several of them indebted to Agamben—a 'new subaltern', or an 'incarnation of rightlessness', or an 'archetype of the state of exception', or an 'embodiment of the crisis of political community', or a combination of the above (see Morton in this section; also Dhawan and Randeria in Part V).

As these examples suggest, 'the refugee' is nothing if not an overdetermined figure, but to their credit Farrier and Tuitt are well aware of the limitations of this kind of high-abstract thinking, which runs the risk of further reinforcing the already stereotypical perception of refugees as helpless victims of the modern security state. They are also conscious of the risk of over-relying on Agamben. Tuitt, for example, finds at least as much value in Fanon's 'native' as in Agamben's 'refugee' for the theorization of agency in contexts of violent expropriation and disempowerment, and more use in Fanon than in Agamben for setting up those oppositional forms of critical thinking—those 'minor jurisprudences', in Peter Goodrich's legalistic terms (Goodrich 1996)—that characterize postcolonial thought.

However, there is more at stake here than just critique for, as Tuitt suggests, both Fanon's 'native' and Agamben's 'refugee' register nothing less than the attempt to reinvent modern political relations, e.g. by gesturing towards unmarked forms of 'pure' or 'absolute' violence which, terrifying to behold, may yet sever the bonds that tether violence to the law, and both of these to the foundational principles, themselves violent, of the modern nation state. This envisioning of the refugee is very different, Farrier and Tuitt contend, from the grand spectacles of disaster into which global media representations of refugees are routinely co-opted, at least some of which convey the spectral image of the refugee as death-in-waiting, seeking to 'claim a share of the earth [only to find] a share of the grave'. What is needed, Farrier and Tuitt suggest, is a way to think refugees free from the destructive biopolitical categories in which they continue to be captured. The historicizing function of postcolonial critique is vital to this exercise. However, whether it is enough is a moot point (see Abeysekara in Part IV of this volume); and perhaps the best a postcolonial approach can do is to accord the refugee's 'desperate acts' the dignity they deserve, and to offer in the process 'a glimpse of future political horizons in which these same acts … we sometimes tend to dismiss as impotent recover their legitimate force'.

The section's final chapter, by the New Zealand-based academics Jo Smith and Stephen Turner, also offers perhaps its furthest-reaching critique of Agamben in the context of the colonial present. Smith and Turner's more immediate emphasis is on the continuing reluctance to accord sovereignty to Māori despite the nation's official commitment to biculturalism. Part of the problem, Smith and Turner suggest, is a persistently colonial mindset in New Zealand that adheres to imported western political models within which Indigenous people are *included* (co-opted) and *excluded* at the same time. This mindset has recently manifested itself in different ways: in ongoing battles over native title; in media wars over the 2011 Rugby World Cup; and perhaps above all in the dogged adherence to political models of citizenship and statehood into which Māori are conscripted, despite their different, self-monitored understandings of identity, law, and not least, sovereignty itself. As Smith and Turner show, western political understandings of sovereignty and the law are at odds with what they call Māori 'consubstantial sovereignty', which is based on the mutually constitutive co-presence of 'lands, waters, and peoples', and which operates according to wholly different imaginative geographies than those that govern colonial (settler-invader) conceptions of space and of the relationship between people, place, and time.

This is the basis, as well, for their disagreement with Agamben. For the 'originary political relation of western politics' that Agamben's work challenges is confronted, in turn, with an Indigenous political ontology that is both fundamentally incompatible with it and indisputably anterior to it in terms of the 'long histories' of First peoples it instantiates and performs. As Smith and Turner succinctly put it: 'The consubstantial political ontology of lands, waters, and peoples gives the process of Indigenous exclusion a sovereign agency that exceeds the originary political relation described by Agamben, or at least cannot be recuperated by it'. This agency is related to what Smith and Turner call a form of 'Indigenous presencing' through which prior relations to the land are continuously reasserted—an ontological assertion that cannot be incorporated into, or explained away by, the regulatory procedures of western law.

It is worth emphasizing here that Smith and Turner do not see this ontology in separatist terms; Māori, after all, have been shaped by centuries of colonial encounter with Pākehā (New Zealanders of European origin). However, they point out forcefully that 'long-standing Māori collectives (*tangata whenua*) do not need Pākehā to tell them who they are'; indeed, in the twin political and commercial contexts of national rebranding in contemporary Aotearoa/New Zealand, it is the other way round. As for alternatives to the colonial present—opportunities to go beyond what Agamben might call the exceptional spaces of colonial sovereignty—these cannot be satisfied by the exercise of plural sovereignties. Rather, they must involve a 'coterminous relationship' in which Indigenous 'inhabitations'—ways of living in place—are conditioned by continuing encounters, and in which a different model of Indigenous sovereignty is acknowledged: one where 'the indivisible relationship between land and people is the locus of sovereign power'. The section thus ends, as it began, by appealing to *alternative* epistemologies and ontologies and the imaginative geographies that inform them, which have the capacity to challenge the orthodoxies of the colonial present and to 'open up possibilities of living other than those mandated by the status quo'. This is certainly idealism of a kind, but—to revert one last time to Gregory—it is not 'empty relativism'; instead it suggests, as does Gregory himself, that 'if we are to cease turning on the treadmill of the colonial present ... it will be necessary to explore other [ways of spatial thinking] that can enlarge and enhance our sense of the world and enable us to situate ourselves within it with concern, humility [and] care' (Gregory 2004: 262).

References

Duffield, Mark (2007). 'Getting Savages to Fight Barbarians: Development, Security and the Colonial Present', *Conflict, Security & Development*, 5.2: 141–59.

Fanon, Frantz (2005 [1961]). *The Wretched of the Earth*, trans. R. Philcox. New York: Grove Press.

Goodrich, Peter (1996). *Law in the Courts of Love: Literature and Other Minor Jurisprudences*. London: Routledge.

Gregory, Derek (2004). *The Colonial Present: Afghanistan, Palestine, Iraq*. Oxford: Blackwell.

Harvey, David (2003). *The New Imperialism*. New York: Oxford University Press.

Mukherjee, Pablo (2006). 'Surfing the Second Wave: Amitav Ghosh's Tide Country', *New Formations*, 59: 144–58.

Said, Edward W. (1978). *Orientalism*. New York: Vintage.

Smith, Neil (2003). *American Empire: Roosevelt's Geographer and the Prelude to Globalization*. Berkeley: University of California Press.

CHAPTER 7

VIOLENCE, LAW, AND JUSTICE IN THE COLONIAL PRESENT

STEPHEN MORTON

INTRODUCTION

Over the last decade, postcolonial studies has increasingly moved to address pressing political concerns about the relationship between sovereignty, law, and human rights for understanding contemporary structures of colonial power (see Farrier and Tuitt in this section of the volume; also Smith and Turner). In so doing, postcolonial scholars have sought to challenge the prevailing view that systems of colonial rule and economic exploitation are a thing of the past. In *The Colonial Present* (2004), for example, the social geographer Derek Gregory emphasizes the continuities as well as differences between nineteenth- and early twentieth-century formations of European territorial colonialism, on the one hand, and contemporary formations of colonial power, on the other. Through a series of case studies of colonial interventions in Palestine, Afghanistan, and Iraq, Gregory traces the ways in which 'imaginative geographies' of those territories have been produced by 'regimes in Washington, London, and Tel Aviv' (13) in and through a performative discourse of terrorism that 'produces the effects that it names' (18). The 'spatial stories' (13) that Gregory narrates in order to make sense of these 'imaginative geographies' also entails an account of 'a complex genealogy that reached back into the colonial past' (13). The use of the Nietzschean term 'genealogy' is apposite here. For just as Nietzsche sought to demonstrate how modern moral values are predicated on truth claims that distort the relationships between causes and effects, e.g. in *The Genealogy of Morals*, so Gregory reveals how the dominant discourse of counter-terrorism is founded on a metalepsis in which the terrorist is presented as the cause of violent counter-insurgency, and the complex and overlapping histories of imperial interests that produced such acts of violence are effaced. In this respect, *The Colonial Present* raises urgent questions about the colonial histories underpinning western foreign policy in the Middle East. In what ways have the framing of Osama Bin Laden and al-Qaeda in the dominant discourse of counter-terrorism worked to eclipse the history of US foreign policy in Afghanistan during the Cold War, a policy which contributed to the formation and training of the *mujahideen*? To what extent has the figure of the Palestinian suicide bomber been invoked by the western media and the Israeli authorities to justify Israel's military interventions in the occupied Palestinian territories, and to further America's support for those policies with little reference to the history of Israel's continued military occupation of the West Bank since 1967? (See Hazbun in this section of the volume.) And how did the demonization of Saddam Hussein and the humanitarian argument for war in the build-up to the US and British invasion of Iraq in 2003 serve to ignore the importance of Hussein's repressive Ba'athist regime to Anglo-American interests during the Cold War and the Iranian revolution?

It is in part this masking of the colonial history of the present that such 'spatial stories' seek to challenge. As this chapter suggests, a focus on the relationship between narratives of law, geography, and human rights can help to make sense of the complex genealogy of contemporary formations of violent colonial sovereignty such as the United States' military interventions in Afghanistan and Iraq, or Israel's siege of Gaza in 2008–9. But the colonial present—as we will see—also presents interesting challenges to the prevailing concepts and categories of postcolonialism. The use of human rights as a justification for violent colonial interventions like the war in Iraq or the siege of Gaza raises questions about the meaning and value of human rights as a political concept for anti-colonial resistance. And the Indian national government's use of emergency laws against its own population in areas that are deemed to be 'disturbed' raises questions about the way in which postcolonial nation states have used violent techniques of colonial governmentality against their own populations. In the face of such new formations of lawful colonial violence, it is imperative that postcolonialism attends to the narratives and voices of the oppressed. For it is precisely such narratives that allow us to imagine the conditions of possibility for justice, however difficult such a task might appear.

Spatial Stories and Histories of the Colonial Present

One of the most significant 'spatial stories' of contemporary colonial power that Gregory recounts, in an essay that appeared shortly after the publication of *The Colonial Present*, concerns the global war prisons in Guantánamo Bay and Abu Ghraib. In this essay, Gregory emphasizes the importance of the law as a technique of colonial power in the context of the 'war on terror'. Against the framing of the prison camp at Guantánamo Bay as a "'lawless place" that is "beyond the reach of national and international law", a place where sovereign power has been mobilized "outside the rule of law"' (63), Gregory traces the ways in which Guantánamo has been produced through a series of legal and quasi-legal narratives that define the prison camps as a space that is simultaneously inside and outside the law. The reasons for this elaborate legal framing of Guantánamo Bay, as Gregory explains, are related to the Bush administration's sovereign power over the bodies of the detained prisoners and its attempt to circumvent the terms of the Geneva Convention: 'Through this contorted legal geographing [sic], Guantánamo was *outside* the United States in order to foreclose habeas corpus petitions from prisoners held there and *inside* the United States in order to forestall prosecutions for torturing them' (69; emphasis in the original). This ambivalent form of sovereignty over the bodies of the prisoners detained at Guantánamo Bay parallels the ambivalent status of United States' sovereignty over the territory of Guantánamo Bay, which can be traced to America's war with Spain over its colonial territories in the late nineteenth century and Cuba's subsequent independence in the early twentieth century. According to the terms of a lease signed in 1903 as a condition of Cuba's independence, "'Cuban sovereignty over Guantánamo Bay [is] contingent on the acknowledgement of the United States, in exchange for which Cuba agrees to cede sovereignty over part of the territory it never controlled'" (65). As a consequence, 'the lease also locates Guantánamo in an ambiguous space between the "ultimate sovereignty" of Cuba and the "complete jurisdiction" of the United States' (65).

LAW-PRESERVING VIOLENCE
IN THE COLONIAL PRESENT

Gregory's colonial genealogy of US territorial sovereignty over Guantánamo has important implications for understanding the ways in which the Bush administration was able to exploit the ambivalent legal status of Guantánamo Bay. By situating colonial spaces such as the detention camps at Guantánamo Bay at the interstices of multiple jurisdictions, the US government was able to legitimate repressive and violent practices of counter-insurgency that would not be acceptable within the legal space of the metropolitan centre. It is within the context of multiple jurisdictions such as these that Gregory has compared 'Taliban fighters and Al-Qaeda terrorists, Afghan refugees and civilians' to the figure of bare life that Giorgio Agamben describes in *Homo Sacer: Sovereign Power and Bare Life* (1998). In Agamben's account, bare life, or the form of human life that is stripped of the rights and freedoms associated with citizenship, is produced by the sovereign power of the state, and is epitomized in the classical political thought of the Romans. The figure of *homo sacer* denotes a masculine figure from Roman law who is cast out from the political community, and who can be killed without being sacrificed to the gods because his life is deemed by the political community to be of no value to the gods. Agamben clarifies the political significance of this example from Roman law with reference to Aristotle's distinction between *zoë* (the form of biological life that is common to all living things) and *bios* (the form of life that is proper to members of a given political community). For Agamben, the figure of *homo sacer* reveals how *bios* is defined and constituted by the exclusion of certain forms of life from its political community, and the relegation of those forms to a space in which the law has been suspended. In this sense, the exclusion of bare life from the political community exemplifies the hidden foundation of the political. That is to say, it is the 'capacity' of human life 'to be killed' that forms the 'first foundation of political life' (89). For Agamben, this foundation of political life is not limited to the specific historical context of the Roman republic; on the contrary, the figure of *homo sacer* serves to exemplify a metaphysics of power that underpins modern as well as classical forms of political sovereignty (see Farrier and Tuitt in this section of the volume; also Turner and Smith). Against the common assumption that events of state terror and genocide such as the Holocaust are an aberration or an exceptional case of human atrocity associated with totalitarian governments, Agamben suggests that all modern nation states—whether totalitarian or liberal-democratic, colonial or postcolonial—are founded on a 'state of exception', where it is possible to define a group of people as bare life: people who can be killed without being sacrificed. 'At once excluding bare life from and capturing it within the political order', says Agamben, 'the state of exception actually constituted, in its very separateness, the hidden foundation on which the entire political system rested' (9).

By invoking Agamben's reflections on bare life in the context of the 'war on terror', Gregory reveals how spaces such as the detention camps at Guantánamo Bay disclose the violent political foundations of modern liberal-democratic nation states such as the United States. This is not to suggest, however, that the detention camps at Guantánamo Bay offer a straightforward example of the suspension of the law that has come to be associated with the state of exception. For as Gregory emphasizes, the production of global prison camps such as Camp Delta at Guantánamo Bay as a space of exception historically involved a concrete political struggle over the law 'in its formulation, interpretation and application', as well as in its suspension (Gregory 2009: 58). The recourse to different legal precedents that either justified the suspension of *habeas corpus* for detained prisoners or enabled the US military to justify the use of interrogation techniques on the grounds that they did not satisfy the narrowly defined meaning of what constitutes torture clearly exemplifies the way in which the law provided the Bush administration with a technique of sovereignty over the bodies of the prisoners detained at Guantánamo. Yet the production of a biopoliticized form of bare life in the prison camps at Guantánamo was not only an effect of the law that defined these prisoners as enemy combatants; it was also an effect of the colonial stereotypes that framed the bodies of those subjects as dangerous individuals. If postcolonial studies is to intervene in and contest the neo-Orientalist discourse of terrorism, then it needs to take account of the mutually reinforcing relationships between colonial narratives of law, legality, and the state of exception; the imaginary geographies of Afghanistan, Iraq, and Palestine that are projected onto those spaces by western governments; and the cultural representations and stereotypes that stabilize such legal narratives and spatial fictions.

CULTURAL STEREOTYPES IN THE COLONIAL
STATE OF EXCEPTION

Since the attacks on America of 11 September 2001, the western media has been replete with Islamophobic stereotypes that associate Muslims with terrorism, Sharia law, the practice of veiling, and the preaching of global jihad (see Gopal in this section of the volume). From the depictions of the Prophet Muhammad as a violent figure in some of the provocative cartoon illustrations published in the Danish newspaper *Jyllands-Posten* and the representation of the Muslim cleric Abu Hamza al-Masri as a synecdoche for the British Muslim population, to the television images of Palestinians cheering in response to the attacks of 11 September 2001, the representation of Muslims in the western media reconfigures an Orientalist conceit. As Edward W. Said already emphasized some time ago in *Covering Islam* (1981), the dominant, western-based global media and government experts tend to reproduce damaging verbal and visual images of the Muslim world in order to justify western economic and foreign policies towards Iran, Iraq, Palestine, Pakistan, or Afghanistan (1997: 144).

The prevalent image that Said refers to describes certain verbal and visual stereotypes that are routinely reproduced by the western media and foreign policy to stand in for the Muslim world (147). Read in the context of the colonial present, Said's reflections seem strikingly prescient, and it is this prescience that Derek Gregory gestures towards in his reflections on the imaginative geographies that underpin the discourse of terrorism. If, as Gregory suggests, Agamben's account of the spaces of exception 'radicalizes the imaginative geographies that Said describes in *Orientalism*' (62) by revealing how these 'imaginative geographies' contribute to the legal sanctioning of state forms of violence, it is also true that Said's account of the ways in which the military, political, and economic dimensions of western colonial power are secured through cultural representations of 'the Orient' requires a rethinking of Agamben—one that takes account of the specific historical function of cultural representation in the maintenance of colonial sovereignty. It is the specific historical function of cultural representations of Muslims in the contemporary global conjuncture that Peter Morey and Amina Yaqin have addressed in their recent study *Framing Muslims* (2011). In their argument, 'Said succinctly captures what we would call the frame governing representations of Muslims and the resulting attenuation of real knowledge about what is in fact a heterogeneous set of cultural systems, when he suggests that there is an "incitement to discourse" about Islam, which "canonizes certain notions, texts and authorities" confirming its "medieval", "dangerous" and "hostile" nature' (146). Following Maxwell McCombs' 2004 analysis of the media frame, Morey and Yaqin go on to claim that in the global discourse of terrorism, Muslims are framed in the terms of 'belonging, "Otherness" and threat' (147). In mainstream popular cultural narratives such as Fox's televised US thriller series, *24*, for instance, the figure of the 'Muslim terrorist' is framed as a dangerous enemy within: a westernized Muslim, who is marked as a threatening 'other' even though that figure also performs the rituals associated with the Protestant work ethic and the heteronormative nuclear family (Morey 2010).

The framing of Muslims in the dominant discourse of terrorism has also provided the justification for political techniques such as the suspension of human rights for Muslims in the diaspora, the 'rendition' of Muslims suspected of terrorism to locations beyond the jurisdictions that guarantee the rights of such prisoners, and the indefinite detention of so-called 'enemy combatants' at global war prisons such as Camp Delta, Guantánamo Bay. Judith Butler has shown how the 'racial and ethnic frames by which the human is currently constituted' (2004: 90) were also crucial to the techniques of US imperial sovereignty deployed during the height of the 'war on terror'. Citing the Bush administration's argument that 'the involuntary hospitalization of mentally ill people who pose a danger to themselves and others' provides a 'legal precedent' for the detention of suspected terrorists without criminal charge, Butler argues that such an analogy has broad and significant implications (72). In so doing, she suggests that the imagery and rhetoric framing the stereotype of the 'Muslim terrorist' as an irrational and dangerous other is as important to the techniques of 'extraordinary rendition', indefinite detention, and torture employed during the 'war on terror' as the laws that are invoked to justify such techniques.

LIFE WRITING AND SOVEREIGN POWER

It is precisely this mutually reinforcing relationship between cultural representations of Muslims and the techniques of law and sovereign power used to frame and detain Muslims that former prisoners who were arrested and detained at Guantánamo Bay have sought to question and challenge through the conventions of life writing. In his vivid prison memoir *Enemy Combatant* (2006), Moazzam Begg details the circumstances that led to his arrest and imprisonment and that surrounded the lived experience of detention. Following his abduction by American and Pakistani intelligence services from his family home in Islamabad, Begg describes how the British secret service appears to be both indifferent to his treatment and complicit with the American intelligence service in his detention and framing. The stony-faced response of one MI5 agent to Begg's request for access to the British Consulate after his arrest, and the feeling that the British intelligence service has abandoned him, prompt Begg to surmise that the agent regards him as 'a Paki' rather than a British citizen (10). Begg implies here that the production of subjects as enemy combatants in the global war on terror is bound up with a racist discourse that excludes certain groups of people from the category of (British) citizen—a form of exclusion that enables enemy combatants to be detained indefinitely and tortured with impunity. Indeed, Begg's lived experience of state kidnapping and detention works to destabilize the legal rights he would normally take for granted as a British citizen: 'I didn't know what the parameters of the law were anymore: everyone had said that after '9/11', new laws had taken immediate effect in the US, and that was frightening. How could American laws apply, in retrospect, to a British citizen, who had never travelled west of Dublin, for crimes that never existed in the first place?' (200). After his journey in a US military aircraft from Islamabad to Afghanistan, Begg evokes the experience of being 'under military jurisdiction': of being verbally and physically abused by US troops, being forcibly strip-searched, and having his beard removed. For Begg, what was 'most humiliating … was witnessing the abuse of others, and knowing how utterly dishonoured they felt' (112). 'These were men', he says, referring to the other prisoners, 'who would never have appeared naked in front of anyone, except their wives; who had never removed their facial hair, except to clip their moustache or beard; who never used vulgarity, nor were likely to have had it used against them. I felt that everything I held sacred was being violated, and they must have felt the same' (112).

Against the sovereign power of the Bush administration and the US military, which sought to define him as an enemy combatant who must be stripped of the legal rights defined by the terms of the Geneva Convention and international law, Begg uses the techniques of life writing to construct a writerly self that persistently questions the authority of his captors and the suspension of his political rights, and affirms his cultural identity as a British Muslim. In a letter addressed to the military administration in Guantánamo, for example, Begg presses his captors for 'an explanation of all [his] rights'; 'access to a telephone that is able to call [his] family in the UK'; 'a full inventoried list, detailing all items seized from his residence in Islamabad, Pakistan on January 31st 2002'; and 'a full and legitimate explanation as to why [he has] been held in solitary confinement since [his] arrival in Cuba on 8 February 2003' (60–1). By demanding his rights as a British citizen 'under US and international law pertaining to detention' (260), when it is precisely those rights to have rights that have been withdrawn by the US military in redefining his body as enemy combatant 'number 00558', Begg draws attention to the performative contradiction of making a formal legal demand as a British citizen who has been stripped of the very rights associated with citizenship. Despite this contradiction, Begg uses the conventions of life writing to construct a narrative of his own embodied life during his detention that circumvents the constraints of the military regime in the camp. Begg's account of his daily exercise regime and his confession that this made him 'very fit' (319); his outspoken refusal to recognize the military terminology that is used to describe him and to justify his detention (324); and his fearless defiance of his interrogators, all exemplify the ways in which he attempts to construct a self that refuses the sovereignty of the US military over his bodily life.

ISRAEL AND THE COLONIAL PRESENT

The framing of Muslims as terrorists during the US-led 'war on terror' has also provided the Israeli government with a language for justifying its policies against the Palestinian population. Following the attacks on America of 11 September 2001, the former Israeli prime minister Ariel Sharon was moved to compare Israel's attacks on the occupied territories with America's military assault on Afghanistan. In one statement, Sharon insisted that "[a]cts of terror against Israeli citizens are no different from bin Laden's terror against American citizens' (quoted in Gregory 2004: 108). Such superficial comparisons not only illustrate how the discourse of terrorism collapses differences between places and histories; they also serve to demonstrate how the rhetoric of the state of exception has masked colonial histories such as the occupation of Palestine, and has elided the laws and regulations that have been invoked to justify that occupation. The 'discourse of modern Zionism', Derek Gregory argues, 'constructed Palestine as a space empty of its native Arab population' (2004: 78). In Theodor Herzl's 1896 pamphlet *Der Judenstaat* (Herzl 1934), for instance, the Jewish state was imagined as 'a rampart of Europe against Asia, an outpost of civilisation as opposed to barbarism' (Gregory 2004: 29). Such a view is echoed in S. Yizhar's literary representation of the military dispossession of the fictional Palestinian village of Khirbet Khizeh during the 1948 war as part of a Jewish civilizing mission: by declaring the land surrounding the village to be uncultivated—'a putrid patch of disgusting dirt' (2008 [1949]: 12)—Yizhar's narrator suggests that the *raison d'être* of Zionism was to modernize the landscape though new agricultural techniques.

If cultural representations of Israel were to provide a narrative to justify the colonization of Palestinian land, British colonial law furnished the emergent Jewish state with a technique of sovereignty through which to implement that Zionist settler narrative. The emergency laws introduced in British Mandatory Palestine provided a legal and political framework for Israel's claims on Palestinian land and its policies towards the Palestinian population (see Hazbun in this section of the volume). The Emergency Defence Regulations 'were originally devised and implemented in Palestine by the British to be used against the Jews and Arabs' during the mandate period, and especially during the Arab revolt of 1936–9. But after 1948, Israel retained the emergency regulations 'for use in controlling the Arab minority', and 'forbade Arabs the right of movement, the right of purchase of land [and] the right of settlement' (Said 1992: 36). In this context, the declaration of a state of emergency was used as the legal pretext for a large-scale land grab: 'the Emergency Defense Regulations were used to expropriate thousands of acres of Arab lands, either by declaring Arab property to be in a security zone or by ruling lands to be absentee property' (Said 1992: 105). In a certain sense, then, Israel's territorial sovereignty is predicated on the indefinite extension of the Defence (Emergency) Regulations of 1945. As Uri Davis explains:

> The vast properties of the Palestinian Arab people inside the State of Israel remain vested with the Custodian of Absentee Property under the Absentees' Property Law of 1950 so long as 'the state of emergency declared by the Provisional Council of State in 1948' has not been declared to have ceased to exist. Presumably, when the said 'state of emergency' is declared to have ceased to exist, all 1948 Palestinian refugees' property vested with the Israeli Custodian of Absentees' Property could be claimed back by its 'absentee' owners. (2003: 126)

The inference that Davis draws from Israel's use of the 1945 Regulations raises questions about why these supposedly temporary rules have not been repealed over sixty years after they first became law, and why a state of emergency has become normalized in a modern nation state that claims to be a liberal democracy. The specific connections between the emergency regulations of the British mandatory government in Palestine and Israel's use of those emergency powers to assert sovereignty over Palestinian land and to control the Palestinian population point to a specifically colonial regime of power, law, and sovereignty—one which is immanent to the political foundation of Israel. In this respect, Ariella Azoulay's (2011) use of Walter Benjamin's term 'constituent violence'—a term denoting the connection between state violence and the law—to describe the legal foundations of the state of Israel seems wholly appropriate if one considers that the Defence (Emergency) Regulations of 1945 were used to appropriate territory from the Palestinian population and to defend Israeli sovereignty over that territory against the very refugee population that had been dispossessed (see Farrier and Tuitt in this section of the volume). In the context of the occupied Palestinian territories, the connection between what Benjamin called 'law-making' violence and 'law-preserving' violence is palpable.

The use of the law as a technique of preserving colonial sovereignty in Israel-Palestine is mediated through a series of mutually reinforcing institutions and practices, such as the military court system in the West Bank and Gaza, and the proliferation of military checkpoints in the West Bank. The sociologist Lisa Hajjar explains how the military court system in the occupied Palestinian territories is 'part of a broader array of governing institutions and practices in which Palestinians are enmeshed and tracked in grids of surveillance, subjected to restrictive codes of conduct and interaction, physically immobilized through the use of permits, closures, curfews, checkpoints, and walls, and incarcerated in huge numbers' (2005: 186). Palestinian writers and filmmakers have powerfully evoked the specific ways in which these multiple techniques of colonial governmentality work to control the everyday lives of Palestinians. For example, in her novel *Wild Thorns* (1976; translated 1985), Sahar Khalifeh registers the condition of Palestinians living in the West Bank under occupation from the perspective of Usama, a young man who returns to Palestine from Syria five years after the Six Days War and the occupation of the West Bank in 1967 in order to participate in the resistance movement. Khalifeh establishes the conditions of life for Palestinians in the occupied territory in the second chapter of the novel through the description of an Israeli military checkpoint. The Israeli soldiers' interrogation of Usama, and their beating of a young woman suspected of smuggling a coded message to the resistance movement, highlight the way in which the colonial space of the checkpoint is experienced as a space of state terror: 'Usama found himself in such a turmoil of pain and nervous energy that for a moment he lost all sense of where he was' (1985: 11). Moreover, Usama's response to a question posed by an Israeli soldier as to why he was fired from his job as a translator in Amman reveals his sense of non-being as a Palestinian in the Middle East: '"Because I'm Palestinian, Palestinian," he shouted angrily ... "That was the only charge"' (15). In a similar vein, Annemarie Jacir's short film *Like Twenty Impossibles* (2003) stages the impossibility of making a Palestinian film in a space that is subject to a complex network of checkpoints, roadblocks, and 'forbidden roads' (B'Tselem 2005). After the closure of a military checkpoint between the West Bank and Jerusalem, the film crew travel down a dirt road, only to encounter a temporary military checkpoint. During a dramatic scene in which the film crew are detained and interrogated by Israeli soldiers at the checkpoint, the director is separated from the sound recorder, the cameraman, and the leading actor. As a consequence, the different signifying elements of the film are fragmented as the sound track is separated from the image track, the actor is detained, and the director is forced to leave the checkpoint in search of assistance. In this way, Jacir foregrounds the spatial and legal constraints placed on the civilian population in the colonial context of the occupied Palestinian territories.

The postcolonial theorist Achille Mbembe has suggested that the colony is 'the location par excellence where the controls and guarantees of judicial order can be suspended—the zone where the violence of the state of exception is deemed to operate in the service of "civilization"' (2003: 24). In the colonial present, 'the controls and guarantees of judicial order' have also been appropriated to legitimate military violence and occupation under the guise of protecting liberal values such as democracy and human rights (see Gopal in this section of the volume). If the emergency legislation of the British mandatory government in Palestine historically provided the Israeli state with a legal framework through which to enact practices such as forced expropriation, house demolitions, curfews, permit regimes, torture, and targeted assassinations, it is also significant that international humanitarian law seems powerless to prevent such repressive measures. This is perhaps unsurprising when one considers that contemporary forms of colonial rule have adopted the very discourse of human rights as a technique of governmentality. In a powerful and illuminating analysis of Israel's invasion of Gaza in 2008–9, the architect and theorist Eyal Weizman has considered how '[n]ew frontiers of military practice are being explored via a combination of legal technologies and complex institutional practices that are now often referred to as "lawfare", the use of law as a weapon of war' (2012: 92). By employing international lawyers, the Israeli military finds particular ways of violating the terms of international humanitarian law in order to change that law. Citing the work of a leading professor of ethics at Tel Aviv University on the Israeli military's use of targeted assassinations in the occupied Palestinian territories, Weizman suggests that the global war on terrorism provides an international framework for this military use of the law:

> We in Israel have a crucial part to play in the developing of this area of the law [international humanitarian law] because we are at the forefront of the war against terror, and [the tactics we use] are gradually becoming acceptable in Israeli and in international courts of law … The more often Western states apply principles that originated in Israel to their own non-traditional conflicts in places like Afghanistan and Iraq, then the greater the chance these principles have of becoming a valuable part of international law. What we do becomes the law. (2012: 93)

There is a striking parallel here between the way in which the Israeli military has attempted to bend the rules of international law in order to legitimate its use of force against the Palestinian population and George W. Bush's attempt to find a loophole in international law to legalize the use of torture. In the aftermath of Israel's invasion of

Gaza in 2008–9, the Goldstone investigation identified reports and testimonials from Israeli soldiers as well as Palestinian civilians detailing blatant violations of human rights, including the denial of medical aid to wounded Palestinians, the use of white phosphorus against the Palestinian population, and soldiers firing at women and children with white flags (Weizman 2012: 94–5). Like the public revelations of torture at Abu Ghraib and Guantánamo Bay, such reports and testimonials do not merely illustrate the way in which the Israeli military has violated the human rights of the Palestinian population; they also demonstrate how the violation of humanitarian law is part of a military strategy that aims to test 'the limits of the law … and the limits of violence that can be inflicted by a state and be internationally tolerated' (2012: 96).

INTERNATIONAL LAW AND HUMANITARIAN INTERVENTION IN THE COLONIAL PRESENT

To understand further how this relationship between law, violence, and sovereignty operates in the colonial present, it is helpful to consider how international humanitarian law has worked to support western political hegemony. In *Victors' Justice* (2009), Danilo Zolo has identified a dual-standard system of international law that has been in operation since the formation of the United Nations in 1945. Under the terms of the Charter of the United Nations, 'aggressive war is considered a crime and the Security Council is charged with using force to prevent or punish it'. And yet there are exceptions to these rules. As Zolo emphasizes, it was the victors in the Second World War— particularly the United States, Great Britain, and the Soviet Union—who accorded themselves 'the power of veto … to make free use of military force' (2009: x). As a consequence, the United States, Great Britain, and the Soviet Union have all been able to commit war crimes with impunity, while international criminal tribunals are held to try enemies that have been defeated in military conflicts, such as the various Nazi leaders and high-ranking members of the Japanese administration who were tried after the Second World War (2009: xi, xii).

The systematic double standard in the international law of war is particularly exemplified by the way in which no individual was held accountable for war crimes such as the atomic bombing of Hiroshima and Nagasaki in August 1945 or the military invasion of Afghanistan and Iraq in the early twenty-first century. And while recent military interventions such as NATO's aerial bombardment of Serbia and Kosovo in 1999, or the American and British invasion of Iraq in 2003, did so in the name of human rights, it is important to ask which human lives such 'humanitarian interventions' serve to protect or benefit? In a communiqué that was disseminated by one of the Sunni jihadist militant groups fighting against the United States coalition forces during the Iraq war, the military wing of the Jaish Ansar al-Sunna claimed responsibility for the assassination of Nafia Nafeh 'Aziz, a Kurdish local government official and a respected women's and human-rights activist. This communiqué also questioned and challenged the universality of the human rights claims invoked by George Bush and Tony Blair as a justification for the war in Iraq:

> Where are human rights when more than two hundred Muslims are rotting for months in your prisons in a 4 x 5 meter room, without any of them finding a place even to sit down? Where are human rights when every day prisoners are tortured at the hands of drunken pagans? Where are human rights when Muslims are killed as a result of the torture of your executioners, and their bodies are thrown out in the open? (Quoted in Keenan 2007: 57)

In a commentary on this communiqué, Thomas Keenan has argued that the 'sardonic' tone of this statement and its critique of the humanitarian imperatives of US military intervention in Iraq 'exploit[s] the gap between the discourse of democratization and the practice of the occupation' (2007: 60). What the communiqué implies without explicitly stating is that the torture and murder of Iraqis detained in prisons and detention centres is the means by which occupying forces from Britain and the United States define and delimit human rights by exercising their sovereign power over the lives and deaths of the Iraqi population. In this struggle over the meaning of human rights, the assassination of Nafia Nafeh 'Aziz could be understood as a non-sectarian attempt by the military wing of the Jaish Ansar al-Sunna to reassert sovereign power over the lives and deaths of the Iraqi population.

If, as Adi Ophir has suggested, 'humanitarian intervention ... calls into question the very foundation of political sovereignty' (2007: 171), the military use of humanitarian discourse in the colonial present raises pressing political questions about the relationship between human rights and contemporary formations of imperial power. This relationship was made palpable during the US military intervention in Afghanistan in 2001, when American planes dropped food packages over Afghanistan while others dropped cluster bombs. The visual similarity between the food parcels and the cluster bombs not only highlighted the way in which humanitarian aid was contiguous with the military tactics of contemporary imperialism; it also showed that humanitarian aid had itself become a part of western imperialism's military techniques. It is this relationship between humanitarianism and imperialism that the American-based Pakistani artist Alia Hasan-Khan explored in her 'distributional sculpture' *Gift* (2002).[1] In response to the military instrumentalization of humanitarian aid, Hasan-Khan produced a series of small, yellow dessert boxes modelled on the food packages that had been randomly dropped from US military planes flying at a high altitude over Afghanistan in October 2001. The original food packages contained instructions in English, French, and Spanish, languages not widely spoken or understood in Afghanistan. The packages

---

[1.] *Gift* first appeared at the 16 Beaver Street Artist-Run Collective in the financial district of Lower Manhattan, New York City on 1 May 2002, and was subsequently shown at the Apex Art exhibition 'Playing with a Loaded Gun: Contemporary Art in Pakistan' (6 September–4 October 2003), curated by Atteqa Ali. The term 'distributional sculpture' is Yates McKee's. See McKee (2006: 100).

also displayed a diagram of how to eat the food ration of 2,200 calories contained inside the box, which included items such as peanut butter and jelly, bean salad, and short-bread, all of which are unfamiliar to the majority of the Afghan people. What is more, they resembled in shape and colour the small, yellow cluster bombs that were simultaneously being dropped by the same military planes over areas of Afghanistan that were already littered with around ten million unexploded land mines left over from the war with Russia. The perilous consequences of the US government's cynical aid campaign during the attacks on Afghanistan thus prompted the nation's military to release a radio broadcast emphasizing the difference between food packages and cluster bombs.

In *Gift*, Hasan-Khan inverts the geopolitical structure of 'First World' aid to 'Third World' countries by 'donating' fake food packages to an American audience as part of a series of lunchtime seminars, held in the financial district of Lower Manhattan, about the US response to the terrorist attacks. On the outside of each yellow dessert box is an untranslated Urdu inscription and a diagram instructing the target-subject how to eat. Inside each box are more Urdu instructions and a fake explosive device made up of *gulab jamun* (a piece of dessert made with sweet curdled milk) with wire and metal hardware inserted inside it. By concealing such a device within the packaging of a 'Third World' gift, Hasan-Khan foregrounds the paradoxical relation of violence that has underwritten the gift economy of US aid to Afghanistan, in particular, and of 'First World' financial aid as a whole. Instead of providing the means for economic independence, 'First World' development loans to nations in the global south continue to perpetuate a relation of economic dependence on 'First World' banks and industry-rich donor countries in the north (see Sharp in this part of the volume). During the war in Afghanistan of 2001, as Hasan-Khan powerfully demonstrates, the US aid programme did not even provide short-term relief for Afghanistan's civilians; instead it placed their lives in further danger.

Yet Hasan-Khan's fake devices refuse simply to represent a tragic stereotype of post-colonial subjectivity. By imitating the visual rhetoric of a terrorist threat, Hasan-Khan creates and documents a series of theatrical situations or events that encourage viewers to question the rhetoric of terrorism and its economic and geopolitical agenda. Without denying the violence of state democracies, extremist groups, and military regimes in Pakistan, the recycled devices also encourage viewers to think critically about the violence that is historically embedded in the western-based discourses of universal human rights and representative democracy: discourses which are increasingly subordinated to the economic and political imperatives of western imperialism.

The Politics of Mourning
in the Colonial Present

If the discourse of human rights provided the British and American war machine with an important technique of biopolitical sovereignty during the wars in Iraq and Afghanistan, political theorists such as Judith Butler have asked important questions about why some forms of human life are deemed to be more valuable than others. Against President George W. Bush's assertion on 21 September 2001 that 'we have finished grieving and… *now* it is time for resolute action to take the place of grief' (quoted in Butler 2004: 29), Butler argues that grief can be a 'resource for politics' if it leads to 'a consideration of the vulnerability of others' (30) and a questioning of the political norms that determine why the lives of Americans are grievable and the lives of Iraqis, Palestinians, and Afghans are not (34). Furthermore, by arguing that 'the world itself as a sovereign entitlement of the United States must be given up, lost and mourned' (40), Butler offers a radical democratic vision of global power relations in the twenty-first century. If, as Danilo Zolo has suggested, the predominant system of international law and the liberal discourse of humanitarian intervention aids and abets the violence of contemporary forms of imperialism, Butler contends that narratives of mourning can help us to interrogate contemporary forms of imperialist violence that are committed in the name of human rights.

An exemplary case of such a narrative of mourning can be found in Kamila Shamsie's epic novel *Burnt Shadows* (2009). Much of the novel is focalized through the consciousness of Hiroko Tanaka, a Japanese survivor of the US atomic bombing of Nagasaki in 1945, and chronicles her transnational movements from Nagasaki to Delhi, Karachi, and New York over a period of fifty years. This narrative is juxtaposed with an account of how her son, Raza, came to be framed as a suspected terrorist in the aftermath of the attacks on America of 11 September 2001. By decentring these attacks and situating them in relation to a broader history of western imperialism that includes the nuclear bombing of Nagasaki, the partition of India after independence, the Soviet invasion of Afghanistan, and the US war in Afghanistan, *Burnt Shadows* uses Hiroko's narrative of mourning and trauma to offer a counter-history of the colonial present from the standpoint of the oppressed.

It is Hiroko's own experience of mourning and violence during the bombing of Nagasaki that leads her to question the framing of Muslims in the 'war on terror'. Hiroko's painful memories of Nagasaki are not only inscribed in the scars on her back, but also shape and determine her fears about whether she will be able to have children following a miscarriage. As well as being marked by the discourse of the bomb, Hiroko's narrative is haunted by the image of her dead fiancé, Konrad Weiss. As she explains to her husband Sajjad: "'Those nearest the blast were eradicated completely, only the fat from their bodies sticking to the walls and rocks around them like shadows … I looked for Konrad's shadow. I found it. Or I found something that I believed was it. On a rock. Such a lanky shadow. I sent a message to Yoshi Watanabe and together we rolled the rock to the International Cemetery … And buried it'" (2009: 76–7). By commemorating the death and injury caused by the atomic bombing of Nagasaki, Shamsie encourages readers to question predominant American histories of the Second World War, which frame the atomic massacres in Hiroshima and Nagasaki as a necessity and consequently imply that the deaths of those killed in the massacres are not worth grieving. The parallel here with the violent response to the 11 September 2001 attacks is striking. Just as Hiroko's post-Nagasaki narrative of mourning and trauma raises questions about the framing of the Japanese population as dispensable, racialized bodies in the necropolitical logic of America's atomic war machine, so the novel implies that the Bush administration rehearses this necropolitical logic by framing Muslims as dispensable, racialized bodies in its 'war on terror'.

How, though, can such narratives of mourning help to make sense of the colonial present? The analeptic narrative structure of *Burnt Shadows* demands a recursive reading that can address the question posed in the novel's prologue by an as yet unnamed protagonist as he waits to be clothed in an orange jumpsuit: '*How did it come to this?*' (1; emphasis in the original). If we take this masculine figure to be Raza, and the orange jumpsuit to be an iconic metonym of contemporary global war prisons such as those at Guantánamo Bay, then the question and the context in which it is posed can be read as a rhetorical statement about the way in which Muslims have been framed in the 'war on terror'. But if we reread the prologue in light of the multiple narratives that follow it, the question can also be read as a reflection on the way in which the colonial present and the 'war on terror' are overdetermined by the violent legacies of western imperialism in the twentieth century such as the atomic bombing of Nagasaki and Hiroshima, India's partition, the CIA's covert war against the Soviet military in Afghanistan, and the proliferation of nuclear weapons in India and Pakistan. In this way, *Burnt Shadows* can be seen to engage readers in a collective work of mourning that offers an important historical counterpoint to dominant narratives of the 'war on terror'—narratives which have ignored the historical role of the United States in the training of groups such as the *mujahideen* during the Cold War (Burke 2004 and 2011; Coll 2004; Derrida and Habermas 2003; Esposita 2002; Gregory 2004). Judith Butler has suggested that the political dimension of mourning resides in its capacity to foster a shared recognition of vulnerability and dependency across cultures (Butler 2004: 41). Butler's rethinking of mourning and the recognition of a common corporeal vulnerability as a political and critical form of memory work is presented in part as a challenge to the Bush administration's cynical transformation of 'the liberation of women into a rationale for its military actions against Afghanistan' (Butler 2004: 41). Mourning work can also help to make sense of other genealogies of colonial violence that are eclipsed by the narratives surrounding the 'war on terror', as I will now suggest in my concluding reflections in this chapter.

CONCLUSION

For Derek Gregory, the British and American wars in Afghanistan and Iraq, and Israel's military occupation of the West Bank and its siege of Gaza, are 'the central modalities through which the colonial present is articulated' (2004:13). This is not to say that the colonial present is exclusively defined through the Bush administration's 'war on terror'. For if, as Gregory has argued, one of the critical tasks of postcolonial studies in the twenty-first century is to disentangle the multiple temporalities of the colonial past, and its reiteration in the colonial present, a crucial part of this task involves addressing the ways in which postcolonial states have also used techniques of colonial sovereignty against their own populations. Contemporary forms of state violence in India, for example, are informed and inflected by legal regimes and practices of counter-insurgency that have their provenance in the British colonial past. The Armed Forces (Jammu and Kashmir) Special Powers Act of 1990, for example, can be traced back to the British colonial government's 'Armed Forces (Special Powers) Ordinance' (1942)—an act that provided the British army with extraordinary powers such as the authority to shoot-to-kill civilians in order to suppress the Quit India movement. While the Armed Forces (Jammu and Kashmir) Special Powers Act of 1990 confers similar powers on the Indian army, one of the significant differences between the 'Armed Forces (Special Powers) Ordinance' of 1942 and the 'Armed Forces (Jammu and Kashmir) Special Powers Act' of 1990 lies in the geographical delineation of emergency powers. Whereas the British colonial government's Special Powers Ordinance applied to the 'whole of British India' (*The Gazette of India Extraordinary* 1942: 935), the 'Armed Forces (Jammu and Kashmir) Special Powers Act' limited these special powers to so-called 'disturbed areas'. By defining Jammu and Kashmir as a 'disturbed area', the later Act defines Jammu and Kashmir as a space of exception in which the Kashmiri population can be raped, tortured, kidnapped, and murdered in custody with impunity. What is more, by framing Kashmiri civilians as Pakistani infiltrators, the Indian military has been able to present the extrajudicial killing of a Kashmiri civilian as part of a legitimate struggle to protect the security of the Indian nation state (Duschinski 2009 and 2010).

Activists and writers have challenged the way in which the Indian army has constructed these 'fake encounters' with enemy insurgents. In Mirza Waheed's novel *The Collaborator* (2011), for instance, the first-person narrator, a young man from a Kashmiri village, recounts how he is employed by an Indian captain to collect identity documents, watches, and other personal valuables from the corpses of Kashmiri civilians who have been killed by the Indian army. By detailing how the Indian captain renames the corpses by giving them Pakistani names, Waheed's narrator foregrounds the way in which the Indian military represents the extrajudicial killing of Kashmiri civilians as lawful in the terms of the 'Armed Forces (Jammu and Kashmir) Special Powers Act'. Against this use of emergency law to justify the routine violence of the Indian state, the narrator attempts to commemorate the deaths of Kashmiris killed by the Indian army by cremating some of the human remains he finds around the line of control. In so doing, he tries to give voice, meaning and dignity to the precarious lives and deaths of the Kashmiri population at large.

If the spatial stories and legal narratives of emergency in Guantánamo Bay, Afghanistan, Iraq, and Kashmir help to make sense of the relationship between violence, law, and sovereignty in the colonial present, literary and cultural texts can help to shed light on the condition of possibility for justice in a way that the law cannot. As this chapter has suggested, literary narratives such as *Burnt Shadows* and *The Collaborator*, prison narratives such as *Enemy Combatant*, and films such as *Like Twenty Impossibles* all offer valuable narrative resources for imagining an alternative to a colonial present in which exceptional violence has become the norm, and humanitarianism has become subordinated to the exigencies of a militarized colonial sovereignty. This is not to suggest that such narratives offer a blueprint for effective political intervention. Yet in so far as they convey the fragmented and often traumatic experience of violent colonial sovereignty, these narratives allow us to mourn the lives and deaths of the oppressed, and to imagine a form of justice beyond the liberal fictions of human rights, democracy, and the normal rule of law.

Acknowledgement: This chapter expands and develops some of the arguments presented in my book *States of Emergency: Colonialism, Literature and Law* (Liverpool University Press, 2013).

References

Agamben, Giorgio (1998). *Means Without Ends: Sovereign Power and Bare Life*, trans. Daniel Heller-Roazen. Stanford: Stanford University Press.

Azoulay, Ariella (2011). *From Palestine to Israel: A Photographic Record of Destruction and State Formation, 1947–1950*. London: Pluto.

Begg, Moazzam (2006). *Enemy Combatant: A British Muslim's Journey to Guantanamo and Back*. London: Free Press.

B'Tselem (2005). 'Restriction of Movement: Statistics on Checkpoints and Roadblocks', *B'Tselem—The Israeli Information Center for Human Rights in the Occupied Territories*. Online source: <http://www.btselem.org/freedom_of_movement/checkpoints>, accessed 27 November 2012.

Butler, Judith (2004). *Precarious Life: The Powers of Mourning and Violence*. London: Verso.

Burke, Judith (2004). *Al-Qaeda: The True Story of Radical Islam*. London: Penguin.

Burke, Jason (2011). *The 9/11 Wars*. London: Allen Lane.

Coll, Steve (2004). *Ghost Wars: The Secret History of the CIA, Afghanistan, and Bin Laden, from the Soviet Invasion to September 10, 2001*. London: Penguin.

Davis, Uri (2003). *Apartheid Israel: Possibilities for the Struggle Within*. London: Zed.

Derrida, Jacques and Jürgen Habermas (2003). *Philosophy in a Time of Terror: Dialogues with Jürgen Habermas and Jacques Derrida*, interviewed by Giovanna Borradori. Chicago and London: University of Chicago Press.

Duschinski, Haley (2009). 'Destiny Effects', *Anthropological Quarterly*, 82.3: 691–717.

Duschinski, Haley (2010). 'Reproducing Regimes of Impunity', *Cultural Studies*, 24.1: 110–32.

Esposito, John L. (2002). *Unholy War: Terror in the Name of Islam*. Oxford: Oxford University Press.

Gregory, Derek (2004). *The Colonial Present*. Oxford: Blackwell.

Gregory, Derek (2009). 'Vanishing Points: Law, Violence, and Exception in the Global War Prison', in E. Boehmer and S. Morton (eds), *Terror and the Postcolonial*. Oxford: Wiley-Blackwell, 55–98.

Hajjar, Lisa (2005). *Courting Conflict: The Israeli Military Court System in the West Bank and Gaza*. Berkeley: University of California Press.

Herzl, Theodor (1934 [1896]). *The Jewish State*. London: Central Office of the Zionist Organization.

Jacir, Annemarie (dir.) (2003). *Like Twenty Impossibles*. New York: Philistine Films. 17 min, colour, 35 mm, Arabic and Hebrew with English subtitles.

Keenan, Thomas (2007). 'Where are Human Rights ...?': Reading a Communiqué from Iraq', in Michael Feher with Gaëlle Krikorian and Yates McKee (eds), *Nongovernmental Politics*. New York: Zone, 57–71.

Khalifeh, Sohar (2005 [1976]). *Wild Thorns*, trans. Trevor LeGassick and Elizabeth Fernea. London: Saqi.

Mbembe, Achille (2003). 'Necropolitics', trans. Libby Meintjes, *Public Culture*, 15.1: 11–40.

McCombs, Maxwell (2004). *Setting the Agenda: The Mass Media and Public Opinion*. Oxford: Wiley.

McKee, Yates (2006). 'Suspicious Packages', *October*, 117: 99–121.

Morey, Peter (2010). 'Terrorvision', *Interventions*, 12.2: 251–64.

Morey, Peter and Amina Yaqin (2011). *Framing Muslims: Stereotyping and Representation After 9/11*. Cambridge, Mass.: Harvard University Press.

Ophir, Adil (2007). 'The Sovereign, the Humanitarian, and the Terrorist', in Michael Feher with Gaëlle Krikorian and Yates McKee (eds), *Nongovernmental Politics*. New York: Zone, 161–81.

The Gazette of India Extraordinary (1942). Saturday 15 August: 935–6.

Said, Edward W. (1992). *The Question of Palestine*. London: Vintage.

Said, Edward W. (1997 [1981]). *Covering Islam: How the Media and the Experts Determine How We See the Rest of the World*. London: Vintage.

Shamsie, Kamila (2009). *Burnt Shadows*. London: Bloomsbury.

Waheed, Mirza (2011). *The Collaborator*. London: Viking.

Weizman, Eyal (2012). *The Least of All Possible Evils: Humanitarian Violence from Arendt to Gaza*. London: Verso.

Yizhar, S. (2008 [1949]). *Khirbet Khizeh*, trans. Nicholas de Lange and Yaacob Dweck. Jerusalem: Ibis Editions.

Zolo, Danilo (2009). *Victors' Justice: From Nuremberg to Baghdad*, trans. M. W. Weir. London: Verso.

CHAPTER 8

RENEGADE PROPHETS AND NATIVE ACOLYTES

Liberalism and Imperialism Today

PRIYAMVADA GOPAL

INTRODUCTION

Critical discussions of colonialism as a contemporary formation driven by the militarized expansion of the United States' spheres of influence—or what David Harvey calls 'the New Imperialism'—have tended to engage with formations broadly understood to be right wing or 'neoconservative' in nature (2003: 1; see also Morton in this section of the volume). During the George W. Bush era, which brought with it the invasions of Afghanistan and Iraq, this emphasis was strengthened by documents such as the notorious manifesto of the Project for a New American Century (PNAC) and the prominence of conservative think tanks such as the American Enterprise Institute and the Heritage Foundation.[1] Yet, as the first Obama presidency drew to a close with the trophy killing of Osama bin Laden on its ledger of credits, Guantánamo Bay, where hundreds of Muslim men remain illegally detained, was yet to shut, the war in Afghanistan continued to take a bloody toll, American troops were yet to be fully withdrawn from Iraqi soil, drone attacks on sovereign Pakistani soil had escalated, and the slow but certain drumbeats of war with Iran had begun to beat. Far

---

[1.] The Project for the New American Century defines itself as 'a non-profit educational organization dedicated to a few fundamental propositions: that American leadership is good both for America and for the world and that such leadership requires military strength, diplomatic energy and commitment to moral principle. Through issue briefs, research papers, advocacy journalism, conferences, and seminars', the PNAC commits to rallying 'support for a vigorous and principled policy of American international involvement and to stimulate useful public debate on foreign and defense policy and America's role in the world'. Online source: <http://www.newamericancentury.org>, accessed 24 November 2012.

from winding it down, the last few years have brought, if anything, an intensification of the 'war on terror' which, as some of its advocates themselves indicate, is integral to the new imperialism: 'what else can you call America's legions of soldiers, spooks and special forces straddling the globe?' (Michael Ignatieff, quoted in Harvey 2003: 3).

To the attentive, the intensification of the American imperial project under a presidency realized by the liberal vote in America should not come as a surprise. For quite some time now, what has been resurgent in Anglo-American discourse on empire is not so much conservatism as a so-called 'hard-headed liberalism' or 'liberal fundamentalism' expounded by ideologues calling for a return to the specifically European Enlightenment roots of liberalism defined in part as 'the tradition of thought whose central concern is the liberty of the individual' (Losurdo 2011: 1). As a political and discursive formation, liberal imperialism—with its claims to 'defending values about democracy, freedom, the ability to respect people of different faiths, races and creeds, and a belief that we will create a better world'—has been more influential, more durable, and far more adept both at manufacturing consent and narrowing political possibilities than episodic bouts of militant conservatism (Tony Blair, quoted in Gilroy 2004: 68). At its heart is a refiguring of the idea of the west in relation to the world, partly in the mode of an older European imperialism but with America, rather than Europe, as progenitor and guarantor of 'freedom'.

Since it is no longer 'easy to justify imperial conquest by [recourse] to the overtly racist pieties of the past', Colin Mooers has argued in a perceptive analysis of US imperialism, empire must now resort to the language of 'democracy and human rights; of freedom and dignity; of inclusiveness and respect for difference; of gender equality and the alleviation of poverty; of good governance and sustainable development' (2006a: 2). For Mooers, this catalogue of policy jargon suggests that contemporary imperialism has 'had to drape itself in new ideological clothes', using liberalism as a façade (3). In fact, the intertwining of liberalism and empire is neither new nor, despite its modernist avatars, does it necessarily gesture towards a 'momentous ideological shift' (3). Indeed, scholarship on eighteenth- and nineteenth-century British political thought has demonstrated the 'extended and deep' ways in which 'liberal and progressive thinkers ... notwithstanding—indeed on account of—their reforming schemes, [endorsed] empire as a legitimate form of political and commercial governance ... and fashion[ed] arguments for the empire's at least temporary necessity and foreseeable prolongation' (Mehta 1999: 4, 2). The list of liberals who advocated or justified British imperialism is long, including, besides Locke and the two Mills, some of the leading luminaries of English liberal thought: Thomas Babington Macaulay, Walter Bagehot, John Morley, Henry Maine, John Bright, James Fitzjames Stephen. For all its difficulties in reconciling egalitarian rhetoric with asymmetries of power, 'the liberal involvement with the British empire', Uday Mehta has convincingly demonstrated, can be considered 'coeval with liberalism itself' (1999: 4).

If, as Mehta contends, the links between nineteenth-century liberal thought and British imperialism have been insufficiently theorized, present-day links between liberalism and imperialism are often assumed to be, if not impossible, then at least troublingly

contradictory. In actuality, the close match between liberal thought and neoliberal economics in foreign policy, allied to the lack of a formal empire, 'has allowed the American
state to present itself to the world as a non- or even anti-imperialist power', which
intervenes in other countries in the interest of securing their sovereignty and freedom
(McNally 2006: 88). The rhetoric of political and social liberalism—democracy, human
rights, individual choice, freedom, and global free markets—is integral to this presentation, which has been around for some time now under the more benign moniker of 'LI'
or 'Liberal Internationalism'.[2] As Mooers points out, defences of 'empire' have become
acceptable currency not only within the mainstream media, but also in liberal intellectual quarters such as the *New York Review of Books*, where the self-described 'liberal fundamentalist' Niall Ferguson's call for a renewed American empire—'the imperialism of
anti-imperialism'—has been discussed approvingly in terms of 'the orderly, prosperous
and equitable world for which liberals since Woodrow Wilson have hoped' and which
can only be provided under the 'tutelage' of the United States (Gaddis, quoted in Mooers
2006b: 117). Wilson, of course, had declared famously of the US: 'I believe that God has
planted in us visions of liberty … that we are chosen and prominently chosen to show
the way to the nations of the world how they shall walk in the paths of liberty' (quoted in
Williams 2006: 2). Significantly, current liberal polemics in favour of one form or other
of US global domination have tended to call for the resurgence, not just of empire but,
concomitantly, of liberalism itself.[3]

If the post-Berlin Wall capitalist triumphalism of the late twentieth century consolidated the ground for a latter-day recasting of Wilsonian liberal imperialism, the
September 2001 attacks on New York's World Trade Centre sponsored the emergence
of a distinct kind of liberal narrative which is the main subject of this chapter. Treating
'9/11' as a politically clarifying watershed, this influential narrative, which underpins
several recent liberal polemics, makes the case for a restitution of western civilizational
values under the aegis of a relatively benign American imperium. Each individual
polemic constitutes a variation, *mutatis mutandis*, of the following set of linked claims:

a) '9/11' constitutes an epistemological and political rupture.
b) This necessitates western self-examination.
c) This reveals postcolonial guilt and anti-imperialism to be the problem.
d) Both are pointless because the age of imperialism is really over.
e) A real and greater enemy is Islamism, the new imperialism.

[2.] The literature on Liberal Internationalism is fairly compendious. For an introduction, see Williams
(2006).
[3.] While the definition of 'liberal' in this context becomes clear in the course of the polemics discussed
here, I use the term broadly to mean a normative if often contested Anglo-American philosophy that
asserts the primacy of the individual over the collective and a concomitant insistence on 'liberty'
(defined within a capitalist, market-driven framework) as a resource on which it is possible for all
members of society to draw. This is not to deny that there are varieties of liberalism as well as differences
within its practice since its emergence as a coherent framework of thought. That liberalism is riven by
contradictions is apparent from the argument itself.

f) This can only be fought by liberalism under American leadership.

g) Anti-Americanism must therefore be challenged.

h) Western liberalism must triumph.

To configure these mythemes into various overlapping narratives, contemporary liberal imperial discourse—which at once denies the fact of contemporary imperialism and makes the case for a kinder, gentler American imperium—has thrown up two complementary prototypes of narrator-protagonist. In their self-construction and presentation of the case for the benign imperialism of a reinvigorated Pax Americana, they might be thought of, respectively, as 'The Renegade Liberal Prophet' and 'The Self-Representing Native Acolyte'.

THE RENEGADE LIBERAL PROPHET

Risking all to speak truth to the power of multiculturalism and academic postcolonialism, the Renegade Liberal Prophet figures himself as a lone voice hurling salutary imprecations into the dawn of the twenty-first century, warning of further doom and destruction unless the west changes its ways and returns to the fundamentals of liberalism. Having recognized the error of his own juvenile detour into left-wing anti-imperialism, the Prophet presents himself as an embattled true humanist who 'ponders the dilemmas of the human condition and throws in his reluctant lot with empire only after deep reflection' (McNally 2006: 87). Exemplars include novelists Martin Amis and Ian McEwan (misleadingly referred to as 'Blitcons' or 'British Literary Conservatives'), the Canadian academic-turned-politician Michael Ignatieff, the American former student radicals and writers Paul Berman and Todd Gitlin, and the British journalists Andrew Anthony, Nick Cohen, and the late Christopher Hitchens. The repudiation of a former radical and anti-imperialist self, combined with an impassioned advocacy of western civilizational values and American leadership, is central to all of these men's writings, which have found their way into print in liberal forums like *The New York Times* and *The Guardian*. Liberal Prophets share a hostility to anti-colonialism, dismissed as an outdated project, and multiculturalism, defined as 'the guileless preference for any group or idea that stands opposed to liberal democracy' (Anthony 2008: 116). *Guardian* columnist Jonathan Freedland articulates the official Liberal Prophet position when, sharing Anthony's sense that 'petty corruption, sexism, homophobia, tribalism and patriarchal authoritarianism [are] characteristic of many traditional cultures in the Third World' (2004: 124), he calls for

> today's liberals to be honest—and admit that the ideals they have clumsily bolted together for three decades often chafe badly … Better to admit it and to decide consciously which value we are preferring in this case or that than to pretend there is no conflict. Hard-headed liberalism means hard choices. (124)

'9/11' AND MILLENARIAN LIBERALISM

Although shifts in their thinking may have begun before that date, the dramatic events of 11 September 2001 provided many liberal ideologues with an occasion for a personal conversion to born-again liberalism. For the Liberal Prophet, this date constitutes a millenarian rupture that requires the radical rethinking of existing liberal and left-wing concerns. Andrew Anthony's book *Fallout: How a Guilty Liberal Lost his Innocence* (2008) features the twin towers on its cover, comprising the two 'll's of 'fallout'. The titular 'fall' alludes not only to the destruction of the towers but also the falling of liberal scales from the author's eyes; the author's own fall from a prelapsarian 'good liberalism' to the soft cultural relativism that characterizes the liberal-left; the fallout his apostasy has created with friends and employers; the felling of liberal values; and the fall of western civilization itself at the hands of its crazed enemies and their deluded liberal allies. The intimate relationship between memoir and polemic that marks this particular genre, with its tropes of crisis and rejuvenation as well as the ritualized repudiation of a younger self, is illustrated here when the author's midlife crisis seamlessly morphs into that of western culture at large:

> Over the years, I had absorbed a notion of liberalism that was passive, defeatist, guilt-ridden. Feelings of guilt governed my worldview: post-colonial guilt, white guilt, middle-class guilt, British guilt. But if I was guilty, 9/11 shattered my innocence ... For while I realized almost straightaway that 9/11 would change the world, it would be several years before I accepted that it had also changed me. (Anthony 2008: 19)

It is also on the strength of a radical past, and a decisive break from it in the wake of '9/11', that Todd Gitlin crafts his own particular version of the Liberal Prophet as the Socratic author of *Letters to a Young Activist*. Professing anxiety that others will repeat mistakes his younger activist self made, Gitlin insists that he is still deeply concerned about injustice and inequality, feminism, the environment, people power, and even imperialism: 'I know how it feels when your nerve endings go out to the Salvadoran coffee picker, the Bangladeshi textile worker, the battered wife, the unemployed steel worker, the child at the wrong end of the cruise missile, so that acting on their behalf feels like breathing' (Gitlin 2003: 64). But liberalism, unlike radicalism, tempers idealism with steady doses of realism, and this in turn entails recognizing '9/11' for the attack on liberal values that it is. Meanwhile, for the writer Paul Berman '9/11' serves as a clarion call in a civilizational clash, not explicitly between Islam and Judaeo-Christianity but between 'Terror and Liberalism'. As Elleke Boehmer and Stephen Morton point out, 'the vocabulary of terror has in recent years become the bass note' to a great deal of policy and journalistic rhetoric which simultaneously justifies 'a war waged on an abstract concept' while denying the 'fundamental point that terrorism as political violence is the ground upon which sovereignty is in many cases defined in the colonial present' (2010: 6). The binary invoked by Berman not only maps on to the implicit (at times explicit) opposition between 'east' and 'west', but also enables him, like Gitlin, to minimize or elide altogether the violence inflicted by capitalist globalization and imperialism, both past and present. The iterative sense of the west as defined by an originary liberalism is central to Berman's argument: 'The Western countries seemed to have discovered the secret of human advancement … This idea was, in the broadest sense, liberalism—liberalism not as rigid doctrine but as a state of mind, a way of thinking about life and reality' (37–8). Similarly, Anthony argues that 'a major thrust of the British story over the centuries has been emancipation: religious, political and increasingly in the last century, social and sexual' (2008: 123).

While the aggressive Eurocentrism of these pronouncements could be dismissed as just so much recidivism, the teleology of progress, so familiar to us from nineteenth-century European colonial discourse, should give us pause for thought. If for nineteenth-century philosophers like Hegel (1899), 'world history' [*Weltgeschichte*] moved from despotic east to monarchical west, culminating in the freedom and sovereignty of the European nation state which, in turn, justified the colonization of lands 'without History', the apparent persistence of 'un-freedom' in the Middle East and Africa now provides the justification for its continued domination by an imperialism of freedom (see Hazbun and Sharp in this section of the volume). The apocalyptic claim at the heart of 'hard-headed' liberal rhetoric is that for all of America's faults, there are malign forces at work in the world that trump American misdemeanours. For Gitlin, 'power can be for the good as well as for the bad … is frequently both, and … some sorts of power are worse—far worse, unspeakably much worse—than others' (2003: 146). The 'real' threat of imperialism comes from the darker corners of the globe, from forces willing to kill in the name of their own version of empire and which can only be outstripped by a better, kinder empire: 'Indisputably there are forces in the world that, if victorious, would leave the world far worse off than American power' (145). For unlike the Nazis and the Japanese, unlike Soviet Russia and al-Qaeda, the US fights wars with due 'decent respect for the opinions of mankind' by '[declaring] the cause which impelled them to belligerence' (146).

Berman's justification for American empire against what he deems to be the far-worse imperialism of 'Terror' in the abstract entails the construction of an elaborate if fantastical genealogy for Islamist violence as deriving from totalitarian ideologies in the European past. Al-Qaeda and the Taliban are, in these terms, directly descended from both Hitler and Stalin, and Islamism from communism and Nazism. (This is, of course, in material contradiction of the facts, which include the US's sponsorship of the Taliban in a war *against* Soviet communism.) Berman argues that Islamism represents the new face of totalitarianism, an ideology the east has adopted from the west, with the latter having long expunged its versions—Nazism and communism—from its body politic. Unlike the 'rational' violence of the US or Israeli Zionism, Islamism supposedly resembles its western predecessors in its constitutive irrationality, its practice of cruelty and violence for their own sake. Suggesting that the Germans should 'go door to door throughout [the Middle East] issuing a product recall', Berman insists that only the US and its military can provide a safeguard against the irrational and illiberal, whenever and wherever these are to be found in the world.

The most advanced template for the liberal advocacy of western 'intervention', more specifically US militarism in the name of humanitarianism and extending the liberal democratic political model, was issued by the most controversial of the Renegade Liberal Prophets. Once a leading intellectual light of the British New Left, in the years leading up to his death in 2012 Christopher Hitchens turned into the poster boy for twenty-first-century Liberal Internationalism, inviting denunciation by the left for apostasy, a position he revelled in as proof of his own intellectual honesty. Laying claim to nothing less than the mantle of the European Enlightenment, Hitchens insisted that his own break from the left was undertaken in the name of 'real' revolutionary values: 'The real test of a radical or a revolutionary is not the willingness to confront orthodoxy and arrogance of the rulers but the readiness to contest illusions and falsehoods among close friends and allies' (cited in Cottee and Cushman 2008: 4).

Despite his apparent confidence in the self-evident superiority of western civilizational values over others, Hitchens was preoccupied with the dangers posed by hypothetical postcolonial apologists for Islamism and terrorism. The anti-colonial left's putative 'abdication of its commitment to think' is exemplified by what he believes to be the widely held view that 'the September 11 crime is a mere bagatelle when set beside the offenses of the Empire' and by an insistence on 'chang[ing] the subject ... to Palestine or East Timor or Angola or Iraq' during discussions of the attacks on New York (2008: 56). Insisting that none of these situations are actually colonial in nature, Hitchens ventures a convoluted refutation of comparisons between, for instance, colonial Algeria and present-day Iraq, insisting that the 'more serious analogy' is just between the FLN's resistance to French colonialism and the Kurdish *peshmarga* 'fighting very effectively on the coalition side' (2008: 124). In other words, imperialism itself is in the past, an anachronistic preoccupation for the left, but nevertheless may be handily deployed as a term of a denunciation for the contemporary aspirations of Islamism, 'a totalitarian and medieval ideology' (2008: 125). In a move which replicates George W. Bush's false allegation that Iraq was behind the destruction of the twin towers, Hitchens conflates Saddam's determinedly secular, if violent, Ba'athism with al-Qaeda's brand of militant Islam. American intervention in Iraq is figured as a series of liberal triumphs, each of which echoes older liberal justifications of empire. The 'imperialist plot' in Iraq, Hitchens sneers, has resulted in religious freedom on an unprecedented scale, a brand new economy, and a concerted effort in the face of 'theological barbarism' to 'try and create something that is simultaneously federal and democratic ... to continue to deny Iraq to demagogues and murderers and charlatans' (2008: 129). Then, like other Liberal Prophets, he clinches his point by underscoring the glories of western cultural influence: 'Those Arab Iraqis who take a pro-American line do have a tendency to be secular, educated and multicultural' (2008: 129).

For the Liberal Prophet, the key stumbling block towards achieving a desirable global order is 'anti-Americanism', a capacious term which covers everything from attitudes to American tourists to protests against Guantánamo Bay; from Graham Greene novels to Michael Moore documentaries; and from Edward Said and Noam Chomsky to John Berger and the Muslim Council of Britain. The glossing of the west as constitutively American is a key shift from the nineteenth-century liberal tradition in which Britain and Europe represent the apogee of Enlightenment thought, the exemplary sites of free-dom and sovereignty; with the formal end of European empires and the post-war rise of the United States as defender of 'the free world', to be 'western' is also to be constitutively pro-American. This shift, echoed in the famous *Le Monde* headline in the wake of the 2001 New York attacks—'We are all Americans'—is glossed by Prophets as follows: 'The life I've lived in a Western European liberal democracy, with all its unprecedented free-dom and security, I owe in large part to the existence and support of the United States of America' (Anthony 2008: 276). This claim is routinely followed by counterfactual medi-tations in the following vein:

> It's fine and good to adopt an anti-American bias but what liberals are then obliged to ask themselves is what the world would be like with a different superpower. If we look at the real world alternatives the twentieth century threw up—the British and French empires, Nazi Germany and the Soviet Union—then the United States begins to look quite benign ... Would the lot of humanity improve were China to become the most powerful nation on earth, as some on the left seem fervently to wish? (Anthony 2008: 284)

Raising the philosophical stakes, Hitchens rests his case for a US-led world order on a denunciation of what he insists is left-relativism or so-called 'moral equivalence', a con-cept much favoured by Liberal Prophets by way of denouncing the apparent relativism of critics of US imperialism. His argument runs something like this: America, like Britain before it, may have earned a few black marks historically, but in a world shaped by '9/11', it is incumbent on us not just to make distinctions but actively to elect the force for real good, which is—palpably and properly—the US. To interrogate the limits of this good-ness is to commit the sin of attributing moral equivalence to, say, Saddam's invasion of Kuwait and the Iran-Contra scandal. Within this strictly Manichaean framework, even the likes of Edward Said, whom Hitchens acknowledges to be anything but an appeaser of fundamentalist Islam, fail the relativism test. The same man who, Hitchens concedes, refused to be 'an apologist for jihadism', who 'was ready to attack insularity and tribalism in the Arab world as he was to excoriate condescension in the Anglo-American pro-fessoriate', and who 'repeatedly confronted his Arab readership with stern criticism of their own shortcomings, and of the abject failures and horrible crimes of their regimes and their leaders' is nevertheless, when it comes to the US, culpable of 'silly demagogy' and 'sub-literate violence' (2008: 194, 196). Why is this? Because 'never once did [Said] allow that American or British policy, directed at changing [Middle Eastern] regimes, could be justified' (196). In other words, Said is capable of complexity when critiquing the Arab world but guilty of moral equivalence when he criticizes western policies.

Gitlin's advocacy of anti-anti-Americanism takes a more layered and superficially emollient form. Listing liberal causes he supports—Greenpeace, Amnesty International,

landmine abolition, and the Rainforest Action Network's 'campaigns against corporate abominations' (2003: 95)—Gitlin notes: 'Read history with an open eye and it is
hard not to notice an American empire. On grounds of justice, you have to oppose it'
(2003: 144). Manifest Destiny, the doctrine that justified the conquest of the west is, he
notes critically, 'a robust defense of righteous empire' (144). And yet it turns out these
are preparatory concessions towards a different goal, one that seeks both to mitigate
the effects of past European imperialism and to suggest that, of those empires Gitlin
identifies as being operative in the present, the US's 'imperial reach' is the least bad and,
in many ways, the most desirable option. No sooner is imperialism in America's past
acknowledged than Gitlin hastens to qualify his criticism: 'You need not subscribe to
the Left's grandest claims that America from its birth is—*essentially*—genocidal and
indebted to slavery for much of its prosperity to acknowledge that white colonists took
the land, traded in slaves and profited immensely thereby' (145, emphasis in the original). Deploying 'essentially' where 'constitutively' might have sufficed (for how else can
one read the establishment of the thirteen expanding colonies on land inhabited by slain
indigenes?), Gitlin's satire of anti-Americanism begins to shade into a justification of
American imperialism: 'In the cartoon view ... nothing is worse than American power—not the women-enslaving Taliban, not the unrepentant al-Qaeda committed to kill
Americans anywhere just as they please ... the bitter-end anti-American thinks nothing is complicated about America and its works' (152–3).

AMERICAN GOODS AND THE GLOBAL GOOD

While Prophets rarely address the material underpinnings of US imperialism, restricting themselves to providing ideological support for military and political interventions,
Gitlin is an exception. Acknowledging that 'long-time properties such as the Philippines
and Latin America ... guarantee cheap resources and otherwise line American pockets', he insists that this is not 'colonialism in the strict sense' but something more nebulous and benign—'lording it over' (2003: 145). Imperial reach, however, does not justify
academic critiques of US foreign policy and economic practice. 'In some university
precincts, when you say *empire, power, colonial, dominant, hegemonic,* behold! A bolt
of lightning flashes with a crash of cymbals, and the words are supposed to settle the
question of what to think or do—oppose them!' (2003: 147). While liberals 'dispute
American policies too', they understand that it is 'far better to acknowledge and wrestle
with the strange and perverse dualities of America: the liberty and arrogance twinned,
the bullying and tolerance, myopia and energy, standardization and variety, ignorance
and inventiveness, the awful heart of darkness and the self-reforming zeal' (147).

   While it is not unreasonable to posit these contrapuntal notions to describe the US
as an actual existing geopolitical and social formation, why do Liberal Prophets not
grant the same ontological complexities to Middle Eastern polities rather than paint
them in terms of absolute brutality and backwardness? If the United States is entitled

to be defended from caricatures that depict it as 'uniformly brutal' and as an 'oil-greedy, Islam-disrespecting oppressor', then why do these standards of nuance not apply to Afghanistan or Iraq? It is the reverse crudity of refusing 'strange and perverse' dualities to other contexts that renders Gitlin's 'anti-anti-Americanism' suspect. Unsurprisingly, the last chapters of his Socratic monologue culminate in a paean to the virtues of a global American Republic: 'We might even stand on the edge of an auspicious turn in world history. The ideas of the Enlightenment, which were the founding ideas of the American republic, conceived of human beings as possessed of rights by virtue of being born human … [and] secure life, liberty and the pursuit of happiness' (2003: 167).

This revitalized liberal vision of America and the global good life under the Pax Americana is glossed more fully in the writings of Salman Rushdie, who joined Hitchens, Amis, and other 'liberal hawks' in support of the 2001 US invasion of Afghanistan, though not the 2003 invasion of Iraq: 'America did, in Afghanistan, what had to be done, and did it well' (Rushdie 2003: 399). Rushdie embodies key elements of both the Prophet and—discussed in the next section—the Acolyte. Since 11 September 2001 his writings have reprised the central preoccupations of Liberal Prophets:

> There has been a lot of sanctimonious moral relativism around lately … Let's be clear about why this bien-pensant anti-American onslaught is such appalling rubbish. To excuse such an atrocity by blaming US-government policies is to deny the basic idea of all morality: that individuals are responsible for their actions. (2003: 392)

'All morality' here is sweepingly defined in purely liberal individualist terms and demands an elision of causality and historicity. In the wake of '9/11', Rushdie, whose talent once was to hold both imperialist and postcolonial tyrants to account, sets up a familiar 'us and them' opposition where the 'us' is determinedly western and liberal. His own list of 'what matters' is studded with parochial proclivities masquerading as desirable cultural universals: 'kissing in public places, bacon sandwiches, disagreement, cutting-edge fashion, literature, generosity, water, movies, music, freedom of thought, beauty, love' (2003: 393). Indeed, Rushdie is so insistent on the universal good constituted by American goods—'sneakers, burgers, blue jeans and music videos'—that he deems *all* those who interrogate 'the globalizing power of American culture' to belong to an 'improbable alliance which includes everyone from cultural-relativist liberals to hardline fundamentalists, with all manner of pluralists and individualists, to say nothing of flag waving nationalists and splintering sectarians, in between' (2003: 297–8). Deploying the singularly inappropriate trope of 'apartheid' to describe movements seeking to protect local economies and cultures from the destructive sweep of multinational capitalism, Rushdie seems oblivious to the possibility that globalization—which he describes rather contradictorily as at once American and universal—has so far been neither global nor diverse but rather a form of economic fundamentalism with global ambitions, which operates largely through corporate homogenization. And, like the Liberal Prophets, Rushdie invokes the liberation of Europe by American armed forces, suggesting that any critique of America from Europe constitutes a form of ingratitude and bad faith.

Though his work is distinguished by its enthusiasm for the new, Rushdie's pronouncements on the US tend to fall back on obligatory and predictable forms of counterfactual
which narrow rather than open out imaginative possibilities:

> And if by chance there were a universal value which might, for the sake of argument,
> be called 'freedom' whose enemies—tyranny, bigotry, intolerance, fanaticism—were
> the enemies of us all; and if this 'freedom' were discovered to exist in greater quantity
> in the countries of the West than anywhere else on earth; and if in the world as it
> actually exists, rather than in some unattainable Utopia, the authority of the United
> States were the best current guarantor of that 'freedom', might it not follow that to
> oppose the spread of American culture would be to take up arms against the wrong
> foe? (2003: 297–8)

In keeping with Liberal Prophet assertions, Rushdie identifies an element called 'freedom', mysteriously and hypothetically to be found only in the west for the purposes of
polemical speculation while still reserving the right to make claims on the basis of 'the
world as it actually exists'. Economics, meanwhile, is characterized by a lack of alternatives: 'Globalization isn't the problem, the inequitable distribution of global resources
is', he says, as though the cultural and the economic were easily separable (2003: 415).
In an actually existing world where market fundamentalism with the concomitant subordination of all human life to the workings of the free market has such dominance, we
must ask, as Rushdie does not, whether meaningful counterfactuals can be posed where
genuine alternatives have been closed off.

In his pithy account of the workings of economic neoliberalism, David Harvey asks
a pertinent question of the kinds of liberalism that provide it with ideological cover by
equating unregulated markets with human emancipation: 'If we were able to mount
that wondrous horse of freedom, where would we seek to ride it?' (Harvey 2003: 198).
'What is astonishing', he adds, 'about the impoverished condition of contemporary
public discourse in the US as well as elsewhere is the lack of any serious debate as to
which of several divergent concepts of freedom might be appropriate to our times'
(2003: 184). Instead of opening the grounds for a genuinely cosmopolitan and open
debate, Liberal Prophets have displaced the quest for freedom—in an old imperial
gesture—to the grounds of the unfree 'other'. Unsurprisingly, women and feminized
minorities in need of rescue and rehabilitation are at the heart of this displacing gesture. Berman's bizarre description of the 2001 invasion of Afghanistan as 'the first feminist war' would be more startling were it not for a time-honoured tradition of justifying
western colonial and military missions in the region not just as humanitarian endeavours of emancipation but as specifically *gendered* liberation. The Bush administration,
too, rebranded its retaliatory military mission against the Taliban as a war for Afghan
women's rights, notwithstanding its open anti-feminism in relation to domestic wom-
en's issues. It was the same administration that proceeded later to suggest, even less
credibly, that Operation Enduring Freedom, as it termed the intervention in Iraq, was
underwritten by feminist goals.

THE SELF-REPRESENTING NATIVE ACOLYTE

Regardless of whether or not such emancipatory claims were given credence by the tax-payers who funded these wars, the last decade has witnessed a surge of interest in the topic of Islamic societies and Muslim women, as evidenced in a number of literary and critical texts and media discussions. While the likes of Hitchens and Berman occupied prominent positions as commentators on the topic, a new and increasingly influential category of author in the west, the self-representing Muslim, has also entered the arena. The Self-Representing Native Acolyte not only offers critiques of Islam, assuming authenticity and authority based on personal experience, but typically insists on the superiority of western culture as evidenced by the European Enlightenment and contemporary liberal democracies. The writings of Muslim commentators of Middle eastern or south Asian descent such as Ibn Warraq, Fouad Ajami, Kanan Makiya, and Irshad Manji have been influential in the battle to win hearts and minds within the west for the British and American occupations of Afghanistan and Iraq and intervention in Muslim polities more generally. Speaking with articulate authority, these commentators work to allay liberal anxieties about paternalism and the imposition of western values by adopting a position of equality and partnership in the project of transforming their homelands through western intervention and the spread of liberal values. Their writings are widely represented in popular press and publishing outlets and, in the case of literary works such as Khaled Hosseini's *The Kite Runner* (2003) and Azar Nafisi's *Reading Lolita in Tehran* (2004), have also taken on a pedagogical role, widely taught as sensitively authoritative sources on the predicaments of their respective countries.

If the subjugated Oriental woman in need of rescue constitutes an ongoing trope in liberal imperial discourse, the emergence of the heroic female renegade fleeing repressive Islamic societies represents something of an early twenty-first century shift from traditional styles of representation. Unlike her veiled and silent forbear, who excited the interest of nineteenth-century colonial feminists and travellers, this woman speaks eloquently about her own tribulations which are also those, implicitly, of all other women in her society. Her reader is assumed to be a member of a democratic western polity and is addressed in a European language (usually English). As Fatemeh Keshavarz (2008) has noted, the position of the narrator as insider and eyewitness is crucial for a liberal readership, which sees itself as post-imperial, culturally sensitive, and self-reflexively aware of the politics of cultural encounter. The self-representing Muslim woman's narrative emerges as a story not so much of rescue as of a flight to safety and refuge whereby the west and its values are not imposed but embraced voluntarily, then disseminated, by a woman figured as both naturally rebellious and beautiful to behold. The poster child for this phenomenon is the controversial Dutch-Somali politician, Ayaan Hirsi Ali, advocate of an 'enlightenment project' and author of books such as *Infidel* (2007) and *Nomad* (2010a), vivid memoirs intended to illustrate her claim that Islam has a 'moral framework not compatible with the modern westernised way of living' (Ali 2010b). Feminism has won in the west and must now 'focus on issues faced by non-western women, because they are the biggest issues. To own your own sexuality, as an adult woman; to choose your own lifestyle; to have access to education ...' (Ali 2010b).

LIPSTICK AND LIBERATION: READING (MORE THAN) LOLITA IN TEHRAN

Around the time that Hirsi Ali's appeal to European and American liberals was being undermined by her close links with the Dutch right as well as the unmasking of parts of her story as fake (she resigned from the Dutch parliament in 2006 after admitting to lying on her asylum application), Azar Nafisi's *Reading Lolita in Tehran* (2004) became something of a publishing phenomenon, spending a hundred weeks on the bestseller lists and garnering glowing reviews throughout the western world. Such was its popularity in university curricula and book clubs that publishers attached questions for discussion to the paperback edition. However, the putatively feminist pedagogy of the text bears closer scrutiny. *Reading Lolita*'s frame narrative is the author's account of a private reading group, which meets in her Tehran home between 1995 and 1997. Having resigned her academic post, Nafisi decides to fulfil a dream by 'discussing harmless works of fiction' with several of her most gifted former students although, as it transpires, fiction is anything but 'harmless' in her own deployment of it. Interspersed with an account of the group's discussions are reflections on the Revolution of 1979, which overthrew the unpopular and authoritarian US-backed Shah and instituted an Islamic Republic, though this history plays no actual part of Nafisi's narrative. (Eliding historical detail in favour of generic enunciations of tyranny and misrule is a key feature of liberal arguments for empire.) *Reading* is absorbing, even compelling, as an account of everyday life for the Tehranian upper-middle class under an autocratic regime and an elaboration of the experience of femininity and sexuality in an environment that is repressive of both. Literature, Nafisi insists, must provide a refuge from such a depressing reality as well as 'epiphanies' about its 'truth'.

While Nafisi's encomiums to the joys of reading appear bland, even unexceptionable, literature and reading actually have determinate political resonances in her text. She imagines the reading group as 'a place of transgression' that would 'give me the freedoms denied in the classes I taught in the Islamic Republic' (2004: 6, 10). Remarkably, given the stated intention to seek 'epiphanies' about their shared condition, she and her students will read only one non-European text and that, the most iconic Orientalist one of them all, *The Arabian Nights* (in English translation), which seems to be the only resource the class can draw on to discuss images of Iranian womanhood. Strikingly, Nafisi makes no reference to modern Iranian writers, artists, or numerous contemporary works by women and feminists. Margaret Atwood's scandalously uninformed description of *Reading Lolita*, in a blurb for the soft cover of its Random House edition, as 'a literary raft on Iran's sea of fundamentalism' is enabled by the text's deliberate elision of even modern

Iranian cinema, which features directors such as Kiarostami and Makhmalbaf who are household names even in parts of the west. As Keshavarz demonstrates, also missing are the names of well-known modern women writers such as Forugh Farrokhzad, Parvin Etesami, and Shahrnush Parsipur, all of whom would have posed problems for the delineation of Iran as a cultural wilderness, void of resisting voices. Nafisi nominally grants Iran a classical past but its present is unremittingly tyrannical and empty of thought. In the present, it is the west and the west alone that is the zone of freedom.

This carefully constructed absence of thinking, questioning, writing, and resistance within Iran (and by clear implication, all Muslim societies) is integral to the figuring of the west not just as a resource for change but the *only* possible one. The few allusions to local and feminist resistance in the text are those inspired by *Lolita*: 'And like Lolita, we took every opportunity to flaunt our insubordination: by showing a little hair from under our scarves, insinuating a little colour into the drab uniformity of our appearances, growing our nails, falling in love, listening to music' (2004: 25–6). The redemptive discourse of liberal western intervention requires a reification of the commonplace understanding that freedom and freedom of expression are uniformly absent outside of European–American cultures, an assumption which constitutes the grounds for intervention. Nafisi's account relies on the widespread liberal assumption that: 'The ability to do things such as speak one's mind, make a film, write a story, or publish a book are … inherently Western qualities', albeit ones that can be adopted in other contexts (Keshavarz 2008: 122). Beyond advocating capitalist globalization in general terms, liberal imperial discourse rarely discusses the economic content of 'freedom' and any meaningful choices that might emerge from a debate around it, choosing instead to emphasize sexual and cultural freedoms.

If Nafisi's enthusiasm for the writers she teaches—Nabokov, Fitzgerald, and James, with a smattering of Austen—appears genuine enough, it is also clear that this sliver of the western (mainly American) canon functions to figure the west not just as a zone of singular aesthetic achievement (Macaulay's proverbial 'single shelf') but as the *only* possible site of imaginative freedom. Thus, the 'Magician', Nafisi's mentor, who resists curriculum change, insists: 'What he could teach was Racine … Whenever they decided they wanted to run a proper university and reinstate Racine, that was up to them' (2004: 139). Of course, even within the west, distinctions must be made between the truly good and the merely impassioned ('coarse emotions not worthy of true literature'): 'one single film by Laurel and Hardy was worth more than all … revolutionary tracts including those of Marx and Lenin' (2004: 140). The discourse on imaginative freedom as constitutive of and unique to the west (and in turn underpinning modernity) then leads to another, equally troubling and self-Orientalizing claim: 'We in ancient countries have our past—we obsess over the past. They, the Americans have a dream: they feel nostalgia about the promise of the future' (2004: 109). Even so, very little of Iran's rich and variegated literary and cultural past actually makes it into Nafisi's narrative.

Even as it laments anti-Americanism and satirizes anti-imperialist rhetoric, Nafisi's memoir also elides the details of Iran's recent history, scrupulously avoiding references either to American involvement in the authoritarian regime of the deposed Shah or to its participation in the 1953 overthrow of the democratically elected Prime Minister, Mohammad Mosaddeq. The implied reader is merely informed that 'a far more reactionary and despotic regime' replaced the Shah and involved both the Iranian people and the intellectual elite in a 'serious error of judgement' (2004: 102). Again, the US is nominated at the outset as the lesser evil, if not the outright winner, in a discursive battle fought against both Islam and socialism. Revolution is wrong, but 'rebellion', defined purely in terms of individual liberties, is worthy. The point, as Hamid Dabashi argues is not that Islamists in Iran are benign. But evacuating history and context from the discussion with the aim of portraying Iran itself as an oppressive monolith constitutes 'the systematic abuse of legitimate causes' such as 'the unconscionable oppression of women living under Muslim laws' (2006: n.p.). The opposition between ostensibly past-driven cultures (Asian and African) and freedom-loving, future-oriented democracies (Europe and North America) is itself monologic. Nafisi's attribution of female agency and resistance solely to Austen's heroines and Henry James's Daisy Miller entails a discursive silencing of those many Iranian female and feminist voices that have been engaged in social and political struggles through the Shah's regime and the Islamic Revolution that deposed him.

Reading Lolita also polemicizes against what it sees as being an untenable anti-Americanism. Like Liberal Prophets, Nafisi figures herself as possessed of experience and wisdom through having outgrown her necessarily juvenile revolutionary past. It is her engagement with the domain of the aesthetic and the literary, however, that is the book's unique feature, allowing its author to play 'on the ambiguity of the generic territory it occupies between fact and fiction' (Keshavarz 2008: 137). Indeed, what is striking about the text is not what it tells us about Iranian women under an authoritarian patriarchy but how *little* it tells us about their sufferings beyond the upset of upper-class women at not being able to wear lipstick and blush: 'I felt helpless as I listened to their endless tales of woe … In between bursts of tears, she explained that she was late because the female guards at the door, finding a blush in her bag, had tried to send her home with a reprimand' (2004: 9). These are not insignificant humiliations but they constitute little more than the surface of a far more substantial and complicated story. Rather, Muslim women are reduced in Nafisi's narrative—as they are both by the liberal interventionist discourse she supports and by Islamist patriarchs—to physical features: hair, lips, and eyes.

'There is a Way to Be Good Again': *The Kite Runner*

A powerful and politically more intricate text than Nafisi's memoir, *The Kite Runner* (since turned into a Hollywood film), is a work of fiction that has also moved swiftly up the best-seller lists, becoming a staple for reading groups and university curricula (and duly accompanied in some editions, like Nafisi's text, by a reading guide). Received at once as a familiar narrative of individual redemption and a documentary representation of the collapse of Afghanistan under the Taliban, the novel's politics are subtler than *Reading Lolita*'s, and its ideological cards played much closer to the author's chest. If Nafisi constantly foregrounds the US as a land of freedom and opportunity, 'America' in Hosseini's novel constitutes for the most part an eloquent silence at the narrative's heart. The story of an Afghan boyhood damaged in a moment of cowardice, of failure to protect a weaker child, and of an adulthood subsequently spent in emotional and geographical exile, is arranged uneasily around this silence. Written in the mode of Ian McEwan's *Atonement*, where a childish act of injustice haunts the protagonist who seeks to make amends later in life, *The Kite Runner* also tells a compelling story about fathers, sons, fraternal bonds, and love in times of war.

However, what might have been a powerful tale of missed opportunities and broken families cannot—especially in the context of its publication not long after the invasion of Afghanistan—be easily assimilated into the universalist mode in which fiction from the non-west is often received. This much is clear from routine critical commentary, especially in the US, that hailed the novel as 'an incredible story of [Afghan] culture' (*Denver Post*, quoted in Hosseini 2003) or as offering 'a lesson on [the author's] culture and the history of his beloved homeland' (*San Antonio Express-News*, quoted in Hosseini 2003). At the same time, anything resembling informed specificity is undermined by what Dabashi calls the novel's 'strategy of selective memory', which is itself predicated on an 'empire lacking, in fact requiring an absence of, long term memory' (2006: n.p.). *The Kite Runner* is thus able to rewrite a contemporary conflict both in the mould of a timeless narrative of a good overcoming evil *and* figure Afghanistan as a place of incommensurable and ancient enmities that have no immediate resonance in the west's own historical record. As a result, the United States' own long-standing military and political presence in the region is elided to the point where nearly every geopolitical force behind the Taliban is enumerated except for the superpower responsible for its emergence and militarization in the first place: 'The people behind the Taliban. The real brains of this government if you can call it that: Arabs, Chechens, Pakistanis' (Hosseini 2003: 232).

If women are the objects of oppression and liberation in *Reading Lolita*, Hosseini's novel speaks to a less prominent though also long-standing argument within liberal colonial discourse: the claim that endemic ethnic strife in non-western polities frequently invites the benign intervention of a more enlightened imperial power to keep the peace. In the case of *The Kite Runner*, the benevolence of American protection is extended towards the disenfranchised Persian-speaking ethnic group known as the Hazaras, feminized in the raped figure of the boy Hassan and, later on, his son. Although Hassan's treatment at the hands of the child-protagonist is clearly the result of a combination of childish cowardice and feudal entitlement, it is soon developed into an allegory of the treatment of ethnic minorities under the Taliban and at the hands of Afghans more generally. 'You come all the way from America for a … Shi'a?' asks one character, with surprise, of the protagonist who returns to make amends to his childhood friend's son (2003: 266). While the marginalization and maltreatment of ethnic groups such as the Hazaras is clearly a problem within Afghanistan, the point here is the restitution and privileging of the US, which, in the middle of a brutal war, is portrayed not just as essentially innocent but as an exemplary moral force: 'In the west, they have an expression for that. They call it ethnic cleansing' (284). Only in the west, we are given to understand, is injustice recognized for what it is, providing the moral grounds and pedagogical agenda for a lamentable, but still necessary, war.

At the same time, the personal morality tale of a man who belatedly attempts to make amends for a past injustice also works as a moral allegory for America's role as a liberal rather than traditional imperial power, its latest intervention in the region figured as a form of atonement for past interference: 'Sometimes, I think everything he did, feeding the poor on the streets, building the orphanage, giving money to friends in need, it was all his way of redeeming himself. And that, I believe, is what true redemption is, Amir jan, when guilt leads to good' (263). In addition to being redeemed by its own international interventions, the US also—in a more familiar literary and political image—offers its immigrants shelter, freedom, and the chance to redeem themselves in their turn: 'I see America has infused you with the optimism that has made her so great. That's very good. We're a melancholic people, we Afghans, aren't we? Often we wallow in too much *ghamkhori* and self-pity. We give in to loss, to suffering, accept it as a part of life, even see it as necessary' (175–6). While in America, 'you could step into a grocery store and buy any of fifteen or twenty different types of cereal', Afghanistan is marked by stasis: 'Wars were waged, the Internet was invented, a robot had rolled on the surface of Mars, and in Afghanistan we were still telling Mullah Nasruddin jokes' (232–3). While America gives barbaric cultures the term 'ethnic cleansing' to describe the evil they do and that it will fight, Afghans are marked by a distinct lack of self-reflexiveness and instinctual barbarism: 'maybe what people said about Afghanistan was true. Maybe it *was* a hopeless place' (233).

Intersecting with the forms of liberal imperial discourse discussed above, *The Kite Runner* opposes America's flawed goodness and redeemable mistakes to genealogically allied forms of evil that are absolute and irredeemable. The novel's strutting villain, Assef who is, almost incredibly, a half-German votary of Hitler, intones with cartoonish menace: 'Ethnic cleansing. I like it. I like the sound of it' (2003: 249). Amir's and America's victory over him must be decisive and brutal: 'There are bad people in this world, and sometimes bad people stay bad. Sometimes you have to stand up to them … You gave him what he deserved, and he deserved even more' (278). Like *Reading Lolita*, *The Kite Runner* serves liberal imperialism by 'facilitating the operation of a far more insidious global domination' in 'the disguise of a legitimate critic of localised tyranny' (Dabashi 2006: n.p.).

CONCLUSION

Even as the relationship between liberalism and empire has deep historical roots, the colonial present is served by a vast and sophisticated ideological apparatus—one that serves to elicit and consolidate consent for the workings of militarism and corporate globalization. The triumphal post-Cold War rhetoric of freedom-as-capitalism has, as some scholars have argued, produced a new liberal Orientalism that works, not so much with difference as with an 'economy of sameness' deployed in the interests of producing a consensual assimilation into corporate globalization under the 'benign' leadership of the US. As Daniel Vukovich shows in relation to new forms of Orientalism around China, there is a shift here from the Orientalism previously discussed by Said, which entailed figuring the east as essentially 'other', to one where the east must become *generally equivalent* to the West' (2009: 2, emphasis in original; see also Vukovich in Part V of this volume). Although recent uprisings in Egypt, Libya, Tunisia, Syria, and elsewhere in the Middle East have posed a challenge to the narrative of the west as the originator of ideas of freedom, liberal imperialism has not been slow in appropriating them for its own purposes. Thus, social media originating in the United States— Twitter and Facebook—are given more than their share of credit for fomenting dissent while Christopher Hitchens was able to opine, shortly before his untimely death, that Arabs took their inspiration from the 'assisted' overthrow of Saddam Hussein in Iraq. Similarly, President Obama, addressing Britain's parliament, can claim western inspiration that 'what we saw in Tehran, Tunis and Tahrir Square is a longing for the same freedoms that we take for granted at home'.[4]

The liberal narratives I have examined in this chapter work within this framework of 'spreading or confirming an ideology and practice that has become increasingly self-consciously universal in aspiration and impact' (Williams 2006: 1). Liberalism's universalist aspirations are enabled by a positioning of itself as the sensible middle between 'anarchist utopias envisioned by anti-globalization activists' and 'the stern theocracies envisioned by fundamentalists' (Massey 2006: 39). In this regard, as Douglas Massey insists, liberalism must 'unabashedly adopt the language of market economics' (2006: 39). To the extent that a great deal of postcolonial studies draws on that strand of liberalism which 'includes a purported respect for human rights, non-intervention, anti-imperialism, freedom of commerce and exchange and religious and political tolerance', the field must negotiate the quagmire generated by liberalism's entanglements with contemporary empire (Williams 2006: 21). This is not just about documenting, as Ranajit Guha (1997) puts it, 'liberalism's failure to act up to its profession of freedom when the crunch comes', but a necessary and reflexive engagement with the 'politically expedited collective amnesia—of manufacturing consent and discarding history at the speed of one major military operation every two years' (Dabashi 2006: n.p.). These convenient amnesias are intrinsic to the workings of capitalism, a term which, as Neil Lazarus points out, 'tends to be conspicuous largely by its absence' in postcolonial discussion (2011: 17; see also Lazarus in Part III of this volume). As the financial crises of the present strongly suggest, at the root of the problem is a widespread culture of

---

4 See <http://www.newstatesman.com/2011/05/nations-rights-world-united>, accessed 24 November 2012.

support for 'neoliberalism as the exclusive guarantor of freedom' (Harvey 2003: 4). The time has come for postcolonial studies to begin the work of undoing this tenacious and damaging ideological regime.

REFERENCES

Ali, Ayaan Hirsi (2007). *Infidel*. London: Free Press.

Ali, Ayaan Hirsi (2010a). *Nomad: A Personal Journey Through the Clash of Civilizations*. London: Simon and Schuster.

Ali, Ayaan Hirsi (2010b). 'Why are Muslims so Hypersensitive?' *The Guardian*, 8 May.

Anthony, Andrew (2008). *Fallout: How a Guilty Liberal Lost his Innocence*. London: Vintage.

Boehmer, Elleke and Stephen Morton (2010). 'Introduction: Terror and the Postcolonial', in E. Boehmer and S. Morton (eds), *Terror and the Postcolonial*. Oxford: Wiley-Blackwell, 1–24.

Cottee, Simon and Thomas Cushman (2008). 'Introduction: Terror, Iraq, and the Left', in S. Cottee and T. Cushman (eds), *Christopher Hitchens and his Critics: Terror, Iraq and the Left*. New York: New York University Press.

Dabashi, Hamid (2006). 'Native Informers and the Making of the American Empire', *Al-Ahram Weekly*, 797 (1–7 June). Online source: <http://weekly.ahram.org.eg/2006/797/special.htm>, accessed 12 May 2012

Freedland, Jonathan (2004). 'The Limits of Liberalism', *The Guardian*, 22 December.

Gilroy, Paul (2004). *After Empire: Melancholia or Convivial Culture?* London: Routledge.

Gitlin, Todd (2003). *Letters to a Young Activist*. New York: Basic Books.

Guha, Ranajit (1997). 'Not at Home in Empire', *Critical Inquiry*, 23.3: 482–93.

Harvey, David (2003). *The New Imperialism*. Oxford: Oxford University Press.

Hegel, G. W. F . (1899). *Philosophy of History*. New York: Colonial Press.

Hitchens, Christopher (2008a). 'Stranger in a Strange Land' in S. Cottee and T. Cushman 'Introduction: Terror, Iraq, and the Left', in S. Cottee and T. Cushman (eds), *Christopher Hitchens and his Critics: Terror, Iraq and the Left*. New York: New York University Press, 56–9.

Hitchens, Christopher (2008b). 'Guerillas in the Mist', in S. Cottee and T. Cushman (eds), *Christopher Hitchens and his Critics: Terror, Iraq and the Left*. New York: New York University Press, 122–4.

Hitchens, Christopher (2008c). 'Fallujah', in S. Cottee and T. Cushman (eds), *Christopher Hitchens and his Critics: Terror, Iraq and the Left*. New York: New York University Press, 125–7.

Hitchens, Christopher (2008d). 'Vietnam?' in S. Cottee and T. Cushman (eds), *Christopher Hitchens and his Critics: Terror, Iraq and the Left*. New York: New York University Press, 128–30.

Hitchens, Christopher (2008e). 'Polymath with a Cause: A Review of *From Oslo to Iraq and the Road Map* by Edward W. Said', in S. Cottee and T. Cushman (eds), *Christopher Hitchens and his Critics: Terror, Iraq and the Left*. New York: New York University Press, 193–6.

Lazarus, Neil (2011). *The Postcolonial Unconscious*. Cambridge: Cambridge University Press.

Losurdo, Domenico (2011). *Liberalism: A Counter History*. London: Verso.

Hosseini, Khaled (2003). *The Kite Runner*. London: Bloomsbury.

Ikenberry, G. John (2009). 'Liberal Internationalism 3.0: America and the Dilemmas of the Liberal World Order', *Perspectives on Politics*, 7: 71–87.

Keshavarz, Fatemeh (2008). *Jasmine and Stars: Reading More than Lolita in Tehran*. Chapel Hill, NC: University of North Carolina Press.

Massey, Douglass S. (2006). *Return of the 'L' Word: A Liberal Vision for the New Century*. Princeton: Princeton University Press.

McNally David (2006). 'Imperialist Narcissism: Michael Ignatieff's Apologies for Empire', in C. Mooers (ed.), *The New Imperialism: Ideologies of Empire*. Oxford: Oneworld Publications, 87–109.

Mehta, Uday Singh (1999). *Liberalism and Empire: A Study in Nineteenth-Century British Liberal Thought*. Chicago: University of Chicago Press.

Mooers, Colin (2006a). 'Introduction: The New Watchdogs', in C. Mooers (ed.), *The New Imperialism: Ideologies of Empire*. Oxford: Oneworld Publications, 1–8.

Mooers, Colin (2006b). 'Nostalgia for Power: Revising Imperial History for American Power', in C. Mooers (ed.), *The New Imperialism: Ideologies of Empire*. Oxford: Oneworld Publications, 87–110.

Nafisi, Azar (2004). *Reading Lolita in Tehran: A Memoir in Books*. New York: Random House.

Rushdie, Salman (2003). *Step Across This Line*. London: Vintage Books.

Vukovich, Daniel F. (2009). 'Uncivil Society, or, Orientalism and Tiananmen, 1989', *Cultural Logic: An Electronic Journal of Marxist Theory and Practice. Online source:* <http://clogic.eserver.org/2009/Vukovich.pdf>, accessed 1 May 2012.

Williams, Andrew (2006). *Liberalism and War*. London: Routledge.

CHAPTER 9

THE GEOPOLITICS OF KNOWLEDGE AND THE CHALLENGE OF POSTCOLONIAL AGENCY

International Relations, US Policy, and the Arab World

WALEED HAZBUN

INTRODUCTION

On 19 May 2011, US President Barack Obama gave a landmark speech at the State Department that sought 'to mark a new chapter in American diplomacy'. He recounted how 'for six months, we have witnessed an extraordinary change taking place in the Middle East and North Africa. Square by square, town by town, country by country, the people have risen up to demand their basic human rights'. Obama referred to this as a 'story of self-determination', declaring that 'there must be no doubt that the United States of America welcomes change that advances self-determination and opportunity ... After decades of accepting the world as it is in the region, we have a chance to pursue the world as it should be'. Obama's language and the dramatic events across the region he depicts suggest a changed world; they also signal a different American approach towards the Middle East from the one depicted in Derek Gregory's *The Colonial Present* (2004). In a text that burns with passion and anger, Gregory tells the spatial stories of ordinary people in Afghanistan, Palestine, and Iraq victimized by state violence unleashed in the wake of the September 11, 2001 attacks. Gregory draws heavily on Edward Said's notion of 'imaginative geographies' that fold distance into difference to generate what Gregory calls 'architectures of enmity'. State policies, he argues, were defined by practices that 'mark other people as irredeemably "Other" and that license the unleashing of exemplary violence against them' (2004: 16; see also Said 1979).

This chapter offers an epilogue to *The Colonial Present* by analysing the early phases of the US reaction to the 2010–11 Arab uprisings and the geopolitical changes they triggered. After an initial phase of confusion and indecision, in speeches and policy pronouncements President Obama and Secretary of State Hillary Clinton seemed to transcend the exclusionary, dehumanizing security logic of the 'war on terror'. Obama claimed to seek a 'new beginning' for US policy in the region, suggesting a narrative of mutual recognition between the US and the newly democratizing societies in the Arab world. As we will see, however, this 'new' narrative resonates with those found in *The Colonial Present* by adopting albeit more subtle strategies of exclusion and hierarchical ordering. Obama's vision for how this 'new' Arab world can be incorporated into the evolving liberal international order functions, I argue, as a form of colonial modernity. As Gregory explains in the book's final pages, 'colonialism's promise of modernity has always been deferred—always skewed by the boundary between "us" and "them"' (2004: 255). This chapter traces the development, and then highlights the persistence, of the partitions erected between the US and the Arab world that suppress and deny the agency of postcolonial actors in international politics. In the end, Obama attempts to frame the 'Arab Spring', as did Bush the 'war on terror', in such a way as to define a 'new global narrative in which the power to narrate is vested in a particular constellation of power and knowledge within the United States of America' (Gregory 2004: 16).

Rather than detailing the numerous continuities between the Bush and Obama administration policies towards the Middle East, this chapter maps the 'constellation of power and knowledge' within American scholarship about international politics and US policy in the Middle East. These discourses tend to privilege certain forms of global order while ignoring the hierarchical power relations and means of violence deployed to sustain them. At the same time, they reject the legitimacy of the subjectivity, history, and memory of political actors external to this order (for a brief elaboration, see Grovogui 2010). As Arlene Tickner and Ole Waever observe, the Arab world 'was the original object of "Orientalist" knowledge practices' (Said 1979), and again today it is (for large parts of western debate) the primary global exception: an exception to the global security order, to modernity, to secularism, to forms of knowledge and reason that constitute the "we" talking about these very exceptions (Pasha 2007)' (Tickner and Wæver 2009: 172; see also Hazbun 2011). American scholarship about international politics and US policy in the Middle East (even before '9/11') tends to deny the agency of Arab actors or to recognize it only when measured in reference to western-imposed orders. Arab regimes that support such orders are represented as enlightened autocrats or reformist modernizers. By contrast, Arab states and societies that oppose such orders are viewed as unacceptable threats, not only to regional (US-aligned) states but also to western powers and the global order more generally. As a result, Arab actors are never viewed as legitimate actors with their own interests playing an autonomous regional role or having a voice in shaping the regional or international order (outside of externally drafted scripts).

Such a broad critique of international relations and US foreign policy scholarship of the Middle East is a project that exceeds the scope of this chapter. Instead, I will begin by drawing on that broader critique in order to sketch some crucial threads of argument within the scholarship that help illustrate how the Obama administration's initial reaction to the democratic revolutions of the Arab uprisings have conformed to rather than transcended earlier constructions that 'mark other people as irredeemably "Other"'. The first thread reveals how the discourse of international relations evolved from the internal micro-history of politics across the European continent to view the consolidated, ethnically and racially homogenous nation state as the normal key actor in international politics. The 'deficiencies' of postcolonial states are thus constructed as a source of insecurity and threat to global order. A second thread, which emerged particularly with the end of the Cold War, views the increasing power of such Third World states exclusively as a source of insecurity generating heightened anxiety. These perspectives highlight an underappreciated aspect of the genealogy of Samuel Huntington's 'clash of civilizations' argument (1993, 1996), which I argue was just as much driven by a realist fear of the rising power of Third World states as it was an 'Orientalist', some might add Islamophobic, reading of the emerging post-Cold War order.

The remainder of the chapter suggests that the Obama administration might not be as motivated as Huntington or the George W. Bush administration to build 'architectures of enmity', but that its policies and visions for the Middle East still fail to embrace the agency of regional forces even as local actors are asserting themselves in new and often democratic ways. I show how, instead, major speeches and policies have attempted to position the US on the side of the Arab peoples while offering little room for accommodating their agency at a time when its effects are most apparent. Obama has recently sought to redefine the logic for the strong American presence in the region by arguing that the US is a necessary force for the realization of Arab goals. His statements suggest that the US still privileges US-dominated forms of global order, ignores their hierarchical power relations, and fails to fully recognize the agency of Middle East states and societies as actors in the international system. I conclude by briefly outlining some of the emerging forces attempting to redefine regional politics through the realization of new sources and forms of postcolonial agency.

POSTCOLONIAL STATES AND THE PRODUCTION OF INSECURITY IN THE MIDDLE EAST

Most narratives recounting the development of international relations (IR) as a field of study begin at the end of World War II (see, for example, Kahler 1997). This timeframe privileges as its master narrative the US-led effort to forge a 'liberal' international order to govern global economic and security relations as well as the rise and eventual decline of the Cold War (see Gopal in this section of the volume). At the same time, this framing removes from view the racial hierarchies and imperial geopolitics that characterized the development of the field before 1945. Few readers of the respected journal *Foreign Affairs* (published by the Council on Foreign Relations) know that this, the world's first journal of international relations, was founded in 1910 as the *Journal of Race Development* (Vitalis 2010: 928–9). During the post-war evolution of international relations as a field, these traces were erased in part by the dominance of neorealist approaches that mapped international politics in units of the nation state and their power capabilities (Waltz 1979; Keohane 1986; Mearsheimer 2003). In its most simplified expression, neorealism views global politics as a billiard table with balls of different masses (based on their power capabilities) struggling to survive in an environment of anarchy, that is, with no enforceable global law. Neo-realism attempts to determine how the structure of the 'system-level' environment (consisting of rival states seeking to increase their relative power and making alliances) shapes patterns of state behaviour. For example, according to neorealism, the nature of polarity—if there are one, two, or three-plus great powers in this system—is the most important factor shaping these patterns. Neorealism viewed the bipolar Cold War order as a stable, mostly peaceful system because states tended to align with one or the other great power, leading to rival sides with relatively equal capabilities and thereby preventing a conflict between the two major powers.

Throughout the Cold War, American policymakers, security analysts, and IR scholars generally discussed US policy and interests in the Middle East using the tools and language of neorealism. While neorealism's statist billiard ball imagery tends to discount the role of domestic politics and ideology, in scholarship about the Middle East Arab states and societies are nevertheless repeatedly marked as 'other' while their agency is denied. Most recent efforts to modify the prevailing neorealist framework to better represent the legacies of colonialism, the challenges of postcolonial state formation, and contemporary patterns of politics in the Middle East, have failed to escape a Eurocentric framework. One consequence is that such frameworks, by highlighting the domestic sources of instability in these states, generally obscure the role the US often plays as a generator of insecurity (see Smith and Turner in this section of the volume). Take for example 'subaltern realism' or other similar notions developed by neorealists to better explain the behaviour of Third World states (Ayoob 1998). In accepting the European model of a nation state as the normal unit within the international system, such notions depict the vast diversity of Third World states in terms of their common lack of fully consolidated state structures and homogenous national identity. After identifying this as a defect, these units are measured against the European template to suggest that Third World states are more likely to be led by regimes that lack legitimacy and to experience political instability. As a result, they are less likely to follow the behaviour patterns that produce stable regional balances of power and instead encourage an unstable, threatening, and war-prone international environment.

Efforts to modify the neorealist framework have often been consciously developed with intentions to better reflect ('describe, explain, and predict') the behaviour of non-western states (Ayoob 1998: 32). More critically, they seek to counter international relations scholarship that fails to recognize how weaker states might shape the international or system-level environment (Ayoob 1998: 33). This effort to recognize the agency of postcolonial states is limited, however, by its focus on measuring it in terms of how it might impact on the security concerns of the great powers (Bilgin 2008: 11). A stark example of the deployment of this logic is the work of scholars like Steven David who published a 1992/3 essay in the leading journal of international relations and security studies *International Security* entitled 'Why the Third World Still Matters'. David's essay provides an ominous map of post-Cold War global politics. It seeks to counter a view common in much neorealist scholarship that with the end of global superpower competition, which had exaggerated the strategic importance of the Third World, US policymakers should focus American policy and resources on regions of critical strategic importance such as the advanced industrialized states of Europe (see Van Evera 1990). By contrast, writing in the wake of the 1990–1 Gulf War, David calls for continuing and extending the American projection of power into the Middle East.

At a time when neorealist was facing challenges, and as many scholars were beginning to suggest that the end of the Cold War and prospects for increasing global economic interdependence were making the world safer for the US, David attempts to reanimate neorealism's Hobbesian vision of the dangers of international anarchy through his depiction of the threats posed by Third World states. He notes the 'growing likelihood that Third World States will act in ways inimical to American interests, due to the persistence of instability often leading to war' (129). David argues that 'leaders of these states may be unable or unwilling to follow "rational" policies that would safeguard American interests' (129). Foreshadowing the claims of the George W. Bush administration, he suggests that deterrence may be an unworkable strategy against such states. In sum, the essay offers a logic for the expanded American projection of power based on 'the increasing capability of many Third World states to threaten American interests, particularly in the areas of nuclear proliferation and supply of oil' (129).

In outlining the causes of instability, this portrait recognizes select aspects of the legacy of colonialism. The European colonial powers, David notes, promoted political divides along ethnic lines and imposed arbitrary borders on peoples who shared little common history and culture. Drawing on Samuel Huntington's earlier work *Political Order in Changing Societies* (1968), David argues that, unlike western European states, Third World states witnessed the emergence of mass political participation before a 'well-educated citizenry' arose to build institutions to channel participation and govern populations. David effectively transposes Huntington's warning about the destabilizing aspects of increased political participation at the domestic level to make similar claims at the international level. Huntington's critique of modernization theory, in which he highlights the likelihood of populist social mobilization leading to 'political decay' in Third World states, resembles David's anxiety about the dangers posed by Third World states, which are either due to the likelihood of political instability or because they are not effectively incorporated into the American global security architecture. Again generalizing vastly, David claims that Third World leaders do not face the institutional restraint of popular consent and are thus more likely than western states to engage in war when it serves their personal interest and maintenance of power even if war might be inimical to popular and national interests. He also claims that Third World states have more war-prone cultures since 'enemies are vilified and dehumanized in the press and textbooks … [while the] glories of military struggle are celebrated' (136), and asserts that 'the religious beliefs of many Third World states may also make them less resistant to going to war' (136). On top of this analysis, David goes on to outline 'the bleak future of the Third World' suffering economic decline, rapid population growth, environmental disasters, and massive inequality gaps that impede the rise of democracy (140–2). This approach does not recognize how interventionist policies by the US and the structure of the northern-dominated liberal international economic order pose threats to Third World states and societies (see Niva 1999). Rather, it suggests that Third World states cannot be trusted as constituent members of international society and that the US must, especially after the end of the Cold War, continue to project power across the globe to ensure its own safety and security.

REREADING THE 'CLASH OF CIVILIZATIONS' AND THE EARLY POST-COLD WAR ORDER

In *The Colonial Present*, Gregory identifies the 'at once extraordinary and dangerous claims' (57) Huntington makes about 'Islam' in *The Clash of Civilizations and the Remaking of World Order* (1996). As in other insightful and penetrating critiques, Gregory highlights Huntington's insidious deployment of the concepts of identity, culture, and religion to construct an intense, exclusionary map of global politics that 'mark other people as irredeemably "Other"' (Gregory 2004: 16, as above; see also Mignolo in Part I of this volume). Huntington's focus on culture and the idea of civilizations as units in international politics has led many scholars of international relations to read his work in terms of how these units diverge from neorealist international relations theory. They highlight Huntington's suggestion that nation states will no longer be the principal actors in global politics and that 'culture' rather than rival ideologies or economic interests will become the basis of conflict. Huntington's original 1993 essay was published months after David's *International Security* article, which was written within the idiom of neorealist international relations theory. However, the two essays (by a scholar and his former student) share a common thread that has often been missed amongst the reaction and debate about Huntington's crude use of the concept of culture. They are both driven by anxiety about the rising power and agency of Third World states. And at the same time, both assume that the only acceptable global order is one shaped and dominated by the US.

David begins his essay by stating his concern that 'many Third World states are becoming increasingly powerful' (127). His anxiety about future patterns of global politics in which Third World states have increased agency is only amplified by the uncertain nature of the global order at the end of the Cold War. While many 'defensive realists' saw increased stability and decline of conflict, in part because the US no longer needed to project power so extensively into regions of limited strategic value (Van Evera 1990), others suggested a teleological path towards the consolidation of a US-led liberal international order as more states adopted various forms of capitalist democracy (most emphatically, Fukuyama 1989; for a sophisticated version, see Deudney and Ikenberry 1999). Rereading Huntington with this debate in mind, it is striking how his argument is driven by a recognition of the desire of non-western states to become actors in global politics, which is at every moment countered by an anxiety—we might copy his quote from Bernard Lewis and call it a 'perhaps irrational … reaction' (quoted in Huntington 1993: 32)—that makes him unwilling to accept or accommodate it. He justifies his unwillingness to imagine what such accommodation would look like by resorting to his concept of civilizations that are defined by fundamental, incommensurable differences (25–9) that will shape future patterns of global conflict. As aspects of the neorealist approach to international relations were facing numerous challenges due to shifts in global politics—the end of the Cold War, the erosion of nation state sovereignty, globalization—Huntington developed the concept of 'civilizations' to reanimate select elements of the neo-realist approach that tended to sustain American militarism and unilateralism and the American quest for global primacy. He rejuvenated the notion that the structure of the international system continually poses existential security threats to states, thus compelling them to do anything necessary to survive in this hostile environment.

Lost in much of the debate provoked by Huntington's 'clash of civilizations' thesis is the fact that he was addressing a critical question of concern to scholars of postcolonialism. Like David, at the centre of Huntington's concern and anxiety is the realization that increasingly, non-western states will seek to assert their own agency and will not readily concede to being socialized into a US-defined and dominated order. Huntington exposes the contradictions in claims that the US-led liberal international order is truly inclusive and non-hierarchical. 'The West in effect', Huntington writes, 'is using international institutions, military power and economic resources to run the world in ways that maintain Western predominance, protect Western interests and promote Western political and economic values' (1993: 40). He recognizes that 'decisions made at the U.N. Security Council or in the International Monetary Fund that reflect the interests of the West are presented to the world as reflecting the desires of the world community' (39). A critical example is that 'in the post-Cold War world the primary objective of arms control is to prevent the development by non-Western societies of military capabilities that could threaten Western interests' (46). But 'the West', he notes, 'promotes non-proliferation as a *universal* norm' (46; emphasis mine).

Huntington ends the first section of his essay by suggesting that with the decline of the Cold War, international politics will no longer be centred in the west; 'the centerpiece' of the next phase of global politics will be defined rather by 'interactions between the West and non-Western civilizations and among non-Western civilizations' (1993: 23). Ignoring for a moment the problematic nature of his civilizational ontology, Huntington was addressing a question largely marginalized by the central debate amongst international relations scholars during the early 1990s, which was focused on the implications of the end of the Cold War for the rise of US regional hegemony and the Arab-Israeli peace process. Huntington's more wide-ranging suggestion was that 'the peoples and governments of non-Western civilizations no longer remain the objects of history as targets of Western colonialism, but join the West as movers and shapers of history' (23). He concludes from this that 'international relations, historically a game played out within Western civilization, will increasingly be de-Westernized and become a game in which non-Western civilizations are actors and not simply objects' (48; for a different reading of the 'de-westernization' process, see Mignolo in Part I of this volume). While Huntington takes note of the need for mutual understanding and coexistence, since cooperation and the development of collective norms and governance is not possible across civilizations, he warns that the west must 'maintain the economic and military power to protect its interests in relation to these civilizations' (49).

Across the Middle East, US policy followed the strategic logic suggested by Huntington and David and expanded the American projection of its military and diplomatic power in order to sustain its position within the potentially hostile Islamic world. This period is sometimes referred to as the 'American era' in the Middle East, echoing the period of British hegemony in the first half of the twentieth century. With no global challenger or other major power that regional states could seek aid and support from, the US quickly came to dominate regional politics. During the 1990–1 Gulf War, the US mobilized a broad coalition of Arab states to defeat Iraq. In the war's aftermath, the US was able to foster an Arab–Israeli peace process that resulted in the Oslo Process between Israel and the Palestinians (begun in 1993) and the signing of the Israel-Jordan peace treaty in 1994. At the same time, with an unchallenged military force in the Gulf, the US was able to sustain a policy of 'dual containment' against Iraq and Iran anchored by bases in Turkey, Kuwait, Saudi Arabia, Bahrain, and Qatar, and a naval fleet circulating in Gulf waters.

By 2001, however, this US-backed regional order was coming undone. The Arab-Israeli peace process had collapsed and Palestinians and Israelis were engaged in a low-intensity war. The post-Gulf War containment regime over Iraq was falling apart as regional support for maintaining harsh sanctions diminished (Lynch 2000). Meanwhile, Iran was expanding its regional influence and secretly developing a nuclear programme. Even the limited experiments with political liberalization and democratization of the late 1980s and early 1990s offered by US allies, including Jordan, Egypt, and Tunisia, had been reversed. Several states faced increasing societal opposition— often led by Islamist forces—to their regime's dependence on external support from the US that made them beholden to American regional security interests. Moreover, the American military presence in the Gulf and its sanctions regime over Iraq was provoking domestic opposition and anti-Americanism within key pro-US states such as Jordan, Egypt, Saudi Arabia, and the smaller Gulf states.

The American invasion of Iraq in 2003 can be understood in part as a reaction to this destabilized position. Following the logic of Huntington, David, and neoconservative policy analysts, Bush was unwilling to allow an erosion of US influence or a contraction in the American ability to project power in the region. Gregory's *The Colonial*

Present graphically documents this era and its violence. Gregory's discussion of the Iraq war ends by noting the rising insurgency against 'America's Iraq'. The Iraq war failed, however, to realize the Bush administration's strategic vision for regional transformation and resulted in what many have come to suggest is the end of the 'American era' of dominance over the Middle East (Haass 2006; see also Walt 2011). The years since 2003 have witnessed the steadily declining ability of the US to shape regional politics. The 2003 Iraq war was conducted without broad regional support and led to the breakdown of political order verging on sectarian civil war in Iraq. Any post-war Iraq is likely to remain a weak, divided state, increasingly influenced by Iran and the anti-American forces of the Sadrist movement. Moreover, the Arab-Israeli peace process has remained effectively dead, while the 'two-state solution' is viewed by many as no longer being viable. The breakdown of the peace process led to the re-polarization of regional politics along an Arab-Israeli axis, with US support for Israel eroding Arab support for US policies and mobilizing popular dissent in Egypt and Jordan which had in turn, with US backing, signed peace agreements with Israel. The US-led order also rotted from within as pro-US state elites seemed increasingly disconnected from the interests and concerns of their societies while non-state actors, such as Hamas and Hizballah (with Iranian backing), evolved as popular, powerful movements challenging US influence and US allies in the region (see Hazbun 2008: 252–6). These trends were most starkly illustrated during the 2006 war between Hizballah and Israel. By the late period of the Bush administration, US allies in the region had become threatened by instability and Islamist forces while regional states, such as Iran, and outside powers, such as Russia, China, and the European Union, looked to play an increasingly important role in the region.

THE ARAB UPRISINGS AND OBAMA'S 'MOMENT OF OPPORTUNITY'

On 4 June 2009 Obama gave a long awaited speech at Egypt's Cairo University in which he declared:

> I've come here to Cairo to seek a new beginning between the United States and Muslims around the world, one based on mutual interest and mutual respect, and one based upon the truth that America and Islam are not exclusive and need not be in competition. Instead, they overlap, and share common principles—principles of justice and progress, tolerance and the dignity of all human beings.

Among its other features, this speech can be read as a direct challenge to the 'clash of civilizations' thesis. It even highlights the notion of shared, overlapping values between American and Muslim societies. Since Barack Obama began his run for president many observers expected he would seek to define a new role for the US in the Middle East while attempting to undo destructive elements of the Bush administration's legacy in the region. Obama wrote, for example, that American security and wellbeing depend 'on the security and wellbeing of those who live beyond our borders … in the understanding that the world shares a common security and a common humanity' (Obama 2007; for a contradictory assessment, see Hazbun 2008).

These expectations, however, remained largely unmet before the Arab uprisings. As Ryan Lizza documents in his revealing report in the *New Yorker,* early in his administration Obama was influenced by 'realist'-oriented advisors who sought to redirect American policy in the Middle East away from military engagements and democracy promotion while cautiously holding on to the status quo (Lizza 2011). Obama's initial reaction to the protests in Egypt in early 2011, as it had been to those in Iran two years before, was an attempt to avoid the impression that the US was taking sides. Obama was aware of the limits of Bush's democracy promotion efforts and recognized that the US's regional position was heavily tied to Mubarak's willingness to support US (and Israeli) interests. Writing after the US engagement in Libya but before Obama's 19 May 2011 speech, Lizza traces how events across the Arab world throughout the spring of 2011 led Obama towards increased re-engagement with the Middle East. Lizza highlights the pre-uprising internal debates between the 'realists', who emphasized stability and had been dominating policymaking, and the more liberal internationalists, who recognized the negative implications of American ties to repressive regimes and recommended a strong push for reform. While Lizza, based on his inside sources, highlights the role of insiders advocating policy change, a close reading of events reveals that shifts in US policy at each moment were responses to changing political realities over which the US had little control. Years of debate about the trade-offs between stability and democracy were effectively trumped by massive protests in Tunis, Cairo, and elsewhere. The US publicly backed Egyptian President Mubarak, a long-term ally, right up until protests and shifts in the attitude of the Egyptian military made his position untenable. Thus, while the US might have supported democratic reform before, it only seemed to embrace political revolution after the fact.

Meanwhile, during the early months of the Arab protests the participants appeared secular and non-ideological in nature. American media coverage focused on tech-savvy youth and noted the absence of Islamists and anti-American slogans. This depiction allowed many Americans finally to view the Arab world with empathy and identification rather than as hostile and other. The British Foreign Secretary suggested that the uprisings could mark 'the greatest advance for human rights and freedom since the end of the cold war' (quoted in Kurlantzick 2011), and Francis Fukuyama remarked that 'there's something very gratifying about the Middle East demonstrating that Islam is not at odds with the democratic currents that have swept up other parts of the world' (quoted in Bast 2011). Similarly, Secretary of State Clinton would later note that 2011 saw 'the first Arab revolution for democracy' (2011) and ask 'after 2011, how can anyone honestly say that civil society is not indigenous to the Middle East and North Africa?' (2012). The revolutions accomplished what Obama in his 2009 Cairo speech did not: they overturned the exclusionary construction of otherness and visions of a 'clash of civilizations' that had previously dominated

American and European images of the region. In his 19 May 2011 speech titled 'A Moment of Opportunity', Obama accordingly attempted to craft a new narrative of American relations with the Arab world. He refers to the ongoing events as a 'story of self-determination', which he said would 'mark a new chapter in American diplomacy' in which we 'have a chance to pursue the world as it should be'. Former US Ambassador Daniel Kurtzer went so far as to suggest that 'Obama [has] articulated a radical definition of change, a kind of political "liberation theology" that he says will guide US policy' (2011).

THE 'NEW' MIDDLE EAST AND THE IDEAL OF A LIBERAL INTERNATIONAL ORDER

Obama's approach seemed to transcend the exclusionary construction of otherness found in Huntington and David. However, he studiously avoided addressing their 'postcolonial' concerns over the rising power and agency of Third World states while attempting to displace concerns about the end of the American era in the Middle East. To date, Obama and other members of his administration have notably failed to recognize the agency of the forces mobilized by the Arab uprising as actors in international politics. He may defend the dignity of individuals, but he makes little if any reference to the collective dignity of the peoples of postcolonial societies who have long sought to realize national self-determination in a global system dominated by western powers. Additionally, rather than suggesting that the US will accommodate emerging political forces and voices in the region, he persists in outlining a reinvention of the American rationale for its continued presence in the region even as events have further eroded its influence. He defends the US position in the region by restating American 'core interests' that include 'countering terrorism and stopping the spread of nuclear weapons; securing the free flow of commerce and safe-guarding the security of the region; standing up for Israel's security and pursuing Arab–Israeli peace' (Obama 2011). Seeking to justify an American role as a hegemon (strategically defined as a provider of public goods: see Vitalis 2006), Obama declares that these are not exclusively American interests but rather universal ones, in the interest of all states. He also argues that these interests are by no means 'hostile to [the Arab] people's hopes' and even claims that the American pursuit of these interests are '*essential* to [their hopes]' (Obama 2011, emphasis mine).

In his effort to address what he refers to as the 'broader aspirations of ordinary people' in the Arab world, Obama narrowly recognizes not rival geopolitical interests, but a liberal interpretation of basic human rights. He neglects to add that it is only in societies that have undergone revolutions that these rights seem attainable. He repeatedly refers to US support for political and economic reform in the region, but seems to ignore the fact that many Arab protestors are not interested in economic aid and technical advice but rather in renegotiating the terms of the Washington Consensus and US backing for neoliberal economic reforms which have been thoroughly exploited by local regimes and economic elites. In the end, he tries to outline a set of 'values' to complement the set of 'interests' that drives US policy in the region. These values, however, are those that define the basis for a liberal international order dominated by the US and western powers. The uprisings and the American recognition of an Arab democratic imaginary allows Obama to speak about the possible incorporation of the Arab world into a liberal international order defined by economic independence and mutual security arrangements and regulated by global norms and international institutions.

What Obama fails to consider is how one force currently driving social and political movements in the Arab world is the view that the terms of the US-backed liberal international order are unjust or that much insecurity in the Arab world is *caused* by external powers and pro-US regimes like Israel's. Moreover, the Middle East sits in a very awkward position in relationship to the liberal international order. The Middle East contains regions of vital security and economic interest to the US and other western powers. The Arab states, however, have remained outside the community of states that practise its collective and cooperative governance. At the same time, the Middle East has also been a deeply penetrated space, repeatedly suffering from great-power intervention and from numerous external efforts to divide and order the region, such as the British and French Mandate system after World War I.

American IR scholars such as John Ikenberry who celebrate the idea of a US-backed liberal international order, argue that global US hegemony serves the interests of other states since 'for most countries, the US-led order is a negotiated system wherein the United States has sought participation by other states on terms that are mutually agreeable' (Ikenberry 2004: 146). Ikenberry has more recently argued that 'the rise of the non-Western powers and the growth of economic and security interdependence are creating new constituencies and pressures for the liberal international order' (2011: 2). In a direct challenge to Huntington, he suggests that states like China have an interest in the maintenance of such a rule-based order because it can best protect its own interests and global influence (see Vukovich in Part V of this volume).

By contrast, others like Charles Kupchan observe that 'if India and Brazil are any indication, even rising powers that are stable democracies will chart their own courses, expediting the arrival of a world that no longer plays by Western rules' (Kupchan 2012). As Robert Vitalis points out, Ikenberry's vision of the liberal international order is dismissive of the relevance of past colonial experiences and what Ikenberry refers to as the 'crude imperial policies [of the US], most notably in Latin America and the Middle East' (Ikenberry 2004: 146, quoted in Vitalis 2006: 30). And to the degree that other non-western countries have become integrated into the liberal international order, it is in terms and within institutions already established by the North Atlantic states. The NATO-led war in Libya highlights these tensions as the Arab League originally sought to back a narrow UN mandate for a no-fly zone, but the US pushed to promote a very extensive military intervention leading to regime change, which was supported by only some Arab states. More broadly, in the Middle East the US has often worked to suppress, or very selectively to deploy, international institutions and international law as mechanisms for governing its own behaviour and that of other states in the region. For example, America's key ally Israel is frequently shielded from sanction by the actions of the Security Council. The Arab Gulf states remain critical US allies but have yet fully to embrace international norms regarding human rights, labour standards, freedom of expression, and democracy (Ulrichsen 2011). And, oddly, populations within what have been some of the most democratic polities—including Lebanon, Palestine, Iraq, and even Israel itself—tend to look to the UN as a body that has failed to protect their security and well-being.

DEMOCRACY, US INTERESTS, AND 'HISTORY'

US Secretary of State Hillary Clinton recently addressed these and other issues in a 7 November 2011 speech to the National Democratic Institute (NDI). In the speech, she stated that the US strongly supports democratic change in the Arab World as 'democracies make for stronger and stable partners'. She explained how such states fit within a liberal order, noting that 'they trade more, innovate more, and fight less'. Clinton delivered these remarks at a time when there was mounting concern about the rise of Islamist forces and about the commitment of new power holders—like the Egyptian military—to democratic change. She reveals, though, the highly conditional and contingent bases on which the US backs democratic change. In short, while the US will back democratic reform (in allied states) when it promotes stability and contains dissent, it backs revolutionary democratic change only when the status quo is unsustainable, or when it targets a regime not aligned with the US. Clinton's underlying concern seems to be to avoid a worst-case scenario such as that in the wake of the Islamic revolution in Iran. Democracies, she notes, 'channel people's energies away from extremism and towards political and civic engagement'.

Clinton also considers the question of 'how will America respond if and when a democracy brings to power people and parties we disagree with?' In her reply, she exclusively addresses domestic political and social concerns. The US, she notes, will certainly want to push for political and social rights, such as women's equality. Her only reference to regional and geopolitical dimensions to this question is her statement to the effect that 'nobody wants to see political parties with military wings and militant foreign policies gain influence'. Through such thinly veiled references to movements like Hamas and Hizballah, which had recently gained increased political power through free elections, Clinton implies that such forces do not represent legitimate voices in shaping the political future of the Arab world since they oppose US efforts to define a regional order sympathetic to its own interests. At the same time, she recognizes that the US maintains conflicting short-term interests, such as relying on non-democratic regimes to support national interests in the Gulf and host the American ability to project military power. These concerns came to the fore when the US took only limited actions in response to the Saudi-backed crackdown on the democracy protests in Bahrain. More generally, in the later phases of the Arab uprisings the US has not opposed the growing influence of non-democratic Gulf States such as Qatar and Saudi Arabia over the course of the uprisings in Libya, Yemen, and Syria.

In the end, the speeches by Obama and Clinton are best seen as ongoing attempts to pivot from the previous US strategy that viewed the uprisings against pro-US regimes as a severe threat to US security architecture in the region, to a strategy that seemingly embraces the changes as vehicles for transforming the region in a way that might establish a new, more liberal order under US guidance and protection. Not only is this 'new-look' American approach largely unconvincing and rife with contradictions, but neither Obama nor Clinton has made much effort so far to depict what the regional geopolitical implications of the Arab uprising might be, being content instead to suggest only that an expanded American role in the region (economic, diplomatic, military) is essential for Arabs to realize self-determination.

A key line in Clinton's NDI speech, echoing a resonant phase also used by Obama, is that 'fundamentally, there is a right side of history. And we want to be on it' (Clinton 2011; for Obama's usage, see also Halloran and Shapiro 2011). The early phase of the American reaction to the Arab uprisings I have been documenting here was driven by the embarrassing recognition that the uprisings had once again exposed the association of US alliances and interests with increasingly repressive regimes and unpopular policies. Clinton and Obama responded to this by arguing that US support for democratic change (in *some* countries) meant the US was now on the 'right side of history'. Many aspects of US policy during the uprisings, such as its support for stability in the Gulf, have led critics to suggest that the US has backed the forces of counter-revolution. Clinton's statement, however, exposes a more critical issue. What is that future, and who is going to have the power and voice to shape it? The question of what the 'right side of history' is must inevitably remain an open one because the future path of global politics is contested. Such questions urgently require a sustained engagement with the geopolitical visions and interests of the peoples and states in the region. These must be understood *prior* to addressing which side the US is really on. If the US wants to be on the 'right side', it will need to embrace the agency and autonomy of Arab societies, to allow them to debate and determine for themselves what they wish to make of their future, and to support their role in shaping the regional and global order.

MAPPING NEW PATHWAYS OF POSTCOLONIAL AGENCY

In their programmatic 2006 essay 'The Postcolonial Moment in Security Studies', Tarak Barkawi and Mark Laffey not only reconfirm how 'security studies [has generally been] by and for western powers' (344), but also suggest a series of moves that might help pluralize the fields of security studies and international relations. As they argue, 'the politics of a non-European security studies … necessarily stands … with the weak against the strong, with the many against the few'; and they embrace the notion that 'the weak' must be viewed as being equal to 'the strong' in their 'right to bear arms' (2006: 351; see also the General Introduction to this volume). Even when the violence of 'the weak' is characterized as terrorism or insurgency, and even when, by the standard definitions of western security and policy discourses, their actions are viewed as unacceptable or illegitimate, postcolonial security studies should refrain from passing normative judgement (351; see also Smith and Turner in this section of the volume). Gregory would seem to embrace this turn. He notes in his preface to *The Colonial Present* that the book sets out 'to trace the connections between the modalities of political, military, and economic power—the grand strategies of geopolitics—and the spatial stories told by the lives of ordinary people' (2004: xv). The Arab uprisings, however, may turn out to be a moment when recording these stories allows us to do more than report on the victims of state violence; it may also give us access to ordinary people's imaginings of domestic, regional and global politics, offering us alternative 'geographical imaginations that can engage and enhance our sense of the world and enable us to situate ourselves within it with care, concern, and humility' (Gregory 2004: 262).

Any effort to outline a postcolonial approach to international relations and security studies would do well to follow Gregory's statement that 'people make geographies' (2004: xv). Barkawi and Laffey wryly note that in the recent development of alternative critical approaches to international relations and security studies, 'the agent of emancipation is [still] almost invariably the West, whether in the form of Western-dominated international institutions, a Western-led global civil society, or in the "ethical foreign policies" of leading Western powers' (2006: 350). Many of these alternatives to neorealism have gained titles associated with geographical locations outside the US. These include the IR approach referred to as the 'English School' as well as the 'Copenhagen', 'Wales', and 'Paris' schools of security studies (Buzan and Hansen 2009: 187–225). Perhaps the next turn in security studies and international relations theory will lead to the proliferation of research developed by scholars situated in the postcolonial states, especially those exposed to the violence of colonial modernity. These new forms of knowledge production might someday be referred to as the 'Cairo School', the 'Beirut School', and the 'Palestinian School'. In an insightful essay reflecting on the implications of the Arab uprisings on Palestine, the journalist Adam Shatz gives a sense of what some of these alternative parameters might look like:

> The old Arab order was buried in Tahrir Square. Young revolutionaries rose up against a regime which for three decades had stood in the way of Palestinian aspirations. It seemed too good to be true and some pundits in Palestine wondered whether it wasn't an American conspiracy. But it wasn't, and Palestinians began to re-examine what had been one of their most disabling convictions: the belief that the US controls the Middle Eastern chessboard, and that the Arab world is powerless against America and Israel. 'There has been a kind of epistemic break,' a young Palestinian said to me. (2011: 8)

Within the ongoing Arab uprisings there has been a proliferation of alternative voices and a mobilization of popular social opinion that seeks to redefine 'national security' away from a US-dominated regional architecture and towards concerns with human security, dignity, and participatory government. In the next phase of regional geopolitics, the most influential states will likely be those able to accommodate and mobilize, rather than suppress, these popular social forces. However, as these trends toward the regional diffusion of power become more clear, it will become *less* clear to what degree the US will be willing to accommodate the rise of more autonomous regional actors. It is worth noting, finally, that these new forces operate within a regional system that has long been resiliently multipolar (see Hazbun 2010). No regional or external power has been able to establish itself as a hegemon, and even the US has failed in its efforts. Not only do rival regional powers tend to cancel each other out (often with the support of external patrons), but power is also wielded by a variety of non-state and transnational actors. A broader trend is the increasing assertiveness of regional 'middle powers' such as Iran and Turkey, Qatar and Egypt. Each of these states will doubtless use a range of tools to project its influence and articulate competing visions for the emergence of a multi-actor regional order; but none of these rival visions will likely match the American ideal of a liberal order or envision the maintenance of a US-dominated regional order in the Middle East.

A region with multiple autonomous actors always runs the risk of becoming unstable with continually shifting alliances. I fear that in such a consolidated multipolar system, the US will be even less willing to rely on 'soft power' or to accept the short-term trade-offs needed to invest in a long-term vision for democratic order as it faces an increasing number of competitors in the regional contest over hearts and minds; over alternative visions of the future. So far, the US has shown little willingness to consider developing a more inclusive regional security framework that might address the varied interests of both its allies and its rivals. Its interests in the region seem too 'vital'. Recent events suggest, though, that the US will again have to choose whether it wants to exert influence through persuasion and diplomacy, which would mean a retreat from its current posture, or whether it wishes to forgo such influence in a renewed effort to impose control through projecting power.

REFERENCES

Ayoob, Mohamed (1998). 'Subaltern Realism: International Relations Theory Meets the Third World', in S. G. Neumann (ed.), *International Relations Theory and the Third World*. New York: St Martin's Press, 31–54.

Barkawi, Tarak and Mark Laffey (2006). 'The Postcolonial Moment in Security Studies', *Review of International Studies*, 32: 329–52.

Bast, Andrew (2011). 'The Beginning of History', *Newsweek*, 10 April.

Bilgin, Pinar (2008). 'Thinking Past "Western" IR?' *Third World Quarterly*, 29.1: 5–23.

Buzan, Barry and Lene Hansen (2009). *The Evolution of International Security Studies*. Cambridge: Cambridge University Press.

Clinton, Hillary Rodham (2011). 'Keynote Address at the National Democratic Institute's 2011 Democracy Awards Dinner', Washington, DC, 7 November. Online source: <http://www.state.gov/secretary/rm/2011/11/176750.htm>, accessed 25 November 2012.

Clinton, Hillary Rodham (2012). 'Remarks at the United Nations Security Council', United Nations, New York City, 12 March. Online source: <http://www.state.gov/secretary/rm/2012/03/185623.htm>, accessed 25 November 2012.

David, Steven R. (1992/3). 'Why the Third World Still Matters', *International Security*, 17: 127–59.

Deudney, Daniel and G. John Ikenberry (1999). 'The Nature and Sources of Liberal International Order', *Review of International Studies*, 25: 179–96.

Fukuyama, Francis (1989). 'The End of History?' *The National Interest*, 16 (Summer): 3–18.

Gregory, Derek (2004). *The Colonial Present: Afghanistan, Palestine, Iraq.* Oxford: Blackwell.

Grovogui, Siba N. (2010). 'Postcolonialism', in Tim Dunne, Milja Kurki, and Steve Smith (eds), *International Relations Theories: Discipline and Diversity.* Oxford: Oxford University Press, 238–56.

Haass, Richard (2006). 'The New Middle East', *Foreign Affairs*, 85.6: 2–11.

Halloran, Liz and Ari Shapiro (2011). 'Obama: U.S. is "On Right Side of History" in Mideast', National Public Radio. Online source: <http://www.npr.org/2011/02/15/133779423/obama-u-s-is-on-right-side-of-history-in-mideast>, accessed 25 November 2012.

Hazbun, Waleed (2008). 'Beyond the Bush Doctrine', *Middle East Report*, 249: 38–44.

Hazbun, Waleed (2011). 'The Middle East through the Lens of Critical Geopolitics: Globalization, Terrorism, and the Iraq War', in Michael E. Bonine, Michael Gasper, and Abbas Amanat (eds), *Is There a Middle East?* Stanford: Stanford University Press, 207–30.

Hazbun, Waleed (2010). 'US Policy and the Geopolitics of Insecurity in the Arab World', *Geopolitics*, 15.2: 239–62.

Huntington, Samuel (1968). *Political Order in Changing Societies.* New Haven: Yale University Press.

Huntington, Samuel (1993). 'The Clash of Civilizations?' *Foreign Affairs*, 72.3: 22–50.

Huntington, Samuel (1996). *The Clash of Civilizations and the Remaking of World Order.* New York: Simon and Schuster.

Ikenberry, G. John (2004). 'Illusions of Empire: Defining the New American Order', *Foreign Affairs*, 83.2: 144–56.

Ikenberry, G. John (2011). 'America's Challenge: The Rise of China and the Future of Liberal International Order', *New America Foundation*, 12 July.

Kahler, Miles (1997). 'Inventing International Relations: International Relations Theory after 1945', in Michael W. Doyle and G. John Ikenberry (eds), *New Thinking in International Relations Theory.* Boulder, Col.: Westview, 20–53.

Keohane, Robert O. (ed.) (1986). *Neorealism and its Critics.* New York: Columbia University Press.

Kupchan, Charles A. (2012). 'America's Place in the New World', *New York Times*, 7 April.

Kurlantzick, Joshua (2011). 'The Great Democracy Meltdown', *The New Republic*, 19 May.

Kurtzer, Daniel (2011). 'Obama's Emerging Philosophy of Self-determination'. Online source: <http://www.bitterlemons-international.org/inside.php?id=1388>, accessed 25 November 2012.

Lizza, Ryan (2011). 'How the Arab Spring Remade Obama's Foreign Policy', *The New Yorker*, 2 May.

Lynch, Marc (2000). 'The Politics of Consensus in the Gulf', *Middle East Report*, 215: 20–3.

Mearsheimer, John (2003). *The Tragedy of Great Power Politics.* New York: Norton.

Niva, Steve (1999). 'Contested Sovereignties and Postcolonial Insecurities in the Middle East', in Jutta Weldes et al. (eds), *Cultures of Insecurity.* Minneapolis: University of Minnesota Press, 147–71.

Obama, Barack (2007). 'Renewing American Leadership', *Foreign Affairs,* 84.4: 2–16.

Obama, Barack (2009). 'Remarks by the President on a New Beginning'. Cairo University, Egypt, 4 June. Online source: <http://www.whitehouse.gov/the_press_office/Remarks-by-the-President-at-Cairo-University-6-04-09/>, accessed 25 November 2012.

Obama, Barack (2011). 'Remarks by the President: A Moment of Opportunity in the Middle East and North Africa'. State Department, 19 May. Online source: <http://www.whitehouse.gov/the-press-office/2011/05/19/remarks-president-middle-east-and-north-africa>, accessed 25 November 2012.

Pasha, Mustapha Kamal (2007). 'Human Security and Exceptionalism(s)', in Giorgio Shani, Makoto Sato, and Mustapha Kamal Pasha (eds), *Protecting Human Security in a Post-9/11 World.* London: Palgrave Macmillan, 177–92.

Said, Edward (1979). *Orientalism.* New York: Vintage.

Shatz, Adam (2011). 'Is Palestine Next?' *London Review of Books,* 14 July.

Tickner, Arlene B. and Ole Wæver (2009). 'Arab Countries: Editors' Introduction', in *International Relations Scholarship Around the World.* New York: Routledge, 172–3.

Ulrichsen, Kristian Coates (2011). 'Rebalancing Global Governance: Gulf States' Perspectives on the Governance of Globalisation', *Global Policy,* 2.1: 65–74.

Van Evera, Stephen (1990). 'Why Europe Matters, Why the Third World Doesn't: America's Grand Strategy After the Cold War', *Journal of Strategic Studies,* 13.2: 1–51.

Vitalis, Robert (2006). 'Theory Wars of Choice: Hidden Casualties in the "Debate" Between Hegemony and Empire', in Charles Philippe David and David Grondin (eds), *Hegemony or Empire? The Redefinition of American Power under George W. Bush.* Aldershot: Ashgate, 21–31.

Vitalis, Robert (2010). 'The Noble American Science of Imperial Relations and its Laws of Race Development', *Comparative Studies in Society and History,* 52: 909–38.

Walt, Stephan (2011). 'The End of the American Era', *The National Interest,* 25 October.

Waltz, Kenneth (1979). *Theory of International Politics.* New York: McGraw Hill.

CHAPTER 10

....

AFRICA'S COLONIAL PRESENT

Development, Violence, and Postcolonial Security

....

JOANNE SHARP

INTRODUCTION

....

> I think of civilization as a constant creation whereby we gradually expand the
> boundaries of community, the boundaries of those with whom we share the world—
> this is why it is so grotesque to see bombs and food parcels raining on the defenseless
> people of Afghanistan from the same source. (Mamdani 2001)

Since '9/11' and the subsequent 'war on terror', it has been 'harder than ever to see our
world as simply "postcolonial"' (Loomba 2005: 213). The very moniker highlights the
ongoing universalism of western (US) notions of history where '9/11' was the moment
when everything changed; the people without history were presumably also without terror. In this linguistic move to mark a temporally and spatially specific moment, the Bush
administration depicted 'terrorism as exceptional in order to discursively construct an
enemy through the polarized boundaries of "us" as good—the civilized—and "them" as
evildoers—barbarians' (Smith 2010: 11; see also Elden 2007).

   A number of commentators have questioned what it is that postcolonialism can
contribute to this analysis. Shohat has suggested that while postcolonialism has influenced a range of disciplines, it is this very acceptability that 'serves to keep at bay more
sharply political terms such as "imperialism" or "geopolitics"' (Shohat 1993: 99, quoted
in Loomba 2005: 3; see also Hazbun in this section of the volume). In an attempt both to
politicize the postcolonial and to embed postcolonial concerns at the centre of geopolitics, Gregory (2004) adopts the term 'the colonial present'. He does this 'to "colonize" the

constellations of power, knowledge, and geography [by tracing] connections between the modalities of political, military, and economic power—the grand strategies of geo-politics—and the spatial stories told by the lives of ordinary people' (2004: xv). Drawing on Said's 1978 classic *Orientalism*, Gregory argues that colonial modernity produces and privileges itself by reconstructing others through the processes of 'colonial memory' (2004: 9). These processes may be divided into two strands: colonial nostalgia, which idealizes the difference of the other, deferring to this difference even as it dominates it; and colonial amnesia, where otherness is seen as deviation, to be subjugated and con-trolled. It is this tension that so horrifies Mamdani in his reaction to US intervention in Afghanistan, and that drives both the 'white man's burden' of development aid and the militarism of the 'war on terror'. This pairing will be used here to discuss the experience of the colonial present in Africa. The chapter will address the geopolitics of Africa in the 'war on terror' by exploring the grotesque tensions that exist between biopolitical processes of security and development. It will conclude with a discussion of alterna-tive modernities, which suggests that other forms of biopolitics are being practised—in Africa and elsewhere—that subvert the imperial ambitions of the colonial present, even if they do not always succeed in resisting it.

Africa and the 'War on Terror'

With the focus of the 'war on terror' so firmly fixed on Afghanistan, Pakistan, and Iraq, it is easy to forget that what could be considered to be the opening gambit in this geopoliti-cal conflict actually took place in Africa. On 7 August 1998, car bombs were detonated simultaneously in the US Embassies in Nairobi, Kenya and Dar es Salaam, Tanzania. While twelve American citizens were killed, more than two hundred East Africans lost their lives and many more were injured (many in surrounding buildings, which were not as well able to resist the blast force as the embassies). In response to the commemo-ration of American deaths and the fact that East Africans and their families were com-pensated to a much lower degree than their US counterparts, Paul Muite, chairman of the Parliamentary Committee on Administration of Justice and Legal Affairs in Kenya, argued that the 'attacks on the US embassy were targeted at the Americans. Kenyans were regarded as collateral damage' (quoted in Muhula 2007: 49). In the colonial present, there is a geopolitics of worth; quite literally, East African lives were not considered to be equal, to be equally grievable in Butler's (2009) terms.

The bombers were linked to al-Qaeda and Osama bin Laden. The US president at the time, Bill Clinton, ordered a strike on the Sudanese al-Shifa factory, which he insisted had been producing chemical weapons (but was later shown to be manufacturing noth-ing more threatening than aspirin) and further air attacks on Afghanistan. To many African commentators, this powerful state violence enacted upon the poor of Sudan and Afghanistan seemed perversely out of proportion. Thus, when news of al-Qaeda's attacks on the US in 2001 was reported in Africa, there was horror at the human cost of the actions, but little surprise. As one Tanzanian newspaper put it:

> Is America humble enough to admit that it has been wrong in its dealings with the rest of the world and that it must change in the interests of lasting peace? The fact is that the war did not start with Tuesday's murderous strike on American soil. It simply changed the rules, the battlefield, the ugly scorecard and the balance of evil power in a contest that has been raging for a long time. To many observers, it is America's smug, arrogant isolationism that has begotten this disaster. (Makali 2001: 8)

Coverage in the Tanzanian press highlighted the United States' disregard for the views of others: articles reminded readers of US withdrawal from international treaties before the September 2001 attacks and their wilful defiance of international etiquette. There was animated discussion of the US's undermining of arms treaties and its flagrant lack of concern for the impacts of global environmental change in its refusal to ratify the Kyoto Treaty, and criticism of the fact that US representatives had walked out of the UN anti-racism conference in Durban days before the attacks, provoking widespread claims of racism and bolstering the widely held view that US foreign policy privileged the 'white nations' (Sharp 2011). It was argued, in short, that America had created its enemies through the interventionist and imperialist policies it enacted around the world. Some went so far as to place the origins of modern jihad at the feet of the Americans. Echoing Tanzanians' historically critical views on the impact of Cold War geopolitics around the globe, one article in *The African* newspaper explained matter-of-factly that President Reagan had previously supported the Afghan Mujahídeen, thereby giving 'a new and ominous lease of life to the medieval concept of jihad' (Mathiu 2001: 8).

What was clear in East African media coverage of the events of 11 September 2001 was that the main fear was not so much of international terrorism, but rather of the likely consequences of America's revenge. To many, it was the disproportionate after-effects of the initial attacks that threatened those in the Third World, rather than terrorism per se; and media coverage duly insisted that 'pulverizing' one of the poorest countries in the world (Afghanistan) could only be counterproductive, breeding anti-American fundamentalism. Bringing it closer to home, one author asked ominously: 'Shall we be terrorists when we disagree with Americans in the future?' (Ochieng 2001: 12).

The vast majority of deaths from acts of terror in Africa come from internal sources; international terrorism does not feature as a significant menace. Nevertheless, despite the fact that no such action had been taken after the 1998 bombings, in 2002 Tanzania introduced the Prevention of Terrorism Act (based on the US Patriot Act), a move which prompted further accusations that US deaths were valued and grievable while those of East Africans were not (Smith 2010: 11). This led to claims that the act was being used to repress certain groups within the country. Muslims complained that racial profiling was permitted by the Act and that they were being targeted disproportionately (Tamim and Smith 2010: 102). The Arusha Declaration, Tanzania's landmark statement of socialist independence in 1967, which celebrated the value of all citizens regardless or race or religious affiliation, faced a major constitutional challenge.

Relations between Africa and the west since '9/11' have become increasingly militarized (Abrahamsen 2005), and a significant western military presence has emerged across the continent in addition to support for anti-terrorism legislation. Tanzania's police, military, and other security forces have been trained in anti-terrorism by the US. Although Kenyans were not so quick to adopt their own version of the Patriot Act, accusations followed in Kenya, too, of opportunism on the part of the ruling party. In response, the country's Justice and Constitutional Affairs assistant minister, Robinson Njeru Githae, insisted that the effective fight against terrorism required the overturning of some rights, arguing that changed legislation 'may be taking away a few fundamental rights of Kenyans [but that] this may be justified by the very nature of terrorism, which is basically done in secret and by unknown people who do not advertise themselves' (quoted in Tamim and Smith 2010: 106). For most Africans, '9/11' was nothing surprising and certainly nothing new, but international governance—and as a direct corollary, the domestic governance of African states—did change. Though not as starkly and obviously as in Afghanistan, Africa is now caught within a geopolitics of colonial memory that is managed around both aid and security, two apparently separate mechanisms that on closer inspection turn out to be entangled, as Mamdani (2001) among others suggests.

The western geopolitical imaginary of Africa has been reignited in the current 'war on terror'. While, at the end of the Cold War, Africa was relegated to the margins as development funding and political attention were focused on the countries of the former Soviet Union and eastern Europe, the more recent refiguring of relations after the 2001 attacks on the US has drawn Africa back into the colonial geopolitical fold. Orientalist representations of the 'dark continent' have persisted through geopolitical representations of a continent of failed states, rampant disease, and poverty. Mbembe highlights the negative presence of Africa in the western imagination:

> African human experience constantly appears in the discourse of our times as an experience that can only be understood through a negative interpretation. Africa is never seen as possessing things and attributes properly part of 'human nature'. Or, when it is, its things and attributes are generally of lesser value, little importance, and poor quality. It is this elementariness and primitiveness that makes Africa the world par excellence of all that is incomplete, mutilated, and unfinished, its history reduced to a series of setbacks of nature. (Mbembe 2001; see also Barkawi and Laffey 2006)

Whether through the 'white man's burden' of colonial nostalgia, drawing on crisis images of starving women and children dying and passively waiting for 'our' help, or through the apparently chaotic violence of failed states in colonial amnesiac representations, the predominant and indeed overwhelming metanarrative is one of lack. This narrative has scripted the role of western powers as 'reluctant imperialists', forced to transgress the sovereign territory of African states in order to offer humanitarian aid or military support to the needy. Some authors have even gone so far as to suggest that the threat of terrorism in Africa has been reinscribed into contemporary geopolitics in such a way as to invite the US and its allies into this African 'absence'. Keenan (2009) insists this has been a direct and unashamed manipulation; others suggest it is the result of a longer and subtler process. Whether direct or indirect, it has led to increased fears that priorities for aid budgets will shift from poverty reduction to issues of geopolitical strategy and that Africa will be approached as 'a security concern rather than a developmental or humanitarian challenge, [with] policy [being] guided by the desire to ensure more and better security for "us"' (Abrahamsen 2005: 73–4).

COLONIAL NOSTALGIA AND THE
MORAL HIGH GROUND OF AID

When we hear about 'Africa' today, it is usually in urgent and troubled tones. It is never just Africa, but always the crisis in Africa, the problems of Africa, the failure of Africa, the moral challenge of Africa to 'the international community', even (in British Prime Minister Tony Blair's memorable phrase) Africa as 'a scar on the conscience of the world'. (Ferguson 2006)

The journalists' trips take them to crushingly hopeless post-bellum territory. The chosen backdrops more or less speak for themselves: homes for war orphans, aid projects for amputees and feeding stations for the starving. Not a single healthy person features in their reports, aside from white aid workers. Africans are guaranteed to be shown tottering half naked through crammed refugee camps. They have nothing to do but wait for Western aid. Children have flies in their eyes and swollen bellies and mothers have breasts like used tea bags. Victims are universal and stripped of anything that might frighten off donors, such as political convictions or tainted pasts. They're the obvious good guys: 'women and children', 'the elderly and babies', 'defenceless civilians'. In these stories they do what you'd expect victims to do. They suffer, full stop. (Polman 2010)

The inception of the Millennium Development Goals marked the point in a trajectory where aid had become beyond partisan or party politics, beyond the purview of any one state or ideology, beyond debate. With the exception of a few dissenting voices, such as those of Glennie (2008) and Moyo (2009a), aid has since been placed beyond critique in a space of moral certainty, as something necessary to assuage Blair's scarred conscience. Kapoor notes that aid is conceived, philosophically and linguistically, as a gift from a rich and enlightened western country whose 'privileged status makes it incumbent upon it to act with kindness and generosity, while its superior wealth and knowhow situate it as exclusive agent of development' (2008: 79). He goes on to note the Christian inflection in this concept, which is 'associated with good conscience, charity, benefaction, salvation' (79). The recipient is constructed, through this binary logic, as a victim, vulnerable and lacking, and dependent on 'the benevolence and altruism of the Western donor' (79).

As many have argued, this 'benevolent' view translates development into a profoundly depoliticizing concept (Ferguson 1990; Ng 2006; Sharp, Campbell, and Laurie 2010, 2011). Ferguson provocatively labels it 'the anti-politics machine', which depoliticizes 'everything it touches, everywhere whisking political realities out of sight, all the while performing, almost unnoticed, its own pre-eminently political operation of expanding bureaucratic state power' (1990: xv). As Polman suggests, a billion-dollar development industry has emerged, the very life of which is predicated on the difference between north and south (Polman 2010).

Duffield critiques liberal conceptualizations of human security when these take a language of freedom and rights to insist upon a form of development arguing that 'the alleviation of poverty must come before politics; people must be taken out of politics, reduced to a life of exception, if they are to be helped' (2007: 44; see also Gopal in this section of the volume). Through this modern form of governance—biopolitics—entire populations are administered and managed (see Chow and Rangan in Part III of the volume; also Smith and Turner in this section). Biopolitical regimes are required to deal with the 'surplus population' created by modern neoliberal global society—those people who are unable or unwilling to be incorporated into modern, industrial urban life. Aid is provided to manage these populations. However, by putting aid recipients into a state of exception, a sense of urgency is created—what Sharp, Campbell, and Laurie (2010), following Žižek, call 'SOS aid'—that allows for the bypassing of political or critical thought in the interests of immediate action. For all the apparent focus on human security, this way of understanding humanitarian intervention 'is not simply about the avoidance of harm; instead, its defining feature is the ability to place an issue above the normal rules of liberal democratic politics, and hence justify emergency action to do whatever is necessary to remedy the situation' (Abrahamsen 2005: 59). The normal rules do not apply; a situation is created outside of the conventions of international law, in which bodies are already marked out as dead (but for emergency aid) and are rendered *homo sacer*, neither able to be killed directly nor grievable if killed through inaction (Agamben 1998; see also Farrier and Tuitt in this section of the volume). Dutton sees such an interventionist stance as 'post-political':

> That [those intervening] simultaneously and invariably deny that there is anything political in their quick and decisive actions is, one might say, a very political way of being apolitical. Such a post-political stance is political in that it reveals the underlying utopian dream-desire of all liberal democratic forms of governance. Reason, not politics, it argues, is what drives its actions. (Dutton 2009: 307)

This 'post-political' logic runs through international development agents and states, military and civilian actors, the block mechanisms of geopolitics and humanitarianism. The refiguring of *development* as *security* has led to new biopolitical regimes of development governance, effecting a 'blurring of lines between civilian and military, and humanitarian aid workers and intelligence, security and other military personnel who [all] became part of the operational delivery of aid' (Smith 2010: 22). Following Agamben, Mbembe regards these sites of western neoliberal imperialism as 'the location[s] par excellence where the controls and guarantees of judicial order can be suspended—the zone[s] where the violence of the state of exception is deemed to operate in the service of civilization' (2003: 24). Such sites also belong to a more general western perception of Africa as an absence; African security and politics are defined in terms of lack. Stripped of everything but the basic human need to survive—stripped naked of culture, religion, personality— the bare life of African peoples, seen as being in desperate need of humanitarian care and security intervention, is placed outside of regular political space; the bypassing of local laws and governance structures thus allows for a 'colonization-through-development' enabled by the global penetration of NGOs. As Shivji puts it, 'Donor-driven policy making only shows how much our states and our people have lost their right to self-determination under the domination of post-Cold War imperialism, euphemistically called globalisation' (Shivji 2004: 690; see also Part V of this volume).

Such 'receiving' states are reduced to *performing* the roles of sovereignty and statehood, so acute and encompassing is the penetration of external power through the nominally supportive mechanisms of budget assistance and development aid. For instance, in 2009–10 foreign assistance made up 33 per cent of the Tanzanian budget (Ng'wanakilala 2010), rising to perhaps as much as 90 per cent in Ethiopia (Moyo 2009b), and leading to arguments that in effect many African states are internationally controlled, which suggests that 'it would be more useful to conceive of donors as *part of the state itself*' (Harrison 2004, quoted in Duffield 2007: 169; emphasis in the original). The irony, of course, is that at the same time as they preach democracy and good governance, western governmental and non-governmental organizations have become increasingly entangled in African state affairs, the agents of which are beyond the reach of national electorates. Mbembe links this to the erosion of postcolonial African states' ability to 'build the economic underpinnings of political authority and order' in the 1970s, followed by the loss of value of local currencies in the 1980s, leading to hyperinflation and their replacement with outside hard currencies (2003: 33).

While there have been moves in the west to cancel some debt (e.g. the announcement made at the G8 summit in Gleneagles in 2005), the status of this gift to the south has been questioned. Numerous studies have demonstrated that net flows of wealth are from global south to global north; a character in Malian director Abderrahmane Sissako's film *Bamako* claims that not only has Africa paid back its debts many times over, but that the repeated failures of western policies tied to aid should mean that Africa owes the west nothing at all. For Sissako and many others, the implication is that the debt cancellation had much more to do with improving the image of the G8 than it did with helping Africa. Aid, seen this way, is part of the colonial present of the global north as well as of its southern counterpart. The notion of aid as gift focuses attention on the benign and generous action of the donor while simultaneously drawing attention away from how the privileges of the giver are maintained. Donors are not asked to reflect too fully on the situation that has given them privilege, only to understand that the other is vulnerable. However, vulnerability is always *created*, whether deliberately or through persistent neglect (Philo

2005). The placing of western development aid beyond politics 'acts to deflect attention from critical engagement with the nature of globalisation, power and aid itself, hiding both economic and epistemological violences behind the apparently benevolent act of giving' (Sharp, Campbell, and Laurie 2010: 1125). Meanwhile, new forms of giving and aid are emerging that allow the private donor, rather than the state, NGOs, or communities themselves, to choose how money is spent. From Oxfam's 'unwrapped' schemes to Kiva (which connects individuals and organizations in the south with wealthy donors in the north, effectively providing western publics with the choice to decide who to save), Orientalist images of the passive African awaiting the benevolent actions of the western subject are literally and repeatedly reinforced. Although some of these images do present proactive communities using resources to better themselves, there are limits to the agency that can be assigned to aid recipients. The UK *Guardian*'s Katine Project, for example, had to be curtailed when visitors to the newspaper's website complained that the villagers were no longer eligible for aid, being too empowered and well off (Sharp, Campbell, and Laurie 2010).

COLONIAL AMNESIA AND THE VIOLENCE OF AID

Africa, as already noted, is presented in the western imagination as absence (Mbembe 2001). Thus,

> When mass slaughter takes place in locales seemingly more removed from the West, as in Africa, it is also attributed to non-Western factors such as the absence of modern political, economic and social arrangements, as in discourses of quasi- and failed states and of 'underdevelopment as dangerous', or to the peculiarities of local ethnic identities, as in the 'new barbarism' thesis. (Barkawi and Laffey 2006: 342)

Development narratives offer development—neoliberal, capitalist development—as the salvation from violence. Development is posited as the opposite of violence: hence the UK Conservative Party's argument that 'capitalism and development [are] Britain's gift to the world', and their insistence that the 'rewards' of this system 'will be clear: a better life for millions of people, and a safer, more prosperous world for Britain' (Conservative Party UK 2009: 3).

While the linkage of poverty and vulnerability to political destabilization is hardly new (in the Cold War, poverty was seen as a possible weakness that would lead to communist seduction or insurgency), the strength of the connection between development and security has never been perceived as being so strong, nor have the chains of cause and effect been demonstrated so starkly. Increasingly, the geopolitical discourse has changed from one focused upon the threat posed by strong states to one that concentrates on the challenges presented by weak ones. NATO Deputy Supreme Allied

Commander, Admiral Sir Ian Forbes, contends that this has led to a significant strategic change since September 2001, arguing that future threats will come 'not from conquering states, but from failed or failing ones' (quoted in Mills 2007: 18). Moreover, according to the German Federal Ministry for Economic Cooperation and Development:

> Twenty of the world's poorest countries are engaged in an armed conflict. This statistic shows that the poorer a country, the greater its risk of violent conflict. Research by the World Bank and others also reveals that a country with an annual per capita income of 250 US dollars has a 15% chance of civil war within five years, whereas in a country with an annual per capita income of 5000 US dollars, the probability is less than 1%. (Quoted in Chandler 2007)

Although Chandler (2007) argues that there is little empirical evidence for this connection,[1] the 'security–development nexus' has elevated Africa in the US foreign-policy imagination to such a degree that despite initially infamously mistaking Africa for a country, in the post-'9/11' period George W. Bush gave greater rhetorical attention and financial support to the continent than any previous president. Under Bush's leadership, the US state established a number of continental strategy and military organizations, most prominently the US military's Africa Command (AFRICOM), whose duty it was to articulate the relevance to the US of current events taking place in Africa. In its recent 2011 report, it is clearly stated that the first 'theatre objective' of AFRICOM is to 'ensure that the al-Qaida networks and associated violent extremists do not attack the United States' (AFRICOM 2011). The report makes the globalized nature of the threats from weak African states abundantly clear and creates causal geopolitical links between Africa and the west, insisting for example that the 'increasing operational reach of Somali pirates vividly illustrates that dangers emanating from ungoverned spaces rarely remain local'.

Such lurid claims suggest that the location of danger in Africa is no longer something to be dismissed as was sometimes argued in the early 1990s, most starkly articulated in Robert Kaplan's (1994) paranoid announcement of 'the coming anarchy' in Africa, which suggested simply closing down connections to the continent. More recent

---

[1.] Despite the geopolitical rhetoric of inside and outside, it is the margins, in bell hooks' (1990) terms, that remain the most vulnerable, and which have been the recipients of most attention and most aid. However, this reveals a contradiction in the narration of failed states as a threat. For a successful and sufficiently high-profile attack, international terrorists need aspects of a modern state: transport, communications, and connections to international finance (Mills 2007). It is not the truly failed states that have provided the sites for al-Qaeda's attacks but those on the margins: Kenya and Tanzania, for instance, where enough of the connections are in place. As one East African newspaper put it:

> But why Kenya? Experts say basically the country is a 'soft target', a chink in the West's armour. It is affluent enough, by African standards, to have Western investments and interests but without enough money to buy world class security, sufficiently democratic—and corrupt—to allow the terrorists and their equipment to move around and with good communication to put the terrorists' handiwork on to the big media networks. (Mathiu 2002: 13)

discourses on globalization and the networked nature of the globe have highlighted the threats and dangers, as well as the opportunities, of an interconnected planet (see Part V of this volume). According to this logic, 'if underdevelopment causes conflict and we live in an interconnected and shrinking world, we cannot rest secure that such conflict will be easily contained within national boundaries' (Abrahamsen 2005: 64). Even it were not the case that the US government has specifically reinscribed parts of Africa as the 'second front' in the 'war on terror' (Keenan 2009), it increasingly perceives the threat of terrorism as a global concern: weakness *over there* becomes cause for concern *over here*. UK Secretary of State for Development, Andrew Mitchell, also makes this connection clearly:

> *Not all conflicts have equal resonance for the UK, nor do we have the resources, historical ties or the ability to prevent them all.* So it is important that when we in the National Security Council look at the many conflicts that may arise, we concentrate on those countries and regions that are at greatest risk; *those that are of greatest interest to us*; and those where the UK as a whole is likely to have the greatest impact. (Mitchell 2010, emphasis mine)

According to this definition, development is first and foremost about the security of the west, about managing populations surplus to the needs of international capitalism 'over there' from threatening the privileges of those who benefit from it 'over here'. Geopolitical narratives of threat typically locate danger in the villainous figures of pirates, warlords, and other physical manifestations of failed states; thus, while Duffield argues that development 'has always existed in relation to a state of emergency or exception', this is all the more so in the current geopolitical regime (2007: viii): development is not about 'them', but about 'us':

> Rather than development being concerned with reducing the economic gap between rich and poor countries, or extending to the latter the levels of social protection existing in the former, as a technology of security it functions to contain and manage underdevelopment's destabilizing effects, especially its circulatory epiphenomena such as undocumented migrants, asylum seekers, transborder shadow economies or criminal networks. Since decolonization, the biopolitical division of the world of peoples into developed and underdeveloped species-life has been deepening. Today it shapes a terrain of unending war. (Duffield 2007: ix)

The UK Conservative-Liberal Democrat coalition has made much of its commitment to ring-fencing the development budget, even as government spending has been reduced in other sectors. The lines of distinction between development and military budgets are increasingly blurred, however. Officials in the UK Department for International Development currently insist on the need to trust and work together with their colleagues in Defence, while Foreign Secretary William Hague has recently argued that in Afghanistan, 'where our soldiers are working so hard, clearly our development aid should be working hard as well to assist them in their task, and we're bringing those things together, and I think it's high time that happened'. USAID has long exhibited such dual purpose:

> AEI's [USAID's Africa Education Initiative] development assistance in Tanzania is consistent with broader foreign policy goals. The U.S. national interests in Tanzania are two-fold. First, Tanzania plays a constructive role among its east and central African neighbors in leading efforts to resolve regional conflicts peacefully. Second, (and more importantly, for AEI) development assistance to Tanzania offers avenues for outreach to a large Muslim population. (USAID 2005: 9)

The convergence of development and security in states projected as being key strategic locations in the geopolitics of danger has gradually shifted from the Cold War to the Axis of Evil to a new 'rimland' geopolitics scattered around the Indian Ocean (Kaplan 2010; Barnett 2004). Kaplan locates Zanzibar—historically at the centre of Indian Ocean trade and cultural exchange—as the new motif for this emergent geopolitics. Accordingly, USAID interest in the Indian Ocean rim countries of East Africa has increased, leading perhaps most controversially to new investment in Muslim education, including the high-profile funding of the al-Rahma madrassa (USAID 2005). Many East African Muslims have understandably objected to this blatant colonialist act, which they see as an 'American promoted brand of Islam designed to produce "good Muslims"', a performance of identity presumably also designed to foist the label 'bad Muslims' on those who practise a different, less palatable version of Islam (Tamim and Smith 2010: 123; see also Mamdani 2001).

   Žižek has recently highlighted the increasingly systemic nature of violence, which is 'no longer attributed to concrete individuals and their "evil" intentions, but is purely objective, systemic, anonymous' (2008: 9). For him, violence is dispersed through global capitalist relations, which are strategically hidden from view by the embodiment of violence in the specific figures of Somali pirates, Sierra Leonian warlords, Congolese child soldiers: readily identifiable villains. The violence of neoliberal globalization is nevertheless visible when viewed from below. Just as had been the case during the Cold War, the concerns of the dominant powers have come to eclipse the fears faced by the rest of the world; as one East African journalist wryly puts it, the US now fears 'terrorists, flying, night clubs, parcels, white powder, shoes, metal cutlery [and, above all,] Muslims'; while the 'rest of the world … fears starvation, military invasion [and] being rocketed, captured and detained' (Lyimo 2003a: 6). The same author continues his attack in a later article:

> If AIDS, malaria, maternal/child diseases and deaths, drought and floods are not weapons of mass destruction, then these words have truly lost their meaning … What I mean is this: you don't have to go and unilaterally invade Iraq if you want to see WMDs the way 80% of the world population see and know them. After all, it is this majority that lives with those weapons in their own destitute, afflicted way day in, day out—and dies from them, too! (Lyimo 2003b: 6)

Following Duffield and Žižek, such African views see violence not in the spectacle but, more importantly, in an entire system of development governance—one that looks to functions efficiently in 'managerial', biopolitical terms. In the consensual language of biopolitical policy discourse, 'not only has conflict been delegitimated, [but] political violence has been cast as a systemic threat to development' (Duffield 2007: 118); violence in this sense, which may be 'rational and effective for the weaker party, is systematically delegitimated by the West' (Barkawi and Laffey 2006: 350).

LIVING IN THE COLONIAL PRESENT

On Saturday 18 December 2010, Mohamed Bouazizi set fire to himself in Tunis, creating the spark that would ignite protest—ongoing at the time of writing—throughout the Middle East and North Africa. Through this visceral act, Bouazizi's death became grievable on an international scale, illustrating a third dimension to the colonial present that exists in excess of western projections of colonial memory: the embodied reality of life. For Bouazizi and for thousands of North Africans like him, protesting, marching through, and occupying the streets have offered ways of asserting agency when their voices are not heard through systemic forms of representation and governance. Violence and embodied displays of subjectivity, often as a last resort, force their bodies to count, force them to be recognized, and force them to be celebrated and, sometimes, grieved.

Challenges to dominant biopolitical regimes can take radically different forms, and most of these are considerably less dramatic than the self-immolating actions of Mohamed Bouazizi. Most Africans, suggests Paolini,

> ... get on with the task of living, all the while cognizant of the limitations and openings that exist in the unsettling embrace of modernity and tradition. There is an everyday scanning and monitoring of modernity that takes place. Africans cope with the conditions of modern living and make do ... Mostly this action is far removed from the grand narratives of resistance in postcolonialism and equally distant from projections of homogeneity in globalization. (Paolini 1999: 17–18)

'A multitude of narratives [exists] about how ordinary people in the South connect imaginatively with the possibility of a global life from which they are effectively excluded' (Darby 2006: 49). Many have articulated these narratives as 'alternative modernities', a concept that sits neatly with Gregory's temporal challenge embedded within the colonial present (see Hindess in Part IV of this volume). Such subaltern reworkings of biopolitical systems are emerging to challenge those forms of governance enabled by the practices of development and enacted by externally controlled states. They highlight the inherent ambivalence of development as a technology of power and governance (Gidwani 2008), suggesting that just as Homi Bhabha (1994) has stated for the case of colonialism, the geographies of development might themselves foster the conditions necessary for reworking contemporary modalities of biopolitical governmentality.[2] For example, a range of 'traditional' beliefs is being recognized in terms of the reworking of modernity rather than as relics from the past; as Moore and Sanders put it, 'for many people in Africa, witchcraft is not so much a "belief" about the world as it is a patent feature of it, a force that is both self-evident and solemnly real' (2001: 14). This is a clear example of a deeper indigenous knowledge—what Evans-Pritchard once called 'African epistemology'—that cannot simply be 'value-added' to the kinds of development-as-usual that are currently favoured by western neoliberalism and its primary financial support mechanism, the World Bank.[3]

'[African] witchcraft [has traditionally] offered explanations for misfortunes, explanations that address the "why" more than the "how" questions' (Moore and Sanders 2001: 6): to accept these explanations requires the recognition, not just of different ways of knowing, but of different ways of being in the world. Western discourse offers explanations of *how* things happen (from poor crops to contracting AIDS to becoming wealthy) but not necessarily *why*, e.g. why this has happened to one member of the community and not others. However, these different ways of understanding the world, and the self in the world, are not usually seen as being to the west's benefit, while the one-size-fits-all version of modernity supported by development demonstrates that there is a wide gap between what is promised by development and what, for the majority of Africans, lies within their actual reach. Numerous studies have demonstrated that neoliberal development has led to increasing differences between rich and poor while still taunting people with the promise of wealth and modernity. Increasing differences between levels of wealth mean that, rather than becoming irrelevant, witchcraft and other 'African epistemologies' present a useful set of explanations for these growing disparities, providing people with potential courses of action to intervene in situations that might otherwise seem to be outside their control. Ayinde (2010) highlights the rise of 'mega churches' in Africa promising success and wealth, while others have suggested that cuts in public services, especially educational provision, have made people more susceptible to such schemes' illusory and venal promises. The nature of African Islam is changing too. Most East African Muslims are from the 'moderate Suwarian tradition of Sufi Islam' (Mills 2007: 21). More recently, however, *Wahhabist* Imams have been brought in from the Gulf to preach in new mosques constructed with money from wealthy Saudi families, and satellite TV politicizes youth in Zanzibar and Mombassa about the plight of fellow Muslims in Palestine. The increasing number of unemployed youth in African countries is proving a receptive audience for such radicalization.

While it is Orientalist to dismiss traditional beliefs and resistance to neoliberal globalization as so much superstition and traditionalism, it is equally Orientalist to suggest that *all* such reactions should be unquestioningly valorized (see Briggs and Sharp 2004). For instance, the idea that 'people often experience modernity as a lack, as something

---

[2.] I would like to thank Wes Attewell for drawing my attention to this argument.

[3.] Of course, as Spivak (1988) famously warned with regards to the practice of *sati* in colonial India, such performances are all too readily reincorporated into dominant narratives.

from which they are "abjected" (Ferguson 1999), or that others have access to via nefarious means' (Moore and Sanders 2001: 16), has led to the reconfiguration of African modernities with destructive outcomes. A belief that albino body parts can be used to conjure up success has led to a market in bodies and to the terrorization of this particular minority in Tanzania and surrounding countries. Meanwhile, recent reactions to western aid being tied to sexual equality have insisted that homosexuality is alien to African culture, leading to the persecution of sexual minorities; thus at the same time that research demonstrates that it is women and other marginalized groups who are most economically impacted by the implementation of Structural Adjustment Policies, it now emerges that they are the most vulnerable to the reworking of cultural identities similarly affected by globalization as well.

Conclusion

> To even think about a war on *terror* is to articulate a space and perpetual moment outside of the constitutional legal order, a state of exception, but also a radically new conceptual imaginary. (Smith 2010: 10)

While Smith suggests that the 'war on terror' has led to a 'radically new conceptual imaginary', this chapter has argued that it has acted to reinforce a more entrenched Orientalist conception of lack in Africa's colonial present: an 'empty' space of African (bare) life, beyond politics, in the morally charged space of victimhood, that invites humanitarian intervention to fill it before it leads to terrorism. The colonial present in Africa shows that '9/11' did not change everything at all; rather, it allowed for business-as-usual with a recharged moral justification (see Morton in this section of the volume).

Postcolonialism has highlighted the epistemic violence of colonialism. This has been central to the production of more nuanced accounts of imperial pasts and their lingering effects in westernized culture, knowledge, and even identities (see Part I of this volume). Without doubt, this epistemic violence continues in the colonial present, whether in the US-centrism of marking history ('9/11'), or in the American production of 'good Muslims' in Zanzibari madrassas, or in the self-rationalizations of western development praxis. What the idea of the colonial present forces us to do is to confront the embodied—material and visceral—violence that goes along with these epistemologies; the geopolitics of the colonial present, while reproducing and being reproduced through colonizing knowledge systems, also has the potential to inscribe bodies, creating precarious, bare life.

To begin to challenge the language of security from a postcolonial perspective requires the abandonment of forms of identity that rely upon binaries and boundaries (a language of 'or') and that embrace multiplicity instead (a language of 'and'). Beeson and Bellamy dispute the realist version of the state and argue for an understanding of security that is based not on states but on humans: 'human security' (2003: 346). This involves protecting people from poverty, malnutrition, and the state itself, in addition to the usual 'outside' threats perceived by realists. As they argue:

> Neo-realist security practices are predicated upon a conceptualisation of international order that remains centred on sovereign boundaries and clear distinctions between 'self' and 'other'. What 11 September demonstrates is that not only are those boundaries theoretically and practically insecure, so too is the security politics that is based upon them. (Beeson and Bellamy 2003: 353; see also Stoler in Part I of this volume)

However, it is also evident that such forms of human security have themselves been open to recolonization, for example, and as previously argued, through the biopolitical management of 'surplus' populations in the south. However, contra Duffield, this chapter has argued that this is not the end point, for in the convergence of development and security, and in the range of responses to western biopolitical management, we can see the emergence of a politics of the colonial present that rethinks 'security', but also contains the potential for a dialectical recognition of its opposite. In recognizing the shared vulnerability of populations in the global south, Tanzanian popular responses to the attacks on the US in September 2001, along with the shared hope for North African futures in the public spaces of the 'Arab Spring', echo Butler's hope for an 'awareness of dependence upon anonymous others' that is based on the experience of vulnerability and loss, thereby offering the opportunity to imagine different forms of political community (Darby 2009: 106). This is an inherently postcolonial ethics: one which, rather than adopting a masculinist form of cosmopolitanism that 'accepts normative framings of liberal democratic deliberation, and choice-making, self-reflective subjects', sees subjects as 'endlessly reconstituted through dialectical processes of recognition, within multiple networks of power' (Mitchell 2007: 6).

Acknowledgements: I would like to thank Wes Attewell, Sara Koopman, and Jeff Whyte for their careful and insightful engagements with an earlier draft of this chapter.

REFERENCES

Abrahamsen, Rita (2005). 'Blair's Africa: The Politics of Securitization and Fear', *Alternatives*, 30: 55–80.

AFRICOM (2011). United States African Command before the House Armed Services Committee, 5 April.

Agamben, Giorgio (1998). *Homo Sacer: Sovereign Power and Bare Life*. Stanford: Stanford University Press.

Ayinde, Oladosu Afis (2010). 'Beyond 9/11: Histories and Spaces of Terrorism in Africa', in M. Smith (ed.), *Securing Africa*. Aldershot: Ashgate, 51–65.

Barkawi, Tarak and Mark Laffey (2006). 'The Postcolonial Moment in Security Studies', *Review of International Studies*, 32: 329–52.

Barnett, Thomas (2004). *The Pentagon's New Map*. New York: Putnam Publishing Group.

Beeson, Mark and Alex Bellamy (2003). 'Globalisation, Security and International Order after 11 September', *Australian Journal of Politics and History*, 49.3: 339–54.

Bhabha, Homi (1994). *The Location of Culture*. London: Routledge.

Briggs, John and Joanne Sharp (2004). 'Indigenous Knowledges and Development: A Postcolonial Caution', *Third World Quarterly*, 25: 661–76.

Butler, Judith (2009). *Frames of War: When is Life Grievable?* London: Verso.

Butler, Judith (2004). *Precarious Life: The Powers of Mourning and Violence*. London: Verso.

Chandler, David (2007). 'The Security-Development Nexus and the Rise of "Anti-Foreign Policy"', *Journal of International Relations and Development*, 10: 362–86.

Conservative Party UK (2009). *One World Conservatism: A Conservative Agenda for International Development*, Policy Green Paper No. 11. Conservative Party, London.

Darby, Phillip (2006). 'Rethinking the Political', in P. Darby, (ed.), *Postcolonializing the International: Working to Change the Way We Are*. Honolulu: University of Hawai'i Press, 46–72.

Darby, Phillip (2009). 'Recasting Western Knowledges about (Postcolonial) Security', in D. Grenfell and P. James (eds), *Rethinking Insecurity, War and Violence: Beyond Savage Globalization?* London: Routledge, 98–109.

Davis, John (ed.) (2007). *Africa and the War on Terrorism*. Aldershot: Ashgate.

Duffield, Mark (2007). *Development, Security and Unending War: Governing the World of Peoples*. Cambridge: Polity Press.

Dutton, Michael (2009). 'The After-life of Colonial Governmentality', *Postcolonial Studies*, 12.3: 303–14.

Elden, Stuart (2007). 'Terror and Territory', *Antipode*, 39: 821–45.

Ferguson, James (1990). *The Anti-Politics Machine*. Cambridge: Cambridge University Press.

Ferguson, James (1999). *Expectations of Modernity: Myths and Meanings of Urban Life in the Zambian Copperbelt*. Berkeley: University of California Press.

Ferguson, James (2006). *Global Shadows: Africa in the Neoliberal World Order*. Durham, NC and London: Duke University Press.

Gidwani, Vinay (2008). *Capital, Interrupted: Agrarian Development and the Politics of Work in India*. Minneapolis: University of Minnesota Press.

Glennie, Jonathan (2008). *The Trouble with Aid: Why Less Could Mean More for Africa*. London: Zed.

Gregory, Derek (2004). *The Colonial Present*. Oxford: Blackwell.

Harrison, Graham (2004). *The World Bank and Africa: The Construction of Governance States*. London: Routledge.

hooks, bell (1990). 'Marginality as a Site of Resistance', in R. Ferguson et al. (eds), *Out There: Marginalization and Contemporary Cultures*. Cambridge, Mass.: MIT Press, 341–3.

Kaplan, Robert (2010). *Monsoon: The Indian Ocean and the Future of American Power*. New York: Random House.

Kaplan, Robert (1994). 'The Coming Anarchy', *The Atlantic Monthly*, 273.2: 44–76.

Kapoor, Ilan (2008). *The Postcolonial Politics of Development*. London: Routledge.

Keenan, Jeremy (2009). *The Dark Sahara*. Cambridge: Pluto Press.

Loomba, Ania (2005). *Colonialism/Postcolonialism*, 2nd edn. London: Routledge.

Lyimo, Karl (2003a). 'One Either for Bush, or for Evil Axis: Non-alignment Concept Takes on New, Ominous Meaning', *The African*, 4 April, p. 6.

Lyimo, Karl (2003b). 'Africa's Weapons of Mass Destruction? They are Famine, Disease, Corruption and More!' *The African*, 25 April, p. 6.

Makali, David (2001). 'Lessons from US Humiliation', *The African*, 17 September, 8–9.

Mamdani, Mahmood (2001). 'Good Muslim, Bad Muslim—An African Perspective', *Social Science Research Council*. Online source: <http://essays.ssrc.org/sept11/essays/mamdani.htm>, accessed 28 October 2011.

Mathiu, Mutuma (2002). 'Countdown to Kenya Elections: Why Kenya is Target of Terrorists', *The African*, 2 December, p. 13.

Mathiu, Mutuma (2001). 'The World has Changed, So Must America', *The African*, 10 October, p. 8.

Mbembe, Achille (2001). *On the Postcolony.* Berkeley: University of California Press.

Mbembe, Achille (2003). 'Necropolitics', *Public Culture*, 15.1: 11–40.

Mills, Greg (2007). 'Africa's New Strategic Significance', in J. Davis (ed.), *Africa and the War on Terrorism.* Aldershot: Ashgate, 17–27.

Mitchell, Andrew (2010). 'Development in a Conflicted World', speech at the Royal College of Defence Studies, on 16 September 2010, online source: <http://www.dfid.gov.uk/news/speeches-and-statements/2010/development-in-a-conflicted-world/>, accessed 4 August 2011.

Mitchell, Katharyne (2007). 'Geographies of Identity: The Intimate Cosmopolitan', *Progress in Human Geography*, 31.5: 706–20.

Moore, Henrietta and Todd Sanders (eds) (2001). *Magical Interpretations, Material Realities: Modernity, Witchcraft and the Occult in Postcolonial Africa.* London: Routledge.

Moyo, Dambisa (2009a). *Dead Aid: Why Aid is Not Working and How There is Another Way for Africa.* London: Allen Lane.

Moyo, Dambisa (2009b). 'Why Foreign Aid is Hurting Africa', *The Wall Street Journal*, 21 March, online source: <http://online.wsj.com/article/SB123758895999200083.html>, accessed 21 December 2011.

Muhula, Raymond (2007). 'Kenya and the Global War on Terrorism: Searching for a New Role in a New War', in J. Davis (ed.), *Africa and the War on Terrorism.* Aldershot: Ashgate, 43–60.

Ng, Edgar (2006). 'Doing Development Differently', in P. Darby (ed.), *Postcolonializing the International: Working to Change the Way We Are.* Honolulu: University of Hawai'i Press, 125–43.

Ng'wanakilala, Fumbuka (2010). 'Donors to Slash Tanzania Budget Aid', *Reuters Africa*, 15 April, online source: <http://af.reuters.com/article/topNews/idAFJOE64D0FI20100514>, accessed 20 December 2011.

Ochieng, William (2001). 'KENYA: What Happens When we Disagree with the US in the Future?' *The African*, 1 October, pp. 12–14.

Paolini, Albert, Anthony Elliott, and Anthony Moran (eds) (1999). *Navigating Modernity: Postcolonialism, Identity and International Relations*, Critical Perspectives on World Politics. Boulder Col.: Lynne Rienner.

Philo, Chris (2005). 'The Geographies that Wound', *Population, Space and Place*, 11.6: 441–54.

Polman, Linda (2010). *War Games: The Story of Aid and War in Modern Times.* London: Viking.

Said, Edward W. (1978). *Orientalism.* New York: Vintage.

Sharp, Joanne (2009). *Geographies of Postcolonialism: Spaces of Power and Representation.* London: Sage.

Sharp, Joanne (2011). 'A Subaltern Critical Geopolitics of the "War on Terror": Postcolonial Security in Tanzania', *Geoforum,* 42: 297–305.

Sharp, Joanne, Patricia Campbell, and Emma Laurie (2010). 'The Violence of Aid?' *Third World Quarterly,* 31.7: 256–72.

Sharp, Joanne, Patricia Campbell, and Emma Laurie (2011). 'Securing Development', *Area,* 43.4: 507–8.

Shivji, Issac (2004). 'Reflections on NGOs in Tanzania: What We Are, What We Are Not, and What We Ought to Be', *Development in Practice,* 14.5: 689–95.

Shohat, Ella (1993). 'Notes on the Postcolonial', Social Text, 31/32: 99–113.

Smith, Malinda S. (ed.) (2010). *Securing Africa: Post-9/11 Discourses on Terrorism.* Aldershot: Ashgate.

Smith, Malinda S.(2010). 'Terrorism Thinking: "9/11 Changed Everything"', in M. Smith (ed.), *Securing Africa.* Aldershot: Ashgate, 1–28.

Spivak, Gayatri Chakravorty (1988). 'Can the Subaltern Speak?', in C. Nelson and L. Grossberg (eds), *Marxism and the Interpretation of Culture.* Chicago: University of Chicago Press, 271–313.

Tamim, Faraj Abdullah and Malinda S. Smith (2010). 'Human Rights and Insecurities: Muslims in Post-9/11 East Africa', in Malinda S. Smith (ed.), *Securing Africa.* Aldershot: Ashgate, 99–125.

USAID (2005). 'Africa Education Initiative—Tanzania Case Study', online source: <http://pdf. usaid.gov/pdf_docs/PNADG233.pdf>, accessed 15 November 2011.

Žižek, Slavoj (2008). *Violence.* London: Profile Books.

CHAPTER 11

....

BEYOND BIOPOLITICS

Agamben, Asylum, and Postcolonial Critique

....

DAVID FARRIER AND PATRICIA TUITT

INTRODUCTION: WHAT POSSIBLE FUTURE?

Seeking refuge is a speculative act: the pursuit of a better future than can be envisaged at the present moment. The purpose of the following dialogue is to consider the question of what possible futures are available to the refugee and to those engaged in the production of refugee discourse. In diagnosing the colonial present, Derek Gregory has made extended use of the 'metaphysics of power' in Giorgio Agamben's description of biopolitical relations (Gregory 2004: 63). But it also seems essential to consider whether Agamben's diagnostic value is accompanied by viable solutions to the problems of the colonial present (see Smith and Turner in this section of the volume).

Each of the four sections of the dialogue below represents an attempt to see beyond the biopolitical order Agamben describes. In the first, Farrier explores Agamben's work on potentiality in the context of lip sewing as a resistance strategy deployed by asylum seekers, while, in the second, Tuitt examines how far such strategies can be said to exemplify the 'law-destroying' force that will bring about the end of the biopolitical order. Threaded through the whole is the question of how the biopolitical is engaged in contemporary theory and, specifically, how different modes of engagement serve to sustain or disturb it (see Chow and Rangan in Part III of this volume). The third (Farrier) and fourth (Tuitt) sections apply these questions to the example of the wreck of SIEV-221 off Christmas Island in December 2010 and to the many images of the disaster that have circulated since then. Both sections contemplate the role of what might loosely be called spectators of the biopolitical, whether these are theorists like Agamben or others who merely look upon images of disaster for whatever reasons of their own. That this chapter takes the form of a dialogue between a legal scholar (Tuitt) and a literary one (Farrier) is important. For supplementary to the question of refugee futures is our awareness that, as it meets the challenges of the colonial present, the future of postcolonial studies is in a kind of disciplinary cosmopolitanism (see Part IV of this volume). The outcomes of such a discussion are not neat, nor can they ever hope to be, but our common horizon is constituted by a conviction that the refugee's future lies beyond the biopolitical order—as will be demonstrated below.

READING ASYLUM AFTER AGAMBEN (FARRIER)

> Through the wire
> one last time
> please observe
> I am sewing my lips together
> that which you are denying us
> we should never have
> had to ask for.

Mehmet Al-Assad, 'Asylum' (2002)

In early 2002, Mehmet Al-Assad was one of seventy asylum seekers, including three children, detained in Woomera Immigration Reception and Processing Centre in the western Australian desert, who sewed shut their lips in protest at the unspecified duration of their detention. Since then, lip sewing has become a recursive modality in asylum discourse: in May 2003, in Nottingham, UK, an Iranian called Abas Amini sewed shut his eyes, ears, and lips for nine days to protest the government's decision to appeal his refugee status; in October 2010, 25 asylum seekers in Greece sewed their lips, followed the next month by 10 detainees on Christmas Island (part of the Australian government's estate of extra-territorial processing centres); and in April 2011, again in the UK, four Iranian men sewed their lips as part of a month-long hunger strike in protest at plans to return them to Iran. Lip sewing occurs as the embodiment of an imposed abjection; in postcolonial terms, it represents the appropriation in the body of the language of asymmetrical power relations, offering in the most compelling fashion the configuration of the asylum seeker as the new subaltern (see Dhawan and Randeria in Part V of this volume). Such gestures dramatically qualify assumptions about the location of agency, obscuring as they do the boundary between speech and silence. As Joseph Pugliese (2002) has observed, lip sewing 'reflects back on the nation the gestures of refusal and rejection that it violently deploys in the detention, imprisonment and expulsion of refugees and asylum seekers' (n.p.). Lip sewing demands a response: as an interlocutory act predicated on a visual statement, it asks the viewer to consider both what is *right* and what are *rights*—as can graphically be seen in Al-Assad's poem.

These urgent questions also create disciplinary anxiety (see Part IV of this volume). How should lip sewing be read as an instance of the colonial present? The asylum seeker presents a formidable problem for postcolonial studies. As deterritorialized subjects defined by an appeal to a territorial sovereign, asylum seekers undermine what Simon Gikandi has called the 'redemptive narrative' of postcolonial cosmo-politanism (2010: 24). To claim asylum is to speak simultaneously 'the language of adherence to authority and the language of resistance' (Farrier 2011: 6); that is to say, asylum challenges both the tenets of nationalism and the trans- or even anti-national sentiment of postcolonial criticism. These difficulties emphasize the importance of testing postcolonial studies' ongoing commitment to the pursuit of liberating prac-tices (see the Introduction to this volume; also Part III). But to cast the asylum seeker as *only* emblematic of disciplinary traction risks replicating the essentialism that has dogged some postcolonial discourse on migration. It is critical, therefore, to establish methods of reading that can move between paradigm and person without the former absorbing the latter. It is widely acknowledged that Giorgio Agamben's work on the refugee figure presents crucial paradigms by which to read the troubling proliferation of contexts of rightlessness (see Smith and Turner in this section of the volume); but his prescience as a reader has received far less consideration to date. Antonio Negri has dismissed Agamben's early writing on literature as little more than juvenilia, and critics have generally preferred to dwell on the bold statements in his trilogy on con-temporary biopolitics, *Homo Sacer* (1998), *Remnants of Auschwitz* (1999c), and *State of Exception* (2005). However, closer scrutiny shows that Agamben's work also pro-vides reading strategies that are deeply committed to realizing the insurgent potential in moral statements like Al-Assad's poem.

Agamben's method follows Foucault in investigating a series of paradigms, epistemo-logical figures (the exception, *Homo Sacer*, the concentration camp, the *Musselmann*) that, despite their socio-historical specificity, still 'allow statements and discursive prac-tices to be gathered into a new intelligible ensemble and in a new problematic context' (2009: 18). Agamben's discussion of the refugee begins with Hannah Arendt's seminal treatise on the production of rightlessness in *The Origins of Totalitarianism*, published in the same year as the 1951 UN Convention Relating to the Status of Refugees. Arendt argues here that because it emancipated the concept of Man rather than any particu-lar individual, the 1789 Declaration of the Rights of Man marked Man's historical sub-sumption by the Citizen. Momentarily the source and guarantor of his own dignity, Man almost immediately vanished 'into a member of a people' (Arendt 1951: 291). The mass statelessness that followed the 1939–45 conflict demonstrated the stark consequences of this: that the loss of citizenship effectively entailed an expulsion from humanity. For Agamben, Arendt's analysis illustrates what he calls the 'decisive fact' of modernity: the biopolitical structuring of power relations around a zone of indistinction between what is inside and outside the political order, which he calls the exception. In the exception, life itself, the subject of the 1789 declaration, is revealed as constituting, 'in its very sepa-rateness', the hidden basis of the political order (1998: 9). Thus, for Agamben, rights are where life is inscribed in the organization of power. His analysis offers a vital paradigm for reading the mechanisms that reinforce nation state sovereignty via the reproduction of the asylum seeker as criminal. Possessing rights and rightlessness are equally states of being captured by the biopolitical order; the distinction is that the former is made pos-sible by the incorporation of the latter (see Rangan and Chow in Part III of this volume).

Agamben calls this political relation the 'ban': a relation of simultaneous inclusion and exclusion (or inclusion via exclusion) in which the subject is cast out but remains held on the threshold of the political order by a vested interest in its exclusion. Asylum seekers in indefinite detention or threatened with a liminal existence of imminent-but-never-realized removal are subjects of the ban. Agamben's critics suggest, however, that the value of his analysis goes only so far (in identifying structures of power) but no further (in offering a viable platform for resistance). Jacques Rancière, for example, charges Agamben's reading of Arendt with merely converting an 'archipolitical statement into a depoliticised approach' (Rancière 2004: 299); while for Judith Butler, Agamben's retention of a vocabulary of sovereignty and bare life prevents the very renewal of categories he seeks to establish (Butler and Spivak 2008: 41–2).

These might appear, on the face of it, to be valid criticisms. Agamben, after all, freely confesses to being more concerned with 'the refugee' as an archetype than with asylum seekers per se, positing the refugee as a 'limit concept' on the 'blood-and-soil' logic of the nation state, which will inaugurate 'a long-overdue renewal of categories' of political belonging and power in times to come (1998: 134). Still, what motivates this particular passage is not explicitly addressed, and a postcolonial reader might well take issue with Agamben's failure to consider either the influence of race or the heritage of colonialism in his otherwise convincing deconstruction of the contemporary nation state. However, careful reading of Agamben's literary criticism, as well as his work on potentiality, both of which are coeval with his work on the refugee in *Homo Sacer*, reveals a method of reading that seems more explicitly oriented towards emancipatory movements—as I aim to show in more detail below.

Agamben's thought is largely the product of his work as an attentive reader of others (Arendt, Aristotle, Foucault, Levi, Schmitt); his work on potentiality (the non-figurative element of the 'coming community', his yet-to-be-realized paradigm of what succeeds the biopolitical order) emerges principally from his engagement with paradigmatic figures drawn not from *history*, but from *literature*. It is telling that he begins one essay on potentiality with an account of the Russian poet, Anna Akhmatova. While waiting outside Leningrad prison for news of her son, Akhmatova was once asked by the woman next to her, 'can you speak of this?' Akhmatova's response, 'without knowing how or why', was in the affirmative; and for Agamben, this 'I can', which 'does not refer to any certainty or specific capacity but is, nevertheless, absolutely demanding', is 'the experience of potentiality' (Agamben 1999b: 177–8). But perhaps the most iconic of Agamben's literary paradigms is the figure of Bartleby in Herman Melville's eponymous tale, the scribe whose preference not to write demonstrates Aristotle's proposition that potentiality is most fully realized through its opposite. Bartleby's famous formula 'I would prefer not to' is, for Agamben, the realization of potential apart from action where agency originates in a negation. 'To be potential', he states, 'means to be one's own lack' (1999b: 182), an observation which—to hark back to my previous example—has clear implications for how lip sewing can be read as a statement of the potential to have rights and a voice through the incarnation of silence and rightlessness (see Al-Assad's poem).

The value of Agamben's work on potentiality in relation to asylum is in providing a measure of agency in acts of despair rather than repeating (and thus reaffirming) the terms of biopolitical power or fixing the subaltern subject as eternally abject. Just as reading Agamben is to encounter emergent forms of new political relations, reading, *for* Agamben, constitutes an engagement with the politics of liberation in literary form. In an essay on 'The End of the Poem', he traces a parallel between the exception and enjambment as a threshold of indistinction in poetic form. As the point at which a line breaks according to metrical rather than syntactical sense, enjambment leaves a poem poised (Agamben's term is 'abandoned') on the threshold of itself. Ultimately, enjamb-ment, like the exception, presupposes a crisis: confronted with the imminent coinci-dence of sound and sense in its final line, the poem enters a condition of suspense that resembles the exception: 'At the point in which sound is about to be ruined in the abyss of sense, the poem looks for shelter in suspending its own end in a declaration, so to speak, of the state of emergency' (Agamben 1999a: 113). A state of exception, whether inclusive or exclusive of poetry and prose, thus registers the poem's only response to its crisis of form.

This concept of poetic crisis provides a method for reading the emancipatory urgency in Al-Assad's poem and, by extension, in the act of lip sewing. The poem ends with a complex accusation: 'that which you are denying us / we should never have / had to ask for'. In the hesitation they produce between syntactic and metrical meaning, these final lines articulate the split experienced by the subject denied 'the right to have rights'; they convey in their syntactic meaning a sense of human rights, albeit denied, as inalienable ('that which you are denying us we should never have had to ask for'), but simultane-ously cross this with a far more ambivalent metrical meaning. The final enjambment— 'we should never have / had to ask for'—contests the syntactic meaning by describing the logic of the exception (that the asylum seeker is excluded from the sphere of rights by his/her exclusion from the polis; that rights are what 'we should never have'). It is this logic that forces individuals, as in Al-Assad's poem, to adopt such extreme measures to assert their right to have rights. Embedded within a statement of the inalienability of human rights is an acknowledgement of the force of the exception, creating a kind of warp or torsion within the poem which, as its variant meanings work against each other, suspends it in a state of crisis that also recalls the effect of the ban on the asylum seeker.

Perhaps inevitably, this reading raises as many questions as it answers. Al-Assad's poem reveals the contemporary resonance of Homi Bhabha's observation that mimicry is a form of colonial discourse uttered 'between the lines...both against the rules and within them' (1994: 128). But if the value of Agamben's work is in indicating the passage into politics via the agency of potentiality, how can such a reading take account of the profoundly violent nature of gestures such as lip sewing without reproducing the refu-gee as passive victim; and what responsibilities does the reader, as more or less willing spectator of the biopolitical, bear? With this in mind, it seems that the success of a strate-gic reading of the violence to which the refugee is exposed is determined by the extent to which it looks beyond the biopolitical order.

AGAMBEN AND POSTCOLONIAL CRITIQUE
(TUITT)

From the first section of this chapter we have seen how postcolonial critique enters into a dialogue with Agamben's thought in an effort to correct a thesis that views the refugee as merely emblematic of a crisis of political community. Questions over the sufficiency of Agamben's paradigms remain, however, and a postcolonial critique at once exposes the limits of Agamben's analysis of the refugee condition and begins the process of completing it. For Agamben, the refugee is the 'only thinkable category for the people of our time' (2000: 18). So categorical a statement inevitably calls attention to what is possible in Agamben's thoughts: to the philosophical enquiries he permits himself; and to the worlds he is able, or indeed willing, to explore. Specifically, it calls attention to the work of others that Agamben explicitly engages. The refugee condition intimates no less than a political community that has reached the limits of its efficacy, the response to which can only be an ushering in of the end of present social and political life. But accurate diagnosis and appropriate cure are both conditional upon openness to philosophical experimentation; and, at least from the point of view of the postcolonial, such experimentation is not evident in Agamben's work. Is 'the refugee' the category from which we should begin to gesture towards the reinvention of political community, or do equally compelling paradigms lurk within the work of others that Agamben has not read? More pertinently, perhaps, what is the relation between the world Agamben critiques and the works he cannot or will not read? In the following, I want to draw out some of these themes by putting a reading of Frantz Fanon's *The Wretched of the Earth* (1961) in dialogue with Agamben's musings on the political, especially in *Homo Sacer: Sovereign Power and Bare Life*. For Fanon, it is the 'native' who brings knowledge of a crisis of political community, and I want to see how this figure works in tension with Agamben's exemplar. Next, in a return to the beginning of the chapter, and the case of Mehmet Al-Assad, I will advance the claim that lip sewing is one of many ways in which Agamben's notion of 'pure violence' is instantiated. Agamben develops this notion from a reading of Walter Benjamin's seminal essay 'Critique of Violence' (1921), but it is Fanon's treatment of the native in *The Wretched of the Earth* (which Agamben does not 'read') that arguably provides an appropriate theoretical frame within which to interpret agency in the desperate acts of asylum-seekers like Mehmet Al-Assad.

Taken as a whole, Agamben's work is concerned with the conditions that might allow us to imagine, and then make real, other ways of being and belonging than those allowed by the present biopolitical order. Like Benjamin, from whom he draws rich inspiration, it is the law, which has become everywhere a brute force—a set of meaningless marks upon the body—that Agamben indicts.[1] So when Agamben speaks directly of the

---

[1.] Agamben refers to this condition as a law 'in force without significance' (Agamben 1998: 35).

refugee, he poses a particular challenge to the nation state; but it is also clear from other references—especially to Benjamin and Schmitt—that it is to the primary *condition* that made the state system possible that the weight of his analysis is trained. This condition, taken from Schmitt, is nothing less than the 'law of the earth'—a fundamental law which decrees that the very existence of political community, and all civic rights and responsibilities derived from it, is predicated on the taking of territory, the working on territory, the attachment to territory: the various 'ways of being' with territory for which Schmitt deploys the composite term 'land-appropriation' (2006: 48). The distinction between the basic law of the earth and the rules and regulations to which this one law gives rise is at the core of legal theory and is usually expressed in the distinction between the law as *nomos* (as opposed to *norm*) and the law as *thesis* (as opposed to *legislation*).

Frantz Fanon's *The Wretched of the Earth* was published (in French) just eleven years after Carl Schmitt's *Nomos*. Unlike Schmitt's, however, Fanon's discussion of *nomos* is from the point of view of the colonized and not that of the colonizer. The law of the earth gives legitimacy a legal and political entity and is determinative of civic rights: basic social and economic entitlements, rights of political participation, and so forth. The question of how social rights are distributed between peoples is one that is foreclosed at the emergence of political community. Thus, whatever informal groupings we might construct for ourselves and for others, a law of the earth can know only four fundamental categories. Individuals are 'discoverers', 'settlers', 'nomads', or 'natives' and are more or less included in the social fabric according to these hierarchically structured groupings. In alighting on the 'native' as the paradigmatic case of a crisis of political community, Fanon comes closer to a realization of the true crisis of political community than does Agamben; as I hope to show, while the primary context for *The Wretched of the Earth* is the Algerian struggle for independence, Fanon is far from insensible towards the political and ethical concerns that inform Schmitt's and, later, Agamben's work.

The Wretched of the Earth is a relevant point of reference for the development of Agamben's thoughts on the political community to come (see Smith and Turner in this section of the volume; also Abeysekara in Part IV). But I am less concerned here with the fact that *The Wretched of the Earth* is the absent text in Agamben's philosophy and more interested in explaining why it is *necessarily* silent. To appreciate this, one must understand that the law of the earth is not just a marker of the legitimate sphere of action but also of the sphere of thought, form, and expression. If, *pace* Schmitt, the first act to constitute the *nomos* is a cutting—an act of appropriation and closure—then the first thought must perforce be of one of distinction: a thought of *judgment*.

Seen this way, the law of the earth does not merely assign people to a particular order and distribute land in the furtherance of sovereign claims, it also produces particular ways of *thinking*, particular forms and modes of expression from which other expressive possibilities are effectively cut off. What I will call here the '*nomos* of thinking' alludes to the process in which the original act of closure determines what can be imagined or thought in relation to the future; it also suggests that there are forms of 'rebel thinking' that have outsider status given to them as law enters the world. Peter Goodrich (1996) refers to such outsider or rebellious forms of thinking as 'minor jurisprudences'. For Goodrich, literature sits in such an oppositional relation to dominant or major jurisprudences, occupying the wrong side of the cut between what is considered permissible in thought and what is not. It is among these minor jurisprudences that I would place postcolonial criticism. This might be a rather ponderous way of echoing the criticism that Agamben tends to 'recreate the categories he is trying to destroy', but I believe the length of the explanation to be warranted. My suggestion is that Agamben must be prepared to align himself with minor jurisprudences, which alone can unsettle or deconstruct the law; and among these minor jurisprudences are the tools that enable philosophical experimentation.

Returning now to Fanon, the creation of the 'settler' and the 'native' are inventions that expose the limits of what we have since come to speak of as the biopolitical. While the reversal of these categories is the driving force behind *The Wretched of the Earth*, the settler/native opposition also gestures towards the very origins of political community. For Fanon then, we might say, the question of the colonial is ultimately and necessarily a question of the *nomos*; and when he argues that 'the immense majority of natives want the settler's farm. For them, there can be no question of entering into competition with the settler. They want to take his place' (1961: 19), he is calling into question not just the colonial order but the order of the world itself. In the idea of the native who takes the settler's place without entering into competition with the settler, Fanon folds in conventional ideas of revolution—the rise of the new nation—with the potential for a radically new beginning: one in which settlement is emphatically denied as either the 'absolute beginning' or the 'unceasing cause' (40).

In classic understandings of colonialism, there is a seizure and settlement of territory by an external power that renders the colony subordinate to the metropole and its indigenous inhabitants subordinate to the colonizer. But seizure and settlement also happen in places that are not colonies. Colonialism is a precipitating cause for critical theory's contemplation of the end of the present world—of an escape from the colonial present— precisely because colonialism is a distortion upon an original distortion: that the legitimacy of community can be reduced to the blunt fact of settlement; that it is a matter of *political fact*. To be sure, the original distortion—what Fanon speaks of as 'numb violence everywhere'—is made more ugly with the advent of colonialism; but overlaying this is the originary violence that 'will only yield when confronted with greater violence', violence 'in its natural state' (Fanon 1961: 48).

The category of the 'native' is—it seems to me—at least as compelling a place as Agamben's refugee figure from which to begin to reimagine political community. In this context, it would not be straining language too much to see Mehmet Al-Assad as one of Fanon's natives, caught between 'suicide and madness' (Fanon 1961: 104). Like Fanon's native, Agamben's refugee represents a form of agency that might bring about the force that severs the connection between violence and law. Putting Agamben into conversation with Benjamin, as well as Fanon, might help explain this. Agamben, as we have seen, effectively seeks a new invention of the political, which can only occur from the 'pure violence' that severs the connection between violence and law. Lip sewing, I want to argue here, is one such form of 'law-destroying' violence. Here, Agamben is following Benjamin, who in 'Critique of Violence' lends criticism a *theory of law*—one that serves as an overarching critical frame when spurred to action by atrocity. For Benjamin, this theory, which seeks to issue forth a force that is 'law-destroying', is one of *divine* violence.

For Benjamin, divine violence is by definition 'law-destroying': it 'expiates [in lethal fashion, but] without spilling blood' (Benjamin 1986 [1921]: 250). Agamben likewise speaks of a force that destroys both 'law-creating' and 'law-preserving' violence (1998: 41). Fanon, on the other hand, prefers to speak of 'absolute violence'. Although Fanon alludes time and again to the revolutionary potential of the proletariat—marked now by race and not specifically class—it is not towards the proletariat that we should look to understand the particular forms of force that critical theory must deploy to usher in the end of the colonial present. Rather, it is when Fanon speaks of the 'death reflex'— the spontaneous, involuntary motion of the person who, caught between suicide and madness, forgets that colonialism exists—that we come closer to an appreciation of the nature of the force that is divine, pure, or absolute and of why such force can only be harnessed by those excluded from the *polis*.

Slavoj Žižek, for his part, has criticized the spectral or transcendental quality that interpretation has given to Benjamin's concept of divine violence, urging instead that critical theory 'fearlessly identify divine violence with positively existing historical phenomena' (2008: 170, 167). The only known historical phenomenon Žižek seems to appreciate is terror in the conventional sense. And yet the battered woman who has suffered years of physical and emotional abuse and who, just once, in a violent act that is no way proportional to the violence she has suffered, strikes back against her tormentor, *is* a known phenomenon. Her response is absolute in its completeness; it is absolute insofar as it is uncontaminated by any frame of meaning that might logically assert that counter-violence, to be complete, must be equivalent violence. Absolute violence is such because it is independent of the social restrictions and conditions that might defeat its particular purpose; it is such because it is independent of the contexts and understandings that have persuaded us down through the centuries that certain forms of violence achieve no discernible ends.

With all due respect for Žižek's desire to see a less 'decaffeinated' Fanon in contemporary criticism, violence in Fanon's work retains a spectral, ghost-like quality. In a sense, the impact of the woman beaten near to death who still musters sufficient force to strike her abuser *must* have a spectral quality to it, in keeping with the death reflex. The death reflex brings to the fore fears that the dead might yet be capable of movement: this is not terror in the conventional sense that Žižek understands it, but it is terrifying nonetheless. I find the distinction between 'terror' and the 'terrifying' to be a useful one in contemplating the kind of violence that can 'expiate … without spilling blood' (Benjamin 1921: 250; see also Morton in this section of the volume). Lip sewing, in this context, is not simply an expression of agency in the refugee; it produces precisely the terrifying spectacle that might bring about the end of his/her degradation—it is an example of 'absolute violence' (Fanon 1961).

SPECTRAL FUTURES (FARRIER)

The question that haunts our discussion is the place of violence in the passage to a possible future for the refugee figure. Discourse around asylum is often shadowed by discrepant visions of spectral futures—of communities 'swamped' or alternatively energized by immigrants—in which violence is implicitly encased. One version of the asylum seeker's spectral double is, after all, the terrorist (see the essays by Morton and Gopal in this section of the volume). If, as Tuitt suggests, lip sewing is not simply a seizing of agency by the refugee, but also involves the production of a spectacle of violence that challenges received assumptions of power and powerlessness, then I am led to ask: what is the *time frame* for such terrifying scenes? So far we have considered how lip sewing ordains a reordering of forces via an incarnation of that most spectral quality, silence. But does lip sewing, in its instantiation in a poem like Al-Assad's, represent the moment of terror as a perpetual present or as a way of negotiating the competing demands of traumatic pasts and unrealized (spectral) futures? Can other scenes, where refugees are exposed to the threshold of disaster, somehow inaugurate a reinvention of political relations?

I want to argue here for a connection between territoriality and spectrality as a way of thinking through what might be the forms of 'minor jurisprudences'—literature, for example, or aesthetic activity in general—best suited to thrive outside the *nomos*. More specifically, and with reference to media images of the wreck of SIEV (Suspected Illegal Entry Vessel) 221 on Christmas Island on 15 December 2010, I will extrapolate Agamben's description of the photograph as a demand for redemption (Agamben 2007), placing this alongside Elleke Boehmer's portrayal of postcolonial cultural production as being generally characterized by 'a commitment to *life*, the continuation of life' (Boehmer 2007: 4). Territoriality, Schmitt's law of the earth, was described in the preceding section as a form of cognitive closure, a trammelling of which futures are conceivable. The ground zero of our debate, Arendt's reading of the 1789 Declaration of the Rights of Man—itself a moment marked by multiple scenes of terror—also hints at the spectral quality of territoriality. The 1789 Declaration is, we are told, the moment when Man 'vanished' into a member of the polity. As the foundational moment of the biopolitical order, the rise of the Citizen demonstrates that it is possible to locate a spectral value embedded within the law of the earth. Just as the exception occurs as a kind of spectral law, so territoriality is both haunted by and haunts the refugee; and while the *unheimlich* presence of the refugee threatens territoriality with the unhomeliness of place, as Ariella Azoulay has indicated, 'the refugee' is itself a term 'haunted by the spectre of nationalism' (Azoulay 2008: 80). This spectral territoriality is realized most forcefully in the various, often drastic actions that have been taken by the Australian government in the past decade to curtail access to sanctuary within its borders: from the events surrounding the MV *Tampa* in August 2001 and the subsequent 'Pacific Solution', to the 2011 attempt to exchange 800 'boat people' for 4,000 so-called 'genuine' refugees already resident in Malaysia. What I will suggest in the following is that Australia's pursuit of the enforcement of territoriality via extra-territorial means presents us, in effect, with a spectral law of the earth.

On 26 August 2001, the MV *Tampa*, a Norwegian freighter, rescued 438 Iraqi and Afghan migrants in distress 246 miles off the coast of Indonesia. Because of the weakened condition of those rescued, the *Tampa* set a course for Christmas Island, an area of Australian sovereign territory only 75 miles distant. Permission to enter Australian waters was refused, however, and this command being ignored by the captain, forty-five SAS troops boarded the vessel. Following a three-day standoff, Australia conceded that the migrants could be transferred and detained on Nauru and Manus Island in Papua New Guinea until a more lasting solution could be found. This was the so-called 'Pacific Solution', under which (until 2008) asylum applications were processed on offshore territories, and multiple Australian territories including Christmas Island, Ashmore Reef, and the Cocos Islands were excised from its official migration zone.

The *Tampa* incident coincided with Australia's pursuit of the most parsimonious asylum policy in the western world. Anti-asylum seeker rhetoric sought to cast asylum seekers as an undesirable presence, often coded as 'queue jumpers' or 'potential terrorists'. Indeed, the *Tampa* affair can be seen in retrospect as a harbinger of the conflation of asylum seeker and terrorist that was to crystallize alarmingly only a month later, following the September 11 attacks on the United States. However, the official response to *Tampa* also functioned in effect as a denial of Australia's colonial history. John Howard, the then prime minister, hysterically declared that 'no asylum seeker arriving by boat would ever again be permitted to land on Australian soil' (Manne 2002: 29). Tough dealing with new migrants operated dually, both as a means of exorcizing the ghosts of contemporary Australia's difficult past and of excising 'undesirables' from its future. If postcolonial studies can be said to have a singular message, however, it is surely the lesson of history as *revenant*.

To appreciate this more fully, it is necessary to turn to a subsequent occasion when migrants attempted to reach Australia by boat, this time fatally: the wrecking of SIEV-221 at Rocky Point on the coast of Christmas Island in December 2010, during which at least thirty (but possibly as many as fifty) people perished. The images of SIEV-221 crumpling under the force of massive waves while its stricken passengers floundered in the water were broadcast around the world, with many news reports focusing on the number of children lost as the boat broke apart.[2] However, despite global media emphasis on the most horrifying elements of SIEV-221, the disaster was allowed only a qualified capacity to terrify. The capacity of lip sewing to terrify lies in the irruption of violence in the boundary between citizen and non-citizen (the refugee's body); when violence can be dismissed as simply a 'hazard' (e.g. Pacific crossings in unfit vessels), it ceases to convey the same fear of the intrusion of the uncanny. Azoulay describes this in terms of the difference between disasters that involve citizens and those that befall non-citizens.

[2.] Reporting on the inquest into the tragedy, *Perth Now* carried the headline, 'Screams to Save Infants in Christmas Island Rescue Effort' (Jones 2011).

Such is the urgency attendant upon the former, she suggests, that such disasters become subject to an 'emergency claim' that testifies to their uniqueness; disasters which afflict non-citizens, on the other hand—such as the passengers on board SIEV-221—are not afforded the necessary distinctiveness to qualify as an emergency claim and are thus only allowed the intermediate status of 'threshold catastrophes' (Azoulay 2008: 67–69, 198–207). Reconfigured as a prolonged exposure to violence—as a way of being in the world—terror lacks the force to properly terrify because it is hypostasized (see Morton in this section of the volume). It would be instructive here to compare '9/11' or '7/7' as signifiers of the iconic distinctiveness of an emergency claim with the anonymous and timeless denominations for disasters that have befallen migrants in the Pacific since *Tampa*, notably SIEV-X, in which 353 migrants drowned en route to Christmas Island on 19 October 2001.

It goes without saying that looking upon spectacles of violence involving refugees does not automatically inaugurate change; but I would still contend that it is possible to go beyond the framing of these images as moments of normalized, even banalized violence, and to restore their distinctiveness via a latent sense of 'deep history', which, as Boehmer says, is central to postcolonial enquiry and also essential to a proper realization of spectral futures (Boehmer 2007: 7). The recent history of boat arrivals in Australia has been exhaustively historicized (see, for example, Suvendrini Perera's trenchant observation that *Tampa* had 'a distinctly nineteenth-century feel' (2002: 24)). Similarly, behind the images of SIEV-221 is the *longue durée* of indentured labour, racism, and colonial violence on Christmas Island. The island was settled in 1888 by the British on account of its rich phosphate deposits, which were mined in the absence of an indigenous population by labour imported from China and Malaysia. Sovereignty was transferred to Australia in 1958, which introduced a three-year restricted term of residency for Asian workers as part of the racist 'White Australia' policy. There followed a period of effective apartheid, with separate schools, public transport, swimming pools, and social clubs. Resistance to this emerged in the 1970s, however, with the formation of the Union of Christmas Island Workers (UCIW).[3] It was this union that issued one of the most compelling statements in protest at the government's response to *Tampa*, compelling because it was informed by historical consciousness: it was because many Christmas Islanders had 'lived the experience of a racist, colonial regime', union members asserted, that they understood that 'humanitarian values must come first' (Dimasi and Briskman 2010: 210).

The solidarity expressed by UCIW is in itself a powerful retort to the exclusionary stance of the Australian government. But it also squares with a more general sense of civic solidarity, which Azoulay among others has identified as a particular consequence of looking at photographs of disaster and, as such, presents us with one particular form that Goodrich's 'minor jurisprudences' might take (see, however, the next section of this chapter by Tuitt). Azoulay states that citizen and non-citizen alike are equally subject to

---

[3.] See Dimasi and Briskman (2010). It is worth noting that following the closure of the Nauru and Manus Island detention centres in 2008, a new detention centre was established on Christmas Island.

forms of governance, in the context of which citizenship is both an obligation and a struggle. She advocates reading images of injury as a 'civic skill'; photography, she suggests, engenders a 'civil contract' between photographer, subject, and spectator that exists, like a minor jurisprudence, apart from dominant forms of governance (2008: 33, 14). Azoulay's argument seems equally applicable to a poem such as Al-Assad's, whose invitation to observe also appeals to the viewer to restore a sense of responsibility to the act of observing (2008: 17). Photographs present a demand that requires the viewer to go beyond aesthetic appreciation, to recollect (Agamben 2007). Yet Azoulay goes further to posit a 'civil contract' of photography which, consisting of multiple minor jurisprudences bursting out here and there, acts as an alternative to Agamben's coming community. While the 'pure violence' of lip sewing offers a passage to a new politics via the spectacle of the terrifying, the images of SIEV-221 perform a different but related task. The photographs bear witness to a dual scene. This scene is one of muted terror, where the violence attendant on those who live at the limit is assumed and hypostasized. But it also presents the spectral flashes of an alternative future unmarked by the violence attendant upon the law—a scene in which threshold catastrophe gives way to a civil contract between viewer and subject. This latter scenario, to paraphrase what Boehmer says about postcolonial writing, has the capacity to seize the right to define the moment without negating the future (Boehmer 2007: 7). To put this another way: the spectrality of territoriality need not lead to the dead end of dispossession, but may gesture instead towards the emerging presence of a new political order. In 2003, six migrants were washed ashore on Tiwi Island, which led to the island's excision from Australia's migration zone. As one islander commented at the time: 'they said that [asylum seekers] didn't land here, but six men were on the beach'. The islanders' spirited response, 'We know what it means to be non-Australians' (Dimasi and Briskman 2010: 210), suggests that encountering scenes and times of terror as a civic skill can be a means of realizing alternative—spectral—futures.

Territory, Death, and Responsibility (Tuitt)

Farrier reminds us that the question of the refugee condition is often a question of death—of his/her violent end—so it seems fitting that the final segment of this chapter should address further the question implied in our joint enterprise of writing: whither is the refugee bound? The notion that the figure of the refugee signals someone in flight has assumed the status of an axiom. As we theorize the refugee condition, we sometimes see (but more often imagine) flows and tides of refugees in perpetual motion, between states and camps, between communities, tenuously clinging to the social order. We encounter the refugee first in his/her escape from territorial violence at home, but we, for whom territory provides stability and security, cannot see that this something towards which he or she moves is a 'territorial spectre' (see the previous section by Farrier). The normative state of the refugee is one in which territory is a place of death. 2011—the year of this writing—has brought to global media attention numerous instances of a promise of territorial security that remains elusive, suspended, apparently leaving death as the inexorable end point of the refugee's long flight. For example, the first weekend in May brought the knowledge that 2,000 Libyan migrants had reached the Mediterranean island of Lampedusa. Amid tales of hostile reception by the Italian authorities, we learned of twenty-five bodies found in the engine room of a boat carrying over 200 escapees. The dead—all men—had died from asphyxiation.

I have alluded already to the contrast Fanon draws between the 'settler' and the 'native', but the condition of the refugee produces an equally important opposition: that between the 'nomad' and the 'settler' (see the previous section by Tuitt). These categories are all embraced, though seldom explicitly so, within the status we call 'citizenship'. An important task for postcolonial theory is to ascertain the practical effects of a conceptual distinction between citizen and non-citizen. If, according to Fanon, 'native citizens' are challenged in their effort to take the place of 'settler citizens', enjoying some of the fruits of their forced labour on the land, 'nomads' (most starkly represented today in the refugee figure) can see their share of the land only in death. Drowning, burning, asphyxiation: these are the fates that far too often mark the violent end of the refugee's 'escape from violence'. Let us continue with our sad chronicle. On 2 June 2011, 250 Libyan refugees were presumed drowned off Tunisia's east coast. (So many refugee disasters have occurred since, in January 2002, twenty-four Burundian refugees were burned alive after attempting to leave refugee camps in Tanzania that we are in danger of forgetting the children and pregnant women that perished.) More recently still, in July 2011 the transitional government of Somalia was moved to approach the South African government to take steps to protect South African-based Somali merchants from threats to life and safety by local gangs.

The examples I have described here are not tragic exceptions to the refugee's normative progress towards the territorial safety that the Refugee Convention promises; on the contrary, they provide compelling (if also customarily overstated) evidence that refugees, in claiming their share of the earth, find only a share of the grave. For the refugee, there is no sense in which his/her death can ever be thought of as *premature*; rather, it is *timely*. So-called 'refugee catastrophes' show how territory doubles as life and death and, Janus-like, reveals different faces to the 'citizen settler' and the 'citizen nomad'. However, it is only when the death face turns, as it occasionally does, to the 'citizen settler' that full-fledged disaster arrives on the scene. This is disaster not because of any present loss or destruction—though both may be great—but because of what of the past it shatters; of that past, and the present it shadows, postcolonial criticism has done much to reveal (see the General Introduction to this volume). Colonialisms of both past and present hold out territory as something that can be acquired, maintained, and nurtured in the interests of good governance and economy. For the colonist, land is fertile: it is a source of life and, above all, it is exploitable territory, capable of cultivation and amenable to control. Territory, in this arch-colonial sense, is that which can be mastered, and those that can master territory are also likely to be able to master others. While death comes eventually to all, 'disaster' is a term reserved for *untimely* death, but in death as in life one is bound to the law of the earth, and one's death upon the earth, at whatever moment it may occur, is simply in obedience to this greater law. The unpalatable truth, though, is that the refugee's death is *timely*; as with Fanon's native, the disturbance that comes closest to a disaster is when he/she assumes the place of the settler, thereby disrupting—disastrously—the normative conditions of the law of the earth. Who is this refugee, however, neither caught in perpetual flight nor settled in death; neither drowned nor burned nor asphyxiated? And what is it like to see her? It is with these questions in mind that I turn to Farrier's gentle provocations on the subject of the photograph.

Knowing little of the history of this particular cultural form, I come to this discussion via Bruno Latour and the possibilities his works open up for an experience of 'heterogeneous temporalities' (2002: 249). These temporalities are produced, Latour suggests, via interaction with technologies that are approached not as mere things but as subjects for philosophy.[4] Before and always apart from the image it contains, the photograph sits within a world of meaning that tells us that some events are to be attended to and others to be discarded—a world in which images are relentlessly priced. Writing of a technological form considerably blunter than the photograph, Latour says:

> The hammer that I find on my workbench is not contemporary to my action today. It keeps folded heterogeneous temporalities: one of which has the antiquity of the planet because of the mineral from which it has been moulded, while another has that of the age of the 10 years since it came out of the German factory which produced it for the market. When I grab the handle, I insert my gesture in a 'garland of time', which allows me to insert myself into a variety of temporalities or time differentials, which account for (or rather imply) the relative solidity that is often associated with technical action. What is true of time holds for space as well. For this humble hammer holds in place heterogeneous spaces that nothing before the technical action could gather together: the forest of the Ardennes, the mines of the Ruhr, the German factory, the tool van which offers discounts every Wednesday on Bourbonnais streets, and finally the workshop of a particularly clumsy bricoleur. Every technology represents what surrealists call 'an exquisite cadaver'. If, for pedagogical reasons, we would remove the movement of the file for which the hammer is but the end product, we would employ an increasing assemblage of ancient times and dispersed spaces: the intensity, the dimension, the surprise of the connections, invisible today, which would thus have become visible, and, by contrast, would give us an exact measure of what the hammer accomplishes today. (Latour 2002: 249)

The responsibility we have towards the refugee is the responsibility that comes in relation to all who are not permitted to die a natural or mature death: the refugee, but also that wide-ranging gallery of individuals that Agamben presents as exemplifying bare life (see Smith and Turner in this section of the volume). Before we behold the scene of death, the disaster held within the photograph, we must ask ourselves whether the photograph can ever really know what it has been asked to capture. When I take hold of

---

4. See also Latour (1991).

a photograph, it is the gloss of *Vogue* I feel through my fingertips; I think little of the life of the indifferent student who delivers the magazine to my door. Am I more likely to be transported to a refugee camp in Tasmania or to the arresting beauty of a Trafalgar Square gallery? The photograph is too full of carefully calculated life to hold the ordinary experience of the refugee: so full of life that even the most horrific death scene is elided. And yet is it not the ordinary—the premature—death of the refugee that we must hold in memory if the revolution that Agamben is looking for is to be realized? The photograph, after all, provides numerous opportunities to celebrate the refugee who escapes both a premature death and a risk-filled nomadic existence. Why should we not look for refugees among the fashion pages? Why should we not quietly rejoice when the face of terror is turned away from them? For the rest, we turn not to the gallery but the graveyard.

CONCLUSION

The figure of the refugee has long served as an important reference point in critical theory. Refugees today are probably most often seen as emblematic of the modern political condition, and our intervention in this chapter has been made, accordingly, within this particular conceptual frame. As we hope to have shown, Agamben's work on the refugee in his analysis of the sovereign sphere has become well-nigh indispensable, but it has become increasingly apparent that it is in want of a critical supplement if it is to guide us to a place beyond biopolitics (see Rangan and Chow in Part III of this volume). In common with other contributors to this volume, we see postcolonial critique as the missing element in a range of critical discourses that joins the two great reference points in the critique of biopolitics: Foucault and Agamben (see Morton and Smith and Turner in this section of the volume; also Rangan and Chow in Part III). In this chapter, we have tried not only to recuperate some of the founding voices of postcolonial criticism, such as Fanon, but also to embed our dialogue in a critical frame, which, from its earliest articulation, has defined itself in relation to the transformative achievements of those who exist at the margins of political community.

Perhaps, to this end, the aspect of our dialogue that resonates most with Agamben's thoughts on the refugee condition is to be found in the belief that the putative end of the biopolitical will be signalled by those who, like the refugee, do most to expose its foundational violence. Faced with such an aim, the narrative we have presented cannot fail to be rather bleak. It is postcolonial critique, however, that at once gives concrete expression to a phenomenon that can often seem to disappear behind grand abstractions and ensures that refugees are not reduced to mere victims. Our stark portrayal of what may seem at one level to be desperate acts and hopeless actions offers, at another, a glimpse of future political horizons in which those same acts and actions that we sometimes tend to dismiss as impotent recover their legitimate force.

References

Agamben, Giorgio (1998). *Homo Sacer: Sovereign Power and Bare Life*, trans. Daniel Heller-Roazen. Stanford: Stanford University Press.

Agamben, Giorgio (1999a). 'The End of the Poem', in *The End of the Poem: Studies in Poetics*, trans. Daniel Heller-Roazen. Stanford: Stanford University Press, 109–15.

Agamben, Giorgio (1999b). 'On Potentiality', in *Potentialities: Collected Essays in Philosophy*, trans. Daniel Heller-Roazen. Stanford: Stanford University Press, 177–84.

Agamben, Giorgio (1999c). *Remnants of Auschwitz: The Witness and the Archive*, trans. Daniel Heller-Roazen. New York: Zone Books.

Agamben, Giorgio (2000). *Means without End: Notes on Politics*, trans. Vincenzo Binetti and Cesare Casarino. Minneapolis and London: University of Minnesota Press.

Agamben, Giorgio (2005). *State of Exception*, trans. Kevin Attell. Chicago and London: University of Chicago Press.

Agamben, Giorgio (2007). 'Judgement Day', in *Profanations*, trans. Jeff Fort. New York: Zone Books, 23–27.

Agamben, Giorgio (2009). *The Signature of All Things*, trans. Luca di Santo, with Kevin Atwell. New York: Zone Books.

Al-Assad, Mehmet (2002). 'Asylum', *Borderlands* 1.1. Online source: <http://www.borderlands.net.au/vol1no1_2002/alassad_asylum.html>, accessed 1 August 2008.

Arendt, Hannah (1973 [1951]). *The Origins of Totalitarianism*. New York: Harvest.

Azoulay, Ariella (2008). *The Civil Contract of Photography*. New York: Zone Books.

Benjamin, Walter (1986 [1921]). 'Critique of Violence', in *Reflections: Essays, Aphorisms, Autobiographical Writings*, trans. E. Jephcott. New York: Schocken Books, 277–300.

Bhabha, Homi (1994). *The Location of Culture*. London and New York: Routledge.

Boehmer, Elleke (2007). 'Postcolonial Writing and Terror', *Wasafiri*, 22.2: 4–7.

Butler, Judith and Gayatri Chakravorty Spivak (2008). *Who Sings the Nation-State? Language, Politics, Belonging*. New York: Seagull Books.

Dimasi, Michelle and Linda Briskman (2010). 'Let Them Land: Christmas Islander Responses to Tampa', *Journal of Refugee Studies*, 23.2: 199–218.

Fanon, Frantz (1961). *The Wretched of the Earth*, trans. Constance Farrington. Harmondsworth: Penguin.

Farrier, David (2011). *Postcolonial Asylum: Seeking Sanctuary Before the Law*. Liverpool: Liverpool University Press.

Gikandi, Simon (2010). 'Between Roots and Routes: Cosmopolitanism and the Claims of Locality', in Janet Wilson et al. (eds), *Rerouting the Postcolonial: New Directions for the New Millennium*. London: Routledge, 22–36.

Goodrich, Peter (1996). *Law in the Courts of Love: Literature and Other Minor Jurisprudences*. London: Routledge.

Gregory, Derek (2004). *The Colonial Present*. Oxford: Blackwell.

Jones, Lloyd (2011). 'Screams to Save Infants in Christmas Island Rescue Effort', *Perth Now* 23 May. Online source: <http://www.perthnow.com.au/news/western-australia/screams-to-save-infants-in-christmas-island-rescue-effort/story-e6frg13u-1226061377503>, accessed 7 June 2011.

Latour, Bruno (1991). *We Have Never Been Modern*, trans. C. Porter. Cambridge, Mass.: Harvard University Press.

Latour, Bruno (2002). 'Morality and Technology: The Ends and Means', trans. C. Venn, *Theory, Culture & Society*, 19.5–6: 247–60.

Manne, Robert (2002). 'Reflections on the Tampa Incident', *Postcolonial Studies*, 5.1: 29–36.

Perera, Suvendrini (2002). 'A Line in the Sea', *Race & Class*, 44.2: 23–39.

Pugliese, Joseph (2002). 'Penal Asylum: Refugees, Ethics, Hospitality', *Borderlands*, 1.1: §53. Online source: <http://www.borderlands.net.au/vol1no1_2002/pugliese.html>, accessed 8 May 2011.

Rancière, Jacques (2004). 'Who is the Subject of the Rights of Man?', *South Atlantic Quarterly*, 103.2–3: 297–310.

Schmitt, Carl (2006). *The Nomos of the Earth in the International Law of the Jus Publicum Europaeum*, trans. G. L. Ulmen. New York: Telos Press.

Žižek, Slavoj (2008). *Violence: Six Sideways Reflections*. London: Profile Books.

CHAPTER 12

....

INDIGENOUS INHABITATIONS AND THE COLONIAL PRESENT

....

JO SMITH AND STEPHEN TURNER

INTRODUCTION

....

The colonial project of settlement is necessarily ongoing; and it involves techniques and practices that work to regulate, discipline, and at times expunge expressions of Indigenous sovereignty, in Aotearoa/New Zealand and elsewhere. A more recent global love of all things Indigenous disguises continuing colonialism: New Zealand is probably a world leader here. More critical consideration of the country's benign biculturalism is bound to expose self-serving settler interest. In this context, postcolonialism describes new as well as more established measures of controlling a Māori body that will ultimately not be governed in non-Māori terms. The will-to-invasion that has historically been inscribed in settler nation states like New Zealand has recently manifested itself in attempts to repel perceived threats to the state's indivisible authority. These attempts have both changed the local landscape and challenged an implanted western political model in Indigenous contexts. This chapter will look at recent events in the New Zealand context that mark out the country's colonial present in thanatopolitical terms.[1]

In 2004, the Foreshore and Seabed Act (FSA) extinguished the possibility of Māori establishing customary title over parts of the country's foreshore, sections commonly misconstrued as the 'beach'. Widespread resistance to this move led to the creation of the Māori Party in parliament. In 2007, a 300-strong paramilitary police force locked down an area of land within the upper central North Island domain of Tūhoe people in order to arrest alleged 'terrorists'.[2] National media coverage of the two events worked to produce

---

[1] Thanatopolitics (after the Greek *thanatos*) is politics oriented around death.

[2] See the collection of essays on the raids *Terror in our Midst?* (Keenan 2008) and the more recent documentary *Operation 8* directed by Errol Wright and Abi King-Jones (2011).

both a 'performative unison' and a rearguard action against the sizeable Indigenous presence (around 15 per cent of the total population) and the force of its long history of inhabitation. The first event was designed to preserve access to beaches as the birthright of all New Zealanders, though this had never been threatened in the first place. In the second, by contrast, 'beaches' were opposed to interior 'badlands' whose inhabitants were designated by the anti-terror raids as enemies of the state.

Settler-Indigenous relations in Aotearoa/New Zealand today are increasingly shaped by the technoculture of national media, which, characterized as it is by a form of constructive amnesia, persistently remaps the imaginative geography of the nation state. But the media cartography of national imagining, as we will demonstrate later, is neither coherent nor unchallenged. Our focus here, thirdly, will be on the particular role played by Māori Television, the country's first Indigenous broadcaster, in articulating the political ontology of Indigenous inhabitation. In 2009 it too was subjected to political management by the New Zealand government when it made a bid for exclusive broadcast coverage of the 2011 Rugby World Cup.

If the foreshore and seabed represent the 'last frontier' for colonial New Zealand, media practices surrounding the anti-terror raids and the emergence of Māori Television suggest that contemporary struggles between the settler state and Indigenous collectivities are increasingly played out via technologically mediated communication landscapes. While the technocultural project of settlement involves the emptying out and management of Indigenous presences so as to ensure viable settler futures, there persists a disavowed force that works to unsettle the project of settlement and call into question established geometries of power. This disavowed force is a form of Indigenous presencing that is consistently worked over, erased, and reaffirmed in the colonial present of Aotearoa/New Zealand.

In many ways, the active and ongoing reconfiguration of Indigenous presences that operates in Aotearoa/New Zealand echoes Derek Gregory's analysis of the distorted imaginative geographies that characterize contemporary representations of Islamic worlds (Gregory 2004). For Gregory, the performative force of colonial modernity lives on in the ordering of social, political, and economic spaces. His more particular project is to counter the imaginative geographies surrounding the events of 11 September 2001, by outlining the longer histories of place, people, and power entangled in 'the west's' encounter with 'the east'. These geographies thrive on the capacity to truncate the longer histories of a place and its peoples and to operate an organizing logic that oscillates between the erasure of prior presences (colonial amnesia) and the valorization of cultural difference (colonial nostalgia) (2004: 9; see also Sharp in this section of the volume).

While the performative force of colonial modernity codifies and regulates social spaces and conceptual orderings in ways that suppress contemporary articulations of cultural difference, Gregory reminds us of the radical potential of the idea that people's actions literally 'take place' (2004: xv). He cites the case of the physical choreography behind Islamic prayer rituals, which includes kneeling in 'a never-ending wave of synchronised prayer' (209). This public orchestration of bodies, voices, and movements exemplifies a radically different way of being and seeing in relation to western social practices, performing an alternative ontology that both eludes and exceeds western meaning-making systems. When seen from the viewpoint of 'the west', such practices destabilize orthodox power relations and affirm other histories of time and place; for Gregory, the colonial present works to eradicate, tame, and domesticate these alternative social orders. While Islam and Indigeneity in the context of Aotearoa/New Zealand may seem worlds apart, the distorted imaginative geographies that seek to account for both collectivities—imaginary and actual—can be countered by illuminating the longer histories disavowed by the colonial present.

The performative force of the Islamic *Ummah* is an overt example of taking up time and place in ways that scramble received Eurocentric wisdom (see also Sayyid in Part I of this volume); in a contemporary settler nation such as New Zealand, the performative force of a long-standing Māori presence conditions the ongoing project of settlement in less obvious ways. Dealing with this Indigenous presencing (an alternative ordering of time and place that is itself a matter of sovereignty) is not a task for critical theory, nor even a matter of rhetorical persuasion; rather, it requires listening or attending—in the sense of attending a Māori gathering (*hui*)—and of feeling the *hau* (life-affirming breath) of long Indigenous history (by contrast with the short history in the same place of non-Māori settlement). In this manner, one might register the disavowed force of Indigenous presencing and enter a space for engaging, articulating, and negotiating cross-cultural differences.[3]

Contrary to the manufactured consensus of a short settler history, Indigenous sovereignty is not something that Indigenous peoples can be talked out of. Such wishful thinking deeply structures settlement. On the contrary, the self-presencing of Indigenous gathering insists upon a constitution, formed by a long history of Indigenous inhabitation that is inadmissible to settler nationalism.[4] Indigenous sovereignty, in this sense, involves the presencing of long history and the experiential acknowledgement, in Aotearoa/New Zealand, of a fully Māori place, since shaped, honed, and transformed by colonial encounters. While the organizing logics of the colonial present work to expunge this longer history, settler modes of organization never succeed completely; for the residue of these encounters—the self-presencing of Indigenous gathering that is increasingly enabled by media technologies—open out political ontologies that challenge the settler status quo. This question of visibility and invisibility—of half-glimpsed presences and incoherent objects—looms large in a settler context where images, articulations, and expressions of Indigenous culture are part and parcel of settler national identity.

---

[3] Elizabeth Povinelli might call this kind of registering of difference a form of 'immanent obligation' (2011: 28).

[4] Irene Watson makes a similar claim about Aboriginal sovereignty when she writes, 'For more than 200 years the colonial paradigm has lectured us on the impossibility of Aboriginal laws and sovereignty. Yet for many Aboriginal people, Aboriginal laws, or sovereignty, simply exist, perhaps not in the ivory towers, or the power houses, of the Australian state, but elsewhere; Aboriginal laws live' (2007: 24).

INDIGENOUS PRESENCING

If earlier forms of colonization involved military force, economic exploitation, and cultural imposition, the colonial present of Aotearoa/New Zealand is perhaps most fully characterized by its continuing exploitation of the *use value* of things Māori, particularly images and articulations of Māori-ness. In an officially bicultural nation Māori must labour to secure the belonging of non-Māori, while Māori-ness is extracted as surplus profit for a brand-conscious corporate nation. The domesticated image of Indigenous presence (think of the film festival hit *Whale Rider* or the national rugby team haka) is used to shore up the borders of a nation within a globalized economy and to help retell the successful story of Pākehā settlement. In this and other ways, bicultural policies have made a mantra of things Māori. State bodies (the armed forces, the police, government departments, etc.) all bear bicultural insignia that promise shared sovereignty between Pākehā and Māori. Meanwhile, biculturalism as state policy hinges retrospectively on the 1840 Treaty of Waitangi, signed between the British Crown and numerous, though not all, Māori tribal collectives (*iwi*). Quasi-constitutional in status—New Zealand does not have a written constitution—the Treaty fuels intranational claims to Indigenous sovereignty, and has dominated Māori and state relationships during the last few decades. Assuring non-Indigenous New Zealanders of their belonging, it has also been considered a management technique for controlling more insurgent forms of political resistance (Fleras and Spoonley 1999; O'Sullivan 2007; Sharp 1997). While official biculturalism ostensibly offers Māori certain forms of cultural and political visibility, the over-representation of Māori in poverty, crime, and violence statistics, and underperformance in health and education by comparison with non-Māori, attest to continuing social and economic struggles. Domesticated forms of Māori cultural difference shore up the insecurities of a settler nation while more autonomous bids for self-expression are promptly rejected. This is consistent with a controlling logic within the national setting of 'inclusive exclusion' (Turner 2007). On the one hand, the government funds initiatives that showcase the nation's cultural differences on the world stage (framed in terms of things Māori); on the other, the state consistently negates more structural economic and political changes that might address Indigenous sovereignty.

The logic that operates within this particular socio-cultural context involves the dissemination, distribution, and circulation of Māori cultural differences. Yet, for all the local talk of world-beating race relations, Māori are still being asked to be Māori for the nation's sake, and not for the sake of the multiple peoples that Māori are. Māori do bicultural work for all New Zealanders in order to secure official policy; and yet some Indigenous presences are cut off from national life. The Tūhoe terror raids are a case in point and will be discussed below. Though the raids generated a good deal of local concern about unwarranted police action, it seems unlikely that majority Pākehā (the most used Māori word for non-Māori) will be persuaded by our view of the event, given that the New Zealand government is an expression of majority interest in settlement and works explicitly to secure the nation state from which that same majority draws down a national identity. The New Zealand public, understood to include Māori, must therefore reckon with another prospect: Māori *sovereignty*.

REFIGURING GROUNDS

An attribute of Indigenous story is that the Indigenous sovereignty for which it is a vehicle cannot be extracted in theoretical form. Indigenous articulations *take place* and occur in time in ways that are embedded in particular circumstances.[5] There can be no packaging of Indigenous sovereignty for postcolonial studies. Its acknow-ledgement in the place from which the power-that-it-is emanates (more properly *tino rangatiratanga* or absolute chieftainship, discussed below) requires instead a recon-struction of the *short* history of non-Indigenous terms in view of a *long* history of Indigenous presence. The reverse anthropology of Pākehā studies may be an object of critical theory, but not the Indigenous presence that requires it (all Indigenous peoples similarly require that the peoples who have invaded their land are able to see them-selves through Indigenous eyes, thereby multiplying, differentiating, and specifying settler-colonial studies—a route seldom taken in academic writing).

We take as given an unbounded Māori world of which Māori sovereignty was and is constitutive. But this givenness is predicated on the shared predicament of colonization and the leap of faith required to imagine otherwise (Mikaere 2011). To acknowledge a fully present Māori-ness involves a negotiation with settler sovereignty, and requires reciprocity, imagination, and multiple acts of hospitality (Smith 2007). These are clearly conditions that have not yet been achieved. Settler invasion, the appropriation of Māori land, and the degradation of Māori people all involve a process of 'cultural colonization' (Gibbons 2002) or Pākehā-fication, that stretches from the 'better-Briton' colonialism of nineteenth-century settlers to a benign and official biculturalism today. Understood as the historiographical revision of long Māori history in terms of short Pākehā (settler) history, which is the national history-making project, the continued home-making of Pākehā describes the colonial present. Making a colonial past 'past' for settlers conflicts with the enduring presence of long history for First peoples. The differential between long Indigenous history and a shorter settler one in the same place is a foundational truth that escapes the originary relation of western politics, as described by the Italian philosopher Giorgio Agamben (1998), and suggests different grounds, literally and physically, for the constitution of a settler nation. This refiguring of foundational truths can also be understood as a form of *taking place*.

Long history suggests an entwining of *insistence* and *resistance* (MacDonald 2008) that characterizes Māori responses in a majoritarian Pākehā context. Indigenous

---

[5.] For a deeper understanding of the relationship between place and people in Aotearoa/New Zealand, see Russell (2006) and Stephenson, Abbott, and Ruru (2010).

political ontology, registered as a more positive insistence or presencing of long history, is something more than the remainder or residue of settler exclusion. By 'presencing', we mean the insistence of First peoples on a prior relation to place, understood in First peoples' terms and no one else's. Such presencing may be juxtaposed with the colonial present just as insistence may be conjoined with resistance. Indigenous political ontology requires no recognition from non-Indigenous people of its substance in order to be the power-that-it-is; that is what we mean by taking it as given. This presupposition (the givenness of the given) also enfolds a mode of being—and *doing*—that expresses sovereign capacities.

Indigenous sovereignty has always existed in places of non-Indigenous settlement. Settlement in Aotearoa/New Zealand describes the process by which a universalizing, nation-making, rights-bearing western political regime came to intrude into the *tikanga* law contexts of a local Māori presence (*tikanga* describes the Indigenous law practices that distinguish Māori collectives; more will be said about it below). This thanatopolitical regime can be placed in the context of a much longer local history whose basis—the sense of being and belonging it articulates—is nothing less than a constitutional drive for Indigenous life.

At stake is the survival and flourishing of First peoples as such, though relations since established with settlers make the future of Indigenous countries a shared one. As Linda Tuhiwai Smith argues, the term 'indigenous' takes on new meaning when applied to a settler society where it 'has been coopted politically by the descendants of settlers' who claim an 'indigenous' identity based on long-term occupation of land or by being born there (1999: 7). Settler indigeneity depends on the use of Māori imagery to shore up settler belonging, a process that is undeniably exploitative, but one which still inserts the inassimilable being of Māori sovereignty into the national fabric. Mediated images of Indigenous lands, waters, peoples, and practices may have been appropriated and subjected to a regulatory settler order, yet they also posit a prior political ontology that haunts the colonial present. This *consubstantial* sovereignty differentiates itself from the biopolitical western sovereignty of recent theorizing (as described by Farrier and Tuitt in this section of the volume), and is strictly inassimilable to the juridical structures of self-recognition that Māori have been forced into for the nation's sake. Māori *mana motuhake* (autonomous power) insists on the long history of Indigenous inhabitation as much as it resists circumscription within settler history's short form.

GOOD AND BAD POLITICAL BODIES

In this part of the chapter, we show how the distorted imaginative geographies of the colonial present work to secure the health or purity of the contemporary settler nation. The logic beyond these imaginings casts certain collectivities as outside of, and threatening to, the whole that is considered to be at issue. This mode of organization may be demonstrated in contemporary New Zealand in terms of beaches and badlands, good and bad political bodies. Beaches today suggest to settlers a place of homecoming, relaxation, and recreation, the epitome of the good life that emigration promised them; and these beaches are opposed by the badlands (Jutel 2007) where abandoned people roam. As Giorgio Agamben suggests, the principle of abandonment, a person bereft of legal protection being removed beyond the city walls, is internal to the constitution of the city itself and articulates the originary political relation of the western *polis*.[6] According to the same logic, the 'inclusive exclusion' of Tūhoe/Māori is internal to the settler state. This process can be seen in numerous historical instances of confiscation, from the nineteenth-century confiscation of Tūhoe lands, when Tūhoe were considered 'rebels' by a settler government less than fifteen years in existence, to the twentieth-century appropriation of Māori lands for the national 'good' under various Public Works Acts. However, the consubstantial political ontology of lands, waters, and peoples—their entwined relations, attributes, and properties—gives the process of Indigenous exclusion a sovereign agency that exceeds the originary political relation of the west described by Agamben, or at least cannot be recuperated by it. In the case of the Foreshore and Seabed Act, the long Māori presence in the country was disavowed by the government's refusal to grant Māori claimants due legal process. If the claim was inadmissible in law, it was because settler culture required that a longer Indigenous history be forgotten. Our attention now shifts to the story of insistence/resistance it generated in turn.

The Foreshore and Seabed Act (FSA), passed in 2004 by the centre-left Labour government, ensured state ownership of land below the high tide mark. This Act was a response to the New Zealand Court of Appeal's ruling that the Māori Land Court could investigate claims of Māori customary rights in this area. By declaring this land New Zealand Crown-owned, the government prevented Māori from exercising their rights as guaranteed under the 1840 Treaty of Waitangi.[7] By restricting the notion of Indigenous customary law, the FSA demonstrated the limits of state-sanctioned bicultural politics, which promises the official recognition of two separate peoples. The most significant Indigenous response to these restrictive practices was Labour MP Tariana Turia's break with the party and the establishment of New Zealand's first Indigenous political party, the Māori Party.

---

[6]. See Agamben, 'The Ban and the Wolf' (1998: 104–11).

[7]. According to the second article of the Treaty, 'Ko te Kuini o Ingarani ka wakarite ka wakaae ki nga Rangatira, ki nga hapu, ki nga tangata katoa o Nu Tirani, te tino Rangatiratanga o o ratou wenua o ratou kainga me o ratou taonga katoa. Otiia ko nga Rangatira o te Wakaminenga, me nga Rangatira katoa atu, ka tuku ki te Kuini te hokonga o era wahi wenua e pai ai te tangata nona te wenua, ki te ritenga o te utu e waka-ritea ai e ratou ko te kai hoko e meatia e te kuini hei kai hoko mona' ('The Queen of England agrees to protect the chiefs, the subtribes and all the people of New Zealand in the unqualified exercise of their chieftainship over their lands, villages and all their treasures. But on the other hand the chiefs of the Confederation and all the chiefs will sell land to the Queen at a price agreed to by the person owning it and by the person buying it, the latter being appointed by the Queen as her purchasing agent.' For a very large local literature on the texts, interpretations, and legal provenance of the Treaty, see 'The Three Articles of the Treaty of Waitangi' (Te Ara, Online Encyclopaedia of New Zealand. Online source: <http://www.teara.govt.nz/en/government-and-nation/1/2>, accessed 17 September 2010).

The hallmark of settler governmentality in this particular context was the exclusion of Indigenous lives from the life of the general populace. The 'general public' were effectively being asked to choose between upholding rights to the somewhat mythic notion of 'the beach' (an image and ideal that today encompasses 'Kiwi' baches [beach-homes], holidays in the sun, and instant access to the sea) or recognizing Indigenous customary law. The choice was not hard for most. Anti-Māori sentiments were further exploited by the centre-right National Party election campaign, which used billboard messages to sum up the ideological positions of both National and Labour. To the left of signs that read 'Who Owns the Beaches?' the campaigners placed an image of then Labour Prime Minister Helen Clark alongside the word 'Iwis' (tribes), while the image of National Party leader Don Brash, to the right, was connected to 'Kiwis'. Brash's 'Nationhood' speech of January 2004, delivered to a conservative constituency at the Orewa Rotary Club, just north of Auckland, amplified this message. In the speech, Brash argued that too much weight had been placed on granting political recognition to the Treaty of Waitangi and that this had contributed to divisive race-based legislation that granted special privileges to Māori. The logic behind such arguments rested on the notion of a 'level playing field' where all citizens were granted an equal opportunity to improve material and social conditions. The question of how that level playing field came to be was never raised: it was simply a field without history and context and without Indigenous presence.

Like the beaches and baches that ground the 'Kiwi' lifestyle, the logic of settler colonialism attempts to eradicate all trace of prior occupations. The FSA not only eradicated Indigenous rights in customary law; it also separated out customary law from the space of national citizenship. Such was its violent affront to existing law that prominent Māori academic Margaret Mutu suggested it might incite civil war in some parts of the country (Goldsmith 2004). The FSA demonstrated two conflicting drives at the heart of current state practices in relation to Indigenous issues. On the one hand, state practices seek to 'preserve' and 'revitalize' those aspects of Māori culture that can provisionally settle intranational tensions; on the other, it shores up 'Brand NZ' on the international stage. A 'necrophilic' national love (Hage 2004) of the Indigenous lavishes attention on an 'other' that conforms with and facilitates settler sovereignty. Meanwhile, the state seeks to expunge insurgent Indigenous articulations, banishing their perpetrators to the badlands in the interests of preserving the 'greater good' of national unity.

On 15 October 2007, a large-case paramilitary police operation saw seventeen putative 'terrorists' arrested under the 2002 Terrorism Suppression Act in Auckland, Wellington, and Christchurch and in Te Urewera, the interior forested domain of the Tūhoe people. Those arrested were mostly but not all Māori and consisted of Indigenous rights activists, environmentalists, and anarchists. The small rural town of Ruatoki in particular was closed off by police as locals were stopped, searched, and photographed. The charges were subsequently withdrawn by the New Zealand Solicitor-General, who declared the Act to be fatally compromised. Tūhoe were hardly arbitrary targets of the 'terror raids', as these quickly became known, for they had long asserted their independence, had never signed the 1840 Treaty of Waitangi, and had suffered the invasion of armed constabulary at least twice before (Binney 2009). First, in the 1870s settler militia with allied Māori pursued the 'rebel prophet' Te Kooti Arikirangi Te Turuki into Tūhoe land, where he was being sheltered, and adopted a scorched earth policy; then, in 1916, armed police invaded and destroyed the independent settlement of Maungapōhatu, established by the later 'prophet' Rua Kēnana. Tūhoe have thus long been perceived as constituting a threat to national unity, at least since the nation itself constituted an entity that an internal element could threaten by declaring its difference. In 2007, this 'threat' to the nation re-emerged.

In his analysis of the events, Vijay Devadas describes 'media necropower' in terms of the creation of a racialized panic that made it seem that the safety and security of the whole nation was truly being threatened.[8] Necropower, derived from the work of Achille Mbembe (2003), refers to the capacity to kill so that others may live, and is con-nected to the biopolitical ordering of subjects into categories of 'human' and 'non-hu-man', a practice Mbembe identifies with slavery and the social schema of the plantation as well as colonial outposts at different times in different parts of the world. Integral to this ordering is the suspension of western juridical law in the name of a form of life that must be preserved and another form of life that must be negated. In necropolitical terms, the power of the media worked in the 2007 terror raids to 'kill' an Indigenous people in order to preserve—and Police Commissioner Howard Broad replicated this language—the health and safety of the nation as a whole.[9] Leading local and interna-tional papers fell in line with the biopolitical logic of the police raids, the purpose of which was seen to be the 'management' of Indigenous people for the sake of properly national citizens. Following Michel Foucault, Devadas considers the development of a disciplinary regime, focused on individual bodies for the purpose of making them useful, into a biopolitical regime whose compass includes the whole population. For Devadas, the key constituent of the view of a fragmented biopolitical field, instigating the sovereign reflex, is racism.

While middle New Zealand allowed itself to be shocked by the sight of balaclava-clad, machine-gun-carrying paramilitary stopping cars in small-town New Zealand—reminiscent of the Mohawk (Kanesatake) stand-off with provincial and federal Canadian forces at Oka, Quebec, in 1990—no gun-toting defenders of Māori territory were to be detected. Many New Zealanders assumed the police must be 'on to some-thing', helped by leaked 'evidence', but many others were dismayed by the glaring dis-regard of civil liberties. Tūhoe, non-Māori New Zealanders like to think, should have the same liberties as other New Zealanders. But Tūhoe do not necessarily think they are New Zealanders at all.[10] The colonial present, for Tūhoe, is not just about being subject to the withdrawal of the legal protection afforded to other New Zealanders; it is also about not being free to be Tūhoe. The ongoing regulation of Indigeneity seeks to deprive peoples of the capacity to say who they think they are and to organize

---

[8.]   Devadas draws on the work of Goldie Osuri (2006) in making this point.
[9.]   According to the Police Commissioner, as reported in *The New Zealand Herald*, 'the raids were carried out in the interests of public safety' (Devadas 2008: 9).
[10.]   See TVOne's 'Sunday Extra: Tamati Kruger Interview' (2007).

themselves accordingly. Because majoritarian New Zealanders can only see colonialism as brutal incarceration—and the anti-terror raids certainly gave them a glimpse of their own invasiveness—they are more likely to wonder, benignly, what Māori really have to complain about. This is due in no small part to the myth of biculturalism: its self-insulating benevolence masks stark racism and continuing colonization. This sense of benign invisibility is a crucial mode of regulation and control for the contemporary settler nation. If the anti-terror raids were an example of the extremities of media necropower, the Māori Television bid in 2009 for coverage of the Rugby World Cup, while less politically charged, represents the insidiously benign dimensions of settler governmentality—as will now be shown below.

Media Cartographies
of National Imagining

The case of Māori Television enables us to address the national imaginary as a fully mediated cartography. The national television system comprises state broadcaster TVNZ, private corporations such as MediaWorks and the global SKY network, and, after some twenty years of struggle, the government-supported broadcaster, Māori Television. As long as state-funded broadcasters are compelled to make a profit, the appeal made to a national audience differs little from private ones. Māori are fully part of this appeal, but Māori Television also redefines the nation as a mixed constituency, and—as we will see—its disruptive power to reconfigure the national space has periodically sparked government intervention, demonstrating a sovereignty in excess of those forms of 'inclusive exclusion' that continue to characterize and consolidate New Zealand's settler-colonial regime today.

In October 2009, Māori Television caused a stir when it attempted to secure exclusive free-to-air broadcasting rights to the 2011 Rugby World Cup (a tournament eventually won by the host nation). The possibility of having 10 per cent of the World Cup commentary spoken in the Māori language (*te reo Māori*) was enough to generate a public outcry that went far beyond the confines of the nation's television industry, with many complaining vociferously that Māori Television could only transmit to 90 per cent of the population, a complaint that conveniently overlooked the fact that two other broadcasters (the privately owned TV3 and Prime) have similar transmission restrictions (*The Dominion Post*, 15/10/09). Other questions were raised about the financial backing that Māori Television had received from the Minister of Māori Affairs, Pita Sharples, and the government department, Te Puni Kōkiri. The government of the centre-right National Party quickly responded by offering financial backing to a rival state broadcaster, TVNZ, a move that threatened to create a bidding war between the two institutions. Māori Television CEO Jim Mathers subsequently expressed disappointment over the level of political management that occurred around the bid.

The then National Party leader and Prime Minister John Key ultimately prevented a bidding war by offering Māori Television symbolic leadership of a three-way deal with TVNZ and TV3—a resolution which, while still claimed as a political victory, fell far short of Māori Television's original bid for exclusive rights. Pita Sharples drew attention to the fact that the 2011 World Cup event would occur in election year—as indeed it did—seeing the government's panicky reaction as being about control and fear of the impact of rugby commentary including an element of *te reo Māori*. The controversy epitomizes a long-standing practice of managing Māori cultural difference for the sake of the settler nation, as discussed above.

In the context of short settler history, rugby has played a prominent role in binding classes and races to the developing ideal of national unity (Philips 1996). Yet it seems somewhat inaccurate to suggest, as one political commentator did at the time, that Māori TV's bid threatened 'to put a Māori *face* to the Pākehā nation's pre-eminent cultural icon, rugby';[11] rather, advertising campaigns featuring warrior iconography and the ritual haka suggest that the New Zealand Rugby Union was once again seeking to capitalize on a Māori *brand*, characterized by commodified trappings of Māori-ness and media-friendly simulations of Māori cultural style (Jackson and Hokowhitu 2002).

Māori Television's World Cup bid, while ostensibly a business move, might also be seen in terms of making an attempt to inhabit symbolic space within the national imaginary. Coterminous with fights over material space—the land struggles ignited by colonization, the more recent foreshore and seabed controversy, and current off-shore drilling for energy reserves—Māori Television's bid threatened to reorient dominant cartographies of the national imaginary by turning the tables on existing uses of Māori cultural difference. As one local political commentator put it: 'Harmless ethnic tokenism was one thing, assertive ethnic commerce was something else altogether.'[12] However, the real controversy stirred up by Māori Television's bid for World Cup coverage was its seemingly audacious belief that it had something to offer to a kind of *public* not yet able to be imagined by TVNZ and National Party ministers. Indeed, the subsequent success of Māori Television's World Cup coverage suggests that Māori Television asserted—and continues to assert—its contribution not just to Māori culture, but to New Zealand's national culture in general (Smith and Abel 2008; Smith 2011).[13] If the New Zealand government has benevolently bestowed the gift of broadcasting rights to *iwi Māori* for the purpose of 'preserving' language and culture, it does so within an environment where the liveliness of Indigenous articulations can be taken up and disseminated as part of the

[11.] Chris Trotter, 'Without Prejudice', *The Independent*, 22 October 2009.

[12.] Trotter, ibid.

[13.] According to media surrounding the event, Māori Television had a ratings success with their coverage—a success that bodes well for the health of the nation. See *The New Zealand Herald*, 'Rugby World Cup nets Māori Television record audience', Monday 12 September 2011, <http://www.nzherald.co.nz/entertainment/news/article.cfm?c_id=1501119&objectid=10751300>; or Cath Winks's 'Māori Television Trumps Rugby World Cup Ratings', *Idealog*, 11 October 2011, <http://www.idealog.co.nz/news/2011/10/maori-tv-trumps-rugby-world-cup-ratings>, both accessed 9 November 2012.

national brand. It becomes a very different story when *iwi Māori* make a bid to rewrite orthodox narratives of nationhood and national identity, and yet it is Māori Television's potential to do just this—to expand and multiply existing modes of articulation—that has made the broadcaster such a prime target of government management and regulation in the recent past.

Māori Television's struggle to gain exclusive rights to the World Cup event should also be situated within a global mediascape where national boundaries are consistently contested. After all, media technologies play a significant role in constituting and regulating political publics. Where the nation's state-funded broadcaster focuses in its advertising on the 'one-ness' of the nation (TVOne), the Māori Television logo offers up another form of collectivity (*mā ratou, mā mātou, mā koutou, mā tātou*—for them [those who have gone before], for us, for you, for everyone), which addresses the nation without being nation-centric. Its aspirational mode of address both gestures to and invokes other forms of collectivity (*mā mātou*) beyond the reified distinction between Māori and Pākehā, insider and outsider. While the media necropower of the Tūhoe anti-terror raids worked to separate Māori from the national space, Māori Television's mode of address seeks to imagine another kind of nation altogether and to envisage new sets of relations between Māori and the nation. Above all, the differences and similarities that are the hallmark of Māori Television's programming strategies crucially produce inclusive counter-publics to other television providers, offering Indigenous articulations that operate in response to prevailing relations of power, while providing viable alternatives.

The Rugby World Cup broadcast bid can thus be seen as having demonstrated a struggle over a communication landscape in much the same way that the foreshore and seabed controversy expressed a struggle over access to part of the natural landscape, while the Tūhoe terror raids showed how Indigenous presences can be conceived as threatening in terms of the dominant national imaginary. At stake in each case was an attempt to monopolize existing imaginative geographies of the nation space and a counter-initiative to produce new narratives of New Zealand identity and community, both intra- and international, both local and global. The case studies treated in this chapter show why the struggle for access to electronic and digital technologies is integral to the cause of Indigenous autonomy, while the implication of Māori sovereignty in Māori imagery for non-Māori also suggests the potential for liberation from the national yoke. In cases such as these, sovereignty and autonomy are bound up with gaining access to the media technologies that constitute, regulate, and discipline the national body. If television is a dominant means of talking about ourselves, then the public it configures can hardly be made 'safe' from its diverse constituencies, still less from an actually existing Indigeneity. Rather, such protective and exclusionary strategies are effectively a denial of the full life that Indigenous presences make conceivable. Bearing in mind Agamben's concept of 'bare life'—which is limited by a political relation that is allegedly western in origin—what does 'full life' mean if not that of those who are denied representation of their own flourishing and their own freedom in their own terms? And if Māori are not free in this sense, then non-Māori are also bound to the terms of the circumscribed life that the structural intent of their collective majority has imposed on Māori.

Consubstantial Sovereignty

We have been suggesting here that the basis of another kind of nation includes the disavowed force of Indigenous presencing and a form of *taking place* as an expression of sovereignty. This consubstantial sovereignty effectuates the presencing of a future place beyond the 'inclusive-exclusion' logic of a westernizing *polis*. Looking as much to the future as to the past, it combines the prior political ontology of Indigenous inhabitation with contemporary communication technologies and mediated landscapes. Māori Television, in this regard, is but an extension of Māori modalities of expression; and Indigenous sovereignty, which involves the redoubling of long history rather than the redaction of short history, consequently needs to be understood in extensional, not exclusivist, terms. Considered as such, the parasitical dependency of colonial bondage is inverted: now it is the master's power that is made to appear derivative. Long-standing Māori collectives (*tangata whenua*) do not need Pākehā in order to be who they are; it is rather Pākehā who appear to need *tangata whenua* in order to be who *they* are. Thinking about the time and space of long history—beyond the coming of Pākehā and Pākehā-fication, beyond the exception of colonial sovereignty—does not necessarily imply plural sovereignties; rather, it involves a coterminous relationship enfolding Indigenous inhabitations and conditioned by ongoing encounters.

Indigenous sovereignty entails a different mode of organization where the indivisible relationship between land and people is the locus of sovereign power. For Māori, the mutual and simultaneous organization of land and people developed according to epistemological, economic, and esoteric knowledges and practices. That is to say, *tangata* (people) and *whenua* (land) are inseparable: *iwi* and *hapū* life (*hapu* being the sub-tribal, extended family unit) is based on the maintenance and esteem of the relationship between land and people. Colonization subsequently introduced a system of law that reduced geographical territories to consumer goods, translated Māori attributes of place into the property of imperial markets, and conscripted the free activity of local peoples to labour in a coercive economic system of circulation and exchange. The bonds between *tangata* and *whenua* were thus eroded and a different law asserted in their place.

To say this is to both acknowledge and assert a prior or 'first law' (Mikaere 2005: 330). The substance of this law does not consist in the lingering resistance to colonization but in the perpetual assertion of a differently configured time and place. First law confirms an Indigenous presence long instantiated by the relationships understood to pertain among lands and peoples; today this nexus also includes communicative landscapes. The idea that the political ontology of earth-bodies might themselves be rights-bearing has recently been given substance in the new constitution of Ecuador

(2008), which instantiates the natural law of Mother Earth (Pachamama), whose flourishing is the foundational basis of all entitlements. The agency of 'earth-based beings', says Marisol de la Cadena, by which she means 'an insurgence of indigenous forces and practices' (2010: 336), both exceeds the human–nature divide of the modern western constitution, and returns politics, quite literally, to the immanent ground of Indigenous cosmogony. Bolivia, too, a country in which Indigenous people have the more usually non-Indigenous power to assert a majority view, similarly constitutionalizes collective earth-based well-being (*buen vivir*), suggesting for Arturo Escobar the real possibility of post-capital, or non-capital-centred, post-liberal and post-statist bases of governance.[14] In Indigenous terms, this is a constitutional matter, in the first instance, of *who you are*, which is to say, how one is constituted as such, which, without being admitted, makes politics moot. If the Quechua *allyu* (community) refers to the identity-giving specificity of a socio-natural, or long-inhabited landscape, the Māori *marae* (tribal meeting area and buildings), where *hui* (formal gatherings) take place, also makes a claim deeper and other than state-oriented politics to be the premier site of constitutional power in Aotearoa/New Zealand. Indigeneity, in this sense, implies in every Indigenous place a law of land itself, whose relational or long-peopled properties and attributes ground collective wellbeing,[15] rather than the triumvirate of western political theory: property/capital/rights.

For *tangata whenua* there is a right way in every place that is articulated by *tikanga* (*tika* means 'right'). The assertion of this right—this 'right of way'—over and against settlers, indeed any outsiders, suggests the withdrawal of western notions of sovereignty and the continuous assertion of an alternative expression of sovereignty in their place. The source of this Indigenous sovereignty is expressed in terms of *rangatiratanga*, the power of the *rangatira* or chief. 'At various times', Roger Maaka and Augie Fleras assert, 'reference to rangatiratanga has included Māori sovereignty, Māori nation, iwi nationhood, independent power, kingdom, full chiefly authority, chiefly mana, strong leadership, independence, supreme rule, self-reliance, Māori autonomy, tribal autonomy, absolute chieftainship, self-management, and trusteeship' (Maaka and Fleras 2005: 101–2). Taking the term primarily to imply Indigenous rights to self-determination, Maaka and Fleras offer Native American scholar Kirke Kickingbird's umbrella definition of *tino rangatiratanga* as 'the supreme authority from which all specific powers and rights derive their legitimacy or effect (102)'. The authors note that *tino rangatiratanga* is the Māori variant of all Indigenous claims. There is no space here to explore the rich covenant of constitutionality suggested by this definition, understood by the authors in

---

[14.] 'In other words, the "post" signals the notions that *the economy is not essentially or naturally capitalist, societies are not naturally liberal, and the state is not the only way of instituting social power as we have imagined it to be*' (Escobar 2010: 12, emphasis in the original).

[15.] In the context of an interview about constitutional change in Aotearoa/New Zealand, Moana Jackson makes reference to Bolivia and the presence of the earth mother (Pachamama) in its constitution: 'We [Māori also] started with the earth, the rivers, the seas, the forests and the mountains because they are a part of us' (Jackson 2010: 334).

terms of reciprocity and reconciliation rather than rights. Given the ongoing regulation of Indigenous presence that continues through hostile actions of national governments toward Indigenous people, we ask instead how 'supreme authority' relates to a sovereign power dedicated in the first instance to itself.

In relation to Māori sovereignty, constituting power lies with the ancestors of Indigenous story, and the cosmological world of deep history on whose recognition through genealogy (*whakapapa*) Māori flourishing has long depended, and for which Māori have been constituted as guardians. A constitution in any authentically juridical sense must flow from an understanding of Māori being so constituted, which is to say from an Indigenous understanding. The political ontology of this consubstantial sovereignty has the substance of supreme power. Specific powers and rights, Kickingbird notes, are derived from the consubstantial presencing—the very *taking place* of Māori *hui*—of past, people, and place. Seen in this context, the constituting power of Indigenous sovereignty cannot be the passive object of legal procedures, nor can Indigenous peoples be properly constituted by such procedures. In New Zealand, the Treaty settlement process demands certain forms of cultural, legal, and political visibility, providing a set of institutional constraints that corporately shape *iwi* identity (see Bargh 2007). Yet *tino rangatiratanga* bears no such circumscription. The figure of the *rangatira* embodies a literally grounded 'constitution' (*mana whenua* or substance of the land) that historically did not separate people and land; rather, it is the relations *among* people and local lands as configured in the *rangatira* that constitute Māori as *tāngata whenua* (people of the land). 'Such was the strength of this connection', says Anne Salmond, 'that a *rangatira* (or a group of chiefs) might describe the land as their own body' (2011: 15). The health of those relations has always measured the *mana* of the *rangatira*, suggesting an alternative—and prior—sovereignty.

In the life of the *rangatira*, power is the conglomerate mana of the collective, including its guiding spirits (*atua*), ancestors (*tupuna*), and land (*whenua*). 'Rangatiratanga' (chieftainship), says Māori Marsden, 'is the natural heritage of every Māori through *mana atua, mana tupuna, mana whenua*' (Marsden 2003: 154). It is a 'supreme' power, greater than a *rangatira* who is its vehicle, because it is this power that has established the lifeways of such people and that also ensures their continuance as such. As that people's very constitution this power is both law and life. The very shape and pattern of belief and behaviour which has long sustained *iwi* and *hapu* is one way of describing local law or *tikanga*. 'The law', said Māori film-maker and writer Barry Barclay in the title of one talk, 'is my breathing' (2006). Given this law rather than law-giving, the *rangatira* is more properly a guardian.

Kickingbird's 'supreme power' is then manifest as local law. Going about the place 'rightly', in a way that preserves and enhances an established set of relations, human and natural, is at the basis of *tikanga* and First law. The very idea that *Māori tikanga* has more than 'customary' political substance has only recently challenged legal thinking in New Zealand (see Tomas 2006) and has raised the spectre for Pākehā of an alternative 'real' constitution, where the quasi-constitutional Treaty of Waitangi currently acts as a placeholder. The very word 'constitution' is a foreign concept, as the editors of a significant recent collection note, quoting Moana Jackson in the same volume, and needs to be understood in terms of the *kawa* (operative rules) of the *marae*, which is to say, 'Māori law' (Mulholland and Tawhai 2010: 2). The very form of the *hui* that takes place there suggests an alternative constitution that goes beyond notions of the juridical to the composition, organization, and establishment of a time and space (one might say the refiguring of grounds or a form of *taking place*) that is expressive of Indigenous sovereignty.

This networked, expansive, and consubstantial form of sovereignty gestures towards an open-ended enfolding of people and place within the fluctuating motion of long history. Aotearoa/New Zealand is a land of many, not one, and of many-to-many relations. Pākehā, a new 'many' since added, are now asked to think about themselves in terms of that fold. Thus the layered and mediated counter-publics of communicational landscapes suggest new ways of being and organizing life, locating Pākehā within an Indigenous commons and life-giving law that their colonization has cut up and enclosed.

At the beginning of this chapter, we invoked Derek Gregory's analysis of the colonial present as a performative force that regulates social spaces and conceptual orderings in such a way that articulations of cultural difference are suppressed. As we have demonstrated here, the ongoing regulation of Indigenous cultural differences also persists within a contemporary settler nation such as Aotearoa/New Zealand, as witnessed in such disparate examples as the Foreshore and Seabed Act, the Tūhoe Terror Raids, and institutional responses to Māori Television's Rugby World Cup bid. The colonial present, within the context of contemporary Aotearoa/New Zealand, is ordered in any number of different if interrelated ways (exclusive–inclusive, benign–belligerent, passive–aggressive, etc.). Yet behind all of these social orderings lies the disavowed force of Indigenous inhabitation. As we have demonstrated in this chapter, Indigenous inhabitations posit alternative sites of cultural difference; and they do so by continually reasserting the rightness and givenness of place. The assertion of this 'right of way' over and against settlers suggests the retraction of western notions of sovereignty and the articulation of alternative expressions of sovereignty in their place. In the residue of such encounters, alternative political ontologies challenge the orthodoxies of the colonial present, and open up possibilities of living other than those mandated by the state and settler status quo.

References

Agamben, Giorgio (1998). *Homo Sacer: Sovereign Power and Bare Life*, trans. Daniel Heller-Roazen. Stanford, Calif.: Stanford University Press.

Arturo, Escobar (2010). 'Latin America at a Crossroads: Alternative Modernisations, Post-liberalism, or Post-development?', *Cultural Studies*, 24.1: 1–65.

Barclay, Barry (2006). 'One Country/Two Laws'. Paper presented at a symposium held at Old Government House, University of Auckland, 22 July.

Bargh, Maria (2007). *Resistance: An Indigenous Response to Neoliberalism*. Wellington: Huia Press.

Binney, Judith (2009). *Encircled Lands: Te Urewera 1820–1921.* Wellington: Bridget Williams Books.

De la Cadena, Marisol (2010). 'Indigenous Cosmopolitics in the Andes: Conceptual Reflections beyond "Politics"', *Cultural Anthropology,* 25.2: 334–70.

Devadas, Vijay (2008). '15 October 2007, Aotearoa: Race, Terror and Sovereignty', *Sites,* 5.1: 124–51.

Fleras, Augie and Paul Spoonley (1999). *Recalling Aotearoa: Indigenous Politics and Ethnic Relations in New Zealand.* Melbourne and Oxford: Oxford University Press.

Gibbons, Peter (2002). 'Cultural Colonisation and National Identity', *The New Zealand Journal of History,* 36.1: 5–17.

Goldsmith, Rosie (2004). 'New Zealand Embroiled in Race Row', BBC Radio 4, *Crossing Continents,* 28 October. Online source: <http://news.bbc.co.uk/2/hi/programmes/crossing_continents/3956265.stm>, accessed 10 May 2012.

Gregory, Derek (2004). *The Colonial Present: Afghanistan, Palestine and Iraq.* Malden, Mass.: Blackwell.

Hage, Ghassan (2004). 'On Loving Dead Others: Colonialism and Social Necrophilia'. Paper presented at the conference *Dialogue Across Cultures: Identity, Place, Culture,* University of Melbourne, Melbourne, 12–14 November.

Jackson, Moana (2010). 'Constitutional Transformation', in Malcolm Mulholland and Veronica Tawhai (eds), *Weeping Waters: The Treaty of Waitangi and Constitutional Change.* Wellington: Huia Publishers, 325–37.

Jackson, Steven J. and Brendan Hokowhitu (2002). 'Sport, Tribes, and Technology: The New Zealand All Blacks' Haka and the Politics of Identity', *Journal of Sport and Social Issues,* 26.2: 125–39.

Jutel, Thierry (2007). 'Why Are There No Badlands in New Zealand?'. Paper presented at the *MEDIANZ* conference, Victoria University of Wellington, Wellington, 8–10 February.

Keenan, Danny (ed.) (2008). *Terror in Our Midst? Searching For Terror in Aotearoa New Zealand.* Wellington: Huia Publishers.

Maaka, Roger and Augie Fleras (2005). *The Politics of Indigeneity: Challenging the State in Canada and Aotearoa.* Dunedin: University of Otago Press.

MacDonald, Amanda (2008). 'If Everybody Could Just Settle Down: Representational Insistence in Lieu of Resistance in the Pre-Post-Colony of New Caledonia'. Paper presented at the *Conditions of Settler Colonialism* symposium, University of Chicago, Chicago, 25–6 April.

Marsden, Māori (2003). *The Woven Universe: Selected Writings of Rev. Māori Marsden.* Masterton: Estate of Māori Marsden.

Mbembe, Achille (2003). 'Necropolitics', *Public Culture,* 15.1: 11–40.

Mikaere, Ani (2005). 'The Treaty of Waitangi and Recognition of Tikanga Māori', in Michael Belgrave, Merata Kawharu, and David Williams (eds), *Waitangi Revisited: Perspectives of the Treaty of Waitangi,* 2nd edn. Auckland: Oxford University Press, 330–48.

Mikaere, Ani (2011). *Colonising Myths–Māori Realities: He Rukuruku Whakaaro.* Wellington: Huia Publishers.

Mulholland, Malcolm and Veronica Tawhai (2010). *Weeping Waters: The Treaty of Waitangi and Constitutional Change.* Wellington: Huia Pubishers.

O'Sullivan, Dominic (2007). *Beyond Biculturalism: The Politics of an Indigenous Minority.* Wellington: Huia Publishers.

Osuri, Goldie (2006). 'Media Necropower: Australian Media Reception and the Somatechnics of Mamdouh Habib', *Borderlands,* 5.1. Online source: <http://www.borderlands.net.au/vol5no1_2006/osurI_necropower.htm>, accessed 10 May 2012.

Philips, Jock (1996). *A Man's Country? The Image of the Pākehā Male, a History.* Auckland: Penguin.

Povinelli, Elizabeth (2011). 'The Governance of the Prior', *Interventions,* 13.1: 13–30.

Russell, Khyla (2006). 'Landscape: Perceptions of Kai Tahu I mua, aianei, a muri ake', *Spasifika,* 12: 72–3.

Salmond, Anne (2011). 'Ontological Quarrels: Indigeneity, Exclusion and Citizenship in a Relational World'. Online source: <https://researchspace.auckland.ac.nz/docs/uoa-docs/rights.htm>, accessed 10 May 2012.

Sharp, Andrew (1997). *Justice and the Māori: The Philosophy and Practice of Māori Claims in New Zealand since the 1970s.* Auckland and New York: Oxford University Press.

Smith, Jo (2007). 'Postcultural Hospitality: Settler-Native-Migrant Encounters', *Arena,* 28: 65–86.

Smith, Jo (2011). 'Postcolonial Māori Television? The Dirty Politics of Indigenous Cultural Production', *Continuum,* 25.5: 719–29.

Smith, Jo and Sue Abel (2008). 'Ka Whawhai Tonu Mātou: Indigenous Television in Aotearoa/New Zealand', *New Zealand Journal of Media Studies,* 11.1: 1–14.

Stephenson, Janet, Mick Abbott, and Jacinta Ruru (eds) (2010). *Beyond the Scene: Landscape and Identity in Aotearoa New Zealand.* Dunedin: Otago University Press.

TVOne (2007). 'Sunday Extra: Tamati Kruger Interview', *TVOne* (New Zealand), 2 November. Online source: <http://tvnz.co.nz/content/1426283>, accessed 7 October 2010.

Tomas, Nin (2006). 'Key Concepts of Tikanga Māori (Māori Custom Law)'. PhD thesis, University of Auckland.

Tuhiwai Smith, Linda (1999). *Decolonising Methodologies: Research and Indigenous Peoples.* London: Zed Books.

Turner, Stephen (2007). 'Inclusive Exclusion: Managing Identity for the Nation's Sake in Aotearoa/New Zealand', *Arena,* 28: 87–106.

Watson, Irene (2007). 'Aboriginal Sovereignties: Past, Present and Future (Im)possibilities', in Suvendrini Perera (ed.), *Our Patch: Enacting Australian Sovereignty Post-2001.* Perth: Network Books, 23–43.

Wright, Errol and Abi King-Jones (dirs) (2011). *Operation 8: Deep in the Forest.* Cutcutcut Films.

⋯⋯⋯⋯⋯⋯⋯⋯⋯⋯⋯⋯⋯⋯⋯⋯⋯⋯⋯⋯⋯⋯⋯⋯⋯⋯⋯⋯

TOWARDS AN
ANTI-COLONIAL FUTURE

⋯⋯⋯⋯⋯⋯⋯⋯⋯⋯⋯⋯⋯⋯⋯⋯⋯⋯⋯⋯⋯⋯⋯⋯⋯⋯⋯⋯

PETER HALLWARD

The colonial present described in this part of the Handbook is shaped above all by brute imperial power. Drawing on a substantial body of new work in fields ranging from geography and security studies to political theory and literary criticism, the contributors to this section paint a stark picture of a world structured in dominance and oppression, a world every bit as Manichean as that implacably divided settler regime famously denounced in Frantz Fanon's *The Wretched of the Earth* (1961).

Denunciation of the ways in which our colonial modernity legitimates itself by demonizing its 'other' (while disguising its own Eurocentric and racist reflexes) is common, of course, to virtually all anti- or postcolonial criticism. But compared with the more discourse-oriented and deconstructive perspectives associated with an earlier phase of postcolonial theory—one that devoted much effort to blurring or questioning the apparent binaries inherited from colonialism—these essays have a more materialist inflection. Here the focus is firmly on newly intensive mechanisms of oppressive power, operating in an era of newly open-ended war. This new colonial present is a time marked by shock and awe, by Guantánamo and Abu Ghraib, by extraordinary rendition and all-too-ordinary targeted killings, by drone assassinations, security perimeters, and continuous surveillance, as well as by more subtle forms of population control: neoliberal austerity measures, full-spectrum marketization of public goods and services, the deliberate cultivation of mass debt, political assaults on organized labour and immigration. Understood here primarily through reference to thinkers like Giorgio Agamben and Judith Butler, our colonial present figures as a time of maximum vulnerability and exposure to power.

It is also a time, as several of the essays point out, when such forms of power tend once again to be justified and legalized in the broadly liberal terms of an ethical or humanitarian responsibility to protect populations deemed vulnerable to objectionable forms of instability. Stabilizing colonial power, as much in our neoliberal present as in our liberal past, determines its own norms, such that—to repeat Eyal Weizman's (2012) phrase—'what we do becomes the law' (quoted in Morton's chapter; see also Losurdo 2011).

Waleed Hazbun draws attention to the ways in which the more 'accommodating' rhetoric of Barack Obama and Hillary Clinton serves to blunt criticism of underlying US objectives; and as Priyamvada Gopal points out, the field of postcolonial studies remains obliged to 'negotiate the quagmire generated by liberalism's entanglements with contemporary empire', couched in the consensual terms of human rights and 'respect for difference'. Meanwhile, Joanne Sharp's critique of aid-induced, NGO-brokered passivity and depoliticization offers further confirmation of Paulo Freire's old insight that 'true generosity consists precisely in fighting to destroy the causes which nourish false charity' (Freire 1976: 29).

What is comparatively underdeveloped, however, in these rich descriptive accounts of contemporary imperial power is, first, an explanation of its underlying causes and, second and more importantly, a strategic analysis and critical assessment of the various forms of resistance it encounters. In the colonial past, to condemn colonialism was usually at one and the same time to affirm and support a struggle for national liberation; in the colonial present, things do not seem so clear-cut.

On the first point, a number of far-reaching questions are occasionally evoked but generally left unanswered. Are the latest bursts of US aggression best understood, as Noam Chomsky likes to imply, in terms of an effectively age-old form of 'mafia' politics, whereby 'the strong do as they wish while the poor suffer as they must?' Or is the new phase of imperialism better seen as a distinctively neoliberal variant of the 'highest phase of capitalism'? More precisely, to what extent is the 'war on terror' part of a broader contemporary crisis in global capital accumulation, one that combines predatory forms of so-called primitive accumulation or appropriation with newly fluid and destructive forms of overaccumulation? In a conjuncture marked by far-reaching financial deregulation and generalized marketization, by structural unemployment and mass debt, to what extent should the assault on Third World populations generally and Middle Eastern populations more specifically be understood as part of a wider campaign of 'population pacification', in which what is ultimately at stake is not only military supremacy and control of natural resources but also the preservation of a suitably docile, deferential, and defenceless global labour force? In other words, how far should the deployment of new imperial power be understood in the end, more or less as Marx predicted, in terms of an increasingly intensive effort, suitably channelled and differentiated across the global economic system, to compel precariously employed or underemployed people to work harder and harder for less and less?

The way we answer this first question will also orient our approach to the second. Given the harrowing brutality of the forms of domination they describe, it is striking that most of the contributors to this section limit their counter-proposals to relatively modest accounts of resistance and political or cultural alternatives, a tendency that hints at what might be called the underlying 'postcolonial' inflection to this particular account of our colonial times. For example, after considering Māori attempts to play a more active role in the 'technologically mediated communication landscapes' that regulate 'contemporary articulations of cultural difference' in New Zealand, Jo Smith and Stephen Turner conclude their contribution with an evocation of 'possibilities of

living other than those mandated by the status quo'. They argue that 'Indigenous inhabitations posit alternative sites of cultural difference', asserting a 'right of way' over settler
or Eurocentric 'notions of sovereignty and the articulation of alternative expressions of
sovereignty in their place'—but they do little to say how such an articulation might be
distinguished from other appeals to established customs and practices.

Sharp's contribution offers a glimpse of the ways in which 'other forms of biopolitics
are being practised—in Africa and elsewhere—that subvert the imperial ambitions of
the colonial present, even if they do not always succeed in resisting it', and she duly notes
how, in the wake of Mohamed Bouazizi's self-immolation in December 2010, for thousands of north Africans 'protesting, marching through and occupying the streets have
offered ways of asserting agency when their voices are not heard through systemic forms
of representation and governance'. Citing Butler and Mitchell, Sharp concludes with a
call for an 'inherently postcolonial ethics: one which, rather than adopting a masculinist
form of cosmopolitanism that "accepts normative framings of liberal democratic deliberation and choice-making", ... sees subjects as "endlessly reconstituted through dialectical processes of recognition, within multiple networks of power"'. Stephen Morton
also draws on Butler to show how literary forms of testimony and mourning can 'foster
a shared recognition of vulnerability and dependency across cultures'. Mirza Waheed's
novel *The Collaborator* (2011), for instance, serves to 'give voice, meaning, and dignity
to the precarious lives and deaths of the Kashmiri population at large', and 'in so far as
they convey the fragmented and often traumatic experience of violent colonial sovereignty, [such] narratives allow us to mourn the lives and deaths of the oppressed, and to
imagine a form of justice beyond the liberal fictions of human rights, democracy, and
the normal rule of law'.

David Farrier and Patricia Tuitt are more directly concerned with militant agency and
resistance, and ponder how Fanon's assault on colonialism might supplement Agamben's
critique of sovereign power. However, their decision to focus on 'what may seem at
one level to be desperate acts and hopeless actions' like self-mutilation offers at best a
'glimpse of future political horizons in which those same acts and actions that we sometimes tend to dismiss as impotent recover their legitimate force'. Hazbun likewise evokes
a neo-Fanonian theme when he cites Tarak Barkawi and Mark Laffey's argument that
'even when the violence of "the weak" is characterized as terrorism or insurgency, and
even when, by the standard definitions of western security and policy discourses, their
actions are viewed as unacceptable or illegitimate, postcolonial security studies should
refrain from passing normative judgement' (Barkawi and Laffey 2006: 351, quoted in
Hazbun's chapter). Along these lines, Hazbun suggests, the Arab uprisings of 2011–12
may provide access to ordinary people's imaginings of domestic, regional, and global
politics, offering us alternative 'geographical imaginations that can engage and enhance
our sense of the world and enable us to situate ourselves within it with care, concern,
and humility' (Gregory 2004: 262, quoted in Hazbun).

Fanon himself, by contrast, made his point in more forceful terms. Given what he
is up against, Fanon argues, 'the colonized man finds his freedom in and through violence' pure and simple. In the colonial present that was French Algeria, once isolated

urban revolutionaries and intellectuals finally turned their attention to the rural areas they 'discover[ed] that the mass of the country people [had] never ceased to think of the problem of their liberation except in terms of violence, in terms of taking back the land from the foreigners, in terms of national struggle, and of armed insurrection. It [was] all very simple' (Fanon 1968 [1961]: 86, 127).[1] The Algerian revolutionaries then found themselves obliged to resort to violence for the same reason as the Jacobins in 1793 or the Bolsheviks in 1918: by 1956, 'the revolutionary leadership found that if it wanted to prevent the people from being gripped by terror it had no choice but to adopt forms of terror which until then it had rejected' (Fanon 1970 [1959]: 40).[2] Since colonialism is itself a form of violence, so then the partisans of the national liberation struggles came to the conclusion 'it [would] only yield when confronted with greater violence' (Fanon 1968 [1961]: 61).[3] By the same token, when Fanon issues an appeal for solidarity from anti-imperialist forces in France, he does not ask them merely to 'refrain from passing normative judgement' or to enhance their sense of place in the world; on the contrary, after noting that 'certain French democrats are at times shocked by the sincerity of the Algerian fighter', he is shocked in turn by their 'unendurably painful' reluctance to take sides. Now that the Algerian people has 'expressed its will to set itself up as a sovereign nation', and now that the stakes of the conflict are clear, Fanon concludes, for everyone concerned the political question boils down to a basic choice: whether or not to support that will (Fanon 1967 [1964]: 87–9; see also the General Introduction to this volume).

A version of this choice is part and parcel of every great confrontation with established power. Some of those who, like Rousseau or Robespierre, denounced tyranny in the late eighteenth century also affirmed the 'will of the people' as the source and agent of sovereign power. Some of those who, like Marat or Toussaint L'Ouverture, denounced slavery also affirmed the right of the enslaved to overthrow it. Some of those who, with and after Marx, denounced capitalism also devoted themselves to the organization and education of the people who would eventually win the opportunity to dig its grave. And some of those who denounced colonialism in its previous incarnation, with and around Fanon (or Mao, Che, Giáp, Mandela, Martin Luther King ...) likewise investigated and affirmed the popular mobilizations that took shape to overcome it. As Vietnam's general Võ Nguyên Giáp would repeatedly argue at the height of the most intensive colonial war in history, critique of the self-evident obscenities of imperial power is only pertinent if it

---

[1] As Fanon argues, 'The starving peasant, outside the class system, is the first among the exploited to discover that only violence pays. For him there is no compromise, no possible coming to terms; colonization and decolonization are simply a question of relative strength' (1968 [1961]: 61).

[2] For Fanon, 'The naked truth of decolonization evokes for us the searing bullets and bloodstained knives which emanate from it. For if the last shall be first, this will only come to pass after a murderous and decisive struggle between the two protagonists' (Fanon 1968 [1961]: 37).

[3] In a colonial context, 'violence alone, violence committed by the people, violence organized and educated by its leaders, makes it possible for the masses to understand social truths and gives the key to them. Without that struggle, without that knowledge of the practice of action, there's nothing but a fancy-dress parade and the blare of the trumpets. There's nothing save a minimum of readaptation, a few reforms at the top, a flag waving: and down there at the bottom an undivided mass, still living in the middle ages, endlessly marking time' (Fanon 1968 [1961]: 147).

helps clarify and win the 'people's war', in line with appeals to 'mobilize the entire people, arm the entire people and fight on all fronts' (Giáp 1970: 264). Che Guevara's famous call to 'create two, three, many Vietnams' needs to be understood in this context.[4]

An important difference between the colonial present as diagnosed here and the colonial past that was the 1960s would seem to be the relative reluctance of analysts of the former to make unequivocal declarations of solidarity with at least some of those who are currently fighting for decolonization (see Lazarus in Part III of this volume). No doubt today the issues are more murky, the warring parties more diverse and more difficult to assess; it would make no sense to condemn today's colonial present while also endorsing al-Qaeda-style terrorism, for instance, not least because the latter has been—and still is—part and parcel of this very present. There is all the more need, then, for detailed assessment of the various groups who are struggling against present forms of colonial power. There are indeed some general discussions of agency in this section, and some brief references to the 'Arab Spring' and the Palestinians. But despite the evocation of Fanon as 'the most lucid analyst of neocolonialism' (Huggan), no clear discussion can be found here of the pros and cons of Fanon's general approach to decolonization. Sharp and Hazbun both refer to Barkawi and Laffey's pointed suggestion that 'the weak' should be viewed as being equal to 'the strong' in their 'right to bear arms', and consider how violence that may be 'rational and effective for the weaker party', is systematically delegitimated by the West' (Barkawi and Laffey 2006: 351, 350). But they fail to complement a critique of this delegitimation with consideration of its actual deployment in any of the numerous places (Afghanistan, Haiti, Palestine, Colombia, Syria, central India) where, for good or ill, the issue has become a pressing political concern. Similarly, Gopal is sensitive to the way 'partitions erected between the US and the Arab world suppress and deny the agency of postcolonial actors in international politics', showing for instance how the 'carefully constructed absence of thinking, questioning, writing, and resistance within Iran (and by clear implication, all Muslim societies)' staged in Azar Nafisi's *Reading Lolita in Tehran* is an integral part of 'the figuring of the west not just as a resource for change but the *only* possible one'. But here again she neglects to correct this misrepresentation with an account of anti-imperial agency per se. Smith and Turner go further down this route when they suggest that the 'presencing' of Indigenous peoples and their non-negotiable claims to territorial sovereignty effectively transcends the relational domain of political struggle, such that 'Indigenous political ontology requires no recognition from non-Indigenous people of its substance in order to be the power-that-it-is; that is what we mean by taking it as given'. However, leaving aside the markedly European origins of the concept, I am not sure what it might mean to take other un- or underrecognized (e.g. Arawak or Carib) claims to sovereignty as 'given' in this sense.

As far as understanding resistance to colonial power is concerned, it is not clear that we have moved much past Edward Said's awareness, dating back to the 1980s if not well before then, that the basic problem in the Middle East is 'Arab powerlessness'. Nowhere

---

4. Che Guevara, 'Message to the Tricontinental' (16 April 1967). Online source: <http://www.marxists.org/archive/guevara/1967/04/16.htm>, accessed 27 November 2012.

in this section is there a strategic analysis of Hamas or Hezbollah, for instance, or a critical evaluation of the insurgencies in Iraq or Afghanistan; nor is much discussion to be found of the actual political organizations and campaigns (and their ideological inflection, class composition, historical trajectory) that have taken shape along the various fault lines of our colonial world. There is little discussion, for instance, of the mobilization of popular power in Tunisia and Egypt in 2011, still less consideration of the more divisive questions frequently asked of the mobilizations in Libya and Syria (which must at least complicate an interpretation *en bloc* of the Arab uprisings as *simply* anti-imperialist). Nor is there reference to the Maoist legacy in parts of Asia, to the ongoing campaigns of landless and homeless people in various parts of the contemporary world, or (apart from a passing reference to Bolivia) to recent and far-reaching popular mobilizations in Latin America—and thus no intervention in the animated debates that now divide, within the broad anti-colonial camp, supporters and critics of the current governments of Bolivia, Venezuela, and Ecuador.

The prominence of Giorgio Agamben as a privileged point of theoretical reference is one symptom of this difficulty. Several of the contributors to this section have drawn on interpretations of Guantánamo as a space of exception and, to some extent, on what the section introduction summarizes as 'Gregory's loose likening of Taliban fighters, al-Qaeda terrorists, and Afghan refugees and civilians to Agamben's exclusionary figures of "bare life"' (Huggan). To move from anti-imperial fighters to the utterly exposed and disposable animality that is 'bare life', however, is no small shift. For while the former continue to wage a political struggle that merits strategic evaluation and judgement, leading to solidarity, neutrality, or opposition, the latter have been stripped of any capacity for agency, and in the end can solicit only an 'ethical' response. Farrier and Tuitt, while conceding that 'Agamben's work on the refugee in his analysis of the sovereign sphere has become well-nigh indispensable', sensibly point out that 'it has become increasingly apparent that it is in want of a critical supplement if it is to guide us to a place beyond biopolitics'. They duly look to Fanon, acknowledging his recognition that the 'narrow world' of colonialism 'can only be called in question by absolute violence' (Fanon 1968 [1961]: 37), to provide that supplement. But it is all the more curious in this context that their most striking illustration of 'Fanonian' agency—lip sewing[5]— is one that draws attention, in spectacular fashion, to its own exclusion and impotence. More than a strategy for directly breaking down the resistance of the colonizer, it seems easier to make sense of lip sewing as a demand for recognition or an appeal to the colonizer's guilty conscience: an approach that the Fanon of *The Wretched of the Earth* explicitly discounts. It is not easy, in my view, to supplement Agamben's post-Heideggerian ontology with an account of deliberate political resistance.

Rather than dwell on current configurations of such resistance, the essays collected here tend to focus instead on western policy and liberal *mauvaise foi*, compensated with

---

[5.] 'Lip sewing, in this context, is not simply an expression of agency in the refugee; it produces precisely the terrifying spectacle that might bring about the end of his/her degradation—it is an example of "absolute violence"' (Farrier and Tuitt).

an emphasis—familiar to anyone versed in the recent postcolonial past—on the complexity, multiplicity, and fragmentation of colonial experiences. This raises two further questions. First, although they certainly all discuss varied and longer-term patterns of power and oppression, several of the essays' analyses of recent western aggression and liberal self-justification appear to some extent to accept the underlying assumption, vigorously advanced by these same western propagandists, that some 'central modalities' of our colonial present—to use Gregory's phrase—did indeed begin to take shape in September 2001 (or perhaps, as Sharp suggests, a couple of years before that). Would it not be more accurate, however, to situate analysis of the past decade in terms of an ongoing colonial *continuum*, one that reaches back through earlier declarations of a 'war against terror' and across earlier sequences of metropolitan-sponsored state terror, e.g. across much of Latin America, to say nothing of Algeria, Kenya, Mozambique, East Timor? And second, is it not time that we submit the almost instinctive (intrinsically 'ethical'?) valorization of complexity and pluralism itself to critical scrutiny; that we consider such a perspective in the rather unforgiving light cast by earlier anti-imperial and anti-capitalist struggles?

In short, the analyses proposed in this part make a compelling case for understanding our political present as a continuation of older and deeper forms of colonialism by other means, and compounded by many of the same means. There is all the more reason, then, to hope that the near future will be understood in more explicitly *anti-* rather than evasively postcolonial terms.

References

Barkawi, Tarak and Mark Laffey (2006). 'The Postcolonial Moment in Security Studies', *Review of International Studies*, 32: 329–52.

Fanon, Frantz (1967 [1964]). *Toward the African Revolution*, trans. Haakon Chevalier. New York: Grove Press.

Fanon, Frantz (1968 [1961]). *Wretched of the Earth*, trans. Constance Farrington. New York: Grove Press.

Fanon, Frantz (1970 [1959]). *A Dying Colonialism*, trans. Haakon Chevalier. London: Pelican Books.

Freire, Paulo (1976). *Pedagogy of the Oppressed*. Boston: Bergin and Garvey.

Giáp, Võ Nguyên (1970). *The Military Art of People's War*. New York: Monthly Review.

Gregory, Derek (2004). *The Colonial Present: Afghanistan, Palestine, Iraq*. Oxford: Blackwell.

Losurdo, Domenico (2011). *Liberalism: A Counter-History*, trans. Gregory Elliott. London: Verso.

Weizman, Eyal (2012). *The Least of All Possible Evils: Humanitarian Violence from Arendt to Gaza*. London: Verso.

PART III

THEORY AND PRACTICE

INTRODUCTION

GRAHAM HUGGAN

The question mark at the end is probably the least surprising element in the title of Ato Quayson's 2000 book *Postcolonialism: Theory, Practice or Process?* Its interrogative value, as the composite implies, is as much relational as definitional, with the fraught relationship between theory and practice, in particular, being integral to most current understandings of the postcolonial field. For many—both within the field and outside it—postcolonial studies is marked by a profound, even constitutive, disparity between theory and practice: hence increasingly routine criticisms that postcolonial theory is merely an end in itself or that, in primarily serving the needs of the western academy, it paradoxically silences the voices of those for whom it wishes to advocate: the economically exploited, the socially marginalized, the historically oppressed.

Such criticisms are hardly new; indeed, the postcolonial field has long since generated momentum by inviting them. For several decades now, the field has made a virtue of its own embattlement; a large part of that battle has been the continuing attempt to interrogate itself. Theory—in Jonathan Culler's characteristically generous understanding of the term as a more-or-less systematic way of disputing 'common-sense' views of meaning, representation, and experience (1997: 3)—has been at the centre of postcolonial studies since most versions of its first beginnings. For Culler among others, theory is defined in terms *both* of its potential to adjust its own intellectual horizons—in terms of its heightened capacity for critical self-reflexivity—*and* in relation to the material consequences of those adjustments, i.e. theory, in so far as it seeks to change the way people think, is necessarily determined by its 'practical effects' (1997: 4).

One prominent version of the practical effects of postcolonial theory would be what the Kenyan writer Ngũgĩ wa Thiong'o once famously called the 'decolonisation of the mind' (Ngũgĩ 1980): the challenge to European and other western knowledge systems and ways of thinking that have historically supported imperial authority, e.g. the view that imperial rulers are both culturally different to and morally superior to those they rule. The 'decolonisation of the mind' both underpins and supplements those forms of material transformation that postcolonial theorists like to call for: a radical overhauling of global social and economic inequality; an increased and appropriately legislated respect for what Young calls 'the generative relations between different peoples and their cultures' (2003: 7); a concerted political move towards establishing and developing broad-based participatory democracies no longer bound to the authoritarian power of the state.

'Radical' is perhaps the key term here. The radicalism of postcolonial theory and criticism has often tended to be taken for granted, not least by postcolonial practitioners themselves; as Moore-Gilbert et al. breezily put it, 'in terms of its political orientation, [postcolonial studies offers] a site of radical contestation and contestatory radicalism'

(1997: 3)—as if neither of these mutually supportive radicalisms were seriously in doubt. Just how radical, however, is postcolonial studies? Moore-Gilbert et al.'s directly preceding suggestion already seems to undermine the brazenness of their declarative statement: postcolonial studies, they say, is the product of the poststructuralist turn and, as such, is best situated 'between theory and practice, between literary and cultural studies, between Marxism and existentialism, between localism and universalism, between personal and public, between self and state' (1997: 3). Seen this way, postcolonial studies' radical potential is indexed to its self-perpetuating capacity for rethinking the relationship between theory and practice rather than being generated by the capacity of its own theories to produce and/or be produced by 'real-world' material effects.

The field's troubled relationship to Marxism offers further if not necessarily conclusive evidence of this dilemma. For several Marxists engaging with the field, postcolonial theory has singularly failed in what should amount to its own greatest commitment, the 'praxis of producing knowledge ... in the terrain of popular struggle' (San Juan, Jr. 1998: 70). Instead, reliant as it is on the eternal equivocations of poststructuralist philosophy, it has performed the elaborate conjuring trick by which 'the objective asymmetry of power and resources between hegemonic blocs and subaltern groups (racialized minorities in the metropoles and in the "third world"), as well as [their] attendant consequences, disappear' (San Juan, Jr. 1998: 7). However, even doctrinal Marxists of this kind are not necessarily 'against' postcolonialism per se; rather, they tend to see postcolonial theory and practice as being fundamentally disjoined and as lacking the political purchase of more systematic philosophies, like Marxism, which posit a properly dialectical relationship between theory and practice within a 'coherent and unitary conception of the world' (Gramsci, quoted in San Juan 1998: 95).

As argued elsewhere (see the General Introduction to this volume), vehement disagreements between Marxists and poststructuralists have been one of the most characteristic features of postcolonial theory from the outset. Some Marxists, like E. San Juan, Jr., view the ideological goals of Marxism and poststructuralism as being incompatible with or even antithetical to one another; while others, like Gayatri Spivak, see postcolonial theory as combining Marxist and poststructuralist elements in the pursuit of sophisticated anti-colonial critique. A balanced view, if one from outside Marxism, is that of Leela Gandhi, who contends that 'neither the assertions of Marxism nor those of poststructuralism ... can account for the meanings and consequences of the colonial encounter' (1998: ix). Instead, says Gandhi, the 'poststructuralist critique of Western epistemology and theorisation of cultural alterity/difference is indispensable to postcolonial *theory* [while] materialist philosophies, such as Marxism, seem to supply the most compelling basis for postcolonial *politics*' (ix; emphasis in the original). As such, she concludes, the postcolonial critic has to work toward 'a synthesis of, or negotiation between, both modes of thought' in order to stay true to the 'theoretical and political integration' to which postcolonial studies is committed and for which it is academically known (ix).

While Gandhi's formula is admirably clear, it runs the risk of ceding politics to Marxism while attaching theory too closely to poststructuralist philosophy—a questionable dichotomy that several postcolonial theorists, keen as they are to establish theory as *itself* a kind of politics, have made it their business to contest. Robert Young's contention, for example, is that postcolonialism—which he appears to see in terms of the suturing of theory to practice—names both 'a politics and [a] philosophy of *activism* that contests [contemporary global disparities] and so continues in a new way the anti-colonial struggles of the past' (2003: 4; emphasis mine). However, whether postcolonial studies is seen as activist or not depends on whether work mostly produced from within the western academy is seen as matching its own perhaps too-ready claims to be interventionist; on whether theory is seen as complementary with rather than supplementary to practice; and on whether both of these are seen as being harnessed to socially emancipatory goals.

This section of the Handbook, strategically placed at its centre, assesses the claim to activism via a multifaceted exploration of the relationship between theory and practice in postcolonial studies, seeking to cover a wide range of its main theoretical concerns. These concerns—racism, sexism, language, translation, memory, the problems of speaking of and for others—are of obvious relevance to anti-colonial struggles of both past and present, and are generally accepted as underpinning the material realities of these struggles; a different case however obtains when the primary object of postcolonial theory is, or at least appears to be, itself. The self-reflexivity of postcolonial theory can be seen of course as beneficial, since an analysis of the terms in which any struggle is conducted is an integral part of the struggle itself. Still—to take one prominent example—there seems to be quite a wide discrepancy between Homi Bhabha's hypertheoretical notion of 'critical resistance' (Bhabha 1994) and the *actual* resistance practised by anti-colonial freedom fighters and other subaltern insurgent groups.

The need to distinguish between these groups is more important than ever in the context of today's 'war on terror' in which theoretical differences can have huge practical consequences, and whether one person's freedom fighter is another person's terrorist is in part a *philosophical* question to resolve (see Morton's and Hazbun's chapters in Part II of this volume). Similarly, *national* issues of race and cultural difference, whether acknowledged as such or not, have a broad bearing on the current (ill) treatment of migrants and asylum seekers in a number of contemporary western societies that are given to rephrasing the 'problem' in uniquely *practical* terms. Further complications arise when the response is or is perceived to be 'emotional'—as if the language of affect somehow short-circuits the need for rational analysis or is incompatible with it; or as if all that is needed is to present complex socio-political issues in the uncontroversial language of 'common sense' (see Culler's definition of theory above). Such 'common-sense' arguments for oppression are integral to the colonialist mindset, and—as Ngũgĩ implies—it is arguably the greatest task of postcolonial criticism to 'unthink' the biases of colonialist thought. The essays in this section seek, accordingly, to unpack the profoundly practical implications of attitudes that are wont to present themselves as 'non-theoretical', thereby re-establishing postcolonialism's theoretical credentials. However, they remain alert at the same time to the practical limitations of what is after all primarily an academic discipline, and to the dangers—different versions of the theory/politics nexus notwithstanding—of simply substituting theoretical insight for political work.

Elleke Boehmer's opening chapter sets the tone by suggesting that one way of going beyond the manufactured theory/politics divide might be to focus on the historical figure of the anti-colonial activist-intellectual, whose life may then be read as an exemplary instance of 'resistance theory … produced on the job'. Her chosen focus is on Nelson Mandela as twentieth-century-spanning anti-apartheid activist, political prisoner, and, later, democratically elected leader of his own country: both a multifaceted man and an inspirational embodiment of the democratic and liberationist values inscribed within the morally exemplary 'anti-colonial life'.

Mandela's life is simultaneously used as a representative case of what Boehmer calls the practical 'antecedents-in-resistance' of postcolonial theory and as an experiential counterpoint to academic works within the postcolonial field, notably Ashcroft, Griffiths, and Tiffin's now-dated but still-influential 1989 primer—itself nominally designed to bridge theory and practice—*The Empire Writes Back*. Contrary to Lazarus (see his chapter in this section), Boehmer reads Ashcroft, Griffiths, and Tiffin's book as belonging to a celebratory historical moment that might help account for its heady enthusiasm for the supposedly subversive properties of postcolonial literature, though—closer in spirit this time to Lazarus—she also reiterates standard criticisms of the book's lack of historical depth and its potential 'deradicalization' of the very 'resistance it reads and for which it wishes to enlist respect'. *The Empire Writes Back*, Boehmer suggests, skates over the pain of situated anti-colonial struggle while also failing notably to account for 'the irregular penetration of colonial capital across the globe'. These are familiar criticisms; less orthodox is the view that Mandela's life can be used, not necessarily to invalidate Ashcroft, Griffiths, and Tiffin's theories, but to provide a working instance of them in the wider context of postcolonialism's 'radical antecedents within anti-colonial struggles across the world'.

In charismatic anti-colonial leaders like Mandela, Boehmer suggests, there are no clear boundaries between intellectual and political interests, and theory is wedded to practice within the framework of an overarching moral vision (though one by no means opposed to the use of violence for revolutionary ends). Boehmer reads in Mandela a complex mixture of retaliatory and reconciliatory impulses—'chameleon skills' equally adapted for the forging of populist solidarities and the outflanking of political foes. Mandela is seen, accordingly, as an incarnation of the 'supremely tactical postcolonial leader' and as a compelling case of 'postcolonial theory-in-practice', in which anti-colonial resistance is both lived and thought, and theoretical/ practical forms of liberationism are strategically brought together to assert what Boehmer calls—echoing to some extent the upbeat message of *The Empire Writes Back*—an empowering, African-centred postcolonial humanism for our times.

In Neil Lazarus's polemical chapter, 'liberation' is also the key term, but it is interpreted very differently than in Boehmer's essay. Without attacking Boehmer's celebratory left-liberalism directly, Lazarus—one of postcolonial studies' most combative Marxists—suggests that the field's primary commitment to 'the pursuit of liberation after the achievement of political independence' (Robert Young's on-the-face-of-it unobjectionable phrase) has not necessarily been reflected in what he sees as its

dominant 'Third Worldist' tendencies, which if anything have 'roll[ed] back the challenge represented by "Third World" insurgency at the peripheries'. This is in keeping,
Lazarus provocatively contends, with the general move *against* anti-colonial nationalism and revolutionary anti-imperialism in the immediate post-independence decades
(the 1970s and 1980s) and 'the demise of the [liberationist] ideologies that had flourished during the decolonizing years'.

Postcolonial studies, Lazarus suggests, is not necessarily anti-liberationist, but
'anti-anti-liberationist' in the modified sense that many of its practitioners see the liberation movements of the decolonization era as having been rendered anachronistic
by globalization, and the idea of the 'Third World' as a genuine political alternative as
having become obsolete (for a dissenting view, see Boehmer; also some of the essays in
Parts II and V of this volume). 'Third Worldism', Lazarus insists, has little in common
with that earlier politico-historical project; instead, it signals a decisive conceptual shift
towards post-nationalist and post-Marxist ways of understanding a world structured
in the interests of capitalism—a world often mystifyingly encoded in terms of 'north–
south' relations or, even more problematically, the dominance of the 'west'. Like Diana
Brydon (see Part IV of this volume), whose politics he no more shares than Boehmer's,
Lazarus sees the insufficiencies of these obfuscatory geopolitical categories and their flagrant inadequacy in the face of the new liberation movements—notably those associated
with the 'Arab Spring'—of our age. These movements, he argues, belong to 'a long and as
yet unbroken counter-history [the counter-history of resistance to capitalist imperial-
ism] that postcolonial studies in its incorporated form wrongly supposes to have come
to a close around 1975'.

Whereas for Lazarus the conspicuous inequalities of the contemporary globalized
world still require—require more than ever—a rigorous class analysis, for Susan Bassnett
they focus attention rather on those *translation* processes—social and cultural rather
than narrowly linguistic—that have accompanied 'a marked increase of mobility for
populations that had previously been more constrained'. These practices involve both
literal and metaphorical forms of translation embedded within, e.g., Homi Bhabha's
influential work on migrant discourse or James Clifford's equally well-known notion of
'travelling cultures', though Bassnett—issuing a salutary warning not always heeded by
either Bhabha or Clifford—highlights the problem of using a 'primarily linguistic concept in a broad "cultural" sense'. Broad-based 'cultural' understandings of translation,
Bassnett insists, may overlook the harsher realities of language contact (e.g. the 'ethnocentric violence' that often accompanies translation from one language to another),
though, over and against this, she also stresses the transformative potential contained
within and disseminated by translated texts.

Bassnett's chapter makes it clear that postcolonial translation studies, understandably enough, has tended to focus on translation in the context of unequal power relations and assumptions of cultural superiority; indeed, as she points out, the 'colony can
itself be seen as a translation of … a "superior" original that had come into being somewhere else and at another point in time'. Translation, however, can equally serve the
cause of decolonization, e.g. in the subversive 'cannibalist' theory/ practice of the early

twentieth-century Brazilian modernists, or in the various, potentially liberating possibilities offered nearly a century later by cross-linguistic and cultural exchanges within what Emily Apter intriguingly calls a global 'translation zone' (Apter 2008). Bassnett ends, on this last note, with some largely optimistic thoughts on what she calls, after Bachmann-Medick, the 'translational turn' in the humanities in general: a turn represented, for example, by the self-consciously inclusive 'planetarity' of World Literature (though what some critics see as the reinscribed 'Anglo-globalist' hegemony of World Literature might well be worth a chapter in its turn; Arac 2002; Huggan 2011).

Just as Bassnett gauges the implications of translating from one *text* to another—an intersemiotic rather than strictly interlinguistic process—Michael Rothberg looks at the implications of translating from one *time* to another; at the multiple and multidirectional ways in which memory refashions relationships between the present and the past. Memory studies, like translation studies, is of growing importance to postcolonial criticism, with a recent raft of monographs—making up lost time as much as recovering lost memory—seeking to engage with disparate memories of the colonial past. Memory addresses the 'post' in postcolonial, which is usually acknowledged as registering both continuity and break (see the General Introduction to this volume), by considering what Rothberg calls the 'disjunctive temporalities of colonial legacies—colonialism's ability to colonize not just space, but time as well'. The back-and-forth movements of memory prove useful for disrupting the linear narratives of progress with which, e.g., Enlightenment versions of modernity have been associated; and for recuperating and reinvigorating the anti-colonial struggle, e.g. by rereading archives of imperial dominance (as Ann Laura Stoler does in her opening chapter in Part I of this volume) or by reinstating, without necessarily romanticizing, pre-colonial pasts effectively erased by colonialism's claiming of the grand narrative of History for itself (as Kennedy and Hindess do in their respective chapters in Part IV).

Much of the 'memory work' done in postcolonial studies—which, as other chapters in this volume make clear, is by no means limited to or dominated by imperial historians—has inevitably been *traumatic* given both the destructive nature of colonial encounter and the inescapable fact that violence 'fundamentally shapes the temporality of modern memory' itself. However, postcolonial memory studies also has an opportunity, not least through Rothberg's own excitingly innovative work on multidirectional memory, to forge unexpected solidarities in the face of destruction and violence. As Rothberg insists, memory 'constitutes one of the [most] significant fronts in the struggle against empire'. As many of the best-known anti-colonial intellectuals of the decolonization era were quick to recognize, collective memory—especially *cultural* memory—is a highly effective weapon in combating the violence of colonial erasure and in counteracting those forms of strategic amnesia that often go hand in hand with it; in confronting what Rothberg calls, after the great Martinican intellectual-activist Aimé Césaire, the colonial 'forgetting machine'. This struggle, which continues apace today, takes in a wide variety of textual and medial forms, as well as an extensive range of different ways of and strategies for remembering; it also brings together different 'communities of remembrance', as in Rothberg's fascinating account of the triangulated memories associated with the

Holocaust, the Algerian war of independence, and the struggle for civil rights in the United States.

In keeping with the remit of the section, Rothberg insists throughout on the *activist* potential of cultural memory, its ability to create oppositional solidarities both in the short term and in long-term struggles carried out over generations. While he makes no mention of those more recent liberation struggles in North Africa and the Middle East that have been popularly associated with the 'Arab Spring', it is clear that these too have worked with the cross-fertilizing properties of memory, and with the transnational and transcultural dynamics that are a feature, not just of the contemporary world order, but of the intertwined histories of empire itself.

Like Bassnett and Rothberg, Simon Featherstone draws attention to a subfield within postcolonial studies that has arguably been neglected until recently: the study of popular culture. Featherstone's wide-ranging chapter begins by reading Edward Said's high-handed dismissal of popular culture—'[it] means nothing to me except as it surrounds me'—as symptomatic of a general scepticism in postcolonial studies towards 'the capacity of popular material to sustain cultural and political interrogations': a scepticism, it has to be said, that has sometimes been matched by those relatively few to have worked in postcolonial popular-cultural studies, e.g. the sport historians John Bale and Mike Cronin, who peremptorily see postcolonial literature as 'subjective ... placeless and contrived'.

Featherstone, looking for a balance between these two views, sees the assumed opposition between literary 'subjectivity' and popular 'performativity' as a major impediment to understandings of the place of popular culture in postcolonial studies, turning initially to the Trinidadian Marxist intellectual C. L. R. James—who was equally at home writing about French-Caribbean revolt and Anglo-Caribbean cricket—to show how 'high' and 'popular' cultural interests may fruitfully intersect. James's inclusiveness, Featherstone convincingly suggests, is a useful rallying call for a postcolonial critical practice that incorporates *all* cultural activities, whether textual or performative, and for a properly democratized postcolonial cultural studies in which popular culture, in challenging methodological priorities and assumptions, can act as a 'creatively intrusive presence in the field'.

Featherstone's own examples come from the areas of sport (international competitive athletics) and Caribbean popular music (reggae), the former of which is used to open up a subtle performative critique of the values and meanings of late-imperial British 'body culture', and the latter of which raises the possibility of an organic or vernacular intellectualism, shaped though never fully determined by global communications networks, through which anti-colonial liberationist politics and black diasporic consciousness can be rearticulated in the non-orthodox practices of 'symbolic atonement' and 'spiritual dissent'. Featherstone finds in the work of Bob Marley and one of his successors, the Jamaican dancehall artist Buju Banton, viable alternatives to more orthodox forms of emancipatory postcolonial rhetoric, though he remains critical of both musicians' endorsement, whether implicit (Marley) or explicit (Banton), of the 'illiberal gender politics of Rastafarianism' and of the tendency of the cultural industries that support them to distil their wayward creativity into more readily marketable, internationally recognizable forms. The issues surrounding Banton's work, in particular, suggest the need for cultural performances of all kinds to be 'taken seriously even when they are evidently problematic or seemingly irrelevant to the major questions of power'; they also demonstrate the potential of music—and of performance cultures in general—not only to open up the acknowledged range of oppositional postcolonial cultural practices, but also to generate new, possibly unexpected, vernacular theories of their own.

In Featherstone's essay, both race and gender—but especially race—are factors in twentieth-century discursive constructions of the Kenyan athlete and the Jamaican musician, respectively. Pooja Rangan and Rey Chow's chapter looks more broadly at tropes of race, and the persistence of racism, in the production of postcolonial cultural identities, from the anti-racist polemics of Fanon and Memmi through the poststructuralist turn of Gates and his contemporaries, to biopolitical considerations of contemporary genetic manipulation inspired by, among others, Foucault.

For several generations of postcolonial thinkers, racism has obdurately served as a structure of power and injustice, forged in a crucible of colonial relations stretching from the so-called 'Age of Discovery' to the present day. For both Fanon and Memmi, racism is first and foremost a pathological condition that entraps colonizer and colonized alike, while for Gates and others (who certainly would not deny this pathology) racial alienation is underpinned by language, for which it functions as 'both the medium and the sign'. Returning to the scene of Boehmer's opening chapter, Rangan and Chow draw on the example of South African apartheid—'racism's last word', as Derrida melodramatically describes it, which goes beyond race to demonstrate the complicity between social acts of exclusion and those formative exclusions that constitute the basis of language itself. Foucault, like Derrrida, is seen as an important interlocutor with theories of race and racism, though Foucault's approach moves away from the poststructuralist emphasis on language to look at the ways in which power—including the power to define and police racial identity—is disseminated across a series of institutional sites. Foucault traces a link between racist biopower and neoliberal economics (see Gopal's chapter in Part II of this volume), which can be seen in such diverse practices as the self-help industry, the medicalization of consumer bodies, and the racialized designation of less-than-human 'intruders' (see Farrier and Tuitt's discussion of refugees and asylum seekers in Part II) and 'enemies of the state'.

In this last context, Rangan and Chow give credence to what Balibar and Wallerstein collectively call the 'new racism'—those racisms born of globalization and the post-independence reversal of population flows between the metropoles and the colonies, both of which processes have increasingly created the 'division of humanity into a single political space'. Culture rather than biology is the index of the new racism, with the notion of 'cultural difference' lying at the heart of, e.g., *both* ostensibly liberal European projects of citizenship and integration *and* their demonstrably illiberal counterparts, which are often ranged against those cast as inassimilable or threatening to traditional-minded European national polities despite mounting global evidence of the erosion of the nation state (see Schulze-Engler in Part V of this volume).

In 'cultural differentialism' of this kind—as visible in the US as in Europe—the earlier colonial dynamics that inspired Memmi and Fanon fan out across a series of increasingly deterritorialized settings in which the violence of racialization, normalized in a similarly wide variety of institutional contexts, becomes part-and-parcel of the 'mechanisms through which [people] inhabit [their] positions as subjects and enter into [the] relationships of exchange' that characterize everyday social life. This sobering thought returns us at the end of the section to some of the controversies that had animated the previous two parts: the lingering presence of the colonial past; its spectral reformulation in the guise of globalist neoliberalism; and the maddening persistence of racially discriminatory attitudes towards designated 'others' in all walks of social and political life. Postcolonial critics are not alone in making these points, nor—with some notable exceptions—do they offer a cure for the diagnoses they present. But they remain alert to theories which, whether academically treated or not, are anything but academic in their practical implications; and which, for better or worse, have the capacity to determine the mechanisms and procedures of everyday life.

REFERENCES

Apter, Emily (2008). *The Translation Zone: A New Comparative Literature*. Princeton, NY: Princeton University Press.

Arac, Jonathan (2002). 'Anglo-Globalism?' *New Left Review*, 16: 35–45.

Ashcroft, Bill, Gareth Griffiths, and Helen Tiffin (1989). *The Empire Writes Back: Theory and Practice in Post-Colonial Literatures*. London: Routledge.

Bhabha, Homi (1994). *The Location of Culture*. London: Routledge.

Culler, Jonathan (1997). *Literary Theory: A Very Short Introduction*. Oxford: Oxford University Press.

Gandhi, Leela (1998). *Postcolonial Theory*. New York: Columbia University Press.

Huggan, Graham (2011). 'The Trouble with World Literature', in A. Behdad and D. Thomas (eds), *A Companion to Comparative Literature*. New York: Wiley-Blackwell, 490–506.

Moore-Gilbert, Bart, Gareth Stanton, and Willy Maley (eds) (1997). *Postcolonial Criticism*. London: Longman.

Ngũgĩ wa Thiong'o (1980). *Decolonising the Mind: The Politics of Language in African Literature*. London: James Currey.

Quayson, Ato (2000). *Postcolonialism: Theory, Practice, or Process?* New York: Wiley-Blackwell.

San Juan, E. (1998). *Beyond Postcolonial Theory*. New York: Palgrave.

Young, Robert J. C. (2003). *Postcolonialism: A Very Short Introduction*. Oxford: Oxford University Press.

CHAPTER 13

....

REVISITING RESISTANCE

*Postcolonial Practice and
the Antecedents of Theory*

....

ELLEKE BOEHMER

THE EMPIRE WRITES BACK: POSTCOLONIAL STUDIES ASCENDANT

....

It is now over two decades ago, at a time of infectious historical optimism, that Bill Ashcroft, Gareth Griffiths, and Helen Tiffin's co-written work *The Empire Writes Back: Theory and Practice in Post-Colonial Literatures* (1989) was published, and rapidly became—at least in the western academy—the key foundational work of what is now widely termed postcolonial studies. For this reason, the book is taken in the first part of this chapter as a representative case to open my discussion of the still underacknowledged antecedents-in-resistance of postcolonial theory. The second half of the chapter then goes on to explore the biography and political practice of South African anti-apartheid warrior and first democratic president Nelson Mandela as a case study of how anti-colonial practice might generate the values and perceptions that we now term postcolonial, and on which postcolonial critique is based.

The Empire Writes Back was exemplary of the spirit of that *annus mirabilis* 1989: of *glasnost*, the unfreezing of the Cold War, and the breaking down of barriers and walls in Berlin, eastern Europe as a whole, and soon, apartheid South Africa—developments reflected in the upbeat mode of the work, its celebration of worldwide and almost inevitable cultural syncretism and hybridity, and in the collaborative make-up of its writing team (for a different view, see Lazarus in this section of the volume). These developments were also embodied in the authors' predominant conviction that empire—for which read British colonialism—could be written back to from the margins, from the spaces at its edges; indeed, in its firm sense that such spaces of textual and cultural resistance actively existed and might eventually be expanded. And in the years since publication, it is fair to say, this conviction, firing the left-leaning interests and sensitivities of would-be postcolonial critics in the academy, became the driving engine of the exponential growth and academic success of postcolonial literary studies across North America, Britain, the rest of Europe, and various parts of the formerly colonized world.

In its first incarnation, appearing as part of a Routledge 'New Accents' series designed to introduce new movements in critical theory, *The Empire Writes Back* had relatively modest ambitions. It set out to be little more than a descriptive introduction to a field, namely the study of literatures in English from around the once-colonized world, earlier referred to as Commonwealth literary studies or Third-World writing, whose textual subject matter was already perceived to be burgeoning exponentially. Yet at the time of the linguistic and poststructuralist turn in literary criticism, the field was perceived to be lacking in analytical tools. The significant achievement of the book was that, by leaning on the critical and imaginative insights of non-metropolitan writers like Wilson Harris and Salman Rushdie (albeit citizens of the metropolis), it offered a persuasive approach to these newly defined 'post-colonial texts': it demonstrated a series of borne-across ways of reading which themselves, like the texts they purported to analyse, had successfully travelled or been translated across cultural borders, and certainly were promoted and marketed as such.[1] Much like the impact of Rushdie's *Midnight's Children* (1981) in the field of the modern late twentieth-century novel, *The Empire Writes Back* became in the domain of literary and cultural criticism a watershed text for its time, committed to the task of comparison and to a respect for plurality, complexity, and difference in their manifold manifestations across cultures over both time and space.[2]

In its awareness of cultural plurality as well as the predicaments of 'othering', *The Empire Writes Back* was perceptibly built on critical perceptions inaugurated in Edward Said's *Orientalism* (1978), to which it paid due homage. The co-authored book not only presented overwhelming evidence to the effect that English as a literary language had conclusively gone global and that new critical languages and new epistemologies were required to deal with this pluralization. Along with the other introductory primers that quickly followed in its wake, it also compiled—if it fell short of wholly generating—an analytical language for approaching the many texts of the cultural and national 'other'. It did so in the first instance pragmatically. In part, it gleaned a heuristic vocabulary from writers and critics operating in different Anglophone regions, gathering together in an amalgamated bibliography influential critical articles by inter alia Homi Bhabha, Gayatri Spivak, and Anne McClintock, which to date had appeared only in piecemeal

---

[1.] I refer to Pascale Casanova's exhaustive analysis of the competitive making of literary value within the transnational 'world republic of letters', *The World Republic of Letters* (Casanova 2004).

[2.] Graham Huggan makes a related point in his critical adaptation of Peter Hallward's subtitle in *Absolutely Postcolonial*, when he notes that the postcolonial field wavers warily, and sometimes unconvincingly, between the singular and the specific (Hallward 2001; see also the General Introduction to this volume).

fashion in edited collections and journals.[3] Critical terms and phrases like 'mimicry and man/the mimic man', 'heterogeneous community', 'counter-discourse', double or triple subjection, and 'subalternity', among many others, were now brought together in transformative interaction between the covers of one book.

And yet it was in response to that same, at first influential and persuasive critical recognition from Ashcroft, Griffiths, and Tiffin of cross-cultural plurality and complexity that the charge emerged that is still routinely levelled not merely at the three authors, but at postcolonial studies more generally. From as far back as the early 1990s it was frequently argued that postcolonial theories of cultural and textual hybridization had the tendency paradoxically to homogenize and flatten out local anti-colonial particularities in their very deference to an overriding, hypostatized specificity.[4] In effect, *The Empire Writes Back* offered a one-size-fits-all perspective on a global postcolonial poetics through what seemed a wide angle yet, in practice, was the reductively narrow aperture of particularity. As Graham Huggan also suggests in his General Introduction to this volume, an approach that reaches out to highly particularized if not recondite and untranslatable cultural difference, such as is found in *Empire Writes Back*, can have the effect of collapsing this difference into an overarching Difference that subsumes them all.

Aggravating the situation further is the fact that postcolonial critics, many of them located in the west, have found themselves in the contradictory situation of imposing their interpretative frameworks of otherness and difference from above and outside the postcolonial cultures and texts they are describing, thus operating in effect as did colonial systems of knowledge, in oppressive and hegemonic ways. In this sense, postcolonial critique is not only homogenizing and universalizing in its heuristic effects, it is also depoliticizing, even deradicalizing, in relation to the resistance it reads and for which it wishes to enlist respect. It draws attention away from, or pays insufficient heed to, the contexts of political struggle against empire from which the recalcitrant texts with which it is concerned have in many cases emerged. In the words of Benita Parry, one of the sterner proponents of this materialist critique of postcolonial discourse, conflict and violence arising out of 'incommensurable interests and aspirations immanent in

[3] One of the more influential of these precursor collections was Henry Louis Gates, Jr. (ed.), *'Race', Writing and Difference* (1986), which first appeared as two special issues of the journal *Critical Inquiry*, and contains keynote essays from all those critics named in this paragraph, including Homi Bhabha, whose reputation it launched. Bhabha's own complete collection of critical essays *The Location of Culture* appeared only in 1994 from Routledge. As regards other introductions to the field, the following list is representative but by no means exhaustive: Elleke Boehmer, *Colonial and Postcolonial Literature* (1995, 2005); Leela Gandhi, *Postcolonial Theory* (1998); Ania Loomba, *Colonialism/Postcolonialism* (1998); John McLeod, *Beginning Postcolonialism* (2000). A significant number of postcolonial Readers, published in partial imitation of the Gates collection, including one edited by the authors of *The Empire Writes Back*, also appeared in regular fashion from across the range of mainstream academic publishers in the decades following.

[4] Some of the most prominent of these countervailing voices include the highly influential and combative Aijaz Ahmad, *In Theory: Classes, Nations, Literatures* (1992), Arif Dirlik, *The Postcolonial Aura: Third World Criticism in the Age of Global Capitalism* (1998), and the later, more philosophically derived Peter Hallward, *Absolutely Postcolonial* (2001).

colonial situations' are thus 'vaporised' or ignored, and 'a historical project of invasion, expropriation and exploitation [is rewritten] as a symbiotic encounter'; illiberal domination is replaced with equalizing exchange (Parry 2004: 4–6).

In spite of its self-nomination as postcolonial (or, more specifically, *post-colonial*: coming after, yet inextricably a part of, colonial history), a third charge, bound up tightly with the first two of homogenization and depoliticization, has been that postcolonial criticism is not only ideologically separated from, but also blithely dismissive of what Said, in *Culture and Imperialism*, calls the 'gravity of history' (Said 1993: 366–7). It is true that, as in *The Empire Writes Back*, postcolonial readings of cultural and literary developments are often free of in-depth historicization. In this, the critical discourse is very much a creature of its late twentieth-century moment: the era that saw Francis Fukuyama's infamous proclamation, with the fall of communism, of the 'end of history' itself (see Fukuyama 1993). Running contrary to the historical reference points indicated by the term 'postcolonial', and even more the hyphenated formulation 'post-colonial', postcolonial critics have seemingly been happy to join with Michel Foucault to 'cast doubt on the claims of an objective historical consciousness' (Ashcroft, Griffiths, and Tiffin 1989: 162).

Rising from this lack of concern with respect to historical evidence, postcolonial critical discourse has at the same time been silently content to assume an onwards-and-upwards narrative trajectory in its understanding of history, one moving from oppression to freedom, from the draconian pure to the happy impure, from empire to a world without empire (see Hindess in Part IV of this volume). As David Scott writes, citing Reinhart Koselleck, in *Conscripts of Modernity*, such heroic story-forms offer a 'congealed' and 'singular' view of the decolonization project, one that is single-stranded, end-directed, and limited, and that overlooks contingency and recursion in favour of an inevitable and highly idealized freedom—a freedom that is projected as coterminous with the future (Scott 2004: 89 and 135).

Across the 1990s and 2000s, these combined charges of homogenization, depoliticization, and a neglect of history, have been sobering for postcolonial critics. They have also at times appeared unfair and distorting, especially given the critics' political commitment to social justice and their attempt to engage actively in the historical struggles they analyse in their work. Postcolonial discourse '[makes] hybridity and syncreticity the source of literary and cultural redefinition', Ashcroft, Griffiths, and Tiffin spiritedly wrote in manifesto mode in 1989, thereby establishing hybridity as the wellspring of new postcolonial meaning. However, with their emphasis firmly placed on the global peripheries over the metropolitan centre (though with an Anglo-centrality still at times assumed), they also submitted that 'the syncretic and hybridized nature of post-colonial experience refutes the privileged position of a standard code in the language and any monocentric view of human experience' (Ashcroft, Griffiths, and Tiffin 1989: 78 and 41). The concern with the dissident, heterogeneous, anti-authoritarian, canon-deforming and remaking energies of postcolonial cultures that is reflected in this statement, and in many postcolonial propositions like it since, is unquestionable. As irrefutable, too, is another of their primary critical interventions, one related to the emphasis on the 'syncretic' peripheries, which reflects in turn their interest in what might roughly be described as 'home-grown' critical protocols—the quest to uncover resistant hybridizing energies at work not only within local, regional, and marginal communities, but also in 'native' and indigenous cultural and political practice from across the Anglophone world (see Smith and Turner in Part II of this volume). Moving in the opposite direction to the tendencies of homogenization and westernization, this quest involves decoding the ways in which cultural practitioners, whether from Nigeria or India, Vanuatu or Trinidad, 'abrogate' the master's tools and voice and creatively 'appropriate' English structures and meanings in order to translate and transmit their own cultural, social, and political points of view (Ashcroft, Griffiths, and Tiffin 1989: 83).

But even on the margins, an epistemological stumbling block arises. Integral to centripetal postcolonial investigations, as well as to centrifugal ones, is the colonial encounter. As a scan through some of the key postcolonial interventions of the late 1980s and 1990s reveals—from Mary Louise Pratt and Sander Gilman, through Homi Bhabha and Robert Young, to Anne McClintock—the colonial encounter still generates the definitive terminologies of postcolonial studies (Pratt 1992; Gilman 1985; Bhabha 1994; Young 1990, 1995; McClintock 1995). The stand-off of black and white, the confrontation of colonial master and colonized slave, shapes the vocabulary of even postcolonialism's most seemingly subversive formulations; though to say so is to generalize grossly, the relationship of the west with the rest, of self and other, is still fundamental to how the postcolonial is understood. The critical focus here tends to be on the (post)colonial interactive relationship rather than on native cultures as the main site of hybridity, and on the signifying process over political struggle as the most dynamic source of resistance (by which is meant overt opposition to oppression and inequality). The effects of privileging colonial exchange over opposition in this way, of favouring reciprocity over division, are nothing if not marginalizing and oppressive. As this implies, the consequences of the critical emphasis on the hybrid have in many cases become deeply ironic and negative, running counter to the seemingly anti-hegemonic and democratizing impacts emanating from the postcolonial vision of a world in perpetual creolizing and pluralizing mode.

In short, despite postcolonial theory's own oft-issued warnings about the universalizing thrust of European poststructuralism, and despite the repeated insistence on refracting concepts from metropolitan colonial discourse through the lens of local difference, dominant definitions of the postcolonial, such as *The Empire Writes Back*'s own defence of the hyphen in the term 'post-colonial', imply that hybridizing, 'impurifying' effects are produced throughout the imperial process more or less smoothly and evenly. This picture of what might be called an emolliated hybridity chooses almost wilfully to ignore the jagged and irregular penetration of colonial capital across the globe and the highly differentiated operation of anti-colonial liberation movements, to say nothing of the steep hierarchies and sharp national conflicts and stand-offs which also govern the international domain of letters—as will now be seen in my examples below.

MANDELA AGAINST EMPIRE

In an effort to depart from, if not redress, some of the more egregious historical and political occlusions that have been performed within postcolonial discourse to date, the second part of this chapter makes an analytical return to a particular history of anti-colonial struggle in order to engage critically with the particular forms of resistance it represents and to draw from them the dimensions-in-formation of an epistemology of anti-colonial subversion and contestation. In Benita Parry's words, it is vitally important to reground concepts of freedom in histories of dissent, so that perceptions from the margins are restored to their place as 'the primary form and substance of anticolonial understanding' (see Parry 2004: 42 and 9). It is crucial, in other words, at once to *radicalize* and to *theorize* our understanding of anti-colonial history. My discussion in this part of the chapter therefore collaborates with widely applauded if still relatively tentative postcolonial efforts to displace the hegemonic master–slave relationship, as will shortly be detailed. My main aim in what follows is to reconnect critical concepts and subjects in the postcolonial studies field to their radical antecedents within anti-colonial struggles around the world and, more particularly, within the formative, anti-apartheid activities of one of the twentieth century's greatest liberationists, South Africa's Nelson Mandela. My secondary objective is to participate in and encourage new and emerging investigations in the genealogy of postcolonial influences and ideas, leading from the time of the late nineteenth- and early twentieth-century resistance and liberation movements up to the present day.[5] For, as Robert Young strongly reminds us, postcolonialism is not merely a critical treatment of new and old imperialisms; it is also, at least ideally, 'a politics and philosophy of activism that ... continues in a new way the anti-colonial struggles of the past' (2003: 1–4).

As was suggested earlier, postcolonial subjectivities, agencies, texts, and testimonies from different contexts have to be stretched, even misperceived, in order to match an overarching one-size-fits-all theory of postcolonial hybridity. Accepting this to be the case, the contention that runs through this critical overview of Mandela as anti-apartheid activist, political prisoner, and, later, his country's democratically elected leader is that, by contrast, the careful 'reading' of a particular case of anti-colonial intervention helps to give proper critical recognition to the diverse progressive and transformative histories of struggle from which postcolonial critique has in part emerged and with which it shares important resources and perspectives. This goes further than just tracing the antecedents of deconstruction back to, say, movements of resistance to the colonial state; the aim is rather to investigate the abrogation of hegemonic cultures within postcolonial

---

[5.] This genealogy is plotted, for example, by Edward Said's *Culture and Imperialism* (1993). See also Elleke Boehmer, *Empire, the National and the Postcolonial: Resistance in Interaction, 1880–1920* (2002); Laura Chrisman, *Rereading the Imperial Romance* (2000); Leela Gandhi, *Affective Communities: Anticolonial Thought, Fin-de-Siècle Radicalism, and the Politics of Friendship* (2006).

cultural practices and their adaptation and integration of the local as well as the distant, so as to realign the centre–periphery hierarchies and flows of influence that still tend to shape postcolonial theory today. The aim, in other words, is to reanimate some of the radical concerns with which *The Empire Writes Back* authors began, concerns which were however compromised to a degree by their overemphasis on poststructuralist (particularly deconstructionist) techniques at the expense of working out a grounded materialist approach to the field.

From this perspective, the anti-colonial life can be read as a parable teaching national and liberationist values, as a moral lesson in democracy building, or a lived analysis of colonialism's illegitimacy. The anti-colonial life, in effect, both performs and interrogates postcolonial principles. To give an example taken from a different but related biography of decolonization, that of M. K. Gandhi: the political writings of the Indian leader of non-cooperation, in particular *Hind Swaraj* (1910), can be seen with the benefit of postcolonial hindsight to shadow forth the definitive postcolonial idea of the mimic man or imperfect copy, the seeming opponent of empire who constitutes himself (subversively but also compromisingly) in the image of the imperialist (Gandhi 1997).[6] Certainly, a prominent idea in Gandhi's thought is that unless India strip away from itself every integument of imperialist thinking, independence will simply bring another form of imperial rule (Gandhi 1997: 26–9).

To put the point more boldly, across the twentieth century the analysis produced by the leaders of liberation movements pitted against empire, as expressed for example in their speeches, pamphlets, manifestos, and position papers, worked in subterranean but still underacknowledged ways to help shape the academic interrogation of colonialism and imperialism. In related ways, the practices and vocabularies of native and nationalist resistance were diffused through, and often foundational for, the formation of colonial discourse theory. In its most practical manifestation, at the high schools, universities, and colleges that the pioneering men of independence or 'interpreters' (Wole Soyinka's term) attended, a lively osmosis of anti-colonial and subversive ideas took place between budding writers, scholars, activists, and would-be politicians, with the activists and politicians offering terms of resistance to the writers and scholars, and vice versa (Soyinka 1965).[7] In the case of leaders like Agostinho Neto (Angola) or Léopold Sédar Senghor (Senegal) in Africa and Jawaharlal Nehru in India, writer, intellectual, and politician were all wrapped up in one person. In each case, however, the point is that the leaders produced their liberation and resistance theories on the job, much as women across the centuries have worked out ideas of slow-burn opposition in the confined yet networked spaces of the home (Burton 2003).

[6.] On mimicry, see Homi K. Bhabha, 'Of Mimicry and Man', *The Location of Culture* (1994). The term 'mimic man' is derived by Homi Bhabha from his reading of V.S. Naipaul's mordant novel of postcolonial retreat, *The Mimic Men* (1967).

[7.] Soyinka coined the collective noun to describe that generation of nationalist intellectuals in Nigeria who first experienced and then gave expression to the mixed elation and seemingly inevitable let-down of postcolonial independence.

From this point on in the chapter, where Mandela's political example and his involvement in the African National Congress (1913), of which he was a long-time leader, are
taken as object lessons, the discussion will set out to demonstrate that his anti-colonial
practice was at least potentially knowledge-making, even theory-making, for his fellow activists and followers, right up until the time that he stepped into power as president of a neoliberal state. Mandela's distinctly Africanist yet broad-church anti-colonial
politics, though composed on the ground in an ad hoc way, was culturally and socially
transformative on a broad scale. What is now enshrined as his liberationist ethic was
developed both on the job and in close collaboration—through discussion with comrades and colleagues on the struggle front line, in the courtroom, in the kitchens and
offices of the various dwellings he inhabited, and in the various 'seminar' discussions
and debates held on Robben Island.[8] Indeed, with the benefit of historical hindsight it
is clear that Mandela's political work shaped the critical and creative parameters of at
least two generations of South African writers: the poet Dennis Brutus (a fellow Robben
Island inmate), critic and novelist Njabulo Ndebele, poet and critic Jeremy Cronin, and
novelist Achmat Dangor, to name just a few.

The biographical trajectory of Nelson Rolihlahla Mandela has been thoroughly traced
elsewhere (see for example Boehmer 2008; Lodge 2006; Meer 1990; Sampson 2000).
Here, a critical commentary on the outline of his life will suffice to highlight key areas
of his political and intellectual development. These will be cast as formative for several
of what we now understand to be orthodox postcolonial ideas of resistance and subversion, especially in sub-Saharan Africa: among them cross-national interaction, mass
defiance and non-cooperation, resistant appropriation, and the complicated lineaments
of negotiation, 'talks about talks'.[9]

When in 1943–4 Mandela together with Walter Sisulu, Oliver Tambo, and others
launched the ANC Youth League, he was a committed African nationalist concerned
to campaign first and foremost against black oppression and for black political rights in
his country by borrowing ideas and strategies from, amongst others, the Indian independence struggle and, later, African American civil rights campaigns. However, the
1949 communal riots in Durban between African and Indian communities became the
trigger for Mandela, guided by Sisulu, to espouse a more multiracial or broad-front politics and to explore wider channels of collaboration, in particular with the South African
Indian Congress (SAIC). Already at this early point in his career, Mandela proved that
in response to a crisis he could be a flexible and far-sighted strategist for political freedom. As he saw it, combating the state-sanctioned racism of apartheid with a politics

---

[8.] Fredrick Cooper, in *Colonialism in Question: Theory, Knowledge, History* (2005: 16) claims that
histories of decolonization often tend to overlook the history and sociology of the people who lived
in the colonies, and so fail their own emancipatory objectives. My reading of Mandela's micro-history
determinedly runs counter to this tendency.

[9.] Though homologies exist, mass defiance in Mandela's time as an activist represented a very different
phenomenon than the mass defiance that generated the 2011 'Arab Spring', at least in technological and
hence also inter-generational terms.

that sought to override racial distinctions and to interrogate narrow definitions of the nation represented a strong if not impregnable moral position in these circumstances. Significant advantage was to be gained by forging cross-national political collaborations with other liberationists (communists, socialists, advocates of women's rights, as well as nationalists of different stripes) on the basis of clear principles held in common against a common enemy.

The ANC's collaboration with the SAIC, led by Mandela and others, built to a success-ful climax with the 1952 Defiance Campaign of non-cooperation against apartheid laws, in which M. K. Gandhi's ideas again proved influential. Yet to recognize the influence of Gandhi (or Nehru) on Mandela's political philosophy is not to imply that his thought was belated or borrowed. On the contrary, he demonstrated a deft 'postcolonial' adapta-bility in translating influences and approaches that had proved effective in other cultural and political contexts, and in tactically grafting these on to local practices to suit South African conditions at the time. He found, for example, that while the mass march and the silent protest rallied activists across racial divides, police retaliation tended to reim-pose racial distinctions (as detention centres and gaols were segregated). The march was therefore effective only in a circumscribed way and could be carried out, by and large, only in urban centres.

In the final years of the 1950s, faced with continuing government intransigence, Mandela moved determinedly though still gradually towards a more militant approach. In 1960, after the devastating Sharpeville Massacre and a series of failed mass walkouts and strikes, he came after lengthy and considered deliberation with other Congress lead-ers to an endorsement of armed struggle—albeit armed struggle in a graduated form. At the same time, by becoming the leader of the armed wing, Umkhonto we Sizwe, he made his way to the front of the militant flank within the ANC, coming to define and direct its new cutting edge. Once again, Mandela demonstrated as a leader not only political flex-ibility and insight, but also a keen, ethically driven responsiveness to, and responsibility for, the sensitivities and frustrations of both the leadership and the rank and file within the movement. His capacity for finding aims in common with other parties (including nationalist and pan-nationalist groupings in Africa) in order to forge the ground for strategic collaboration was also clearly in evidence. At a time when he could in all likeli-hood not yet have read Frantz Fanon (*The Wretched of the Earth* was first published in French in 1961), his convinced sense was that the only recourse for the South African majority in the face of the repressive state apparatus was resistance in kind: the cleans-ing process of fighting fire with fire (Fanon 1983). Against a government that responded with escalating levels of violence to whatever opposition it encountered, there was, in the view of the ANC high command, no possible alternative.

For Mandela, this was a significant departure from the to-date highly effective Gandhian script that, in his opinion, had become outmoded in the polarized apartheid context. As he saw it, political violence alone, in a staged form, would—in these circum-stances at least—work to transformative or revolutionary ends. Colonial brutality had exhausted the options available to non-violence. Though this is a perception that might be deemed 'Fanonian' today, Mandela reached it more or less independently, through his political efforts on the ground and in debate with his comrades. In place of Gandhi's idea that to resort to the tools and strategies of the oppressor is to become like him, Mandela arrived at a position that the later Black Consciousness leader Steve Biko, though not otherwise an ANC supporter, might have found congenial: that an oppressed group cannot be given or granted freedom; it can only be freed by its own hands (Biko 1978).

It is possible to see Mandela at this point as authoring an innovative 'postcolonial' approach to resistance in two key aspects. First, from his perspective two choices alone were available to the oppressed people of his country: 'submit or fight' (but submission, he immediately conceded, was not in effect an option) (Mandela 1965: 118–19; Meli 1988: 214). National self-expression, he believed, could come only through polarization and the destruction of the colonizer. And fighting back had the advantage of tapping into black South Africans' buried histories of resistance. In advocating outright armed struggle in this way, Mandela was among the few anti-imperial leaders who pitted themselves against colonial-style authorities in the former British Empire in the second half of the twentieth century, *and* who later came to power. Yet at the same time, in respect to his second 'postcolonial' intervention, that process of violent resistance was always to proceed in a modulated manner. Retaliation was to be divided into four categories of incremental intensity: sabotage, guerrilla warfare, terrorism against civilians, and open revolution. Even during the dark days of the early 1960s, he urged that the first stage alone should be developed. Though armed resistance was unavoidable, retaliation had to be disciplined and as bloodless as possible. To resort immediately to terroristic approaches, such as those being propagated by the state, was to risk losing the moral high ground that had so far been won; it was, as Gandhi too might have said, to stoop to the oppressor's tactics.

From the point of view of the South African government, however, such distinctions were merely academic; any calibration of armed resistance was viewed as armed resistance pure and simple and was equated with treason. Mandela was arrested in 1962 after a period of travelling in Africa to seek military training, and then charged with sabotage in 1963. In 1964, he and seven of his fellow Rivonia trialists were sentenced to life imprisonment on Robben Island. An important new phase in his political and intellectual development now began to unfold, the reconciliatory 'walk to freedom', a phase that might also be described as his self-conversion into an iconic 'rainbow warrior' for peace with justice. It is this phase that is highlighted by the post-2000 heroic myth that attaches to Mandela's name, though it represents only one period, albeit a long one, in the history of resistance and struggle with which he is associated. Ironically, given the destructive intentions of the South African state, the twenty-seven-year period of isolation and incarceration, together with like-minded African nationalists, communists, and pan-Africanists, made possible on Mandela's part an important though once again incremental regrouping of political strategies, approaches, and ideas.

Viewed with the benefit of hindsight, it was during the near-three decades of his imprisonment that Mandela came to express some of his most paradigmatic 'postcolonial' shifts, turns, and approaches: his capacity for the long game of defeating his enemy not by patience alone, important as that was, but also by the ability to see from the point of view of the other; his finely honed skill of weighing a problem from various different angles, both oblique and direct; his deliberate yet subtle movement away from armed struggle and towards structured negotiation, though always supported by the uncompromising threat of a return to violence should negotiation fail. Working as an African lawyer in Johannesburg in the 1950s, Mandela had already self-consciously cast himself as a thoroughly modern and urban individual, a role that involved the canny yet non-cynical manipulation of the part of 'civilized black gentleman' his post-Edwardian education in 1930s South Africa had instilled in him. It also involved a continual shuttling between different frames of cultural reference and/or the 'discrepant temporalities' of the postcolonial condition that Dipesh Chakrabarty insightfully outlines in his study *Provincializing Europe* (2000). But if deft political and social footwork was an ability that Mandela had brought with him to Robben Island, the challenging and variegated conditions of life in prison—which involved now protesting against his treatment as a black prisoner, now bargaining with white warders for small privileges—vastly expanded and fine-tuned these chameleon skills. In a word, Mandela on Robben Island, and later in Pollsmoor and Victor Verster prisons, outmimicked both friend and foe in the interests of forging solidarity and a path beyond conflict. A mission school product, he had long ago discovered that to gain the upper hand in any situation of conflict meant outmastering the master. On Robben Island, he found he could most successfully survive the rigours of prison life by internalizing them completely.

During his years in prison Nelson Mandela came by his own admission to realize that most problems and disagreements—including complex political and economic ones post-apartheid—could be solved through the judicious balancing and counterbalancing of different options, just as if the problem were an impasse in an Island board-game. On Robben Island, the political prisoners, all intellectually disciplined, experienced men, were in the unique position of being able to ponder political issues and processes (resistance, negotiation, nationalization) in detail and from every available angle, on and on for years. In effect, as Fran Buntman suggests in her analysis of the Island's political culture, the prisoners' efforts to set up through their interactions and discussions an orderly political microcosm, transformed their incarceration in recognizably 'postcolonial' or dialogic ways from a reactive, prohibitive experience into a productive social contract (Buntman 2003).

As one of the more charismatic and politically adept of the leaders present, Mandela was central to this process of transformation; yet the converse situation also pertains. The political prisoners' culture of dialogue, the interactive codes of attentive listening and slow considered response they developed across the years, were fundamental to how Mandela arrived at what he called his 'negotiating concept' in the mid-1980s: his decision to begin to deal with the Afrikaner government by planning for extensive talks (Boehmer 2008: 149–69). This decision led more or less directly to his release in February 1990. The more public talks that proceeded from that time eventually resulted in South Africa's first democratic elections of April 1994, when he became President.

Across his long period of imprisonment, Mandela in effect translated a practice of interpersonal accommodation into a lived theory of national and cross-national reconciliation, something that must count as the primary postcolonial achievement of his life. In this respect, it is no surprise that the writer Njabulo Ndebele, in part inspired by Mandela's example, has generated a subgenre in South African writing and criticism in praise of the everyday, 'the rediscovery of the ordinary' that followed upon the extraordinary scandal that was the apartheid state (Ndebele 2006). In prison, Mandela worked on developing amicable if always watchful dealings with his warders, sparked by day-to-day likes and dislikes held in common. He later adapted and expanded these into the painstaking vigilance with which he approached his government interlocutors, introducing his views to them, engaging them in social chit-chat, finding out contiguous political ideals, keeping them talking yet at the same time consulting with the ANC, remembering always that the one shared ideal on which he might find common ground with his Afrikaner enemy was their mutual devotion to the nation, South Africa. Whereas on matters of common interest (armed struggle, negotiation, reconciliation) Mandela always made a point of speaking clearly and directly to his people, in certain situations he recognized that one effect of his commitment to consensus building was to see apartheid conflict from the point of view of the hated Afrikaner other, as well as from the perspective of his own party.

To put this in another way, Robben Island honed Mandela's capacity for active symbolization, which he had already learned skilfully to manipulate for the purposes of legal advocacy in his political work. Now he found a conceptual space where his political intellect could move with special facility, as when he attempted to approach others' perspectives, including his warders', on their own merits, or when he identified at different levels with both Creon and Antigone in a Robben Island production of Sophocles's eponymous play. Difficult debates, such as those between the ANC and Black Consciousness adherents, he liked to imagine literally in 3D, as a drama might be played out in a theatre. Fellow prisoner Mac Maharaj once summarized his leader's style of debate as 'proceeding from *their* assumptions and carefully marshalling arguments to move them to his conclusions. His line of advance [was] developed on the other party's line of attack': it was an intensely strategic, spatialized approach closely resembling that of a chess game or Socratic dialogue (Maharaj 2001: 32; emphasis his). What this suggests is that, shut away together with a group of trusted interlocutors committed to one-to-one dialogue, Mandela moulded out of the situation he found himself in his eventual rules of engagement with the Afrikaner government. His theory of consensus building, in effect, was hammered out through the day-to-day practice of incremental accommodation during the Robben Island years.

The period 1994–9, Mandela's time as South Africa's first democratic president, was less a new political or strategic departure than an extension and consolidation (though for critics like Neville Alexander a compromise) of the approaches and practices that had gone before (Alexander 1993). He continued to pursue the multi-targeted politics espoused by the ANC since 1962, something he particularly admired in Gandhi. Just as his shift towards a dialogic ethic never involved a complete renunciation of political violence, so the ANC government under Mandela was now content to make accommodations with neoliberal capital on the international stage, all the while pushing for social justice and reconstruction at home. Throughout this time, Mandela continued as before to try to be all things to all people, an African nationalist among nationalists, a South African patriot among Afrikaners, a revolutionary when in conversation with Fidel Castro, though his taking of accommodating and at times compromising positions sent out mixed signals in a way that had not been the case before. In the sphere of public life, Mandela succeeded in transforming his flair for accommodation into a credo for political action, so achieving what one of his cabinet ministers described as the total politicization of his political being (Sampson 2000: 412). In many ways he incarnated the role of the adaptive, supremely tactical postcolonial leader.

Conclusion: New Humanism

As the foregoing suggests, Nelson Mandela's political career presents the twenty-first-century postcolonial critic with a compelling case of an anti- or postcolonial *theory in practice*, that is to say, with an intensely *practical* discourse of anti-colonial resistance. Throughout, the long trajectory of his work as an activist, revolutionary, and politician was marked by undertakings and achievements that invite description as 'typically' postcolonial: hybridizing, appropriative, recreative. Mandela demonstrated that a colonial legacy of power could be overcome by adopting and then subverting the languages and the laws of that power in order to effect its overcoming; that an oppressive situation could be withstood through the process of strategically repeating and exceeding the oppressor's self-justifying discourses of rationality or belonging, as the case might be. One of Mandela's strong points of contrast with M. K. Gandhi was that he was never as reluctant as was the Indian leader to articulate his opposition to the repressive state in the selfsame cultural terms as those deployed by it. Thus he selectively invoked the priority of Europe including its notions of modern progress and 'civilized' values, as well as a respect for British traditions of justice and democracy, in order to frame his own particular critique of apartheid: his is a classic case of outmimicking the role of the colonial mimic man. Yet even so, in every one of its historical phases, Mandela's struggle against apartheid represented a dynamically evolving anti-colonialism.

If postcolonialism is defined as an attempt by the marginalized of the world to lay claim to its centres of meaning, then Mandela's efforts to promote African cultural values and indigenous histories of freedom struggle are unequivocally postcolonial. Yet so, too, was his pragmatic empathy for the rival nationalist position of South Africa's Afrikaner minority in the 1980s—an empathy that pushed him towards the risky bid for cross-race and cross-nationalist reconciliation. For him, the intrinsically African qualities of reciprocal brotherhood and consensualism were, at the same time, intensely human qualities: *Africanness* and *humanness* were coextensive, not oppositional, and could thus be shared by his Afrikaner opposition. Such redemptive inclusiveness represents a distinctly postcolonial vision for our times, though one that his critics might still condemn as fatally accommodating.

As for the seeming contradiction in Mandela's career between his willingness to espouse armed struggle in the late 1950s and the 1960s, and his tendencies both earlier and later to pacifism and negotiation, this can be seen once again as representing a peculiarly postcolonial set of strategic responses, which were always pitched as contingent upon circumstance. Across his long life in politics, Mandela worked both active and passive modes of resistance interdependently. Like Gandhi, he was keenly aware that non-violence operated in dialectical tandem with outbreaks of violence or what the ANC called armed propaganda—the presentation of a front (and often only a front) of armed resistance (Legassick 2002: 42). So rather than being a conclusive shift away from passive resistance, Mandela's move to armed struggle, when it occurred, entailed a tacit recognition that non-cooperation could not thrive as politics without the accompaniment of some form of militancy; but that militancy, likewise, had to be counterbalanced with more passive and accommodating forms of resistance when the time came.

If Mandela the life asks to be read critically as a postcolonial practice, as a theory of political resistance and social transformation in action, it also invites recognition as the assertion of a new postcolonial humanism for our age.[10] For if colonialism involves separating human beings from their inclinations, then a postcolonial response is to restore a sense of self-belief to people. As all his biographers in their different capacities observe, Mandela over the years found a way of converting his respect for the human dignity in each and every person into a political practice through dialogue. He turned interactive, cross-border conversation into a culture-wide expectation and a productive means of mapping common ground and mutual regard. For him, national reconciliation involved convincing South African citizens, by example, to base their actions and interactions on the same premise of mutual respect.

Completing a development that began with his turn to multiracialism *circa* 1950, Mandela began to shift the ground of his concept of human identity from the partial and racialized to something more universal and reciprocal. Moving through diverse situations of one-to-one interaction, Mandela increasingly approached others, not as members of a certain group or party, but as human beings first and foremost: unpredictable and complicated yet always ethical (or potentially ethical) in their acts. He became more interested in likeness than in difference, focusing on interaction, not distinction or separation. With respect to postcolonial thought in Africa, which has conventionally focused on the polarized conflict of oppressed and oppressor, Mandela promoted the idea of the fellow human being—the human perceived not as fixed but as fluid, multifarious, defined through the reciprocity of their and others' acts. His political vision grew out of anti-colonial and anti-apartheid practice, yet it developed through his prison dialogues

---

[10.] Though Mandela was probably not aware, before he went to prison, of Frantz Fanon's call for a new humanism on the part of colonized people, as expressed in the closing pages of *The Wretched of the Earth*, in the 1990s, the decade of his achievement of power, his views would have been profoundly affected by the influential Christian approach to building a new sense of humanity in South Africa that was propagated by Archbishop Tutu. Mandela himself however is not a practising Christian.

and the negotiations with his adversary into a hope for involvement that defied enmities and antimonies of all kinds.

Although Mandela never disregarded the risk and uncertainty that accompanies the process of approaching the other, his expanded understanding of the fellow human being coordinates to an extent with the Christianized humanist concept of *ubuntu* popularized by Desmond Tutu. This is reflected in Tutu's Nguni saying *umntu ngumntu ngabantu*, which means: a person is a person through other people; or, my selfhood is contingent upon your selfhood, I am well if you are well. In Mandela's case, the thought directly translates into his 1985 speech refusing P. W. Botha's conditional release, when he told his people: 'Your freedom and mine cannot be separated' (Mandela et al. 2003: 47). Such a reciprocal recognition of contingency, an adventurous openness to the other's humanness, was self-evidently anathema to the apartheid system—and to other oppressive systems, both of yesterday and today.

Towards the end of Fanon's canonical call-to-arms *The Wretched of the Earth*, he looks forward to the day when the emergent postcolonial nation will produce 'new men'. His conclusion speaks urgently of how the Third World must rehumanize the masses of humankind and rewrite history; not by imitating Europe, which always proceeds by way of deadly oppositions, but rather by making new, intensified connections, the Third World will create a humanity that exceeds and cancels the colonial experience. Through his tentative dialogic practices both in prison and beyond, Mandela contributed forcefully to the postcolonial redefinition of the human as proclaimed by Fanon, yet at the same time pulled it in a new direction. In his view, postcolonial life was not necessarily defined in contrast with colonial death. He disposed of Fanon's 'irrepressible violence' as a sole means of making history, instead championing conversation, trust, and listening; and he also subtly but determinedly Africanized his definition of a reshaped—a more fully inclusive—humanism. Reminding supporters and enemies alike of his Africanness, Mandela brought his humanism in line with the values of social harmony and mutual support that, in his view, had always been at the heart of African socialism. As the pan-nationalist Aimé Césaire might have said, his was a humanism made to the measure *both* of Africa *and* of the world more generally, defined from the perspective of those whose humanity had historically been denied. Radically, the African was at the centre of his concept of the human, not the margin or outside against which the human was understood.

References

Ahmad, Aijaz (1992). *In Theory: Classes, Nations, Literatures*. London: Verso.

Alexander, Neville (1993). *Some Are More Equal Than Others: Essays on the Transition in South Africa*. Cape Town: Buchu Books.

Ashcroft, Bill, Gareth Griffiths, and Helen Tiffin (1989). *The Empire Writes Back: Theory and Practice in Post-colonial Literatures*. London: Routledge.

Bhabha, Homi K. (1994). *The Location of Culture*. London: Routledge.

Biko, Steve (1978). *I Write What I Like*. London: Bowerdean.

Boehmer, Elleke (2002). *Empire, the National, and the Postcolonial, 1890–1920: Resistance in Interaction*. Oxford: Oxford University Press.

Boehmer, Elleke (2005). *Colonial and Postcolonial Literature: Migrant Metaphors*, 2nd edn. Oxford: Oxford University Press. Original edition, 1995.

Boehmer, Elleke (2008). *Nelson Mandela: A Very Short Introduction*. Oxford: Oxford University Press.

Buntman, Fran Lisa (2003). *Robben Island and Prisoner Resistance to Apartheid*. Cambridge and New York: Cambridge University Press.

Burton, Antoinette M. (2003). *Dwelling in the Archive: Women Writing House, Home, and History in Late Colonial India*. New York and Oxford: Oxford University Press.

Casanova, Pascale and M. B. DeBevoise (2004). *The World Republic of Letters*, trans. M. B. DeBevoise. Cambridge, Mass. and London: Harvard University Press.

Chakrabarty, Dipesh (2000). *Provincializing Europe: Postcolonial Thought and Historical Difference*. Princeton, NJ: Princeton University Press.

Chrisman, Laura (2000). *Rereading the Imperial Romance: British Imperialism and South African Resistance in Haggard, Schreiner, and Plaatje*. Oxford: Clarendon Press.

Cooper, Frederick (2005). *Colonialism in Question: Theory, Knowledge, History*. Berkeley, Calif. and London: University of California Press.

Fanon, Frantz (1983 [1961]). *The Wretched of the Earth*. Harmondsworth: Penguin.

Fukuyama, Francis. (1992). *The End of History and the Last Man*. Harmondsworth: Penguin.

Gandhi, Leela (1998). *Postcolonial Theory: A Critical Introduction*. Edinburgh: Edinburgh University Press.

Gandhi, Leela (2006). *Affective Communities: Anticolonial Thought, Fin-de-Siècle Radicalism, and the Politics of Friendship*. Durham, NC and London: Duke University Press.

Gandhi, M. K. (1997). 'What is Swaraj?', in *Hind Swaraj and other writings*, ed. A. J. Parel. Cambridge: Cambridge University Press, 1–126.

Gates, Henry Louis, Jr. (1986). *'Race', Writing, and Difference*. Chicago and London: University of Chicago Press.

Gilman, Sander L. (1985). *Difference and Pathology: Stereotypes of Sexuality, Race, and Madness*. Ithaca and London: Cornell University Press.

Hallward, Peter (2001). *Absolutely Postcolonial: Writing Between the Singular and the Specific*. Manchester: Manchester University Press.

Legassick, Martin (2002). *Armed Struggle and Democracy: The Case of South Africa*. Uppsala: Nordiska Afrikainstitutet.

Lodge, Tom (2006). *Mandela: A Critical Life*. Oxford: Oxford University Press.

Loomba, Ania (1998). *Colonialism/Postcolonialism: New Critical Idiom*. London: Routledge.

Maharaj, Mac (2001). *Reflections in Prison. Robben Island Memories Series*. Cape Town: Zebra and the Robben Island Museum.

Mandela, Nelson (1965). *No Easy Walk to Freedom: Articles, Speeches and Trial Addresses of Nelson Mandela*. London: Heinemann.

Mandela, Nelson, Kader Asmal, David Chidester, and Wilmot Godfrey James (2003). *Nelson Mandela: From Freedom to the Future: Tributes and Speeches*. Johannesburg: Jonathan Ball.

McClintock, Anne (1995). *Imperial Leather: Race, Gender and Sexuality in the Colonial Contest*. New York and London: Routledge.

McLeod, John (2000). *Beginning Postcolonialism*. Manchester: Manchester University Press.

Meer, Fatima (1990). *Higher than Hope: A Biography of Nelson Mandela*. London: Hamish Hamilton.

Meli, Francis (1988). *South Africa Belongs to Us: A History of the ANC*. Harare: Zimbabwe Publishing House.

Naipaul, V. S. (1967). *The Mimic Men*. London: A. Deutsch.

Ndebele, Njabulo S. (2006). *Rediscovery of the Ordinary: Essays on South African Literature and Culture*. Scottsville, South Africa: University of KwaZulu-Natal Press.

Parry, Benita (2004). *Postcolonial Studies: A Materialist Critique*. London: Routledge.

Pratt, Mary Louise (1992). *Imperial Eyes: Travel Writing and Transculturation*. London: Routledge.

Rushdie, Salman (1981). *Midnight's Children*. London: Cape.

Said, Edward W. (1978). *Orientalism*. London: Routledge & Kegan Paul.

Said, Edward W. (1993). *Culture and Imperialism*. London: Chatto & Windus.

Sampson, Anthony (2000) *Mandela: The Authorised Biography*. London: HarperCollins.

Scott, David (2004). *Conscripts of Modernity: The Tragedy of Colonial Enlightenment*. Durham, NC and London: Duke University Press.

Soyinka, Wole (1965). *The Interpreters*. London: A. Deutsch.

Young, Robert (1990) *White Mythologies: Writing History and the West*. London: Routledge.

Young, Robert (1995). *Colonial Desire: Hybridity in Theory, Culture and Race*. London: Routledge.

Young, Robert (2003). *Postcolonialism: A Very Short Introduction*. Oxford: Oxford University Press.

CHAPTER 14

'THIRD WORLDISM' AND THE POLITICAL IMAGINARY OF POSTCOLONIAL STUDIES

NEIL LAZARUS

Rehearsals of the intellectual and theoretical antecedents of the academic initiative that goes by the name of 'postcolonial studies' have been staged so many times now as to amount almost to a literature in themselves. Commentators—especially those reporting on postcolonial studies from beyond its boundaries—often draw attention to the fact that a high percentage of these rehearsals have taken the form of repudiation or thoroughgoing disavowal. In his witty review of Gayatri Chakravorty Spivak's 1999 study *A Critique of Postcolonial Reason*, for instance, Terry Eagleton suggests that

> [t]here must exist somewhere a secret handbook for post-colonial critics, the first rule of which reads: 'Begin by rejecting the whole notion of post-colonialism'. It is remarkable how hard it is to find an unabashed enthusiast for the concept among those who promote it … The idea of the post-colonial has taken such a battering from post-colonial theorists that to use the word unreservedly of oneself would be rather like calling oneself Fatso, or confessing to a furtive interest in coprophilia. (1999: 3)

Certainly, we must concede that 'the idea of the post-colonial' has been fiercely contested by 'post-colonial theorists' themselves. One might cite in this respect Kwame Anthony Appiah, who defined 'postcoloniality' as 'the condition of what we might ungenerously call a comprador intelligentsia' (1991: 348); Arif Dirlik, who revised Appiah's definition to propose instead that 'postcoloniality is the condition of the intelligentsia of global capitalism' (1994: 356); Edward Said, whose work—at least from the time of *The World, the Text, and the Critic* (1983) onwards—was severely critical of the prevailing emphases in the field; that cohort of materialist critics (myself included) who have sought to criticize the culturalism and historical ungroundedness of much postcolonialist scholarship;[1] and such other variously affiliated critics as Anne McClintock and Ella Shohat, whose identifications of 'pitfalls of the term "post-colonialism"' (McClintock 1992) and 'theoretical and political ambiguities of the "post-colonial"' (Shohat 1992) have represented milestones in the emergent field's consciousness of itself.

The level of critical self-consciousness expressed in these contributions might seem unusually high when compared to the situation in, say, Shakespeare studies or romanticism; but it is surely to be expected in what is essentially a revisionist mode of critical practice,[2] whose signature commitment is—in the words of one of the more senior postcolonialists—to 'the pursuit of liberation after the achievement of political independence' (Young 2001: 11).[3] The observation that many scholars working in postcolonial studies have been sharply critical of the methodological procedures and epistemological and ideological assumptions prevailing in the field is true. But because it is a purely descriptive observation, it does not provide a particularly good platform for thinking about the defining characteristics of postcolonial studies as an intellectual (or, more narrowly, an academic) formation. In this latter respect, the supplementarity of postcolonial studies to poststructuralist theory has of course frequently been registered; and some of the defining theoretical and ideological dispositions in the field have correctly been identified and assessed by critics, accordingly, through reference to poststructuralism.[4] Yet it seems to me that if we are to identify and begin to understand the distinctive emphases and investments of postcolonial theory, we must do more than offer an intellectual

[1.] See, for example, Ahmad (1992, 1995); Brennan (1997, 2006); Chrisman (2003); Larsen (2001, 2005); Lazarus (1999); Parry (2004b); San Juan, Jr. (1998). See also the essays by Brennan, Larsen, Parry, and San Juan, Jr. in Bartolovich and Lazarus (2002) and by Lazarus and Parry in Lazarus (2004).

[2.] Postcolonial studies has been centrally concerned from the outset to challenge pre-existing and hitherto dominant representations and modes of knowledge production. It would not be too much to suggest, in fact, that one defining gesture of scholarship in the field has consisted precisely in its critique of the specific set of representations famously addressed by Edward W. Said under the rubric of 'Orientalism'. Building upon Said's canonical formulation, scholars working in postcolonial studies have produced a considerable amount of valuable work over the past thirty-odd years on 'western' conceptions of the 'non-west', in which they have sought to demonstrate not only the falsity or inaccuracy of these conceptions but also their systematicity and their capacity to ground, engender, or constitute social practices, policies, and institutions.

[3.] Young attributes this missionary conception to Amilcar Cabral—a misattribution if ever there was one, since it disregards the abyss separating Cabral's writings, produced in the heat of a revolutionary struggle for national liberation, from academic 'postcolonial critique'. See my discussion of Young's 'Third Worldism', to follow.

[4.] Benita Parry, for instance, observes that '[t]he institutionalization of postcolonial studies took place at a time when the linguistic turn was in the ascendant within philosophy and literary theory, and at the moment when cultural studies was in the process of turning its back on its materialist beginnings ... The stage was then set for the reign of theoretical tendencies which Edward Said, among others, has deplored for permitting intellectuals "an astonishing sense of weightlessness with regard to the gravity of history". In the realm of postcolonial studies where premises affording analytic priority to formations of discourse and signifying processes were already to the fore, discussion of the internal structures of texts, enunciations, and sign systems became detached from a concurrent examination of social and experiential contexts, situations, and circumstances' (Parry 2004a: 74; the citation is from Said 1993: 366–7).

genealogy, no matter how astute or compelling; we need in addition to put forward a credible sociological account of the relation between the problematic of postcolonial studies and developments in the wider social world.

What, then, is the problematic of postcolonial studies? (I use the term 'problematic' here not in any strict Althusserian sense,[5] but more loosely, to designate an epistemological-ideological framework, a specific and determinate line of sight or way of seeing.) My own view is that postcolonial studies in its dominant aspect (consolidated as a dedicated field of study and institutionalized within literature and other humanities departments in universities across the mostly Anglophone world) is to be understood as a 'Third Worldist' tendency—but as a 'Third Worldism' of a conjuncturally distinct kind. Shaped, as are all variants of 'Third Worldism', by the vicissitudes of the Cold War, and seeking to carve out a space of critical non-alignment in the battle between 'capitalist' 'west' and 'communist' 'east'—seeking to reconceptualize the 'east'/'west' contest in terms of an opposition between 'north' and 'south' (see Brydon in Part IV of this volume)—the 'Third Worldism' of the postcolonialist imaginary is also profoundly informed by the decisive collapse, at the beginning of the 1970s, of the global dispensation that had prevailed since the end of the Second World War. Emerging at the end of the 1970s and incorporating itself over the course of the following decade and a half, postcolonial studies is very much a creature of its time or, better, a creature *of* and *against* its time. Just behind it lies the post-1945 boom: the 'golden age', as Eric Hobsbawm has called it, of a quarter-century or so of explosive global economic growth, accompanied in the core capitalist countries by a historically unprecedented democratization of social resources and in the 'Third World' by insurgent demands for decolonization and self-determination (Hobsbawm 1994). This boom period came to an end at the beginning of the 1970s, when the world system stumbled into economic recession and attendant political crisis, from which it has yet to recover. The thirty-plus years since the puncturing of the boom—the 'long downturn', to use Robert Brenner's term (2006)—have been marked not only by economic crisis, but also by political reaction: a forced restructuring of class relations in the interests of capital in the core capitalist countries; a rolling back of the challenge represented by 'Third World' insurgency at the peripheries.

The thought-figure of '1975' is crucial, in these terms, to the 'political unconscious' of postcolonial studies (or the 'postcolonial unconscious', the shorthand formula I use in

---

5. The Althusserian concept of *problématique* designates the total framework (epistemological, ideological, cultural, and historical) within which particular terms, concepts, theories, and ideas are generated. In the 'glossary' to his translation of Althusser's *For Marx*, Ben Brewster writes that: 'A word or concept cannot be considered in isolation; it only exists in the theoretical or ideological framework in which it is used: its problematic. A related concept can clearly be seen at work in Foucault's *Madness and Civilization* ... It should be stressed that the problematic is *not* a world-view. It is not the essence of the thought of an individual or epoch which can be deduced from a body of texts by an empirical, generalizing reading; it is centred on the *absence* of problems and concepts within the problematic as much as their presence; it can therefore only be reached by a symptomatic reading ... on the model of the Freudian analyst's reading of his patient's utterances' (Althusser 1969 [1966]: 252–3).

my recent book of that title).[6] '1975' might be said to mark a break between the initial, more widely recognized form of 'Third Worldism' and another version of the tendency. Where the 'Third World' is concerned, the three decades from 1945 to 1975 constitute the decolonizing era—years of insurgency, revolution, nationalism and national liberation struggle, the radical and insurrectionary politics of emancipation. One can identify this era unmistakably by reciting the names of such countries as Algeria, Cuba, and Vietnam, or of such charismatic political leaders as Ché, Gandhi, Ho Chi Minh, Nasser, and Nkrumah. '1975' was the moment at which the globally popular and uplifting 'Third Worldist' narrative of self-determination—think of Fanon: 'The people of Africa have only recently come to know themselves. They have decided, in the name of the whole continent, to weigh in strongly against the colonial regime … [A] coordinated effort on the part of two hundred and fifty million men to triumph over stupidity, hunger and inhumanity at one and the same time' (1977 [1961]: 132)—began to founder in the face of complementary and powerful counter-offensives. On the one hand, 'externally', there was the unremitting hostility of the United States in the context of the Cold War, bent on securing its global hegemony and working ceaselessly—at times directly, at other times covertly—to undermine, subvert, and overthrow regimes, movements, and initiatives it deemed to stand in opposition to its own interests and political philosophy. On the other hand, 'internally', within the postcolonies[7] themselves, there was the institutionalization of the various 'revolutions', which is to say the petrification of them: the subordination of 'social' imperatives touching on the distribution of capital, resources, and services to 'statist' requirements of elite entrenchment. So independent Algeria, as David Macey has written, 'soon came to look more like a sclerotic one-party despotism … [than] a beacon of hope' (2000: 21); in Vietnam, the war was won but the peace was lost; in Indonesia, Sukarno was removed from office and replaced by Suharto; in Chile, Allende was assassinated in the coup that installed Pinochet at the head of a military dictatorship; in India, Nehruvian socialism gave way to Mrs Gandhi's autocracy and the Emergency of 1975–7, which in turn opened on to the neoliberalism of the early 1980s; and in Lusophone Africa, the remarkable liberations of Guinea-Bissau, Angola, and Mozambique from Portuguese 'ultra-colonialism'[8] resulted not in peace, prosperity, and social justice, but in renewed warfare, despoliation, and social violence.

[6] The idea of a 'postcolonial unconscious' is derived and adapted from Fredric Jameson's 'political unconscious', as elaborated in his book of that title (Jameson 1981). In my own book (Lazarus 2011), I use the term to designate the unique and historically specific complex of ideas, attitudes, and presumptions that might be said to underlie postcolonial theory as a consolidated field of scholarly production.

[7] I use the term 'postcolonies' to refer to territories—formerly colonized—that have undergone a process of decolonization and have emerged, through this process, as nation states in a world system of such states. One could, of course, refer to these formally decolonized territories as 'nation states' or 'countries', but the term 'postcolonies' is useful in suggesting that the colonial order (institutions, regimes of accumulation and regulation, forms of governance, patterns of thought and understanding) continues to exert a powerful—even, in some instances, defining—influence beyond the formal transfer of power. What is celebrated in the various 'Independence Days' is rarely 'independence' as that term is commonly understood.

[8] I derive this term from Perry Anderson's 1962 essay.

Postcolonial studies emerged as an institutionally specific, conjuncturally determined response to these global developments. Germinating initially in the elite universities of the United States and Britain, the emergent field breathed the air of the general
reassertion of imperial dominance, whose metropolitan ideologists reached powerfully for hegemony in what Stuart Hall once memorably characterized as 'The Great
Moving Right Show' of the middle and late 1970s (Hall 1979). A major precondition of
this new imperialist drive for hegemony was the containment and recuperation of the
historic challenge from the 'Third World' that had been expressed in the struggles for
decolonization in the boom years following 1945. After 1975, the prevailing political
sentiment in the west turned sharply against anti-colonial nationalist insurgency and
revolutionary anti-imperialism. Especially after the collapse of historical communism
in 1989, commentators in the west were disposed to pronounce Marxism finally dead
and buried also.

The substance and trajectory of the work produced in postcolonial studies has been
strongly marked by this epochal reversal of the fortunes and influence of revolutionary
ideologies and insurgent national liberation movements in the 'Third World'. The decisive defeat of liberationist ideologies within the western (or increasingly western-based)
intelligentsia, including its radical or dissident elements, was fundamental to the emergent field, whose subsequent consolidation during the 1980s and early 1990s must be
seen, at least in part, as a function of its articulation of a complex intellectual response to
this defeat. On the one hand, as an initiative in tune with its times, postcolonial studies
was party to the general anti-liberationism then rising to hegemony in western societies. The field not only emerged in close chronological proximity to the enforced end
of the decolonizing era, the era of 'Third World' insurgency; it also characteristically
offered, in the scholarship it fostered, something approximating a monumentalization
of this moment—not a celebration but a pragmatic rationalization of, and intellectually resourceful adjustment to, the demise of the ideologies that had flourished during
the decolonizing years. On the other hand, however, as a self-consciously *progressive* or
radical initiative, postcolonial studies was, and has remained, opposed to the dominant
forms assumed by anti-liberationist policy and discourse in the politically bleak years
since the mid-1970s: years of neoliberal austerity, structural adjustment, and political
rollback. What Homi K. Bhabha influentially described as 'the postcolonial project'
(1994: 171) might thus be conceptualized (in analogy with the liberal Cold War discourse of 'anti-anti-communism') as 'anti-anti-liberationism'. Itself predicated on a recoil
from liberationism, which it understands to have been rendered historically anachronistic by the advent of the new world order represented by 'globalization',[9] postcolonial
studies has nevertheless stood as a firm opponent of imperialist anti-liberationism, as
expressed both in the language of leading politicians, policymakers, and intellectuals

---

[9.] For discussion of 'globalization' in relation to postcolonial studies, see the essays in Part V of this
volume. See also Timothy Brennan's important dissenting commentary (Brennan 2004). For my own
views on globalization theory, see Lazarus (1998–9).

in the core capitalist states, and through the punitive and disciplinary policies enacted by such corporate and parastatal agencies as the International Money Fund, the World Trade Organization, and the World Bank.[10]

Reflecting on this transition from the liberationist or insurrectionary 'Third Worldist' discourse of the decolonizing era to the altogether more tortuous 'Third Worldism' that finds expression in postcolonial studies ('anti-liberationist' but, as I have just suggested, 'anti-anti-liberationist' also), Aijaz Ahmad speaks of a 'shift' in the 'governing theoretical framework … from Third World nationalism to postmodernism' (1995: 1). He quite properly accords representative significance to Bhabha's writings, in which, as he points out, the 'post' in 'postcolonial'

> becomes a 'post' not only of colonialism but also of an indeterminate larger thing. At the same time, the term 'postcolonial' also comes to us as the name of a *discourse* about the condition of 'postcoloniality' … Following on which is the attendant assertion that only those critics, who believe not only that colonialism has more or less ended but who also subscribe to the idea of the end of Marxism, nationalism, collective historical subjects and revolutionary possibility as such, are the true postcolonials, while the rest of us, who do not quite accept this apocalyptic anti-Marxism, are not postcolonial at all. In this formulation, then, that which is designated as postcolonial discourse presumes the prior consent to theoretical postmodernity. (1995: 9–10)

The diagnostic critique here is substantially correct, in my view. It is clear that in Bhabha's thinking, 'postcolonial' has ceased to be a historical category. The term does not designate what it sounds like it designates: that is, the moment, or more generally the time, *after* colonialism. There *are* temporal words and phrases in Bhabha's general formulation, but these do not appear to relate in any discernible way to *decolonization* as a historical event, that is, to decolonization as a 'cut' or break in historical time, such that one could speak of a colonial 'before' and a postcolonial 'after'. Bhabha writes in one of the essays collected in *The Location of Culture* that 'postcolonial criticism' concerns itself with 'social pathologies' that can 'no longer' be referred to the explanatory factor of class division: 'postcolonial criticism' is thus opposed to (and for Bhabha evidently comes after or supersedes) class analysis. But no explanation is given as to why the term 'colonial' is implicated in the putative obsolescence of class analysis. Indeed, on the basis of what Bhabha says, 'postcolonial criticism' could as easily be called 'post-Marxist criticism'. Or indeed 'postmodern

---

[10.] The account of the emergence of postcolonial studies offered here differs sharply from that presented by Elleke Boehmer in this part of the volume. Organizing her account around the cultural zeitgeist of 1989, Boehmer invokes 'glasnost, the unfreezing of the Cold War, and the breaking down of barriers and walls, in Berlin, in eastern Europe as a whole, and, soon, in apartheid South Africa'. However, she fails to place these heady developments in the wider context of the post-1945 period, with the result that she both overstates their epochal character and takes their own progressivist rhetoric too much for granted. Her narrative does not register with sufficient clarity the fundamental differences between the prevailing ideological casts of the 'decolonizing' and the 'end-of-the-Cold-War' moments; and it is much too quick to allow that what is phrased as 'resistance' in postcolonial theory is the necessary form of appearance of resistance in the world—that is to say, in the supposedly post-cold War, post-communist, post-Marxist, post-colonial, and post-revolutionary world—today.

criticism', since he is also at pains to emphasize that the 'post-' in 'postcolonial criticism'
is directed against the assumptions of the 'ideological discourses of modernity', which
are declared categorically (and I believe wrongly) to flatten out complexity, to simplify
the sheer heterogeneity and unevenness of real conditions, to reduce these to 'a binary
structure of opposition'. For Bhabha, 'postcolonial' is a fighting term, a theoretical weapon
that 'intervenes' in existing debates and 'resists' certain political and philosophical constructions. 'Postcolonial criticism', as he understands and champions it, is constitutively
anti-Marxist, departing not only from more orthodox Marxist scholarship but even from
'the traditions of the sociology of underdevelopment or "dependency" theory"; it disavows
nationalism as such and refuses an antagonistic or struggle-based model of politics in
favour of one that emphasizes 'cultural difference', 'ambivalence', and 'the more complex
cultural and political boundaries that exist on the cusp' of what 'modern' philosophy had
imagined as the determinate categories of social reality (1994: 171, 173).

Ahmad uses the term 'postmodern' to describe the complexion of 'Third Worldist' discourse after the 'break' represented by '1975'. Sharper-edged, it seems to me, is the vocabulary mobilized by Neil Larsen, who observes that what tends in the new (post-'1975')
discourse to be referred to as the 'postcolonial' is a 'euphemism' for what used to be
referred to as the 'Third World'—'euphemism' because the political meaning of the 'Third
World', which used to 'conjure ... up an entire historical conjuncture and accompanying
political culture, in which one naturally went on to utter the ... slogans of national liberation', has now been eclipsed. '[W]e who once unself-consciously said "third world"
now hesitate, if only for a second, to utter it in the same contexts. This hesitation reflects
the decline of the national liberation movements of the "Bandung era" ... leaving us with
the question of why and with what effect this decline has occurred' (Larsen 2005: 25).[11]

Larsen's formulation allows us to register that what we might now call postcolonialist 'Third Worldism' takes its warrant from the conviction that between the era within
which the great wave of post-1945 decolonization unfolded and the post-1975 dispensation there has been an epochal transformation from one overarching global dispensation into another. Hence the suggestions in the critical literature that the grand
'Bandung era' narratives of revolution, emancipation, and national liberation are not
merely arguable or susceptible to criticism, but have become definitively *obsolete*. Even
Arif Dirlik, usually cited as a spokesperson for the 'Marxist' line in postcolonial scholarship, in the midst of his wide-ranging and influential 1994 critique of 'the postcolonial
aura', nevertheless concedes that what he calls 'postcoloniality' 'represents a response to
a genuine need':

> the need to overcome a crisis of understanding produced by the inability of old
> categories to account for the world. The metanarrative of progress that underlies two

---

[11.] The reference here is to the historic conference in Bandung in 1955, at which leaders of the decolonizing world (among them Nehru of India, Nasser of Egypt, and Sukarno of the host country Indonesia,
with Tito of Yugoslavia 'as the sole European interloper and Zhou-En-Lai [of China] the somewhat anxiously tolerated guest of honor') had launched the Non-Aligned Movement (2005: 33).

centuries of thinking is in deep crisis. Not only have we lost faith in progress but also progress has had actual disintegrative effects ... The crisis of progress has brought in its wake a crisis of modernization ... and called into question the structure of the globe as conceived by modernizationalists and radicals alike in the decades after World War II, that is, as three worlds. (1994: 352)

Notwithstanding the astringency of his critique of postcolonial theory, Dirlik shares with its leading proponents key assumptions as to the eclipse of 'modernity'[12] and the correlative 'metanarrative of progress that underlies two centuries of thinking'. Like them, he takes it as read that Marxism has been obliterated as an enabling political horizon[13] and that the eclipse of the original 'Third Worldist' idea of the 'Third World' as a historico-political project is part of a wider—epochal—shift from an 'old' order, whose constituent features and aspects—unevenness, revolution, the centrality of the nation, even imperialism—are seen to have lost their explanatory power, to the 'new world order' of fully globalized capitalism.[14]

Dirlik is at one here with other influential contributors to the postcolonial discussion, whose work is in other respects widely disparate. What all of these theorists have in common, I believe, is a particular set of presuppositions which, recognizably 'Third Worldist' in tenor, is nevertheless clearly to be distinguished from the insurrectionary 'Third Worldism' of the decolonizing era. Both in its insurrectionary and its postcolonialist avatars, 'Third Worldism' involves a conceptual displacement from 'class' to 'nation' to 'globe' and from 'capitalist' social relations to 'core'/'periphery' (or 'First World'/'Third World', or 'north'/'south') ones. I note in passing that this displacement has as its inevitable consequence the mystification of the agency and geopolitical vectors of imperialism (see Lazarus 2002). A steady drift in description of anti-imperialist and anti-colonial nationalist politics, which moves from the vocabulary of 'class struggle' to that of 'Third World revolution', can already be discerned between the mid-1950s and the early 1970s. In the African context, for example, the initial phase might be identified through reference to Kwame Nkrumah's *Neo-Colonialism: The Last Stage of Imperialism*,

[12.] I have argued elsewhere that the dominant 'postcolonialist' construction of 'modernity'—like the construction of 'modernity' disseminated generally in poststructuralist theory—is reductive and misconceived. The routine conflation of 'modernity' with 'the west' is a particular source of error. See Lazarus (1999: 16–67) and Lazarus (2002).

[13.] It is noteworthy that Dirlik sees no need explicitly to identify Marxism in his diagnosis of the contemporary 'crisis of progress', a crisis he sees as imposing upon us the burden of rethinking 'the structure of the globe'. This is a pity, for had he done so, he might have been led to recognize that many Marxist scholars have never had much time for 'three worlds theory'—not even in the years of its relative ascendancy—always preferring to conceptualize 'modernity' through reference to the *capitalist* world system. For these theorists, what Dirlik sees as a 'crisis of progress' might be taken precisely to *confirm* their understanding of 'the structure of the globe', rather than to enjoin them to 'question' or rethink it.

[14.] In this respect, as Timothy Brennan has suggested, postcolonial studies can be regarded as a cousin of globalization theory as well as a child of poststructuralism. See Brennan (2004).

published in 1965. A transitional phase might then be represented by Walter Rodney's 1972 study, *How Europe Underdeveloped Africa*, in which a theoretical project and vocabulary derived from dependency theory exists uneasily alongside a project and vocabulary defined in classical Marxist terms. Thus, on the one hand Rodney writes that his key term, underdevelopment, 'expresses a particular relationship of exploitation: namely, the exploitation of one *country* by another' (1982 [1972]: 14; emphasis mine); but then on the other he points out that 'most of the people who write about underdevelopment … confuse the issue [by placing] all underdeveloped countries in one camp and all developed countries in another camp irrespective of different social systems; so that the terms capitalist and socialist never enter the discussion' (23). The latent contradiction between these two modes of conceptualization is never finally resolved in *How Europe Underdeveloped Africa*. By the time of Chinweizu's *The West and the Rest of Us: White Predators, Black Slavers and the African Elite*, published in 1975, the erstwhile Marxist problematic has been definitively displaced by a polemical 'Third Worldism' that eschews any focus on capital and class in favour of a thoroughly culturalist (or civilizational) definition of the neocolonial world order. Here is how *The West and the Rest of Us* begins:

> For nearly six centuries now western Europe and its diaspora have been disturbing the peace of the world. Enlightened, through their Renaissance, by the learning of the ancient Mediterranean; armed with the gun, the making of whose powder they had learned from Chinese firecrackers; equipping their ships with lateen sails, astrolabes and nautical compasses, all invented by the Chinese and transmitted to them by Arabs; fortified in aggressive spirit by an arrogant, messianic Christianity of both the popish and Protestant varieties; and motivated by the lure of enriching plunder, white hordes have sallied forth from their western European homelands to explore, assault, loot, occupy, rule and exploit the rest of the world. And even now, the fury of their expansionist assault upon the rest of us has not abated. (1975: 3)

In its representation by a theorist like Homi Bhabha, postcolonialist 'Third Worldism' takes shape quite explicitly as both post- and anti-nationalist and post- and anti-Marxist: hence the definitional citation of Bhabha in Ahmad's critique of the tendency. But consider by contrast the formulation to be found in Robert Young's *Postcolonialism: An Historical Introduction*, a volume to which I have already made passing reference. This is a beguiling work, whose central rhetorical strategy, as Sarika Chandra and Neil Larsen have pointed out in their deft critique of it, is to insert a silent apology for postcolonial studies as it actually exists into a purported historicization of something called 'postcolonialism' (Chandra and Larsen 2006). It might seem churlish to insist on criticizing a book that so clearly wants to be liked, and that seems, on the face of it at least, to be so ecumenical in its referential embrace. Surely only a misanthrope or a misery guts could find something to cavil at when confronted by an intellectual programme that sets out to articulate itself with different forms of emancipatory politics, to synthesize different kinds of work towards the realization of common goals that include the creation of equal access to material, natural, social and technological resources, the contestation of forms of domination, whether economic, cultural, religious, ethnic or gendered, and the articulation and assertion of collective forms of politics and cultural identity. (Young 2001: 11)

Postcolonialism: An Historical Introduction pivots on the rather breathtaking claim that the demonstrable and indeed constitutive anti-Marxism of postcolonial studies as represented in the work of nearly all of its most influential proponents is in fact not anti-Marxism at all but rather a reconstructive extension and internal, or at least solidaristic, strengthening of Marxism. Here is how this circle is squared in Young's upbeat account of things:

> The assumption of postcolonial studies is that many of the wrongs, if not crimes, against humanity are a product of the economic dominance of the north over the south. In this way, the historical role of Marxism in the history of anti-colonial resistance remains paramount as the fundamental framework of postcolonial thinking. Postcolonial theory operates within the historical legacy of Marxist critique on which it continues to draw but which it simultaneously transforms according to the precedent of the greatest tricontinental anti-colonial intellectual politicians. (2001: 6)

The first sentence here situates 'postcolonial studies' unambiguously as a variant of 'Third Worldism'. Underlying the structural asymmetry of the modern world system, we are told, and therefore at the heart of the 'wrongs ... against humanity' for which this asymmetry is responsible, is the conflict between the geopolitical blocs of 'north' and 'south'. Despite its gesture to the premise of '*economic* dominance', this formulation removes capitalism from the centre of the frame. Even on the best postcolonialist accounts, such as Said's in *Culture and Imperialism*, we can already observe the tendency to cast imperialism as pre-eminently a political dispensation and to refer it, in civilizational terms, to 'the west', rather than to the specific dynamics of capitalist development. Young's preference for the distinctively 'Third Worldist' term, 'north', compounds this problem still further. While the construction of a homogenized and vilified 'north' standing in the way of the autonomy and self-determination of a homogenized and valorized 'south' enables the critic to include the Soviet Union in addition to the core capitalist states in his preview, it renders the actual determinants of historical development in the twentieth century even more inaccessible to analysis than they are when the euphemism of 'the west' is used. Since 'north' is not 'west' (and since 'west' is evidently not—or at least not in the first instance—'capitalist'), the domination of the 'south' by the 'north' is evidently to be registered in terms of something like physical conquest or coercion rather than through reference to the specific dialectics of capitalist development: combined and uneven development, imposition of generalized commodity production, development of markets for the selling and buying of labour power, expropriation of surplus value, exploitation.

The sentence that follows this first one in Young's formulation, which at first glance seems altogether mystifying, may now be deciphered. The key to unlocking it is provided by its first three words: 'In this way'. These serve to pull away from Marxism in advance what the rest of the sentence appears to concede to it. The claim being made is that, in taking the domination of the south by the north as its central problem, postcolonial studies is continuing to ground itself in a Marxist lineage. A big problem for Young here is that across the range of its articulations, Marxism has in fact seldom rooted its analyses of colonialism and imperialism (or, more generally, of 'domination') in the conceptual soil of 'north' and 'south'. So it is not clear how or why Marxism—a theory and practice centred on class struggle—should have been or should remain 'paramount' to postcolonial studies, a theory and practice whose conceptual scaffolding is, quite demonstrably, radically different. However, the genius of the phrase 'in this way' is that it allows Young to have his cake and eat it too, enabling him to argue simultaneously that 'Third Worldist' discourse (he himself prefers to call it 'tricontinentalism') does not simply share a deep-seated affinity with Marxism but is rather the very face of Marxism in the 'Third World', and that the tendency's various reformulations of and explicit breaks with 'classical' Marxist theory are therefore to be grasped not as *ideologically* but as *geohistorically* mandated. Young's suggestion, in other words, is that the shift within 'Third Worldist' discourse from 'class' to 'race' or 'nation' and on to 'globe', or from 'capitalist' to 'west' to 'north', accurately registers the contingencies of the social order in the colonial (and subsequently the postcolonial) 'Third World'. Hence his argument that 'Third Worldist' discourse represents 'a Marxism which has been pragmatically modified to suit non-western conditions and which does not, as a result, altogether coincide with that of the classical mainstream' (6–7).

This is very convenient, of course, and it nicely sets up the third of the sentences in the passage previously quoted, in which Young proposes not merely that 'tricontinentalist' discourse represents a pragmatic modification of received Marxist theory but that 'postcolonial theory' is a pragmatic modification of 'tricontinentalist' discourse in its turn. Marxism is still there, as the wellspring of 'postcolonial theory', but it has been changed as and where necessary, 'according to the precedent of the greatest tricontinental anti-colonial intellectual politicians'. Similarly, the ideas of the greatest tricontinentalist anti-colonial intellectual politicians are still there, also as a bedrock, but they too have been changed—modified, refunctioned, junked—as and where it is considered to be necessary, in the passage from 1955, say, or 1968, to the fully globalized present day.

It is hard to know how to take this statement, whose rather sensational hubris seems to be the least of its problems. Does Young seriously want us to entertain the proposal that the revolutionary legacies of Lenin and Luxemburg (classical Marxist) and of Castro and Cabral (tricontinentalist) are now incarnate in the work of the embattled postcolonial scholar courageously advancing the struggle against 'the forces of oppression and coercive domination that operate in the contemporary world' from his or her base in

Oxford or New York? There ought to be a limit to the lengths to which a critic can go in order to pander to the illusions of his readers or make them feel good about themselves.

At one level, when Young argues that the great tricontinental anti-colonial intellectual politicians found themselves revising and sharpening, not merely confirming, received Marxist theory in their various political applications of it, he is merely stating a truism. For it is not, of course, only tricontinental anti-colonial intellectual politicians whose close attention to the specificity of local conditions and local circumstances leads them to the reformulation of received Marxist theory. The writings and political activism of Lenin, Luxemburg, Trotsky, Bauer, Gramsci, Korsch, Lukács, Kollontai, Labriola, Tito, and Preobrazhensky, for instance, are all critically reflexive in just this sense. It is, after all, precisely his detailed investigations into the conditions prevailing in the Russian hinterland and in China that prompts Trotsky to put forward his law of combined and uneven development. But Young wants to suggest that something other than critical reflexivity is involved in tricontinental intellectuals' testing and adapting of Marxist theory in the Bandung era. What he wants to propose, in fact, is that between the 'classical' Marxists and the 'tricontinentalists' there is a world-historical fault line. A single sentence tells the story in full: 'The contribution of tricontinental theorists was to mediate the translatability of Marxist revolutionary theory with the untranslatable features of specific non-European historical and cultural contexts' (2001: 6). The formulation splits the world on its axis to propose a 'classical' Marxism whose conceptual horizon is 'Europe' on one side and its necessary complement, a 'tricontinental' Marxism that is alert to 'non-European' specificities, on the other. The essentialism of this conception, whose demonstrable homogenization of 'Europe' cannot but fail to take into account the differences between the various peoples, histories, societies, and states implicated, is remarkable. Equally arresting, however, is Young's failure to make anything significant of the fact that throughout the Bandung era—that is to say, even at the high tide of 'Third Worldism'—there were many actively engaged Marxist intellectuals in the 'Third World' who had no time at all for 'three worlds theory' or for the politics to which it gave shape. These 'Third World' Marxists wrote decisively against the former and campaigned tirelessly against the latter. One might reference in passing, for example, the various critiques of Fanon's radical voluntarism that were voiced in the context of the Algerian liberation struggle, or the different Marxist rejoinders to the philosophy of 'black consciousness' in South Africa (see Boehmer in this section of the volume). Even in the intellectual contexts of anti-imperialist struggle, the 'Third Worldist' jettisoning of the specifically Marxist legacy of class struggle, communism, and revolutionary internationalism is not mandated by the instantiation of the idea of the 'Third World' itself as a rallying point. It is enough to compare Young's theory with that of a contemporary 'tricontinentalist' like Samir Amin to begin to appreciate the tendentiousness and radical selectivity of his purported historicization of 'postcolonialism' in this respect (see, for example, Amin 2011).

Seeking to emphasize the intrinsic connection between the 'Third Worldist' imaginary and Marxism, Young writes that 'Marxism, which represents both a form of revolutionary politics and one of the richest and most complex theoretical and philosophical movements in human history, has always been in some sense anti-western, since it was developed by Marx as a critique of western social and economic practices and the values which they embodied. The Bolsheviks themselves always identified their revolution as "Eastern"' (2001: 6). In light of what I have just written, I hope it is possible to see that the construction of Marxism here has untenably been co-opted in advance by 'Third Worldist' assumptions. In point of fact, Marx develops his thought as a critique, not of '*western* social and economic practices and the values … they embodied' (emphasis mine), but of *capitalism* and the bourgeois practices and values it brings in its train. Marx's massive late work is not entitled *The West: A Critique of Political Economy* but *Capital: A Critique of Political Economy*; and its opening sentence does not read: 'The wealth of western societies appears as an "immense collection of commodities"', but 'The wealth of societies in which the capitalist mode of production prevails appears as an "immense collection of commodities"' (1990 [1867]: 125). In the *Manifesto of the Communist Party*, similarly, Marx and Engels are absolutely insistent that their narrative's central historical protagonist is not 'the west' but the *bourgeoisie*. 'The bourgeoisie, historically, has played a most revolutionary part', they write: 'The bourgeoisie … has put an end to all feudal, patriarchal, idyllic relations … The bourgeoisie has stripped of its halo … The bourgeoisie has torn away from the family … The bourgeoisie has disclosed … The bourgeoisie cannot exist without … The bourgeoisie has through its exploitation of the world market … ' (Marx and Engels 1988 [1848]: 35–7). Even when colonial social relations are explicitly evoked in this text, and the language of 'east' and 'west' is used, the bourgeoisie continues to be phrased as the decisive historical agent: it is the bourgeoisie which 'has made barbarian and semi-barbarian countries dependent on the civilised ones, nations of peasants on nations of bourgeois, the East on the West' (Marx and Engels 1988 [1848]: 38).

The suggestion that Marxism 'has always been in some sense anti-western' is simply not true; nor is it true that '[t]he Bolsheviks themselves always identified their revolution as "Eastern"' (Young 2001: 6). In fact, it would be more accurate to say the reverse, although the truth is inevitably more complex, requiring among other things an internal distinction, which Young does not provide, between 'Europe' and 'the west'.[15] Already in the fierce debates between 'Slavophile' and 'Westerner' intellectuals in Russia in the mid-nineteenth century, as Christopher Gogwilt has explained, it was clear that the myth of 'Europe' as the unified, secularized, enlightened cognate of 'Christendom' had broken down irretrievably (1995: 233). To the Slavophiles, Christendom needed to be protected *from* 'the west', the godless world of humanism, modernity, and industrial capitalism. Capitalist modernity had driven a wedge into the heart of 'Europe', sundering 'east' from 'west' *within* the concept just as decisively as the Great Schism had done. There was no integral 'European civilization' to be differentiated primarily from its non-European 'others' in the world beyond. The anti-capitalist Bolshevik Revolution then thickened

---

[15.] For more on the different histories and meanings of the ideas of 'Europe' and 'the west', see the commentaries in Lazarus (2002) and Lazarus (2012).

and compounded the terms of this intra-European division. Reactionary ('Europeanist') thinkers in Russia simply extended their critique of modernity, folding Bolshevism into the hated ideal of 'the west' that they had earlier identified with capitalist culture, but that could easily be broadened now to include the post-capitalist socialist order.

'The central task enjoined upon scholars working in the field of postcolonial studies', Priyamvada Gopal and I wrote in 2006, introducing a special issue of the journal *New Formations* on the subject of 'Postcolonial Studies after Iraq', 'is to work towards the production of a new "history of the present"—a new reading above all of the twentieth century, liberated from the dead weight either of the Cold War or of a compensatory "Third Worldism"' (2006: 9). If anything, that injunction seems even more urgent today than it did when it was written several years ago. For I am writing now, in 2011, in the midst of extraordinary developments currently unfolding in Bahrain, Egypt, Libya, Syria, Tunisia, and Yemen—all of which seem quite evidently to demand an interpretation that exceeds the parameters of Atlanticist or 'Third Worldist' discourse. Saree Makdisi has recently drawn my attention to an old Palestinian slogan, '*Thawra, thawra, hatta'l nasr*' ('Revolution, revolution, until victory'), which serves well to indicate that we might find the resources to construct this necessary interpretation by looking again at our history. Our task as postcolonial critics today, I believe, is to attempt to rejoin the conjuncture in and through which we are living to a long and as yet unbroken history—and, even more important, to a long and as yet unbroken *counter-history*—that postcolonial studies in its incorporated form wrongly supposes to have come to a close around '1975'. This is the history of a specifically capitalist imperialism and the counter-history of resistance to it.

REFERENCES

Ahmad, Aijaz (1992). *In Theory: Classes, Nations, Literatures*. London: Verso.

Ahmad, Aijaz (1995). 'The Politics of Literary Postcoloniality', *Race & Class*, 36.3: 1–20.

Althusser, Louis (1969 [1966]). *For Marx*, trans. B. Brewster. Harmondsworth: Penguin.

Amin, Samir (2011). 'The Trajectory of Historical Capitalism and Marxism's Tricontinental Vocation', *Monthly Review*, 62.9: 1–18.

Anderson, Perry (1962). 'Portugal and the End of Ultra-Colonialism', part 1, *New Left Review*, 15: 83–102; part 2, *New Left Review*, 16: 88–123; part 3, *New Left Review*, 17: 85–114.

Appiah, Kwame Anthony (1991). 'Is the Post- in Postmodern the Post- in Postcolonial?' *Critical Inquiry*, 17.2: 336–57.

Bartolovich, Crystal and Neil Lazarus (eds) (2002). *Marxism, Modernity and Postcolonial Studies*. Cambridge: Cambridge University Press.

Bhabha, Homi K. (1994). *The Location of Culture*. London: Routledge.

Brennan, Timothy (1997). *At Home in the World: Cosmopolitanism Now*. Cambridge, Mass.: Harvard University Press.

Brennan, Timothy (2004). 'From Development to Globalization: Postcolonial Studies and Globalization Theory', in N. Lazarus (ed.), *The Cambridge Companion to Postcolonial Literary Studies*. Cambridge: Cambridge University Press, 120–38.

Brennan, Timothy (2006). *Wars of Position: The Cultural Politics of Left and Right*. New York: Columbia University Press.

Brenner, Robert (2006). *The Economics of Global Turbulence: The Advanced Capitalist Economies from Long Boom to Long Downturn.* New York: Verso.

Chandra, Sarika and Neil Larsen (2006). 'Postcolonial Pedigrees', *Cultural Critique*, 62: 197–206.

Chinweizu (1975). *The West and the Rest of Us: White Predators, Black Slavers and the African Elite.* New York: Vintage.

Chrisman, Laura (2003). *Postcolonial Contraventions: Cultural Readings of Race, Imperialism and Transnationalism.* Manchester: Manchester University Press.

Dirlik, Arif (1994). 'The Postcolonial Aura: Third World Criticism in the Age of Global Capitalism', *Critical Inquiry*, 20.2: 328–56.

Eagleton, Terry (1999). 'In the Gaudy Supermarket', *London Review of Books*, 21.10: 3–6.

Fanon, Frantz (1977 [1961]). *The Wretched of the Earth*, trans. C. Farrington. Harmondsworth: Penguin.

Gogwilt, Christopher (1995). *The Invention of the West: Joseph Conrad and the Double-Mapping of Europe and Empire.* Stanford: Stanford University Press.

Gopal, Priyamvada and Neil Lazarus (2006). 'Editorial', *New Formations*, 59: 7–9.

Hall, Stuart (1979). 'The Great Moving Right Show', *Marxism Today* (January): 14–20.

Hobsbawm, Eric (1994). *The Age of Extremes: A History of the World, 1914–1991.* New York: Pantheon Books.

Jameson, Fredric (1981). *The Political Unconscious: Narrative as a Socially Symbolic Act.* Ithaca, NY: Cornell University Press.

Larsen, Neil (2001). *Determinations: Essays on Theory, Narrative and Nation in the Americas.* New York: Verso.

Larsen, Neil (2005). 'Imperialism, Colonialism, Postcolonialism', in H. Schwarz and S. Ray (eds), *A Companion to Postcolonial Studies.* Oxford: Blackwell, 23–52.

Lazarus, Neil (1998–9). 'Charting Globalization', *Race & Class*, 40.2–3: 91–109.

Lazarus, Neil (1999). *Nationalism and Cultural Practice in the Postcolonial World.* Cambridge: Cambridge University Press.

Lazarus, Neil (2002). 'The Fetish of "the West" in Postcolonial Theory', in C. Bartolovich and N. Lazarus (eds), *Marxism, Modernity and Postcolonial Studies.* Cambridge: Cambridge University Press, 43–64.

Lazarus, Neil (ed.) (2004). *The Cambridge Companion to Postcolonial Literary Studies.* Cambridge: Cambridge University Press.

Lazarus, Neil (2011). *The Postcolonial Unconscious.* Cambridge: Cambridge University Press.

Lazarus, Neil (2012). 'Spectres Haunting: Postcommunism and Postcolonialism', *Journal of Postcolonial Writing*, 48.2: 117–29.

Macey, David (2000). *Frantz Fanon: A Life.* London: Granta Books.

Marx, Karl (1990 [1867]). *Capital: A Critique of Political Economy*, vol. 1, trans. B. Fowkes. London: Penguin.

Marx, Karl and Friedrich Engels (1988 [1848]). *Manifesto of the Communist Party.* Beijing: Foreign Languages Press.

McClintock, Anne (1992). 'The Angel of Progress: Pitfalls of the Term "Post-colonial"', *Social Text*, 31/2: 84–98.

Nkrumah, Kwame (1980 [1965]). *Neo-Colonialism: The Last Stage of Imperialism.* New York: International Publishers.

Parry, Benita (2004a). 'The Institutionalization of Postcolonial Studies', in N. Lazarus (ed.) *The Cambridge Companion to Postcolonial Studies* (Cambridge: Cambridge University Press), pp. 66–80.

Parry, Benita (2004b). *Postcolonial Studies: A Materialist Critique*. London: Routledge.

Rodney, Walter (1982 [1972]). *How Europe Underdeveloped Africa*. Washington, DC: Howard University Press.

Said, Edward W. (1983). *The World, the Text, and the Critic*. Cambridge: Harvard University Press.

Said, Edward W. (1993). *Culture and Imperialism*. New York: Knopf.

San Juan, Jr., E. (1998). *Beyond Postcolonial Theory*. New York: St Martin's Press.

Shohat, Ella (1992). 'Notes on the "Post-Colonial"', *Social Text*, 31.2: 99–113.

Young, Robert J. C. (2001). *Postcolonialism: An Historical Introduction*. Oxford: Blackwell.

CHAPTER 15

POSTCOLONIALISM AND/AS TRANSLATION

SUSAN BASSNETT

INTRODUCTION

Translation in the twenty-first century has acquired global significance with the movement of millions more people around the planet than at any time in the past. Since the early 1990s, the end of the Cold War, the opening of China to the rest of the world, and the end of apartheid in South Africa have been just some of the major social and political turning points that have led to a marked increase of mobility for populations that had previously been more constrained. Where previous generations remained relatively static, with only a privileged (or desperate) minority willing to travel, today large numbers move in search of employment; to escape from famine, persecution, or natural disasters; or simply for leisure purposes, with a surge of tourism enabled by low-cost transportation to all corners of the world.

When people move, they take with them their languages, cultural practices, and belief systems, and consequently their encounters with others necessarily involve translation in some form. Since such negotiations take place in both the linguistic and cultural spheres, it is hardly surprising that there should be great interest in the theory and practice of translation at present. That interest has been developing in two nominally separate yet related fields, one of which can loosely be termed postcolonial theory and the other translation studies, and both of which rose quickly to prominence during the latter decades of the twentieth century. However, significant differences in approach, both in how translation is perceived and how the terminology of translation is utilized, have led some scholars to perceive the two fields as inimical to one another. This chapter will seek to trace these two broad lines of theorizing about translation, and will suggest that research is now moving towards a greater integration between them—an integration that offers exciting new possibilities for the future of both fields.

In-Betweenness

In his essay 'How Newness Enters the World' in *The Location of Culture*, Homi Bhabha posits a theory of 'in-betweenness' that involves 'a new international space of discontinuous historical realities' (1994: 217). This is a migrant or nomadic space where continuities are disrupted and where identities are unmade and remade in a vortex of change and uncertainty but—despite or possibly because of this—in a highly creative way. Bhabha's essay is prefaced by a quotation from Walter Benjamin, whose work on translation has been so significant since its first appearance in the early twentieth century: 'Translation passes through a *continua* of transformation, not abstract ideas of identity and similarity' (Benjamin 1996 [1916], quoted in Bhabha 1994: 212). Here as elsewhere, Benjamin draws attention to the constant process of change that is intrinsic to translation; since no two languages are identical, it follows that no translation can be identical to the original from which it derives. Translation implies movement; it *is* transformation in so far as it involves the recreation of a text elsewhere, in another context, where it will become another text altogether. Bhabha begins with Benjamin so as to focus on this idea of infinite movement and transformation, but also to highlight the *ambivalence* of translation, which takes place between two sites in a liminal space that does and does not belong to both 'source' and 'target' cultures. The contradiction at the heart of translation is that although the translator may set out to bring a text constructed in one context into another as effectively as he or she can manage, nevertheless the very act of translating forces the translator to confront those aspects of a text that actively resist being translated. The task of the translator is, at one level, to engage with the problem of the untranslatable. For as Edward Sapir, the American linguist, has argued, no two languages are ever sufficiently similar to be considered as representing the same social reality. The worlds in which different societies live are distinct worlds, not merely the same world with different labels attached (1956: 79).

Difference, then, is at the heart of any translation endeavour, for texts implicitly resist assimilation, and sentences constructed in one language refuse to be transposed in exactly the same way into another language, for what can be said in one language cannot simply be straitjacketed into another. Equivalence between languages is thus always a matter of negotiating the in-between, a highly charged space that 'carries the burden of the meaning of culture' (Bhabha 1994: 38). Bhabha argues that this is also the space in which translation occurs; after all, a frequent metaphor for the space occupied by the translator is no-man's-land, with all the associations of the battlefield that the phrase carries with it. Bhabha adapts Benjamin's idea of translation as interlingual activity to describe the back-and-forth movement between different cultural processes; he also takes Benjamin's idea of the untranslatable as resisting assimilation and applies it to what he perceives to be a new global reality: those migrant cultures he sees an inhabiting the differential spaces of the 'in-between'. These cultures, embodying a minority position, dramatize the activity of culture's untranslatability and, in so doing, move the question of culture's appropriation beyond the possibility of a full transmission of subject matter—the racist's nightmare or the assimilationist's dream (Bhabha 1994: 224; see also Benjamin 1992 [1923]).

Bhabha deploys the terminology of translation to write about the phenomenon of postcolonial 'migrant culture'. Postcolonial migration is, for him, above all else a *translational* phenomenon—a state in which meaning is constantly remade through encounters with other cultures. It is the opposite of historical colonialism, part of whose self-given task was to reproduce an original culture and to map the political, social, ethical, and aesthetic frameworks of that original onto other cultures. Seeking a language with which to describe migrant culture, Bhabha uses in-between terms like 'hybridity', 'liminality', and 'diversity'. The newness he writes about is a newness of migrant or minority discourse, one brought about by 'cultural translation'. The newness that enters the world comes about through encountering, challenging, interpreting, absorbing, juxtaposing, transposing, reformulating, forgetting, inventing, imagining—it comes about, in short, through the variegated, often conflicting activities and processes of *translation*. By the mid-1990s, translation had thus come to acquire a broad-based metaphoric significance in postcolonial writing as a term indicating movement, intercultural encounters, and the continual juggling of identities. Benjamin had previously posited the idea of translation as survival, as a means of ensuring the afterlife of a text that might otherwise cease to be read and remembered. This idea now came to acquire a new relevance in the postcolonial world, particularly in the light of Bhabha's work on 'migrant cultures' and Jacques Derrida's rereading of Benjamin, which extended the latter's idea of survival to the idea of living on the boundary, on borderlines, on the edge.

Cultural Translation

Distinct from postcolonial theory and practice, but running to some extent in parallel with it, cultural anthropology was also increasingly using the terminology of translation during the last couple of decades of the twentieth century. James Clifford (1997) and Clifford Geertz (1986) both problematized the facile representation of other cultures within anthropological discourse, arguing that the anthropologist constructs a version of another culture in a similar way to the task undertaken by a translator. Just as the translator plays a key role in shaping the translation, so the ethnographer plays a key role in shaping his or her research findings. The term 'cultural translation' came into vogue, both as a specific means of facilitating discussion of the complex processes in which anthropological researchers were entangled, and as a kind of rhetorical (and in turn sometimes facile) catch-all for processes of interpretation of the multiple sign systems across and between cultural borders in which numerous differentiating factors were at work.

At roughly the same time, the ideological implications of using the terminology of translation in this way were taken up in Talal Asad's important essay, 'The Concept of Cultural Translation in British Social Anthropology' (1986). Asad derives equivalences between anthropology and translation, but expresses concern about the power inequalities between languages, reminding us that non-western languages 'are more likely to submit to forcible transformation in the translation process than the other way round' (1986: 142). Asad's warning is important because he challenges the assumption that translation can take place on a horizontal axis, with source and target languages occupying equal positions of status. He also takes up the problem of using a primarily linguistic concept in a broad 'cultural' sense:

> One difference between the anthropologist and the linguist in the matter of translation is perhaps this: that whereas the latter is immediately faced with a specific piece of discourse produced within the society studied, a discourse that is *then* textualized, the former must construct the discourse *as* a cultural text in terms of meanings *implicit* in a range of practices. (1986: 149; emphasis in the original)

Asad highlights the difference here between translation conceived of metaphorically, as a way of talking about a physical experience of cultural encounter, and translation as it refers to the transfer of texts across linguistic boundaries. This is a crucial difference and failure to recognize it can lead—has led—to terminological and methodological confusion in both translation studies and postcolonial fields.

A decade later, in 1992, the US-based Indian scholar Tejaswini Niranjana published *Siting Translation: History, Post-Structuralism and the Colonial Context*, a landmark book in the dialogue between translation and postcolonial studies. Niranjana echoes Asad in challenging assumptions about translation in both literary studies and ethnography that fail to take into account the unequal power relations between languages. She suggests that the view of translation as a transparent and unbiased medium is not only naïve but can also be used detrimentally for hegemonic purposes. Translation, she insists, has 'reinforced hegemonic versions of the colonized, helping them to acquire the status of what Edward Said calls representation of objects without history' (1992: 176). She calls for greater recognition of the cultural contexts in which translations occur, arguing that they need to be seen as reciprocal, both informing and transforming established notions of culture and identity at large.

From these various examples it can be seen that the terminology of translation, and in particular cultural translation, can be employed in very different ways in different contexts. The word 'translation' has been used loosely, and nowhere more so than by Salman Rushdie when he declares that he and other diasporic postcolonial writers are 'translated men' (1991: 16). Here, of course, Rushdie is trying out some of the same ideas as Bhabha—translation conceived of as identity shift, as a form or process of cultural transposition—but the fact that he employs the terminology of translation is surely significant, as is his broad metaphorical usage of the key term.

Challenging Cultural Translation

The use of translation as a figurative term to explore postcolonial contexts has not found universal acceptance. For one thing, it fails to take account of the notion of translation as the transfer of texts across languages; cultural translation may be an exciting notion, but it focuses on the idea of exchange, not the reality of language contact. Harish Trivedi unequivocally attacks the use of a metaphorics of translation by monolinguals:

> In current theoretical discourse, then, to speak of post-colonial translation is little short of tautology. In our age of (the valorization of) migrancy, exile and diaspora, the word translation seems to have come full circle and reverted from its figurative literary meaning of an interlingual transaction to its etymological physical meaning of locational disrupture; translation itself seems to have been translated back to its origins. (Bassnett and Trivedi 1999: 13)

Trivedi's position is that of a multilingual scholar, well acquainted with western post-modernist and postcolonial theories and with debates about translation within India, a country with some of the greatest linguistic diversity anywhere in the world. He is understandably concerned by what he sees as the appropriation of a discourse of translation by scholars who are unable to translate because they can only function in a single language. In an unpublished lecture from 2007, he goes further and declares that what Bhabha means by translation is nothing less than 'the condition of Western multiculturalism brought about by Third World migrancy' (2007: 11). Trivedi's is a harsh indictment of cultural translation by an Indian scholar, concerned about the survival of what are perceived by many western scholars to be 'minority' languages and equally anxious about the hegemony of global English in its turn:

> Migrancy, often upper-class elite migrancy as for example from India, has already provided the First World with as much Newness as it needs and can cope with, and given it the illusion that this tiny fraction of the Third World has already made the First World the whole world, the only world there is. Those of us still located on our home turf and in our own cultures and speaking our own languages can no longer be seen or heard. (Trivedi 2007: 18)

Trivedi's critique of what he sees as being little more than a fashionable intellectual trend that marginalizes translation between languages is provocative and thought-provoking. But in his 2007 paper, he also attacks another group of scholars—those who define themselves as coming from within translation studies—for a failure to engage with translation discourse's increasing metaphoric spread. He refers here to the work of Bassnett and Lefevere and, particularly, to their 1998 study *Constructing Cultures*, where they express the hope that translation studies research and cultural studies (understood in its broadest sense) might work more closely together to investigate ways in which texts become cultural capital across cultural boundaries, and to explore the politics of translating and the ethnocentric violence that sometimes accompanies it. According to Trivedi, this cooperation simply has not happened and the two fields, despite the collaborative claims they like to make for themselves, do not appear to be moving in the same direction at all.

THE CULTURAL TURN IN TRANSLATION STUDIES

As postcolonial studies was starting to gain an institutional foothold—mostly in the English-speaking world—during the latter part of the twentieth century, so too was research in what has since come to be known as the 'translation studies' field. It is generally agreed that the American scholar James Holmes coined the term in his 1972 essay, 'The Name and Nature of Translation Studies', in which he argued that academic interest in translation was inexorably rising, with the Second World War operating as the crucial turning point. Though Holmes offers no further explanation for this, we can assume he had in mind the failure of machine translation as 'instant access' to other cultures, hailed as the new utopian solution for a Cold War world where timely communication was the goal. The project failed because of the narrow concept of equivalence that characterized machine translation—the naïve assumption that anything written in one language could be translated meaningfully and instantaneously into another. Ever since ancient times it had been accepted that there were two basic ways of translating: word for word or sense for sense, as Cicero and St Jerome put it, so a project based on the idea of absolute linguistic equivalence was doomed from the start.[1]

Rejecting the notion of equivalence as sameness between languages, Holmes focused instead on the complex processes of intersemiotic negotiation that take place whenever texts are translated. His views were shared by a small group of international researchers from a variety of different disciplines, and gradually the field gained credibility and status.[2] Central to early research in translation studies was an insistence on two issues: first, the vital importance of considering texts in context; and second, the need to move away from old-fashioned evaluative concepts of translation so as to explore the role played by translated texts as a force for innovation and renewal.

An essay published six years later, in 1978, by the Israeli scholar Itamar Even-Zohar then laid down the basis for the next stage of development of the fledgling discipline. In his awkwardly titled 'The Position of Translated Literature Within the Literary Polysystem', Even-Zohar set out a method for investigating the role of translated texts in literary history. He noted that there are periods when a great deal of translation activity takes place and other periods when little or nothing is translated, and observed that

---

[1.] See the relevant passage from Marcus Tullius Cicero's *De optimo genere oratorum*, trans. L. G. Kelly, in Weissbort and Eysteinsson (2006: 21). See also the two key texts by Eusebius Hieronymus (St Jerome), the Preface to *Chronicles* of Eusebius, and Letter 57 to Pammachius, 'On the Best Method of Translating', trans L. G. Kelly, in Weissbort and Eysteinsson (2006: 30–3).

[2.] These included Itamar Even-Zohar, Gideon Toury, José Lambert, Raymond van de Broek, André Lefevere; Susan Bassnett and Theo Hermans also took part in the Leuven seminar of 1975.

some cultures translate more than others. He also argued that translated texts vary both in the way in which they are received and in the influence they may exert, with some translations becoming a major force for innovation. From these observations he formulated a theory that posited three basic conditions for high levels of translation: (a) when a literature is 'young', in the process of being established; (b) when a literature is either 'peripheral' (within a large group of correlated literatures), or 'weak', or both; (c) when there are turning points, crises, or literary vacuums in a literature (Even-Zohar, in Venuti 2000: 194). The impact of these propositions was considerable and led, in the first instance, to dedicated research into the history of translation in different contexts, which posed an immediate challenge to established histories of literature that had previously tended to marginalize or disregard the significance of translation as a shaping force in individual national literatures. The explanation for this is easy to see: histories of literature are intimately bound up with issues of national identity, and to acknowledge the influence of translation is to recognize the hybridity of literary systems instead of seeing them as 'native' products. Moreover, the national model of literary history had a vested interest in guarding its own frontiers. André Lefevere neatly sums up the nationalist bias that underpinned the writing of much literary history during the nineteenth and twentieth centuries:

> Literary histories, as they have been written until recently, have had little or no time for translations, since for the literary historian translation had to do with 'language' only, not with literature—another outgrowth of the 'monolingualization' of literary history by Romantic historiographers intent on creating 'national' literatures preferably as uncontaminated as possible by foreign influences. (1992: 39)

Lefevere is referring here to monolingualization, but the issue is far broader. For example, it is only quite recently that the term 'English Literature' has come to mean literature written by English writers, one of many literatures written in English. Previously, the term had been used in a highly elitist manner, with a hierarchy of value that meant that anything not deemed to be acceptable as 'English Literature' was likely to be excluded (see McLeod in Part IV of this volume). The Nobel-winning Nigerian playwright Wole Soyinka recounts how, when he was Visiting Fellow at Cambridge in the 1970s, he was compelled to offer his lectures on African literature via the Department of Social Anthropology, since the Department of English simply 'did not believe in any such beast as "African literature"' (1976: vii). The drive to preserve the boundaries of English Literature led to what we would today consider to be a series of absurd territorial skirmishes, but these took place in the 1970s, not the 1930s—not long ago at all.

By focusing on the impact of translations in the receiving system, research in translation studies shifted the ground away from previous debates about whether a translation was a 'faithful' equivalent of the original. Such debates were untheorized and subjective, since criteria for assessing the faithfulness of textual transfer cannot be established once any notion of absolute linguistic equivalence is discarded and different times evolve different aesthetics. Translation studies drew upon reception theory, cultural studies, and cross-disciplinary approaches to intertextuality, effectively introducing an ideological dimension into discussions of translation by insisting on the importance of looking at it in its double contexts—original or 'source', and destination or 'target'—so as to take into account the manipulative processes that are intrinsic to textual transfers of all kinds.

By the early 1990s, translation studies had become a significant field of academic research. Programmes were emerging in colleges and universities, journals and monographs were proliferating, and international conferences and doctoral dissertations were flourishing across the world. The new approach to translation appealed to a younger multilingual, multicultural generation, and the insistence of translation studies that theory should be linked to and tested against practice ensured interdisciplinarity, with social and cultural history meeting linguistic philosophy through close textual analysis. Probably the keyword for this phase of translation research was *visibility*: visibility of the translator creating the text, visibility of the mechanics of textual production and dissemination, visibility of the strategies employed by the translator within the text itself. Lawrence Venuti's 1995 book, *The Translator's Invisibility: A History of Translation*, sought to effect a paradigm shift in the way in which translation and translators were perceived, stressing the role of the translator as a rewriter, not merely as a filter through which the material of a text, by some mysterious alchemical process, is anonymously transferred. Venuti called for a change in contemporary thinking about translation—a recognition, not only of the historical significance of translations, but also of the complexity of translation as a literary practice.

This call for greater visibility (of both translations and translators) was one of two major developments in translation studies in the 1990s. The other was the so-called 'cultural turn', exemplified by a collection of essays edited by Susan Bassnett and Andre Lefevere, *Translation, History and Culture* (1990). In their introduction, Bassnett and Lefevere state that 'what the development of Translation Studies shows is that translation, like all (re)writings, is never innocent. There is always a context in which the translation takes place, always a history from which a text emerges and into which a text is transposed ... Translation has been a major shaping force in the development of world culture, and no study of comparative literature can take place without regard to translation' (1990: 12). The central propositions of the cultural turn were straightforward enough: translation should be recognized as a literary activity central to the growth and development of individual literatures; it should be acknowledged that literatures are interconnected through translation; and it should also be accepted that translations do not happen in a vacuum since there is always a dual historical context.

POSTCOLONIAL TRANSLATION STUDIES

As translation studies developed, lines of enquiry exploring the links between gender and translation, power relations and translation, globalization and translation proliferated. A further major strand emerged: the postcolonial. In *The Poetics of Imperialism:*

Translation and Colonization from The Tempest *to* Tarzan (1991), Eric Cheyfitz, for example, considers some of the ways in which European colonizers used translation as a means of obtaining land rights. Analysing a seventeenth-century pamphlet, *A True Declaration of the Colonie in Virginia*, Cheyfitz shows how legal grounds for obtaining land from the Algonquian tribe were established via a document that gave a crown and sceptre to a local chief, Paspehay, in exchange for 'land to inherit and inhabite'. He then notes:

> In the first instance the English translate Paspehay into English property relations (and into English political relations as well, with his nomination as a 'king', a typical English translation of the Algonquian *weroance*) so that the English can recognize him as having sold 'his' land to the English, who following the 'legal' logic of their language can thus claim 'title' to this land. The English convert the land that Paspehay and his people use that nobody 'owns' (at least not in the Algonquian languages) into Paspehay's property. (1991: 60)

Cheyfitz points out that the legal repercussions of that translation were to last into the twentieth century, as for that matter have the legal ramifications of the Treaty of Waitangi, signed in 1840 by more than five hundred Māori chiefs and a representative of the British Crown (see Keown and Murray in Part V of this volume; also Smith and Turner in Part II). The treaty was regarded for some time (but no longer) as a model of cooperation between colonizer and colonized, and in a fascinating essay that traces the history of its translation, Sabine Fenton and Paul Moon show how concerns about the accuracy and viability of the translated document led to great bitterness and, ultimately, legal strife. A retranslation of the Treaty in 1869 to deal with the 'execrable Māori' of the first version revealed significant differences and opened the way for challenges to the terms of the 1840 document. It was not until 1975 that the Waitangi Tribunal was established to deal with grievances arising from errors in the original translation, which may or may not have been intentional. As Fenton and Moon put it, the case of the translation of the Treaty of Waitangi

> confirms the view that translations reflect the imperatives of their context, their time and their culture. Translators, caught in a web of often contradictory relationships, will resolve the tensions according to their understanding of their own position and role within their culture ... translation becomes even more problematic when source and target cultures are substantially different. Once the divide between two cultures includes great power disparities, culture becomes untranslatable. (Fenton and Moon 2002: 41–2)

Both the Algonquian and Māori cases are examples of ways in which translation can disempower not just individuals but entire cultures through the unequal power held by different languages. Another example is the way in which Native American names came to be regularly translated in the nineteenth century, the English versions serving to accentuate 'civilized' opinions about the barbarity and infantilism of tribespeople

named after animals or birds. The significance of translation as an instrument in establishing colonial systems and structures is huge, though it has received relatively little
scholarly attention until recently. Translation studies has useful tools at its disposal here.
It is able, for example, to engage directly with the problem of unequal linguistic power
relations, exposing the manipulative processes that underpin the act of translating. Even
where the political purpose of a translation is less apparent, it is clear that translators
produce texts specifically designed for a target readership, hence the dominant norms
of production are those that belong to that readership. As Ovidio Carbonell puts it in his
essay on translation and exoticism:

> When the actual procedure of cultural transmission takes place, the linguistic,
> as well as the overall semiotic structures of the source (object) culture are made to
> cohere in the light of the structures of the target (subject) culture. Rather than textual
> translation, a contextual translation takes place. A context is sought to be reproduced
> [sic] by making the linguistic fragments of the alien culture make sense, that is, fit
> into the context of the target culture. (Carbonell 1996: 85)

Here as elsewhere, translation becomes a means of shaping the alien into textual
forms that are acceptable to the target culture. This can be accomplished in many different ways, and increasingly postcolonial translation scholars have drawn attention
to examples of this particular kind of textual manipulation. One of the best-known
cases is Edward FitzGerald's translation of *The Rubáiyát of Omar Khayyam*, first published in 1858 and one of the rare cases of a translation to have entered the English
literary canon. FitzGerald famously wrote that a live sparrow was better than a dead
eagle and a live dog better than a dead lion; in other words, he recognized that his
translation was a lesser creature than the Persian original. However, a few years before
his translation appeared, he wrote to a friend expressing his less than flattering opinion of Persian poetry in general: 'It is an amusement to me to take what liberties I like
with these Persians, who (as I think) are not Poets enough to frighten one from such
excursions, and who really do want a little Art to shape them' (FitzGerald, quoted in
Bassnett 2002: 3). With *The Rubáiyát*, Fitzgerald produced a poem that, after a halt-
ing start, became one of the most popular works of the nineteenth century, appealing to a readership eager to encounter the fabulous East. It is beautifully done, full
of striking images, composed in strongly rhymed quatrains with a distinct rhythm,
though it diverges substantially from the original, especially in terms of the poem's
underlying philosophical basis. The Sufi mysticism of the original has been changed
in FitzGerald's version into a poem spoken by a hedonist, with the underlying message of *carpe diem*. It is a fine example of translation as rewriting: the problem is not
the reshaping as such, but the translator's expressed sense of superiority over the culture of the original.

Mahasweta Sengupta examines this very issue in her essay, 'Translation as
Manipulation: The Power of Images and Images of Power' (1995). She draws attention
to the image-making process that leads translators to construct notions of the other that

will preserve or extend the hegemony of the dominant culture, and notes that the selection of texts for translation is the first stage in this manipulative process:

> By formulating an identity that is acceptable to the dominant culture, the translator selects and rewrites only those texts that conform to the target culture's 'image' of the source culture; the rewriting often involves intense manipulation and simplification for the sake of gaining recognition in and by the metropole. (1995: 160)

In this way, a homogeneous image of another culture is constructed, and expectations are created that subsequent translators will strive to meet. In the case of *The Rubáiyát*, a twentieth-century attempt to produce a translation that tried to bring across to English-language readers the religious philosophy of the original was an utter failure, for FitzGerald's version had created a set of expectations that had become effectively unalterable (Franklin 2011). Once an image of a culture created by a successful translation is established, it becomes extremely difficult to change, regardless of how that image was initially formed. Focusing on Indian literatures, Sengupta argues that over time, a problematic image of Indian writing was built up through a selective process of (English) translation—an image of Indian culture foregrounding its simplicity, naturalness, and childlike innocence. English translators from Sir William Jones onwards erased the explicitly erotic from many texts and, choosing instead to translate works that were either religious or spiritual, reinforced the image of India as 'safely tame, singularly other-worldly, and quite domesticated in relation to the self of the dominant power' (Sengupta 1995: 162).

THE COLONY AS TRANSLATION

Benjamin reminds us in his essay that the original is closely connected to the translation: indeed that the two are intimately linked, for without an original a translation cannot exist. Simply put, there has to be a prior text for there to be a translation, since in translating there is always a point of origin somewhere else. Translation is an act that takes place between languages and cultures, hence an intercultural process, but it is also intertemporal since the original came into being in some other place at some other moment in time. This means there is a memory implicit in translation, for however divergent the translation may be from an original the memory of that original is always present. Translation, in this sense, can be seen as a process of transformation, a kind of journey from source to target and an act of remembrance. Elsewhere in this part of the volume, Michael Rothberg argues for closer links between postcolonial studies and memory studies; translation as memory is another important element in this discussion.

One of the concerns of postcolonial translation research is, as suggested above, the unequal power relations between cultures and hence between languages. This has resulted in a one-way traffic of translations, since during the colonial period the tendency was for literary texts to be translated into European languages for consumption by European readers, effectively foreclosing on the possibility of mutual exchange. Translation from European languages during this period mainly involved missionary activity, the Bible and other sacred texts being the principal translations undertaken. The positive side to this kind of translation was the preservation of numerous indigenous languages, since early Bible translators often compiled bilingual dictionaries and grammars of the languages into which they were translating, though on the negative side, this also meant that in the preservation process indigenous languages were reformulated so as to conform to European codification systems. Such endeavours were frequently collaborative, involving first-language converts as well as European missionary-translators, the result of their labour being what Isabel Hofmeyr in her illuminating book *The Portable Bunyan: A Transnational History of The Pilgrim's Progress* describes as 'a mission-made language not always fully recognizable to its speakers and a world of racially supervised literary and cultural production' (2004: 22).

The relative one-sidedness of translation activity between European and non-European languages raises a fundamental issue regarding the significance of translation today. Prior to the seventeenth century, the status of translation was by no means inferior to that of 'original' writing; indeed, the concept of originality is arguably an innovation that came into force at some point in the seventeenth century, in an age when textual property rights began to take on force. Once translations were perceived as somehow inferior to other forms of writing, their status dropped, and this can be seen through the changes in figurative language used to talk about translation. Whereas in the sixteenth century metaphors for the translation process included searching for treasure or exchanging clothing, a century later the figurative language was more pejorative, with translations being seen as 'copies' or 'mirrors' held up to a clearly superior original. Translations were now viewed as second-hand and second class, and it is hardly coincidental that this shift should have occurred during the great age of colonial expansion. For the colony itself can be seen as a translation of the great European Original; what was exported was a vision of Europe, with the colony destined to be a translation of a superior original that had come into being somewhere else and at another point in time. Though linked to an original, both the translation and the colony were seen as mere copies or reflections of a greater source.

RESISTANCE THROUGH CANNIBALISM

One of the most provocative postcolonial contributions to discussions about translation has come from writers and theoreticians in Brazil. For more than a century in Latin America, intellectuals have been arguing about how to rethink the exchange between their cultures and those of their European former colonizers. One perceived problem was the relationship between their own developing literary traditions and the European literatures they had read, admired, and absorbed. Writers across the continent felt the need to find ways to assert themselves without being labelled as mere 'copyists' of European models, but without simply rejecting either everything of value that had originated in Europe. The celebrated *Manifesto Antropófago* (1928) of Oswald de Andrade offered a way forward for Brazilian intellectuals via a witty yet at the same time wholly serious rethinking of an infamous episode from Brazilian history.

The episode in question, from the sixteenth century, refers to the indigenous Tupinamba, members of which tribe killed and ate Bishop Sardinha, a missionary Catholic priest. The incident appalled his contemporaries, cannibalism being the ultimate taboo for European Christians. Yet, for the Tupi, eating a respected alien was not only not barbaric, it was an act of homage, a way of recognizing the priest's importance. In a sense, the Tupi had literally translated the Christian message of the Eucharist, when the body and blood of Christ are ritually and symbolically devoured. In returning to this well-known episode, de Andrade was also concerned to rethink it, noting that Brazilians were descended from the tribes of both devourers and devoured and proposing an alternative way to reassess their relationship with Europe. His conclusion was that whatever came from Europe could be used to strengthen Brazilian culture if it was 'devoured' on Brazilian terms. Else Ribeiro Pires Vieira sums up de Andrade's radical proposition, noting that in his manifesto he plays with the phonic similarity between 'Tupi' and the English 'to be'. 'Tupi or not Tupi' ('To be or not to be') is thus a cannibalized quotation from Shakespeare:

> The devouring of Shakespeare and the revitalization of Hamlet's dilemma in the *Manifesto* points to the assimilative perspective of cannibalism both as a programme and a praxis: foreign input, far from being denied, is absorbed and transformed, which brings cannibalism and the dialogical principle close together.
> (Vieira 1999: 98)

The manifesto had a massive impact on Brazilian critical discourse and, a few decades later, on translation theory and practice in particular. During the 1960s, two leading poets and translators, Haroldo and Augusto de Campos, began to break away from the binary association of original and translation, using the cannibal metaphor as a way of talking about translation as a creative act in its own right. Brazilian literature, they insisted, constitutes the 'non-origin', and the translator has the right to devour and remake any so-called 'original'. Translation, Haroldo de Campos claimed, needs to break with the ties that bind it to a source if it is to be truly creative—it needs to be 'parricidal dis-memory':

> Any past which is an 'other' for us deserves to be negated. We could say that it deserves to be eaten, devoured. With this clarification and specification: the cannibal was a polemicist (from the Greek polemos, meaning struggle or combat) but he was also an 'anthologist': he devoured only the enemies he considered strong, to take from them the marrow and protein to fortify and renew his own natural energies.
> (1999: 103)

The notion of translation as cannibalism has spread rapidly in the last few decades since it offers a particularly effective postcolonial strategy for dealing with what had long been seen as an epistemological stalemate: the implicit power of the (European) original over its translation. The work of the de Campos brothers has inspired a whole generation of writers and translators, not just in their own country and across Latin America, but around the world. Edwin Gentzler looks at the impact of the cannibal theory of translation across the Americas in his 2008 book *Translation and Identity in the Americas*, suggesting that the cannibal metaphor has become a primary tool for the expression of independent identity, an independence that 'creates new cultural conditions that allow for the possibility of rethinking one's own past' (2008: 107).

THE TRANSLATION ZONE

As previously suggested, the cultural turn in translation studies expanded the boundaries of research into translation from the narrowly linguistic to the socio-cultural. Research into the history of translation exposed the ways in which translators had manipulated texts in the interests of the receiving culture, most notably when translations were being made into European languages from non-European languages, and also revealed gaps or lacunae in national literary historiography that could only be explained by recognizing the significance of translation at particular times. The cultural turn served a purpose in bringing ideological issues back into discourse about translation, and marked a clear break from earlier methods of approaching translation built around decontextualized ideas of fidelity and accuracy.

However, it would be wrong to assume that the kind of translation studies that has developed in the west is universally acceptable. There is a long-standing tradition of local translation theory in China, but there has also been a boom in translation activity since the late 1980s when China began to open up to the rest of the world. Xie Ming summarizes the Chinese dilemma as follows:

> Globalization in the modern Chinese context has largely been a continuous movement of attraction and attrition … Modern China is forced to globalize under the sign of the West, even while it has never relinquished its own traditional assumptions of Chinese universal culture (and empire). (2008: 17; see also Vukovich in Part V of this volume)

Chinese translation studies must therefore wrestle with its own traditions in relation to the influx of thinking about translation coming from the west, e.g. as a product of the cultural turn, and must ask serious questions about the applicability of western models and western postcolonial translation discourse. Translation is an important issue for contemporary Chinese academics: the shift in China towards greater global involvement, commercially and politically, has led to high demand for translators, hence the training of translators is paramount and it is essential to have a good grasp of what translation actually involves.

But while China moves towards greater linguistic awareness, the epochal events of '9/11' highlighted the dearth of skilled translators in Middle Eastern languages in the United States and revealed another side to the apparent global hegemony of English. Concerned by the exposure of her country's monolingualism at this time of crisis, Emily Apter produced an important book, *The Translation Zone*, significantly subtitled *A New Comparative Literature* (2006). In the book, Apter draws on the influential idea of the 'contact zone', previously formulated by Mary Louise Pratt, as a space of encounter between peoples in which discursive transformations occur as different groups seek to represent themselves to one another.[3] The contact zone may be a site of violence and disruption, but it remains an enabling theoretical space where cultural differences and their imaginative possibilities can be explored. Apter ambitiously attempts a broad intellectual topography that does not belong to any single nation but is rather 'a zone of critical engagement that connects the "l" and "n" of transLation and transNation' (2006: 5). She defines translation in this context as an act both of love and of disruption, pointing out that translating takes individuals out of their 'comfort zone' of national space and forces them to engage with otherness. The experience of learning another language challenges expectations, while the recognition of the untranslatable compels individuals to confront the question of what belongs, or does not belong, to any one language in particular. Translation is therefore 'a significant medium of subject re-formulation and political change' (2006: 6): there are both personal and political dimensions to it.

Apter's book broke new ground in reclaiming translation as a fundamental aspect of contemporary communication, and in positioning the study of translation at the heart of what she argues is a new comparative literature. Significantly, in her view there is no contradiction between translation as metaphor and translation practice. Similarly, she acknowledges the importance of both practical research within translation studies and the work of those theorists from Derrida to Spivak who have offered postcolonial rereadings of Benjamin, her dual aim being to assert the value of learning other languages (she is, after all, a professor of French) and 'to imagine a field in which philology is linked to globalization, to Guantanamo Bay, to war and peace, to the Internet and "Netlish" and to "other Englishes" spoken worldwide, not to mention the languages of cloning and computer simulation' (2006: 11). Translation thus becomes the primary tool in a contemporary vision that seeks to encompass multiple forms of communication.

[3.] Mary Louise Pratt's concept of the 'contact zone' as a border territory or no-man's-land, understood both literally and metaphorically, has been widely used in translation studies and in the study of travel writing.

TRANSLATION AND WORLD LITERATURE

Equally large claims for the significance of translation have been made by another comparativist scholar, Bella Brodzki, in her 2007 book *Can These Bones Live? Translation, Survival, and Cultural Memory*. Brodzki insists that translations do not belong to a separate sphere of literary production; rather, translations are rewritings and, as such, necessarily involve reading and rereading. Translations are texts that reflect the changing conditions of the socio-political contexts in which they are created. In this sense, translation is not simply a technical process of rendering a text written in one language into another, but is a phenomenon that underpins 'all cultural transactions, from the most benign to the most venal' (2007: 2), and it deserves the kind of seminal critical attention that is given to considerations of gender in cultural analysis:

> Just as it has become impossible, for example, to explore authorship, agency, subjectivity, performativity, multiculturalism, postcolonialism, transnationalism, diasporic literacy, and technological literacy without considering the impact of gender as an intersecting category of analysis, so should it be inconceivable to overlook translation's integral role in every discursive field. (2007: 2)

Brodski and Apter are two key figures taking comparative literature into a new era. Spivak's critique of traditional models of comparative literature, *Death of a Discipline*, had previously appeared in 2003, when she called for an end to the ritual battle between comparative literature and cultural/ethnic studies, and for a renewed emphasis on the centrality of translation together with a move towards a new 'planetary' approach to global issues and problems. That call has been echoed in the rapid development of World Literature as a field of investigation (particularly in the US) that seems set to expand in the twenty-first century. Spivak highlights the problematic status of the nation in traditional comparative literature, as well as the marginalization of translation, and argues that the time has come to move on. Critical exponents of World Literature see themselves as part of this revolutionizing process.

Mads Rosendahl Thomsen's *Mapping World Literature: International Canonization and Transnational Literatures* (2008), for example, sets out the parameters of the field, explaining its relationship both to comparative literature and to postcolonialism through the influential work of such scholars as Casanova, Damrosch, and Moretti. Thomsen ventures into tricky terrain, suggesting that postcolonialism 'has not come up with particularly convincing ideas and methods for dealing with the literature of the traditional centres of literature, the old colonizers' (2008: 25). In his view, and echoing Spivak, this had led to the 'irrational divide' (25) between objects of study in comparative literature and in postcolonial studies. If we choose to see translation studies as being more closely linked in terms of its development to comparative literature, we can consider this divide to be another aspect of the same conflict between translation as practice and translation as theory—as philosophical conceptualization—that Trivedi has attacked.

For if postcolonial theorists have on the whole ignored translation studies, it is also the case that translation studies has been more closely aligned with traditional comparative literature methodologies. Approaching the study of literary translations from within a World Literature model represents one way of working towards a resolution of these conflicts, since literature is studied in terms of global flows and translation is at the heart of these (see, for example, Casanova 2004; Damrosch 2003, 2008; d'Haen 2011; d'Haen et al. 2012; Moretti 1996, 1998).

In her introduction to a special issue of the recently established journal *Translation Studies*, Doris Bachmann-Medick discusses what she calls 'the translational turn' in the humanities in general. She argues that the horizon of translation is expanding and differentiating and that translation can and should serve as an analytical concept for social theory, cultural theory, history, and theories of interculturality that no longer remains on a metaphorical level but is worked out on the basis of demonstrable empirical processes (2009: 4). The translational turn coincides with calls for a new 'planetarity'—a vision of World Literature that no longer revolves around European models and in which translation plays a crucial role in facilitating the multiple linguistic/cultural encounters of the contact zone.[4] Perhaps most importantly, it reflects a greater recognition of the importance of translation in *all* cultural transactions, both metaphorical and literal, which might serve as the vital prelude to breaking down artificially constructed divisions between analytical fields.

References

Apter, Emily (2006). *The Translation Zone: A New Comparative Literature*. Princeton: Princeton University Press.

Asad, Talal (1986). 'The Concept of Cultural Translation in British Social Anthropology', in J. Clifford and G. Marcus (eds), *Writing Culture*. Berkeley: University of California Press, 140–61.

Bachmann-Medick, Doris (2009). 'Introduction: The Translational Turn', *Translation Studies*, 2:1: 2–16.

Bassnett, Susan (2002). *Translation Studies*, 3rd edn. London: Routledge.

Bassnett, Susan and André Lefevere (eds) (1990). *Translation, History and Culture*. London: Cassell.

Bassnett, Susan and André Lefevere (1998). *Constructing Cultures*. Clevedon: Multilingual Matters.

Bassnett, Susan and Harish Trivedi (eds) (1999). *Postcolonial Translation: Theory and Practice*. London: Routledge.

[4.] Gayatri Chakravorty Spivak develops the notion of 'planetarity' as an alternative to globalization in the following terms: 'as presumed collectivities cross borders under the auspices of a Comparative Literature supplemented by Area Studies, they might attempt to figure themselves—imagine themselves—as planetary rather than continental, global or worldly ... The globe is on our computers. No one lives there. It allows us to think that we can aim to control it. The planet is in the species of alterity, belonging to another system, and yet we inhabit it, on loan' (2003: 72).

Benjamin, Walter (1996 [1916]). 'On Language as Such and the Language of Man', trans. E. Jephcott, in Marcus Bullock and Michael W. Jennings (eds), *Walter Benjamin: Selected Writings*, Vol. I. Cambridge, Mass.: Harvard University Press (Belknap), 62–74.

Benjamin, Walter (1992 [1923]). 'The Task of the Translator', trans. Harry Zohn, in Rainer Schulte and John Biguenet (eds), *Theories of Translation: An Anthology of Essays from Dryden to Derrida*. Chicago and London: University of Chicago Press, 71–82.

Bhabha, Homi (1994). *The Location of Culture*. London: Routledge.

Brodzki, Bella (2007). *Can These Bones Live? Translation, Survival, and Cultural Memory*. Stanford: Stanford University Press.

Carbonell, Ovidio (1996). 'The Exotic Space of Cultural Translation', in R. Álvarez and C.-Á. Vidal (eds), *Translation, Power, Subversion*. Clevedon: Multilingual Matters, 79–88.

Casanova, Pascale (2004). *The World Republic of Letters*. Cambridge, Mass.: Harvard University Press.

Cheyfitz, Eric (1991). *The Poetics of Imperialism: Translation and Colonization from* The Tempest *to* Tarzan. New York and Oxford: Oxford University Press.

Clifford, James (1997). *Routes: Travel and Translation in the Late Twentieth Century*. London and Cambridge Mass.: Harvard University Press.

Damrosch, David (2003). *What is World Literature?* Princeton: Princeton University Press.

Damrosch, David (2008). *Teaching World Literature*. New York: Modern Language Association.

De Andrade, Oswald (1928). 'Manifesto Antropófago', *Revista da Antrópofago*, 1.

De Andrade, Oswald (1991). 'Oswald de Andrade's Cannibalist Manifesto', trans. L. Bary, *Latin American Literary Review*, 19.38: 335–47.

Derrida, Jacques (1985). 'Des Tours de Babel', trans. J. F. Graham, in J. F. Graham (ed.), *Difference in Translation*. Ithaca: Cornell University Press, 165–248.

D'Haen, Theo (ed.) (2011). *The Routledge Concise History of World Literature*. London: Routledge.

D'Haen, Theo, César Domínguez, and Mads Rosendahl Thomsen (eds) (2012). *World Literature: A Reader*. London: Routledge.

Dingwaney, Anuradha and Carol Maier (eds) (1995). *Between Languages and Cultures: Translation and Cross-Cultural Texts*. Pittsburgh and London: University of Pittsburgh Press.

Even-Zohar, Itamar (2000 [1978]). 'The Position of Translated Literature within the Literary Polysystem', in L. Venuti (ed.), *The Translation Studies Reader*. London: Routledge, 192–7.

Fenton, Sabine and Paul Moon (2002). 'The Translation of the Treaty of Waitangi: A Case of Disempowerment', in M. Tymoczko and E. Gentzler (eds), *Translation and Power*. Amherst: University of Massachussetts Press, 25–44.

Franklin, Michael J. (2011). *Orientalist Jones*. Oxford: Oxford University Press.

Geertz, Clifford (1986). 'The Uses of Diversity', *Michigan Quarterly Review*, 25.1: 105–23.

Gentzler, Edwin (2008). *Translation and Identity in the Americas*. London: Routledge.

Hofmeyr, Isabel (2004). *The Portable Bunyan: A Transnational History of* The Pilgrim's Progress. Princeton: Princeton University Press.

Holmes, James (2000 [1972]). 'The Name and Nature of Translation Studies', in L. Venuti (ed.), *The Translation Studies Reader*. London: Routledge, 172–85.

Lefevere, André (1992). *Translation, Rewriting and the Manipulation of Literary Fame*. London: Routledge.

Moretti, Franco (1996). *Modern Epic: The World System from Goethe to García Márquez*. London: Verso.

Moretti, Franco (1998). *Atlas of the European Novel, 1500–1900*. London: Verso.

Niranjana, Tejaswini (1992). *Siting Translation: History, Post-Structuralism, and the Colonial Context*. Berkeley: University of California Press.

Pratt, Mary Louise (1992). *Imperial Eyes: Travel Writing and Transculturation*. London: Routledge.

Rushdie, Salman (1991). *Imaginary Homelands: Essays and Criticism 1981–1991*. London: Granta.

Sapir, Edward (1956). *Culture, Language and Personality*. Berkeley: University of California Press.

Schulte, Rainer and John Biguenet (eds) (1992). *Theories of Translation: An Anthology of Essays from Dryden to Derrida*. Chicago and London: University of Chicago Press.

Sengupta, Mahasweta (1995). 'Translation as Manipulation: The Power of Images and Images of Power', in A. Dingwaney and C. Maier (eds), *Between Languages and Cultures: Translation and Cross-Cultural Texts*. Pittsburgh and London: University of Pittsburgh Press, 159–80.

Soyinka, Wole (1976). *Myth, Literature and the African World*. Cambridge: Cambridge University Press.

Spivak, Gayatri Chakravorty (2003). *Death of a Discipline*. New York: Columbia University Press.

Thomsen, Mads Rosendahl (2008). *Mapping World Literature: International Canonization and Transnational Literatures*. London: Continuum.

Trivedi, Harish (2007). 'Translating Culture vs. Cultural Translation'. Unpublished paper.

Tymoczko, Maria and Edwin Gentzler (eds) (2002). *Translation and Power*. Amherst: University of Massachussetts Press.

Venuti, Lawrence (1995). *The Translator's Invisibility: A History of Translation*. London: Routledge.

Venuti, Lawrence (ed.) (2000). *The Translation Studies Reader*. London: Routledge.

Vieira, Else Ribeiro Pires (1999). 'Liberating Calibans: Readings of *Antropofagia* and Haroldo de Campos' Poetics of Liberation', in S. Bassnett and H. Trivedi (eds), *Postcolonial Translation: Theory and Practice*. London: Routledge, 95–113.

Wang Ning and Sun Yifeng (eds) (2008). *Translation, Globalisation and Localisation: A Chinese Perspective*. Clevedon: Multilingual Matters.

Weissbort, Daniel and Astradur Eysteinsson (eds) (2006). *Translation—Theory and Practice: A Historical Reader*. Oxford: Oxford University Press.

Xie Ming (2008). 'Transvaluing the Global: Translation, Modernity and Hegemonic Discourse', in W. Ning and S. Yifeng (eds), *Translation, Globalisation and Localisation: A Chinese Perspective*. Clevedon: Multilingual Matters, 15–30.

CHAPTER 16

REMEMBERING BACK

*Cultural Memory, Colonial Legacies,
and Postcolonial Studies*[1]

MICHAEL ROTHBERG

The field of postcolonial studies has had a paradoxical relation to cultural memory. On the one hand, the most influential monographs, anthologies, companions, and guidebooks to postcolonial studies have largely left the category of memory out of their theory and practice of the field. A scanning of the indexes of field-defining books, such as Edward Said's *Orientalism* (1978), Bill Ashcroft, Gareth Griffiths, and Helen Tiffin's *The Empire Writes Back* (1989), Kwame Anthony Appiah's *In My Father's House* (1993), Homi Bhabha's *The Location of Culture* (1994), and Gayatri Spivak's *A Critique of Postcolonial Reason* (1999), along with influential anthologies and textbooks, such as Ashcroft, Griffiths, and Tiffin's *The Post-Colonial Studies Reader* (1995), turns up almost no mention of memory.[2] Conversely, memory studies has largely avoided the issues of colonialism and its legacies, both in its founding texts and in many of its more recent assessments. Even a cutting-edge and comprehensive compendium such as Susannah Radstone and Bill Schwarz's *Memory: Histories, Theories, Debates* (2010) contains no entry for postcolonial studies and only scattered references to colonialism, although it foregrounds related debates in the politics of memory.[3]

[1]. I am grateful to Graham Huggan for comments on early drafts and to Cristina Stanciu for research assistance.

[2]. Spivak's *In Other Worlds* (1988b) does not have an index, but memory as such is not an explicit concern there either. In all of the books mentioned above, only *The Post-Colonial Studies Reader* includes 'memory' in its index. There it appears three times, with two references pointing to an extract from Derek Walcott's *The Muse of History* and the final one to Dipesh Chakrabarty's influential essay 'Postcoloniality and the Artifice of History'.

[3]. Colonialism also appears only marginally in Olick, Vinitzky-Seroussi, and Levy's large anthology of writings on collective memory (2011). More attention to postcolonial studies is given in the introduction to Michael Rossington and Anne Whitehead's useful collection of source texts *Theories of Memory* (2007).

Despite this surprising deficit of references, it can easily be argued that issues related to cultural memory make up some of the core concerns of postcolonial studies. One of the signal controversies that accompanied the emergence of postcolonial studies as an interdisciplinary academic field in the late 1980s and early 1990s, for instance, concerned the meaning of the 'post' in postcolonial studies. Influential essays by Kwame Anthony Appiah (1993), Anne McClintock (1992), and Ella Shohat (1992), among others, questioned the temporality of the 'post' and its relation to other 'post' discourses, especially postmodernism. At stake in such debates was whether the moniker 'postcolonial' suggested a clean break from the colonial past—a meaning very few scholars have actually embraced—or whether the 'post' indicated some other relation to colonialism, either a temporal 'hang-over' or 'lag' or, alternatively, an oppositional 'against' or 'in response to'. As the 'post' debates indicate, the self-critical reflection of postcolonial studies on its own conditions of possibility, which has always accompanied the development of the field, has concerned above all that field's fundamental relation to the *disjunctive temporality* of colonial legacies— colonialism's ability to colonize not just space, but time as well. Such disjunctive temporality also indicates the field's proximity to debates in memory studies, where concern with the relative weight and 'mixture' of past and present in a temporality beyond any notion of linearity or 'homogenous empty time' has been an originary and ongoing source of productive dispute.[4]

To get a first sense of the potential overlapping concerns of postcolonial studies and memory studies, consider such matters as: the erasure of the pre-colonial past by the invasion of colonialism, the reappropriation of that past by anti-colonial struggles, and its subsequent reconfiguration by postcolonial regimes; the cultural legacies of colonialism in the postcolonial present embodied in matters of language and education; the nostalgia for empire or pre-contact conditions in film, literature, and scholarship; the production of memoirs and autobiographical essays by leading scholars in the field (including Appiah, Diawara, Said, Spivak, and Suleri); and the rereading of the archives of imperial dominance by contemporary historians and critics. The understanding of such phenomena—taken both from the postcolonial world and the world of postcolonial studies—ought to benefit from an analytic lens honed by memory studies, but both that field and postcolonial studies itself have in the past largely avoided such an approach. Nevertheless, the easy enumeration of such phenomena signals that further reckoning with the relation between cultural memory, colonial legacies, and postcolonial studies is certain to be fruitful for scholars in a variety of fields.

Indeed, such a project is especially timely because both cultural memory studies and postcolonial studies are presently showing an increased convergence around shared

---

⁴ Walter Benjamin's critique of 'homogenous, empty time' (Benjamin 1968: 261) is a commonplace in both postcolonial studies and memory studies, an overlap perhaps traceable in part to Benedict Anderson's appropriation of the term as a way of talking about the time of the nation (Anderson 2006). Bill Schwarz emphasizes that modern memory is defined above all by its disjunctive temporality and 'perpetual dysfunctions' (Schwarz 2010: 42).

themes and problems. If the founding texts of cultural memory studies were surprisingly silent about the significance of colonialism and its after-effects, a current turn toward various forms of transnational and transcultural memory practices has begun to bring questions of empire and globalization to the forefront of the field.[5] Meanwhile, although the initiating texts of postcolonial studies do not employ an explicit vocabulary of memory, a turn toward practices of remembrance can be seen among postcolonial scholars in recent years. Numerous essays and monographs since the turn of the millennium have studied the impact of colonialism, decolonization, and postcolonial recalibration on conceptions of the colonial and pre-colonial past, and on practices of remembrance by the colonized and the colonizer as well as their postcolonial and post-imperial avatars.[6]

This chapter attempts both to explain the missed encounter that attended the formation of the fields of memory studies and postcolonial studies in the 1980s and 1990s and to map out productive sites of overlap between them as they grow increasingly proximate to each other. I first briefly describe the field of cultural memory studies and point out its failure to address colonial legacies, and then turn to the ways in which anti-colonial and postcolonial thinkers have addressed the presence of the past without necessarily employing the term 'memory'. In a subsequent section, I provide a literary example of what imperial memory looks like from a postcolonial perspective, a perspective that also suggests the usefulness of a media studies approach to remembrance. I end by turning to the context of the Algerian War of Independence in order to recommend a 'multidirectional' model attuned to the transnational and transcultural politics of memory. The emerging proximity of postcolonial and memory studies helps to shed light on both fields as discourses that seek to mediate the past in the present: while memory studies predominantly investigates the cultural mediation of temporality, postcolonial studies predominantly attends to the cultural and political mediation of imperial and neo-imperial violence. The benefit of considering these two overarching forms of mediation together lies in a new understanding of how violence fundamentally shapes the temporality of modern memory and how regimes of memory help propagate and potentially resist violence through the creation of unexpected solidarities.

[5.] In addition to work cited elsewhere, see Assmann and Conrad (2010); Crownshaw (2011); Levy and Sznaider (2010); Rothberg (2009).

[6.] One of the earliest attempts to synthesize memory studies and postcolonial studies—albeit from a particular disciplinary and area studies perspective—comes in Werbner 1998. As Werbner writes at the end of his introduction: 'Here lies the challenge of our contribution: *Memory and the Postcolony* locates politicized memory at the very heart of postcolonial studies' (15). Although much work has taken up this challenge in the years since then, I would not say that postcolonial studies as a whole has embraced this vision of the field. But see Huggan (2002) as well as the following collections: Mageo (2001); Hargreaves (2005); and Sengupta (2009). Recent monographs emerging from a variety of disciplines and areas include Cole (2001); Winston (2001); Woods (2007).

CULTURAL MEMORY STUDIES AND THE
AVOIDANCE OF COLONIALISM

I begin by surveying three of the most significant points of departure for contemporary memory studies in order to assess their possible articulations with a postcolonial lens. The study of cultural memory has a variety of sources and draws on diverse theoretical predecessors, but its most obvious beginning in the modern period lies in the work of the French sociologist Maurice Halbwachs, a student of Durkheim. Writing in the 1920s, Halbwachs considered what he called 'collective memory' in relation to 'social frameworks' (*cadres sociaux*) (see Halbwachs 1992). He argued that social forces shape even seemingly individual memories by providing a framework or 'language' through which subjects recall their pasts. Emphasis on the shaping forces of social frameworks opens the study of memory to politics, for—as those working in the Halbwachsian tradition argue—those forces wed the articulation of memory to the interests and conflicts of the present. The frameworks of memory rely in turn on the existence of groups of various kinds: individuals exist not in isolation but in a series of interlocking communities—families, religions, regions, professions, civil society organizations—that contour their social identities and consequently their practices of remembrance. As this incomplete list of groups in which Halbwachs locates the social frameworks of collective memory attests, he did not weld collective memory to any privileged scale of social life, but located it in groups 'up to and including the nation' (J. Assmann 1995: 127). Indeed, for Halbwachs, subjects always belong to diverse groups and thus also possess multiple schemata of collective memory. Yet, at the same time, he understood groups as relatively homogenous and closed entities. Such a conceptualization ultimately limits (without by any means foreclosing) Halbwachs's usefulness for a memory studies interested in questions of colonialism and globalization, since these are conditions that dislocate the organically defined groups that interested Halbwachs and that continue to interest many students of memory today.

When—in what might be the most important founding gesture of contemporary memory studies—Pierre Nora reanimates the Halbwachsian heritage of collective memory by connecting it to the classical tradition of *loci memoriae*, he also strongly reterritorializes Halbwachs's attention to multiplicity through a defining emphasis on the *nation* as the ultimate modern 'social framework'. Nora's massive collective project on *Les Lieux de mémoire*—seven volumes in the original (1984–92)—brilliantly explores 'sites of memory' that preserve and reproduce French identity in the face of the eroding flux of modernity.[7] Nora depicts modernity as a force that tends to wipe out the organic

---

[7] Pierre Nora (ed.), *Les Lieux de mémoire* (Paris: Gallimard, 1984–92). In English: *Realms of Memory: The Construction of the French Past*, 3 volumes, under the direction of Pierre Nora, edited by Lawrence D. Kritzman, translated by Arthur Goldhammer (New York: Columbia University Press, 1996–8); and *Rethinking France*, under the direction of Pierre Nora, translated by Mary Trouille (Chicago: University of Chicago Press, 2001–6).

communities in which Halbwachs situated collective memory and to replace them with a compromise formation based on cultural monuments or 'sites' of various sorts (from war memorials to cookbooks and novels to the geography of Paris). In other words, Nora energized the study of cultural memory despite declaring the death of 'real' collective memory as it had been conceived until then.

Notwithstanding Nora's avowed interest in a 'polyphonic' approach (*Realms*, 1.xxiii), his project ultimately puts forward a starkly limited conception of the nation purged of its imperial adventures and minoritarian inflections (a further carry-over of Halbwachs's organicism into a late modern moment). Despite an emphasis on the local and the heterogeneous—on what volume 3 of *Les Lieux de mémoire* calls 'Les France'—the project has surprising absences. Perry Anderson has pointed out that the effect of the project's admitted 'Gallocentrism' and its unease with certain social divisions has been that 'the entire imperial history of the country ... becomes a *non-lieu*' of memory, subject to forgetting. As Anderson asks with respect to one of the turning points of the era of decolonization: 'What are the *lieux de mémoire* that fail to include Dienbienphu?' (P. Anderson 2009: 161–2).[8] Despite its debt to new directions in critical historiography, the project under Nora's direction ends up reproducing a reified and ironically celebratory image of the very nation state it set out to deconstruct, as even Nora seemed to recognize in his afterword 'The Era of Commemoration' (*Realms*, 3.609–37).

Although less well known in the English-speaking world than Halbwachs and Nora, the German scholars Jan Assmann, an Egyptologist, and Aleida Assmann, a literary critic, provide a systematization of the study of collective memory that draws on and adds nuance to the approaches of Halbwachs and Nora, without, however, eliminating the problems associated with a predominantly metropolitan-oriented account. The Assmanns' contribution begins with a distinction between two forms of collective memory: they suggest that Halbwachs's use of the term refers to what they call 'communicative memory', 'varieties of collective memory that are based exclusively on everyday communications' (J. Assmann 1995: 126). What they call cultural memory, on the other hand, represents 'an externalization and objectivation of memory', which is 'evident in symbols such as texts, images, rituals, landmarks and other "lieux de mémoire"' (J. Assmann 2010: 122). While communicative memory has a duration that the Assmanns specify as 'three interacting generations or 80–100 years', they believe canonical cultural memory has a 'typical time-range ... [of] 3000 years' (J. Assmann 2010: 122). Although obviously indebted to Nora, the concept of cultural memory does not suppose the narrative of the decline of 'authentic' memory that limits Nora's perspective. Unlike Nora, the Assmanns are also more forthright about the fact that cultural memory, as they use it, refers to *canonical* memory—those monuments (broadly understood) of a given civilization that have a shaping force over a long duration (see A. Assmann 2008). Like the theory of *lieux de mémoire*, the Assmanns' theory of cultural memory provides important tools for understanding

---

[8.] See also Rothberg, Sanyal, and Silverman (2010).

and ultimately deconstructing the configurations of nationalist and imperial power embedded in representations of the past. However, despite their acknowledgement that official archives and repositories of memory 'have their own structural mechanisms of exclusion in terms of class, race, and gender' (A. Assmann, 2008: 106), their theory has not generally sought to uncover alternative archives or seek out non-canonical memory traditions, although recent work by Aleida Assmann suggests that this path may become more central to their work as it continues to develop (see A. Assmann 2009).

Each of the major figures in the development of cultural memory studies provides resources for thinking productively about the politics of the past in colonial and postcolonial contexts, but this brief survey also suggests some of the reasons why this important intellectual tradition has largely remained marginal to the concerns of postcolonial studies. Indeed, taken together, Halbwachs's organicism, Nora's purified national frame, and the Assmanns' preponderant focus on canonical archives suggest that throughout the twentieth century—the era of colonialism's apotheosis, collapse, and reconfiguration in neo- and postcolonial guises—cultural memory studies may have inadvertently done as much to reproduce imperial mentalities as to challenge them. In particular, the emphasis of so much memory studies on the construction of continuity over time and the coherence of cultural groups—whether defined as small-scale, national, or civilizational—appears in the postcolonial mirror as a kind of fetishism that disavows the structural dislocations produced by an imperial world system. Communities of memory in metropolitan locations have always been shadowed by apparently distant colonial realities, but memory studies (with some exceptions) has yet to investigate what such a situation entails for the memory cultures of either the colonizer or the colonized.[9] A memory studies available for the understanding of colonial and postcolonial realities would require more than just attention to the shaping force of the present and the accretion of power-laden memory in national and civilizational canons of memory, although these latter would certainly play a significant role. It would also require an understanding of the relations between memory, identity, and violence—the trauma and rupture produced by conquest, occupation, and genocide—as well as techniques for recovering the traces of non-dominant pasts.[10] Despite its limits, memory studies can contribute important insights into the mediation of trauma and violence to postcolonial studies, for not all forms of violence are experienced, integrated, or remembered in identical ways.

[9]. Fredric Jameson (1990) has helped conceptualize the way that colonialism 'shadows' modern metropolitan daily life.

[10]. The field of trauma studies, which overlaps with but is not identical to memory studies, offers greater attention to the dislocations of violent histories. Yet, as critics have pointed out in recent years, it too has largely disavowed engagement with colonialism and its legacies and has thus failed to engage with structural, systemic forms of violence. For an influential volume on trauma and memory, see Caruth (1995). For a postcolonial critique of this version of trauma studies, see Craps (2010).

Decolonizing the Past: From Anti-Colonialism to Postcolonial Studies

Although the absence of reflection on colonialism in cultural memory studies may help explain the neglect of memory as an explicit issue in postcolonial studies, the anti-colonial source texts of postcolonialism are in fact deeply and urgently engaged with the problem of memory as with its twin—forgetting. Such engagement arises from a recognition common to all movements of decolonization—that the struggle against colonialism involves, in part, a struggle over collective memory. Both dimensions of collective memory theorized by the Assmanns are key here: colonialism involves a break in the intergenerational communicative memory of a colonized group at the same time as it involves the imposition of a foreign canon of cultural memory. In other words, colonialism ruptures both the past-present continuities embedded in the practices of everyday living and the larger symbolic systems that give shape, continuity, and coherence to cultures over time.

Whatever their political differences, anti-colonial theorists such as Aimé Césaire, Frantz Fanon, and Amilcar Cabral share a sense that memory constitutes one of the significant fronts in the struggle against empire. As Fanon writes in *The Wretched of the Earth*, 'Colonialism is not satisfied merely with holding a people in its grip and emptying the native's brain of all form and content. By a kind of perverted logic, it turns to the past of the oppressed people, and distorts, disfigures, and destroys it. This work of devaluing pre-colonial history takes on a dialectical significance today [i.e., in the anti-colonial struggle]' (Fanon 1968 [1961]: 210). Cabral similarly recognizes the past as a stake in colonial and anti-colonial processes: 'The colonialists usually say that it was they who brought us into history: today we show that this is not so. They made us leave history, our history, to follow them, right at the back, to follow the progress of their history' (Cabral, quoted in Young 2001: 288). For Cabral, this destructive dimension of colonialism necessitates that cultural praxis join armed struggle for independence and reclamation of productive forces as axes of the fight for national liberation: 'A people who free themselves from foreign domination will be free culturally only if, without complexes and without underestimating the importance of positive accretions from the oppressor and other cultures, they return to the upward paths of their own culture ... Thus, it may be seen that if imperialist domination has the vital need to practice cultural oppression, national liberation is necessarily an act of *culture*' (Cabral 1973: 43). The act of culture Cabral imagines as part of national liberation is also an act of collective memory: a 'return' not to some essential identity but to a historical itinerary that colonialism displaced without fully erasing. Similarly, Fanon, while sceptical that 'the past existence of an Aztec civilization' or 'all the proofs of a wonderful Songhai civilization' will benefit Mexican or Songhai peasants in the present, nevertheless considers the 'passionate search for a national culture' in the collective memory of a decolonizing society an essential moment of struggle (Fanon 1968 [1961]: 209).

In his powerful polemic *Discourse on Colonialism* (1950/1955), Fanon's teacher Césaire also embraces the claims of cultural memory against the violence of colonial erasure. For Césaire, the colonial project relies on a 'forgetting machine'. As he writes in a bitterly ironic passage from his anti-colonial pamphlet,

> Before the arrival of the French in their country, the Vietnamese were people of an old culture, exquisite and refined. To recall this fact upsets the digestion of the Banque d'Indochine. Start the forgetting machine!
> These Madagascans who are being tortured today, less than a century ago were poets, artists, administrators? Shhhhh! Keep your lips buttoned! And silence falls, silence as deep as a safe! Fortunately, there are still the Negroes. Ah! the Negroes! Let's talk about the Negroes! ... About the Sudanese empires? About the bronzes of Benin? Shango sculpture? (Césaire 2000 [1950/1955]: 52)

While strategically staging a potentially nostalgic and idealized vision of pre-colonial cultures, Césaire also anticipates Fanon and Cabral in stating clearly that the anti-colonial project does not entail a simple nativism or 'return' to the past (despite the title of his most famous poem, *Cahier d'un retour au pays natal*): 'It is not a dead society that we want to revive. We leave that to those who go in for exoticism ... It is a new society that we must create' (2000 [1950/1955]: 52). Yet, for all three of these anti-colonialist theorists, the new postcolonial society will be one that remembers—recalls and reconfigures—resources that predate the imposition of foreign domination. In drawing attention to the 'cultures trampled underfoot, institutions undermined, lands confiscated, religions smashed, magnificent artistic creations destroyed, extraordinary possibilities wiped out'—in 'see[ing] clearly what colonization has destroyed'—the theory of anti-colonial practice made memory a tool in the struggle against the colonial 'machine' (2000 [1950/1955]: 42–3).

In the move from the moment of anti-colonial struggle to a postcolonial present in which most former colonies have attained formal independence (if without the full 'national liberation' Cabral and others called for), the problematics of temporality shift. In its institutionalized form, postcolonial studies draws on the classic anti-colonial texts discussed above and addresses many of the same questions of violence, erasure, and reconstruction, but without the same urgency surrounding the moment of decolonization. Rather, postcolonial studies provides a long view that helps explain the tenacity of colonialism beyond formal colonization, but also the instabilities that have always resulted from (and made possible) resistance to empire. Insights about memory can assist in clarifying both the shaping of mentalities over the *longue durée*, which takes place through the production of the Assmanns' cultural memory, and the opposition such imposition engenders, which emerges in various forms of counter-memory.[11]

[11.] The term 'counter-memory' derives from the work of Michel Foucault, although many uses of it do not necessarily follow Foucault to the letter (cf. Foucault 1977). Counter-memory is closely allied to the genealogical approach Foucault develops in his critical reading of Nietzsche. For the French philosopher, 'counter-memory' functions to strip history and memory of their metaphysical trappings: their investment in a teleological notion of time and a sovereign notion of subjectivity. The forms of discontinuity Foucault associates with genealogy and counter-memory do indeed run against the grain of the Assmanns' canonical understanding of cultural memory. Often, however, counter-memory is used in a less philosophical, more explicitly political context to refer to forms of memory that oppose hegemonic constructions of empire and nation but do not necessarily oppose teleology and sovereign subjectivity.

The academic field of postcolonial studies generally traces its origins to the 1978 publication of Edward Said's *Orientalism*. Without explicit invocation, Said describes *avant la lettre* the Assmanns' concept of canonical cultural memory and reveals—as the two German scholars themselves generally do not—its implication in colonial power relations. Drawing on Foucault's notions of the archive and discursive formation, Said reveals how centuries of knowledge production about 'the Orient' have constructed geo-cultural regions as targets for European (and later US) colonial intervention. He argues that scholarly investigations and cultural texts have 'enclosed' the Orient in a theatrical representational space: 'the Orient is the stage on which the whole East is confined. On this stage will appear figures whose role it is to represent the larger whole from which they emanate. The Orient then seems to be, not an unlimited extension beyond the familiar European world, but rather a closed field, a theatrical stage affixed to Europe' (Said 1978: 63). Although Said does not use such terminology, this is a stage constructed out of, and in turn constructing, the canons of cultural memory:

> In the depths of the Orientalist stage stands a prodigious cultural repertoire whose individual items evoke a fabulously rich world: the Sphinx, Cleopatra, Eden, Troy, Sodom and Gomorrah, ... and dozens more ... The European imagination was nourished extensively from this repertoire: between the Middle Ages and the eighteenth century such major authors as Ariosto, Milton, Marlowe, Tasso, Shakespeare, Cervantes, and the authors of the *Chanson de Roland* and the *Poema del Cid* drew on the Orient's riches for their productions, in ways that sharpened the outlines of imagery, ideas, and figures populating it. (1978: 63)

This 'repertoire' of early Orientalist 'stagings', along with scholarly reference works such as the *Bibliothèque orientale*, helped conveyed 'Orientalism's power and effectiveness, which everywhere remind the reader that henceforth in order to get at the Orient he must pass through the learned grids and codes provided by the Orientalist' (1978: 67). In so doing, they also helped set the stage for conquest of precisely those 'staged' and 'enclosed' lands.

Said's field-defining critique of the cultural memory of empire provides a crucial corrective to memory studies scholarship that considers canons and archives to be outside the field of power. Yet as the many revisions and correctives that followed suggest, Said may have fallen prey to canonical cultural memory's self-conception as an enclosed system of knowledge. Said's generative model of Orientalism soon seemed to have foreclosed all oppositional cross-currents and acts of resistance, both within the 'west' and especially in the colonized lands themselves, as he himself came to admit. In reflecting back on his project in *Culture and Imperialism* (1993), Said would contribute to a more flexible model by stressing a 'contrapuntal' reading strategy dedicated to uncovering 'intertwined and overlapping histories' (1993: 18). Now the very canons of cultural memory, as well as the intertextual and intermedial links that help constitute them, are turned against empire, although Said's vocabulary stresses 'narrative' and 'stories' over 'remembrance' as such: 'my basic point [is] that stories are at the heart of what explorers and novelists say about strange regions of the world; they also become the method colonized people use to assert their own identity and the existence of their own history' (xii).[12] Similarly, in the well-known move of 'writing back' to empire, postcolonial writers revise the European canon, simultaneously confirming and displacing the colonial cultural memory it underwrites.[13]

In the essays of Homi Bhabha collected in *The Location of Culture* (1994), Said's contrapuntal technique emerges as fundamental to the colonial encounter and, more generally, to the logic of cultural production. Bhabha only occasionally discusses memory as such (although a more recent lecture addresses 'global memory' and traumatic violence),[14] but his frequent references to the thought of Walter Benjamin as well as his attention to questions of temporality signal an ongoing interest in the '"in-between" space' of a 'past-present' that resembles memory (Bhabha 1994: 7). As Susan Bassnett's essay in this section of the volume demonstrates, this past-present hybrid is also a figure of translation: 'Translation is an act that takes place between languages and cultures, hence it is an intercultural process, but it is also intertemporal since the original came into being somewhere else at some other moment in time'. Although seemingly wedded to canonical notions of the 'original' and the past, translation and memory—especially when thought through a postcolonial lens—share a transformative potential that links them with novelty and resistance. For Bhabha, the potential of culture lies in its ability to 'creat[e] a sense of the new as an insurgent act of cultural translation' (7).[15] Postcolonial and minoritized cultural production acts, that is, as a form of counter-memory—a resignification of the past in the present—that unsettles canonical cultural memory.

Even more radically, Bhabha's work repeatedly reveals how the very attempt to instantiate canonical cultural memory runs up against a structural 'ambivalence' and 'hybridity'. The work of missionaries, for instance, sought to bring 'the Word of God and Man—Christianity and the English language' to the colonized, but such an attempted implantation of the canon ran up against the structural hybridity of cultural translation, as the colonized rewrote the sacred texts in their own terms (1994: 32–3). Working with the structuralist distinction between the subject of the *énonciation* and the subject of the *énoncé*, Bhabha suggests that the very attempt to institute a canonical 'pedagogic' message or *énoncé* runs up against the dislocating necessity of the contingent 'performative', which defines every act of *énonciation* (1994: 36, 148). In more recent work, he connects this model explicitly to the issue of memory. He draws on Benjamin to suggest that cultural memory in its oppositional guise seeks not simply to resurrect a repressed past but to 'displace the angle of vision' through which we approach history. It thus makes

---

[12.] In some of his late work, Said turned even more explicitly to memory in the telling of his own life story (1999) and in exploring remembrance as both a source of conflict and contest and as a potential resource for the production of solidarity and the imagination of coexistence (2000).

[13.] If most postcolonial critics have moved away from this seemingly 'reactive' mode of 'writing back', it remains an important part of the genealogy of postcolonial studies and an important dimension of postcolonial literatures.

[14.] See Homi Bhabha, 'On Global Memory: Thoughts on the Barbaric Transmission of Culture', lecture given at the Townsend Center for the Humanities, University of California, Berkeley, 14 April 2008. Available online: accessed 18 December 2010.

[15.] For more on cultural memory and translation in postcolonial contexts, see Brodzki (2007).

possible a 'new relation to the past' based not on 'resemblance' but on 'recognition' of our ethical implication in traumatic violence ('On Global Memory').

Like Bhabha, Gayatri Chakravorty Spivak, the final theorist of postcolonial studies I touch on here, draws much more significantly on poststructuralist critique than the humanist Said. At the same time she returns us to Said's less 'ambivalent' reading of the colonial archive. Although far less totallizing than Said's initial vision of Orientalism, Spivak's consideration of colonialism's 'epistemic violence' throughout her work doubles as a critique of canonical cultural memory. In her most famous essay, 'Can the Subaltern Speak?' (1988a), as well as in her engagements with the subaltern studies school of historians, Spivak rigorously cautions against the assumption of a too easy counter-memory of the lives of colonized subjects; her emphasis instead is on the erasures colonial memory regimes foster. In 'Subaltern Studies: Deconstructing Historiography', for instance, she rejects the presumption that contemporary scholars can capture the 'voice-consciousness' of the subaltern (see Spivak 1988b). Meanwhile in 'Can the Subaltern Speak?' she demonstrates at length how 'the palimpsestic narrative of imperialism' overwrites subaltern histories, thus leading to her infamous and frequently misunderstood conclusion—later recontextualized in *A Critique of Postcolonial Reason*—that 'the subaltern cannot speak' (Spivak 1988a: 281, 308).[16] As two astute commentators on Spivak's work have suggested, the silence of the subaltern has to do with overlapping traditions of canonical cultural memory: 'Spivak's archive is a diachronic "palimpsest" whose textual layers enfold not only the synchronic court documents of British legal power/knowledge, but also the texts of Hindu antiquity, themselves palimpsestic layers of mistranslation and errant commentary' (Shetty and Bellamy 2000: 28). Spivak's project is thus a deconstruction of hegemonic archives, but a deconstruction that does not readily offer the subversive possibilities proffered by Bhabha; rather, her work ceaselessly maps the contours of imperial cultural memory as an ongoing version of what Césaire had called a half-century earlier the 'forgetting machine' (2000: 52).

LITERATURE AND THE MEDIA OF (POST) COLONIAL MEMORY

No less than the anti-colonial and postcolonial theorists discussed here, postcolonial writers have also explored the ruptures produced by the imposition of imperial cultural memory and the erasure of pre-colonial histories. Such ruptures produce new constellations, as when colonial pedagogy elicits what Alison Landsberg (2004) calls in another context 'prosthetic memories' of the colonizing country—think of the infamous French colonial education in which children from the colonies learned about 'nos

---

[16.] See also Spivak (1999).

ancêtres, les Gaulois' (see Ha 2003). The Antiguan/American writer Jamaica Kincaid explores the institution and unravelling of such prosthetic memories in her brilliant and much-anthologized essayistic deflation of imperial culture, 'On Seeing England for the First Time' (1991).[17] In Kincaid's essay, the cognitive dissonance of reading at school in Antigua about daffodils and the 'white cliffs of Dover' results in a disabused view of Britain during the author's first visit to the metropole as an adult (1991: 35, 40; cf. A. Assmann 2009: 163). Although amusing in its ironies, the stakes of such cultural memory are also deadly serious. As Kincaid writes, 'the reality of my life was conquests, subjugation, humiliation, enforced amnesia. I was forced to forget' (1991: 36). One of her examples is the provenance of place names, such as 'Hawkins Street' in St John's, Antigua, where she grew up. John Hawkins, she points out,

> was knighted after a trip he made to Africa, opening up a new trade, the slave trade. He was then entitled to wear as his crest a Negro bound with a cord. Every single person living on Hawkins Street was descended from a slave. John Hawkins's ship, the one in which he transported the people he bought and kidnapped, was called The Jesus. He later became the treasurer of the Royal Navy and Rear Admiral. (1991: 36)

Kincaid's essayistic practice, like its novelistic counterpart, both maps the complicity of memory and forgetting in colonial and metropolitan *lieux de mémoire*, such as Hawkins Street or the cliffs of Dover, and dialectically reads those *lieux* against themselves through a practice of counter-memory that stages the colonized 'remembering back' to empire (just as, in an earlier moment, many postcolonial texts were understood as 'writing back' to empire: cf. Ashcroft, Griffiths, and Tiffin 1989; also Bassnett on translation as rewriting in this section of the volume).

Indeed, one way to read Kincaid's essay is as an illustration of what Nora's *lieux de mémoire* project would look like when viewed from the 'displaced angle' (Bhabha 2008: n.p.) of colonized vision. Visiting post-imperial England decades after having been introduced to its overweening power through education and the everyday consumption of goods 'Made in England' (1991: 33) during the colonial period, Kincaid observes a Nora-esque alienation from 'authentic' national memory among the residents of the metropole: 'There were monuments everywhere; they commemorated victories, battles fought between them and the people who lived across the sea from them, all vile people, fought over which of them would have dominion over the people who looked like me. The monuments were useless to them now, people sat on them and ate their lunch. They were like markers on an old useless trail, like a piece of old string tied to a finger to jog the memory' (1991: 37–8). Here Kincaid produces a double profanation of imperial cultural memory, exposing both the forgetting of violence that always underwrote it and its contemporary, postcolonial 'uselessness'. The 'contrapuntal' performance of memory

---

[17.] On Kincaid and cultural memory, see also A. Assmann (2009: 163–5). Here Assmann explores briefly how colonial and postcolonial contexts have the potential to reshape thinking about cultural memory by foregrounding 'contrasting and irreconcilable narratives' and 'contestation' over memory sites (161).

in the present—Kincaid's, but also that of the casual diners—undermines the pedagogical message of the greatness of empire the monuments were originally intended to produce. As Bhabha would predict, the necessity of iteration in the performance of cultural memory—'there were many times of seeing England for the first time', writes Kincaid (1991: 34)—proves to constitute both the force of that memory and the 'site' of its weakness. And yet, as Spivak might warn, even the undoing of imperial memory does not necessarily lead to the emergence of a 'subaltern' memory in the public sphere. Kincaid's essay ends with a fantasy of destruction, unmitigated by the recovery of any kind of alternative Antiguan archive: 'I wished every sentence, everything I knew, that began with England, would end with "and then it all died; we don't know how, it just all died"' (1991: 40). While the anti-colonial moment of Césaire, Fanon, and Cabral still seemed to offer the possibilities for a 'liberated' cultural memory, Kincaid's disabused postcolonial memory can only gesture towards the wished-for 'death' of ongoing colonial hegemony.

If the activist possibilities of earlier eras seem absent here, Kincaid's essay is nonetheless suggestive for furthering the project of a postcolonial memory studies. In particular, her essay anticipates the contemporary convergence of memory studies with media studies and suggests how such a pairing can contribute to our understanding of colonial and postcolonial cultures, while also pointing out potential lacunae in studies of cultural memory. Kincaid's deconstruction of metropolitan cultural memory refers not only to particular images and stories, but to a host of *media forms* through which imperial power makes itself felt: the map of England, canonical poetry, street names, royal crests, ship names, biblical texts. In a study of the afterlife of the 1857 Indian uprising or 'Mutiny', memory studies scholar Astrid Erll draws on the concepts of 'premediation' and 'remediation' developed by the media theorists Jay David Bolter and Richard Grusin and applied to the work of remembrance by Ann Rigney.[18] For Erll, 'it is the "convergence" of medial representations which turns an event into a *lieu de mémoire*', and that convergence takes place through two fundamental processes of 'intermedial network[ing]': in 'premediation', existing media images and narratives 'provide schemata for new experience and its representation'; conversely, in 'remediation', the now-constituted event circulates through a variety of media forms, so that 'what is known about an event which has turned into a site of memory … seems to refer not so much to what one might cautiously call the "actual event," but instead to a canon of existent media constructions' (Erll 2009: 111). As Erll's work would predict, Kincaid's essay hints at both the 'premediation' of colonial memory and the remediation of 'England' as colonial power. Religion 'premediates' the 'transportation' medium of the slave trade—as in Hawkins's ship the *Jesus*—while English culture seems to premediate all of Antiguan colonial life: from table manners and clothing (her father's inappropriate felt hat: Kincaid 1991: 33) to literature's depiction of weather and urban lifestyles. Similarly, acts of remediation are everywhere in the essay, from Hawkins's slave-depicting crest to the commemoration of the slave trade in street names. Erll's work helps us notice the specific media that

---

[18.] See Erll (2007, 2009). Erll draws on Bolter and Grusin (1999) and Rigney (2005).

transport colonial meaning even into the postcolonial period, and thus establishes pre- and remediation as two of the material forms taken by the 'post' in postcolonial. But Kincaid supplements this story by putting greater emphasis than does Erll on the forms of *power* that articulate with those media. Thus, what interests Kincaid about Hawkins, for instance, is not only the media that carry his image across time, as he once carried slaves across the abyss of the Middle Passage; she also notes that he 'later became the treasurer of the Royal Navy and Rear Admiral' (Kincaid 1991: 36). Memory lives on through its circulation in media forms, but premediation and remediation are themselves made possible through articulation with the channels of economic and military power.

THE FRENCH-ALGERIAN CONNECTION: MEDIA, MEMORY ACTIVISM, AND MULTIDIRECTIONALITY

Although indelibly contoured by economic and military power—the driving forces of empire—cultural memory cannot be reduced to these factors. Indeed, Erll's attention to the circulation of memory in media forms suggests new ways of thinking about the activist potential of memory in struggles against empire. To illustrate such potential I turn in this final section of the chapter to one particularly dense knot of memory in the era of decolonization and suggest that it is memory's relative autonomy from determination by power or limited notions of group identity that constitutes its value as a resource for resistance. While, in her chapter for this volume, Elleke Boehmer uses the 'anti-colonial life' of Nelson Mandela as an emblem of postcolonial 'theory-in-practice', I draw here on a particular 'anti-colonial conjuncture'—the struggle against French colonialism in Algeria—to illustrate the simultaneously theoretical and activist potential of cultural memory work.

As we have seen via the texts of anti-colonial activist-intellectuals, imperialism interrupts the development of colonial societies, but the process is by no means one-way, as Césaire in particular theorized with his notion of the *choc en retour* or 'boomerang effect'.[19] Even before the postcolonial migrations that radically transformed the texture of life in places like Great Britain and France, the free or coerced flow of people, goods, and ideas accompanying colonial expansion created new constellations of histories and temporalities. Such flows constitute and institute memory's 'multidirectionality', a dynamic in which multiple pasts jostle against each other in a heterogeneous present, and where communities of remembrance disperse and reconvene in new, non-organic forms not recognizable to earlier theorists of memory like Halbwachs and Nora. Like empire, memory is both disjunctive and combinatorial: it both disassembles and

---

[19.] On Césaire's notion of the *choc en retour*—a way of explaining how imperial violence returns 'home' to the metropolis, see Rothberg (2009: chapter 3).

reassembles. This 'multidirectionality' of memory in the colonial/postcolonial age does not come with a guaranteed political vision—indeed it tends to trouble the 'camp' mentality that seeks to corral politics into a simplified identitarian topography—but it is also an unavoidable component of political struggle and a potential resource in ongoing movements for decolonization and justice in today's globalized world.[20]

The Algerian War of Independence (1954–62) was one of the most brutal and bloody wars of decolonization, but the excess of violence that accompanied it should not blind us to the cultural dimensions that informed the fight, in particular the forms of collective memory that served as sources of mobilization among a range of participants.[21] Like the French war in Indochina before it, as well as other wars of decolonization in the 1950s and 1960s, the Algerian War was fought against the backdrop of World War II, an event etched, however unevenly, in the minds of combatants on all sides of the struggle, many of whom took part in both wars. Indeed, from the very inauguration of the post-war era, World War II and Algerian struggles for independence have been interlinked. On 8 May 1945, a demonstration in the Algerian city of Sétif took place to mark the end of the war and to call for decolonization. After several dozen *pieds noirs* were killed in ensuing violence, the French army took part in reprisals that included the massacre of thousands (if not tens of thousands) of Algerians. At least in the formerly colonized world, that massacre has forever soldered together the liberation of Europe from fascism and the reluctance of liberated Europe to let go of its own forms of extreme violence—a connection that leaves clear traces in the writings of Césaire, Fanon, and Cabral.[22] The memory of Sétif and of massacres in Madagascar and elsewhere as well as their links to European barbarism 'at home' would echo through anti-colonial struggles. For metropolitan anti-colonial activists, their engagement frequently arose out of and further propagated memories of the world war and, specifically, the Nazi persecution of Jews.[23]

Response to and memory of the massacre of peacefully demonstrating Algerians in Paris on 17 October 1961 demonstrate the multidirectional dynamics of media and memory activism. When the FLN called for a march in the heart of the French capital to protest a racist curfew and show their strength in the metropole, the French police responded with violence, killing dozens and arresting 11,000 protestors, who were rounded up and taken to makeshift camps in sports stadiums at the edges of the city. The police response was directed by the prefect Maurice Papon, who, it later transpired, had collaborated with the Nazis in the deportation of Jews from Bordeaux; but even before those revelations inextricably linked the 1961 events to the Holocaust, contemporary

---

[20.] See Paul Gilroy's critique of 'camp' mentalities in *Between Camps* (2000). Also relevant to the project of joining memory studies and postcolonial studies are two other books by Gilroy: *The Black Atlantic* (1993) and *Postcolonial Melancholia* (2006).

[21.] Most of the examples in the following paragraphs are explored at greater length in Rothberg (2009: chapters 6–9), but they are all recast here for present purposes.

[22.] On the Sétif massacre, see Benot (2001).

[23.] For an oral history of French anti-colonial activists that emphasizes in many cases memory of the Nazi period, see Evans (1997: esp. 31–72).

observers already experienced 17 October as 'premediated' by the round-up of Jews in Paris. For instance, a week after the event, the New Left newsweekly *France-Observateur* published an article by the Algerian-French writer Henri Kréa called 'Le racisme est collectif, la solidarité individuelle' ('Racism is collective; solidarity individual'), which was accompanied by a photograph of Algerians being held in the Palais des Sports. Underneath the image a caption reads, 'Cela ne vous rappelle rien?' ('Doesn't that remind you of something?') (Kréa 1961: 14–15). The caption clearly references the round-ups of Jews during the Nazi occupation and, in particular, the infamous July 1942 *rafle du Vel' d'Hiv'*, in which thousands of 'foreign' Jews were arrested by French police and held in a velodrome before being deported to Auschwitz. Premediation plays a significant role here, for the photograph resembles a famous image thought to be of Jews imprisoned by the Nazis in the Vel' d'Hiv', which would have been known to many Parisian readers of *France-Observateur* through its inclusion in Alain Resnais's 1955 camp documentary *Nuit et brouillard* (*Night and Fog*). Although, decades later, that image turned out to have been misidentified—it actually depicts suspected *collaborators* held after the war—the remediation of the image in Resnais' film as well as its premediation of similar images during the Algerian War demonstrates the powerful links that accrue between media forms and acts of memory.[24]

In fact, the dynamics of mediation and memory surrounding this event went on to acquire further layers of complexity. In addition to the implicit visual reference to the 1942 *rafle*, one of Kréa's Algerian interviewees refers to *Exodus*, the 1960 Otto Preminger film based on Leon Uris's novel about Jewish refugees from Hitler on their way to Palestine, which was showing at the time in Paris and which the interviewee uses to juxtapose audiences' sympathy for Jewish victims with their relative indifference toward Algerians (Kréa 1961: 15). Even more interesting, the *form* of Kréa's article—interviews with Algerian workers—seems to call upon another film just opening in Paris at that time, Jean Rouch and Edgar Morin's *cinéma-vérité* experiment *Chronique d'un été* (*Chronicle of a Summer*, 1961). *Chronique* was the only film released during the Algerian War that made reference to the conflict—albeit briefly and cryptically—and, in addition to interviews with workers and African students, it also featured at its centre an unprecedented testimony by an Auschwitz survivor, Marceline Loridan, a testimony that emerges from discussions of decolonization and racism and allegorically stands in for the many censored testimonies of Algerians (and French activists) tortured or held at that time in detention camps.

Chronique d'un été's role in mediating the Algerian struggle through juxtaposition with what was only then beginning to be understood as the 'unique' Holocaust is even more striking in another *France-Observateur* response to the October 17 massacre. Marguerite Duras's 'Les deux ghettos' (The Two Ghettos) also uses the interview form, this time juxtaposing discussions with two Algerians and a survivor of the Warsaw Ghetto, whom Duras dubs 'M' (a possible echo of Marceline) (Duras 1961: 8–10). Again images play a role, as the cover of the newsweekly displays parallel images of an Algerian

---

24. On the mistaken identification of this image, see Lindeperg (2007: 59).

and a Jew wearing a yellow star. The text of the interviews itself draws connections between the plight of Algerians and Jews, but offers a more differentiated picture of the relation between these different forms of violence than the title and photographs suggest. Such connections were not unique to the metropolitan resistance. Not only did the FLN itself also recognize the strategic usefulness of such analogies, as the research of Jim House has demonstrated, but individual FLN combatants also experienced the events themselves as untimely echoes of the recent past. House quotes an FLN document in which an Algerian 'report[s] to his FLN superiors what he saw when he was taken to the *Palais des Sports*: "There we made a macabre discovery. The [*Algerian*] brothers were lying on the ground, their heads split open and limbs dislocated. All these horrors were comparable to those endured by the Jews in the Nazi concentration camps"' (House 2010: 30).[25] Strikingly similar connections are also made in another text that seems to remediate *Chronique*, William Gardner Smith's novel *The Stone Face* (1963), the first novel to treat the Paris massacre, which also features a female Holocaust survivor whose name begins with 'M' at its centre and adds still another resonant multidirectional link: in nuanced and differentiated fashion, the novel constellates both the Holocaust and the Algerian revolution with the struggle for civil rights in the United States.

Whatever the historical accuracy of such comparisons (or even the sources of such images, as in the *Nuit et brouillard* case), what emerges from the October 1961 moment is a strong sense of the *mobilizing* nature of cultural memory, its ability to create solidarities through the very channels of the media and regardless of the 'immediacy' of one's own experiences. This lesson continues into the afterlife of October 17 memory. After having been suppressed by the French state, downplayed by the communist left in favour of its own losses during the temporally proximate Charonne violence, avoided by Algerian families, and instrumentalized by the nascent Algerian state, memory of October 17 re-emerged in migrant youth movements in the 1980s. Interestingly, though, the transmission of the events to this 'post-memory' generation happened in non-organic fashion.[26] As House and MacMaster write, 'these descendants of Algerians often came across 17 October via the resilient counter-memories of French former anti-colonial activists rather than memory transmission within their own families' (2006: 19). Those French activists were in turn precisely the generation motivated by their own sense—either directly experienced or inherited—that the Algerian events disturbingly echoed the Nazi period. In the most recent remediations of October 17, such as Michael Haneke's *Caché* (2005), the Holocaust/Algeria link remains as a haunting subtext even as new multidirectional links—Abu Ghraib and the invasion of Iraq—come to join the decades-old constellation. As this brief genealogy suggests, the activation of memory can produce

[25.] See also House and MacMaster (2006).

[26.] Marianne Hirsch initially coined the term 'post-memory' to refer to the aesthetic production of children of Holocaust survivors. Since then, in her work and that of others, it has grown in scope to refer more generally to second (and subsequent) generations who live in the shadow of some defining, often traumatic event that they did not directly experience. For the invention and genealogy of the term, see Hirsch (2008).

immediate, short-term resistance, but it can also set the stage for longer-term struggles carried out over generations.

Conclusion: New Visions of Solidarity

The French-Algerian example stands at an angle to 'classical' considerations of cultural memory, while also supplementing postcolonial accounts in interesting ways. Taking into account the transnational and transcultural dynamics of empire disrupts models of memory premised on the boundedness of groups and nations and provides a 'displaced angle' on the canons of cultural memory. Anti-colonial and postcolonial practices of memory reveal the intimacy of metropole and colony—the 'tensions of empire' identified by Ann Laura Stoler and Frederick Cooper (1997)—as well as civilization and barbarism. Memory emerges not only from the closed field of organically defined groups and the sacred sites of national monumentality, but also in the very tensions and ruptures of imperial conquest and traumatic violence that dislocate space, time, and identity. Such insights also render the boundaries of postcolonial studies itself uncertain since, as the French-Algerian example illustrates, acts of memory overrun boundaries between 'Europe and its Others' or 'the west and the rest'. Even more radically, the multidirectional nature of memory—its spiralling, echoing tendencies—makes it difficult to know what the 'proper' terrain of a postcolonial memory studies could ever be. The haunting presence of Nazi genocide in both foundational texts such as Césaire's *Discourse* and in the activist memory work of the FLN and its French allies, along with the traces of colonial violence that can be found in some responses to the Holocaust, suggests the possibility of new directions: future projects in memory studies and postcolonial studies will want to remain open to surprising forms of difference and unexpected visions of solidarity.

References

Anderson, Benedict (2006). *Imagined Communities: Reflections on the Origin and Spread of Nationalism*, new edition. New York: Verso.

Anderson, Perry (2009). *The New Old World*. New York: Verso.

Appiah, Kwame Anthony (1993). *In My Father's House: Africa in the Philosophy of Culture*. New York: Oxford University Press.

Ashcroft, Bill, Gareth Griffiths and Helen Tiffin (1989). *The Empire Writes Back: Theory and Practice in Post-Colonial Literatures*. London: Routledge.

Ashcroft, Bill, Gareth Griffiths and Helen Tiffin (eds) (1995). *The Post-Colonial Studies Reader*. London: Routledge.

Assmann, Aleida (2008). 'Canon and Archive', in Astrid Erll and Ansgar Nünning (eds), *Cultural Memory Studies: An International and Interdisciplinary Handbook*. New York: Walter de Gruyter, 97–107.

Assmann, Aleida (2009). 'How History Takes Place', in Indra Sengupta (ed.), *Memory, History, and Colonialism: Engaging with Pierre Nora in Colonial and Postcolonial Contexts*. London: German Historical Institute, 151–65.

Assmann, Aledia and Sebastian Conrad (eds) (2010). *Memory in a Global Age*. New York: Palgrave Macmillan.

Assmann, Jan (1995). 'Collective Memory and Cultural Identity', trans. John Czaplicka, *New German Critique*, 65 (Spring/Summer): 125–33.

Assmann, Jan (2010). 'Globalization, Universalism, and the Erosion of Cultural Memory', in Aleida Assmann and Sebastian Conrad (eds), *Memory in a Global Age*. New York: Palgrave Macmillan, 121–37.

Benjamin, Walter (1968). *Illuminations: Essays and Reflections*, ed. Hannah Arendt and trans. Harry Zohn. New York: Schocken.

Benot, Yves (2001). *Massacres coloniaux: 1944–1950: La IVe République et la mise au pas des colonies françaises*. Paris: La Découverte.

Bhabha, Homi (1994). *The Location of Culture*. New York: Routledge.

Bhabha, Homi (2008). 'On Global Memory: Thoughts on the Barbaric Transmission of Culture'. Lecture given at the Townsend Center for the Humanities, University of California, Berkeley, 14 April 2008. Online source: <http://www.youtube.com/watch?v=5Fp6j9Ozpn4>, accessed 18 December 2012.

Bolter, Jay David and Richard Grusin (1999). *Remediation: Understanding New Media*. Cambridge, Mass.: MIT Press.

Brodzki, Bella (2007). *Can These Bones Live? Translation, Survival, and Cultural Memory*. Stanford: Stanford University Press.

Cabral, Amilcar (1973). *Return to the Sources: Selected Speeches by Amilcar Cabral*. New York: Monthly Review Press.

Caruth, Cathy (ed.) (1995). *Trauma: Explorations in Memory*. Baltimore: Johns Hopkins University Press.

Césaire, Aimé (2000 [1950/1955]). *Discourse on Colonialism*, trans. Joan Pinkham. New York: Monthly Review Press.

Cole, Jennifer (2001). *Forget Colonialism? Sacrifice and the Art of Memory in Madagascar*. Berkeley: University of California Press.

Craps, Stef (2010). 'Wor(l)ds of Grief: Traumatic Memory and Literary Witnessing in Cross-Cultural Perspective', *Textual Practice*, 24.1: 51–68.

Crownshaw, Richard (ed.) (2011). 'Transcultural Memory', special issue of *Parallax*, 17.4.

Duras, Marguerite (1961). 'Les deux ghettos', *France-Observateur*, 9 November: 8–10.

Erll, Astrid (2007). *Prämediation-Remediation: Repräsentationen des indischen Aufstands in imperialen und post-kolonialen Medienkulturen (von 1857 bis zur Gegenwart)*. Trier: WVT.

Erll, Astrid (2009). 'Remembering Across Time, Space, and Cultures: Premediation, Remediation, and the "Indian Mutiny"', in Astrid Erll and Ann Rigney (eds), *Mediation, Remediation, and the Dynamics of Cultural Memory*. Berlin and New York: Walter de Gruyter, 109–38.

Evans, Martin (1997). *The Memory of Resistance: French Opposition to the Algerian War (1954–1962)*. Oxford: Berg.

Fanon, Frantz (1968 [1961]). *The Wretched of the Earth*, trans. Constance Farrington. New York: Grove.

Foucault, Michel (1977). *Language, Counter-Memory, Practice*, ed. Donald Bouchard. Ithaca: Cornell University Press.

Gilroy, Paul (1993). *The Black Atlantic: Modernity and Double Consciousness.* Cambridge, Mass.: Harvard University Press.

Gilroy, Paul (2000). *Between Camps: Nations, Culture, and the Allure of Race.* London: Allen Land.

Gilroy, Paul (2006). *Postcolonial Melancholia.* New York: Columbia University Press.

Ha, Marie-Paule (2003). 'From "Nos ancêtres, les Gaulois" to "Leur Culture Ancestrale": Symbolic Violence and the Politics of Colonial Schooling in Indochina', *French Colonial History,* 3: 101–17.

Halbwachs, Maurice (1992). *On Collective Memory,* trans. Lewis Cosner. Chicago: University of Chicago Press.

Haneke, Michael (dir.) (2005). *Caché.* Paris: Les Films du Losange.

Hargreaves, Alec G. (ed.) (2005). *Memory, Empire, and Postcolonialism: Legacies of French Colonialism.* Lanham, Md.: Rowman & Littlefield.

Hirsch, Marianne (2008). 'The Generation of Postmemory', *Poetics Today,* 29.1: 103–28.

House, Jim (2010). 'Memory and the Creation of Solidarity During the Decolonization of Algeria', *Yale French Studies,* 118–19: 15–38.

House, Jim and Neil MacMaster (2006). *Paris 1961: Algerians, State Terror, and Memory.* Oxford: Oxford University Press.

Huggan, Graham (2002). 'Cultural Memory in Postcolonial Fiction: The Uses and Abuses of Ned Kelly', *Australian Literary Studies,* 20.3 (May): 132–45.

Jameson, Fredric (1990). 'Modernism and Imperialism', in Terry Eagleton, Fredric Jameson, and Edward Said, *Nationalism, Colonialism, and Literature.* Minneapolis: University of Minnesota Press, 43–68.

Kincaid, Jamaica (1991). 'On Seeing England for the First Time', *Transition,* 51: 32–40.

Kréa, Henri (1961). 'Le racisme est collectif, la solidarité individuelle', *France-Observateur,* 26 October, pp. 14–15.

Landsberg, Alison (2004). *Prosthetic Memory: The Transformation of American Remembrance in the Age of Mass Culture.* New York: Columbia University Press.

Levy, Daniel and Natan Sznaider (2010). *Human Rights and Memory.* University Park, Pa.: Penn State University Press.

Lindeperg, Sylvie (2007). *'Nuit et Brouillard': Un film dans l'histoire.* Paris: Odile Jacob.

Mageo, Jeannette Marie (ed.) (2001). *Cultural Memory: Reconfiguring History and Identity in the Postcolonial Pacific.* Honolulu: University of Hawai'i Press.

McClintock, Anne (1992). 'The Angle of Progress: Pitfalls of the Term "Post-Colonialism"', *Social Text,* 31/32: 84–98.

Nora, Pierre (ed.) (1984–1992). *Les Lieux de Mémoire.* Paris: Gallimard.

Nora, Pierre (ed.) (1996–1998). *Realms of Memory: The Construction of the French Past,* 3 vols, English language edition, ed. Lawrence D. Kritzman and trans. Arthur Goldhammer. New York: Columbia University Press.

Nora, Pierre (ed.) (2001–2006). *Rethinking France,* trans. Mary Trouille. Chicago: University of Chicago Press.

Olick, Jeffrey K., Vered Vinitzky-Seroussi, and Daniel Levy (eds) (2011). *The Collective Memory Reader.* New York: Oxford University Press.

Radstone, Susannah and Bill Schwarz (eds) (2010). *Memory: Histories, Theories, Debates.* New York: Fordham University Press.

Resnais, Alain (dir.) (1955). *Nuit et Brouillard.* Paris: Argos Films.

Rigney, Ann (2005). 'Plenitude, Scarcity and the Circulation of Cultural Memory', *Journal of European Studies*, 35.1: 11–28.

Rossington, Michael and Anne Whitehead (eds) (2007). *Theories of Memory*. Baltimore: Johns Hopkins University Press.

Rothberg, Michael (2009). *Multidirectional Memory: Remembering the Holocaust in the Age of Decolonization*. Stanford: Stanford University Press.

Rothberg, Michael, Debarati Sanyal, and Max Silverman (eds) (2010). *Noeuds de Mémoire: Multidirectional Memory in Postwar French and Francophone Culture*, special issue of *Yale French Studies*, 118–19.

Said, Edward (1978). *Orientalism*. New York: Vintage.

Said, Edward (1993). *Culture and Imperialism*. New York: Vintage.

Said, Edward (1999). *Out of Place: A Memoir*. New York: Knopf.

Said, Edward (2000). 'Invention, Memory, and Place', *Critical Inquiry*, 26 (Winter): 175–92.

Schwarz, Bill (2010). 'Memory, Temporality, Modernity: *Les lieux de mémoire*', in S. Radstone and B. Schwarz (eds), *Memory: Histories, Theories, Debates*. New York: Fordham University Press, 41–58.

Sengupta, Indra (ed.) (2009). *Memory, History, and Colonialism: Engaging with Pierre Nora in Colonial and Postcolonial Contexts*. London: German Historical Institute.

Shetty, Sandhya and Elizabeth Jane Bellamy (2000). 'Postcolonialism's Archive Fever', *diacritics*, 30.1: 25–48.

Shohat, Ella (1992). 'Notes on the "Post-Colonial"', *Social Text*, 31/32: 99–113.

Smith, William Gardner (1963). *The Stone Face*. New York: Farrar, Straus, and Co.

Spivak, Gayatri Chakravorty (1988a). 'Can the Subaltern Speak?', in Cary Nelson and Lawrence Grossberg (eds), *Marxism and the Interpretation of Culture*. Urbana, Ill.: University of Illinois Press, 271–313.

Spivak, Gayatri Chakravorty (1988b). *In Other Worlds*. New York: Routledge.

Spivak, Gayatri Chakravorty (1999). *A Critique of Postcolonial Reason*. Cambridge, Mass.: Harvard University Press.

Stoler, Ann Laura and Frederick Cooper (eds) (1997). *Tensions of Empire: Colonial Cultures in a Bourgeois World*. Berkeley: University of California Press.

Werbner, Richard (ed.) (1998). *Memory and the Postcolony: African Anthropology and the Critique of Power*. London: Zed Books.

Winston, Jane Bradley (2001). *Postcolonial Duras: Cultural Memory in Postwar France*. New York: Palgrave.

Woods, Tim (2007). *African Pasts: History and Memory in African Literatures*. Manchester: Manchester University Press.

Young, Robert J. C. (2001). *Postcolonialism: An Historical Introduction*. Oxford: Blackwell Publishers.

....

CHAPTER 17

POSTCOLONIALISM AND POPULAR CULTURES

....

SIMON FEATHERSTONE

'Popular culture means absolutely nothing to me except as it surrounds me', Edward Said told Jennifer Wicke and Michael Sprinker in 1992, and despite recent suggestions that his tastes ranged more widely, this forthright statement is generally confirmed by his published work (Said, Wicke, and Sprinker 2004: 145; Valassapoulos 2010). Though Said's dismissal of the popular is thoroughgoing, the terms of the rejection nevertheless remain instructive for a more general consideration of the place of popular culture in postcolonial studies. So, whilst he dissociates himself in the interview from Theodor Adorno's (1991) 'hideously limited and silly remarks' about popular music he also comes close to affirming Adorno's sense of the exceptional status of the western classical tradition. 'I wouldn't call it an autonomous realm', he tells his interviewers, using Adorno's terminology, 'but I certainly think one can talk about it as having a kind of relatively autonomous identity' (144). Such discrimination is highlighted in Said's relatively rare references to music in a postcolonial context, the most extended of which is the discussion of *Aida* in *Culture and Imperialism* (1993). Verdi's opera, commissioned by the client ruler of Egypt for the Cairo Opera House in 1871, is shown to embody the 'web of affiliations, connections, decisions, and collaborations' that constituted European imperial control of both the government and cultural representation of Egypt (Said 1993: 151). This detailed examination of operatic Orientalism can be compared to Said's brief engagement with Egyptian music proper. In *Musical Elaborations* (1991), he recalls attending a performance by Umm Kalthoum, the celebrated popular singer. Only when he was 'able to associate what she did musically with some features of Western classical music', could he appreciate her virtuosic technique, he comments (Said 1991: 98). European opera, because of the complexity of its Orientalizing role, is integrated into a postcolonial project on the representational strategies of colonialism. Popular music, on the other hand, even the 'classical' popular music of Umm Kalthoum, is meaningful only by reference to the traditions of which *Aida* is a part.

The detailed presence of Verdi and the virtual absence of Kalthoum is significant not for the pursuit of the arguments of Said's 'elitism' voiced by Aijaz Ahmad and others, but rather because they suggest a more general scepticism about the capacity of popular material to sustain cultural and political interrogations (see Ahmad 1992). None of the major anthologies and course readers which mapped the theoretical and pedagogic priorities of postcolonial studies in the 1990s devote much attention to the study of popular culture, and more recent reassessments have generally maintained this inattention, even as they have established a case for the significant revision and development of politics and purpose in the field (see Williams and Chrisman 1993; Ashcroft, Griffiths, and Tiffin 1995; and Castle 2001). In *Postcolonial Studies and Beyond* (2005), for example, Ania Loomba and her fellow editors identify a 'moment of doubt, renewal, and expansion' for the discipline and argue for a renewed 'gathering of scholarly, critical political energies that is no longer detained by recycled debates and institutional jockeying, but instead is methodologically complex and eclectic, extroverted, experimental, and engaged in multiple sites of investigation and contest' (Loomba et al. 2005: 29, 33–4). The essays in the collection, however, do not extend eclecticism and experiment to popular materials or to new academic disciplines that have developed their study in directions congruent with postcolonial studies: sports history and popular music studies, to name just two.

In their turn, these disciplines have had difficulties in achieving fruitful dialogues with the key concerns of postcolonialism. John Bale and Mike Cronin's *Sport and Postcolonialism* (2003), for instance, perhaps the first sustained attempt to connect sports history and postcolonial studies, reveals fundamental discrepancies between the two fields' respective disciplinary perspectives. In their introduction the editors assert that 'postcolonial theory has been dominated by a consideration of literature, an essentially subjective form that can be highly individual, placeless and contrived'. 'Sport and bodily practices offer a potentially more fruitful vehicle for considering postcolonialism than literature', they argue, 'as they are mass happenings made "real" through performance' (Bale and Cronin 2003: 2). An assumed opposition between literary 'subjectivity' and performative 'reality' (however discreetly the latter is hedged by quotation marks) is just one example of the obstacles to a broader conception of postcolonial studies inherent in diverse traditions of scholarship and in disciplines with popular cultures at their centre. At such moments of misunderstanding, it is helpful to recall the legacy of C. L. R. James.

James, celebrated historian of the Haitian revolution, Marxist theorist, author of a study of Herman Melville, and cricket correspondent of the *Manchester Guardian*, advocated and enacted just the extrovert experiment that the editors of *Postcolonial Studies and Beyond* anticipate. Significantly, perhaps, the very diversity of his interests, his non-institutional alignments and modes of writing, and a perceived inattention to some now central concerns of the discipline—gender, most obviously—have made James's presence in postcolonial studies at best partial. Yet his passionate adisciplinarity makes him an important point of reference for any project to expand the field, and for including popular cultures in that expansion. James insisted on the capacity of popular forms, especially performative modes such as sport and music, not only to express historical struggle, but also to theorize and develop it. To denigrate the popular as commodified affect while limiting the discussion of music to the western classical tradition would be, for James, unnecessarily to restrict engagement with societies in which oral and physical cultures had rich and complex traditions. At the same time, though, to render literature as 'subjective' and 'placeless' and hence beyond historical and social analysis would be an unthinkable limitation of intellectual endeavour. As his own work amply demonstrated, James envisaged a critical practice that worked towards an inclusive sense of the potential for meanings to be made from all cultural activities, textual or performative, and which allowed a generous dialogue to take place between novels, cricket matches, calypsos, and philosophy, and, by extension, between the diverse theories that underpin their study.

Like other admirers, Said made the journey to visit the elderly James at his flat in Brixton during the 1980s and, in retrospect, the encounter between the two prominent activist-scholars seems emblematic of a moment of transition. The previously unformed concept of 'postcolonial studies' represented in one aspect by James's writings (only then beginning to be collected in accessible editions) was in this period being realized as the academic discipline heralded by the publication of Said's *Orientalism* in 1978. Said admired the older man's confident appropriation and redirection of the intellectual materials of imperialism and his deployment of scholarship in the cause of political objectives, twin commitments he sought to maintain in his own work. In Brixton, though, James made him think about other things, or rather about the same things in a different way. 'He was obsessed with cricket', Said recalled, 'and, of course, I grew up in a cricket-playing culture, and so there was a little bit of that to talk about' (Said 2004: 265).

That 'little bit' of talk is unrecorded in Said's account of the meeting. However, it hints at a dialogue latent within postcolonial studies and the possibility of an inclusive space of cultural reference and performance in which Said talks about cricket and James at last enters the university classroom. What follows is conceived in the spirit of their dialogue, bringing performance cultures (though not the particular one that 'obsessed' James) to the centre of the discipline that Said effectively inaugurated. Its aim is to suggest ways in which popular culture can act as a creatively intrusive presence in the field, challenging methodological assumptions, priorities, and discourses, in the same way that James made Said remember that he came from a 'cricket-playing culture'. Using the examples of two relatively obscure Kenyan athletes of the 1950s, Lazaro Chepkwony and Nyandika Maiyoro, and two well-known Jamaican musicians of a later period, Bob Marley and Buju Banton, it explores the ways in which their performances, physical and oral, press upon the interpretative resources of the discipline. These performances also bring with them a scholarship that has not yet been fully integrated into postcolonial studies: the work of sports historian John Bale, for example, along with that of the cultural theorist Paul Gilroy and the scholars of Caribbean popular culture associated with the Mona Campus of the University of the West Indies (UWI). Equally significant, though, is the capacity of popular performers to improvise responses to moments of political change and crisis and, through those performances and improvisations, to develop interpretative strategies and structures on their own terms.

In July 1954 Lazaro Chepkwony and Nyandika Maiyoro became the first Kenyans to take part in the Amateur Athletic Association championships, held that year at London's White City stadium. Chepkwony competed in the six miles race where he ran against the future Olympic medallist Gordon Pirie, while Maiyoro ran the three miles in a field that included Christopher Chataway, who was soon to hold the 5,000 metres world record. The races were briefly reported in *The Times* where the main focus was on the retirement through injury of Pirie and on the world record set by Fred Green in a race in which Chataway, placed second, also broke the previous record (*The Times* 1954a). The performances of the Kenyans were treated in ambivalent terms, with the six miles event described as 'enlivened and also robbed of its customary rhythm and stately order by L. Chepkwony … who, lap after lap and half-mile after half-mile, persisted in challenging anyone who tried to set up a reasonably comfortable lead'. His 'down-fall', it concluded, was his 'lack of balance' which led him to fall and then retire three miles into the race (*The Times* 1954b). A similar unease to that expressed about 'the hapless Chepkwony' marked *The Times*'s account of the three miles. 'One of the numerous Africans who had entered for the championships, N. Maiyoro of Kenya, set such a pace and went so far ahead … that for nearly a third of the way Chataway … almost looked to be losing ground', it reported. Nevertheless, the Englishmen recovered to pass the 'barefooted Maiyoro', breaking the record, with the Kenyan finishing third (a fact omitted in *The Times* article). These moments of African running suggest, not least in the brevity and partiality of their record, some of the scholarly challenges that performance culture represents for contemporary postcolonial studies.

Implicit in the *Times* reports are codes and contests that informed imperial sporting traditions in a period of political uncertainty. Antony Ward, reflecting ten years later upon Chataway's performances in 1954, identified the qualities of the successful middle-distance athlete of the period as 'knowledge of pace judgement, knowledge of one's own ability and knowledge of one's opponents' (Ward 1964: 75). Sharing the lead represented one means of achieving and using such knowledge. It enacted temporary agreement on a communal endeavour that allowed individual athletes time and space to assess opponents and conserve energies before eventually pressing for individual advantage. By persistently maintaining the lead, the Kenyans breached this implicit custom and so, by reference to the consolidated practices of European athletic competition, proved themselves hopelessly out of their depth. This failure of mimicry, as it might be termed, elicited discrepant responses. Chepkwony, in particular, is said to have been 'taken to heart by the spectators', presumably for displaying qualities that might then have been described as 'pluck'. But the less generous view of the *Times* correspondent was that the athletes had disrupted the classical aesthetics of English body culture, its 'customary rhythm and stately order', a veiled indication of the relevance of amateur athletics to the anti-colonial struggles of the post-Second World War period.

Chepkwnony and Maiyoro visited London as representatives of the Kenya Amateur Athletic Association en route to the Empire and Commonwealth Games in Vancouver. As such, they were intended to contribute to a new national identity that was being rapidly constructed in response to a perceived revolutionary threat to British rule in the

East African colony. An Emergency had been declared in 1952 to counter armed resistance to colonial policy in the Central Highlands by the predominantly Kikuyu Land Freedom Army. The conflict resulted in the imprisonment of Kikuyu leaders (including the future president Jomo Kenyatta), the militarization of large areas of the Highlands, and the mass deportation and 're-education' of large numbers of the populace. Military operations reached their climax in April and May of 1954 with the detention of 19,000 adult males in Nairobi (see Percox 2003; Berman 1990). In the course of the rebellion, an essentially localized political conflict over land distribution was presented by the colonial government as an uprising that combined nationalist ambitions and regressive primitivism. As Robert Young has argued, 'nationalism ... has always been the language in which the power struggle between colonizer and colonized for domination or self-determination operated' (Young 2001: 173). In the Kenya of 1954, however, such aspiration to modern statehood was also associated with 'Mau Mau', a quasi-religious concept that, as Carl Rosberg and John Nottingham suggest, was represented as an 'atavistic rejection of modern civilization and an attempt to revert to a degraded savagery' (Rosberg and Nottingham 1966: 353). The military response to the Land Freedom Army was accompanied by initiatives that attempted to delineate alternative civic structures of Kenyan identity, offering 'progressive' models for an anticipated future nationhood to be established within imperial borders. It was in this spirit that the Kenya Amateur Athletic Association, founded in 1951, sent Chepkwony and Maiyoro to London and North America.

The political purpose of Kenyan athletics was outlined by KAAA president, Derek Erskine, in a letter to *The Times* in May 1954 announcing the Association's participation in the Commonwealth Games. Erskine anticipated 'the coming of a new and vigorous spirit of national unity—the merging of old tribal and racial loyalties, religious and colour prejudices in a healthy and integrated nationalism'. 'As yet we can produce no Roger Bannisters', he continued, 'but we aim to hold our position as her Majesty's premier Crown Colony, and we may even give one or two of the Dominions something to think about' (Erskine 1954). In this late imperial version of a public-school house competition, Chepkwony and Maiyoro—who, like most subsequent Kenyan athletes, were non-Kikuyu—were deemed to represent a newly emergent colonial 'Kenyan-ness'. *The Times*'s reportage of their performance certainly meshed with contemporary analyses of the 'Kenyan problem' and its solution. The apparent inability of the athletes to cope with the technical demands of modern racing, for instance, reflected the conclusions of Louis Leakey, the leading colonial commentator on 'Mau Mau', who argued that the conflict was rooted in the imposition of an imported modernity upon an essentially traditional people. The 'speed of progress has been so rapid that it has made a part of the population unbalanced in their outlook', he wrote in 1952, using the same term that the *Times* correspondent was to apply to Chepkwony's running (Leakey 1952: 85). For Leakey and the colonial government, the remedy for this 'imbalance' was what one administrator termed 'the medicine of rehabilitation ... a mixture of education, religion and recreation' (Askwith 1958: 78). Competitive athletics formed one part of this, encouraged, as Mohamed Amin and Peter Moll suggest, as a cheaply resourced 'relief to the boredom and frustrations of village life under restrictive curfews', as well as a means of civic reconstruction (Amin and Moll 1972: n.p.). But if the athletes' way of running could be interpreted as an understandably flawed work-in-progress, it also demonstrated an unexpected capacity to compete with the imperial elite and to provide a performative critique of the values and meanings of late imperial English body culture.

Derek Erskine's reference to Roger Bannister in his letter to *The Times* is significant in its implicit assurance of English sporting supremacy. Bannister had run his sub-four-minute mile two months before the White City meeting, marking what Peter Lovesey, the official historian of the Amateur Athletic Association, termed the 'sublime achievement of British athletics' (Lovesey 1979: 106). But as John Bale has argued, Bannister's record represented competing rather than unifying versions of post-Second World War national sporting culture (Bale 2004). The record was readily interpreted, not least by the athlete himself, as a reassertion of the relevance of classic traditions of English amateurism in sport. In his autobiography, *First Four Minutes* (1955), Bannister set out his reaction to what he perceived as the corruptive Cold War politics that had shaped a professionalized athletic competition at the Helsinki Olympic Games of 1952. 'To regard sport as a hobby is surely more of a virtue than a vice', he writes, 'and is much closer to the Greek ideal of the complete man than is the athletic machine [of the USA and USSR]' (Bannister 1955: 162). However, although Bannister remained economically independent of his sport, his determined pursuit of the decidedly un-amateurish goal of a timed record suggests the kind of pressures that were accruing upon older categories of sporting practice. Whilst Bannister rejected the timetables and demeanour of the professional sportsman, his outcome-based training and willingness to push at some key limits of performative propriety to achieve his objective, notably in the use of pacemakers in the ostensibly competitive race in which the record was broken, suggested a technical sophistication and hard-nosed methodical application foreign to earlier versions of amateurism. Chepkwony and Maiyoro's 'lack of balance', by contrast, represented a style of running that interrogated both the Cold War 'athletic machine' and the British technocratic ideal through a circumvention of established strategies of competition. Their 'running with élan', John Bale and Joe Sang suggest, was 'something which had become suppressed in the rational world of restraint occupied by "modern" runners', Bannister included (Bale and Sang 1996: 178).

C. L. R. James, writing about the performances of the Caribbean cricketers Rohan Kanhai and Garfield Sobers in the post-war period, argued that their innovations in the body cultures of imperial sport were similarly expressions of and agents in wider political aspirations and achievements (James 1989: 165–71; 218–32). The invention of 'Kenyan-ness' to which Chepkwony and Maiyoro contributed was intended to serve existing structures of control and development, and to reinforce the status of colonial subjects as a focus for development in implicit contrast to the avowedly regressive trajectory of 'Mau Mau'. However, their running styles, developed through the hybrid convergence of indigenous and colonial approaches and sporting organizations, instead predicted an athletics that would embody a postcolonial 'Kenyan-ness', just as, in James's argument, Kanhai and Sobers performed as confidently independent West Indians.

Kipchoge Keino famously developed their 'unbalanced' running style into a method that established world records in the 3,000 and 5,000 metres soon after Kenya's independence in 1963. However, also embedded in Chepkonwy's and Maiyoro's London performances was a later challenge to the integrity of that national body culture. The very dominance of Kenyan runners in middle-distance events established, post-Keino, in the globalizing athletics competitions of the 1970s, combined with faltering economic and infrastructural development in Kenya, meant that Chepkwony's and Maiyoro's Atlantic journeys, as well as their running techniques, anticipated the migrant future of the African athlete. The body of the 'Kenyan runner' was commodified in what Andrew Simms and Matt Rendell have termed the 'global trade in muscle', resulting in 'Kenyan-ness' itself becoming a portable body culture in the global economy of athletics (Simms and Rendell 2004). In exchange for enhanced training and educational facilities, athletes traded that identity, merging it into those of European (and, later, Gulf) states to compete in the Olympic and World championships that still nominally represented the securities of nationhood. If, as James argued, sporting theatre is also political theatre, the running that anticipated the emergence of new postcolonial identities in the 1950s also predicted their later migrant formations in a sport defined by a more intensive globalization than that staged at the British Empire and Commonwealth Games of 1954 (see Jarvie 2007; Wirz 2006; Giulianotti and Robertson 2007).

Whilst Chepkwony and Maiyoro provide an example of the ways in which the colonial body is simultaneously determined by and resistant to colonial politics of representation, the career of Bob Marley suggests a considered intervention in and articulate commentary upon that process. Marley has long been an object of global attention, of course, and has also been the subject of some academic analysis, though, as noted earlier, that analysis has not been conducted in the foreground of postcolonial studies: he warrants just one page reference in the combined indexes of Castle's, Ashcroft's, and Williams and Chrisman's readers (Castle 2001; Williams and Chrisman 1993; Ashcroft, Griffiths, and Tiffin 1995). Instead, studies of Marley have been developed in disparate disciplinary contexts, from Paul Gilroy's cultural studies to Kwame Dawes's literary-critical celebrations of the songs and Jason Toynbee's sociological monograph on the singer (see Gilroy 1987, 2000, 2010; Dawes: 1999, 2002; Toynbee 2007). To this political and cultural criticism can be added Marley's own self-conscious theorizing as a 'vernacular' intellectual, to use Grant Farred's term (Farred 2003).

Gilroy's reflections on Marley, developed over a period of twenty-five years, provide the most thoughtful guides to the musician's elusive significance for postcolonialism. In his first extensive discussion of the singer in 'There Ain't No Black in the Union Jack' (1987), Gilroy is primarily concerned with the implications of Marley's entry into the corporate structures of global capitalism following his decision in 1974 to reconstitute the original singing trio of The Wailers, and to allow Island Records to shape a new sound and imagery that would allow his music to be promoted beyond Jamaica. In 1962, the year of Jamaican independence, C. L. R. James had celebrated popular cultures of the Caribbean as expressions of an already-achieved modernity—'the mass of the people are not seeking a mass identity', he wrote, 'they are expressing one'

(James 1963: 417). Just over ten years later, abandoning the corruption and marketing limitations of the Jamaican music industry, Marley wagered such expressive achievement against a political advantage that James might have understood and appreciated. What Gilroy judges to be Marley's 'obvious compromises'—the addition of new instrumentation and performance styles to attract rock audiences, for example, and a complicity in his own projection as a kind of radical 'other' within a rock sensibility—are weighed against the 'solidification of communicative networks across the African diaspora' (Gilroy 1987: 170). Trusting the resilience of the expressive potential of a musical form born of that diaspora and of Third World liberation movements against the totalizing impetus of corporate management, Marley accepted many of the entailments of western stardom. Yet as Gilroy notes quizzically in *Between Camps* (2000), that negotiation was pursued as much by reference to religion as to revolutionary politics. 'On what scale of cultural analysis do we make sense of [Marley's] reconciliation of modern and postmodern technologies with mystical antimodern forces?' he enquires, a question of critical method that has relevance to postcolonial studies more generally (Gilroy 2000: 132).

Marley's Rastafarianism was important for Island's initial marketing campaigns, with their prominent display of dreadlocks and ganja on record sleeves and posters establishing a somatic otherness that equated to rock's rebellious 'authenticity' even as it implicitly exploited older colonialist derogations of indigenous custom. But the role of Rastafarianism in the cultural production of Marley's music and performance presents a different challenge to a discipline that might be eager to assimilate his involvement in anti-colonial activism within its own traditions of secular analysis. Bob Marley as eloquent supporter of the latter stages of Third World liberation struggles is one thing; Bob Marley as equally eloquent proselytizer for the living God Selassie-I is something else. Yet his insistent conflation of those roles suggests that the unexpected answer to Gilroy's question is that 'mystical antimodern forces' provided theoretical and discursive means for both a vernacular appraisal of imperialist history and an unprecedented popular critique of postcolonial modernity. Marley's engagement with the 'culture industry', for example, was developed and defused by a rendering of its secular routines as, in some sense, sacred. Ian McCann notes that Marley 'rarely refused an interview', and his responses to the generally banal questioning that he endured transformed the predictable discourse of the rock star into a challenging reasoning through which he explicated the practice and strategy of his faith (McCann 1993: 5). Marley's interviews make consistently unnerving reading for anyone attempting to co-opt him to secular postcolonialist politics. 'Me don' understand politics … me don' understand big words like "democratic socialism"', he told *New York Magazine* in 1977. 'What me say is what de Bible say, but because people don' read de Bible no more, dey tink me talk politics' (Bradshaw 2004: 109). Such insistence upon a biblical hermeneutics that is foreign to postcolonial studies nevertheless provides a frame for the complex popular theatre that Marley developed in the 1970s. Two events in particular provide material for thinking about his performative theology: his appearance with the warring political leaders of Jamaica in the One Love Peace Concert in Kingston in April 1978 and his contribution to Zimbabwe's independence ceremony in Salisbury/Harare two years later. Both were testimonies to an extraordinary global status in the final years of his life, but both also demonstrated an integration of political action within a practice of spiritual dissent.

The 'One Love' concert, which also featured the ex-Wailer Peter Tosh and other reggae stars such as Jacob Miller and Big Youth, indicated the political significance of popular culture, particularly popular music, in post-independence Jamaica. Both Edward Seaga and Michael Manley, the political leaders whose violent competition had provoked the 'peace concert', exploited music in their campaigns, and their reluctant agreement to share a stage with Marley was a mutual recognition of his local and international stature. The chaotically choreographed (and latterly much-reproduced) climax of the concert featured a tableau of Seaga and Manley uncomfortably joining hands with the singer as The Wailers played 'Jamming', that easy-rhythmed paean to creative co-operation. As such it is evidently a theatre of reconciliation, intended perhaps to recall the chorus of the Marley song that gave the concert its name, with its injunction 'let's get together and feel alright'. In this interpretation of the scene a new form of popular music is seen, momentarily at least, to have superseded the corruption of the postcolonial national ideal and coerced those responsible for that corruption into symbolic atonement in the new popular cultural space of the music festival.

However, as his interviews suggest, Marley's relationship with postcolonial politics was neither close nor secular, and his methodology of engagement was ill-suited to humanitarian gesture. The band played 'Jamming', not 'One Love', while the politicians came on stage and though, at first hearing, it is one of Marley's simpler songs, it nevertheless established a lyrical context that complicated the events that ensued. 'We are the living sacrifice', the song asserts, and it is not Jamaicans who 'must unite' but 'Jah Jah children' (Marley 1977). The emphasis upon that theological injunction, reiterated in Marley's 'blessing' when Manley and Seaga met, counterpoints the banality of political 'reconciliation' in a context as riven as Jamaica in 1978; in truth, the term is as foreign a notion to Rastafarianism as it was to the politicians and gunmen of the Jamaica Labour Party and People's National Party. In one of his interviews, Marley had mused that the 'devil ain't got no power over me ... The devil come, and me shake hands with the devil. Devil has his part to play' (Palmer 2004: 169). If the 'devils', Manley and Seaga, were playing their part and shaking hands with Marley on his Kingston stage, the singer's role was to 'come between the politicians and become something else for the people', as he put it. (170). The presence of Marley on stage literally 'between' the Prime Minister and Leader of the Opposition realized the prophetic role that this implied: Marley offered his audience not reconciliation but a manifestation of that 'something else', a role reiterated in the song that he performed when the devils had departed. 'Jah Live' had been written as a polemical reassertion of Rastafarian belief at the moment of its most profound crisis, the death of the 'living god' Selassie in 1975. Three years later, in another crisis, it restated Marley's only (theocratic) alternative to the evident failures of postcolonial politics.

Marley's performance in Zimbabwe provides further evidence of his strategy of harnessing Babylonian communication systems to sufferers' ends. That 'solidification of communication networks across the African diaspora' that Gilroy defines as its political objective found a vivid climax in a Jamaican's participation in the formal declaration of an African nationhood. However, Marley's attendance combined postcolonial national-ist celebration with pan-Africanist dissidence in an act of astringent questioning rather than unequivocal affirmation. The terms of that interrogation were already embedded in the song 'Zimbabwe', which Marley had written in Ethiopia in 1978. Despite being a favourite of the guerrilla armies and consequently a major factor in the invitation to the ceremony, the song's iteration of the fact that 'Africans a liberate Zimbabwe' is hedged with questions about the outcomes of that liberation and of a menacing 'internal power struggle'. The cryptic prophecy, 'soon we will find out / who is the real revolutionary', cautions rather than anticipates, and exhibits the wariness that always characterized Marley's dealings with secular politics (Marley 1979). 'Never make a politician, grant you a favour', he had sung in 'Revolution', 'They will always want to control you forever', and in this spirit he paid his own and his band's passage to Africa (Marley 1974). Marley's concern to act as untrammelled witness of pan-African spirituality that was evident in the theatre of the 'One Love' concert also conditioned his response to the chaotic events in Salisbury where veteran revolutionaries were excluded from the independence cel-ebrations and tear-gassed by the police of the new regime. When hastened to conclude his interrupted set, he responded by singing 'War', the setting of a Haile Selassie speech addressing the consequences of all political iniquity, before concluding with the ques-tioning uncertainty of 'Zimbabwe' itself (Davis 1993: 226–8; Boot, Salewicz, and Marley 1995: 261). 'Africa is more revolutionized today than yesterday', he told an interviewer, before adding the characteristic qualification that the 'real thing is that Africa [doesn't] unite as Rasta. They unite as Marx and Lenin' (Blount 2004: 203).

Bob Marley, the pan-Africanist Rastafarian outsider in both Jamaica and Zimbabwe, acted alternately as witness and warner in the latter stages of postcolonial nation-building. That it was Rastafarianism rather than Marxism that provided the frame and discourse for his celebratory critiques is indicative of the more general challenges that popular culture, with its hybrid resources and improvised performance practices, brings to post-colonial studies. Rastafarianism might be a 'mystical antimodern force', as Gilroy sug-gests, but it also provided the means for astute evaluations of modernity and innovative engagements with its globalizing projects. In *Darker Than Blue* (2010), Gilroy's most recent—and most elegiac—treatment of Marley, he laments the 'disaggregation and iconisation of the old rebel culture', situating the singer's work as the 'twentieth centu-ry's last effective contribution to the forms of black consciousness that could span the divisions of colonial development and speak in different but complementary ways to dispersed and remote populations' (Gilroy 2010: 127, 53). However, the effective depo-liticization of Marley's work in an afterlife of digital reproduction and decontextualized recycling of a selective repertoire was also a process of de-theologizing, a fact that only intensifies the theoretical demands that such popular cultural expressions make of their interpreters.

These demands are differently inflected but no less pressing in the work of Buju Banton, a performer who represents the generation of Jamaican musicians that succeeded Marley, and who brings the problematic that Gilroy defines into the twenty-first century. Marley's death in 1981 coincided with radical changes in the dominant styles, preoccupations, and trajectories of reggae, all of which are represented by Banton's *Mr Mention* (1992), one of the key recordings of what was by then known as 'dancehall'. The packaging of the original LP instantly establishes Banton's distance from Marley's role as spiritual sufferer, with the young DJ, wearing leopard-print shirt and cap, pictured glancing coyly at the camera over designer sunglasses, numerous gold accoutrements—necklace, wristwatch, personalized ankle-bracelet—on prominent display. Such worldly concern with consumption and style is also reflected in the tunes, with their avid interest in fashion ('Batty Rider'), female objectification ('Love How the Gal Flex'), and sexual boasting ('Have to Get You Tonight'). Banton, later to become the self-proclaimed 'voice of Jamaica', expressed dancehall's retreat from the internationalist politics that defined Marley's later work, emphasizing instead discourses of sexuality, masculinity, and material consumption performed in unmediated Jamaican speech over indigenous dance rhythms (Banton 1993). The music explores a highly localized cultural geography and advertises a privatized politics of the body, fascinations which, as Carolyn Cooper and Alison Donnell put it, appear to be 'complicit with the conditions of the very global capitalist system that postcolonial studies has directed its intellectual energies against' (Cooper and Donnell 2004: 13). If Marley's work confronts that discipline with finding a way to engage with spiritual discourse as political agency, Banton and dancehall more generally confront it with a popular discourse that evidently attacks the grounds of its progressive project in its embodiment and celebration of insular commodification.

The biggest local hit on *Mr Mention*, 'Love Me Browning', suggests the interpretative problems that dancehall poses. Like many such tunes, it is a sexual narrative, but one that flags in its title a conjunction of desire and intra-ethnic demarcation. Such discrimination is unthinkable in the work of Marley for whom 'blackness' was an indivisible marker of origin in concerted opposition to colonial legacies of epidermic categorization and evaluation. Banton's casual articulation of sexual attraction defined by this very value system signals dancehall's general unwillingness to engage with emancipatory postcolonial rhetoric. 'Me love me car, me love me bike / Me love me money and ting / But most of all me love me browning', Banton chants, installing the racially defined woman in the role of prized commodity. The relocation of sexuality to the political centre of Jamaican music was emphasized—and given unintended international prominence—later in 1992 when Banton's 'Boom Bye Bye' was released. The song is one of many violent dancehall derogations of homosexuality, with its chorus voicing a seemingly unambiguous declaration: 'Boom bye bye inna battyboy head / Rude boy no promote no nasty man / Dey haffi dead' (Banton 1992; see Chin 1997). Such sentiments were not uncommon in Jamaican dancehall either before or after its release, but 'Boom Bye Bye' came to have particular significance because it coincided with the DJ joining the American record company, Mercury, one of the first suggestions that the genre, like Marley's music, could reach international markets. The subsequent cancellations of Banton's appearances in North America and Europe in response to publicity concerning the song's homophobic call to violence, along with the DJ's initial refusal to revoke its sentiments, focused attention on the status of an evidently reactionary politics articulated in an equally evidently vibrant postcolonial cultural form.

The 'problem' of dancehall politics has revived the tone if not the methodology of Adorno's minatory evaluations of popular music's implication in the bleak operations of capital. Gilroy, for example, writing of cognate developments in American hip-hop, laments the 'dismal process in which public politics become unspeakable and a body-centred biopolitics [begins] to take hold' (Gilroy 2000: 272). By reintegrating uncritically racialized discourse into popular music and foregrounding a violently moralistic reaction against both women and groups defined exclusively by their sexuality, it reactivates the virulent discourses of an imperialist past through the pervasive systems of contemporary culture industries. Even Banton's shift towards more 'spiritual' concerns on later recordings such as 'Til Shiloh (1995) and Inna Heights (1997) served to emphasize the illiberal gender politics of Rastafarianism, something that Marley, through a mastery of the conventions of American soul music, generally elided (though, as Jason Toynbee notes, it was nevertheless evident in his biography and elements of his performance practice) (Toynbee 2007: 155). The startling conjunction of the spiritual politics of 'Untold Stories' and the sexual confrontation of 'Champion' on 'Til Shiloh is just one example of the permissive discontinuities in discursive performances that, in Gilroy's analysis, reflects the etiolation of the long tradition of black Atlantic radical expression (Banton 1995). Thirty years after Marley's participation in the independence of Zimbabwe, Banton's incarceration in an American prison for trading cocaine can appear as a dark inversion of Marley's postcolonial journey, representative of what Gilroy terms the 'final commodification of the extraordinary cultural creativity born from the slave populations of the New World' (Gilroy 2000: 272).

A contrasting approach to such premises of the expressive degeneration and political regression of musical forms that had previously been at the centre of radical postcolonial projects has been developed in Jamaican scholarship of dancehall. Once again, this is a body of work shaped outside and in some measure in tension with postcolonial studies, its stress upon a radical localism of expressive and performative strategies providing an implicit, at times explicit, critique of the discipline's cultural politics. Patricia Saunders, for example, argues that the Jamaican DJ needs to be viewed as an oral interpreter and public legislator of '"unofficial" cultural codes of conduct' rather than a purveyor of the banalities of consumption and of reactionary gender politics (Saunders 2003: 106). Unlike Marley's music, dancehall makes little or no concession to 'international' audiences, and its retreat from the black Atlantic ambitions of earlier reggae is accounted in this reading as a return to an intimate expression of the everyday conflicts of local audiences, as distinct from the more expansive modes of transnational cultural expression to which Marley aspired. Such reconfiguration of audience and objective has consequences for the interpretative methodology of its study. Carolyn Cooper, whose Sound Clash (2004) was one of the first extended scholarly treatments of dancehall, emphasizes the agonistic orality of the DJs, rejecting what she represents as the overliteral interpretation of lyrics which, unlike the carefully transcribed versions accompanying Marley's recordings, are generally non-textual and hence actively engaged with and dependent upon the contexts of their performance and reception. The extravagance of the verbal play and gendered positioning of the popular DJ, she argues, invite argument and laughter as much as serious approbation, an interpretative possibility that allows her to characterize apparently derogatory sexual statement as also offering a 'radical, underground confrontation with the patriarchal gender ideology and the duplicitous morality of fundamentalist Jamaican society' (Cooper 2004: 3).

In such performative contexts, Banton's praise for his 'browning' could be critiqued by the lyrics' own sly and evasive narrative, which implies a more critical perspective on the speaker's motives and values than the speaker himself is willing to admit—a comic investigation rather than an expression of the 'duplicitious morality' that Cooper defines. More controversially, Cooper renders Banton's rhetoric of weaponry as 'lyrical guns' rather than as incitements to murder, verbal appropriations that may allude to material realities of everyday violence and prejudice in the island but operate on discursive and performative levels. To limit the interpretation of 'Boom Bye Bye' to the 'hate speech' of its chorus, she argues, ignores the 'theorizing' of the rest of the lyrics, which locate judgement in a celebration of heterosexual pleasure. 'To Jamaican ears', Cooper suggests, provocatively quoting from the lyrics, Banton's performance is as much about '"the sweetness between women's legs" as it is an indictment of homosexuality' (173). 'Jamaican ears' are important here, for part of the implicit critique of the broad postcolonialist project that marks dancehall scholarship centres on an inattention to the deep culture that generates particular popular expressions, and the fierce independence that such expressions imply. 'The homogenizing imperative of global political correctness effaces cultural difference in a new imperialism of "liberal" ideology', Cooper asserts (177). Banton himself told an interviewer in 1995 that 'it's good when cultures meet, but I have to deal with my people and stay true to my people', an argument developed by Deborah Thomas who suggests that his refusal to suppress 'Boom Bye Bye' should be seen as a stance that 'mediated the hegemonic force of economic (market) values by refusing to compromise what has been seen as a Jamaican cultural value' (Zabihyan 1995: 14; Thomas 2004: 242). That such a 'cultural value' devolves to a national consensus on the sinfulness of homosexuality and the need for its eradication situates such localizing arguments at a dangerous political crux, of course. Even as dancehall is read as enacting a militant resistance to culturally appropriative forces of global commerce, the return of music to the national popular assertiveness that C. L. R. James identified at the time of the independence of Caribbean states, exposes a politics which, viewed from the perspective of the secular liberal scholarship instituted by Said, is defined not by nationalist optimism but by a reactionary positioning that colludes with the very forces it purports to resist.

The arguments that surround the performances of the dancehall DJs suggest some of the risks and disruptions that popular culture and its accompanying disciplines inject into postcolonial studies. The challenges set by the particular examples used in this chapter—the meaning of the fragmentary record of Lazaro Chepkwony's and Nyandika Maiyoro's running, the spiritual discourse underlying Bob Marley's negotiations with capitalist industries and postcolonial politics, and the illiberal biopolitics of Buju Banton's music—illustrate the range of questions that somatic and oral traditions and innovations bring to what have been predominantly textual concerns. Their demands upon existing disciplinary resources recall James's own emphasis in his later work on the value of performative improvisation for the practice and study of postcolonial politics: his critique of Kwame Nkrumah's rule in Ghana in the 1960s and his assessment of Walter Rodney's opposition to Forbes Burnham's regime in Guyana both devolve upon failures to react flexibly and imaginatively to changing circumstances (James 1977, 1983). By extension, James's insistence on supple response and inclusive curiosity in the intellectual endeavours demanded by colonial and postcolonial history reflected his mistrust of fixed and replicated interpretative positions. His requirement that cultural performances be taken seriously even when they are evidently problematic or seemingly irrelevant to the major questions of power—the point perhaps of his cricketing conversation with Said—suggests his continuing relevance for a still young and developing discipline. The inclusion of sport, music, dance, and other performance cultures as central concerns, and the recognition of such vernacular materials' capacity to generate theory as well as to be objects of theorizing, present abundant possibilities for a postcolonial studies that is open to dialogue across disciplines and across the varieties of cultural production.

REFERENCES

Adorno, Theodor (1991). *The Culture Industry*, ed. J. M. Bernstein. London: Routledge.

Ahmad, Aijaz (1992). *In Theory: Classes, Nations, Literatures*. London: Verso.

Amin, Mohamed and Peter Moll (1972). *Kenya's World Beating Athletes: A Photohistory*. Nairobi: East African Publishing House.

Ashcroft, Bill, Gareth Griffiths, and Helen Tiffin (eds) (1995). *The Post-Colonial Studies Reader*. London and New York: Routledge.

Askwith, T. G. (1958 [1953]). *Kenya's Progress*. Nairobi: Eagle Press.

Bale, John (2004). *Roger Bannister and the Four-Minute Mile*. Abingdon and New York: Routledge.

Bale, John and Joe Sang (1996). *Kenyan Running: Movement Culture, Geography and Global Change*. London and Portland, Or.: Frank Cass.

Bale, John and Mike Cronin (eds) (2003). *Sport and Postcolonialism*. Oxford and New York: Berg.

Bannister, Roger (1955). *First Four Minutes*. London: Putnam.

Banton, Buju (1992). *Mr Mention*. Penthouse.

Banton, Buju (1992). *Boom Bye Bye*. Shang.

Banton, Buju (1993). *Voice of Jamaica*. Mercury.

Banton, Buju (1995). *'Til Shiloh*. Loose Cannon.

Banton, Buju (1997). *Inna Heights*. Island Records.

Berman, Bruce (1990). *Control and Crisis in Colonial Kenya: The Dialectic of Domination*. London, Nairobi, and Athens, OH: James Currey, Heinemann, and Ohio University Press.

Blount, Rose (2004). 'Bob Marley—Rastaman, Reggae Musician', in H. Bordowitz (ed.), *Every Little Thing Gonna Be Alright: The Bob Marley Reader*. Cambridge, Mass.: Da Capo Press, 201–4.

Boot, Adrian, Chris Salewicz, and Rita Marley (1995). *Bob Marley: Songs of Freedom*. London: Bloomsbury.

Bradshaw, J. (2004 [1977]). 'The Reggae Way to "Salvation"', in H. Bordowitz (ed.), *Every Little Thing Gonna Be Alright: The Bob Marley Reader*. Cambridge, Mass.: Da Capo Press, 96–109.

Castle, Gregory (ed.) (2001). *Postcolonial Discourses: An Anthology*. Oxford and Malden, Mass.: Blackwell.

Chin, Timothy S. (1997). '"Bullers" and "Battymen": Contesting Homophobia in Black Popular Culture and Contemporary Caribbean Literature', *Callaloo*, 20.1: 127–41.

Cooper, Carolyn (2004). *Sound Clash: Jamaican Dancehall Culture at Large*. New York and Basingstoke: Palgrave Macmillan.

Cooper, Carolyn and Alison Donnell (2004). 'Jamaican Popular Culture', *Interventions*, 6:1: 1–17.

Davis, Stephen (1993). *Bob Marley: Conquering Lion of Reggae*. London: Plexus.

Dawes, Kwame (1999). *Natural Mysticism: Towards a New Reggae Aesthetic in Caribbean Writing*. Leeds: Peepal Tree.

Dawes, Kwame (2002). *Bob Marley: Lyrical Genius*. London: Sanctuary.

Erskine, Derek (1954). 'Athletes from Kenya', *The Times*, 22 May: 7.

Farred, Grant (2003). *What's My Name? Black Vernacular Intellectuals*. Minneapolis and London: University of Minnesota Press.

Gilroy, Paul (1987). *'There Ain't No Black in the Union Jack': The Cultural Politics of Race and Nation*. London: Hutchinson.

Gilroy, Paul (2000). *Between Camps: Race, Identity and Nationalism at the End of the Colour Line*. London: Allen Lane/Penguin Press.

Gilroy, Paul (2010). *Darker Than Blue: On the Moral Economies of Black Atlantic Culture*. Cambridge, Mass. and London: Belknap Press of Harvard University.

Giulianotti, Richard and Roland Robertson (2007). *Globalization and Sport*. Oxford: Blackwell.

James, C. L. R. (1963). *The Black Jacobins: Toussaint L'Ouverture and the San Domingo Revolution*, 2nd edn. New York: Vintage Books.

James, C. L. R. (1977). *Nkrumah and the Ghana Revolution*. London: Allison and Busby.

James, C. L. R. (1983). *Walter Rodney and the Question of Power*. London: Race Today Publications.

James, C. L. R. (1989). *Cricket*, ed. A. Grimshaw. London: Allison and Busby.

Jarvie, Grant (2007). 'The Promise and Possibilities of Running In and Out of East Africa', in Y. Pitsiladis, J. Bale, C. Sharp, and T. Noakes (eds), *East African Running: Towards a Cross-Disciplinary Perspective*. London and New York: Routledge, 24–39.

Leakey, L. S. B. (1952). *Mau Mau and the Kenyans*. London: Methuen.

Loomba, Ania, Suvir Kaul, Matti Bunzl, Antoinette Burton, and Jed Esty (eds) (2005). *Postcolonial Studies and Beyond*. Durham, NC and London: Duke University Press.

Lovesey, Peter (1979). *The Official Centenary History of the Amateur Athletic Association*. Enfield: Guinness Superlatives.

Marley, Bob (1974). *Natty Dread*. Island Records.

Marley, Bob (1977). *Exodus*. Island Records.

Marley, Bob (1979). *Survival*. Island Records.

McCann, Ian (1993). *Bob Marley: In His Own Words*. London: Omnibus Press.

Palmer, Robert (2004 [1994]). 'One Love', in H. Bordowitz (ed.), *Every Little Thing Gonna Be Alright: The Bob Marley Reader*. Cambridge, Mass.: Da Capo Press, 160–9.

Percox, David A. (2003). 'Mau Mau and the Arming of the State', in E. S. Atieno Odhiambo and J. Lonsdale (eds), *Mau Mau and Nationhood: Arms, Authority and Narration*. Oxford, Nairobi, and Athens, OH: James Currey, East African Educational Publishers, and Ohio University Press, 121–54.

Rosberg, Carl G., Jr and John Nottingham (1966). *The Myth of 'Mau Mau': Nationalism in Kenya*. New York and London: Frederick A. Praeger and Pall Mall Press.

Said, Edward (1978). *Orientalism*. London: Routledge & Kegan Paul.

Said, Edward (1991). *Musical Elaborations*. London: Chatto and Windus.

Said, Edward (1993). *Culture and Imperialism*. London: Chatto and Windus.

Said, Edward, Jennifer Wicke, and Michael Sprinker (2004). 'Criticism and the Art of Politics', in Edward Said, *Power, Politics, and Culture: Interviews with Edward W. Said*, ed. G. Viswanathan. London: Bloomsbury, 118–63.

Saunders, Patricia (2003). 'Is Not Everything Good to Eat, Good to Talk: Sexual Economy and Dancehall Music in the Global Marketplace', *Small Axe*, 7.1: 95–116.

Simms, Andrew and Matt Rendell (2004). 'The Global Trade in Muscle', *New Statesman*, 9 August: 24–5.

The Times (1954a). 'Green and Chataway Break the Three Miles World Record', 12 July: 3.

The Times (1954b). 'Pirie Retires in Six Miles', 10 July: 4.

Thomas, Deborah A. (2004). *Modern Blackness: Nationalism, Globalization, and the Politics of Culture in Jamaica*. Durham, NC and London: Duke University Press.

Toynbee, Jason (2007). *Bob Marley: Herald of a Postcolonial World?* Cambridge: Polity Press.

Valassopoulos, Anastasia (2010). '"Long, Languorous, Repetitious Line": Edward Said's Critique of Arab Popular Culture', in A. Iskandar and H. Rustom (eds), *Edward Said: A Legacy of Emancipation and Representation*. Berkeley: University of California Press, 191–203.

Ward, Antony (1964). *Modern Distance Running*. London: Stanley Paul.

Williams, Patrick and Laura Chrisman (eds) (1993). *Colonial Discourse and Post-Colonial Theory: A Reader*. Harlow: Prentice Hall.

Wirz, Jürg (2006). *Run to Win: The Training Secrets of the Kenyan Runners*. Oxford: Meyer and Meyer.

Young, Robert J. C. (2001). *Postcolonialism: An Historical Introduction*. Oxford: Blackwell.

Zabihyan, Kimi (1995). 'A Roar from the Lion's Den', *The Guardian Tabloid*, 8 December: 14.

CHAPTER 18

....

RACE, RACISM, AND POSTCOLONIALITY

....

POOJA RANGAN AND REY CHOW

INTRODUCTION

....

The arrest of Prof. Henry Louis Gates, Jr. in the summer of 2009 outside his home in Cambridge, Massachusetts instigated outraged responses from a wide variety of different quarters, with a substantial portion of the discourse from both conservative and liberal commentators being focused on speculations as to whether or not race had had an operative role to play. On the surface, the stakes seemed quite simply to be colour-coded—the arresting officer in question happened to be a white man, and Gates a black one. Taking the issue of class into account, however, adds another dimension to the incident. The attention received by the arrest was due in no small part to the fact that the party who was presumed to be guilty is a professor at one of the world's most prestigious universities, an institution where discrimination or setting-apart, albeit of a different kind, is the rule of admission. The complications of analysing the incident then increase in manifold fashion when we consider that the stakeholders in the event were not limited to Gates, the policeman, and the vigilant neighbour who summoned the police to the scene, but included academic communities at Harvard and beyond, as well as television, radio, print and internet publics, all of whom were discursively involved in the extended 'scene' of the arrest.

As with other accounts that have attempted to come to terms with this event, we can begin by dealing with the economy of stereotypes underpinning the incident. Here, the figures of the black perpetrator and the white law enforcer readily offer themselves as footholds for taking stock of the encounter between Gates and the police officer. But while the alarming ease with which we can recognize and apprehend these figures demonstrates that race can still be reduced to stereotypes to the exclusion of other factors, it is more difficult to talk about the role these stereotypes play within the expanded discursive universe that such incidents bring to the fore. As stereotypes generally have a negative or repressive connotation—of someone being victimized and stigmatized because of their race, for instance—it might seem perverse, but is nonetheless pertinent, to ask if and how these devices served a *productive* function within the encounter between Gates and the policeman. This would amount to asking what ideological mechanisms are engaged when we apprehend and take up our places in society in response to the 'interpellation' of the racialized subject—the process in which institutions or figures of authority 'hail' us to recognize ourselves in subject positions that strengthen the dominant ideological structures of society (Althusser 1971). In other words, this would imply asking how racism is not simply repressive but is in fact essential to the production, regulation, and governance of 'good citizens'. While it is nearly impossible to discuss this neutrally, it is ultimately what is at stake in talking about race under postcolonial circumstances, as will also be seen in some of the other instances and incidents we analyse below.

This chapter is devoted to questions of the persistence of racism in the production and maintenance of postcolonial cultural identity. More specifically, it looks at how the notions of race and racism have been conceptualized over the past several decades of postcolonial critical theory, beginning with its conception as a major analytical rubric in the anti-colonial writings of Frantz Fanon and Albert Memmi, through the poststructuralist turn in race theory marked by Henry Louis Gates Jr.'s influential edited volume, *'Race', Writing, and Difference*, to more recently the move toward questions of biopolitics, as enabled by the later writings and lectures of Michel Foucault. Rather than summarizing the last sixty years of postcolonial theory—an impossible task—or adopting a narrowly schematic view, we will attempt instead to approach some of the broader rubrics under which race and racism have been hypothesized. While evaluating the significance of positing racism as a negative and repressive structure, we will also explore how useful it is to think through the generative functions that racism serves as a technology of government within modern society as a whole.

The Early Moment of Anti-Colonial Reflection

As Michael Omi and Howard Winant have argued, anti-colonial and postcolonial studies are important interlocutors with the subject of race, since they take as their point of departure racism and racialization as phenomena cultivated within the colonial encounter, rather than beginning, as other sociological or anthropological approaches to racial theory do, with epiphenomena such as ethnicity or class (1994: 37–47). Indeed, postcolonial theory has played a seminal role in dislodging questions of race from the ethnological domain of evolutionary theory, not least by elaborating the treacherous ramifications of deploying race as a self-evident concept of natural hierarchy for the purpose of justifying imperialism. In this regard, the anti-colonial writings of Frantz Fanon and Albert Memmi represent an earlier moment in the encounter between race and postcoloniality in which racism is seen as a structure of power and injustice, enforced and perfected within the circumstance of colonial relations.

For Fanon, writing in the 1940s as a colonial émigré from French Martinique educated in the metropole, racism results in the psychic injury that the colonized black subject is forced to endure at the hands of his white oppressors, in such a manner that the experience of loss or 'alienation' becomes the defining character of black identity. Fanon draws on Jacques Lacan's notion of 'misrecognition' to describe the process of being set in motion by the visual stereotype of 'Negro', arguing that the *gestalt*, which Lacan describes as being the founding feature of ego-formation, cannot be better understood than in the colonial context (Lacan 1977). The 'mirror stage' is, so to speak, always already mediated by race, so that the black man's relationship with his self-image is doubly marked by loss and fracture; identification with the white oppressor is both necessary and impossible. This internal fragmentation, Fanon reflects, is reinforced by denigrating interactions in the colonial world, in which the black subject is regularly reduced to his skin and hailed as such—as lesser-than, lacking, resolutely other—to the extent that these internal fractures gravitate outwards, creating psychic schisms within the colonized population as a whole (Fanon 1967). Fanon thereby anticipates Louis Althusser's description of 'interpellation' in his illustration of a quotidian street scene of racial interpellation ('Look! A Negro!'). This encounter, we should add, is no less constitutive of the self-image of the white child who cries out in wonder and terror at the sight of the black man; for this child, the category of the absolute other is resolutely and ineluctably racialized.

In Fanon's writing, racism resembles an Oedipal scenario, with the white man occupying the position of the father who must be deposed in order for his reign of tyranny to end and for the black man to gain a sense of positive cultural identity. Accordingly, injury can only be countered with another injury; violent overthrow is the only means by which the black man can externally make good his internal loss, repossess what was taken from him, and assume what Lacan terms an 'orthopaedic' totality (1977: 4). Racism is therefore symptomatic of the repressive logic that, for Fanon, defines the functioning of power; it heralds the sign of castration, a perpetually internalized negativity that can only be ameliorated through periodical eruptions of revolutionary violence.

Albert Memmi, the other major theorist of colonial racism and proponent of the ineluctability of violent struggle, also conceptualizes racism as a pathological condition that entraps both the colonized *and* the colonizer within a vicious circle that is ultimately debilitating to both parties. Straddling the Manichaean tradition of Fanon and the poststructuralist bent of the next generation of postcolonial scholars, Memmi's work represents a series of tentative attempts at defining racism, which he describes variously as an ideological structure resembling Barthesian myth and as a discourse akin to Edward Said's notion of Orientalism (Memmi 2000; see also Memmi 1965; Barthes 1972; Said 1979). At the same time, Memmi is reluctant to endorse the idea that racism has any rational basis, arguing rather that the fundamental character of racism is its irrationalism. As he writes at one point, 'racist reasoning has no secure foundation, is incoherent in its development, and is unjustified in its conclusions ... racism is not simply of the order of reason ... [it] is called forth and maintained, in its essence and goals, by something other than itself' (2000: 21). In his nuanced and rich analysis, Memmi refers to racism as sharing common elements with both normal physiological instincts and irresistible, self-destructive drives. Racism resembles, on the one hand, 'the onset of an allergic reaction toward the other. Indeed the word "allergy" derives from *allas*, the Greek for "other," and *ergon*, which means reaction' (2000: 27). On the other hand, we are drawn towards otherness even as we recoil from it, for '[u]ndeniably, difference is disquieting; it reflects the unknown, and the unknown often seems full of danger. Difference disturbs even when, at times, it seduces' (27). Memmi concludes that racism, or the impulse to single out a scapegoat or victim on the basis of biological differences that are deemed unacceptable, is a subset of the more pervasive modern condition of heterophobia, or the generalized and pathological fear of difference, which he calls a 'refusal of the other' (101). Subsequently, the solutions he settles on for combating this condition of negativity are also acts of negation: both violent overthrow and empathy essentially negate the 'refusal of the other'.

THE POSTSTRUCTURALIST TURN

Memmi's writing, particularly in his later work, draws on the assumption that the coherence of racism is defined and borne out by the dyadic structure internal to the relationship between colonizer and colonized, one that traps the racist and the victimized in a co-dependency of dominance–subjugation. This emphasis on the structural foundations of racism defines the impetus of the next generation of scholarship on race, which remains indebted to the binary thinking of structuralism even as it attempts to deconstruct it. With the advent of poststructuralism, the emergent discipline of postcolonial studies concerns itself not only with the primary figures of Fanon and Memmi, but crystallizes around Marxist poststructuralist scholars such as Edward Said, Gayatri Chakravorty Spivak, Homi Bhabha, and Henry Louis Gates, Jr. in a series of conversations that coalesce in questions regarding the determinant role of language in the repression of the other. Said, for example, in his famous discussion of Orientalism, deals with the systematic and structural relationship between textual power and economic-political power, and interrogates the material prehistory of the representational traditions that have contributed toward constructing 'the Orient' as an entity that is racially distinct from—and inferior to—the western world. Arguing that the east and the west are discursive rather than ontological categories, Said demonstrates that the two comprise a dialectical pair wherein the definition of each is propped up—and 'oriented'—by the other (Said 1979). Building upon Said's insights, Bhabha has argued more recently that the book, as a discursive form and linguistic commodity, not only behaves as an emblem of western empiricism, idealism, and monoculturalism, but also functions as the surface that stabilizes the agonistic space of colonial discourse, instrumentalizing language as a vehicle for regulating 'the ambivalence between origin and *Entstellung*, discipline and desire, mimesis and repetition' (Bhabha 1986: 171). Spivak, for her part, is committed to investigating the feedback mechanisms that make the enterprise of intellectual work complicit with the logic of western economic expansion. She writes that while subalternity is the product of very real conditions of material difference, it is secured and compounded by textual production—which would include not just historiography but all practices of academic writing. According to Spivak, the work of interpretation inevitably occludes subaltern subjectivity, condemning it to what she calls, following Jacques Derrida, a space of 'text-inscribed blankness' (1988a: 294; see also 1988b).

To borrow a phrase from Gates Jr's 1986 introduction to 'Race', Writing, and Difference, the tendency among poststructuralist theorists has been to emphasize language as 'both the medium and the sign' of racial alienation (1986: 6). The exchange between Derrida and co-authors Anne McClintock and Rob Nixon on the question of apartheid is an excellent instance of how the relationship between theories and practices of racism, or the 'word' and the 'world' as Spivak puts it, is played out within postcolonial contexts. McClintock and Nixon criticize Derrida's attention to the word 'apartheid' as anachronistic, urging attention to be paid instead to the shifting linguistic strategies of racism of the South African government. The discriminatory 'no' of apartheid, they argue, has given way to the rhetorically benign 'yes' of democratic federalism (McClintock and Nixon 1986). Derrida's response to this charge of ahistoricality is to argue that these emerging rhetorics of positivity merely represent a new liberalist alibi for apartheid. But something more is at stake in Derrida's strategic insistence on apartheid's currency: according to him, the avoidance of the word 'apartheid' in political parlance redoubles language's tendency to repress the mechanisms of its own functioning, and, moreover, stages the violent ramifications of similar repressions in the social arena. As 'racism's last word', apartheid preserves, as he puts it, 'the archival record of a failure' (1986: 332). 'Apartheid', for Derrida, crystallizes the complicity between racism as a social practice of exclusion and the exclusion that constitutes the theoretical basis of language. That is to say, the word 'apartheid' is not just a name that denotes the meaning of racist segregation; it also serves as a reminder of another kind of setting-apart, a process of differentiation without which human signification itself cannot materialize. Derrida's work offers an important reminder of the responsibility of theoreticians of race to interrogate the idioms through which they intervene in racism's historical manifestations, thereby acknowledging their role in the ongoing complicity between language and the act of prohibition (Derrida 1986).

THE PROBLEM OF BIOPOLITICS

Derrida's commitment to working within the limits of language, words, and etymologies as a means of addressing the relationship between theories and practices of power stands in contradistinction with the methodology adopted by French theorist and philosopher Michel Foucault, who has perhaps contributed the most towards thinking about the generative (as opposed to repressive) dimensions of discourse and power. Although to many he remains more famous for his writings on the history of sexuality and the emergence of institutional and disciplinary power, Foucault has been acknowledged as an important interlocutor with theories of race and racism, especially with the publication of the English-language translations of his 1976–9 lecture series at the Collège de France. Here, he explicitly discusses the subjects of state racism and what he terms 'biopolitics': the mode of governance specific to the modern state, the regulatory purview of which extends not just to civic or administrative functions, but to the social ecology of life as a whole (Foucault 2008). Unlike many of his contemporaries, Foucault shifts his critical gaze away from an exclusive emphasis on language, disseminating it instead among a diverse network of institutions, including hospitals, prisons, schools, asylums, and states. He argues that rather than operating through one exclusive or primary site, power in the modern era tends to 'swarm' these institutional spaces, whose organization allows them to function both internally and in conjunction with one another as discursive sites or 'apparatuses'. Defined in this sense, power is immanent in the discursive 'force relations' (economic, sexual, informational) subtended by these apparatuses, with subjects, individuals, and citizens as embodiments of its effects (Foucault 1990: 92).

One of Foucault's major innovations has been to theorize power by rejecting what he calls the 'repressive hypothesis', according to which Marxism and psychoanalysis, two of the main cornerstones of structuralist and poststructuralist thinking, derive some of their most important conceptual breakthroughs. Foucault argues that the notion of power-as-law or repression—whether attributed to the father who forbids, the prince who arbitrates rights, or language which censors—takes the juridical form of sovereignty. He disagrees with this formulation of power on two fronts: first, the repressive hypothesis imagines power to be an alienable possession rather than as something that is immanent within the social field. This kind of thinking tends to be limited in its outlook because it can imagine the subject only as a submissive or passive victim of power rather than as a vehicle that actively produces and channels it (1990: 15–50). Moreover, according to Foucault, the repressive view of power is outdated. He contends that the juridical logic of sovereignty best characterizes how power functioned in the fifteenth and sixteenth centuries, when the sovereign had a monopoly on power, which gave him the right to 'have people put to death or let them live' (2003: 240). With the advent of industrialization and the accompanying demographic explosion in the seventeenth and eighteenth centuries, a new modality of power emerged, which Foucault dubs 'discipline' (1995: 135–69). Operating through a generalized system of surveillance, discipline spreads virally by way of specialized institutions (including schools, prisons, hospitals, asylums, and the like). Such a system represents a vast improvement in efficiency over sovereign power in that individuals are now enlisted to regulate themselves by internalizing discipline. Rather than enforcing a prohibition on discourse, disciplinary power relies on an incitement to discourse, holding out the promise of a 'free' subjecthood as the incentive for acquiescing to subjection. Consequently, the complex libidinal desire to become a subject is harnessed and put to work in the institutionalization of a new economy of social relations that seems to function automatically, by people's free will, so to speak, rather than depending on force or law.

In his 1978–9 lecture series, *The Birth of Biopolitics*, Foucault argues that the issues of biopolitics cannot be thought outside liberalism, the 'framework of political rationality within which they appeared and took on their intensity' (2008: 317). However, he spends little time in these late lectures on the connection between racist biopower and neoliberal economics, emphasizing only that biopolitics and neoliberalism are both guided by the dictum of governing as little as possible, reducing the intervention of the state to an efficient minimum. While he takes care to dispel the notion of any easy parallel between economic and governmental rationality, his insistence that neoliberalism provides an impetus to biopower remains suggestive. The driving *economic* principle behind neoliberalism is Adam Smith's notion of a self-regulating market. According to this theory, the market, guided by the self-interest of private individuals, will regulate itself without requiring state intervention, as if steered by an 'invisible hand' (Smith 1976: 456).

The key to neoliberalism's success as a mode of governance, therefore, lies in its way of privatizing the burden of regulation, which releases the state from the onerous task of supervision. Indeed, if there can be a Foucauldian summation of neoliberalism, we might call it the 'privatization of the soul'. To that extent, letting people be—*laissez faire*—really means letting them (believe that they) have ownership over their soul, self, property, sexuality, or ethnicity. This is consistent with a technology of power that authorizes individuals to observe and monitor themselves, maintaining relations among one another through a network of 'private link[s], which is a relation of constraints entirely different from [the] contractual obligations' that would have mechanized the older sovereign regime of power (Foucault 1995: 222). This logic of a systemic investment in the self—as an entity that has been worked over by and must 'live' or 'survive' in correspondence to institutional surveillance—can be witnessed historically in the emergence of bourgeois individualism, and in the proliferation of entire industries and commodified practices devoted to self-help, self-liberation, and self-augmentation (the recent work of Nikolas Rose (2006) on the medicalization of consumer bodies as vehicles of biopower is edifying in this regard).

We can also return to Foucault's earlier writings to understand his unfinished work on the mutual implication between biopower and neoliberalism. Towards the end of *The Order of Things*, Foucault writes that the modern epoch is signalled in part by the appearance of the figure of 'Man' as an 'empirico-transcendental doublet' (1994: 318). A symptom of this is the rise, in the realm of knowledge production, of the 'human sciences'—disciplines that specialize in the objectification and scrutiny of 'Man' as an empirical entity. But while these disciplines, which include economics, biology, and linguistics, ostensibly generate empirical data, they are simultaneously performing the function of adjudicating the boundary between the human and the non- or subhuman. The soul, the transcendental part of the empirico-transcendental doublet and the traditionally definitive quality of man, is thus produced—and privatized—in the same process that weeds out that data which is deemed to be insufficiently human. From a postcolonial perspective, the data disqualified as less-than-human also tends to be used to discriminate against peoples identified as being the west's racial others. When Foucault's earlier observations are studied in light of his later lectures, we can see a consistent argument of how the social controls typical of modern society intensify in tandem with the galvanizing of new apparatuses for biopower. The executive uses of racism are disseminated beyond the domain of the state to the realms of intellectual exchange and discourse, and the production of a private individual with a soul is reinforced with classificatory techniques that are thoroughly implicated in the discursive politics of racialization.

As briefly noted earlier, biopolitics marks the birth of a new and specifically modern kind of governmental rationality, whereby the object of the state is no longer government for its own sake or the aggrandizement of its own sovereignty. Rather, *life itself* becomes the object and stake of power, the conservation, purification, and invigoration of which is now carried out in the name of an abstract entity, a mass body known as a 'population'. Consequently, the onus shifts from individual bodies to the human species as an economic and political problem, and the mechanisms of life at the level of the population—such as sexuality, reproductive health, fertility, morbidity, life expectancy, hygiene, health, birth and death rates, security, scarcity, ecology, and the environment— become key variables to be managed and monitored. Henceforth, the imperative of the state is to develop technologies of administration and management in response to these large-scale phenomena.

Racism presents itself as just such a technology and proves to be a remarkable fit with the problems specific to regulation at the level of the population. Like the abstract category 'population', race lends fixity to flexible and nebulous qualities such as the nature, character, and potential of a group. It does this by locating these invisible traits in visible physical attributes such as skin colour, body build, physiognomy, and behaviour, all of which can be 'scientifically' observed and documented. This in turn makes race convenient for such tasks as statistical mapping of groups, scientific modelling, and long-term demographic forecasts and planning. Moreover, race updates the pre-modern agonistic impulse of war between human groups by allowing war to thrive, indeed become permanent, by way of the modern emphasis on life. By reconfiguring the older warlike relationship between groups as a struggle for life itself, (the) race (war) becomes a question of the health and future of the species as a whole—and racism, the biopolitical state's means of establishing a caesura within the population so that the extermination of the bad part—the 'enemy within'—becomes the very condition for improving life for the rest. Killing is now regenerative rather than repressive, rational rather than arbitrary, for the purpose of life rather than death, and 'peace itself is a coded war' (Foucault 2003: 51). For Foucault, this is how the discourse of race struggle in modern times converges with the discourse of power. For that reason, he concludes, the race thematic is 'no longer a moment in the struggle between one social group and another; it will promote the global strategy of social conservatisms' in the appearance of a 'State racism: a racism that society will direct against itself, against its own elements and its own products. This is the internal racism of permanent purification, and it will become one of the basic dimensions of social normalization' (2003: 61–2).

NEOLIBERALISM AND NEO-RACISM

Foucault's intervention contributes in a unique manner to discourses of race and racism in postcolonial studies. While the notions of exclusion, censorship, and discrimination have been central to the theories of racism we have considered thus far in this chapter, Foucault is arguably the first to make the following two provocative claims: first, that to talk about the specificity of racism in the context of twentieth-century neoliberalisms entails addressing it as a technology of rationalization rather than as an irrational or pathological condition, as Fanon and Memmi have tended to argue; and second, that we have moved into an era in which power operates through the 'yes' rather than through the 'no'. In other words, as a technology of rationalization, racism does not depend on a strictly negative logic but does its work as part of an enabling disciplinary economy with infinite potential for proliferation. Accordingly, analyses of racism need to be attentive not just to questions of subjection or repression but also to racialization's positive and endlessly multiplying capacities.

This linkage of racialization and power offers an innovative rubric for understanding recent geopolitical developments that demonstrate the striking continuity of imperialist dynamics when it comes to the question of race. Within the frame of the USA, these might include the 'oversight' of the Bush government in its response to the 2006 Hurricane Katrina relief operation, in a move which strategically permitted some to die; the ubiquitous sound bites of defence and security after '9/11' that emphasize the identification and rooting out of internal enemies and intruders; and the legislative phenomenon of 'affirmative action', which came under fresh scrutiny with the appointment of Sonia Sotomayor to the US Supreme Court (see the essays by Morton and Sharp in Part II of this volume). Expanding our purview to phenomena of a more global nature would mean taking note of such disparate situations as McClintock and Nixon's aforementioned account of the shift in the official presentation of South African racism from a language of overt discrimination to the positive rhetorics of democratic federalism; the political and economic significance of genocide in the twentieth century, with such salient examples as the Soviet gulag, the Nazi death camps, the Japanese atrocities in East and South East Asia, and the Turkish massacre of Armenians; the relationship between the consolidation of the European Union and the treatment of immigrant and stateless refugee populations seeking employment or asylum within western European states (Balibar 2003); and the transnational interest in monitoring 'global' epidemiological phenomena such as avian and swine flu.

While Foucault, who was unashamedly Eurocentric in his political and historical perspective as a scholar, might seem an unlikely figure to take up for questions of postcolonial study, his writings on biopower have been fecund in generating theorizations pertaining to race in fields as varied as science and technology studies (Nikolas Rose, Kaushik Sunder Rajan), anthropology (Paul Rabinow, Didier Fassin), new media theory (Jussi Parikka), queer theory (Jasbir Puar), and philosophy (Roberto Esposito, Giorgio Agamben, Achille Mbembe, and Eugene Thacker). While all of these inquiries impinge on our current topic, a particularly relevant set of issues is that posed by anthropologist and historian Ann Laura Stoler's *Race and the Education of Desire*, which explores the relationship between biopower and the cultivation of colonial subjectivity. Focusing on the case of the Dutch East Indies, Stoler argues that the colony served as a 'laboratory of modernity', a site where disciplinary strategies of industrial production and social behaviour were rehearsed prior to being imported to the metropole as bourgeois norms (1995: 15; see also Stoler in Part I of this volume). Taking her cue from Said's still-influential work on the discursive construction of colonial regimes of power, Stoler argues that Foucault, even as he attends to the details of European bourgeois sexuality, is notably negligent of the extent to which 'an implicit racial grammar', rehearsed in the imperial context of European colonies, 'underwrote the sexual regimes of bourgeois culture in more ways than he explored and at an earlier date' (1995: 12). Crucially, while Foucault focuses on the deployment of sexuality as a type of discursive formation, Stoler examines the more unruly terrains of desire—namely, those quotidian activities whose affective dimensions in the colonies might have served to discipline and regulate 'proper' European bourgeois citizens 'back home'. Colonizers' subjectivities, she argues, were cultivated in relation to colonized bodies, through sexual and service relations that converged at sites such as language use, attire, sexual moralities, lifestyles, schooling, church membership, childcare, pedagogy, cultural affiliations, self-discipline, and spending habits.

Stoler's study advocates attention to the gentle, the everyday, the domestic, and the intimate—one might even say the softly feminine—over and against the more overtly coercive aspects of the colonial relationship as sites for the 'education' of colonial desire. This calls to mind the early work of Memmi, whose sympathetic psychological portraits of the 'colonizer' and the 'colonized' as ideal social types suggest that racism is socialized as a mundane aspect of collective life under colonial circumstances, and therefore represents the norm rather than the exception in social formations marked by (post)coloniality. Consequently, he argues, anti-racist work needs to address a spectrum of racist attitudes, ranging from brutal and discriminatory acts to 'civilized' expressions of prejudice such as benign tolerance and paternalistic benevolence, which deflect charges of reactionary violence by staking claim to a more 'liberal' position. According to Memmi, paternalism founds a 'new moral order', a kind of gift economy that permits the colonizer to 'stretch racism and inequality farther' while abnegating any duties or responsibilities to his wards. As he explains: 'It is, if you like, a charitable racism—which is not thereby less skilful nor less profitable. For the most generous paternalism revolts as soon as the colonized demands his union rights, for example' (1965: 76). This veneer of benevolence—which absolves the colonizer of guilt while allowing him to hold the colonized at a distance, as an outcast—rehearses at a gentler level the expiatory functions of scapegoating violence, which too is ultimately a drama of the colonizers' 'self-absolution' through collective 'self-purification' (2000: 65). By addressing the ways in which the colony is, *de facto*, a training ground for experimenting with liberalism as a mode of governmentality, Memmi's argument presciently anticipates the work of Foucault, and later Stoler, and most directly Étienne Balibar.

In their co-authored 1991 volume *Race, Nation, Class: Ambiguous Identities*, Balibar and Immanuel Wallerstein address the systemic transformations in dominant forms of racism in the contemporary world. Methodologically, they argue the significance of his-toricizing the relationship between the economic stage of capitalism on the one hand, and, on the other, social and cultural formations such as racism, nationalism, and class struggles. By charting epistemic shifts in the tactics of racialization and racism, Balibar and Wallerstein's work provides an important point of dialogue with Foucault. Not only do they present such shifts as being intrinsic to modern society's mode of operation, but the stresses they put on cultural formations also—much like Foucault's writings on biopower and neoliberalism—steer us away from Marxism's more economistic empha-ses, encouraging us to rethink political economy itself as a condition of possibility rather than as a determining force that ultimately instrumentalizes the subject.

Balibar's work is particularly instructive in this regard. In 'Is there a Neo-Racism?' (Balibar and Wallerstein 1991), he raises the issue of whether neoliberalism inaugurates the evolution of newly rationalized expressions of prejudice that have become the hege-monic form of racism in the post-World War II era (17–28). His thesis, which is central to the present discussion, is worth quoting in full:

> The new racism is a racism of the era of 'decolonization', of the reversal of population movements between the old colonies and the old metropolises, and the division of humanity within a single political space. Ideologically, current racism, which in France centres upon the immigrant complex, fits into a framework of 'racism without races', which is already widely developed in other countries, particularly the Anglo-Saxon ones. It is a racism whose dominant theme is not biological heredity but the insurmountability of cultural differences, a racism which, at first sight, does not postulate the superiority of certain groups or peoples in relation to others but 'only' the harmfulness of abolishing frontiers, the incompatibility of life-styles and traditions; in short it is what P.A. Taguieff has rightly called a *differentialist racism*. (21)

Like Foucault, Balibar identifies Nazism as a turning point in the history of racism. According to him, World War II precipitated movements within Europe toward the 'cul-turalist' or 'differentialist' mode of racism that had already achieved predominance in North America. Significantly, this post-war embrace of discourses of cultural relativism represents an *improvement* in the efficiency of racialization as a technique of governance, rejecting expensive and extreme measures such as genocide and adopting affirmative measures such as cultural diversity instead (in ways that are consistent with the post-war ethos of democratic liberalism). The usefulness of 'culture' lies in its Janus-faced flex-ibility: the universality of culture can be deployed as a category of inclusion (we are all cultural beings, and hence the same) but cultural difference can at the same time be a matter of irreconcilable divergence, serving as grounds for separation, discrimination, exclusion, and even, in the extreme case, death. The liberal emphasis on both the differ-ence and equality of cultures simultaneously authorizes the recent European project of post-national integration and citizenship; by the same token it can be mobilized in the service of discrimination, of setting-apart or cultural distancing, and herein lies the fer-tility—and resilience—of the coupling of 'culture' and 'life'. For Balibar, this regulation of what he calls 'thresholds of tolerance' is not only still in force, but has also intensified with the unification of the European Union; and this flexible biopolitics has become a stand-in for the disintegration of traditional state sovereignty in the age of globalization today (2003: 37; see also Farrier and Tuitt in Part II of this volume).

Meanwhile, in the contemporary political climate of the United States, the rise of dis-courses of multiculturalism, together with the last decade's resurgence of official and unofficial ethnic fundamentalisms, attests to the fact that today's Americans are very much operating under the sign of differentialist culturalism. In the multicultural era, there has been a tendency to overwrite the repressive connotations of the term 'race' with the discourses of 'ethnicity'. Ethnicity positively emphasizes aspects of cultural diversity such as nationality, cultural heritage, language, lifestyle, behaviour, and mores while circumventing the biological and eugenic connotations of race. Indeed, some postcolonial theorists, too, have escalated their efforts to disarm biological and evolu-tionary racisms, drawing on the latest developments in molecular and genetic science in order to de-naturalize the link between racial classification at the biological level and its socio-political implications (Gilroy 2002). But despite these initiatives—or perhaps in concert with them—ethnicity, as the cultural counterpart of racial science, seems to provide racialization with less systematic but nonetheless highly generative and sophis-ticated new forms through which to persist in the twenty-first century. It is urgent that we turn our attention to ethnicity for this very reason. While this means on the one hand that race has emerged again as an analytic of biological truth, 'viewed ... through a molecular gaze', and needs to be theorized as such, as Foucault scholars Rose and Rabinow have argued (2006: 204), what needs to be emphasized is that ethnicity has become a privileged line of force within present-day global biopolitical flows, a line that possesses a chimerical currency not unlike Balibar's specialized conception of differen-tialist culturalism. Unlike race, which in current genomic discourses is located within the logic of biological determinism, ethnicity functions within a complex, because con-stantly shifting, symbolic economy, confronting us with a whole range of biopolitical antagonisms at multiple, cross-cultural levels.

Thinking the notion of neo-racism together with Stoler's excursus on the racialized education of desire is particularly helpful at this juncture, as it helps us address the intertwined global economies of ethnic labour and ethnic violence. If interpellation in multicultural times functions by hailing the subject through a stereotype that is always already ethnicizing, then it is necessary to acknowledge that the libidinal labour of assuming subjecthood in a neoliberal multicultural society is, in the last instance, also a biopolitical event. In this sense, Gates Jr.'s arrest is exemplary of the kind of racial-izing interpellation that has become normative in current times, and which—as was evidenced by the 'good sense' of his neighbour, whose vigilant surveillance of the neigh-bourhood precipitated the arrival of the police and Gates Jr.'s eventual arrest—allows us to assume our roles as good citizens. Althusser's argument about the interpellation of citizen-subjects by authority figures plays out here as a drama of racialization, where ethnic identity is ritualistically enforced by a mutual play of call and response, or surveillance and confession. The difficulty of theorizing the labour of assuming ethnic citizenship is that this labour is driven by a desire for the positive benefits of inclusion associated with the benevolent, universal dimensions of ethnicity. But this expression of desire can simultaneously be construed as a confession—whether voluntary or not—of difference that warrants discrimination, exclusion, and persecution (Chow 2002: 1–49; 95–127). Similarly, we can think of the ritual function of 'ethnic cleansing', for which the paranoid imperative to watch, identify, and call out the other takes on more extreme proportions. Such momentous instances of violence are instructive in alerting us to the stakes of drawing on ethnicity whenever the obligations of (collective) self-reflection, rejuvenation, and improvement are placed on society as a whole.

CONCLUSION

Biopolitics and neoliberalism, then, may provide postcolonial studies with an astute perspective on the epistemic changes taking place within the very functioning of race in modern society. Whereas previously racism may have served to legitimize the divisive dynamic between colony and metropole, Foucault's insights compel us to examine the increasingly deterritorialized and rationalizing roles played by racism as a motor that propels, manages, and refines the everyday social workings of an entire population. The writings we have considered here argue that the violence of racialization has become normalized and internalized within social institutions and apparatuses, including the very mechanisms through which we inhabit our positions as subjects and enter into relationships of exchange.

This is, of course, far from a definitive statement on the multiple ways in which race and racism continue to operate in contemporary societies. We have not, for instance, considered the writings of the Italian philosopher Giorgio Agamben, which have exerted a considerable appeal in recent years for scholars of the postcolonial condition (see Morton, Farrier and Tuitt, and Smith and Turner, all in Part II of this volume). Against Foucault, for whom the repressive hypothesis does not adequately describe the discursive promiscuity of modern power, Agamben argues that the sovereign right to kill has been institutionalized and intensified in modernity as 'thanatopolitics': a politics of death. In Agamben's model, power is defined by the capacity for arbitrating the separation of *zoē* (the objective or biological fact of living) and *bios* (the subjective way of living or being-in-the-world proper to any group or individual) (Agamben 1998). Once stripped of *bios*, the entirety of its cultural and political dimensions, life is rendered 'bare', abject, and vulnerable to sovereign power. But unlike Foucauldian biopolitics, in which even death is a means to the enhancement and regeneration of life, for Agamben extermination means that 'bare life' is bereft of political or social consequence. In this view, the concentration camp serves as a transcendent universal condition as opposed to a logical culmination of biopolitics, the point at which rationality turns on itself and becomes madness (as is the case with Foucault). In his apocalyptic view of the present, Agamben implies that death, abjection, and loss have been internalized as the principle of existence and the motivating force behind a power that is fundamentally negative in its functioning.

Agamben's suggestion, in work such as 'Beyond Human Rights' (1996), that the figure of the refugee—the dispossessed, rightless, and stateless person—increasingly represents the paradigm of contemporary political consciousness, coincides with the turn in postcolonial studies toward theories of loss, abjection, and grief as ways of theorizing postcolonial racial politics. In recent decades, various scholars have drawn on Freud's notion of melancholy—a process of mourning that remains incomplete—for arguing the damaging and hostile psychic dimensions of racialization. Building on Judith Butler's seminal schema of melancholic gender formation (Butler 1990), Anne Anlin Cheng, for instance, has argued in her 2000 book *The Melancholy of Race* that the psychical 'wound' inflicted by racism plays a similarly constitutive role in racial or ethnic subject-formation, the outcome of which is that normative racial identity is fundamentally melancholic in constitution, while marginal racial subjects are rendered doubly abject as the suspended, abandoned objects of white desire. Other theorists have found this model of the racialization of desire to be productive of hostile differences, and the British sociologist Paul Gilroy has argued, accordingly, in favour of a 'post-racial' optic for the sake of thinking about multiculturalism as a joyous convivial condition, without hierarchy of any kind (Gilroy 2004).

In the work of theorists like Butler and Cheng, postcolonial melancholy offers an updated psychoanalytic reading of a scenario not entirely different from Frantz Fanon's description of racial injury—it is the wound or castration that is responsible for the production of fractured and schizophrenic colonial subjects. Strangely enough, while Fanon upholds the white subject as the mimetic standard and ideal of an unattainable totality, the recent turn to questions of melancholy seems to regard sexual or racial otherness (or, in the case of Gilroy, cultural diversity or polymorphism) as representative of some original, lost condition—a move that, for obvious reasons, deserves more in-depth interrogation (Chow 2008). These issues of bare life and melancholic subjectivity are major areas in which the controversies of race, racism, and postcoloniality are likely to continue in the foreseeable future. They cannot be resolved easily in relation to any discussion of neoliberalism, the market, and biopower; rather, it is the *nexus* of these conversations that demands further informed theorization and critical debate.

REFERENCES

Agamben, Giorgio (1996). 'Beyond Human Rights', in Paolo Virno and Michael Hardt (eds), *Radical Thought in Italy: A Potential Politics*, trans. Cesare Casarino. Minneapolis: University of Minnesota Press, 159–65.

Agamben, Giorgio (1998). *Homo Sacer: Sovereign Power and Bare Life*, trans. Daniel Heller-Roazen. Stanford: Stanford University Press.

Althusser, Louis (1971). 'Ideology and Ideological State Apparatuses (Notes Towards an Investigation)', in *Lenin and Philosophy and Other Essays*, trans. Ben Brewster. New York: Monthly Review Press, 127–86.

Balibar, Étienne (2003). *We, the People of Europe? Reflections on Transnational Citizenship.* Princeton: Princeton University Press.

Balibar, Étienne and Immanuel Wallerstein (1991). *Race, Nation, Class: Ambiguous Identities.* London and New York: Verso.

Barthes, Roland (1972). *Mythologies*, trans. Annette Lavers. New York: Hill and Wang.

Bhabha, Homi (1986). 'Signs Taken for Wonders: Questions of Ambivalence and Authority under a Tree Outside Delhi, May 1817', in H. L. Gates, Jr. (ed.), *'Race', Writing, and Difference.* Chicago: University of Chicago Press, 163–84.

Butler, Judith (1990). *Gender Trouble: Feminism and the Subversion of Identity.* New York: Routledge.

Cheng, Anne Anlin (2000). *The Melancholy of Race.* New York: Oxford University Press.

Chow, Rey (2002). *The Protestant Ethnic and the Spirit of Capitalism.* New York: Columbia University Press.

Chow, Rey (2008). 'Translator, Traitor; Translator, Mourner (or, Dreaming of Intercultural Equivalence)', *New Literary History*, 39.3: 565–80.

Derrida, Jacques (1986). 'Racism's Last Word', in H. L. Gates, Jr. (ed.), *'Race', Writing, and Difference.* Chicago: University of Chicago Press, 329–38.

Esposito, Robert (2010). *Bios: Biopolitics and Philosophy*, trans. Timothy Campbell. Minneapolis: University of Minnesota Press.

Fanon, Frantz (1967). *Black Skin, White Masks.* New York: Grove Press.

Fassin, Didier (2007). 'Humanitarianism as a Politics of Life', *Public Culture*, 10.3: 499–520.

Foucault, Michel (1990). *The History of Sexuality, vol. 1, An Introduction*, trans. Robert Hurley. New York: Vintage Books.

Foucault, Michel (1994). *The Order of Things: An Archaeology of the Human Sciences.* New York: Vintage Books.

Foucault, Michel (1995). *Discipline and Punish*, trans. Alan Sheridan. New York: Random House.

Foucault, Michel (2003). *Society Must Be Defended: Lectures at the Collège de France, 1975–1976*, trans. David Macey. New York: Picador.

Foucault, Michel (2008). *The Birth of Biopolitics: Lectures at the Collège de France, 1978–79*, trans. Graham Burchell. New York: Palgrave Macmillan.

Gates, Henry Louis, Jr. (1986). 'Writing "Race" and the Difference It Makes', in H. L. Gates, Jr. (ed.), *'Race', Writing, and Difference.* Chicago: University of Chicago Press, 1–20.

Gilroy, Paul (2002). *Against Race.* Cambridge: Harvard University Press.

Gilroy, Paul (2004). *Postcolonial Melancholia.* New York: Columbia University Press.

Lacan, Jacques (1977). 'The Mirror Stage as Formative of the Function of the I', in *Ecrits*, trans. Bruce Fink, Héloïse Fink, and Russell Grigg. New York: Norton, 1–7.

McClintock, Ann and Rob Nixon (1986). 'No Names Apart: The Separation of Word and History in Derrida's "Le Dernier Mot du Racisme"', in H. L. Gates, Jr. (ed.), *'Race', Writing, and Difference.* Chicago: University of Chicago Press, 339–53.

Mbembe, Achille (2003). 'Necropolitics', trans. Libby Meintjes, *Public Culture*, 15.1: 11–40.

Memmi, Albert (1965). *The Colonizer and the Colonized.* New York: Orion Press.

Memmi, Albert (2000). *Racism.* Minneapolis: University of Minnesota Press.

Omi, Michael and Howard Winant (1994). *Racial Formation in the United States from the 1960s to the 1990s*. New York: Routledge.

Parikka, Jussi (2010). *Insect Media: An Archaeology of Animals and Technology*. Minneapolis: University of Minnesota Press.

Puar, Jasbir (2007). *Terrorist Assemblages: Homonationalism in Queer Times*. Durham, NC: Duke University Press.

Rabinow, Paul (2007). *Marking Time: On the Anthropology of the Contemporary*. Princeton: Princeton University Press.

Rajan, Kaushik Sunder (2006). *Biocapital: The Constitution of Postgenomic Life*. Durham, NC: Duke University Press.

Rose, Nikolas (2006). *The Politics of Life Itself: Biomedicine, Power, and Subjectivity in the Twenty-First Century*. Princeton: Princeton University Press.

Rose, Nikolas and Paul Rabinow (2006). 'Biopower Today', *Biosocieties*, 1: 195–217.

Said, Edward (1979). *Orientalism*. New York: Vintage Books.

Smith, Adam (1976). *An Inquiry into the Nature and Causes of the Wealth of Nations, vol. 1, book IV*, ed. R. H. Campbell and A. S. Skinner. Oxford: Oxford University Press.

Spivak, Gayatri Chakravorty (1998a). 'Can the Subaltern Speak?', in Cary Nelson and Lawrence Grossberg (eds), *Marxism and the Interpretation of Culture*. Urbana, Ill.: University of Illinois Press, 271–316.

Spivak, Gayatri Chakravorty (1988b). 'Deconstructing Historiography', in Ranajit Guha and Gayatri Chakravorty Spivak (eds), *Selected Subaltern Studies*. New York: Oxford University Press, 3–34.

Stoler, Ann Laura (1995). *Race and the Education of Desire: Foucault's History of Sexuality and the Colonial Order of Things*. Durham and London: Duke University Press.

Thacker, Eugene (2010). *After Life*. Chicago: University of Chicago Press.

THEORY AND PRACTICE IN POSTCOLONIAL STUDIES

LEELA GANDHI

The charge of a breach between theory and practice in postcolonial studies unites all adversaries of the field. It can also get personal. Scholars who ply their craft in postcolonial locations raise eyebrows at a vehement critique of the west so comfortably housed in the west; and western scholars turn irate for similar reasons. It is important to wag a defensive finger in the direction of these complaints from time to time. Perhaps there is a touch of the old anxiety about overreaching in the western critic's unease about the postcolonial assault on *theoria* itself—that cast of mind (retroactively) said to travel a fixed route from ancient Greece through western Europe, with a short hop across the Atlantic. The nationalist intellectual's objections to so harmless a pursuit as theoretical reflection upon the evils of imperial history are, likewise, disingenuous. Why not pick on the brain-draining and wealth-amassing software programmers of Silicon Valley? Border-crossing arms dealers and drug lords? But this degree of petulance is about as far as our objections should go because even the most hostile expectations of singular and first-order accountability from postcolonialism's theory are generative and, ultimately, profound.

Graham Huggan puts it well in his introduction to this section when he argues that postcolonialism has 'for several decades now … made a virtue of its own embattlement'. This is the case not only because any attention is good attention, but for reasons of genealogy. Various nineteenth- and twentieth-century anti-colonialisms are animated by the view that an accord between theory and practice is crucial for improved collective coexistence. In these articulations, the terms 'theory' and 'practice' acquire synonyms and become placeholders for a dizzying array of kindred terms and concepts. Here I want to foreground three such past taxonomies that attach to the theory/practice dialectic. All three belong to the world of transnational twentieth-century imperialism; more precisely, to the time when the first two world wars quite literally brought home the devastating effects of internecine European imperial rivalry and created fertile conditions for oppositional collaboration across colonizer/colonized lines. They cohere around the emergence of what we might term a global phenomenology.

TRANSCENDENTAL PHENOMENOLOGY

In the early decades of the twentieth century, the transcendental phenomenologist Edmund Husserl issued a clarion call for a restitution of the theoretical attitude, believing this to be the best solution to the crisis of imperialist and capitalist Europe (Husserl 1965; 1970). In due course, one circuit of the Husserlian hypothesis passed through the residual utopian and ethical socialisms of the time, and substantiated their energetic anti-colonial anti-materialism. Figures like R. H. Tawney and G. D. H. Cole, amongst others, railed against the dehumanizing acquisitiveness of post-imperial consumer cultures. They reasoned, à la Husserl, that a theoretical deportment—an intensified ethical curiosity about pure obligations, services, and principles—was the only cure for the prevailing profit-driven and pragmatic attitude. Another set of circuits connecting these thinkers to M. K. Gandhi enabled the latter to refine his own perception of the east–west colonial encounter as a conflict between historically and socially reformist soul-force, on the one hand, and historically and socially deforming brute force, on the other. In a corollary to this schema, Gandhi also reconceived the theoretical disposition as a politically exigent commitment to ideals. We can see this in his view that the impossible perfection of Euclidean geometry was a lodestar for *satyagraha* or non-violent anti-colonial practice. Gandhi often observes that non-violence, much like the Euclidean line that cannot even be drawn on a blackboard, shows up the limitations of the world in which it cannot be realized. Yet its work does not stop with critique. When invoked often enough, ideational *ahimsa* may well encourage the emergence of adaptive and improved social, ethical, and psychological technologies. Thus, over time, disappointed at encountering no resistance to his violence even the worst tyrant might learn to extend recognition rather than brutality toward his victims.

EXISTENTIAL PHENOMENOLOGY

The transmissions of Husserl's call-to-theory are pedagogic. Their engaged anti-positivism requires subjects to swerve from a habitual or given course of action (though not from action itself) at the behest of an impossible and strictly unrealizable project, or one at least which defies final satisfaction. Many of the chapters in this section of the volume touch upon this theme in different ways. The multidirectional paths of cultural memory summoned by Rothberg, for instance, do not counter imperial epistemology through a different set of verifiable facts. Rather, cultural memory disorients totalizing narratives through its defiance of facticity itself: challenging what is said to have happened with a cloudy picture of what might have happened, and which can never be recovered entirely. Featherstone's chapter does similar work in its reflections upon improvisation as a postcolonial mode whose operation consists in loosening the hold of set or received practices in favour of more supple, flexible, and imaginative modes of life. All of this is material which can be accommodated within the familiar postcolonial tropes of hybridity, interstitiality, instability, the in-between, and so on.

Theory and practice interact somewhat differently, albeit sympathetically, in the path taken by mid-twentieth-century existential phenomenology. Here, theory's participation in the world no longer consists in the ambush—and thence external liberation from external false command—of given life forms. Rather, theory is held out as the authentic promise of each individual life: the conditions whereby it rises of its own accord, and by its own example, above its desperate circumstantiality. Such is the distinct emphasis of Jean-Paul Sartre's somewhat thunderous *Existentialism and Humanism* (2007 [1946]), with its claim that each life will achieve definition or form through the conditions of its signatory phenomenal abandonment: anguish, despair, or other bad affect. The long shadow of Hegel's slave—achieving freedom by doggedly working through its own materiality—is readily visible in Sartre's hypotheses. Always less visible is the fact of his rich investments in anti-colonial thought and (as evinced by his bristling prefaces for Frantz Fanon's *The Wretched of the Earth* and Albert Memmi's *The Colonizer and the Colonized*) dialogues with leading anti-colonial thinkers of the time. It is in the polemic of these latter thinkers—Fanon especially, as Elleke Boehmer points out in her chapter—that the theoretical attitude manifests as the effort simply and beautifully to rise above harsh historical materialities into something like self-belief and humanity. Or to put this differently, bare life can sometimes defy its instrumentalization by turning itself defiantly into reflective-ethical life. This mutation almost always involves, as Boehmer suggests, a movement away from the bounded self (bounded because suffering) toward 'common ground and mutual regard'.

SPIRITUAL PHENOMENOLOGY

At the scenes we have been surveying there is a great deal of openness to the critical requirement that thinkers of social justice must cultivate a contiguous fidelity to the object of their analysis. This does not necessarily imply that personal suffering is the sole precondition for thinking philosophically about suffering. It does, however, carry the following charge: in order to to earn their stripes revolutionary thinkers, however sedentary, must concretely embody and give life to the impossible abstraction of their desire for a reformed world. And they must do so in their own person.

Such a requirement was at the very heart of a spiritual phenomenology of *karmayoga*, revived in the course of early twentieth-century South Asian anti-colonialism. The oxymoronic term *karmayoga*, which combines the mental abstractions of spiritual life (*yoga*) with a call to practice or action (*karma*), was a mixed bag in the context under review. For most exponents it signalled a masculinist and culturally recidivist call to arms consistent with the glory of a mythic unconquerable Hindu past. Yet in the hands of a few thinkers, such as M. K. Gandhi and Aurobindo Ghosh, *karmayoga* declared the irreducible unity of theory and practice, idea and action, and also described the thinker who would best exemplify these unities. The project is perhaps best elaborated in 'The Karmayogin', Aurobindo's incomplete commentary on the ancient *Isha Upanishad*.

Aurobindo's *karmayogin* is a theoretical worker who can accomplish his/her work in any condition or posture: who is 'busy doing good to all creatures by his very nature, even though he does not lift a finger or move a step' (Aurobindo 2003: 206). This does not, of course, disqualify more energetic personalities from *karmayoga*, but it does call for an ultimately idiosyncratic conception of work (or of 'works') as a reckless carelessness with regard to the self combined with an exorbitant care for the world. Work or practice, in other words, designates the *yogi*'s radical identity with the phenomenal world. It commences as such with the axiom that everything *is*: no one thing more real or substantial than the other. Thus, thought itself is saturated with an inescapable phenomenality that renders even its greatest abstractions into types of action or labour. Conversely, the most insignificant of phenomena are invested with philosophical density. Theory is practice, and vice versa, but one from which the *yogi* must accrue no personal benefit. She must inhabit the world entirely whilst abandoning her own interest in it: 'as a king merely touching the nazzarena passes it on to the public treasury, so shall the Karmayogin, merely touching the wealth that comes to him, pour it out for those around him, for the poor, for the worker, for his country, for humanity ... Glory, if it comes to him, he will veil in many folds of quiet and unobtrusive humility and use the influence it gives not for his own purposes but to help men more effectively in their needs ...' (Aurobindo 2003: 191). Enough said. Why should this be an impossible ask of those who think meaningfully about social justice? And why should it be inadmissible within academic postcolonial studies? Isn't there a distant echo of Sri Aurobindo's *Karmayogin* in Edward Said's complicated call, in his *Orientalism*, for disinterested knowledges which are borne exclusively from the capacity 'to identify with human experience' (2007: 328)?

REFERENCES

Husserl, Edmund (1965). *Phenomenology and the Crisis of Philosophy: Philosophy as Rigorous Science and Philosophy and the Crisis of European Man*, trans. Quentin Lauer. New York: Harper Torchbooks.

Husserl, Edmund (1970). *The Crisis of European Sciences and Transcendental Phenomenology: An Introduction to Phenomenological Philosophy*, trans. David Carr. Evanston: Northwestern University Press.

Said, Edward (2007). *Orientalism*. Harmondsworth: Penguin Books.

Sartre, Jean-Paul (2007 [1946]). *Existentialism is a Humanism*, trans. Carol Macomber. New Haven: Yale University Press.

Sri Aurobindo (2003). *Isha Upanishad*, in *The Complete Works of Sri Aurobindo*, vol. 17. Pondicherry: Sri Aurobindo Ashram Trust.

PART IV

ACROSS THE DISCIPLINES

INTRODUCTION

GRAHAM HUGGAN

Postcolonial studies is increasingly acknowledged to be a multidisciplinary field, taking in a number of new disciplinary perspectives drawn from, e.g., environmental studies and religious studies, as well as consolidating the forms of disciplinary knowledge now generally accepted as contributing to it: those belonging to any one or combination of literary studies, history, geography, modern languages, political science, anthropology, sociology. Whether it is an *inter*disciplinary field is, however, moot and to date there has been considerably more achieved by individuals with training in a similar discipline than in the type of work, more common to the sciences than the humanities, done in collaborative research teams. To some extent, it could be said, postcolonial studies to date has been more inter*discursive* than inter*disciplinary*, i.e. it has been characterized by the work of individual humanities researchers who draw on the knowledge and protocols of, without necessarily having intellectual training in, other fields.

This recognition frequently obtains within a field that has historically been alert (though not always as alert as it claims to be) to the limitations of its own methods. Gayatri Spivak, for example, has repeatedly voiced her belief that postcolonial studies 'cannot be fully contained within English' and 'should yoke itself to other disciplines', but she has been equally firm in disclaiming her own expertise as, e.g., a historian, a philosopher and a South Asianist (1999: 198, 267). Thus while Spivak, like many postcolonial critics and theorists, is eager to combat disciplinarity as what she sees as being an exemplary manifestation of the academic division of labour, she is keenly aware of her own disciplinary grounding, and conscious too that much of what passes as postcolonial interdisciplinary practice amounts to little more than 'neutralizing the vocabulary from another discipline and taking to describe yet again what happens between reader and text' (1990: 55).

While Spivak's is by no means an isolated case, the postcolonial field at large still tends to confuse 'interdisciplinarity' with its non-identical semantic correlates, 'intertextuality' and 'interdiscursivity', and those instrumental forms of institutional cooperation that some see as characterizing interdisciplinarity proper are belied by both the 'textual excesses' of humanities studies and the 'continuing inhibitions' of the social sciences towards an analysis of the aesthetics of cultural forms (Wolff 1992: 714; see also Huggan 2002). Semantic distinctions of this kind are less important, no doubt, than the quality of the work that continues to be produced by postcolonial scholars, but they still cast doubt on routine claims to interdisciplinarity in the field. Some postcolonial scholars go further still, claiming that traditional disciplinary regimes have been complicit in the imperial enterprise, and that to challenge disciplinary boundaries is, at one level, to challenge the divisive tendencies of imperialism itself. Consider, for example, Edward Said's bold claim that the traditional academic disciplines represent 'an extension of the imperialism that decreed the principle of divide-and-rule' (1997: 142), or his no less provocative view that a 'decentered [critical] consciousness' is needed to combat the 'paradigmatic fossilization' of disciplinary regimes (1997: 139).

Said's is utopian thinking of a kind described by Ato Quayson (2000) as 'synoptic interdisciplinarity'—the attempt not only to produce synthetic theories that have the capacity to cross particular disciplines, but also to work towards a counter-traditional model of knowledge that effectively combines them all. Over and against this, Quayson posits 'instrumental interdisciplinarity'—the need for cross-disciplinary dialogue in the identification and confrontation of problems and issues considered to be central to their field. It is important to recognize that 'synoptic' and 'instrumental' forms of interdisciplinarity—as can be seen in Said's work—are not mutually exclusive, but a discrepancy still remains between general, 'post-disciplinary' claims to new knowledge and those free-ranging, broadly 'interdiscursive' borrowings and collocations that are particular to the postcolonial field.

A further slippage arguably exists between what might be called, after Julie Thompson Klein (1990), 'additive' (multidisciplinary), 'integral' (interdisciplinary), and 'transcendent' (transdisciplinary) approaches, though such distinctions imply a progressivist route to the 'post-disciplinary' to which most postcolonial critics—wary as they are of all forms of progressivist logic—would be unlikely to subscribe (and a route that Klein herself demonstrates is neither as smooth nor as desirable as it seems). Thus, while grand claims continue to be made about postcolonialism's potential to undermine the authority of the disciplines—to challenge the disciplinary imperialism of institutionalized knowledge systems—it is more usual to find work that *combines* different disciplinary knowledges in 'additive' rather than 'integrative' terms. Similarly, the methodological eclecticism of postcolonial theory, 'far from gesturing towards the "post-disciplinary" curriculum, sometimes amounts to little more than simulacra of institutional transgression, to a series of sparsely conceived but expansively celebrated "border crossings" in which ideas and methods, freely borrowed from other more or less established fields and subjects, are retooled to meet the requirements of anti-imperialist critique' (Huggan 2002: 263). It would therefore be fair to say that the field of postcolonial studies has tended so far towards 'synoptic' rather than 'instrumental' models of interdisciplinarity, i.e. it has registered 'the collective desire for cross-disciplinary modes and procedures of analysis rather than [being marked] by genuinely collaborative initiatives of the sort pursued by affiliated educational programmes or task-oriented 'think-tanks' and research teams' (Huggan 2002: 263).

Whether this balance will shift is too early to predict, though there is recent evidence of team building, while postcolonial scholars are responding—grudgingly in some cases—to the increasing pressures being placed on the academy to work in tandem with, as well as demonstrate accountability for, the various regional, national, and international communities it ostensibly serves. Reasons for their reluctance are not hard to see given the present climate of economic rationalism, which has amplified fears that intellectual autonomy might be at threat, that collaborative work might be more easily manipulated, and that interdisciplinarity, far from being rewarded, might become 'the siren-song university management uses to lure departments and other larger administrative units into [a variety of] Machiavellian cost-cutting schemes' (Huggan 2002: 245).

On the other hand, it is increasingly recognized that many of the world's most pressing problems today cannot be solved either by scholars working in isolation or scholars working within single disciplines; collaborative work seems urgently to be necessary, whether or not the more abstract commitment to interdisciplinarity is met. Aware of these competing demands, and alert to the slippery rhetoric that underlies them, this section of the Handbook understandably steers a cautious path between 'synoptic' and 'instrumental' views of postcolonial interdisciplinarity, looking both at those more narrowly defined kinds of problem-solving that require going beyond single disciplinary formations, and at those broader issues that may even involve a radical testing of the boundaries of disciplinary knowledge itself. At the same time, the section also looks at the specific contributions that disciplines, both established and emerging, have made to postcolonial studies, and at debates *within* those disciplines about the validity of postcolonial theories and methods and the vocabularies on which they draw. Finally, it looks at debates *across* the disciplines, some of which—postcolonial theory and imperial history for instance—have tended to treat each other with suspicion, reflecting a wider 'anxiety of interdisciplinarity' (Coles and Defert 1998) across the university sector at large. These arguments can be territorial and petty; but behind them is the larger question of how to make university study more relevant to the world in which we live without surrendering to policy-driven instrumentality—and this is a question that no socially committed scholar, postcolonialist or not, can afford to ignore.

For Diana Brydon, in the opening chapter of the section, postcolonial studies today needs to recognize 'alternative modes of social organization in a world facing unprecedented challenges'. This shift entails a move away from the binary theoretical models and nation-based imaginaries that informed earlier, determinedly oppositional versions of postcolonial studies towards more interactive critical practices based on transnational alliances and networks; it also requires the consolidation and expansion of cross-disciplinary forms of cultural critique. As Brydon suggests, the current social, economic, and environmental challenges posed by neoliberal globalization—those attached to climate change for example—urgently require the overhauling of traditional discipline-based postcolonial models and the intensification of dialogue between the academy and other knowledge producers. These challenges also require a rethinking of the spatial configuration of postcolonial studies in keeping with a growing awareness within the field that the old binaries—east and west, west and non-west, even the more economically oriented north and south—no longer hold. Two intriguing conceptual possibilities Brydon explores are 'tidalectics' (which works according to a maritime rather than terrestrial grammar) and 'planetarity' (which acknowledges a world system characterized by a high degree of multiplicity and intermixture); while further opportunities are supplied by indigenous knowledges and perspectives that have more often been invoked than actually implemented—an admonitory view that squares with Mount and O'Brien's later chapter in the section, and with several other chapters (Smith and Turner in Part II, for instance) in the Handbook as a whole.

Like many postcolonial critics, Brydon is committed to the view that postcolonial studies must intervene in the world—as throughout her work, she insists on the dialectical relationship between theory and practice—but she is disappointed at the same time that it has not achieved the political purchase, within let alone beyond the academy, that its potentially transformative insights deserve. Part of this failure, she suggests, is down to the privileging of individual over collaborative achievement—hence the academy's exaggerated rewarding of the 'lone scholar'—while part also owes to the privileging of academic over other kinds of knowledge production—hence the academy's frequent reluctance to engage with civil society. However, the chapter ends on a more hopeful note by suggesting that as new dialogues between different knowledge producers begin to emerge, and as new revolutionary energies in today's globalized world begin to manifest themselves, there will be further opportunities for the implementation of 'non-traditional' practices, and for the featuring of new locations—possibly even new knowledges—in postcolonial cultural work.

This balance between institutional scepticism and individual optimism is maintained in John McLeod's capacious chapter on the value of the literary in postcolonial studies, a value seen by some as diminishing even though many—probably most—contemporary postcolonial critics would still recognize that it is vitally necessary to uphold. McLeod rightly insists on the diversity of postcolonial responses, not least by creative writers themselves, to imaginative literature, which has not always been 'crudely oppositional in its spirit [or] progressively political in its cause'. This diversity—not always recognized in the field—then becomes the basis for his measured discussion of postcolonial literary studies as a discipline (perhaps the formative discipline in so far as many of the so-called 'first wave' of postcolonial critics were literary scholars). McLeod's tracing of the disciplinary development of postcolonial literary studies is largely appreciative, stressing the role it has played in analysing the discursive as well as material effects of colonialism and the particular forms colonialism has used to perpetuate itself; but he also sees the limitations of emphasizing the discursive at the possible expense of the material, and the literary over other representational forms. Similarly, he shows how the more recent shift to diasporic and 'migrant' writing has granted new and exciting forms of imaginative access, but has also had the less positive side-effect of turning an institutionalized 'postcolonial literature' into a complacently 'cosmopolitan and indeed bourgeois affair'.

McLeod's account draws attention to some of the problems involved in seeing postcolonial literary studies as a dominant discipline: the reduction of a vast and heterogeneous field into a palatable canon; the mistaking of textual innovation for political radicalism; the downplaying of popular cultural forms. Postcolonial literature, he insists, should not be seen as intrinsically radical, nor should postcolonial literary critics automatically congratulate themselves on their own radicalism; but it still has transformative potential and the capacity to destabilize assumptions about 'literature' and 'the literary' themselves. Postcolonial literature is many things and should not be reduced by disciplinary mechanisms to one or other institutionalized version of 'postcolonial literature'; however conceived, 'postcolonial literature' needs to take its place 'within a wider cultural terrain'. The chapter ends, notwithstanding, by reasserting the capacity of postcolonial literature—literature in general—to ask awkward questions; and perhaps its primary value is, paradoxically by taking us away from it, to bring us closer to and open up possibilities for critical reflection on the world we only think we know.

While literature, until quite recently, has been integral to most institutional versions of postcolonial studies, the same cannot necessarily be said of history, which has had a somewhat troubled, at times fractious, relationship to the postcolonial field. At the beginning of his chapter, the American-based British imperial historian Dane Kennedy recalls the confusion—consternation even—with which imperial historians first greeted postcolonial studies, an attitude that has gradually shifted if not definitively changed. Most of the rest of the chapter is taken up with an informed overview of this shift, taking in the work of—among others—the Subaltern Studies Collective, diverse feminist historians, and historical anthropologists, and dividing this work into three broad thematic categories: identity, geography, and epistemology. Taken together, much of this work falls into the loose category of the 'new [British] imperial history', which has sought to show how 'the domestic realm was … shaped by its imperial interests and colonial dependencies' (see also Part I of this volume). Kennedy lauds the efforts of these historians, but also shows that their views and methods have been far from uniform, the response to their work not always positive, and the innovative value of their research sometimes overdrawn. His is an equally mixed view of the debate between historians and historical geographers around the spatial dimensions and implications of empire, though he gives due credit to the attempt to account for subaltern peoples whose interests are often divorced from those of the state; to those 'transnational processes that [lie] beyond the grasp of national histories'; and to the general trend towards a 'decentring' of empire that acknowledges its dispersal across multiple sites. He also points out, though, that the decentring of empire may not be sufficient to account for the wide variety of local power struggles that have taken place within it, while the postcolonial critique of nation-centred history might itself be accused of being western-centred in its orientation.

'Epistemological' approaches to empire, Kennedy suggests, are perhaps best suited to analysing these specific power relations, to checking the Eurocentric and historicist biases that still generally obtain within the discipline, and to teasing out complex connections between 'imperial' and 'modernizing' projects in India, Africa, and elsewhere. At the same time, he notes—like several other contributors to this volume—that key terms such as 'modernity' and 'development', along with key methodological processes such as 'historicizing', have multiplied and ramified to the extent that they risk being emptied of meaning; and adds the obvious if still salutary caveats that (1) historical approaches to different regions may require different methods, and (2) imperial historians, whether influenced by postcolonial theory or not, remain divided to the bone on method (cf. equal and opposite views of the archive as a 'neutral repository of information' and as a 'creation and instrument of the state': see Stoler in Part I of this volume). Kennedy thus understandably calls for caution, but he still reiterates the importance of postcolonial theory to imperial history while emphasizing—as a check against self-congratulatory postcolonial presentism—that the economic, military, and political manifestations of empire that were the focus of 'pre-postcolonial' versions of imperial history will never go out of date.

In the next chapter, the Australian-based political scientist Barry Hindess makes explicit what is strongly hinted at in Kennedy's essay: that understandings of modernity and the politics of temporality underlying it are central to postcolonial concerns. Indeed, one of the foundational aims of postcolonial studies is to challenge what Hindess aptly calls, at the beginning of his chapter, the 'temporalizing pretence' that some of us belong to the present while others have yet to reach it. Much of what follows is given over to different instantiations of this pretence, one of the categories being that of the developmental understanding of human progress which, buoyed by the discoveries of the Enlightenment, has been a 'general feature of western thought', surfacing again more recently in disparaging western accounts of the Islamic world (see the essays by Mignolo and Sayyid in Part I of this volume). Particular attention is given to the 'temporalizing pretence' as this has been applied to Australia's Aboriginal people, who continue to be assumed, partly following Weber's linkage of traditionalism and irrationalism, as not being fully rational and therefore less fully modern than 'we' are—a distinction long since used, in a variety of contemporary and historical contexts, to justify colonial rule.

Underlying the continuing mistreatment of Aboriginal people, Hindess persuasively suggests, is the Eurocentric myth of a western-centred modernity that provides one of the most obvious historical and philosophical targets of postcolonial critique. Hindess shifts focus, accordingly, to the 2000 study *Provincializing Europe*, probably the most influential recent example of such critique, citing its author Dipesh Chakrabarty's argument to the effect that while the 'so-called European intellectual tradition is the only one alive in the social science departments of most, if not all, modern universities', it is as 'inadequate' as it is 'indispensable', its inadequacies being particularly marked by its penchant for *historicist* thought. For Chakrabarty, historicism refers primarily to Europe as an originating presence, such that 'historical time [is conceived to be] a means of the cultural distance ... assumed to exist between the West and the non-West'. According to this historicist model, people in the 'non-west' are always behind their western counterparts; history effectively happens 'for the first time' in the west. Like Chakrabarty, Hindess sees historicism as informing 'much of the current work of major development agencies, the international human rights regimes, and other aspects of the west's interactions with the non-west'. Historicism clearly informs the disciplinary protocols of social science (and their practical consequences for social and cultural policy) as well; however, Hindess recognizes that, as 'inadequate' as social science is, it still carries the capacity *both* to 'promote prejudicial observation' *and* to 'provide a partial remedy for such prejudice', as can be seen—to some extent at least—in the varied case studies he draws from the present and the past.

Hindess's critical account of historicism is taken a stage further in Ananda Abeysekara's provocative attack on postcolonial studies' lack of critical reflection on its own methods, not least as these pertain to the relationship between the occult processes of historicization and one of their most visible end products, critique. For Abeysekara, postcolonial studies can be understood as a 'broad-based discipline' in so far as it deploys the methods of historicization—but herein also lies its greatest problem, for these methods imply a *separation* from their subject, embedded in turn in the notion of critique, which paradoxically impedes historical thinking at large. Abeysekara's issue with postcolonial studies is thus not so much that it has failed to account for the institutional effects of its own disciplinary status, but that it remains insufficiently attentive to the metaphysical underpinnings of its own methods—it is not 'disciplinary' enough.

Nor has postcolonial studies been vigilant enough to the implications of its own secular legacies: not for the first time, Said is seen here as a foundational figure. By putting Said's work into dialogue with that of diverse philosophers and religious-studies scholars, Abeysekara suggests, following Gil Anidjar, that the 'Christian secularized religion' that was one of the original—if not always acknowledged—critical targets of *Orientalism* has historically been 'rooted in [western] democratic capitalism and its attendant inequalities, e.g. those around gender, ethnicity, and race'. Abeysekara then goes even further by positing a link between the Christian history of self-critique and Derrida's 'promise' of democracy—a 'promise' which, despite its continuing connection with histories of racism, exclusivist nationalism, and sexual inequality, cannot simply be withheld. Maintaining this promise requires an alternative to historicization; it also demands a much more vigilant attitude to critique and its attempt to separate its own object of analysis (e.g. religion) from itself. This calls for, among other things, thinking about religion, religious studies and, by risky extension, postcolonial studies 'otherwise', positioning them 'at the limit of [their] own internal critique' rather than assessing their 'critical traditions'. Abeysekara does not deny the value of historical critique, but—like Brennan in Part I—he argues strongly for the need to understand postcolonial studies *genealogically* rather than *historically*, seeking to account for the metaphysical implications of its methods and laying less stress on the field's institutional 'development' than on its scattered, at times contradictory, disciplinary effects.

The closing chapter in the section, by the Canadian scholars Dana Mount and Susie O'Brien, returns us to the scene of McLeod's earlier chapter by considering literature as the disciplinary dominant of postcolonial studies, but then strategically aligns *literary* studies with *environmental* studies, one of the newer—and itself internally differentiated—disciplines to enter into the postcolonial fray. Mount and O'Brien skilfully chart the ongoing conversation between literary and environmental studies in terms of indigenous cultural politics, the rise and development of western (colonial) environmentalism, the not always friendly dialogue with feminism, and intensifying debates around consumption, climate change, sustainability, genetics, and human/animal rights. These variegated elements are seen as embodying the cross-disciplinary work that postcolonial studies is capable of producing, but—characteristically—they produce aporia of their own, e.g. the continuing American bias of ecocriticism, the corresponding neglect of alternative voices, and the tacit reinforcement of white privilege and other forms of 'environmental racism' in a hotly contested research field.

Implicit in Mount and O'Brien's work are several of the issues raised in other chapters in this section: how to convert textual politics into 'politics proper' (Brydon, McLeod);

how to broaden constituencies for, as well as participants within, postcolonial critical projects (Brydon, Kennedy); how to counteract western ideologies of progress and development (Hindess); how to make postcolonial studies more aware of its own disciplinary procedures, as well as more politically efficient (Hindess, Abeysekara). Above all, Mount and O'Brien ask a question that resonates, not just through this particular section but through the Handbook as a whole, one that has obvious ramifications for both the disciplinary and cross-disciplinary practice of postcolonial studies: how to make the field more inclusive in a general sense, confirming the value of non-human as well as human life-worlds; and how to ensure in the process that it remains fully committed to 'the [twin] goals of social and environmental justice, [which] can only be voiced as one'.

REFERENCES

Coles, Alexia and A. Defert (eds) (1998). *The Anxiety of Interdisciplinarity.* London: Blackdog Publishing.

Huggan, Graham (2002). 'Postcolonial Studies and the Anxiety of Interdisciplinarity', *Postcolonial Studies*, 5.3: 245–75.

Huggan, Graham (2008). *Interdisciplinary Measures: Literature and the Future of Postcolonial Studies.* Liverpool: Liverpool University Press.

Klein, Julie Thompson (1990). *Interdisciplinarity: History, Theory, Practice.* Detroit: Wayne State University Press.

Quayson, Ato (2000). *Postcolonialism: Theory, Practice, or Process?* Cambridge: Polity Press.

Said, Edward W. (1997). 'Orientalism Reconsidered', in B. Moore-Gilbert, G. Stanton, and W. Maley (eds), *Postcolonial Criticism.* London: Longman, 131–42.

Spivak, Gayatri Chakravorty (1990). *The Post-Colonial Critic.* London: Routledge.

Spivak, Gayatri Chakravorty (1999). *A Critique of Postcolonial Reason: Toward a History of the Vanishing Present.* Cambridge, Mass.: Harvard University Press.

Wolff, Janet (1992). 'Excess and Inhibition: Interdisciplinarity in the Study of Art', in L. Grossberg, P. Treichler, and C. Nelson (eds), *Cultural Studies.* New York: Routledge, 706–18.

....

CHAPTER 19

MODES AND MODELS OF POSTCOLONIAL CROSS-DISCIPLINARITY[1]

....

DIANA BRYDON

INTRODUCTION

Frederick Cooper's assertion that 'questions of poverty and exploitation that were once imperial have become both national and international' (2005: 233) names the general shift in context in which postcolonial critique takes place today. While historians certainly continue to study the imperialisms and colonialisms of the past, even they now do so from the vantage point of the present, in which globalization and transnational relations are reframing the posing of postcolonial questions and redirecting the modes and models through which postcolonial scholars work. This chapter charts some of those transformations and the challenges they present with a focus on the way in which older debates within the field, posed in various ways as theory versus practice or cultural politics versus politics proper, continue to shape postcolonial cross-disciplinary discussions but are also yielding to newly framed problematics that seem more urgent as Benedict Anderson's imagined national communities disintegrate and proliferate and newly imagined forms of global community as 'communities of shared fate' emerge (Williams 2009: 33–52). Nation states are not disappearing, as once predicted, but the frames through which they are understood are changing.

Postcolonial thinking has been framed since its origins by tensions produced between the modes of scholarly engagement developed within the academy, with its privileging of theory above practice on the one hand, and those formed through political struggle

[1] The research for this chapter was supported by the Canada Research Chairs programme and conducted while I was a visiting fellow at the Institute for the Humanities at the Australian National University in 2010. I am also grateful to Sandy Annett, my research assistant, for her prompt and thorough support.

within capitalist/imperialist economic structures and an international system based on the Westphalian nation state on the other. These positions are sometimes described as contestations between postcolonial and anti-colonial positioning respectively, but since each addresses questions of power through attention to colonialism and its aftermath, and since each professes a commitment to decolonization, it seems best to recognize that they are skirmishing within a similar terrain. While verbal battles between these positions continue to be fought, and while each still generates its own publications, the rise of globalization as a competing and more successful cross-disciplinary frame through which to understand contemporary struggles has also enabled new modes of postcolonial analysis to emerge, some of which attempt to move beyond these structuring dichotomies or at least to encourage these two warring factions to consider collaborating under the banner of a shared goal.

This chapter surveys some of these transformations and considers their implications. In the most general sense, this shift might be described as a move away from binary models that stress purely oppositional formations towards interactive models of relations that can still embrace an agonist or contestatory politics when necessary, but which also recognize a need for strategic coalitions and negotiations across genuine points of disagreement. Anna Lowenhaupt Tsing's proposed model of 'friction' to designate 'the sticky materiality of practical encounters' (2005: 1) and the 'awkward, unequal, unstable, and creative qualities of interconnections across difference' (4) captures some of the ways in which postcolonial cultural work now challenges neoliberal globalization's rhetoric of liberating and unimpeded global flows. Her suggestion is that as 'a metaphorical image, friction reminds us that heterogeneous and unequal encounters can lead to new arrangements of culture and power' (5). Feminist, critical race, and postcolonial critique have chipped away at the legitimating models governing inequitable social interaction in the twentieth century, but with the global financial and environmental crises of the early twenty-first century, more radical reimagining seems necessary. If postcolonial critique once concentrated its energies on itemizing the ways in which the physical violence of colonialism interacted with epistemic, ontological, and psychic violence (Venn 2006: 11), thereby constituting 'the dark side of modernity' (Mignolo 2007), the pressure now is to reimagine alternative modes of social organization for surviving in a world facing unprecedented challenges.

There are many ways of responding to such pressures. Leela Gandhi, for example, seeks to complicate perspectives on colonial encounter by engaging in a project of historical redress that discovers affinities between a variety of movements loosely gathered under what she calls 'the overriding grammar' (2006: 177) of late nineteenth-century anti-colonial utopian socialism, which shares certain characteristics with social movements today. Her attention to the 'promiscuous alliances ... among unlikely ideological bedfellows' (177) leads her to theorize a 'politics of friendship' (9) and a self-consciously 'immature politics' (177–89) that, in her view, might more productively engage the challenges of the present than do the formalized, nation-based politics of politics proper. This turn to exploring transnational and heterodox alliances in refutation of the 'compartmentalization of causes' (188) that seems to characterize corporate governance as well as the divisions of the disciplines marks one response within postcolonial studies to what Gandhi describes as the 'unsatisfactory theoretical choice between the oppositional but repetitive forms of cultural nationalism on the one hand and the subversive but quietist discourse of hybridity or contrapuntality on the other' (6). While her framing of these postcolonial choices differs somewhat from mine, she too seems to lament their troubling affinity with 'imperial binarism' (5). Her story of colonialism and the challenges to it, as Cooper suggests, reserves 'a large place for political struggles that crossed lines of geography and of self-identification or cultural solidarity, partly through the mobilization of political networks, partly through the coming together of different strands of political action in critical conjunctures' (Cooper 2005: 232).

To the extent that such views are becoming a new orthodoxy within postcolonial studies, it remains valuable to remain alert to dissident voices within the field. Not everyone believes it will be either possible or desirable 'to liberate alternative understandings of "the political"' (Gandhi 2006: 12) through the kind of postcolonial resituating advocated by Gandhi, Cooper, or in a different vein, myself in later sections of this chapter. At least two influential publications over the last decade or so have expressed caution about literary postcolonialism's desire for the political: Peter Hallward's *Absolutely Postcolonial: Writing between the Singular and the Specific* (2001) and Chris Bongie's *Friends and Enemies: The Scribal Politics of Post/Colonial Literature* (2008). Each continues to see the tensions between the textualist and materialist, the literary and the political, dimensions of the field as constituting its problematic identity. The main difference between their focus and my own derives from my interest in postcolonial studies as an inherently *cross-disciplinary* enterprise, whereas Hallward and Bongie engage the politics of postcolonial *literary* studies specifically. Each expands on Graham Huggan's insight that this tension between textualism and materialism within postcolonial literary and cultural studies may be seen as 'further evidence of the field's unresolved attempt to reconcile political activism and cultural critique' (2001: 261). Current debates within feminist philosophy and political studies; indigenous, resilience, and environmental studies; international relations, human rights, and globalization studies; educational and social justice movements: all of these are now in negotiation with postcolonial studies as a means of rearticulating understandings of global connections in ways that insist on the co-production of theory and practice (see Part III of this volume). In an age when 'there is growing agreement that knowledge is now at the very core of economic welfare and development' (Archibugi and Lundvall 2001: 1), attention to dominating forms of knowledge and their corresponding production of 'the power of ignorance' (Code 2007: 213–29; Sullivan and Tuana 2007) is more essential than ever. Such a task can only succeed through concerted, collaborative cross-disciplinary and transnational work.

Within postcolonial literary studies, Hallward and Bongie make important arguments about why literary scholars should value and nurture what they bring to such debates rather than try to move into non-literary spheres of engagement on their own. In arguing that 'the realm of the aesthetic invariably solicits the exercise of a *thoughtful* freedom', Hallward deplores the tendency of '[b]oth postcolonial theorists and their more stringent Marxist critics [to] too often deny or downplay these opportunities' (2001: 334, emphasis in the original). He continues: 'Less than its undeniable but hardly surprising inflation of literary values over socio-materialist ones, what is perhaps more peculiar about postcolonial criticism as a genre is just how *little* it has to say about its own "home" discipline, about literature proper' (335–6, emphasis in the original). Without address- ing here how much (or how little) of 'literature proper' postcolonial criticism addresses, I do not believe it is possible any longer to describe literature as the home discipline of the postcolonial (see, however, McLeod in this section of the volume). Even if literary studies is recognized as one of the first sites of entry of postcolonial studies into the US and UK academies, there have been alternative routes, within many different discipli- nary and geopolitical sites, into postcolonial analysis. My argument is that if we are to understand postcolonial cultural work in its productive multiplicities, then we need to recognize more fully its multiple sites of origin and address (because even in a global world the imagined audience matters) as well as how these sites interact, or fail to inter- act, with one another.

Nonetheless, what Bongie picks up from Hallward's argument is the other side of his modest defence of the possibilities offered by the realm of the aesthetic: his scathing critique of the pretensions and complicities of postcolonial literary and cultural theory. Bongie praises 'Hallward's bracingly dismissive account of postcolonial theory', his ques- tioning of the way it privileges 'the interminable "negotiations" of culture and psychol- ogy' over the 'collective principles' without which 'the political pursuit of justice' would be quite simply unthinkable (3). It is precisely these collective principles that I wish to stress here. Bongie's book asks: 'What if a radical thinker like Peter Hallward is right about postcolonial studies? Where does his damning critique leave us?' (3). His answer, like Hallward's, seeks to reclaim the literary as a valuable perspective within the postco- lonial without exaggerating its utility. Hallward and Bongie both call for finer distinc- tions to be drawn between cultural politics and politics proper; and this is clearly one of the more important challenges for our times.[2] While Bongie expresses some anxiety that an emphasis on the autonomy of these separate spheres may imply a continued complic- ity with discredited modernist preferences, his vigilance against simplistic claims for the political agency of postcolonial literary studies is a salutary reminder of the complicated terrain within which claims to postcolonial politics operate today (see Part III of this volume).

Whereas Hallward and Bongie see the turn to globalization as yet another sign of the postcolonial's ineffectuality as a radical project, its complicity with capitalist com- modification, and its surrender to the endless search for the new within academia, this chapter sees such complicity as one part of a larger dynamic that is also creat- ing new spaces for the revisioning of cross-disciplinary and global political engage- ments. David Slater discusses some of these new spaces in his book, *Geopolitics and the Post-colonial* (2004). In posing postcolonial questions for global times as a way of

[2.] I have sought to address this problem through the lens of autonomy: see Brydon (2009a). Povinelli (2005) takes a more sceptical approach to the term.

trying to think beyond the imperialism of knowledge, Slater develops an approach consonant with Brent Hayes Edwards's suggestion that 'the term *postcolonial* may have proven itself to be most useful precisely when it is placed under severe pressure … as a task or problematic rather than a method or map' (quoted in Slater 2004: 1). In accepting this assessment of the postcolonial project, I agree with those who still find value in the postcolonial while also believing it has largely failed in influencing either political discussion or institutional change, even within the academy let alone outside it. Part of that failure may derive from the methods and maps most closely associated with the field over the last three decades of its practice.

Current challenges associated with neoliberal globalization and climate change, however, offer possibilities for rethinking these modes and models. Opportunities for renewal exist in the increased pressures to expand postcolonial dialogue beyond humanities and social science domains into closer interaction with the sciences within university structures of knowledge production (see, for example, Harding 1998, 2006; Santos 2007a, 2007b), and beyond the university into discussion with other knowledge producers, such as civil society and indigenous communities, educators and policymakers.[3] Current rethinking of social contracts and democratic practices at both sub- and supranational scales can benefit from postcolonial input, but postcolonial approaches will be just one of several justice-seeking modes within a larger dialogue of voices (see Smith and Turner in Part II of this volume).

FROM TWENTIETH-CENTURY POSTCOLONIALISMS TO GLOBALIZATION STUDIES

During the last two decades of the twentieth century, binary framings of the postcolonial dominated across the disciplines, with two major positions locked in contestation in ways that simultaneously defined and divided the field. For one influential group of thinkers, the postcolonial field could not allow itself to be overly distracted by theoretical attention to discursive representations when major injustices and imbalances in power relations remained to be corrected in the material world (see Bartolovich and Lazarus 2002, Parry 2004, and San Juan, Jr. 1998 for classic statements of this position, but also Scott 1999 for the argument that the end of the twentieth century marked an appropriate time to shift the balance from an overemphasis on representations back toward the more properly political). In an ideologically nuanced variation on this framing, Simon During describes the major split within the postcolonial field at this time as

[3] The potential within such trans-sectoral partnerships is what has drawn me to work with the Ford Foundation-funded 'Building Global Democracy' programme and to my current team research, funded by the Social Sciences and Humanities Research Council of Canada, 'Brazil/Canada Knowledge Exchange: Developing Transnational Literacies'.

one between those who wished to develop it as 'a critical, anti-colonialist category' and those who were shaping it as a 'reconciliatory' category in alignment with postmodern thought (During 2000). Ashcroft, Griffiths, and Tiffin, along with Homi Bhabha, are mentioned as exemplars of this latter trend. During also argues though that by the millennium both kinds of postcolonial approaches had effectively been superseded by globalization. These developments, he says, have shifted attention back towards capitalism, democracy, and ethics, but in ways that enable a deeper historical and wider global framing of postcolonial concerns with the impact and legacies of empire. Globalization, in other words, has forced postcolonial analysis to move away from an Anglocentric emphasis on the British Empire and its colonies towards multilingual and multicultural analyses of empires old and new (see Parts I and V of this volume).

This enlarged frame, in turn, draws renewed attention to the idea that the starkly alternative choices between theory and practice, discursive analysis and political engagement, the local and the global, which had shaped postcolonial debates throughout the 1980s and 1990s, had themselves been shaped by culturally specific, dominant modes of Eurocentric thought running throughout the disciplines while regulating their various zones of responsibility. I stress that this involves a renewed attention because this critique of what Bernard S. Cohn terms 'colonialism and its forms of knowledge' (1996) has been an area of postcolonial concern from its beginnings, wherever one locates them. According to this critique, these apparently divergent fields of engagement have each been framed within epistemologies that privilege Eurocentric modes of knowing at the expense of those alternative knowledge systems produced within indigenous and other colonized cultures (see Chakrabarty 2000 and Pieterse and Parekh 1995 for various articulations of this position). Furthermore, these Eurocentric epistemologies, posing as timeless universals, continue to foreclose on humanity's ability to imagine alternative futures (see Lazarus in Part II of this volume).

Postcolonial critiques of Eurocentric imaginaries, their unnamed biases and spheres of sanctioned ignorance, can trace their roots back to different genealogies. Whereas postcolonial thinking has been most closely associated with the engagements of Said with Foucault and Spivak with Derrida, and with their regions of expertise, the Middle East and India respectively, Walter Mignolo locates his 'decolonial' project of border thinking within Latin American critiques of colonial modernity (2007: 163; see also Mignolo in Part I of this volume). Meanwhile, and in common with both streams of engagement with the legacies of colonial modernity, the recent social emancipation research enterprise coordinated by the Portuguese scholar Boaventura Sousa de Santos has identified western epistemologies as the source of the persistent and intensifying divides between theory and practice, the academy and the world, the universal and the particular, that can be witnessed today. These divides are currently blocking efforts to deal with the complex connectivities that shape globalization; to accept them, and the established autonomies of the literary, economic, social, and political they regulate, is, in this mode of thinking, to remain within the confines of Eurocentric habits of mind.

If there is agreement on the need to 'decolonise the mind' (Ngugi 1986) and to deconstruct 'the colonial matrix of power' that blocks decolonized thinking, as Mignolo among others calls for (2007: 156), there is less agreement on how such a task might be accomplished or even whether or not it is possible at all. Each of the loose groupings within the postcolonial field tends to accuse the other of complicity with Eurocentric modes of thinking even though their definitions of the Eurocentric are by no means always the same. The main differences seem to lie in the perceived ideological orientation, e.g. towards resistance or reconciliation/complicity, and in the estimated degree of difficulty that such revisionary tasks might entail. Postcolonial scholarship is beginning to revisit its key terms in recognition of how intertwined such oppositions can be (see Povinelli 2005 on freedom; Jefferess 2008 on resistance; McGonegal 2009 on reconciliation; and Crichlow 2009 on the post-Creole imagination for examples from different contexts). Those influenced by poststructuralist modes of thinking find the task most challenging—witness Spivak's famous lament (1988), since revisited (1999), that 'the subaltern cannot speak'. Those committed to anti-colonial struggle or social justice initiatives argue on the contrary that alternative knowledges remain within reach, either within surviving indigenous traditions, an emergent pluriversalist approach (de Costa 2010: 49), or what Spivak hopefully terms 'the precapitalist cultures of the planet' (2003: 101) and other differently grounded locations (see, for example, Parker, Samantrai, and Romero 2010). The renewed emphasis on the transformative power of the imagination across the disciplines reflects this hope (Appadurai 2001, 2006; Kenway and Fahey 2009; Pieterse and Parekh 1995).

Not everyone believes it is possible to move outside the perceived conflation of colonial/modern and Eurocentric ways of knowing. While Santos and Chakrabarty provide similar diagnoses of the ways in which globalization has shifted understanding of the problem, Santos remains more sanguine about the possibility of leveraging the emancipatory potential within western modernity in dialogue with other traditions, thereby 'democratizing democracy' and generating other knowledge that might come closer to achieving 'cognitive justice' (2005: viii). Santos suggests that 'ours is a time of modern problems (the unfulfilled promise of modernity) for which there are no modern solutions (those based on the above-mentioned dichotomies are now in disarray)' (viii). His 'above-based dichotomies' are the divisions between 'capitalists and socialists, reformists and revolutionaries, nationalists and internationalists' (vii); and these have their counterparts in the various framings of textualist versus materialist approaches described above. For Dipesh Chakrabarty (2000), working within the different genealogical tradition of subaltern studies, the problem is similar (see Dhawan and Randeria in Part V of this volume). In Chakrabarty's *Provincializing Europe*, as Barry Hindess reminds readers in this volume, western modes and the models they project are both inadequate and inescapable. Accepting Derridean assertions that there is no 'outside the text', this group of theorists, among whom Bhabha and Spivak have been the most influential, has engaged in 'the setting to work of deconstruction' (Spivak 1999: 423–31). While this approach was to dominate postcolonial studies right up until the end of the twentieth century, challenges have since emerged, for example from within resurgent indigenous movements and from the Latin American school that engages colonial modernity (Morana et al.

2008; see also Mignolo (2000); Mignolo and Escobar (2010); Santos (2007a, 2007b), with arguments being made for alternative epistemologies in parallel with the World Social Forum's motto that 'another world is possible'.

SPATIAL MODELS OF ANALYSIS AND THE MODALITIES OF ENGAGEMENT THEY SUPPORT

Such challenges are renewing the field, shifting its attention away from the dynamics of once-dominant models, such as those framed by the dialectics of the colonized/colonizer relation and centre/periphery models, towards civil society, politics, and also alternative spatial metaphors such as tidalectics (Kamau Brathwaite's portmanteau coinage from tidal/dialectic, explicated by DeLoughrey 2007), Ngũgĩ wa Thiongo's (2010: 120) globalectics (merging global and dialectic), and planetarity (Spivak's 2003 model for displacing globalization) and the alternative communal models for cooperative endeavour they support. Importantly, each of these spatial metaphors includes a recognition of alternative understandings of temporality, Derek Walcott's 'the sea is history' being the best-known example (Walcott 1986). While not everyone within the field applauds these moves, the interdependencies made visible by globalization are leading to changes in 'imaginative geography' (Said 1978: 55), in social relations, and in temporal understandings, including those promoted through academic practices.

Spatially, the entire world is currently being reconfigured. For some, increasing divisions between rich and poor merit the metaphorical naming of 'global apartheid' (Alexander 1996; Mutasa 2004) in recognition of the ways in which neoliberal globalization seems to act as a form of colonialism by other means. These divisions no longer match inherited geographical distinctions between east and west, north and south, First and Third Worlds. Meanwhile, 'Earth', 'world', and 'planet' offer different, equally problematic attempts to remap global space in its entirety (Brydon 2009b; see also Part V of this volume). For postcolonial thinking, Edward Said's *Orientalism* (1978) has long since named and challenged the symbolic imaginary that constructed the Orient, the Near and Middle East, from the point of view of the west, which in turn constructed itself as the knower in opposition to what it knew through the practices of Orientalism. Similarly, oppositions between east and west have long shaped colonial imaginaries based on the incommensurability of opposites, as articulated in Kipling's poem asserting that 'never the twain shall meet', even though, as Ngũgĩ wa Thiongo (2000) asks, 'is this really true in a world that ultimately is round?' (120). The answer, of course, is that it is only true in a world in which the powerful assume the right to deny coevalness to those they deem their inferiors. As power shifts, so too do its imaginaries. The shift from thinking in terms of flat maps and Mercator projections to conceiving of the earth as a globe (as seen from outer space) is one of the fundamental shifts in perspective associated with the recent turn to globalization studies and the rise of discourses of planetarity in the early twenty-first century.

Tellingly, when writing of the west and its others, critics often write of the west and the non-west, expanding the Orientalizing imaginary beyond association with the east alone. These appellations draw attention to the power imbalances that constitute colonial modes of knowing across the various modalities identified by Cohn in terms of historiography, observational travel, demographic surveys, museum studies, and surveillance—modalities that had come to distinguish the different areas of disciplinary responsibility by the onset of the twentieth century (1996: 3–15). Interestingly, the only mention of postcolonial theory in Joe Moran's study *Interdisciplinarity* (2002) addresses Said's challenge to the supposed neutrality of geography, cartography, and travel writing by exposing their complicities with imperial imaginaries (167–8). This reinforces my view that postcolonial cultural work, while boundary crossing in many ways, has been far more influential within individual disciplines than it has been to date in theories of inter-, trans-, or cross-disciplinarity (see also Huggan 2002).

In contrast to those dominant models of the west and the non-west, the west and the rest, that were previously employed in twentieth-century postcolonialisms, contemporary globalization discourse offers the alternative conception of global north and south (see Part V of this volume). But how much of a difference is there in this reorientation of focus and what actual difference does it make? 'North' and 'south', after all, are broadly metaphorical constructions that should not be confused with literal (i.e., physical) geographies, and while they represent a well-intentioned attempt to describe globally unequal relations, they do so in terms that tend, ironically if inadvertently, to flatten world relations of power. They retain some validity, however, precisely *because* they are metaphorical designations. Australia, for example, clearly belongs in the global north, despite the continent's physical location in the southern hemisphere. Similarly, one can speak of pockets of the global south within the global north, thereby designating relative relations of privilege in a way that is not possible for the more monolithic 'east' and 'west'. And whereas these latter tend all too often to be used as polarizing opposites, global south and north are contained within complex models of global circulation, friction, and flow that describe the ways in which cultures meet, influence, and cross-fertilize each other over time, and where 'exclusion' (another binary term) may be paradoxically understood to be a form of differential and disadvantaged *inclusion* within a larger system that operates within conspicuously unequal relations of power. The more politically engaged term 'global apartheid' perhaps captures best this sense of differential inclusion within a global system in so far as it focuses on the structuring principles of the system rather than on its component parts. Caroline Levander and Walter Mignolo, however, make a persuasive case for exploring 'the possibilities—institutional, disciplinary, geopolitical—of "global south" as an emergent conceptual apparatus' (2011: 1). For them, 'global south can be seen at the confluence of conflicts between systems of knowledge and ways of conceptualizing space, cultures, and ways of knowing' (9). Raewyn Connell's *Southern Theory* (2007) finds similar value in this construction as a starting point for devising 'a new path for social theory that will help social science to serve democratic purposes on a world scale' (vii).

This is not to say that north and south have effectively replaced east and west as the orienting compass points of contemporary postcolonial imaginaries; rather, these terms coexist—confusingly at times, but also productively—in shaping how contemporary global patterns and power relations are understood. Eve Darian-Smith, for example, examines 'the endurance of myths of "East" and "West" and the role national and international law plays in affirming and legitimizing these myths' in contemporary Hong Kong (2002: 294); while in a more extended critique, Neil Lazarus argues that 'the concept of "the West", as it is used in postcolonial theory … has no coherent or credible referent. It is an ideological category masquerading as a geographic one' (2002: 44). In Lazarus's analysis, as the west comes to signify a civilization, it becomes dangerously culturalized and dematerialized: as a stand-in for imperialist power, its usage within certain kinds of postcolonial cultural work ultimately functions 'as [an] alibi in the determinate absence of a plausible conceptualization of capitalism and imperialist social relations' (57). Lazarus's essay equates these uses of 'the west' in postcolonial theory with the similar ways in which designations of 'Europe' and the 'Eurocentric' have made a fuller analysis of the world's problems that much more difficult. In showing how the spatial imaginaries surrounding such terms seem to support a 'culturalist' mode of analysis that obscures the material contexts of any given situation, he reminds postcolonial critics of the dangers of naturalizing these models and literalizing their referents. The term 'Eurocentric', for instance, names the origin of a particular epistemology that claims universality, modernity, and objectivity for its own, decidedly partial perspective on how to understand the world. That perspective, however, no longer has (and perhaps never had) its exclusive frame of reference in Europe; nor should it be expediently assimilated into a world model of civilizational clash (see Mignolo in Part I of this volume).

Globalization's production of a transnational and complexly connected globe has led to a shift away from the nation-based imaginaries that previously inspired the major anti-colonial movements towards thinking in terms of transoceanic circulations, as evidenced in Paul Gilroy's seminal study *The Black Atlantic* (1993). Cross-disciplinary research, both within and beyond postcolonial studies, now works at least partly within the encompassing frames of Atlantic, Indian Ocean, Mediterranean, and Pacific worlds. These revised spatial configurations, along with those that attach themselves to 'networked' global cities, have provided new models for the contact zones that were initially made central to postcolonial analysis through Mary Louise Pratt's groundbreaking 1992 study *Imperial Eyes* (revised by her in 2008). These models stress global flows and the interaction of 'global scapes' (Appadurai 1996) in conjunction with renewed attention to 'global friction' (Tsing 2005); they emphasize the points of interaction *among* differences rather than the points of separation *between* them, in ways quite similar to those that have come to be associated with Mignolo's influential 'border thinking' (Mignolo 2000). Taking his cue from Fanon, Imre Szeman (2003) names these 'zones of instability'.

Perhaps the pre-eminent example here is Gilroy's combination of 'roots' and 'routes'—historical/geographical paradigms previously more likely to be set apart or even contrasted—in *The Black Atlantic* (2003). A few years later, yoking Glissant's 'complicity of relation' to Brathwaite's 'tidalectics', Elizabeth DeLoughrey moves a step beyond Gilroy in comparing two forms of transoceanic imaginary—Caribbean and Pacific—in her *Routes and Roots: Navigating Caribbean and Pacific Island Literatures* (2007). Preaching a 'diversity that [neither] romanticize[s] indigeneity nor pathologize[s] diaspora', DeLoughrey describes her approach in terms of a 'tidalectic model of roots and routes that … works against the rigid claims of ethnic nationalism' (xi) and that establishes a new 'maritime grammar' (30) in which the open Deleuzean metaphors of deterritorialization and reterritorialization prove more productive than those conventionally associated with bounded communities or sovereign states. Ocean metaphors have also marked a recent shift in current metropolitan imaginaries of knowledge production. Some historians are currently embracing a 'new thalassology' (Horden and Purcell 2006), a Greek-derived term describing a mode of study focused on oceanic circulations. The turn to transoceanic imaginaries replaces continent-based regionalisms with an emphasis on mobility that seems more appropriate to global imaginaries but is not necessarily attuned to power imbalances.

Whereas *tidalectics* privileges immanent forms of critique, *planetarity* might initially seem to privilege a panoptical view from on high, such as that enabled when the earth is seen from the perspective of outer space. As it is currently theorized, however, planetarity seems more designed to work across different scales of engagement, replacing hierarchies with 'heterarchy', described by O'Brien in terms of 'a system of organization characterized by overlap [and] multiplicity, and [with] no rankings or mixed rankings among elements' (O'Brien et al. 2009). Such modes of engagement can recognize a 'wider group of stakeholders interacting across different levels, perhaps drawing on principles of coalition building or deliberative democracy' so as to address some of the problems that cross conventional disciplinary and state boundaries (O'Brien et al. 2009). As the above citation suggests, so-called 'resilience theorists' are increasingly recognizing the need to rethink social contracts, revisiting the building blocks—democracy, forms of imagined community, citizenship, and the human—on which the current world order rests.

I still wonder whether this kind of shift, productive though it is, in theoretical understandings of the spatial dynamics of postcolonial relations will be reflected in changing modes of cross-disciplinary practice. After all, while the various postcolonial theories of the twentieth century crossed disciplinary boundaries at will, they also largely reinforced their conventional divisions of responsibility. Even as staunchly idiosyncratic a text as Spivak's *Critique of Postcolonial Reason* (1999) might be read as solidifying conventional disciplinary boundaries, and though it ranges impressively across philosophy, history, and culture from its customary bases in feminism and comparative literature, Spivak also proclaims her lack of erudition for performing interdisciplinarity, choosing instead to play up her break with clannishness and her ability to 'break rules' (xiii). Even here, Spivak acknowledges her profound debt to other feminist theorists, while in later works such as *Death of a Discipline* (2005) and *Other Asias* (2008) she either self-consciously grounds herself in the (combined) traditions of comparative literature and area studies or rigorously commits herself to 'deep language learning in the collectivity of the classroom', an activity she argues leads 'toward all those words that policy studies conjure with: peace, justice, the rights of humanity' (2008: 2). While postcolonial theory is alert to the misuse of these words, it is also wedded to the universal ideals they embody and to their potential for replacing the oppositional structures of 'us' and 'them' that colonialism employed with alternative visions of collaborative work.

Spivak's turn to deep language learning and the collectivity of the classroom marks an implicit rejection of the academic star system that has made her, along with Said and Bhabha, one of the chief representatives of the postcolonial project as it has been understood to date. The star system, in its selectivity and aggressive individualism, has arguably led postcolonial critique away from its multiple origins towards a misleading emphasis on perspectives derived from the specific histories of India and the Middle East. In contrast, the emergent colonial-modernity analysts, in differentiating their work from that of postcolonial scholars, have attached alternative genealogies and practices to themselves. The broad-based group gathered around Walter Mignolo at Duke University, for example, is involved in an ongoing collective project on modernity/coloniality; while, in a similar fashion, the research team of Boaventura de Sousa Santos has produced a multi-volume series under the overarching title, 'Reinventing Social Emancipation: Toward New Manifestos' (see my introductory section). Ambitious cross-disciplinary projects such as these are certainly aware of postcolonial approaches and they do employ them selectively, but within frames they see as being more encompassing than those explicitly associated with postcolonial critique. The best example of a long-term, collective, cross-disciplinary initiative that has made a significant impact on postcolonial studies is the subaltern studies group, seen in this volume by Dane Kennedy (Part IV) and Nikita Dhawan and Shalini Randeria (Part V) as essentially a historical project while also representative of the kinds of border crossings that have been enabled by postcolonial imaginaries. But border crossings, of course, as Mignolo points out, are not the same as actually *inhabiting* the border regions of the world (Mignolo 2000; see also Mignolo in Part I of this volume).

Until now, postcolonial cross-disciplinarity has largely constructed itself around Saidian notions of travelling theory (Said 1982, 1994) and border crossings. As a result, the challenge it has posed to conventional disciplinary formations has been largely illusory. It has readily been assimilated into traditional disciplinary models in an add-on fashion without necessitating any large-scale structural changes. For example, just as postcolonial theory has institutionalized an academic star system of theorists, so too has it institutionalized a star system of modernist and high modernist authors whose works seem most amenable to postcolonial analysis and commercial viability (see Bongie (2008), Brouillette (2007), and Huggan (2001) for elaborations of this argument). Can the recent emergence of collective cross-disciplinary academic projects be seen as a challenge to these institutionalized arrangements? It is too early to tell. There are strong pressures within the academy to maintain publication hierarchies and citation systems that buttress these hierarchical arrangements. While the move toward open-access publication may eventually help to democratize the field, in the shorter term it is ironic that the kind of collaborative enterprise represented by the *Oxford Handbook of Postcolonial*

Studies—in which this chapter appears—is one of the most established approaches to the field and yet one of the least valued, being far less likely to be cited (though statistics are not available to confirm this) than the single-authored work.

Typical of recent moves to consign postcolonial approaches to the past, as being 'overly concerned with a vertical analysis confined to one nation-state, such as the effect of British colonialism in India, where the vertical power relationship between the colonizer and the colonized is the main object of analysis' (11), is Françoise Lionnet and Shu-mei Shih's *Minor Transnationalism* (2005). Born out of dissatisfaction with 'the disciplinary boundaries that would ordinarily keep us on very different professional tracks' (1), this international team project maintains that in contrast to postcolonialism, 'globalization increasingly favors lateral and nonhierarchical network structures, or what Gilles Deleuze and Félix Guattari call a rhizome' (2). (Clearly the rhizome bears interesting similarities to the aforementioned tidalectics.) In their introduction, the editors argue that 'while postcolonial studies has proven to be an important tool for the exploration of colonized cultures, sociocultural developments since decolonization now call for better contextualization using transcolonial perspectives' (11). Nonetheless, despite these disavowals and the transnational framing, the volume continues to employ more-or-less conventional postcolonial models (west and non-west, Eurocentric knowledges, Orientalism, creolization, the struggle for coevality, etc.) and to engage with more-or-less standard postcolonial issues. And like so many collections of postcolonial essays, it lacks a conclusion, making the book seem more like a heterogeneous collection of diverse work than a focused collective project with shared questions to address.

THEMATIC AND GENERIC SHIFTS

My argument thus far has been that while the most influential schools within twentieth-century postcolonial studies situated themselves within either colonial discourse analysis or models derived from Marxism, with world system theories and subaltern studies being the most prominent among these, the beginning of the twenty-first century has seen each of these two major trends reinvent, sometimes cross-fertilize, themselves. Colonial discourse analysis is now turning increasingly toward Levinasian ethics, storytelling, memorializing, and witnessing, and is engaging more centrally with historical memory (Cheah 2003), environmental movements (Huggan and Tiffin 2010), and discourses of the law, including human rights (Slaughter 2007). Meanwhile, Marxists, post-Marxists, and cultural materialists have begun to engage more directly with established versions of globalization studies, attending to politics and economics and putting pressure on international relations (Agathangelou and Ling 2009; Chowdhry and Nair 2004; Darby 1998, 2006) and development studies (McEwan 2009). As in the first wave of postcolonial theory, however, current anthologies linking the postcolonial and the global look to represent both discursive and materialist orientations (e.g. Desai and Nair 2005; Krishnaswamy and Hawley 2008) and introductory texts still seek to link the two, even if a particular approach and/or thinker is privileged (e.g. Levinas in Hiddleston 2009). Furthermore, certain influential theorists such as the cultural materialist Peter Hitchcock (1999, 2003, 2010) and the rhetorician Pheng Cheah (2003, 2006) continue to work within the border territories where these approaches meet, as do many feminist postcolonial thinkers of both present and past.

A good example of this continuing trend is Andrea Lunsford and Lahoucine Ouzgane's collection, *Crossing Borderlands: Composition and Postcolonial Studies*, which defines itself as moving 'beyond a Eurocentric view of post-colonialism, considering the position of Mexican Americans, African Americans, and Native Americans, and hence tracing colonialist economies of power in America' (2004: 4). The anthology is exemplary of contemporary attempts to crosshatch multicultural and postcolonial projects (see also Narayan and Harding 2000) and to include white settler colonies, the US in particular, within the purview of postcolonial studies. The tendency of what Lunsford and Ouzgane term Eurocentric postcolonial analysis to bracket out what it terms 'the "white" Anglophone settler colonies of Canada, New Zealand, and Australia' (Lazarus 2004a: xiv) from analysis within the postcolonial domain has meant that the field has been slow to see the relevance of indigenous concerns within these and other invader-settler contexts. Henry Schwarz and Sangeeta Ray's *A Companion to Postcolonial Studies* (2000) was path-breaking in this regard in its inclusion of Jace Weaver's essay, 'Indigenousness and Indigeneity'; while John McLeod's *Routledge Companion to Postcolonial Studies* (2007) devotes attention to indigenous issues by including Australasia, Canada, and Latin America within its categories of postcolonial locations. Still far too typical, however, is *The Cambridge Companion to Postcolonial Literary Studies* (Lazarus 2004b), which neglects indigenous perspectives on colonialism and postcolonialism entirely; and it remains the case that indigenous movements have found more support for their decolonizing initiatives within the shifting international political scene (Henderson 2008; Kymlicka 2007) than they have within academic postcolonial studies to date.

What indigenous engagements with postcolonial theory do exist, are perhaps inevitably fraught. A relatively early example, Bob Hodge and Vijay Mishra's *Dark Side of the Dream: Australian Literature and the Postcolonial Mind* (1990), raised the importance of understanding Australia as 'still thoroughly marked by its role as an agent of imperialism' (xiii), stressing throughout the urgent need to recognize Aboriginal perspectives in framing Australian postcoloniality. However, indigenous academics within Australian academia and elsewhere have tended to find more purchase within the modes and models of critical race studies than they have within postcolonial analysis (see, for example, Moreton-Robinson 2004, 2007; Riggs 2007; and Grossman 2003, the last of whom characteristically writes that 'even though some Indigenous writers have used tools made available by postcolonial literary theory, it would be a mistake to assume that Indigenous critical writing and postcolonial analysis are one and the same thing' (23)).

Non-Australian indigenous interventions include those of the Māori scholar Linda Tuhiwai Smith, whose *Decolonizing Methodologies* (1999) has been both locally and transnationally influential in recognizing the usefulness of postcolonial theory for indigenous critics interested in revising the power relations built into research to reshape the disciplines in accord with indigenous knowledges; and the Mi'kmaw scholar Marie Battiste's *Reclaiming Indigenous Voice and Vision* (2000), one of the early sustained Canadian engagements across indigenous and postcolonial concerns. In her introduction to this latter collection, which emerged from a 1996 summer institute at the University of Saskatchewan, Battiste explains that indigenous thinkers currently use the term postcolonial to indicate an 'aspirational practice, goal, or idea that the delegates used to imagine a new form of society that they desired to create' (2000: xix). Typically however, she stresses that 'postcolonial Indigenous thought should not be confused with postcolonial theory in literature. Although they are related endeavours, postcolonial Indigenous thought emerges from the inability of Eurocentric theory to deal with the complexities of colonialism and its assumptions' (xix). James Sakej Youngblood Henderson duly elaborates the strategies of Eurocentric thinking in one of his chapters in the volume, 'Postcolonial Ghost Dancing', and begins to answer the question, 'How do Indigenous peoples create a postcolonial society?' (2000a: 161), in a later chapter, 'Postcolonial Ledger Drawing: Legal Reform'. Here, he provides a case study to indicate how 'our postcolonial visions are … enfolded in legal codes, nonnarrative legal documents, rather than in philosophical manifestos or grand narratives' (2000b: 161). While his chief focus as an indigenous lawyer (Chickasaw and Cheyenne) lies with constitutional reform, he also insists on the way in which university disciplines deny the holistic character of indigenous knowledge, arguing that 'the Eurocentric curriculum and methods must renounce their assumed higher authority' (164). (Torres Strait Islander Martin Nakata makes a similar point, without explicitly referencing postcolonialism, in his influential *Disciplining the Savages, Savaging the Disciplines*, 2007.)

Examples such as these suggest that whereas indigenous scholars have been prolific in articulating their views on colonialism and decolonization, they have seldom engaged directly with postcolonial theory. This is an area where little cross-disciplinary engagement has as yet occurred. However, recent evidence suggests that sites of contention are beginning to emerge between some versions of postcolonial theory and certain articulations of indigenous perspectives, particularly around questions of identity, cultural politics, and sovereignty within the US context (see Acoose et al. 2008; Byrd 2011; Morgensen 2011). A major point of shared concern has been found in reimagining curricular, pedagogical, and research practices. In this context, Yatta Kanu's collection, *Curriculum as Cultural Practice: Postcolonial Imaginations* (2006) marks an important cross-disciplinary attempt to begin translating postcolonial theory into institutionalized practice (see Part III of this volume). While recognizing the diversity of its usages, Kanu employs postcolonial primarily to designate 'the site where educational/curricular assumptions and norms are called into question in the struggle for more democratic social relations' (8).

Conclusion

In this chapter, I have argued that postcolonial studies currently operates both within and across the conventional disciplinary divisions, engaging scholars trained within anthropological, geographical, historical, literary, philosophical, political, and sociological studies, and slowly entering the more traditionally resistant fields of development studies and international relations as well as the professional schools of architecture, business, education, engineering, medicine, and law. Other late twentieth-century enterprises such as cultural studies and feminism have long interacted with postcolonial ideas if they have taken care to retain their own intellectual and social focus, while the newly resurgent fields of indigenous studies and human rights studies began their own engagements with postcolonialism at the millennial turn. Yet while postcolonial studies has often assumed itself to be inherently interdisciplinary, many publications within the field continue to operate within established disciplinary conventions. Within these conventions, writers draw on other disciplines as they are needed, but genuinely collaborative work across the disciplines remains rare (see Huggan 2002, 2008). Furthermore, what cross-disciplinary anthologies there are, are by and large eclectic compilations in which each chapter maintains its own disciplinary or area studies emphasis.

By the beginning of the twenty-first century, postcolonial studies had already begun to move beyond its initial Anglophone focus, expanding into Francophone, Lusophone, and Hispanic domains. Calls for a more multilingual and diversely situated postcolonial criticism, including greater engagement with comparative literature and area studies, have similarly resulted—in conjunction with globalizing pressures—in certain changes within the field of American comparative literature. The shift in focus from the 1995 Bernheimer report to the Saussy volume ten years later is instructive. Whereas the Bernheimer report addressed American multiculturalism with minimal attention to global issues, Saussy's 2006 collection consciously addressed itself to broader global themes. Interestingly, though, postcolonial approaches remain muted in both anthologies. Postcolonial criticism is influencing work on past and more recent empires, such as the post-Soviet empire (Shkandrij 2001; Moore 2005), and it continues to address the special problem of Israel/Palestine (Mufti 2007). Troublingly, however, it holds a marginal position within the new US-based world literature studies (Damrosch 2003, 2009a, 2009b). The 2009 MLA volume on *Teaching World Literature*, for example, includes a chapter by Michael Palencia-Roth describing how he has moved away from using colonization as the skeleton on which his cross-cultural courses are based: 'Today one might present the issue without using the term colonization and in the form of a question, "What is the history of humanity if not the history of cross-cultural encounter?"' (149). This bland formulation, reminiscent of some versions of the earlier Commonwealth literary studies, seems set to replace the historically specific attention to the violence that attended colonization and that now continues into what Derek Gregory provocatively names the 'colonial present' (see Gregory 2004; see also Part II of this volume). Yet if literary study in such mainstream venues appears to have tired of the postcolonial—even though it continues to valorize its stars—book history (Brouillette 2007; Fraser 2008) and children's literature (Bradford 2007; Cannella and Viruru 2004) have been re-energized through their recent engagements with postcolonial theory, while the nation-, region-, and language-specific study of those literatures described as postcolonial, or those newly presented as interacting with the postcolonial, continues apace. Finally, the utopian promise and revolutionary energies made possible by the asking of postcolonial questions in earlier times may now be more insistently, and one hopes more influentially, asked within non-traditional locations for postcolonial engagement. As civil society groups assert their own knowledge-producing capacities both in dialogue with the universities and in opposition to them, postcolonial scholars are increasingly being challenged to rearticulate the goals of our research to meet the needs of a changing global scene.

References

Acoose, Janice et al. (2008). *Reasoning Together: The Native Critics Collective.* Norman: University of Oklahoma Press.

Agathangelou, Anna M. and L. H. M. Ling (2009). *Transforming World Politics: From Empire to Multiple Worlds.* London: Routledge.

Alexander, Titus (1996). *Unravelling Global Apartheid.* Cambridge: Polity Press.

Appadurai, Arjun (1996). *Modernity at Large: Cultural Dimensions of Globalization.* Minneapolis: University of Minnesota Press.

Appadurai, Arjun (2001). 'Grassroots Globalization and the Research Imagination', in A. Appadurai (ed.), *Globalization.* Durham: Duke University Press, 1–21.

Appadurai, Arjun (2006). 'The Right to Research', *Globalization, Societies, and Education,* 4.2: 167–77.

Archibugi, Daniele and Lundvall, Benge-Åke (eds) (2001). *The Globalizing Learning Economy.* Oxford: Oxford University Press.

Bartolovich, Crystal and Neil Lazarus (ed.) (2002). *Marxism, Modernity and Postcolonial Studies.* Cambridge: Cambridge University Press.

Battiste, Marie (ed.) (2000). *Reclaiming Indigenous Voice and Vision.* Vancouver: University of British Columbia Press.

Bernheimer, Charles (ed.) (1995). *Comparative Literature in the Age of Multiculturalism.* Baltimore: Johns Hopkins University Press.

Bongie, Christopher (2008). *Friends and Enemies: The Scribal Politics of Post/Colonial Literature.* Liverpool: Liverpool University Press.

Bradford, Clare (2007). *Unsettling Narratives: Postcolonial Readings of Children's Literature.* Waterloo: Wilfrid Laurier University Press.

Brouillette, Sarah (2007). *Postcolonial Writers in the Global Marketplace.* New York, Palgrave.

Brydon, Diana (2009a). 'Competing Autonomy Claims and the Changing Grammar of Global Politics', *Globalizations,* 6.3: 339–52.

Brydon, Diana (2009b). 'Earth, World, Planet: Where Does the Postcolonial Critic Stand?', in C. Prentice, H. Johnson, and V. Devadas (eds), *Cultural Transformations: Perspectives on Translocation in a Global Age.* Amsterdam: Rodopi, 3–29.

Byrd, Jodi A. (2011). *The Transit of Empires: Indigenous Critiques of Colonialism*. Minneapolis: University of Minnesota Press.

Cannella, Gaile S. and Radhika Viruru (2004). *Childhood and Post-Colonization: Power, Education, and Contemporary Practice*. New York: RoutledgeFalmer.

Chakrabarty, Dipesh (2000). *Provincializing Europe: Post-Colonial Thought and Historical Difference*. Princeton: Princeton University Press.

Cheah, Pheng (2003). *Spectral Nationality: Passages of Freedom From Kant to Postcolonial Literatures of Liberation*. New York: Columbia University Press.

Cheah, Pheng (2006). *Inhuman Conditions: On Cosmopolitanism and Human Rights*. Cambridge, Mass.: Harvard University Press.

Chowdhry, Geeta and Sheila Nair (eds) (2004). *Power, Postcolonialism and International Relations: Reading Race, Gender and Class*. London: Routledge.

Code, Lorraine (2007). 'The Power of Ignorance', in S. Sullivan and N. Tuana (eds), *Race and Epistemologies of Ignorance*. Albany: State University of New York Press, 213–29.

Cohn, Bernard S. (1996). *Colonialism and its Forms of Knowledge: The British in India*. Princeton: Princeton University Press.

Connell, Raewyn (2007). *Southern Theory: The Global Dynamics of Knowledge in Social Science*. London: Polity.

Cooper, Frederick (2005). *Colonialism in Question: Theory, Knowledge, History*. Berkeley: University of California Press.

Crichlow, Michaeline A. (2009). *Globalization and the Post-Creole Imagination: Notes on Fleeing the Plantation*. Durham, NC: Duke University Press.

Damrosch, David (2003). *What is World Literature?* Princeton: Princeton University Press.

Damrosch, David (2009a). *How to Read World Literature*. Chichester: Wiley-Blackwell.

Damrosch, David (ed.) (2009b). *Teaching World Literature*. New York: Modern Language Association of America.

Darby, Phillip (1998). *The Fiction of Imperialism: Reading Between International Relations and Postcolonialism*. London: Cassell.

Darby, Phillip (ed.) (2006). *Postcolonizing the International: Working to Change the Way We Are*. Honolulu: University of Hawai'i Press.

Darian-Smith, Eve (2002). 'Myths of East and West: Intellectual Property Law in Postcolonial Hong Kong', in D. T. Goldberg and A. Quayson (eds), *Relocating Postcolonialism*. Oxford, Blackwell, 294–319.

De Costa, Ravi (2010). 'Afterword', in M. R. Blaser, R. de Costa, D. McGregor, and W. D. Coleman (eds), *Indigenous Peoples and Autonomy: Insights for a Global Age*. Vancouver: University of British Columbia Press, 241–9.

DeLoughrey, Elizabeth M. (2007). *Routes and Roots: Navigating Caribbean and Pacific Island Literatures*. Honolulu, University of Hawai'i Press.

Desai, Gaurav and Supriya Nair (eds) (2005). *Postcolonialisms: An Anthology of Cultural Theory and Criticism*. New Brunswick: Rutgers University Press.

During, Simon (2000). 'Postcolonialism and Globalization: Towards a Historicization of their Inter-relation', *Cultural Studies*, 14.3–4: 385–404.

Fraser, Robert (2008). *Book History Through Postcolonial Eyes*. London: Routledge.

Gandhi, Leela (2006). *Affective Communities: Anticolonial Thought, Fin-de-Siècle Radicalism, and the Politics of Friendship*. Durham: Duke University Press.

Gilroy, Paul (1993). *The Black Atlantic: Modernity and Double Consciousness*. Cambridge, Mass.: Harvard University Press.

Glissant, Edward (1997). *Poetics of Relation*, trans. B. Wing. Ann Arbor: University of Michigan Press.

Goldberg, David Theo and Ato Quayson (eds) (2002). *Relocating Postcolonialism*. Oxford: Blackwell.

Gregory, Derek (2004). *The Colonial Present*. Oxford: Blackwell.

Grossman, Michele (ed.) (2003). *Blacklines: Contemporary Critical Writing by Indigenous Australians*. Melbourne: Melbourne University Press.

Hallward, Peter (2001). *Absolutely Postcolonial: Writing Between the Singular and the Specific*. Manchester: Manchester University Press.

Harding, Sandra (1998). *Is Science Multicultural? Postcolonialisms, Feminisms, and Epistemologies*. Bloomington: Indiana University Press.

Harding, Sandra (2006). *Science and Social Inequality: Feminist and Postcolonial Issues*. Urbana: University of Illinois Press.

Hayes Edwards, Brent (2004). 'The Genres of Postcolonialism', *Social Text*, 78/22.1: 1–15.

Henderson, James Youngblood (2000a). 'Postcolonial Ghost Dancing: Diagnosing European Colonialism', in M. Battiste (ed.), *Reclaiming Indigenous Voice and Vision*. Vancouver: University of British Columbia Press, 57–76.

Henderson, James Youngblood (2000b). 'Postcolonial Ledger Drawing: Legal Reform', in M. Battiste (ed.) *Reclaiming Indigenous Voice and Vision*. Vancouver: University of British Columbia Press, 161–71.

Henderson, James Youngblood (2008). *Indigenous Diplomacy and the Rights of Peoples: Achieving UN Recognition*. Saskatoon: Purich.

Hiddleston, June (2009). *Understanding Postcolonialism*. Stocksfield: Acumen.

Hitchcock, Peter (1999). *Oscillate Wildly: Space, Body, and Spirit of Millennial Materialism*. Minneapolis: University of Minnesota Press.

Hitchcock, Peter (2003). *Imaginary States: Studies in Cultural Transnationalism*. Urbana: University of Illinois Press.

Hitchcock, Peter (2010). *The Long Space: Transnationalism and the Postcolonial Form*. Stanford: Stanford University Press.

Hodge, Bob and Vijay Mishra (1990). *The Dark Side of the Dream: Australian Literature and the Postcolonial Mind*. Sydney: Allen & Unwin.

Horden Peregrine and Nicholas Purcell (2006). 'AHR Forum: The Mediterranean and "the New Thalassology"', *American Historical Review*, 111.3: 722–40.

Huggan, Graham (2008). *Interdisciplinary Measures: Literature and the Future of Postcolonial Studies*. Liverpool: Liverpool University Press.

Huggan, Graham (2001). *The Postcolonial Exotic: Marketing the Margins*. London: Routledge.

Huggan, Graham (2002). 'Postcolonial Studies and the Anxiety of Interdisciplinarity', *Postcolonial Studies*, 5.3: 245–75.

Huggan, Graham and Helen Tiffin (2010). *Postcolonial Ecocriticism: Literature, Animals, Environment*. London: Routledge.

Jefferess, David (2008). *Postcolonial Resistance: Culture, Liberation and Transformation*. Toronto: University of Toronto Press.

Kanu, Yatta (ed.) (2006). *Curriculum as Cultural Practice: Postcolonial Imaginations*. Toronto: University of Toronto Press.

Kenway, Jane and Johannah Fahey (eds) (2009). *Globalizing the Research Imagination*. London: Routledge.

Krishnaswamy, Revathi and John C. Hawley (eds) (2008). *The Post-Colonial and the Global.* Minneapolis: University of Minnesota Press.

Kymlicka, Will (2007). *Multicultural Odysseys: Navigating the New International Politics of Diversity.* Oxford: Oxford University Press.

Lazarus, Neil (2002). 'The Fetish of "the West" in Postcolonial Theory', in C. Bartolovich and N. Lazarus (eds), *Marxism, Modernity and Postcolonial Studies.* Cambridge: Cambridge University Press, 43–64.

Lazarus, Neil (2004a). 'Indicative Chronology', in N. Lazarus (ed.), *The Cambridge Companion to Postcolonial Literary Studies.* Cambridge: Cambridge University Press, pp. xii–xvi.

Lazarus, Neil (ed.) (2004b). *The Cambridge Companion to Postcolonial Literary Studies.* Cambridge: Cambridge University Press.

Levander, Caroline and Walter D. Mignolo (2011). 'Introduction: The Global South and World Dis/Order', *Global South,* 5.1: 1–11.

Lionnet, Françoise and Shu-mei Shih (eds) (2005). *Minor Transnationalism.* Durham: Duke University Press.

Lunsford, Andrea and Lahoucine Ouzgane (eds) (2004). *Crossing Borderlands: Composition and Postcolonial Studies.* Pittsburgh: University of Pittsburgh Press.

McEwan, Cheryl (2009). *Postcolonialism and Development.* London: Routledge.

McGonegal, Julie (2009). *Imagining Justice: The Politics of Postcolonial Forgiveness and Reconciliation.* Montreal: McGill-Queen's University Press.

McLeod, John (ed.) (2007). *The Routledge Companion to Postcolonial Studies.* London: Routledge.

Mignolo, Walter D. (2000). *Local Histories/Global Designs: Coloniality, Subaltern Knowledges, and Border Thinking.* Princeton: Princeton University Press.

Mignolo, Walter D. (2007). 'Introduction: Coloniality of Power and De-colonial Thinking', *Cultural Studies,* 2.3: 155–67.

Mignolo, Walter D. and Arturo Escobar (eds) (2010). *Globalization and the Decolonial Option.* London: Routledge.

Moore, David Chioni (2005). 'Is the Post- in Postcolonial the Post- in Post-Soviet? Toward a Global Postcolonial Critique', in G. Desai and S. Nair (eds), *Postcolonialisms: An Anthology of Cultural Theory and Criticism.* New Brunswick: Rutgers University Press, 514–38.

Moran, Joe (2002). *Interdisciplinarity.* London: Routledge.

Moraña, Mabel, Enrique D. Dussel, and Carlos A. Jáuregui (eds) (2008). *Coloniality at Large: Latin America and the Postcolonial Debate.* Durham: Duke University Press.

Moreton-Robinson, Aileen (ed.) (2004). *Whitening Race: Essays in Social and Cultural Criticism.* Canberra: Aboriginal Studies Press.

Moreton-Robinson, Aileen (ed.) (2007). *Sovereign Subjects: Indigenous Sovereignty Matters.* Sydney: Allen & Unwin.

Morgensen, Scott Lauria (2011). *Spaces Between Us: Queer Settler Colonialism and Indigenous Decolonization.* Minneapolis: University of Minnesota Press.

Mufti, Aamir R. (2007). *Enlightenment in the Colony: The Jewish Question and the Crisis of Postcolonial Culture.* Princeton: Princeton University Press.

Mutasa, Charles (2004). 'Global Apartheid', *Global Policy Forum.* Online source: <http://www.globalpolicy.org>, accessed 2 January 2010.

Nakata, Martin N. (2007). *Disciplining the Savages, Savaging the Disciplines.* Canberra: Aboriginal Studies Press.

Narayan, Uma and Sandra Harding (eds) (2000), *Decentering the Center: Philosophy for a Multicultural, Postcolonial, and Feminist World*. Bloomington: Indiana University Press.

Ngũgĩ, wa Thiong'o (1986). *Decolonising the Mind: The Politics of Language in African Literature*. London: James Currey.

Ngũgĩ, wa Thiong'o (2000). 'Borders and Bridges: Seeking Connections Between Things', in F. Afzal -Kahn and K. Seshadri -Crooks (eds), *The Pre-Occupation of Postcolonial Studies*. Durham: Duke University Press, 119–25.

Ngũgĩ wa Thiong'o (2012). *Globalectics: Theory and Politics of Knowing*. New York: Columbia University Press.

O'Brien, Karen, B. Hayward, and Fikret Berkes (2009). 'Rethinking Social Contracts: Building Resilience in a Changing Climate', *Ecology and Society*, 14.2. Online source: <http://www.ecologyandsociety.org/vol14/iss2/art12/ES-2009-3027.pdf>, accessed 2 February 2010.

Palencia-Roth, Michael (2009). 'Pioneering Cross-cultural Studies and World Literature at Illinois', in D. Damrosch (ed.), *Teaching World Literature*. New York: MLA, 145–54.

Parker, Joe, Ranu and Mary Romero (eds) (2010). *Interdisciplinarity and Social Justice: Revisioning Academic Accountability*. Albany: State University of New York Press.

Parry, Benita (2004). *Postcolonial Studies: A Materialist Critique*. London: Routledge.

Pieterse, Jan Nederveen and Bhikhu Parekh (eds) (1995). *The Decolonization of Imagination: Culture, Knowledge and Power*. London: Verso.

Povinelli, Elizabeth A. (2005). 'A Flight from Freedom', in A. Loomba, S. Kaul, M. Bunzl, A. Burton, and J. Esty (eds), *Postcolonial Studies and Beyond*. Durham: Duke University Press, 145–65.

Pratt, Mary Louise (2008 [1992]). *Imperial Eyes: Travel Writing and Transculturation*. 2nd rev. edn. London: Routledge.

Riggs, Damien W. (ed.) (2007). *Taking up the Challenge: Critical Race and Whiteness Studies in a Postcolonising Nation*. Adelaide: Crawford House.

Said, Edward W. (1978). *Orientalism*. London: Penguin.

Said, Edward W. (1982). 'Traveling Theory', *Raritan: A Quarterly Review*, 1.3: 41–67 .

Said, Edward W. (1994). 'Traveling Theory Revisited', in R. H. Polhemus and R. Henkle (eds), *Critical Reconstructions: The Relationship of Life to Fiction*. Stanford: Stanford University Press, 251–65.

San Juan, Jr., E. (1998). *Beyond Postcolonial Theory*. New York: St. Martin's Press.

Santos, Boaventura de Sousa (2005). 'Preface', in B. S. Santos (ed.), *Democratizing Democracy: Beyond the Liberal Democratic Canon*. London: Verso, vii–xvi.

Santos, Boaventura de Sousa (ed.) (2007a). *Another Knowledge is Possible: Beyond Northern Epistemologies*. London: Verso.

Santos, Boaventura de Sousa (ed.) (2007b). *Cognitive Justice in a Global World: Prudent Knowledges for a Decent Life*. Lanham, Md.: Lexington.

Saussy, Haun (ed.) (2006). *Comparative Literature in an Age of Globalization*. Baltimore: Johns Hopkins University Press.

Schwarz, Henry and Sangeeta Ray (eds) (2000). *A Companion to Postcolonial Studies*. Oxford: Blackwell.

Scott, David (1999). *Refashioning Futures: Criticism After Postcoloniality*. Princeton: Princeton University Press.

Shkandrij, Miroslav (2001). *Russia and Ukraine: Literature and the Discourse of Empire from Napoleonic to Postcolonial Times*. Montreal: McGill-Queen's University Press.

Slater, David (2004). *Geopolitics and the Post-Colonial: Rethinking North–South Relations.* Oxford: Blackwell.

Slaughter, Joseph R. (2007). *Human Rights, Inc.: The World Novel, Narrative Form, and International Law.* New York: Fordham University Press.

Smith, Linda Tuhiwai (1999). *Decolonizing Methodologies.* London: Zed.

Spivak, Gayatri Chakravorty (2003). *Death of a Discipline.* New York: Columbia University Press.

Spivak, Gayatri Chakravorty (1988). 'Can the Subaltern Speak?', in C. Nelson and L Grossberg (eds), *Marxism and the Interpretation of Culture.* Urbana: University of Illinois, 271–313.

Spivak, Gayatri Chakravorty (1999). 'Appendix: The Setting to Work of Deconstruction', in G. C. Spivak, *A Critique of Postcolonial Reason.* Cambridge, Mass.: Harvard University Press, 423–31.

Spivak, Gayatri Chakravorty (2008). *Other Asias.* Oxford: Blackwell.

Sullivan, Shannon and Nancy Tuana (eds) (2007). *Race and Epistemologies of Ignorance.* Albany: State University of New York Press.

Szeman, Imre (2003). *Zones of Instability: Literature, Postcolonialism, and the Nation.* Durham, NC: Duke University Press.

Tsing, Anna Lowenhaupt (2005). *Friction: An Ethnography of Global Connection.* Princeton: Princeton University Press.

Venn, Couze (2006). *The Postcolonial Challenge: Towards Alternative Worlds.* London: Sage.

Walcott, Derek (1986). 'The Sea is History', in *Derek Walcott: Collected Poems 1948–1984.* New York: Noonday Press, Farrar, Straus & Giroux, 364–7.

Williams, Melissa S. (2009). 'Citizenship as Agency Within Communities of Shared Fate', in S. Bernstein and W. D. Coleman (eds), *Unsettled Legitimacy: Political Community, Power, and Authority in a Global Era.* Vancouver: University of British Columbia Press, 33–52.

CHAPTER 20

POSTCOLONIALISM AND LITERATURE

JOHN MCLEOD

POSTCOLONIAL LITERATURE

In 1950, a young Martinican writer, Joseph Zobel, published a semi-autobiographical novel in Paris called *La Rue Cases-Nègres* (later translated as *Black Shack Alley*). The novel depicts the fortunes of a young boy, José, who grows up amidst the plantation poverty of early twentieth-century rural Martinique, and who works hard to pursue an education which eventually sees him move to Fort de France to pursue the *baccalauréat*. In Fort de France he discovers books and begins a lifelong passion for reading literature. He dreams of becoming a novelist but admits that the thought is fanciful as the world as depicted in literary fiction is so removed from his own: 'I had never frequented those people with blond hair, blue eyes, pink cheeks, that were put in novels' (1997: 135). Novels transport him from his immediate environment to the realm of hotels, cars, crowds, 'ocean liners, trains, mountains and plains' (135), so distant from his own modest background. 'I was only familiar', he recalls, 'with Black Shack Alley, Petit Bourg, Sainte-Thérèse, men, women and children, all more or less black. Now, certainly that was not the stuff novels were made of, since I had never read any of that color' (135).

In the same year, a young student from Trinidad, V. S. Naipaul, arrived in England with a fierce ambition to become a writer. Precocious, bright, and inspired by the encouragement of his journalist father Seepersad, the young Naipaul began his studies at Oxford, keen to embark upon his chosen career. He soon got stuck. As he reflected as a much older man, looking back over his literary career, in those early days 'in my fantasy of being a writer there had been no idea about how I might actually go about writing a book' (2003a: 15). His childhood reading of English literary classics gave him, as with Zobel, the sense of entering a fantasy world: 'The language was too hard; I lost my way in social or historical detail … When it came to the modern writers their stress on their own personalities shut me out: I couldn't pretend to be Maugham in London or Huxley or Ackerley in India' (2003a: 6). The form of the novel, in particular, seemed remote from his experience of his Trinidadian past or his exiled present in Oxford and London. In its conventional shape, it articulated the mores and subtleties of western societies, imperial and established, and seemed to offer little scope for colonized societies or the colonials who hailed from such places. 'The English or French writer of my age', he reflected, 'had grown up in a world which was more or less explained. He wrote against a background of knowledge. I couldn't be a writer in the same way, because to be a colonial, as I was, was to be spared knowledge' (2003b: 66). In attempting to write about the world as he saw it, from his vantage as a 'colonial', Naipaul had no substantial literary models to turn to. Literature took him away from the world towards the experiences of others than his, leaving him with a sickening feeling of anxiety when he contemplated the task of writing (2003b: 64).

As both Zobel and Naipaul discovered in the mid-twentieth century, postcolonial locations seemed at a far remove from the rarefied atmosphere of 'literature'. Literary representations of colonized places did exist, but these were predominantly written by visitors or western outsiders, often as brief portraits and travel narratives, and communicated little native sense of how life actually passed in the colonies. The principal literary forms emerged from and spoke to colonizing, not colonized, cultures: their languages, styles, attitudes, assumptions of aesthetic beauty, and protocols of artistic genius and craft were anchored in the imperial metropolis. For an aspiring postcolonial writer to commence the task of writing, then, two immediate challenges presented themselves. The first concerned subject matter and content—the task of putting into words the environments, languages, social codes, issues, and struggles of colonized peoples: of depicting Black Shack Alley and Miguel Street rather than Piccadilly Circus or the Champs Élysées. But perhaps more importantly, the second challenge revolved around style: how to find a mode of writing that would give the realities of these places and experiences proper expression, rather than using conventional forms which seemed fated only to capture, in Naipaul's telling phrase, 'the externals of things' (2003a: 25).

When we think about literature and postcolonialism, an awareness of these two challenges must never be far away for the simple reason that the advent of postcolonial literature since the mid-twentieth century has involved a perpetual wrestling with the concept of the literary. In seeking to articulate local experiences using non-local models and conventions, postcolonial writers have had to contend with, to resculpt and refashion, a sense of what constitutes the literary: its genres, languages, themes. This has led to the development of some remarkable new modes of literary creativity, both between and beyond conventional generic boundaries; but it has also resulted in the academic institutionalization of literary experimentation as characteristically 'postcolonial', often to the critical detriment of the work of postcolonial writers whose engagement with conventional forms has often been more reverent than contentious, more subtle than dramatic. Debates continue to this day among postcolonial writers and academics as to the very category of the 'literary', especially as regards literature's alleged complicity in the vexed relationship between culture and imperialism or its mystical ability to transcend the material circumstances of its production and speak 'universally'. This chapter is concerned with discerning just some of the key elements of this still-evolving debate, primarily by attempting to keep open a distinction between postcolonial literature—as it has been variously and divergently practised—and the critical category of 'postcolonial literature' which, it might be argued, maps only imperfectly the literary terrain it is intended to describe. As I will argue, the mismatch between postcolonial literature as a cultural practice and 'postcolonial literature' as a critical category has meant that the complexity and variety of the former has not always been captured in the latter, even if the emergence of 'postcolonial literature' in literary studies at the end of the twentieth century was of major intellectual and indeed political significance—a significance that still obtains today.

As suggested above, Zobel's character José has an acute sense of the improbability of his ever becoming a writer owing to the perceived gulf between the humdrum surroundings of Black Shack Alley and the cultured world of metropolitan France. This sentiment should remind us of just how momentous it was for writers from once-colonized countries to dare to think of themselves as writers in the first place, and how much social and psychological conditioning they had to overcome in order to make the business of literature their own. To take as one's subject colonized peoples, places, cultural practices, and social mores was no mean feat; and in making these the stuff of literature, writers were involved in a radical act. Another Caribbean writer from the mid-century, George Lamming, captures vividly the immensity of deciding to write in *The Pleasures of Exile* (1960), in which he portrays the inevitable challenge to the cultural and political assumptions of colonialism made by the native writer:

> Books, in that particular colonial conception of literature, were not—meaning, too, not supposed to be—written by natives. Those amongst the natives who read also believed that; for all the books they had read, their whole introduction to something called culture, all of it, in the form of words, came from the outside: Dickens, Jane Austen, Kipling and that sacred gang ... [A] writer cannot function; and, indeed, he has no function as writer if those who read and teach reading in his society have started their education by questioning his very right to write. (1960: 27)

Lamming's insistence on claiming the 'right to write' indicates how the very act of writing was itself bound up in a wider cultural and political contest, primarily against a colonial sensibility, internalized by the colonized, which saw no value in local cultures and modes of cultural expression since the values—and cultures—that mattered were perceived as being elsewhere.

When one speaks of *postcolonial* literary practices emerging in various parts of the world as opposed to *literature* arising from colonized or once-colonized countries, it is just this sense of mounting a challenge that the adjective 'postcolonial' helps articulate: that occasion for speaking against the power of metropolitan, European-derived culture, often by taking on and engaging dynamically with its creative forms. In Lamming's case, his intervention in the cultural ascendancy of British literature took the form of a series of formally complex, deeply meditative novels that sought to reshape the novel form by working both with and against received models. While Lamming's example is by no means indicative, most postcolonial writers have at one time or other had to address what the novelist Caryl Phillips calls 'the conundrum of form' (Swift 2009: 15), even if the result has been the decision by some to accept more than reject the protocols provided by received literary modes. As Phillips suggests, it is the *level* of the writer's self-conscious engagement with form that really matters—one which safeguards against a blithe acceptance of 'that particular colonial conception of literature'—rather than the decision to write an experimental literary text which dismisses by default the tradition of 'that sacred gang' (Lamming 1960: 27). The postcolonial encounter with conventional literary forms and values is never so predictable, narrow, or tidy—as will shortly be seen.

Postcolonial literature is often motivated to a greater or lesser extent by reflexes of engagement with forms of metropolitan literary representation and with the worldly horizons of their content. In settler colonies like Australia, New Zealand, and Canada, the writing of literary texts from the late nineteenth and early twentieth centuries was one way in which European settlers and their descendants could attempt to distinguish themselves, both culturally and nationally, from the colonial motherland and to support the political contestation of European legislature overseas. In so-called Third World countries in the Caribbean, South Asia, and Africa, literary creativity during the period of decolonization in the mid-twentieth century was often geared to cultural regeneration and national redefinition: it was part of a deliberate cultural and political attempt to break from the orbit of colonial and neocolonial dependency. Linking such literary activity in countries which shared a common European colonial connection was the sense that to create literature was to challenge the view, allegedly embedded in metropolitan literatures, of colonial people and places as essentially devoid of any meaningful history, culture, and creativity of their own. Literature offered colonized peoples the chance to shape representations of the world on their own terms; and it gave them an opportunity to fashion a sense of national and cultural distinctiveness that escaped metropolitan dictates, ironically by using metropolitan literary models to new ends.

One consequence of these various activities was the emergence of a fresh sense of the meaning of 'literature' and its functions, which suggested in turn a much closer relationship between the world and the literary text. It is remarkable how often the political processes of decolonization were energized by the creation of new literatures in English, which were involved, in Kenyan novelist Ngũgĩ wa Thiong'o's influential phrase, in 'decolonising the mind' of all those subject to colonial circumscription (Ngũgĩ 1986). Perhaps the most eloquent statement to this effect, still cited today by writers and intellectuals, was the Nigerian writer Chinua Achebe's essay 'The Novelist as Teacher' (1965), in which he set out his sense of the purpose of the writer in the decolonizing nation. In arguing that 'it is part of my business as a writer to teach … that there is nothing disgraceful about the African weather, that the palm tree is a fit subject for poetry' (1988a: 30), Achebe described the educative impact of literature that many have taken since as integral to postcolonial writing:

> Here then is an adequate revolution for me to espouse—to help my society regain belief in itself and put away the complexes of the years of denigration

and self-abasement.... I would be quite satisfied if my novels (especially the ones I set in the past) did no more than teach my readers that their past—with all its imperfections—was not one long night of savagery from which the first Europeans acting on God's behalf delivered them. Perhaps what I write is applied art as distinct from pure. But who cares? Art is important but so is the education of the kind I have in mind. And I don't see that the two need be mutually exclusive. (1988a: 30)

It is important to note that Achebe is describing both an ideological and an aesthetic revolution in the production of literature. At stake here, as he saw it, was a challenge not just to the conventional representation of Africans in metropolitan literature, but also to received notions of 'literariness' in twentieth-century Europe as a mystical property that somehow transcended the contingencies of circumstance to explore universal themes of suffering, love, and pity that remained true and constant for all people at all times. Achebe rejected such liberal sentiment, provocatively so, and in the process he seeded the beginnings of a different way of thinking about literature, literariness, and the literary. At the same time, the beginnings could be glimpsed of a longer, at times controversial, critique of the literary as deeply complicit in colonialism, which would later be taken up in the scholarly work of postcolonial literary critics.

It might well seem, then, that postcolonial literature has historically been shaped by a stubborn contestation of metropolitan literatures and notions of literariness due to the close material connections between cultures and imperialisms, in Europe and elsewhere (Said 1993). But things are more complex than this, and it seems vitally necessary to understand the *multifariousness* of postcolonial attitudes to literature, as it is here we find evidence for postcolonial literature as neither crudely oppositional in its spirit nor progressively political in its cause. First, we need to be alert to the debates that have emerged between writers regarding the pros and cons of engaging with metropolitan models of literature. To be sure, some writers have clearly identified metropolitan literary conventions as ideologically tainted, fit only for rejection by those keen to create new postcolonial cultural forms. Most famously, Ngũgĩ has written at length of his disdain for the damage wrought by the teaching of First World literatures in his native Kenya, and of the necessity for grounding a truly revolutionary literature in the indigenous languages and cultural practices—songs, folklore, orality—of dispossessed peoples (practising what he preaches, he now no longer writes in English but in Gikuyu, his native tongue). In his 1973 essay 'Literature and Society', for example, he castigated European literatures for their narrowness and cultural exclusivity and condemned English as 'the most racist of all human languages' (1981: 14). At the other end of the spectrum is the view that European languages and literary practices, once established in colonized locations, no longer belong to the colonizing nations, nor should they be considered as essentially foreign or invasive phenomena. In parts of South America, North Africa, the Caribbean, South Asia, and elsewhere, languages such as English, French, and Spanish have become part of the linguistic make-up of the complex societies existing there, while writers from these and other places feel they have as much right to the literary resources of these language contexts as do Europeans.

Although postcolonial literature is inseparably bound to the legacies of colonialism and is inevitably shaped by the historical and cultural impact of these legacies, the *nature* of such bonds defies neat political positioning. Evidence of this can be seen, on the one hand, in the disjunction between writers' differing attitudes to European culture and European imperialism, differences still often bypassed or ignored by literary critics; and on the other, in the highly critical position that some writers have taken towards the independence movements and political intrigues of once-colonized countries during and after formal decolonization.

Achebe provides a good example of the first of these. In his essay 'Named for Victoria, Queen of England' (1973), he recalls reading Shakespeare for the first time as a young Ibo boy in Nigeria:

> I remember *A Midsummer Night's Dream* in an advanced stage of falling apart. I think it must have been a prose adaptation, simplified and illustrated. I don't remember whether I made anything of it. Except the title. I couldn't get over the strange beauty of it. *A Midsummer Night's Dream*. It was a magic phrase—an incantation that conjured up scenes and landscapes of an alien, happy and unattainable land. (1988b: 24)

This sense of metropolitan literature as magical, as a captivating incantation that is inspiring rather than enslaving, describes another side to postcolonial literature where the rejection of metropolitan imperialism does not go hand in hand with the dismissal of metropolitan culture. Indeed, literatures from colonizing countries have arguably been as much inspirational as objectionable to postcolonial writers, who have sought to engage creatively with received forms in order to fulfil the rubric of art as 'man's constant effort to create for himself a different order of reality from that which is given to him' (Achebe 1988c: 95). Similarly, the Caribbean poet Derek Walcott has written vividly of his indebtedness to his schooling in the classical texts of European civilization as well as to the vernacular languages and African-derived cultural practices of St Lucia and the performances of Indian-descended texts such as the *Ramayana* in rural Trinidad. Each is his heritage, and all combine in his epic attempt to shape a new poetry for the Caribbean by working as much with as against this mixed aesthetic inheritance. 'Those who break a tradition', he counsels, 'first hold it in awe' (1998: 36). Walcott's epic poem of Caribbean creative becoming, *Omeros* (1990), owes as much to the formal traditions of high English poetry as it does to the voices and feelings of St Lucia's fisherfolk; while Achebe's most salient example of the novelist as teacher, *Things Fall Apart* (1958), draws upon the traditions of classical western tragedy as well as the poetry of W. B. Yeats in its depiction of the fortunes of its hero Okonkwo and the Ibo village of Umuofia.

Even when it seems exclusively involved in a particular locale, postcolonial literature is often a distinctly hybridized literary endeavour, calling upon a range of literary influences and practices, whether critically or dutifully. Indelibly stamped by the inevitable contacts and conflicts between cultures forged by colonialism, postcolonial literature is something other than a blanket rejection of all things European or a naïve return to an original state magically unsullied by colonialism's advent (or, later, colonialism's demise). Nor have postcolonial writers been much given to falling reverently into line behind a political movement or offering wholesale support for a particular culture or nation. The capacity of literature to function as an interrogative way of thinking, calling into question not just the values of colonizing cultures but also those of the colonized themselves, has meant that postcolonial literature has become one of the most important spaces where the social and political machinations of postcolonial peoples have been held up for intense questioning. Thus, Achebe's *Things Fall Apart* is as much a critique of the pitfalls and problems of Nigeria's Ibo peoples as it is of British colonial dispossession; George Lamming's magisterial novel of Caribbean cultural awakening, *In the Castle of My Skin* (1953), paints a bleak picture of anti-colonial politicians keen to feather their nests while seeming to challenge British colonialism in the name of the dispossessed peasantry; and one of the most powerful novels from mid-century sub-Saharan Africa, Ayi Kwei Armah's *The Beautyful Ones Are Not Yet Born* (1968), offers a horrifying representation of the corruption and impoverishment of Ghana in the first years of independence from British rule. Likewise, Salman Rushdie's early novels of India and Pakistan, *Midnight's Children* (1981) and *Shame* (1983), rebuked the governments of each for their political failures and violent conduct against their own people, while his critique of the political appropriation of Islam in *The Satanic Verses* (1988) became a major international incident and saw him condemned to death in 1989. Last but not least, V. S. Naipaul has written extensively about the alleged failures, depredations, and dismay he sees as being characteristic of India, Africa, and the Caribbean, a state of decay in which once-colonized peoples are wholly complicit—with the result that some writers and critics have rushed to judge his work as being as odious as that of the worst British colonialist.

To repeat: we need to recognize the cultural hybridity and ideological complexity of postcolonial literature right from the start—its wide range of political standpoints, its intense variety of attitudes to what constitutes literature and literariness—not least because many postcolonial critics have struggled to capture these complexities in attempting to define 'postcolonial literature' as a whole. Postcolonial writers have more often than not worked critically with, rather than aggressively against, metropolitan literary forms, representations, and linguistic protocols, as a way of finding appropriate ways to shape and express cultural and intellectual independence. As Rushdie put it in his 1982 article 'The Empire Writes Back With a Vengeance', for 'escapees from colonialism' like himself, 'the language, like so much else in the newly independent colonies, needs to be decolonized, to be remade in other images, if those of us who use it from positions outside Anglo-Saxon culture are to be more than artistic Uncle Toms' (1982: 8). This remaking has ranged from Rushdie's avant-garde experimentalism and hyperbole to the elegant neo-Victorian prose of V. S. Naipaul, freshly turned to contemporary purposes. It is thus vital to understand that there is no one aesthetic style or ideological standpoint that postcolonial literature consistently adopts; as Robert Fraser argues in his study of the poetics of postcolonial fiction, 'to talk of a uniform postcolonial grammar, syntax or form would … be insufferably glib. What might realistically be claimed, however, is that, as societies pass through successive phases in their history—into colonialism and then out again and beyond—different grammars, syntaxes and structural forms come into existence, and then maybe fade out' (2000: 10). While we must resist the programmatically diachronic vision of post-colonial poetics being implied here, Fraser rightly insists that we remain attentive to the inseparable relationship between postcolonial literature and history, as well as to the essential heterogeneity of the postcolonial literary field.

However, there is a considerable difference between postcolonial literature as it has been variously and creatively practised and 'postcolonial literature' as it has been defined, prescribed, and in some cases condemned since the early 1980s—not least because many postcolonial critics (unlike Fraser) have been much less at ease with the range of styles and standpoints that have made postcolonial literature such an internally varied and excitingly heterogeneous field. For if postcolonial *writers* have worked in fascinating ways with the tensions between political ideology and aesthetic form, post-colonial *critics* have at times been much less sophisticated in their thinking about this relationship—as will be seen in the next section below.

'Postcolonial Literature'

It is quite possible to argue that postcolonial studies began life as postcolonial *literary* studies. The critical conceptualization of 'postcolonial literature' acted as the primary vehicle for opening up discussions of postcolonial issues across the arts and humanities from the early 1980s onwards. While some of the major initial texts of postcolonial critique to emerge in the late twentieth century—Edward Said's *Orientalism* (1978) and *Culture and Imperialism* (1993), Gayatri Chakravorty Spivak's *In Other Worlds* (1987), Homi K. Bhabha's *The Location of Culture* (1994)—certainly engaged across history, philosophy, politics, critical theory, and cultural studies more broadly, each was written by a scholar trained in literary studies and each often featured examples from literature to illustrate key points. Much of the initial energy unleashed by such major intellectual works was felt first in literary studies, where the category of 'postcolonial literature' became well established as quickly as the late 1980s—much to the chagrin of some. Some of the critical questions brought into focus by 'postcolonial literature', especially those concerning the relations between literary cultures and European imperialism, impacted beyond the immediate remit of the field, and joined a wider critique of literature and literariness in the arts and humanities at large.

It is probably fair to say that the emergence of a distinct field of 'postcolonial literature', deemed worthy of academic nomenclature and scholarly attention, was indebted to two key intellectual manoeuvres. The first concerned the emergence of the idea—central to the 'cultural turn' of the period—that representation formulated reality and experience rather than simply expressed or reflected it, a notion formulated by Michel Foucault in his concept of discourse, where power and knowledge are inextricably fused. Under the influence of Foucault and other major poststructuralist thinkers like Jacques Derrida and Jacques Lacan, postcolonial intellectuals began to suggest that colonialism was in essence discursive, and that it was fundamentally reliant on modes of representation in order to perpetuate itself—modes such as *literary* representation. Said's notion of Orientalism, Bhabha's formulation of 'colonial discourse', and Spivak's concept of 'worlding' were each indebted in different ways to this intellectual atmosphere. Critics of literature from once-colonized countries became quickly sensitized to these ideas concerning the primacy of the discursive, especially the notion that the conventional forms and languages of literary representation were inevitably imbued with the colonialist values of the metropolitan locations from whence they came. In this emergent scholarly environment, postcolonial writing that seemed especially innovative, experimental, or irreverent now came to appear ideologically radical, not just aesthetically fresh: 'counter-discursive' and resistant to colonialist representation. A postcolonial text deemed to be 'disobedient' at the level of form seemed automatically to be ideologically defiant: texts which functioned to disrupt discursive norms acquired the glamour of political critique, even if no declared political or ideological standpoint could be readily identified at the level of content or theme.

In addition, critical enthusiasm for the discursive radicalism of unconventional forms of postcolonial writing was fuelled by a new generation of postcolonial critics, theoretically informed and indefatigably enthusiastic, who were eager to dispense with the older liberal assumptions concerning literature's function as a repository of eternal values, a treasure house of timeless truths. On this last point, critics were in concert with many writers: in his 1981 essay 'Literature and Society', for example, Ngũgĩ decried the tendency of critics of the new African literatures to recycle the usual 'phrases about the anguish of the human condition, universal values that transcend race, class, economics, politics and other social activities of ordinary living' (25). Since the early 1960s, Anglophone literature from once-colonized countries had often been discussed in terms very much like these, under general headings such as 'Commonwealth Literature' or more regional monikers like 'African literature' and 'Australian literature'. But despite this seeming sensitivity to location, much of this criticism had seen matters of cultural and regional specificity as being firmly secondary to literature's alleged exploration of universal issues. (In their rush to demonize Commonwealth literary studies, the fundamental significance of establishing scholarly legitimacy for writing that was both recent and from outside Europe was tragically forgotten by postcolonial critics during this new phase.) Hence, 'postcolonial literature' was created very much in opposition to an older critical paradigm, and this fact had as big a part to play in its definition as the literary texts with which it was meant to be concerned. The naming of 'postcolonial literature' was as much a reaction against scholarly practices as it was inspired by an enthusiasm for literature from colonized or once-colonized countries.

For this new generation of poststructuralist-inspired critics, postcolonial texts necessarily articulated a defiant response to the specific colonial or neocolonial conditions of a location, not transcendence of them. Many critics simply assumed the default radicalism of aesthetic innovation, which more often than not was taken as read rather than carefully scrutinized. One early yet still extraordinarily influential attempt to formulate the theory and practice of postcolonial literature in these terms came from three

Australian critics, Bill Ashcroft, Gareth Griffiths, and Helen Tiffin, in their book *The Empire Writes Back* (1989; see also Boehmer in Part III of this volume). Engaging with a wide range of postcolonial writing from across the globe, these critics cheerfully rejected previous comparative or race-centred accounts of the new literatures in English, prioritizing instead writers' apparent innovations with time and space and received language use as well as the fecund hybridity of their literary endeavours. Postcolonial texts, these critics argued, effectively resisted the colonialist attitudes embedded within metropolitan literary discourse. Disjunctions *within* these texts, e.g. between aesthetic shape and ideological stance, were conveniently bypassed, as was a more prolonged enquiry into the specifics of both texts and authors. Contesting colonialism, it seemed, was fundamentally discursive: 'the process of literary decolonization', Ashcroft, Griffiths, and Tiffin confidently concluded, 'has involved a radical dismantling of the European codes and a post-colonial subversion and appropriation of dominant European discourses' (1989: 195). The prescriptive definition of postcolonial literature promoted in *The Empire Writes Back* had little meaningful to say about the tensions between aesthetic form and ideological standpoint in postcolonial writings; it also seemed curiously uninterested in the specific, at times highly conflicted, positions of the writers whose work was being discussed. Hence V. S. Naipaul's work was approached as being similarly 'subversive' to that of R. K. Narayan and both of theirs to that of Timothy Findley: the kind of sensitivity to specificity advocated by Robert Fraser was precious hard to find. For these reasons, I would argue that while *The Empire Writes Back* did much to highlight the significance of postcolonial literature in literary studies, its programmatic rendering of literary materials actually inhibited the critical assessment and sophisticated appreciation of postcolonial literature's range.

Ashcroft, Griffiths, and Tiffin's equation of discursive novelty with anti-metropolitan resistance was part-influenced by the theorist Homi K. Bhabha, who in the 1980s published a series of challenging essays that sought ingeniously to tether postcolonial critique to the disruption of conventional discursive modes. Revised and collected as *The Location of Culture* (1994), these essays did much to fuel a growing sense of the postcolonial as a deliberately 'disorderly' mode of thought that sought to break down and bring to crisis the forms, structures, and conventions of all forms of discourse: literary, historical, philosophical. If colonialism fetishized binary thinking (master/slave, self/other) and notions of wholeness and purity—as Bhabha averred—then its postcolonial counterpart revelled in hybridity and heterogeneity; it aimed at nothing less then the deliberate frustration of received patterns of representation and thought. Postcolonialism was a 'border logic' that confused and confounded the boundaries of colonialist discourses: 'the postcolonial perspective resists the attempt at holistic forms of social explanation. It forces ... recognition of the more complex cultural and political boundaries that exist on the cusp of these often opposed political spheres' (Bhabha 1994: 173). Crucially, Bhabha's sporadic examples of literary texts that defy holistic forms of thinking were often by postcolonial migrant writers, notably Rushdie, or writers whose work displayed a distinctly cosmopolitan sensibility that had brought it to the attention of readers around the globe. Bhabha's thought (energized no doubt by his own migrant background) frequently took as its key theme the disruptive impact of migrants to those homogenizing forms of thinking beloved of colonialism and modernity, such as ideas attached to 'nation' and 'race'.

If criticism of Commonwealth Literature had tended to prioritize the national or regional when approaching new literatures in English, Bhabha's postcolonialism now shifted the focus markedly towards migration and postcolonial diasporas. This transition from the national and nationalist to matters of migration and diaspora would have a huge impact on larger understandings of 'postcolonial literature', which now seemed less concerned with the decolonizing revolutions of the Third World than with the argot of metropolitan migrants, whose border-crossing exploits were engendering distinctly experimental, irreverent literary texts that often seemed more magical than real. If literature from the ex-colonized countries of the Commonwealth had previously seemed revolutionary, in the Achebean sense, and preoccupied with the cultural regeneration and mental decolonization of the colonized, the new 'postcolonial literature' seemed a much more cosmopolitan and indeed bourgeois affair, produced by middle-class, well-educated migrants like Rushdie and Okri and critically endorsed by a new intelligentsia for whom anti-colonial resistance and its legacies, material and symbolic, were primarily a matter of 'discursive transformation'. For some critics, even those sympathetic to the emergent field of 'postcolonial literature', this limited formulation of the postcolonial was deeply problematic. As Kwame Anthony Appiah pithily put it, 'Postcoloniality is the condition of what we might call a *comprador* intelligentsia: of a relatively small, Western-style, Western-trained, group of writers and thinkers, who mediate the trade in cultural commodities of world capitalism at the periphery' (1992: 240).

By the mid-1990s, then, the newly moulded 'postcolonial literature' seemed preoccupied with two major issues: the allegedly radical power of discursive disruption, especially at the level of form, and the apparently subversive propensity of migrants and diasporic communities across the globe to challenge some of modernity's biggest myths: 'cultural purity', 'nation', 'race'. Coupled with the remarkable popularity of Rushdie's fiction after the landmark publication of *Midnight's Children* in 1981, 'postcolonial literature' came to be identified with virtuoso displays of verbal pyrotechnics and a migratory literary sensibility that emphasized border-crossing and mobility—travelling theory—rather than national interests or political dissent.

While this revised way of conceiving 'postcolonial literature' became and in many ways still remains fundamental to wider scholarly understandings of the term's meaning, it also attracted a number of hostile responses from critics who also believed themselves to be invested in the fortunes of once-colonized peoples, migrants or otherwise, especially those on the political left. This fierce attack on 'postcolonial literature' turned on a number of issues, but four were salient: the fetishization of literary experimentalism, the privileging of discursive over more material realities of power and struggle, the focus on 'border thinking' at the expense of local or nationalist standpoints, and the critique of 'literature' itself as a bourgeois category of elite culture (perpetuated by the *comprador* class of middle-class postcolonial cosmopolitans: see Appiah 1992). The ascendancy of a 'high' postcolonial literary style, avant-garde and formally challenging, also meant that the work of those postcolonial writers who seemed more conventional in spirit and form attracted much less critical attention—and in some cases was upbraided for not being 'postcolonial' enough.

Some of these concerns were crystallized in Aijaz Ahmad's pugnacious 1992 study *In Theory*, which launched a stinging attack on the institutionalization of postcolonial thought from a stringently Marxist position just as the field was beginning to occupy secure ground. Ahmad's more immediate target was the poststructuralist rejection of modernity during the 'cultural turn' and the postcolonial vogue for dismissing all forms of nationalism (European or anti-colonial, cultural or political) as reductive and homogenizing. For Ahmad, postcolonial intellectuals, frequently migrants making their way in the metropoles, were fixated on joining the First World middle class and had effectively abdicated their responsibility towards the wretched of the earth in once-colonized locations outside Europe. A corollary to this was the scholarly tendency to privilege 'modernist' texts—that is, writing which self-consciously pursued innovative formal strategies—that asked certain kinds of questions about the representation of colonialism, corrupt rulers, and the like. Texts from ex-colonized countries which preferred a more 'realist' mode of literary representation, or which wanted to raise alternative issues less immediately concerned with colonialism and its aftermath, were neglected. Irritatingly, the apparently small handful of literary texts that seemed to fit the bill of 'postcolonial literature', 'Third World Literature', or the like were too quickly read as representative or indicative of the region as a whole; indeed, Ahmad's more specific critique of 'Indian literature' exposed a major gap between the nation's dizzyingly diverse literary and linguistic milieu and the handful of English-language Indian literary texts that had come to serve almost as a national canon—especially for readers and critics based elsewhere. For Ahmad, in short, 'postcolonial literature' was a bourgeois affair confined to a select few with nothing to say about, or on behalf of, those who had suffered the most under colonialism and its legacies. Matters of class inequality and gender difference, and concomitant concerns of power and discrimination, were rarely raised in such writing, Ahmad argued. 'Postcolonial literature' might wish to declare matters of ideological radicalism and transformation at its core, but to Ahmad's way of thinking, it achieved nothing of the sort.

While Ahmad's intervention was as steadfastly programmatic as the literary-critical terrain he surveyed—for him, migrant postcolonial writing appeared to have no meaningful transformative potential at all—his critique exposed in important ways how quickly postcolonial literary critique had absorbed, in Eli Park Sorensen's words, 'the uncritical assumption that a set of politically subversive concepts corresponds [neatly] to formal disruption, meta-fictive strategies and labyrinths of narrative structures' (2010: 10). Even today, this assumption has not necessarily been dislodged: as Sorensen rightly argues, postcolonial literary critique still struggles to read judiciously 'literary forms such as realism, which has often been misread and caricatured by many postcolonial critics' (2010: xii). Whether or not one agrees with Ahmad's militant Marxist position, his exposure of a significant fracture between the dismal material conditions of ex-colonized peoples and their transformative representation in 'postcolonial literature' remains important, not least because the lazy assumption persists that 'postcolonial literature' of a certain kind is intrinsically radical.

Ahmad's contempt for what he takes to be the bourgeois nature of postcolonial thought has since been developed by a number of like-minded critics who regard the academic institutionalization of 'postcolonial literature' as fundamentally at odds with more militant forms of intellectual practice, e.g. those concerned with materialist matters: neocolonialism, exploitation, dispossession, class struggle (see Lazarus in Part III of this volume). Many of the debates about 'postcolonial literature' since the early 1990s remain shaped by an unresolved conflict between those 'culturalist' postcolonial critics who remain faithful to the transformative promise of literature's disruption, and those for whom 'postcolonial literature' is complicit with an ideological conservatism that is more attuned to bourgeois sentiment than social and political unrest. In decrying the formation of a canon of 'postcolonial literature' which prefers magic-realist writing over realist modes and local, non-Anglophone languages, Benita Parry notes the 'privileging of novelistic styles which animate postcolonial identity as fissured, unstable and multiply located' and points out how 'the rapt interest of Western academics in migration and exile has led to a neglect of developments and realities in post-independence nation-states' (2004: 73).

BEYOND 'POSTCOLONIAL LITERATURE'

From its inception, the field of postcolonial studies has often sought to radicalize and destabilize assumptions about the classification and role of literature. In recent years, this destabilization has continued on a number of fronts. First, and most familiarly, postcolonial critiques of the literary have spread into the reading of literature per se, with postcolonial literary critics reading back into the canon in order to expose the tryst between culture and imperialism embedded within it (Said 1993). Second, a new sensitivity has emerged to the literariness of postcolonial literature which goes beyond uncritical assumptions regarding the agency of innovative form, and which has sought to think more imaginatively about the specificity of literary materials in postcolonial contexts rather than applying a 'one-size-fits-all' model of literary interpretation and explanation, like 'writing back'. Third, the continued popularity of postcolonial literature in the global marketplace has led some to question the extent to which it has made any kind of transformative renegotiation of knowledge (Brouillette 2007; Huggan 2001). Postcolonial writers may or not have an 'adequate revolution to espouse', to cite Achebe again, but are any such intentions actually bearing fruit when 'marketing the margins' (Huggan 2001) has proven to be such a lucrative business for publishers and writers across the world?

As John Marx has argued, postcolonial writing can be 'credited with fundamentally altering how literature in general is thought of and how it is taught. It has become difficult for even the most recalcitrant critics to ignore imperialism when teaching European literary history, or to maintain that the canon is simply a record of what Matthew Arnold dubbed "the best that is known and thought in the world"' (2004: 83). The postcolonial critique of the literary canon has been especially controversial, not least because it has angered many critics who do not welcome awkward questions being asked about writers and texts revered for centuries, but also because it can seem distinctly at odds with the self-declared practices of postcolonial writers for whom European literary texts can be welcomed as inspirational rather than antithetical (see my first section).

Postcolonial writers themselves have sometimes been culpable of fuelling an unproductive critical response to European literature. A classic example is Achebe's 1975 lecture, 'An Image of Africa: Racism in Joseph Conrad's *Heart of Darkness*', in which he condemned Conrad's literary representation, ironic or otherwise, of African subjects and dismissed Conrad as a 'thoroughgoing racist' (1988d: 10) while anxiously pointing out his continued popularity on university literature courses in the US and elsewhere. Both Conrad and his 1899 novella have suffered ever since, and in their critical fortunes we can discern something of the postcolonial retort to the value of canonical literature. Much of this work has centred on challenging the assumption that a literary text can slip its ideological or cultural moorings and exist beyond history. To borrow Edward Said's term, postcolonial literary studies demands that all texts are considered as 'worldly' (1991: 39); that is, the material circumstances surrounding their production must not be elided. Said urges critics accordingly to recognize 'the ways in which texts impose constraints upon their interpretation' (1991: 39); but critical accounts of the *nature* of these constraints have differed. For those like Achebe, there can be no excuse for Conrad's articulation of racist discourse: it is not enough to say that racist thinking was the norm in the late nineteenth century, as plenty of other Europeans chose to represent Africa in a different light. This view raises all kinds of questions concerning literature's connection to ways of thinking which are now discredited: do we condone or condemn a canonical text if its ideological underpinnings today look suspect? Should matters of ideological standpoint be more important than the aesthetic qualities of a text? For others such as Said, a responsible intellectual reads such texts less judgementally and with an eye to their complexity. In contrast to Achebe's view, Said's account of *Heart of Darkness* in *Culture and Imperialism* exposes the novella's critique of colonialism, although it only goes so far (Said 1993: 20–35). Here, further questions arise: is a literary text valuable to the extent that it critically investigates its own ideological circumstantiality? And what of texts which seem to champion colonialism: are they insufficiently 'literary' in their uncritical representation of colonial relations? A whole subfield of postcolonial literary studies has opened up that is devoted to the task of reading canonical literature *historically*, rather than judgementally through the narrow lens of ideological fashion. In an attempt to think beyond the attitude of Achebe, critics such as Benita Parry, Laura Chrisman, and others have mounted intelligent readings of canonical texts and the complexities of their materiality in colonial contexts (Chrisman 2003; Parry 2004). Similarly, in *Postcolonial Criticism* (2003) Nicholas Harrison performs a detailed reading of *Heart of Darkness* as part of the wider attempt to move postcolonial literary criticism away from naïve, historically ill-informed judgements. As Harrison persuasively argues, 'for the postcolonial critic wishing to grasp the text historically and understand the work it does (or did), giving due weight to the historical complexities of reception and remaining alert to that indeterminacy that marks literature as such may seem frustratingly pernickety and at times apolitical tasks' (2003: 150).

Harrison's reference to literature's indeterminacy, its relative autonomy from other discourses such as politics or social theory, points to a renewed attempt by critics to resist the neat synchronization of literary representation with ideological stance in orthodox models of 'postcolonial literature'. A growing body of work is paying attention to the aesthetic elements of postcolonial literary texts, which require critical consideration beyond a metanarrative of sanctioned postcolonial poetics in which 'textual radicalism … is seen as equivalent to political radicalism' (Sorensen 2010: 42). In addition to the work of Harrison (2003) and Sorensen (2010), Elleke Boehmer has recently asked if we might identify a 'postcolonial aesthetic' that recognizes 'postcolonial writing *qua* writing, as not simply reducible to testimony, tract, or manifesto' (2010: 171). Boehmer poses a series of questions which have frequently been anathema to postcolonial critics, including the vexed issue of aesthetic universality, in order to approach a more intellectually responsible account of how a text might oscillate between 'the aesthetic as autonomous, in-and-for-itself, and the aesthetic as deeply complicit' in cultural and material conditions (2010: 172). Matters of literary 'style, imaginative transformation, generic choice, singular language, modes of poetic attention' require proper consideration, in all their variety and singularity (Boehmer 2010: 176). Peter Hallward's work on the specificity and singularity of postcolonial writings also captures this new commitment to textual detail. Hallward's engagement with postcolonial literature, while theoretically resourced, is underwritten by an attempt *not* to second literature to overarching theoretical models: 'we should not defer our normative aesthetic and political choices to theory. It is worth defending literature as one of the few fields that actively discourages this deference' (2001: 335).

To my mind, the future of postcolonial literary studies lies in such attempts to think beyond the orthodoxies of 'postcolonial literature' as it has been critically formulated, not least because these attempts have the potential to be properly sensitive to the myriad modalities of postcolonial writing. Others have moved beyond 'postcolonial literature' by dethroning literary materials as the primary subject matter of postcolonial critique, perhaps in response to the accusation that postcolonialism is an elite discourse in both its creative and critical modes. Graham Huggan has described 'the "first wave" of postcolonial criticism (the period between, roughly, the mid-1980s and the mid-1990s), [in which] literary modes of analysis were central, and most of the key figures to emerge from this period were trained literary critics' (2008: 10). Since then, he suggests, 'it would probably be true to say that the status of literature and the literary has shifted with the move to a more culturally oriented analysis' (12), although 'literature continues to play an important role' (11). This shift from literary to cultural studies has not been wholesale, but it has facilitated some important work in which some of the wisdom of postcolonial literary critique has been expended on arguably more popular cultural forms: film, television, dance, sport. For example, while acknowledging how 'the serious predicaments of postcolonialism are more normally read through high cultural discourses of literature and philosophy', Simon Featherstone has engaged instead with the 'fluid, contested performances of popular culture [that] allow an exploration of points of rupture in dominant culture'—performances which include football, cricket, film, the museum, and popular representations of the beach (2005: 29–30; see also Featherstone in Part III of this volume). In a parallel fashion, Paul Gilroy's exploration of British culture after empire engages with popular television, sporting events and celebrities, and the spoof fictional rapper 'Ali G' in exploring the extent to which contemporary postcolonial Britain may be caught in the grip of a counterproductive melancholia that blocks the progressive opportunities of postcolonial multicultural conviviality (Gilroy 2004). Postcolonial cultural studies does not signal the ending or supersession of postcolonial literary studies, and in many ways literary texts still predominate in current discussions of postcolonial culture; but this broadening of horizons has contributed to a sense of postcolonial literature as being constellated within a wider cultural terrain rather than as aloof from it, which has been of benefit to postcolonial literary critics and cultural studies scholars alike.

Part of literature's centrality to postcolonialism as a critical practice has not just been due to its academic institutionalization, but also to its contemporary commodification by international publishers and patronage, e.g. via the awarding of prestigious literary prizes and lucrative book deals. Some important critical work has been expended on the realities of 'postcolonial writers in the global literary marketplace' (Brouillette 2007). The fashionable promotion of postcolonial writing has been regarded by some as a strategy of containment that converts radical literary endeavour into palatable exotica for First World readers (Brouillette 2007; Huggan 2001). The emergence of an international canon of postcolonial literature—featuring a select band of sanctioned writers whose clutch of work is held to represent the postcolonial world in its entirety—is as much a concern for today's critics as it was for Ahmad over twenty years ago, and amongst postcolonial critics of many different political stripes. Graham Huggan, for example, has written about the tensions between the literary and ideological aims of postcolonial writers, which may be pitted against metropolitan standards and values, and the economic structure in which their texts circulate where their alleged marginality and cultural novelty are problematically reinscribed. His influential concept of the 'postcolonial exotic' captures this persistent dilemma, which faces writers and critics alike (2001: 32). As this line of enquiry suggests, postcolonial literary critics must contend not only with the ambiguous links between literary representation and historical materiality, but also with the current economic realities of global capital and markets. Edward Said once famously demanded that we recognize the connections between the world, the text, and the critic; in the twenty-first century, the 'world' seems increasingly defined by the vicissitudes of the international marketplace and the global production and consumption of literary texts.

It is many years since the likes of Zobel, Naipaul, and Lamming dared to think that postcolonial realities and writers might become a preoccupation of literary studies.

They, and others like them, have clearly been vindicated over time: the ascendancy of postcolonial writing and the institutionalization of 'postcolonial literature' show the progressive impact that postcolonialism has had on the production and conceptualization of literature, within postcolonial contexts and beyond. To be sure, the glib celebration of postcolonialism's supposedly transformative capacities should be resisted; and we might well have good reason to be suspicious of the popularity of postcolonial literature today. But the capacity for literature to ask critical questions about the world is a central part of its singularity, and in a current milieu that can often seem more imperial than postcolonial, literature maintains a vital role. As Caryl Phillips has written in the wake of terrorist attacks in London on 7 July 2005, fictional writing can 'force us to engage with a world which is clumsily transforming itself, a world that is peopled with individuals we might otherwise never meet in our daily lives ... Literature *is* plurality in action; it embraces and celebrates a place of no truths, it relishes ambiguity, and it deeply respects the place where everybody has the right to be understood' (2011: 17). Here then is an adequate revolution for us all to espouse.

References

Achebe, Chinua (1958). *Things Fall Apart*. London: Heinemann.

Achebe, Chinua (1988a [1965]). 'The Novelist as Teacher', in *Hopes and Impediments: Selected Essays 1965–87*. Oxford: Heinemann, 27–31.

Achebe, Chinua (1988b [1973]). 'Named for Victoria, Queen of England', in *Hopes and Impediments: Selected Essays 1965–87*. Oxford: Heinemann, 20–6.

Achebe, Chinua (1988c). 'The Truth of Fiction', in *Hopes and Impediments: Selected Essays 1965–87*. Oxford: Heinemann, 95–105.

Achebe, Chinua (1988d [1975]). 'An Image of Africa: Racism in Conrad's *Heart of Darkness*', in *Hopes and Impediments: Selected Essays 1965–87*. Oxford: Heinemann, 1–13.

Ahmad, Aijaz (1992). *In Theory: Classes, Nations, Literatures*. London: Verso.

Appiah, Kwame Anthony (1992). *In My Father's House: Africa in the Philosophy of Culture*. London: Methuen.

Armah, Ayi Kweh (1968). *The Beautyful Ones Are Not Yet Born*. London: Heinemann.

Ashcroft, Bill, Gareth Griffiths, and Helen Tiffin (1989). *The Empire Writes Back: Theory and Practice in Post-Colonial Literatures*. London: Routledge.

Bhabha, Homi K. (1994). *The Location of Culture*. London and New York: Routledge.

Boehmer, E. (2010). 'A Postcolonial Aesthetic: Repeating Upon the Present', in J. Wilson, C. Şandru, and S. L. Welsh (eds), *Rerouting the Postcolonial: New Directions for the New Millennium*. London and New York: Routledge, 170–81.

Brouillette, Sarah (2007). *Postcolonial Writers in the Global Literary Marketplace*. Basingstoke: Palgrave Macmillan.

Chrisman, Laura (2003). *Postcolonial Contraventions: Cultural Readings of Race, Imperialism and Transnationalism*. Manchester and New York: Manchester University Press.

Featherstone, Simon (2005). *Postcolonial Cultures*. Edinburgh: Edinburgh University Press.

Fraser, Robert (2000). *Lifting the Sentence: A Poetics of Postcolonial Fiction*. Manchester and New York: Manchester University Press.

Gilroy, Paul (2004). *After Empire: Melancholia or Convivial Culture?* London and New York: Routledge.

Hallward, Peter (2001). *Absolutely Postcolonial: Writing Between the Singular and the Specific.* Manchester and New York: Manchester University Press.

Harrison, Nicholas (2003). *Postcolonial Criticism: History, Theory and the Work of Fiction.* Cambridge: Polity.

Huggan, Graham (2001). *The Postcolonial Exotic: Marketing the Margins.* London and New York: Routledge.

Huggan, Graham (2008). *Interdisciplinary Measures: Literature and the Future of Postcolonial Studies.* Liverpool: Liverpool University Press.

Lamming, George (1953). *In the Castle of My Skin.* London: Michael Joseph.

Lamming, George (1960). *The Pleasures of Exile.* London: Michael Joseph.

Marx, John (2004). 'Postcolonial Literature and the Western Literary Canon', in N. Lazarus (ed.), *The Cambridge Companion to Postcolonial Literary Studies.* Cambridge: Cambridge University Press, 83–96.

Naipaul, V. S. (2003a). 'Prologue: Reading and Writing: A Personal Account', in *Literary Occasions: Essays.* London: Picador, 3–31.

Naipaul, V. S. (2003b). 'Prologue to an Autobiography', in *Literary Occasions: Essays.* London: Picador, 53–111.

Ngũgĩ wa Thiong'o (1981). 'Literature and Society', in *Writers in Politics: Essays.* London: Heinemann, 71–81.

Ngũgĩ wa Thiong'o (1986). *Decolonising the Mind: The Politics of Language in African Literature.* London: James Currey.

Parry, Benita (2004). *Postcolonial Studies: A Materialist Critique.* London and New York: Routledge.

Phillips, Caryl (2011). 'Colour Me English', in *Colour Me English.* London: Harvill Secker, 1–18.

Rushdie, Salman (1981). *Midnight's Children.* London: Jonathan Cape.

Rushdie, Salman (1982). 'The Empire Writes Back With a Vengeance', *The Times,* 3 July: 8.

Rushdie, Salman (1983). *Shame.* London: Jonathan Cape.

Rushdie, Salman (1988). *The Satanic Verses.* London: Viking.

Said, Edward W. (1978). *Orientalism.* London: Routledge and Kegan Paul.

Said, Edward W. (1991). *The World, the Text, and the Critic.* London: Vintage.

Said, Edward W. (1993). *Culture and Imperialism.* London: Chatto and Windus.

Sorensen, Eli Park (2010). *Postcolonial Studies and the Literary: Theory, Interpretation and the Novel.* Basingstoke: Palgrave Macmillan.

Spivak, Gayatri Chakravorty (1987). *In Other Worlds: Essays in Cultural Politics.* London: Methuen.

Swift, Graham (2009). 'Caryl Phillips Interviewed by Graham Swift', in R. T. Schatteman (ed.), *Conversations with Caryl Phillips.* Jackson: University Press of Mississippi, 11–18.

Walcott, Derek (1990). *Omeros.* London: Faber and Faber.

Walcott, Derek (1998). 'The Muse of History', in *What the Twilight Says: Essays.* London: Faber and Faber, 36–64.

Zobel, Joseph (1997). *Black Shack Alley*, trans. Keith Q. Warner. Boulder and London: Lynne Rienner Publishers.

CHAPTER 21

···

POSTCOLONIALISM AND HISTORY[1]

···

DANE KENNEDY

INTRODUCTION

···

For more than a few historians, the advent of postcolonial studies, with its strange language and theoretical promiscuity, appeared akin to an invasion by a barbarian horde. These historians manned the barricades, determined to defend their discipline against the alien invaders. Some patrol the parapets still, though their redoubt is now much diminished. Postcolonialism has managed over time to infiltrate the borders of history and mix with the natives. While important pockets of resistance and points of disagreement remain, the discipline's stance toward this alien interloper has for the most part shifted from suspicion and antagonism to tolerance and even fraternization.

Perhaps nowhere has this change of attitude been more dramatic than in British imperial history, a field that was once among the most hidebound in its insistence on an austere empiricism that stressed the official archive and the political, military, and economic concerns of the state. The gulf between this historiography and postcolonial studies was so great in the first decade of their encounter that it seemed all but unbridgeable. From the mid-1990s onwards, however, it became increasingly apparent that postcolonialism had struck a chord with a cohort of scholars for whom imperial history as it was then constituted had ceased to address issues they found meaningful (Kennedy 1996). Others who remained sceptical of postcolonialism's merits found it necessary nevertheless to rethink and reframe their own aims in response to its challenge. The result has been a remarkable revival of imperial history, transforming it into one of the most active and intellectually invigorating fields of study within the

[1] I am grateful to Mrinalini Sinha and Andrew Thompson for their insightful comments on an earlier version of this chapter.

profession at present. The hybridization of British imperial history provides us with an especially striking example of the broader impact of postcolonialism on the historical discipline (Bush 2006).

BORDER CROSSINGS

Postcolonial studies found several distinct avenues of entry to history as a discipline. One important source of intercession came from subaltern studies (see Dhawan and Randeria in Part V of this volume). This group of historians from India was frustrated with a historiography that seemed incapable in its then dominant schools of thought—the hagiographic approach adopted by nationalist historians, Marxist historians' preoccupation with the proletariat, and the Cambridge school's Namier-like analysis of interest-based politics—of coming to grips with the experience and consciousness of the vast majority of the Indian populace, that is to say the illiterate peasantry as well as other subjugated or 'subaltern' parties. This frustration extended to the archives that supplied the evidence most historians relied upon, since these products of the colonial and postcolonial state seemed to have left frustratingly few traces of subaltern voices. Ranajit Guha, the founder of subaltern studies, devised a different approach in his seminal study, *Elementary Aspects of Peasant Insurgency in Colonial India* (1983), which made use of semiotic analysis, seeking out verbal clues, physical signs, and other symbols that might give insights into peasant grievances and political aims. Contributors to the early subaltern studies volumes, which Guha edited, drew on a wide array of analytical strategies and theoretical influences, ranging from the cultural Marxism of Antonio Gramsci and E. P. Thompson to the linguistic and poststructuralist approaches associated with Ferdinand de Saussure, Jacques Derrida, and Michel Foucault. Its intellectual trajectory gradually passed from investigations of the social world of the subalterns to a critique of historical practices and historicism, drawing it ever closer to key concerns of postcolonial studies (see Chaturvedi 2000; also Chakrabarty 2002, esp. ch. 1). The publication in 1988 of *Selected Subaltern Studies*, with an introduction by Gayatri Charkravorty Spivak (who also co-edited the volume with Guha), was simultaneously an important marker of the collective's turn toward a more avowedly postcolonial perspective, one that entailed a self-reflexive preoccupation with the politics of knowledge, and its highly successful coming out on the international intellectual stage.

Many feminist historians also found established historical practices increasingly unsatisfactory. In their determination to examine the social construction of women's roles, the cultural formation of gendered identities, and the political regulation of sexuality and gender relations, they had to confront the evidentiary limitations of public archives and the methodological limitations of conventional modes of historical analysis. Joan Wallach Scott (1986), Judith Butler (1990), and other feminist critics exposed some of the problems with existing scholarly practices and pointed the way to new approaches. Perhaps because gender difference intersected with racial difference in such striking and revealing ways in the colonial realm, this became a particularly productive area of inquiry (see Ghosh 2004). A number of feminist historians began to explore the discursive and institutional interactions of gender, race, and sexuality in the colonial context, initiating what would become one of the most influential areas of engagement with postcolonial studies.

Border crossings by postcolonial studies into history occurred at various other locations as well, including the work of historical anthropologists such as Bernard Cohn (1990, 1996), Talal Asad (1973), and Jean and John Comaroff (1991), and historical geographers like J. B. Harley (2001) and David Harvey (1989). The intellectual influences, then, were complex, multifarious, and impossible to trace to a single lineage. This is a point worth stressing, especially in light of the reputation that Edward Said's *Orientalism* (1978) enjoys as the founding text for postcolonial studies. While Said's work certainly influenced much of the newer historical scholarship on empire, it is all too often allowed to serve as a placeholder for many other sources of inspiration (as it does in Abeysekara's chapter in this section of the volume). Indeed, Said's impact was in many respects a negative one, serving as a lightning rod for criticism by historians suspicious of literary studies' prominence in the postcolonial turn (see for example MacKenzie 1995; Irwin 2006). What Graham Huggan has referred to in the General Introduction to this volume as the 'slipperiness' of postcolonialism as a school of thought is abundantly apparent in its multiple routes of access to historical studies.

To understand the appeal that postcolonialism exerted with a certain cohort of historians we should also consider the role played by the sociology of knowledge. A disproportionate number of postcolonialism's initial proponents within the discipline were female scholars and scholars of colour, most of them either Americans or émigrés from non-western countries (see Ahmad 1992: ch. 2; also Cannadine 2005). This was especially true for those who ventured into British imperial history, a field then dominated by white male British historians who remained for the most part wedded to the concerns and methods that John Gallagher and Ronald Robinson had introduced in the 1950s and early 1960s (Kennedy 2001). For women and men who felt professionally marginalized because of their backgrounds or interests, postcolonial studies provided them with an instrument to remake the study of imperialism and colonialism for their own purposes.

How they did so is the subject of this chapter. In it, I will divide imperial history's engagement with postcolonial studies into three thematic categories—identities, geographies, and epistemologies. Attention will be directed towards some of the leading scholarship in each category, indicating its main themes and arguments and noting objections that have been and can be lodged against it. The unevenness of postcolonialism's influence on historians specializing in different regions of the world will receive notice as well, highlighted in the contrast between its transformative effect on colonial Indian historiography and African scholars' much more muted response. Finally, I will speculate on the future of this association between postcolonial studies and imperial history.

IDENTITIES

One of the principal ways in which postcolonialism gained purchase among historians engaged in the study of British imperialism, especially those who saw themselves as historiographical outsiders, was as a result of its approach to the problem of identity, particularly racial and gender identity. A key component of its contribution to the 'cultural turn' in the humanities (see for example Hunt 1989; Ortner 1999) was the emphasis it placed on the intersection of culture and power and the determinative role it gave to difference, which served to delineate categories of identity—race, gender, class, religion, and so forth—and to embody them in individuals and groups. These categories were seen as cultural constructs, not primordial instincts, and it was stressed that they served specific social and political interests. Identity, then, was understood as enmeshed within structures of power and susceptible to shifts as those structures altered or collapsed. These insights gave impetus to several important lines of historical inquiry.

One issue that attracted a great deal of interest was the colonial state's use of its classificatory powers to define and differentiate subject peoples, imposing on them much more rigid and mutually exclusive categories of identity than they might have acknowledged or embraced in the past (see Hindess in this section of the volume). Bernard Cohn laid much of the analytical groundwork for this analysis with his influential series of essays on the colonial census and other state projects that sought to count and classify Indian peoples (Cohn 1990, 1996). Among those who developed this line of analysis was Cohn's student, Nicholas Dirks, whose *Castes of Mind* (2001) argued that the Indian caste system as the British presented it was largely a construct of their own, distorting and simplifying a complex, shifting set of social relationships in order to divide and subjugate Indians. Others argued that Indian communal tensions were made much worse, if not caused, by British policies that institutionalized and politicized distinctions between Hindus and Muslims (Freitag 1990; Pandey 1990). Africanists noted similar patterns in that continent's colonial experience, observing that so-called tribal identities were far more fluid in pre-colonial Africa than they would later become under colonial rule, which they credited in many instances with actually creating tribalism and its attendant conflicts. Although some of those who pursued this line of analysis adopted an avowedly postcolonial perspective, as did David William Cohen and Atieno Odhiambo in their co-authored work, most did not (Cohen and Odhiambo 1989, 1992). Leroy Vail and his contributors, for example, relied on the standard tools of social history and cultural anthropology to trace the role that colonial regimes played in *The Creation of Tribalism in Southern Africa* (1991).

Some of the most interesting work on identity focused on the cultural uses of gender, race, and sexuality. Lata Mani's influential essay on the early nineteenth-century debate about *sati*, the Hindu practice of burning widows on their husbands' funeral pyres, opened the door to a number of studies of colonial gender discourse, many of them expanding on Mani's argument that collusion occurred between male colonizers and colonized elites to speak for and subordinate colonized females (Mani 1987; see also

Sangari and Vaid 1990). Some African historians came to similar conclusions about the patriarchal politics of colonialism, though once again they did so for the most part without recourse to postcolonial theories or methods. The South Asian debate about gender also took an important turn with Mrinalini Sinha's *Colonial Masculinity* (1995), which showed that both British officials and Indian nationalists deployed competing notions of masculinity and effeminacy, the former by casting the latter as lacking the manliness to govern themselves, the latter by conceding their effeminacy but attributing it to colonial dependency. Sinha stressed the historical particularities of this debate, avoiding any appeal to an overarching discursive framework such as Said's Orientalism and grounding her study instead in a specific set of political struggles that exposed the connection between assertions of masculinity and claims to power.

Another scholar who did important work on gender and sexuality in the colonial context was the historian/anthropologist Ann Laura Stoler, who wrote a series of groundbreaking essays and books on the management of the intimate domain in the colonial context, comparing British, Dutch, and other European colonizers' practices. Stoler demonstrated that debates about concubinage, poor whites, miscegenation, child-rearing practices and other issues associated with personal conduct revealed that gender, race, and sexuality were inextricably woven together and that the policies meant to regulate such conduct were integral to colonial regimes' strategies of rule. Drawing on Foucault's concept of biopower, which concerned the state's regulation of sexuality (Foucault 1980), she exposed the political stakes invested in the control of intimate behaviour (see for example Stoler 1989, 1995, 2002; also Stoler in Part I of this volume). Philippa Levine made a similar point in her ambitious comparative study of the regulation of prostitution in four British colonies—India, the Straits Settlements, Hong Kong, and Queensland (Levine 2003). Historians of Africa took up these issues as well, examining the social significance of 'white peril panics' and other manifestations of colonial sexuality's racialized politics (see for example McCulloch 2000).

The body itself came to be seen as a culturally pliant indicator of identity (Ballantyne and Burton 2005). As David Arnold, Warwick Anderson, and Megan Vaughan among others have shown, British medicine encoded racial differences in the classification and treatment of the diseases that afflicted the bodies of both colonizers and colonized (Anderson 2006; Arnold 1993; Vaughan 1991). Elizabeth Collingham's examination of 'imperial bodies' in British India revealed that even such seemingly mundane matters as style of dress, food preferences, and personal hygiene were important—and shifting—markers of difference, establishing gender and racial distinctions as well as moral judgements about the bodies of both colonizers and colonized (Collingham 2001). Similarly, Timothy Burke's fascinating study of soap, domesticity, and bodily discipline in colonial and postcolonial Zimbabwe pointed to some of the contested meanings that a commodity culture attached to the African body (Burke 1996).

Some of the historians mentioned above came to be identified with the 'new imperial history', which sought to place 'metropole and colony in a single analytic field' (Stoler and Cooper 1997: 4). Its main intent was to bring the British Isles back into the story of empire, showing how the domestic realm was itself shaped by its imperial interests and colonial dependencies. This line of inquiry shed new light on what it meant to be British. Here was an identity that transcended the ethnic particularisms of the home islands' various peoples and found its most meaningful frame of reference in the context of the larger world, especially the Empire. Postcolonial studies, it should be stressed, was hardly the only avenue of entry into this subject. Once again, mainstream social and cultural history provided another option, as John MacKenzie demonstrated in his own pioneering work and in the book series he edited for Manchester University Press, 'Studies in Imperialism' (see esp. MacKenzie 1984). Linda Colley's *Britons* (1992; see also Samuel 1989) was in many ways as responsible as any work in recent decades for the renewed interest in the historical construction of a British identity, and although Colley identified the Empire as an important aspect of that identity, postcolonialism had little if any influence on her approach to the subject. J. G. A. Pocock's earlier plea for a more expansive understanding of British history that acknowledged the connections with and contributions of British communities overseas provided another important antecedent to the recent interest in the imperial dimensions of Britishness (Pocock 1975).

Still, most of the scholars who took up the new imperial history banner embraced the aims and methods of postcolonialism. This was especially true of certain feminist historians, whose interest in issues of gender increasingly drew their attention to the wider set of discursive practices and institutional structures that informed women's roles and opportunities (see for example Hall 2000; Hall and Rose 2006; Wilson 2004). Antoinette Burton led the way with her provocative challenge to the celebratory historiography on Victorian and Edwardian feminists, showing that these mainly middle-class women made their bid for rights by constructing an identity for themselves as imperial citizens whose moral authority was deemed essential to the British civilizing mission abroad, and especially to the task of saving seemingly degraded and helpless Indian women from their own oppressive society (Burton 1994). Catherine Hall, whose earlier work had examined women in British middle-class culture, produced a richly documented study of the Baptist missionaries from Birmingham who sought to transform the lives of ex-slaves in post-emancipation Jamaica, revealing the ways that race, gender, religion, and other categories of identity were formed and reformed through the mutually constitutive constructions of difference in imperial metropolis and colony (Hall 2002). Among the most forceful advocates of the view that 'empire was ... the frontier of the nation' was Kathleen Wilson, who sought to show that Britain's worldwide reach informed its sense of self as early as the eighteenth century (Wilson 2003: 17).

If British identity was constituted at least in part through its connections to empire, what about the identities of settlers and their offspring in places like Canada, Australia, and New Zealand? Reacting against several decades of historical scholarship that had focused on the development of separate and insular national identities in these settler dominions, a new cohort of historians, many of them associated with the 'British World' conferences that took place between 1998 and 2007, insisted on settlers' enduring allegiance to a broader British imperial identity (Bridge and Fedorowich 2003; see also Ward 2008). Some of the impetus behind this 'British World' scholarship was generated by an antagonism to postcolonial studies, both on methodological grounds and because of the undue emphasis it was said to place on the dependent empire of non-western peoples. Yet the British Worlders' preoccupation with the problem of identity was itself indicative of the shift of orientation that postcolonialism had helped to produce in imperial history. And it soon became apparent that any analysis of a pan-British imperial identity had to confront the issue of race, which manifested itself most visibly in privileged claims to 'whiteness' that marginalized indigenous peoples within these settler states and restricted entry into the colonies by non-white immigrants. It is here that historians informed by a postcolonial perspective were especially influential in shaping research into British settler societies. They gave new analytical rigour to the study of race relations between white settlers and indigenous peoples, identifying their various terms of interactions, which ranged from miscegenation and assimilation to segregation and extermination, and assessing their implications for the construction of racial difference (see Perry 2001). In addition to the numerous case studies of race and identity in particular settler states, the groundwork for a broader comparative analysis was laid by Patrick Wolfe in his brilliant essay on the different criteria that Australia, the United States, and Brazil employed to delineate racial categories, revealing the strategic nature of these notions of difference (Wolfe 2001). Moreover, Marilyn Lake and Henry Reynolds have traced the transnational construction of 'whiteness' as the source of a greater British identity in *Drawing the Global Colour Line* (2008).

Critics of this postcolonial-inflected body of work on the imperial construction of identities adopted several distinct lines of attack. Bernard Porter took to task the new imperial historians' methodological practices and challenged their claims that empire had a significant influence on the national consciousness of the British public (Porter 2006; see also Thompson 2005). Although Porter marshalled an impressive body of evidence in support of his argument, it ultimately rested on too narrow a definition of imperialism to be persuasive. David Cannadine was more sympathetic to the view that the British sense of self was shaped by empire, but he objected to the new imperial historians' emphasis on racial identity, which he believed obscured the importance of class and status as categories of difference within the Empire (Cannadine 2001). Yet the case he made for them was sketchy and at least as selective as the one he objected to regarding race. A far more penetrating critique came from Frederick Cooper, who insisted that the term 'identity' was being used by historians in so many different and often contradictory ways that it had lost all analytical value. He was particularly critical of the tendency in postcolonial scholarship to refer to the fragmented and fluid nature of identity, which seems to subvert the term's nominal associations with sameness, connection, or fixity (Cooper 2005: ch. 3).

This problem derives in some respects from the tendency to apply 'identity' both to individual consciousness and group allegiance, corresponding respectively to what Cooper in his critique referred to as 'soft' and 'hard' identities. While group allegiance is grounded in conformity to a prescribed set of cultural norms and presumes a sameness and stability in identity, individual consciousness implies far greater pliability and often entails shifting or multiple identities. Quite apart from complaints about the divergent implications of these two conceptions of identity, questions can be raised about whether either of them has inspired as much genuinely new and original scholarship as their proponents have trumpeted. The interest so many postcolonial-inspired historians have shown in the construction of group identity is hardly new, as evidenced by previously mentioned work by various Africanists, as well as Colley, Mackenzie, and others. In so far as these historians have suggested that categories of identity such as race, tribe, caste, and religion hardened in the colonial period, are they really telling us much more than social historians had already revealed? And in so far as they attribute that hardening almost exclusively to the actions of the colonial state, aren't they denying the agency of those peoples who embraced and mobilized around identities that promised them some form of security or power?

Meanwhile, much of the recent scholarship on individual identity, which stresses the subjective self, has perhaps unavoidably taken on a biographical thrust. Though this work rarely assumes the form of a conventional biography that narrates a single life from birth to death, it often relies on serial or group biographical sketches. Catherine Hall's *Civilizing Subjects* opens with a lengthy prologue on the imperial career of Edward Eyre, and biographical accounts of its other protagonists are central to the book's narrative structure. Antoinette Burton has framed many of her books around the lives, experiences, and perceptions of a select group of individuals, and one of her most recent studies focuses entirely on what she calls the 'postcolonial careers' of Santha Rama Rao (2007). My own work took a biographical turn with an intellectual study of Richard Burton (Kennedy 2005). Indicative of what may be taken as a trend is the collection of essays edited by David Lambert and Alan Lester, *Colonial Lives Across the British Empire* (2006), which consists of a series of essay-length biographical studies. There is surely some irony in the fact that so many practitioners of the 'new' imperial history have been drawn to biography, one of the most old-fashioned ways of telling stories about the past. As yet, no one seems to have seriously grappled with the significance or implications of this development. Does this postcolonial preoccupation with individual consciousness risk recapitulating conventional biography's limitations as a mode of historical analysis, above all its foregrounding of the biographical subject's own subjectivity? Does it confirm the complaint of critics who suggest that postcolonialism's rejection of master narratives leaves historians with little more than a fragmentary array of singular lives to investigate and interpret? (Bayly 2004: 106). These remain open questions.

GEOGRAPHIES

A second important aspect of postcolonialism's influence on history arose from its challenge to the spatial assumptions or geographies that informed how most historians plied their trade. This challenge took at least two distinct forms. One derived from Edward Said's analysis of the 'imaginative geographies' that differentiated the 'west' from the 'Orient' (Said 1978: ch. 1). Said showed that the territorial spaces with which these

POSTCOLONIALISM AND HISTORY   475

binary categories were associated became imbued with contrasting cultural meanings and political significance, making them discursive repositories of imperial efforts to exert power. The other aspect of postcolonialism's approach to the issue of geographical space was provoked by frustrations with the way the nation was privileged as the primary locus of historical scholarship (Chakrabarty 2000: 41). It launched a sustained critique of the limitations of national historiographies and provided at least some of the intellectual impetus for a heightened interest in mobility, migration, and the multiple circuits through which peoples, practices, and ideas moved across space.

The Saidian concern with imperial representations of space generated a huge scholarly industry, bringing historians into dialogue with historical geographers, literary specialists, art historians, and others. A large body of work directed attention to the ways in which European explorers, officials, missionaries, and others imbued strange and exotic environments with meanings. Some of these meanings derived from traditional European aesthetic models like the picturesque, the pastoral, and the sublime, which supplied a familiar frame of reference for unfamiliar landscapes (Bishop 1989). But other meanings carried connotations of difference, often expressed in terms of danger and desire, as Said demonstrated in his study of the 'Orient' in western thought and as others observed about the 'tropics', 'darkest Africa', and other morally freighted geographical categories. David Arnold showed how India came to be conceived as part of the tropics after the mid-nineteenth century, a designation that carried connotations of decay and degeneration. Medical theories, botanical categories, and other aspects of British scientific knowledge were coloured by this preoccupation with geographical difference (Arnold 2006). Timothy Mitchell's *Colonizing Egypt* portrayed that country as succumbing to a European disciplinary order that 'inscribe[d] in the social world a new conception of space', one that differentiated between reality and representation and created a 'world-as-exhibition' (Mitchell 1988: x). Works such as these exposed the culturally constructed character of Europeans' notions of space and place, which came into correspondence with their notions of time by equating other lands with an earlier stage in their own historical development (as Hindess highlights in this section of the volume). Among the more intriguing lines of inquiry in recent years is one that focuses on the intentions and assumptions embedded in British scientific mapping of colonial territories. Thought-provoking studies of Captain Cook's naval surveys of the Pacific, the Great Trigonometic Survey of India, and various other cartographic endeavours have shown that these scientific practices operated in discursive contexts that served to legitimate imperial ambitions (Burnett 2000; Edney 1997; Etherington 2007; Richardson 2005).

Space also assumed importance for postcolonial historians of the British colonial world because of their frustrations with the influence exerted by nation-centred histories, which they came to view as arbitrary and ideologically imposed constraints on the spatial scope of their inquiries. Subaltern studies arose in large measure as a challenge to those historians who saw India as their sovereign subject, and similar objections were raised in Britain, with Antoinette Burton, for example, pointedly asking, 'Who Needs the Nation?'(1997; see also Burton 2003b). In both instances, this discontent came to a head in the context of political crises that shook the foundations of the two nations, evidenced in India by the state of emergency and the Sikh separatist campaign and in Britain by civil war in Northern Ireland and demands for devolution in Scotland and Wales. Those historians who adopted a postcolonial approach to the problem of the nation pursued two distinct strategies. One was to direct attention, as we have already seen, to those subaltern peoples whose interests and identities seemed divorced from the state within which they resided, thereby disaggregating the nation into what Partha Chatterjee referred to as 'its fragments' (Chatterjee 1993). The other response was to shift attention to diasporas and other transnational processes that lay beyond the grasp of national histories. Postcolonial historians were certainly not the only ones to move in this direction, as was evident from the preoccupations of the 'British World' contingent, as well as the increasing attention economic historians gave to the imperial engines of globalization (Hopkins 1999, 2002; see also Ferguson 2003). But the contribution made by those who shared postcolonialism's interest in the cultural and epistemological dimensions of imperialism was distinctive and important.

This turn to the transcolonial-cum-transnational aspects of British imperialism stirred new interest in the cultural plaiting that tied the various strands of empire together. Social and demographic historians had, to be sure, produced a large and distinguished body of work that tracked the movements of particular groups of peoples— British settlers, African slaves, Indian indentured servants, and so forth—from their homelands to foreign shores, and economic historians had done much the same for capital and commodities. Surprisingly little attention had been given, however, to the transnational networks that made the movement of these peoples and products possible, and their equally important service in circulating ideas, institutions and cultural practices around the globe had gone all but unnoticed. This began to change with Paul Gilroy's *The Black Atlantic* (1993), which examined the transnational cultural ramifications of the African diaspora. Among historians of the British colonial world, Alan Lester and Tony Ballantyne became two of the leading proponents of the idea that a network or web (their respective metonyms) supplied a more flexible and productive analytical framework for understanding imperial processes than the nation state, with its unilateral limits, or the bilateral binary of metropole-and-colony. Ballantyne in particular showed in his first book how an idea (Aryanism) and in his second a people (Sikhs) circulated through the Empire, their meanings or identities shifting as they moved from place to place (Ballantyne 2002, 2006; see also Lester 2001). Others have directed attention to the technological lineaments of these networks—steamships, railways, telegraphs, the press—and observed the influence they exerted on the idea of empire and the contending uses to which it was put by colonized peoples (see for example Bell 2007a; Potter 2007).

As a consequence of this reconceptualization of space, some standard assumptions about the unidirectional flow of imperial power were challenged, resulting in what has been termed the 'decentring' of empire (Ghosh and Kennedy 2006). This was not simply an assertion of the limits of imperial power, but an acknowledgement of its dispersal across multiple locations. Jessica Harland-Jacobs traced the transnational and transracial imperial bonds forged by Freemasonry (Harland-Jacobs 2007). Thomas Metcalf examined the subimperial system that operated out of India and extended across the Indian Ocean to South East Asia, Arabia, and Africa (Metcalf 2007). Similarly, Eve Troutt Powell showed that Egypt pursued imperial ambitions of its own in the Sudan both before and after it came under British control (Troutt Powell 2003). Other historians made the important point that the circuits of empire also aided in the circulation of anti-colonial agents and ideas, expanding their influence and establishing common ground with opponents of British rule elsewhere (see for example Bose 2006; Ho 2006; Sinha 2006).

Various objections can be made to these interpretations of imperial space. The sheer range of 'imaginative geographies' that scholars have attached to European representations of various parts of the non-European world at various points in time has raised questions about whether the dichotomies between the west and the Orient (or the tropics or 'darkest Africa' or such like) were quite as clear, categorical, and enduring as the Saidians have drawn them. The turn towards a decentred approach to empire that traces its circuits of exchange and disaggregates its drive for expansion can be seen in some sense as an effort to overcome the essentializing tendencies of the 'imaginative geographies' model. But it runs risks of its own, most notably as a result of its tendency to downplay the importance of power. Unlike the standard view of empire that sees it projecting outwards from a metropolitan centre, a decentred empire is one where power is in some sense diffused and geographically dispersed. It has been noted, too, that the networks this empire creates also facilitate connections between the anti-colonial forces arrayed against it, thereby equalizing or neutralizing their power effects.

Finally, the postcolonial critique of nation-centred histories can be criticized for being itself too western-centred in its orientation. The title of a 2003 essay by the Australian historian Ann Curthoys aptly illustrates the problem: 'We've just starting making national histories, and you want us to stop already?' While nation-centred histories may have established a stranglehold on historiographical practices in Britain and powerful postcolonial states such as India, it is doubtful whether the same can be said of the many small, fragile countries in Africa and elsewhere that emerged from colonial rule without the institutional means to propagate a strong sense of national pride or consciousness among their populations. This may help to explain why Africanists have been less susceptible than South Asianists to postcolonial critique— its objections seem misdirected if not meaningless for their subject, given the limited influence that most African states exert over historical memory and the production of historical knowledge (see Quayson in Part V of this volume). More broadly, much of the weight of contemporary concern about the nation state has shifted from anxiety about its strength to worries about its weakness, with Afghanistan, Pakistan, Somalia, and, most recently, some of the countries of North Africa and the Middle East serving as the latest examples (see Hazbun and Morton in Part II of this volume). In this regard, the postcolonial challenge to histories that privilege the nation can be seen as very much a privilege of its own.

EPISTEMOLOGIES

A third contribution that postcolonial studies made to the new histories of British imperialism came about as a result of its critique of the intellectual underpinnings of the west's claims to power. This epistemological inquiry encouraged some historians to re-evaluate the ideological rationales offered on behalf of British imperial rule and to expose their own discipline's complicity in the consolidation of its practices. Postcolonial theorists placed particular importance on the universalist ambitions of European thought, especially as manifested in the Enlightenment, which was charged with having advanced its own standard of rationality and model of modernity as templates for other peoples (see Hindess in this section of the volume). Its teleological conviction that all societies passed through uniform stages of development provided Europeans, who saw themselves as leading the way in this march to progress, with the justification to impose their will on those they considered less civilized.

While the ideological origins of the British Empire have been traced by David Armitage and others to the composite monarchy that arose in Britain in the sixteenth and seventeenth centuries (Armitage 2000), most of the postcolonial-inflected studies of British imperial ideology have focused on the period from the late eighteenth century onwards, with particular attention being paid to how nineteenth-century liberal theorists rationalized autocratic rule in India. Thomas Metcalf's masterful *Ideologies of the Raj* (1994) traced the tension within imperial thought between notions of similarity and notions of difference with respect to Indians, showing how British attitudes and policies oscillated from one position to the other as the circumstances of their rule changed over time. Although Metcalf's analysis owed something to postcolonial insights, the scholar who brought its influence most directly to bear on the question of imperial ideology was Uday Mehta, a historian of political theory, who argued in *Liberalism and Empire* (1999) that the leading lights of liberalism, James and John Stuart Mill foremost among them, defended imperial polices that thwarted freedom for Indians by equating them to children who required the tutelage of adults—or, in this context, the British. Mehta presented Edmund Burke as the main exponent of an alternative liberal tradition, an abortive one that opposed empire and its universalist premises. More recently, however, Burke has been portrayed by Nicholas Dirks as the true progenitor of liberal imperialism, rescuing Britain from a sense of complicity in the scandals that arose out of East India Company rule in late eighteenth-century India. In Dirks's view, Burke laid the foundations for Britain's subsequent sense of mission to bring the benefits of western civilization to the subcontinent (Dirks 2006). Either way, most scholars agree that nineteenth-century liberalism accommodated itself to empire (see Pitts 2005; also Mantena 2010). Although much of the empirical evidence for this accommodation had already been marshalled by mainstream historians (Semmel 1970; Zastoupil 1994), the postcolonial perspective brought a new urgency to the inquiry into liberal imperialism, not least because its nineteenth-century proponents could be characterized as the direct antecedents of the neoliberalism that informs contemporary United States foreign policy (see Gopal in Part II of this volume).

A related measure of the postcolonial influence on historical inquiries into British imperialism's epistemological premises can be discerned in the attention it has given to the relationship between empire and modernity. Most defenders of the British Empire portrayed it as the agent of modernity, which they understood to entail civil society, free trade, the rule of law, private property, monogamy, science and technology, and so on—that is to say, those characteristics that were credited with having contributed to Britain's success on the world stage. The conviction that this model of modernity was universally applicable informed British colonial policies in India, Africa, and elsewhere, and its traces lingered on in western aid and development projects following decolonization (Hodge 2007; see also Hindess in this section of the volume). For historians inspired by postcolonial theory, it became important to expose these universalist claims for what they were, the particularistic products of a European cultural and intellectual tradition. The aim, as Dipesh Chakrabarty provocatively put it, was to 'provincialize' Europe. Chakrabarty did not reject the idea of modernity per se, but he sought to show that Bengalis negotiated their own distinctive agreement with 'the angel of progress' (Chakrabarty 2000; see also McClintock 1994). Other historians of India, as well as many of their South East and East Asian counterparts, pursued a similar line of inquiry, creating a cottage industry concerning the indigenous sources of colonial and postcolonial modernity across the region (see for example Alu and Perdue 2009; Duara 2003; Prakash 1999; Tsin 1999).

Given the remarkable economic and political progress that Asian nations have experienced in recent decades, this scholarly interest in the culturally variable origins of modernity is understandable. The lack of any equivalent progress in most of Africa and the Middle East may help to explain the very different tack that historians of those regions have taken toward this issue. Long before postcolonial studies entered the arena, Africanists in particular felt a need to explain why their continent was so politically troubled and economically enfeebled. What the postcolonial turn produced was a move away from explanations that stressed material forces, such as the sway of the military on politics or the constraints of global systems of trade on wealth production, towards those that highlighted cultural and ideological factors. Mahmood Mamdani, for example, argued that the British reliance on indirect rule in Africa institutionalized the authority of local chiefs, whose powers derived from their ability to maintain and reinforce a sense of 'tribal' identity. This 'decentralized despotism' survived decolonization and sustained the polarizing ethnic rivalries that have continued to plague the African pursuit of modernity (Mamdani 1996). Similar charges were made about Britain's reliance on princely rule in the Middle East, though Priya Satia has taken this critique a step further with her 2008 analysis of the British agents who laid the foundations for that rule, suggesting that they themselves forsook modernity and its assertion of rationality in favour of an intuitive ethos that embraced the very primitivism they attributed to the 'Arab mind'.

Lastly, the postcolonial challenge led historians to question the epistemological foundations of their own discipline. Some gave scrutiny to the archive, rejecting the view that it was a neutral repository of information about the past that made objective historical knowledge possible. The charges that postcolonial scholars had issued against colonial information-gathering practices and institutions like the census, the cadastral survey, and the museum were equally applicable to the archive—that it was the creation and instrument of the state, reflecting its interests and concerns (Dirks 2001: ch. 6). Antoinette Burton gave this critique a feminist thrust, arguing that even though the state's panoptic ambitions were manifested in this 'archive fever', it failed to take into account women's historical perspectives, which were usually private and passed on through memory (Burton 2003a; also 2005).

Others focused on what they saw as the failure of the discipline to extricate itself from a mode of historical reasoning arising from the Enlightenment, which posited Europe's past as the master narrative against which all other societies' histories could be measured. This historicist tradition, Chakrabarty argued, 'enabled European domination of the world in the nineteenth century' by establishing the premise that its own historical experience provided the roadmap for all other societies, a roadmap that only Europeans were qualified to read (Chakrabarty 2000: 7). Even if historians can overcome historicism, according to Chakrabarty, they can never reconcile their understanding of the past with the enchanted version found in many traditional peasant communities, which made no room for reason or evidentiary rules. He also concedes, however, that modern historiography, for all its limitations, remains indispensable. Ranajit Guha, by contrast, seems in a recent work to reject it altogether. Identifying western-style history as an innately imperial system of thought that originated with Hegel, Guha urges its rejection in favour of stories that recover some of the wonder evoked by traditional epics like the *Mahabharata* (Guha 2002).

It is hardly surprising that Guha's radical recommendations, which would dismantle historical practices as they are currently constituted, have had few takers within the discipline. The more moderate stance adopted by Chakrabarty has generated greater interest and admiration, though it too has stirred uneasiness and even bafflement in some circles. And almost every aspect of the critique advanced by a number of postcolonial scholars about the intellectual framework that sustained British (and, more broadly, European) imperialism has provoked criticism. The charges it has lodged against the Enlightenment as the nursery of modern imperial ideologies and their universalist doctrines have been challenged by scholars who have demonstrated that many of the leading *philosophes*—Bentham, Condorcet, Diderot, Herder, Kant, Smith—were outspoken in their objections to European imperial expansion (Muthu 2003; see also Pitts 2005: intro.). Even as the Enlightenment descended into nineteenth-century liberalism, it continued to harbour far more varied views on imperialism than the preoccupation with James and John Stuart Mill would suggest (Bell 2007).

A similar objection has been raised against the preoccupation with modernity as the principal manifestation of the liberal imperial project. Given the range of alternative modernities that historians working from a postcolonial perspective have identified as emerging across much of the colonial and postcolonial world, Frederick Cooper has rightly asked whether the term retains any serviceable meaning (Cooper 2005). Adding to the confusion is the countervailing argument associated with Mamdani, Satia, and others, which attributes to the British an anti-modern attitude and agenda in certain parts of their empire. Is there, then, any instrumental association between modernity and imperialism?

As for the postcolonial critique of the historical discipline and its practices, this is a stance that seems open to objection on two grounds—its derivativeness and its exaggeration. There are few if any historians active today who are naïve enough to suppose that the historical records housed in archives provide full and objective insight into the past. The profession has been cognizant for decades of the need to seek out other sources of information, ranging from archeological artifacts to visual records such as painting and photographs to oral traditions and interviews. And the postcolonial charge that subaltern peoples have been rendered invisible in the archives is seriously exaggerated. Resourceful historians have found ways to extract from the archives a great deal of information and insight about women, peasants, and other subordinated and marginalized groups. To take only one of many recent examples, Durba Ghosh's *Sex and the Family in Colonial India* (2006) has drawn from court records, church registers, personal papers, and other archival sources a remarkably rich body of evidence about the lives of the indigenous women who married or were mistresses of British officials in late eighteenth- and early nineteenth-century India.

Future Directions

What does the future hold for the postcolonial turn in British imperial history (and in history more generally)? It is always risky to predict scholarly tastes and trends, and that risk seems especially great at this juncture, when the global forces that do so much to shape the kinds of questions academics ask seem in such flux. That said, the number of noteworthy books cited in this chapter that have appeared just in the past few years suggests that postcolonial approaches to the history of empire are far from flagging. To appreciate how prevalent they have become, one need only consider Patrick Kelley's *Imperial Secrets* (2008), a postcolonial critique of the limitations of imperial intelligence, written by a US army major and published by the National Defense Intelligence College! With so many new imperial historians, subaltern studies scholars, and other postcolonial- inflected historians of imperialism and colonialism now ensconced in secure and often prominent places in the academy, we can expect much more scholarship to build upon their already substantial body of work.

But will historians' relationship to postcolonial studies remain the same? The inspiration that the early proponents of a postcolonial approach to the history of imperialism and colonialism drew from theorists and critics in other disciplines—figures such as Michel Foucault, Edward Said, and Gayatri Spivak—may well have run its course.

Arguably the most influential voice within postcolonial circles at present is a historian, Dipesh Chakrabarty; and the work of other historians interested in aspects of the British imperial world has become essential reading among the broader community of postcolonial scholars as well. Insofar as a cross-disciplinary dialogue continues to characterize the postcolonial enterprise, much of its energy and insight is likely to come from history itself.

What remains to be seen is whether this work will retain the same edge and sense of purpose that made its intellectual interventions so compelling and influential during the past decade or two. Recent events may precipitate a rupture in the way historians approach the problem of empire in the future. The American invasions of Afghanistan and Iraq have reminded us of the role that naked military force, with its desire to induce 'shock and awe', still exerts in world affairs, while the subsequent insurgencies in those countries have reminded us of the limits of imperial power, as well as the resourcefulness—and often ruthlessness—of those who resist it. Postcolonial studies and its allies in history are not well suited to addressing the military manifestations of imperialism. And the sudden collapse of the global economic system in 2008–9 has alerted us to the fact that capitalism itself remains a far more vital and volatile factor in shaping our future than the recent bland pronouncements about globalization and its decentring effects would have had us believe. Michael Hardt and Antonio Negri's *Empire* (2001), only recently acclaimed for its analysis of the new post-national imperialism of globalization, now reads like an artifact from a bygone era.

Will we return, then, to the pre-postcolonial version of imperial history, with its emphasis on the military, economic, and political manifestations of empire? It seems more likely that historians of empire will adopt strategies that integrate the material, cultural, and epistemological dimensions of imperialism into a post-postcolonial synthesis. The growing interest in the history of consumerism, commodities, and material culture may be one indication of such a move (see for example Belich 2009; Prestholdt 2008; Thompson and Magee 2011). Still another is the renewed attention being given to the ideological lineaments of the imperial state (Heath 2010; Stern 2011; Travers 2007). Even if the collaboration between postcolonial studies and imperial history does begin to wane, its contribution to the renewal of the latter field over the past two decades cannot be denied. It has helped to create a richer and more nuanced understanding of the effects of imperialism, exposing its manifold cultural and epistemological implications, not least for historical practice itself.

REFERENCES

Ahmad, Aijaz (1992). *In Theory: Classes, Nations, Literatures*. London: Verso.

Alu, I. and P. Perdue (eds) (2009). *Shared Histories of Modernity: China, India, and the Ottoman Empire*. London: Routledge.

Anderson, Warwick (2006). *The Cultivation of Whiteness: Science, Health, and Racial Destiny in Australia*. Durham, NC: Duke University Press.

Armitage, David (2000). *The Ideological Origins of the British Empire.* Cambridge: Cambridge University Press.

Arnold, David (1993). *Colonizing the Body: State Medicine and Epidemic Disease in Nineteenth-Century India.* Berkeley: University of California Press.

Arnold, David (2006). *The Tropics and the Traveling Gaze: India, Landscape, and Science, 1800–1856.* Seattle: University of Washington Press.

Asad, Talal (eds) (1973). *Anthropology and the Colonial Encounter.* London: Ithaca Press.

Ballantyne, Tony (2002). *Orientalism and Race: Aryanism in the British Empire.* New York: Palgrave.

Ballantyne, Tony (2006). *Between Colonialism and Diaspora: Sikh Cultural Formations in an Imperial World.* Durham, NC: Duke University Press.

Ballantyne, Tony and A. Burton (eds) (2005). *Bodies in Contact: Rethinking Colonial Encounters in World History.* Durham, NC: Duke University Press.

Bayly, Christopher (2004). *The Birth of the Modern World 1789–1914: Global Connections and Comparisons.* Oxford: Blackwell.

Belich, James (2009). *Replenishing the Earth: The Settler Revolution and the Rise of the Anglo World, 1783–1939.* Oxford: Oxford University Press.

Bell, Duncan (1970). *The Idea of Greater Britain: Empire and the Future of World Order, 1860–1900.* Princeton: Princeton University Press.

Bell, Duncan (ed.) (2007). *Victorian Visions of Global Order: Empire and International Relations in Nineteenth-Century Political Thought.* Cambridge: Cambridge University Press.

Bishop, Peter (1989). *The Myth of Shangri-La: Tibet, Travel Writing and the Western Creation of Sacred Landscape.* Berkeley: University of California Press.

Bose, Sugata (2006). *A Hundred Horizons: The Indian Ocean in the Age of Global Empire.* Durham, NC: Duke University Press.

Bridge, C. and K. Fedorowich (eds) (2003). *The British World: Diaspora, Culture and Identity.* London: Frank Cass.

Burke, Timothy (1996). *Lifebuoy Men, Lux Women: Commodification, Consumption, and Cleanliness in Modern Zimbabwe.* Durham, NC: Duke University Press.

Burnett, D. Graham (2000). *Masters of All They Surveyed: Exploration, Geography, and a British El Dorado.* Chicago: University of Chicago Press.

Burton, Antoinette (1994). *Burdens of History: British Feminists, Indian Women, and Imperial Culture, 1865–1915.* Chapel Hill, NC: University of North Carolina Press.

Burton, Antoinette (1997). 'Who Needs the Nation? Interrogating "British" History', *Journal of Historical Sociology,* 10.3: 227–48.

Burton, Antoinette (2003a). *Dwelling in the Archive: Women Writing House, Home, and History in Late Colonial India.* New York: Oxford University Press.

Burton, Antoinette (ed.) (2003b). *After the Imperial Turn: Thinking With and Through the Nation.* Durham, NC: Duke University Press.

Burton, Antoinette (ed.) (2005). *Archive Stories: Facts, Fictions, and the Writing of History.* Durham, NC: Duke University Press.

Burton, Antoinette (2007). *The Postcolonial Careers of Santha Rama Rao.* Durham, NC: Duke University Press.

Bush, Barbara (2006). *Imperialism and Postcolonialism.* Harlow: Pearson Longman.

Butler, Judith (1990). *Gender Trouble: Feminism and the Subversion of Identity.* New York: Routledge.

Cannadine, David (2001). *Ornamentalism: How the British Saw Their Empire*. New York: Oxford University Press.

Cannadine, David (2005). '"Big Tent" Historiography: Transatlantic Obstacles and Opportunities in Writing the History of Empire', *Common Knowledge*, 11.3: 375–92.

Chakrabarty, Dipesh (2000). *Provincializing Europe: Postcolonial Thought and Historical Difference*. Princeton: Princeton University Press.

Chakrabarty, Dipesh (2002). *Habitations of Modernity: Essays in the Wake of Subaltern Studies*. Chicago: University of Chicago Press.

Chatterjee, Partha (1993). *The Nation and its Fragments: Colonial and Postcolonial Histories*. Princeton: Princeton University Press.

Chaturvedi, Vinayak (ed.) (2000). *Mapping Subaltern Studies and the Postcolonial*. London: Verso.

Cohen, D. W. and E. S. A. Odhiambo (1989). *Siaya: The Historical Anthropology of an African Landscape*. London: James Currey.

Cohen, D. W. and E. S. A. Odhiambo (1992). *Burying SM: The Politics of Knowledge and the Sociology of Power in Africa*. London: James Currey.

Cohn, Bernard S. (1990). *An Anthropologist Among the Historians and Other Essays*. Delhi: Oxford University Press.

Cohn, Bernard S. (1996). *Colonialism and its Forms of Knowledge: The British in India*. Princeton: Princeton University Press.

Colley, Linda (1992). *Britons: Forging the Nation 1707–1837*. New Haven: Yale University Press.

Collingham, E. M. (2001). *Imperial Bodies: The Physical Experience of the Raj, c.1800–1947*. Cambridge: Polity Press.

Comaroff, Jean and John L. Comaroff (1991). *Of Revelation and Revolution: Christianity, Colonialism, and Consciousness in South Africa*, vol. 1. Chicago: University of Chicago Press.

Cooper, Frederick (2005). *Colonialism in Question: Theory, Knowledge, History*. Berkeley: University of California Press.

Curthoys, Ann (2003). 'We've Just Started Making National Histories, and You Want Us to Stop Already?', in A. Burton (ed.), *After the Imperial Turn: Thinking With and Through the Nation*. Durham, NC: Duke University Press, 70–89.

Dirks, Nicholas (2001). *Castes of Mind: Colonialism and the Making of Modern India*. Princeton: Princeton University Press.

Dirks, Nicholas (2006). *The Scandal of Empire: India and the Creation of Imperial Britain*. Cambridge, Mass.: Belknap Press.

Duara, Prasenjit (2003). *Sovereignty and Authenticity: Manchuko and the East Asian Modern*. Lanham: Rowman and Littlefield.

Edney, Matthew H. (1997). *Mapping an Empire: The Geographical Construction of British India, 1765–1843*. Chicago: University of Chicago Press.

Etherington, Norman (ed.) (2007). *Mapping Colonial Conquest: Australia and Southern Africa*. Crawley: University of Western Australia Press.

Ferguson, Niall (2003). *Empire: The Rise and Demise of the British World Order and the Lessons for Global Power*. New York: Basic Books.

Foucault, Michel (1980). *The History of Sexuality, vol. 1: An Introduction*. New York: Vintage.

Freitag, Sandria B. (1990). *Collective Action and Community: Public Arenas and the Emergence of Communalism in North India*. Delhi: Oxford University Press.

Ghosh, Durba (2004). 'Gender and Colonialism: Expansion or Marginalization?', *The Historical Journal*, 47.3: 737–55.

Ghosh, Durba (2006). *Sex and the Family in Colonial India: The Making of Empire*. Cambridge: Cambridge University Press.

Ghosh, Durba and D. Kennedy (eds) (2006). *Decentring Empire: Britain, India and the Transcolonial World*. Hyderabad: Orient Longman.

Gilroy, Paul (1993). *The Black Atlantic: Modernity and Double Consciousness*. Cambridge, Mass.: Harvard University Press.

Guha, Ranajit (1983). *Elementary Aspects of Peasant Insurgency in Colonial India*. Delhi: Oxford University Press.

Guha, Ranajit (2002). *History at the Limit of World-History*. New York: Columbia University Press.

Guha, Ranajit and G. C. Spivak (eds) (1988). *Selected Subaltern Studies*. New York: Oxford University Press.

Hall, Catherine (2000). 'Introduction: Thinking the Postcolonial, Thinking the Empire', in C. Hall (ed.), *Cultures of Empire: A Reader*. New York: Routledge, 1–33.

Hall, Catherine (2002). *Civilizing Subjects: Metropole and Colony in the English Imagination, 1830–1867*. Chicago: University of Chicago Press.

Hall, Catherine and S. Rose (2006). 'Introduction: Being at Home with the Empire', in C. Hall and S. Rose (eds), *At Home with the Empire: Metropolitan Culture and the Imperial World*. Cambridge: Cambridge University Press, 1–31.

Hardt, M. and A. Negri (2001). *Empire*. Cambridge, Mass.: Harvard University Press.

Harland-Jacobs, Jessica (2007). *Builders of Empire: Freemasons and British Imperialism, 1717–1927*. Chapel Hill, NC: University of North Carolina Press.

Harley, J. B. (2001). *The New Nature of Maps: Essays in the History of Cartography*, ed. Paul Laxton. Baltimore: Johns Hopkins University Press.

Harvey, David (1989). *The Condition of Postmodernity: An Enquiry into the Origins of Cultural Change*. Oxford: Blackwell.

Heath, Deana (2010). *Purifying Empire: Obscenity and the Politics of Moral Regulation in Britain, India and Australia*. Cambridge: Cambridge University Press.

Ho, Engseng (2006). *The Graves of Tarim: Genealogy and Mobility Across the Indian Ocean*. Berkeley: University of California Press.

Hodge, Joseph (2007). *Triumph of the Expert: Agrarian Doctrines of Development and the Legacies of British Colonialism*. Athens: Ohio University Press.

Hopkins, A. G. (1999). 'Back to the Future: From National History to Imperial History', *Past and Present*, 164: 198–243.

Hopkins, A. G. (ed.) (2002). *Globalization in World History*. London: Pimlico.

Hunt, Lynn (ed.) (1989). *The New Cultural History*. Berkeley: University of California Press.

Irwin, Robert (2006). *Dangerous Knowledge: Orientalism and its Discontents*. Woodstock, NY: Overlook Press.

Kelley, Patrick A. (2008). *Imperial Secrets: Remapping the Mind of Empire*. Washington, DC: National Defense Intelligence College.

Kennedy, Dane (1996). 'Imperial History and Post-Colonial Theory', *The Journal of Imperial and Commonwealth History*, 24.3: 345–63.

Kennedy, Dane (2001). 'The Boundaries of Oxford's Empire', *The International History Review*, 13.3: 604–22.

Kennedy, Dane (2005). *The Highly Civilized Man: Richard Burton and the Victorian World.* Cambridge, Mass.: Harvard University Press.

Lake, M. and H. Reynolds (2008). *Drawing the Global Colour Line: White Men's Countries and the International Challenge of Racial Equality.* Cambridge: Cambridge University Press.

Lambert, D. and A. Lester (eds) (2006). *Colonial Lives Across the Empire: Imperial Careering in the Long Nineteenth Century.* Cambridge: Cambridge University Press.

Lester, Alan (2001). *Imperial Networks: Creating Identities in Nineteenth-Century South Africa and Britain.* London: Routledge.

Levine, Philippa (2003). *Prostitution, Race, and Politics: Policing Venereal Disease in the British Empire.* London: Routledge.

Mamdani, Mahmood (1996). *Citizen and Subject: Contemporary Africa and the Legacy of Late Colonialism.* Princeton: Princeton University Press.

Mani, Lata (1987). 'Contentious Traditions: The Debate on Sati in Colonial India', *Cultural Critique,* 7: 119–56.

Mantena, Karuna (2010). *Alibis of Empire: Henry Maine and the Ends of Liberal Imperialism.* Princeton: Princeton University Press.

McClintock, Anne (1994). 'The Angel of Progress: Pitfalls of the Term "Post-colonialism"', in P. Williams and L. Chrisman (eds), *Colonial Discourse and Post-Colonial Theory: A Reader.* New York: Columbia University Press, 291–304.

McCulloch, Jock (2000). *Black Peril, White Virtue: Sexual Crime in Southern Rhodesia, 1902–1935.* Bloomington: Indiana University Press.

MacKenzie, John (1984). *Propaganda and Empire: The Manipulation of British Public Opinion, 1880–1960.* Manchester: Manchester University Press.

MacKenzie, John (1995). *Orientalism: History, Theory and the Arts.* Manchester: Manchester University Press.

Mehta, Uday (1999). *Liberalism and Empire: A Study of Nineteenth-Century British Liberal Thought.* Chicago: University of Chicago Press.

Metcalf, Thomas R. (1994). *Ideologies of the Raj.* Cambridge: Cambridge University Press.

Metcalf, Thomas R. (2007). *Imperial Connections: India in the Indian Ocean Arena, 1860–1920.* Berkeley: University of California Press.

Mitchell, Timothy (1988). *Colonizing Egypt.* Berkeley: University of California Press.

Muthu, Sankar (2003). *Enlightenment against Empire.* Princeton: Princeton University Press.

Ortner, Sherry (ed.) (1999). *The Fate of 'Culture': Geertz and Beyond.* Berkeley: University of California Press.

Pandey, Gyanendra (1990). *The Construction of Communalism in Colonial North India.* Delhi: Oxford University Press.

Perry, Adele (2001). *On the Edge of Empire: Gender, Race, and the Making of British Columbia 1849–1871.* Toronto: University of Toronto Press.

Pitts, Jennifer (2005). *A Turn to Empire: The Rise of Imperial Liberalism in Britain and France.* Princeton: Princeton University Press.

Pocock, J. G. A. (1975). 'British History: A Plea for a New Subject', *Journal of Modern History,* 47: 601–28.

Porter, Bernard (2006). *The Absent-Minded Imperialists: Empire, Society and Culture in Britain.* New York: Oxford University Press.

Potter, Simon J. (2007). 'Webs, Networks, and Systems: Globalization and the Mass Media in the Nineteenth- and Twentieth-Century British Empire', *Journal of British Studies,* 46.3: 621–46.

Powell, Eve M. Troutt (2003). *A Different Shade of Colonialism: Egypt, Great Britain, and the Mastery of the Sudan*. Berkeley: University of California Press.

Prakash, Gyan (1999). *Another Reason: Science and the Imagination of Modern India*. Princeton: Princeton University Press.

Prestholdt, Jeremy (2008). *Domesticating the World: African Consumerism and the Genealogies of Globalization*. Berkeley: University of California Press.

Richardson, Brian W. (2005). *Longitude and Empire: How Captain Cook's Voyages Changed the World*. Vancouver: University of British Columbia Press.

Said, Edward W. (1978). *Orientalism*. New York: Vintage.

Samuel, Raphael (1989). *Patriotism: The Making and Unmaking of British National Identity*, 3 vols. London: Routledge.

Sangari, K. and S. Vaid (eds) (1990). *Recasting Women: Essays in Indian Colonial History*. New Brunswick, NJ: Rutgers University Press.

Satia, Priya (2008). *Spies in Arabia: The Great War and the Cultural Foundations of Britain's Covert Empire in the Middle East*. New York: Oxford University Press.

Scott, Joan Wallach (1986). 'Gender: A Useful Category of Historical Analysis', *American Historical Review*, 91.5: 1053–75.

Semmel, Bernard (1970). *The Rise of Free Trade Imperialism: Classical Political Economy and Empire of Free Trade and Imperialism 1750–1850*. Cambridge: Cambridge University Press.

Sinha, Mrinalini (1995). *Colonial Masculinity: The 'Manly Englishman' and the 'Effeminate Bengali' in the Late Nineteenth Century*. Manchester: Manchester University Press.

Sinha, Mrinalini (2006). *Specters of Mother India: The Global Restructuring of an Empire*. Durham, NC: Duke University Press.

Stern, Philip J. (2011). *The Company-State: Corporate Sovereignty and the Early Modern Foundations of the British Empire in India*. New York: Oxford University Press.

Stoler, Ann Laura (1989). 'Making Empire Respectable: The Politics of Race and Sexual Morality in 20th-Century Colonial Cultures', *American Ethnologist*, 16.4: 634–59.

Stoler, Ann Laura (1995). *Race and the Education of Desire: Foucault's History of Sexuality and the Colonial Order of Things*. Durham, NC: Duke University Press.

Stoler, Ann Laura (2002). *Carnal Knowledge and Imperial Power: Race and the Intimate in Colonial Rule*. Berkeley: University of California Press.

Stoler, Ann Laura and F. Cooper (1997). 'Between Metropole and Colony: Rethinking a Research Agenda', in F. Cooper and A. L. Stoler (eds), *Tensions of Empire: Colonial Cultures in a Bourgeois World*. Berkeley: University of California Press, 1–56.

Thompson, Andrew (2005). *The Empire Strikes Back? The Impact of Imperialism on Britain from the Mid-Nineteenth Century*. Harlow: Pearson Longman.

Thompson, Andrew and G. Magee (2011). *Empire and Globalisation: Networks of Peoples, Goods and Capital in the World c.1850–1914*. Cambridge: Cambridge University Press.

Travers, Robert (2007). *Ideology and Empire in Eighteenth-Century India: The British in Bengal*. Cambridge: Cambridge University Press.

Tsin, Michael (1999). *Nation, Governance, and Modernity in China*. Stanford: Stanford University Press.

Vail, Leroy (ed.) (1991). *The Creation of Tribalism in Southern Africa*. Berkeley: University of California Press.

Vaughan, Megan (1991). *Curing their Ills: Colonial Power and African Illness*. Stanford: Stanford University Press.

Ward, Stuart (2008). 'Imperial Identities Abroad', in S. Stockwell (ed.), *The British Empire: Themes and Perspectives.* Oxford: Blackwell, 219–43.

Wilson, Kathleen (2003). *The Island Race: Englishness, Empire and Gender in the Eighteenth Century.* London: Routledge.

Wilson, Kathleen (2004). 'Introduction: Histories, Empires, Modernities', in K. Wilson (ed.), *A New Imperial History: Culture, Identity, and Modernity in Britain and the Empire, 1660–1840.* Cambridge: Cambridge University Press, 1–26.

Wolfe, Patrick (2001). 'Land, Labor, and Difference: Elementary Structures of Race', *American Historical Review,* 106.3: 866–905.

Zastoupil, Lynn (1994). *John Stuart Mill and India.* Stanford: Stanford University Press.

CHAPTER 22

'SLIPPERY, LIKE A FISH'

The Discourse of the Social Sciences

BARRY HINDESS

This chapter addresses two related concerns: first, what are the costs of considering differences between contemporaries in terms of temporal categories like 'modern' and its various synonyms and contraries; and, second, can we avoid resorting to temporal categories in considering these differences? My use of the term 'contemporaries', which usually carries the sense of belonging to the same moment or short period, suggests a negative answer to the second question. Yet at least it avoids the destructive temporalizing pretence that some of us (the moderns) belong to the present while others (the pre-modern, modernizing, developing, industrializing, traditional, tribal, etc.) have yet to reach it. To indicate what may be at stake in this pretence, I begin with two examples.

The first consists of passages from one of the classics of Enlightenment historiography, 'The Nature and Value of Universal History', Friedrich von Schiller's inaugural lecture as professor of history at the University of Jena in 1789. Schiller observes that European voyages of discovery had provided his audience with

> a spectacle which is as instructive as it is entertaining. They show us societies arrayed around us at various levels of development, as an adult might be surrounded by children of different ages, reminded by their example of what he once was and whence he started. A wise hand seems to have preserved these savage tribes until such time as we have progressed sufficiently in our own civilization to make useful application of this discovery, and from this mirror to discover the lost beginning of our race. (1972 [1789]: 325)

If we leave the reference to entertainment to one side, the two most striking features in this passage are, first, the barbed suggestion that many of Schiller's contemporaries were anachronisms (cf. Chakrabarty 2002: 238–9); and second, his reference to children, which implies that people belonging to an earlier time had relatively undeveloped intellectual and moral capacities and were less than fully mature. The view that many contemporaries really belong in the past suggests that some, perhaps all, of the different human conditions that make up universal history—feudal, peasant, slave, and hunter-gatherer societies, for example—can be seen by moving elsewhere on the surface of the earth. Universal history thus becomes a kind of descriptive human geography (see also Thornton 2001).

As for the reference to children: 'How embarrassing and dismal', Schiller later confesses, 'is the picture of our own childhood presented in these peoples'. Many of them, he observes, are

> unacquainted with the most elementary skills, without iron, without the plough, some even without fire... Here there is not even the simplest marriage tie; there no knowledge of property; here the indolent mind cannot learn even from experience that is repeated daily. (1972 [1789]: 325)

'Others', he admits, 'have reached a higher level of civilization, but their slavery and despotism still present a horrible picture' (325–6).

Schiller's lecture is of interest today only to a few historians concerned with the history of their own discipline. Schiller himself is perhaps more widely known for his influential essay 'On Naïve and Sentimental Poetry' (1795), which played an important part in the history of European Romanticism in the early development of German sociology (see, for example, Tönnies's (1955) distinction between *Gemeinschaft* and *Gesellschaft*—community and association). Departing from the claims of his inaugural lecture, Schiller's essay makes a different, if no less problematic, use of the image of childhood, suggesting that the primitive has something that he and his readers lack: the primitive, like the idealized child, is closer to nature than the civilized adult. The essay treats the Homeric Greeks as representing 'the historic childhood' of humanity and humanity's acquisition of civilization as analogous to the process of maturation in an individual. In both cases, Schiller suggests, the earlier condition is that of unity, of individuals within themselves in the one case and of humanity with the world around it in the other. As the individual matures and humanity becomes more civilized, this original unity is disrupted. What remains, in Schiller's view, is a 'striving after unity. The correspondence between his feeling and thought which in his first condition actually took place, exists now only ideally' (1985 [1795]: 194). Consequently, the conditions of childhood and of civilization produce entirely different kinds of poetry, and of art in general, with the unpretentious naïvety of the first representing an unattainable ideal for the second.

The dark side of this developmental understanding of humanity is examined in Edward Said's *Orientalism* (1978) and again, in rather different terms, by the anthropologist Johannes Fabian in his *Time and the Other* (1983). Fabian writes of anthropology's 'denial of coevalness', its tendency to treat the people it studies as if they belonged to another time. While the anthropologist and the people studied are contemporaries in the moment of fieldwork, he suggests, the written report too often places the latter in the past of the anthropologist's readers. Fabian uses the term 'coevalness' to invoke the biblical view that all surviving portions of humanity are descended from the children of Noah, and have thus developed over the same historical period, but his argument against treating contemporaries as if they belong in the past works equally well if we start from the conventional archaeological view that we are all descended from the family of a prehistoric East African Lucy.

In their introduction to *Orientalism and the Postcolonial Predicament* (1993), Carol Breckenridge and Peter van der Veer observe that, compared with their colleagues in the humanities,

> social scientists have been particularly recalcitrant when it comes to self-reflection on their *representational* strategies in respect to the non-Western world…The humanities are not the only realm of scholarship that has facilitated the construction of an enfeebled, subservient, and sometimes oppositional other. (1993: 16)

I can hardly pretend that social scientists in general are no longer recalcitrant, but as the Breckenridge and van der Veer collection shows (see also Asad 1973; Cooper 2005; Wolf 1982), parts of anthropology at least have moved on significantly since Said's and Fabian's books appeared, in part under the influence of contemporaneous and more recent postcolonial critiques.

Fabian could hardly avoid noting that the denial of coevalness is not peculiar to anthropology but is a more general feature of western thought, which is the aspect of his argument that most interests me in this chapter. This aspect can also be found in classical political economy and sociology (Smith, Comte, Durkheim, Marx, Weber) and their modern successors, economics and twentieth-century social theory. Where it appears in anthropology or the other social sciences, the denial of coevalness reflects a developmental understanding of humanity of roughly the kind set out in Schiller's inaugural lecture. While there have been several critical studies of the narcissistic west's vision of its own progress (see, for example, Burrow 1991; Haas 1997; Mittelstrass et al. 1997; Nisbet 1980; Rae 2002), the history and influence of the developmental understanding of humanity is one of those few important areas of western political thought which, with rare exceptions (Inayatullah and Blaney 2004; O'Brien 1997; Pocock 2010; Tully 1995), mainstream political theorists and historians of political thought have yet seriously to address.

This relegation of non-western ways of life to the status of anachronisms is not merely of historical interest. Social science discourses of modernity, modernization, and development divide the contemporary world into those who are fully of our time and those who have yet to reach it and even those who are considered, more playfully perhaps, to have moved beyond the modern (Cooper 1996; Lyotard 1984). Nor is the problem confined to academia, for the developmental perspective remains influential in the work of international financial and development agencies and in several other aspects of the west's interactions with the non-western world. Here, for example, is a passage from one of Thomas Friedman's op-ed pieces in the *New York Times* (3 July 2002): 'America and the West have potential partners in [Islamic] countries who are eager…to move the

struggle to where it belongs: to a war within Islam over its spiritual message and identity'. What Friedman has in mind is not, he insists, a war against Islam but one 'between
the future and the past, between development and underdevelopment, between authors
of crazy conspiracy theories versus those espousing rationality'. Like Schiller's reference
to children, Friedman's comments suggest that those who belong to the past are less than
entirely rational.

My second illustration of the divisive effects of the temporalizing pretence is taken
from the recent history of Australia. Around the middle of 2006, the government
of Australia's Northern Territory appointed a Board of Inquiry into the Protection of
Aboriginal Children from Sexual Abuse, which reported in the following June. Its report
(Anderson and Wild 2007) noted that though there had been several earlier government inquiries into this issue in Australia, these had not led to significant action by the
governments concerned. In its first recommendation, the report insisted that both the
federal and NT governments should treat the issue of 'Aboriginal child sexual abuse in
the Northern Territory...as [one] of urgent national significance' (22). In considering
what might be done about it, the report focused on the improvement of education, the
building of community trust, the provision of family support services, and the empowerment of Aboriginal communities. Although the inquiry had been established by the
NT government, the federal Australian government took up its call for urgent action
and established the Northern Territory National Emergency Response—an initiative
generally known as the Intervention—which ignored the report's advice that action
should be organized in consultation with local communities. To enforce its policies,
the Intervention sent military forces into NT indigenous communities, thereby turning Australia, in the sardonic words of one commentator, into 'the first member of the
Coalition of the Willing to invade itself'.[1]

The Intervention involved a variety of measures that were widely regarded as both racist and oppressive, including significant changes in welfare provision, law enforcement,
indigenous land tenure, and partial suspension of the 1975 Racial Discrimination Act,
which prohibited discrimination on the basis of race in many areas of public life. The
Australian Labor Party, which, like its British Labour counterpart, sits just a little to the
left of the decidedly right-wing centre it has done so much to establish, was elected to government later that year and, to the disappointment of many of its supporters, it has continued with the Intervention. This is now rebadged as 'Closing the Gap in the Northern
Territory', to indicate that this version of the Intervention, unlike that of the previous
government, seriously intends to bring conditions in NT indigenous communities up to
the standards of 'mainstream' Australia.[2] While, in its election campaign, the Party had

---

[1] Guy Rundle, quoted in Burnside (2009).

[2] A monitoring report issued in November 2009 by FAHCSIA (the Commonwealth Department of
Families, Housing, Community Services, and Indigenous Affairs) indicates limited progress, at best, on
a number of measures since the Intervention began. Reported domestic violence incidents and breaches
of domestic violence orders, for example, have both increased between 2006–7 (pre-Intervention) and
2008–9 (post-Intervention) (35–6), while figures for school attendance have barely changed (20).

promised to reinstate the Racial Discrimination Act, it took its time over doing so,[3] but it quickly moved to reduce the discriminatory effects of the Intervention by extending its controls over indigenous welfare recipients in the NT to many other welfare recipients.

While its authors did not support the Intervention triggered by their report, the report itself is hardly a radical document: its findings were already familiar to welfare workers and researchers in the area and to the relevant government departments, and it used conventional social science concepts and research methods. Yet the authors were critical of the paternalism that had characterized relationships between indigenous people and government agencies, insisting instead that both the NT and Australian governments should commit to 'genuine consultation with Aboriginal people in designing initiatives for Aboriginal communities' (6).

For the most part, the report is careful to avoid suggesting that Aboriginal society is in any way inferior to Australia's larger, mostly white, settler society. It refers, for example, to 'Aboriginal culture' and 'European or mainstream society' as 'the two branches of society' (12). While not representing one branch as superior to the other, it notes that there is a 'major difference' between them and specifically that, as earlier commentators had also noted, there was an ongoing 'breakdown of Aboriginal culture'. And again, for the most part, the word 'mainstream' is used to refer to 'European society' without invoking the invidious distinction between those who are 'modern' and others who are not; without directly asserting, in other words, that 'Aboriginal culture', in contrast to 'mainstream society', is not yet modern.

However, in spite of its authors' best intentions, there are too many places in the report where the contrast between 'modern' and 'not really modern' seems to slip in. For example, the report cites approvingly a 1998 coronor's inquest into four young Aboriginal suicides in the Tiwi Islands that notes 'a weakening of the *traditional* and cultural values in *modern* Australian society' (13, emphasis mine). Here *traditional*, in contrast to *modern*, is presented as a feature of Aboriginal culture. The same contrast between traditional and modern reappears later in the report:

> *Traditional* marriage practices as they once existed cannot continue in the *modern* world, especially when they conflict with modern international human rights. Practices such as accepting goods in exchange for a 'wife', for example, are not consistent with *modern* international human rights. (71, emphasis mine)

This passage manages to damn traditional ways for not being modern and for conflicting with human rights; without precisely saying so, it suggests that human rights are associated with the modern and, conversely, that contravening them is a feature of the pre-modern world.[4] Finally,

> [t]he Inquiry observed that many Aboriginal people are struggling to understand the 'mainstream' modern world and law. They therefore do not know how to change

---

[3.] The Act was eventually reinstated in August 2010.
[4.] Rejali (1994) addresses one version of this modernist prejudice, specifically in relation to torture.

Aboriginal law so that it works positively within the framework of the modern 'mainstream' world. (179)

The modern is presented here as a framework to which the non-modern has to adapt. To illustrate the difficulty facing 'many Aboriginal people', the report cites two Aboriginal elders:

1. 'In the old days we were going in a straight line, now we turning around and going in different directions'.
2. 'Whitefella law is very slippery, like a fish'.

This second comment hardly distinguishes indigenous people from others in the Australian population. Non-indigenous people, including the present author and many practising lawyers, also have problems making sense of modern 'mainstream' law, but few of them would be able to make the point so forcefully (see also Farrier and Tuitt and Turner and Smith in Part II of this volume).

At this point, I should note that while in Australian public life 'modern' and 'traditional' are commonly seen as distinct and opposed, the contrast between them does not always involve a disparaging perception of the latter. At times, traditional ways are regarded as serving to sustain indigenous communities or, like many endangered species, as things to be preserved, if only for the benefit of tourism; while, at others, they are seen as obstacles to be overcome. (At still other times, and again like endangered species, they are seen as both.) Either way, they are seen as opposed: tradition is thought to be undermined by the modern—and is seen accordingly by modern observers as in the process of breaking down—and to stand in the way of its development. However, since the report plays this opposition both ways, it is not clear why its authors insist on 'genuine consultation' (16). On the one hand, consultation might seem to offer some defence against the destructive impact of modern ways of life. Yet, on the other, if tradition is seen as resisting the modern, consultation can only provide another obstacle to modernization.

For the most part, as noted earlier, the report remains neutral, offering neither a positive nor a negative assessment of what it sees as traditional, the strange references to 'modern "mainstream" world' and '"mainsteam" modern world' (both on p. 179, as if the order of 'modern' and 'mainstream' were inconsequential) and the counter-position of *traditional* marriage and '*modern* international human rights' (p. 71, emphasis mine) being the most notable exceptions. Nevertheless, the overall effect of the report's contrast between traditional and modern is to suggest that tradition, however valuable, makes it difficult for indigenous people to cope with the (modern) world in which they live.

The sorry tale of the original Intervention and its continuation under a new government raises many issues that deserve further consideration. The one that concerns me most here is the shifting import of the report's distinction between traditional and modern. This distinction draws on two contrasting usages of the term 'tradition'. Raymond Williams notes that while the English term 'tradition' was once, and is sometimes still, associated with 'ceremony, duty and respect', it is now 'often used dismissively' to indicate hostility 'to virtually any innovation' (1983: 319–20). The latter usage is perhaps the more influential. The social sciences have rarely advanced beyond Max Weber's treatment of traditional action as irrational. In his discussion of the types of social action (1978: 24–6), for example, Weber identifies two types of rational action, instrumental and value, focusing respectively on the efficient achievement of given ends and the realization or implementation of values, and two others, affective and traditional. He adds that action of the latter type 'is determined by ingrained habituation' (25). This dismissive treatment of tradition reflects the tendency of the modern social sciences and of modern social thought more generally to treat many non-western peoples as if, unlike us, they are dominated by tradition and can therefore be viewed as living in the past.

Despite its service in the rationalization of colonial rule, this unpleasant tendency probably has its origins, not simply in Enlightenment Orientalism (Halbfass 1988: 60), but also in conflicts between Protestants and Catholics in early modern Germany. Among the many issues at stake in these conflicts were the claims of the Papacy and the Holy Roman Empire to be eternal. Since their claims to legitimacy were based on continuity over a long period, they also maintained that many decisions made in the past continued to hold in the present. Against these claims, Protestant historians argued that they misrepresented what happened in the past, and that whatever had in fact occurred should not be allowed to dominate conduct in the present. One outcome of this revolt, Constantin Fasolt argues, is the radical modern distinction between past and present, which suggests that the former is somehow less 'rational' than the latter, and that there was a time in which people were dominated by the past, allowing themselves to be ruled by custom and tradition in a manner best summarized as 'irrational' (Fasolt 2004). While, in its original form, this crude perception was turned mainly against European Catholics whose communities were contemptuously seen as priest-ridden, it has also surfaced recently in no less dismissive western accounts—such as Friedman's—of the Islamic world (see the chapters by Mignolo and Sayyid in Part I of this volume).

The second usage of the term 'tradition' is what Williams presents to us as the earlier English version, the one associated with 'ceremony, duty and respect'. Just as Dalits in India and members of target populations in the west (e.g. in the area of sexuality: homosexual, transgender, transsexual, queer—see Bhagavan and Feldhaus 2008; Hacking 2006) have sometimes adopted pejorative categories as positive identities, indigenous peoples in Australia have given a positive spin to the 'traditional' categories to which they have been assigned. Thus, inverting the conventional valorization of the modern, they celebrate a culture that has continued for 40,000 years or more and deliberately market selected aspects of that tradition to 'mainstream' Australians and foreign tourists (see Smith and Turner in Part II of this volume).

Thus, while in one familiar usage the divide between traditional and modern reflects poorly on the former, there is another in which the latter is devalued; it may even be possible to find cases in which the divide serves as little more than a conventional marker of difference between the two. Yet it is difficult overall to avoid a sense of opposition. Homi Bhabha urges us to unsettle conventional oppositions, but this is easier said than done; and in one of the most interesting attempts to tackle the traditional/ modern opposition directly, Eric Hobsbawm and Terence Ranger's *The Invention of Tradition* (1983), which contains some fine essays on the traditions fabricated by imperial authorities in Africa, India, and various parts of the British Isles, the opposition is inadvertently reproduced in a slightly different form (Hobsbawm and Ranger 1983; see also Bhabha 1994). Hobsbawm's introduction notes that modern societies have their own traditions, which seems to undermine the usual contrast between modern and traditional. He describes these 'invented traditions' as 'responses to novel situations which take the form of reference to old situations' (2) and continues by noting that 'tradition in this [invented] sense must be distinguished from "custom" which dominates so-called "traditional" societies' (2). While this seems to suggest that there are societies with invented traditions and others that are dominated by 'custom', Hobsbawm insists that 'there is probably no time or place...which has not seen the invention of tradition' (4). Yet if the invention of tradition is universal, it seems to appear more in some societies than in others: 'Societies since the industrial revolution have naturally been obliged to invent, institute or develop new networks of...convention or routine more frequently than previous ones' (3). In place of the opposition between modern and traditional, we now have one between post-Industrial Revolution societies undergoing rapid change and societies that have yet to reach that condition.

We might note that in its appeal to 'the industrial revolution', this approach takes Europe as a model for the rest of the world: it is a version of Dipesh Chakrabarty's 'first in the west and then elsewhere' paradigm, which I will go on to consider in more detail below (see also Brydon in this section of the volume). On the other hand, the Argentine-Mexican philosopher Enrique Dussel undermines the traditional/modern opposition indirectly by confronting its second term and, specifically, the conventional Eurocentric myth of modernity (Dussel 1995, 1993; see also Mignolo in Part I of this volume). Dussel argues that where most accounts of modernity treat it as developing first in Europe and then affecting other regions, it should be seen as relational, embracing both Europe and those regions subjected to European imperialism. Modernity begins with the Spanish invasion of the Americas in 1492 and with Portuguese military/colonial ventures into Africa and Asia at around the same time. In this sense, one would have to say that contemporary Europe and postcolonial societies elsewhere are all equally modern. Despite its religious/metaphysical foundations, this approach displays interesting parallels with dependency theory (Amin 1976; Gunder Frank 1967) and with Wallerstein's view that the origins of the contemporary world system can be traced to the period immediately following the European discovery of the Americas (Wallerstein 1974). However, the approach has had little impact on the social sciences outside the Americas.

Moreover, while there may be no option but to describe the position of indigenous people within 'mainstream' Australian society in terms of the opposition between modern and traditional, or something uncomfortably like it, it is hard to do so without also enabling, if not actively promoting, the perception that they are both unable to cope with the present and living in the past. The difficulty to be faced here is that certain concepts can be unavoidable and yet still have potentially damaging consequences. Significant versions of this difficulty have been addressed by postcolonial social scientists. In the opening chapter of his self-consciously 'postcolonial' *Provincializing Europe*, for example, the Indian historian Dipesh Chakrabarty observes that 'European thought…is both indispensable and inadequate in helping us to think through the various life practices that constitute the political and the historical in India' (practices he goes on to analyse in the book's later chapters). He then says that 'exploring…this simultaneous indispensability and inadequacy of social science thought is the task this book has set itself' (2000: 6).

Sanjay Seth's 2008 study of education in colonial/postcolonial India presents a variation on this theme, noting first that 'almost all serious "respectable" and officially disseminated knowledge about the non-western world shares the presumptions and guiding categories of modern western knowledge' (3), and then proceeding to put these categories and presumptions into question. Still other versions appear in Bhabha's celebration of hybridity and the unsettling of conventional oppositions, and a decade later in the prologue to Scott (Bhabha 1994; Scott 2004). For ease of exposition, the following discussion will focus on Chakrabarty's argument.

Taken out of context, Chakrabarty's phrase 'simultaneous indispensability and inadequacy' might seem to denote some kind of poststructuralist paradox, a contemporary version of the Kantian antinomies in which reflection on the impossibility of accepting either of two apparently opposed positions is expected to induce in the reader a craving for metaphysical speculation (Hunter 2001). Indeed, Amit Chaudhuri's review of *Provincializing Europe*, after citing the same lines I have quoted above, signals a possible parallel with poststructuralism by asserting that this is not very far from Derrida who, at an important point in *Writing and Difference* (1978), writes of Lévi-Strauss's cautious handling of the nature/culture distinction

> conserving all these old concepts within the domain of empirical discovery while here and there denouncing their limits, treating them as tools which can still be used. No longer is any truth attributed to them, there is a readiness to abandon them, if necessary, should other instruments appear more useful. In the meantime, their relative efficacy is exploited, and they are employed to destroy the old machinery to which they belong and of which they themselves are pieces. This is how the language of the social sciences criticizes itself. (1978: 359)

Derrida's *Writing and Difference* is best seen as a loosely structured collection of papers on related themes, with the paper quoted here, 'Structure, Sign and Play in the Discourse of the Human Sciences', being the last and most influential chapter, possibly because it first appeared at an early stage in poststructuralism's invasion of the American academy (Macksey and Donato 1970: 245–67). The passage itself comes from Derrida's aggressive caricature of Lévi-Strauss's tortured reflections on the distinction between nature and culture. To cite a classic Lévi-Straussian example: prohibitions on conduct are normally seen as human inventions, and thus as phenomena that vary between cultures (Hindu cultures, for example, discourage the eating of beef while western cultures encourage it).

Yet, as Lévi-Strauss notes in *The Savage Mind* (1966), the prohibition of incest seems to be both cultural and natural. On the one hand, as a prohibition, it appears to be a phenomenon of culture, so if it appears at all we would expect to find it in some cultures and not in others. On the other hand, the fact that some version of the prohibition appears in all cultures suggests that it cannot be an invention at all, but is rather a natural feature of the human condition. While the universality of the prohibition seems to undermine the conventional distinction between nature and culture, Lévi-Strauss argues that this distinction is nevertheless of great methodological importance for the social sciences.

Lévi-Strauss's argument, and Derrida's detailed metaphysical critique of it, need not detain us here. In fact, the real parallel suggested by Chaudhuri's review is not between Chakrabarty and Derrida, but between Chakrabarty and Lévi-Strauss. Chaudhuri describes the view criticized by Derrida as follows: Lévi-Strauss, 'when confronted with South American myths, finds the tools of his trade obsolete but still indispensable' (2004: 8). He adds that the 'idea of Chakrabarty registering a similarly self-reflexive moment about thirty years later…is poignant and ironic' (8), his point being that Chakrabarty was more likely to have been seen in Lévi-Strauss's time as an object of social science inquiry than as one of its originators.

Chakrabarty's argument is in fact as far removed from Lévi-Strauss's structuralism as it is from Derrida's poststructuralism.[5] Derrida aims to seduce his readers into speculation about the limitations, not simply of the tools of Lévi-Strauss's trade, but also those of western metaphysics in general, and it is partly for this reason that he is able to conclude with a reference to 'a kind of question, let us still call it historical, whose conception…we are only catching a glimpse of today' (Derrida 1978: 267). In contrast, Chakrabarty's concerns over European social science thought are less with its metaphysical tendencies—though some readers may find his reliance on Heidegger disturbing—than with what he calls its 'historicism' (Chakrabarty 2000; see also Abeysekara, who offers a more positive view of Heidegger and Derrida, in this section of the volume). Moreover, as he uses them, the terms 'indispensable' and 'inadequate' are hardly able to sustain a Derridean aporia, let alone the polarity of a Kantian antinomy.

The sense in which he regards social science thought as indispensable can be gathered from Chakrabarty's earlier claim that 'the so-called European intellectual tradition is the only one alive in the social science departments of most, if not all, modern universities' (5). Here he uses 'tradition' in the more respectful of the various senses of the term previously identified by Williams. While not denying that the idea of a 'European intellectual tradition' stretching back from today to the ancient Greeks is a fabrication (as traditions often are), he suggests that other intellectual traditions have been killed off

---

[5.] This is not to suggest that there are no connections between postcolonialism and poststructuralism. A strong historical case for the importance of these connections is made by, among others, Ahluwalia (2011). Whatever the merits of that argument, it may be tempting to read Derrida's and Heidegger's critique of western metaphysics as signalling a potential alliance with postcolonialism's rather different critique of western pretensions. My own view is that metaphysics plays a lesser role in these pretensions than such an alliance might suggest.

by colonialism, not simply by their contact with the modern.[6] As a result of 'European colonial rule in South Asia', he suggests, 'intellectual traditions once unbroken and alive in Sanskrit or Persian or Arabic are now only matters of historical research for... social scientists in the region. They treat these traditions as truly dead, as history' (5). European social science thought is indispensable, then, in the sense that it is the only serious tradition of intellectual inquiry we have left to deal with. This reluctant confession of the conditions in which one has to work has little in common with Lévi-Strauss's discomfort—the immediate target of Derrida's attack—with the distinction between nature and culture or with his claim that this distinction is 'of primarily methodological importance' (Lévi-Strauss 1966: 247, quoted in Derrida 1978: 285).

Social science thought is 'inadequate' because its historicism leads to misleading views on significant questions of Indian history, several of which Chakrabarty addresses in later chapters (his discussion of the Bengali practice of *Adda*, 180–213, is especially revealing). Like many English words ending in 'ism', 'historicism' has several meanings, as Chakrabarty notes (22–3), but in his argument it primarily refers to 'the idea that to understand anything it has to be seen both as a unity and in its historical development' (6). Of course, this reference to 'historical *development*' is itself open to interpretation. The historicism that concerns Chakrabarty is the one that takes the development of Europe as its point of reference and consequently posits 'historical time as a measure of the cultural distance... that is assumed to exist between the West and the non-West' (7). In practice, this measure of distance only works in one direction, adopting the temporal structure of the statement 'first in the West and then elsewhere' (6). According to this view, people in the 'non-west' are always some distance in time behind the west, and never ahead.

Partha Chatterjee, for his part, views this temporal perspective from a different, more obviously Marxist, perspective:

> Empty homogenous time is the time of capital. Within its domain, capital allows for no resistance to its free movement. When it encounters an impediment, it thinks it has encountered another time—something out of pre-capital, something that belongs to the pre-modern. (2005: 925–6)

Here, too, temporal difference is seen as working backwards from the western present. We should not think of this strange temporal perspective on the non-west as if the latter were to be seen as homogeneous. Indeed, for those who take the contemporary west as a reference point, there are many earlier positions that could be identified on the imagined temporal continuum that runs behind the western present. For example, reflecting on his experiences as Lieutenant-Governor in Northern Nigeria, C. L. Temple writes in his *Native Races and Their Ruler* (a title that deserves an essay of its own):

[6.] Indeed, Chakrabarty has argued elsewhere that, in addition to western modernities, there are several alternative modernities in the contemporary world: see, for example, Chakrabarty (2002).

The native is a human being like ourselves, but in a different stage of development. Some natives are, even today, in the stage of our Druidical ancestors, whereas others are in the stage which we passed through in about the Middle Ages. The whirligig of time has brought us from five hundred to a thousand years ahead of them in the process of evolution... (1918: 310)

This plurality of past locations in which western thought has been tempted to place non-western peoples suggests the possibility of what the American demographer Arland Thornton calls 'reading history sideways' (2001). In other words, one can either investigate the history of some place by studying another where the same history appears to be happening today, or alternatively, as Chakrabarty's 'historicism' suggests, by reading about how this history happened for the first time in the west. Thornton gives several examples of demographers following this misleading practice. Outside demography, perhaps the most prominent example of this approach is Lewis Henry Morgan's *Ancient Society* (1877), a study that was to provide the foundations for Friedrich Engels's equally influential historicist argument in *The Origins of the Family*. Morgan's work moves both ways, using the reported behaviour of contemporaneous American Indians to shed light on puzzles about peoples in western antiquity, and using Caesar's and Tacitus's reports on German savages in their time to shed light on the behaviour of American Indians in his.

In addition to its impact on nineteenth-century anthropology and the writing of history, historicism has had—and continues to have—important political implications, an aspect not directly covered by Chakrabarty's formula of 'indispensability and inadequacy'. Were it not for the neatness of the formula, it would be tempting to add 'unsavoury' or 'injurious'. I noted earlier that this historicist approach, or something like it, informs much of the current work of major development agencies, the international human rights regime, and other aspects of the west's interactions with the non-west, while Thornton shows that this perspective has also had significant implications for social policy in various parts of the modern world (see Abeysekara in this section of the volume).

Chakrabarty wryly notes that 'historicism... came to non-European peoples in the nineteenth century as somebody's way of saying "not yet" to somebody else' (8). In support of this point, he refers to two influential liberal essays from the era of direct colonial rule, John Stuart Mill's *On Liberty* (1975 [1859]) and *Considerations on Representative Government*, which argues that the peoples of British India and, by implication, Britain's other non-European possessions are not yet sufficiently advanced 'to be fitted for representative government' (1977 [1865]: 567). Yet here, too, the issue is more complex than Chakrabarty suggests; for Mill's essays were mainly written for British readers and his 'not yet' was effectively telling these readers (along with anyone else who happened upon his work) that the peoples of Britain's non-European colonies could not be trusted to govern themselves and would be better off under British rule. Since, like his father, Mill spent most of his adult life as a senior officer of the British East India Company, it is hardly surprising that he concludes by suggesting that the Indian people would have fared best under the rule of the British East India Company, whose Indian possessions had been taken over in the aftermath of the 1875 rebellion by the Crown.[7]

A second point derived from Mill is that if non-Europeans are not yet like Europeans, it might be a bad idea to govern them in the way that Europeans should be governed. Similarly, Alexis de Tocqueville, writing in 1847 on how to govern the indigenous peoples of Algeria, maintains that 'the same rules of administration and justice that seem to the European to be guarantees of liberty and property, seem an intolerable oppression to the barbarian' (2001: 145). Moreover, if some non-Europeans are closer to European ways than others, then a mode of government that seems appropriate for one group of non-Europeans may not be appropriate for the rest. Here is Lord John Russell writing to George Gipps, governor of the colony of New South Wales in Australia on 25 August 1840:

> We should run the risk of entire failure if we should confound in one abstract description of aborigines the various races of people, some half-civilized, some little raised above the brutes; some hunting over vast tracts of country, others with scarcely any means, or habits, of destroying wild animals at all, who have encountered the discovering or invading races of Europe all over the face of the globe. One tribe in Africa differs widely in character from another at 50 miles distance; the red Indian of Canada and the native of New Holland are distinguished from each other in almost every respect. We indeed, who come into contact with these various races, have one and the same duty to perform towards them all; but the manner in which this duty is to be performed must vary with the varying materials upon which we have to work. (Russell 1968: 73)

Perhaps the most important way in which colonial rulers attempted to take account of what they believed to be the characteristics of these 'varying materials' was the decision to rule through what were thought to be indigenous institutions and structures of authority, a practice which, in the British case, eventually came to be known as indirect rule. The result was the empowerment, even invention, of what were thought to be indigenous structures of authority. Mahmood Mamdani argues that South African apartheid epitomized this system of 'decentralised despotism' (Mamdani 1996; see also Ntsebeza 2005).[8] Decolonization undermined the white/black structures of the colonial state, but it generally left in place those of decentralized despotism. Thus, the postcolonial state in Africa and the patterns of resistance to it can be seen as legacies of late colonial rule (see Quayson in Part V of this volume).

---

[7] In the final paragraph of *Representative Government*, Mill laments: 'It has been the destiny of the government of the East India Company to suggest the true theory of the government of a semi-barbarous dependency by a civilised country, and after having done this, to perish' (575).

[8] If the practices of 'indirect rule/decentralized despotism' take up one aspect of the historicism that Chakrabarty disputes, another is taken up by the view that what happens first in the west should happen later elsewhere. Partha Chatterjee has taken up this issue in his reflections on the appropriateness of the model of the 'nation state', and more generally of the western image of civil society, to conditions in the non-western world (Chatterjee 1993, 2004).

In an essay designed to demonstrate that his discipline would be useful in the government of the subject peoples of Africa, the anthropologist Bronisław Malinowski maintains that the real difference between direct and indirect or dependent rule

> consists in the fact that direct rule assumes that you can create at one go an entirely
> new order, that you can transform Africans into semi-civilised pseudo-Europeans
> within a few years. Indirect rule, on the other hand, recognises that no such magical
> rapid transformation can take place, that in reality all social development is very
> slow, and that it is infinitely preferable to achieve it by a slow and gradual change
> coming from within. (1929: 23)

A few pages later, Malinowski insists that 'an old system of traditions, of morals or
laws' cannot simply be replaced 'by a ready-made new morality and sense of right; the
result invariably will be what might be called "black bolshevism"' (28)—a condition
he seems to understand in terms of pure abandonment, unrestrained by any sense
of morality or law. The reference to bolshevism here is clearly intended to frighten
colonial authorities. This lack of restraint, in Malinowski's view, is what happens when
an established culture breaks down. Similarly, Temple maintains that if you free the
African from the hold of native institutions 'he becomes at once like a kite without a
tail' (1918: 37). This consideration suggests that rather than attempt the rapid dismantling of indigenous institutions, colonial administrators would do better to proceed at
a slow and gradual pace.

I want to bring this chapter to a close by returning one last time to Chakrabarty's
central theme of the 'simultaneous indispensability and inadequacy of social science thought'. I have already complicated this theme by suggesting that the dyad
'indispensable and inadequate' might be joined by a third term, e.g. 'unsavoury' or
'injurious'. I also noted that Chakrabarty regards social science thought as 'indispensable' in the sense that, after the colonial destruction of other intellectual traditions, it is the only serious tradition of intellectual inquiry we have left. Yet if we are
stuck with this tradition, we should also recognize that it is divided against itself.
Certain aspects of the tradition, for example, are clearly 'inadequate'. For example,
the chapters that make up the second part of *Provincializing Europe* show how easy
it is to be led astray by historicist perceptions of Indian cultures and peoples. In
demonstrating this, they demonstrate the capacity of social science thought *both* to
promote prejudicial observation and data collection *and* to provide a partial remedy
for such prejudice.

The difficulty this leaves us with is the one I mentioned earlier in relation to the
Intervention in the Northern Territory of Australia. While it may be tempting, even
valuable, to describe the situation of indigenous peoples in Australia in terms of the
contrast between modern and traditional ways of life, it is not easy to determine how
these terms will be used by others. And as the authors of the report that precipitated the
Intervention were to discover, what unscrupulous, or simply thoughtless, politicians do
with the words of others can be as slippery as any fish.

References

Ahluwalia, Pal (2011). *Out of Africa: Poststructuralism's Postcolonial Roots.* London: Routledge.

Amin, Samir (1976). *Unequal Development: An Essay on the Social Formations of Peripheral Capitalism.* New York: Monthly Review Press.

Anderson, Patricia and Rex Wild (2007). *Ampe Akelyernename Meke Mekarle: 'Little Children are Sacred'.* Report of the Northern Territory Board of Inquiry into the Protection of Aboriginal Children from Sexual Abuse. Darwin: Northern Territory Government.

Asad, Talal (1973). *Anthropology and the Colonial Encounter.* New York: Humanity Books.

Bhagavan, Manu and Anne Feldhaus (eds) (2008). *Claiming Power From Below: Dalits and the Subaltern Question in India.* New Delhi: Oxford University Press.

Bhabha, Homi K. (1994). *The Location of Culture.* London: Routledge.

Breckenridge, Carol A. and Peter van der Veer (1993). *Orientalism and the Postcolonial Predicament.* Philadelphia: University of Pennsylvania Press.

Burnside, Sarah (2009). 'Macklins Special Treatment', *New Matilda,* 4 November. <http://newmatilda.com/2009/11/04/macklins-special-treatment>, accessed 23 October 2012.

Burrow, John (1991). 'Henry Maine and Mid-Victorian Ideas of Progress', in Alan Diamond (ed.), *The Victorian Achievement of Sir Henry Maine: A Centennial Reappraisal.* Cambridge: Cambridge University Press, 55–69.

Chakrabarty, Dipesh (2000). *Provincialising Europe: Postcolonial Thought and Historical Difference.* Princeton: Princeton University Press.

Chakrabarty, Dipesh (2002). *Habitations of Modernity. Essays in the Wake of Subaltern Studies.* Chicago: University of Chicago Press.

Chatterjee, Partha (1993). *The Nation and Its Fragments: Colonial and Postcolonial Histories.* Princeton: Princeton University Press.

Chatterjee, Partha (2004). *The Politics of the Governed: Considerations on Political Society in Most of the World.* New York, Columbia University Press.

Chatterjee, Partha (2005). 'The Nation in Heterogeneous Time', *Futures,* 37.9: 925–42.

Chaudhuri, Amit (2004). 'In the Waiting-Room of History', *London Review of Books,* 26.12 (24 June): 3–8.

Cooper, Frederick (2005). *Colonialism in Question: Theory, Knowledge, History.* Berkeley: University of California Press.

Cooper, Robert (1996). *The Post-Modern State and the World Order.* London: Demos.

Derrida, Jacques (1978). *Writing and Difference.* London: Routledge.

Dussel, Enrique D. (1993). *The Underside of Modernity: Apel, Ricoeur, Rorty, Taylor and the Philosophy of Liberation.* New Jersey: Humanities Press.

Dussel, Enrique D. (1995). *The Invention of the Americas: Eclipse of 'the Other' and the Myth of Modernity.* New York: Continuum.

Fabian, Johannes (1983). *Time and the Other: How Anthropology Makes its Object.* New York: Columbia University Press.

FAHCSIA (2009). *Closing the Gap in the Northern Territory (previously the NTER) Monitoring Report, Part Two—Progress by Measure.* Canberra: Department of Families, Housing, Community Services and Indigenous Affairs (2 November). Available online at: <http://www.fahcsia.gov.au/sa/indigenous/pubs/nter_reports/Pages/closing_the_gap_nter.aspx>, accessed 24 October 2012.

Fasolt, Constantin (2004). *The Limits of History.* Chicago: University of Chicago Press.

Friedman, Thomas L. (2002). 'Arabs at the Crossroads', The New York Times, 3 July 2012.

Gunder Frank, Andre (1967). Capitalism and Underdevelopment in Latin America: Historical Studies of Chile and Brazil. New York: Monthly Review Press.

Haas, Ernst B. (1997). Nationalism, Liberalism and Progress, 2 vols. Ithaca, NY: Cornell University Press.

Hacking, Ian (2006). 'Making up People', London Review of Books, 28: 16–17, 23–6.

Halbfass, Wilhelm (1988). India and Europe: An Essay in Understanding. Albany: State University of New York Press.

Hobsbawm, Eric and Terence Ranger (eds) (1983). The Invention of Tradition. Cambridge: Cambridge University Press.

Hunter, Ian (2001). Rival Enlightenments: Civil and Metaphysical Philosophy in Early Modern Germany. Cambridge: Cambridge University Press.

Inayatullah, Naeem and David L. Blaney (2004). International Relations and the Problem of Difference. London: Routledge.

Lévi-Strauss, Claude (1966). The Savage Mind. London: Weidenfeld & Nicolson.

Lyotard, Jean-François (1984). The Postmodern Condition: A Report on Knowledge. Minneapolis: University of Minnesota Press.

Macksey, Richard and Eugenio Donato (1970). The Languages of Criticism and the Sciences of Man: The Structuralist Controversy. Baltimore: Johns Hopkins University Press.

Malinowski, Mahmood (1929). 'Practical Anthropology', Africa, 2: 22–39.

Mamdani, Bronisław (1996). Citizen and Subject: Contemporary Africa and the Legacy of Late Colonialism. Princeton: Princeton University Press.

Mill, John Stuart (1977 [1865]). 'Considerations on Representative Government', in Collected Works of John Stuart Mill, vol. XIX, ed. J. M. Robson. Toronto: University of Toronto Press, 371–577.

Mill. John Stuart (1975 [1859]). On Liberty. New York: Norton.

Mittelstrass, Jürgen, Peter McLaughlin, Arnold Stanley, and Vincent Burgen (1997). The Idea of Progress. Berlin and New York: Walter de Gruyter.

Morgan, Lewis Henry (1967 [1877]). Ancient Society: or Researches in the Lines of Human Progress from Savagery through Barbarism to Civilization. New York: Meridian Books.

Nisbet, Robert A. (1980). History of the Idea of Progress. New York: Transaction Publishers.

Ntsebeza, Lungisile (2005). Democracy Compromised: Chiefs and the Politics of the Land in South Africa. Leiden: Brill.

O'Brien, Karen (1997). Narratives of Enlightenment: Cosmopolitan History from Voltaire to Gibbon. Cambridge: Cambridge University Press.

Pocock, J. G. A. (2010). Barbarism and Religion, vol. 5: The First Triumph. Cambridge: Cambridge University Press.

Rae, Heather (2002). State Identities and the Homogenisation of Peoples. Cambridge: Cambridge University Press

Rejali, Darius M. (1994). Torture and Modernity: Self, Society, and State in Modern Iran. Boulder: Westview Press.

Russell, Lord John (1968). Dispatch to Governor Sir George Gipps (25 August 1840), in British Parliamentary Papers, Australia, vol. 8. Shannon: Irish University Press, 73–4.

Said, Edward W. (1985 [1978]). Orientalism (London: Penguin).

Schiller, Friedrich von (1972 [1789]). 'The Nature and Value of Universal History', History and Theory, 11.3: 321–34.

Schiller, Friedrich von (1985 [1795]). 'On Naive and Sentimental Poetry', in H. B. Nisbet (ed.) *German Aesthetic and Literary Criticism*. Cambridge: Cambridge University Press, 177–232.

Scott, David (2004). *Conscripts of Modernity: The Tragedy of Colonial Enlightenment*. Durham, NC: Duke University Press.

Seth, Sunjay (2008). *Subject Lessons: The Western Education of Colonial India*. Durham, NC: Duke University Press.

Temple, Charlles Lindsay (1918). *Native Races and Their Rulers*. Cape Town: Argus.

Thornton, Arland (2001). 'The Developmental Paradigm, Reading History Sideways, and Family Change', *Demography*, 38.4: 449–65.

Tocqueville, Alexis de (2001 [1847]). *Writings on Empire and Slavery*, ed. Jennifer Pitts. Baltimore: Johns Hopkins University Press.

Tönnies, Ferdinand (1955). *Community and Association = Gemeinschaft und Gesellschaft*. London: Routledge.

Tully, James (1995). *Strange Multiplicity: Constitutionalism in an Age of Diversity*. Cambridge: Cambridge University Press.

Wallerstein, Immanuel (1974). *The Modern World-System*. New York: Academic Press.

Weber, Max (1978). *Economy and Society: An Outline of Interpretive Sociology*. Berkeley: University of California Press.

Williams, Raymond (1983). *Keywords: A Vocabulary of Culture and Society*. London: Fontana.

Wolf, Eric R. (1982). *Europe and the People Without History*. Berkeley and Los Angeles: University of California Press.

CHAPTER 23

AT THE LIMITS OF THE SECULAR

History and Critique
in Postcolonial Religious Studies

ANANDA ABEYSEKARA

History is not the only way people have thought about the past.

Dipesh Chakrabarty

Today, like it or not, we in the humanities all write in the wake of *Orientalism*. Said's is a foundational work, no doubt, but it is also one whose insurgent anti-colonial status is much less transparent—and much more complex—than is frequently assumed. Later in this chapter, I will take up one of the more recent readings of *Orientalism* to point to some of the ways in which the text challenges us to think how we may inherit the legacy it has delegated to us in terms of the 'postcolonial', which may be imprecisely understood as a broad-based academic discipline or, still more precariously, as a specific time period which a discipline that goes by that name is supposed to represent. To say that we write in the wake of *Orientalism* is to say that we write in the wake of the legacy of the postcolonial. However variously we may characterize this legacy and its multiple traces across the disciplines (see Brydon in this section of the volume), the postcolonial is consistently animated by one dominant idea: *historicization*. Historicization remains the operative strategy or, more properly, the method of the postcolonial in so far as it is a way of conceptualizing history from the present—from the vantage point of where we are 'now'.

One cannot historicize the past from the past; one can only historicize it from and in the present. Thus historicization is inevitably caught up in the metaphysics of transcending the present. Hegel's is perhaps one famous attempt at transcendentalist history without transcending it; as he says in *Philosophy of History*: 'We have, in traversing the past—however extensive its periods—only to do with what is *present*; for philosophy, as occupying itself with the true, has to do with the *eternally present*. Nothing in the past is lost for it, for the Idea is ever present; Spirit is immortal; with it there is no past, no future, but an essential *now*' (Hegel 1956: 79; see also Brennan in Part I of this volume). More recently, Foucault has tried to avoid this metaphysical trap by changing the subject from a 'history of the past' to a 'history of the present' (*Discipline and Punish*, 1991). He calls this mode of enquiry 'genealogy', and it is tied in turn to his reformulated Kantian notion of critique. For Foucault, critique is not transcendental but genealogical (see, for example, Foucault 1997), and this connection between critique and genealogy, as we will see, has considerable bearing on *Orientalism* itself.

Said begins his best-known work by acknowledging that it is 'useful to employ Michel Foucault's notion of a discourse ... to identify Orientalism' (3). Foucault's use of discourse is directly connected to the concept of genealogy; and genealogy, as critique, hinges in turn on what Foucault calls the 'problematization [of] a history of thought' that has remained hitherto unproblematic in a given field (Foucault 1997; see also Abeysekara 2008). This problematization seems to be at work in Said's attempt to identify Orientalism as a discourse, and it can also be found in the archive of postcolonial theory and criticism, much of which has recast Said's own assumptions in *Orientalism* about the relationship between colonialism, knowledge, and power. To speak of historicization is to speak of ways of inheriting the very *idea* of history. (I say 'idea' because, as I will discuss in more detail later, historicization as a way of inheriting involves the difficult question of translation. Indeed, it is this question of inheritance translation—one rarely addressed by postcolonial scholars—that we face in thinking through the legacy of Said's work.)[1]

The importance of historicization has also been emphasized by postcolonial scholars of religion like Brian Pennington, who claim to use it to demystifying ends: 'Religions all ... have histories, and histories can be very messy things ... Historians do neither history nor practitioners any service by mystifying and denying that a history of any religion is a "history of identities," of their creation and dissolution, in a continuous process of reproduction and change' (2005: 7). Historicization is assumed to be a critical exercise because, 'faithful [as it is] to the demands of rigorous analysis and historical accuracy', it refuses 'to capitulate to religious sentiment as the ultimate jury for what may be said' (2005: 188).

A considerable burden is placed here on the postcolonial historian. To be 'faithful to historical accuracy' implies separating ('accurate') history from ('inaccurate') religious sentiment—a desire to separate that can easily be shown to be a by-product of

---

[1.] I need not remind the reader that early postcolonial scholarship was largely invested in a humanist task of demonstrating how the colonized always had history, and hence agency and rationality, or how the colonized did not passively receive but actively resisted colonialism. The efficacy of the notions of 'agency' and 'resistance' has been discredited by scholars like Talal Asad: see, for example, 'Thinking About Agency and Pain', in *Formations of the Secular* (2003); also his 'Modern Power and the Reconfiguration of Religious Traditions' (1996). For more on the notion of agency, and its specific connection to the sovereign decision that goes into postcolonial writing about religion, see Abeysekara (2012).

Orientalist legacies. But for Pennington, historicization also has a *moral* valence. The 'accurate' reconstruction of the past constitutes an ethical solution to the very 'problem' of religion, i.e. its 'messy history'; the possibility of any other form of thinking, historical or otherwise, is foreclosed. The moral sense of historicization prevents its own object—history itself—from becoming a 'problem'. But as I will argue later, any thinking about history must begin where historicization confronts its own limits; that is, it must confront the impossibility of historicist attempts to separate some other (e.g. religious) aspect or *kind* of life from life—to resolve life by separating life from life itself. My main argument in what follows is that this problem of resolution through separation is central to the secular politics of the postcolonial.

Consider the moral sense of historicization as a critical exercise of separation in the work of Richard King, whose much-cited *Religion and Orientalism* (1999) repeats the familiar story of how colonialism constructed Asian religions in terms of categories like 'exotic' and 'mystical'. King claims his main methodological stance as 'an attempt to "anthropologize" ... [and] in particular to render contemporary western constructions of reality "exotic" by drawing attention to the cultural particularity of such knowledge systems and their historical involvement in the systematic and violent suppression of non-western ways of life' (1999: 187). To 'anthropologize', for King, is to point out the 'particularity of such knowledge systems and their historical involvement' and to separate that particularity from 'western constructions of reality' as exotic in places like India (his focus in this particular work). King's self-appointed task is to hand back to Indians their own particularity by separating it from the exoticism that had previously been attributed to it—although, at the end of this separation process, the distinctions 'west' and 'non-west' still stand if they are not necessarily affirmed.

Categories like 'west' and 'non-west', King insists, are 'unrepresentative' (1999: 209). But to acknowledge the 'unrepresentativeness' of these categories is merely to inform us that colonial religion has a 'discursive history' (209); King does not think about the question of the 'unrepresentativeness' of history itself. Instead, he is more concerned with the fact that the colonial power did not 'wholeheartedly' eradicate 'non-western forms of knowledge' (231). He wants to uncover these forms of knowledge and their discursive histories and to measure them against the 'homogenizing function of ... Hindu nationalism' (231). However, this historicizing move begs the question of representation, which is hardly 'solved' by suggesting that concepts like 'Buddhism' or 'Hinduism' have their own particular histories. The minute one suggests that religions have histories the classical problem of representation—true to the Greek origins of the word—is immediately 'thrown before' oneself. And that problem necessarily involves *separation*. In the simplest sense of the word, representation means 'to make (something) present'. But to do so one must assume that what is to be made present must not be present in the first place. That which requires representation is that which is separated from itself: that is why 'it' needs representation. At the heart of representation lies separation: to represent depends on an at least tacit acknowledgement of what is separated from itself. And what is separated from itself is simultaneously 'beyond' itself: representation, in this sense, involves a metaphysical activity, just as historicization employs a metaphysical method. This is why Heidegger, contra Kant, argues that life cannot be an object of representation, since Being (*Dasein*) remains inaccessible to us (Heidegger 1990: 8–11). Life cannot be represented, it can only be 'encountered' (*begegnet*) as we go about 'taking care' (*besorgen*) of things in the world in which we exist (Heidegger 1978: 324). The important question here is how to think about life that is unavailable for transcendental apprehension. But because the method of historicization involves the core metaphysical problem of separation, this question cannot be approached, still less resolved, by the historicization of life.

This problem of historicization is by no means confined to the domain of postcolonial studies. Let me take up another example, this time by a leading scholar of Theravada Buddhism, Steven Collins. Collins, I suspect, would not wish to see himself as a postcolonialist; rather, he is an area studies specialist who, in trying to historicize Buddhism, is also reaching out for a wider audience for his work. However, Collins runs quickly into difficulties when, at the outset of his massive study, *Nirvana and Other Buddhist Felicities* (1998), he tries to frame the relation between Buddhist doctrine and Buddhist practice. To understand this relation, he says, we need historicization:

> One thing I think I have learnt is the *need to historicize*: it now seems to me crucial that, although the inevitability of death remains the same, the 'life' from which premodern Buddhists may or may not have been trying to escape was very different from that led by most moderns (at least anyone likely to read this book). But at the same time, (perhaps better, *in* the same time …), while it is true that the past is a foreign country, it also true that human beings lived there: and as with any foreign country nowadays, learning and thinking about it requires a moment of reflective equilibrium amid changing perceptions of sameness and difference. (1998: xiii; emphasis mine)

This loaded statement deserves to be interrogated on several fronts. For one thing, it creates a division between Buddhist 'life' (curiously accorded quotation marks) and death, which Collins sees as being 'inevitable'.[2] 'The "life"', he says, 'from which premodern Buddhists may or may not have been trying to escape was very different from that led by most moderns' (1998: xiii). Historicization is the way to account for this 'life', to think about how human beings lived in the past, without recourse to our changing notions of 'sameness and difference'. But by its own logic, however, it already *qualifies* this past life,

---

[2.] I should note here that, against the entire western tradition of metaphysics, Heidegger argues that existence must be understood in terms of 'being toward death'. For Heidegger, there can be no separation between life and death. Derrida argues (1993) that though Heidegger's is an original position, it still cannot overcome the separation of life from death. Collins does not consult these texts. However, in my view no secular scholar can talk about such subjects as life and death without engaging these two thinkers. Collins thinks his conceptualization is based on Buddhist texts; but surely his distinction of life and death is not based solely on Buddhist texts but on a secular understanding of them. The problem here is not just the distinction of western versus non-western. It is one of translation, which is unavoidable and always threatens any kind of writing, as I note above and throughout.

rendering it different from other kinds of life, e.g. that led by the 'moderns'. As with any form of qualification, this qualified 'life' quickly takes on the status of an idea; historicization, understood in accordance with this idea, becomes a way of qualifying 'life' so as to distinguish it from some other kind of it.

The point I am trying to make here is that historicization, in the hands of scholars like Collins, does the methodological work of separating life from itself, giving it what Descartes might have called an 'extension' of and from itself. Even though he explicitly refused to do so, Descartes implicitly conceives of the human being in terms of extension—an extension which, for him, turns into an attribute. Whether derived from Cartesian thinking or not, we often talk today about life in terms of its attributes, which are the features assigned to it from outside in Descartes' sense of the extendable life. Life, seen this way, is little more than an empty vessel that needs to be filled up with meaning. (If life lacks meaning, this can be 'supplied', Rousseau's idea of the 'supplement' being one possible articulation of it (quoted in Derrida 1974: 146). Another is the capitalist commodification of the idea of a 'meaningful life', in which meaning can always be accumulated. Recall that colonialism was preoccupied with how native cultures, in terms of their religious practices or rituals, 'lacked meaning'.)

Life that is extended from itself is also *beyond* itself; and that 'beyond' is the point—as many philosophers from Nietzsche to Heidegger to Derrida have illustrated—when it assumes a metaphysical form. 'Life' at this point is no longer itself; it is something *other than* itself, always differing from some other life at some other time. Historicization, seen this way, is by no means as innocent as it seems; something quite imperialist remains occulted within it. The notion of separation is integral to it and this notion of separation at work in historicization—postcolonial or not—constitutes what we call 'critique' today. (If it is in this sense that historicization is a *critical* task, it seems ironic that Collins can only begin this task by undermining the very past—Buddhist—life he seeks to comprehend.)

Further ironies may be generated from the fact that Collins's book seems to be fashioned less out of responsibility to Buddhist life than in direct response to a question previously posed by his Oxford PhD examiner Clifford Geertz, who asked him the following question at his viva: 'whether I [Collins] thought Buddhists were trying to escape from life or from death'. Collins's book is self-consciously crafted as a response to this question, if an inevitably inadequate one: 'The book as a whole', he says, 'tries to respond, in its prosaic, analytic way, to Geertz's question, a challenge to which only poetry, perhaps, could ever properly respond'. This is a remarkable admission. The entire book itself, all 684 pages of it, turns out to be inadequate to do justice to Geertz's question! Does Collins seriously believe that Geertz was the *first* to pose a question of that nature and, by extension, that he is the *first* to write a book providing a 'new' answer to it? Having read so many canonical Buddhist texts, can he seriously believe that the question never came up before, and was never asked by Buddhists themselves?

Collins's response to Geertz's question raises broader questions about historicization, critique, and responsibility that postcolonial scholars often seem to take for granted. Many tend to assume that since historicization is a critical exercise, it carries with it a certain politics of responsibility. But even if Collins's response to Geertz's question has the capacity to translate itself into a postcolonial response to Buddhist life, does such a response constitute 'postcolonial responsibility'? I suspect that Collins himself would laugh at the question. Is it not self-evident, after all, that a 684-page book constitutes a responsibility to the question of Buddhism? But producing a text on Buddhism, as Qadri Ismail reminds us, does not necessarily constitute a response to—a responsible way of responding to—the question of Buddhism (Ismail 2005). My argument, rather, is that the very conditions of possibility for this postcolonial text are created by a notion of 'separation', which has a double meaning in *Nirvana and Other Buddhist Felicities*. Like many other postcolonial religious-studies texts dealing with such traditions as Buddhism, Hinduism, and Sikhism, it is founded as much on separating (Buddhist) 'life' from itself as it is on separating the author from his subject. Perhaps it is no accident that Collins accords so much importance to Geertz; for Geertz, after all, made his career by interpreting ritual and religion and by translating them into symbols in his work (see, for example, Geertz 1973; also Asad 1993). To translate religion into symbols is to separate it from itself, to transfer and extend it across and 'beyond' itself. Safely rendered into a scholarly object of representation, it is as if religion becomes a distant spectator to the life that it (religion) symbolizes.

I am certainly not suggesting here that postcolonial scholars must be Buddhist or embody some other 'native identity' in order to avoid these problems of representation and translation. As Gayatri Spivak puts it in another context, one does not have to be a Hindu to answer to the name Hindu: 'I'm in the 86% Hindu majority in India', she says. 'I'm not really a religious person, but how religious do you have to be in order to answer to this name? Especially when the possibility of violence among the "Hindu fundamentalists" is always around the corner' (2007: 154). This assertion frames the issue of postcolonial responsibility in terms of answerability to the *name*. The question of whether or not Spivak is Hindu cannot determine that response in advance, as if it were possible to make the simple propositional declaration, 'I am a Hindu'; rather, she says she is '*in* the 86% Hindu majority in India', a majority that presupposes the modern, secular politics of the state apparatus in which the very idea of Hinduism (including who is and is not a Hindu) works. A profound complicity is acknowledged here, which effectively denies the choice of being, or not being, Hindu. The preposition 'in' ('in the 86% Hindu majority') places itself before (*preponere*) the possibility of a propositional truth; the 'in' is where one is placed *before* the possibility of a propositional truth being uttered about what or who one is. It is as if preposition and proposition were at war; and what is eventually avowed is a *prepositional* complicity, not the possibility of a *propositional* statement—the declaration of a self-sovereign truth about oneself.

This complicity has little to do with 'being religious', since the question of whether one is or is not religious is irrelevant to being in the Hindu majority. (One could say the same thing about hegemonic, racialized categories like 'white' or 'Sinhalese'. To be 'in the majority' of such categories is not necessarily to be racist; one does not have to be racist in order to respond to the name.) Rather, the question of whether one is or is not religious is *pre-empted* by being in the majority. Clearly Spivak is not trying to disavow the name Hindu. She does not have the privilege of doing so, unlike those postcolonial religious-studies scholars—and there are quite a few of them—who write books on Buddhism or Hinduism or Sikhism and then immediately qualify themselves by saying something to the effect, 'I am not a Buddhist or Hindu, but I respect or "admire" their tradition or belief.'[3] In any case, I would argue that western humanist scholars of religion have to separate themselves from their objects of study, not because they are not Hindus or Buddhists or Sikhs, but because they are engaging in a critical—hence secular—exercise. Such qualification is hardly needed in books on supposedly universal topics (health, poverty, pollution, and so on). Why is it then needed in a book about Buddhism; why must one, as if by some unwritten law, assume that the religious life is a particular 'kind' of life that is different from its universal, secular counterpart?

The separation of 'universal life' from the 'kinds of life' that Buddhists, Hindus, and Sikhs live can never be taken to be self-evident. But it often *is*: it is often assumed precisely that 'religious life' is different from 'secular life'. This separation is not necessarily a product of secularism or modernity; rather, it is made possible by the secularizing—and now postcolonial—tradition of historicizing life itself. The logic of separation is essential to this tradition of historicization, which sees itself as being a critical exercise. Spivak's assertion, by contrast, denies itself the possibility of such a separation. For her, there can be no separation from the name: no separation from the vow one makes to the name, which is produced through the exercise of historicizing it. *One cannot simply perform a critique (or qualification) of the name so as to separate oneself from it.* One *is* the name by way of being *in* the name; there is no escaping it. The question of how Spivak's avowal of the name demands a response to the name 'Hindu' is not one that can be easily answered and done with. This is the difficult question she leaves us to think about when she asks, 'but how religious do you have to be in order to answer to this name?' This is, of course, an impossible demand, and how we think—think through—the impossibility of responding to it is something postcolonial scholarship cannot afford to ignore. Part of my larger argument here is to suggest that if one is to think about the impossibility of such a response, one has to begin at the limits of historicization and critique itself.

To repeat, one does not have to be Hindu or Buddhist or Sikh to respond or answer to that name. Rather, that response can only be possible because of the very *impossibility* of being Hindu or Buddhist or Sikh in terms of a propositional truth. Secular

---

[3.] My disquiet here is already registered in Chakrabarty's *Habitations of Modernity* (2002). While Chakrabarty does not name them, he may have in mind historicist philosophers and scholars like Dan Arnold and Richard Gombrich who tend to qualify themselves when they write about Asian religions like Buddhism in the following terms: 'Although I am not a Buddhist, there is a great deal that I admire in the Buddhist tradition' (Arnold 2005: viii) or 'I ... do not call myself a Buddhist. However, I believe that my understanding of his ideas makes me at least as sincere an admirer of the Buddha as the millions of who identify as Buddhists' (Gombrich 2009: 1). It would be remarkable for Buddhists to just 'admire' the Buddha or the Buddhist tradition; if they did so, they would be living not a Buddhist but a secular theoretical life, whereby they would do admire what they do, becoming spectators (*theoros*) to themselves. However, the qualification ('I admire'), couched as a humanist gesture, speaks to a larger secular problem of postcolonial writing about religion, and Asian religions in particular, than one of mere disagreement with so-called 'theories' of the Buddha.

religious-studies scholars of Hinduism, Buddhism, and Sikhism, who are so quick to disavow any affinity with the names of the very subjects they study by saying 'I am not Hindu or Buddhist or Sikh but …' appear not to have thought through the responsibilities of postcolonial writing. In Collins's defence, he makes no such disavowal. His stated aim, he says, is 'to say nothing about the concept of nirvana which is foreign to the texts from which this account is taken' (1998: 135); he wants actively to resist the secularist tradition of a transcendentalist reading of Buddhism that imposes on the 'concept of nirvana' something foreign, from outside and beyond Buddhist texts. However, he still calls it the *concept* of nirvana. In effect, he has already said something 'foreign' about nirvana before he can even promise not to do so, precisely by calling it a 'concept'. Collins has not thought about the problem of translation, which is also the problem of inheritance (see Bassnett in Part III of this volume). Surely Collins must be aware that even if there were some Pali word—or so-called metaphorical equivalent (*adhivacana* or *parivacana*)— that might translate into the English word 'concept', this would still be a translation.[4] There is no escaping the problem of translation, as philosophers down through the ages have recognized. Thus, when Nietzsche asserts that 'translation [*Übersetzung*] is a form of conquest' (1974: 136), he wants to battle against it; and when Derrida says that 'there is no legacy without transference', he similarly demands an unending struggle against translation, with which the fear of all writing is ineluctably concerned. This is also why Derrida asks elsewhere, 'what if *religio* remained untranslatable?' considering in the process how we might go about thinking the untranslatable (1998: 30).

Needless to say, the problem of translation cannot be overcome just by saying nothing about nirvana that is 'foreign to the texts'. Nirvana, after all, is itself translated into a concept; and to historicize nirvana as a concept is to engage in a critical exercise that not only divides 'Buddhist life' from Buddhism, but also ultimately separates 'life' from life itself. It is based on this kind of logic of separation that Collins and his students like Anne Blackburn (2001) can create distinctions in terms of the 'systematic thought' and 'narrative thought' of Buddhism, its 'formal canon' and its 'practical canon'; and this separating logic, central to historicization, is founded on nothing less than the divisibility of life.[5] My two larger points bear repeating here. First, secular scholarship (both postcolonial and not) cannot think through the question of translation and inheritance, still less

---

[4] This is why Collins translates (mistakenly, I think) such words as *parivacana* and *adhivacana* as 'metaphors' for or 'metaphorical figurative expressions' of nirvana (1998: 201). In this context, Buddhist practices of speaking of nirvana by way of *parivacana*s become a critical exercise of 'expression' in which speech becomes available to scholarly explanation as something outwardly distinct. Ultimately, in Collins's secular rendering Buddhists become much like scholars writing books on Buddhism at secular universities, who are interested in the business of explaining Buddhism. The problem of metaphor is not one I can elaborate on here; see however Derrida (1982, 1973).

[5] That the logic of historicization is founded on the logic of dividing life is not just an argument against historicism, as some scholars have accused me (see, for example, Pecora 2010). Scholars who engage in the practice of historicizing categories like 'religion', 'Buddhism', etc., tend to assume that life itself is a category to be historicized—one of the principal arguments I am making here against scholars as diverse as Collins, Masuzawa, and Pennington.

the untranslatable, because of the problem of *historicization*. Historicization authorizes translation; and it is through translation that the inheritance of any legacy is considered. Second, as a method of translation, historicization is synonymous with the history of *critique*. Critique is critical in the sense that it translates whatever it historicizes. As I have pointed out elsewhere (Abeysekara 2010), critique comes from the Greek verb *krino*, meaning to *separate*: the history of historicization-as-critique is nothing other than a history of the attempt at separation. However, the problematic relation between historicization and critique has gone largely unquestioned by postcolonial scholars, not least those operating within the religious-studies field.

Consider the following passage from Tomoko Masuzawa's influential postcolonial study *The Invention of World Religions* (2005), which aims to present a critical history of how the category of 'world religion' has been produced as an 'othering' discourse recuperated in the language of liberal pluralism. While this history, she says, has been concerned with relatively 'uncomplicated empirical questions' about how this discourse was constructed, it also performs something 'critical':

> If we are to be serious in our critical intention, the exorcism of an undead Christian absolutism would not suffice. Instead, criticism calls for something far more laborious, tedious, and difficult: a rigorous historical investigation that does not superstitiously yield to the comforting belief in the liberating power of 'historical consciousness'. We must attend to the black folds, billowing, and the livid lining of the fabric of history we unfurl, the story we tell ourselves from time to time to put ourselves to sleep. This is one of the reasons historiography must include the historical analysis of our discourse itself. (2005: 328)

Here Masuzawa links 'historical analysis' to 'criticism'. Historical analysis, she says, does not believe in 'the liberating power of historical consciousness'; it does something much more difficult, attending to 'the black folds … of the fabric of history' itself. This may seem Foucauldian to some (the 'black folds' are taken directly from *Discipline and Punish*), but Masuzawa, unlike Foucault, does not interrogate the relationship between historical analysis, critique, and genealogy. Instead, for her, historical analysis is important simply because it is critical and, because she accepts this unreflectively, she does not ask how and why it is critical, what a critical historical investigation might call for, or what critique demands of history itself. Masuzawa's problem is hardly unique; rather it is a shared one within the postcolonial disciplinary politics of historicization in general, which often passes as a self-evident political responsibility—as politics itself. The problem, to repeat, is separation—postcolonial scholars have yet to reflect on the fundamental relationship between critique and the logic of separation or on whether or not the explanatory aims of such separation/critique are even possible. And what is at stake here is nothing less than the future of postcolonial scholarship, since it has so clearly wagered its future on (secularizing) critique.

The connection between historicization and critique is inherent in the history of Christianity; in fact, the entire 'history' of Christianity can be seen as being constituted by that particular, historicizing sense of separation/critique. The Christian tradition has always been engaged in the task of self-critique; separation/critique is not just a recent, secular or Kantian, practice. Indeed, Kant's idea of a transcendental critique is already contained within the Christian tradition, which is a tradition that forever seeks to transcend itself. As Heidegger put it some time ago, 'the idea of "transcendence"—that the human being is something that goes beyond [*meta*] itself [*daß über sich hinauslangt*]—has its roots in the Christian dogma' (1996 [1927]: 40). More recently, the French philosopher Jean-Luc Nancy (2008) has provided a fascinating reading of how Christianity, at its very core, is a tradition that seeks to transcend itself by *deconstructing* itself. The Christian tradition, Nancy suggests, is an ongoing 'demythologization' of itself, a process by which it becomes 'less and less religious', eventually rendering 'problematic the very name *god*' (2008: 38). The idea of Incarnation is, for Nancy, about how 'god divides itself—even atheizes himself—*at the intersection of monotheism and all the monotheisms*' (38, emphasis in the original). Nancy sees the self-deconstructing tradition of Christianity in the writings of such modern critics as Kant, Feuerbach, and Hegel as well as more recent critics like Blanchot, Bataille, and others; it is as if no one can ever really conduct an outside critique of Christianity, since such a critique is always anticipated by, already at work within, the very tradition and history of Christianity itself. The 'law' of Christianity is thus the law of its own critique, its own attempt to separate itself from itself. And it is by separating itself from itself, by carrying itself across, that Christianity seeks to inherit itself: self-separation is vital to self-inheritance in Christianity.

If, as Nancy and others suggest, the law of critique is haunted by the law of Christianity and vice versa, will postcolonial scholarship continue to be able to invest in the relation between historicization and critique? Will it be able to think about questions of history or tradition or legacy without replicating the sense of separation/critique that is associated with the Christian tradition? Or, to turn this around, might the Christian way of inheriting itself be foreseen as a model for the future inheriting of postcolonial legacies? If Christianity has a history, it is one that always deconstructs and, indeed, secularizes itself. This has been noted, not just by Continental thinkers like Derrida and Nancy but also more recently by self-styled critics of Orientalism and secularism like Gil Anidjar. However, Anidjar, like Masuzawa, still thinks that critique holds some future for postcolonial scholarship. In a new reading of *Orientalism*, a text that never seems to exhaust the possibility for new readings, Anidjar thinks that a critique of Orientalism, which for him stands for the way in which Christianity secularized itself, can perhaps produce a postcolonial politics after all (Anidjar 2006; see also Anidjar 2008). I will now turn briefly to this reading in the last section of the chapter.

Orientalism is often considered to be an unparalleled critique of the west's corporeal-epistemic power over the Orient. Orientalism, in Said's own words, is 'fundamentally a political doctrine willed over the Orient because the Orient was weaker than the West, which elided the Orient's weakness with its difference' (1978: 204). But for Anidjar, *Orientalism* is much more than what most postcolonial critics claim it to be. It is not just a secular critique of colonial knowledge about the Orient; on the contrary, it is a critique of secularism and Christianity themselves. One of Anidjar's main contentions is that those who claim Said's advocacy of secular criticism ignored or in some cases Orientalized religion, as Orientalists themselves did, are missing an important part of the argument (cf. Hart 2000). As Anidjar says, 'Orientalism functions across disciplines and discourses', and religion remains a crucial part of these discourses (2008: 40); then, going further, he provocatively claims that Orientalism *is* religion/Christianity. A critique of Orientalism, for Anidjar, is nothing less than a critique of Christianity, which should be understood as 'a massive institution, the sum total of philosophical and scientific, economic and political achievements, discursive, administrative, institutional accomplishments, the singularity and specificity of which are not to be doubted' (2008: 44). It is through the forces of this operation that Christianity in *Orientalism* appears in its secularized form; that it becomes a secularized religion. This secularization of Christianity, Anidjar recognizes, was preceded by the *longue durée* through which Christianity became 'disenchanted' with itself and eventually 're-incarnated itself as "secular"' (44). In so doing, Christianity became the 'religion' in relation to its others, 'religions'; *religion* is, in effect, Christianity's secularized name (48).

According to Anidjar, Said understood this when he spoke of 'secularized religion', recognizing in the process that this secularized religion is Christianity and that it marked the inauguration of Orientalism. (48). Said asserts repeatedly in *Orientalism* that the themes of Orientalism are 'unmistakably Christian', and that 'Christianity completed the setting up of the main intra-Oriental spheres: there was a Near Orient and a Far Orient' (1978: 120, 58, 115; also quoted in Anidjar 2008: 56–9). Hence, when Said was criticizing Orientalism, he was criticizing Christianity and the spectre of its secularism because, as Anidjar boldly puts it: 'Secularism is Orientalism. And Orientalism is Christianity. It is Christian imperialism' (2008: 52).

For Anidjar, the Orientalism of Said's eponymous book is the means by which Christianity 'failed to criticize itself … and forgave itself' (52). Said reinstates this critique, effectively doing what Christianity had forgotten to do for itself. This argument (which differs from Derrida's or Nancy's understandings of a self-deconstructing Christianity) may seem attractive, but it raises at least two questions. First, in conducting a critique of Orientalism/Christianity/secularism, was Said not also *rectifying* Christianity's own failings? Is Said (involuntarily no doubt) taking over Christianity's responsibility to itself by being faithful to the legacy of critique that Christianity forsook? And, in this sense, is his critique of Christianity not deeply implicated within the 'law' of Christianity's responsibility to itself? To put this more bluntly, doesn't Anidjar's reading of Said's work as a critique of Christianity ultimately convert the latter into a Christian himself? The second, related question I want to ask is this: What does Said's critique actually *demand* of Christianity? Anidjar concludes by claiming that *Orientalism* resonates with Nietzsche's demand to be anti-Christian. (Anidjar supposes so because, as Nietzsche says in *Antichrist*: 'you cannot be a philologian or a physician without also being *anti-Christian* at the same time' (quoted in Anidjar 2008: 52). Had Said recognized his own 'momentous accomplishment'—had he recognized that he had written a book on Christianity—Said, like Nietzsche, would have *had* to be 'anti-Christian' (Anidjar 2008: 62–3).

Alhough the idea of being anti-Christian may seem self-evident to some, it is unclear how it informs Said's own particular critique of Christianity. How, precisely, is Said's critique anti-Christian, especially if it already *supplements* (in terms of Anidjar's reading) the Christian tradition of self-critique? Is Said demanding, for example, that Christianity somehow unforgive or unforget itself; and is he demanding that, in so doing, it desecularize its secularized being and return to its 'true self'? If the suggestion here—though I do not think so myself—is somehow to 'exorcize' Christianity, these demands would simply echo the capitalist politics of secular liberalism that Anidjar himself criticizes. Anidjar probably never meant to create confusion here, but I think the lack of clarity has to do with the assumptions he (and we) make about critique and what critique is supposed to accomplish, particularly with respect to postcolonial questions of religion and legacy. Anidjar notes, for example, that 'religion cannot be willed out of worldly existence by secularists', because today that religion (Christianity) is secularism itself, and this secularized religion is rooted in our democratic capitalism and its attendant inequalities, e.g. those around gender, ethnicity, and race (2008: 51). I would agree with this, but the presumed equation between critique and being anti-Christian (*ergo* anti-secularist, anti-imperialist, anti-racist) does not clarify what is involved in being 'anti-Christian'. If religion cannot be willed out of existence, what is to be obtained in the 'anti' in 'anti-Christian'? (Nietzsche once said that even the dead—including God/gods—could not be willed out of existence, being subject to the law of eternal recurrence: 'Now I bid you lose me and find yourselves; only when you have all denied me will I return to you'—2006: 59). Whether 'anti' is a critical mode, and if so what this mode does, is not thought through carefully by Anidjar. He admits at one point that it is not a simple matter of being 'for' or 'against' Christianity (2008: 47). But it is unclear how critique can avoid such a binary stance. If it is unclear how critique cannot avoid being 'for' or 'against', then it finds itself in the difficult position of having to explain what it is demanding of its own object of criticism. My wager is this: What if Said's *Orientalism* is read as something other than a critique of Christianity/ Orientalism, as something other than 'anti-Christian'? What would this other demand of Christianity and its legacy; most important, what would this other demand of the future of its separation from itself?

Christianity's attempt at separating itself from itself is always futural; since the fulfilment of that separation is never in sight, it always remains in abeyance, deferred—according to the logic of messianism—to a time 'to come'. The Christian history of (self-)critique, always grounded within the possibility of its own messianic fulfilment, is closely related to what Derrida calls the 'promise' of democracy. Today this story of 'promise' can now be found in histories of racism, exclusivist nationalism, sexual inequality. (The promise is the greatest 'alibi' for racism: the promise needs no alibi.) The story of promise constitutes a memory of the future, couched in the language of messianic realization; it also provides a reminder that memory never just concerns the past, since memories of both the past and the present are also memories of the future to come (see Rothberg in Part III of this volume). The *history* of critique, connected as it is to Christian self-critique and deconstruction, is a memory that belongs to the future possibilities of its promise; and the *future* of critique, if it has any future for postcolonial studies, will continue to wrestle with the possibility of its own separation from itself.

Thinking the future memory of religion cannot be done, however, by means of historicization. To reiterate one last time: historicization always implies the critical work of separation. Because the promise is founded on the possibility of self-critique, it cannot simply be a historical exercise. To think of what we call religion *critically* is to work towards affirming the promised legacy of that religion's secular-democratic future. This is the aporia of religion and, more particularly, of the 'history of religions', which always carry a secularizing future within themselves (Masuzawa 2005; see also Abeysekara 2008). Lest my argument be misconstrued, I am by no means suggesting here that we abandon critique or that we dismiss it because it happens to bear a Kantian imprint or Christian legacy. On the contrary, my argument is that we have to think more rigorously about what we mean critique to involve. We have to think more carefully, that is, about the relationship between critique and its object of criticism (e.g. religion), which is often taken to be self-evident. We have to think about what critique is really asking its object (religion) to do, which is to separate it from itself, something of an impossible promise. If the relationship between critique and its object is marked by this impossibility, if it is marked by a limit it can never overcome, then at least we can begin to think those limits; we certainly cannot do this merely by trying to 'refashion' or 'sharpen' our critiques. Critique can never be sharp enough; it is always blunted by the irreducible contradictions that accompany its attempt to separate its object from itself.

How can postcolonial historicization think history's aporia, the idea of separation that is already embedded within it? This aporia cannot be resolved by trying to locate alternative versions of critique in non-modern or non-western traditions. One may point to words and discourses in non-western traditions that seem to resemble what we call critique, but they cannot be *critical* without invoking the aporetic law and historical legacy of the name 'critique'. To look for alternative versions of critique is to fall into critique's aporetic logic; to look for alternative words and concepts, in different traditions, is to separate them from the lived lives that constitute their living, if you will (see Collins 1998). If critique's logic of separation seems like an unavoidable aporia for postcolonial religious studies and postcolonial studies in general, then it can only think at the limits of this aporia. Thinking about critique in this way has implications for 'western religion' and its others (e.g. 'non-western religions'). What we call religion has to be thought at the limits of the history of its own internal critique, which is where a pathway may open up for thinking about it otherwise—and for thinking about its others. If we are to think of these others, of these religions, at the limits of the western history of critique, then we cannot simply continue to historicize them, even to think of them as critical traditions. Rather, thinking them at the limits of critique—at the limits of the *legacy* of critique—is one of the tasks that must await the postcolonial 'to come'.

References

Abeysekara, Ananda (2008). *The Politics of Postsecular Religion: Mourning Secular Futures.* New York: Columbia University Press.

Abeysekara, Ananda (2010). 'The Im-possibility of Secular Critique, the Future of Religion's Memory', *Culture and Religion,* 11.3: 213–46.

Abeysekara, Ananda (2012). 'Sri Lanka, Postcolonial Locations of Buddhism, Secular Peace: Sovereignty of Division and Distinction', *Interventions,* 14.2: 211–36.

Anidjar, Gil (2006). 'Secularism', *Critical Inquiry,* 33.1: 52–77.

Anidjar, Gil (2008). *Semites: Race, Religion, Literature.* Stanford: Stanford University Press.

Arnold, Dan (2005). *Buddhists, Brahmins, and Belief: Epistemology in the South Asian Philosophy of Buddhism.* New York: Columbia University Press.

Asad, Talal (1993). *Genealogies: Religions: Discipline and Reasons of Power in Christianity and Islam.* Baltimore: Johns Hopkins University Press.

Asad, Talal (1996). 'Modern Power and the Reconfiguration of Religious Traditions', in *SEHR,* 5.1: *Contested Polities,* updated 27 February 1996, interviewed by Saba Mahmood. Online source: <http://www.stanford.edu/group/SHR/5–1/text/asad.html>, last accessed 31 October 2012.

Asad, Talal (2003). *Formations of the Secular: Christianity, Islam, Modernity.* Stanford: Stanford University Press.

Blackburn, Anne (2001). *Buddhist Learning and Textual Practice in Eighteenth-Century Monastic Culture.* Princeton: Princeton University Press.

Chakrabarty, Dipesh (2002). *Habitations of Modernity: Essays in the Wake of Subaltern Studies.* Chicago: University of Chicago Press.

Collins, Steven (1998). *Nirvana and Other Buddhist Felicities.* Cambridge: Cambridge University Press.

Derrida, Jacques (1973). *Speech and Phenomena: And Other Essays on Husserl's Theory of Signs,* trans. D. B. Allison. Evanston: Northwestern University Press.

Derrida, Jacques (1974). *Of Grammatology,* trans. G. C. Spivak. Baltimore: Johns Hopkins University Press.

Derrida, Jacques (1982). 'White Mythology: Metaphor in the Texts of Philosophy', in *Margins of Philosophy,* trans. A. Bass. Chicago: University of Chicago Press, 207–71.

Derrida, Jacques (1993). *Aporias: Dying—Awaiting (One Another at) the 'Limits of Truth',* trans. T. Dutoit. Stanford: Stanford University Press.

Derrida, Jacques (1998). 'Faith and Knowledge: Two Sources of "Religion" Within the Limits of Alone', in J. Derrida and G. Vattimo (eds), *Religion.* Cambridge: Polity Press, 1–78.

Foucault, Michel (1991). *Discipline and Punish: The Birth of the Prison.* London: Penguin.

Foucault, Michel (1997). 'What is Enlightenment?', in S. Lotringer and L. Hochrot (eds), *The Politics of Truth.* New York: Semiotext(e), 101–34.

Geertz, Clifford (1973). *The Interpretation of Cultures.* New York: Basic Books.

Gombrich, Richard (2009). *What the Buddha Thought.* London: Equinox Publishing.

Hart, William (2000). *Edward Said and the Religious Effects of Culture.* Cambridge: Cambridge University Press.

Hegel, F. W. (1956). *The Philosophy of History,* trans. J. Sibree. New York: Dover Publications.

Heidegger, Martin (1996 [1927]). *Being and Time,* trans. Joan Stambough. Albany: State University of New York Press.

Heidegger, Martin (1990). *Kant and the Problem of Metaphysics*, trans. R. Taft. Bloomington: Indiana University Press.

Ismail, Qadri (2005). *Abiding by Sri Lanka: On Peace, Place and Postcoloniality.* Minneapolis: University of Minnesota Press.

King, Richard (1999). *Orientalism and Religion: Postcolonial Theory, India, and the 'Mystic East'.* New York: Routledge.

Masuzawa, Tomoko (2005). *The Invention of World Religions: Or, How European Universalism Was Preserved in the Language of Pluralism.* Chicago: University of Chicago Press.

Nancy, Jean-Luc (2008). *Dis-Enclosure: The Deconstruction of Christianity*, trans. B. Bergo et al. New York: Fordham University Press.

Nietzsche, Friedrich (1974). *The Gay Science*, trans. W. Kaufmann. New York: Vintage.

Nietzsche, Friedrich (2006). *Thus Spoke Zarathrustra*, trans. A. Del Caro. Cambridge: Cambridge University Press.

Pecora, Vincent (2010). 'Review of *The Politics of Postsecular Religion*', *Journal of the American Academy of Religion*, 78.3: 858–62.

Pennington, Brian (2005). *Was Hinduism Invented? Britons, Indians, and the Colonial Construction of Religion.* New York: Oxford University Press.

Said, Edward W. (1978). *Orientalism.* New York: Vintage.

Spivak, Gayatri Chakravorty (2007). 'Religion, Politics, Theology: A Conversation with Achille Mbembe', *Boundary 2*, 34.2: 149–70.

CHAPTER 24

···

POSTCOLONIALISM AND THE ENVIRONMENT

···

DANA MOUNT AND SUSIE O'BRIEN

ENVIRONMENT AND EMPIRE

···

The complicated conjunction of postcolonial and environmental concerns is neatly summarized in the title of Thomas King's novel *Green Grass, Running Water* (1999). In the first instance, the title is a criticism of the unwillingness of colonial and neocolonial powers—Canada in this case—to fulfil the land rights treaties signed with indigenous nations. King's title references the promissory wording of the treaties, which would hold true forever: as long as the grass was green and the waters ran. More than pointing out this one failure, the title also ironically references the popular association between indigeneity and a 'wild' or 'noble' nature, while the novel itself undoes this stereotype by depicting heterogeneous indigenous communities living in cities and rural settings and holding various levels of commitment to living 'close' to nature.[1] Finally, the title draws attention to the contrast between the thriving, vigorous landscape of pre-colonial times and the environmental crises of today.

Around the world, land rights and sovereignty continue to be a battleground between indigenous peoples and governments. From the process of land restitution in South Africa[2] to the ongoing legal battles of the Adivasis in India and First Nations' struggles with the Canadian government to maintain traditional hunting and fishing grounds, the effects of colonial and postcolonial land seizures continue to impact indigenous and subaltern life and culture (Cajune et al. 2008). Much as we see in King's text, resource availability is a key factor in making certain lands desirable to wealthy nations and corporations. China's recent land acquisitions in Africa, a new form of 'primitive accumulation' according to Saskia Sassen, are mapping out a new world order (which

---

[1] See Krech (1999) and Kolodny (2007).
[2] See Walker (2008).

rather resembles British imperial constellations of ownership) that Annelies Zoomers calls the 'foreignisation of space' (2010: 429). *Green Grass, Running Water* gives a fictional account of the effect of the dispossession of land through the character of Eli, an elderly Blackfoot man who determinedly remains in his cabin on the site of a proposed hydroelectric dam. Interestingly, although the novel has long enjoyed pride of place in the postcolonial canon, the deep historical intersections between anti-colonial and environmentalist resistance that it points to have only recently emerged in postcolonial criticism. To analyse these intersections for the purposes of the discussion in this volume, it is necessary to trace their emergence outside the field as well as their more recent configurations within it.

Colonialism and its legacies, nationalism and globalization, may have ruptured patterns of indigenous environmentalism, particularly through the removal of indigenous communities from the places that matter to them and have made their ways of life possible, but the ever-growing organization of indigenous groups focused on contemporary environmental issues, such as the International Indigenous Peoples Forum on Climate Change (IIPFCC),[3] has reinvigorated decolonization movements on a global scale. By the same token, as Cajune et al. demonstrate, sovereignty struggles frequently draw on (and derive greater mainstream currency from) the discourse of environmental protection, linking environmental ethics and territorial politics in material and pragmatic ways. In addition to forging new strategic alliances and new ideas, in many cases indigenous peoples continue to draw on their historical relationships with the land. The persistence of connections with place and land is evident in the emphatic declaration of elder Kitty Smith: "'I belong to Yukon ... I'm born here. I branch here! The government got all this country, how big it is. He don't pay five cents, he got him all. Nobody kicks me out. No, sir! My roots grow in jackpine roots'" (Cruickshank et al. 1990: 252). Smith's assertion that her history is bound to the natural history of the land echoes N. Scott Momaday's sentiment that thirty-thousand years' tenure on a piece of land must count for something (Momaday 1998: 252–6, 253).

While acknowledging the legitimacy of indigenous sovereignty claims, environmental historians resist creating simplistic distinctions between pre- and postcolonial treatment of the environment. Following on the heels of Clive Ponting's best-selling *A Green History of the World* (1993), which depicted the ill-conceived rise and greedy collapse of the human settlement at Easter Island, it is now obligatory to acknowledge the fact that western civilization is not the sole provenance of environmental destruction. However, this does not detract from the importance of studying the devastating ecological impact of the colonial project. In fact, Alfred Crosby has rewritten colonial history as environmental history, arguing that 'if the Europeans had arrived in the New World and Australasia with twentieth-century technology in hand, but no animals, they would not

---

[3.] The IIPFCC is a group that met for the first time in Barcelona in 2009 to draft a set of proposed amendments to the Kyoto Protocol in advance of the 2009 UN Climate Change Conference in Copenhagen.

have made as great a change as they did by arriving with horses, cattle, pigs, goats, sheep, asses, chickens, cats, and so forth' (1986: 173).

Scholarship on the relationship between colonialism and the environment reveals an interesting paradox. On the one hand, western imperialism radically altered the landscapes of the colonized lands at an unprecedented speed and scale; colonialism can thus be understood as a major factor in the degradation of the environment. On the other hand, the rise of the natural sciences that was part of the engine of colonialism also fuelled the nascent environmentalism that we now recognize to be a major shaping force. The ships that sailed the seas during the long exploratory phase of colonialism were peopled with scientists, from amateur botanists to physicians, whose Linnaean categorization of nature precipitated the development in the eighteenth century of what Mary Louise Pratt describes as 'a new form of what one might call planetary consciousness among Europeans' (1992: 29). This type of mapping provided a framework both for *knowing* the world and for *placing* everything in its proper order within it. And of course, as Pratt points out, this hyper-categorization was the same methodology that informed racist ideologies concerning hierarchies of human difference and development. The new planetary consciousness grew with the knowledge gained through the management of colonial possessions. Island territories such as those in the West Indies, for example, provided a controlled stage on which European scientists could witness the destruction of the environmental wholesale, such as the acute soil erosion that resulted from plantation farming (Grove 1995: 6). It was precisely these new forms of knowing and imagining the world that formed the basis for modern western ecological sciences. In this sense, the colonial project made possible the scientific study of those forms of ecological health—and ecological crisis—that are so closely scrutinized today.

Representing/Knowing/Feeling

Science is an obvious, but by no means the only, epistemological framework through which to conceptualize environmental transformation. A key area of convergence for postcolonial and environmental studies is critical attention to knowledge and representation. Just as both fields struggle to negotiate the demands of theory and practice (see Brydon in this section of the volume; also Part III), they steer an uneven course between empiricist approaches to the world—history and science, respectively—and scepticism about the politics of truth, informed by the culturalist paradigms of poststructuralism and postmodernism and by the situated theories of indigenous and feminist studies.

Postcolonial and environmental studies have not always agreed in their critical stance on the transcendent 'nature' of truth. Both schools, however, have drawn on the structuralist reconfiguration of knowledge that emerged out of the decolonization and ecological movements of the 1960s. These projects unsettled political and educational institutions and the philosophies of knowledge they upheld, replacing an objectively grounded, hierarchical edifice of truth with a subjectively fluid set of relations of difference impelled by political forces. This shift informed the critical insights of Michel Foucault and Jacques Derrida, and in turn of Edward Said, which came collectively to shape postcolonial criticism. It also underwrote the creation of the discipline of ecology, whose rejection of hierarchical models of authority in favour of a focus on relationships and processes reinforced its critique of prevailing ideas of progress (Conley 1996). Meanwhile, this critique expressed a *new* kind of planetary consciousness, building on books like Rachel Carson's *Silent Spring* (1962), which documented the deadly effects of pesticides on communities far from sites of their original production. Such accounts were avowedly political in their critiques of industry and in their insistence on principles of interdependence and corresponding responsibility. However, the smoothness of ecology's view of the world, as a network of flows and biofeedback mechanisms, presents a marked contrast to a postcolonial perspective that focuses on processes of conflict and rupture, struggle and negotiation. These contrasting perspectives do not just prescribe different world views, they also imply a different understanding of looking and knowing. Ecology's nominal anchorage in the physical sciences has often prescribed an uncritically positivist approach to knowledge, coupled with a rejection of historical analysis, which is seen as being inimical to the scientific method (Kingsland 1994: 351).

Some of the biases of ecological thinking were also evident in the development of ecocriticism in US literature departments in the early 1990s. Defined by a focus on the relationship of literature and the environment, much early ecocriticism sought to promote those forms of writing—specifically realist genres of nature writing and non-fiction more generally—that were seen to be conducive to environmental values (Buell 1995; see also Love 2003). As the field grew to prominence, crystallized by the publication of Glotfelty and Fromm's *The Ecocriticism Reader* (1996), ecocriticism faced criticism for its parochial focus on the writing of a select group of Thoreauvian backwoodsmen and on American nature more generally. Challenges to the race, gender, and nationalist bias of the field have been accompanied more recently by efforts to broaden its scope, along with more substantial interrogations of its aesthetic and epistemological foundations (see, for example, Armbruster and Wallace 2001). For instance, Dominic Head (1998) stages a mutual interrogation between ecology and postmodernism in his reading of Coetzee's 1983 novel, *Life & Times of Michael K.* Postcolonialism emerges as a peripheral but promising third term in Head's analysis, which shares 'a connection, as well as a parallel [with] ecologism' in its dialectical movement between anti-authoritarian scepticism and an '[informed] recentring of the enlightened subject, as instigator and agent of change (in ideology and in policy)' (1998: 34, 29). Later efforts to conjoin ecocritical and postcolonial reading practices have inspired a move away from the concept of an idealized nature towards environments in which crisis is represented as constitutive rather than exceptional (Garrard 2004).

Efforts to bring the fields of postcolonialism and ecocriticism into dialogue are perhaps the most visible embodiments of the interdisciplinary work that this chapter and this section of the Handbook as a whole are tracing; but it is also important to qualify the narrative of that work that has gained orthodoxy: that 'ecocriticism started as an insurgency that located itself explicitly with US literary studies ... [and then] spread throughout the Anglophone world and beyond' (Buell 2007: 228). This narrative finds confirmation in the expansion of ASLE (Association for the Study of Literature and the Environment), the pre-eminent scholarly association for literature and the environment, from the US across the Anglophone world and elsewhere. But as Cara Cilano and Elizabeth DeLoughrey caution, 'to suggest that postcolonial ecocriticism is new is to give a normative status to ecocriticism's institutional origins without questioning the limitations of its foundational methodologies and focus' (2007: 73). Focusing too closely on the history of ecocriticism or the activities of ASLE also risks bypassing a significant body of work on literature and environment that has developed along a parallel course with ecocriticism, but has drawn on other national traditions and different conceptions of nature. In Australia, for example, the development of a robust field of environmental humanities has been informed more strongly by the disciplines of history and philosophy than by literary criticism (see, for example, Griffiths and Robin 1997). Moreover, while much of this scholarship on culture and the environment has proceeded in tandem with the dominant strand of ecocriticism, some writers have explicitly rejected it. Thus, while many critics have explored the significance of nature in African writing (Coetzee 1988), William Slaymaker suggests that some are wary of 'ecolit and ecocrit [as] another attempt to "white out" black Africa by coloring it green' (2007: 232). Byron Caminero-Santangelo and Garth Myers, conversely, embrace an ecocritical approach to African literatures in their 2011 collection, *Environment at the Margins: Literary and Environmental Studies in Africa*, stressing the specificity of African discursive as well as physical contexts, while also attending to their interpenetration by global currents. Recent collections of postcolonial ecocriticism are highly conscious of the risk of both 'white-' and 'green-washing'. Bonnie Roos and Alex Hunt, in their recent *Postcolonial Green: Environmental Politics and World Narratives* (2010), argue that counter-imperialist methodology needs to be an integral part of ecocritism in the global context.

As ecocriticism and postcolonial criticism have come together, however uneasily, they have formed part of an important strain of scholarship that works to challenge the disembodied character of European ways of representing the living world. Western cartography, for example, whose abstract rendering of places was key in enabling and legitimating a variety of colonial practices, has been a critical theme in postcolonial literature (Devi 1995) and criticism (Huggan 1994). A number of anthropological studies go further than this, drawing on indigenous ways of knowing and inhabiting place in order to counter the synchronic abstraction of maps with diachronic, situated accounts. For example, Keith H. Basso's investigation of how 'wisdom sits in places' draws on Apache oral narratives to reinterpret the geography of Arizona, granting legitimacy to indigenous ways of dwelling in place while trying to understand how 'places come to generate their own fields of meaning' (1996: 108). This premise also informs Cruickshank's focus on glaciers, and stories about them, as a way to illuminate the Saint Elias mountain region of the northwest, and to intervene in broader discussions about the relevance of local knowledge to environmental policies as a whole. Cruickshank draws on diverse indigenous, European explorer, and scientific accounts to articulate a landscape whose meaning is bound up in (though not reducible to) the processes of inhabitation, exploration, colonization, and artistic creation and experimentation through which various human actors have come to know it (Cruickshank 2005). In addition, DeLoughrey has adopted Kamau Braithewaite's concept of 'tidalectics' (3) as a framework for reimagining 'the worldliness of islands' by employing the connective capacity of the sea as a means of subverting isolationist cartographies (see also Brydon in Part IV of this volume).

As Diana Brydon notes in this volume, postcolonial criticism has overlapped much less with critical indigenous scholarship than its nominal focus would suggest it should; the same is true for the nascent field of postcolonial ecology. In the grow-ing field of indigenous education, postcolonialism and environmental studies have played occasional back-up rather than formative roles, a situation attributable partly to their superfluity: the principles of epistemological decolonization and ecological responsibility—and the fundamental links between them—are already assumed by the project of critical indigenous education. Indigenous scholars stress the 'artificiality' of colonial education (Youngblood Henderson 2000: 57–9), which is hierarchically ori-ented and based on abstraction—an emphasis concretely realized in colonial education policies in Canada and Australia that mandated the removal of indigenous children from their families and local environments. By contrast, in the words of Pueblo scholar Gregory Cajete, 'Indigenous education is, in its truest form, about learning relation-ships in context' (2000: 183). Burgeoning indigenous education programmes at the post-secondary level, such as the Institute of Koori Education at Deakin University and the Saskatchewan Federated Indian College, define their curricula around indigenous law and ethics which, Kanien'kehaka scholar Alfred Taiaiake Youngblood notes, arise from 'observation and experiential learning ... conducted over generations' (2009: 28). Postcolonial and environmental concerns combine in the objective to redefine 'what counts as literacy', recognizing that in Māori cultures, for example, literacy encom-passes 'the ability to communicate and understand the environment including nature, weather patterns, star paths, tides and seasons' (Edwards 2010: 30; see also Smith and Turner in Part II of this volume).

Sometimes implicit, but foundational in the project of decolonizing education, is an emphasis on history, not just as a written record of the past, but as an immanent, living force.[4] The environmental history projects begun by scholars such as Crosby and Ponting take on renewed importance in the construction of a postcolonial ecology that seeks to understand the collaboration of human and other-than-human activities in shaping the global environment. Taking environmental history seriously mandates extending postcolonial scepticism about mimesis to consider the way places shape representa-tion—long a key theme in postcolonial literature, as Elizabeth DeLoughrey and George B. Handley have observed (2011: 6–7). It also requires, historian Dipesh Chakrabarty suggests, a radical rethinking of scales, as climate change signals the definitive end of the fantasy that human history takes place somewhere outside of natural time. Marking

---

[4] For a critique of the process of postcolonial cross-cultural historicization, see Abeysekara in this section of the volume. Also in this section, see Hindness, who questions the labels 'modern' and 'traditional' as they apply to the living Aboriginal culture in Australia.

the magnitude of the shift with the label of a new geological era—the Anthropocene—Chakrabarty calls for a recalibration of postcolonial history in uncomfortable recognition of humans' collective role *as a species*: responsible for, as well as subject to, natural history on a massively broad, indefinitely long scale (Chakrabarty 2009).

SUBJECTIVITY/ENVIRONMENTAL ETHICS

Questions of epistemology are linked in postcolonial and environmental thought to a broader ethics of subjectivity, responsibility, and interdependence. As ethics has come to assume a place of greater prominence in postcolonial studies (following the 'ethical turn' in literary studies more generally), areas of intersection—including many points of antagonism—have arisen with the well-established field of environmental ethics, which considers from a philosophical perspective 'the value and moral status of the environment and its non-human contents' (Brennan and Lo 2009). A tendency to frame the destructive dimension of the human–environment dynamic in universal terms means that the discourse of environmental ethics risks eliding problems of cultural specificity and politico-economic inequality. Deane Curtin underscores this problem in his discussion of the circumstances surrounding a recent green energy project in Manitoba. The Cree who live in the area have derived little benefit from the energy generated by the project, which was primarily produced for southern markets. They have suffered significant impacts, however, including the flooding of traditional hunting and trapping grounds, poisoned fish stocks, social upheaval, and the tragic drowning death of a young boy, described as an unfortunate but inevitable cost of 'green development' by the hydro company. Curtin echoes the words of the boy's family when he cynically asks whether concern over environmental crisis has precipitated a world in which human rights are becoming thought of as a luxury we can no longer afford (2005: 75). A related concern for postcolonial critics is environmentalists'—particularly deep ecologists'—endorsement of ecocentrism.[5] Environmental thought is committed to the idea of 'decentring' the human. In order to confront environmental issues, the argument runs, we need to move beyond anthropocentrism to take non-human life, even non-sentient nature, into our accounting processes. The deep ecology movement, spearheaded by Arne Naess, is the most extreme example of this controversial school of thought. Indian environmental historian Ramachandra Guha criticizes deep ecologists like Naess for their Orientalist methods, including the dehistoricization of non-western peoples and nature—a concern also shared by many feminists (Guha 1989).

The relationship between ecofeminism and postcolonialism is complex to say the least. Early ecofeminist writings often attempted to subvert patriarchal epistemologies which relied on the hierarchical, binary opposition between man/woman and culture/nature by

[5]. See Naess (1973) and Sessions (1995).

reclaiming the positive associations between women and nature. Starhawk, a noted poet and writer of spiritual ecofeminism, employed the birth metaphor as a means to recall to women their connections to life (1989: 175). Such ideas also resonated with other ecofeminist works, such as Vandana Shiva's critique of maldevelopment in the global south and the western scientific ideology that pushes aside women's traditional ecological knowledge (Shiva 1988; see also Sharp in Part II of this volume). In this search for reclaiming ecologically rooted feminist models, Noel Sturgeon points out that ecofeminist projects often involved a celebration of indigenous, Indian, and pre-Christian European women—women from cultures where it was assumed that nature and women were revered. By creating this hybrid 'other' against which to measure the putatively modern white western self, this ecofeminist trope ended up 'reconstituting white privilege' (2009: 113). But as Sherilyn MacGregor counters, much critical response to ecofeminism seems to be 'unfairly' stuck on these old debates, despite the fact that innovative anti-racist and anti-colonial work, often with a focus on collective action, has been done—and continues to be done—under the wide banner of ecofeminism (MacGregor 2006: 113; see also Alaimo 2010; Sandilands 1999; Sturgeon 2009). Viewing the environment through a postcolonial lens can offer new ground for ecofeminism, as in Laura Wright's 2010 collection *'Wilderness into Civilized Shapes': Reading the Postcolonial Environment*, which highlights the historical process by which unruly female bodies and uncivilized 'natures' were subject to masculinist technologies of colonization.

Ecofeminism and postcolonialism converge in their aim to interrogate the invisible lines of privilege (gender, sexuality, race) that demarcate the category of the human—a concern shared, not always happily, with animal studies. Although postcolonialism's interrogation of humanism 'offer[s] immediate entry points for a re-theorizing of the place of animals', the discursive use of "'animal'" as a derogatory term in genocidal and marginalising discourses ... makes it difficult even to discuss animals without generating a profound unease, even a rancorous antagonism, in many postcolonial contexts today' (Huggan and Tiffin 2010: 135). While foundational postcolonial thinkers highlighted the racist underpinnings of the European concept of man, they tended to do so in order to establish in its stead a *truer*, more inclusive humanism (see Fanon 2005 [1961]: 36). This project remains salient for many today, allied with the task of challenging the legacies of colonial discourses in places such as South Africa, in which the dehumanization of black colonial subjects went hand in hand with the sentimentalization of animals and nature (Martin 1994). An increasingly prominent strand of animal studies, however, takes a more broadly critical approach to what Neel Ahuja calls 'animalization, the organized subjection of racialized groups through animal figures' (Ahuja 2009: 557, emphasis in the original), articulating the connection, both philosophical and historical, between racism and speciesism (Wolfe 2003).[6] A particularly

---

[6.] Articulation of these linked forms of discrimination follows the argument advanced by many feminist scholars that women and animals have been objectified in the same terms, to similar ends (Adams and Donovan 1995).

interesting development of this line of thinking is Giorgio Agamben's elaboration of the concept of *zoe*, or 'bare life', which marks the constitutive exclusion that founds the category of the modern human as a bearer of political, social meaning and agency, as distinct from the animal (2003). The category of *homo sacer* ('sacred man') resonates in postcolonial and animal studies in its description of the outlaw, the exception, whose relegation to the fringes of social life (to the concentration camp, the refugee camp) and whose deprivation of human rights, are the essential predicates of modern politics (Agamben 1998; see also Farrier and Tuitt, Morton, and Smith and Turner in Part II of this volume; and Rangan and Chow in Part III).

Political analyses such as that offered by Agamben counter the relatively straightforward argument, advanced by philosophers such as Peter Singer, that inequality should be addressed by extending legal rights to include non-human subjects (1990 [1975]). The posthumanist reflections of Carey and Derrida (2008) as well as Agamben, along with the insights of ecofeminist philosophers such as Val Plumwood (2003), resonate with postcolonial scepticism towards the Euro-American cast of 'universal' human rights discourse and the racialized and gendered notion of autonomous reason on which it is premised. Focusing on the interdependency of humans and other-than-human nature, Plumwood's work is formative of an emerging field of postcolonial animal studies that sees animal and human concerns as interlocking and argues for the need to address them simultaneously (see Huggan and Tiffin 2010; also Elder et al. 2002). As a critical approach that has fundamentally concerned itself with possibilities of flourishing together with difference, postcolonialism will continue to play a key role in discussions about what it might mean to reframe collectivity from 'cosmopolis' to 'zoöpolis' (Wolch 1996).

Environment and Justice

Rob Nixon makes the general point that although 'postcolonial critics understandably feel discomfort' with certain aspects of the environmental movement, they do a disservice to their own cause when they unreflectively characterize environmental discourse as an exclusively elitist, white interest (2005: 235). To do so, he argues, is to overlook the environmental struggles in non-western nations and communities of colour. These struggles, according to Julian Agyeman, have made the environment 'discursively different' 'so that the dominant wilderness, greening, and natural resource focus now includes urban disinvestment, racism, homes, jobs, neighborhoods, and communities' (2005: 2). Renowned as a social justice activist and only later as an environmentalist, Ken Saro-Wiwa articulated a vision of environmental responsibility, seen equally in his life and work, which took into account the health and sovereignty of affected communities. His ultimately fatal public stance against the destruction caused by Shell Oil in the Niger Delta drew attention to the complicity of multinational corporations and governments in exploiting vulnerable minority groups. The Chipko movement in India is another prominent example that illustrates the conjunction of environmental and social activism in the postcolonial world. Brought to global fame through the work of Vandana Shiva, Chipko Andolan was a grass-roots protest, initiated by peasant women in the Himalayan region and inspired by the Gandhian principle of *satyagraha* or peaceful non-cooperation. The women wrapped their arms around trees in order to halt commercial deforestation, not because they were against the felling of trees on principle, but because they relied on the selective harvesting of the trees' products to meet their own needs. Shiva explains that commercial deforestation would have 'reduced [their] primary source of life into a timber mine' (1988: 61).

Despite these histories of environmental activism interlinked with social justice causes in the global south, most scholars locate the birthplace of the environmental justice movement in the US (see McDonald 2002 for a good overview of the field in South Africa). It was there that the movement was first defined as a paradigm, and where an Executive Order was passed in 1994 that brought environmental justice into a juridical framework (Agyeman, Bullard, and Evans 2003). Like its international cousins, the US environmental justice movement began as grass-roots protests. In 1982, the people of Warren County, North Carolina, mounted a large protest against a proposal to dump PCB-laden soil in their community. Residents of the predominantly black, low-income southern community came together to voice their anger and concern over this proposal: with the water table lying only 5–10 feet underground, there was significant potential for leeching and contamination. Their efforts failed to stop the toxic project, but they succeeded in inspiring a new movement. Soon after, working-class black communities and other communities of colour began protesting this newly identified source of discrimination that threatened the health and wellbeing of their communities right where they lived: they called it 'environmental racism'. A landmark 1987 study by the United Church of Christ Commission for Racial Justice confirmed the suspicion that race, rather than simply economics, was the single most determining factor in where a toxic waste dump was likely to be sited in the US. Environmental justice, here as elsewhere, was a response to environmental racism.

The current state of environmental racism in the US can be linked to a troubled history between marginalized communities and the development of a national environmental ethic (Merchant 2003). Racism informed early American land use policy in complex ways: 'Emancipated blacks in the South were expected to pay for land with wages at the same time that free lands taken from Indians were being promoted to whites via the Homestead Act' (Merchant 2003: 381). During the period when the land was to be 'settled', so-called 'wilderness' symbolized the savage and was a place to avoid. Later, as indigenous peoples were forcefully removed from their lands, wilderness was reimagined as a virgin land offering Edenic pleasures for the white tourist—a trope that still exists in popular culture today (see, for example, Carrigan 2011; Cronon 1995; Honey 2008). The phenomenon of 'white flight' from the cities to the suburbs is a more recent example of how race has structured land use and power distribution in North America. African Americans, who had once been associated with the 'wilds' of Africa or the rural south, became symbols of decaying cities. 'Sublime nature', Merchant writes, 'was white and benign, available to white tourists; cities were portrayed as black and malign, the home of the unclean and the undesirable' (2003: 385). Although African Americans were aligned with both the city and the country, in both stereotypes the dominant image of dirt stuck. As Toni Morrison has argued, in the white imagination, African Americans and indigenous peoples are conceptually stained with dirt; the addition of still more dirt, for example in the form of toxic waste or polluted water, is therefore a non-issue (Morrison 1992: xvii).

At the global level, environmental racism can be read through anxiety about over-population, which is constructed almost exclusively as a problem of Third World women. Concern about the size of the world's population has a precedent in the early nineteenth-century works of Thomas Malthus as well as Paul Ehrlich's 1968 text, *The Population Bomb*. Around the same time, the image of the earth taken from space, a brilliant blue marble against the 'sphere of deathly silence' (Sachs 1999: 112), drove home the idea that the Earth is a singular vessel with a finite carrying-capacity and that our unchecked technological and industrial progress, paired with resulting increases in population, has resulted in severe damage to our planet's ability to sustain life. By emphasizing the role of progress and its twin—development—this 'spaceship Earth' model points to a direct relationship between environmental crisis and the postcolonial world in particular. Concern focused on the outcomes of development: if western-style progress inexorably led to large-scale environmental degradation, and development projects like those advanced in the controversial Green Revolution relentlessly sought to foster western-style progress, it followed that environmental degradation would only continue to increase.[7] As Wolfgang Sachs comments, 'the world's poor entered the equation only as future claimants of an industrial lifestyle' (1999: 60). The bodies of women of the global south were targeted for family plan-ning and sterilization (Akhter 1992). Ghanaian author Ama Ata Aidoo takes aim at these issues in her novel *Changes: A Love Story*, when her character Opokuya, a nurse, says:

> Meanwhile, our governments are behaving like all professional beggars ... And they know the givers like one thing very much now: that there should not be too many of us. Under such circumstances, how does the beggar tell the giver to go and stuff his dangerous and experimental contraceptive pills, capsules and injections? Yes, injections. And they call their murderous programmes such beautiful names: 'family planning' and 'mother health' ... all to cover up ... (Aidoo 2001: 15)

Opokuya's words portray the frustration and suspicion felt by many postcolonial writers and critics who are worried about the neo-imperialist tendencies of a western-oriented global environmental agenda, her own solution being to have the children she wanted (three) before getting a tubal ligation on her own terms.

[7.] For critiques of the Green Revolution, see Conway and Barbier (1990), Curtin (1995), and Shiva (1991).

DEVELOPMENT/GLOBALIZATION

Aidoo's novel clearly exposes the combination of racial and environmental Orientalism underpinning those 'forms of environmental conservation that simultaneously seek to protect nature and to vilify Third World poor today' (Agarwal and Sawyer 2000: 71). A variant of the same paradoxical logic animates contemporary debates about climate change. The arguments advanced by countries such as Canada, to the effect that the pain of cutting carbon emissions should be shared equally among developing and developed nations, reinforce connections between global ecology and the politics of uneven development. The cultural and political frameworks that inform the contemporary science and policy of climate change have been subject to critical interrogation, deepened by dialogue with the diverse perspectives of indigenous people (Pettenger 2007). The consequences of global climate change, including the exacerbation of persistent forms of postcolonial displacement with the creation of a new category of 'environmental refugees', exemplify the deadly stakes—unequally distributed—of living in global risk society (Beck 1999). Since at least 1999, when the grass-roots 'Battle in Seattle' successfully disrupted a pivotal World Trade Organization meeting, anti-colonial and environmental activists have found common cause in challenging the forces of economic globalization. As a process of capitalist expansion and intensification, globalization extends the exploitative energies of colonialism from the commodification of all aspects of culture to the cannibalization of life itself. Postcolonial and environmental critiques have converged on several aspects of economic globalization, with an emphasis on three principal areas: place and deterritorialization, food security, and intellectual property conflicts.

Following its original usage in the work of Gilles Deleuze and Félix Guattari, 'deterritorialization' has come, especially in recent works of cultural geography, to refer simply to the detachment of culture from place associated with globalization, an intensification of the unsettling of space and place begun by colonialism (Appadurai 1996; Canclini 1995; Tomlinson 1999). Electronic technologies that facilitate the transmission of information, along with the considerably less fluid movement of people across borders, mean that human lives are lived with increasingly less reference to or engagement with their physical surroundings. While diaspora studies has tended, along with a shift in anthropology's focus from 'roots' to 'routes', to emphasize the more positive aspects of displacement (Said 2003 [1978]: 200), postcolonial literature often highlights the sense of environmental longing that migration produces, in combination with the self-conscious forms of ecological belonging that gradually emerge in new places (see, for example, Brand 1997; Kincaid 2001). Meanwhile, a significant number of critics are calling for a renewed focus on the dynamics—cultural, political, and ecological—of *place* at a time that has been dominated by the privileging of *space* (conceptualized, in Marxist theory in particular, as the arena of movement, political and economic agency: see Brydon in this section of the volume). Doreen Massey, Arif Dirlik, and Arturo Escobar each, in different ways, have complicated universalizing spatial ideals with models of place defined by histories of exploitation, attachment, engagement, and struggle (Dirlik 2007; Escobar

1996; Massey 1995). Every locality, as Massey puts it, is 'a conjunction of many histories and many spaces' (1995: 191). These postcolonial interpretations extend ecological theories of bioregionalism to a more politicized and historical consideration of how places are constructed.

One of the most significant factors in the resignification of contemporary places, which is simultaneously dependent on and disruptive of culture and ecology, is tourism. The myriad issues raised by this theme—home versus world; tradition versus progress (see Hindess in this section of the volume); protection versus exploitation of nature and culture, all muddied by the imperative to make a living—have been the subject of many works of postcolonial fiction (see, for example, Grace 1986; Kincaid 2001). Zakes Mda's *The Heart of Redness* (2002) is exemplary in its representation of the opposing energies that infuse postcolonial debates about tourism: on the one hand there are pro-development forces that want to construct a mega-resort and, on the other, those that want to respect and protect local culture and ecology. The conflict is ultimately resolved in the form of a scaled-down, ecotourist operation that aims to preserve the ecosystem and enrich the economy. A 'win-win' situation, or so it would seem; but ecotourism does not necessarily address local needs and, at its worst, it merely reiterates the economic and cultural inequalities of colonial adventure travel (Mowforth and Munt 1998).

Opposition to this approach to the protection of place informs the growth in localism: the rise of activist groups seeking to galvanize consumer efforts to 'eat (shop, dress: the list is ever-expanding) local'. In their more extreme manifestations, such movements, which echo in rhetoric and sometimes work alongside campaigns to protect indigenous flora and fauna against 'invader species', smack of xenophobic parochialism (Comaroff and Comaroff 2001). Ursula Heise notes that 'there is nothing in the idea of localism itself that guarantees its connection with the grassroots-democratic and egalitarian politics that many environmentalists envision when they advocate place-based communities', advocating instead a vigorous 'sense of planet—a sense of how political economic, technological, social, cultural, and ecological networks shape daily routines' (2008: 48, 55). This 'eco-cosmopolitanism' (Heise 2008: 50–62) has inspired movements that are, in Arif Dirlik's words, 'place-based but not place-bound' (Dirlik 2007: 22) such as the international Slow Food movement, which combines the defence of *terroir*—a conception of place defined by ecology and traditional food cultures—with an emphasis on global fair trade and education, and, increasingly, food sovereignty.

Defined as 'the right of peoples, communities and countries to control their own agricultural, labour, fishing, food and land policies which are ecologically, socially, economically and culturally appropriate to their unique circumstances' (IPC), the cause of food sovereignty was advanced by the international peasant farmers' movement Via Campesina in 1996 against the growing pressure on farmers from a combination of industrialization, climate change, global agribusiness, and biotechnology. Food has long been thematized in postcolonial literature, its production and consumption (or the absence thereof) linked with hunger, memory, and the politics of race, class, and gender (see for example Coetzee 1983; Dangarembga 1989; Markandaya 1982 [1955]). A potent embodiment of the convergence of culture and ecology, food is also thoroughly political, a fact highlighted by repeating histories of famine in Algeria, India, and other former colonies that are now complicated and exacerbated by current processes of globalization (Davis 2001). Rising food prices resulting from these developments have spawned widespread hunger in the global south (and significant pockets of the north) as well as the land grabs by wealthy nations and corporations noted above. Long sidelined by the competing themes of 'urban' culture and 'wild' nature, agriculture and rural issues are becoming key sites for the convergence of postcolonial and ecocritical concern.

A significant target of this concern is a new form of imperialism the reach of which extends to the raw elements of life itself (Shiva 1997). In 2006, for instance, a group of activists embarked on a sixteen-day *Bija Yatra* (seed pilgrimage), walking from Sevagram to Bangalore (India) in protest against the patent and seed laws that prohibit farmers from saving and exchanging seeds. The walkers distributed indigenous seeds to more than six thousand farmers and urged a boycott of Monsanto's Bt Cotton and agrichemicals as part of an effort to stop farmers' suicides and create an 'agriculture of hope'. Vandana Shiva, along with many scholars and activists, understands genetic modification as a kind of perversion of nature by technology, driven mainly by corporate greed. Other scholars, while concurring with the characterization of corporate monopoly as a threat to democracy, reject both the nature/technology and the ecology/economy (money versus life) terms in which the argument against genetic modification is often framed. Donna Haraway and Bruno Latour, for example, dispense with concepts of 'nature' to consider a non-human world that is infused with politics through and through (Haraway 1991; Latour 2004). They neither reify a realm of objective nature nor reduce material reality to culture or ideology: rather, they subscribe to a model of social relations, defined by human/natural/technological assemblages, the actions and perspectives of which are fundamentally interested and partial, but no less real for being so. The world thus described is *biopolitical*, in Foucault's sense when he refers to modern regimes of governmentality that work to maximize 'life' through the amplification and control of practices of health, reproduction, and sexuality (Foucault 2003; see also Part II of this volume). Harnessed for the production of corporate profit, biopower follows the agenda of a still-robust humanism (buttressed by the ideals of rational self-interest, individualism, and private property) while devolving increasingly, via the mechanisms of biotechnology and copyright law, into a *post*humanist landscape of indistinct boundaries separating life from 'non-life', human from 'non-human', and culture from 'nature'. For a number of critics, the goals of social and environmental justice must be pursued not by decrying the forces that have combined to make possible—say—the patenting of the human genome, but by deploying them differently so that biopolitics becomes properly political, serving egalitarian and democratic ends (Didur 2003).

Indra Sinha's novel *Animal's People* (2007) tells a story about 'inappropriate/d others', the term Donna Haraway borrows from Trinh T. Minh-ha to describe 'the personal and collective being to whom history has forbidden the strategic illusion of self-identity' (quoted in Haraway 1991: 329). Sinha's narrator, Animal, inhabits a post-apocalyptic landscape, the result of a massive chemical spill by an American company, which has yet to compensate any of the victims. The echoes of Bhopal are unmistakable. The rough outlines of the narrative, however—environmental catastrophe in the global south; truth and the quest for justice swallowed up by the production of a media spectacle of Third World suffering—have a broader resonance. Science, not least the putatively healing science of medicine, plays an ambiguous role, breaking down the boundaries of human and animal at the same time as it attempts to police them. Technology is inseparable from culture, which is neither evil nor benign, but is bound up in corporeality and subject to fear and desire and also—unexpectedly—humour. Animal (so-called because his spine is so compressed as a result of toxins that he has to walk on all fours) has a dirty mind: he messes with readers' expectations just as Sinha himself breaks with conventions of realism, humanism, and morality in his depiction of twenty-first century environments. Nature is spectrally present, corresponding to what Haraway, echoing Gayatri Spivak,[8] describes with deliberate awkwardness as: 'that which we cannot not desire' (1991: 296). It bears no resemblance to the landscapes of Walden Pond or the American southwest that were celebrated by early ecocritics. However, the 'nature' invoked in postcolonial fiction shares with those images a confirmation of the value of non-human life worlds that exist beside, around, and within us, and a sense that the goals of social and environmental justice can only be voiced as one.

References

Adams, Carol J. and Josephine and Josephine Donovan (eds) (1995). *Animals and Women: Feminist Theoretical Explorations.* Durham, NC: Duke University Press.

Agamben, Giorgio (1998). *Homo Sacer: Sovereign Power and Bare Life.* Palo Alto, Calif.: Stanford University Press.

Agamben, Giorgio (2003). *The Open: Man and Animal.* Palo Alto, Calif.: Stanford University Press.

Agarwal, Arun and Suzana Sawyer (2000). 'Environmental Orientalism', *Cultural Critique,* 45: 71–108.

Agyeman, Julian (2005). *Sustainable Communities and the Challenge of Environmental Justice.* New York: New York University Press.

Agyeman, Julian, Robert D. Bullard, and Bob Evans (2003). *Just Sustainabilities: Development in an Unequal World.* Cambridge, Mass.: MIT Press.

Ahuja, Neel (2009). 'Postcolonial Critique in a Multispecies World', *PMLA,* 124.2: 556–63.

Aidoo, Ama Ata (2001). *Changes: A Love Story.* New York: The Feminist Press.

Akhter, Farida (1992). *Depopulating Bangladesh: Essays on the Politics of Fertility.* Dhaka: Narigrantha Prabartna.

Alaimo, Stacy (2010). *Bodily Natures: Science, Environment, and the Material Self.* Bloomington: Indiana University Press.

Appadurai, Arjun (1996). *Modernity at Large: Cultural Dimensions of Globalization.* Minneapolis: University of Minnesota Press.

---

[8] Spivak has described the emancipatory ideals of liberalism as 'that which we cannot not want' (quoted in Haraway 1991: 45).

Armbruster, Karla and Kathleen R. Wallace (2001). *Beyond Nature Writing: Expanding the Boundaries of Ecocriticism*. New York: Zed Books.

Basso, Keith H. (1996). *Wisdom Sits in Places: Landscape and Language Among the Western Apache*. Albuquerque: University of New Mexico Press.

Beck, Ulrich (1999). *World Risk Society*. Cambridge: Polity Press.

Brand, Dianne (1997). *Land to Light On*. Toronto: McClelland and Stewart.

Brennan, Andrew and Yeuk-Sze Lo (2009). 'Environmental Ethics', in E. N. Zalta (ed.), *The Stanford Encyclopedia of Philosophy*. Stanford, Calif.: Stanford University. Online source: <http://plato.stanford.edu/archives/win2009/entries/ethics-environmental/>, accessed 13 July 2011.

Buell, Lawrence (1995). *The Environmental Imagination: Thoreau, Nature Writing, and the Formation of American Culture*. Cambridge, Mass.: Harvard University Press.

Buell, Lawrence (2007). 'Ecoglobalist Effects: The Emergence of U.S. Environmental Imagination on a Planetary Scale', in W.-C. Dimock and L. Buell (eds), *Shades of the Planet: American Literature as World Literature*. Princeton: Princeton University Press, 227–48.

Cajete, Gregory (2000). 'Indigenous Knowledge: The Pueblo Metaphor of Indigenous Education', in M. Battiste (ed.), *Reclaiming Indigenous Voice and Vision*. Vancouver: University of British Columbia Press, 181–91.

Cajune, June, Vance G., Martin, and Terry Tanner (eds) (2008). *Protecting Wild Nature on Native Lands: Case Studies by Native People from Around the World*. Golden, Colo.: Fulcrum.

Caminero-Santangelo, Byron and Garth Myers (2011). *Environment at the Margins: Literary and Environmental Studies in Africa*. Athens, Ohio: Ohio University Press.

Canclini, Néstor García (1995). *Hybrid Cultures: Strategies for Entering and Leaving Modernity*, trans. C. L. Chiappari and S. L. López. Minneapolis: University of Minnesota Press.

Carrigan, Anthony (2011). *Postcolonial Tourism: Literature, Culture, Environment*. London: Routledge.

Carson, Rachel (1994 [1962]). *Silent Spring*. Boston: Houghton Mifflin.

Chakrabarty, Dipesh (2009). 'The Climate of History: Four Theses', *Critical Inquiry*, 35: 197–222.

Cilano Cara and Elizabeth DeLoughrey (2007). 'Against Authenticity: Global Knowledges and Postcolonial Ecocriticism', *ISLE (Interdisciplinary Studies in Literature and the Environment)*, 14.1: 71–787.

Coetzee, John Michael (1983). *Life & Times of Michael K*. New York: Penguin.

Coetzee, John Michael (1988). *White Writing: On the Culture of Letters in South Africa*. New Haven: Yale University Press.

Comaroff, Jean and John Comaroff (2001). 'Naturing the Nation: Aliens, Apocalypse and the Postcolonial State', *Journal of Southern African Studies*, 27.3: 627–51.

Conley, Verena A. (1996). *Ecopolitics: The Environment in Poststructuralist Thought*. London: Routledge.

Conway, Gordon R. and Edward Barbier (1990). *After the Green Revolution: Sustainable Agriculture for Development*. London: Earthscan.

Cronon, William (ed.) (1995). *Uncommon Ground: Toward Reinventing Nature*. New York: W. W. Norton.

Crosby, Alfred W. (1986). *Ecological Imperialism: The Biological Expansion of Europe, 900–1900*. Cambridge: Cambridge University Press.

Cruickshank, Julie (2005). *Do Glaciers Listen? Local Knowledge, Colonial Encounters, and Social Imagination*. Vancouver: University of British Columbia Press.

Cruickshank, Julie in collaboration with A. Sidney, K. Smith, and A. Ned (1990). *Life Lived Like a Story: Yukon Native Elders*. Vancouver, BC: University of British Columbia Press.

Curtin, Deane (1995). 'Making Peace with the Earth: Indigenous Agriculture and the Green Revolution', *Environmental Ethics*, 17.1: 59–73.

Curtin, Deane (2005). *Environmental Ethics for a Postcolonial World*. Lanham, Md.: Rowman and Littlefield.

Dangarembga, Tsitsi (1989). *Nervous Conditions*. Seattle: Seal Press.

Davis, Mike (2001). *Late Victorian Holocausts: El Niño Famines and the Making of the Third World*. New York: Verso.

DeLoughrey, Elizabeth and George B. Handley (eds) (2011). *Postcolonial Ecologies: Literatures of the Environment*. Oxford: Oxford University Press.

Derrida, Jacques (2008). *The Animal That Therefore I Am*. New York: Fordham.

Devi, Mahasweta (1995). *Imaginary Maps: Three Stories*, trans. G. C. Spivak. New York: Routledge.

Didur, Jill (2003). 'Re-embodying Technoscientific Fantasies: Posthumanism, Genetically Modified Food and the Colonization of Life', *Cultural Critique*, 53: 98–115.

Dirlik, Arif (2007). *Global Modernity: Modernity in the Age of Global Capitalism*. Boulder, Colo.: Paradigm Publishers.

Edwards, Shane (2010). 'Matauranga Māori Literacies: Indigenous Literacy as Epistemological Freedom v. Eurocentric Imperialism', in *Indigenous Voices, Indigenous Research*. Guovdageaidnu, Norway: World Indigenous Nations Higher Education Consortium, 25–37. Online source: <http://www.win-hec.org/files/World_Indigenous_Nations_Higher_Education_Consortium_formatted2.pdf>, accessed 5 September 2011.

Ehrlich, Paul R. (1968). *The Population Bomb*. Cutchogue, NY: Buccaneer Books.

Elder, Glen, Jennifer Wolch, and Jody Emel (2002). 'La Practique Sauvage: Race, Place, and the Human-Animal Divide', in M. J. Dear and S. Flusty (eds), *The Spaces of Postmodernity: Readings in Human Geography*. Malden, Mass.: Blackwell, 431–41.

Escobar, Arturo (1996). 'Construction Nature: Elements for a Poststructuralist Political Ecology', *Futures*, 28.4: 325–43.

Fanon, Frantz (2005 [1961]). *The Wretched of the Earth*, trans. Constance Farrington. New York: Grove Press.

Foucault, Michel (2003). *Society Must Be Defended: Lectures at the Collège de France, 1975–76*, trans. D. Macey. New York: Picador.

Garrard, Greg (2004). *Ecocriticism*. New York: Routledge.

Glotfelty, Cheryll and Harold Fromm (eds) (1996). *The Ecocriticism Reader: Landmarks in Literary Ecology*. Athens: University of Georgia Press.

Grace, Patricia (1986). *Potiki*. Auckland: Penguin.

Griffiths, Tom and Libby Robin (1997). *Ecology and Empire: Environmental History of Settler Societies*. Edinburgh: Keele University Press.

Grove, Richard (1995). *Green Imperialism: Colonial Expansion, Tropical Island Edens and the Origins of Environmentalism 1600–1800*. Cambridge: Cambridge University Press.

Guha, Ramachendra (1989). 'Radical American Environmentalism and Wilderness Preservation: A Third World Critique', *Environmental Ethics*, 11.1: 72–83.

Haraway, Donna (1991). *Simians, Cyborgs, and Women: The Reinvention of Nature*. New York: Routledge.

Head, Dominic (1998). 'The (Im)possibility of Ecocriticism', in R. Kerridge and N. Sammels (eds), *Writing the Environment: Ecocriticism and Literature*. New York: Zed Books, 27–39.

Heise, Ursula (2008). *Sense of Place, Sense of Planet: The Environmental Imagination of the Global*. New York: Oxford University Press.

Henderson, James (Sákéj) Youngblood (2000). 'Postcolonial Ghost Dancing: Diagnosing European Colonialism', in M. Battiste (ed.), *Reclaiming Indigenous Voice and Vision.* Vancouver: University of British Columbia Press, 57–76.

Honey, Martha (2008). *Ecotourism and Sustainable Development: Who Owns Paradise?* Washington, DC: Island Press.

Huggan, Graham (1994). *Territorial Disputes: Maps and Mapping Strategies in Contemporary Canadian and Australian Fiction.* Toronto: University of Toronto Press.

Huggan, Graham and Helen Tiffin (2010). *Postcolonial Ecocriticism: Literature, Animals, Environment.* London: Routledge.

Kincaid, Jamaica (2001). *My Garden (Book).* New York: Farrar, Straus and Giroux.

King, Thomas (1999). *Green Grass, Running Water.* Toronto: HarperCollins.

Kingsland, Sharon E. (1994). 'Essay Review: The History of Ecology', *Journal of the History of Biology,* 27.2: 349–57.

Kolodny, Annette (2007). 'Rethinking the "Ecological Indian": A Penobscot Precursor', *ISLE (Interdisciplinary Studies in Literature and the Environment),* 14.1: 1–23.

Krech, Sheppard III (1999). *The Ecological Indian: Myth and History.* New York: Norton.

Latour, Bruno (2004). *Politics of Nature: How to Bring the Sciences into Democracy,* trans. Catherine Porter. Cambridge, Mass.: Harvard University Press.

Love, Glen A. (2003). *Practical Ecocriticism: Literature, Biology, and the Environment.* Charlottesville: University of Virginia Press.

McDonald, David A. (ed.) (2002). *Environmental Justice in South Africa.* Athens: Ohio University Press.

MacGregor, Sherilyn (2006). *Beyond Mothering Earth: Ecological Citizenship and the Politics of Care.* Vancouver: University of British Columbia Press.

Markandaya, Kamala (1982 [1955]). *Nectar in a Sieve.* New York: Signet.

Martin, Julia (1994). 'New, With Added Ecology? Hippos, Forests, and Environmental Literacy', *ISLE (Interdisciplinary Studies in Literature and the Environment),* 2.1: 1–912.

Massey, Doreen (1995). 'Places and their Pasts', *History Workshop Journal,* 39: 182–92.

Mda, Zakes (2002). *The Heart of Redness.* New York: Farrar, Straus and Giroux.

Merchant, Carolyn (2003). 'Shades of Darkness: Race and Environmental History', *Environmental History,* 8.3: 380–94.

Momaday, N. Scott (1998). 'A First American's View', in R. G. Botzler and S. J. Armstrong (eds), *Environmental Ethics: Divergence and Convergence,* 2nd edn. Boston: McGraw-Hill, 252–5.

Morrison, Toni (1992). 'Introduction', in T. Morrison (ed.), *Race-ing Justice, Engendering Power: Essays on Anita Hill, Clarence Thomas and the Construction of Social Reality.* New York Random House, vii–xxiii.

Mowforth, Martin and Ian Munt (1998). *Tourism and Sustainability: Development and the New Tourism in the Third World.* London: Routledge.

Naess, Arne (1973). 'The Shallow and the Deep, Long-Range Ecology Movement', *Inquiry,* 16: 95–100.

Nixon, Rob (2005). 'Environmentalism and Postcolonialism', in A. Loomba, S. Kaul, M. Bunzl, A. Burton, and J. Esty (eds), *Postcolonial Studies and Beyond.* Durham, NC: Duke University Press, 233–51.

Pettenger, Mary E. (ed.) (2007). *The Social Construction of Climate Change: Power, Knowledge, Norms.* Aldershot: Ashgate.

Plumwood, Val (2003). 'Decolonizing Relationships with Nature', in W. M. Adams and M. Mulligan (eds.), *Decolonizing Nature: Strategies for Conservation in a Postcolonial Era.* London: Earthscan, 51–78.

Ponting, Clive (1993). *A Green History of the World.* New York: Penguin.

Pratt, Mary Louise (1992). *Imperial Eyes: Travel Writing and Transculturation.* New York: Routledge.

Roos, Bonnie and Alex Hunt (eds) (2010). *Postcolonial Green: Environmental Politics and World Narratives.* Charlottesville: University of Virginia Press.

Sachs, Wolfgang (1999). *Planet Dialectics: Explorations in Environment and Development.* Halifax, NS: Fernwood.

Said, Edward W. (2003 [1978]). *Orientalism.* New York: Vintage Books.

Sandilands, Catriona (1999). *The Good-Natured Feminist: Ecofeminism and the Quest for Democracy.* Minneapolis: University of Minnesota Press.

Sessions, George (ed.) (1995). *Deep Ecology for the Twenty-First Century.* Boston: Shambhala.

Shiva, Vandana (1988). *Staying Alive: Women, Ecology and Survival in India.* New Delhi: Zed Press.

Shiva, Vandana (1991). *The Violence of the Green Revolution: Third World Agriculture, Ecology and Politics.* New York: Zed Books.

Shiva, Vandana (1997). *Biopiracy: The Plunder of Nature and Knowledge.* Cambridge, Mass.: South End Press.

Singer, Peter (1990 [1975]). *Animal Liberation.* New York: Avon Books.

Sinha, Indra (2007). *Animal's People.* New York: Simon and Schuster.

Slaymaker, William (2007). 'Ecoing the Other(s): The Call of Global Green and Black African Responses', in T. Olaniyan and A. Quayson (eds), *African Literature: Anthology of Theory and Criticism.* Malden, Mass.: Blackwell, 683–97.

Spivak, Gayatri Chakravarty (1993). 'Woman in Difference', in *Outside in the Teaching Machine.* New York: Palgrave Macmillan, 77–96.

Starhawk (1989). 'Feminist, Earth-based Spirituality and Ecofeminism', in J. Plant (ed.), *Healing the Wounds: The Promise of Ecofeminism.* Philadelphia: New Society Publishers, 174–85.

Sturgeon, Noël (2009). *Environmentalism in Popular Culture: Gender, Race, Sexuality and the Politics of the Natural.* Tucson: University of Arizona Press.

Tomlinson, John (1999). *Globalization and Culture.* Chicago: University of Chicago Press.

Walker, Cherryl (2008). *Land-Marked: Land Claims and Land Restitution in South Africa.* Athens, OH: Ohio University Press.

Wolch, Jennifer (1996). 'Zoöpolis', *Capitalism Nature Socialism,* 7: 21–48.

Wolfe, Cary (2003). *Animal Rites: American Culture, the Discourse of Species, and Posthumanist Theory.* Chicago: University of Chicago Press.

Wright, Laura (2010). *'Wilderness into Civilized Shapes': Reading the Postcolonial Environment.* Athens: University of Georgia Press.

Youngblood, A. T. (2009). 'First Nation Perspectives on Political Identity', *First Nations Citizenship Research and Policy Series: Building Towards Change,* online source: <http://taiaiake.posterous.com/pages/research-papers>, accessed 5 September 2011.

Zoomers, Annelies (2010). 'Globalisation and the Foreignisation of Space: Seven Processes Driving the Current Global Land Grab', *Journal of Peasant Studies,* 73.2: 429–47.

ORIGINS, OUTCOMES, AND THE MEANING OF POSTCOLONIAL DIVERSITY

DAVID ATTWELL

In his introduction to this part of the Handbook, Graham Huggan argues that while postcolonial studies is increasingly seen as *multidisciplinary*, this is still not a fully achieved state of affairs; that it might be more accurate to speak of the field as *inter-discursive*. In his General Introduction to the volume, Huggan also writes—with some qualification—of the shift from an earlier 'text-based approach' to a 'cross-disciplinary, interventionist model' that is more favoured today though not yet wholly realized. Cross-, inter-, and multidisciplinary: all these terms have slightly different implications. The questions that interest me here however are, first, how might we construct the narrative of the field's development differently; and then, what light might a different narrative cast on the question of interdisciplinarity in postcolonial studies?

We might begin by observing that the narrative of increasing disciplinary diversification may not be justified: it all depends on how we construe the question of origins. If one takes the view that Robert Young offers in *Postcolonialism: An Historical Introduction* (2001) to the effect that the roots of postcolonial studies lie in the cultural politics of early to mid-twentieth-century political movements of decolonization, then what we witnessed towards the end of the twentieth century, in the rise of postcolonial theory and criticism as this is conventionally perceived, was a decided *narrowing* of the field. From the careers, intellectual as much as political, of Mahatma Gandhi, C. L. R. James, Frantz Fanon, Amilcar Cabral, and Nelson Mandela—to venture a liberationist canon—to a handful of famously specialized poststructuralist interventions into the Anglo-American literary academy of the 1980s, is a bathetic reduction; so much so that one is tempted to ask whether these modes and moments of cultural-political work can be drawn into the same narrative at all. (The link that enables us to draw the connection with some confidence is, of course, Edward Said, whose 1978 classic *Orientalism* was a founding work of both political advocacy and literary theory.)

The narrative, therefore, could be one of institutionalization, specialization, and attenuation, rather than expansion. The fact that we are eager to see a more interdisciplinary pattern emerging has everything to do with the consequences of institutionalization. The early- to mid-century architects of liberationist thought did not think of themselves as interdisciplinary; they saw themselves, rather, as addressing by every means possible matters of political, social, economic, and cultural sovereignty, and if their attention drifted from one domain of life to another, that was proper to the scale of their aspirations. We who hold office in higher education may well think of moves from the literary to the economic, or from the spiritual to the political or the environmental, as interdisciplinary—but such thinking is surely a sign of the institutional code settling on our shoulders. For a field whose most common self-defining gesture is its authorization by an emancipatory politics, this is embarrassing, however unavoidable it may appear to be. It is possible, then, that the call for greater interdisciplinarity—or the claim that the field already enjoys increasing levels of diversification—could be an expression of the contradiction between postcolonial studies' location and its larger ambitions. The assumption that we will achieve greater social traction through interdisciplinarity, and thereby reconstitute ourselves in our own image, may really turn out to be the gesture of a discipline seeking to rewrite history in the terms of its own conditions of possibility.

Diana Brydon's wide-ranging survey tests these grim reflections precisely by making the argument that interdisciplinarity could be a route to achieving more purchase on the shifting geopolitical scene. As the 'worlding' of the world system intensifies, she argues, and as the politics of decolonization gives way to the politics of globalization, it becomes more and more imperative to seek strategic alliances and to diversify the vocabulary. A similar assessment is made in Dana Mount and Susie O'Brien's account of the relationship between postcolonial studies and environmentalism. While Brydon and Mount/O'Brien make their respective cases with authority and impressive coverage, the underlying positionality remains troubling by implying a febrile, possibly fissiparous scramble for currency. In a contrasting approach, Huggan's General Introduction reformulates and clarifies the field's core focus, showing why the postcolonial as traditionally understood remains a valid category both as advocacy and as an expanding research agenda.

The developmental narrative with which I began could also be challenged on the grounds that there are several points of origin, not one. The notion that postcolonial studies grew out of the metropolitan poststructuralist turn usually associated with Bhabha, Said, and Spivak is at best a partial truth. It could be argued, certainly, that what we perceive as the increasing heterogeneity of the field is less a function of its becoming more interdisciplinary, and more the effect of a growing recognition that the visibility of metropolitan postcolonial theory in the 1980s and 1990s led erroneously to an assumption that the field could be defined in singular terms. In other words, the welcome and developing recognition of heterogeneity is not a function of the field's development but of its changing epistemology.

I would go as far as to suggest that, at the end of the twentieth century, what we witnessed as metropolitan postcolonial theory began running into difficulties of field coverage and reception, was a repetition of events that had already taken place towards the end of the nineteenth, when historical linguistics was in a frenzy over the quest for the origins of language (a quest in which Oriental linguistics was deeply engaged, as we know from Said, although the project reached south as well as east, in its interest in the Khoisan languages of southern Africa). So inconclusive was the nineteenth-century debate about the origins of language that it quickly became discredited as a subject of proper scholarly attention. At the end of the twentieth century, attempts to isolate a phenomenon called the 'postcolonial condition' ran into similar trouble; that is, the idea of a single disciplinary movement called 'postcolonial theory', whose institutional provenance was the northeastern American metropole, became shipwrecked on the shores of seemingly infinite historical variety. Seldom was postcolonial theory able to respond convincingly to the oral and print cultures of non-metropolitan societies, for example. This deficit opened the door to the kind of critique that Neil Lazarus mounts so effectively in his 2011 study *The Postcolonial Unconscious*.

Nevertheless, the *persistence* with which postcolonial theory, and by implication postcolonial studies, continues to be associated with this one instantiation of it is distressing. Surprisingly, some of the field's most authoritative critics commit this error, including Lazarus himself. The essential project of his passionately argued book *The Postcolonial Unconscious* is legitimate and timely (John McLeod's contribution to this section of the Handbook has a similar laudable purpose): it is to confront 'postcolonial theory' with the heterogeneity of postcolonial *writing*, a task that he carries off with an astonishing range of reference. But the animus with which he engages his subject leads to a kind of tunnel vision: the heterogeneity that is granted to postcolonial *writing* is not carried over to a recognition of the actual historical diversity of postcolonial *theory*. There is no obvious willingness on Lazarus's part to disaggregate the field of postcolonial theory and speak of it in its various manifestations, a starting point for which could simply be regional: Latin American, Caribbean, black diasporic, Australasian, west and southern African, etc. It is an odd vulnerability in Lazarus's book—fuelled, one imagines, by genuine *ressentiment*—but to continue to treat metropolitan postcolonial theory (for which Bhabha stands as the prime target) as if it filled the entire space, is to be complicit in the distortions of representation that are being critiqued.

An equally surprising example is to be found in Simon Gikandi's contribution to Jane Elliott and Derek Attridge's recent collection *Theory After 'Theory'* (2011). In his chapter, 'Theory After Postcolonial Theory: Rethinking the Work of Mimesis', Gikandi argues, conventionally enough, that postcolonial theory established itself in the slipstream of poststructuralism, but with an additional emphasis on injecting into metropolitan discourse analysis an element of historical testimony relating to colonialism. As a result of its disciplinary orientation, the argument goes, postcolonial theory contained a contradiction at its heart: its deeper intuitions were unwittingly antipathetic to the work of cultural recovery. Gikandi cites Paul de Man pouring condescension on 'the platitudes of positivistic historicism' (166); but above all he points to 'the persistent difficulties postcolonial theory has in accounting for and providing us with a critical language that can adequately speak about the literature of decolonization as a distinctive event in literary history' (163).

As in Lazarus's case, the focus of critique is Bhabha, whose analysis of V. S. Naipaul's 1961 novel *A House for Mr Biswas* argues that the novel's achievement was to textualize history as a form of 'metonymic displacement' that resists incorporation into literary realism. Gikandi argues that this reading traduces Naipaul: the metonymic playfulness 'is *not* a measure of *mimetic* absence, [because] colonial fantasy [Biswas's desire to enter the middle class] and the narrative disturbances it generates come to function as part of the text's claim to a certain kind of historicity and its auto-referential purpose' (172; emphasis in the original). The text of decolonization, Gikandi continues, 'must be recognized as creating the spaces in which postcolonial criticism would emerge, rather than as insignia of a failed politics of representation' (176). The thrust of Gikandi's argument is thus a call for a form of postcolonial criticism that is responsive to the historical event of decolonization.

What is overlooked in this otherwise helpful analysis is the fact that there have by now been at least two *generations* of critics who have sought to provide exactly the kind of criticism Gikandi is calling into being. The omission is all the more startling because Gikandi *himself* has contributed to it, notably in his work on Chinua Achebe and Ngũgĩ wa Thiong'o. Why does this work, some of it written in universities in west and east Africa, not merit proper attention in *Theory After 'Theory'*? It is as if when arguing with 'postcolonial theory', Gikandi finds it necessary to restrict his range of reference to the metropole—an odd distortion, surely. If disciplinary heterogeneity is to flourish, we need to take seriously the continuing disaggregation of the fields of postcolonial theory and criticism.

On the evidence of the chapters that make up this part of the Handbook, the most productive interdisciplinary relationship shared by postcolonial studies to date is with history. Dane Kennedy's account of postcolonial-inflected work in historical studies, which he organizes around the themes of identities, geographies, and epistemologies, suggests an almost inexhaustible research agenda that is properly in tune with one of the ongoing and fundamental tasks of postcolonial studies, which is to understand and engage with non-metropolitan (or in the metropoles, minority) histories and subjectivities. In this respect, postcolonial and historical studies are natural allies. I would add only one caveat to Kennedy's account (with which he would surely agree), which again has to do with how the narrative of the disciplinary relationship is constructed. Kennedy's colourful opening paragraph suggests that history was initially unaccommodating to the literary and theoretical emphases of postcolonial studies and that this resistance has weakened over time; but it would be more accurate to say that postcolonial-inflected work had already developed in historical scholarship independently of the influence of literary postcolonialism. I would certainly agree with Kennedy's concluding observation that 'as a cross-disciplinary dialogue continues to characterize the postcolonial enterprise, much of its energy and insight is likely to come from history itself'. The more we recognize that theory exists as a range of disaggregated and historically contingent traditions, responsive to unique situations, the more it will become apparent that postcolonial forms of knowledge need to be elicited painstakingly from the historical record.

Ananda Abeysekara's chapter focuses on intriguing issues in the phenomenology of religion, in particular the difficulties of epistemological incommensurability that arise when secular forms of analysis settle on religious consciousness. Would it ever be possible, he asks, for postcolonial studies, as a variety of critique, to slip out of the dualism that defines its positionality and separates it from its object? It is not simply that the tradition of critique is a product of post-Enlightenment rationalism. The tradition of critique has also absorbed a Christian hermeneutic into itself that is continuously self-deconstructing; to separate secular critique from Christian self-scrutiny is neither feasible nor historically accurate. For postcolonial studies to encounter religion in a postcolonial way, therefore, it would have to do so at the limits of its own epistemology. This is a powerful argument, but it gains its force from an implied (if not baldly stated) association between critique, Christianity, and their joint association with western, liberal-democratic power. Postcolonial studies must pay attention to that configuration, obviously, just as it would pay attention to all forms of colonial discourse; but postcolonial religious studies will be just as interested, if not more so, in *transculturated* forms of Christianity where the internal traditions of the church, both epistemological and theological, have been recontextualized and refashioned, and their relationships with secular power have accordingly been redefined. The phenomenological conundrum that Abeysekara discusses has a different moral and political valency in those regions where Christianity is, in fact, strongest: Africa and Latin America.

The theme of alternative knowledge systems provides a useful segue into the chapter by Barry Hindess on postcolonial studies and the social sciences. Hindess's subject is the central postcolonial question of coevalness: what are the gains and losses, he asks, when we use temporal categories (most obviously, 'modern' and its opposites, including 'developing', 'traditional', or 'tribal') in discussions of the relationships amongst contemporaries in a globalized world? He broadly accepts Dipesh Chakrabarty's analysis in *Provincializing Europe* (2000) that, given the reach of global capitalism and western European and North American power (and the critical-philosophical traditions that attend them), 'western historicism' is an indispensable point of reference. To the term 'indispensable' Chakrabarty adds 'inadequate', to emphasize a key contradiction (and reality) of postcolonial cultural epistemology. To these terms Hindess adds a third, namely 'injurious', to emphasize the costs of the conjunction. While the addition and its implications seem bleak, possibly even elegiac, its relevance to the treatment of Aboriginal communities by recent Australian governments might well be appropriate.

Hindess's analysis touches on, but unsurprisingly does not tackle, the great lingering unresolved philosophical problem at the heart of postcolonial studies: whether it is desirable, and then possible, to speak of modernity in terms of the singular or the plural. This is the latest version of the debate over culturalist vs materialist analysis that has been with us since the 1980s, with some new inflections. With ballast provided by Fredric Jameson's *A Singular Modernity* (2002), the materialist position is that the notion of alternative modernities weakens a critical purchase on capitalism as the engine of the world system, with debilitating effects on the intellectual and organizational work of resistance. Measured in those terms, 'alternative' is not the most helpful of adjectives to link with modernity, implying a degree of wishfulness that is simply belied by the facts. But the question remains nevertheless: are modernity and capitalism *entirely* coterminous, and if they are not, can we then speak of representations and practices that have undeniably come to define modern experience in particular contexts (or more accurately, in particular cities, whether this is Kolkata, São Paulo, or Johannesburg)— representations and practices that are not determined, in either the first or last instance, by global capitalism? Put this way, the case for respecting the multiplicity of modern experience seems just a little stronger without having to abandon an adequate sense of history. Without this kind of acknowledgement—without creating sufficient intellectual space for the possibility of coevalness on independent terms—there is no case for a great deal of the work that is done under the sign of the postcolonial.

One last observation: it is not that the postcolonial is a rival paradigm to the current expansion of global-systems analysis. Given its multiple points of origin, and the heterogeneous histories in which postcolonial scholarship and activism have developed, what has brought postcolonial scholars and activists together in the first place is, precisely, those globalized institutional spaces we inhabit and the flows of knowledge to which we contribute. The point of origin for our discipline is not any single microculture of discursive analysis; it is the fact that from our various and splendidly unique situations, we have, by the forces of our contemporary mediatized and globally integrated history, been brought together, for better or worse.

References

Chakrabarty, Dipesh (2000). *Provincializing Europe: Postcolonial Thought and Historical Difference*. Ithaca, NY: Princeton University Press.

Gikandi, Simon (2011). 'Theory After Postcolonial Theory: Rethinking the Work of Mimesis', in Jane Elliott and Derek Attridge (eds), *Theory After 'Theory'*. London: Routledge, 163–78.

Jameson, Fredric (2002). *A Singular Modernity: Essay on the Ontology of the Present*. London: Verso.

Lazarus, Neil (2011). *The Postcolonial Unconscious*. Cambridge: Cambridge University Press.

Said, Edward W. (1978). *Orientalism*. New York: Pantheon Books.

Young, Robert J. C. (2001). *Postcolonialism: An Historical Introduction*. Oxford: Blackwell.

PART V

ACROSS THE WORLD

INTRODUCTION

GRAHAM HUGGAN

Despite those who would see global studies as more fitting than postcolonial studies for the critical analysis of the contemporary era (see for example During 2000; also Loomba et al. 2005), the term 'postcolonial' has always had a global reach to it, and the multiple impacts and legacies of colonialism are nowhere more apparent than in the context of (late) global capitalism today. Postcolonial studies, in this sense, constitutes both a *continuing* engagement with and a *renewed* contestation of globalization within what the sociologist Ankie Hoogvelt (1997) calls the 'reshuffled context' of a global economy in which First Worlds have appeared in the Third World and Third Worlds in the First, confirming a contemporary world order in which earlier binary distinctions—First/ Third, north/south, core/periphery—seem no longer serviceable without necessarily diminishing the economic imperatives that drove them, and without which we could hardly speak of a globalized (or any other kind of) capitalist world at all.

The relationship between postcolonial studies and global studies is perhaps best seen as a dialectical one in which the complementary terminologies of each are understood as being equally inadequate (During 1998, 2000). As Simon During puts it, 'postcolonialism and globalism are reductive, often internally divided, names for forces which work, and long have worked, in transaction with one another'—although he goes on almost immediately to assert that this transaction also has the means to be productive, and that one of the effects of contemporary world unification has been, by 'reconfiguring the past in its own image, [to rekindle the] colonial struggles [that help] keep old pasts alive' (2000: 392). During tacitly recognizes that theories of globalization often contain valuable 'postcolonial content', a content readily identified in the migratory vocabulary—'deterritorialization', 'transnationalism', 'cosmopolitanism'—they commonly deploy (Krishnaswamy 2008: 3; see also Appadurai 1996, Spencer 2011). However, whether the relationship between the postcolonial and the global is oppositional or complicit is moot—hence the ongoing debate as to whether postcolonialism registers an ethical response to globalism or merely presents an economic effect of it: the simplest, though not necessarily most illuminating, answer to this would probably be that it does both. One version of this debate might ask whether postcolonialism unwittingly serves the expansionist needs of neoliberal globalism or whether globalization, seen from a postcolonialist perspective, offers both a platform for coordinated resistance and an opportunity for the world's marginalized and exploited to negotiate modernity in their own terms (Hoogvelt 1997; Stewart-Harawira 2005). Another version might point out the productive overlaps between two fields—postcolonial studies and global studies—that evolved separately but have since fashioned a quasi-symbiotic relationship with one another (Brennan 2008; During 2000). Such overlaps include the reinvigorated call for transnational alliances and affiliations in an era of unprecedented mobility; the powerful if potentially disingenuous recognition that today's global problems (poverty, inequality, disease, climate change, etc.) require global solutions; and the urgent need, pressing beyond this, to address the new and intensified forms of capitalist imperialism that underwrite social and economic conflict in the modern globalized world (Krishnaswamy 2008; see also Part II of this volume).

However the debate is framed, it seems necessary to insist that there are different *kinds* of globalization with very different effects and consequences; also different *scales* and *temporalities* of globalization (Appadurai 1996; Sassen 2008). This emphasis on plurality is needed to counteract the 'presentist' assumptions and polarizing tendencies that are often embedded within contemporary discourses of globalization (globalization 'from above' and 'from below'; 'euphoric' versus 'catastrophist' accounts of globalization; globalization as the latest iteration in the long history of capitalism or as the distinctive signature of our times). It also seems necessary to see globalization in both economic and cultural terms (Hoogveldt 1997), as both a localizing and a de-localizing process (Appadurai 1996), and as both a profoundly divisive ideology ('globalism') and a potentially unifying vision ('global consciousness') of the world as an interconnected whole (Huggan 2009; see also Robertson 1992). This section of the Handbook aims, accordingly, to look at the complex interplay between contemporary postcolonial social/cultural formations and economic globalization without reducing the one to the other or setting up an implacably antagonistic relationship in which postcolonialism is seen as a 'cultural front' against economic globalization-cum-'fiscal imperialism' (Spivak 1999) in the overarching context of today's unevenly developed world. Rather, the section opens out the debate on globalization by considering the extent to which (1) social divisions have largely replaced geographical divisions in a contemporary world order characterized by the politics, and political management, of exclusion (Hoogveldt 1997; see also Part II of this volume); and (2) new transnationally incorporated *regions* have emerged both as the effect of and in response to an economically reorganized world.

In this latter context, both postcolonial and global studies can be situated within the context of what David Harvey (2003) and others have called the 'new regionalism'. The most obvious thing to say about the 'new regionalism' is that it is no longer new—if it ever was. Most commentators ally it with a combination of political and economic elements relating to the immediate post-Cold-War era: the geopolitical move towards a 'multipolar' rather than 'bipolar' world order; the economic ascendancy of the Asia-Pacific; the increasing globalization of finance and concomitant development of 'globe-girdling' (Spivak 1999) free-market ideologies; and the breathless 'rise of new technologies that have [since definitively] reorganized human calculations of time and space' (Larner and Walters 2002: 410). As the political scientists Wendy Larner and William Walters—whose provisional list this is—suggest, the 'new regionalism' may be distinguished from the 'old' by its acceptance of, and capitalization on, the region as part of a fully evolved world system rather than as an economically oriented amalgamation of nation states (2002: 410). But it is no more new than globalization itself is new, and—as with the 'older' nation-state-oriented models it is prematurely argued to have replaced—its political and economic consequences are similarly conflicted. Thus, it may act as a vehicle for democratization, allowing for participatory forms of international politics within the context of a non-hegemonic world order; but it may equally well act as the catalyst for a re-hierarchized world economy in which competitive (and/or protective) regional units square off against one another, thereby re-enacting the centuries-old capitalist struggle for 'global supremacy in terms of economic power' (Stewart-Harawira 2005: 13–14).

Postcolonial critics and theorists have been suspicious, by and large, of the promises held out by the 'new regionalism', seeing it as being intrinsically connected to, though not necessarily reducible to, globalization 'from above' (see Harvey 2003 and his postcolonial followers). Accordingly, one of the most important recent projects of postcolonial studies has been to develop a 'critical regionalism' that is at once attentive to the political and economic hegemony of the current world order and the flagrant injustices that stem from it, and aware of vernacular responses to it in which the region, often understood as an internal alternative to the nation, is reconceived as being largely external to it; as sharing some of the benefits of national identity but also reaching out beyond these to embrace transnational and/or diasporic modes of affiliation and conviviality that would normally be more characteristic of globalization 'from below' (Spivak 2008; see also Mignolo 2000).

Critical regionalism, says Gayatri Spivak, its most vocal postcolonial exponent, is best understood as a device for 'rewriting postcolonialism into globality' (2008: 131). Spivak presents critical regionalism as a set of practices rather than a set of slogans; cooperatively inclined but pragmatically oriented, it is obstinately immune to the blandishments of nationalism and 'post-nationalism' alike. Although critical regionalism, Spivak-style, is anti-programmatic, some of its key aspects can readily be identified: its displacement of ethnic history and primordialist cultural nationalism; its non-discriminatory support for transnational collaboration and cultural pluralism; its resistance to the global managerialism and 'regionalist unilateralism' (235) that underlie regional economic imperatives (2008: 212); and, perhaps above all, its vehement rejection of the global-capitalist mantra of 'growth' (245). It is with this kind of critical regionalism in mind that this section's essays engage with their respective regions ('Asia', 'the Pacific', 'Africa', 'the Americas', 'Europe')—areas which, in radically different ways and from radically different perspectives, are still fighting to free themselves from the triple stranglehold of geopolitical determinism, economic managerialism, and the attitudinal legacies of imperialist cultural myth. In this last context, the essays are attentive to the ways in which these regions have been historically identified, and have attempted to redefine themselves in their own image, but also the ways in which their social realities are structured by the global ideologies within—and against—which most of us currently live.

The section begins with an overview chapter by the social theorists Nikita Dhawan and Shalini Randeria. Dhawan and Randeria offer a series of intersecting, mostly South-

Asian-oriented perspectives on globalization and subalternity in which the latter term provides a further link between globalization and postcolonialism (though this link is not necessarily direct and the chapter vigilantly guards against reductivism, e.g. the uniform view of postcolonial 'resistance' to globalization or the equally sweeping prospect of a subaltern 'globalization from below'). The chapter begins by asking to what extent globalization can be seen as a continuation of the imperial project. The answer, as might be expected, is yes and no, depending on the degree to which globalization is seen as (1) a destructive ideology and (2) an ambivalent vehicle for contemporary processes of accelerated change. Globalization is caught between competing narratives of celebration and crisis. The former is connected to new, enabling global flows and the proliferation of alternative 'modernities in the margins'; the latter, in foregrounding those who have been left out of contemporary globalization processes, advertises the growing 'asymmetries of wealth and power', many of them inflected by colonial legacies, that exist between the global north and the global south.

Globalization is further inflected, Dhawan and Randeria suggest, by *regionalism* (which complicates the local/global binaries that haunt globalization discourse) and by *gender* (which counteracts the common tendency of globalization theory to ignore 'the contradictory consequences of globalization for the [everyday] lives of women across the world'). Most of all, perhaps, it is inflected by *subalternity*: by the continued, sometimes intensified existence of the poor and disenfranchised within a global system that further marginalizes them even as it mobilizes to support them in the name of 'civil society' and 'good governance'. Subaltern agency, Dhawan and Randeria insist, must be uncoupled from those forms of civic engagement that are premised on western normative conceptions of the 'rights-bearing citizen'; it also stands in conflicted relation to those contemporary (left-liberal) activist movements that seek to 'interrogate global hegemony [by] using the languages of global justice and human rights' (see also Farrier and Tuitt in Part II of this volume). Subaltern groups may be paradoxically effective, they suggest, precisely because they operate at levels perceived to be insignificant to national and international politics, although the liberating *possibilities* of subalternity remain pitted against the repressive *production* of subalternity, defined by Spivak in neo-Marxian terms as 'a condition of not being able to represent oneself'.

Following Spivak again, Dhawan and Randeria suggest that the political and economic empowerment of the subaltern is incomplete without 'epistemic change', as much in the global north as the global south; and that one form this might take is a radical rethinking of human rights, which are still far too often seen in Eurocentric terms as a 'western gift to the non-western world'. Arguing against the claim of universal human rights as a western invention (a claim also interrogated elsewhere in this volume, e.g. in the General Introduction), Dhawan and Randeria conclude that human rights discourses—while still routinely exploited by the dominant—remain useful when reattached to ongoing histories of anti-colonial struggle and to all those contemporary subaltern agents who, in the conspicuously uneven contexts of globalization, seek to 'arrest the abuse of public power under conditions of endemic appropriation by the postcolonial state'.

In the first of the section's 'regional' chapters, Daniel Vukovich takes on the impossible task of accounting for Asia and its relationship to both globalization and postcolonialism. This impossibility is announced from the outset. 'Asia' makes little sense,
Vukovich suggests, for the people that actually live there. Nor are people in 'Asia' very
likely to identify as 'Asians'. Rather, the identity of 'Asia' is either bound up in diaspora
(the subject of Quayson's chapter later in the section) or 'arises from, and is dependent on, real or perceived contact with the west'. The term 'Asia' traces its roots to a long
imperialist history in which 'Asia' has been pitted against 'the west'; and this false binary
persists, re-emerging in 'new' Orientalist discourses that have adapted 'older', more
conspicuously racist ways of thinking about Asia to those more social science-based
forms of knowledge, and the 'modernizationist' vocabulary that accompanies them,
that dominate the 'current neo-imperial globalized scene'.

It might be best, in fact, to do without 'Asia' altogether, though its spectral presence
lingers, not least in nominally decolonizing discourses such as those of the Singapore-
based 'inter-Asian' studies project, which looks to study Asia inter-regionally, i.e. comparatively from within. Vukovich is sceptical of such 'home-grown' moves, as he is of
their western neoliberal counterparts, e.g. the oft-recycled global-capitalist fiction of
Asia's 'opening up' to the west. In fact, Vukovich suggests, the rise of Asia, and of the
PRC in particular, has brought with it a newly configured (if still inherently unstable)
world system in which the west has been effectively reprovincialized. In so far as the
provincialization of the west—and of Europe in particular—has always been part of the
postcolonial critical project (see, for example, Chakrabarty 2000), one might think that
opportunities exist here for postcolonialism. However, as Vukovich points out, postcolonial studies has yet to come to terms with China, in part because it is seen as a poor
fit for colonial/postcolonial paradigms. After all, for Lenin and others, China was 'only
ever semi-colonial', while there is a long and insufficiently challenged tradition of area
studies scholarship in which China is categorized as 'not colonized' at all.

Such scholarship ignores the ways in which China has historically been affected by
'imperialist contact as well as by the political brinkmanship of the Cold War'; it also
either represses or reductively moralizes China's past and present status as a global imperial power. The last of these views, Vukovich suggests, is another example of
those forms of globalist Orientalism through which China, (rightly) seen as a serial
violator of human rights, has been strategically grafted onto a liberal 'civil-rights-as-
democratization narrative' that effectively reinforces western authority—an uncritical
'modernizing' narrative sometimes used by self-styled progressives in China itself (see
Dhawan and Randeria in this section of the volume; also Gopal in Part II). Meanwhile,
other contemporary forms of Orientalism can be found in post-Cold-War discourse,
which maps 'new' globalist homogenization onto 'old-style' Asian totalitarianism; in the
persistent assimilation of Chinese and other revolutionary legacies to Eurocentric models; and in anti-communist documents such as Charter 08 which use the language of
human rights while simultaneously drawing on neoclassical economic ideology. In these
and other examples, Vukovich convincingly shows that the PRC, while still presenting
something of an exceptional case to postcolonial studies, exemplifies today's pervasive

triangulation of colonial discourse, globalization *realpolitik*, and the 'unabashed deployment of "universal" modernizationist terms'.

Like 'Asia', the 'Pacific' is a densely mythologized cross-cultural space in which discrepant narratives of the real and the imagined have competed and commingled. Unlike Asia, however, the Pacific has not enjoyed the attention it deserves in postcolonial studies. The primary task of Michelle Keown and Stuart Murray's chapter is to show how this space, far from being distant from postcolonial concerns, is in fact proximate to them: in terms of the complex relationship between the local and the global; in terms of the interwoven histories of Pacific Island communities; in terms of the colonialisms, both past and present, that the Pacific's inhabitants have repeatedly contested; and in terms of the intricately interconnected understandings of themselves, and of each other, that they have continuously evolved. A secondary objective of the chapter is to break down the internal distances that separate the Pacific in order to account for it as a *region*; thus, while Keown and Murray acknowledge that the Pacific Ocean 'contains one of the most heterogeneous groups of cultures and languages in the world', and that these cultures and languages are stretched across vast expanses of space, it has always been productively linked through trade and travel, through politico-economic cooperation, and through home-grown cross-cultural initiatives which, adopting and adapting traditional myths and cosmologies, have helped unite and protect Pacific Islanders against the destructive forces of global capitalism, military imperialism, and—more recently—those expedient forms of 'planetary management' (Ross 1991; see also Mount and O'Brien in Part IV) that have accompanied the global drive to combat climate change.

Pacific regionalism, Keown and Murray insist, has by no means rendered nationalism defunct; on the contrary, it can be seen to have reinvigorated it by supplying a comparative frame for 'nationalist traditions that present the cultural politics of the present through [progressive] reworkings of the past'. However, ongoing histories of Indigenous protest across the region (e.g. in Australia and New Zealand) provide a salutary reminder of the discriminatory legacies of settler nationalism, while longstanding ethnic rivalries (e.g. in Hawai'i and Fiji) have been restoked by a neoliberal global economy which, in intensifying already heavy pressures for migration, has simultaneously freed up opportunities for some and further entrenched the dependency of the rest. Thus, while cooperative models of 'critical regionalism' (Spivak 2008) do exist, they must contend with several complicating factors, which operate across a sliding scale that belies generalization: extreme linguistic and ethnic diversity; considerable economic and environmental fragility; and a long history of incorporation into totalizing cultural and/or economic discourses which, generated from metropolitan centres located well beyond the region, lay false claim to a knowledge and understanding of how the Pacific functions—and can be made to function for those whose livelihoods are not necessarily dependent on it, and whose lives are mostly experienced elsewhere. Caught in a vortex of global flows—money, goods, people—the Pacific remains in many ways a vulnerable space, yet cultural and political autonomy are by no means beyond it. As the Tongan writer and anthropologist Epeli Hau'ofa suggests,

Oceania (his chosen term) may be insular in form but it is not insular in spirit, and, buffeted though it is by globalization, it will continue to draw on the collective 'cultural achievements of its own histories' in order to give shape and meaning to its individual inhabitants' lives.

One of the distinctive features of the Pacific, for Keown and Murray, is that it is a *diasporic* space, imaginatively fashioned in part by people who no longer live there. This emphasis is upheld in Ato Quayson's historically wide-ranging chapter on Africa and its diasporas. As Quayson suggests, how Africa is seen today depends as much on how it is perceived 'from without'—from the vantage point of its diasporas—as on how it imagines itself 'from within', in relationship to the west. However, the concept of 'diaspora' also complicates this 'inside/outside' binary, just as it questions politically expedient notions of bounded territory; similarly, the fashionable invocation of an 'African diaspora' obscures as much as it reveals, e.g. the semantic distinction between 'diaspora' and 'dispersal', the historical entanglement of African and other global diasporas, and the conflicting ideas and ideologies embedded within the term 'Africa' itself.

'Diaspora', for Quayson, is by definition a relational term and needs to be understood both historically and comparatively, within multiple frames of reference. Colonialism provides one of the key frames. Thus, while enforced child migration to North America and Australia, peaking in the mid-nineteenth century, was obviously different in kind (and in degree) to the relocation of London's black poor to Sierra Leone in the late eighteenth century, the colonial structures that underpinned them were broadly similar. Two larger points follow: that the instrumentalization of population dispersal has always been an important part of colonial policy, of whichever form and at whatever historical juncture; and that this policy has created very different diasporic communities, including those fashioned from *within* a given region (e.g. the African continent) as well as those manufactured from 'elsewhere'.

Quayson gathers examples accordingly. The history of indentured labour in Uganda, Kenya, and Tanzania, for instance, has created diasporas that are as 'African' as they are 'Indian'; as he pointedly asks, 'are the descendants of Indian indentured labourers less African, say, than the Zulu or the Gikuyu? Or is it rather that the diasporic culture of the Indians of East Africa marks a cosmopolitan "Africanity" that has not yet been fully understood?' The history of military diasporas likewise suggests a heady blend of 'intra-' and 'extra-African' dispersals, not all of these coalescing into recognizable diasporas. Similar question marks hover over diasporic and non-diasporic constituencies in British colonial ports such as Liverpool. Quayson rightly insists here that there is 'no straightforward way in which we can speak of a singular identification of black Liverpool with Africa'; rather, it seems necessary to speak of multiple identifications, with only some of these being formed within Britain itself. Finally, plantation slavery certainly produced diasporas in, e.g., the American South, Brazil, Cuba, and the Caribbean islands, but far less certain is whether the residues of African culture these diasporas produced were 'sure marks of Africa itself or whether they were creolized products forged out of an altogether new amalgam'. Here as elsewhere, Quayson implicitly critiques homogeneous views of an African diaspora that reinforce colonial myths of Africa as a static space or a lost continent (see Sharp in Part II of this volume). On the contrary, he concludes, Africa is not the bounded entity to which its diasporas attach as so many geographical extensions; rather, both the continent and its diasporas speak to the diversified 'social landscapes that have been forged among peoples of African descent everywhere'—never more so than in today's globalized world.

If African scholarship, by and large, has had an ambivalent relationship with postcolonial theory, then a different if not wholly unrelated set of problems obtains for American scholars. One version of the problem is a not-unjustified perception of the American dominance of the field, of the powerful institutional processes by which postcolonial studies has effectively become an 'Atlantic phenomenon, the result of various strands of thought and theory ... travelling beyond their point of origin [and then] emerging in a new form in the Anglophone academy, most notably in the United States' (see also Schulze-Engler in this section). Another concerns the place of the US itself, and of the Americas more generally, in postcolonial studies. The question is not so much of who is included and who not, although the usual caveats need to be borne in mind about the location and institutional authority of postcolonial criticism. It is rather one of *method*—postcolonialism's ongoing need to extend its range beyond the English-speaking world, to acknowledge alternative critical discourses in alternative European and non-European languages, and to interrogate its own tendencies to nationalist and/or regionalist parochialism, not least by seeking to develop a globally conscious if locally inflected *comparative* approach (see the General Introduction to this volume).

In his chapter Charles Forsdick suggests, after Quayson, that a 'postcolonializing' gaze on America may help, paradoxically perhaps, to do this; and that a retooled form of transcultural comparatism, drawing in part on earlier traditions of Inter-American studies, may prove useful in pursuing this particular critical goal. 'Postcolonializing' the US, specifically, must steer between the twin traps of positing its originary status (the 'first postcolonial nation') and reinforcing its obdurate exceptionalism (America's colonial past is 'like no others'); but it must also work towards correcting the countervailing tendency to see colonialism as having little to do with the historical formation of US national identity and/or the present multiethnic concoction that is 'American culture' at all. 'Postcolonializing' the Americas, more generally, involves broader, 'hemispheric' conceptions of the US and more flexible, 'multidirectional' models that look both east and west (e.g. to the Atlantic and the Pacific), but north and south (e.g. to Canada and Latin America) as well.

Forsdick turns his attention, accordingly, to Quebec, aptly described by Rachel Killick as both 'semi-attached participant and semi-detached observer on the northern fringe of American (US) empire'; and to Haiti, the geopolitical and socio-historical dimensions of which seem actively to require 'post-national, transnational and diasporic' understandings as well as revealing the extent to which 'postcolonial accounts of history and culture are only ever partial if they restrict themselves to [a] national or monolingual [approach]'. As Forsdick suggests, Haiti's importance in 'postcolonializing' the Americas may be disproportionate to its size, but it is 'wholly proportionate to the world-historical significance of its revolution'; similarly, a postcolonial perspective on

Haiti counteracts what some historians have seen as the 'systematic silencing' of Haiti in North American Atlanticist accounts. In advocating a properly inclusive American studies, allied to if not necessarily identical with postcolonialism, Forsdick goes some way towards supporting Spivak's 'critical regionalist' project even though he does not go so far as to name it. He also makes it clear—as does Quayson—that postcolonial studies exists in tandem rather than in competition with the critical paradigms ('diaspora', 'transnationalism', 'globalization') that some prematurely see as having replacing it; and that 'postcolonialization', acting together with these global forces, also works against their 'presentist' tendencies by showing the historical role of empire in underpinning them all.

The last chapter in the section, by the German literary/cultural scholar Frank Schulze-Engler, returns us to a region of the world which, though frequently posited as the (false) origin of postcolonial thinking, has not featured until relatively recently in postcolonial critical debates. 'Postcolonial Europe', as Schulze-Engler admits, is an awkward term in several ways, confronting Europe with a colonial past it often seeks to suppress, but also confronting postcolonial critics with a seemingly amorphous space, 'literally everywhere and nowhere', that belies the persistent critical inclination to 'write Europe out of the idea of a postcolonial world'. Schulze-Engler's chapter resists the temptation to construct 'Europe' as a straw category for postcolonial resistance while examining contemporary processes of 'Europeanization' and their implications for a field he sees as being persistently dominated by Anglo-American transatlantic perspectives (see Forsdick). His primary concerns, accordingly, are to break up the binary thinking he sees as dominating popular left-liberal conceptions of Europe as either high-minded cosmopolitan ideal or crude repository of imperial ideology, and to focus instead on different areas of 'unfinished business'—historical, geographical, cultural, political—that underlie contemporary 'Europeanization' debates. The decisive question for Schulze-Engler is not what Europe is but what kind of Europe is preferable to live in. Here, he sides with Balibar and others in pointing to the alarming discrepancy between Europe's continuing history of diversity and the contemporary 'politics of exclusion' that implicitly denies it (see Part II of this volume); he also draws attention to an equally long history of migration—both external and internal—that contradicts recent attempts to vouchsafe a 'core' European identity, e.g. by creating polarized political narratives of 'Europe and its others', or by shoring up national borders against those perceived to be incompatible with 'European values' and the 'common Christian heritage' of (western) Europe's increasingly fearful nation states.

But if 'postcolonial Europe' cannot be reduced to the 'cleavages and exclusions' it has inherited from its colonial past, nor should it be lazily indexed to the conflicts that surround global hypermobility in the present; it is also an arena of convivial possibility in which what the political philosopher Jürgen Habermas has perhaps optimistically called 'the transnational amplification of civic solidarity across Europe' is set firmly in place. This positive remaking of Europe can be seen, Schulze-Engler believes, in the 'wide-ranging network of transcultural connections to Africa, Asia, the Americas and the Pacific that is re-embedding contemporary European identities in a global setting'. Notwithstanding, Europe remains 'structurally invisible' in much postcolonial theory and criticism, either to be folded into its composite ideological counterpart, Eurocentrism, or to be identified with the equally undifferentiated colonialisms that have historically been constructed as the *raison d'être* for postcolonial studies as it looks to forge 'post-European commonalities' in an incompletely decolonized world. There is no doubting the need for appropriately decentred understandings of the kind that show, for instance, that Europe's is only one among many competing versions of global modernity (see Hindess in Part IV of this volume); but equally needed is the kind of decentring of Europe *from within* that might lead to a renewed appreciation of the region's linguistic and cultural diversity—a diversity also paradoxically missing in the postcolonial studies field, which still operates largely in English with an agenda far too conveniently shaped by dominant Anglo-American concerns. What is needed, Schulze-Engler concludes— and I can think of no more fitting conclusion to this volume—is an alternately decentred and polycentric postcolonial studies which, in complicating the easy binaries that continue to impede it, acknowledges the wide variety of critical-regionalist perspectives ('Asian' and 'African', but also 'European') that might best enable its geographically dispersed practitioners to negotiate the challenges of a globalized world.

REFERENCES

Appadurai, Arjun (1996). *Modernity at Large: Cultural Dimensions of Globalization.* Minneapolis: University of Minnesota Press.

Brennan, Timothy (2008). 'Postcolonial Studies and Globalization Theory', in R. Krishnaswamy and J. Hawley (eds), *The Postcolonial and the Global.* Minneapolis: University of Minnesota Press, 37–53.

Chakrabarty, Dipesh (2000). *Provincializing Europe: Postcolonial Thought and Historical Difference.* Princeton: Princeton: University Press.

During, Simon (1998). 'Postcolonialism and Globalisation: A Dialectical Relation After All?' *Postcolonial Studies,* 1.1: 31–47.

During, Simon (2000). 'Postcolonialism and Globalization: Towards a Historicization of their Inter-relation', *Cultural Studies,* 14.3/4: 385–404.

Harvey, David (2003). *The New Imperialism.* New York and Oxford: Oxford University Press.

Hoogvelt, Ankie (1997). *Globalization and the Postcolonial World.* Basingstoke: Palgrave Macmillan.

Huggan, Graham (2009). *Extreme Pursuits: Travel/Writing in an Age of Globalization.* Ann Arbor: University of Michigan Press.

Krishnaswamy, Revathi (2008). 'Connections, Conflicts, Complicities', in R. Krishnaswamy and J. Hawley (eds), *The Postcolonial and the Global.* Minneapolis: University of Minnesota Press, 2–21.

Larner, Wendy and William Walters (2002). 'The Political Rationality of "New Regionalism": Toward a Genealogy of the Region', *Theory and Society,* 31: 391–432.

Loomba, Ania, Suvir Kaul, Matti Bunzl, Antoinette Burton, and Jed Esty (eds) (2005). *Postcolonial Studies and Beyond.* Durham, NC: Duke University Press.

Mignolo, Walter (2000). 'The Many Faces of Cosmopolis: Border Thinking and Critical Cosmopolitanism', *Public Culture,* 12.3: 721–48.

Robertson, Roland (1992). *Globalization: Social Theory and Global Culture*. London: Sage.

Ross, Andrew (1991). *Strange Weather: Culture, Science, and Technology in the Age of Limits*. New York: Verso.

Sassen, Saskia (2008) 'The Many Scales of the Global: Implications for Theory and for Politics', in R. Krishnaswamy and J. Hawley (eds.) *The Postcolonial and the Global* (Minneapolis: University of Minnesota Press), pp. 82–93.

Spencer, Robert (2011) *Cosmopolitan Criticism and Postcolonial Literature* (Basingstoke: Palgrave Macmillan).

Spivak, Gayatri Chakravorty (1999) *A Critique of Postcolonial Reason: Toward a History of the Vanishing Present* (Cambridge, MA: Harvard University Press).

Spivak, Gayatri Chakravorty (2008) *Other Asias* (Malden, MA: Blackwell).

Stewart-Harawira, Makere (2005) *The New Imperial Order: Indigenous Responses to Globalization* (London and Wellington: Zed Books).

CHAPTER 25

PERSPECTIVES ON GLOBALIZATION AND SUBALTERNITY

NIKITA DHAWAN AND SHALINI RANDERIA

INTRODUCTION

Globalization theory and postcolonial studies constitute two influential paradigms in social sciences and cultural studies that address past and present social, political, and economic transformations in an increasingly interconnected world. Despite partial overlaps and shared concerns the relationship between the two analytical frameworks remains uneasy and complex. While some theorists posit postcolonial studies as a 'critical strain posed within and against, as well as antecedent to, dominant notions of globalization' (Loomba et al. 2005: 8), others argue that in the period spanning Edward Said's *Orientalism* (1978) and Michael Hardt's and Antonio Negri's *Empire* (2000) globalization studies has gradually come to replace postcolonial studies (During 1998). Both of these new academic fields have succeeded in overcoming narrow disciplinary boundaries. Both face the challenge of differentiating between the economic, political, legal, and cultural dimensions of transnational processes and their differing impacts in various periods and regions of the world. Arguing that both fields constitute their own novelty by disowning their own predecessors and prehistories, Brennan contends that of the two, postcolonial studies is more open to a critical self-questioning (2008: 38). In this chapter, we would like to focus on another commonality between the two; namely the 'hostility of both to the nation form (particularly as nation-*state*)' (49, emphasis in the original). Globalization and postcolonial studies diverge, however, in their analyses of whether, and in what ways, contemporary processes of transnationalization constitute a continuation of imperial domination; or whether, and how, these mark a rupture that is currently restructuring the world in unprecedented ways (Krishnaswamy 2008: 10, 15; Brennan 2008: 39). These opposing views rest on a descriptive disagreement as well as a normative variance. For there is little consensus on whether we are currently 'witnessing an intensification of American imperialism' or whether we are in a post-imperial age of 'empire' (Krishnaswamy 2008: 4; see also Part II of this volume).

Globalization is deployed as an analytical category in much current social science scholarship but is also a word widely used in demotic discourse to make sense of one's experiences of the world. Not only has the meaning and significance of the term been contested among scholars, but also its novelty, velocity, extent, and impact on people of various classes, castes, ethnic groups, and genders in various regions have been assessed differently. While globalization constitutes an empirical description of contemporary processes of transformation for some scholars, for others it is an analytical frame-work for understanding these. Some consider it to be an empty signifier, whereas for others it is simply an ideologically loaded term. Definitions of globalization abound. With Held et al. (1999: 14–15) one can define it as a spatio-temporal process of change that deepens, widens, and speeds up horizontal and vertical interconnections between spaces and scales, thereby transforming social relations and the organization of society. Celebratory accounts of globalization view it as enabling a 'global or transnational imaginary' (Bhabha 1994: 205). Yet access to globality is highly uneven. Globalist fantasies and ideas of seamless flows tend to overlook the fact that the vast majority of people in the world are not mobile (Tsing 2005); they continue to live and work throughout their lives in one place even if everyday lives in these places are likely to be affected by distant events to a larger extent than ever before. Contemporary globalization is thus a bundle of profoundly uneven and deeply contradictory processes, which are able continuously to negotiate and incorporate the differences that threaten its hegemony. There seems to be 'no difference that it cannot contain, no otherness it cannot speak, no marginality that it cannot take pleasure out of' (Hall 1997: 182).

With Held et al. (1999: 2) one can distinguish three broad positions on globalization. The first is represented by 'hyperglobalists' for whom contemporary processes of globalization as defined by the forces of global capitalism along with the concomitant weakening of the state are unprecedented. This view may be held both by enthusiastic *advocates* of globalization, who welcome deregulation, privatization, and the free play of unfettered market forces, as well as by ardent *opponents* of neoliberal globalization, who are critical of the new 'market fundamentalism' that corrodes democracy. Both concur in the importance of the rapidity and far-reaching impact of current processes of change even as their judgements on the desirability of the consequences of these changes vary sharply over and against this position, the 'sceptics' not only doubt the novelty of the extent of current economic integration, but also downplay its significance. For 'transformationalists', current processes, patterns, and practices of globalization evince both historical continuities and radical ruptures. They distinguish not only between various forms of globalization that vary with time and place but are also sensitive to the differences in the ways in which these are experienced by communities and individuals. While some scholars stress growing homogenization and standardization due to globalization, others emphasize an increase in diversity, hybridity, and cultural translation. Most would agree that it entails a 'disjuncture' between the economic, the political, and the cultural (Appadurai 1996: 32), whereby 'mediascapes' and 'ideoscapes' become the sites of tension between processes of cultural homogenization and heterogenization. The contemporary relevance of older narratives of 'cultural imperialism' (Randeria 2011), for instance, has been challenged by analyses of polycentric flows of images, ideas, goods, and people that facilitate the emergence of 'delocalized transnations' that have displaced the 'hegemony of Eurochronology' (Appadurai 1996: 172, 30). In contrast to older forms of Euro-American modernity aimed at an instrumental rationalization of the world, in this view it is multidirectional flows rather than hierarchies that characterize the new global culture. Global cultural production has been posited as decentred due to increasing flows within the south as well as from the semi-periphery to the erstwhile centres (Hannerz 1987). The idea of 'subversive consumption' (Krishnaswamy 2008: 14) also questions the billiard ball model of one-way cultural impact, which underlies the thesis of cultural imperialism. It points instead, for instance, to active forms of indigenization by subaltern communities subjected to internal colonialism in the margins of the nation state. Localized communities employ a variety of strategies to domesticate, adapt, or resist ideas, images, and institutions emerging elsewhere (Inda and Rosaldo 2007). While challenging western hegemony and definitional monopolies these local engagements shape 'vernacular modernities' (Knauft 2002).

Older models of explaining global interrelationships such as the three-worlds conception, or the centre–periphery model of world systems theory (Wallerstein 1984), are considered by some scholars to be no longer adequate. Arguably these paradigms have been rendered obsolete after the collapse of the Soviet Union and are in need of revision in the wake of new geopolitical constellations like the G8, BRICS, ASEAN, or China's reach in Africa. Moreover, migration and new communication technologies have rendered the relationship between localities and cultural practices more complex. Stuart Hall (1997: 178) detects the emergence of a 'global culture' in the late twentieth century, while David Harvey speaks of the 'time/space compression' that has shrunk geographical and temporal distance, enabling a condition of instantaneity in human interactions (1989: 240–1). For some scholars the world is thus being reconstituted as a single social, economic, political, and cultural space, even as this global integration allows 'complex and internal variations across an interconnected system of localities and regions' (Brennan 2008: 39). Mobility, material or virtual, facilitates the access of some hitherto excluded groups to the public sphere, thereby disrupting older logics and mechanisms of exclusion. As an analytical framework for the contemporary, globalization thus overcomes the methodological nationalism dominant in the social sciences (Martins 1974: 276) in order to facilitate decentred narratives that emerge in transnational spaces outside the boundaries of the nation states. Nation states can no longer be conceptualized as bounded entities, nor do they constitute an adequate arena for understanding either the dynamics of contemporary capitalism or of resistance to it.

Postcolonial theorists have noted that ideas of 'the world' and 'the globe' are deeply implicated in (neo)colonialism. Given the close connection between colonial conquest and cartography some scholars doubt whether it is possible to imagine 'the

globe' without invoking imperial prospects (Hulme 2005: 45). In view of the significance of colonial and neocolonial relations in the very emergence of the global, postcolonial theory has been a 'major source of a new grammar for rethinking the global'
(Gikandi 2005: 612). Current paths and patterns of globalization thus need to be
situated against the background of European colonial conquest, exploitation, expropriation, and restructuring of relations between people and places in the west and
the rest, to use Hall's (1992) phrase. An understanding of trade, travel, and territorial claims in historical perspective helps to clarify the links between neo-imperialism
today and older systems of colonialism (Loomba et al. 2005: 4). Postcolonial theorists
are of the view that asymmetries of wealth and power between the global north and
global south continue to be inflected by this colonial legacy. Neoliberal globalization
thus reinforces structural disparities and intensifies inequalities put into place during
colonial rule instead of dismantling them. Many of the poor and the marginalized in
postcolonial societies thus experience neoliberal globalization as a process of recolonization (see Vukovich in this section of the volume; also the chapters by Gopal and
Hazbun in Part II).

The paradigm change from 'Third World' to 'postcolonial' marks a decisive shift in
the terms of the debate. In view of the centrality accorded to culture in most postcolonial analyses of transnational experiences, the émigré has emerged as the protagonist of
postcolonial globalism. Critics of this position have interrogated the unequivocal celebration of the liberating potential of the diaspora. They point instead to the ambivalence
of diasporic politics with its 'long-distance' nationalism, which is often conservative, if
not chauvinistic. Feminist and queer theorists in particular have critiqued the hetero-
sexist nationalism emerging within diasporic formations (Gopinath 2005). Moreover,
a privileging of the category of diaspora fails to recognize that a transformation of the
nation state by no means implies its marginality. For the 'diaspora's rise does not necessarily signal nation's fall' (Cooppan 2005: 87; see also Quayson in this section of the
volume).

Neoliberal Globalization
in Postcolonial India

Instead of simply celebrating the post-national as in much of the discourse of globalization, many postcolonial theorists emphasize the dangers of the erosion of the
nation state, national economies, and national-cultural identities. One of the perils
of the decline of the nation state is the recourse to defensive and exclusivist formations of national identities driven by aggressive forms of racism and communalism
(Hall 1997). A telling instance of this is the rise of the Hindu right in India, which
has accompanied the liberalization of the subcontinent's economy. Current processes

of neoliberal globalization in India began in the late 1980s and early 1990s with the country's centrally planned economy being opened up to foreign capital. In the wake of a balance of payment crisis in 1991, the New Economic Policy was launched by executive fiat, bypassing the Indian parliament. If the imperatives of the global capital markets along with the prescriptions of the IMF and World Bank forced the adoption of these new policies and programmes, the Indian elite, which shared this vision, willingly embraced the mantra of deregulation and market-led growth. The new policies permitted and encouraged foreign and domestic capital investment in areas hitherto reserved for the public sector (infrastructure, mineral extraction, telecommunications, media), allowed the privatization of several profitable state enterprises, reduced agricultural subsidies, and led to the restructuring of taxes, tariffs, and the removal of many import restrictions and controls. Imported consumer goods become freely available to the moneyed middle class, spurring an unbridled consumerism that was also founded on the new job opportunities for the well-educated in outsourced global enterprises.

Since the late 1990s there has been an unprecedented boom in mobile telephones and new privately owned satellite television channels, shopping malls have sprung up in all cities, and the music and fashion industries are thriving. The enormous Bollywood cinema industry has successfully entered the global entertainment market by producing films for overseas audiences that incorporate diasporic, middle-class themes and Euro-American locations. As global trends are thus transmuted into a variety of vernacular forms, a globalized imagination has been formed, albeit one that is not marked by cultural uniformity (Appadurai 1996). Regional differences among the middle classes in India remain salient. For instance, there is an increasing demand for English-medium education from kindergarten onwards in communist-ruled West Bengal (Donner 2005). But in the western Indian state of Maharashtra, where English is still regarded as the colonizer's language, the strong preference of middle-class parents for schooling in the mother tongue remains unaffected by the countervailing pressures of the job market (Bénéi 2005).

Paradoxically, economic liberalization in India has been accompanied by the growing popularity of right-wing Hindu nationalist politics (Corbridge and Harriss 2000). This trend has been interpreted as an expression of cultural insecurity on the part of the new urban middle classes (Nandy et al. 1995) or as political assertion by lower and upper middle classes, which have increasingly turned to new media-savvy Hindu religious preachers and organizations (Rajagopal 2001). With their message of a modern, often globalized Hinduism, these cult figures and organizations attract followers of various castes and classes in the country but are equally popular with so-called non-resident Indians (NRIs) overseas. Religious nationalism in India and abroad, which reflects parochial and chauvinistic tendencies rather than cosmopolitan ones, is driven by the desire to turn the country into a modern and powerful superpower with a nuclear weapons arsenal (Assayag and Fuller 2005: 5). The postcolonial Indian state has neither been weakened nor rendered insignificant by the forces of globalization but has been restructured by being partly transnationalized and partly privatized (Randeria 2007a). Power within the state has shifted too, on the one hand from the legislature to the executive and judiciary, and on the other hand from the federal level to regional governments increasingly run by caste-based parties.

Post-liberalization economic growth in India has been highly uneven across regions as well as within each individual region. Urban–rural differentials have widened and inequality has increased. Unemployment in many sectors has risen, as has indebtedness among the rural poor. Regional governments in India have become involved in a competitive federalism to attract domestic and foreign capital by offering 'tax holidays' while making land available to industry at throwaway prices. Vast tracts of agricultural land and commons have been used to set up Special Economic Zones, where labour and environmental laws are kept in abeyance and production of goods and services is tax-exempt. Expropriation by the state has led to large-scale dispossession and destruction of livelihoods of the poor. Rapacious extraction of minerals has eroded the natural resource base, exacerbated environmental pollution (Ahmed et al. 2011: 1–2), and deprived indigenous communities of access to forest habitats. A notable concomitant of rapid industrialization and high rates of economic growth has been the rapid development of infrastructure (privatization of highways, airports, ports, and power plants), which has also led to forced displacement of hundreds and thousands every year, thus rendering destitute those who are economically and socially vulnerable and politically marginalized.

Displacement along with deindustrialization in traditional branches has made urban land readily available to foreign and domestic investors. Real-estate prices have skyrocketed as a result of speculation and investment of unaccounted-for 'black money' into the building sector. The poor have been forced out to the margins of mega-cities in areas without any civic amenities. Whether, and to what extent, poverty has decreased over the past two decades as a result of liberalization continues to be a matter of considerable controversy. With a population of over a billion, India still has as many people living in hunger as sub-Saharan Africa. Among the highly divisive issues which have dominated public debates in the wake of the neoliberal restructuring of the Indian economy, is the erosion of collective rights of farming communities. There has been strong criticism by activists and academics of (i) 'biopiracy' (Shiva 1999) under the World Trade Organization's framework of Trade-Related Intellectual Property Rights (TRIPS), which permits the patenting of biogenetic material like Basmati rice or Neem oil (Randeria 2007a); and (ii) the introduction of genetically manipulated seeds by multinational corporations, which has resulted in widespread rural distress, high indebtedness, and the suicide of thousands of farmers across the country (Sainath 2004). Massive protests against agricultural and plant patents as well as against corporate 'land grab' have accompanied widespread dispossession and destruction of livelihoods. Strategies of contention by the poor have ranged from armed resistance to non-violent mass mobilization and the recourse to courts in a quest for justice against the illegalities of the state. Brutal repression by the armed forces and semi-private militias, indiscriminate arrests, and the killing of activists and ordinary citizens in the name of combating 'terrorism' have been the response of the state to sustained resistance in resource-rich areas inhabited by indigenous communities.

PERSPECTIVES ON CRITICAL REGIONALISM

Despite strong reservations about the actually existing state, many postcolonial scholars have pointed to its indispensability in the quest for rights and justice, a point dealt with in the following section of the chapter. The state remains salient as an agent and an object of development as well as an arena in which actors may pursue a variety of visions of social and economic transformation. As a counterpoint to much recent writing on modernity and development, which shifts the focus to actors at either the local or global level, an emphasis on the nation state is crucial to an understanding of the emergence of 'regional modernities' and trajectories of development (Sivaramakrishnan and Agrawal 2003). As an alternative to the stark binary of 'local/global', Sivaramakrishnan and Agrawal map the space between the two by focusing on the regional, but without assuming its spatial connotations as pre-given. Instead of identifying a 'region' with a specific size or scale, they use the term relationally to trace the practices of individuals, collectivities, and institutions on a variety of spatial levels. Thus, regions are seen as products of socio-political, cultural, and economic forces and ongoing processes. If a consideration of regions avoids the 'endless proliferation of difference that the "local" necessarily produces and in some sense reinforces' (Sivaramakrishnan and Agarwal 2003: 14), it equally eschews the totalizing connotations of an all-encompassing or homogenizing sense of the 'global'. It also serves as a reminder that localities and global processes as well as forms of capitalism are embedded within regional formations (Ong 1999: 240; see also Vukovich in this section of the volume).

Sivaramakrishnan and Agrawal suggest that the focus on regions as social and discursive sites allows for an investigation of variations in paths and patterns in the production of modernities that range from subnational to multi- and supranational formations. Their point of departure is the recognition that modernities are multiple (see the General Introduction to this volume; also Schulze-Engler in this section). Often this plurality has been coupled in Weberian fashion to civilizations defined in terms of religions (Eisenstadt 2000) (as in discourses of Islamic modernity), or to nation states or continents as units (as in studies of Indian or African modernity) (Randeria et al. 2004). Randeria (2002, 2009) has argued instead for a study of the specificities of modernity in different postcolonial societies, which are products of past and present interactions and unequal exchanges. Instead of assuming pre-given spatial units of analysis she suggests tracing the production of structural asymmetries and cultural differences against the background of histories of entangled modernities that have been mutually constitutive of former colonies and metropoles (Conrad and Randeria 2002). Whereas for Partha Chatterjee (1997) modernities in different postcolonial societies vary in form since the very task of the cultural project of nationalism is the production of a distinctly national modernity, for Sivaramakrishnan and Agarwal a particular national modernity is but a variant of the regional. It reflects the 'geographic divergence, varying temporal rhythms, and institutional differences' within the 'historically sedimented social, economic, and spatial structures' of a region (2003: 16). A flexible notion of regions thus facilitates the mapping of processes of differentiation and network formation, but also of shifting constellations of bloc and coalition building both within and across regional (trade) networks and alliances as well as new governance structures. Continuities and disjunctures of power are 'a product of the regional geography of landscapes, institutions, and cultural complexes' (2003: 21). The effects of power and the struggles against it therefore also need to be situated in the context of the historically informed imaginaries and place-making practices of various actors, be these nation states and groups within it or those transcending state boundaries like diasporas or transnational formations.

Pointing to the need to distinguish between 'region' and 'regionalization', Prasenjit Duara (2010) argues that the Asian region does not reflect a cartographic representation of Asia. Whereas a region signifies the historical emergence of patterns of interaction, regionalization connotes an active, often ideologically motivated, political process of regional formation that follows the hegemonic modes of spatial production in every historical period. Addressing the politics of reterritorialization in terms of the complex interplay between these processes, Duara emphasizes that world regions like Asia are products of contemporary place-making strategies as well as entanglements. Postcolonial societies produce national space out of politically and economically dependent colonial territories by truncating, on the one hand, 'external' transnational ties and homogenizing 'internal' diversity, on the other. Created within the framework of imperial projects these territories appear to be 'natural' regions, irrespective and independent of the colonial relations of domination that shaped them. Duara (2010) shows, for example, how the Japanese and British empires in the nineteenth and twentieth centuries created significant regional interdependence in Asia. He explores in particular how British 'imperial regionalism' came not only to shape the interactions that underlie current images of Asia, but also how these new imperial patterns of ties overshadowed and eclipsed earlier regional interrelationships to which Europe had been rather marginal. Regional integration was thus an interactive process undertaken by colonial states and metropolitan capitalists as well as by Asian merchants, who dominated the indigenous financial markets. How was this increasing intertwining of people's quotidian lives and economic practices reflected in representations of the region? Duara suggests that the Asian 'region', with its colonial heritage, served as a point of departure for anticolonial struggles but also as a resource for nationalistic as well as cosmopolitan visions of decolonization. While Rabindranath Tagore, for instance, remained committed to an alternate cosmopolitanism drawn from Asian traditions, nationalism was a necessary component in the conception of pan-Asianism in the intellectual and cultural projects of Zhang Taiyan or Okakura Tenshin, as Duara convincingly shows.

If anti-imperialist thought linked to rising Asian nationalism crafted alternative conceptions of the region that evoked earlier ties between societies of the continent, these conceptualizations of Asia too were predicated on, and enabled by, contemporary imperialist technologies and modes of regional integration (Duara 2010: 969). Given the fact that many world regions are artefacts of colonial rule or products of the cartography of the Cold War, such geopolitically motivated redefinitions of space raise serious questions about the ontological status of territorial units taken for granted in disciplines or interdisciplinary fields like area studies, history, international relations, development studies, anthropology, or literary studies. Tracing the 'conceptual matrix' of the formation of area studies in the US academy, Pheng Cheah in his essay on Asian studies reminds us that an 'area' is by definition 'that which is not universal' but also 'precisely that which is not *capable* of universality' (2008: 54, emphasis in the original). Thus there is an inherent asymmetry built into the relationship between area studies and the 'universal knowing subject of the disciplines' (54).

In an attempt to deconstruct border regimes and identity politics, Gayatri Spivak (2008) has developed the notion of 'critical regionalism' as an alternative both to 'area studies' and to the methodological nationalism that assumes bounded nation states as pre-given units of analysis. In his provocative essay titled 'Does India exist?' Immanuel Wallerstein (1991), too, not only questions the naturalness of nation states as geographical entities but also draws attention to their colonial origins as political entities. He makes a double argument: India, like all other present-day nation states, is a product of the modern world system; for the capitalist world system was predicated on the existence of the 'political superstructure of sovereign states linked together in and legitimated by an interstate system' that had to be built and maintained over 500 years (Wallerstein 1991: 131). Moreover, the geographical and political entity with the boundaries that we know as India today is a result of a complex colonial production of space that was projected backwards in time. Thus 'India's pre-modern history is an invention of modern India' (132).

Making a similar argument in terms of regions, Spivak suggests that even as the word 'Asia' 'reflects Europe's eastward trajectory' (2008: 207), Asia too has come to think of itself today in terms of this totalized representation. Thus the very question of what 'Asia' is, whether in its historical or contemporary form, is a vexed issue (see Vukovich in this section of the volume). Spivak reminds us that 'Asia' does not signify a fixed referent in space or time; it is best understood instead in terms of its plurality as 'Asias'. Over and against the colonial gesture of 'corrective knowledge from above' (211), wherein Asia is postulated as an identifiable region and assigned its geographical and historical position in a Eurocentric world history, Spivak, following Said's idea of 'imaginative geography' (Said 1978), advocates the theoretical-methodological corrective of an 'informed imagination' (2008: 237), one that might do justice to the heterogeneity and complexity of a vast continent. Challenging the uncritical acceptance of regions as 'geographical facts', Appadurai (1996) advances a similar understanding of space as processual. He advocates taking seriously both the historical connections and contemporary trajectories of mobility within and across regions by mapping the orientations and imaginaries of the ordinary men and women who define these spaces through their everyday lives.

GENDERING GLOBALIZATION FROM A POSTCOLONIAL PERSPECTIVE

Processes of globalization have contradictory consequences for the lives of women across the world. Economic globalization increasingly undermines traditional patriarchy by the rapid incorporation of women into wage labour, a trend that has arguably contributed to their financial independence and social empowerment. But these gains have accrued for the most part to women with higher levels of education and ownership of, or access to, resources (Moghadam 2005). Economic liberalization has undoubtedly brought new work opportunities for young women in urban areas of the global south, be these in factories in special economic zones, in the IT industry, or in the service sector. For example, newly established call centres across Indian cities have led to a significant increase in the employment of women at relatively high wages in the formal sector. Yet 94 per cent of the country's female labour force continues to toil in the unorganized sector. Thus not only are a majority of women concentrated in low-skilled, low-wage, temporary, insecure employment, but vast numbers of older women have been rendered redundant due to deindustrialization in other sectors or the decline of industries as a result of economic restructuring. If globalization has meant a feminization of the labour force, it has also meant an informalization of work (Rowbotham and Mitter 1994).

Advocates of neoliberalism argue that the dismantling of state structures creates new employment opportunities for women and other disadvantaged groups in the south. However, there has neither been a corresponding increase in women's education nor do women receive equal pay for equal work. Not only does a gendering of work persist but highly qualified women all over the world are still confronted by a glass ceiling. An increased gendered international division of labour thus goes hand in hand with limited access to wealth, property, resources, and to institutions for women (Balakrishnan 2001). Middle- and upper-class women in both north and south have benefited from new opportunities on the labour market in part due to structural asymmetries that allow a global care chain (Hochschild 2000). But women are also losers when caught between the contesting forces of patriarchal nation states and religious fundamentalisms that are everywhere on the rise parallel to free-market policies (Moghadam 2005).

After more than six decades of failed policies and programmes of development, the neo-imperialism of contemporary discourses and practices of development aid continues to attract critique (see Sharp in Part II of this volume). Some of these discourses serve to legitimize neocolonial interventions in the name of empowering women in the so-called Third World (Dhawan 2009). It has been argued, for instance, that the notion of 'women's interest', common to all women regardless of race, class, religion, and sexuality has led to universal one-size-fits-all solutions being propagated for the emancipation of women worldwide (Dhawan 2011). Mohanty et al. (2003) advocate instead a rethinking of 'global sisterhood' within the international women's movement as a way to eschew the essentialization of gender identity and western feminist hegemony. One aspect that the international women's health movement has highlighted, for instance, is the link between biopolitics and globalization. Ironically, while fertility control for poor women is being implemented through more or less explicit coercion in the global south (Randeria 2007c), not only do health insurance companies pay for assisted conception in Europe, but pregnancies in Euroamerica are also being increasingly outsourced to countries like India. Global gradients of inequality and the commodification of the female body in the so-called Third World through international commercial surrogacy are intimately linked (Hochschild 2012). The deliberately lax regulation of transnational contracting of wombs in countries like India poses urgent ethical and political questions for the agency of poor women in the global south.

Postcolonial feminist theorists also point to the question of subject formation at the heart of neoliberal policies of economic growth (Dhawan 2009, 2011). For example, FTZs (free-trade zones) or SEZs (special economic zones) for exports promotion do not simply employ young women but constitute women's bodies, sexualities, and social relations in specific ways (Ong 1987). Young women workers are disciplined to exhibit 'female' traits such as passivity, patience, and dexterity, thereby producing bodies suited to long hours of labour in confined spaces under strict surveillance (ibid.: 152). The challenge, therefore, is to de-instrumentalize women as efficient economic subjects in the era of globalization. The role of transnational feminism in this regard has been the subject of some controversy. Critics argue that the merging of women's local struggles to a global women's movement comes at the price of further entrenching the hegemony of elite feminist agendas. Advocates of transnational feminism, however, highlight the role of cross-border civil society networks as an outcome of globalization, which facilitate the participation of women in 'global' politics. The UN Cairo Conference (1994) and the Beijing Conference (1995) sparked debate on the complicities of the transnational feminist movement with imperialism (Spivak 1993), as well as the potential of feminism across borders (Mohanty et al. 2003). For most feminist scholars from the global south and north 'decolonizing feminism' remains a matter of urgency. This is, however, no easy task for it would involve 'feminists with a transnational consciousness' acknowledging their own 'agency in complicity' while resisting the role of 'native-informant-cum-hybrid-globalist' (Spivak 1999: 399).

ALTER-GLOBALIZATION AND SUBALTERNITY

Transnationalism is arguably not a monopoly of multinational capital or of multilateral organizations, but is also claimed by several oppositional socio-political formations.

Progressive forms of 'globalization from below' function as a collective countervailing force to the symbolic and material power of 'globalization from above'. Some scholars and activists thus conceive of 'alter-globalization' movements as promising agents of grass-roots social transformation and as a counterweight to the power of corporations, nation states, and international organizations like the IMF, WTO, or the World Bank. Others remain sceptical about using the notion of 'global civil society' to describe actors in the global north and south engaged in contesting neoliberal globalization. Some critics of the term claim that 'civil society' cannot be used meaningfully at the transnational level in the absence of its pendant, the state (Tarrow 2002). Others point to the context of its resurgence after 1989, when 'civil society' was shorn of its critical potential and reduced to a synonym for non-governmental organizations (NGOs). Such a sanitized version of civil society conceptualized and promoted as an apolitical sphere of voluntary associations funded by international donors and by the state, has blunted the critical edge of the concept. However, many of the social actors involved in transnational politics of contention continue to use it as a term of self-reference. Therefore, instead of deploying it as an analytical concept, it seems best to conceptualize global civil society in terms of the 'practices that are shaped in its name' (Amoore and Langley 2004).

Definitions, forms, and the nature of global civil society (Kaldor et al. 2006; Keane 2003; Scholte 2000) as well as the applicability of the concept to societies outside the west (Comaroff and Comaroff 2006; Hann and Dunn 1996; Kaviraj and Khilnani 2001) have been contested over the past decade. In addition scholars in India have raised important issues regarding the politics of transnational civil society activism. Baxi (2002: 41), for instance, has assailed the 'Euro-enclosed imagination' of so-called cosmopolitan ideas of global civil society, just as Chandhoke (2003) has critiqued the role of NGOs as vehicles of westernization. Their dependence on, and accountability to, foreign donors, their transformation from watchdogs to lapdogs of the state, as well as their uncritical acceptance of shifting donor agendas have come in for criticism as well. Reflecting on the asymmetries of power within transnational networks and alliances, Jai Sen has also drawn attention to relations of power among and between non-state actors. He argues that global civil society represents a 'globalization from the middle' (2007: 62), rather than one 'from below', for at its forefront are transnationally networked middle-class activists from the north and the south. Baxi's observation that compared to earlier histories of working-class struggles much of the current global activism around human rights issues remains the work of 'human rights elites and entrepreneurs' (2006: 70) concurs with such a view.

However cross-border activism has opened up spaces for a critique of the neoliberal bias of the new norms being promulgated by international institutions and implemented by more or less willing national elites, especially with regard to economic, fiscal, and trade policies. Critics have nevertheless questioned the possibilities of progressive, emancipatory politics by professionalized NGOs. They have also raised important issues regarding the legitimacy, representation, and autonomy of these unelected, self-appointed guardians and spokespersons, who speak in the name of those whom they claim to represent. Neocolonialism, like colonialism, sustains itself in the name of doing good for 'the people' (Spivak 2007: 177). International civil society and anti-globalization activists often bypass the state by virtue of having gained tremendous influence of late as part of the new architecture of global governance. Global justice and human rights activists, for instance, directly use international alliances and extra-domestic fora to name and shame states or put pressure on them (Randeria 2007a, 2007b; Dhawan 2009, 2011). Strategies for leapfrogging the state weaken the authority and legitimacy of the post-colonial state, from whom activists demand greater answerability to its citizens instead of accountability to international financial and trade organizations or international donors (Randeria 2007a).

Neoliberal discourses of 'good governance', which have replaced demands for substantive democracy, often assume that a vibrant civil society both strengthens and extends the reach of democracy by giving voice and representation to those excluded from participation in state institutions and from access to the public sphere. Following Gramsci, Spivak (2007) complicates this easy equation between democracy and civil society by delineating the manner in which the latter functions as an extension of the hegemonic order rather than a locus of resistance against it. With the integration of NGOs into the new neoliberal architecture of global governance, 'civil society' has become part of a project of the selective dismantling and privatization of the state. Responsibilities that the state is unwilling or unable to fulfil are transferred to NGOs, which are increasingly involved in 'public–private partnerships' with states, international aid organizations, and corporations, in order to ensure efficient and cheaper service delivery to the poor. As the state progressively withdraws from the provision of public services, social security, education, healthcare, and even public security, a notion of civil society compatible with the market emerges.

However, Partha Chatterjee has critiqued the very concept of civil society in post-colonial societies as applicable only to democratic arenas of citizen action, and hence as excluding those without access to full citizenship, who constitute the majority. Civil society, in his view, is thus quintessentially a realm of bourgeois politics of private property, equality of law, and freedom of contract that operates only within a small elite zone (Chatterjee 2004: 69). His influential intervention on the 'politics of the governed' contrasts 'civil society', the domain of middle-class civic engagement premised on a western normative conception of rights-bearing citizens interacting with the state, with 'political society', which encompasses mobilization by the (urban) poor. Sporadic, contextual, and characterized by spontaneous collective action, or by ad hoc negotiations with state representatives through local power brokers and strongmen, the polities of the poor may often verge on illegality.

Such an understanding of subaltern politics resonates well with Jai Sen's (2007) forceful argument contrasting 'civil society' with the domain he provocatively terms the 'incivil' (in the eyes of the state and civil society alike). The former is the realm of 'self-appointed guardians' of civility belonging to middle or upper classes/castes, who not only impose their norms of political actions on others but also attempt to 'colonize and domesticate' those outside the ambit of 'civility' (Sen 2007: 56). 'Incivility' is thus seen to characterize the lives and politics of the lower classes/castes/people of colour, the world of 'second-class denizens' (58). In all societies these groups are forced to resort to what is considered 'illegal' or 'unauthorized' in order to survive and secure a livelihood. Sen distinguishes between the 'incivil' and the 'uncivil'. The former are 'oppressed, victimized, but building insurgent societies, or challenging power structures dominated by the civil', while the 'uncivil' (60) are those who resist and subvert civil society but out of materialist interests, or criminal and exploitative motives. Although the lines between the 'incivil' and 'uncivil' are blurred in the lived experiences of the poor, Sen insists that these three different worlds of 'civility', 'incivility', and 'uncivility' coexist in dynamic tension. For from the point of view of those marginalized and excluded, the sphere of civil society and anti-globalization activism may signal subjugation rather than emancipation. The example of the Dalit (the former 'untouchable castes') movement in India points to just such a divergence of perspectives. In sharp contrast to the assessment of British rule in India by the leadership of the Indian national movement, the Dalit statesman, Dr B. R. Ambedkar insisted that colonialism was not the only, or even the primary, enemy for the communities he represented. Upper castes had for centuries stigmatized and discriminated against the castes confined to the bottom of the social, economic, and religious hierarchy. Their oppression was thus neither rooted in colonial rule nor would it simply disappear with independence from it. Echoing such a divergent position on colonial rule, many Dalit activists and organizations at the 2004 World Social Forum in Mumbai did not share the critique of neoliberal globalization put forward by a majority of participants. They emphasized instead the potential of globalization to open access to education and employment opportunities by dismantling entrenched caste/class structures and privileges.

The intensification of global processes of economic, political, and cultural transformation has radically transformed the nature and politics of international activist networks (Fisher and Ponniah 2003; Escobar 2004). The transnational reach of contemporary social movements is not unprecedented since activists have often cooperated across national borders in the past, as, for instance, in the movement for the abolition of slavery in the nineteenth century. Following Baxi (2006: 70), contemporary movements, which interrogate global hegemony and domination using the languages of global justice and human rights, can be situated in the much longer history of 'anti-systemic' movements (Arrighi and Silver 2000; Balibar and Wallerstein 1991). Many of these cross-border movements in the late eighteenth and nineteenth centuries bore the marks of a Janus-faced imperialism that denied human rights in colonies, while allowing juridical contestation on issues like opposition to slavery in the European metropolis.

The presentist perspective of many a celebratory account of contemporary transnational mobilization overlooks important historical precedents. Recall in this context, for instance, the strength of tiermondism in the late 1970s through the 1980s and its subsequent decline all over Europe (Kössler and Melber 2007: 30–1). Or consider the thought-provoking analogy drawn by Hardt (2002) between the World Social Forum (WSF) meeting in 2002 and the historic Bandung conference in Indonesia in 1955, which is hardly remembered today. This important event had brought together twenty-nine African and Asian nations with a view to forging lateral ties, creating a 'third bloc' within the UN based on a positive 'Third World' identity. It developed a shared postcolonial vision as an alternative both to western imperial hegemony and to the divisive politics of the Cold War (Gupta 1992). The idea of non-alignment was more than a reaction to, or a position of passive neutrality in, the politics of the Cold War. It was an attempt to define newly won sovereignty and independence in a context of cultural imperialism, racism, and continued neocolonial dependence. In terms of economic strategy, however, the Bandung agenda remained one of national autarky. Despite some interesting parallels between the alter-globalization and the non-aligned movement, there are also significant differences. While the World Social Forum offers a space for heterogeneous social movements and networks to discuss alternatives to the present world order, the alternative to the two existing blocs and systems was charted by leading national leaders from the so-called Third World (e.g. Nehru, Nasser, and Sukarno). The latter failed to capture the popular imagination in most postcolonial societies or to forge and foster lasting supranational ties of an imagined community. Unlike the alter-globalization movement, the non-aligned movement, with its interstitial location between the two superpowers, chose to set up a small number of formal institutions in different parts of the world like the Centre for Public Enterprises, the News Agency Pool, the International Centre on Transnational Corporations, the Centre for Science and Technology, or the UN Caucus Group (Gupta 1992); but all of these have been rendered more or less irrelevant today.

It is important to remember that the leaders of the non-aligned movement also envisioned the shared future of their newly independent peoples and countries in larger than purely national terms (Hawley 2008: 289). For as Prashad (2007) points out the project of a Third World was born as much out of the need to combat neocolonialism as to promote 'internationalist nationalism'. Thus from its very inception the movement represented a globalization of the postcolonial imagination. Whereas the non-aligned movement aimed to transform the bipolar world order solely through state action, alter-globalization movements set their hopes instead on civil society activism while being at best ambivalent with regard to the state (see Brydon in Part IV of this volume). Disagreement about the significance of national sovereignty was the most important political difference at the 2002 Porto Alegre Forum. As Hardt (2002) has noted, two opposing positions represented at the Forum on this issue cut across the broad spectrum of alter-globalization movements. Whereas the one identifies unfettered neoliberal globalization in the service of foreign capital as the main problem, the other voices a more fundamental opposition to capital and capitalism itself. While the former invests its hopes in the strengthening of state control and national sovereignty similar to erstwhile anti-colonial and anti-imperial struggles, the latter envisions a democratic alternative beyond the nation state. These debates point to the tensions between national and capitalist space by raising the question of whether, and to what extent, the territorial sovereignty of the nation state can limit or regulate the deterritorializing imperatives of capitalism.

Though non-national, the non-aligned movement's vision of a transnational imagined community immediately after formal decolonization did not include the diaspora, which only became part of the nation state's project in the 1990s in many countries of the south (Gupta 1992: 64). Consequently another important theme today in debates about alter-globalization is the complex relationship of diasporas to subalternity (Dhawan 2007). Yeğenoğlu (2005: 103), for instance, traces how the condition of disenfranchised subaltern groups of the south is linked to that of diasporas in metropolitan centres. Following Spivak, she argues that the focus on diasporic agency is symptomatic of a wider sanctioned ignorance of the subaltern other of capitalist globality (103). Subaltern groups continue to be marginal to nations and nation building even as they bear the impact of neocolonial globalization, both material and symbolic. These groups, for whom international migration is not even an option, bear the consequences of neo-colonial globalism but do not have access to even the basic benefits of citizenship (105). Even as metropolitan diasporics can make claims to democratic rights and equality, the underclass in the global south does not enjoy these even 'at home'. Instead of anti-statism or post-nationalism, resistance for subaltern groups may involve their very insertion into the existing framework of the nation state (Dhawan 2007, 2009).

The postcolonial state is both an agent and an object of neoliberal globalization. It has often come in for severe criticism for the exclusion of large sections of its citizens from its protective measures and from the enjoyment of their rights. It has been equally condemned for its more or less willing compliance with the mandates of transnational capital as well as international financial and trade organizations. Caught between the demands of citizens and the injunctions of global as well as national capital, the cunning state in the south tries to absolve itself of responsibility to both domestic and foreign constituencies by a selective and partial domestication of neoliberal policies and programmes (Randeria 2003, 2007a). Marginalized citizens, social movements, and grassroots NGOs engaged in struggles for justice at the national and transnational levels are forced to rely on the postcolonial state to mitigate the effects of these policies in the absence of another agent capable of mediating between subaltern groups and powerful transnational forces (Beverley 1999: 53). One of the dilemmas faced by activists engaged in processes of counter-hegemonic globalization is, therefore, of developing strategies to deal with a Janus-faced state that must be resisted but is often also needed as an ally to protect the rights of the dispossessed (Randeria 2007a). Although current politics of contention take place, successively or even simultaneously, at a variety of scales as well in various arenas within and beyond the nation state, the state continues to be the prime addressee of protest. While regulation by the state is unlikely to transform a system that operates on a world scale, the national arena remains nevertheless indispensable for those struggling for rights and justice.

The nature of protest with its complex multiscalar character has also undergone a change. Both at national and transnational levels, it is easier for citizens and activists to exercise surveillance, to inspect, name, and shame corporations and governments rather than improve access to, or gain participation and representation in, international institutions (Randeria 2007b). An older politics of representation has been superseded by an increasing judicialization of politics as activists use the law at the level of the state and beyond it as a tool of resistance and of emancipation (Baxi 2002; Randeria

2003, 2007a; Santos and Rodríguez-Garavito 2005). These new forms of legal politics are ambivalent in their implications for democratization and equally uncertain in their outcome. While the shift in power from the legislature to the judiciary at the national level results in 'choiceless democracies' (Mkandawire 1999), the formation of a global legal consciousness around spectacular law is predicated on the growing influence of the media (Mattei 2003). The interventions of activists at a variety of scales compound older problems of access, participation, and legitimacy, which remain unresolved in most western democracies, but have become even more acute in structurally adjusted postcolonial societies. Multiscalar activism in the human rights and global justice movements have led to the emergence of a broader grammar of politics, which has extended the vocabulary of citizenship both within and beyond the nation state. Paradoxically, however, this has paralleled the shrinking of space for politics within (postcolonial) democracies (Randeria 2007b: 39).

Despite the politics of duplicity practised by the more powerful of postcolonial states in the international system (Randeria 2007a) and the crisis of legitimacy of the postcolonial state that many regard as 'last refuge of ethnic totalitarianism' (Appadurai 1996: 159), it would be a mistake to disregard the grave political implications of an anti-statist position for subaltern populations in the south. Instead of a narrow understanding of the state as merely a repressive apparatus, which underlies such a position, several postcolonial theorists emphasize the need to envisage a different state, one that is capable of articulating the will of excluded subaltern populations (Yeğenoğlu 2005: 106). Notwithstanding the widespread disillusionment with the postcolonial state for failing to deliver on its promises, it is important to recall that the current neoliberal ideological opposition posits a false opposition between the ills of state planning and the virtues of the free market. Such an argument elides the fact that neoliberal policies and programmes are predicated on the state for their functioning (114). An emancipatory politics must thus be able to articulate the interests and demands of the disenfranchised in the struggle for hegemony (Beverley 1999: 152) and search for ways to institutionalize anew the redistributive functions of the state (Yeğenoğlu 2005: 114) instead of its currently enabling role for capital.

Alter-globalization activists from the north and south, who have forged strategic, cross-border alliances around common concerns, do not simply oppose globalization. They strive instead to anchor alternative visions of globality that could provide a just alternative to the current processes of corporate-driven cultural and economic globalization, tame its forces, and mitigate its injustices (Sen and Kumar 2003; Sen et al. 2004). Beginning with the indigenous peoples' movement since Zapatismo in 1994 and globally coordinated anti-war demonstrations since 2001, the last two decades have witnessed an upsurge of protest around issues of health, land, water, debt, trade, and development finance (Bond 2007). Successful mobilization against the millennium round of the World Trade Organization (WTO) in Seattle in 1999 marked a new phase and momentum in transnational contestation, which has continued since at annual meetings of the IMF-World Bank, the G8 or WTO summits, and at the World Economic Forum (WEF) at Davos. These protests culminated in the formation of the World Social Forum (WSF), which has become one of the most important arenas to challenge the adverse effects of predatory globalization and militarism. It is also the site of ongoing critique of the systemic crisis of capitalism that involves economic, social, political, and ecological issues. Since its establishment in Porto Alegre, Brazil in 2001, the WSF's annual meetings, complemented by intermediary regional and local forums, have become the most prominent global arena for social movements and networks seeking to transform current economic and political structures by democratic means.

Many activist-academic participants at, and chroniclers of, the WSF have been rather critical of the politics of, and at, the WSF (Sen et al. 2007). The WSF process has advocated a new conception of the political that transcends territorial states and political parties. Though movements under its umbrella have attempted to politicize transnational relations of capitalist production, they have paid less attention to the asymmetries of power among the movements themselves (Teivainen 2007: 72–3). The WSF has also been criticized for a tendency towards depoliticization as reflected, for instance, in the idealization of horizontal networks to the neglect of, or even in opposition to, issues of representation. Some South African activists have been critical of the transformation of the WSF from an 'arena of encounter for local social movements into an organized network of experts, academics and NGO practitioners' (quoted in Bond 2007: 87). Whereas scholars agree on the achievements of the WSF in providing a platform for bringing together a multiplicity of movements fighting neoliberal capitalism and imperialism, many are disappointed by the dilution of its politics in practice (Bello 2007), its inability to converge on strategy or generate joint action across sectors and issues, as well as its exclusion of the ordinary working class and the poor (Bond 2007).

It has been argued that the WSF functions as a 'subaltern counterpublic' (Fraser 1997: 82) that disrupts the universalizing and homogenizing processes of globalization. In contrast to Fraser's usage of the term 'subaltern', Spivak argues that a sort of subalternity is produced when a citizen is unable to access the public sphere, which is, of course, itself a product of colonial history. The use of the Gramscian category of the 'subaltern' to denote non-hegemonic groups has gained wide currency in historical and social science scholarship following the 'subaltern studies' school (Guha and Spivak 1988), which constituted a radical intervention into Indian historiographical debates in the 1980s. The wide reception of its ideas and methodology in scholarly circles in Africa and Latin America has led to a global interest in analyses of semi-autonomous subaltern politics in colonial and postcolonial contexts. Perceived by the organized left parties as 'pre-political' and sporadic, the subaltern was seen to operate at 'local' levels that were insignificant for national or international politics. Given that the 'norms of recognition' militate against subaltern groups, their political claims appear unintelligible and illegible to the dominant class and the state (Dhawan 2012). Thus subalternity for Spivak (2009) is a condition of not being able to represent oneself, articulate one's interests, or make one's claims count in face of the lack of institutional validation.

Even as the WSF has been celebrated as an open space largely located in the global south as well as a platform for disenfranchised groups and communities to voice their critique (Santos 1995), the continual production of subalternity within these spaces of dissidence remains a serious challenge for alter-globalization movements. An important issue in this context is the relationship between seemingly discrete dissident spaces and autonomous struggles in order to articulate demands, which are simultaneously economic, political, and cultural. Questions have been raised about the weakness of the WSF's internal democratic structures and the resulting opacity of decision-making (Klein 2001). Feminists and indigenous activists, in particular, have pointed out that relations of inequality, racism, and coloniality have not been overcome within the WSF or alter-globalization movements more generally (Conway 2011; Patomäki and Teivainen 2004). Another strand of criticism against transnational civil society in general, and the WSF in particular, has been the hegemony of institutionalized critique and dissent due to the trend towards 'NGO-ization', co-option, and marginalization of vulnerable groups. Spivak goes so far as to accuse international civil society and its vanguardism of engaging in a politics of representation plagued by paternalism that reproduces a 'Feudality without Feudalism' (2008: 8).

GLOBAL JUSTICE AND RESPONSIBILITY

Several postcolonial scholars have critiqued the contemporary politics of human rights or humanitarian activism with a view to reconceptualizing issues of global justice and responsibility. The writings of Upendra Baxi and Gayatri Spivak exemplify such a critique. Moving away from globality, Spivak poses the question of what it would mean to rethink the postcolonial in terms of 'planetarity' (Sharpe and Spivak 2003). She suggests reconsidering our ethical, political, and epistemic commitments as planetary subjects inhabiting an earth merely on 'loan' to us. The notion of planetarity thus allows her to address not only the materiality of the world but also our collective place and responsibility as humans within it. But it also allows her to rethink the notion of responsibility in terms of responsibility *to* the other rather than the duty of the 'fitter self' *for* the other (2004: 537). In a trenchant critique of a humanitarian ethic, which limits itself to the provision of relief for distant suffering by merely organizing aid, she argues that transnational activism of this kind reduces the deprived to their material needs, which are understood as transparent to our western and/or middle-class reading practices. In seeking to transform the world, activists and intellectuals must learn to learn instead from the singular and unverifiable, which defies universal blueprints. Planetary ethics thus entails forsaking formulas for solving global problems. Instead of situating ourselves as altruistic problem-solvers of the world's troubles, she urges us to learn to see ourselves first as part of the problem. A practice of decolonization must, for Spivak, thus engage with the imagination and desires of the dispensers as well as the receivers of global justice (Dhawan 2009, 2011, 2012).

Economic empowerment of the subaltern is incomplete without an accompanying 'epistemic change' in the global north as well as the global south (Spivak 1993: 177).

Alter-globalization activists are insufficiently oppositional in Spivak's view as they only attempt to manage the crisis of capitalist globalization. Decolonization requires more than crisis-driven corporate philanthropy or human rights interventions, which in Spivak's view patronize the disenfranchised. Programmes of corporate social responsibility (CSR) are one response by multinational corporations (MNCs) to the legal action, public protest, and shaming campaigns, including calls for divestment or consumer boycott, being organized by activists and ordinary citizens at various sites and on different scales. These have targeted the cooperation of MNCs with oppressive regimes, exploitation of labour, inhuman working conditions, violations of environmental norms, or destruction of indigenous cultures and habitats.

While Spivak critiques the idea of human rights, arguing for the impossibility of realizing justice under capitalism, Upendra Baxi (2007) emphasizes the important transformations that ideas of human rights have undergone through practices of resistance in the time-spaces of the postcolony. It would therefore be a serious mistake, in his view, to conceive of human rights as a western gift to the non-western world. The very idea of the fundamental rights of the people, for instance, was as foreign to imperial power as the idea of constitutionalism in the colony, he argues. For Spivak, considering human rights to be Eurocentric would be disingenuous since in the global south, 'the domestic human rights workers are, by and large, the descendants of the colonial subject, often culturally positioned against Eurocentrism' (2004: 525). Baxi (2000) makes a powerful case against the mainstream Eurocentric genealogy of the idea and practice of human rights on different grounds. He shows how postcolonial constitutions are saturated with ideas of justice and redistribution as well as human rights that have been extended well beyond western liberal templates. The very idea of rights, development, and justice had to be forged in postcolonial societies in and through peoples' struggles, so that for Baxi anti-colonial struggles contributed a great deal to the imagination and practice of human rights.

In his view human rights constitute ethical or moral as well as juridico-political inventions, which engender new systems of values, principles, and languages but also give rise to new practices, movements, and institutions (Baxi 2012). However, he also cautions against the trend towards the 'disinvention' of many languages of human rights under conditions of unfettered capitalism, which not only subverts rights but also reverses their logics. For example, languages of radical self-determination, which were so important in the anti-/postcolonial context, stand dismantled today as do socialist languages of distributive justice or proletarian languages of affirming the collective rights of working classes. With their disappearance, the social worlds they once signified have also been lost and replaced by new vocabularies of 'representation', 'recognition', and 'participation', as Baxi argues. But he also points to the 'reinvention' of some forms of human rights. The conversion of basic human rights into instruments of global social policy such as the Millennial Development Goals constitutes one such example. Such a transformation, however, not only renders rights within this new framework to be non-justiciable, but in his view also renders the notion of 'progressive implementation' of social and economic rights meaningless by stretching the timeline for global efforts to promote the realization of basic rights to healthcare, shelter, or education. Such practices of 'reinvention', Baxi (2012) contends, amount to a 'disinvention' of human rights that signal their future demise.

The paradigm shift from universal human rights to 'trade-related market-friendly human rights' (Baxi 2006) in the service of capital imperils the future of human rights through such ingenious dilutions of human rights by multinational corporations. In face of such strategies of subversion how can the impoverished and the disenfranchised make their voices heard, Baxi (2012) asks? And from whom may they demand answerability? What human rights obligations do 'the state-like and yet state-transcendent' multinational corporations have (2012: 25)? What responsibilities does national and transnational business and industry owe, and to whom? A state-centric conception of human rights leaves out of its ambit a host of rightless people like those internally and forcibly displaced, political refugees, or asylum seekers, on the one hand, as well as the agents of global capital, on the other (see Farrier and Tuitt in Part II of this volume). But Baxi (2006) also warns against a colonization of the language, logics, and rhetoric of human rights by multinational corporations. The task of resistance would then be to achieve the decolonization of these new market-friendly human rights. His incisive analyses demonstrate how multinational corporations have used so-called Corporate Social Responsibility programmes to render themselves free of all obligation by signing non-binding codes of conduct. Using voluntary self-regulation by way of non-enforcable standards, corporations try to pre-empt or diffuse demands for compensation for the harms caused by their activities. These codes of conduct entail the systematic evasion of responsibility by privileging instead what Baxi (2006) calls 'corporate legal humanity', i.e. the extension of rights to corporations while ensuring that their obligations remain at best 'soft' law. Corporations like Union Carbide, which was responsible in 1984 for the worst ever industrial disaster at its chemical plant in Bhopal (India) that led to the death of some 25,000 people and permanent injuries to more than 100,000 people, are not the only actors who enjoy immunity and impunity today, as Baxi shows. The 'rendition' of terror suspects, and the killings of civilians in the south in drone attacks by hegemonic state actors in the name of security and the 'war on terror', for example, bear ample testimony to the mechanisms by which other powerful actors can render themselves immune from international and domestic law.

Baxi (2012) contrasts these serious and systematic violations by dominant states and corporations with the recent efforts by human rights activists and new social movements to 'reinvent' human rights. These players have sought, for instance, to expand the scope of human rights and extend the categories of the bearers of these rights. They have suggested including in the ambit of human rights those no longer alive, as in the case of reparations for slavery, or to extend them to the 'collective species-rights' of present and future persons, populations, and generations with a view to sustainable development and to mitigate the impact of climate change. Such a conception leads to the proliferation of human rights through 'the continual translation of human needs into human rights' as well as 'the practices of insurgent human rights reason' (2012: 17). It not only entails a reimagination of 'the conditions of both predation and vulnerability' (17), but also the continued survival of the earth and its peoples.

Baxi advances a powerful argument against the claim of universal human rights as a western invention based on what he calls the 'regional metaphysic' of the 'great' American and French declaration (2012: 18; see also the General Introduction to this volume). The claim to 'greatness' has historically involved complete irresponsibility towards the non-European others, be they slaves, indigenous peoples, or the colonized. All of these others have contested the inherent epistemic racism of the Euro-American conception of liberalism and rights whose logic of violent social exclusion denied their humanity. Baxi argues that it is through their struggles that the rights of subjugated peoples for self-determination won recognition during anti-colonial movements, thereby establishing human rights values, norms and principles much before the Universal Declaration of Human Rights. While striking a cautionary note about the futures of human rights, Baxi also explores their pasts outside Euro-America in order to trace an alternative postcolonial genealogy. This is done not with a view to offering another history, but rather in order to address critiques of human rights that see these as being tainted by the legacy of European Enlightenment. Against those who proclaim the end of human rights by pointing to their continual abuse and appropriation by the dominant, Baxi insists instead on the recognition of the significant contributions of struggles outside the west to the historical establishment as well as contemporary reappropriation of human rights by the subaltern. Pointing to the many and varied continuing struggles for rights across the globe, he makes a compelling case for the inclusion of the suffering, the impoverished, and the rightless, of all those subjected to the 'microfascism of quotidian "terror"' (2012: 28), and of all those who seek to arrest the abuse of public power under conditions of endemic appropriation or challenge the normality of everyday states of exception in postcolonial societies.

CONCLUSION

The appropriation of languages of hybridity, difference, and mobility along with those of democracy and of human rights in the service of capital has blunted the critical potential of these emancipatory discourses. Neoliberalism has meant the free movement of capital along with ever more restrictions on the movement of people with few resources as powerful nation states increasingly strengthen and police their boundaries. Emerging new forms of subalternization render illegible, unintelligible, and illegitimate the perspectives of oppressed and marginalized groups in the global south. Many in the postcolonial world therefore experience current processes of neoliberal globalization, which reinforce structural disparities and intensify inequalities both within and between societies of the north and south, as a recolonization of their futures. The fruits of decolonization—parliamentary democracy, economic and social justice, civil and political rights—remain accessible to an elite minority in postcolonial societies, whereas the vast majority is engaged in a struggle for survival, dignity, and enfranchisement. As several postcolonial scholars point out, it is urgent to reimagine mechanisms for dispensing justice and claiming rights that address the needs and aspirations of the most vulnerable citizens of the global south as well as north. Ending their subalternization entails the insertion of disenfranchised individuals and groups into the enabling institutional structures of democracy, rights, and justice, even as these must be purged of their exclusionary legacies in order to accommodate the interests and demands of those prevented from inhabiting them so far. Herein lies the challenge and responsibility of transnational politics in a postcolonial world.

REFERENCES

Ahmed, Waquar, Amitabh Kundu, and Richard Peet (eds) (2011). *India's New Economic Policy: A Critical Analysis.* London and New York: Routledge.

Amoore, Louise and Paul Langley (2004). 'Ambiguities of Global Civil Society', *Review of International Studies,* 30.1: 89–110.

Appadurai, Arjun (1996). *Modernity at Large: Cultural Dimensions of Globalization.* Minneapolis: University of Minnesota Press.

Arrighi, Giovanni and Beverly J. Silver (2000). 'Workers North and South', *The Socialist Register,* 2001: 53–76.

Assayag, Jackie and Christopher J. Fuller (eds) (2005). *Globalizing India: Perspectives From Below.* London: Anthem Press.

Balakrishnan, Radhika (ed.) (2001). *The Hidden Assembly Line: Gender Dynamics of Subcontracted Work in a Global Economy.* Sterling, Va.: Kumarian Press.

Balibar, Étienne and Immanuel Wallerstein (1991). *Race, Nation, Class: Ambiguous Identities.* London and New York: Verso.

Baxi, Upendra (2000). 'Human Rights, Suffering Between Movements and Markets', in R. Cohen and S. Rai (eds), *Global Social Movements.* London: Athlone Press, 33–45.

Baxi, Upendra (2002). *The Future of Human Rights* (2nd edn 2006). Oxford: Oxford University Press.

Baxi, Upendra (2007). *Human Rights in a Posthuman World: Critical Essays.* Oxford: Oxford University Press.

Baxi, Upendra (2012). 'Public and Insurgent Reason: Adjudicatory Leadership in a Hyperglobalizing World', in S. Gill (ed.), *Global Crises and the Crisis of Global Leadership.* Cambridge: Cambridge University Press, 161–78.

Bello, Walden (2007). 'The Forum at the Crossroads', *Foreign Policy in Focus,* 19.2. Online source: <http://www.tni.org//archives/act/16771>, accessed 27 December 2012.

Bénéi, Véronique (2005). 'Of Languages, Passions and Interests: Education, Regionalism and Globalization in Maharashtra, 1800–2000', in J. Assayag and C. Fuller (eds), *Globalizing India: Perspectives From Below.* London: Anthem Press, 141–62.

Beverley, John (1999). *Subalternity and Representation: Arguments in Cultural Theory.* Durham: Duke University Press.

Bhabha, Homi K. (1994). *The Location of Culture.* London and New York: Routledge.

Bond, Patrick (2007). 'Linking Below, Across and Against—World Social Forum Weaknesses, Global Governance Gaps and the Global Justice Movement's Strategic Dilemmas', *Development Dialogue,* 49: 81–95.

Brennan, Timothy (2008). 'Postcolonial Studies and Globalization Theory', in R. Krishnaswamy and J. C. Hawley (eds), *The Postcolonial and the Global*. Minneapolis: University of Minnesota Press, 37–53.

Chandhoke, Neera (2003). *The Conceits of Civil Society*. New Delhi: Oxford University Press.

Chatterjee, Partha (1997). *Our Modernity*. Rotterdam and Dakar: SEPHIS, CODESRIA.

Chatterjee, Partha (2004). *The Politics of the Governed: Reflections on Popular Politics in Most of the World*. New York: Columbia University Press.

Cheah, Pheng (2008). 'Universal Areas: Asian Studies in a World of Motion', in R. Krishnaswamy and J. C. Hawley (eds), *The Postcolonial and the Global*. Minneapolis: University of Minnesota Press, 54–68.

Comaroff, Jean and John L. Comaroff (eds) (2006). *Law and Disorder in the Postcolony*. Chicago: University of Chicago Press.

Conrad, Sebastian and Shalini Randeria (eds) (2002). *Jenseits des Eurozentrismus: Postkoloniale Perspektiven in den Geschichts- und Kulturwissenschaften*. Frankfurt am Main: Campus Verlag.

Conway, Janet (2011). 'Cosmopolitan or Colonial: The World Social Forum as "Contact Zone"', *Third World Quarterly*, 32.2: 217–36.

Cooppan, Vilashini (2005). 'The Ruins of Empire: The National and Global Politics of America's Return to Rome', in A. Loomba, K. Suvir, M. Bunzl, A. Burton, and J. Esty (eds), *Postcolonial Studies and Beyond*. Durham: Duke University Press, 80–100.

Corbridge, Stuart and John Harriss (2000). *Reinventing India: Liberalization, Hindu Nationalism and Popular Democracy*. Cambridge: Polity Press.

Dhawan, Nikita (2007). 'Can the Subaltern Speak German? And Other Risky Questions: Migrant Hybridism Versus Subalternity', *translate. Beyond Culture: The Politics of Translation*, webjournal of eipcp—European Institute for Progressive Cultural Policies, April 2007, <http://translate.eipcp.net/strands/03/dhawan-strands01en#redir#redir>, accessed May 2012.

Dhawan, Nikita (2009). 'Zwischen Empire und Empower: Dekolonisierung und Demokratisierung', *Femina Politica, Schwerpunktheft: Feministische Postkoloniale Theorie—Gender und (De)Kolonisierungsprozesse*, 2: 52–63.

Dhawan, Nikita (2011). 'Transnationale Gerechtigkeit in einer Postkolonialen Welt', in M. Castro Varela and N. Dhawan (eds), *Soziale (Un)Gerechtigkeit: Kritische Perspektive auf Diversität, Intersektionalität und Anti-Diskriminierung*. Münster: LIT, 12–35.

Dhawan, Nikita (2012). 'Hegemonic Listening and Subversive Silences: Ethical–Political Imperatives', in A. Lagaay and M. Lorber (eds), *Destruction in the Performative*. Amsterdam: Rodopi, 47–60.

Donner, Henrike (2005). 'Children are Capital, Grandchildren are Interest: Changing Educational Strategies and Kin-Relations in Calcutta Middle-Class Families', in J. Assayag and C. J. Fuller (eds), *Globalizing India: Perspectives From Below*. London: Anthem Press, 119–39.

Duara, Prasenjit (2010). 'Asia Redux: Conceptualizing a Region for Our Time', *Journal of Asian Studies*, 69.4: 963–83.

During, Simon (1998). 'Postcolonialism and Globalisation: A Dialectical Relation after All?', *Postcolonial Studies*, 1.1: 31–47.

Eisenstadt, Shmuel N. (2000). *Die Vielfalt der Moderne*. Weilerswist: Velbrück Verlag.

Escobar, Arturo (2004). 'Beyond the Third World: Imperial Globality, Global Coloniality and Anti-Globalization Social Movements', *Third World Quarterly*, 25.1: 207–30.

Fisher, William F. and Thomas Ponniah (eds) (2003). *Another World is Possible: Popular Alternatives to Globalization at the World Social Forum.* London and New York: Zed Books.

Fraser, Nancy (1997). *Justice Interruptus: Critical Reflections on the 'Postsocialist' Condition.* New York: Routledge.

Gikandi, Simon (2005). 'Globalization and the Claims of Postcoloniality', in G. G. Desai and S. Nair (eds), *Postcolonialisms: An Anthology of Cultural Theory and Criticism.* New Brunswick: Rutgers University Press, 608–34.

Gopinath, Gayatri (2005). *Queer Diasporas and South Asian Public Cultures.* Durham: Duke University Press.

Guha, Ranajit and Gayatri C. Spivak (eds) (1988). *Selected Subaltern Studies.* New York and Oxford: Oxford University Press.

Gupta, Akhil (1992). 'The Song of the Nonaligned World: Transnational Identities and the Reinscription of Space in Late Capitalism', *Cultural Anthropology*, 7.1: 63–79.

Hall, Stuart (1992). 'The West and the Rest: Discourse and Power', in S. Hall and B. Gieben (eds), *Formations of Modernity.* Cambridge: Polity Press, 275–331.

Hall, Stuart (1997). 'The Local and the Global: Globalization and Ethnicity', in A. McClintock, A. Mufti, and E. Shohat (eds), *Dangerous Liaisons: Gender, Nation, and Postcolonial Perspectives.* Minneapolis: University of Minnesota Press, 173–87.

Hann, Chris and Elizabeth Dunn (1996). *Civil Society. Challenging Western Models.* London and New York: Routledge.

Hannerz, Ulf (1987). 'The World in Creolization', *Africa: Journal of the International African Institute*, 57.4: 546–59.

Hardt, Michael (2002). 'Porto Alegre—Today's Bandung?', *New Left Review*, 14: 112–18.

Hardt, Michael and Antonio Negri (2000). *Empire.* Cambridge, Mass.: Harvard University Press.

Harvey, David (1989). *The Condition of Postmodernity: An Enquiry into the Origins of Cultural Change.* Oxford: Basil Blackwell.

Hawley, John (2008). 'Postscript: An Interview with Arjun Appadurai', in R. Krishnaswamy and J. Hawley (eds), *The Postcolonial and the Global.* Minneapolis: University of Minnesota Press, 289–94.

Held, David, Antony McGrew, David Goldblatt, and Jonathan Perraton (1999). *Global Transformations: Politics, Economics and Culture.* Cambridge: Polity Press and Stanford: Stanford University Press.

Hochschild, Arlie R. (2000). 'Global Care Chains and Emotional Surplus Value', in W. Hutton and A. Giddens (eds), *On The Edge: Living with Global Capitalism.* London: Jonathan Cape, 130–46.

Hochschild, Arlie R. (2012). *The Outsourced Self: Intimate Life in Market Times.* New York: Metropolitan Books.

Hulme, Peter (2005). 'Beyond the Straits: Postcolonial Allegories of the Globe', in A. Loomba, K. Suvir, M. Bunzl, A. Burton, and J. Esty (eds), *Postcolonial Studies and Beyond.* Durham: Duke University Press, 41–61.

Inda, Jonathan X. and Renato Rosaldo (eds) (2007). *The Anthropology of Globalization: A Reader.* Oxford and Malden, Mass.: Blackwell.

Kaldor, Mary, Helmut K. Anheier, and Marlies Glasius (eds) (2006). *Global Civil Society 2006/7.* London: SAGE.

Kaviraj, Sudipta and Sunil Khilnani (2001). *Civil Society. History and Possibilities.* Cambridge: Cambridge University Press.

Keane, John (2003). *Global Civil Society?* Cambridge: Cambridge University Press.

Klein, Naomi (2001). 'Reclaiming the Commons', *New Left Review*, 9: 81–9.

Knauft, Bruce (ed.) (2002). *Critically Modern: Alternatives, Alterities, Anthropologies.* Bloomington: Indiana University Press.

Kössler, Reinhart and Henning Melber (2007). 'International Civil Society and the Challenge for Global Solidarity', *Development Dialogue*, 49: 30–1.

Krishnaswamy, Revathi (2008). 'Connections, Conflicts, Complicities', in R. Krishnaswamy and J. Hawley (eds), *The Postcolonial and the Global.* Minneapolis: University of Minnesota Press, 2–21.

Loomba, Ania, Kaul Suvir, Matti Bunzl, Antionette Burton, and Jed Esty (2005). 'Beyond What? An Introduction', in A. Loomba, K. Suvir, M. Bunzl, A. Burton, and J. Esty (eds), *Postcolonial Studies and Beyond.* Durham: Duke University Press, 1–40.

Martins, Herminio (1974). 'Time and Theory in Sociology', in J. Rex and P. Kegan (eds), *Approaches to Sociology: An Introduction to Major Trends in British Sociology.* London and New York: Routledge, 246–94.

Mattei, Ugo (2003). 'A Theory of Imperial Law: A Study on US Hegemony and the Latin Resistance', *Indiana Journal of Global Legal Studies*, 10.1: 383–449.

Mkandawire, Thandika (1999). 'Crisis Management and the Making of "Choiceless Democracies" in Africa', in R. Joseph (ed.), *The State, Conflict and Democracy in Africa.* Boulder, Col.: Lynne Rienner, 119–36.

Moghadam, Valentine (2005). *Globalizing Women: Transnational Feminist Networks.* Baltimore: Johns Hopkins University Press.

Mohanty, Chandra T., Ann Russo, and Lourdes Torres (2003). *Third World Women and the Politics of Feminism.* Bloomington: Indiana University Press.

Nandy, Ashis, Shikha Trivedi, and Achyut Yagnick (eds) (1995). *Creating a Nationality: The Ramjanmabhumi Movement and Fear of the Self.* Delhi and Oxford: Oxford University Press.

Ong, Aihwa (1987). *Spirits of Resistance and Capitalist Discipline: Factory Women in Malaysia.* Albany: State University of New York Press.

Ong, Aihwa (1999). *Flexible Citizenship: The Cultural Logics of Transnationality.* Durham: Duke University Press.

Patomäki, Heikki and Teivo Teivainen (2004). *A Possible World: Democratic Transformation of Global Institutions.* London: Zed Books.

Prashad, Vijay (2007). *The Darker Nations: A People's History of the Third World.* New York: The New Press.

Rajagopal, Arvind (2001). *Politics After Television: Religious Nationalism and the Reshaping of the Indian Public.* Cambridge: Cambridge University Press.

Randeria, Shalini (2003). 'Globalization of Law: Environmental Justice, World Bank, NGOs and the Cunning State in India', *Current Sociology*, 51.3–4: 305–28.

Randeria, Shalini (2007a). 'The State of Globalization: Legal Plurality, Overlapping Sovereignties and Ambiguous Alliances between Civil Society and the Cunning State in India', *Theory, Culture & Society*, 24.1: 1–33.

Randeria, Shalini (2007b). 'De-politicization of Democracy and Judicialization of Politics', *Theory, Culture & Society*, 24.4: 38–44.

Randeria, Shalini (2007c). 'Staatliche Interventionen, Bevölkerungskontrolle und Gender: Indien und China im Vergleich', in C. Klinger, G.-A. Knapp, and B. Sauer (eds), *Achsen der Ungleichheit: Zum Verhältnis von Klasse, Geschlecht und Ethnizität.* Frankfurt am Main and New York: Campus Verlag, 235–56.

Randeria, Shalini (2009). 'Entangled Histories of Uneven Modernities: Civil Society, Case Councils, and Legal Pluralism in Postcolonial India', in H.-G. Haupt and J. Kocka (eds), *Comparative and Transnational History*. New York: Berghahn Books, 77–104.

Randeria, Shalini (2011). 'Kulturimperialismus', in F. Kreff, E.-M. Knoll, and A. Gingrich (eds), *Lexikon der Globalisierung*. Bielefeld: Transcript Verlag, 209–13.

Randeria, Shalini et al. (eds) (2004). *Konfigurationen der Moderne: Diskurse zu Indien*, Soziale Welt Sonderband, 15. Baden-Baden: Nomos Verlag.

Rowbotham, Sheila and Swasti Mitter (eds) (1994). *Dignity and Daily Bread: New Forms of Economic Organization Among Poor Women in the Third World and the First*. London and New York: Routledge.

Said, Edward W. (1978). *Orientalism*. New York: Random House.

Sainath, Palagummi (2004). 'Seeds of Suicide', *The Hindu*, 20 July. Online source: <http://www.hindu.com/2004/07/20/stories/2004072003071200.htm>, accessed May 2012.

Santos, Boaventura de Sousa (1995). *Toward a New Common Sense: Law, Science, and Politics in the Paradigmatic Transition*. New York: Routledge.

Santos, Boaventura de Sousa and Cesar A. Rodriguez-Garavito (eds) (2005). *Law and Globalization from Below: Toward a Cosmopolitan Legality*. Cambridge: Cambridge University Press.

Scholte, Jan A. (2000). *Globalization: A Critical Introduction*. London: Macmillan.

Sen, Jai (2007). 'The Power of Civility', *Development Dialogue*, 49: 51–67.

Sen, Jai, Anita Anand, Arturo Escobar, and Peter Waterman (eds) (2004). *World Social Forum: Challenging Empires*. New Delhi: Viveka Foundation.

Sen, Jai and Madhuresh Kumar (eds) (2003). *Are Other Worlds Possible? The Open Space Reader on the World Social Forum and Its Engagement with Empire*. New Delhi: National Foundation for India.

Sen, Jai, Madhuresh Kumar, Patrick Bond, and Peter Waterman (2007). *A Political Programme for the World Social Forum? Democracy, Substance, and Debate in the Bamako Appeal and the Global Justice Movements—A Reader*. New Delhi: CACIM.

Sharpe, Jenny and Gayatri C. Spivak (2003). 'A Conversation with Gayatri Chakravorty Spivak: Politics and the Imagination', *Signs: Journal of Women in Culture and Society*, 28.2: 609–24.

Shiva, Vandana (1999). *Biopiracy: The Plunder of Nature and Knowledge*. Boston, Mass.: South End Press.

Sivaramakrishnan, Kalyanakrishnan and Arun Agrawal (eds) (2003). *Regional Modernities: The Cultural Politics of Development in India*. Stanford: Stanford University Press.

Spivak, Gayatri C. (1993). *Outside in the Teaching Machine*. London and New York: Routledge.

Spivak, Gayatri C. (1999). *A Critique of Postcolonial Reason: Toward a History of the Vanishing Present*. Cambridge, Mass.: Harvard University Press.

Spivak, Gayatri C. (2004). 'Righting Wrongs', *The South Atlantic Quarterly*, 103.2–3: 523–81.

Spivak, Gayatri C. (2007). 'Feminism and Human Rights', in N. Shaikh (ed.), *The Present as History: Critical Perspectives on Global Power*. New York: Columbia University Press, 172–201.

Spivak, Gayatri C. (2008). *Other Asias*. Oxford and Malden, Mass.: Blackwell.

Spivak, Gayatri C. (2009). 'They the People: Problems of Alter-Globalization', *Radical Philosophy*, 157: 31–6.

Tarrow, Sidney (2002). 'From Lumping to Splitting: Specifying Globalization and Resistance', in J. Smith and H. Johnston (eds), *Globalization and Resistance: Transnational Dimensions of Social Movements*. Lanham: Rowman and Littlefield, 229–50.

Teivainen, Teivo (2007). 'The Political and its Absence in the World Social Forum—Implications for Democracy', *Development Dialogue,* 49: 69–79.

Tsing, Anna L. (2005). *Friction: An Ethnography of Global Connection.* Princeton: Princeton University Press.

Wallerstein, Immanuel (1984). *The Modern World System.* New York: Academic Press.

Wallerstein, Immanuel (1991). *Unthinking Social Science: The Limits of Nineteenth-Century Paradigms.* Cambridge: Polity Press.

Yeğenoğlu, Meyda (2005). 'Cosmopolitanism and Nationalism in a Globalized World', *Ethnic and Racial Studies,* 28.1: 103–31.

CHAPTER 26

POSTCOLONIALISM, GLOBALIZATION, AND THE 'ASIA QUESTION'[1]

DANIEL VUKOVICH

INTRODUCTION

Beyond the problem of attributed common experience or shared history, Asia's relationship to postcolonialism is complicated by what both of these deeply ambiguous terms, especially the former, might possibly signify. Even as a cartographic designation, 'Asia' only makes sense through force of habit. And even if one leaves out West Asia or the Middle East, themselves ambiguous designations, a simple glance at a map and Asia stands revealed as a clear example of the age-old Orientalist bifurcation of the world. 'Asia' denotes a civilizational concept more than anything else and a misleading one at that—as if all Confucian or Buddhist societies (which are clearly not coextensive with the various spaces named by 'Asia' on any map) were somehow to be considered the same in Oriental essence or even within themselves. This culturalist designation is of little use in any case in thinking through, e.g., South Asia—and not only because Confucianism and Buddhism are either absent there or are (depending on location) relatively minor. As Ravi Palat has argued, India has gone from being powerfully identified with Asia in the past to being left out of prevailing notions of it (Palat 2002). This has everything to do with global capitalism and its imagined associations with what used to be called the 'Asian tigers' (South Korea, Taiwan, Hong Kong, Singapore), Japan, and, by the 1990s, China. India was certainly not 'shining' at that point, and even with its recent economic success it is still not quite part of what counts as 'Asia'. The various crises of the above-mentioned national economies, save of course for that of the PRC,

[1.] This chapter draws briefly on the first chapter of *China and Orientalism* (Routledge, 2012) and is included here with their permission.

have meant that it is now China that stands metonymically for 'Asia'. Similarly, the composite category 'Asia Pacific' raises as many problems as it solves, both with reference to the terms themselves and to the relationship between them; for the Oceanic or island territories of the Pacific region often have little connection—or at least a deeply ambivalent connection—to the nations, mainlands, and federations that bind them, still less to some gargantuan landmass called 'Asia' that seems, to all intents and purposes, to straddle the world (see Keown and Murray in this section of the volume).

Even within an East Asian context it is hard to find people *within* Asia who identify as 'Asians'. 'Asia' is far more likely to be invoked by people in conversation with or relation to Caucasians or foreigners. In that sense—and also in the sense of such western-based academic disciplines as Asian American studies—the identity of Asia today seems largely to be bound up with diasporas in western countries or is a term that arises from, and is dependent on, real or perceived contact with the west. The by now defunct discourse of 'Asian values' was mostly a Singaporean creation; it was also more a sustained media event than a significant cultural marker. (Despite affinities between Deng Xiaoping and Lee Kuan Yew, 'Asian values' were rarely talked about in China itself.)

Why is this the case? It is, in large part, because the term 'Asia' has its roots in a long imperialist history that pitted Asia against the west in an imaginary but dialectically real binary that in some ways still persists today. Nobody wants to be called an Asian. As Naoki Sakai among others has argued, there is not only an interpellating force to the Asia/west binary (in which Asians are constructed as other to whites and Occidentals), but in terms of the production of knowledge and political culture, Asia has historically featured as a space of negative and/or exotic difference from the west (Sakai 2000). To put it simply, Asia is what the west is not; the west is defined by its qualitative difference from Asia. No doubt this all sounds too vulgar to the poststructuralist critic; it might even register an affront to fashionable notions of postcolonial hybridity; and more importantly, it risks underestimating the palpable extent to which Asia today is significantly less exoticized and demonized (but perhaps even more commodified and banalized) than in times gone by. But that traditional 'Asian' difference, or more precisely the *function* of that difference and of the image of western superiority associated with it, are still very much with us. Recall, for example, Zack Snyder's 2007 box office mega-hit *300*, which pitted the 'free Greeks' of Sparta against the 'hordes of Asia'. One might easily substitute 'Asia' for 'the Orient' along the lines of Edward Said's 1978 classic *Orientalism* and miss only the subtlest beats even if, for Said, it was arguably 'Islam' (the Middle East) and not 'Asia' (the Far East) that was the main target (see Sayyid in Part I of this volume). When one recalls who uses the concept of 'Asia' today—predominantly governmental, military, financial, and multilateral agencies of latter-day empire as well as area studies departments in western universities—then the continuing relevance of Said's work stands in sharp relief. We are, in some crucial ways, still at the crossroads described in the last chapter of *Orientalism*, gravitating uneasily from a traditional, philological, overtly 'othering' if not necessarily racist way of thinking about Asia towards more empirical, social science-based forms of knowledge in the context of the Cold War and the current neo-imperial globalized scene. These forms of knowledge became even stronger after the fall of the Soviet Empire and with the rise of China since the mid-1970s; and globalization—in this and other respects—might well be seen as masking a neo-imperial politics and Eurocentric world view (see Dhawan and Randeria in this section of the volume).

As many commentators have noted, Said's relationship to postcolonial studies was always ambivalent (Brennan 2006; see also the General Introduction to this volume). There is a sense in which *Orientalism* both predates the field and somehow manages to go beyond it. Just as Palestine could not be *post*colonial, Orientalism and the larger phenomenon Said was trying to account for in his eponymous book—the divisive politics of knowledge, the lineaments of an imperial political culture—preceded modern colonialism and continued after it into a late-Cold-War geopolitical context which, despite the rise of the Chinese economy and the fall of the Soviet bloc, in some ways still looked strikingly familiar (see Part II of this volume). Even that rise is often overstated. China's economy may be the world's second largest, but its GDP per capita places it below at least a hundred other nations. And while China may have 'awakened' (just as Napoleon feared) in terms of the production of knowledge—of what 'we' know about it and about the difference it makes in global intellectual-political culture—the PRC is still a relative pauper, to say nothing of the challenges (inequalities, protests, rampant corruption) it has in maintaining a stable, let alone a globally influential, state.

INTER-ASIAN STUDIES: MULTILATERALISM OR EUROPEAN POSTSTRUCTURALISM?

The common thread connecting Orientalism to Asia is an imperial-cum-globalist mode of knowledge production—one which, while admittedly combined and multilateral, is still fundamentally unjust and uneven. This mode accounts for the fact that Asia can be a realm of dazzling data but never a source of illuminating theory; for if Asia is by and large what the west is not (i.e. a space of reason, individuality, capitalism-inspired liberal democracy), then its primary role is to help constitute and consolidate the identity and political culture of the west. *In fact, it might be a good idea to do without the term 'Asia' altogether.* This would be a form of philosophical and historical hygiene; for, as the Japanese historian Harry Harootunian bluntly puts it: 'it has been one of the enduring ironies of the study of Asia that Asia itself, as an object, simply doesn't exist' (2000: 25). But it is also warranted because even within the allegedly 'de-imperializing' inter-Asian cultural studies project, 'Asia' remains an impossible object. How could anyone claim to know or study such a massive thing; how could anyone hope to account for its immense differences, its labyrinthine tributary systems, its formidably long histories? It is striking in this regard that the few attempts to date to use postcolonial theory to study Asia (by which I primarily mean East Asia) have had so little to say about mainland China other than to see it as akin to the modern British or French Empires. Thus, just as the latter empires produced Anglo- and Francophone literatures, China produced Sinophone writing; in place of overseas western imperialism, insert Chinese 'internal colonialism' (Shih 2011). Certainly 'Chineseness' should be seen as a contested and tendentious construct, both inside China and abroad (for a sharp critique of the notion, see Chun 1996). And certainly Mao's strictures against Han chauvinism have been conveniently 'forgotten' by the Party in its pursuit of legitimacy through growth and patriotic gore, just as there is a long-standing internal 'Orientalism' or more simply an 'othering' process towards China's own 'national minorities' (Mao 1956; Schein 2000). These are necessary forms of postcolonial critique. But the assumption that China, ancient or modern, fits the standard poststructuralist, 'postcolonial' template—as Shih's work suggests—also runs the risk of a facile assimilation through non-recognition. Can we just add China and stir? Modern colonialism's legalized racial discrimination and monopolistic economic extraction will not be found in China's imperial past—or its present for that matter.

If there is anything like an Asian imaginary today, as opposed to yesterday's pan-Asianism (infamously incorporated into Japanese fascism) or the too reverentially invoked 'Bandung', then it exists predominantly within the states and agencies listed above. It is worth recalling here that area studies were born of the Cold War against the PRC and 'Asiatic' Stalinist Russia. For these and several other reasons, it seems best not to study Asia itself, but rather the specific regional and subregional links between various nation states within the eastern hemisphere. This can and must include inter-referencing *from within* 'Asia', including scholarly work, which can help provincialize Euro-American knowledges and protocols of scholarship. This reorientation is the project of the 'inter-Asian cultural studies' movement that is loosely based in Asian universities (chiefly 'greater China' and Japan, but not the PRC or India). It also—perhaps ironically—incorporates many American and Australia-based scholars.

Asian identity and some real space called Asia are at the heart of this project, as articulated by one of its founding scholars, Chen Kuan-Hsing (Chen 2010, 1998). Chen's call for using 'Asia as method' draws on Japanese pan-Asianist intellectuals, the basic idea being to multiply points of reference within Asia so as to de-emphasize, if not necessarily abandon, the orthodox preoccupations of the west. (He offers detailed readings of Takeuchi, for example, but also Chatterjee, connecting these to pressing issues in Taiwanese film and politics.) But in reading Chen one is struck by how little of his work is noticeably Asian other than the specific (often national) contexts it discusses or the people it refers to. Even the theory he draws on is palpably western in many cases: Freudianism, poststructuralism. (Asia needs to heal, it seems, through a type of talking cure based in 'theory', while dualities and overarching terms are strenuously to be opposed, aside that is from 'inter-*Asia*'.) Chen is clearly opposed to elite, Eurocentric, and nationalist conceptions of culture; but this is not enough to produce a pan-Asian identity. One has to ask: where is the theory of social space here, and what is the basis of the identity other than being 'not-western'? One can ask the same questions of Spivak's foray into the prospect of 'other Asias' (2008). There, the call is for a 'position without identity' and a 'critical regionalism' that deconstruct national and other identities

(2008: 239–56). But if this is clearly less essentialist than the pan-Asian project, it is also a fairly plain pluralism that—as Spivak is much more ready to acknowledge than Chen—has very little to say about China and the PRC.

Politically, there is no need to try to reinvent pan-Asianism in the radically different historical and ideological circumstances that obtain under globalization. At one level, globalization seems to hold out the possibility of thinking, abstractly or imaginatively, of Asia as a unified entity. But in reality there has been a recent resurgence of competing nationalisms and regional conflicts as well as class struggles within particular Asian nations, from north–south tensions within Vietnam to 'red shirt'–'white shirt' skirmishes in Thailand, to the massive floating population of rural-to-urban migrant workers in the PRC. It is hard to see how the inter-Asian cultural-political project, which might be described as a postcolonial cosmopolitanism modelled on the European Union, can substitute for nationalist and other sharply aligned polities that remain bounded by powerful (if also at times failing) states. What we have to think through are still multilateral or simply bilateral relations and histories as well as national ones. Politically, *internationalism* remains the more rigorous idea (see Lazarus in Part III of this volume).

China, Asia-as-ASEAN +3, and Postcolonial Theory

Let me turn now to another influential designation of 'Asia', one broadly defined by the Chinese sphere of economic and political influence. This 'Asia' is sometimes described as ASEAN +3 (i.e., the Association of Southeast Asian Nations, plus Korea, China, and Japan, that was formed initially in 1997). What this formation simultaneously reflects is a shift away from American global influence and a realization of the need to deal with China: to take China seriously not just as a potential hegemon but a political and economic opportunity, a mediating influence on both the region and the globe. (The fact that ASEAN +3 excludes Taiwan is instructive here, though Taiwanese capital is as rampant in Southeast Asia as it is in the PRC.)

Learning to deal with China is obviously something that postcolonial criticism and theory have yet to come to terms with. It is in humanities fields that that this non-engagement has been most evident. World systems theory, by contrast, has been wrestling with China for some time, albeit at a high level of generality; and it was the late Giovanni Arrighi and, above all, Andre Gunder Frank, drawing in turn on the more specialized work of others such as Roy Bin Wong (1997) and Kenneth Pomeranz (2001), who argued forcefully that our world system had shifted and was no longer situated in the 'US–west' core (albeit leaving aside the question of military-political hegemony). Imperial China was once the centre of the global economy (alongside what is now India) and is now well under way to returning there after a century and a half of intense and conflicted encounter with capitalist modernity and a drawn-out sequence of hot and cold imperial wars. Europe's ascendancy, Frank notes, was due in no small part to selling silver to China after it had been 'freed' from the Americas, alongside 'free' slave labour from Africa (Frank 1998). The shift to a European- and then American-dominated world system ultimately had to do not just with military superiority but with Europe's and America's respective positions (locations) within a mutating world system that was driven by the globalization of capital from its very beginnings (Frank 2007; see also Lazarus in Part III of this volume). Frank's main point here is to underscore the US–west's short-lived and ultimately arbitrary centrality in terms of economic power. For Frank, as for other world systems theorists, the old core has effectively been reprovincialized by the rise of Asia, and especially China, within a newly configured world system. This new system requires new methods to examine it. Vocabularies of national and regional exceptionalism, modernist teleologies of progress and democracy, notions of civilizational clash and the autonomous development or take-off of Europe—all of these are of little use in figuring the rise, fall, and rise again of a China-centred Asia within the ever-shifting capitalist world system.

More recently, Li Minqi has argued that China's rise may well lead to the demise, or at least the radical transformation, of that system due to environmental havoc and the increasing costs associated with a growing Chinese workforce (Li 2009). In short, the world-historical growth of China (which even the most committed Chinese Marxist must admit has lifted millions of people out of poverty) may be unsustainable, in financial terms but also in human ones. If Li and others are correct, then China will have moved from directly challenging the global capitalist system under Mao (not without success) to inadvertently bringing it to the brink of ruin, forcing it to change into some other kind of system. Such a view obviously departs from other analyses, such as official Chinese ones and neoliberal ones that celebrate the rise of China as saving global capitalism from itself or even teaching the west a lesson or two about the limits of democracy and Keynesianism. Li certainly departs from the previous optimism of Arrighi, who argues powerfully that China, as opposed to many other postcolonial nations, has maintained control over its own economy and has been able to direct it towards real growth within a 'non-capitalist' market system that will eventually prove to be far more competitive globally than the US–west (2007).

As for neoliberalism proper, David Harvey's work has been useful in situating China's rise *alongside* the global deployment of neoliberalism while not *reducing* it to that either (Harvey 2005). There is much in Deng Xiaoping and later leadership that resonates with full-scale privatization, entrepreneurialism, and the 'greed-is-good' mentality. The smashing of the 'iron rice bowl' (Maoist welfare system), decollectivization, and other like-minded strategies certainly fit this mould, as do Deng's horribly compelling slogans: 'some must get rich first'; 'black cat, white cat, what does it matter so long as it catches mice'; 'to get rich is glorious'. But China cannot quite be called neoliberal, at least not yet. For one thing, it developed under a socialist mode of production that in some ways still obtains (as Arrighi and Li note); and for another, there is much in the culture that is too civilized and 'communal' for it. In sum, the rise of China poses some deep and challenging questions for postcolonial and global studies in so far as it challenges our received notions of development, progress, and political legitimacy (including 'democracy') as well as classical accounts of vegetative, poor, and pre-modern Asia. Western modernity, and its place at the summit of world history, turn out to be reversible. What does the west do when China and ASEAN +3 start to look wealthier, more modern, and more future-oriented than it does? The west has always been a social or imaginary construct; but it has also been what counts as the dominant political culture. The now seriously outdated proclamation of the 'end of history' after the fall of the Soviet Union has been matched more recently by the unravelling of the 'clash of civilizations' thesis. There is no clash between Confucius and Jesus, only a triumph of capitalist developmentalism and transnational class collaboration under the guise of globalization (see the introduction to this section; also some of the chapters in Part II). At the same time, the 'China difference' remains, at the very least in the form of a question.

In the more properly political realm it was Walden Bello and Nicola Bullard of the think-tank activist NGO 'Focus on the Global South' who, despite their critical position on Chinese capitalism, welcomed the entry of China into the WTO when few others did (2001). They did so precisely because it would likely spell the effective demise of the WTO and its anachronistic and hierarchical rules about free trade. But to their great credit, Focus's position was also aimed against anti-Chinese and anti-PRC rhetoric from progressive, labour, and other anti-globalization groups in the west and elsewhere (e.g. Bullard 2000). These latter were almost unanimously opposed to China being allowed into the WTO, which speaks to the ongoing legacies of Cold War politics. Based primarily in Thailand but also the Philippines and India, Focus does not propagate an Asian identity so much as a social-democratic and anti-capitalist or 'de-globalization' one. This is its lesson for Asian studies. China is one of five thematic areas and the only country mentioned by name in its mission statement (Focus on the Global South 2012). Work such as this shows that it *is* possible to work out a nuanced position in response to China's global ascendancy. This involves steering a course between the baldly antagonistic 'progressive' position, which sees the PRC as the new empire one must implacably oppose, and the grossly corporate or neoliberal agenda represented by, among others, ASEAN +3.

Postcolonial theory, to repeat, has been singularly reluctant to address this new conjuncture. If, on the ground, Asia has come to mean China—and the PRC's rise has after all been one of the most significant narratives of the last thirty years—postcolonial studies has yet to register the difference this might make for how we understand Asia, the west, or for that matter colonialism and imperialism. We need to ask why this has been the case. One reason is that area studies has remained a largely empiricist enterprise holding out against the theoretical and reflexive turns that have swept most of the other disciplines. This applies less to work on South Asia, perhaps, which, as in the case of subaltern studies, has been one of the principal inspirations for postcolonial studies (see Dhawan and Randeria in this section of the volume). But if there are deep roots in critical South Asian scholarship that retrace the experiences of modern British and French colonialisms, this in turn poses—or at least should pose—an analytical problem for developing postcolonial approaches to the PRC and *that* Asia, which is probably also the 'Asia' that most people have in mind by the word. Meanwhile, the fact that it was Japanese imperialism that arguably did most damage throughout East and South East Asia, again under the degraded banner of 'Asianism', must also give one pause.

One of the arguments against postcolonialism within area studies, and even in some Chinese scholarship within the PRC, has been that China simply does not fit the paradigm: it never lost its sovereignty. China's problems are modernity and revolution. As Lenin put it first, to be followed by Mao et al., China was *semi*-colonial; though even this suggestion is far stronger than most area studies scholars would care to admit. Instead, in post-World War II area studies China is generally slotted into the category of the 'not-colonized'. While the chaos and poverty of China as a whole from the Opium Wars to 1949 is beyond question, it retained its political sovereignty at all times aside from various cantonments and concessions. This freedom is true in a formal sense, and China's is obviously a different scenario than that endured by the (future) nations of South Asia, Africa, and Latin America (or even Hong Kong, whose colonial liberalism is a point of pride for much of the city's intelligentsia). Given that our working definitions of colonialism turn on this very distinction, there are logical grounds for seeing China's 'problematic' as being closer to *modernization* than *colonialism*. Alternatively, for the radical and Mao era intellectuals, there was a third term, i.e. the dominant problematic was *revolution* and this incorporated the modern and anti-imperialist dimensions. The rise of depoliticization and de-Maoification in turn eviscerates this of content; modernization reigns supreme, via liberalism and/or developmentalism. This is the dominant coding of China inside and abroad, where the notion of 'colonial modernity' has yet to disrupt the dominant ways in which the country is written (Barlow 1997; see also some of the chapters in Part II of this volume). This also seemingly undercuts the received critical theories of colonialism and empire that flow out of British and French experiences of empire and colonial rule. The iconoclasts of the May 4th period as well as the early Communist Party all embraced 'westernization' in a very conscious and deliberate, if also inevitably misinformed and utopian, manner. (This is why the Maoist Sinification of Marxism and the shift towards the rural peasantry and not the urban proletariat proved so difficult to achieve.) One certainly cannot say they were *forced* to think in the manner of the typical colonial subject.

Even here, however, is it not obvious that the concept of ideology or discursive power, let alone imperialism, is lacking in such China studies perspectives? Hence one can readily find histories of opium in China, accounts of an age of openness before the so-called 'takeover' in 1949, narratives of Hong Kong developing more or less flawlessly prior to 1997, or eulogies to Shanghai's singular cosmopolitanism—all of which avoid the capitalist/imperialist problematic entirely (Dikotter 2008; Lee 1999). One can contrast this, for example, with the largely unknown historical work of the Chinese radical historian Hu Sheng (1918–2000). Readily available in English but predictably dismissed as an official Party voice during the Mao era, Hu's work on the destructive effects of imperialism from the later Qing through the Republican periods is serious, impassioned scholarship that is emblematic of a considered and considerable mainland perspective on key

'China–west' questions (Hu 1981, 1991). It seems worth adding that if postcolonial studies can read, say, Frantz Fanon or Aimé Césaire as inspirational historical figures, it is high time it did the same with Chinese and other Asian voices, from Hu Sheng or Mao himself to Ho Chi Minh. Nor is there any good reason to define colonialism as primarily an issue of political sovereignty and its loss or recapture. Sovereignty and the global interstate system remain important, as any number of recent humanitarian-imperialist adventures illustrate. But modern twentieth-century imperial conflicts and discourses are too complex and messy to be demarcated so clearly (as might be said to some extent of their earlier colonial counterparts: see Stoler in Part I of this volume). For one thing, as Robert Young has noted, the practical differences between the modern French and British empires made little difference from the standpoint of colonized subjects (Young 2001). Young's point is directed against recent efforts to disaggregate colonialism to the point of making it go away as a unified whole or to defend it in the Niall Ferguson manner. But his point also obtains for modern China and even for current nationalist Chinese reactions to western media discourse (witness the infamous anger of the 'netizens' of China against continuing western government and media bias, or high-profile protests against foreign embassies and French supermarket chains). While China might appear to occupy an exceptionalist space vis-à-vis postcolonial theory, it was deeply affected by imperialist contact as well as by the political brinkmanship of the Cold War. In an important sense, it is not the details of sovereignty and occupation that matter, so much as the cultural-ideological conflicts and the politics of knowledge and 'face'. Recall the anger of Chinese people over anti-Olympics and 'free Tibet' protests, the awarding of Nobel prizes to exiled dissidents, currency devaluation pressures from the west, and so on. What is at stake here is not the truth about, say, Tibet but a certain paternalist, even colonial arrogance from abroad along with—for non-western identified, non-diasporic Chinese—the lack of permission to participate in global narratives. Thus, while either only 'semi-colonial' (for the classical left) or simply 'not-colonized' (for area studies), the PRC has nonetheless been strongly affected by 'coloniality' (an admittedly broad term) and western-imperial political culture (Mignolo 2000; see also Mignolo in Part I of this volume). The fact that the Party-state also speaks of the relatively brief but anguishing era of 'national humiliations' does not make this any less true.

But the details matter too. As Hevia has argued, and as was the case in colonial India, the production of an imperial archive of texts, translations, and knowledge about China was integral to the global colonial project of the foreign powers during the later Qing Republican periods (1998: 236). Prominent within this history are missionary activities before and after the Boxer Movement and a larger discourse that lives on today 'in the pious moral tone of American foreign policy toward China' (Hevia 1997: 325). This, it will be recalled, is the problem of orientalism and colonial discourse. After the Revolution, the knowledge produced by China studies would take on more social science-oriented and modernizing forms including anti-communist and gung-ho capitalist theory, as in the notion that freeing China's markets would inexorably usher the polity into democracy. We might also recall the impact of an older philological Sinology in changing Chinese perceptions and practices of their own language: no less a radical Chinese patriot than Lu Xun, for instance, would claim that unless the Chinese language were radically altered and 'westernized' it, and the nation along with it, would perish. All in all, then, contact with the west certainly left its mark on China, materially and culturally, as did the later Cold War. The Cold War was in some sense the continuation of western (mainly American) imperialism by other means: at the level of discourse, rhetoric, and knowledge as much as at the more familiar *realpolitik* level. As Barlow summarizes it, notwithstanding empirical differences between 'real' colonialism in South Asia and Africa and 'not-colonized' China, 'the fact of multiple imperialist adventures in China [as opposed to a single conquest] should not distract attention away from the fact that already well-established colonial knowledges [significantly] informed the Great Powers' experiments and contributed to "development" in their "spheres of influence"' (2005: 277).

ORIENTALISM AND OCCIDENTALISM
WITHOUT COLONIZATION

All of this leads us to three problems that remain insufficiently addressed in studies of China in particular, but also the ASEAN countries more broadly: (1) orientalism, (2) Occidentalism, and (3) the Cold War as an imperial formation after the age of decolonization. These are apt terms for the study of 'coloniality' since none of them presupposes an actual scene of formal colonization. China studies scholars have largely dismissed the phenomenon as inapplicable to their field. John King Fairbank got the ball rolling in the 1950s by transcoding western imperialism and cantonments as bilateral relations and forms of 'dyarchy' or joint rule between the Qing dynasty and their western partners (Fairbank 1953; see also Barlow 1997). Much of the rest of this institutional history has been ably analysed by James Peck (2002) and Bruce Cummings (2006). Specific engagements with Said were largely non-issues owing to the resolute empiricism and liberal humanism of the field (for examples, see Huang 1998; Schwarz 1980; Zhang Longxi 1992). Even in the one significant *rapprochement*, by Paul Cohen, the call for a 'China-centred' method hardly amounted to a postcolonial turn. Cohen criticized the Eurocentrism of past approaches (with China always responding to the west) and even claimed that Said's basic insight about intellectual inquiry partaking 'of a kind of "imperialism" [especially] when the inquirer's milieu helped shaped "the object of inquiry"' was sound (1984: 150).

This apt distillation is followed, however, by a conventional alternative. 'China-centred' analysis seems a more-or-less orthodox historicism that simply seeks to be more sensitive to the Chinese context. This is a decent and humane suggestion surely, but what of it? Harry Harootunian argues that Cohen's model 'rejects theory out of hand for the "facts" and thus [fails to acknowledge] the authority of native knowledge and experience'

(1999: 138). The area, he suggests, has still not been defined intellectually, but rather linguistically and geographically. In addition, however much we might centre ourselves in China, this begs the question of *which* China. Finally worth considering are the global and transcultural dimensions of both China and the west that complicate what a 'China-centred' analysis might look like. In short, while the China field in general has been no more welcoming of critique than Middle Eastern studies were to Edward Said's initial volley, it is nonetheless increasingly hard to deny that Orientalism applies not only to popular and literary imaginings of China (which has never been in doubt) but, more importantly in terms of academic and professional work, to knowledge production proper. What has happened has been a transformation of the logic of Orientalism from one of essential difference (as in Said's model or Rudyard Kipling's 'East is East, West is West') to one of *sameness*. Under globalization, the logics of modernization, progress, bourgeois development, and civil society have become triumphant. The booming cities of Asia are becoming 'just like us': modern, wealthy, free, liberal, and at least vaguely democratic. And even if this has not happened uniformly it eventually will; there is no alternative since communism, revolution, and national liberation have either failed or been co-opted. What is essential here, in turn, is that the other *can* be the same; the only thing holding China back from fully achieving modernity is the Communist Party. This, in a nutshell, is the dominant, teleological coding of the PRC since Tiananmen, 1989—the civil society-as-democratization narrative, which can include generic human rights and 'social movement' discourses. It is as if the classic logic of colonial discourse or colonial difference—what Chakrabarty once memorably coined as the colonizer saying 'not yet' to the colonized—has subtly shifted: the moment has arrived already, or is just around the corner. Contemporary Sinological Orientalism represents, in part, a redeployment of missionary and civilizing discourses, including their logic of sameness and equivalence (Vukovich 2012). But this is, from a Marxist perspective, also a capitalist logic that harmonizes perfectly with the homogenizing logic of exchange value. It is no accident that capital has been most active and dominant in China and in East Asia more generally as the world globalizes. All of this has happened *without* formal colonialism or a loss of formal political sovereignty but *with* the globalization of capital, 'developmentalism', and the global reach of western educational and media flows.

This brings us to Occidentalism: the imaginary understanding of the west as not just a real and singular thing but as the Orient's necessary opposite. Most often, in the postcolonial era, this has been a favourable comparison. As already suggested, China (and later the PRC) have been powerfully influenced by Occidentalism. One might argue that the PRC, especially in the post-Mao era, has been defined by an embrace of Occidentalism from the early Republican period and a later, Maoist-communist anti-Occidentalism. This has manifested itself, on the one hand, in a critique of traditional China through the lens of western science, economics, and democracy; and on the other, in a Sinification of Marxism and the Soviet system from 1949–79 and a later, post-Tiananmen attempt to revitalize Confucianism and discover a 'China model'. Much the same struggle could be shown in regard to other 'not-colonized' places of contemporary Asia, including Taiwan, South Korea, and Japan. As Beijing-based scholar Sun Ge aptly puts it:

> For the Asians engaged in the discussion of the Asia question [i.e. what is Asia, how does it mean?], though one cannot say there is precisely something called 'Occidentalism' worked out by them, there indeed exists, and not without reason, in abstraction an ambiguous single entity named the 'West' ... Occidentalism had, at least in the modern history of East Asia, once played a key role in mediating the self-knowledge of the nations within the East with important questions being stirred up in the process. (2000: 13)

Such Occidentalist knowledges on the part of the (male) elite and urban intellectuals were the result of colonial/imperial contact between the west and Asia. This last point is not really addressed by Sun, who focuses instead on Japanese–Chinese intellectual contributions to the concept of 'Asia'. Sun goes on to note that some Asian versions of Orientalism ('self-Orientalisms') are directed not just against the west but also towards Asian Occidentalists. The point, following Japanese intellectual Tenshin Okakura, is that 'Orientals have their own way of knowing and evaluating themselves, totally different from [Western] Occidentals' idea of Asia' (Sun 2000: 21). This might be called, at best, a strategic essentialism mobilized around the spectral entity of 'Asia'. But does it really take us beyond the purview of postcolonial theory and Saidian anti-Orientalism? Is this autonomous 'Asia' not the same bifurcation of the world bequeathed by Orientalism and imperial culture? And in either case, given the history of imperialism and fascism within Asia by Asians, is the dream of Asia really worth reimagining today?

Chen Xiaomei has argued that the existence of Occidentalism effectively negates the applicability of Orientalism as postcolonial critique to China. Chen adroitly unpacks the occidentalism of various post-Mao writers, noting how this is used to challenge the Party-state and mainstream discourse. She also notes the post-Mao state's own 'official' Occidentalism. It is worth pausing to consider the most significant of Chen's (2002) examples of 'good' Occidentalism. This was a highly influential text in the 1980s that received the extra cachet of having been banned in the wake of the Tiananmen incident: *He Shang* or *River Elegy*, a long documentary series that was broadcast by official television (CCTV). The film expresses heartfelt enthusiasm for the post-Mao programme of western-style 'reform and opening up' to global capitalism. In the final minutes, it calls for further political reform and transparency. At the same time, the bulk of the script contains vulgar Orientalist views of ancient or 'yellow' China (stagnant, despotic, doomed in its encounter with modernity) and fervently Occidentalist ones about the west and 'blue' free-trade zones of China like Shanghai and Hong Kong. *He Shang* describes contemporary Chinese rural people in this way:

> In the vast, backwards rural areas, there are common problems in the peasant makeup [*suzhi*] such as a weak spirit of enterprise, a very low ability to accept risk, a deep psychology of dependency and a strong sense of passive acceptance of fate. (Su and Wang 1991:169)

Such statements diagnose the 'feudal' mentality of the peasants and 'the national character' and contrast this with the entrepreneurial spirit and scientific rationality of modernity. This is the type of sanctioned discourse that the Chinese revolution had to overcome, and it has known a new lease of life since the mid 1980s. Outside of the a priori belief that the communist government is an unmitigated evil whose dissolution is to be desired by all right-thinking people, it is hard to understand exactly why this type of anti-peasant Occidental cosmopolitanism is to be valued, other than it being of value just because it is anti-Party/state. *He Shang* makes clear that Occidentalism does not disprove Saidian postcolonial critique or even serve as a counter-discourse to it, but is merely internalized Orientalism. This speaks more generally to the survival, even escalation, of the Oriental/Occidental dyad under globalization. For all the talk of a rising China and the return of Asia to global economic centrality, it is important to keep in mind which political cultures get globalized. For every Confucius Institute being established in American universities, there are longer-standing Goethe Institutes, not to mention thousands of western NGOs and think tanks (many of them inside China) that operate in anything but Cohen's 'China-centred' ways.

COLD WAR, HOT POSTCOLONIALISM

However much it might be over in terms of 'recognized' politics and mass movements, the Cold War remains central to the question of China and, if one recalls the plethora of US military bases across the Pacific, to Asia in general. US attempts to contain China, to maintain its military might in Asia, to 'save' Taiwan and Tibet, and to act as 'Asian leader', are by now well known, as is its reluctance to follow similar practices in Japan and South Korea. Less known, but more pressing, are the conceptual and theoretical aspects of the Cold War and its legacies in Asia. Even in Taiwan, Chen Kuan-Hsing has called for the need to 'de-Cold War' in the crucial sense that decolonization within Asia was left incomplete, interrupted by new Cold War structures that amounted to fresh forms of imperialism (2010: 4). For Chen, the confrontation of these ongoing tensions is therapeutic; it is also properly political in so far as it can guard against future events like those of 11 September 2001, moving Asia (China, Korea, Taiwan, Vietnam) away from the 'anti-communism, pro-Americanism structure' that has dominated Asian politics, even dissident culture, in China in the recent past (2010: 8).

There is more to be said here in terms of theory and method. Perhaps the most important point is that we can no longer separate the twinned histories of postcolonialism and the Cold War. Decolonization was caught up in the Cold War; the Cold War was caught up in colonialism. While it seems clear, at the moment, which side won that particular battle, we are still left with the global political culture it bequeathed us. What the more particular case of China shows is the imbrication of colonial discourse and anti-communism and the unabashed deployment of 'universal' modernizationist terms (democracy, civil society, development) to explain China but also other regions of Asia. Cold War discourse and the lynchpin concept of totalitarianism in particular are part and parcel of this formation. 'Oriental despotism' became 'totalitarianism'; passive and irrational Chinese minds were easily brainwashed and manipulated into being 'Mao's army of blue ants'; and even today this mythology lives on in the figure of 'the Chinese' being uniform, whether through consumerism and the pursuit of wealth or through a homogenous nationalism.

In a 1988 essay, early enough in the development of postcolonial studies to be almost entirely neglected, William Pietz unpacks the racialized, Orientalist thinking of the founders of Cold War discourse and the concept of 'totalitarianism'. Arendt's 1951 *Origins of Totalitarianism* had previously endowed the concept with academic respectability. Pietz argues that Cold War discourse displaced colonial discourse in the aftermath of World War II (when, not least thanks to China, decolonization was the order of the day); Cold War discourse effectively substituted itself for 'the language of colonialism' (1988: 55). Cast in a less immediately racist, modified guise, Cold War discourse became not just intelligible but popular and persuasive. Note that it is not that colonial discourse disappeared but that it was rearticulated to the Cold War. The two combined, making colonial discourse 'vanish' in a relative sense while living on as a constituent part of Cold War political culture. For George Kennan among others, totalitarianism was 'traditional Oriental despotism plus modern technology' (58); it lay in the Oriental mind (recall that Stalin/Russia were already half-'Asiatic').

But it is Arendt who establishes, at the same time, the centrality of a racist understanding of African 'tribalism' to her theory of totalitarianism. Racism—which she clearly wishes to oppose—and totalitarianism have their origins in colonialism and in European (Boer) contact with Black Africa and Africans:

> When the Boers, in their fright and misery, decided to use these savages as though they were just another form of animal life they embarked upon a process which could only end with their own degeneration into a white race living beside and together with black races from whom in the end they would differ only in the color of their skin. They had transformed themselves into a tribe and had lost the European's feeling for a territory, a *patria* of his own. They behaved exactly like the black tribes who had roamed the Dark Continent for centuries. (Quoted in Pietz 1988: 68)

Arendt points to Black Africa's 'tribal' effect on the Boers and thence, so the diffusionist argument goes, on Europe. 'We' degenerate into a race-based, primitive, and nomadic tribe, no better than 'them'. Due to this contact with the primitive, not only do 'we' come to think in terms of race but this later morphs into a tribal nationalism that in turn becomes modern anti-Semitism and totalitarianism: 'a whole outlook on life and the world ... [rooted] in tribalism rather than in political facts and circumstances', Arendt calls it (quoted in Pietz 1988: 69).

Totalitarianism, seen this way, comes equipped with a colonial genealogy. In the case of China, it assumes a striking lack of human agency on the part of hundreds of millions of people: as if they all said and did whatever they were told and as if this was always false consciousness; as if there were a massive uniformity of experience across so much diverse, complex social territory; as if there were such an Oriental surfeit of power that this was possible. But to speak of the Cold War as a residual discourse is still to speak of revolution and its aftermath. The coding of China and Asia as inevitably 'becoming the same' under globalization (i.e., modern, free, democratic, liberal, wealthy) hearkens back to the original desires of the Cold War from the western/northern angle. The Cold War, in fact, was decidedly hot in much of Asia, from China's own borders to Vietnam and much of South East Asia. For Taiwan and South Korea, decolonization and national liberation may already have been compromised by those countries' dependence on the west; but in China and elsewhere the liberations were self-understood as far more actual and accomplished: not just postcolonial but revolutionary, they carved out self-reliant and alternative modernities that attempted, and to some extent are still attempting, to cut a path that is fundamentally different from either the *Pax Americana* or the former Soviet bloc (see the General Introduction to this volume).

Another fundamental aspect of this legacy lies in the competing political cultures of the region. Anti-imperialist nationalisms (now sometimes directed against one another) are alive and well and can even trouble the depoliticizing ambit of developmental states like the PRC; the 'masses' and 'netizens' are often angrier and more anti-imperialist and patriotic than their states. Part of the same heritage has been an appropriately dyadic understanding of politics as a life-and-death struggle between 'friends' and 'enemies' seen in class and revolutionary terms (see Schmitt 2007). This radical legacy also helps explain—and de-pathologize—the frequently noted 'irrational' or 'excessive' quality of political rhetoric and argument in China and the region. This quality is not to be understood as the sign of underdevelopment or a rough initiation into the 'cooler' political modernity of the west, but rather as an impassioned mode of commitment politics that sits uneasily within depoliticized states that do not, in fact, want to see revolution or the passions of the masses (for an opposite view, see Barmé 2000).

The revolutionary legacy contains not only a residual anti-imperialism but also an insistence that Eurocentric models or theories cannot adequately explain fundamental aspects of Chinese history and politics. This insistence stretches back to Sino- and other 'Asian'-centrisms, but its impetus is modern. A particularly striking example, opposed to more essentialist versions of neo-Confucianism, is Wang Hui's recent work against the Eurocentric hierarchy between empires (bad) and nation states (good) (Wang 2011). Perhaps the most controversial plank within this is Wang's argument that the western fascination with Tibet and its independence as a free nation state is a product of Orientalism, British colonialism, and, especially, Cold War politics. Wang suggests that the complex tributary relations of the past between Tibet and China, as between and among other states and empires within Asia, are worth recovering, as are Zhou Enlai's original plans for relative but real autonomy for Tibet and other 'national minority' areas. This is *not* because the final Qing dynasty boundaries (of 1911) must be kept on principle. Nor is it because colonial discourse resolutely sets up China as the inferior, infantilized subject that must learn correct ways and models. Wang's point is rather that the modern nation state, especially in its western-developmentalist form, is precisely the problem and will only make things worse. This includes the PRC state, especially in its post-Mao moment, and the attempt to resolve the Tibet and Taiwan problems not only through force (or the threat of it) and the imposition of the modern (Chinese) nation state form, but also through commodification or economic incorporation to the point where no one will imagine independence. It is the latter that is eroding Tibetan culture and history, as capital does everywhere whether it is directed by the Chinese or by other states. The larger problem is that of capitalist modernity.

It is in this wider sense that Wang Hui's and others' attempts to rethink the Tibet (or conceivably Taiwan) issue in terms of past relations of suzerainty, Asian tributary relations, and Zhou Enlai's 'unity in diversity' are importantly *not* a form of Sinocentric triumphalism (see the debate in Tsering and Wang 2009; also Sautman 2006). A path will have to be found between pre-modern Chinese imperialism and the Westphalian model of the world. Short of the collapse of the PRC, an outcome that is neither likely nor desirable, the independence of Tibet (or Xinjiang) is more or less unthinkable in realist terms. And while the PRC's occasional threats to use force to reunify Taiwan can certainly seem like imperialistic bullying, it must also be said that the mainland's claim that China-Taiwan is an unresolved issue of (revolutionary) civil war also explains a good deal. Some type of negotiated political settlement must be fought for—this, rather than a simulation of past national liberation movements, velvet revolutions, or the independence dreams of the exiles and émigrés. It is either real politics in this sense or more of the same: the awful solution of commodification/incorporation.

Furthermore, it is also not at all clear what subaltern Tibetans *in Tibet* want in terms of independence, Beijing, and politics generally. Admittedly this is due to Chinese censorship. But the assumption that the Dalai Lama or even monks within China and Tibet can speak for all Tibetans is striking. It is easy enough to see Chinese state rhetoric as interested and self-serving, but far more difficult to see the 'interests' of the Tibetan exiles or 'Free Tibet' groups. The ambivalence of at least large parts of the Taiwanese populace in regard to independence is also a knotty issue that includes, but is not reducible to, the fear of Chinese (and American) missiles (for more on Taiwan see Cumings 1999; Johnson 2004). For better or for worse, long-standing 'Asian' notions of the primacy of material livelihood may well outweigh postcolonial desires for political independence. (This has long been the case in Hong Kong, which is only now, thanks to the 1997 handover, becoming a broadly politicized society.) 'Livelihood' in this sense is typically rendered as quasi-Confucian but is as much a rural legacy and common-sense materialism. Construing this as false consciousness can only get one so far. Postcolonial thinking can have a role here in wrestling with China's alleged 'internal colonies' by refusing ethnic nationalisms on all sides and reminding us of the baleful consequences of (colonial) modernity and an imperious sovereignty. This would be a different approach than the standard one, which maps modern European colonialism (and thus a generic anti-colonial/liberation politics) onto Asia, and which ironically replicates the obsession with clear boundaries and compartmentalized peoples. In so far as the PRC was in pursuit of an alternative socialist modernity, imagined against Han chauvinism as well as capitalist inequalities and cultural imperialism, it too is relevant here as a founding myth and, indeed, a still extant constitution.

The postcolonial and the revolutionary, then, are not necessarily opposed (see also the General Introduction to this volume). Postcolonial theory—including orientalism and often lumped together with postmodernism—made a limited but important impact in the PRC during the 1990s. It was still largely about introducing western academic work; it was culturalist rather than Marxist; but it still gave a regionally adaptable fillip to the critique of Eurocentrism and cultural imperialism as well as to the rise of nationalisms (Wang Hui 2003). This also made it controversial among liberal intellectuals. It was a small but not insignificant part of the counter-movement of the 1990s against the development of neoliberalism after Tiananmen. Here, postcolonial theory met a longer Chinese revolutionary and 'Sinocentric' history; it became part of the reaction against the cultural fever for all things western in the 1980s.

With the more recent rise of the New Left intellectuals and their heated but important debates with their liberal counterparts, the best postcolonial questions and issues—universalism versus Eurocentrism, cultural and political-economic imperialism, nationalism—may not necessarily be named as 'postcolonial' at all but are nonetheless stronger than ever (see, for example, Cao 2005; Davies 2001; Wang, C. 2003). Perhaps the best instance of this—and a fittingly complex note on which to end—is the case of the imprisoned dissident Liu Xiaobo and the 'human rights and democracy' Charter 08 document he principally authored (Liu et al. 2008). There is something inspiring and seductive about the classical liberal language of the Charter (calls for freedom of speech, assertions of the legitimacy of protest in the context of the current Party-state) and it certainly demonstrates Liu's great courage. But the Charter, not unlike *He Shang*, also works from an anti-Maoist and anti-communist position that argues for the removal of the state from the economy, for an end to state-owned enterprises (which protect key industries and are usually the best jobs for the working class), and for a reduction of state involvement in favour of the market and individual entrepreneurs and consumers. The Charter draws on neoclassical economic ideology, arguing emphatically for the privatization of land and for the natural right to private property. It clearly evidences the presence of western 'China experts' and Cold War discourse. The author has received large sums from the US National Endowment for Democracy, funded by the Congress. Liu has notoriously insisted that the mainland lacked western colonization and could still use a three-hundred-year period of that to catch up with Hong Kong (see Sautman and Yan 2011). Of course, none of this in itself justifies the imprisonment of Liu, regardless of the content of the Charter. And it is supremely ironic that many of these views—especially the economic ones—are shared by leading functionaries within the Party. At least one noted and heterodox liberal intellectual, Qin Hui, refused to sign the Charter (Qin 2009). What we have with the Charter and with Liu's imprisonment is a complex confluence of political, ideological, and historical streams that is ripe for analysis yet simultaneously resists it, whether this analysis takes the shape of postcolonial critique or any other critical form. It is also a return, but with a difference, to the problem of colonial liberalism and the ongoing search for a form of state that fits a post-revolution-ary or 'liberated' society.

REFERENCES

Arendt, Hannah (1973 [1951]). *The Origins of Totalitarianism*. New York: Harcourt, Brace, Jovanovich.

Arrighi, Giovanni (2007). *Adam Smith in Beijing: Lineages of the Twenty-First Century*. New York: Verso.

Barlow, Tani (1997). 'Colonialism's Career in Postwar China Studies', in T. Barlow (ed.), *Formations of Colonial Modernity in East Asia*. Durham, NC: Duke University Press, 373–411.

Barlow, Tani (2005). 'Eugenic Woman, Semicolonialism, and Colonial Modernity as Problems for Postcolonial Theory', in A. Loomba et al. (eds), *Postcolonial Studies and Beyond*. Durham, NC: Duke University Press, 359–84.

Barmé, Geremie (2000). *In the Red: On Contemporary Chinese Culture*. New York: Columbia University Press.

Bello, Walden F. and Anuradha Mittal (2000). 'Dangerous Liaisons: Progressives, the Right, and the Anti-China Trade Campaign', *Focus On Trade Index*, No. 50. Online source: <http://www.tni.org/archives/archives_bello_china>, accessed 14 April 2012.

Brennan, Timothy (2006). *Wars of Position: The Cultural Politics of Left and Right*. New York: Columbia University Press.

Bullard, Nicola (2000). 'China: The Country Everyone Loves to Hate', *Focus On Trade*, No. 51. Online source: <http://www.focusweb.org/publications/FOT%20pdf/fot51.pdf>, accessed 14 April 2012.

Cao, Tian Yu (ed.) (2005). *The Chinese Model of Modern Development*. New York: Routledge.

Chen, Kuan-Hsing (ed.) (1998). *Trajectories: Inter-Asia Cultural Studies*. New York: Routledge.

Chen, Kuan-Hsing (2010). *Asia As Method: Toward Deimperialization*. Durham, NC: Duke University Press.

Chen, Xiaomei (2002). *Occidentalism: A Theory of Counter-Discourse in Post-Mao China*, 2nd edn. Lanham, Md.: Rowman & Littlefield.

Chun, Allen (1996). 'Fuck Chineseness: On the Ambiguities of Ethnicity as Culture as Identity', *boundary 2*, 23.2: 111–38.

Cohen, Paul A. (1984). *Discovering History in China: American Historical Writing and the Recent Chinese Past*. New York: Columbia University Press.

Cumings, Bruce (1999). *Parallax Visions: Making Sense of American-East Asian Relations*. Durham, NC: Duke University Press.

Cumings, Bruce (2002). 'Boundary Displacement: The State, the Foundations, and Area Studies During and After the Cold War', in H. Harootunian and M. Miyoshi (eds), *Learning Places: The Afterlives of Area Studies*. Durham, NC: Duke University Press, 261–302.

Davies, Gloria (ed.) (2001). *Voicing Concerns: Contemporary Chinese Critical Inquiry*. Lanham, Md.: Rowman & Littlefield.

Dikotter, Frank Ö. (2008). *The Age of Openness: China Before Mao*. Hong Kong: Hong Kong University Press.

Fairbank, John K. (1953). *Trade and Diplomacy on the China Coast: The Opening of the Treaty Ports, 1842–1854*. Cambridge, Mass.: Harvard University Press.

Focus on the Global South [NGO] (2012). 'Who We Are'. Online source: <http://www.focusweb.org/content/who-we-are>, accessed 24 April 2012.

Frank, Andre Gunder (1998). *Re-Orient: Global Economy in the Asian Age.* Berkeley: University of California Press.

Frank, Andre Gunder (2007). 'No Civilization/s: Unity and Continuity in Diversity; or, Multilateral and Entropic Paradigms for the World Today and Tomorrow', *positions: east asia cultures critique*, 15.2 (Fall): 225–49.

Harootunian, Harry (1999). 'Postcoloniality's Unconscious/Area Studies' Desire', *Postcolonial Studies*, 2.2: 127–47.

Harootunian, Harry (2000). *History's Disquiet: Modernity, Cultural Practice, and the Question of Everyday Life.* New York: Columbia University Press.

Harvey, David (2005). *A Brief History of Neoliberalism.* New York: Oxford University Press.

Hevia, James (1997). 'Leaving a Brand on China: Missionary Discourse in the Wake of the Boxer Movement', in T. Barlow (ed.), *Formations of Colonial Modernity in East Asia.* Durham, NC: Duke University Press, 113–39.

Hevia, James (1998). 'The Archive State and the Fear of Pollution: From the Opium Wars to Fu-Manchu', *Cultural Studies*, 12.2: 234–64.

Hu, Sheng (1981). *Imperialism and Chinese Politics.* Beijing: Foreign Languages Press.

Hu, Sheng (1991). *From the Opium War to the May 4th Movement.* Beijing: FLP.

Hui, Wang (2003). *China's New Order: Society, Politics, and Economy in Transition*, trans. T. Huters. Cambridge, Mass.: Harvard University Press.

Huang, Philip (1998). 'Theory and the Study of Modern Chinese History: Four Traps and a Question', *Modern China*, 24.2: 183–206.

Johnson, Chalmers (2004). *Blowback: The Costs and Consequences of American Empire*, 2nd edn. New York: Holt.

Lee, Leo Ou-fan (1999). *Shanghai Modern: The Flowering of a New Urban Culture in China, 1930–1945.* Cambridge, Mass.: Harvard University Press.

Li, Minqi (2009). *The Rise of China and the Demise of the Capitalist World Economy.* New York: Monthly Review Press.

Liu, Xiaobo et al. (2008). 'Charter 08: a blueprint for China', trans. Perry Link. Online source: <http://www.opendemocracy.net/article/chinas-charter-08>, accessed March 2012.

Mao, Zedong (1977 [1956]). 'On the Ten Major Relationships', *Selected Works of Mao Tse-tung.* Beijing: Foreign Languages Press.

Mignolo, Walter D. (2000). *Local Histories/Global Designs: Coloniality, Subaltern Knowledges, and Border Thinking.* Princeton: Princeton University Press.

Palat Ravi (2002). 'Is India Part of Asia?' *Environment and Planning D: Society and Space*, 20.6: 669–91.

Peck, James (2006). *Washington's China: The National Security World, the Cold War, and the Origins of Globalism.* Amherst, Mass.: University of Massachusetts Press.

Pietz, William (1988). 'The "Post-colonialism" of Cold War Discourse', *Social Text*, 19–20: 55–75.

Pomeranz, Kenneth (2001). *The Great Divergence: China, Europe, and the Making of the Modern World Economy.* Princeton, NJ: Princeton University Press.

Qin, Hui (2009). 'Critique of Charter 08: Democratic Debate and Renewed Enlightenment is More Necessary for China', trans. David Kelly, *Boxun News.* Online source: <http://www.boxun.us/news/publish/china_comment/Qin_Hui_s_Critique_of_Charter_08_Democratic_Debate_and_Renewed_Enlightenment_is_More_Necessary_for_China.shtml>, accessed January 2012. For a full report in Chinese, see <http://rwjch.blogbus.com/logs/39445413.html>.

Said, Edward W. (1978). *Orientalism.* London : Routledge and Kegan Paul.

Sakai, Naoki (2000). '"You Asians": On the Historical Role of the West and Asia Binary', *South Atlantic Quarterly*, 99.4: 789–817.

Sautman, Barry and Hairong Yan (2011). '"The Right Dissident": Liu Xiaobo and the 2010 Nobel Peace Prize', *positions*, 19.2: 581–613.

Sautman, Barry (2006). 'Colonialism, Genocide and Tibet', *Asian Ethnicity*, 7.3: 243–65.

Schein, Louisa (2000). *Minority Rules: The Miao and the Feminine in China's Cultural Politics*. Durham, NC: Duke University Press.

Schmitt, Carl (2007). *The Concept of the Political: Expanded Edition*, trans. George Schwab. Chicago: Chicago University Press.

Schwartz, Benjamin (1980). 'Presidential Address: Area Studies as a Critical Discipline', *Journal of Asian Studies*, 40.1 (November): 15–25.

Shih, Shu-mei (2011). 'The Concept of the Sinophone', *PMLA*, 126.3: 709–18.

Snyder, Zach (dir.) (2007). *300*. Warner Brothers, 117 min.

Spivak, Gayetri Chakravorty (2008). *Other Asias*. Oxford: Blackwell Publishing.

Su, Xiaokang and Luxiang Wang (1991). *Deathsong of the River: A Reader's Guide to the Chinese TV Series Heshang*, trans. R. W. Bodman and Pin P. Wan. Ithaca, NY: Cornell University Press.

Sun, Ge (2000). 'How Does Asia Mean? (Part I)', trans. Hui Shiu-Lun and Lau Kinchi, *Inter-Asia Cultural Studies*, 1.1: 13–47.

Tsering, Shakya and Lixiong Wang (2009). *The Struggle for Tibet*. New York: Verso.

Vukovich, Daniel (2012). *China and Orientalism: Western Knowledge Production and the PRC*. London: Routledge.

Wang, Chaohua (ed.) (2003). *One China, Many Paths*. London: Verso.

Wang, Hui (2011). *The Politics of Imagining Asia*. Cambridge, Mass.: Harvard University Press.

Wong, R. Bin (1997). *China Transformed: Historical Change and the Limits of European Experience*. Ithaca: Cornell University Press.

Young, Robert J. C. (2001). *Postcolonialism: An Historical Introduction*. Oxford: Blackwell.

Zhang, Longxi (1992). 'Western Theory and Chinese Reality', *Critical Inquiry*, 19.1: 105–30.

CHAPTER 27

OUR SEA OF ISLANDS

*Globalization, Regionalism,
and (Trans)Nationalism
in the Pacific*[1]

MICHELLE KEOWN AND
STUART MURRAY

INTRODUCTION

The Pacific has always been a cross-cultural space, one in which various narratives of the real and the imagined have coexisted. From the expansion of those ancestral peoples of today's contemporary indigenous populations, whether Australian Aborigines and Torres Strait Islanders or the later movement of the precursors to Melanesian, Polynesian, and Micronesian communities, to the arrival of the Europeans and the colonial and postcolonial complexities that followed, the region has continually suggested both the promise and cost of exchange. Impossible ever fully to articulate because of its immense size and diversity, the Pacific has necessarily been conceived of in terms of absence and presence, the global and the local, and the contested idea of what might constitute any kind of regional identity. Central to ideas of developing European modernity in the late eighteenth century, when exploration carried powerful ideas of philosophy

[1] Michelle Keown wishes to thank the Carnegie Trust for the Universities of Scotland for funding that enabled her to complete research for this chapter within New Zealand.

and the natural sciences, it was also a space that, for Europeans, came to be defined by what was *not* there: the absence of the Great Southern Continent that might rival earlier myths created by Marco Polo's journey to Central Asia and China, or the fantastic promise of El Dorado. By way of contrast, indigenous Pacific communities have resisted the idea that the region is only composed of tiny islands separated by immense space, preferring to stress the continuities across the water that is itself firmly located in local cosmologies and oral narratives.

Continuing the idea of 'absence', the Pacific has largely been marginalized in any of the various narratives that speak of the development of postcolonial studies or theory. Given the points made above about modernity (and its corollary, capitalism), this might constitute a surprise, but the centrality of the Caribbean/African/South Asian axis in shaping the subject matter of institutionalized thinking about the postcolonial has pushed questions raised by Australia, New Zealand, and the wider Pacific (whether these concern old or new settlement, indigenous responses, or recent demographic patterns of transnational cultural exchange) to the periphery of the key formations of the postcolonial as they have emerged over the last thirty years. The 'first wave' of postcolonial theorizing included the outline of critical ideas surrounding what Stephen Slemon termed 'second world' colonies, and in the work of figures such as Slemon and Alan Lawson spaces such as Canada, Australia, and New Zealand gained a foothold in mainstream postcolonial thought, something underscored by the Australian location of the three authors of *The Empire Writes Back* in 1989 (Ashcroft et al. 1989; Lawson 1995; Slemon 1990). The later 1990s, however, failed to see a consolidation of such a position, and the Pacific largely disappeared from central debates surrounding the postcolonial. The recent rise of 'Settlement Studies', in Australia and New Zealand in particular, works within a somewhat strained relationship to mainstream postcolonial theorizing, being anxious about the larger subject's global claims and seeking to do justice to located specifics without resort to a too-easy frame of nation or region (Calder and Turner 2002; Neumann et al. 1999). The simple fact that this chapter comes in the final section of this Handbook is perhaps a certain proof of the standing of the region in relation to the wider argument of which it might form a subset.

Nevertheless, we remain convinced that both old and new formations of the Pacific do, in fact, speak centrally to the various experiences of the postcolonial, be they physical and material, or epistemological and relational. As we intend to show, the key concerns of this Handbook—in terms of relations between the global and local, multilingual and multicultural forms of regionalism, post- and transnational patterns and anxieties, and the longevity of pre-contact communities—inform the complex nature of Pacific cultural production. From the discussions of Tahiti amongst the *philosophes* in the salons of eighteenth-century Paris, to the space that nuclear testing and new forms of colonialism occupy in emerging contemporary debates surrounding postcolonial ecocriticism, the Pacific exemplifies that which we might properly understand as the postcolonial.

REGIONALISM AND GLOBALIZATION
IN THE PACIFIC

Regions are amorphous entities, based partly in geographical space but also products of ideology, with their boundaries shifting in response to changing geopolitical dynamics (Dirlik 1997: 129; Larner and Walters 2002: 393; Spivak 2008). The watery realm of Oceania epitomizes this spatio-conceptual mutability: spread across one third of the globe, the Pacific Ocean contains one of the most heterogeneous groups of cultures and languages in the world, and its geographical and conceptual limits have shifted many times in response to the vicissitudes of global politico-economic relations. Prior to European imperial incursions into the Pacific (inaugurated by Spain in the sixteenth century and continued by Britain, France, the Netherlands, Germany, and the US in the eighteenth and nineteenth centuries), indigenous Pacific island communities were interlinked through multiple networks of trade and oceanic travel, sharing in common a vast 'sea of islands' known to the Māori (indigenous New Zealanders) as 'Te Moana Nui ā Kiwa' (the great ocean of Kiwa, legendary Polynesian explorer and guardian of the sea) (Hau'ofa 2008; Keown 2007). From the late eighteenth century, however—when advances in maritime technology expedited European exploration and settlement in the region— European forms of geographical and conceptual mapping compartmentalized the Pacific into various racial categories and colonial spheres of influence. The French explorer Dumont D'Urville, for example, inaugurated the racial division of indigenous Pacific peoples into Polynesians, Melanesians, and Micronesians in 1832, and the imposition of English, French, and Spanish as languages of colonial administration created linguistic as well as geopolitical barriers between previously interlinked Pacific communities.

Yet in addition to dividing Oceania into separate imperial realms, western representations of the Pacific have also generated various regional models and paradigms. Eighteenth-century French explorers named the region l'Océanie (Oceania), while their British counterparts described it as the 'South Seas' or the 'South Sea Islands', terms which quickly became synonymous with Romantic conceptions of the Pacific as a utopian paradise, and which endured well into the twentieth century (Hau'ofa 2008: 44; Keown 2007: 11). Since the Second World War, various other regional paradigms have come into circulation: the term 'South Pacific' was first used by the western Alliance military forces during the war in the Pacific and was then popularized through US ex-serviceman James Michener's *Tales of the South Pacific* (1946), a collection of wartime adventure romance narratives adapted by Rodgers and Hammerstein into the hugely successful stage musical *South Pacific* (which opened in 1949). The film version of the musical, shot on location in a heavily militarized Hawai'i and released the year before Hawai'i became the fiftieth US state (in 1959), dramatizes what Teresia Teaiwa has termed the 'militourist' complex: a milieu in which fetishized images of the Pacific as a tourist 'paradise' accompanied the consolidation of nuclear imperialism in Oceania during and beyond the Cold

War, when the Pacific was viewed as an important strategic site protecting the US and its allies from communist military incursion (Teaiwa 1999: 249; see also Hau'ofa 2008: 45 and Wilson 2000).

Recent studies of globalization have suggested that the 'bipolar' politico-economic relations that characterized the Cold War era have been largely superseded by 'new regional' formations that have played 'a more powerful role in the reorganization of global capitalism than the blanket term "globalization" tends to imply' (Harvey 2005: 37; see also Breslin et al. 2002 and Mittelman 2000). Where dependency theorists of the post-war era interpreted globalization as an inimical force that intensified socio-economic inequalities between (once-)colonized peoples and the west, many postcolonial 'developing' states have embraced the new regionalism as a means by which to foster local or regional alliances while simultaneously participating in the wider global economy (Breslin et al. 2002: 8; Hoogvelt 1997: 39). However, the era of 'new regionalism' has proved problematic for the Pacific Islands, which have become increasingly marginalized following the rise of the 'Asia-Pacific' as a global economic giant. The Asia-Pacific Economic Cooperation (APEC), formed in 1989 to promote open trade and practical economic cooperation in the region, includes in its membership wealthy 'developed' nations such as Australia, New Zealand, and the United States, yet excludes all Pacific Island countries except Papua New Guinea (one of the largest Pacific islands and endowed with rich mineral deposits). Within this context, the area now commonly designated 'the Pacific Islands region' has been described as 'the hole in the doughnut', dismissed as an economic 'backwater' or space of erasure within the boundaries of the affluent Pacific Rim (Dirlik 1997; Hau'ofa 2008; Spivak 2008). As Australia and New Zealand have increasingly aligned their economic objectives towards Asia, many indigenous peoples have come to view APEC as an invidious instrument of economic globalization that has served to intensify the marginalization and exploitation of indigenous peoples and resources in the Pacific Islands region (Stewart-Harawira 2005: 185).

Within the 'Rim', however, there are regional politico-economic organizations that actively involve and serve the Pacific Islands: prominent among these is the South Pacific Forum, formed in 1971 to allow independent and self-governing Pacific states a greater role in regional affairs. While the Forum's decolonizing agendas have been compromised at times by the inclusion of Australia and New Zealand—regional 'hegemons' (and former colonial powers)[2] whose funding and logistical support have been vital to the survival of the organization—regional cooperation between Australia, New Zealand, and Pacific Island nations has nevertheless resulted in some significant acts of resistance against military imperialism in the Pacific (see Keown 2007). Notable examples include the establishment of the South Pacific Nuclear-Free Zone (with the signing of the Treaty of Rarotonga in 1985) and the mobilization of regional and international opposition to the French resumption of nuclear testing in French Polynesia in 1995, which led to the cessation of the tests and to the US, UK, and France becoming Treaty signatories in 1996.

Further, regional cooperation has often allowed newly independent Pacific Island states to play a much more active role in international affairs and the global economy

[2] See Keown (2007) for an overview of these colonial histories.

than would have been possible on an individual basis: their negotiation of the 1982 UN Convention on the Law of the Sea, for example, led to the establishment of large exclusive economic zones that have generated significant revenue from foreign fishing vessels as well as domestic fishing industries, and the Lomé convention of 1975 (superseded by the Cotonou Convention of 2000) gave the Pacific Islands' agricultural exports preferential access to EU markets (Frazer and Bryant-Tokalau 2006: 8; Lockwood 2004: 23).

Other involvements in the global economy, however, have contributed to the advancement of neocolonial agendas in the region: the extraction of mineral resources in Melanesia, and tourist industries in many parts of Polynesia and Micronesia, have been dominated by foreign multinational companies, while the maintenance of French and US military facilities (in exchange for economic aid) in French Polynesia and Micronesia has brought environmental damage, health problems, and widening socio-economic inequalities to the people of these islands (Lockwood 2004: 23). Significantly, while the majority of Pacific Island states are now independent, a substantial number of the heavily militarized Pacific Islands remain under US and French colonial jurisdiction,[3] and a large body of indigenous protest literature (against nuclear and other imperialisms) has emerged from these locations (see inter alia Barclay 2002; Ishtar 1994; Santos Perez 2008, 2010; Spitz 2007).

Indigenous discursive interventions into debates about regionalism and neocolonialism in the Pacific have gathered momentum since the 1960s in particular, when the decolonization era officially began (with Western Samoa the first to achieve independence in 1962). Much of this activity has emerged from within the University of the South Pacific (USP), a regional organization (established in Fiji in 1968) that primarily serves those islands formerly under British colonial jurisdiction, but has also fostered links with many other parts of the Pacific. Founded by Britain and New Zealand as a means by which to expedite Pacific Island self-sufficiency, the USP has become a distinctly postcolonial institution, spawning a range of philosophical, critical, and creative paradigms and movements that have—as Samoan writer (and former USP academic) Albert Wendt argues in a seminal essay on Pacific literature—sought to create a 'new Oceania' that is 'free of the taint of colonialism' (1976: 53).

Early attempts to foster a regional identity within (and beyond) the university were focused around the political philosophy of the 'Pacific Way', which advocated ideological unity amongst Pacific Islanders against the 'colonial powers', and emphasized cultural commonalities between Pacific peoples (including putatively 'Pacific' values such as communalism, reciprocity, and love and respect for the land and other people) (Va'ai 1999: 33–5). The 'Pacific Way' ideology gave impetus to USP-based organizations—such as the South Pacific Creative Arts Society (founded in 1972), which provided publishing opportunities for a wide range of emerging 'postcolonial' Pacific writers—as well as inspiring other subregional ideologies such as the 'Melanesian Way' (Narokobi 1980). As Tongan scholar (and former USP academic) Epeli Hau'ofa has noted, however, the 'Pacific Way' ideology sat uneasily alongside concurrent attempts to celebrate the

---

[3.] French territories include French Polynesia, Wallis and Futuna, and the settler colony of New Caledonia. American Samoa and Guam are still US territories, while the northern Mariana Islands became a Commonwealth of the US in 1986.

diversity of Pacific cultures (including support for student cultural groups and events based on nationality and race), and the right-wing military coups that took place in Fiji in the 1980s and 1990s further exposed the interracial tensions that have hampered attempts to foster a regional identity (2008: 43).

In an attempt to transcend these divisions, in the 1990s Hauʻofa produced a series of influential essays advocating a new regional 'Oceanic' politico-ideological identity that would not only help unite and protect Pacific Islanders against the vicissitudes of global capitalism and climate change (a significant consideration given that Pacific Islanders are among the earliest casualties of rising sea levels), but could also serve as a source of inspiration to contemporary Pacific artists and creative writers. While some Pacific scholars have criticized the more utopian or idealist elements of Hauʻofa's arguments (Edmond and Smith 2003; Teaiwa 2008), his theories have taken hold throughout the indigenous Pacific, debated by writers, artists, and theorists of many Pacific nations and linguistic groups (see Mateata-Allain 2008; Santos Perez 2010; Subramani 2003; Waddell et al. 1993). One of the key reasons for the wide appeal of Hauʻofa's work is its interdisciplinary range of reference (drawing, inter alia, on his expertise in anthropology, economics, politics, and literature), while another compelling element of his writing, particularly in the context of this Handbook, is his recognition of the complex and interweaving local, regional, and global networks that shape the lives of contemporary Pacific peoples:

> The development of new art forms that are truly Oceanic, transcendant [*sic*] of our national and cultural diversity ... allows our creative minds to draw on far larger pools of cultural traits than those of our individual national lagoons. It makes us less insular without being buried in the amorphousness of the globalised cultural melting pot ... We learn from the great and wonderful products of human imagination and ingenuity the world over, but the cultural achievements of our own histories will be our most important models, points of reference, and sources of inspiration (Hauʻofa 2000: n.p.).

Such a formulation offers a new method by which to locate 'unity in diversity', resonating with the work of other critical regionalists (such as Arif Dirlik and Gayatri Spivak) who have argued for the importance of recognizing plurality and difference within 'new regional' constructs such as 'Asia' or the 'Asia-Pacific' (Dirlik 1997; Spivak 2008; see also Appadurai 2001 and Wilson 2000). Since Hauʻofa's death in 2009, however, the difficulties of striking a balance between national, regional, and global imperatives have again become apparent in events such as the suspension of Fiji from the Pacific Islands Forum and the Commonwealth (following the refusal of the military-led interim government to fulfil its earlier pledge to restore democracy by 2009), which has had a deleterious effect on Pacific regional trade and tourism, as well as the failure to agree a legally binding international treaty on minimizing climate change at the 2009 Copenhagen summit, despite vigorous lobbying by various Pacific delegates following a series of natural disasters in the region during that same year.

Nationalism Again: Beyond
and Back Around

These ideas, complex and contested as they are, of a 'new regionalism' in the Pacific pose specific challenges to the construction of Australia and New Zealand in particular as national spaces, bringing as they do potential configurations of culture in which the nation is no longer an obvious or normative unit. From the late nineteenth into the twentieth century, the centrality of nationalism as what appeared to be the automatic ideology of development out of colonial status dominated political, social, and cultural formations of place (Sinclair 1986; White 1981; Williams 1997). Each country saw in nationalism both an efficacious set of arguments that allowed for the assertion of continued distance from British control, and an approach to the specificity of the local that provided what appeared as 'realist' narratives of self-articulation.

The hegemony of nationalism in Australia and New Zealand took many local forms, such as—to cite but one example—a reverence for the memory of participation in the European wars of 1914–18 and 1939–45 and the subsequent elevation of the returned serviceman to the status of national icon. It also became focused on specific large-scale events—the 1940 centennial celebration, and 1990 sesquicentennial, of the signing of the Treaty of Waitangi in New Zealand, and the marking of the 1988 bicentenary of British colonization in Australia. These occasions, however, themselves produced multiple challenges to the national status quo even as they attempted to champion its achievements (Bennett 1992; James 1992; Murray 1998: 20–47; O'Brien 1991). By the 1980s in particular, with increased opposition to nuclear testing in the Pacific and the rise of coordinated indigenous protests centred on land claims and human rights, the seemingly ubiquitous nature of nationalism's rhetoric was firstly dissected and finally dethroned.

The accounts of the national that followed in the late 1980s were multiple. Supply-side macroeconomic theory, especially in New Zealand, advocated fiscal and economic flexibility, as opposed to regulation, in a manner that fostered transnational connections and the development of regional economic models such as APEC. In cultural narratives, nationalism itself became the subject of an increasing irreverence that typified creative output. In Australia, Lisa Matthews's 1994 short film *Rosie's Secret* produced a hoax version of the building and opening of the Sydney Harbour Bridge in March 1932 through the fictional 'rediscovery' of Rosie Foster, who the film claims was the first to cut the ribbon during the bridge's opening ceremony. In an almost identical vein, Peter Jackson's and Costa Botes's 1995 'mockumentary' film *Forgotten Silver* celebrated the 'rediscovery' of New Zealand film pioneer Colin McKenzie, who not only invented any number of film techniques—the use of colour and tracking shots among others—but also filmed the first example of powered flight (by another New Zealander) and shot a vast production of *Salome*, of which Cecil B. DeMille would have been proud, in the

South Island bush. *Forgotten Silver* ends with the (faked) screening of the 'restored' version of McKenzie's lost classic, but as with *Rosie's Secret*, the real force of the film lies in the subtle unpicking of national pride and the desire for exceptionalism that accompanies it (Conrich and Smith 1998). On television, series such as *Summer Heights High* (2007) and *Flight of the Conchords* (2007–9) were highly popular satirical approaches to national culture, exposing both old and new rhetorics of community and belonging.

In the 1990s, then, the kinds of nationalism that had dominated social, cultural, and political life for decades in both Australia and New Zealand had dissipated. But for all the new transnational formations and processes of indigenous claim that had challenged national hegemony, arguably what developed in its wake was as much a reconfigured nationalism as it was post-national difference. New Zealand, for example, emerged out of the 1980s with a bicultural nationalism that still sought to assert local exceptionality, but now did so with a vision of Māori being at the heart of the nation's new spiritual and cultural formations (for a critical view of this, see Smith and Turner in Part II of this volume). The shift from a Commonwealth identity to one that stressed new connections to Polynesia and the Pacific more widely aimed to combine the best of both legacies in a new model of citizenship.

In Australia, the key word as the 1990s developed was 'reconciliation', the desired end product of national unity that came from the full realization of the ways in which two centuries of settlement had devastated Aboriginal cultures. In 1992, following representations that had lasted ten years, the High Court of Australia adjudicated in the Mabo v Queensland case that Aborigines and Torres Strait Islanders possessed common-law title over their lands, rejecting previous legal opinion that had declared the primacy of English law in Australia following the processes of colonization. The Mabo ruling, as it came to be known, paved the way for the Native Title Act of 1993, which sought to address indigenous/native title claims. Earlier, in 1991, the Australian Parliament passed an Act that brought into being the Council for Aboriginal Reconciliation, an organization charged with establishing unity between indigenous and non-indigenous Australians. In the words of the legislation, the government recognized that Aborigines and Torres Strait Islanders had settled in the region for 'thousands of years' before the arrival of the British First Fleet in 1788 and had 'suffered dispossession and dispersal from their traditional lands' as a consequence of this new settlement. 'To date', the Act continued, 'there has been no formal process of reconciliation between Aboriginals and Torres Strait Islanders and other Australians' and 'it is most desirable that there be such a reconciliation' (Council for Aboriginal Reconciliation Archive 1991). In 2000, the Council for Aboriginal Reconciliation became Reconciliation Australia, and that year also saw the Sydney Olympic Games, an event that provided the opportunity for a showcasing of new national unity, especially around the success of Aboriginal athlete Cathy Freeman.

As with New Zealand's biculturalism, Australia's moves towards reconciliation were not seamless and without problems. The 2010–15 Reconciliation Australia strategic plan notes, for example, that 'there remains more work to be done before national reconciliation between the First Australians and other Australians is achieved'. What emerges from these processes is the clear sense of a *desire* for a national reassessment that is also a reassessment of the legacy of settlement more generally. The cultural production that has surrounded and expressed this sentiment mixes anxiety with revisionist detail. From a novel like David Malouf's *Remembering Babylon* (1993) to Kate Grenville's contemporary fictionalization of early Australian settlement in *The Secret River* (2005) and *The Lieutenant* (2008), and in the re-evaluation of state policy towards Aborigines as displayed in Phillip Noyce's 2002 film *Rabbit-Proof Fence*, Australian narratives that discuss place and location in the reconciliation era continue nationalist traditions that present the cultural politics of the present through reworkings of the past. For all that many aspects of culture in both New Zealand and Australia eschew and ignore old forms of national formation, especially in an era of changing immigration patterns, a continuing focus on the consequences of settlement has not been lost.

Another reconfiguration of the national has come through what might be seen as the continuing institutionalization of the arts and cultural production within policies of state-sponsored support and promotion. Through the development of initiatives such as national book and film awards, and the encouragement of foreign investment in the arts sector, both Australia and New Zealand have seen new formations of the nation space as it has been constituted in cultural and heritage industries. In New Zealand, Helen Clark, who was Prime Minister across three terms between 1999 and 2008, was also Minister for Arts, Culture, and Heritage during the same period, a configuration that allowed for the Arts portfolio to assume national significance. The global success of *The Lord of the Rings* trilogy (2001–3) was tied into government initiatives that not only sought to create the infrastructure of an international film industry, but also formed a central part of a national tourism campaign. Tourism New Zealand, the official website of the New Zealand Tourist Board, advertises *Lord of the Rings* location tours, while other high-profile tourism outlets emphasize the link further. 'Middle Earth is New Zealand', claims the New Zealand Tourism Guide (2005–6), making additional links to ideas of national creativity and environmentally friendly filmmaking. Within this kind of campaign, the national is packaged in terms of innovation (often aligned with other attributes, such as health and a sense of spectacle) for international consumption (Lawn and Beatty 2006).

The persistence of the national in Australia and New Zealand, even as both countries embrace their position within a newly formulated Pacific, signals both the continuity of traditional historical concerns over legitimacy and the response of successive governments to the international development of neoliberal thinking. Settlement and market dynamics have found common cause in a nationalism that is outward-facing as much as it is concerned with the local, and it is not a picture that seems likely to change in the near future.

INDIGENOUS CLAIM AND PRESENCE

For many indigenous communities across the Pacific, as with those in other postcolonial locations, settlement is refigured as invasion. A history of dispersal and dispossession has stretched from the beginnings of settlement in the late eighteenth century to the mid-twentieth-century development of island locations for nuclear testing. Throughout, assumptions of the 'inevitability' of the decline of indigenous populations, as well as that of the social and cultural infrastructure of such communities, have played a paramount part in the assumptions governing relations between non-indigenous and indigenous Pacific societies. Even given the period of official decolonization cited earlier, the collective memory of imperialism has enacted processes of prejudice and exclusion, with indigenous peoples cast as the subjects of research or denied access to resources (Smith 1999). In Australia and New Zealand, recent moves towards bi- and multicultural community, and the language of reconciliation, have marked a turning point in relations and have brought members of indigenous communities into high-level positions in government and society, but it is still the case that in both locations indigenous populations often constitute an economic underclass. Official Australian government statistics record that in data collected between 1996 and 2004, average ages of death for both Aboriginal men and women were nearly twenty years lower than those for the total Australian population (Australian Institute of Health and Welfare 2010). In New Zealand, similar statistics show life expectancy for Māori to be, on average, seven years less than for non-Māori (Statistics New Zealand/Te Tari Tatau 2010; see also Reid and Robson 2006).

The global civil rights movements of the 1970s saw an accompanying rise in indigenous protest in the Pacific, as political and cultural groups inherited the language and methods practised, in particular, by black and Native American advocacy associations. The major focus of such protest was land: in 1975, after nearly a decade of strikes and protest, land was handed back to the Gurindji people in Australia's Northern Territory in a landmark settlement, while the Mabo proceedings began in the Australian High Court in 1982; in New Zealand 1976 saw a major protest march, centred around land claims, across the North Island to Wellington; and the 1981 Springbok rugby tour by South Africa was marked by widespread protest as opposition to apartheid created a process of national self-reflection about relations between Māori and Pākehā (European New Zealanders). In the 1980s, the Waitangi Tribunal (established in 1975) oversaw the airing of Māori claims and Crown omissions under the terms of the 1840 Treaty of Waitangi, now seen as the founding document of modern New Zealand not solely in terms of British possession, but rather as a guide to reciprocity and a bicultural future (Orange 1987).

In Hawai'i, indigenous protest over the continued occupation and despoliation of Hawai'ian land by the US military became focused in 1976 on the island of Kaho'olawe (off the southwest coast of Maui), a site of traditional Hawai'ian religious worship that had been used as a US military bombing target since 1941. Protest occupations led by the Protect Kaho'olawe 'Ohana (family/clan group), bolstered by a range of protest literature, resulted in the demilitarization of the island in 1990, and the return of the title of the island to native Hawai'ians in 1994 (see Keown 2007: 94–6). Despite such developments, debate and anger continue surrounding the issue of land: ongoing legal hearings surrounding the lands of the Noongar people in western Australia highlight Aboriginal claims over the nation's major cities, while debates surrounding Māori rights to customary land title over New Zealand's foreshore and seabed created a national crisis in 2004, with the government passing an Act restricting the power of the Māori Land Court to determine Māori title and asserting Crown ownership (Hingston 2006), a decision not repealed until 2010. In Bougainville (an island incorporated into German New Guinea in 1884, and retained as a province of Papua New Guinea even after the latter achieved independence from Australia in 1975), local resentment over foreign exploitation of its rich copper reserves helped trigger a civil war that raged between 1988 and 1997.

The overall effect of such disputes projects the injustices of the past into the present for the indigenous peoples of the Pacific. In Australia, the scars of dispossession are not limited to questions of land; the state-sanctioned removal of Aboriginal and Torres Strait Islander children from their families, which continued up until the late 1960s, constituted a blatant racism that still feeds into the heart of contemporary society. The issue of the 'Stolen Generations' exposes the continuing fault lines in Australian race relations, with *Bringing Them Home*, the official 1997 report on the removals, and the 2008 apology on the topic by Prime Minister Kevin Rudd revealing an acknowledgement of state culpability that cannot yet undo decades of prejudice. At the same time, countering the assumption that they are only the victims of injustice, indigenous activists have pressed for the right to assert indigenous understanding of both these events and other questions of place and location, and the acceptance of such stances as being legitimate is increasingly widespread (Barclay 2005; Grossman et al. 2003; Huggins 1998). For all that the effects of settlement continue to be deep and enduring, the presence of indigenous peoples—once thought to be an anachronism in a Pacific future—now finds sophisticated and extensive expression.

As a result, and despite the legacies of traumatic histories, it is not possible to generalize about indigenous experience in the contemporary Pacific. For example, in addition to the kinds of organized protest around the continuities of the past that are still part of contemporary political expression, other indigenous groups sit more comfortably within the new neoliberal economies of the region. Financial reparations made following rulings by the Waitangi Tribunal, for example, have made some *iwi* (tribes) in New Zealand into what are, in effect, companies that oversee the economic future of their communities, with considerable profits produced as a consequence. Likewise, a vibrant cultural scene, in the arts and music especially, showcasing indigenous creativity and responses to global artistic trends is complemented by more inward-looking perspectives that stress conservative attitudes towards indigenous social practices and expectations (Duff 1993; Keown 2008). Although the market for indigenous cultural productions is still small, with many important and high-profile projects (such as documentary film or art exhibitions) made possible by direct state support from ring-fenced funding, it is nevertheless the case that the visibility of these events and narratives is greater than it has ever been.

Indigenous communities also have to face the changes in society and culture that have come with the increased mobility of peoples. Migration patterns from the Pacific Islands and from Asia to Australia and New Zealand have produced substantial changes in those nations' non-white populations. Indigenous responses to this have been varied. The development of pan-Pacific communities in major cites such as Sydney and

Auckland has brought both social tensions and artistic innovations, but in both countries these developments have been seen by some to threaten the special status of indigenous peoples as 'first residents' (what in New Zealand is called *tangata whenua*—'people
of the land'). The development of official multicultural policies, produced as a response
to new demographic configurations, has faced opposition from some prominent indigenous leaders, concerned that their primary status within the region might come under
threat with the potential result of lost access to resources (Keown 2008: 46). If the start of
the twenty-first century has seen the social and cultural systems of the indigenous peoples of the Pacific recognized as a question of rights, it is still the case that there remain
a multitude of challenges to the full expression of those who have lived in the region for
centuries.

MIGRATION/DIASPORA

As noted above, and in keeping with Epeli Hau'ofa's arguments on globalization and
the wider development of neoliberal economies, much contemporary Pacific cultural
production is inflected by the large-scale dispersal of Pacific Islanders to neighbouring
settler-invader colonies (such as New Zealand, Australia, Canada, New Caledonia, and
the United States) since the Second World War, when there was a demand for manual
labour during a time of industrial expansion. By this time, western economic imperialism in the Pacific had made many island nations heavily reliant upon their powerful
neighbours for imports and financial aid, and many islanders went abroad for employment and education opportunities, sending money back to their home countries in
order to keep their fragile economies afloat. The acronym 'MIRAB'—conflating 'migration, remittances, aid, and bureaucracy'—was coined as a label for Pacific Island cultures
characterized by these conditions, which continue today (Goss and Lindquist 2000;
Watters 1987). Even by the mid-1980s, over 37 per cent of ethnic Polynesians were living
outside their home countries, and in countries such as Niue, the Cook Islands, Rotuma,
and Tokelau, the number of expatriates currently far exceeds those remaining at home
(Hayes 1991: 3; Subramani 2003: 7).

These international migrations are largely a product of continuing politico-economic links between island nations and their (former) colonial administrators:
French Polynesians have access to metropolitan France; Micronesians and American
Samoans to the US; (Western) Samoans, Cook Islanders, Niueans, and Tongans to
New Zealand; and so on (Lockwood 2004; Keown 2007). The fact that many of these
migrants have been channelled into low-skilled labour has helped perpetuate some
of the socio-economic and racial inequalities of the colonial era, and a wide array
of indigenous Pacific writers and scholars have explored the negative aspects of
Pacific Island out-migration. Notable examples include Albert Wendt and Sia Figiel's
fictional representations of alienated Samoan émigrés in New Zealand and the US
(Figiel 1999; Wendt 1973); Teresia Teaiwa's analysis of military colonialism, which

has (inter alia) resulted in the forced evacuation of the Bikini islanders to expedite US atomic tests during the Cold War; and, more recently, the despatching of Native Hawai'ian and other Pacific military forces as US allies in the global 'war on terror' (Teaiwa 2008).

However, various scholars have also emphasized the positive aspects of the global distribution of Pacific peoples. Hau'ofa, while acknowledging that not all Pacific migration has been voluntary or beneficial, has also described post-war migration as an enabling continuation of pre-colonial patterns of Oceanic cultural expansion and exchange, enabling what Arjun Appadurai terms 'grassroots globalization' or 'globalization from below' (Hau'ofa 2008: 34; Appadurai 2001: 3). Similarly, numerous social scientists have documented the strong kinship ties (and associated mutual socio-economic benefits) that link many Pacific diasporas with their home communities, with traditions of material reciprocity perpetuated through the multidirectional flow of gifts and commodities (Ferguson et al. 2008; Lockwood 2004: 26). 'Virtual communities' created through internet news websites and discussion forums (such as the Tongan site 'Kava Bowl' and the Rotuma Web) have also played a vital role in maintaining transnational links amongst widely dispersed Pacific peoples (Howard 2000: 405; Lee 2004: 139). As Appadurai notes, these electronic media circuits can foster 'long-distance nationalism', but can also become the 'crucibles of a postnational political order', creating new 'imagined communities' that transcend former geographical boundaries (1996: 22, 4; see also Quayson in this section of the volume).

Such transformations are evident in the increasing currency of pan-ethnic labels such as 'Pacific Islander', 'Pacific Island American', or 'Polynesian' amongst Pacific diasporic communities. When used by bureaucratic organizations within the host countries, such labels can prove alienating and homogenizing (Lee 2004: 145), but these terms have also been embraced by Pacific peoples as a means by which to forge new pan-Pacific cultural affiliations and creative projects (see Keown 2007: 194). The increasing numbers of Pasifika scholars securing posts in metropolitan universities, for example, have generated intense debates about how 'Pacific epistemologies' might transform the ways in which Oceania is perceived and represented within the academy (see Huffer and Qalo 2004; Prasad 2006). Within New Zealand, Pacific Island creative practitioners are also forging stronger links with other immigrant communities, such as the large numbers of East and South-East Asians who have arrived in the country as a result of strengthening alliances between New Zealand and other APEC countries from the late 1980s. The animated television comedy series *Bro' Town*, a collaboration between Pacific Island, Chinese, and Pākehā New Zealanders, is a revealing index of the ways in which transnational migration has transformed the cultural landscape of New Zealand. Revealing both indigenous Māori and Pākehā resistance to Pacific Island and Asian immigrants as perceived threats to the unique bicultural relationship that has long shaped understandings of New Zealand 'national' identity, much of *Bro' Town*'s comedy centres around ethnic stereotypes, exposing and (partly implicitly) critiquing pejorative representations such as the 'dumb Islander' or the avaricious, 'inscrutable' Asian (see Keown 2008). Similar strategies are evident in the Australian mockumentary series *We Can Be Heroes* and, as mentioned earlier, *Summer Heights High*, in which actor/scriptwriter Chris Lilley exposes the fault lines in Australian official multiculturalism by adopting an array of racially inflected comic personas. These include Jonah, a breakdancing Tongan teenager (who appears to embody, but also challenges, the common stereotype of the violent, socially dysfunctional Polynesian male); Ja'mie, a snobbish white Australian schoolgirl who sponsors Sudanese refugees purely for public recognition; and Ricky, a second-generation Chinese physics student who rebels against his father's ambitious plans for his career by becoming an actor (thus confounding the stereotype of the studious Asian), but suffers discrimination within the white-dominated Australian television and drama industry. Such productions bespeak the increasingly complex diasporic dynamics and rivalries that have emerged as a consequence of expanding Asian settlement and investment in the Pacific. Such tensions are not restricted to Australia and New Zealand: notably, indigenous Pacific concerns over Asian labour mobility in the region erupted into anti-Chinese arson, looting, and brawling in the Solomon Islands, Tonga, and Papua New Guinea during 2006 and 2009 (see Maclellan 2010).

Multilingualism in the Postcolonial Pacific

Multiethnic diversities and tensions in the Pacific are also apparent within the realm of language politics. The Pacific is marked by extraordinary linguistic diversity, with one quarter of the world's languages (some 1,200) concentrated in Melanesia alone (Crocombe 2001). None of the indigenous Pacific languages was written prior to the arrival of Europeans in the Pacific, and while the development of orthographies (by missionaries and linguists) has given rise to a corpus of written material in these languages, colonial incursions into the region frequently resulted in imperial metropolitan languages becoming the main vehicles of communication and publication, with separate Anglophone, Francophone, and Hispanophone enclaves established in the region. While many Pacific Islanders speak at least one indigenous Pacific language (and/or contact languages such as pidgins, creoles, and koinés), the vast majority of written material in the region has been published in the colonial metropolitan languages (see Keown 2007; Lynch 1998).

It has been widely acknowledged that postcolonial studies has, until relatively recently, been focused primarily upon Anglophone texts and contexts (Forsdick and Murphy 2003; Huggan 2008; see also Bassnett in Part III of this volume), and the Pacific is no exception to this general rule, due in no small part to the dominance of English as the main language of trade, diplomacy, and interregional communication. Further, Francophone and Hispanophone Pacific Islanders—the former concentrated in French Polynesia, New Caledonia, Wallis and Futuna, and Vanuatu, and the latter in the Chilean colony of Easter Island—represent a very small minority of the overall regional population: some 5 per cent are Francophone, with even fewer speaking Spanish (Crocombe 2001).[4]

However, the kinds of regional collaborations between Pacific Islanders discussed earlier in this chapter have at times transcended linguistic barriers between the Anglophone and non-Anglophone Pacific. In 1982, for example, the SPCAS journal *MANA* deviated from its usual focus on Anglophone Pacific writing by publishing a trilingual Tahitian, French, and English special issue featuring poetry by three Māʻohi (French Polynesian) poets: Hubert Brémond, Henri Hiro, and Charles Manutahi. Many of the poems in the issue contained anti-colonial and anti-nuclear themes also evident in indigenous Anglophone Pacific writing of the period, opening up a dialogue between the Francophone and Anglophone Pacific that has intensified in the first decade of the new millennium, with the publication of a number of French and English-language texts in (reciprocal) translation. Some of these initiatives have been inspired by Hauʻofa's 'Oceanic' theories: Māʻohi (Tahitian) scholar Kareva Mateata-Allain, for example, draws upon his work to posit Māʻohi writing as a metaphorical *vaʻa* (voyaging canoe) that can reunite Anglophone and Francophone Pacific peoples through a process of 'intellectual cross-fertilization' (2008: 41), and similar sentiments were expressed by the editors of *Vārua Tupu*, an anthology of contemporary Māʻohi writing in English translation (Stewart et al. 2006: xx).

Like Anglophone Pacific authors, writers of the French Pacific have remained marginal to international postcolonial studies, notably absent among the signatories to the 2007 *Le Monde* manifesto celebrating the contributions non-metropolitan authors have made to the expanding field of '"littérature-monde" en français' (see Keown 2010). Yet it is arguably the international expansion of 'Francophone postcolonial studies' that has contributed to a burgeoning interest in Francophone Pacific writing in English translation within Anglophone Pacific metropolitan centres such as Hawaiʻi, Australia, and New Zealand. Given the location of these readerships, it is perhaps no coincidence that some of these Francophone authors had already established strong affiliations with Anglophone Pacific writers at the time their translated works were published. Māʻohi author Chantal Spitz, for example, whose anti-nuclear novel *L'Île des Rêves Écrasés* (1991) was published in English translation by Huia of New Zealand in 2007 (under the title *Island of Shattered Dreams*), had recently published a series of articles urging stronger connections between Francophone and Anglophone Pacific writers, as well as editing a special 1997 issue of the Māʻohi journal *Littéramaʻohi* (with the theme 'Rencontres Océaniennes') featuring a range of Francophone and (translated) Anglophone Pacific writing (see Keown 2010: 246–7). Similarly, Kanaky (New Caledonian) writer-activist Déwé Gorodé—a selection of whose poetry and prose was published in English translation by Pandanus of Australia in 2004—has been active within regional feminist and anti-nuclear movements in the Pacific, and in 1997, she published her own translation (into French) of selected poetry by the Anglophone ni-Vanuatu poet and fellow feminist Grace Mera Molisa (see Keown 2010).

----

4. The countries listed here are ones in which French or Spanish are official languages.

Such projects are evidence of the regional political agendas that unite Pacific Islanders despite linguistic differences, and it is significant that both Spitz's and Gorodé's work are marked by a strongly conservationist and anti-nuclear sensibility also evident in the work of Anglophone Pacific writers such as Patricia Grace and Hone Tuwhare (of Aotearoa/New Zealand), Robert Barclay (based in Hawai'i), and Craig Santos Perez (of Guam). While some of the unique stylistic qualities of the source texts may be lost through the process of translation, this same process can open up new channels of multilingual experimentation and subversion. Both Gorodé's and Spitz's source texts, for example, alternate between metropolitan and indigenous Pacific languages, and the fact that indigenous words remain untranslated and intact within the main body of each translation (with any explanatory matter relegated to footnotes and translator's notes) poses a challenge to the dominance of the two 'metropolitan' languages, creating new 'plurilingual' dynamics that problematize 'conventional notions of linguistic equivalence or ideas of loss and gain' elaborated within translation theory (Mehrez 1992; see also Keown 2010 and Bassnett in Part III of this volume).

While translingual dialogues between the Francophone and Anglophone Pacific are well established, Hispanophone Pacific writing remains peripheral to regional debates thus far. However, Easter Island, the main locus of Spanish-speaking Pacific Islanders, has—like Hawai'i and Aotearoa/New Zealand—recently witnessed an indigenous language revival programme, following the development of an orthography for the Rapanui language in the 1980s (Keown 2007: 137). These revival initiatives have given rise to an expanding corpus of indigenous-language (or bilingual) publications, from dictionaries and grammars to creative writing, and the increasing recognition given to non-metropolitan languages (and dialects) in the Pacific is also evident in the publication of other works such as Indo-Fijian writer Subramani's *Dauka Puraan* (2001), the first Fiji Hindi novel. Written in a direct protest against the local marginalization of Fiji Hindi as a written language, the novel also offers a subversive challenge to subcontinental Indian literary culture by replacing the gods and mythical heroes of the Hindu religious scriptures with the 'subaltern' Indian indentured labourers transported to Fiji under British colonialism (Subramani 2003: 11; see also Keown 2007: 160). Subramani, like Gorodé (and other Pacific authors), thus signals a critical awareness of the 'marginal' status of Pacific literature within international postcolonial studies, while also seeking to make an intervention into global literary debates. Significantly, it is only when the field is widened to include the regional 'hegemons', Australia and New Zealand, that global 'celebrity' authors such as Peter Carey can be identified within the Pacific region (see Huggan 2001).

CONCLUSION

Throughout much of the region's post-contact history the peoples of the Pacific have become accustomed to the ways in which their experiences and environment have been implicated in totalizing discourses, generated from metropolitan centres beyond the ocean, which lay claim to a knowledge and understanding of how such an immense space functions. From the cartographic and philosophical, through ideas of adventure and the touristic, to the erasure of place that is inherent in nuclear testing, the Pacific has been a testing ground for more than Euro-American military technology alone. In the contemporary era, in which a considerable degree of self-determination has been established within indigenous Pacific communities across the region, the sweeping transnational logic of the juggernauts of international capital and trade still leaves many of these communities in a fraught position with regard to the day-to-day nature of their self-expression. This juxtaposition of independence and fragility necessitates a careful balancing act, especially within Island communities, if a secure future is to be obtained for the people who call such spaces home.

At the same time, the sheer variety of what is called the Pacific, from the confidence of cosmopolitan Sydney to the dependency of the Federated States of Micronesia (which draws the bulk of its revenue in financial assistance from the US), makes generalizations about the region largely impossible. In the range of historical, socio-political, and cultural events and movements we have discussed here, often there appears little commonality of contemporary experience. And yet the divergent trajectories that have sprung from the earliest moments of sustained cross-cultural contact in the region can be adequately and properly seen within the broad remit of the postcolonial. All such issues of settler nationalism, indigenous claim, and contemporary migrancy, or of political sovereignty, financial connectivity, and environmental concern, can be assessed within the various critical languages that have grown to become part of modern postcolonial studies. In fact, we would claim that the Pacific can and should be seen as a quintessentially postcolonial space as that term is best understood. Though the Pacific region has hitherto been marginalized within much international postcolonial scholarship, its particular imbrications in both local and global (neo)imperial configurations, including its acute vulnerability to the depredations of climate change and contemporary military imperialism, bespeak its importance to any considered analysis of the complexities of contemporary postcolonial experiences across the globe.

References

Appadurai, Arjun (1996). *Modernity at Large: Cultural Dimensions of Globalization.* Minneapolis: University of Minnesota Press.

Appadurai, Arjun (2001). 'Grassroots Globalization and the Research Imagination', in A. Appadurai (ed.), *Globalization.* Durham, NC: Duke University Press, 1–21.

Ashcroft, Bill, Gareth Griffiths, and Helen Tiffin (1989). *The Empire Writes Back: Theory and Practice in Post-colonial Literatures.* London and New York: Routledge.

Australian Institute of Health and Welfare (2010). 'Indigenous Australians'. Online source: <http://www.aihw.gov.au/indigenous/health/mortality.cfm>, accessed December 2010.

Barclay, Barry (2005). *Mana Tuturu: Ma ori Treasures and Intellectual Property Rights.* Auckland: Auckland University Press.

Barclay, Robert (2002). *Meḷaḷ: A Novel of the Pacific*. Honolulu: University of Hawai'i Press.

Bennett, Tony (1992). 'Introduction: National Times', in Tony Bennett (ed.), *Celebrating the Nation: A Critical Study of Australia's Bicentenary*. St Leonards, New South Wales: Allen & Unwin, pp. xiii–xviii.

Breslin, Shaun, Richard Higgott, and Ben Rosamond (2002). 'Regions in Comparative Perspective', in S. Breslin, C. H. Hughes, N. Phillips, and B. Rosamond (eds), *New Regionalism in the Global Political Economy*. London and New York: Routledge, 1–19.

Calder, Alex and Stephen Turner (eds) (2002). *Settlement Studies*, special issue of the *Journal of New Zealand Literature*, 20.

Conrich, Ian and Roy Smith (1998). 'Fool's Gold: New Zealand's *Forgotten Silver*, Myth and National Identity', *British Review of New Zealand Studies*, 11: 57–65.

Council for Aboriginal Reconciliation Archive (1991). Online source: <http://www.austlii.edu.au/au/other/IndigLRes/car/2000/16/text02.htm>, accessed January 2011.

Crocombe, Ron (2001). *The South Pacific*. Suva, Fiji: Institute of Pacific Studies.

Dirlik, Arif (1997). *The Postcolonial Aura: Third World Criticism in the Age of Global Capitalism*. Boulder, Col.: Westview.

Duff, Alan (1993). *Maori: The Crisis and the Challenge*. Auckland: Harper Collins.

Edmond, Rod and Vanessa Smith (2003). 'Editors' introduction', in R. Edmond and V. Smith (eds), *Islands in History and Representation*. London and New York: Routledge, 1–18.

Ferguson, Kathy E., Sally Engle Merry, and Monique Mironesco (2008). 'Introduction', in K. E. Ferguson and M. Mironescu (eds), *Gender and Globalization in Asia and the Pacific*. Honolulu: University of Hawai'i Press, 1–12.

Figiel, Sia (1999). *They Who Do Not Grieve*. Auckland: Vintage.

Forsdick, Charles and David Murphy (2003). *Francophone Postcolonial Studies: A Critical Introduction*. London: Arnold.

Frazer, Ian and Jenny Bryant-Tokalau (2006). 'Introduction: The Uncertain Future of Pacific Regionalism', in I. Frazer and J. Bryant-Tokalau (eds), *Redefining the Pacific: Regionalism Past, Present and Future*. Aldershot: Ashgate, 1–23.

Goss, J., and B. Lindquist (2000). 'Placing Movers: An Overview of the Asian-Pacific Migration System', *The Contemporary Pacific*, 12.2: 285–414.

Grossman, Michelle, with I. Anderson, M. L. Langton, and I. Moreton-Robinson (eds) (2003). *Blacklines: Contemporary Critical Writing by Indigenous Australians*. Carlton, Vic.: Melbourne University Press.

Harvey, David (2005). *The New Imperialism*. Oxford: Oxford University Press.

Hayes, G. (1991). 'Migration, Metascience, and Development in Policy in Island Polynesia', *The Contemporary Pacific*, 3.1: 1–58.

Hau'ofa, Epeli (2000). Opening address for the Red Wave Collective exhibition at the James Harvey Gallery, Sydney, 27 September. Unpublished pamphlet.

Hau'ofa, Epeli (2008). *We Are the Ocean: Selected Works*. Honolulu: University of Hawai'i Press.

Hingston, Ken (2006). 'Foreshore and Seabed', in Malcolm Mulholland (ed.), *State of the Māori Nation: Twenty First Century Issues in Aotearoa*. Auckland: Reed, 107–14.

Hoogvelt, Ankie (1997). *Globalization and the Postcolonial World*. London: Macmillan.

Howard, Alan (2000). 'Pacific-Based Virtual Communities: Rotuma on the World Wide Web', in D. Hanlon and G. M. White (eds), *Voyaging Through the Contemporary Pacific*. Lanham, Md.: Rowman and Littlefield, 403–18.

Huffer, Elise and Ropate Qalo (2004). 'Have We Been Thinking Upside-Down? The Contemporary Emergence of Pacific Theoretical Thought', *The Contemporary Pacific*, 16.1: 87–116.

Huggan, Graham (2001). *The Postcolonial Exotic: Marketing the Margins*. London and New York: Routledge.

Huggan, Graham (2008). *Interdisciplinary Measures: Literature and the Future of Postcolonial Studies*. Liverpool: Liverpool University Press.

Huggins, Jackie (1998). *Sister Girl: The Writings of Aboriginal Activist and Historian Jackie Huggins*. St Lucia, Queensland: University of Queensland Press.

Ishtar, Zohl de (1994). *Daughters of the Pacific*. Melbourne: Spinifex Press.

James, Colin (1992). *New Territory: The Transformation of New Zealand, 1984–92*. Wellington: Bridget Williams Books.

Keown, Michelle (2007). *Pacific Islands Writing: The Postcolonial Literatures of Aotearoa/New Zealand and Oceania*. Oxford: Oxford University Press.

Keown, Michelle (2008). '"Can't We All Just Get Along?" *Bro' Town* and New Zealand's Creative Multiculturalism', *Moving Worlds*, 8.2: 44–58.

Keown, Michelle (2010). '*Littérature-monde* or *Littérature Océanienne*? Internationalism versus Regionalism in Francophone Pacific Writing', in C. Forsdick, A. Hargreaves, and D. Murphy (eds), *Transnational French Studies: Postcolonialism and Littérature-Monde*. Liverpool: Liverpool University Press, 240–57.

Larner, Wendy and W. Walters (2002). 'The Political Rationality of the "New Regionalism": Towards a Genealogy of the "Region"', *Theory and Society*, 31.3: 391–432.

Lawn, Jennifer and Bronwyn Beatty (2006). 'On the Brink of a New Threshold of Opportunity: *The Lord of the Rings* and New Zealand Cultural Policy', in Ernest Mathijs (ed.), *The Lord of the Rings: Popular Culture in Global Context*. London: Wallflower, 43–60.

Lawson, Alan (1995). 'Postcolonial Theory and the "Settler" Subject', *Essays on Canadian Writing*, 56: 20–36.

Lee, Helen M. (2004). 'All Tongans are Connected: Tongan Transnationalism', in V. S. Lockwood (ed.), *Globalization and Culture Change in the Pacific Islands*. Upper Saddle River, NJ: Pearson, 133–48.

Lockwood, Victoria (2004). 'The Global Imperative and Pacific Island Societies', in V. S. Lockwood (ed.), *Globalization and Culture Change in the Pacific Islands*. Upper Saddle River, NJ: Pearson, 1–39.

Lynch, John (1998). *Pacific Languages: An Introduction*. Honolulu: University of Hawai'i Press.

Maclellan, Nic (2010). 'The Region in Review: International Issues and Events, 2009', *The Contemporary Pacific*, 22.2: 400–14.

Mateata-Allain, Kareva (2008). *Bridging Our Sea of Islands: French Polynesian Literature within an Oceanic Context*. Saarbrücken: Verlag Dr. Müller.

Mehrez, Samia (1992). 'Translation and the Postcolonial Experience: The Francophone North African Text', in L. Venuti (ed.), *Rethinking Translation: Discourse, Subjectivity, Ideology*. London: Routledge, 120–38.

Mittelman, James H. (2000). *The Globalization Syndrome: Transformation and Resistance*. Princeton, NJ: Princeton University Press.

Murray, Stuart (1998). *Never a Soul at Home: New Zealand Literary Nationalism and the 1930s*. Wellington: Victoria University Press.

Narokobi, Bernard (1980). *The Melanesian Way*. Boroko: Institute of Papua New Guinea Studies.

New Zealand Tourism Guide (2005–6). 'Lord of the Rings—New Zealand'. Online source: <http://www.tourism.net.nz/lord-of-the-rings.html>, accessed January 2011.

Neumann, Klaus, Nicholas Thomas, and Hilary Ericksen (eds) (1999). *Quicksands: Foundational Histories in Australia and Aotearoa New Zealand*. Sydney: University of New South Wales Press.

O'Brien, Denis (1991). *The Bicentennial Affair: The Inside Story of Australia's 'Birthday Bash'*. Crows Nest, New South Wales: Australian Broadcasting Corporation.

Orange, Claudia (1987). *The Treaty of Waitangi*. Wellington: Bridget Williams Books.

Prasad, Mohit (ed.) (2006). *Dreadlocks* Special Issue. Vaka Vuku. Proceedings of the Pacific Epistemologies Conference, 2006. Suva, Fiji: Pacific Writing Forum, The University of the South Pacific.

Reconciliation Australia (2000). 'About Reconciliation Australia'. Online source: <http://www.reconciliation.org.au/home/about-ra>, accessed January 2011.

Reid, Papaarangi and Bridget Robson (2006). 'The State of Māori Health', in Malcolm Hulholland (ed.), *State of the Māori Nation: Twenty-first-Century Issues in Aotearoa*. Auckland: Reed.

Santos Perez, Craig (2008). *from unincorporated territory [sacha]*. Honolulu: Tinfish.

Santos Perez, Craig (2010). *from unincorporated territory [saina]*. Richmond, Calif.: Omnidawn Publishing.

Sinclair, Keith (1986). *A Destiny Apart: New Zealand's Search for National Identity*. Wellington: Allen & Unwin.

Slemon, Stephen (1990). 'Unsettling the Empire: Resistance Theory for the Second World', *World Literatures Written in English*, 30.2: 30–41.

Smith, Linda Tuhiwai (1999). *Decolonizing Methodologies: Research and Indigenous Peoples*. London and New York: Zed Books; Dunedin: University of Otago Press.

Spitz, Chantal (2007). *Island of Shattered Dreams*, trans. Jean Anderson. Wellington: Huia. First published in 1991 as *L'île des Rêves Écrasés*. Papeete: Au Vent des îles.

Spivak, Gayatri (2008). *Other Asias*. Malden, Mass. and Oxford: Blackwell.

Statistics New Zealand/Te Tari Tatau (2010). 'Life Expectancy and Death Rates'. Online source: <http://www2.stats.govt.nz/domino/external/web/nzstories.nsf/3d7ba81fd31d11adcc256b16006bfcf3/82dfd788a5ad21c1cc256b180004bacf?OpenDocument>, accessed December 2010.

Stewart, Frank, Kareva Mateata-Allain, and Alexander Dale Mawyer (2006). 'Te Ao Mā'ohi: An Overview', in F. Stewart, K. Mateata-Allain, and A. D. Mawyer (eds), *Vārua Tupu: New Writing from French Polynesia*. Honolulu: University of Hawai'i Press, xi–xxi.

Stewart-Harawira, Makere (2005). *The New Imperial Order: Indigenous Responses to Globalization*. London and New York: Zed.

Subramani (2001). *Dauka Puraan*. New Delhi: Star Publications.

Subramani (2003). *Pacific Epistemologies, Monograph Series 1*. Suva, Fiji: Pacific Writing Forum, 1–14.

Teaiwa, Teresia (1999). 'Reading Paul Gauguin's *Noa Noa* with Epeli Hau'ofa's *Kisses in the Nederends*: Militourism, Feminism, and the "Polynesian" Body', in V. Hereniko and R. Wilson (eds), *Inside Out: Literature Cultural Politics, and Identity in the New Pacific*. Lanham, Md.: Rowman and Littlefield, 249–63.

Teaiwa, Teresia (2008). 'Globalizing and Gendered Forces: The Contemporary Militarization of the Pacific/Oceania', in K. E. Ferguson and M. Mironescu (eds), *Gender and Globalization in Asia and the Pacific*. Honolulu: University of Hawai'i Press, 318–32.

Va'ai, Sina (1999). *Literary Representations in Western Polynesia: Colonialism and Indigeneity.* Apia: National University of Samoa.

Waddell, Eric, Vijay Naidu, and Epeli Hau'ofa (eds) (1993). *A New Oceania: Rediscovering Our Sea of Islands.* Suva, Fiji: School of Economic and Social Development.

Watters, R. (1987). 'Mirab Societies and Bureaucratic Elites', in A. Hooper, S. Britton, R. Crocombe, J. Huntsman, and C. Macpherson (eds), *Class and Culture in the South Pacific.* Suva, Fiji: Institute of Pacific Studies, 32–54.

Wendt, Albert (1973). *Sons for the Return Home.* Auckland: Longman Paul.

Wendt, Albert (1976). 'Towards a New Oceania', *Mana Review,* 1.1: 49–60.

White, Richard (1981). *Inventing Australia: Images and Identity 1688–1980.* London: Allen & Unwin.

Williams, Mark (1997). 'Crippled by Geography? New Zealand Nationalisms', in Stuart Murray (ed.), *Not On Any Map: Essays on Postcoloniality and Cultural Nationalism.* Exeter: University of Exeter Press, 19–42.

Wilson, Rob (2000). *Reimagining the American Pacific.* Durham and London: Duke University Press.

CHAPTER 28

AFRICA AND ITS DIASPORAS

ATO QUAYSON

INTRODUCTION

Africa is normally interpreted under the sign of crisis. In both scholarly and popular discourses, since the oil crisis of the 1970s the continent has been viewed as a test case for forms of intervention, whether humanitarian, political, economic, or otherwise (see Sharp in Part II of this volume). While these crisis perspectives have been robustly challenged from both African studies and postcolonial studies more generally, one element that has often eluded the commentaries on Africa until fairly recently is the issue of its relationship to its variant diasporas and the implications this has for understanding the socio-cultural and economic changes taking place in the continent itself.[1] From the perspective of its diasporas a number of questions are automatically implicated: the dimensions of nation and citizenship; the significance of both intrinsic and extrinsic migration ebbs and flows that have served to structure African society over the past four centuries; the relation of these to transnationalism and globalization. All these help refocus our attention on a simple question but one whose answer carries significant implications: what is Africa in the world today? The answer to this ostensibly simple question will be quite different if pursued exclusively from the perspective of the continent's internal social dynamics or that of its external relations with the west or that of its implicit and explicit ties to its different diasporas. In this chapter, I propose to tackle the question of Africa mainly from the constitution of its diasporas and to explore the variety of ways in which these have shaped and continue to shape African societies today. This focus also serves to break or at least redirect attention away from the fixation with Africa's relations with the west, which have been a dominant thematic in discussions of Africa

---

[1.] By Africa's variant diasporas I mean to indicate a purview that goes well beyond studies of the black diaspora in the New World. It is important to place these diasporas in the historical context of processes of diasporization that have taken place incessantly upon the continent itself since at least the mid-nineteenth century. As we will come to see, this perspective produces a different understanding of the black and African diasporas and of Africa's current place within them.

within scholarly circles, whether from the purview of modernization theory, theories of core/periphery relations, or the discursive relations unearthed by postcolonial studies (Chinweizu 1975; Mudimbe 1988; Rodney 1972; Wallerstein 1961).

Let us begin by imagining ourselves before a gigantic billboard of rotating headlines drawn from events that have taken place in the past thirty years that, though seemingly disparate, speak collectively to Africa's shifting relation to its diasporas:

- In 2005 the African Union declared its African Diaspora the 'sixth region' of the continent.[2]
- The current chairperson of the Commission of the African Union is Jean Ping, of mixed Chinese and Gabonese parentage. Among his many distinctions was persuading Hu Jintao, president of China, to visit Gabon as part of Jintao's four-nation tour of Africa in 2004. Hu Jintao has toured Africa six times since 2000, covering twenty countries in all.[3]
- There is currently a fast-growing African trading community in Guangzhou, China (Bodomo 2010; Morais 2009).
- There have been more African-born Africans migrating to the United States annually since 1970 than were sent there each year throughout the 400-year period of slavery. This amazing fact was posted on Barack Obama's campaign website during the Democratic Party presidential nomination contest in 2008, but had previously been given wide circulation from an article by Sam Roberts published in *The New York Times* in 2005.[4]
- The World Bank estimates that in 2010 there were 30.6 million Africans living outside their homelands. France is the highest recipient of African migrants at 9 per cent of the total, followed closely by the Ivory Coast at 8 per cent, with the UK and the US at 4 per cent each (Ratha 2011: 9–11, 15–26).

[2] The process to make the diasporas the 'sixth region' started in May 2003 when President Wade of Senegal moved for its adoption at the first extraordinary meeting of the assembly heads of state in Addis Ababa, Ethiopia. The Council of Ministers then made a declaration at its ordinary meeting in May in 2005 in Addis Ababa and the first African Union Diaspora Ministerial Conference was held in Johannesburg, South Africa from 16 to 18 November 2007. The most significant development was the decision to amend the Constitutive Act of the AU to include Article 3(q), which 'invites and encourages the full participation of the African Diaspora as an important part of our Continent, in the building of the African Union'. I am grateful to my colleague Thomas Tieku at the University of Toronto for pointing me to the relevant sections of the AU documents regarding the declaration.

[3] Guo Quian, 'Decade-Old China-Africa Cooperation Forum Yields Abundant Fruits', English. xinhuanet.com./English.news.cn, 21 December 2010, online source: <http://news.xinhuanet.com/english2010/china/2010–12/21/c_13657292.htm>, accessed 20 June 2011.

[4] Sam Roberts, 'More Africans Enter US Than in the Days of Slavery', *The New York Times*, 21 February 2005. See also William A. Kandel, 'The U.S. Foreign-Born Population: Trends and Selected Characteristics', CRS Report for Congress, 18 January 2011, online source: <http://www.fas.org/sgp/crs/misc/R41592.pdf>, accessed 21 June 2011; and the United States Census Bureau, 'Profile of Selected Demographic and Social Characteristics: 2000, People Born in Africa', online source: <http://www.census.gov/population/cen2000/stp-159/STP-159-africa.pdf>, accessed 21 June 2011.

- A recent report released by the World Bank and the African Development Bank has recommended that African governments should issue 'African Diaspora Bonds'. The World Bank report suggests that Africans outside their home countries have annual savings of $40bn and that African governments might be able to raise up to $10bn a year on the sale of such bonds to their various diasporas.[5]
- Finally, the black British musician Dizzee Rascal (Dylan Kwabena Arthur Mills) was born to a Nigerian father, but on his death when Dizzee was quite young he was brought up in a single-parent household by his Ghanaian mother Priscilla in East London. Dizzee takes inspiration for his music style from garage, hip hop, and Caribbean influences, rather than from African cultural influences as such.[6]

The African Union's declaration of the Diaspora as its 'sixth region' is understandable given the fact that the continent has gained a great deal from remittances and will continue to do so into the foreseeable future. However, it is also clear that both the African Union and indeed most of the economists who try to tap into the economic potential of the continent's widespread diasporas have a rather simplified idea of the term 'African diaspora'. The overarching invocation of an African diaspora obscures the question of who is African in today's world and, concomitantly, of how a diasporic African identity is formed. Fundamental conceptual problems clearly not attended to by the AU's declaration lie worryingly just beneath the surface. As a starting point to our discussion, we should note that the different routes by which Africans were dispersed in its diasporas actually produce not just disparate forms of black cultural identity (as opposed to African identity), but also different forms of identification with the African continent itself. There are two dominant route metaphors of African diasporic identity formation that seem pertinent to this discussion: the 'maritime' and the 'plantation' route metaphors, respectively.[7] To be sure, the description of diasporic routes in terms of metaphors is unsatisfactory, but in settling on these terms I wish to draw inspiration from the Greco-Latin etymology of *metapherein,* which originally meant to 'carry or transfer over'. This etymology suggestively captures the transfers that take place in the formation

5. Teo Kermeliotis, 'Diaspora Bonds Can Tap into Migrant Wealth, Say Economists', CNN, 7 April 2011, online source: <http://edition.cnn.com/2011/BUSINESS/04/07/diaspora.bonds.africa/index.html>, accessed 19 June 2011. Even though the figures look fantastic, in reality they are quite modest. Given their own estimates of the number of Africans resident outside their home countries, the World Bank figures suggest that 30.6 million Africans save on average just over $100 each a year, a scandalously small amount when you think about it.

6. Ian Burrell, 'Streets Ahead: Dizzee Rascal', *The Independent,* 19 September 2009, and Ed Marriott, 'Dizzee Rascal, Rebel with a Cause', *The Times,* 17 May 2008.

7. Trade provides a potential third route metaphor; in the present period this would take us into an examination of the rapidly growing African trade diasporas in Guangzhou, Hong Kong, Bangkok, and New York, among other places. However, African trade diasporas have a long history and must be pursued through at least five centuries of trade across the Sahara on the one hand and across the Indian Ocean as far afield as the coastal regions of India on the other. This rich metaphor has to be set aside for now for lack of space.

of diasporic identities. The two route metaphors are not to be seen as mutually exclusive, but rather as interdependent and interanimating. Most of what follows will be of a historical nature, and will concentrate predominantly on the period between the early 1800s to roughly the 1960s, the period in which the current forms of diasporic African and black identities came to be consolidated in the ways in which we recognize them in the world today.

A preliminary methodological distinction needs to be drawn between dispersals and diasporas, for not all dispersals lead to diasporas. For example, the dispersals that took place in Libya and Ivory Coast in 2011 due to the political turmoil in those two countries may not necessarily lead to the formation of diasporas as such. For a diaspora to emerge out of the dispersal of a given population a number of conditions have to be met. These include the time depth of dispersal and settlement in other locations; the development of a myth of the homeland (note the emphasis on myth here); the attendant diversification of responses to homeland and host nation; the evolution of class segmentation and conflict within a given diaspora; and the ways in which contradictions among the different class segments end up reinforcing different forms of material and emotional investment in a utopian ideal of the homeland. Sometimes the utopian impulse serves to place the quest for the homeland in the vicinity of an active nationalism, as in the well-known cases of Israel and of Palestine; but the stake in a spatial homeland is not always consonant with the interests of a diaspora. It is the utopian idealization that gives the homeland ultimate salience within diasporic consciousness, whether this ensues in a return-to-homeland movement or not (Armstrong 1976; Brah 1996; Clifford 1997; Cohen 1996; Dufoix 2008; Sheffer 2003; Tölölyan 2000). A diaspora, whether African or otherwise, should not be perceived as a discrete entity but rather as being formed by a series of often contradictory convergences of peoples, ideas, and even cultural orientations. This last point raises a significant methodological issue as it determines in a fundamental way the manner by which we delimit a diaspora research field and the ways by which we establish causal relationships among the various elements that fall within it. Finally, it is important not to attempt to see African diasporas as being completely separate from the shaping of other global diasporas. There are major lessons to be learned from a comparative perspective, as will be seen in the section that follows.

DISPERSALS AND DIASPORAS

The early modern period was distinguished by several key phases of population dispersal, marked most distinctively by the major European migrations that took place from the sixteenth to the nineteenth centuries, and the transatlantic slave trade in the same period that coincided and overlapped with it. These major European and African dispersals were later to be followed by population dispersals within the colonial world itself from the 1800s to around 1960. These latter dispersals took place between colonial locations and were largely the product of colonial trade and bureaucratic processes.

The major dispersal of Jews from Europe from the late nineteenth until the first half of the twentieth century forms another important population movement in the modern period, with the final major phase being that of the movement of economic migrants and refugees from the global south to the global north that started in the late 1970s and is still ongoing today.[8] From the earliest phase of population dispersals in the early modern period, dispersal was sometimes deployed as a handy instrument of demographic control in Europe, especially with regard to the regulation of race, crime, and poverty. Thus, while West Africa had long been considered unsuitable for a British penal colony—the choice was eventually made in favour of Australia—a settlement was still established in Sierra Leone for the settlement of London's black poor from 1786–91. These Londoners were subsequently joined by a number of black Nova Scotians. The term 'Nova Scotians' did not refer at the time to persons originating from what is now a Canadian province; rather a large majority of those who migrated to what was later to become a West African colony in 1808 were ex-slaves from Virginia and South Carolina, who had moved as Black Loyalists to British Nova Scotia in 1783, before leaving again in 1787 and then in 1792 because of broken promises of free land (Byrd 2008; Walker 1992). Sierra Leone will feature again later in the discussion; suffice to note for now that for much of the first part of the eighteenth century the province was a stronghold for pirates. It took till late into the eighteenth century for the Royal Navy to completely secure the trade routes around the coast of Sierra Leone. As Linebaugh and Rediker (2000) have shown, sailors tired of the harsh conditions on board slaving ships often abandoned their merchant vessels to sail under the black flag, with Sierra Leone and Madagascar being the most favoured pirate locations on the African continent.

The resolution of issues of poverty in Britain through the movement of segments of its own population was not limited exclusively to the plight of the black poor; it also included the dispersal of poor children to Australia, South Africa, and the Americas. As early as 1618 a hundred 'vagrant' children in London were rounded up and transported to the colony of Virginia. The policy of enforced child migration continued piecemeal throughout the colonial period, with orphaned children being sent off to the Cape of Good Hope in South Africa and the Swan River Colony in Australia in 1832, and to New Brunswick and Toronto in Canada in 1833. They were set to work in indentured labour and slave-like conditions. Over 150,000 children are estimated to have been so dispersed from 1618 until the 1920s (Bagnell 2001; Bean and Melville 1989).[9] It would be

[8.] Scholars of colonialism and empire generally concede that the period from the sixteenth century represents the largest movement of human population in world history, with some estimates placing the figure as high as 60 million. But these population movements are usually detailed in segments, focusing on the emigration of Europeans to other parts of the world, or on variant migrations around the edges of empire such as between Australia and New Zealand, or on the transatlantic slave trade. The 1905 Census of the British Empire was to detail for the first time many of these population dispersals. See Maas (2003: 479–81); also Christopher (2008: 268–85).

[9.] See also, 'Child Immigration', National Maritime Archives and Library Information Sheet No. 9, National Museums Liverpool, online source: <http://www.diduknow.info/emigrants/media/child_emigration.rtf>, accessed 31 May 2010.

speculative, but not untoward, to surmise that several Abolitionists of the eighteenth and nineteenth centuries may have come from this cohort of hitherto dispersed children and their descendants.

While some revisionist imperial historians with an eye on identifying some of the positive effects of empire have argued that colonial policy was often confused and unsystematic (Darwin 2009; Ferguson 2002), it remains the case that the British created and implemented conditions for the transfer of large chunks of its colonial populations during the colonial period, and that these were dispersed between different regions of the Empire.[10] In fact, it would not be hyperbolic to suggest that colonialism relied essentially on the instrumentalization of population dispersal as a key component of colonial governmentality. Whether with the direct establishment of colonial administrative and bureaucratic arrangements in the conversion of what were initially trade outposts (as in much of Africa, India, and Southeast Asia), or in the context of settler colonialism (as in Australia, Canada, Latin America, and arguably Ireland), or in that of colonialism in post-plantation economies (as in Sri Lanka, Jamaica, and Malaysia), colonial governmentality invariably involved the creation of conditions for the dispersal of populations, some of which came to coalesce into diasporas. And in several instances, as in the indentured labour policies that took effect from the 1830s, population dispersal was systematic and designed to meet particular economic ends.

Thus in the specific case of Africa the processes of population dispersal under colonialism led to the establishment of quite disparate diasporic communities both within the continent and elsewhere. These dispersals were both extra- and intra-African. A distinctive case of extra-African dispersals, which means the relocation of populations from outside of Africa onto the continent, is provided by the Indians of East Africa. The British indentured labour policy that operated in East Africa from the 1880s till the 1920s was to have a major impact on the demographic constitution of the region (Tinker 1974). The indentured labour policy was designed as a response to the abolition of slavery to take account of the needs of plantation owners, who now felt their plantations were under threat of collapse due to the loss of slave labour. When the policy was extended to East Africa it was mainly to provide non-African labour for building the Uganda Railway, which was to link the interiors of Uganda and Tanzania with the Indian Ocean at the Kenyan port of Mombasa. Of the estimated 32,000 Indian men brought into the region, roughly 6,700 stayed behind to work in the commercial and business sectors after the termination of the indentured labour programme. Colonial policy then encouraged family reunion along with more voluntary migration from South Asia. By the end of World War II the Indians in East Africa were an estimated 360,000, with many of them firmly in control of the commercial trade in Uganda, Kenya, and Tanzania. After the independence of these three countries in the 1960s, the Indians had not only become a central part of the civil service administration but also considered themselves African

---

[10.] The notion of the messiness of the British colonial enterprise is somewhat balanced by the implications of systematicity in the expansion and consolidation of the trade and business interests of the nineteenth century. See Cain and Hopkins (2001).

(Bhachu 1985; Ghai and Ghai 1970). The ill-advised policy of Africanization in the region and the racially based economic policies aimed at wealth redistribution were later to lead to the migration of this population to other parts of the world, with the ascension to power in 1971 of Idi Amin, the Ugandan dictator, entrenching their violent diasporization. Additionally, another 25,000 Indian indentured labourers were to be transported to French Mauritius by 1840, thus forming an Indian majority on the island off the coast of Southern Africa (Allen 2006). The presence of large non-African communities on the continent such as the Indians of East and Southern Africa and the Lebanese of West Africa also raises questions for understanding Africa's diasporas, for all these constituencies still maintain symbolic and material links with India and Lebanon respectively (as well as to Malaysia in the case of South Africa), and thus provide important bridges to social realities well beyond the continent (Torabully and Carter 2002). Furthermore, and perhaps even more fundamentally, these communities do not consider themselves as anything other than African; they have established firm relationships and cultural identities that define them as African and are fully invested in the development of the continent. They have contributed to cuisine and literary cultures and have even helped establish distinctive models of African advertising. After over 150 years of continuous residency and interethnic relations with African groups, are the descendants of Indian indentured labourers less African than, say, the Zulu or the Gĩkũyũ? Or is it rather that the diasporic culture of the Indians of East Africa marks a cosmopolitan 'Africanity' that has not yet been fully understood? [11]

Though not on the same scale as the indentured labour policies, military campaigns also help to illustrate the intra-African variety of population dispersals. The Hausa Constabulary was formed in 1865, made up initially of runaway Hausa slaves from Northern Nigeria. These were recruited mainly because of their facility in horse riding; a platoon of them was later to be transferred to the Gold Coast to fight against the Ashanti in the war of 1873–4. The Hausa Constabulary subsequently went through various name changes but was to remain in the Colony as an arm of law enforcement until the start of World War I, when they were incorporated into the then fledgling army. After the end of the Ashanti war, they along with a large number of recruits from the Northern Territories (now Northern Ghana) were settled at the current Accra neighbourhood called Cantonments. Hausa had been adopted as the language of military command for the West African Frontier Force from the 1870s until 1937, when it was finally replaced with English; thus despite the members of the fledgling armed forces

---

[11] In urban Kenya what passes for authentic Kenyan food is clearly derived from Indian cuisine, while the literary production of East African Indian writers such as M. G. Vassanji, Yusuf Dawood, and Shiva Naipaul (brother of the Nobel Prize winner) is heavily flavoured with the sense of East African locations. The 2005–6 TIGO cell phone advertising campaign that was launched in Tanzania, Ghana, Senegal, and other places, on the other hand, promoted a version of Pan-Africanist youth culture that bore no resemblance to the better known political version, yet was saturated with recognizable images of black urban chic. Creative Eye, the firm behind the television and outdoor advertising for TIGO in East Africa as well as Ghana and Senegal, was first established by an East African Indian based in Dar es Salaam. See Quayson (2010: 77–96).

being from a polyglot background, it was Hausa that was associated with a muscular masculinity for much of the colonial period in the region. Given that Hausa was and still is a language spoken in a large geographical belt across much of the northern part of West Africa, the members of the relocated Hausa Constabulary were duly assimilated to migrant Hausa-speaking populations from the Northern Territories, at least from the late nineteenth century onwards. Recruitment into the fledgling army for World War I, and later also in the lead up to World War II, was drawn heavily from the Northern Territories; in time, no distinction could be made between the Hausas that had originally come from Northern Nigeria and those from the Northern Territories (Adae 2005; Austin 1985; Schleh 1968).[12] Among other things, the first local-language dictionary was compiled for teaching the members of the Hausa Constabulary and the first metropolitan bus service in Accra was developed, initially to service their interests. This bus service was commissioned in 1926 to carry soldiers and workers on an urban route from Cantonments to the General Post Office in the CBD.

On a much wider scale, and moving African military populations outside of the continent, West African *tirailleur* (light infantry) regiments were recruited to fight alongside the French in their various campaigns from as early as the Napoleonic period. Many of these would progressively end up in Paris and its suburbs to impact upon the racial character of France well before the wave of migrants from its former colonies were to arrive after the Second World War. The *Tirailleurs Sénégalais* conscription supplied an estimated 170,000 troops for France in the First World War alone, with many of them fighting and dying in Europe (Echenberg 1990). Finally, the West Indian Regiment provides us with an example of a mixed intra- and extra-African dispersal dynamic. First raised in 1795 and initially made up of both freed slaves and slaves bought from the slave plantations in the West Indies, one battalion of the BWIR was sent to Sierra Leone in 1819 to quell a rebellion of the 'settlers' or freed slaves (also known as Creoles). As might be recalled, these freed slaves had themselves been drawn from among London's black poor as well as the freed Black Loyalists from the American South. After the rebellion was quelled, many members of this regiment remained in the colony and intermarried with the Creoles of Sierra Leone. The WIR was to be augmented by more detachments and remained in active service in West Africa for much of the nineteenth century. It was used to maintain law and order in various parts of the region, including fighting in the Ashanti War of 1873–4 alongside the Hausa Constabulary (Ukabi 1974; Buckley 1979; Dyde 1997). Though the members of the WIR were originally 'African', having been taken from the continent itself they and their descendants subsequently became 'West Indian' before being relocated back to Africa as part of the WIR. However, if they returned 'home', home itself was really the crucible of their diasporic condition that was multiply intertwined with various locations engendered out of the processes of a colonial governmentality that had no interest in placing them 'at home' in the first place.

[12.] For the implications of the Hausa Constabulary for the invention of ethnicity, see Lentz and Nugent (2000: 121–7).

While the remnants of the *Tirailleurs Sénégalais* in France gradually coalesced into a diaspora, the evidence suggests that other military groups such as the Hausa Constabulary and the remainder of the BWIR were eventually assimilated into their local contexts within Africa itself. We are obliged then to draw a distinction suggested in the differences among the military groups just discussed, one that also lies implicit in the current figures regarding African immigration to France and the Ivory Coast. While the World Bank report's 2010 estimate of 9 per cent of African migrants going to France seems almost indistinguishable to the 8 per cent that find themselves in the Ivory Coast for the same period, the two figures actually conceal some sharp differences between the two African groups. With time, the ones in France may be considered as having coalesced into a diaspora, while those in the African nation cannot be said to have been converted into a diaspora without some further heavy qualifications. These distinctions arise for a number of reasons. Diasporas, as Avtar Brah suggests, are the product of *diaspora space* and the best way of conceptualizing such space is by understanding the series of relationalities that continually structure and restructure that space. As she puts it: 'My central argument is that *diaspora space* as a conceptual category is "inhabited" not only by those who have migrated and their descendants but equally by those who are constructed and represented as indigenous. In other words, the concept of *diaspora space* (as opposed to that of diaspora) includes the entanglement of genealogies of dispersion with those of "staying put"' (1996: 18, emphasis in the original). While all the military groups we have discussed will have maintained social networks from the different parts of the imperial landscapes from which they were recruited, they came to be settled in different diaspora spaces that impacted upon their identities. Racial, cultural, and language differences have their part to play in the shaping of diaspora space as do the politics of the ruling elites of the recipient nations. These factors determine whether migrant military and other groups are partially or indeed completely assimilable to the local communities in which they find themselves (the Hausa Constabulary and the BWIR in West Africa; African migrants in the Ivory Coast) or the formation of diasporic identities (*Tirailleurs Sénégalais* in France; African migrants in Europe and North America in general).[13]

[13.] Though South Africa is considered an African country, its settler European colonialism, race relations, and subsequent apartheid ideology have meant that the diaspora space constituted within its borders has overlapped with various other realities that cannot be described exclusively in African terms. Thus the rabid xenophobia expressed in the mass lynching of foreign African workers in 2009 indicates that its diaspora space is constituted quite differently from, say, that of the Ivory Coast or even Nigeria. For native black South Africans are still just as alienated from their own economy as the African migrants that were attacked. However, this economic alienation is masked by a nationalist sentiment that dictates that there *must* be outsiders distinctive from an 'us' and upon whom the bewilderment and anger of the insiders can be projected, sometimes in very violent forms. This means that alien Africans can never really be assimilated into the local, and will always have to bear the imprint of their alienness. The 2009 film *District 9* is a magnificent allegory of precisely this interplay between alienation, xenophobia, and violence toward the alien. On this see Quayson (2009).

THE MARITIME ROUTE METAPHOR
OF IDENTITY FORMATION

Paul Gilroy's suggestion in *The Black Atlantic* (1993) that the circulation of ideas and activists on slave and merchant ships provided the basis for cosmopolitan forms of modern consciousness coincides with the observations made by maritime historians such as Linebaugh, Rediker, and others. This gives us an entry into the maritime route metaphor of African diasporic identity formation. Not only did the ships act as crucibles of transnational cosmopolitan identity, but the ports these ships docked at were themselves heavily impacted by the embryonic transnational cultures incubated on the merchant ships. Nowhere is this more evident than in the history of black Liverpool, as Jacqueline Nassy Brown has adroitly shown in her *Dropping Anchor, Setting Sail* (2005). Genealogically varied, this community dates from the middle of the eighteenth century. After the abolition of slavery, and beginning in the 1870s, shipping firms in Liverpool were to hire West and East Africans in great numbers, along with Afro-Caribbeans, demobilized Indian soldiers known as Lascars, and Chinese, Arab, and Somali seamen (Brown 2005: 17–31; Frost 1995: 24–5). By the beginning of the twentieth century, Liverpool had come to dominate the British trade with West Africa and indeed much of the colonial world. Estimates are that up to a third of the labour force on British ships from 1901 to the 1950s, or roughly 66,000 men, were from the aforementioned regions (Tabili 1994: 42).

It was general practice at the time that seamen would settle on shore to await a new consignment of goods, but it was not unusual for large numbers of seamen to jump ship, either awaiting better conditions on other ships or casually mingling with the population on shore. Significantly, however, the numbers of coloured seamen hired by British ships changed according to the availability of their white counterparts. The two world wars saw a shortage of white seamen and a concomitant rise in non-Europeans for the shipping industry; the popularity of the latter also fell just after the wars (Brown 2005: 19; Rich 1986: 21). The foreign seamen were to be joined by demobilized black soldiers after World War I and both these groups were to face significant racism and violence. Thus in June 1919 Charles Wooton was murdered by a white mob in Liverpool, provoking an uprising of blacks in almost all areas where they had settled. Indeed it is this first race riot in Liverpool that was to reveal the intricate connections between domestic social relations in Liverpool and Britain and the politics of colonial governance in Britain's colonies. Given that the seamen in Liverpool from different parts of the Empire were male, by settling down and entering amorous relationships with white women (typically poor Irish women, themselves a long-standing diasporic community in Liverpool and other port cities in the country), the seamen introduced a sexual dynamic into metropolitan Britain whose results subsequently came to raise problems for colonial policymakers. After the 1919 riots, policymakers struggled unsuccessfully to accommodate the requests made by African seamen to return home with their white wives. This created considerable headaches for the Home Office, the Colonial Office, and the local colonial governments respectively, with the governments in the colonies being especially nervous about the deleterious effect that the sight of white women living in impoverished conditions with their black husbands might have on white respectability. Every imaginable effort was exerted to prevent the women from travelling back with their husbands, with sometimes damaging implications for the health of both the Africans and their wives (Ray 2009).

It was the docking of the now iconic *Empire Windrush* at Tilbury in 1948, carrying 492 passengers from Jamaica, that marked a shift in the cultural tide of black immigration in the UK (see McLeod in Part IV of this volume). From the 1950s more women began migrating from the Caribbean, Africa, and Asia into Britain and helped to change the gender dynamic of black Britain. Liverpool and other colonial ports like it thus became significant portals through which to examine the different dimensions of black Britishness. However, a nagging question still persists. Given the varied provenance of black immigrants in Liverpool, the extensive nature of interracial marriages that have taken place there since the start of the twentieth century, and the character of interactions that they as a community have had with other diasporic and non-diasporic constituencies there and in the UK more generally, to what degree is it possible to speak of this Liverpool community as an 'African', as opposed to simply a black diaspora? There is no straightforward way in which we can speak of a singular identification of black Liverpool with Africa. Rather, it is better to speak of multiple identifications of blackness, some of them forged within Britain itself, but others fed heavily from the cultural input of the American Civil Rights and hip hop movements and the cultures of the Caribbean, with only a residual Pan-Africanism to suggest any links between black Britishness and Africa itself.

Caribbean cultural forms have arguably been the most influential single factor in the formation of black identities in Liverpool and other parts of the UK. Reggae, for example, has been so powerful as to have spawned utterly contrasting yet now classically British styles. These classic styles can be seen in the markedly different reggae orientations of UB40 on the one hand and Steel Pulse on the other. Formed in Birmingham in 1978 and fronted by local white brothers Ali and Duncan Campbell, UB40 helped to globalize a brand of romantic reggae ballad that appears to have nothing to do with African culture. Contrastingly, Steel Pulse, an all-black group also formed in Birmingham in 1975, has been unremittingly Pan-Africanist from its inception, with tracks such as 'Dub Marcus Say' (from their 1982 *True Democracy* album) becoming a standout Pan-Africanist anthem in its own right. Add to this the fact that the dominant black cultural voices in the UK over the past thirty or so years such as Stuart Hall, Paul Gilroy, Trevor Nelson, Trevor MacDonald, Benjamin Zephaniah, and various others have been from the Caribbean registers and we see that black British identification is much more with the Caribbean islands than with Africa as such. It is not for nothing, then, that Dizzee Rascal has styled himself musically as Caribbean, but with a heavy infusion of hip hop influences. In this he falls in line with black youth in western metropolises like London, Toronto, New York, Amsterdam, and various others who typically identify with a polyglot Caribbean and hip hop culture as the signature of their difference from a white hegemonic mainstream. Africa features only dimly in such identifications.

The Plantation Route Metaphor
of Identity Formation

For good reasons, by far the greatest emphasis in studies of the black diaspora has been placed on the effects of plantation slavery and its aftermath. Most scholars of black Atlantic dispersals agree that the cultures that took seed in the New World had residues of Africa in them. This is not in doubt. The problem emerges with the question of 'how' these African elements were retained. Melville Herskovits (1941) and his followers argued forcefully that the African cultures of the American South, Cuba, Brazil, and the Caribbean islands revealed certain African cultural features that made them decisively part of an African diaspora. The key issue, however, was whether these residues of African culture were sure marks of Africa itself or whether they were creolized products forged out of an altogether new amalgam. Probably the best adjudications of this question are provided by Sidney Mintz and Richard Price in their slim but highly regarded *The Birth of African-American Culture* (1976), and by J. Lorand Matory in the Herskovits-Award-winning *Black Atlantic Religion* (2005). Mintz and Price's central contribution is to have focused attention on the relationship between culture and social relations in the formation of African cultures in the New World and to have pointed out the significance of the early slaves and their encounter with novel social conditions that required them to create cultural models relevant to the negotiation of these social conditions. For them, these novel social conditions also made a necessity out of accepting borrowings from the external environment. Thus, as they point out:

> All slaves must have found themselves accepting, albeit out of necessity, countless 'foreign' cultural practices, and this implied a gradual remodeling of their own traditional ways of doing many things. For most individuals, a commitment to, and engagement in, a new social and cultural world must have taken precedence rather quickly over what would have become before long largely a nostalgia for their homelands ... A 'culture', in these terms, becomes intimately linked to the social contexts within which affective ties are experienced and perceived. With the destruction of those ties, each individual's 'cultural set' is transformed phenomenologically, until the creation of new institutional frameworks permits the refabrication of content, both based upon—and much removed from—the past. (47)

Despite the conceptual brilliance of Mintz and Price's discussion, their model suffers from one irresolvable contradiction: the fact that the New World is conceptualized as a receptacle of peoples and influences from an Africa that seems to have remained stable and unchanging. This idea is deeply problematic, especially as such a model of non-coevalness is never applied to the relationship between the white immigrant settler communities of the New World and their metropolitan counterparts in Europe. Ultimately their model implies that European settlers have History, while their African counterparts only have Culture.

Matory, for his part, stands out for refining a thoroughly transnational model of cultural exchange between the West African coast and the New World, in his case specifically Afro-Brazilian Bahia and, to a lesser degree, Cuba. Matory's work is both conceptually and methodologically distinctive on the question of how Africans in the New World reproduced African cultural forms. Though his focus is predominantly on the Afro-Brazilian Candomblé, the conclusions he arrives at have suggestive resonances for thinking about Africa and its variant diasporas more generally. He suggests, first of all, that we see Africa and the New World as coeval: in other words, history was not frozen in Africa during the course of slavery. Second, he insists on seeing the creation of African cultures in the New World as the product of active human agency that is fully conscious of its historicity, as opposed to being merely the reflex reproduction of nostalgia for a lost continent. The implicit move here is to try to discern the conversion of plantation colonies into crucibles of transnational social experimentation specifically tied to the West African homeland. Third—the most dramatic proposition he puts forward—is that not only did cultural entrepreneurs in the Afro-Brazilian context actively and self-consciously produce an African culture, but this production had a recursive effect in the (re)production of an 'African' culture in the West African homeland itself. That is to say, through a process of transnational exchange diasporic cultures were produced by the descendants of African slaves that, in their turn, impacted directly upon the production of African cultures on the continent.

Matory's specific example for this brilliant insight is the cultural renaissance that took place in Lagos between the 1890s to the 1930s. Several convergences make themselves visible in the Lagos of the period, all of which go to show the translocal factors that fed into the formation of this colonial city. As he points out, as many as 8,000 manumitted slaves from Bahia returned to West Africa between 1822–99, with many of these settling in colonial Lagos. Some of these were also Candomblé cultic specialists—the redoubtable 'English Professors of Brazil'—who themselves came to study and proselytize in the Yoruba homeland for many years before returning back to Brazil (Matory 2005: 46–50). The main reason for the resettlement of returnee Afro-Brazilians in this specific location, however, is that from the first decade of the nineteenth century the British had shown an active interest in freeing slaves that had been ensnared in the residual slave trade after its abolition in 1807. By 1890 one in seven of Lagos residents was a returnee from Brazil or Cuba. These returnees contributed to the architectural and technical life of the city and added to its cosmopolitan bustle.[14]

[14.] Accra would also feel the impact of these Afro-Brazilian returnees. The Tabon, as they were called following a corruption of one of their greeting responses, were excellent tailors and carpenters. They were also responsible for the circulation of the colourful trade beads that have now become a defining feature of sartorial wardrobes among Ghana's most prominent chiefs. The evidence is not conclusive but, being avid gardeners, they may also have been responsible for introducing tomatoes into the local diet, thus radically transforming not just local Ga cuisine, but also the diet of most Ghanaians in the process. The evidence for these conclusions is drawn from various sources, but predominantly from the interviews and observations I conducted during fieldwork for my own Canadian SSHRC-funded research project on the social history of Accra in the summers of 2009–12.

British efforts to prevent slavery also involved intercepting slave ships along the West African coastline. A large number of slaves sold by the mighty slave-trading Kingdom of Benin had been members of various constituent Yoruba tribes. The slaves freed by the British were normally taken to Sierra Leone, which by this period already had a highly active missionary community. The missionaries in Sierra Leone set about converting the freed slaves to Christianity and giving them a thorough western-style education. Many of these freed slaves returned to Lagos, where they were known by the generic name of Saros, a corruption of their Sierra Leonean provenance. The Saros were however no ordinary returnees. Armed with the education they had received from the missionaries, they set about making themselves useful, translating the Bible into local languages, starting up newspapers and reading groups, entering into commerce and trade, and generally providing some of the most skilled members of the then embryonic colonial civil service. This group of returnees included the renowned Bishop Ajayi Crowther, first Anglican bishop of Nigeria and one of the most gifted translators and thinkers that Africa has ever produced. It was Bishop Ajayi Crowther, along with the Rev. Samuel Johnson, another redoubtable Saro returnee, who were responsible for forging the idea of a pan-Yoruba identity from the fragmented Oyo, Ifé, Ibadan, Ekiti, Ijebu, and Anago groupings that formed the Yoruba, thus creating a completely new template of self-representation for peoples that had hitherto conceived of themselves primarily as part of largely autonomous ethnic groups. Even the standardization of the orthography and language of the Yoruba was undertaken by the Saros (Matory 2005: 50–61; see also Doortmont 1990; Peel 1989, 2000; Quayson 1997).

The third main actor in this heady cosmopolitan Lagos renaissance was of course the British colonial apparatus. The CMS missionaries and the British administration had an early interest in promoting Yoruba identity as the most coherent and pronounced among the collectives they governed in West Africa. Not only that, the colonial administration expressed a strong interest in maintaining links between the cultures of Lagos and Atlantic Brazil. In 1890 and 1891 Alfred Moloney, governor of Lagos Colony, subsidized a trial shipping line between Lagos and Brazil. He also made a speech in which he extolled the values of the returnee Afro-Brazilians, insisting that they were not to be referred to as Afro-Brazilians but as Yoruba (Matory 2005: 55–6). The central proposition Matory makes with respect to the relationship between the Yoruba of West Africa and the strong Yoruba cultural elements and recensions that were evident in the Afro-Brazilian cults of Candomblé is that the influences cut both ways. The many layers of slaves brought from the Yoruba hinterland and later augmented by scores of Nigerian commercial entrepreneurs in the nineteenth century helped to strengthen the Yoruba 'authenticity' of Candomblé in Bahia, down even to the ritual language and discourse their practitioners deployed. But the 'English Professors of Brazil' were also to travel to Yorubaland to learn and to proselytize and, along with the mass of returnee Afro-Brazilians and Saros, they came to shape the identity of what we know as the 'Yoruba' today. The Yoruba may not have come to see themselves in a pan-ethnic light until much later, if indeed at all, had it not been for the convergences instigated by their African diasporas from the New World and Sierra Leone.

Matory's model for understanding the processes of cultural transfer between Africa and its various diasporas is extremely suggestive, since it refuses to give agential priority to either 'sending' or 'receiving' cultures but rather sees them as working in tandem within specific historical configurations for the production of what comes to pass for an 'African' identity. As he puts it later in the book:

> Because the most purist and self-consciously traditional 'folk' cultures are often taken as proof of local cultural closure and isolation, Candomblé and other similarly African-inspired African-American practices provide perhaps the best proof that broadly translocal and cosmopolitan fields of migration, commerce, and communication are the normal conditions of human culture and its reproduction (2005: 267)

In other words, these are living cultures and not museumized residues of cultures existentially transcended in space and time.

We are obliged to ask a similar set of questions to those previously posed in discussing the maritime metaphor and the formation of black Liverpool, namely to what degree can we assume that the Afro-Brazilians of Bahia identify with Africa and how far do Yorubas in today's Nigeria think of their Afro-Brazilian counterparts as diasporic brothers? One thing for certain is that what Matory describes as the mutual co-production of the cultures of the New World and of Yorubaland is rarely noted by contemporary scholarship on the Yoruba. The model of Yoruba cultural formation is considered in the critical literature to have been partially instigated by the Saro cultural elite and driven by the internal dynamics of Yoruba war and state formation, as well as more extensively in relation to the later formation of the Nigerian nation state. Powerfully evident today is the continuing importance of Yoruba cosmology, ritual practices, and symbols to the self-understandings of both locations. Yorubaland appears to be more of a symbolic homeland than the location of real material desire: it remains salient for Afro-Brazil as the seat of cultural symbols and not as a place of substantive social relations and desire for utopian reconstruction.[15] With the passage of time and the progressive disorientation of the Nigerian nation state, Yorubaland has provided a rich payout of symbol, metaphor, and cultic status, but without becoming translated into the site of a material homeland for Afro-Brazilians. This represents a sharp change from the conditions detailed in Matory's book.

[15.] Like South Africa, Brazil provides another complex test of any model of diaspora, especially in its relationship to Africa. While Matory is generally correct in asserting the overall correspondences and exchanges that took place between Afro-Brazil and West Africa during the later part of the nineteenth century and first half of the twentieth, by the start of the twenty-first century Brazil's interest in Africa was driven mainly by economic and political considerations, as opposed to cultural ones. Thus it is not present-day Nigeria that is the beneficiary of Brazilian interest but rather Angola. And even here we see an illustration of what might be termed as a loose form of interethnic elite identification between the descendants of Portuguese settler colonialists of Brazil and those of Angola. In other words, it is possible to trace forms of translocal and interdiasporic relations between the two countries, but this time through an entirely different diasporic vector from the one stipulated by Matory.

A Conclusion by Way of Pan-Africanism

If the various African diasporas discussed thus far have had any particular identification with Africa, this must be attributed more to the rise and fall of Pan-Africanism as a global cultural and ideological phenomenon in the twentieth century than to any other single factor. Marcus Garvey's ill-fated arrangements in 1919 to repatriate Africans from America back to Africa were only the start of a long and steady series of political, as opposed to exclusively cultural, attachments to the continent. The 1930s and '40s saw the emergence of Negritude, spearheaded mainly by intellectuals from Francophone Africa and the Caribbean. Among its leaders was Léopold Sédar Senghor, who was later to become the first president of independent Senegal. But Negritude's styling of Africa in terms of feeling and passion—in opposition to Europe's cold reason—was soon to face criticism from the likes of Chinweizu, Fanon, Soyinka, and several others (Irele 2011). Negritude was rapidly superseded by a more robust form of Pan-Africanism, which was tied to the political and social liberation of black peoples everywhere. The clarion call for this was encapsulated in Ghanaian President Dr Kwame Nkrumah's famous words at Independence: 'Ghana's Independence is meaningless unless it is tied to the total liberation of the African continent'. From the early 1950s Nkrumah was to pursue an active Pan-Africanist project, inviting various writers and thinkers, including Fanon, Richard Wright, George Padmore, and W. E. B. Du Bois, to Accra. Du Bois went originally to complete his ambitious *Africana Encyclopedia*; he arrived in 1961 but in the same year the US government refused to renew his expired passport. Nkrumah gave him and his wife safe haven, but Du Bois passed away after a short illness in 1963. On his wishes, his remains were buried (along, later, with those of his wife) in the home Nkrumah provided for him at Cantonments in Accra. It is now called the Du Bois Cultural Centre and receives thousands of visitors every year from all over the world.

It was also in this period of political Pan-Africanism that many people from Africa's diasporas decided to come and help in the nation-building project. Hundreds of African Americans and Black Caribbeans came to Ghana to make their home there—a heady voluntary repatriation of a professional class of diasporic Africans that was actively encouraged by Nkrumah. However, Nkrumah himself was not immune from the temptations of self-aggrandisement that afflicted many of the early post-Independence statesmen in Africa. While actively cultivating the ideology of Pan-Africanism he also rapidly alienated internal political constituencies inside his own country. He was eventually overthrown in a military coup in 1966 (spearheaded by the CIA). His demise was accompanied by that of a main plank of Pan-Africanist ideology, namely the project of national liberation and its role in galvanizing a specific form of diasporic identification with Africa. The salience of national liberation struggles for Africa's diasporas was articulated most cogently by Richard Wright on his visit to Ghana in 1955. As Wright put it, rather bluntly, he had no particular affinity with the cultures of Africa. Indeed, he felt that culture and tradition were the real enemies of Africa's future, since they seemed to him to stand in stark opposition to technological progress. Rather, what he completely identified with was the project of national liberation that was taking place across the continent at the time (Wright 1995 [1954]; see also Olaniyan 2009). In the African struggles for liberation from colonialism its diasporas show in a palpable way African agency attempting to carve out a space in history on its own terms. African liberation struggles were later to inspire various cultural expressions, including Bob Marley's famous rendition of the words of a speech by Ethiopia's Haile Selasse in the song 'War' (from the 1976 album *Rastaman Vibration*): 'Until the philosophy, which holds one man inferior than another, is finally, and permanently, discredited and abandoned/Until the colour of a man's skin, is of no more significance than the colour of his eyes/ It is a war'.

Sung during the heyday of apartheid and the liberation wars in Angola, Zimbabwe, South Africa, and Mozambique, Marley's words resonated loudly in the consciousness of black youth everywhere (see Featherstone in Part III of this volume). Even as he sang this heady Pan-Africanist anthem to liberation, it could be argued that Pan-Africanism as a political ideal was itself drawing its last breath. The events that were to unfold in Africa in the 1980s were to reverse the gains of decolonization and the nationalist struggles. The list of factors makes for sober reflection: the collapse of African economies and the contraction of the state apparatus following the adoption of IMF policies; the evisceration of any form of African social welfarism or leftist thinking during that period; the rise of deadly kleptocracies from what was then Zaire to Nigeria, Kenya, Gabon, and other places; and the unmasking of brutal dictatorships in Uganda, Malawi, and Zimbabwe from the 1980s through to the 1990s and beyond. These were to produce an image of Africa that even African-born Africans living on the continent felt repulsed by and were obliged to denounce. Thus, in contrast to the Pan-Africanism of Marley we find the sharp scepticism of Fela Ransome-Kuti, whose brand of juju music generated memorable critiques to guide a post-Independence generation of disaffected African youth throughout the 1970s and '80s, in the same period that Bob Marley was forging his global soundtracks to Pan-Africanist consciousness (Olaniyan 2004). Fela was closely followed by his cousin and Nobel laureate Wole Soyinka, who, in powerful plays such as *Kongi's Harvest* (1965), *Madmen and Specialists* (1971), and in many of his other writings, excoriated the moral bankruptcy of the Nigerian and African ruling classes. Africa's diasporas were not immune to the despair that afflicted the continent: the exhausted cynicism we find in Saidiya Hartman's *Lose Your Mother* (2007), a memoir of her quest for roots in Ghana in the mid-1990s, provides an illustrative case. The various social and political upheavals that have taken place on the continent since independence provide ample justification for the equivocal response to Africa's fate by Africans, both locally and in its diasporas.

To think properly of Africa in this second decade of the twenty-first century, then, is to be obliged to approach from many directions simultaneously. If the diasporic 'sixth region', as the AU declaration drafters have named it, is no straightforward geographical extension of the continent, it still speaks to the diverse landscapes of social relations that have been forged amongst peoples of African descent everywhere. These must command our serious attention, not least in order to define what Africa means today; and also to help us envision how the continent and its diasporas, both external and internal, might move forward to multiple yet intricately connected futures in a globalized world.

REFERENCES

Adae, Stephen (2005). *General History of the Ghana Armed Forces.* Accra: Ministry of Defence.

Allen, Richard (2006). *Slaves, Freedmen and Indentured Laborers in Colonial Mauritius.* Cambridge: Cambridge University Press.

Armstrong, John (1976). 'Mobilized and Proletarian Diasporas', *American Sociological Science Review,* 70.2: 393–408.

Austin, Dennis (1985). 'The Ghana Armed Forces and Ghanaian Society', *Third World Quarterly,* 7.1: 90–101.

Bagnell, Kenneth (2001). *The Little Immigrants: The Orphans Who Came to Canada.* Toronto: Dundurn Press.

Bean, Phillip and Joy Melville (1989). *Lost Children of the Empire.* London: Unwin Hyman.

Bhachu, Parminder (1985). *Twice Migrants: East African Sikh Settlers in Britain.* London: Tavistock.

Bodomo, Adams B. (2010). 'The African Trading Community in Guangzhou, China: An Emerging Bridge for Africa-China Trade Relations', *China Quarterly,* 203: 693–707.

Brah, Avtar (1996). *Cartographies of Diaspora: Contesting Identities.* London: Routledge.

Brown, Jacqueline Nassy (2005). *Dropping Anchor, Setting Sail: Geographies of Race in Black Liverpool.* Princeton: Princeton University Press.

Buckley, Roger Norman (1979). *Slaves in Red Coats: The British West India Regiments, 1795–1815.* New Haven: Yale University Press.

Burrell, Ian (2009). 'Streets Ahead: Dizzee Rascal', *The Independent,* 19 September.

Byrd, Alexander X. (2008). *Captives and Voyagers: Black Migrants Across the Eighteenth-Century British Atlantic World.* Louisiana: Louisiana State University Press.

Cain, P. J. and A. G. Hopkins (2001). *British Imperialism, 1688–2000,* 2nd edn. London: Longman.

'Child Immigration', National Maritime Archives and Library Information Sheet No. 9, National Museums Liverpool, online source: <http://www.diduknow.info/emigrants/media/child_emigration.rtf>, accessed 31 May 2010.

Chinweizu (1975). *The West and the Rest of Us.* New York: Random House.

Christopher, A. J. (2008). 'The Quest for a Census of the British Empire, 1840–1940', *Journal of Historical Geography,* 34.2: 268–85.

Clifford, James (1997). *Routes: Travel and Translation in the Late Twentieth Century.* Cambridge, Mass.: Harvard University Press.

Cohen, Robin (1996). *Global Diasporas: An Introduction.* 2nd edn, 2008. London: Routledge.

Darwin, John (2009). *The Empire Project: The Rise and Fall of the British World System, 1830–1970.* Cambridge: Cambridge University Press.

Dilip Ratha et al. (2011). *Leveraging Migration for Africa: Remittances, Skills, and Investments.* Washington, DC: IBRD/World Bank.

Doortmont, Michel R. (1990). 'The Invention of the Yorubas: Regional Pan-African Nationalism versus Ethnic Provincialism', in P. F. de Moraes Farias and Karin Barber (eds), *Self-Assertion and Brokerage: Early Cultural Nationalism in West Africa.* Birmingham: Centre for West African Studies, 101–8.

Dufoix, Stéphane (2008). *Diasporas*, trans. William Rodamor. Berkeley: University of California Press.

Dyde, Brian (1997). *The Empty Sleeve: The Story of the West India Regiment of the British Army.* London: Hansib Publications.

Echenburg, Myron (1990). *Colonial Conscripts: The Tirailleurs Sénégalais in French West Africa, 1857–1960.* Portsmouth, NH: Heinemann.

Ferguson, Niall (2002). *Empire: The Rise and Demise of the British World Order and the Lessons for Global Power.* New York: Basic Books.

Frost, Diane (1995). 'Racism, Work and Unemployment: West African Seamen in Liverpool, 1880s–1960s', in Diane Frost (ed.), *Ethnic Labor and British Imperial Trade: A History of Ethnic Seafarers in the UK.* London: Frank Cass, 22–33.

Ghai, Dharam P. and Yash P. Ghai (eds) (1970). *Portrait of a Minority: Asians in East Africa.* Nairobi: Oxford University Press.

Gilroy, Paul (1993). *The Black Atlantic: Modernity and Double Consciousness.* Cambridge, Mass.: Harvard University Press.

Hartman, Saidiya (2007). *Lose Your Mother: A Journey Along the Atlantic Slave Route.* New York: Farrar, Strauss and Giroux.

Herskovits, Melville (1941). *The Myth of the Negro Past.* New York: Harper.

Irele, Abiola (2011). *The Negritude Moment: Explorations in Francophone and Caribbean Literature and Thought.* Trenton, NJ: Africa World Press.

Kandel, William A. (2011). 'The U.S. Foreign-Born Population: Trends and Selected Characteristics', CRS Report for Congress, 18 January, online source: <http://www.fas.org/sgp/crs/misc/R41592.pdf>, accessed 21 June 2011.

Kermeliotis, Teo (2011). 'Diaspora Bonds Can Tap into Migrant Wealth, Say Economists', CNN, April 7, online source: <http://edition.cnn.com/2011/BUSINESS/04/07/diaspora.bonds.africa/index.html>, accessed 19 June 2011.

Lentz, Carola and Paul Nugent (2000). *Ethnicity in Ghana: The Limits of Invention.* London: Palgrave Macmillan.

Linebaugh, Peter, and Marcus Rediker (2000). *The Many-Headed Hydra: Sailors, Slaves, Commoners, and the Hidden History of the Revolutionary Atlantic.* Boston: Beacon Press.

Maas, Willem (2003). 'Population and Demographics', in Melvin E. Page (ed.), *Colonialism: An International Social, Cultural, and Political Encyclopedia.* London: ABC-CLIO, 479–81.

Marriott, Ed (2008). 'Dizzee Rascal, Rebel with a Cause', *The Times*, 17 May.

Matory, Lorand J. (2005). *Black Atlantic Religion: Tradition, Transnationalism, and Matriarchy in the Afro-Brazilian Candomblé.* Princeton: Princeton University Press.

Mintz, Sidney and Richard Price (1976). *The Birth of African-American Culture: An Anthropological Perspective.* Philadelphia: Institute for the Study of Human Issues.

Morais, Isabel (2009). '"China Wahala": The Tribulations of Nigerian "Bushfallers" in a Chinese Territory', *Transtext(e)s / Transcultures: Global Journal of Cultural Studies*, 5: 1–22.

Mudimbe, V. Y. (1988). *The Invention of Africa: Gnosis, Philosophy and the Order of Knowledge.* Bloomington and Oxford: Indiana University Press and James Currey.

Olaniyan, Tejumola (2004). *Arrest the Music! Fela and his Rebel Art and Politics.* Bloomington: Indiana University Press.

Olaniyan, Tejumola (2009). 'Thinking Afro-Futures: A Preamble to an Epistemic History', *South Atlantic Quarterly*, 108.3: 449–57.

Peel, J. D. Y. (1989). 'The Cultural Work of Yoruba Ethnogenesis', in Elizabeth Tonkin, Maryon McDonald, and Malcolm Chapman (eds), *History and Ethnicity.* London: Routledge, 198–215.

Peel, J. D. Y. (2000). *Religious Encounter and the Making of the Yoruba*. Bloomington: Indiana University Press.

United States Census Bureau (2000). 'Profile of Selected Demographic and Social Characteristics: 2000, People Born in Africa', online source: <http://www.census.gov/population/cen2000/stp-159/STP-159-africa.pdf>, accessed 21 June 2011.

Quayson, Ato (1997). *Strategic Transformations in Nigerian Writing*. Oxford and Bloomington: James Currey and Indiana University Press.

Quayson, Ato (2009). 'Unthinkable Nigeriana: The Social Imaginary of District 9', JWTC Blog, 16 October, online source: <http://jhbwtc.blogspot.com/2009/10/unthinkable-nigeriana-s ocial-imaginary.html>.

Quayson, Ato (2010). 'Signs of the Times: Discourse Ecologies and Street Life', *City & Society*, 22.1: 77–96.

Ray, Carina (2009). '"The White Wife Problem": Sex, Race and the Contested Politics of Repatriation to Interwar British West Africa', *Gender and History*, 22.3: 628–46.

Rich, Paul (1986). *Race and Empire in British Politics*, 2nd edn. Cambridge: Cambridge University Press.

Roberts, Sam (2005). 'More Africans Enter US Than in the Days of Slavery', *The New York Times*, 21 February.

Rodney, Walter (1972). *How Europe Underdeveloped Africa*. London: Bogle L'Ouverture Publications.

Schleh, Eugene P. A. (1968). 'The Post-War Careers of Ex-Servicemen in Ghana and Uganda', *Journal of Modern African Studies*, 6.2: 203–20.

Seria, Nasreen (2011). 'African Development Bank May Sell Nigeria Diaspora Bonds', *Bloomberg Businessweek*, 4 May, online source: <http://www.businessweek.com/news/2011-05-04/african-development-bank-may-sell-nigeria-diaspora-bonds.html>, accessed 19 June 2011.

Sheffer, Gabriel (2003). *Diaspora Politics*. Cambridge: Cambridge University Press.

Soyinka, Wole (1974 [1965]). *Kongi's Harvest*, in *Collected Plays*, vol. 2. Oxford: Oxford University Press.

Soyinka, Wole (1974 [1971]). *Madmen and Specialists*, in *Collected Plays*, vol. 2. Oxford: Oxford University Press.

Tabili, Laura (1994). *'We Ask for British Justice': Workers and Racial Difference in Late Imperial Britain*. Ithaca: Cornell University Press.

Tinker, H. (1974). *A New System of Slavery: The Export of Indian Labour Overseas 1820–1920*. Oxford: Oxford University Press.

Tölölyan, Khachig (2000). 'Elites and Institutions in the Armenian Transnation', *Diaspora*, 9.1: 107–36.

Torabully, Khal and Marina Carter (2002). *Coolitude: An Anthology of the Indian Labour Diaspora*. London: Anthem Press.

Ukabi, S. C. (1974). 'West Indian Troops and the Defence of British West Africa in the Nineteenth Century', *African Studies Review*, 17.1: 133–50.

Walker, James St G.W. (1992). *The Black Loyalists: The Search for a Promised Land in Nova Scotia and Sierra Leone, 1783–1870*. Toronto: University of Toronto Press. First published in 1976.

Wallerstein, Immanuel (1961). *Africa, the Politics of Independence: An Interpretation of Modern African History*. New York: Vintage Books.

Wright, Richard (1995 [1954]). *Black Power: A Record of Reactions in a Land of Pathos*. New York: HarperPerennial.

CHAPTER 29

....

POSTCOLONIALIZING THE AMERICAS

....

CHARLES FORSDICK

> To put 'postcolonial' theory and 'the Americas' into the same title is imme-
> diately to exacerbate some of the problems that accrue to the very idea of
> postcolonial theory ... 'America' is the spoon I stir with, in order to keep
> the debate fluid.
>
> (Hulme 2008: 389)

> We are struggling to decipher the new formations as they emerge from the
> debris of eroding traditions and worlds.
>
> (Edwards and Gaonkar 2010: 6)

INTRODUCTION: POSTCOLONIALISM AND THE AMERICAS

....

The emergence of postcolonial studies was accompanied, almost from the outset, by a series of assaults on the epistemological assumptions, institutional structures, and geographical frames according to which the field was being built and regulated. Early essays by critics such as Kwame Anthony Appiah (1991), Aijaz Ahmad (1992), and Arif Dirlik (1994) interrogated what they saw as the mismatch between the selected objects of study gathered under the term 'postcolonial' and the analytical apparatus deployed to investigate them. Rapidly anthologized, such critical interventions became part of a core of key, even canonical, postcolonial texts. This process of collection revealed either the enabling capacity of postcolonialism to accommodate a broad range of often apparently opposed and even contradictory critical positions, or its disabling propensity to recuperate and integrate criticism in a process that led to often paralysing degrees of taxonomic anxiety.

With hindsight, over the past decade a clearer institutional history of postcolonial studies has begun to emerge, developed by critics such as David Scott and Graham Huggan, who have unpicked the genealogies of the field, tracked its development through various subfields, and reflected on the possible twenty-first-century futures of postcolonialism as a growing and sustainable critical project (Huggan 2008; Loomba et al. 2005; Scott 1999).

Central to any such institutional history are issues of location, voice, and power, as well as associated questions relating to sites of articulation. Ahmad was one of the first to express a Marxist critique of a postcolonial 'comprador' class, scholars employed predominantly in the United States academy, but often with origins outside North America, whose criticism dominated the field and allowed privileged access to the means of production of critical discourse. A cognate critique, which similarly engages with issues of location, is evident in, for instance, French resistance to postcolonial thought. According to a predominant strand of French critique, postcolonialism is associated with what Pierre Bourdieu and Loïc Wacquant see as the more general 'cunning of imperialist reason' (1999), the imposition of a foreign and even exotic body of thought onto a context for which it is not appropriate and where it is not welcome (Bayart 2010, 2011; for a response, see Young 2011). While such an observation highlights a pitfall evident in (but by no means restricted to) postcolonial studies (i.e. the way in which the elaboration of knowledge unwittingly reflects predominant structures of geopolitical power), it is linked here more specifically to the privileged place of North America in the institutional emergence of that loose body of work federated under the label 'postcolonial studies'. In these terms, postcolonial studies may be understood—despite its initial focus in the works of its key early practitioners on subjects, cases, and phenomena relating to South Asia and the Middle East—as an Atlantic phenomenon, the result of various strands of thought and theory (particularly poststructuralism and anti-colonialism) travelling beyond their points of origin in often unexpected and unpredictable ways, and then emerging in a new form in the Anglophone academy, most notably in the United States. Such a process is to be associated with the more general invention of 'French theory' in North America, particularly evident in the repercussions of key events such as the Johns Hopkins conference in 1966 (van der Poel and Bertho 1999). However, this 'postcolonial turn' reflects at the same time a critique of these wider intellectual developments, revealing their fundamental Eurocentrism, but also illuminating the ways in which key thinkers such as Barthes, Derrida, and Foucault were themselves influenced by the colonial context in which their work developed (Hargreaves 2005; Hiddleston 2009, 2010; Syrotinski 2007).

Outlining this narrative of emergence is certainly not an attempt to deny the existence of those increasingly acknowledged alternative postcolonialisms (and associated sets of concepts and terms) that were evident from an early stage of the postcolonial debate, not least in the work of the subaltern studies collective, intellectuals from Latin America, and also from other groups of scholars and writers such as Édouard Glissant and the *créolistes* in Martinique. The predominant role of the United States in the emergence of postcolonial studies as an institutional and intellectual phenomenon is nevertheless evident, and, as I shall explore below, this association has created a striking sense of resistance to postcolonialism and the critical practices it betokens, most notably in those zones in the

Americas sensitive to the pressures of US neo-imperial power and of the Anglosphere more generally. In Latin America and Quebec in particular, the often lukewarm response to the postcolonial has been linked to unease regarding the historical ambivalence of the term as well as over its applicability to nations and regions whose long-standing, chronologically 'post-colonial' status has been tempered by continued asymmetries of power in the Americas (see the essays by Mignolo and Seed in Part I of this volume).

Although these considerations of location, points of emergence, and more general genealogies of intellectual analysis are essential to the self-critical deployment of any body of thought as unwieldy as postcolonialism, they should not blind readers and critics to an equally important question in the field, epistemological more than chronological, regarding the determination of appropriate objects of study. Huggan (2001) has identified the risk that 'postcolonial' may have become a contemporary synonym of 'exotic', especially if the boundaries of the term's purview are restricted to sites, situations, and phenomena associated with historical colonialism or with its contemporary, neocolonial manifestations. In one of the field's foundational texts, Sartre warned that the Algerian War of Independence related to the decolonization of France as much as it did to that of North Africa (1964: 48), suggesting that the intellectual, political, and cultural resonances of the independence movements of the post-war period were to be seen as global as opposed to localized. The aim of this chapter is to generalize that observation in order to reflect on the implications of postcolonialism for analyses not only of the United States, an area that has already attracted considerable attention and generated heated debate, but also of the wider transnational, hemispheric, and Atlantic frames in which that nation, with the discourse and mythology of its exceptionalism increasingly challenged, is to be placed.

As such, and as my title suggests, the aim of the chapter is to reflect on the ways in which recent, current, and future criticism has sought or should endeavour to seek—in Ato Quayson's terms—to 'postcolonialize' the Americas. For Quayson, 'postcolonializing' entails not a specific theory or practice, but rather the recognition of an analytical process that eschews any implications of 'chronological supersession' and implies instead a 'notion of the term as a process of coming-into-being and a struggle *against* colonialism and its after effects' (2000: 9, emphasis in the original). Such an understanding not only allows acknowledgement of the existence of the chronologically 'post-colonial' within resistance to the colonial itself, but also provides a clear justification of one of the key aspects of the postcolonial project: the search for continuities between often seemingly (and actually) discontinuous sets of circumstances, 'drawing on a notion of the centrality of colonialism for understanding the formation of the contemporary world' (2000: 10). Quayson's aim in such a manoeuvre is not to designate certain situations or phenomena as somehow essentially 'postcolonial', but instead to 'suggest creative ways of viewing a variety of cultural, political and social realities both in the West and elsewhere via a postcolonial prism of interpretation' (2000: 21). He echoes a number of earlier critics when he rejects as 'simplistically chronological' (2000: 10) the claim by Ashcroft, Griffiths, and Tiffin (1989) that the USA may itself be seen as postcolonial because it was at one point part of the British Empire, and focuses additionally on the tensions between such a claim and the persistent status of the independent country as an imperial and imperializing nation state. His response is to suggest an alternative approach, primarily comparative, that permits interrogation of any reductive or singularizing designation of the nation as either 'postcolonial' or 'imperial':

> [L]ooked at in another way, the social and cultural configurations of the United States today do bear comparison with situations in real postcolonial societies. Think of the mutually illuminating comparisons that can be established between sociocultural conditions affecting both majority and minority populations in the United States, South Africa, Australia and Canada. Or consider what insightful work could be achieved if the condition of micro-minority 'tribals' in India were compared not to their aborigine counterparts in Australia, but to the conditions of native Americans in the United States itself, or to that of other micro-minorities in Africa and Latin America. Factors such as multiculturalism, ethnicity, diaspora and transnationalism as they apply in the West can only be fully understood if seen in tandem with the realities of real postcolonial societies, precisely because some of these factors are actually the effects of global population and cultural flows after colonialism. (Quayson 2000: 10–11)

As such, Quayson echoes the suggestion in two significant collections of essays similarly published at the turn of the century (King 2000; Singh and Schmidt 2000) that there is a need to turn a postcolonial gaze onto the United States, not least to challenge the idea that the US serves primarily as the site of production of knowledge that may be dubbed 'postcolonial'. The danger of such a self-fulfilling analysis is that it structures postcolonialism into traditionally concentric patterns of knowledge construction, positing the North American academy as the world-making centre of intellectual capital and replicating in the process structures of colonial power. Quayson evokes instead the potential of a 'postcolonializing' gaze on the United States, and also, as I shall suggest, on the Americas more generally. Such an approach foregrounds the importance of the experience of colonialism, and of its past impact and present effects, for both colonizer and colonized, recognizing that in the Americas, as elsewhere, defining such categories of relative agency is not always clear-cut. At the same time, this method underlines the need for recognition of alternative discourses, either from different communities or articulated in different languages, emphasizing in Harish Trivedi's terms (despite the very different context to which he originally referred) that the postcolonial should not have 'ears only for English' (1999: 272). The chapter will suggest that the comparatism central to an earlier tradition of Inter-American studies may indeed serve a useful purpose in the exploration of such ideas. The ultimate reliance of such a practice on national units, despite a willingness to explore their diversity and even fragmentation, increasingly requires the recognition of new configurations and new narratives in which the national persists, but where it is supplemented by other ways of understanding the interconnections and entanglements inherent in colonial contact and its postcolonial afterlives (see Lazarus in Part III of this volume). The extent of the ideological, theoretical, and analytical refinement that such a process implies merely serves to highlight the ways in which postcolonial studies may yet be in its infancy as an academic field. In Peter Hulme's terms, drawn from one of the epigraphs to this chapter, '"America" is the spoon I stir with, in order to keep the debate fluid' (2008: 389).

Postcolonializing the USA

In *The Empire Writes Back* (1989), rightly seen as one of the first coherent attempts to articulate an intellectual and institutional project that may be identified as postcolonialism, Bill Ashcroft, Gareth Griffiths, and Helen Tiffin make a clear case for the inclusion of the United States in the purview of the field whose early contours they go on to outline. In light of the catholic understanding of the 'postcolonial' around which their analyses are built—'We use the term post-colonial, however, to cover all the culture affected by the imperial process from the moment of colonization to the present day' (1989: 2)—there is an opening attempt to federate a range of very different traditions of cultural production under the umbrella term:

> [T]he literatures of African countries, Australia, Bangladesh, Canada, Caribbean countries, India, Malaysia, Malta, New Zealand, Pakistan, Singapore, South Pacific Island countries, and Sri Lanka are all post-colonial literatures. The literature of the USA should also be placed in this category. Perhaps because of its current position of power, and the neo-colonizing role it has played, its post-colonial nature has not been generally recognized. But its relationship with the metropolitan centre as it evolved over the last two centuries has been paradigmatic for post-colonial literatures everywhere. What each of these literatures has in common beyond their special and distinctive regional characteristics is that they emerged in their present form out of the experience of colonization and asserted themselves by foregrounding the tension with the imperial power, and by emphasizing their differences from the assumptions of the imperial centre. It is this which makes them distinctively post-colonial. (1989: 2)

Central to the volume as it develops is an exploration of the distinction between the 'settler' and the 'settled' colony, and although the authors acknowledge the very different processes associated with the emergence of literary production in each of these broadly defined historical situations, they nevertheless present the US as 'the first post-colonial society to develop a "national" literature', and go on to grant this body of material a foundational status: 'In many ways the American experience and its attempts to produce a new kind of literature can be seen to be the model for all later post-colonial writing' (1989: 16). This conclusion is based not least on the attempt of US literary texts 'to constitute a literature separate from that of the metropolitan centre' (1989: 133). Setting out a postcolonial model that Peter Barry has subsequently and succinctly described as 'adopt, adapt, adept' (1995: 196), Ashcroft, Griffiths, and Tiffin go on to describe the emergence of US literature according to a staged process of imitation, progressive rejection, and eventual autonomy:

> Like early American tourists, American writers and critics at first had to choose the 'European model' of literary history, interpreting their concern with their own literature as a sign of 'immaturity', and this model has been successively applied since to other post-colonial literatures. Post-colonial literatures would apparently demonstrate their maturity when they stopped talking about themselves and got on with more 'universal' (i.e. European) concerns. The radically subversive questions

raised for British literature and European philosophy by, for instance, Melville's *Moby Dick* or Hawthorne's *The Scarlet Letter*, and later by Joseph Furphy's *Such Is Life* or G. V. Desani's *All About H. Hatterr*, went largely unrecognized. (1989: 138)

In such an analysis, the addition of postcolonial concerns to debates where, in the 1980s, postmodernism and poststructuralism tended to predominate, seemed to offer a new context of clarity and specificity to understandings of the subversive tendencies in US literature: 'Whilst the recent American critical models have been profoundly influenced by Europe, with Derridaian and Foucaultian theories being whole-heartedly adopted by American critics, the Americans are now beginning to recognize that their own post-coloniality had already provided the ground for similarly subversive views of language and culture' (1989: 163). In a clear case of a historically postcolonial nation that—like Brazil in the Lusophone world and unlike any cases in the French-speaking world—had, through the reversal of power structures, rapidly outstripped in size and influence its original colonizers, the USA had ceased to view its relationship with Britain in terms of imperial legacies, a tendency particularly apparent in the aftermath of the Second World War. The authors of *The Empire Writes Back* countered this tendency and suggested that '[a]n acceptance of post-coloniality as part of the American formation is then no longer a badge of shame or of immaturity, but a sign of distinction and difference, a difference which has been potent in American culture as a creative force' (1989: 163).

As the above discussion of Quayson's work makes clear, the reaction to the mooted integration of the USA into a postcolonial frame was robust, both in the emerging field of postcolonial studies itself and in that of American studies. Ashcroft, Griffiths, and Tiffin had been careful, despite their attempt to grant the US a foundational status in discussions of postcoloniality, to avoid the ahistorical singularization of understandings of the 'postcolonial', a tendency arguably evident in, for instance, the work of Lawrence Buell on the 'marks of postcolonialism in American Renaissance writing' (1992: 427; Buell responded to his critics in a revised version in 2000). Although Ashcroft, Griffiths, and Tiffin did their best to distinguish between often very different imperial processes and postcolonial formations, the risk of apparent equivalence remained, and the response to them was a firm rejection of claims to any US postcoloniality that might be equated with that condition as it manifested itself in other formerly colonized regions and countries. Anne McClintock, for example, linked such identification to protests against the Columbus quincentenary: 'By what fiat of historical amnesia can the United States of America, in particular, qualify as "postcolonial"—a term which can only be a monumental affront to the Native American peoples currently opposing the confetti triumphalism of 1992' (1992: 87; see also Mignolo in Part I of this volume). To such critics, particularly unsavoury in such an intimation was the apparent sleight of hand according to which the designation of the US as itself 'postcolonial' might be seen to lessen the nation's status as an imperial power in its own right, not least because the regularly cited and resilient exceptionalism of the American experience was often seen as antithetical to the experience of imperialism in US history. Such a manoeuvre may indeed be seen to perpetuate a state of denial regarding the US historical past, and to forget that its contemporary world role had already been critiqued over fifty years ago in the revisionist historiography of scholars such as William Appleman Williams, whose work on the euphemistic rhetoric of the US as a 'World Power' revealed the underlying mechanisms of neo-imperialist expansion and control (see also Part II of this volume).

Building on such traditions, I would suggest that postcolonializing the US itself, a key driver within as well as an integral part of a wider process of postcolonializing the Americas, involves the search for approaches to history and culture that avoid the tendency to 'colonize postcolonial theory by implicitly positing the United States as the original postcolonial nation' (Kaplan 1993: 21) while at the same time rejecting any trap of persistent exceptionalism that seeks to deny the importance of a postcolonial engagement by stating 'that colonialism had little or nothing to do with the formation of the U.S. national identity and that the study of U.S. culture will not affect their understanding of postcoloniality' (Pease 2000: 208). Despite the inclusive approach of *The Empire Writes Back*, it is the latter stance that has predominated, tacitly accepting what C. Richard King, in his 2000 collection *Post-colonial America*, calls 'the public, popular and professional assumptions that (1) colonialism has never occurred within the United States; (2) imperialism and its aftermath have had little or nothing to do with the formation of distinctly American identities, institutions, and idioms; and (3) postcoloniality cannot refer to American culture' (2000: 3).

Postcolonial studies was for a period wholly unsuited to such a task, for it regularly tended to forget the neo-imperial niche, characterized by the displacement of European hegemony with that of the US, in which it emerged as an intellectual practice. It often also celebrated as liberatingly post-national such contemporary phenomena as globalization, transnationalism, and cultural hybridity without acknowledging the ways in which these phenomena reflect the continuation of asymmetries of power traditionally associated with historical imperialism (Behdad 2005). The challenge for scholars and readers today is to avoid the taxonomic dilemma that scholars such as Gesa Mackenthun have identified: 'Compared to recently decolonized states in Africa or India, the United States of course cannot be called "postcolonial" in any easy sense' (1996: 264), and to seek instead an approach that builds on Peter Hulme's insight, in his important 1995 essay-manifesto, 'Including America':

> [T]he adjective [postcolonial] implies nothing about a postcolonial country's behaviour. As a postcolonial nation, the United States continued to colonize North America, completing the genocide of the Native population begun by the Spanish and British ... [A] country can be postcolonial and colonizing at the same time. (1995: 122)

Solutions have been identified at the interface of postcolonialism with other fields, most notably American studies where a number of significant interventions regarding these interdisciplinary connections have appeared over the past two decades (Hulme 1995; Mackenthun 1996; Schueller and Watts 2003; Schueller 2004). This work has addressed the three areas of silence or even denial identified by Amy Kaplan in the seminal essay on the occlusion of empire in the study of American culture that introduces the volume of essays on *Cultures of United States Imperialism* that she co-edited with Donald E. Pease: 'the absence of culture from the study of U.S. imperialism; the absence of empire from the study of American culture; and the absence of the United States from the postcolonial study of imperialism' (1993: 11). Such debates are in part disciplinary, and relate to the nature and evolution of (North) American studies as a field of enquiry (related intimately and perhaps even inextricably to the nation state that serves as its object of enquiry, the USA). As Amy Kaplan notes, the implications of the imperial elements of one of the foundational narratives of the field—Perry Miller's attempt, in the preface to his *Errand into the Wilderness* (1956), to locate the epiphanic emergence, in the Congo that he visited in the 1920s, of a modern American studies, rooted in a notion of exceptionalism and based on a clear distance between the US and colonized regions such as sub-Saharan Africa—are yet to be fully explored (1993: 5). For Kaplan, Miller fails to recognize, in his immediate context, the post-war US expansionism into West Africa, relating in particular to the extraction of essential minerals in the Congo; he contributes as a result to 'the unacknowledged interdependence of the United States and European colonialism' (1993: 8). These are the very aspects of the American experience that compete with and challenge the story of Puritan origins that Miller had outlined and dismissed as the 'warp and woof' (1956: viii) of American history, brusquely summarized by Kaplan as 'European colonization, slavery, westward expansion, overseas intervention, and cold war nuclear power' (1993: 4).

Postcolonializing the USA directs critical attention towards the country's status, both past and present, as an imperial nation state; at the same time, it illuminates 'the narratives, discourses, and myths that center the formation of America as an imagined community and nation' (King 2000: 5). There is still a need to focus on internal issues within a national frame: after all, the US emerged from a process of colonial conflict and engagement, and while its independence may have marked an end to external colonialism, it is to be associated with those forms of internal colonialism that are inherent in the institution of slavery as well as in the silencing of indigenous histories and cultures. As scholars such as Robert Rydell (1984) have illustrated, it is not possible to understand key events in modern US history, such as the great expositions of the later nineteenth and early twentieth century, without acknowledging the place of imperialism, and the interconnections between nation-building and the wider, global colonial project in relation to which—through outlandish phenomena such as 'human zoos' (Blanchard et al. 2008)—notions of race were constructed. Such an approach also highlights the need for renewed study and continued historicization of counter-discourses such as Black Power and the Chicano movement and the oppositional practices related to them such as the civil rights movement and Native American activism.

The key question in such approaches is not, however, whether the United States may be designated 'postcolonial' in a sense that associates that term with countries and cultures emerging from post-war decolonization, but rather what happens to our understandings of the country—and, I would add, of the term 'postcolonial' itself—when the US is approached postcolonially, with that adverb encompassing the variety of analyses that the term implies. Such critical manoeuvres are not possible without an acknowledgement of the equally important need to look beyond the nation state, often relating the diverse fragments of dynamic and contested national identity to other external points of origin, and engaging in a process whereby one nation, despite its apparent power, is progressively relativized and even provincialized as it is pulled into different networks of relating. Hulme concludes that:

> [T]he field of postcolonial studies *needs* to find a place for America.... At the moment, the United States has a role as the world's leading imperialist power; the Caribbean is home to a rich tradition of postcolonial theory—Fanon, James, Glissant, Lamming, Fernández Retamar; Latin America is still trying to come to terms with postmodernity; and Canada—as usual—is overlooked. (Hulme 1995: 209; emphasis in the original).

For Hulme, there is no need to denounce the reduction of 'America' to the US; he uses the term automatically in a continental sense (i.e. inclusively, hemispherically, and multilingually), and implies in this outlining of an intellectual project a set of concerns that are yet to be fully understood. The results are twofold: on the one hand, the United States is provided 'with a nineteenth- and twentieth-century imperial and colonial history that helps in the understanding of its current stance within the world' (1995: 120; see also Hulme 2008); on the other, the nation no longer represents a sufficient unit on which to base a postcolonial approach to the Americas—in the case of the US, there is a need to look not just to the east, transatlantically, and to the west, transpacifically, but also to the north and the south. A useful starting point in such an investigation is to focus on two very different zones in the study of which the integration of postcolonialism has been illuminatingly problematic: Quebec, and Latin and Central America, and to consider the ways in which the integration of these into a frame that is both hemispheric and postcolonial contributes to the ongoing project of postcolonializing the Americas.

Exploring the French Atlantic: Postcolonial Quebec

The concept of a postcolonial America restricted to the national boundaries is challenged and disrupted by alternative hemispheric, transnational, transcontinental, and Atlanticist models that stress the permeability and even redundancy of national frames. Reflecting on an American studies that places transnational considerations at its core, Shelley Fisher Fishkin highlights the place of Quebec in such considerations: 'French, of course, is to the northern border of the United States what Spanish is to our southern one; both the Quebeçois [sic] and New England economy and culture have been shaped by the cross-border transits of French-speaking Canadian workers' (2005: 28). Bill Marshall, in his explorations of the French Atlantic (2005, 2009), has sought to supplement the already coloured models of the Ocean—most notably black and red (Gilroy 1993; Rediker 2003)—with a challenge to the Anglophone emphases on which these understandings tend to rely; his acknowledgement of a specifically 'French' Atlantic, defined in terms of what he classes as a 'diasporic Frenchness', rejects the linguistic over-determination of Francophonia (as a political or cultural model) and gestures instead towards what may be seen as an Atlantic 'Francosphere', a designation that 'privileges the spatial over the linguistic in an attempt to widen the range of experiences and influences included under its umbrella' (Dutton 2011: 7). The postcolonial implications of such an approach are evident, for this model foregrounds multiple questions regarding the nature of postcoloniality, and depends on recognition of the afterlives of colonial desire, contact, and loss in ways that permit the exploration of contemporary asymmetries of power and influence. Central to such an analysis, for reasons to be discussed below, remains Haiti, not least because—despite the pitfalls of conjectural history—it is evident that had Haitian independence not been won and the Louisiana purchase not become inevitable (Dubois 2009), then the political, linguistic, and cultural constitution of North America might have been fundamentally different. At the same time, such an observation historicizes contemporary discussions of the fragility of English as the first language of the USA, and may be seen to provide evidence for an additional criticism of a number of early key works of postcolonialism: their inherent monolingualism. Mary Louise Pratt has gone so far as to claim that the 'failure of metropolitan scholars to learn Spanish or Portuguese is … a symptom of the neo-colonial dimensions of the postcolonial project' (2008: 462), and this is a critique directed equally at American studies (Wai Chee Dimock 2006), a field in which US literature has often been presented in terms of a predominantly and self-sufficiently English-language canon.

Although the scope of Marshall's work is transatlantic and hemispheric, linking Nantes and Cayenne as well as St Pierre and Miquelon and Uruguay, privileged in his analysis is Quebec, the relation of which to studies of postcolonialism remains as ambiguous as it is illuminating. Mary Jean Green describes the challenges of 'locating Quebec on the postcolonial map' (2009), noting that although US scholars with an interest in Québécois literary and cultural production had been keen to deploy postcolonial analyses, in French Canada itself such a manoeuvre had been met with a suspicion similar to that in France itself regarding the perceived hegemony of Anglophone critical practices. Réjean Beaudoin, for instance, claims that 'putting [Quebec] in the postcolonial ragbag is a desperate attempt to normalise it' (cited in Gauvin 2007: 433). Vincent Desroches, in a special issue of *Quebec Studies* (2003), was the first to offer a sustained reflection on the ways in which Quebec may be understood as 'postcolonial' in historical terms as well as in relation to the oppositionality created by the voices permitted articulation in its literature (see also Gauvin 2007; Killick 2006). As Green notes (2009: 249), the identification of postcolonial debates in the context of Quebec may be tracked back to the 1960s, when the Tunisian writer Albert Memmi visited French Canada, and described the culture he discovered and the people with whom he interacted as 'dominés' (significantly not 'colonisés') by the majority Anglo-American culture of Canada (as well as by the persistent soft power of France, of which Quebec remained a settler colony into the twentieth century, and the proximity of the USA). He identified the power relationship evident in the 'colonial diglossia' and recourse to traditional phenomena such as Catholicism that he encountered (Green 2009; see also Randall 2003: 77). Moreover, political thought and literary activity associated with the 'Quiet Revolution' was regularly inspired by a globalized Francophone solidarity that drew on the models of the Algerian War of Independence as well as anti-colonial debates in the Caribbean.

It is not insignificant that Memmi, his own identity as a member of the Tunisian Jewish community rendering more complex the binaries he identified, had been drawn to the comparative situation in Quebec. In a pioneering article on such 1960s responses to the Patriots' Rebellion of 1837–8, Marilyn Randall highlights the ambiguities inherent in such processes of political and cultural definition, noting that the French in Canada have 'been at times united against a common enemy and at others divided among themselves' and outlining the 'confusing range of subject positions' in which this situation has resulted: 'colonizer and colonized; victim and political partner; collaborator in their own oppression and active rebel' (2003: 86–7). The French Canadian experience lends itself to analysis in the light of what Kate Marsh, in the context of the French in India, has called the 'subaltern colonizer' (Marsh 2007). The community that would eventually identify itself as Québécois was reduced to minority status after the imposition of British rule in 1763, and responded to colonial domination through periodic rebellion and a firm resistance rooted in the protection of values relating to the pre-conquest period (bound up with an ideology dubbed *survivance*). The decolonization evident in Quebec culture in the 1960s was accordingly double: a resistance to Anglophone assimilation, but also an attempt to challenge the asphyxiating effects of an adherence to traditional cultural values. At the same time, Québécois postcoloniality encompasses minority Francophone populations within Canada, most notably the Acadian communities of Nova Scotia and New Brunswick, and in Quebec's own diasporic communities, especially isolated in Manitoba, Saskatchewan, and Alberta; it also focuses on the at times troubled relationship of the original French settlers to the indigenous populations (the Inuit and Indian nations) they encountered.

What is striking is the way in which, once Quebec began to move beyond this emphasis—now perceived as being increasingly outdated—on a colonized status, an alternative postcoloniality has emerged, associated with the now well-established communities of migrant origin, most notably Haitian and Chinese, whose impact on Francophone literary production is progressively evident. Authors such as Ying Chen, Marie-Célie Agnant, and Dany Laferrière have developed, often from the multilingual and translational context of Montreal (Simon 2006), distinctive voices that partake in Quebec's own identity debates whilst—especially in the case of Laferrière—engaging with the wider frame of the Americas. The debates in the 1960s about the status of Québécois literature as a form of national literary production have given way in the thinking of some intellectuals to more explicitly transnational understandings, not least in the concept of a representative *américanité*, presented most notably by novelist Noël Audet, who identifies in Quebec a hybrid, Francophone community where Native Americans, the French,

POSTCOLONIALIZING THE AMERICAS   659

the British, and those who have arrived through more recent processes of migration 'all intimately and inextricably unite to create a distinct and distinctive North American cultural identity' (Killick 2006: 186). Audet also highlights the strategic advantages of Quebec's ex-centric location, both linguistic and geographical, 'semi-attached participant and semi-detached observer on the northern fringe of American (US) empire' (Killick 2006: 186). The emergence of a postcolonial perspective on Quebec—and on French-speaking Canada more generally—has accordingly forced recognition of the multidirectional nature of a postcolonial understanding of the Americas. It has not least revealed the ways in which the hemispheric underpinnings of such approaches are less focused on 'simply replacing nationalist essentialism predicated upon state autonomy with a geographical essentialism predicated on physical contiguity' (Giles 2006: 649–50), and are more concerned with multiple axes and alternative connections that 'dislocate the United States from the center of the hemisphere's academic purview' (McClennan 2005: 394). What such approaches reveal are the afterlives of colonial histories and the persistent efforts to acknowledge and renegotiate these in the present.

POSTCOLONIALISM AND NEOLIBERALISM: LATIN AMERICA AND THE CARIBBEAN

Just as Quebec provides a model to the north of the US the history, location, and culture of which are very different, while also drawing the US into a set of questions about language and influence, so a postcolonial engagement with Latin and Central America similarly draws the US into comparative and increasingly hemispheric debates about imperialism (encompassing its historical legacies and contemporary manifestations). It is significant to note at this stage that one of the major shifts in (North) American studies—and a key element in the field's postcolonialization—has been the emergence of Chicano/a studies, a clear instance of alliance between political praxis and theoretical investigation, as a substantial area in its own right (see Part III of this volume). Displacing the key concept of the 'Frontier', an often reductively understood site of binary relationships relating to expansion and conquest, Chicano studies began in the 1980s, with work by pioneering scholars such as Gloria Anzaldúa (1987), to explore contested sites at the limits of, as well as often firmly within, the nation state: 'borderlands, crossroads, and contact zones that disrupt celebratory nationalist narratives' (Fishkin 2005: 19). Drawing on concepts such as the 'contact zone' (Pratt 1992), such approaches build on the implication that colonial contact and its postcolonial afterlives generate unpredictably new and hybrid cultures. New emphases are accordingly permitted (e.g. on ethnicity, immigration, and other phenomena to which postcoloniality is integral), foregrounding questions of empire and its contemporary manifestations, and challenging in the process centripetal, self-sufficient, and even essentialist notions of national identity.

Caroline Levander and Robert Levine describe the privileged role of Latin American studies in 'crossing ... national and disciplinary boundaries and creating research fields that were organized around rubrics other than the nation' (2008: 6), but the resistance to engagement with postcolonial debates in the area has been marked (Coronil 2008). Early critical confrontations, expressed by scholars such as J. Jorge Klor de Alva (1992; revised 1995) rehearsed arguments evident in and about other regions and zones, stating the inappropriateness of using 'tools and categories of analysis developed in the twentieth century for understanding British colonialism, especially in India and Africa, to make sense of the experiences of sixteenth to eighteenth century Latin America' (1992: 264) and seeing such a critical practice as a form of intellectual recolonization. Along these lines, Walter Mignolo similarly proposed the foundations of a 'decolonial' knowledge that was multiple, multilingual, and decentred, seeking to use postcolonialism as a productive space in which to engage with 'vernacular' intellectual traditions that reveal the epistemological assumptions of a postcolonial critique as it had been elaborated in different locations for the analysis of very different subjects (Mignolo 1993; see also Mignolo in Part I of this volume). The integration of the colonial history—the 'coloniality' (Moraña, Dussel, and Jáuregui 2008)—of Latin America similarly extends the genealogies of contact, conquest, and resistance originally understood in the postcolonial field, and invites reflection on relationships not only with European powers (most notably Britain, France, Spain, and Portugal), but also, from the late nineteenth century onwards, with the US. For Fernando Coronil, these are debates not about 'Latin American postcolonial studies' but about 'postcolonial studies in the Americas' (2008: 397), and this widening of frame allows him to imagine an expansion of postcolonial studies more generally:

> Capitalism and modernity, so often assumed both in mainstream and in postcolonial studies to be a European process marked by the Enlightenment, the dawning of industrialization, and the forging of nations in the eighteenth century, can be seen instead as a global process involving the expansion of Christendom, the formation of a global market, and the creation of transcontinental empires since the sixteenth century. A dialogue between Latin American and postcolonial studies ought not to be polarizing, and might range over local histories and global designs, texts and their material contexts, and subjective formations and structures of domination. (2008: 415)

Alternative models have emerged, a number of which I have alluded to above, including most notably an emphasis on hemispheric and transnational approaches in which nations persist as units, but with their importance progressively relativized or even provincialized; at the same time, as has also been signalled above, there has been growing attention paid to the importance of borderlands and to the study of external connections and internal reconfigurations that these imply. These developments are evident not only in the field of Chicano/a studies, but also more generally in an increasingly expanding Atlantic studies paradigm, moving beyond its traditional North Atlantic axis, and encompassing interconnections, collisions, and flows between peoples and cultures in Europe, Africa, and North and Latin America. They are also apparent in the emergence of a growing academic interest in the Pacific Rim, a field that has itself undergone a process of intellectual decolonization (Thaman 2003). Meanwhile, there has been a rapid transformation in the subjects of study, most notably with the recognition of the importance of African American literature, culture, and history, but also with the wider acknowledgement of multiculturalism and diasporas as phenomena and experiences that undermine earlier emphases on the vectors of immigration and emigration and the narratives of assimilation to which these lent themselves. Central to such developments, as the discussion above has already made clear, has been a reinterrogation of the place of the nation as a structuring category—what Edwards and Gaonkar dub 'an anxious vacillation between expanding and rejecting the national frame for organizing American literary studies' (2010: 11). Levander and Levine identify 'the complex ruptures that remain within but nonetheless constitute the national frame, while at the same time moving beyond the national frame to consider regions, areas, and diasporan affiliations that exist apart from or in conflicted relation to the nation' (2008: 2).

If there is a place—and an associated set of ideas (Nesbitt 2009)—that may be seen as central in such understandings of the Americas, both historical and contemporary, it is Haiti. The critique central to postcolonial studies has often been elaborated from specific sites and zones, most notably in its preliminary stages from the Indian subcontinent. Whilst the universalization of such paradigms is a hazardous process, the privileging of Haiti in a hemispheric American context is linked to its foundational status in understandings of postcoloniality:

> Two of the processes that came to distinguish the twentieth century were invented in Haiti: decolonization and neocolonialism. Haiti was the first to demonstrate that the colonized can take hold of their own historical destiny and enter the stage of world history as autonomous actors, and not merely passive, enslaved subjects. Less happily, newly independent Haiti also demonstrated to the world the first instance of what would later be called neocolonialism, as ruling elites (both mulatto and black) united with the military and merchant class to create an instable balance of power. (Nesbitt 2005: 6)

In one of first comprehensive studies of Haiti and the US, Ludwell Montague described the close entanglements that linked the two countries, but highlighted also the persistent ignorance by which these were often obscured: 'Although Haitian history has been closely related to that of the United States for more than two centuries, to the American mind Haiti remains a land of foreboding and mystery—*terra incognita*' (Montague 1940: 4). Saint-Domingue was the American colonies' main trading partner. John Adams commented in 1783: 'We are necessary to them, and they are to us' (quoted in Sepinwall 2009: 319), and this interdependence has persisted and continues to persist, often in radically different and refracted forms, across the intervening two centuries.

To this end, Robin Blackburn claims that '[t]he Haitian Revolution is rarely given its due, yet without it there is much that cannot be accounted for' (2006: 643; see also the General Introduction to this volume). The study of this event and its unfinished afterlives has major implications—multifocal, multidirectional, and multidimensional—for postcolonial studies and the Americas, and necessitates approaches that are transhistorical, translingual, and transcultural (see Keown and Murray in this section of the volume). The geopolitical reality of the divided island of Hispaniola is itself a concrete meeting place of the French and Iberian Atlantics, and a reminder of the tendency of history and culture to spill beyond accounts that attempt to restrict them to the national. The chaotic series of events subsequently tidied up under the name of the 'Haitian Revolution' involved combinations of French, Spanish, and British troops struggling, within the sphere of influence of the newly independent and still expanding USA, against ever-shifting alliances of black slaves and free coloured rebels (Dubois 2004); the independence struggle triggered the mass displacement of peoples, many of whom, both enslaved people and their owners, left Saint-Domingue and Santo Domingo for Cuba, Venezuela, Colombia, and Puerto Rico (Geggus 2001). As the limitations of disciplinary fields mapped closely onto the boundaries of the nation state become increasingly clear, the study of Haiti, its revolution, and its revolutionary afterlives provides a definitional case study. The aim is not to expose a further instrumentalization of Haiti in postcolonial studies, although there is a need to be acutely aware of the risks of such 'uses' (Farmer 1994). The intention is to suggest instead the ways in which the study of Haiti reveals the extent to which postcolonial accounts of history and culture are only ever partial if they restrict themselves to the national or monolingual. The recent foregrounding of Haiti in postcolonial studies epitomizes a shift in our objects of study, traditionally—especially at the outset—linked to nation states, but now increasingly post-national, transnational, and diasporic (see Quayson in this section of the volume).

In their introduction to an influential collection of essays on hemispheric American studies, it is significant that one of the figures privileged by the editors in the opening pages is Frederick Douglass, analysed as an example of an author relegated in the 1973 anthology, *American Literature: The Makers and the Making*, to the oxymoronic category of 'Literature of the Nonliterary World', a taxonomy in which non-literariness was accompanied by an apparent 'non-national' status since most of the authors included were African American or Native American (Levander and Levine 2008: 1–2). The editors foreground Douglass's fascination with Haiti, a republic to which he considered emigration and where he served as US minister-resident and consul general from 1889 to 1891, following which the Haitian government appointed him its commissioner to the Chicago World's Columbian Exposition of 1893. Discussing Douglass's role at the fair, Levander and Levine suggest that, through engagement with Haiti in his speeches and other interventions, he was already operating in a hemispheric frame, deploying 'his keen interest in the interconnections among nations, peoples, institutions and intellectual and political movements in the larger context of the American hemisphere' (2008: 2). Douglass's aim was to question a commemorative event whose role as a tool of nation-building and roadmap for the American society in the coming century cannot be underestimated:

> Douglass's very interest in those interconnections, as disruptive as such thinking may have been to his U.S. nationalism, helped him to see the nation's potential and limitations within a fuller history of race in the Americas. For Douglass, to move beyond the nation was not to abandon it but instead, through an engagement with overlapping histories and geographies, to better understand it. At the Columbian Exposition, Douglass holds up a Haitian black republican mirror to Chicago's White City of 1893 in order to represent the larger inconsistencies underpinning late nineteenth-century U.S. racialized nationalism. (2008: 2)

The implications of Haiti to a postcolonial approach to the Americas are perhaps disproportionate to its size and population, but they remain wholly proportional to the world-historical significance of its revolution and of the wider impact of its subsequent independence. Michel-Rolph Trouillot (1995) has described, in what has become a key work of postcolonial historiography, the systematic silencing of Haiti in accounts of Atlantic history (and most notably in the narratives of the American and French Revolutions, and their international impacts, with which these are closely associated). Such a process ignores the historical processes that saw, for instance, images of the Haitian revolutionaries serving as one of the triggers of the Aponte Rebellion in Cuba in 1812 (Childs 2006). Aponte's sketch of Toussaint Louverture, supposedly based on an image brought to the island by Spanish-allied Saint-Domingue troops forced to leave Fort-Dauphin in 1795, is one of those material artefacts emblematic of the translingual, transcultural circulations of objects and ideas emergent of Atlantic cultures, as well as the perpetuation of their challenge to modernity; with slavery reimposed in the French Caribbean, key figures such as Toussaint became an exemplum in abolitionist debates and in their literary manifestations, most notably in North America, and this representational tradition continues throughout the twentieth century, reaching a clear point of intensity in the 1930s in the Harlem Renaissance and its immediate aftermath (Jackson 2008).

The impact of the Haitian Revolution in nineteenth-century North America was considerable, and is evident in particular in the inspiration it provided in US abolitionist debates and the Civil War as proof of a 'terrifying alternative universe' or of a 'flicker of inspiration and hope' (Sepinwall 2009: 317). Alfred N. Hunt has studied the ambivalent afterlives of the revolution and its role in strengthening the institutions of slavery as the idea of progressive emancipation emerged (Hunt 1988; see also White 2004). More recent studies have further illuminated this context, shifting the emphasis from the place of Haiti in white (anti-)abolitionist discourse to its role in the agency of the enslaved (Clavin 2010). The persistence of the revolution in the period following the Civil War and abolition is striking, not least in the processes whereby it has been commemorated, represented, and put to a variety of political purposes by African Americans. The revolution has operated as 'a vehicle through which collective memory and identity has been created and transformed and [as] an event that has inspired and influenced black nationalism, abolitionism, black socialist and revolutionary thought, and Pan Africanism' (Jackson and Bacon 2010: 2), and may as such be seen as a central force in understandings of the Americas that are at once hemispheric and postcolonial.

A particular moment of intensity in such processes was the US occupation (1915–34) and its immediate aftermath, a period that saw a rising prominence of African American responses to Haiti, especially in the work of Langston Hughes. In his poem 'Always the Same', Hughes calls for solidarity connecting a range of sites, including 'the coffee hills of Haiti' and 'the streets of Harlem' (1994: 165). He accordingly encapsulates the types of connections central to this chapter. Haiti played a key role in what Mary Renda, in her study of the US occupation, calls the desire to 'remake race' in North America (2001: 263). Renda describes the ways in which Haitian history and culture were deployed to 'challenge hegemonic conceptions of "America"' and to elaborate 'new discourses on

American national identity' (2001: 288): processes which, in light of the presence of a growing diasporic community in North America and of US and Canadian intervention in Haiti over the past decade (Hallward 2007), continue today.

CONCLUSION

The emergence and evolution of the postcolonial debates on which this chapter has focused coincided with a series of major political shifts that marked the final decades of the twentieth century and the opening ones of the twenty-first: the collapse of the Eastern bloc and the end of the Cold War, as well as the first and second Gulf Wars, the US intervention in Afghanistan, and the Haitian earthquake of January 2010. It might be argued that the most significant historical context for these contemporary events was provided by the ideological, intellectual, and historiographic controversies surrounding the Columbus Quincentenary in 1992, a date now remembered less for the commemorations originally envisaged than for widespread protests against celebration of an event associated with conquest, colonization, and environmental exploitation throughout the Americas (Summerhill and Williams 2000). Donald E. Pease creates a link between these geopolitical shifts and the commemorative processes that served as its wider cultural context: 'clashes over the celebration of the Discovery made visible an absent imperial history that the Gulf War, in its renewal of an imperial synthesis, threatened again to eclipse' (1993: 22). In the same volume, Amy Kaplan unpacks the shifting focus and rhetorical justifications of a US exceptionalism that presents itself as essentially anti-imperialist, in contrast to an evolving series of opponents—the Old World, the Eastern bloc, fascism, Iraq, radical Islam—whose objectives, despite their differing historical moments and political contexts, are associated with the threat of empire construction (1993: 12–13). In the yoking of postcolonialism to such questions she sees mutual benefits to our understandings of the US, but also to the nuancing and even reactivation of the postcolonial project:

> The history of American imperialism strains the definition of the postcolonial, which implies a temporal development (from 'colonial' to 'post') that relies heavily on the spatial coordinates of European empires, in their formal acquisition of territories and the subsequent history of decolonization and national independence. (Kaplan 1993: 17)

Such definitional 'straining' reveals the need to avoid any teleological view of intellectual history, reliant on the ultimate disorientation inherent in a series of 'turns', that suggests, for instance, that a postcolonial focus was subsequently replaced by transnational and diaspora studies, which themselves yielded to a contemporary focus on the global (see the General Introduction to this volume). Postcolonialism is not to be seen as a time-ended intellectual moment, but rather as a persistent project or (to return to Quayson's term) a 'process' that may be seen to underpin any approach to transnationalism, diasporization, and globalization as well as, most significantly, the persistent asymmetries of the power with which all these are associated (Lazarus 2006). The function of a postcolonial critique is to underline the historical role of empire in the understandings of such phenomena, as well as the complex persistence of empire's afterlives in their contemporary functioning.

REFERENCES

Ahmad, Aijaz (1992). *In Theory: Classes, Nations, Literatures*. London: Verso.

Anzaldúa, Gloria (1987). *Borderlands/La Frontera: The New Mestiza*. San Francisco: Spinsters/ Aunt Lute.

Appiah, Kwame Anthony (1991). 'Is the Post- in Postmodernism the Post- in Postcolonial?', *Critical Inquiry*, 17.2: 336–57.

Ashcroft, Bill, Gareth Griffiths, and Helen Tiffin (1989). *The Empire Writes Back: Theory and Practice in Post-Colonial Literatures*. London: Routledge.

Barry, Peter (1995). *Beginning Theory: An Introduction to Literary and Cultural Theory*. Manchester: Manchester University Press.

Bayart, Jean-François (2010). *Les Études postcoloniales: un carnaval académique*. Paris: Karthala.

Bayart, Jean-François (2011). 'Postcolonial Studies: A Political Invention of Tradition?', *Public Culture*, 23.1: 55–84.

Behdad, Ali (2005). *A Forgetful Nation: On Immigration and Cultural Identity in the United States*. Durham, NC: Duke University Press.

Blackburn, Robin (2006). 'Haiti, Slavery and the Age of Democratic Revolution', *William and Mary Quarterly*, 63.4: 633–44.

Blanchard, Pascal, Nicolas Bancel, Gilles Boetsch, Eric Deroo, Sandrine Lemaire, and Charles Forsdick (eds) (2008). *Human Zoos: Science and Spectacle in the Age of Colonial Empire*. Liverpool: Liverpool University Press.

Bourdieu, Pierre, and Loïc Wacquant (1999). 'On the Cunning of Imperialist Reason', *Theory, Culture & Society*, 16.1: 41–58.

Buell, Lawrence (1992). 'American Literary Emergence as a Postcolonial Phenomenon', *American Literary History*, 4.3: 411–42.

Buell, Lawrence (2000). 'Postcolonial Anxiety in Classic U.S. Literature', in Amritjit Singh and Peter Schmidt (eds), *Postcolonial Theory and the United States*. Jackson: University Press of Mississippi, 196–219.

Childs, Matt (2006). *The 1812 Aponte Rebellion in Cuba and the Struggle against Atlantic Slavery*. Chapel Hill: University of North Carolina Press.

Clavin, Matthew (2010). *Toussaint Louverture and the American Civil War: The Promise and Peril of a Second Haitian Revolution*. Philadelphia: University of Pennsylvania Press.

Coronil, Fernando (2008). 'Elephants in the Americas: Latin American Postcolonial Studies and Global Decolonization', in Mabel Morana, Enrique Dussell, and Carlos A. Jáuregui (eds.), *Coloniality at Large*. Durham, NC: Duke University Press, 396–416.

Desroches, Vincent (ed.) (2003). 'Quebec and Postcolonialism' (special issue), *Quebec Studies*, 35.

Dimock, Wai Chee (2006). *Through other Continents: American Literature Across Deep Time*. Princeton, NJ: Princeton University Press.

Dirlik, Arif (1994). 'The Postcolonial Aura: Third World Criticism in the Age of Global Capitalism', *Critical Inquiry*, 20.2: 328–56.

Dubois, Laurent (2004). *Avengers of the New World: The Story of the Haitian Revolution*. Cambridge: Belknap Press of Harvard University Press.

Dubois, Laurent (2009). 'The Haitian Revolution and the Sale of Louisiana; or, Thomas Jefferson's (Unpaid) Debt to Jean-Jacques Dessalines', in Peter J. Kastor and François Weil (eds), *Empires of the Imagination: Transatlantic Histories of the Louisiana Purchase*. Charlottesville, VA, and London: University of Virginia Press, 93–116.

Dutton, Jacqueline (2011). 'Francophonie and its Futures: Utopian, Digital, Plurivocal', *Australian Journal of French Studies*, 48.1: 3–18.

Edwards, Brian T. and Dilip Parameshwar Gaonkar (eds) (2010). *Globalizing American Studies*. Chicago: University of Chicago Press.

Farmer, Paul (1994). *The Uses of Haiti*. Monroe, Me.: Common Courage Press.

Fishkin, Shelley Fisher (2005). 'Crossroads of Cultures: The Transnational Turn in American Studies', *American Quarterly*, 57.1: 17–57.

Gauvin, Lise (2007). 'Post ou péricolonialisme: l'étrange modèle québécois (notes)', *International Journal of Francophone Studies*, 10.3: 433–8.

Geggus, David (ed.) (2001). *The Impact of the Haitian Revolution in the Atlantic World*. Columbia: University of South Carolina Press.

Giles, Paul (2006). 'Commentary: Hemispheric Partiality', *American Literary History*, 18.3: 648–55.

Gilroy, Paul (1993). *The Black Atlantic: Modernity and Double Consciousness*. Cambridge, Mass.: Harvard University Press.

Green, Mary Jean (2009). 'Locating Quebec on the Postcolonial Map', in C. Forsdick and D. Murphy (eds), *Postcolonial Thought in the French-Speaking World*. Liverpool: Liverpool University Press, 248–58.

Hallward, Peter (2007). *Damming the Flood: Haiti and the Politics of Containment*. London, Verso.

Hargreaves, Alec (2005). 'A Neglected Precursor: Roland Barthes and the Origins of Postcolonialism', in H. Adlai Murdoch and Anne Donadey (eds), *Postcolonial Theory and Francophone Literary Studies*. Gainesville: University Press of Florida, 55–64.

Hiddleston, Jane (2009). *Understanding Postcolonialism*. Stocksfield: Acumen.

Hiddleston, Jane (2010). *Poststructuralism and Postcoloniality: The Anxiety of Theory*. Liverpool: Liverpool University Press.

Huggan, Graham (2001). *The Postcolonial Exotic: Marketing the Margins*. London: Routledge.

Huggan, Graham (2008). *Interdisciplinary Measures: Literature and the Future of Postcolonial Studies*. Liverpool: University of Liverpool Press.

Hughes, Langston (1994). *Collected Poems*, ed. Arnold Rampersad. New York: Vintage Classics.

Hulme, Peter (1995). 'Including America', *Ariel: A Review of International English Literature*, 26.1: 117–23.

Hulme, Peter (2008). 'Postcolonial Theory and the Representation of Culture in the Americas', in Mabel Moraña, Enrique Dussell, and Carlos A. Jáuregui (eds), *Coloniality at Large*. Durham, NC: Duke University Press, 388–95.

Hunt, Alfred N. (1988). *Haiti's Influence on Antebellum America*. Baton Rouge: Louisiana State University Press.

Jackson, Maurice (2008). '"Friends of the Negro! Fly with Me, The Path is Open to the Sea": Remembering the Haitian Revolution in the History, Music and Culture of the African American People', *Early American Studies*, 6: 59–103.

Jackson, Maurice and Jacqueline Bacon (eds) (2010). *African Americans and the Haitian Revolution*. New York: Routledge.

Kaplan, Amy (1993). '"Left Alone in America": The Absence of Empire in the Study of American Culture', in Amy Kaplan and Donald E. Pease (eds), *Cultures of United States Imperialism*. Durham, NC: Duke University Press, 3–21.

Kaplan, Amy and Donald E. Pease (eds) (1993). *Cultures of United States Imperialism*. Durham, NC: Duke University Press.

Killick, Rachel (2006). 'In the Fold? Postcolonialism and Quebec', *Romance Studies*, 24.3: 181–92.

King, C. Richard (ed.) (2000). *Post-colonial America*. Urbana and Chicago: University of Illinois Press.

Klor de Alva, J. Jorge (1992). 'Colonialism and Postcolonialism as (Latin) American Mirages', *Colonial Latin American Review*, 1.1–2: 3–23.

Klor de Alva, J. Jorge (1995). 'The Postcolonization of the (Latin) American Experience: A Reconsideration of "Colonialism", "Postcolonialism" and "Mestizaje"', in Gyan Prakash (ed.), *After Colonialism: Imperial Histories and Postcolonial Displacements*. Princeton: Princeton University Press, 241–75.

Lazarus, Neil (2006). 'Postcolonial Studies After the Invasion of Iraq', *New Formations*, 59: 10–22.

Levander, Caroline and Robert Levine (eds) (2008). *Hemispheric American Studies*. New Brunswick, NJ and London: Rutgers University Press.

Loomba, Ania, Suvir Kaul, Matti Bunzl, Antoinette Burton, and Jed Esty (eds) (2005). *Postcolonial Studies and Beyond*. Durham, NC: Duke University Press.

McClennan, Sophia A. (2005). 'Inter-American Studies or Imperial American Studies?', *Comparative American Studies: An International Journal*, 3.4: 393–413.

McClintock, Anne (1992). 'The Angel of Progress: Pitfalls of the Term "Post-Colonialism"', *Social Text*, 31–2: 84–98.

Mackenthun, Gesa (1996). 'Adding Empire to the Study of American Culture', *Journal of American Studies*, 30.2: 263–9.

Marsh, Kate (2007). *Fictions of 1947: Representations of Indian Decolonization 1919–1962*. Oxford and New York: Peter Lang.

Marshall, Bill (ed.) (2005). *France and the Americas: Culture, Politics and History*, 3 vols. Santa Barbara, Calif.: ABC-CLIO.

Marshall, Bill (2009). *The French Atlantic: Travels in Culture and History*. Liverpool: Liverpool University Press.

Mignolo, Walter (1993). 'Colonial and Postcolonial Discourse: Cultural Critique or Academic Colonialism?', *Latin American Research Review*, 28.3: 120–31.

Miller, Perry (1956). *Errand into the Wilderness*. Cambridge, MA: Belknap Press of Harvard University Press.

Montague, Ludwell Lee (1940). *Haiti and the United States, 1714–1938*. Durham: Duke University Press.

Moraña, Mabel, Enrique Dussell, and Carlos A. Jáuregui (eds) (2008). *Coloniality at Large*. Durham, NC: Duke University Press.

Nesbitt, Nick (2005). 'The Idea of 1804', *Yale French Studies*, 107: 6–38.

Nesbitt, Nick (2009). *Universal Emancipation: The Haitian Revolution and the Radical Enlightenment*. Charlottesville: University of Virginia Press.

Pease, Donald E. (1993). 'New Perspectives on U.S. Culture and Imperialism', in Amy Kaplan and Donald E. Pease (eds), *Cultures of United States Imperialism*. Durham, NC: Duke University Press, 22–40.

Pease, Donald E. (2000). 'U.S. Imperialism: Global Dominance Without Colonies', in Henry Schwartz and Sangeeta Ray (eds), *A Companion to Postcolonial Studies*. London: Basil Blackwell, 203–20.

Pratt, Mary Louise (1992). *Imperial Eyes: Travel Writing and Transculturation*. New York and London: Routledge.

Pratt, Mary Louise (2008). 'In the Neocolony: Destiny, Destination, and the Traffic of Meaning', in Mabel Moraña, Enrique Dussell, and Carlos A. Jáuregui (eds), *Coloniality at Large*. Durham, NC: Duke University Press, 459–75.

Quayson, Ato (2000). *Postcolonialism: Theory, Practice or Process?* Cambridge: Polity Press.

Randall, Marilyn (2003). 'Resistance, Submission and Oppositionality: National Identity in French Canada', in C. Forsdick and D. Murphy (eds), *Francophone Postcolonial Studies: A Critical Introduction*. London: Arnold, 77–87.

Rediker, Marcus (2003). 'The Red Atlantic, or, "a Terrible Blast Swept Over the Heaving Sea"', in Bernhard Klein and Gesa Mackenthun (eds), *Sea Changes: Historicizing the Ocean*. New York: Routledge, 111–30.

Renda, Mary A. (2001). *Taking Haiti: Military Occupation and the Culture of U.S. Imperialism, 1915–1940*. Chapel Hill and London: University of North Carolina Press.

Rydell, Robert (1984). *All the World's a Fair: Visions of Empire at American International Expositions, 1876–1916*. Chicago: University of Chicago Press.

Sartre, Jean-Paul (1964). 'Le colonialisme est un système', in *Situations V.* Paris: Gallimard, 25–48.

Schueller, Malini Johar (2004). 'Postcolonial American Studies', *Journal of American History*, 16.1: 162–75.

Schueller, Malini Johar and Edward Watts (eds) (2003). *Messy Beginnings: Postcoloniality and Early American Studies*. New Brunswick, NJ: Rutgers University Press.

Scott, David (1999). *Refashioning Futures: Criticism after Postcoloniality*. Princeton, NJ: Princeton University Press.

Sepinwall, Alyssa Goldstein (2009). 'The Specter of Saint-Domingue: American and French Reactions to the Haitian Revolution', in David Patrick Geggus and Norman Fiering (eds), *The World of the Haitian Revolution*. Bloomington and Indianapolis: Indiana University Press, 317–38.

Simon, Sherry (2006). *Translating Montreal: Episodes in the Life of a Divided City*. Montreal: McGill-Queen's University Press.

Singh, Amritjit and Peter Schmidt (eds) (2000). *Postcolonial Theory and the United States: Race, Ethnicity and Literature*. Jackson: University Press of Mississippi.

Summerhill, Stephen J. and John Alexander Williams (2000). *Sinking Columbus: Contested History, Cultural Politics, and Mythmaking during the Quincentenary*. Gainesville: University Press of Florida.

Syrotinski, Michael (2007). *Deconstruction and the Postcolonial: At the Limits of Theory*. Liverpool: Liverpool University Press.

Thaman, Konai Helu (2003). 'Decolonizing Pacific Studies: Indigenous Perspectives, Knowledge, and Wisdom in Higher Education', *The Contemporary Pacific*, 15: 1–17.

Trivedi, Harish (1999). 'The Postcolonial or the Transcolonial?', *Interventions*, 1.2: 269–72.

Trouillot, Michel-Rolph (1995). *Silencing the Past: Power and the Production of History*. Boston: Beacon Press.

van der Poel, Ieme and Sophie Bertho (eds) (1999). *Traveling Theory: France and the United States*. Madison, NJ: Fairleigh Dickinson University Press; London: Associated University Presses.

White, Ashli (2004). 'The Limits of Fear: The Saint Dominguan Challenge to Slave Trade Abolition in the United States', *Early American Studies*, 2.2: 362–97.

Young, Robert J. C. (2011). 'Bayart's Broken Kettle', *Public Culture*, 23.1: 167–75.

CHAPTER 30

IRRITATING EUROPE

FRANK SCHULZE-ENGLER

England has changed. These days it's difficult to tell who's from around here and who's not. Who belongs and who's a stranger. It's disturbing. It doesn't feel right.

Caryl Phillips, *A Distant Shore*

Each of the major European nations has experienced a flourishing of imperial power and, more importantly in the present context, has had to come to terms with the experience of the loss of an empire ... With growing distance from imperial domination and colonial history, the European powers have also had the opportunity to *achieve a reflexive distance towards themselves*. In this way, they could learn to see themselves from the perspective of the defeated in the questionable role of victors who were called to account for the violence of an imposed and disruptive process of modernization. This may have contributed to the repudiation of Eurocentrism and have inspired the Kantian hope for a future global domestic politics.

Jacques Derrida and Jürgen Habermas, 'February 15, or:
What Binds Europeans'

INTRODUCTION

Postcolonial Europe is an awkward term. Postcolonial people, politics, and ideas continue to irritate Europe. They confront Europe with a colonial past it often seeks to forget, and with a transnational present which forces it to reconsider the meaning and direction of its own project of unification. How is Europe to respond to the presence of millions of people of non-European descent—citizens, migrant workers, refugees, 'illegals'—within its borders? Should it turn itself into a fortress, rally round a 'core identity' based on shared history, culture, and beliefs, and insist that the 'New Europeans' assimilate themselves to this identity? Or should it perceive the transnational dynamics of 'Europeanization' enacted in the process of European unification as a cosmopolitan project, orient itself towards an ideal of diversity, and develop a self-understanding beyond traditional confines of cultural, ethnic, and religious difference?

Postcolonial *Europe* is an equally awkward term. Europe continues to irritate post-colonial studies because it is literally everywhere and nowhere. It is everywhere because traditions of 'provincializing Europe'—of combating Europe's Orientalism, of dismantling Europe's intellectual, political, and economic legacies of Empire, of analysing how postcolonial literatures 'write back' to the former European centres of colonial and imperial power—have long been central to the academic and political concerns of postcolonial studies worldwide. At the same time it is nowhere because Europe has effectively been written out of the idea of a 'postcolonial world', which in many varieties of postcolonialism continues to function as a half-defiant, half-nostalgic latter-day synonym of the 'Third World', and because postcolonial discourse has largely abstained from addressing the consequences of the complex and contradictory dynamism of contemporary European unification for its own intellectual and institutional practice.

This chapter explores the uneasy relationship between 'Europe' and the 'postcolonial'. It investigates the significance of postcolonial perspectives for the self-understanding of an emerging 'New Europe'; it also charts the implications of 'postcolonial Europe' and contemporary processes of 'Europeanization' for the theory and practice of a postcolonial studies increasingly dominated by transatlantic perspectives. By examining emerging contact zones between Europeanization and postcolonial studies, it hopes to contribute towards a dialogue that turns mutual irritations into resources for an urgent and overdue reappraisal of both Europe and the postcolonial.

POSTCOLONIAL EUROPE: HISTORICAL, GEOGRAPHICAL, CULTURAL, AND POLITICAL TRAJECTORIES

Contemporary European discourses are often predicated on a categorical distinction between the 'old national' and the 'new cosmopolitan' Europe (Beck 2006: 165); between a 'continent divided by national hatred, ravaged by war, and bereft of a firm psychological basis' and 'an increasingly peaceful, prosperous, and confident polity in which various nation-states are experimenting with a novel kind of international relations' (Checkel and Katzenstein 2009: 4). The 'New Europe' that emerged after the ravages of World War II is notoriously hard to grasp, however: it is a multitiered conglomerate of national, transnational, and supranational entities and institutions, a model of government beyond the nation state, a bureaucratically regulated everyday reality shared by some 500 million EU citizens (and an estimated 20 million legal and illegal 'third country nationals'), a largely realized dream of former enemies becoming neighbours, and—despite recurring setbacks in the process of political integration—arguably 'the last politically effective political utopia' (Beck and Grande 2007: 2). In view of these complexities, a number of recent commentators have suggested that Europe cannot possibly be grasped in terms of a 'fixed geographical unity', but should be seen rather as 'a spatial and social construct' (Wagner 2005: 93) or, as Étienne Balibar puts it, 'a project of active European citizenship' (Balibar 2004: 3). In one of the most incisive attempts to come to terms with the realities of the 'New Europe', Ulrich Beck and Edgar Grande have suggested that Europe can only be understood in terms of an open-ended process of 'Europeanization':

> Whether one equates Europe with the European Union and its member states or understands it as a larger geographical and political space, Europe as such does not exist, only *Europeanization* in the sense of an institutionalized process of permanent change. What 'Europe' includes and excludes, the location and direction of its territorial boundaries, its institutional form and what institutional architecture it should have in the future—none of this is clear. Europe is not a fixed condition. Europe is another word for variable geometry, variable national interests, variable involvement, variable internal-external relations, variable statehood and variable identity. (Beck and Grande 2007: 6)

While the categorical distinction between 'old' and 'new' Europe is saturated with historical experience and is part of an ongoing process of redefining the trajectories and objectives of Europeanization, it nevertheless remains partial and incomplete with regard to the questions raised by Europe's colonial and postcolonial 'unfinished business'. The following section of this chapter will look at these questions in term of (i) history, (ii) geography, (iii) cultural identity, and (iv) politics, exploring in the process the various trajectories by which the 'old' Europe has become sutured to the 'new'.

(i) *History*: In historical terms, it is salutary to remember that the birth hour of the new, post-war Europe did not coincide with the end of colonialism. The founding creed of the first moves towards a democratically reconciled Europe in the 1950s was 'never again fascism' and 'never again war'; for obvious reasons, 'never again colonialism' was not part of this fundamental consensus since Britain, France, Belgium, and the Netherlands (to name only the four most pertinent examples) were still in possession of vast portions of their colonial empires. While the foundations of a peaceful, cosmopolitan post-war order were being laid in Europe with the founding of the European Coal and Steel Community (1951), the Treaty of Paris (1954), and the Treaty of Rome (1957), some of the most violent twentieth-century colonial conflicts took place in other parts of the world: the French War in Indochina culminating in the disastrous defeat at the Battle of Dien Bien Phu (1954), the Mau Mau War in Kenya (1952–7), the Malayan Emergency (1948–60), and the Algerian War of Independence (1954–62). While European nations like France and Britain were heavily engaged in colonial wars that eventually became catalysts of an accelerating decolonization process, others such as Germany were only too eager to banish their own colonial history from a cultural memory preoccupied with coming to terms with the ravages of World War II and the Holocaust.

The emergence of a new cosmopolitan Europe was thus based on a decisive break with a legacy of fascism and war, but not with the legacy of colonialism. There were no Nuremberg trials to deal with Europe's colonial crimes, nor was there a Truth and

Reconciliation Commission to make the voices of Europe's colonial victims heard. As Étienne Balibar has pointed out, it took several decades before Europe began to come to terms with the significance of colonialism for its own history and the legacy of colonialism for its own culture and politics:

> Only recently, and with considerable difficulties, have we become conscious of the fact that 'barbarity' indeed circulated for centuries between the dominant center and the dominated periphery. The critical labour of memory concerning the violence of European conquest and rule did not immediately start with decolonization but long after the event, as in the case of the French War in Algeria. It was clearly encouraged by the massive presence, increasingly legitimate in spite of all the remaining discriminations, of 'postcolonial' populations within the European nations. Much remains to be uncovered and acknowledged, but this growing consciousness of the realities of colonial history, a history that has made Europe what it is, has now profoundly disturbed Eurocentric visions that used to contrast 'our' civilization with 'their' barbarity. (Balibar 2004: 222–3)

Highlighting these continuities between the old colonial and the new cosmopolitan Europe and the 'considerable difficulties' that Europe continues to experience in coming to terms with its not-too-distant colonial past should not be taken to imply that the contradictory processes of Europeanization referred to above are not politically substantial, or that they simply constitute an ideological smokescreen behind which the agenda of 'old' Europe continues unabated. What is at issue, however, is the incompleteness of the conventional story of the emergence of a new European identity based on the end of empire and of European nations that 'instead of looking towards their former Asian and African possessions' decided 'to concentrate on building some institutional agreements destined to prevent another war and to contribute towards Europe's economic recovery' (Guibernau 2007: 108). Not only were colonial possessions and the struggle to retain them still very much an issue when the building of institutional agreements for the emergence of a new Europe began in the 1950s; even more importantly, banishing the re-evaluation of colonialism from the political agenda of this emerging Europe meant that such legacies as racism, the hierarchization of European and non-European peoples and cultures, and the willingness to accept the coexistence of 'internal' drives for democratization and 'external' authoritarian measures to safeguard Europe's new domestic arrangements were carried over from the 'old' to the 'new' Europe. Today, this constitutes a major challenge to the emergence of a cosmopolitan Europe:

> Britain itself, and Europe more generally, is deeply marked by its postcolonial condition, even as—and especially because—it has such difficulty recognizing that condition. For most Europeans, though not all, the postcolonial condition might be grasped by coming to terms with the colonialism that preceded and enabled the establishment of the nation-states we inhabit. (Hulme 2005: 54–5)

(ii) *Geography*: That the story of Europe's 'inward turn' after World War II is incomplete also becomes apparent when its geographical features are taken into consideration.

In 2010, some 4.5 million people or almost 1 per cent of Europe's population lived in the nine 'outermost regions' of the EU, integral parts of political Europe comprising territories such as the Azores, the Canary Islands and Madeira in the Atlantic, Guadeloupe, Martinique and French Guiana in the Caribbean, and Réunion in the Indian Ocean. A further 1.3 million people lived in twenty-one 'overseas countries and territories' with a special relationship to the EU ranging from virtually full integration through different modes of association to virtual independence; these far-flung associates of the EU include Greenland, the Falklands and St Helena in the Atlantic, the Pacific territories of French Polynesia and New Caledonia, and Indian Ocean territories such as Mayotte. Several decades after the great wave of decolonization after World War II, most people in these regions, countries, and territories have opted to remain in the EU or to keep their special relationship to Europe; since it seems improbable that political decolonization is going to change this status quo in the foreseeable future, Europe is likely to maintain these territorial connections. The fact that the European Space Agency, one of Europe's most important future-oriented projects, launches its rockets from Kourou in French Guiana is ample proof of the fact that Europe's overseas presence is anything but an exotic historical residue.

(iii) *Cultural Identity*: A third area of 'unfinished business' relates to the myth of a 2000-year-old European cultural identity that is regularly conjured up in contemporary Europeanization debates. This myth was invoked, for example, in Vaclav Havel's famous address to the European Parliament in 1994 when he claimed that 'the European Union is based on a large set of values, with roots in antiquity and in Christianity, which over 2000 years evolved into what we recognize today as the foundations of modern democracy', going on to assert that 'this set of values has its own clear moral foundation and its obvious metaphysical roots, whether modern man admits it or not' (Havel 1994). The myth of a 2000-year-old Christian tradition as the core of modern Europe has also been called upon in more recent debates on the accession of Turkey to the EU and the role of Cyprus in Europe, where historians have asserted that 'we have a European identity which is based on our joint culture, religion, history, customs and way of life, law, political culture and universal values' and that 'there is no doubt that all Europeans from Brest to the Urals, from the North Cape to Sicily share the universal Graeco-Roman heritage' (Richter 2003: 7).

Given the paramount importance of the negative foundational principles of 'never again fascism' and 'never again war' in the genesis of the 'new' Europe, as noted above, this invocation of a positive principle of European identity is understandable enough; in contemporary Europeanization debates, it nevertheless runs the danger of promoting a sanitized and reductive view of European history and identity. First and foremost, the idea of a 2000-year-old European identity grounded on 'internal' values and a historical continuity unfolding within the spatial boundaries of an alleged continental logic clearly sidelines or even negates the legacies of Europe's involvement in global history, not only for 'other' parts of the world but for Europe itself. The sarcastic comment of one of the protagonists of Salman Rushdie's *Satanic Verses* that 'the trouble with the English is that their ... history happened overseas, so they ... don't know what it means' (1988:

343) thus rings equally true for Europeans trying to reinvent themselves in forgetfulness of the colonial and postcolonial entanglements of their own history.

The story of a 2000-year-old European core identity remains an improbable tale not only because it marginalizes these 'external' entanglements, but also because it fails to come to terms with the past and present 'internal' diversity of Europe on the one hand and the fluid history of the invention and reinvention of Europe over centuries on the other. As Rémi Brague has argued, there are indeed historical continuities that link contemporary Europe through early modern times and the Middle Ages to classical antiquity, but these continuities are not grouped around an essential core, but rather generated by the 'eccentricity' of a Europe whose identity 'is what it has appropriated from what was once foreign to it' (2002: 23). Numerous commentators have pointed out that the classical legend of Europa, the daughter of a Middle Eastern king abducted by Zeus to Crete where she became the ancestral founding mother of the Minoans, constitutes a 'transgressive myth' evoking an 'anti-original, anti-essentialistic, and, in the true sense, cosmopolitan origin' (Beck and Grande 2007: 263), while historians have argued that the history of Europe has unfolded as the result of various discourses and performative acts and that what has been imagined as 'Europe' has not remained the same during the last two millennia, but has undergone a protracted process of shape-shifting (Schmale 2000: 14–15).

The decisive question for contemporary Europeanization processes is thus arguably not what Europe 'is', but what kind of Europe we would like to live in (Beck and Grande 2007: 224). Attempts to tie European identity to a single ethno-cultural principle pave the way for an exclusionary identity politics that not only negates Europe's external entanglements, but also fails to come to terms with the complex and contradictory process of its self-invention and its internal diversity:

> To allow a Christian-occidental principle of ethnic descent to be resurrected from the mass graves of Europe is to fail to understand Europe's *inner cosmopolitanization*. It is to deny the reality of the roughly 17 million people living in the EU who cannot recognize this ethnic-cultural heritage of 'Europeanness' as their own, because they are Muslims or people of colour, for example, yet who understand and organize themselves culturally and politically as Europeans. (Beck 2006: 166, emphasis in the original)

(iv) *Politics*: The 'inner cosmopolitanization' invoked in the above statement points towards a fourth, political, trajectory of postcolonial Europe: the demographic makeover of Europe in the twentieth century through a new transcontinental dynamic of migration and the intricate linkages between the internal diversification of national cultures and the process of Europeanization.

In the course of the twentieth century, Europe underwent a process of transformation from a source area of migration that had for centuries exported settlers and labourers to various parts of the world into a region that, in the second half of the century, became a major focus of global migration flows involving 'a growing number of migrants who are attracted by the vision of a social, prosperous, and peaceful Europe' (Checkel and Katzenstein 2009: 13). These migration flows were generally driven by 'the economic logic of an aging continent that needs migrants but simultaneously fears them' (Checkel and Katzenstein 2009: 226). Some of them were manifestly postcolonial in nature (such as the passage of the 'Windrush generation' from the Caribbean to post-war Britain (Phillips and Phillips 1998), the relocation of large numbers of Algerians and other North Africans from the Maghreb to France, or the resettlement of Indonesians in the Netherlands), while others (e.g. the emergence of a Turkish-German population that today encompasses some 2.6 million people) were not directly related to Europe's colonial history or—as in the case of large-scale labour migration from southern Europe to northern Europe in the 1950s and 1960s—formed part of an intra-European population shift. With the collapse of the communist world and the eastward expansion of the European Union in the 1990s and 2000s, the situation has become even more complex: with 'most of the increase in population in Europe in the past twenty years' originating from 'the cross-border travel of migrants from eastern Europe, Africa, and Asia' (Fligstein 2008: 169), older postcolonial diasporas in western and central Europe (or 'new Europeans' of postcolonial descent) now live side by side with more recent arrivals from eastern Europe,[1] while refugees from Asia, the Arab World, and various parts of Africa seek entry into Europe in order to escape from economic deprivation, war, or political turmoil in their home countries.

These social transformations have had significant political repercussions. All over Europe, they have given rise to the emergence of new transnational networks linking Europe to other parts of the world, new transcultural modes of life involving intense renegotiations of individual and collective identities, and new forms of multicultural politics; at the same time they have become the focus point of an anxious xenophobia, demands to reserve 'Europe for the Europeans', and the emergence of often highly technologized border regimes designed to make Europe's boundaries (which have become porous or have even vanished for European citizens) impermeable for Europe's undesired 'others'.

Framing these complex political realignments within a narrative of 'Europe and its Others' can easily lead to reductive or essentializing responses—as if it was indeed 'Europe' that developed a continental chauvinism or as though non-European migrants 'naturally' triggered off xenophobic responses. What is arguably at issue in the heated debates on migration, border controls, multiculturalism, and European identity (and particularly on the role of Islam in Europe and Turkey's accession to the EU)[2] is nothing less than 'a cultural cleavage ... that pits the winners from globalization and Europeanization—"the Europeans"—against its losers' (Risse 2010: 245), a cleavage that has in turn generated a clash between two very different conceptions of Europe:

> On the one hand, there is the vision of modern, liberal, and cosmopolitan Europe that embodies the values of enlightenment, such as human rights, democracy, and the market economy, that have been constitutive for the European project for the past

---

[1] For an analysis of eastern Europe as a new exotic 'other' in contemporary British culture and literature, see Korte, Pirker, and Helff (2010).

[2] For analytical overviews of and interventions into these debates, see the contributions in Al-Azmeh and Effie Fokas (2007) and Hsu (2010).

fifty years and are still endorsed by a majority of political elites and citizens across the continent. On the other hand, antimodern nationalism increasingly represents itself as a distinct *European nationalism*, as a 'fortress and exclusionary Europe' based on an essentialist interpretation of the European Christian heritage. Interestingly enough, nationalism is less connected to the nation-state as such in this construction but is extended to Europe and the EU. (Risse 2010: 245, emphasis in the original)

It is particularly with regard to the discourse of this 'fortress and exclusionary Europe' that Europe's unfinished colonial and postcolonial business makes its presence felt in contemporary politics (Huggan and Law 2009; see also Back 2009: 329–40). As many commentators have noted, the rhetoric of exclusion mobilized in this discourse has often shifted from an 'older' racism focused on biology and genetics towards new 'postmodern' modes of 'cultural racism' that stress cultural alterity, religious difference, and the 'incommensurability of lifestyles' (Flecha 1999: 150–71). As Paul Gilroy has pointed out, however, the figures of thought employed by this cultural racism are often steeped in a familiarity with a vicious rhetoric of contempt and marginalization going back to older practices of social hierarchization generated during Europe's colonial rule:

> The biopolitical commitments, which were previously mandated by old-style racial hierarchy, persist in the form of common sense ... The residual traces of imperial racism combine easily with mechanistic notions of culture and a deterministic organicism to form a deadly cocktail. (Gilroy 2005: 142)

But 'postcolonial Europe' signifies more than cleavages, exclusions, and the legacies of Europe's colonial past; it also signals the permanent presence in Europe, often extending over several generations, of millions of people of non-European origin. This presence can neither be categorized in terms of 'illegals', 'migrants', 'exiles', 'diasporics', 'multicultural citizens', or 'New Europeans', nor contained in the ubiquitous discourse of 'integration' that has become a focal point of political anxieties across Europe. In political terms, 'postcolonial Europe' stands for an irritation of 'the dense fabric of national culture within individual states' that need 'to become more porous, adaptable and sensitive internally as well as in their external relations', and for a paradoxical civilizational advance whereby Europe's former 'others' carry the potential for 'a transnational amplification of civic solidarity across Europe' (Habermas 2008: 93). As Balibar puts it:

> The *positive* counterpart of all this is a powerful, irreversible phenomenon of hybridization and multiculturalism now transforming Europe ... It started with specific, reciprocal ties between former metropolises and their former empires (France and northern and western Africa, Britain and India, Pakistan, and the West Indies, the Netherlands and Indonesia), but is now quite generalized as a pattern of interaction between Europe as such and its 'exterior.' If the first lesson to be drawn from recent European history could be called a tragic lesson of public order, we might call this other one a lesson of *otherness*. It leads Europe to recognize, albeit with considerable hesitations and drawbacks, that the other is a necessary component of its 'identity', therefore its future vitality, its 'power.' (Balibar 2004: 223 , emphasis in the original)

Postcolonial Europe—Culture, Arts, and Literature

The hybridization of European self-identity remarked upon by Balibar points towards a major facet of postcolonial Europe only noted in passing so far: the transformative potential of what Paul Gilroy has called 'the feral beauty of postcolonial culture, literature, and arts of all kinds [that] is already contributing to the making of new European cultures' (2005: 142). Contrary to the autopoeitic accounts of European cultural identity mentioned above, people of non-European origin have played an important role in Europe's social and cultural make-up for centuries (in the British context, see Dabydeen 1985; Fryer 1984; Visram 1986), and the conspicuous presence of postcolonial literatures and arts in Europe today not only testifies to its cultural transformation, but has also established a wide-ranging network of transcultural connections to Africa, Asia, the Americas, and the Pacific that is re-embedding contemporary European identities in a more global setting.

The most striking feature of Europe's postcolonial literatures and arts is their diversity. Far from giving voice to an archetypal 'postcolonial condition', they relate to—and intervene in—a wide variety of social, political, and cultural contexts. 'Black British/British Asian Literature' as well as 'Beur Literature' in France emerged amidst postcolonial settler populations that had moved from the former peripheries of empire to the colonial 'motherland', but today these literatures explore second- or third-generation struggles for recognition and negotiations of transcultural belonging, often from the perspective of 'new' European citizenship rather than first-generation experiences of migration. In other European countries, 'migrant literatures' have often followed a similar trajectory, although the migrants involved were only partially connected to the host countries' colonial history (e.g. African migrants in Italy or Spain), or had no such connections at all (e.g. Turkish migrants in Germany). At the same time, all over Europe the experiences of refugees, asylum seekers, and 'illegals' are finding expression in literature, film, video art, and new forms of media communication that articulate a more precarious migrant perspective from 'outside' European citizenship—a perspective that often eschews the privileging of national space and is highly attuned to the European scope of contemporary immigration regimes (Helff 2008: 123–32).

Another facet of European postcolonialism relates to a host of 'postcolonial literatures' that have emerged in eastern Europe and the Baltic and that relate to the legacies of the Russian Empire (and later of communist rule under Soviet Russian domination) in Europe rather than to the legacies of European colonialism in other parts of the world (Kelertas 2006; Kolodoziejczyk 2010; Korek 2007; Thompson 2000). While these literatures have generally been studied under the rubric of 'post-communism' rather than 'postcolonialism', recent debates suggest that postcolonial studies might 'help elaborate a general comparative framework for post-communist literary studies' and help overcome the 'habitual national reclusion' that characterizes post-communist eastern European scholarship (Peiker 2006: n.p.). Other participants in these debates have warned, however, that despite similarities and overlaps post-communism and postcolonialism remain distinct fields with their own logics and that, given the fact that post-communism has established itself as a scholarly field in its own right, the challenge for postcolonial studies is 'to negotiate entry into this growing heterogeneous club, rather than to stake out a place all [its] own' (Andreescu 2011: 72).

Finally, European cultures, literatures, and arts have acquired a postcolonial dimension *in toto*, since most European societies were directly affected by the colonialism they practised elsewhere and continue to be affected by its aftermaths, e.g. in the shape of Europe's 'postcolonial melancholia' diagnosed by Paul Gilroy, which will be discussed in more detail later. Somewhat paradoxically, the critical response to these complex entanglements of postcolonial literatures and cultures in the process of Europeanization has often focused on reconfigurations of national rather than European cultural space. This is particularly noticeable in Britain, where the critical reception of first 'Black British' then later 'British Asian' literature and culture has highlighted issues such as the articulation of ethnic minority experiences, the struggle against racism and for meaningful citizenship, the transnational, transcultural, and diasporic linkages between Britain and its former Empire, and the transformation of British society and culture,[3] but has largely abstained from exploring the manifold connections between the 'mongrelization' of Britain (Dawson 2007) or the emergence of a 'BrAsian' population of 'ironic citizens' (Sayyid 2006) on the one hand and the social, political, demographic, and cultural dynamics of Europeanization on the other.

Yet Black British and British Asian literatures have arguably long since begun to move beyond an 'Anglocentric' postcolonialism exclusively based on the legacies of Britain's overseas empire and solely trained on the transformation of British national space. To cite only a few recent examples, Caryl Phillips's *A Distant Shore* (2003) includes a section on the harrowing experiences of the novel's African refugee protagonist witnessing the plight of 'illegals' being trafficked across Europe; Abdulrazak Gurnah's *By the Sea* (2001) dedicates a chapter to the exploits of a Zanzibari student in the GDR who learns about Austrian settlers in Kenya, travels around eastern and central Europe, and finally crosses the Iron Curtain to arrive in Britain as a refugee from communist East Germany; Mike Phillips's *A Shadow of Myself* (2000) sutures an account of Ghanaian nationalists in mid-twentieth-century Britain to the love story of a Ghanaian student in the Soviet Union and embeds these far-flung diasporic connections in a turbulent thriller plot set in Hamburg, Berlin, and Prague that delves deeply into images of a post-1989 European 'Wild East'; while in *The Enchantress of Florence* (2008), Salman Rushdie (once regarded as a postcolonial British, more recently as a cosmopolitan American writer) returns to Indo-European history with a parallel tale of political intrigues, power struggles, and philosophy linking up early modern Florence and the court of Akbar the Great in sixteenth-century India.

[3.] See, for example, Arana and Ramey (2004) Davis and Fuchs (2006); Innes (2002); Murphy and Sim (2008); Nasta (2001); Reichl (2001); Sardar (2008); Sesay (2005); Stein (2004); Upstone (2010).

Not only in Britain, but also in a wide variety of other European countries, writers have produced a substantial body of postcolonial literature in recent decades. France with its long-standing colonial history is a 'classical' and relatively well-known example (Barclay 2011; Cazenave 2005; Hargreaves 2005; Hargreaves and McKinney 1997; Thomas 2007), as are Belgium and the Netherlands (which have attracted much less attention in the English-speaking world: see Bekers 2009; Hoving 2010; Merolla 2009; Ponzanesi and Merolla 2005). In other countries such as Spain or Italy, newly emerging postcolonial literatures have only been partly associated with these countries' colonial histories and often relate to recent migration processes from parts of Africa that were not involved in these histories (Bouchard 2010; De Donno 2006; Hand 2001; Hanley 2010; Mellino 2006; Ponzanesi 2004). Postcolonial literature, art, and culture have also become a hotly debated issue in Germany, where literary postcolonialism has become associated not only with Black Germans, some of whose family histories go back to the times of German colonialism in Africa (Campt 2003; Nganang 2005), but also with more recent population dynamics involving migrants from Asia and North Africa who have no historical connection with German colonialism (Nghi Ha et al. 2007; Reynolds 2008; Steyerl and Rodríguez 2003).

Postcolonial literature and culture in Europe is more than a patchwork of discrete national configurations, however. As Sandra Ponzanesi and Daniela Merolla put it in their introduction to a volume of essays on 'New Cultural and Literary Spaces in Post-Colonial Europe':

> The development of migrant literatures in the European languages reveals indeed that not only people but also ideas have been travelling, transcending, and interconnecting apparently separate colonial legacies ... Within the European scenario it is high time to ask when an idea of European literature will supersede the national literatures, or when migrant literature will be an object of comparison without having to pass via the national canon. (Ponzanesi and Merolla 2005: 3–4)

Literary and cultural studies scholarship has already begun to explore such comparative perspectives. The contributions to a 2009 volume on *Transcultural Modernities: Narrating Africa in Europe* explicitly adopt a transnational and comparative perspective enquiring into

> how African artists, writers, and ordinary people living in Europe experience and explore their transcultural and/or postcolonial environments, and how their experiences and explorations in turn contribute to the construction of modern Euro-African lifeworlds. (Bekers, Helff, and Merolla 2009: xv)

In a similar vein, a 2009 study on 'Afro-Europe' has also stressed the necessity to move beyond national literary paradigms and to develop a comparative perspective capable of assessing the contribution of 'Afro-European' writing to the transformation of European cultural and political identities:

> Exploring Afro-European literature(s) comparatively therefore means tracing diachronic and synchronic connections that reveal new configurations across linguistic and national boundaries ... Afro-Europe should be incorporated into the debate on European identity as a constitutive element of the cultural heritage of the continent and one which contributes to the displacement and reformulation of the concept of Europe such as it has been conceived in centuries of imperialist *Weltanschauung* and Eurocentric practice. (Brancato 2009: 30–1)

Comparative approaches taking Europe as a whole rather than national cultural and literary spaces as their frame of reference for investigations into European postcolonial literatures and cultures are also pursued in a number of recent research projects including the journal *Postcolonial Europe*, published in cooperation with Stockholm University,[4] the 'Postcolonial Europe' network set up by the Universities of Leeds, Munich, and Utrecht,[5] and the 'Postcolonial Europe' project forming part of the Advanced Thematic Network in Activities in Women's Studies in Europe (ATHENA).[6]

One of the most remarkable aspects of European postcolonial arts and literatures is the self-confidence with which they engage in a transformation of European imaginaries. In a 2007 volume of essays on postcolonial Germany, for example, the editors take up the symbolism of the riverine journey in Joseph Conrad's *Heart of Darkness* and transform it into an aquatic fusion of mental geographies that dissolves the obsessive alterity with which the encounter between the European travellers and the indistinguishable and incomprehensible mass of seething 'others' on the riverbank is staged in Conrad's text:

> A postcolonial Germany can only be conceived if the colonial ambivalences of modernity and the crossborder histories of immigration and emigration are taken into account ... Re/visions is a landmark of changed cultural and mental maps, where histories and geographies have long since collapsed into each other: Here the Rhine flows into the Gulf of Guinea and the Elbe into the Bosporus; here the East Frisian Islands are set in the Pacific; here you can view the Mekong Delta from the Ore Mountains; here the Atlantic is no wider than the Spree. The faces of the people on the shore can plainly be seen, their voices can clearly be heard. (Nghi Ha et al. 2007: 15)

'Europe (or the West)': The Structural Invisibility of Europe in Postcolonial Discourse

In many respects Europe has already become 'postcolonial': the enduring historical, geographical, cultural, and political legacies of colonialism and the transnational flows

---

[4.] See <http://www.postcolonial-europe.eu/>.

[5.] See <http://www2.hum.uu.nl/postcolonialeurope/index.html>.

[6.] See http://www.postcolonialeurope.net/index.php?pageid=31.

of migrants, refugees, and 'illegals' continue to erode the false certainties of an 'endog-enous' European identity; postcolonial themes, concerns, and critiques have increas-ingly become part of Europeanization discourses; and postcolonial culture, literature, and art of all kinds are already exploring new European social realities and transform-ing the cultural landscapes of Europe. On the other hand, Europe largely remains 'a blind spot' and 'a hollow signifier in the postcolonial debate' (Ponzanesi and Blaagaard 2011: 4) since postcolonial studies still seems reluctant to confront the intricacies of 'postcolonial Europe'. In the following section of the chapter I argue that (i) this reluc-tance is inextricably linked to the structural invisibility of Europe in much postcolonial theory and criticism—symbolized by the ubiquitous phrase 'Europe (or the West)'—and explore possible reasons for this continuing invisibility related to (ii) the foun-dational suturing of postmodern critique and anti-colonial politics in postcolonial theory, (iii) a reductive response to the seminal issues raised in Dipesh Chakarbarty's *Provincializing Europe* (2000), and (iv) the institutional preponderance of Britain and particularly the USA in postcolonial studies.

(i) Europe's fate in postcolonial theory to some extent resembles that of her mythologi-cal predecessor in ancient Greece: she makes her appearance in the act of being whisked away. In his famous study on Europe's construction of the East, *Orientalism* (1978), Edward Said performed a seminal example of this vanishing act when he outlined the importance of the Orient as 'the place of Europe's greatest and richest and oldest colonies, the source of its civilizations and languages, its cultural contestant' and then went on to argue that 'the Orient has helped to define Europe (or the West) as its contrasting image, idea, per-sonality, experience' (Said 2003 [1978]: 1–2). The term 'Europe' is invoked, but only to be equated with—and subsumed under—the larger category of 'the west', and is thus made structurally invisible in its historical and contemporary specificity (which distinguishes it, for example, from the USA). This epistemological staging of Europe's coeval presence and absence has since become a standard procedure in postcolonial studies, where the figure of 'Europe (or the "west" broadly)' (Gupta 2003: 70) or even the category 'Europe/West' (Brah 1996: 221) is routinely invoked 'to refer not to the continent of Europe but rather to Euro-American hegemony around the world' (Stam and Shohat 2005: 297).

The original object of critical analysis (the staging of 'Europe' as the superior centre of world civilization that was to legitimate Europe's colonial bid for world power) is thus transmuted into a transhistorical subject ('Europe/west') confronting—and confronted by—the 'non-west': 'while it is true that anti-*Eurocentrism* rather than anti-*Europeanism* has usually been postcolonial critics' explicit mandate, the one has tended to be con-fused with the other' (Huggan 2008: 241, emphasis in the original). As Frederick Cooper has argued, 'the occlusion of European history' has emerged as a major structural effect of this transmutation, since for critics of this transhistorical subject 'the metanarrative of European progress is more relevant than the messy and uneven history of post-1789 Europe' (2005: 403). Somewhat paradoxically, Cooper suggests, 'Postcolonial Studies has brought before a large and transcontinental public the place of colonialism in world history, yet it has tended to obscure the very history whose importance it has high-lighted' (2005: 401). This argument can arguably be extended from the perception of Europe's past to the critical confrontation with its present state and future perspectives:

a discipline that continues to rely on a trope like 'Europe/west' that structurally renders the specific political, social, and cultural constellations and contradictions of contemporary Europe invisible will undoubtedly find it difficult to utilize its theoretical insights and methodological expertise for a critical engagement with just these constellations and contradictions.

(ii) A major cause for the eclipse of Europe within postcolonial studies (testified to by the fact that so far no introduction to postcolonial literatures or cultures and no handbook on postcolonial studies has addressed Europe as a region of 'the postcolonial world') lies in the peculiar bond between postmodernist/poststructuralist analysis and anti-colonial politics that has become the hallmark of many varieties of postcolonial theory. A classical example of this bond can be found in *The Empire Writes Back* (1989), where the authors famously use the term 'post-colonial' 'to cover all the culture affected by the imperial process from the moment of colonization to the present day' and declare their concern 'with the world as it exists during and after the period of European Imperial domination and the effects of this on contemporary literatures' (Ashcroft, Griffiths, and Tiffin 2002 [1989]: 2), only to constrict the scope of their study in the next sentence to Britain's former colonies.

As has often been noted, the USA is rather half-heartedly added to this list, but is then factually excluded from the account of 'postcolonial literatures' in the rest of the book (Watson 2000: 61–2; see also Forsdick in this section of the volume). What has usually not been noted is the excision of Europe from this mapping of the postcolonial, although it would be hard to deny that Europe forms part of 'the world as it exists during and after the period of European Imperial domination' and that its culture has been 'affected by the imperial process from the moment of colonization to the present day', as the long-standing presence of postcolonial writers and artists in Europe, along with critical investigations into Europe's canonical literature and culture in the wake of Edward Said's *Culture and Imperialism* (1993), clearly show. The reason for this excision arguably lies in a normative orientation towards the politics of anti-colonialism in *The Empire Writes Back* (and much of the postcolonial scholarship that was to follow in its wake) that continues to rely on the confrontation with European colonialism as the *raison d'être* of postcolonial studies. The desire to identify a 'post-European commonality' in a decolonizing world 'after Europe' (Slemon and Tiffin 1989: ix) understandably generated little interest in engaging with Europe beyond a deconstructive confrontation with 'colonial discourse', but the staging of postcolonialism as an intellectual legatee of the mid-twentieth-century anti-colonial revolutions has meant that the analytical scope of postcolonial studies has been severely curtailed.

(iii) As Graham Huggan has argued, another reason for the marginalization of Europe in postcolonial studies lies in the fact 'that—at least in postcolonial circles—Dipesh Chakrabarty's passionate call for the "provincialization of Europe" has been heeded only too well' (Huggan 2008: 241). This is certainly true with regard to the 'catch-all' metaphor to which Chakrabarty's path-breaking study has often been reduced in postcolonial reception processes based on the gratification of a latent anti-Europeanism rather than on the desire for an analytical engagement with

Eurocentrism. A closer look at Chakrabarty's arguments, however, might warrant the opposite conclusion: that Chakrabarty's argument on 'provincializing Europe' has not been heeded enough.

The pivotal aim of *Provincializing Europe* is neither to engage in an anti-European discourse of dismissal nor to propagate a reverse Indocentrism, but 'to explore the capacities and limitations of certain European social and political categories in conceptualising political modernity in the context of non-European lifeworlds' (Chakrabarty 2000: 20). What is at issue are the historically preposterous claims of European models of modernity: the assumption that European modernity (with its specific historicity and cultural peculiarity) constitutes the universal model of modernity per se and that modernities elsewhere in the world can be measured according to how far they have 'already' or 'not yet' complied with the paradigmatic European pattern (see Hindess in Part IV of this volume). By contrasting the allegedly universal model of European modernity with 'the experience of political modernity in a country like India' (2000: 6), Chakrabarty makes the case for a decentred understanding of modernity that 'provincializes Europe' and shows that the European variety of modernity constitutes only one form of modernity on a global scale. Far from reiterating a conventional postcolonial anti-Europeanism, Chakrabarty's seminal intervention actually opens up new avenues of addressing European modernity in its full complexity: shorn of its hypertrophic claims to universal normativity, European modernity can finally be seen for what it actually is—a specific mode of modernity that is neither more nor less real or relevant than other modes.[7] While taking the analytical challenge of 'provincializing Europe' seriously could pave the way for new critical engagements with Europe's entangled postcolonial present, the habitual reduction of Chakrabarty's taxing concept to a gleeful metaphor of dismissal seems largely to have precluded such engagements so far. Europe continues to remain invisible in the reflexive vanishing act routinely performed in postcolonial discourse, as in Homi Bhabha's injunction to 'Forget Europe!' which dismisses engagements with the concept of Europe as unnecessary ballast and precludes potential postcolonial encounters with the intricate realities of Europeanization by declaring Europe to be nothing but 'a threshold ... a liminal territory to cross over onto other territories' (Bhabha and Çakmak 2008).

(iv) A further reason for the structural invisibility of Europe in postcolonial discourse lies in the continuing stranglehold of Anglo-American academia over the field. As many commentators have noted, the transition 'from commonwealth to postcolonial' in cultural and literary studies effected in the 1980s led to the emergence of a specifically American strand of postcolonialism that relied heavily on celebrity theorists and reshaped postcolonial concerns to fit into a distinctly American agenda (Brydon 1994; Tiffin 1996):

> The crucial difference has been the assimilation of broad-based postcolonial methodologies to current debates on minority cultures within the context of

[7] Similar analytical avenues have been opened up by sociological debates on 'multiple modernities'; see, for example, Eisenstadt (2000).

the *nation* ... A potential side-effect of the narrow focus on national minority cultures is a skewed perception of the global dimensions of postcolonial studies as little more than spatial extensions of prevailing national racial/ethnic concerns. (Huggan 2001: 241)

It is thus hardly surprising that recent debates on the 'potential exhaustion of postcolonialism as a paradigm' have focused exclusively on the institutionalization of postcolonial studies 'as a subfield of English studies in the United States' (Yaeger 2007: 633), or that postcolonial studies is routinely considered as a discipline 'that emerged in the USA' (Gutiérrez Rodriguez 2003: 21). In conjunction with neo-Marxist claims that globalization should be perceived 'in terms of the political renewal and refurbishment of imperial power in what, since the collapse of the Soviet Union in 1989, is today, unprecedentedly, a unipolar world' (Lazarus 2004: 38), this Americocentric perspective in postcolonial studies has tended to play down the political agency and significance of other nations or regions and has largely abandoned the quest for what Edward Said calls 'a new geographical consciousness of a decentered or multiply-centered world' (2002: 470–1). The institutional impact of American academia in postcolonial studies has thus contributed significantly to keeping postcolonial Europe invisible in postcolonial discourse. Paradoxically enough, this even holds true for a remarkable recent study on the making of postcolonial Britain: Ashley Dawson's *Mongrel Nation* presents an intricate account of the hybridization of British society and culture, but resolutely turns its back on Britain's European entanglements in its exclusively transatlantic account of the relationship between British and American minority cultures (Dawson 2007).

BEYOND POSTCOLONIAL MELANCHOLIA: TOWARDS A DIALOGUE BETWEEN EUROPEANIZATION AND POSTCOLONIAL STUDIES

In one of the most incisive accounts of Europe's postcolonial condition yet, Paul Gilroy has argued that Britain and various other European countries have developed a peculiar 'postcolonial melancholia' based on their inability to come to terms with their colonial histories on the one hand and the social and cultural transformations engendered by twentieth-century mass migrations on the other. An analysis of this condition, Gilroy holds, would have to take into account 'the wreckage of their colonial extensions and the injustices of their inconsistent responses to immigration', and would need to be based

upon their obvious difficulties in acknowledging the pains and the gains that were involved in imperial adventures and upon the problems that have arisen from their inability to disentangle the disruptive results supposedly produced by an immigrant presence from the residual but potent effects of lingering but usually unspoken colonial relationships and imperial fantasies. (Gilroy 2005: 100)

In its so far haphazard and hesitant encounters with the realities of the Europeanization process, postcolonial studies has almost exclusively focused on the legacies of colonialism in contemporary European life, on 'old' (biologically founded) and 'new' (culturalist) forms of racism, on European border regimes geared towards the exclusion of migrants and refugees, and on homogenizing and essentializing discourses of European history and identity. All of these critiques are indeed vitally important in coming to terms with the postcolonial dimensions of contemporary Europe, but the sustained Euroscepticism and anti-Europeanism that characterizes much of postcolonialism's engagement with Europe has not been particularly helpful either in developing a precise analysis of the chances and predicaments of Europeanization or in lending political impact to such an analysis. So far postcolonial studies seems content with watching its European 'other' from the outside and with keeping its distance to a Europeanization process that is habitually regarded as a sort of conspiracy against non-Europeans: 'The problem for an open Europe ... is how to close it—against immigrants and refugees from the Third World' (Sivanandan 1989: 86; see also Webber 1991: 11–17). The stock response to this scenario has been to fall back on postcolonial routines of 'deconstructing Europe' (Pieterse 1991: 7–10) and even, in most recent attempts to utilize 'the toolbox of postcolonial theory ... to study the reality of contemporary Europe', to reinvoke the time-honoured postcolonial trope of 'unthinking Europe' (Ponzanesi and Blaagaard 2011: 4–9).

The real challenge for postcolonial studies does not lie in unthinking Europe, however, but in rethinking and transforming it. As Gilroy succinctly puts it, the critique of racist exclusivism in Europe needs to overcome the 'fatalism and resignation' and the 'reified notion of race' of a 'US-centric discourse' that turns race into 'a zone of feeling and being that is considered to be emphatically prior to all merely political considerations' (2005: 145). What is needed instead, Gilroy suggests, is a stubborn hope 'that there are other stories about "race" and racism to be told apart from the endless narrative of immigration as invasion and the melancholic blend of guilt, denial, laughter, and homogenizing violence that it has precipitated' (150), 'a new project ... prepared to break with the notion that racial differences are a self-evident, immutable fact of political life' (151). Taking its inspiration from 'a liberating sense of the banality of intermixture' and 'the chaotic pleasures of the convivial postcolonial urban world' (150–1), Europe thus needs to transform its identity and to develop a self-understanding based on its diversity:

We need to be able to see how the presence of strangers, aliens, and blacks and the distinctive dynamics of Europe's imperial history have combined to shape its cultural and political habits and institutions. These historical processes have to be understood as internal to the operations of European political culture. They do not represent the constitutive outside of Europe's modern and modernist life. They can be shown to be alive in the interior spaces and mechanisms through which Europe has come to know and interpret itself, to define its passions, paths, and habits in opposition to the U.S. models that are identified with an inevitable future of racial conflict. (142–3)

This emphasis on the historical specificity of Europe not only challenges the habitual 'Europe (or the west)' trope in postcolonial discourse, but also opens up new avenues for a productive dialogue between postcolonial studies and critical Europeanization discourses. Such a dialogue would not only strengthen the aspirations of those struggling for a cosmopolitan 'project of active European citizenship' (Balibar 2004: 3), for a vision of 'a Europe free of both colonisers and colonised',[8] and for a political ethos confronting 'the common concerns of all members of European society independently of their origin—an ethos of hope not fear, trust not suspicion, reciprocity not domination, dialogue not condemnation, negotiation not aggression'.[9] It might also help postcolonial studies address some of its own blind spots and unresolved problems, for example with regard to the anti-communist revolutions of 1989/90—which postcolonial critics have by and large chosen to neglect, but which play a major role in current Europeanization debates—and with regard to the grand narratives of anti-colonial resistance that still form the normative backbone of postcolonialism but urgently need to be demystified and 'destabilized' if the postcolonial is to be successfully rerouted and equipped to face the challenges of a globalized world (Wilson et al. 2010: 1–13). Finally, acknowledging Europe as part of 'the postcolonial world' could contribute towards a direly needed decentring of postcolonial studies itself. The preponderance of transatlantic perspectives that has characterized much of recent postcolonial theorizing and has 'become normative, especially in slavery and African diaspora studies', needs to be relativized by a renewed emphasis on the Indian Ocean as a global arena that 'complicates binaries, moving us away from the simplicities of the resistant local and the dominating global and towards a historically deep archive of competing universalisms' (Hofmeyr 2010: 721–2; see also Desai 2010: 715). In a similar manner, comprehending the importance of the *Mediterranean* as a 'postcolonial sea' (Chambers 2004: 423–33; Chambers and Curti 2008: 387–99)—and acknowledging the fact that the 'Black Atlantic' in the twenty-first century has become a site of African migration to Europe rather than the New World (Gebrewold 2007)—could contribute towards an opening up of postcolonial concerns and a significant widening of the scope of the postcolonial field. Ironically enough, coming to terms with a contemporary Europe that is so urgently in need of acknowledging its long-denied postcoloniality in order to safeguard its democratic future may well constitute a major challenge that postcolonial studies needs to meet in order to sustain a viable future for itself.

[8]. Anon, 'Postcolonial Europe: Note of Intent', <http://www.postcolonial-europe.eu/index.php/en/note-of-intent>, accessed 8 March 2011.

[9]. Forum of Concerned Citizens of Europe, 'Living with Diversity: For a Politics of Hope without Fear—A Manifesto for Another Europe', *Dissent Magazine*, 22 July 2010. Online source: <http://www.dissentmagazine.org/online_articles/living-with-diversity-for-a-politics-of-hope-without-fear>, accessed 8 March 2011.

References

Al-Azmeh, Aziz and Effie Fokas (eds) (2007). *Islam in Europe: Diversity, Identity and Influence.* Cambridge: Cambridge University Press.

Andreescu, Liviu (2011). 'Are We All Postcolonialists Now? Postcommunism and Post-colonialism in Central and Eastern Europe', in M. S. Bottez, S. Draga-Alexandru, B. Stef-anescu, with R. Radulescu, *Postcolonialism/Postcommunism: Intersections and Overlaps.* Bucharest: Bucharest University Press, 57–74.

Anon. (2009). 'Postcolonial Europe: Note of Intent'. Online source: <http://www.postcolonial-europe. eu/index.php/en/note-of-intent>, accessed 8 March 2011.

Arana, Victoria R. and Lauri Ramey (2004). *Black British Writing.* Basingstoke: Palgrave Macmillan.

Ashcroft, Bill, Gareth Griffiths, and Helen Tiffin (2002 [1989]). *The Empire Writes Back: Theory and Practice in Post-Colonial Literatures.* London: Routledge.

Back, Les (2009). 'Beaches and Graveyards: Europe's Haunted Borders', *Postcolonial Studies,* 12.3: 329–40.

Balibar, Étienne (2004). *We, the People of Europe? Reflections on Transnational Citizenship,* trans. James Swenson. Princeton: Princeton University Press.

Barclay, Fiona (2011). *Writing Postcolonial France: Haunting, Literature, and the Maghreb.* Lanham, Md.: Lexington.

Beck, Ulrich (2006). *The Cosmopolitan Vision,* trans. Ciaran Cronin. Cambridge: Polity Press.

Beck, Ulrich and Edgar Grande (2007). *Cosmopolitan Europe,* trans. Ciaran Cronin. Cambridge: Polity Press.

Bekers, Elisabeth (2009). 'Chronicling Beyond Abyssinia: African Writing in Flanders, Belgium', in E. Bekers, S. Helff, and D. Merolla (eds), *Transcultural Modernities: Narrating Africa in Europe,* Matatu 36. Amsterdam and New York: Rodopi, 57–70.

Bekers, Elisabeth, Sissy Helff, and Daniela Merolla (2009). 'Introduction', in E. Bekers, S. Helff, and D. Merolla (eds), *Transcultural Modernities: Narrating Africa in Europe,* Matatu 36. Amsterdam and New York: Rodopi, pp. xiii–xx.

Bhabha, Homi K. and E. Efe Çakmak (2008). 'Forget Europe! An Interview with Homi Bhabha', *Eurozine,* 30 December. Online source: <http://www.eurozine.com/articles/2008–12–30-bhabha-en.html>, accessed 8 March 2011.

Bouchard, Norma (2010). 'Reading the Discourse of Multicultural Italy: Promises and Challenges of Transnational Italy in an Era of Global Migration', *Italian Culture,* 28.2: 104–20.

Brague, Rémi (2002). *Eccentric Culture: A Theory of Western Civilization,* trans. Samuel Lester. South Bend, Ind.: St. Augustine's Press.

Brah, Avtar (1996). *Cartographies of Diaspora: Contesting Identities.* London and New York: Routledge.

Brancato, Sabrina (2009). *Afro-Europe: Texts and Contexts.* Berlin: Trafo.

Brydon, Diana (1994). 'Response to Hart', *Arachnē,* 1.1: 100–12.

Campt, Tina M. (ed. and intro.) (2003). 'Reading the Black German Experience', *Callaloo: A Journal of African-American and African Arts and Letters,* 26.2: 288–400.

Cazenave, Odile (2005). *Afrique sur Seine: A New Generation of African Writers in Paris,* After the Empire: The Francophone World and Postcolonial France. Lanham, Md.: Lexington Books.

Chakrabarty, Dipesh (2000). *Provincializing Europe: Postcolonial Thought and Historical Difference.* Princeton and Oxford: Princeton University Press.

Chambers, Ian (2004). 'The Mediterranean: A Postcolonial Sea', *Third Text,* 18.5: 423–33.

Chambers, Ian and Lidia Curti (2008). 'Migrating Modernities in the Mediterranean', *Postcolonial Studies*, 11.4: 387–99.

Checkel, Jeffrey T. and Peter J. Katzenstein (2009). 'The Politicization of European Identities', in J. T. Checkel and P. J. Katzenstein (eds), *European Identity*. Cambridge: Cambridge University Press, 1–25.

Cooper, Frederick (2005). 'Postcolonial Studies and the Study of History', in A. Loomba, S. Kaul, M. Bunzl, A. Burton, and J. Esty (eds), *Postcolonial Studies and Beyond*. Durham and London: Duke University Press, 401–22.

Dabydeen, David (ed.) (1985). *The Black Presence in English Literature*. Manchester: Manchester University Press.

Davis, Geoffrey V. and Anne Fuchs (eds) (2006). *Staging New Britain: Aspects of Black and South Asian British Theatre Practice*. Brussels and Oxford: Lang.

Dawson, Ashley (2007). *Mongrel Nation: Diasporic Culture and the Making of Postcolonial Britain*. Ann Arbor, Mich.: University of Michigan Press.

De Donno, Fabricio (ed. and intro.) (2006). 'Colonial and Postcolonial Italy', *Interventions: International Journal of Postcolonial Studies*, 8.3: 371–539.

Derrida, Jaques and Jürgen Habermas (2006). 'February 15, or: What Binds Europeans', in Jürgen Habermas, *The Divided West*, ed. and trans. Ciaran Cronin. Cambridge: Polity Press, 39–84.

Desai, Gaurav (2010). 'Oceans Connect: The Indian Ocean and African Identities', *PMLA*, 135.3: 713–20.

Eisenstadt, Shmuel N. (2000). 'Multiple Modernities', *Daedalus*, 129.1: 1–29.

Flecha, Ramón (1999). 'Modern and Postmodern Racism in Europe: Dialogic Approach and Anti-Racist Pedagogies', *Harvard Educational Review*, 69.2: 150–71.

Fligstein, Neil (2008). *Euroclash: The EU, European Identity, and the Future of Europe*. Oxford: Oxford University Press.

Forum of Concerned Citizens of Europe (2010). 'Living with Diversity: For a Politics of Hope without Fear—A Manifesto for Another Europe', *Dissent Magazine*, 22 July. Online source: <http://www.dissentmagazine.org/online_articles/living-with-diversity-for-a-politics-of-hope-without-fear>, accessed 8 March 2011.

Fryer, Peter (1984). *Staying Power: Black People in Britain Since 1504*. Atlantic Highlands, NJ: Humanities Press.

Gebrewold, Belachew, (ed.) (2007). *Africa and Fortress Europe: Threats and Opportunities*. Aldershot: Ashgate.

Gilroy, Paul (2005). *Postcolonial Melancholia*. New York: Columbia University Press.

Guibernau, Montserrat (2007). *The Identity of Nations*. Cambridge: Polity Press.

Gupta, Suman (2003). 'Outside Perspectives on Europe After the Second World War', in M. Pittaway (ed.), *The Fluid Borders of Europe*. Milton Keynes: Open University, 66–113.

Gurnah, Abdulrazak (2002 [2001]). *By the Sea*. London: Bloomsbury.

Gutiérrez Rodriguez, Encarnación (2003). 'Repräsentation, Subalternität und postkoloniale Kritik' ['Representation, Subalternity and Postcolonial Critique'], in Hito Steyerl and Encarnación Gutiérrez Rodriguez (eds), *Spricht die Subalterne Deutsch? Migration und postkoloniale Kritik* [Does the Subaltern Speak German? Migration and Postcolonial Criticism]. Münster: Unrast, 17–37.

Habermas, Jürgen (2008). 'Europa und seine Immigranten', [Europe and Its Immigrants], in *Ach, Europa* [Oh, Europe]. Frankfurt/M.: Suhrkamp, 88–95.

Hand, Felicity (2001). 'Postcolonial Studies in Spain', *Links and Letters*, 8: 27–36.

Hanley, Jane (2010). 'Vanishing Empires: Francisco Solano and Spain's Postcolonial Present', in H. G. da Silva, A. P. Martins, F. V. Guarda, and J. M. Sardica (eds), *Conflict, Memory Transfers and the Reshaping of Europe*. Newcastle upon Tyne: Cambridge Scholars, 231–7.

Hargreaves, Alec (ed.) (2005). *Memory, Empire, and Postcolonialism: Legacies of French Colonialism*, After the Empire: The Francophone World and Postcolonial France. Lanham, Md.: Lexington Books.

Hargreaves, Alec and Mark McKinney (eds) (1997). *Post-colonial Cultures in France*. London: Routledge.

Havel, Václav (1994). Speech to the European Parliament, Strasbourg, 8 March. Online source: <http://www.vaclavhavel.cz/showtrans.php?cat=projevy&val=221_aj_projevy.html&typ=HTML>, accessed 10 November 2012.

Helff, Sissy (2008). '"The New Europeans": The Image of the African Refugee in European Literature', *African and Black Diaspora: An International Journal*, 1.2: 123–32.

Hofmeyr, Isabel (2010). 'Universalizing the Indian Ocean', *PMLA*, 125.3: 721–9.

Hoving, Isabelle (2010). 'Review: The Postcolonial Turn in Dutch Literary Criticism', *Journal of Dutch Literature*, 1.1: 114–22.

Hsu, Roland (ed.) (2010). *Ethnic Europe: Mobility, Identity, and Conflict in a Globalized World*. Stanford: Stanford University Press.

Huggan, Graham (2001). *The Postcolonial Exotic: Marketing the Margins*. London: Routledge.

Huggan, Graham (2008). 'Perspectives on Postcolonial Europe', *Journal of Postcolonial Writing*, 44.3: 241–9.

Huggan, Graham and Ian Law (eds) (2009). *Racism—Postcolonialism—Europe*. Liverpool: Liverpool University Press.

Hulme, Peter (2005). 'Beyond the Straits: Postcolonial Allegories of the Globe', in A. Loomba, S. Kaul, M. Bunzl, A. Burton, and J. Esty (eds), *Postcolonial Studies and Beyond*. Durham and London: Duke University Press, 41–61.

Innes, C. L. (2002). *A History of Black and Asian Writing in Britain, 1700–2000*. Cambridge: Cambridge University Press.

Katzenstein, Peter J. and Jeffrey T. Checkel (2009). 'Conclusion—European Identity in Context', in J. T. Checkel and P. J. Katzenstein (eds), *European Identity*. Cambridge: Cambridge University Press, 213–27.

Kelertas, Violeta (ed.) (2006). *Baltic Postcolonialism*. Amsterdam and New York: Rodopi.

Kołodoziejczyk, Dorota (2010). 'Cosmopolitan Provincialism in a Comparative Perspective', in J. Wilson, C. Şandru, and S. L. Welsh (eds), *Rerouting the Postcolonial: New Directions for the New Millennium*. London and New York: Routledge, 151–62.

Korek, Janusz (ed.) (2007). *From Sovietology to Postcoloniality: Poland and Ukraine from a Postcolonial Perspective*. Huddinge: Södertörns Högskola.

Korte, Barbara, Eva Ulrike Pirker, and Sissy Helff (eds) (2010). *Facing the East in the West: Images of Eastern Europe in British Literature, Film and Culture*. Amsterdam and New York: Rodopi.

Lazarus, Neil (2004). 'The Global Dispensation since 1945', in N. Lazarus (ed.), *The Cambridge Companion to Postcolonial Studies*. Cambridge: Cambridge University Press, 19–40.

Mellino, Miguel (2006). 'Italy and Postcolonial Studies: A Difficult Encounter', *Interventions: International Journal of Postcolonial Studies*, 8.3: 461–71.

Merolla, Daniela (2009). 'Poetics of Transition: Africa and Dutch Literary Space', in E. Bekers, S. Helff, and D. Merolla (eds), *Transcultural Modernities: Narrating Africa in Europe*, Matatu 36. Amsterdam and New York: Rodopi, 35–56.

Murphy, Neil and Wai-chew Sim (eds) (2008). *British Asian Fiction: Framing the Contemporary.* London: Cambria.

Nasta, Susheila (2001). *Home Truths: Fictions of the South Asian Diaspora in Britain.* Basingstoke: Palgrave.

Nganang, Patrice (2005). 'Autobiographies of Blackness in Germany', in E. Ames, M. Klotz, and L. Wildenthal (eds), *Germany's Colonial Pasts.* Lincoln, Nebr.: University of Nebraska, 227–39.

Nghi Ha, Kien, Nicola Lauré al-Samarai, and Sheila Mysorekar (2007). 'Einleitung' ['Introduction'], in *Re/visionen: Postkoloniale Perspektiven von People of Colour auf Rassismus, Kulturpolitik und Widerstand in Deutschland* [Re/visions: Postcolonial Perspectives of People of Colour on Racism, Cultural Policy and Resistance in Germany]. Münster: Unrast, 1–21.

Peiker, Piret (2006). 'Post-Communist Literatures: A Postcolonial Perspective', *Eurozine*, 28 March 2006. Online source: <http://www.eurozine.com/article/2006–03–28-peiker-en.html>, accessed 3 August 2011.

Phillips, Caryl (2005 [2003]). *A Distant Shore.* New York: Vintage.

Phillips, Mike (2001 [2000]). *A Shadow of Myself.* London: HarperCollins.

Phillips, Mike and Trevor Phillips (1998). *Windrush: The Irresistible Rise of Multi-Racial Britain.* London: HarperCollins.

Pieterse, Jan Nederveen (1991). 'Fictions of Europe', *Race & Class*, 32.3: 3–10.

Ponzanesi, Sandra (2004). 'Il postcolonialismo italiano: Figlie dell'Impero e letteratura meticcia', *Quaderni dell '900: La letteratura postcoloniale italiana*, IV: 25–34.

Ponzanesi, Sandra and Bollette B. Blaagaard (2011). 'Introduction: In the Name of Europe', *Social Identities: Journal for the Study of Race, Nation and Culture*, 17.1: 1–10.

Ponzanesi, Sandra and Daniela Merolla (2005). 'Introduction', in S. Ponzanesi and D. Merolla (eds), *Migrant Cartographies: New Cultural and Literary Spaces in Post-Colonial Europe.* Lanham, Md.: Lexington Books, 1–52.

Reichl, Susanne (2002). *Cultures in the Contact Zone: Ethnic Semiosis in Black British Literature.* Trier: WVT Wissenschaftlicher Verlag Trier.

Reynolds, Daniel P. (2008). 'The Documentary Critique in Recent German Postcolonial Literature', *German Studies Review*, 31.2: 241–62.

Richter, Heinz A. (2003). 'Introduction', in V. K. Fouskas and H. A. Richter (eds), *Cyprus and Europe: The Long Way Back.* Mannheim and Möhnesee: Bibliopolis, 7–10.

Risse, Thomas (2010). *A Community of Europeans? Transnational Identities and Public Spheres.* Ithaca and London: Cornell University Press.

Rushdie, Salman (1988). *The Satanic Verses.* London: Viking.

Rushdie, Salman (2008). *The Enchantress of Florence.* London: Jonathan Cape.

Said, Edward (1993). *Culture and Imperialism.* London: Chatto & Windus.

Said, Edward (2002). 'History, Literature, and Geography', in *Reflections on Exile and Other Essays.* Cambridge Mass.: Harvard University Press, 453–73.

Said, Edward (2003 [1978]). *Orientalism.* London: Penguin.

Sardar, Ziauddin (2008). *Balti Britain: A Journey through the British Asian Experience.* London: Granta.

Sayyid, S. (2006). 'Introduction: BrAsians—Postcolonial People, Ironic Citizens', in A. Nasreen, V. S. Khan and S. Sayyid (eds), *A Postcolonial People: South Asians in Britain.* London: Hurst, 1–10.

Schmale, Wolfgang (2000). *Geschichte Europas.* Wien: Böhlau.

Sesay, Kadija (ed.) (2005). *Write Black, Write British: From Post-Colonial to Black British Literature*. London: Hansib.

Sivanandan, Ambalavaner (1989). 'UK Commentary: Racism 1992', *Race & Class*, 30.3: 85–90.

Slemon, Stephen and Helen Tiffin (1989). 'Introduction', in S. Slemon and H. Tiffin (eds), *After Europe*. Sydney and Mundelstrup: Dangaroo, pp. ix–xxiii.

Stam, Robert and Ella Shohat (2005). 'Traveling Multiculturalism: A Trinational Debate in Translation', in A. Loomba, S. Kaul, M. Bunzl, A. Burton, and J. Esty (eds), *Postcolonial Studies and Beyond*. Durham and London: Duke University Press, 293–316.

Stein, Mark (2004). *Black British Literature: Novels of Transformation*. Columbus: Ohio State University Press.

Steyerl, Hito and Encarnación Gutiérrez Rodríguez (eds) (2003). *Spricht die Subalterne Deutsch? Migration und postkoloniale Kritik* [Does the Subaltern Speak German? Migration and Postcolonial Criticism]. Münster: Unrast.

Thomas, Dominic (2007). *Black France: Colonialism, Immigration, and Transnationalism*. Bloomington: Indiana University Press.

Thompson, Ewa M. (2000). *Imperial Knowledge: Russian Literature and Colonialism*. Westport, Conn.: Greenwood Press.

Tiffin, Helen (1996). 'Plato's Cave: Educational and Critical Practices', in B. King (ed.), *New National and Post-Colonial Literatures: An Introduction*. Oxford: Clarendon, 143–63.

Upstone, Sara (2010). *British Asian Fiction: Twenty-First Century Voices*. Manchester: Manchester University Press.

Visram, Rozina (1986). *Ayahs, Lascars and Princes: Indians in Britain 1700–1947*. London: Pluto.

Wagner, Gerhard (2005). *Projekt Europa: Die Konstruktion europäischer Identität zwischen Nationalismus und Weltgesellschaft* [Project Europe: The Construction of European Identity between Nationalism and World Society]. Berlin: Philo.

Watson, Tim (2000). 'Is the "Post" in Postcolonial the US in American Studies? The US Beginnings of Commonwealth Studies', *Ariel*, 31.1–2: 51–72.

Webber, Frances (1991). 'From Ethnocentrism to Euro-Racism', *Race & Class*, 32.3: 11–17.

Wilson, Janet, Cristina Şandru, and Sarah Lawson Welsh (2010). 'General Introduction', in J. Wilson, C. Şandru, and S. L. Welsh (eds), *Rerouting the Postcolonial: New Directions for the New Millennium*. London and New York: Routledge, 1–13.

Yaeger, Patricia (2007). 'Editor's Column: The End of Postcolonial Theory? A Roundtable with Sunil Agnani, Fernando Coronil, Gaurav Desai, Mamadou Diouf, Simon Gikandi, Susie Tharu, and Jennifer Wenzel', *PMLA*, 122.3: 633–51.

WHAT WAS GLOBALIZATION?

ALI BEHDAD

The chapters in this section attempt to bring the fields of postcolonialism and global studies into productive dialogue. Although, as Graham Huggan in his introduction to the section points out, the field of postcolonial studies has always maintained a global reach, it is only recently that its practitioners have begun to address the implications of global capitalism for their theoretical considerations of identity, nationalism, and (neo)colonial power. Recent postcolonial scholarship on globalization might thus be described as a belated theoretical practice—belated not just because it emerges well after economists and political scientists have defined the terms and dominated the debates, but also because, in their disparate works, postcolonial theorists elaborate a politico-economic phenomenon that both precedes and goes beyond the assumptions underlying prominent discourses of globalization itself. Zygmunt Bauman's fretful observation that "'[g]lobalization" is on everybody's lips; a fad word fast turning into a shibboleth, a magic incantation, a pass-key meant to unlock the gates to all present and future mysteries' (1998: 1), speaks to the predicament of belatedness as well as the anxiety of postcolonial critics who have jumped aboard the globalization theory bandwagon. Even so, the works of such distinguished postcolonial scholars as Arjun Appadurai, Dipesh Chakrabarty and Gayatri Chakravorty Spivak, have introduced a set of conceptual distinctions that have come to exert considerable influence on sociological, political, and economic discussions of globalization in the academy (see, for example, Appadurai 1996; Chakrabarty 2000; Spivak 1999).

The chapters here, which set out to explore the emergence of new regionalisms as both effects and responses to global capitalism, are remarkable for their broad geographical reach, their even-handed approaches to understanding the relationship between postcolonialism and globalization, and their attentiveness to the uneven development that marks current global cartography. Nikita Dhawan and Shalini Randeria's chapter, for example, offers a careful discussion of subalternity in the age of globalization that thoughtfully attends to the ways in which gender, class, and regionalism interpolate global flows of people and capital. Similarly, Daniel Vukovich's essay astutely problematizes neoliberal discourse concerning China's entry into global capitalism by situating it in the context of the long imperial history that informs China's relationship with the west.

Finally, Michelle Keown and Stuart Murray's wide-ranging piece demonstrates how Pacific regionalism is complicated by linguistic and ethnic diversity, economic instability, and the history of colonialism in the region.

Helpful though these 'regional' chapters are in constructively developing Spivak's notion of 'critical regionalism' in an attempt to link postcolonialism to globalization, they nonetheless arguably privilege a continental regionalism that obscures new regional configurations while leaving out certain regions all together. The most notable absences are the Middle East and, apart from Charles Forsdick's brief discussion, Latin America. (See, however, discussions of these regions in Parts I and II of this volume.) Given the impossibility of covering every region in one short section of a volume, such omissions would be perfectly understandable were it not for the fact that these two regions, especially the Middle East, have been so problematically marginalized, not to mention maligned, in the dominant discourses of globalization. The following statement in an article by Barry Rubin, Director of Global Research in International Affairs, was posted on *Yale Global*, a publication of the Yale Center for the Study of Globalization, and offers a representative example of this tendency: 'Probably no area in the world resists—at least explicitly—globalization to an extent equaling that of the Islamic Middle East. The majority of regimes, opposition movements, and intellectuals in the region are consciously anti-globalization. Moreover, there is no part of the world where violence is more often used in the anti-globalization struggle, most notably by Osama bin Laden but generally by all radical Islamist movements' (2003: 1). Rubin attributes this putative resistance to several factors, including Islam's supposed intolerance of western ideas and values; the influence of an Arab nationalism forged in reaction to 'a profound inferiority complex'; and, last but not least, '[t]he existence of a large and culturally powerful Arabic community [that] builds a linguistic wall against the penetration of Western languages which are such an important aspect of globalization' (2003: 2). Rubin's article presents a symptomatic case of the prevalence of Orientalism in the dominant discourse of globalization forged by economists, political scientists, and political pundits. Viewed as a fanatical, violent, and politically backward region, the Middle East is positioned outside of global temporality even as the region plays a crucial role in the project of global capital, not to mention its utility in mobilizing a neoliberal version of global human rights advocacy, e.g. the narrative of saving the veiled, and thus 'oppressed', Middle Eastern woman. Consideration of the Middle East as a region in this section might have provided a valuable occasion, not only to complicate the relation between socio-cultural formations and global capitalism—consider for example the disturbing coexistence of cultural conservatism, political repression, and global capitalism in countries such as Bahrain and Saudi Arabia—but also to attend to the important issue of uneven development that haunts new regionalism: think here for instance of the role of globalization in producing the varied economic situations presented in occupied Palestine and the United Arab Emirates.

At the same time, an engagement with the issue of globalization in the Middle East might have occasioned a much-needed postcolonial critique of those dominant discourses of globalization that rely on neoliberal notions of growth, productivity, and integration as key terms in mapping circuits of economic and cultural exchange (see

Part II of this volume). Economists and political scientists have often described the challenges facing the integration of the Middle East into the global order in terms that conspicuously avoid discussion of the history of western colonialism and neo-imperialism in the region. For example, in a 2003 publication prepared for the International Monetary Fund, George T. Abed and Hamid Davoodi identify low productivity, population growth, lack of institutional reforms, a large and costly public sector, underdeveloped financial markets, inadequate educational systems, high trade restrictiveness, and inappropriate exchange rate policies as contributing factors to the region's weak performance as measured by the rate of growth and integration into the global economy. Nowhere in their otherwise detailed account, however, do they make reference to, let alone explore, the history of colonization that determined the cartography of the modern Middle East, nor do they discuss the neo-imperial relations of power in which Middle Eastern countries are currently inscribed. A more probing discussion of the region in a global context would surely have engaged the political and economic hegemony of the west in the Middle East today, and, by drawing on postcolonial critiques of orientalism, would have disclosed the lacuna produced by students of global studies who continue to view the region in monolithic and totalizing terms that rely on binary logic and presume western moral and cultural superiority over the 'Orient' (see Hazbun in Part II of this volume).

A discussion of the Middle East in the context of globalization might have been helpful as well in challenging the 'presentist' assumptions of at least some of the work in this section, for well before the rise of European hegemony, the Middle East was already the central locus of a broad and arguably more democratic network of global trade and cultural exchange. In his introduction to this section, Huggan alludes in passing to the tendency to privilege the present in contemporary globalization discourse, and the chapters that follow sometimes (though by no means always) treat globalization as a late twentieth-century phenomenon. But as I have argued elsewhere, in spite of the emphasis on the novelty of today's global flows of people, commodities, and ideas, the condition of globalization is hardly new if viewed historically in the context of colonial relations of power or indeed of the world systems that preceded European hegemony after 1492. To be sure, the scale of economic and cultural connectivity is grander in the contemporary period than it has been in the past due to new technologies of communication and travel, but the flow and interconnection of commodities, peoples, and ideas today—not to mention the conviction that one's present is thoroughly unprecedented—might more accurately be portrayed in terms of a continuity rather than a break with the past (Behdad 2005). As Janet Abu-Lughod (1989), Warren Cohen (2000), and John Whitmore (1977) have all reminded us, even a cursory glance at archaeological discoveries of Polynesian artefacts in Africa or Chinese fragments in the New World is enough to demonstrate that there were global flows and world systems long before the Spaniards began colonizing the Americas: throughout the Mediterranean and in South and East Asia. Cohen, for example, has convincingly demonstrated that, contrary to Orientalist scholars' claims that it was Marco Polo who opened up the 'backward' orient to the 'civilized' Occident, East Asia has had four thousand years of economic, cultural, and political relations with the rest of the world. Citing a broad range of examples, from the extensive sea voyages of Chinese to the Middle East to the important role played by the Ottoman and Egyptian military forces in Indonesia in the struggle against western imperialism, to the influence of Indian cuisine on that of the Chinese, Cohen offers an important corrective to the common misperception of the west as the primary source of globalization.

Abu-Lughod's important but underappreciated book, *Before European Hegemony* (1989), also provides compelling historical evidence for the existence of a complex global network in the thirteenth century. Arguing against the Eurocentric views of Karl Marx and Immanuel Wallerstein, who located the genesis of globalization in sixteenth-century Europe due to the rise of mercantilism and European colonialism, Abu-Lughod documents a network of global flows three centuries before western hegemony; and, as she explains, these networks neither operated through hierarchically structured modes of production, nor did they depend upon a capitalist or colonialist core hegemon. According to Abu-Lughod, the thirteenth-century merchant mariners of Genoa and Venice traded not only with the textile industrialists of Bruges and Ghent, but also with the turquoise merchants of Persia and the craftsmen of Cairo and Baghdad, who themselves bartered with silk and pottery producers of China through the intermediaries of Indian merchants and sailors. These global circuits of capital and trade, which connected Europe with China through the Mediterranean region, the Persian Gulf, and the Indian Ocean, brought into contact a diverse group of people and ethnicities, and thus enabled a vibrant exchange of ideas among them, including the transmission of Aristotle's work on ethics by Arab translators to European philosophers such as Thomas Aquinas.

My critical aim in citing the works of Cohen and Abu-Lughod is not to claim a new origin for contemporary globalization, nor is it to suggest that today's cultural and economic globalization is comparable to its thirteenth-century counterpart. Rather, my point is that today's globalization is built on the ruins of previous networks of global flow; as Abu-Lughod cogently remarks, globalization is a 'cumulative' phenomenon in which 'the lines and connections laid down in prior epochs [tend] to persist even though their significance and roles in the new system may be altered' (1989: 368). This is an important insight for scholars interested in theorizing the imbrication of postcolonialism and globalization. In challenging the ways in which change and novelty have been privileged over processes of restructuring and rearticulation, we are impelled to undertake alternative historical enquiries in the field of global studies. It would surely be unwise, for example, just to dismiss the colonial model of centre/periphery as being irrelevant to the contemporary global order, as many postcolonial critics have been tempted to do; instead, it might be better to consider the political implications of the geographical division of developed and underdeveloped worlds that persists even in 'a world of criss-crossed economies, intersecting systems of meaning, and fragmented identities', to use the words of Roger Rouse (1991: 8). Similarly, it seems critically advantageous to abandon celebratory discourses of diaspora in favour of more historically situated discussions of migration that attend to the similarities between contemporary immigration and the great population movements that occurred during the nineteenth century. In sum, as I have suggested elsewhere (Behdad 2005), the question we might ask as postcolonial critics is not 'What is globalization?' but instead, 'What *was* globalization?'

REFERENCES

Abed, T. George and Hamid Davoodi (2003). *Challenges of Growth and Globalization in the Middle East and North Africa.* New York: International Monetary Fund. Online source: <http://www.imf.org/external/pubs/ft/med/2003/eng/abed.htm>, accessed 27 November 2012.

Abu-Lughod, Janet L. (1989). *Before European Hegemony: The World System A.D. 1250–1350.* Oxford: Oxford University Press.

Appadurai, Arjun (1996). *Modernity at Large: Cultural Dimensions of Globalization.* Minneapolis: University of Minnesota Press.

Bauman, Zygmunt (1998). *Globalization: The Human Consequences.* New York: Columbia University Press.

Behdad, Ali (2005). 'On Globalization, Again', in Ania Loomba et al. (eds), *Postcolonialism and Beyond.* Durham, NC: Duke University Press, 62–79.

Chakrabarty, Dipesh (2000). *Provincializing Europe: Postcolonial Thought and Historical Difference.* Princeton: Princeton University Press.

Cohen, Warren I. (2000). *East Asia at the Center: Four Thousand Years of Engagement With the World.* New York: Columbia University Press.

Rouse, Roger (1991). 'Mexican Migration and the Social Space of Postmodernism', *Diaspora,* 1.1: 8–23.

Rubin, Barry (2003). 'Why Islamic Societies of the Middle East are So Opposed to Globalization'. Yale Global Online, 16 January. Online source: <http://yaleglobal.yale.edu/content/globalization-and-middle-east-part-one>, accessed 27 November 2012.

Spivak, Gayatri Chakravorty (1999). *A Critique of Postcolonial Reason: Toward a History of the Vanishing Present.* Cambridge, Mass.: Harvard University Press.

Whitmore, John K. (1977). 'The Opening of Southeast Asia: Trading Patterns Through the Centuries', in Karl L. Hutterer (ed.), *Economic Exchange and Social Interaction in Southeast Asia: Perspectives from Prehistory and Ethnography.* Ann Arbor: University of Michigan Press, 139–53.

AFTERWORD

STEPHEN SLEMON

A handbook, pronounces the *Oxford English Dictionary*, is 'a compendious book or treatise for guidance in any art, occupation, or study'. It is designed, adds Wikipedia, 'to be easily consulted and provide quick answers in a certain area'. That this particular Handbook does not stay within the formal definitional boundaries of its genre says a lot about the essentially insubordinate nature of postcolonial studies at the level of critical temperament. And it points to a foundational truth about postcolonial studies as a discipline, one that too many of its practitioners have for too long disavowed.

Everywhere in this document one finds evidence of a profound, and in my view enabling, incoherence to the 'art' of postcolonial studies. Graham Huggan, in his General Introduction to the Handbook, suggests alongside R. Radhakrishnan that postcolonialism might usefully be characterized as 'a combination of revisionisms'. Walter Mignolo, in the volume's first section, defines postcolonialism as a 'radical undoing of modernity', while—also in this section—Ann Laura Stoler grounds the practice of postcolonial studies in a principle of critical refusal, of 'unquestioned identification' of any kind. In their means of approach as in their objects of study, the chapters in this Handbook do not sit easily alongside each other at the level of critical argument. Nor do they submit to the demands of methodological unity. They cannot collectively seek to position themselves against the yardstick of global coverage. Instead, they turn again and again, in their methodological singularity, to what Huggan calls 'a continuing obligation to complexity' in the material itself: the cultural backgrounds, the literatures, the histories, the ecologies, the politics. Together, in discordant combination, they eschew the unity of sweep and scope, pursuing instead a rather less visible modality of the scholarship of equity: one that lies implicit in an attention to detail. This Handbook provides no 'quick answers'. Indeed, it abjures the very idea of postcolonial studies as a definable field, a completed project, or designated area. It refuses to map out for its readers a route towards disciplinary occupation.

One answer as to why this is so might be found in the time of the volume's publication. By the second decade of the twenty-first century, the formal discipline of postcolonial studies, as it is generally understood, has grown well beyond its founding moment of academic urgency in the western academy and has now settled into more multiply identified modalities of institutional living. It should go without saying that anything that gestures towards the institutional age of a scholarly field implicitly posits exactly the kind of unity to the discipline that this Handbook so steadfastly refuses; and, in fact, all kinds of critical studies that one might now call 'postcolonial' were already in an advanced state of preparedness within the university system globally, and were doing various work under various disciplinary banners, by that time in the early and mid-1980s when the humanities and social sciences disciplines in the First World collectively discovered postcolonial critique as a necessary complement to their own disciplinary first principles for knowing, and woke up to the long histories and capacious arts of empire's many and different others. The 1980s, however, were also a time when poststructuralist critical theory within the western academy came into a specific cross-disciplinary alignment with, among other confluents, 'Commonwealth' or 'New Literatures' studies, social theory after the Frankfurt school, and the scholarship of Frantz Fanon and Edward Said, and the postcolonial disciplinary formation that arose in the aftershock of *that* particular combination of intellectual forces was shaped profoundly by an internal desire for quick institutional recognition of the discipline itself. That desire was rightly fuelled by a strong sense that the First-World academy had for far too long cognitively traduced those many cultures inflected but not just made by empire: cultures whose peoples were and remain subjects, not objects, of their own histories, social frameworks, and codes of recognition. Still, as a by-product of that early rush to disciplinary stability a lot of what would be seen as standing in for the field of postcolonial studies found itself shaped by a drive for theoretical consistency—as though all things 'colonial' needed somehow to align—and a teleological insistence on disciplinary completion—as though all forms of counter-imperial representation were in political want of procrustean disciplinary inclusion. In that period of rapid, institutionally mercantile, expansion for the field of postcolonial studies, a sizeable part of what counted for postcolonial critical practice repeatedly pushed forward the idea of the discipline itself as a unitary enterprise, designed to bring those many histories encapsulated within 500 years of European global domination—and 500 years of productive resistances—together into a single, and above all teachable, critical master narrative. In the wake of that disciplinary salient, too many of postcolonialism's most enabling tools for critical construction, which had been so carefully elaborated in their first, exploratory scholarly formations—'colonial discourse', 'hybridity', 'the empire writes back', and so forth—found themselves transformed into quasi-universal blueprints for human activity across the registers of modernity's many and variegated forms of imperial domination and postcolonial response.

In the disciplinary lull that followed that early, heady moment of institutional growth, postcolonial studies found itself increasingly challenged by the striking imbalance between postcolonial advance within the academy, on the one hand, and postcolonial retreat in the material world, on the other. At the level of the nation state, the world might have *seemed* to be changing in positive ways. Hong Kong decolonized in 1997, Macao in 1999 ... might a genuine 'end to empire' be in sight or at least conceptually possible? But far from ameliorating the global income gap, the formal political change from colonial to what Kwame Nkrumah once called neocolonial economic relations, or what theorists like Michael Hardt and Antonio Negri have more recently called the economic relations of Big-E, post-national 'Empire', produced greater, not lesser, economic disparity in the world at the millennium. The richest 10 per cent of the world's population now commands 42 per cent of the world's wealth, the poor just 1 per cent (World Economic Forum 2011). By every measure except a temporal one, the political world after the formal end of empire seemed increasingly less 'postcolonial' than it had been before the discipline of postcolonial studies took root within the institution. How could critical work within the university—on critical ethnography, on subaltern historiography, on cultural representation—hope meaningfully to engage with a desperately unequal, and progressively more unequal, material world?

By the end of the twentieth century, postcolonial studies had produced for itself, across the human sciences, a fleet of guidebooks, anthologies, special issues, and gazetteer critical articles. It had long since established its flagship journals, its major research projects, and a place for its own practitioners within the tenure track. Most English departments now scheduled courses on the literatures of empire's others; most anthropology departments taught the cross-cultural politics of critical ethnography; most history departments embedded subaltern historiography within the curriculum; and just about everyone read at least a little 'postcolonial theory'. But it became increasingly difficult within the formal field of postcolonial studies to believe that the fortunes of this now institutionally comfortable discipline could themselves serve as an index to the state of the global dispossessed. With the added fillip of this structural aporia, that once-confident cadre within postcolonial studies that had earlier attempted to advance the discipline as a unitary enterprise now seemed to have surrendered itself to the *longueurs* of identity crisis, as the field's proponents looked intently at their own disciplinary structures and rehearsed the questions that had helped elaborate the discipline's institutional foundation in the first place: what is the meaning of this 'post' in the name we have given ourselves? What is our canon? And who gets 'in'? Much of what now spoke within the institution in the name of postcolonial studies found itself so captured by the self-oriented project of belated field fashioning, so embedded in the practice of disciplinary navel-gazing, that many of the most visibly self-identified manifestations of the postcolonial studies field lost their once-enabling curiosity in the knowledges of others. At the turn of the twenty-first century, postcolonial studies as a formal, predominantly First-World disciplinary enterprise had taken on the look of Salman Rushdie's Midnight Children's Conference at the end of that novel: a group of dreamers who had once possessed a magical belief in transformative possibility, who had begun the work of material change in the disciplinary imaginary, who had begun to locate a form of academic citizenship beyond the myriad designations of identity, but who had then simply lost their way and become vulnerable to the allure of introspection. 'What Was Postcolonialism?' asked Vijay Mishra and Bob Hodge in 2005, in seemingly ironic echo of their own earlier, critical, but still in many ways ebullient article on the discipline's formation, 'What Is Post(-)colonialism?' Their conclusion was that for the political project of the discipline to stay true to itself, postcolonial critique must now rethink its own programme; must reconsider its own internal structural difference from its foundational intentions and

assumptions; must 'turn away' from postcolonialism as a putative platform of engagement and seek instead 'other paradigms' for a critical way of being in the world (Mishra
and Hodge 2005: 399; see also Mishra and Hodge 1991).

This volume, in my view, can be read as part of that greater, more outwardly focused
project of critical 'turning away'. Its writers are not interested in returning to disciplinary
psychomachia: they do not seek reflection in the postcolonial mirror. They position their
separate critical projects not in the mainstream of any singular, methodologically unified academic enterprise but at the intersection between scholarly ventures the names
of which are variable, provisional, strategic: postcolonial studies, globalization studies,
migrancy studies, diaspora studies, transnational and transcultural studies, cosmopolitan studies, subaltern studies, critical race studies, popular culture studies—these and
many more, and all of them both for and against. The writers here commit themselves to
an ethical academic citizenship that is not bound by title.

'So many disciplines have been, so to speak, postcolonialized', writes Robert Young
in a recent article the title of which could serve as both epithet (not epitaph) for the
project of this Handbook: 'Postcolonialism Remains'. Young continues: 'The postcolonial remains: it lives on, ceaselessly transformed in the present into new social and political configurations ... This remarkable dispersal of intellectual and political influence
now makes it difficult to locate any kind of center of postcolonial theory: reaching into
almost every domain of contemporary thought, it has become part of the consciousness of our era' (2012: 22). *That* form of postcolonial critical consciousness will persist,
whatever the institutional fortunes of the postcolonial field; and as it proceeds, it will not
forget this critical first principle: that there is no single motor of historical causality, no
organizing master narrative behind what it is that brought, and still brings, the multiple oppressions of race, ethnicity, class, caste, sexuality, age, and anti-environmentalism
into prominence in the global dispensation, no single disciplinary redress to inequity in
the material real.

I take *this* globally dispersed, non-unified, and ubiquitous intellectual project to be the
real subject of this collection: a modality of the 'postcolonial' that is ultimately no more a
singularity, no more a discipline of study, than this Handbook is an obedient participant
in the genre to which it technically gives its name. 'Postcolonial studies' remains indeed,
but as an omnibus term for what was always an unruly and disruptive set of scholarly
practices—one which held in common a commitment to discern and then keep faith
with an unbreakable, inevitably multiple form of global consciousness that dared to
hope for, if not always believe in, the possibility of real and equitable social change. We
might call that global consciousness postcolonial 'critical thought'—but I would argue
that what we call it does not really matter. Beyond the onomastics, beyond disciplinary
identities, this global consciousness exists everywhere, as fully agential within the margins of neoliberal production as it is within the entitled First-World university. It cannot
be enclosed within disciplinary framing.

Postcolonial critical thought, however it finds itself labelled, will continue to transform the academy. It will not submit to methodological singularity. It will necessarily
interrupt the inculcation of whole-system theories. It will seek out forms of scholarly

recognition that listen before they speak. In turn, those scholarly practices that seek to approach it will have to find more equitable, mutually beneficial forms of collaboration with subaltern individuals and communities in order to do their future work. They will have to remain outwardly positioned, not inwardly administrative—to involve students who bring humility to the seat of learning. Whatever their theoretical take on the multiple hypotheses that inform constructions and conflations of the philosophical, the phenomenological, and the sociological other, postcolonial scholars of the future will have to remain, at least in part, students of other knowledges. For the subaltern knowledges of postcolonial critical thought are ubiquitous, and detailed, and difficult. They remain expansive in their capacity to imagine; and they will continue to prove unstoppable in their power to represent.

References

Mishra, Vijay and Robert Hodge (1991). 'What Is Post(-)colonialism?' *Textual Practice*, 5: 399–414.

Mishra, Vijay and Robert Hodge (2005). 'What Was Postcolonialism?' *New Literary History*, 36: 375–402.

Young, Robert J. (2012). 'Postcolonialism Remains', *New Literary History*, 43: 19–42.

World Economic Forum (2011). The Conference Board of Canada, 'World Income Inequality', World Economic Forum Annual Meeting, Davos. Online source: <http://www.conferenceboard.ca/hcp/hot-topics/worldinequality.aspx>, accessed 30 October 2012.

INDEX

APEC (Asian-Pacific Economic
    Cooperation) 610
Aponte Rebellion (Cuba 1812) 662
Appadurai, Arjun 567–8, 619, 692
Appiah, Kwame Anthony 99 n.9, 324, 359,
    360, 459, 648
Apter, Emily 303, 354, 355
Aquinas, Thomas 695
Arab-Israeli peace process 101, 224, 225, 227
Arab Revolt (1936–9) 186
Arab Spring (2010–11) 1–2, 9, 22, 34, 128 n.3,
    175–6, 214, 217–19, 226–32, 246, 249,
    291, 293, 294, 302, 304, 337
Araucanos Indians 96
archaeology 95, 694
archives 303, 360, 468, 480, 481
    Netherlands Indies 31, 41, 44, 46–51, 53,
        56, 58–61
Arendt, Hannah 3, 5, 22–3, 55, 255, 256, 262, 600
Argentina 72, 99, 104, 120
Aristotle 50, 62, 181–2, 695
Armah, Ayi Kwei 455
Armenian Massacre (1915) 404
Armitage, David 478
Arnold, Dan 512 n.3
Arnold, David 471, 475
Arnold, Matthew 462
Arrighi, Giovanni 591, 592
Asad, Talal 45 n.7, 343, 469, 507 n.1
ASEAN (Association of Southeast Asian
    Nations) 561
    plus Korea, China, and Japan 591–6
Ashcroft, Bill 5 n.1, 301, 307–11, 313, 359,
    432, 458, 608, 650, 651–4, 682
Asia 566, 567
    Cold War in 599
    decolonization of 98
    diaspora 620
    globalization and 552–3, 587–604
    inter-regional studies of 552, see also
        under countries
Asian American Studies 588
ASLE (Association for the Study of Literature
    and the Environment) 524–5
Al-Assad, Mehmet 254, 255, 257, 258,
    262, 265
assassinations 289, 327
Assmann, Aleida 363–4, 366, 367, 370 n.17

Assmann, Jan 363–4, 366, 367
Assyrians 131
Aswany. Alaa Al 22
asylum seekers 244, 253, 404, 579, 677
    lip-sewing strategy 254–8, 260–1, 262, 263,
        265, 291, 294
Athens 133 n.8
athletics 382–6, 392
Attridge, Derek 542
Atwood, Margaret 209
Audet, Noël 658
Austen, Jane 210, 211
Austin, John 59, 60
Australia 94 n.4, 435, 440, 471, 608, 610
    asylum policy of 254, 262–5
    hegemony of nationalism in 613
    Intervention response to Aboriginal child
        sexual abuse 492–4
    multiculturalism in 619–20
    as penal colony 632
    reconciliation policy in 17–18, 614–15,
        see also Aborigines
Austro-Hungarian Empire 122
Ayinde, O. A. 247
'Aziz, Nafia Nafeh 189, 190
Azoulay, Ariella 187, 262, 263, 264–5
Aztecs 95, 96

Bâ, Mariama 99
Baathism 203
Babylonians 131
Bachelard, Gaston 46
Bachmann-Medick, Doris 303, 356
Bacon, Francis 43, 53
Bagehot, Walter 198
Bahrain 128 n.3, 224, 229, 693
Bale, John 304, 381, 382, 385
Balibar, Étienne 305, 405–7, 671, 672, 676, 677
Ballantyne, Tony 476
Bandung conference (1955) 2, 111–12,
    124, 330, 335, 572–3
Bank of England 84
Bannister, Roger 384, 385
Banton, Buju 304, 305, 382, 389–93
Barclay, Robert 622
Barkawi, Tarak 230–1, 291, 293
Barlow, T. 596
Barry, Peter 652